strada lex

How to activate a book online

Identification code

If you have a subscription to our database Strada lex **www.stradalex.com**, Strada lex Luxembourg **www.stradalex.lu**, or Strada lex Europe **www.stradalex.eu** you can activate the digital version of this book* for free by entering the identification code mentioned above.

02525-INTERS702525-49078-0163

If a problem occurs during the activation, you can contact our helpdesk: tel. : **+32(0)2 548 07 20** • fax : **+32(0)2 548 07 22** • **info@stradalex.com**. You will be asked for a proof of purchase.

The identification code can only be used once by one Strada lex subscriber. Once activated, the book can only be consulted on the Strada lex platform in accordance with the terms of the subscription.

If you have not yet subscribed to our databases and would like some more information or a presentation by one of our representatives, please contact us at the following e-mail address: info@stradalex.com.

** If the book is included in one of the mentioned databases. Please visit www.larcier.com to check in which database(s) this monograph is available.*

ARTIFICIAL INTELLIGENCE AND THE LAW

ARTIFICIAL INTELLIGENCE AND THE LAW

Second Revised Edition

Jan De Bruyne
Cedric Vanleenhove
(eds.)

INTERSENTIA
Cambridge – Antwerp – Chicago

Intersentia Ltd
8 Wellington Mews | Wellington Street
Cambridge | CB1 1HW | United Kingdom
Tel.: +44 1223 736 170
Email: mail@intersentia.co.uk
www.intersentia.com | www.intersentia.co.uk

Distribution for the UK and the rest of the world (incl. Eastern Europe):
NBN International
1 Deltic Avenue, Rooksley
Milton Keynes MK13 8LD
United Kingdom
Tel.: +44 1752 202 301 | Fax: +44 1752 202 331
Email: orders@nbninternational.com

Distribution for Europe:
Lefebvre Sarrut Belgium NV
Hoogstraat 139/6
1000 Brussels
Belgium
Tel.: +32 3 680 15 50 | Fax: +32 3 658 71 21
Email: mail@intersentia.be

Distribution for the USA and Canada:
Independent Publishers Group
Order Department
814 North Franklin Street
Chicago, IL60610
USA
Tel.: +1 800 888 4741 (toll free) | Fax: +1312 337 5985
Email: orders@ipgbook.com

First published in hardcover in 2023

Cover design: Danny Juchtmans / www.dsigngraphics.be
Cover image: Production Perig / Shutterstock

ISBN 978-1-83970-252-5 (hardcover)
ISBN 978-1-83970-333-1 (pdf)
D/2023/7849/16
NUR 822

British Library Cataloguing in Publication Data. A catalogue record for this book is available from the British Library.

CONTENTS

Chapter 10.
Tax and Robots

Chapter 18.
Robots and AI in the Healthcare Sector: Potential Existing Legal Safeguards Against a(n) (Un)justified Fear for 'Dehumanisation' of the Physician-Patient Relationship

Chapter 19.
AI and Antitrust: Between Collision and Collusion

FOREWORD

Artificial intelligence (AI) is becoming increasingly more prevalent in our daily social and professional lives. AI can be of benefit to a wide range of sectors such as healthcare, energy consumption, climate change and financial risk management. AI can also help to detect cybersecurity threats and fraud as well as enable law enforcement authorities to fight crime more efficiently.[1] AI systems are more accurate and efficient than humans because they are faster and can better process information.[2] They can perform many tasks 'better' than their human counterparts.[3] Companies from various economic sectors already rely on AI applications to decrease costs, generate revenue, enhance product quality and improve competitiveness.[4] AI systems and robots can also have advantages for the specific sector in which they are to be used. Take the example of autonomous vehicles. Transport will become more time-efficient with autonomous car technology. Self-driving cars will also enable people currently facing restrictions for operating a vehicle – such as the elderly, minors or disabled people – to fully and independently participate in traffic. Traffic will become safer as well. The number of accidents will decrease as computers are generally much better drivers than humans.[5]

At the same time, however, the introduction of AI systems and robots will present many challenges. These will only become more acute in light of the predicted explosive growth of the robotics industry over the next decade.[6] AI

---

1 European Commission, Press Release, IP/19/1893, 'Artificial intelligence: Commission takes forward its work on ethics guidelines', 8 April 2019, https://europa.eu/rapid/press-release_IP-19-1893_en.htm.

2 S.G. Tzafestas, *Roboethics: A Navigating Overview* (Athens: Springer, 2015), p. 147.

3 H.M. Deitel and B. Deitel, *Computers and Data Processing: International Edition* (Orlando: Academic Press, 2014), p. 434. See in this regard the experiment with supercomputer *WATSON* and the identification of lung cancer cases (I. Steadman, 'IBM's Watson is better at diagnosing cancer than human doctors', *Wired*, 11 February 2013, www.wired.co.uk/article/ibm-watson-medical-doctor).

4 S.H. Ivanov, 'Robonomics – Principles, Benefits, Challenges, Solutions', *Yearbook of Varna University of Management*, 2017, vol. 10, pp. 283–285.

5 See for example: J.R. Zohn, 'When Robots Attack: How Should the Law Handle Self Driving Cars That Cause Damages?', *University of Illinois Journal of Law, Technology and Policy*, 2015, vol. 2, p. 471; T. Malengreau, 'Automatisation de la conduite: quelles responsabilités en droit belge? (Première partie)', *RGAR*, 2019, vol. 5, nos. 15578–15607. Also see: J. De Bruyne and J. Tanghe, 'Liability for damage caused by autonomous vehicles: a Belgian perspective', *Journal of European Tort Law*, vol. 8, no. 3, pp. 324–371.

6 R. Calo, 'Robots in American Law', University of Washington School of Law Research Paper no. 2016-04, 2016, p. 3.

has implications for various facets of our society.[7] Some even predict that AI systems can completely eradicate humanity in the long run.[8] There are also several important ethical issues associated with (programming and using) AI systems. The commercialisation of AI will pose several challenges from a legal and regulatory point of view as well.[9]

In this second edition, scholars from various legal disciplines critically examine how AI systems may have an impact on Belgian law. While specific topics of Belgian private and public law are thoroughly addressed, the book also provides a general overview of many regulatory and ethical AI evolutions and tendencies in the European Union. The book additionally explains basic AI-related concepts such as machine learning, robots, Internet of Things and expert systems. Therefore, it is a must-read for legal scholars, practitioners and government officials as well as for anyone with an interest in law and technology. As AI influences a wide range of legal areas, a choice of topics had to be made. We decided to base this selection on several criteria. We included topics that already attracted attention in international scholarship and policy documents (e.g., tort law, consumer protection, human rights and data protection). The second edition of this book builds upon the chapters of the first edition. They were updated where necessary. Two new chapters were included in the second edition.

Chapter 1 provides a broad overview of AI. After some introductory thoughts on how to define AI, the authors focus on the foundations and main paradigms of AI. The current state of the art for a wide range of applications as well as their expected evolutions are discussed. The chapter ends with a glance at the more distant future and some considerations regarding the ethical and safety aspects of AI.

Chapter 2 examines which legal rules are most conducive to the emergence of innovation within a market economy. Western legal systems follow the OECD and the World Bank and welcome tax incentives for research and development (R&D) as sound innovation policy. Based on developments in institutional economics, the chapter illustrates that the proposal of tax incentives for innovation encounters significant information problems. Relying on enriched models of what innovation is, the author argues that the best innovation policy lies in supporting secure, stable and general rules of property and contract.

Chapter 3 provides an overview of the main highlights of the debate on AI ethics and regulation that is currently taking place at various societal levels and

---

7 See: Y.N. Harari, *Homo Deus. A Brief History of Tomorrow* (London: Random House, 2016), 528 p.; J. De Bruyne and N. Bouteca, *Artificiële intelligentie en maatschappij* (Turnhout: Gompel&Svacina, 2021), forthcoming.

8 See: N. Bostrom, *Superintelligence: Paths, Dangers, Strategies* (Oxford: Oxford University Press, 2014), 328 p.

9 R. Leenes et al., 'Regulatory challenges of robotics: some guidelines', *Law, Innovation and Technology*, 2017, vol. 9, no. 2, p. 2.

in various parts of the world. The chapter hopes to give a glimpse of the direction in which the ethical and legal framework on AI might evolve in the coming years.

Chapter 4 discusses the advent of AI techniques such as natural language processing and machine learning within the area of dispute resolution, focusing namely on the development and challenges of quantitative legal prediction applications. It examines some existing applications and highlights the advantages that this new development could bring, whilst shedding light on the challenges that quantitative legal prediction poses to the legal system. The author concludes by critically appraising the situation in Belgium.

Chapter 5 addresses the potential of AI for international arbitration, and, more specifically, the question of whether an AI system could be appointed as an arbitrator. The first part of this chapter goes into the technical (data) requirements which would need to be met in order to develop an AI arbitrator. The second part discusses a number of possible legal obstacles to AI arbitrators. On the basis of the findings of the first two parts, the author goes on to consider how the future of AI-based dispute resolution and arbitration may evolve.

Chapter 6 addresses the relationship between AI and human rights. It explores how AI systems and applications pose risks and opportunities for human rights. The chapter provides an in-depth analysis of the prohibition of discrimination in an AI-context. The authors explore what role human rights can play in fulfilling AI's potential.

Chapter 7 sheds some light on important questions of international law when dealing with robots. The reader is introduced to basic concepts of international humanitarian law and several prima facie concerns regarding their relationship to lethal autonomous weapons (LAWs). The authors then explore the legal aspects of LAWs relating to two themes: the authority awarded to machines in an armed conflict, as well as the processes and procedural safeguards behind targeting and engagement choices. This is followed by a discussion of the current applications of LAWs and their foreseeable developments.

Chapter 8 discusses AI from a data protection perspective by using smart home assistants (SHAs), such as Amazon Alexa and Google Home, as a case study. SHAs are studied through the lens of the data protection framework and the GDPR in particular. The contribution investigates the obligations of data controllers, the rights of data subjects, the remedies the latter can rely on and the enforcement actions that have already been undertaken in relation to SHAs' data protection issues. Specific attention is devoted to the grounds for lawful processing of data, children as 'invisible' data subjects, and concerns regarding automated decision-making.

Chapter 9 deals with the interface of AI and intellectual property (IP) law, with a focus on copyright and patent law. First, the protection of AI technology is discussed. Second, attention shifts to the protection of output generated through or by an AI system. In this context, the author thoroughly analyses the issue of AI authorship and/or inventorship as well as the question of ownership of IP rights associated with AI-generated content.

Chapter 10 focuses on the tax implications related to AI and robots from a domestic and international perspective. In this respect, the chapter firstly analyses the current tax rules applicable in Belgium in relation to AI and robots and discusses whether there is a general need to implement a robot tax. In addition, it analyses the tax challenges posed by AI and smart robots from an international perspective by using a simplified case study and concludes by providing an overview of the opportunities that AI can create for tax authorities, tax practitioners and corporations.

Chapter 11 provides an overview of issues regarding robotisation from a labour law perspective. It explains the concept of robotisation and positions it in the broader context of Industry 4.0. It examines the impact of robotisation on employment with special attention for the Belgian labour market and proposes some recommendations in that regard. Finally, it investigates the impact of robotisation on health and safety, responsibility, privacy and discrimination in the workplace.

Chapter 12 deals with the hypothesis of technological unemployment caused by AI-driven automation and its impact on social security law. This hypothesis is especially relevant for social security systems that either put employment structurally at their centre for determining eligibility or in which employment serves as the legitimation for the rights-based character of social security entitlements. This chapter describes the possible flaws in social security systems that are designed this way when hypothetically confronted with mass technological unemployment.

Chapter 13 focuses on the use of AI systems in Belgian contract law. In the chapter both standard solutions to deal with a faulty contract are discussed. That is, on the one hand, considering AI as a mere communication tool, or on the other hand, granting the AI system legal personality. The goal of this chapter is to come up with a logical framework that would offer a solution to spread the risk of a faulty contract, due to the AI system, more evenly over both contracting parties.

Chapter 14 deals with extra-contractual liability for damage caused by AI systems. It examines whether the existing traditional liability regimes in Belgian tort law are adapted to the reality of AI systems and their unique characteristics such as autonomy and opaqueness. The authors analyse fault-based liability, liability for defective things and products, legal personality for AI systems, and also shed light on causation in an AI context.

Chapter 15 examines the impact of telematics on policy underwriting in vehicle insurance. It provides an analysis of some legal challenges of using telematics in vehicle insurance. The author focuses on the challenges centred around the underwriting policy technique in vehicle insurance and data protection concerns.

Chapter 16 focuses on the automation of creditworthiness assessments, and more specifically on credit scoring systems. Although digitalisation and automation within financial services should be encouraged as they may benefit consumer-borrowers, the fact that this method triggers a lot of challenges and potential ramifications for consumers cannot be ignored. This chapter therefore tries to answer the question whether the current (European) regulation is strong enough to withstand this new digital reality facing consumers and to fully protect consumers against negative effects that may go alongside automated credit decisions.

Chapter 17 analyses consumer law in the era of AI. The author first provides a context for the use of AI in the business to consumer (B2C) context. He then examines the building blocks for an AI consumer policy. Finally, he analyses some of the hurdles AI presents to consumers and how this can be dealt with through consumer law.

Chapter 18 deals with the use of AI in the healthcare sector. One of the major concerns expressed in literature is the 'dehumanisation' of the healthcare sector and the possible negative impact of AI and robotics on the personal relationship between physicians and patients. In this chapter the author nuances this fear of 'dehumanisation' of the physician-patient relationship in light of the current legal framework in Belgium.

Chapter 19 focuses on the implications of AI for the field of EU competition law and provides a comprehensive overview of the current state of the art. The underlying theme within this contribution is 'predictability': while AI is often said to function as a black box, it needs to be borne in mind that algorithms essentially perform a set of steps that any individual could also carry out himself. The ability to retrace these steps offers some solace to competition authorities put in a position to judge the anticompetitive nature of machine intelligence.

Chapter 20 sets the scene with a brief sketch of how AI systems are used in the media sector and of the complex Belgian media law landscape. It subsequently discusses risks and opportunities arising from the use of three AI media applications: recommender systems, content moderation systems and deepfakes. For each of these technologies, it analyses to what extent existing and upcoming rules in Belgian and EU media law (and related frameworks) can address the identified challenges. It formulates concluding thoughts in light of the specificities of Belgian media law and of the crucial role that the media represents for democracy and fundamental rights.

This book would not have been possible without the help of a number of people. First, we would like to thank all contributing authors for their chapters. Second, we are grateful to all peer reviewers that assessed the different chapters and provided excellent and valuable feedback. Their comments increased the quality of each chapter, as well as the overall scientific value of the book. Third, we would like to express our gratitude to Charlotte De Belie and Evi Plettinckx of publishing house Intersentia for their support. Finally, we would like to thank professors Marie-Christine Janssens (KU Leuven, Centre for IT & IP Law), Bart Custers (Leiden, eLaw), Yves Poullet (UNamur, CRIDS) and Paul de Hert (VUB, LSTS).

Dr. Jan De Bruyne
Research expert, KU Leuven Centre for IT & IP Law (CiTiP) – imec
Assistant professor, eLaw Leiden
Senior researcher Knowledge Centre Data & Society
Scientific collaborator Faculty of Law and Criminology Ghent University

Prof. dr. Cedric Vanleenhove
Secretary-General of the Flemish Sports Tribunal
Professor at Ghent University and the HEC Management School of the University of Liège

CONTRIBUTING AUTHORS

Jeffrey Amankwah obtained his Master of Laws degree in law at KU Leuven. He is a lawyer at the Bar of Limburg (Lydian) and a voluntary research associate at the Institute for Insurance Law of KU Leuven. Jeffrey Amankwah is a member of the editorial board of the legal journal Limburgs Rechtsleven.

Alexander Appelmans obtained master's degrees in Modern History (2012) and Law (2015) at KU Leuven and an MSc in Legal Anthropology at the London School of Economics (2016). From 2016 through 2018, he was a financial researcher in London. He is currently a PhD Candidate at the Institute for Property Law (KU Leuven) and was in 2019 a visiting researcher at University College London (UCL). His research focuses on the use of technology in real estate transactions.

Skander Bennis was a teaching assistant at the University of Antwerp and is affiliated with the research unit Business and Law. He studied law at the University of Antwerp and completed his studies *magna cum laude* in 2015. From 2015 to 2018, Skander worked as a litigation attorney at the Brussels Bar.

Marie Beudels is a PhD candidate in energy law at the Université libre de Bruxelles (ULB), Centre de droit public et social (center for public and social law). She holds a Master's degree from the Université de Liège (*magna cum laude*, 2019) and a Master of Laws (LL.M) from Harvard Law School (2020). Before starting her PhD, Marie worked as a researcher at the Centre for IT and IP law (CiTiP) of KU Leuven.

Wannes Buelens, PhD, is a lawyer, a teaching assistant in health law at the University of Ghent and a voluntary academic collaborator at the University of Antwerp. At the latter institution, he worked for three years as an assistant in liability, insurance and health law and obtained a PhD in law with a thesis on the medical accident without liability. His thesis was awarded the 'Wetenschappelijke prijs voor het gezondheidsrecht André Prims' in 2019. Wannes' practice focuses on liability law (both contractual and tort, including product liability and safety) as well as on insurance law in the broad sense (cover disputes and regulatory aspects) and commercial law. He has also expertise in health law (medical devices, clinical trials, patient rights, professional secrecy, etc.). He focuses on dispute resolution, the drafting/review of contracts and providing advice in the aforementioned areas of law.

Charline Daelman is a Social Sustainability Expert at the Strategy & Innovation team of amfori. Charline previously worked as a Business and Children's Rights Expert (UNICEF), Gender & Human Rights Consultant (Enabel) and Associate Attorney (SQ-Law). She was an assistant lecturer in Human Rights at the University of Leuven and guest lecturer in Investment, Business & Human Rights at the University of Pretoria and TEC Monterrey. She holds an LLM from the University of Essex and a PhD from the University of Leuven.

Jan De Bruyne obtained a Master's degree in Political Sciences at Ghent University and a Master's degree in Law at the same university. He successfully defended his PhD in September 2018 on a topic dealing with the liability of third-party certifiers. He was a postdoctoral researcher on robots and liability at the Faculty of Law and Criminology of Ghent University. He currently works as research expert on AI and (tort) law at the KU Leuven Centre for IT & IP Law (CiTiP) and as an assistant professor at eLaw in Leiden. He is also associated with the Knowledge Centre for Data & Society. He is also lecturer of the course 'Electronic Contracts Law' within the Master of Intellectual Property and ICT Law at KU Leuven.

Charles Delmotte is an assistant professor of law at Michigan State University College of Law. He is an affiliate fellow at NYU's Classical Liberal Institute and a scholar at the Center for Intellectual Property and Innovation (C-IP2 at George Mason University).

Rembrandt Devillé obtained his degree in bio-engineering sciences in 2019 at KU Leuven. His focus during his master's degree was on human health engineering with a thesis on the development of a detection algorithm of sedentary behaviour. He is currently researching AI on single board computers, survival analysis and AI for rehabilitation at the Knowledge Center AI of Erasmus University College Brussels.

Michiel Fierens obtained his Master of Laws (*cum laude*) from the KU Leuven in 2018, with a focus on economic and private law. In 2019, he completed the Advanced Master in Intellectual Property Rights & ICT at the KU Leuven (Campus Brussels) (also *cum laude*). Prior to joining CiTiP, Michiel worked as a legal counsel at KU Leuven Research & Development (LRD), supporting companies and researchers of the KU Leuven Association wanting to engage in a research collaboration by offering customized advice throughout the entire collaboration process. Michiel also previously worked for a year as a researcher at CiTiP in the area of (cyber)security & artificial intelligence. Michiel was mainly involved in the Cybersecurity Initiative of Flanders and the ENSURESEC H2020-project (Cybersecurity in e-Commerce).

Thomas Gils is an academic researcher at the KU Leuven Centre for IT and IP law, working for the Flemish Knowledge Centre Data & Society. He studied law and philosophy at the KU Leuven and completed his legal studies (*magna cum laude*) in July 2016. He was an exchange student at the Università di Bologna during the academic year 2013–2014. He then obtained an LL.M in IP/IT law (*cum laude*) at the KU Leuven in 2017. From 2017–2020, Thomas was an associate in an international law firm, practicing in the area of intellectual property, privacy and data protection (GDPR compliance projects), IT-contracting and commercial law.

Julie Goetghebuer is a PhD candidate and academic assistant at the Financial Law Institute of Ghent University. In 2017 she obtained her master's degree in Law at Ghent University, specialising in economic and financial law. In 2017 she started working at KPMG as a Financial Risk Advisor, responsible for offering legal advice to clients regarding diverse financial matters. Since 2018, she has been working on her PhD, analysing the liability of (Belgian) financial institutions when using AI and big data in the credit, investment, and insurance sector.

Maarten Herbosch obtained his Master's degree in Physics in 2016 and his Master's degree in Law in 2019. Subsequently, he started working as an assistant at the Centre for Methodology of Law (KU Leuven), where he is preparing a PhD on the legal implications of the precontractual use of AI systems, under the supervision of Prof. dr. Bernard Tilleman and Prof. dr. ir. Georges Gielen.

Noémie Krack is a researcher at the Centre for IT & IP Law (CiTiP) at imec – KU Leuven Faculty of Law. She joined the Centre in 2020 and focuses on media law, artificial intelligence and the challenges that technology raises for fundamental rights. She holds an LL.M. in IP & ICT Law *cum laude* from the KU Leuven and a Master in law *cum laude* with a specialization in European Law from the Université Catholique de Louvain. Noémie currently works on two European Union funded projects: MediaFutures and AI4Media. Mediafutures is a data-driven innovation hub for reshaping the media value chain and providing innovative solutions to media challenges including disinformation. AI4Media is a project developing an excellence centre about AI for the Society and the Media Industry.

Aleksandra Kuczerawy is a postdoctoral scholar at KU Leuven's Centre for IT & IP Law and currently a visiting research fellow at the Stanford Cyber Policy Center (Program on Platform Regulation). Her research focus is on intermediary liability, content moderation, freedom of expression, AI and platform regulation. She has worked on these topics, as well as privacy and data protection, media law and smart cities since 2010. Aleksandra is the author of the book 'Intermediary Liability and Freedom of Expression in the EU: from concepts to safeguards'. She participated in the works of several Expert Committees at the Council of Europe (on Internet Intermediaries, on Algorithms and Human Rights, on Freedom of Expression and Digital Technologies), responsible for drafting recommendations by the Committee of Ministers. Aleksandra is a lecturer of Media Law at the KU Leuven Master of Intellectual Property and ICT Law, and she supervises CiTiP's Media Law group conducting EU Horizon2020 projects on media and new technologies.

Christof Koolen is a PhD researcher at the KU Leuven, Faculty of Law (Consumer Competition Market). He currently prepares a dissertation on the Internet of Things, focusing on the implications of smart devices on the internal market and, more specifically, on EU consumer law. Before starting with his doctorate, Christof interned at various law firms in Brussels and provided legal advice on IP law issues to start-ups in the high-tech industry. He graduated with distinction from the KU Leuven (Belgium) in 2017 and obtained a Magister Juris degree from the University of Oxford (United Kingdom) in 2018.

Eva Lievens is Associate Professor of Law & Technology at the Faculty of Law and Criminology of Ghent University and a member of the Human Rights Centre, the UGent Human Rights Research Network, the Crime, Criminology & Criminal Policy Consortium, DELTA, ANSER and PIXLES. A recurrent focus in her research relates to the legal impact of the design and deployment of technology in today's society, human and children's rights in the digital environment, and the use of alternative regulatory instruments, such as self- and co-regulation to regulate tech phenomena. At Ghent University, Eva teaches 'European Media Law', 'European Law & ICT', 'Cybercrime, Technology & Surveillance', and 'Data Protection Law'.

Catherine Middag obtained her PhD in Engineering in the field of Speech Processing at Ghent University in 2012. She was the main researcher on the ASISTO project (Automatic Speech analysIs during Speech Therapy in Oncology). After being lecturer in Artificial Intelligence and head of the Knowledge Center AI at Erasmus University College Brussels for some years, Catherine is now senior researcher at Ghent University Hospital investigating the use and generation of synthetic medical data. Catherine is involved in several research projects concerning applications of Artificial Intelligence for healthcare. She works closely together with speech scientists and clinicians worldwide to find a good match between her technological skills and the needs in healthcare.

Ingrida Milkaite is a postdoctoral researcher at the Law & Technology research group at the Faculty of Law and Criminology of Ghent University. She currently focuses on children's rights in the context of children's voice data processing (research project funded by the Flanders Research Foundation (FWO)). Ingrida is a member of the Human Rights Centre, the UGent Human Rights Research Network, PIXLES and the European Communication Research and Education Association (ECREA). She obtained her PhD in 2021. Her doctoral research focused on a children's rights perspective on privacy and data protection in the digital age, and the implementation of the EU General Data Protection Regulation in that context.

Kevin Ongenae is a doctoral researcher at the Center for the Future of Dispute Resolution at Ghent University and a Belgian qualified attorney. He studied law at the universities of Ghent and Leiden and has practised as a commercial disputes lawyer since 2014. His research focuses on the impact of information technology on arbitral procedure.

Stephanie Rossello is a researcher at the Centre for IT and IP law (CiTiP) of KU Leuven. She obtained a Bachelor of Arts in Social Sciences at the Roosevelt Academy in Middelburg (The Netherlands) (*summa cum laude*, 2007), followed by a Master of Law at the KU Leuven (*magna cum laude*, 2011) and an LL.M. at the University of Chicago (2012). Before joining CiTiP, Stephanie practiced as a lawyer, member of the Brussels Bar specialising in Belgian contracts and tort law, complex construction litigation, European and Belgian antitrust law as well as data protection law. Stephanie was also a teaching assistant in public international law at KU Leuven and a legal consultant on GDPR for an international financial institution. At CiTiP Stephanie is currently working on the H2020 MUSKETEER project, where she is providing legal and ethical guidance on the development and use of machine learning algorithms to augment shared knowledge in federated privacy preserving scenarios. Her research interests include liability issues in the digital value chain, privacy engineering and legal analytics.

Dina Scornos is managing associate at Deloitte Legal and a PhD candidate at the Institute of Tax Law at KU Leuven. She studied law at KU Leuven and completed her studies *cum laude* in June 2011. During the academic year 2011–2012, Dina undertook a Masters in Taxation also at KU Leuven which she completed *magna cum laude* in June 2012. During that year she participated in the European and International Tax Moot Court Competition. She and her team won the competition and also several other prizes such as "best pleading team for applicant" and "best defendant memorandum". In 2012, Dina worked as a tax consultant at a large consultancy firm before registering as a lawyer-trainee in 2013 at the Brussels Bar. She became a qualified lawyer in 2016 while she was working at an international law firm dealing with tax matters, specialising in transfer pricing cases. She joined the Institute of Tax Law at the KU Leuven as a PhD candidate in 2017, working on her PhD relating to the impact of AI on international corporate taxation.

Nico Sergeyssels is applied researcher at the Knowledge Center AI of Erasmus University College Brussels. He is an experienced programmer in many languages and frameworks and is specialised in Natural Language Processing, especially topic modelling. His research focused on democratising AI by using Natural Language Processing techniques to facilitate intuitive use of data science tools. Currently, Nico is working as a Senior Software Development Engineer at KBC Bank & Verzekering.

Simon Taes is a PhD Candidate since September 2018 at the Institute for Labour Law (ILL) at KU Leuven. He obtained a Master's degree in Psychology cum laude at KU Leuven (specialisation in labour and occupational psychology). In addition, he obtained a Master's degree in Law cum laude at KU Leuven (specialisation in social and economic law). He attended several conferences and participated in the 36th Pontignano Seminar of Comparative Labour Law on the worker's mobility in the European Union. He also presented his papers about robotisation and labour law on several occasions. In 2019, he was invited to explain the impact of robotisation on the health and safety of employees at the ILO Centenary Conference at KU Leuven in cooperation with the ILO Office of Brussels. In 2021, he participated in the panel "Privacy @ work" at the Fifth Labour Law Research Network Conference organized by the Universities of Warsaw and Lodz. On this occasion, he presented his research about the impact of robotisation on the privacy of workers.

Bruno Van den Bosch is a former researcher at Consumer Competition Market (CCM) and a former affiliated researcher at the University of Leiden. He started his research on the application of mathematics and computational analysis to legal matters in the research master programme in law at KU Leuven, which he completed in 2020. Currently, Bruno is pursuing a degree in bioscience engineering at KU Leuven.

Carl Vander Maelen is a PhD candidate and academic assistant at the research group Law & Technology at Ghent University, Belgium. He commenced his doctoral research in February 2018 and studies codes of conduct based on Articles 40 and 41 GDPR, as well as the impact they have on corporate behavior and global data protection standards. For his work, he has received the 'Young Scholar Award – 1st Prize' during the 2018 Amsterdam Privacy Conference and the award for 'Best Postgraduate Article' during the 2019 BILETA Conference. He has completed internships at the Brussels data protection law firm Time.Lex and the Embassy of Belgium in Washington D.C.

Jozefien Vanherpe is assistant professor in intellectual property law at the KU Leuven Centre for IT and IP law (CiTiP). She studied law at KU Leuven and completed her studies *magna cum laude* in June 2013. During the academic year 2013–2014, Jozefien was enrolled in the LLM program at the University of Cambridge (UK). In June 2014, Jozefien obtained a First Class degree from the University of Cambridge as well as a Bateman Scholarship and the Ian Malcolm Lewis Prize for Law from her college, Trinity Hall. From 2014 through 2018,

Jozefien was active as a litigation attorney specialised in intellectual property law. In March 2022, she successfully defended her PhD at KU Leuven, on the legal framework surrounding contracts in the digitised music industry.

Peggy Valcke is Full Professor of Law and Technology (BOFZAP) at KU Leuven and Vice Dean for Research at the Faculty of Law and Criminology. She is co-director of the Centre for IT & IP Law, executive committee member of Leuven.AI, and principal investigator in the Security & Privacy Department of imec. She has taken up visiting and part-time positions at Tilburg University, Bocconi University, the European University Institute and Central European University. She served as elected Vice-Chair of the Council of Europe's Ad hoc Committee on Artificial Intelligence (CAHAI) and is currently Bureau member of its successor committee, CAI. She is co-director of the Flemish Knowledge Centre on Data and Society and has been assessor/judge at the Flemish Media Regulator since 2008 (and, between 2008 and 2021, assessor/judge at the Belgian Competition Authority).

Matthias Van Der Haegen is judicial trainee within the Belgian judiciary and invited professor of civil procedure at the Free University of Brussels. Until 2021, he was assistant professor at the Maastricht Law & Tech Lab (Maastricht University) and invited professor at Ghent University, where he taught legal history. He obtained his PhD in 2019 at Ghent University as a PhD fellow of the Research Foundation Flanders (FWO). Matthias studied law at the University of Oxford (M.Jur., 2015) and Ghent University (LL.M., 2014).

Elias Van Gool is a Candidate for a Dual PhD degree in law at KU Leuven (Belgium) and Université de Lille (France). He is a member of the research institutes Consumer Competition Market at KU Leuven and Droits et Perspectives du Droit (Équipe René Demogue) at Université de Lille. Elias studied law at KU Leuven (Research Master, 2014) and at Stanford Law School (LL.M., 2022). For his research, he was awarded the 2014 APR Prize and he is also a co-laureate of the 2021 Ius Commune Prize. From 2014 to 2018, he worked as an associate lawyer in the Belgian office of Baker McKenzie. Since 2019, Elias is a part-time teaching assistant and his doctoral research focuses on product liability in the context of circular economy and emerging digital technologies.

Sebastiaan Van Severen is a PhD candidate and academic assistant at the research group Public International Law at Ghent University, Belgium. Before acquiring his Master's Degree in Law at Ghent University, he completed internships at the political desk of the Belgian Embassy in Bangkok, at the UN Directorate of the Belgian Ministry of Foreign Affairs, and at the Human Rights and Law division of UNAIDS. His research focuses on the Russian approaches to public international law, with a recent focus on International Humanitarian Law.

Benjamin Verheye is a part-time post-doctoral researcher at the Institute for Property Law of the KU Leuven (Belgium). In December 2020, he defended his PhD dissertation on land registration in a comparative perspective. Apart from general property law, his research also concerns law and technology, law and sustainability and the crossroads of both. He approaches these topics mostly from a real estate and notarial angle. In 2019, he won the TPR-Price for a contribution on the future circular real estate. Benjamin is also a notarial trainee at the office of notary Dirk Hendrickx in Bruges. Furthermore, he is the managing editor of the European Review of Private law, a member the board of the Belgian Journal for Justices of the Peace and a correspondent for the Belgian Journal for Notaries.

Judith Vermeulen is a voluntary postdoctoral researcher at the Faculty of Law and Criminology of Ghent University, Belgium. There, she is a member of the Law & Technology research group, the Human Rights Centre and PIXLES. Judith obtained her PhD in July 2022 after she successfully defended her doctoral thesis "The Algorithmic State of Mind: A Human Rights Frame for Governing News Recommendation". The main research aim was to establish how existing legal rules, including human rights, apply to news recommendation practices and whether they require further regulation. The research formed part of a larger, interdisciplinary research project called #NewsDNA.

Jakob Markus Werbrouck holds a PhD in social security law from KU Leuven. After working as a doctoral researcher at the Institute for Social Law (ISR) for 5 years, he successfully defended his thesis on the multidimensional nature of the pension concept in December 2021. Prior to his position as a doctoral researcher, he studied law at KU Leuven, Trinity College Dublin, and the University of Cambridge. Jakob Markus currently works as a policy advisor to the Belgian federal Minister for Pensions.

Ellen Wauters holds a master's degree in Political Science (2001) and Law (2010). She has experience in media law, intellectual property and consumer law. Before joining CiTiP, she worked as a legal expert GDPR for the social secretariat for notaries, where she was responsible for GDPR compliance in the notary profession. At CiTiP she is part of the Knowledge Centre Data and Society and also works on the project Spectre, which focuses on smart cities.

Katerina Yordanova is a researcher at KU Leuven's Centre for IT & IP law, working on the intersection between AI, cybersecurity and human rights protection, including in the context of AI regulation. She studied law at Sofia University, acquired an advanced LL.M in International and European Public Law from KU Leuven as well as a postgraduate degree in English Law and EU Law from the University of Cambridge.

CHAPTER 1

BASIC CONCEPTS OF AI FOR LEGAL SCHOLARS

Rembrandt DEVILLÉ*, Nico SERGEYSSELS**
and Catherine MIDDAG***

1. INTRODUCTION

1. Artificial intelligence has become a *hot topic* due to major advances in the field. However, many people participate in the debate without having the necessary understanding of the subject. In this chapter, we will explain some basic concepts of AI that may be useful for legal scholars and practitioners. It will provide readers with the necessary background to fully understand the impact of AI on law.[1]

First, we provide a clear definition of AI and discuss the Turing Test. This test was a first controversial attempt to measure machine intelligence (part 2). We then focus on how AI works. We consider two main AI approaches, namely knowledge-based and data-based learning. The latter is gaining importance every day, mainly due to the massive production of data by the Internet of Things (IoT). Machine learning (ML) can be considered the core of the data-based approach. One very popular ML method is the artificial neural network (ANN), which is described as well. We briefly discuss how it works and focus on its evolution into deep learning (DL). This evolution results from the increased data production and computing power. While DL has been a quantum leap for AI, it also has some drawbacks. These will be covered as well (part 3). AI has several sub-disciplines, many of which rely on ML. We briefly discuss search algorithms, computer vision, natural language processing (NLP), speech processing and agents (part 4). Having touched upon the foundations of AI, we subsequently focus on the wide range of areas and fields in which AI is already used. We discuss the current state of the art and expected evolutions in

* Researcher Knowledge Center AI, Erasmus University College Brussels.
** Senior Software Development Engineer, KBC Bank & Verzekering.
*** Senior Researcher, University Hospital UZ Gent.

transportation, robotics, healthcare, education, public safety and security, art and entertainment, and law. We also look at the more distant future of AI (part 5). We conclude this chapter with some considerations regarding the ethical and safety aspects of AI (part 6).

2. DEFINING AND MEASURING AI

2.1. DEFINITION: WHAT IS AI?

2. Nowadays, AI is ubiquitous in the news. This results in a huge number of articles and (academic) papers on this technology. These texts are usually either overly optimistic or pessimistic[1] regarding the possibilities as well as the dangers and challenges of AI. Most of the time, those claims are a consequence of the fact that people are not properly informed about AI. This lack of knowledge already starts with the name as there is no clear, unambiguous and commonly used definition of the term artificial intelligence.

3. According to Wikipedia, 'AI is intelligence demonstrated by machines, unlike the natural intelligence displayed by humans and animals'.[2] This leaves us with two questions: what is intelligence and how can you demonstrate intelligence? The Merriam-Webster Dictionary defines intelligence as 'the ability to learn or understand or to deal with new or trying situations'.[3] According to David Wechsler, the designer of well-known intelligence tests, intelligence is 'the global capacity of a person to act purposefully, to think rationally, and to deal effectively with his environment'.[4] We can thus define AI as the ability/capacity of a machine to act purposefully, think rationally and deal effectively with its environment, like humans are ideally supposed to do. However, since human thinking and behaviour do not always imply rationality, Russell and others make a clear distinction: machines can either think like humans or think rationally, can either act like humans or act rationally. All these approaches are considered part of AI.[5] Note that intelligence, and thus AI as well, is evolving over time as we are building on knowledge gathered by previous generations.

---

1 L. Steels, 'Artificiële Intelligentie: Naar een vierde industriële revolutie', Koninklijke Vlaamse Academie van België voor Wetenschappen en Kunsten, KVAB standpunten, 2017, vol. 53, 44 p.

2 Wikipedia, 'Artificial Intelligence', http://en.wikipedia.org/wiki/Artificial_Intelligence.

3 Merriam-Webster Dictionary, 'Intelligence', https://www.merriam-webster.com/dictionary/intelligence.

4 D. Wechsler, *The measurement and appraisal of adult intelligence*, 4th edn (Baltimore: Williams & Wilkins Co, 1958), 297 p.

5 S. Russel and P. Norvig, *Artificial intelligence: a modern approach*, 2nd edn (New Jersey: Prentice Hall, 2002), 1080 p.

2.2. THE TURING TEST AND THE LOEBNER PRIZE

4. Considering the aforementioned definition of the concept of AI, the question remains which behaviour, thinking and actions can be qualified as 'human-like'. In 1950, Alan Turing designed a test to determine whether a machine could imitate human intelligence. This is now known as the Turing test.[6] Consider the following setup: person C interviews persons A and B. Person A and B are of opposite genders. All three persons are located in different rooms by means of a screen and keyboard. Person A lies about his/her gender, person B tells the truth. Person C has to guess the gender of person A and B. In the imitation game, a machine takes over A's role. According to Turing, the computer is able to think as a human if it is able to deceive as often as person A in the original game.

5. As can be expected, this test resulted in a lot of criticism from various scientific perspectives. One major critique relates to the question as to what is actually tested with this set-up. Turing's experiment seems to equate verbal communication and the ability to lie with intelligence, which is a rather controversial statement.[7]

6. Another criticism is that the proof of imitation of intelligence does not necessarily imply the proof of intelligence. A well-known thought-experiment used as an argument for this point is the so-called Chinese room. It was designed by the philosopher John Searle.[8] Imagine a person without any knowledge of the Chinese language locked in a room with boxes of Chinese symbols and an instruction book in English explaining how to manipulate the symbols. People outside the room then send Chinese symbols as input. The person inside the room can easily convert this input to a correct Chinese output by using the instruction book. For outsiders, it seems as if the person in the room perfectly understands Chinese even when this is not true. He only mimics this by using the instruction book. Searle concludes that 'The point of the argument is this: if the man in the room does not understand Chinese on the basis of implementing the appropriate program for understanding Chinese, then neither does any other digital computer solely on that basis because no computer has anything the man does not have'.[9]

7. Despite the controversial nature of the Turing test, it has been invaluable to the development of AI. One of the main legacies of the test is the Loebner

---

6 I. Turing, 'Computing machinery and intelligence-AM Turing', *Mind*, 1950, vol. 59, no. 236, p. 433.

7 A. Ayesh, 'Turing Test Revisited: A Framework for an Alternative', *arXiv preprint*, 2019, arXiv:1906.11068.

8 J. Searle, 'Minds, Brains and Programs', *Behavioral and Brain Science*, 1980, vol. 3, pp. 417–424.

9 J. Searle, 'Chinese room argument', *Scholarpedia*, 2009, vol. 4, no. 8, p. 3100.

Prize.[10] This annual competition uses the Turing test, albeit in modified form, to test the capabilities of chatbots in several areas. The most human-like chatbot wins the Prize. The ultimate goal is to find a chatbot that passes the Turing test and is thus capable of making the judge believe that it is a human. However, this goal has not been achieved so far. Although chatbots are increasingly more capable of having a human-like conversation, research by Jacquet and others shows that they lack the capability of answering complex questions and elaborating on their previous answers.[11] Following Turing's arguments, we can thus conclude that machines cannot think yet, although they are becoming increasingly good at learning how to imitate humans.

3. BASIC PRINCIPLES OF AI

3.1. KNOWLEDGE-BASED VERSUS DATA-BASED LEARNING

8. An important question is how AI actually learns to imitate humans. First, computers are designed to process information. AI systems, therefore, approach intelligence as a way of information processing.[12] In order to do so, a computer needs two important components: an internal way of representing this information and a way to transform this information into the desired output. This latter component contains the intelligence as a computer can only transform information into output if it has learned how to do so. Basically, two different approaches exist for this learning step, namely knowledge-based learning and data-based learning.

Knowledge-based approaches initially dominated AI research because data was still scarce. Typically, an expert in the field tried to pour his knowledge into a model (e.g., a set of rules, patterns or logical statements). This model was subsequently implemented as a series of instructions – and thus as an algorithm – in the machine to obtain its goal. Data-driven methods increasingly emerged. Systems were presented with many examples of inputs and the corresponding outputs. The system itself had to find or recognise patterns in order to provide correct answers. This process of deducing patterns and learning from examples/experience is called machine learning. It is considered to be the motor of AI. Nowadays both learning approaches are increasingly combined, for example in

---

10 H. Loebner, 'How to hold a Turing test contest', in R. Epstein, G. Roberts and G. Beber (eds), *Parsing the Turing test* (Dordrecht: Springer, 2009), pp. 173–179.

11 B. Jacquet and J. Baratgin, 'Mind-Reading Chatbots: We Are Not There Yet', *International Conference on Human Interaction and Emerging Technologies*, 2020, pp. 266–271.

12 Steels, 'Artificiële Intelligentie: Naar een vierde industriële revolutie', 44 p.

agents.[13] Whereas a data-based method is used to understand the input, acting upon it is handled by a knowledge-based approach. Both methods have their strengths and weaknesses. Data-based techniques are generally better to make optimal use of the immense amount of data that is now being produced or for performing pattern recognition. Knowledge-based techniques by contrast are better at reasoning rationally to come to the solution or at explaining in language what knowledge they contain or how they arrive at the solution.

3.2. INTERNET OF THINGS AND BIG DATA

9. During the last decade, smart devices have become increasingly more popular. Smart devices consist of a machine (e.g., watch, refrigerator or car) connected to a smaller (mostly electronical) apparatus that is used to detect changes in or around the machine (e.g., movement, heat, light, noise or pressure). This apparatus, also known as a sensor, sends its findings or data to other electronic devices, which can then rely on it. When this machine is able to connect with the user or with other machines through a network such as the internet, it is called a smart device. Typically, smart devices store their data or information in a so-called cloud. This is a cluster of interconnected computers with the purpose of providing massive data storage and processing power for many smaller devices with less memory and weaker computing power.[14]

10. Nowadays, large groups of smart devices are in some way interconnected, often through the cloud. This eventually leads to the Internet of Things in which these devices exchange information with each other without requiring a human to supervise each action.[15] Examples are manifold. Think of a smart watch monitoring the user's health and presenting this data on the user's smartphone. Another example is a smart home in which climate, lights or music are controlled by the user through an agent or smart device that knows all his/her preferences.[16] One can also think of smart cities where all traffic lights are interconnected to optimise traffic flows.[17] The IoT market is growing very

---

13 M.J. Wooldridge and N.R. Jennings, 'Intelligent agents: Theory and practice', The knowledge engineering review, 1995, vol. 10, no. 2, pp. 115–152; L. Padgham and M. Winikoff, *Developing intelligent agent systems: A practical guide*, 1st edn (Chichester: John Wiley & Sons, 2004), 240 p. Also see part 4.5.

14 See also: Z. Mahmood, *Connectivity Frameworks for Smart Devices: The Internet of Things from a Distributed Computing Perspective* (Derby: Springer, 2016), 356 p.

15 L. Atzori et al., 'The internet of things: A survey', *Computer networks*, 2010, vol. 54, no. 15, pp. 2787–2805.

16 D. Pavithra and R. Balakrishnan, 'IoT based monitoring and control system for home automation', *2015 global conference on communication technologies*, 2015, pp. 169–173.

17 P. Rizwan et al., 'Real-time smart traffic management system for smart cities by using Internet of Things and big data', *2016 international conference on emerging technological trends*, 2016, pp. 1–7.

rapidly. A recent study cites staggeringly high numbers regarding the growth of IoT. It also stresses the need to be mindful of privacy and security issues in order to protect the data generated by IoT from being used for malign purposes.[18] The rise of IoT implies that much data is being generated, giving AI the opportunity to learn from so-called big data. Everything that must be learned can be found in many examples (numerous input-output-pairs, called samples) or with a lot of characteristics (called features).

3.3. MACHINE LEARNING

11. An important subfield of AI that benefits from big data is machine learning. As already mentioned, ML aims to develop systems that learn models from data. According to Mitchell, a computer program is said to learn from data for a certain task if its performance with respect to that task improves after gaining experience in solving the specific task.[19] For an image classification task, for instance, the model may be designed to distinguish pictures of dogs from pictures of cats. The task of learning ('training') the model involves identifying parameters, structures and hidden concepts in the presented data ('training data set'). In the case of the previous example, the model would be presented with numerous images of cats and dogs aiming to learn to distinguish between those two categories. The learned model can subsequently be used to make a prediction for any new image of a cat or a dog. Applications of ML are manifold ranging from sales prediction and fraud detection to disease prediction.

12. Two subcategories of ML can be distinguished depending on how the learning happens: supervised and unsupervised learning. In supervised learning, the algorithm learns which output to associate with a certain input ('labelled data'). One can compare it to a child that learns to name animals through a parent showing and naming the specific animal on a picture. In unsupervised learning, the algorithm has only been given input without any output. Its main aim is to discover patterns and structures on its own ('unlabelled data'). Semi-supervised learning is a type of learning that combines both subcategories. For some part of the data, input and output are given, while for other parts only input is available.

In addition to supervised and unsupervised learning, a third subcategory of machine learning models is typically distinguished, namely reinforcement learning. In reinforcement learning, the intelligent agent needs to learn an optimal set of actions – a control policy – to achieve a certain goal. The algorithm

---

18 H. Espinoza et al., 'Estimating the impact of the Internet of Things on productivity in Europe', *Heliyon*, 2020, vol. 6, no. 5, e03935.

19 T. Mitchell, *Machine learning* (New York: McGraw-Hill, 1997), 414 p.

is not told how to do this but only receives feedback in the form of rewards. These rewards can be positive or negative experiences bringing the agent closer to or further away from the (desired) goal. This can be compared to how children learn to ride a bike. Parents typically do not explicitly tell their children how to learn to cycle. Instead, children themselves explore which actions positively or negatively contribute to learning how to ride the bike. They improve their biking skills by learning from these experiences.

3.4. ARTIFICIAL NEURAL NETWORKS AND DEEP LEARNING

13. An important class of supervised learners is formed by artificial neural networks (ANNs), which tend to perform very well in case of a large number of samples. ANNs are loosely inspired by the human neural system. The human nervous system consists of about 86 billion neurons.[20] These neurons receive electrical input signals from neighbouring cells and, depending on the input, produce an output. This output is then propagated to further neurons.

ANNs consist of a large number of artificial neurons that mimic the functioning of the biological neurons by reacting upon the input cells, and thus by letting their output depend on the input. A weighted sum of the input and a threshold is multiplied by a so-called activation function, resulting in the output of the neuron. A typical and simple architecture of an ANN is given in Figure 1. This ANN consists of three layers, being the input layer, the hidden layer and the output layer. The input layer consists of M inputs, called X_1, X_2, …, X_M in the example. Each input can be connected to each of the Q hidden neurons in which the inputs are transformed with linear combinations and an activation function, leading to values Z_1, Z_2, …, Z_Q. Each of the hidden neurons can then be connected to each of the output neurons in which the outputs of the hidden neurons are again transformed to obtain the final output values called Y_1, …, Y_P.

Let us illustrate this with an example. Imagine an ANN designed to forecast tomorrow's weather. Possible inputs could be characteristics of the weather today: hourly statistics of temperature, air pressure or humidity. These are the X_1, X_2, …, X_M in Figure 1. Tomorrow's weather could be defined by tomorrow's minimum and maximum temperature, humidity, hours of sunshine or probability of rain. These are the resulting values Y_1, …, Y_P. The hidden layer could then transform today's hourly statistics into a useful intermediate result such as global statistics of today's temperature or air pressure, which are then the resulting Z_1, Z_2, …, Z_Q. These mean values can then be combined to derive

20 J. Randerson, 'How many neurons make a human brain? Billions fewer than we thought', *The Guardian*, 28 February 2012, https://www.theguardian.com/science/blog/2012/feb/28/how-many-neurons-human-brain.

a forecast for tomorrow. Note that the hidden layer is not user-defined: the user cannot choose which intermediate results or steps are taken. Hence the name hidden layer. One does not know exactly what happens in that layer. Only input, output, and the number of neurons of the hidden layer are determined by the user. The other aspects are determined by the training algorithm. The training itself is done by giving the network many examples (e.g., which weather pattern from a certain day corresponds to which weather pattern for the day after?). The algorithm looks at every example and finetunes all linear combinations of the ANN until it succeeds at simulating the examples as good as possible. At that point, the linear combinations are fixed, and the neural network is ready to be used for new predictions.

Figure 1. Schematic of an artificial neural network with one hidden layer. Every circle denotes a computing node (neuron), resulting in the value marked within the node.[21]

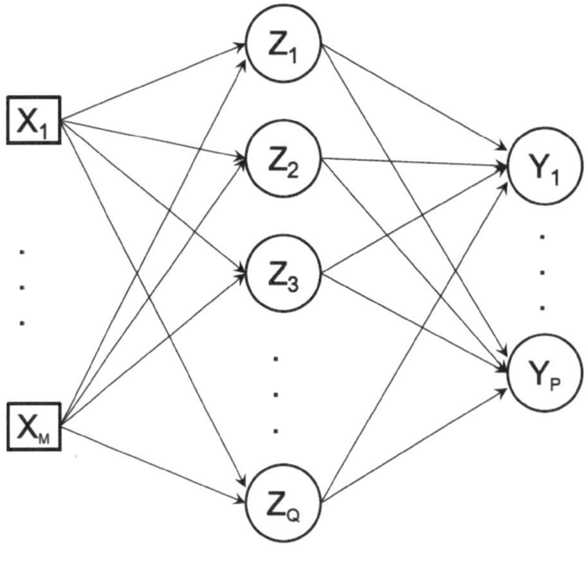

ANNs are used for a wide range of applications such as image recognition and speech recognition. One could, for example, build an ANN to make a distinction ('classify') between male and female voices. For this, thousands of examples of female and male voices would have to be recorded and presented to the ANN. A well-trained ANN will be able to distinguish correctly between all male and female voices it has seen during training. It will also be able to correctly classify new voices, which is of course the whole goal of training: learning how

[21] C. Middag, 'Automatic analysis of pathological speech', Doctoral dissertation UGent, 2012, 180 p., https://biblio.ugent.be/publication/3007443.

to continue to correctly distinguish between new male and female voices after training without any human guidance.

14. ANNs already exist since the 1940s[22] and have been improved ever since. Starting from a two-layered network that was not able to learn logical basic functions, robust training algorithms with a solid mathematical basis have been introduced. The number of layers has also been increased. Several configurations were introduced, including loops to make memory functions available. The biggest improvement, however, occurred only one decade ago. The increase in computing power and the rise of big data resulted in massive datasets to train huge networks on. It suddenly became possible to train ANNs with more than just a few layers. This is referred to as deep neural networks (DNNs). This deep learning technology led to major breakthroughs in several fields within AI.[23] Results in image and speech recognition based on deep learning were remarkably better than any other method that was used before. The results are impressive. Artificial intelligence based on deep learning now outclasses humans for some specific tasks in image recognition[24], which has significant consequences for our society. Suddenly self-driving cars, AI healthcare diagnosis tools and so many other futuristic applications come within reach.[25]

15. Although deep learning is reshaping the future of AI, many experts raise concerns about this technology. First, due to the high number of parameters to be trained in a DNN, the tuning of the parameters can become very complex. Finding the optimal values for all the linear combinations in the neural network can be compared to searching for the lowest point on a very bumpy surface in an extremely high-dimensional space. Often, only a local minimum will be found. As a result, training a DNN on the same data multiple times, thereby starting the search each time on a different random spot, often leads to finding another local minimum and thus to different settings for the network. Consequently, the behaviour of these slightly different networks can affect the overall performance.

A second weakness of DNNs is their brittleness. Slightly different input can lead to another linear combination being the strongest. This can result in a totally different output. Blurring a picture of a cat or slightly changing the background and angle of the picture can (already) lead to a failure of the system

22 R.S. Lee, 'AI Fundamentals', *Artificial Intelligence in Daily Life*, 2020, pp. 19–37.

23 M.R. Minar and J. Naher, 'Recent advances in deep learning: an overview', *arXiv preprint*, 2018, arXiv:1807.08169.

24 A. Krizhevsky et al., 'Imagenet classification with deep convolutional neural networks', *Advances in neural information processing systems*, 2012, pp. 1097–1105.

25 C. Badue et al., 'Self-driving cars: A survey', *Expert Systems with Applications*, 2020, vol. 165, p. 113816; K. H. Yu et al., 'Artificial intelligence in healthcare', Nature biomedical engineering, 2018, vol. 2, no. 10, pp. 719–731. We will briefly discuss this further in part 5.1.

to recognise the cat in the picture.[26] This of course makes it very easy to 'fool' a DNN. Changing only a few pixels in a picture of a lion, for instance, can suddenly make the DNN recognise it as a library.[27] This fragility of DNNs can also lead to dangerous situations[28], which have to be prevented in all cases.

Another concern relates to the fact that DNNs are so-called 'black box' models. Despite their high accuracy, it is very difficult to explain why a certain input leads to the predicted output. It can even be impossible to understand why the output was calculated in that very specific way. This lack of interpretability and explainability makes it sometimes ethically impossible to use these methods. The only information that can be retrieved is a mathematical formula consisting of non-linear combinations of the different inputs, which cannot be converted into an explanation a human would understand. One can easily imagine situations in which this explainability in human language of decisions made by AI is crucial. Take the example of an AI system used in dermatology. When a certain mole is identified as malignant, doctors would like to know why it is identified that way (e.g., size, colour, irregularity, etc.). However, a DNN only provides an answer in the form of benign/malign. Another example occurs when clients of a financial institutions are refused a loan based on a DNN. They of course would want to know the reason(s) of this refusal. In these and many other cases, one needs so-called 'explainable' AI[29], which does not only provide an output (a prediction) but also an explanation. This is a sort of 'followed path' through the flow chart of the model to show how it came to the specific prediction.

3.5. DATA BIAS AND MODEL BIAS

16. Another concern when using DNNs or, more generally, data-based learning algorithm relates to the data which is used to train the model. One simple rule is that the model cannot learn what it has never seen. Imagine training a classifier for tomatoes. Pictures of all kinds of red tomatoes are used to train this model. If this model has learned to identify tomatoes as being *red* objects, it will not be able to classify *yellow* cherry tomatoes as actual tomatoes. One should thus handle training data with care to prevent 'data bias'. This is a deviation of the true variety in the observed object's nature. There are numerous examples of problems associated with data bias, some of which having rather

---

[26] M. Mitchell, *Artificial intelligence: A guide for thinking humans*, 1st edn (Pelican: Penguin UK, 2019), 336 p.

[27] D. Heaven, 'Why deep-learning Ais are so easy to fool', *Nature*, 2019, vol. 574, pp. 163–166.

[28] See in this regard part 5.1.1.

[29] A.B. Arrieta et al., 'Explainable Artificial Intelligence (XAI): Concepts, taxonomies, opportunities and challenges toward responsible AI', *Information Fusion*, 2020, vol. 58, pp. 82–115.

dramatic consequences. Imagine that an algorithm-based passport photo-checker is mainly trained with white people. As a consequence, the pictures of Asian people can be rejected since their eyes seem more closed.[30] Google's image recognition algorithms accidentally categorised two black persons on a picture as gorillas.[31] The algorithm that Amazon used when scanning cover letters also appeared to discriminate against women.[32] To remedy this problem, Google has created a contest to develop better algorithms without racial data bias.[33]

Data-based learning algorithms can also be subject to model bias. Model bias describes how well a model matches the data used for training. If an inappropriate and often too simple a model structure has been chosen (e.g., a linear model for a quadratic curve), the model will not match with the data set. The model bias will be high. A low bias indicates a good match between the training data and the model. A possible solution for this problem is to opt for complex models to decrease the model bias. However, one must be very careful as more complex models tend to memorise every detail of the training data, thereby losing sight of the bigger picture. Consequently, complex models may not be able to generalise towards new data even if this new data is only slightly different from the training data. The latter problem is referred to as 'overfitting'. The balance between these two problems is also known as the bias-variance trade-off problem.[34]

4. AI SUB-DISCIPLINES

17. Before we delve deeper into its numerous applications, we briefly touch upon a few sub-disciplines of AI to clarify a number of concepts. As ML has already been addressed above, we will not discuss it again in the following paragraphs.

---

30 S. Cheng, 'An algorithm rejected an Asian man's passport photo for having "closed eyes"', *Quartz*, 7 December 2016, https://qz.com/857122/an-algorithm-rejected-an-asian-mans-passport-photo-for-having-closed-eyes/.

31 J. Vincent, 'Google 'fixed' its racist algorithm by removing gorillas from its image-labeling tech', *The Verge*, 12 January 2018, https://www.theverge.com/2018/1/12/16882408/google-racist-gorillas-photo-recognition-algorithm-ai.

32 J. Dastin, 'Amazon scraps secret AI recruiting tool that showed bias against women', *Reuters*, 10 October 2018, https://www.reuters.com/article/us-amazon-com-jobs-automation-insight/amazon-scraps-secret-ai-recruiting-tool-that-showed-bias-against-women-idUSKCN1MK08G.

33 T. Doshi, 'Introducing the Inclusive Images Competition', *Google AI blog*, 6 September 2018, https://ai.googleblog.com/2018/09/introducing-inclusive-images-competition.html. Also see Chapter 6 for more information.

34 P. Mehta et al., 'A high-bias, low-variance introduction to machine learning for physicists', *Physics reports*, 2019, vol. 810, pp. 1–124.

4.1. SEARCH ALGORITHMS

18. Search algorithms were among the first AI applications to break through. As the word suggests, search algorithms look for the optimal path to reach a goal, thereby starting from an initial state. These mostly knowledge-based algorithms are used to, for example, solve games (chess, checkers, Go, …), find optimal routes or schedule classes/industrial pipelines. They are also of major importance considering that they are often used to find the best configuration of parameter settings for many ML algorithms.

4.2. COMPUTER VISION

19. Computer vision can be seen as a machine learning problem. The data consists of images or movies. This data is subsequently analysed by using machine learning techniques to understand what can be seen on the image/movie. With the introduction of deep learning, a lot of progress has been made. The progress made since 2015 is even so extensive that computer vision is (already) performing as well as humans for some tasks. The error rate 'of the top 5'[35] in naming objects in images (with thousand classes) decreased from 28.2% in 2010 to 6.7% in 2014.[36] Automatic facial recognition systems are now reliably used in China to provide access to buildings or to transfer money.[37] Moreover, research shows that computer vision can detect skin cancer more accurately than dermatologists.[38] Similarly, it outperforms medical doctors at detecting breast cancer.[39]

4.3. NATURAL LANGUAGE

20. Although DNNs have resulted in major leaps in the capabilities of AI, understanding human language remains a great challenge. The field of Natural Language Processing (NLP), which focuses on processing and understanding written text, is still one of the most challenging sub-disciplines of AI. In addition

---

35 Top 5 means that the correct object has to be in the top 5 of suggested possibilities of the learner.

36 O. Russakovsky et al., 'Imagenet large scale visual recognition challenge', *International journal of computer vision*, 2015, vol. 115, no. 3, pp. 211–252.

37 W. Knight, 'Paying with your face: 10 Breakthrough Technologies', *MIT Technology Review*, 22 February 2017, https://mittr-frontend-prod.herokuapp.com/s/603494/10-breakthrough-technologies-2017-paying-with-your-face/.

38 T.J. Brinker et al., 'Deep learning outperformed 136 of 157 dermatologists in a head-to-head dermoscopic melanoma image classification task', *European Journal of Cancer*, 2019, vol. 113, pp. 47–54.

39 P. Galey, 'AI Is Now Officially Better at Diagnosing Breast Cancer Than Human', *Science Alert*, 3 January 2020, https://www.sciencealert.com/ai-is-now-officially-better-at-diagnosing-breast-cancer-than-human-experts.

to the actual understanding of the written language, AI is also used to generate language. The field of Natural Language Generation (NLG) is relied upon to construct answers for chatbots as well as for summarising or paraphrasing. Although the performances for the parsing of texts, the naming of parts of the sentence and the detection of spam are already quite advanced[40], sentiment analysis and translating texts remain harder to realise for NLP. Interpreting complex speech and having a true conversation are still far from solved problems.[41] Moreover, NLP still struggles with every typical human aspect of language such as emotions, styles, ambiguities, or synonyms.[42]

4.4. SPEECH

21. Whereas NLP deals with the processing of written text, automatic speech recognisers (ASRs) are used to understand spoken language. Similarly to NLP/NLG, speech recognition has a counterpart, namely speech synthesis. It aims to produce speech that is as intelligible and natural as possible. Once again, the use of deep learning has led to a major advance in the field. Recognition errors dropped from 23% to 8% for the English Google ASR.[43] Similar trends are visible in Microsoft's ASR system.[44] As is the case for NLP, however, speech recognition is still far away from achieving a human level. It is also very sensitive to many external factors, which merely are the consequences of training material and data bias.[45] As an ASR learns through data, its results ultimately depend on the quality and variation within the training dataset that is used. An ASR trained on clean speech of native English-speaking adults, for instance, will have difficulties understanding children (who have a higher pitch and less articulation skills) or dialects (cf. unseen is unknown). Such systems will also perform poorly in noisy conditions.

Starting in the 1970s with so-called formant-based synthesisers producing the typical robot-like mechanical voices[46], the clarity and naturalness of the produced speech has been an issue for a long time. A first improvement was the introduction of the waveform concatenation-based methods concatenating

---

40 C. Rădulescu et al., 'Identification of spam comments using natural language processing techniques', *2014 IEEE 10th International Conference on Intelligent Computer Communication and Processing*, 2014, pp. 29–35.

41 Jacquet and Baratgin, 'Mind-Reading Chatbots: We Are Not There Yet', pp. 266–271.

42 Z. Kaddari et al., 'Natural Language Processing: Challenges and Future Directions', *International Conference on Artificial Intelligence & Industrial Applications*, 2020, pp. 236–246.

43 J. Novet, 'Google says its speech recognition technology now has only an 8%-word error rate', *VentureBeat*, 28 May 2015, https://venturebeat.com/2015/05/28/google-says-its-speech-recognition-technology-now-has-only-an-8-word-error-rate/.

44 W. Xiong et al., 'The Microsoft 2017 conversational speech recognition system', *2018 IEEE international conference on acoustics, speech, and signal processing*, 2018, pp. 5934–5938.

45 Also see *supra* part 3.5.

46 Y. Ning et al., 'A review of deep learning-based speech synthesis', *Applied Sciences*, 2019, vol. 9, no. 19, p. 4050.

little pieces of voice together to produce the smoothest possible sentence. Nowadays, mainly statistical parametric speech synthesis methods are used. These methods use some form of data-based learner to predict how the text should sound (e.g., pitch, volume, emphasis, etc.). With the introduction of deep learning, the intelligibility and naturalness of the synthesised speech have improved significantly.[38] Yet, some major challenges (still) remain unsolved. Expressive language or putting the emphasis on the correct word/syllable, for instance, remain difficult. This requires that the text is correctly and rightly interpreted, which brings us back to the challenges related to NLP.

4.5. AGENTS

22. An emerging field in which knowledge-based techniques have become very important is the domain of the autonomous agents. These applications interact with their users – being either humans or other computer programs – and perform certain tasks for them. To do so, they have to understand the meaning and the intent of the user's questions/commands. Therefore, they need a language production/understanding component. They should be able to look up things on the web themselves, give answers in natural language and perform the desired actions such as checking the weather, making reservations or buying products.[47] Famous examples of such agents are SIRI[48], Google Assistant[49], Microsoft Cortana[50] and Alexa.[51] These agents have already been compared in the literature.[52]

5. THE CURRENT AND FUTURE USE OF AI APPLICATIONS

5.1. AN OVERVIEW OF SOME AI APPLICATIONS IN THE PRESENT AND NEAR FUTURE

23. As already mentioned, AI is not new. It has been evolving since the 1940s with ups and downs (cf. AI 'winters' and 'summers').[53] Due to recent

47 Steels, 'Artificiële Intelligentie: Naar een vierde industriële revolutie', 44 p.

48 Apple, 'Siri', https://www.apple.com/siri/.

49 Google, 'Google Assistant', https://assistant.google.com/.

50 Microsoft, 'Cortana', https://www.microsoft.com/en-us/cortana.

51 Amazon, 'Alexa User Guide: Learn What Alexa Can Do', https://www.amazon.com/b?ie=UTF8&node=17934671011.

52 G. López et al., 'Alexa vs. Siri vs. Cortana vs. Google Assistant: a comparison of speech-based natural user interfaces', *International Conference on Applied Human Factors and Ergonomics*, 2017, pp. 241–250.

53 M. Haenlein and A. Kaplan, 'A brief history of artificial intelligence: On the past, present, and future of artificial intelligence', *California management review*, 2019, vol. 61, no. 4, pp. 5–14.

breakthroughs in computing power, data availability and deep learning, however, it is again attracting a lot of attention. The expectations of AI in the future are thus very high. Nevertheless, the media often portray scenarios on the use and capacities of AI systems that may be unrealistic. We will, therefore, focus on more realistic expectations in this part, thereby relying on scientific research. At Stanford University, the 100 Year Study Panel[54] gathers experts in different subfields of AI from both academia and industry. The aim of the Panel is to examine the evolution of AI during a century. Every few years, it meets to review recent changes and trends. Based on this analysis, predictions of future developments in the field are made. In their most recent report dating from 2016, the experts foresee a significant rise of AI applications across a wide range of industries such as transportation, robots, healthcare and education by 2030.[55] Without being exhaustive[56], we discuss some important areas in which AI will arguably be extensively used during the coming decade.

5.1.1. Transportation

24. Experts agree that future transportation will be electric and autonomous.[57] Computer vision used in self-driving cars is less prone to errors than human vision thanks to deep learning. The same goes for a vehicle's responses to traffic risks. Self-driving cars will bring commuters to their workplace allowing them to relax or prepare their working day. This will lead to less stress and safer traffic. Youths, the elderly and disabled will also benefit from an increased mobility. According to Stone and others, autonomous transportation will not be limited to cars but will also involve trucks or drones.[58] As powerful as current computer vision algorithms may be, they still have vulnerabilities that can potentially be very dangerous. These should definitely be addressed before the mass introduction of self-driving cars. Research has shown that simple adversarial crafted stickers can cause errors in road sign and image recognition models.[59] Sometimes, a few pixels can make the difference between a correct and an

54 Stanford University, 'One Hundred Year Study on Artificial Intelligence (AI100)', https://ai100.stanford.edu/.

55 P. Stone et al., 'Artificial Intelligence and Life in 2030. One hundred year study on artificial intelligence: Report of the 2015–2016 Study Panel', Stanford University, September 2016, 52 p.

56 An example is the use of AI for sustainability (see in this regard H. Skaug Sætra, *AI for the Sustainable Development Goals* (London: Routledge, 2022), 120 p.).

57 See: Steels, 'Artificiële Intelligentie: Naar een vierde industriële revolutie', 44 p.; Stone et al., 'Artificial Intelligence and Life in 2030. One hundred year study on artificial intelligence: Report of the 2015–2016 Study Panel', 52 p.

58 Stone et al., 'Artificial Intelligence and Life in 2030. One hundred year study on artificial intelligence: Report of the 2015–2016 Study Panel', 52 p.

59 K. Eykholt et al., 'Robust physical-world attacks on deep learning visual classification', *Proceedings of the IEEE Conference on Computer Vision and Pattern Recognition*, 2018, pp. 1625–1634.

incorrect recognition.[60] Current research focuses on the defence against these and other so-called adversarial attacks.

Another important application domain of AI within transportation consists of transportation planning and the regulation of traffic dynamics. With the rise of IoT, traffic can easily be monitored and thus planned in an optimal way to reduce traffic jams and travel time using among others search and planning algorithms.

5.1.2. Robots

25. Robots are examples of so-called cyber-physical systems (CPS): deeply intertwined combinations of a controlling software component and mechanical or electronic parts.[61] Self-driving vehicles are a special subclass of robots. The control, monitoring, data transfer and data exchange can take place locally, on an embedded computer or over the internet. Other examples of cyber-physical systems are monitored sensor networks or IoT devices. Robots can be seen as a more local CPS application concentrated in one machine and designed specifically to replace humans in one or more situations. One can in this regard also think of 'cloud robotics', which refers to the integration of physical robotic systems with cloud-based services.[62]

There are several views on the breakthrough of robots in our daily life. Stone and others suggest that home robotics will find their way in households because of advances in AI and mechanics.[63] Steels by contrast is somewhat more reserved as some mechanical issues including battery life, safety and production are still unresolved.[64] Therefore, robots are more likely to be found in industrial production environments for assembly and quality control. Robots are very good at accurately and reliably locating, moving and positioning objects. As such, they are often used to automate repetitive and sometimes dangerous jobs. Examples are welding robots, gun painting robots, CNC machines or packaging robots for chocolates.[65] However, manipulation tasks such as folding clothes or emptying the dishwasher remain extremely difficult.

---

[60] T. Maliamanis and G.A. Papakostas, 'Adversarial computer vision: a current snapshot', *Twelfth International Conference on Machine Vision*, 2020, vol. 11433, p. 1143328.

[61] E.A. Lee, 'Cyber physical systems: Design challenges', *2008 11th IEEE International Symposium on Object and Component-Oriented Real-Time Distributed Computing*, 2008, pp. 363–369. Also see: European Parliament, 'Ethical Aspects of Cyber-Physical Systems', Scientific Foresight study, June 2016, 48 p.

[62] See in this regard also E. Fosch-Villaronga and C. Millard, 'Cloud robotics law and regulation: Challenges in the governance of complex and dynamic cyber--physical ecosystems', *Robotics and Autonomous Systems*, 2019, vol. 119, pp. 77–91.

[63] Stone et al., 'Artificial Intelligence and Life in 2030. One hundred year study on artificial intelligence: Report of the 2015–2016 Study Panel', 52 p.

[64] Steels, 'Artificiële Intelligentie: Naar een vierde industriële revolutie', 44 p.

[65] H. Van Brussel et al., 'Naar een inclusieve Robotsamenleving: Robotisering, automatisering en werkgelegenheid', *KVAB Press*, 2016, 47 p. Also see Chapter 11.

While many robots in industrial applications are deployed in the workplace, another smaller type of robot is gradually on the rise: the collaborative robot or 'cobot'. A cobot is specially designed to work with humans. It is often smaller than the average robot and equipped with sufficient safety measures to ensure that cooperation with humans takes place in a responsible way. However, a major problem with cobots is the level of human-computer interaction.[66]

5.1.3. Healthcare

26. Countless AI-based applications are currently being developed or investigated for use in healthcare. Those applications are based on all possible subfields of AI. It has already been mentioned that recent breakthroughs even resulted in computer vision being stronger than doctors for the recognition of some types of cancers. This technology can be relied upon by doctors to diagnose diseases. Genes are being analysed by AI systems to unravel hidden patterns between human constitution and the risk for diseases[67] as well as to develop personalised medicines. These medicines are further refined considering a patient's individual needs.[68] Voices are also being analysed to detect articulation problems[69], depression, drug intake or dementia.[70] All these applications have promising results that can be used in daily practice in the near future.[71]

Moreover, medical insights are gathered automatically from assimilating a large number of medical databases with NLP techniques.[72] Chatbots are being built to help patients find the right care or hospital (e.g., in times of the COVID-19 pandemic[73]). Electronic health records are completed and analysed automatically to ensure a better follow-up of patients.[74] AI-powered robots are

---

66 See for more information J.E. Michaelis et al., 'Collaborative or Simply Uncaged? Understanding Human-Cobot Interactions in Automation', *Proceedings of the 2020 CHI Conference on Human Factors in Computing Systems*, 2020, pp. 1–12.

67 J. Li et al., 'Decoding the genomics of abdominal aortic aneurysm', *Cell*, 2018, vol. 174, no. 6, pp. 1361–1372.

68 E.C. Nice, 'The status of proteomics as we enter the 2020s: Towards personalised/precision medicine', *Analytical Biochemistry*, 2020, p. 113840.

69 C. Middag et al., 'Robust automatic intelligibility assessment techniques evaluated on speakers treated for head and neck cancer', *Computer speech & language*, 2014, vol. 28, no. 2, pp. 467–482.

70 B. Desplanques and K. Demuynck, 'Cross-lingual speech emotion recognition through factor analysis', *19th Annual Conference of the International-Speech-Communication-Association*, 2018, pp. 3648–3652.

71 See for an extensive overview: E. Fosch-Villaronga and H. Drukarch, *AI for Healthcare Robotics* (London: Routledge, 2022), 136 p.

72 C. Luque et al., 'An advanced review on text mining in medicine', *Wiley Interdisciplinary Reviews: Data Mining and Knowledge Discovery*, 2019, vol. 9, no. 3, e1302.

73 A.S. Miner et al., 'Chatbots in the fight against the COVID-19 pandemic', *npj Digital Medicine*, 2020, vol. 3, no. 1, pp. 1–4.

74 P. Yadav et al., 'Mining Electronic Health Records (EHRs): A Survey', *ACM Computing Surveys*, 2018, vol. 50, no. 6, pp. 1–40.

also used to assist doctors during precision surgery.[75] In addition to working with humans, robots can also become part of the human. Powered exoskeletons can be seen as wearable robots designed to restore locomotion of parts of the human body.[76] Researchers are also working towards intelligent prosthetics controlled by neural impulses, which are understood by AI.[77]

27. Although the development and use of AI in healthcare is taking important steps and is indeed looking very promising, a human doctor remains indispensable. To begin with, the doctor must always ensure that no 'wrong' decisions are made by the AI system. Moreover, acting in an empathetic way remains very difficult for AI systems. Ensuring this human element, which is crucial in a doctor-patient relationship, is not feasible by AI yet. Therefore, we wish to emphasise that AI is there to serve humans and not to replace them. Or, to cite Professor Langlotz: 'AI will not replace radiologists, but radiologists who use AI will replace radiologists who do not'.[78]

5.1.4. Education

28. The need for personalised education has been steadily growing for decades. AI is a powerful tool to satisfy this need. Already for a long time, researchers focus on the development of interactive intelligent tutors. These systems are capable of interacting with the student at his/her own pace and level, thereby giving personal feedback and personalising the exercises. Nowadays, the internet is full of Massive Online Open Courses (MOOCs) that provide direct and free education to very large groups of people, including those who normally do not have access to high-quality education. As a result, people from all over the world can now follow courses offered by the world's top universities. Participants are induced to join group discussions and receive automated (AI powered) feedback on their assignments.

On a smaller scale, speech recognition-based tutors teach children how to read[79] or help those with dyslexia by improving their reading skills.[80] Both

---

[75] M.G. Fujie and B. Zhang, 'State-of-the-art of intelligent minimally invasive surgical robots', *Frontiers of Medicine*, 2020, pp. 1–13.

[76] A.S. Gorgey, 'Robotic exoskeletons: The current pros and cons', *World journal of orthopedics*, 2018, p. 112.

[77] J.S. Hussain et al., 'Recognition of new gestures using myo armband for myoelectric prosthetic applications', *International Journal of Electrical & Computer Engineering*, 2020, vol. 9, no. 9, p. 2088.

[78] As reported in S. Reardon, 'Rise of Robot Radiologists', *Nature*, 19 December 2019, https://www.nature.com/articles/d41586-019-03847-z.

[79] J. Duchateau et al., 'Developing a reading tutor: Design and evaluation of dedicated speech recognition and synthesis modules', *Speech Communication*, 2009, vol. 51, no. 10, pp. 985–994.

[80] T. Athanaselis et al., 'Making assistive reading tools user friendly: a new platform for Greek dyslexic students empowered by automatic speech recognition', *Multimedia tools and applications*, 2014, vol. 68, no. 3, pp. 681–699.

ASRs and NLP are increasingly being used to teach students a second language or a specific way of articulating.[81] AI can also be used to automatically subtitle a lecturer's speech and translate his/her presentation. This way, lectures will in the future become available even for those with another mother tongue.

5.1.5. Public Safety and Security

29. Already for some time now, AI is often relied upon in the safety and security domain. Surveillance cameras can recognise license plates, even in suboptimal circumstances.[82] Facial recognition is also used in many places. China deploys this technology in stores, schools, and airports.[83] Computer vision is strong enough to detect anomalies in human behaviour, potentially able to identify criminal acts. In addition to computer vision, AI has proven to be very good and efficient at fraud detection and combatting white-collar criminality in general.[84] Another application of AI in security relates to defence. While computer vision methods can be used to save human lives, for example by deploying drones and robots to explore the terrain, they can also easily be abused for warfare purposes.[85]

5.1.6. Arts and Entertainment

30. AI can also be relied upon to support or create art and entertainment. Applications in this area are manifold. Think of all the video games that use AI to enhance interaction with the player. AI can be used to create the story lines or the game level generation as well. Moreover, AI may be able to learn a certain painting style, create new paintings or learn to transfer styles from one painting to another.[86] AI can even learn how to create music in a specific style. Think of the development of computer programme Experiments in Musical Intelligence (EMI). It can analyse existing music and create new compositions in the style of the original music without any human intervention.[87]

---

81 C.S.C. Dalim et al., 'Using augmented reality with speech input for non-native children's language learning', *International Journal of Human-Computer Studies*, 2020, vol. 134, pp. 44–64; H.T. Bunnell et al., 'STAR: articulation training for young children', Sixth International Conference on Spoken Language Processing, 16–20 October 2020, pp. 1–4.

82 W. Weihong and T. Jiaoyang, 'Research on License Plate Recognition Algorithms Based on Deep Learning in Complex Environment', *IEEE Access*, 2020, vol. 8, pp. 91661–91675.

83 S. Shead, 'Chinese residents worry about rise of facial recognition', *BBC News*, 5 December 2019, https://www.bbc.com/news/technology-50674909.

84 Stone et al., 'Artificial Intelligence and Life in 2030. One hundred year study on artificial intelligence: Report of the 2015–2016 Study Panel', 52 p.

85 T. Walsh, 'Autonomous Weapons: An Open Letter from AI & Robotics Researchers', *Future of Life*, 28 July 2015, https://futureoflife.org/open-letter-autonomous-weapons/. Also see Chapter 7 of this book.

86 L.A. Gatys et al., 'Image style transfer using convolutional neural networks', *Proceedings of the IEEE conference on computer vision and pattern recognition*, 2016, pp. 2414–2423.

87 Also see Chapter 9.

All these learners are based on recent developments in deep learning and succeed quite well in mimicking a human style. Nevertheless, they only do so for a short time (music) or on a particular surface (painting). Learners seem to lack the knowledge of the broader picture. In a recent study, AI-created paintings were evaluated significantly lower than those created by humans.[88] This indicates that the gap between human and computer art is far from bridged. Another example is the movie Sunspring.[89] The script – including stage directions – was completely generated by NLP. With a score of 5.7 on the Internet Movie Database IMDB[90], it is certainly not the worst movie ever made. However, there is still a major difference between movies created by AI and humans.

5.1.7. Law

31. The first applications of AI in the domain of law already stem from 1956. This was the year in which logic was introduced as a tool for drafting and interpreting legal documents.[91] Scholars started to use the phrase AI and law in the 1970s.[92] This was also the moment that Taxman was developed to determine whether or not a given re-organisation of companies was exempt from income tax.[93] Since then, many applications of AI in the legal sphere were developed, eventually leading to the foundation of the International Conference on AI and LAW (ICAIL), which was first held in Boston in May 1987.[94] The International Association for AI and Law (IAAIL) was established in 1991 followed by the launch of the Journal of Artificial Intelligence and Law in 1992. In Europe, the first conference of the 'Stichting Juridische Kennissystemen' (Foundation for Legal Knowledge Systems) was held in 1988.[95] A major overview of AI and law can be found in the work of Bench-Capon and others. They summarise the highlights of 25 years of the ICAIL.[96] The many contributions in this book

---

88 M. Ragot et al., 'AI-generated vs. Human Artworks. A Perception Bias Towards Artificial Intelligence?', *Extended Abstracts of the 2020 CHI Conference on Human Factors in Computing Systems*, 2020, pp. 1–10.

89 A. Newitz, 'Movie written by algorithm turns out to be hilarious and intense', *Arstechnica*, 9 June 2016, https://arstechnica.com/gaming/2016/06/an-ai-wrote-this-movie-and-its-strangely-moving/.

90 IMDB, 'Sunspring', 9 June 2016, https://www.imdb.com/title/tt5794766/?ref_=fn_al_tt_1.

91 L.E. Allen, 'Symbolic logic: A razor-edged tool for drafting and interpreting legal documents', *Yale L.J.*, 1957, vol. 66, no. 6., pp. 833–879.

92 B.G. Buchanan and T.E. Headrick, 'Some Speculation about Artificial Intelligence and Legal Reasoning', Stanford Law Review, 1970, vol. 23, no. 1, pp. 40–62 as reported in F. Coenen and T. Bench-Capon, 'A Brief History of AI and Law', 12 December 2017, AI & Law Workshop, https://cgi.csc.liv.ac.uk/~frans/KDD/Seminars/historyOfAIandLaw_2017-12-12.pdf.

93 L.T. McCarty, 'Reflections on TAXMAN: An experiment in artificial intelligence and legal reasoning', *Harvard Law Review,* 1977, vol. 90, no. 5, pp. 837–893.

94 See: https://dl.acm.org/conference/icail.

95 Coenen and Bench-Capon, 'A Brief History of AI and Law'.

96 T. Bench-Capon et al., 'A history of AI and law in 50 papers: 25 years of the international conference on AI and law', *Artificial intelligence and Law,* 2012, vol. 20, no. 3, pp. 215–319.

illustrate that AI has a major impact on almost every legal domain ranging from intellectual property and human rights to liability, labour, consumer protection, legal procedure and data protection.

5.2. AI IN THE MORE DISTANT FUTURE

32. This chapter shows that AI is on the rise. We, therefore, expect great things from this technology in the near and distant future. Yet, it remains difficult to predict how AI will evolve and what limitations it may have. Some argue that AI will soon reach the point of 'singularity'.[97] This is the point at which AI systems will outsmart humans. Others predict that by the end of the 21st century a so-called superintelligence will emerge. Bostrom defines this as 'any intellect that greatly exceeds the cognitive performance of humans in virtually all domains of interest'.[98] To date, however, there are no indications that artificial general intelligence (also referred to as strong AI) is possible. General AI refers to a system that is intelligent in all domains just like humans. All currently developed AI applications focus on just one domain. They are examples of what is called narrow or weak AI. Such systems can perform a specific task very well, in some cases even better than humans (e.g., facial recognition). All-round AI applications perform very poorly and do not even come close to human performance level. Let us refer to the Chinese room experiment again.[99] The fact that DNNs mimic human intelligence very well does not prove they are intelligent. So-called strong AI that is able to think on its own is still science-fiction. Currently, only weak AI exists. Put differently, 'Unlike in the movies, there is no race of superhuman robots on the horizon or probably even possible'.[100]

6. CONCLUSION

33. Although there is still much room for improvement in almost every sub-discipline, AI has already proven to be a powerful, strengthening, and complementary ally of mankind. This will probably not be different in the future. This chapter started by acknowledging that artificial intelligence is a hype nowadays. The many claims, statements, media coverage and opinions

---

97 R. Kurzweil, *The singularity is near: When humans transcend biology*, 1st edn (New York: Viking Penguin, 2005), 652 p.

98 N. Bostrom, *Superintelligence: Paths, dangers, strategies*, (Oxford: Oxford University Press, 2014), 328 p.

99 See the discussion *supra* part 2.2.

100 See the many experts in: Stone et al., 'Artificial Intelligence and Life in 2030. One hundred year study on artificial intelligence: Report of the 2015–2016 Study Panel', 52 p.

regarding (the capacities of) AI are not necessarily scientifically true.[101] This shows the importance of proper education and the creation of awareness of AI. More people need to be informed about the capacities as well as limitations and challenges of AI.

34. While AI is becoming increasingly important in our society, it is essential to address ethical and privacy issues as well. Although AI may become better than humans for some specific actions, it will (still) make several mistakes a human would never make. AI systems may also unintentionally discriminate or even harm certain categories and groups of the population. A thorough debate should be held regarding the responsibilities for such behaviour and the ethical consequences. Moreover, guidelines and codes of conduct should be adopted. This should not only be done *ex post* once a system is built but should be included right from the start as part of the system design (cf. the 'by design' approach).

---

[101] R. Brooks, 'The Seven Deadly Sins of AI Predictions', *MIT Technology Review*, 6 October 2017, https://www.technologyreview.com/2017/10/06/241837/the-seven-deadly-sins-of-ai-predictions/.

CHAPTER 2

DIFFERENT MODELS OF INNOVATION AND THEIR RELATION TO LAW

Charles DELMOTTE*

1. INTRODUCTION

1. An innovation is the application of a new or significantly improved product (good or service) or process; a new marketing method; or a new organisational method in business practices, workplace organisation, or external relations.[1] It involves the realisation that products, services, means of production, marketing strategies, delivery methods, and business structures do not take a fixed form but rather are subject to change, either incremental or radical. This chapter concerns innovation policy and what governments ought to do to secure the process by which companies inject novelty into the market. Therefore, it deals with different legal rules for commercial innovations. It does not deal with the underproduction of basic research within an economy or, for instance, the task of the state to produce basic research. Our economies have been engaging with innovation at a rapid pace, and research now revolves around the question of how the tax code can streamline and promote this evolution. Governments have adopted this goal: to 'promote innovation, encourage the development of new technologies and increase the fund of human knowledge'. Tax law is seen as one of the main toolkits by lawyers, economists, and policymakers.[2] National economies are competing internationally for the price of the most innovative economy, and our tax codes have been subject to fierce innovation too. In a political environment where governments are pushed to 'create growth', favourable R&D treatment has now turned into the panacea of innovation

* Assistant Professor of Law at Michigan State University College of Law.

1 D. Harper, 'Innovation and Institutions from the Bottom Up: An Introduction', *Journal of Institutional Economics*, 2018, vol. 14, no. 6, pp. 975–1001.

2 D. Burk and M. Lemley, 'Policy Levers in Patent Law', *Virginia Law Review*, 2003, vol. 89, no. 7, p. 1576.

policy.[3] Favourable R&D treatment, such as the allocations of R&D to foreign income, the R&D tax credit, the R&D favourable deduction scheme, and patent boxes, are seldom-contested tax expenditures that are the biggest tax expenditures for many big economies.[4]

2. Western legal systems follow the OECD and the World Bank and welcome tax incentives for research and development (R&D) as a sound innovation policy. In the European Union, nearly all Member States adopted tax subsidies for R&D expenditures.[5] Belgium recently enforced and reformed its incentives for innovation, hereby following the *Base Erosion and Profit Shifting* initiative from the OESO.[6] These research and development benefits are traditionally pushed by international organisations like the IMF, the World Bank, and the OECD, and as tax expenditures on R&D are increasing greatly in most OECD countries (we see an average increase of between 0%–0.1% for 2000 to 0.2–0.3% of GDP for 2016), we can forecast their policy importance for the years to come.[7] In the United States (U.S.), for instance, on an annual basis, federal research and development tax incentives – that is, tax benefits for innovative experiments – amount to more than $10 billion.[8] In comparison, governmental support for agricultural producers – infamous for being the biggest recipients of governmental support – total $29 billion.[9] The current U.S. administration fortifies these policy trends, with favourable R&D treatment being an integral part of the Tax Cuts and Jobs Act of 2017.[10]

---

[3] M. Graetz and R. Doud, 'Technological Innovation, International Competition, and the Challenges of International Income Taxation', *Columbia Law Review*, 2013, vol. 113, pp. 347–445; Obama, 'The President's Framework for Business Tax Reform'; Bush, 'President's Letter on the American Competitiveness Initiative'.

[4] D. Cameron, 'Statutory Construction, Regulatory Interpretation and Policy Incoherence', *Computer Law Review and Technology Journal*, 2004, vol. 9, pp. 63–164.

[5] For data on the European countries' tax expenditures for R&D, see https://taxfoundation.org/rd-tax-incentives-europe-2020/.

[6] The new statute on the tax benefits for R&D can be found in Article 205 of the Belgian Income Tax Code 92.

[7] OECD, 'The OECD Innovation Strategy: Getting a Head Start on Tomorrow', 2010, https://doi.org/10.1787/9789264083479-en; World Bank, 'Innovation Policy: A Guide for Developing Countries', Washington, D.C., 2010. Criscuolo, 'The Effect of R&D Tax Incentives on Location of R&D Investment', January 2009.

[8] Joint Committee on Taxation, 'STAFF OF JOINT COMM. ON TAXATION, 113TH CONG., ESTIMATES OF FEDERAL TAX EXPENDITURES FOR FISCAL YEARS 2012–2017', 1 February 2013, pp. 1–48.

[9] See: https://data.oecd.org/agrpolicy/agricultural-support.htm.

[10] The Tax Cuts and Jobs Act of 2017 decided to maintain the permanent status for Article 41 I.R.C. As from December 21, 2021, research or experimental ('R&E') expenditures under section 174 paid should be capitalised and amortised ratably over a five-year period for research conducted in the United States, beginning with the midpoint of the tax year in which the specified R&E expenditures were paid or incurred. See M. Brossmer et al., 'Tax Reform: And the Winner Is ... R&D', KPMG Report, 12 March 2018, 10 p.

3. Tax incentives for R&D are grounded in a number of standard economic reasonings. First, technological innovation is deemed to be essential for economic growth.[11] Secondly, research is seen as the main driver of technological innovation.[12] Lastly, the gathering of this innovative knowledge, when not subsidised in one way or another, will be underdeveloped in the market. According to the traditional model, without external impetus, pure markets will not produce creative ideas and products.[13] This assumed underproduction of novelty will theoretically be corrected by beneficial treatment of R&D, either through direct subsidies or via tax incentives.[14] And so the credo that dominates the political realm, namely that policies oriented toward growth support innovators by creating tax relief for R&D, has a basis in mainstream economics.

4. This standard economic thinking explains support for strong(er), (more) permanent or more specific R&D tax cuts within the legal literature.[15] Naturally, other policy tools can also be used to compensate for the predicted undersupply of innovative knowledge, notably prizes, IP policy, national labs, and grants.[16] This chapter will join the debate on instrument choice within innovation policy, with a focus on tax incentives. While I am sympathetic to the general endeavour to create a legal framework oriented toward innovation, we perceive a specific gap in the legal literature concerning innovation and tax incentives. Economic policies are a function of the employed economic model and the assumptions on which such models rest. As just explained, legal scholarship on this issue is mainly fuelled by standard economics and equilibrium analysis. However, empirical studies have revealed the ambiguous results of tax incentives for R&D (see *infra*). This chapter will propose a more enriched economic model,

---

11 N. Kaldor, 'A Model of Economic Growth', *The Economic Journal*, 1957, vol. 67, no. 268, p. 591.

12 G. Zachary, *Endless Frontier: Vannevar Bush, Engineer of the American Century*, 1st edn (Cambridge: MIT Press, 1999), 528 p.

13 R. Nelson, 'The Simple Economics of Basic Scientific Research', *Journal of Political Economy*, 1959, vol. 67, no. 3, pp. 297–306.

14 In the spirit of the work of Surrey, deviations from general tax rules can be qualified as 'tax subsidies' or 'tax expenditures'; see S. Surrey and P. McDaniel, *Tax Expenditures* (Boston, MA: Harvard University Press, 1985), 303 p.

15 C. Johnson, 'Capitalize Costs of Software Development', 2009, *Tax Notes*, vol. 124, no. 6, pp. 603–12; W. Natbony, 'Tax Incentives for Research and Development: An Analysis and a Proposal', *Georgetown Law Journal*, 1987, vol. 76, pp. 347–416; E. Wamsley, 'The Definition of Qualified Research Under the Section 41 Research and Development Tax Credit: Its Impact on the Credit's Effectiveness', *Virginia Law Review*, 2001, vol. 87, no. 1, pp. 165–203; S. Mahaffy, 'The Case for Tax: A Comparative Approach to Innovation Policy', *Yale Law Journal*, 2013, vol. 123, no. 3, pp. 530–861; R. Atkinson, 'Expanding the R&E Tax Credit to Drive Innovation, Competitiveness and Prosperity', *The Journal of Technology Transfer*, 2007, vol. 32, no. 6, pp. 617–28; J. Venghaus, 'Tax Incentives: A Means of Encouraging Research and Development for Homeland Security', *Richmond University Law Review*, 2003, vol. 37, pp. 1213–1244.

16 Different policy tools can also be mixed. For instance, the European Innovation Council recently launched a 'blended finance approach', where grants are coupled with equity.

institutional economics, to create an alternative perspective on innovation policy. We will use this model to better understand the failures that arise when governments try to steer innovation via specific fiscal interventions.[17]

5. This chapter proceeds as follows. I will introduce the economic model that is used as the meta-rationale for all OECD countries to adopt tax incentives for innovation, notably the equilibrium-style model that presents innovation as an exogenous shock (part 2). I will then employ more enriched models of innovation to illustrate that governments do not possess the *knowledge* necessary to design tax incentives for innovation. Building on insights from institutional economics, I argue that the best innovation policy lies in supporting the background institutions that drive the market process – being rules of property and contract that take a stable, simple and general form. I extend this thesis to intellectual property (part 3). The final part will deliver the conclusion of this analysis (part 4).

2. STANDARD ECONOMIC MODEL ON INNOVATION

2.1. THE NEOCLASSICAL MODEL

6. To fully grasp the foundations of tax incentives for innovation we have to discuss the standard neoclassical scheme that follows a two-step sequence.[18] Blackboard economics starts off with an *ideal type* of market that depicts an economy as a general equilibrium; that is a simultaneous systematic reconciliation of all individual plans for production, buying, selling and consumption in a set of overlapping fully competitive markets.[19] On the assumption that markets are perfectly competitive because they are populated by rationally optimising self-interested actors with complete shared information, economists like Walras, Marshall, Hicks, Arrow, and Debreu were able to explain why demand and supply will meet each other at an optimal point.[20] Abstracting

---

17 For an expansive treatment of innovation policy that employs public choice economics and offers an application to the US tax system, see C. Delmotte, 'The Case Against Tax Subsidies in Innovation Policy', *Florida State University Law Review*, 2021 (forthcoming), vol. 48, no. 2, pp. 1–55.

18 For a perfect illustration, see K. Arrow, 'Economic Welfare and the Allocation of Resources for Invention', in NBER, *The Rate and Direction of Inventive Activity: Economic and Social Factors* (Princeton: Princeton University Press, 1962), p. 610.

19 J. Hicks, *Value and Capital: An Inquiry into Some Fundamental Principles of Economic Theory*, 2nd ed (Oxford: Clarendon Press, 2001), p. 60; P. Samuelson, *Economic Foundations of Economic Analysis* (Cambridge: Harvard University Press, 1947), 604 p.

20 See L. Walras, *Elements of Pure Economics*, Reprinted [der Ausg.] History of Economic Thought (London: Routledge 2003), p. 20; A. Marshall, *Principles of Economics* (London:

from individual interaction, the wonder of the market, within a world of complete information, is that the impersonal forces of supply and demand mould all this scattered data into a point mass: the price.[21] While temporary deviations from the general equilibrium are expected, they are atypical, produced by exogenous shifts (or 'shocks') in supply and demand. So, within a perfect market, producers respond to perfect information on consumer preferences represented by a stable price. As Don Boudreaux puts it, within perfect markets, producers typically do not influence the price or products.[22] Producers are price-takers, as market forces will deliver competitive prices that reflect their marginal cost, meaning that producers will charge, for each product unit, the addition to the total cost (materials, labour, etc.) of making it.[23] When it comes to product development, entrepreneurs have full access to consumer preferences – which are assumed to be stable and accessible.[24] All that a firm within a perfect market needs to do is choose a product and the level of output; the price and form of the product are mechanically delivered by the over-arching market forces.[25]

7. The second part of the model introduces the realistic case where this ideal scenario of perfectly efficient markets is not met. In reality, the theoretic 'equilibrium', whereby the interests of all market agents are maximally satisfied, will often not be reached.[26] For instance, pure systems of property and exchange will often produce negative externalities, where costs that cannot be properly priced as part of the cost of production cause a mismatch between their marginal benefit and marginal cost. Markets thus incentivise pollutive industries to maximise the outcome, while the negative costs are not accounted for and diffused over society. Unencumbered markets, so goes the theory,

---

Macmillan and Co., Ltd., 1920), 731 p.; Hicks, *Value and Capital*, p. 60; K. Arrow and G. Debreu, 'Existence of an Equilibrium for a Competitive Economy', *Econometrica*, 1954, vol. 22, no. 3, p. 265.

21 D. Boudreaux, 'Schumpeter and Kirzner on Competition and Equilibrium', in P. Boettke and D. Prychitko (eds.), *The Market Process: Essays in Contemporary Austrian Economics* (Aldershot, Hants, England; Brookfield, Vt., USA: E. Elgar, 1994), p. 54.

22 *Ibid.*

23 S. Scotchmer, *Innovation and Incentives* (Cambridge, Mass.: MIT Press, 2004), 357 p.

24 K. Arrow, 'Limited Knowledge and Economic Analysis', *The American Economic Review*, 1974, vol. 64, no. 1, pp. 1–10.

25 The economic model whereby all individual behaviour is dictated from rational maximisation under equilibrium, is sometimes referred to as the 'Walrasian Box'. See T. Cowen, 'Entrepreneurship, Austrian Economics, and the Quarrel Between Philosophy and Poetry', *Public Choice*, 2003, vol. 16, no. 1, p. 5; D. Boudreaux, 'Antitrust and Competition from a Market-Process Perspective', in T. Zywicki and P. Boettke, (eds.) *Research Handbook on Austrian Law and Economics* (Cheltenham: Edward Elgar Publishing 2017), p. 281.

26 The efficiency standard of neoclassic economics is almost never met; see Harper, 'Innovation and Institutions from the Bottom Up', p. 989. This kind of economic exercise, where we compare reality to perfectly competitive markets, has been critised as 'nirvana analysis'; see H. Demsetz, 'Information and Efficiency: Another Viewpoint', *The Journal of Law & Economics*, 1969, vol. 12, no. 1, pp. 1–22.

cannot correct these negative externalities. Consequently, since the second half of the last century, economics as a discipline has specialised as the toolkit to 'correct' for these 'imperfections' of the market, for instance through the imposition of regulations, specific tax rates, public production of specific goods or prohibitions.[27] So the second part of the economic exercise focusses on which political interventions can make sure the economy approximates 'the ideal' as sketched in the first step.[28]

2.2. TAX INCENTIVES FOR INNOVATION

8. Innovation is generally considered to be a desirable economic phenomenon.[29] Alterations within the product structure lead, under competitive conditions, to Pareto-improvements.[30] Scientists spread novel techniques and search for inventions that innovate goods and services, which changes our lives for the better.[31] Under the standard model, however, firms are not expected to engage in innovation.[32] Markets converge in fixed products and services, and individual action does not deviate from the general laws of supply and demand.[33] Once the static point is reached (optimal or suboptimal) there is *no change* in the products, services or means of production, and innovation ceases to exist.[34] Remember, producers are robots that mechanically execute the orders of product

27 A.C. Pigou, *The Economics of Welfare* (London: Library of Economics and Liberty, 1932), 837 p.; W. Baumol, 'On Taxation and the Control of Externalities', *The American Economic Review*, 1972, vol. 62, no. 3, pp. 307–322.

28 Arrow, 'Economic Welfare and the Allocation of Resources for Invention', p. 619 ('To sum up, we expect a free enterprise economy to underinvest in invention and research (as compared with an *ideal*) ... I will first sketch an ideal economy in which the allocation problem can be solved by competition and then indicate some of the devices in the real world which approximate this solution').

29 R. Solow, 'Technical Change and the Aggregate Production Function', *The Review of Economics and Statistics*, 1957, vol. 39, no. 3, p. 312. Solow estimated that about 87,5% of economic growth in America between 1909 and 1949 could be attributed to technological innovation. Also see: Harper, 'Innovation and Institutions from the Bottom Up', p. 989.

30 A Pareto improvement occurs when at least one individual has been made better off and no individual has been made worse off.

31 H. Hovenkamp, 'Restraints on Innovation', *Cardozo Law Review*, 2007, vol. 29, no. 1, p. 253.

32 C. Criscuolo, 'The Effect of R&D Tax Incentives on Location of R&D Investment'.

33 Scotchmer, *Innovation and Incentives*, p. 35.

34 Boudreaux, 'Antitrust and Competition from a Market-Process Perspective', p. 281 ('[N]o actual competition – as that term is popularly understood – occurs in perfectly competitive markets. To attract more customers, no perfectly competitive firm must cut prices, advertise, or build a better mousetrap. Each firm that manages to keep its unit cost low enough to be covered by the market price of its output can sell as much as it wants. All that each firm in perfectly *competitive markets must do is to choose its level of output. And even that choice is mechanical: expand the rate of output produced per period of time* up to, but not beyond, the rate at which marginal cost is made equal to the externally determined and fully known market price').

and price given by the market. Free markets will tell these robots not to engage in innovation and alter price structures or change products.[35] The production of innovative knowledge is traditionally conceptualised as a positive externality – a good that produces benefits that cannot be charged directly to consumers.[36] Although socially desirable, firms will not engage in research and development, or less than what would be socially optimal.[37] Innovative knowledge is not something like bread or cars, excludable goods that can be sold with certainty to consumers.[38] Innovative knowledge is immaterial and hard to fence, and the returns are highly uncertain. Economists like Arrow and Nelson predict 'a free enterprise economy to underinvest in invention and research (as compared with an ideal), because it is risky, because the product can be appropriated only to a limited extent, and because of the increasing returns in use'.[39] Rational and risk-averse individuals will not inject novelty into the economy, which is an endless and unchanging round of activity. Just as for negative externalities, private returns do not match the social benefits. Hence, economists will theorise on the proper mechanisms to approximate the amount of innovative knowledge an ideal market would generate.[40] Next to prizes, or national organisation (via universities), governments compensate the undersupply of innovative knowledge using the tax code.[41]

9. So, innovative knowledge, through research and development, being the source of innovation, is not something we can expect to emerge spontaneously from within a market.[42] The expected equilibrium will fail to properly value

---

35 See, e.g., Hovenkamp, 'Restraints on Innovation', p. 253 (the neoclassical models typically assumed that products were static, and competition meant a state of affairs where prices are as close as possible to cost).

36 Graetz and Doud, 'Technological Innovation, International Competition, and the Challenges of International Income Taxation', pp. 347–445.

37 Harper, 'Innovation and Institutions from the Bottom Up', p. 987 ('The typical diagnosis is that the allocation of resources to innovation in a market economy is socially inefficient and Pareto-suboptimal; real-world market institutions are expected to underinvest in innovation as compared with the ideal norm of perfect competition').

38 Graetz and Doud, 'Technological Innovation, International Competition, and the Challenges of International Income Taxation', pp. 347–445.

39 Arrow, 'Economic Welfare and the Allocation of Resources for Invention', p. 619.

40 R. Nelson, 'The Simple Economics of Basic Scientific Research', *Journal of Political Economy*, 1959, vol. 67, no. 3, p. 298. (But when the marginal value of a 'good' to society exceeds the marginal value of the good to the individual who pays for it, the allocation of resources that maximises private profits will not be optimal. For in these cases private-profit opportunities do not adequately reflect social benefit, and, in the absence of positive public policy, the competitive economy will tend to spend less on that good 'than it should').

41 All these measures are different and are not compared here. See D. Hemel and L. Ouellette, 'Innovation Policy Pluralism', *Yale Law Journal*, 2019, vol. 128, no. 3, pp. 544–614.

42 Growth due to technological change is treated as an exogenous shock within equilibrium analysis. See R. Solow, 'A Contribution to the Theory of Economic Growth', *The Quarterly Journal of Economics*, 1956, vol. 70, no. 1, pp. 65–94; Solow, 'Technical Change and the Aggregate Production Function', p. 312.

research and development, and producers will be stuck with the same products and services. The purpose of tax incentives is to increase the supply of creative knowledge by lowering its costs for the producer and thus inject novelty into the system.[43] The tax code tries to identify the driving investments for innovation and creates a beneficial treatment.

10. According to the equilibrium-model, tax incentives are the *Deus ex Machina* that will bring innovation within the closed system. The policy-goal of a tax incentive is to stimulate the production of creative knowledge so that the optimal amount is reached. Three elements stand out in this line of economic thinking. First, the applied model is *static*, in the sense that it assumes markets necessarily converge into equilibria. In the same way, one can specify a gravity point for a physical object, economics assumes human action will lead to a steady point, and the inquiry is to ask whether that point is the correct one.[44] Second, and flowing from the previous: the neoclassical account is unable to explain the actual emergence of innovation without an external impetus.[45] Markets converge in fixed products and services, and individual action does not deviate from the general laws of supply and demand. That is why the standard model explains the emergence of innovation as an *exogenous shock*.[46] An economy is a closed system, and in the face of uncertainty, rational and risk-averse individuals will stick to what equilibrium dictates.[47] Thirdly, the model is *linear*, in the sense that it assumes a fixed sequence between a number of activities.[48] Research leads to the creation of knowledge, and when this is being injected in the economy, innovation and growth will follow automatically.[49]

---

43 S. Shay, C. Fleming, and R. Peroni, 'R&D Tax Incentives: Growth Panacea or Budget Trojan Horse', *Tax Law Review*, 2016, vol. 69, no. 3, p. 423.

44 R. Wagner, *Politics as a Peculiar Business: Insights from a Theory of Entangled Political Economy. New Thinking in Political Economy* (Cheltenham: Edward Elgar Publishing, 2016), p. 36.

45 Schumpeter was one of the first corrections to the standard equilibrium scheme, to point at the dynamic nature of markets, a process whereby innovations are instigated that create new industries and make others vanish. J. Schumpeter and R. Swedberg, *Capitalism, Socialism, and Democracy* (London: Routledge, 2014), 442 p.

46 Boudreaux, 'Antitrust and Competition from a Market-Process Perspective', p. 281.

47 Cowen, 'Entrepreneurship, Austrian Economics, and the Quarrel Between Philosophy and Poetry', p. 5.

48 Scotchmer, *Innovation and Incentives*, p. 259 ('We have taken on fate that incentives will lead to R&D, that R&D will lead to innovations, and that innovations will lead to improvements in consumer welfare or economic growth'). P. Lewis, 'Technicians and Innovation', Gatsby, King's College London, 2019, p. 3. See also Salzberger, *Law and Economics of Innovation* (Cheltenham: Edward Elgar Pub, 2012), 856 p.

49 Lewis, 'Technicians and Innovation', p. 3.

2.3. DUBIOUS EMPIRICAL TRACK RECORD OF TAX INCENTIVES

11. This theoretical optimism for tax subsidies does not translate to the numbers. Despite the enormous burden on the federal budget, one of its core supporters, the OECD, found that government funding of R&D, for instance via tax incentives, had no or sometimes even a negative impact on economic growth.[50] There are studies that are more optimistic[51], yet the general observation is that 'private R&D has a substantial and significant direct effect on productivity growth which is greater than the impact of total R&D' yet 'public R&D appears to have a much weaker, if not insignificant, direct effect'.[52]

12. While 'many economists and policymakers have grown frustrated with the paucity of systematic statistical evidence documenting a direct contribution from public R&D', the knowledge problem with the operationalisation of tax incentives has surfaced.[53] Studies now admit that while we can measure the effect of tax expenditures on R&D inputs when it comes to effects on innovation *output* and growth more generally, very little can be said with certainty.[54] Shay and others conclude in their recent overview, 'We question whether there is sufficient understanding of the process that leads from research to development to commercialisation to economic growth to be able to specify an appropriate (and appropriately narrow) target for government intervention that can be achieved with a cost-effective tax incentive'.[55] Prominent economists recently presented a model whereby the efficiency of R&D incentives is mediated by factors that *cannot be observed*, such as whether a firm actually invests in the kind of knowledge about which a market failure arises and whether the firm

---

50 OECD, 'The Sources of Economic Growth in OECD Countries', 2003, pp. 64, 84.

51 Dechezleprêtre et al., 'Do Tax Incentives for Research Increase Firm Innovation?', March 2016, Centre for Climate Change Economics and Policy Working Paper No. 260; Grantham Research Institute on Climate Change and the Environment Working Paper No. 230, 41 p.

52 H. Capron and B. van Pottelsberghe de la Potterie, 'Public Support to Business R&D: A Survey and Some New Quantitative Evidence', in OECD, *Policy Evaluation in Innovation and Technology: Towards Best Practices* (OECD: Paris, 1997), pp. 171–188.

53 P. David, B. Hall and A. Toole, 'Is Public R&D a Complement or Substitute for Private R&D? A Review of the Econometric Evidence', *Research Policy*, 2000, vol. 29, no. 4–5, p. 498 (showing how tax incentives lead to a replacement of private R&D and to alterations in its composition such that firms will favour projects that will generate profits in the short run). T. Kealey and O. Al-Ubaydli, 'A Critique of Science and R&D-Based Models of Endogenous Growth', *Knowledge, Technology & Policy*, 2001, vol. 13, no. 4, pp. 37–48.

54 C. Köhler, P. Laredo and C. Rammer, 'The Impact and Effectiveness of Fiscal Incentives for R&D', Nat'l Endowment for Sci., Tech. & the Arts, Working Paper No. 12/01, January 2012, 35 p.; C.I. Jones and J.C. Williams, 'Measuring the Social Return to R&D', *The Quarterly Journal of Economics*, vol. 113, no. 4, pp. 1119–1135; Shay, Fleming and Peroni, 'R&D Tax Incentives: Growth Panacea or Budget Trojan Horse', pp. 419–458.

55 Shay, Fleming, & Peroni, 'R&D Tax Incentives: Growth Panacea or Budget Trojan Horse', p. 424.

under discussion is the kind of firm that is efficient in converting R&D in research productivity.[56] David Schizer argues that governments are not well-positioned to select specific sources of innovation.[57]

13. Building on these empirical indications and the scepticism in the literature, this chapter disentangles the knowledge problem for tax incentives. The empirical literature casts doubt on whether tax incentives for innovation have a positive effect on innovation output and growth. The reason they do so, I will argue, is because the theoretic model that authorises tax incentives for innovation is flawed.

3. INSTITUTIONAL ECONOMICS

14. The neoclassical model has its strengths both in an explanatory sense (why are markets efficient), and an educative sense (how to sketch an initial frame that scholars and students understand). That said, all models have limits. Different models highlight different things. The purpose is to use models for those phenomena which they can explain well. The neoclassical scheme might be useful at explaining static elements of markets, but it has been used to theorise on the prime thing it is not good at, which is modelling *change*.[58] The occurrence of innovation points us at the stochastic component of markets. If we want to engage in normative reasoning on innovation, we have to turn to more dynamic models of economics that manage to properly understand the systematic alterations that characterise products and services in an economy.[59] If we want to understand the dynamic component of markets, we have to rely on theories that explain and conceptualise why products, services, and businesses change within the market.[60] Whereas standard economics depicts the market as 'a place', i.e. a *state* of affairs, several economists rely on a more dynamic and

56 U. Akcigit, D. Hanley and S. Stantcheva, 'Optimal Taxation and R&D Policies', National Bureau of Economic Research, Working Paper 22908, November 2019, 102 p., https://doi.org/10.3386/w22908.

57 D.M. Schizer, 'Limiting Tax Expenditures', *Tax Law Review*, 2015, vol. 68, p. 293.

58 S.S. Metcalfe, 'Systems Failure and the Case for Innovation Policy', in P. Llerena and M. Matt, *Innovation Policy in a Knowledge-Based Economy* (Heidelberg: Springer, 2005), p. 47; R. Koppl, S. Kauffman, T. Felin and G. Longo, 'Economics for a Creative World', *Journal of Institutional Economics*, 2015, vol. 11, no. 1, pp. 1–31.

59 See, e.g., Arrow, admitting that the model could not explain the emergence, over time, of its most central concept. See Arrow, 'Limited Knowledge and Economic Analysis' ('Even if we accept this entire story, there is still one element not individual: namely, the prices faced by the firms and individuals. What individual has chosen prices? In the formal theory, at least, no one. They are determined on (not by) social institutions known as markets, which equate supply and demand').

60 Schumpeter was one of the first corrections to the standard equilibrium scheme to point at the cyclical nature of markets, a process whereby innovations are instigated that create new

process-based account of markets. This group is composed of different streams of thinking, such as Nobel Prize Laureate Paul Romer (endogenous growth theory) and more recent developments within Institutional Economics, that all contested the static model and lay accents which, taken together, enable us to understand the emergence of innovation within markets, not as exogenous shocks but as endogenously embedded essentials of the market process. We can call these economists 'market process theorists', as their work focusses on the specific patterns that emerge *over time* within the market as a function of the underlying system of rules and institutions.

3.1. THE MARKET AS A DYNAMIC PROCESS

15. Within an equilibrium model, the outcome is confused with *the process* that leads to the outcome.[61] Indeed, the neoclassical framework commences the economic exercise at a point where the economic process has already been completed, and the producers have perfect knowledge over the preferences of consumers and the cheapest techniques to satisfy them.[62] We are interested in how the market produces such knowledge in the first place. On such a more procedural account, the emergence of knowledge on consumer preferences and innovative techniques is the explanatory purpose of the model.[63] This account posits a particular role for entrepreneurship in explaining market outcomes. In the neoclassical view, entrepreneurs vanish in the model and function as pure 'price-takers'. As illustrated by Donald Boudreaux, in equilibrium analysis, there is no competitive entrepreneurship:

'... no actual competition – as that term is popularly understood – occurs in perfectly competitive markets. To attract more customers, no perfectly competitive firm must cut prices, advertise, or build a better mousetrap. Each firm that manages to keep its unit cost low enough to be covered by the market price of its output can sell as much as it wants. All that each firm in perfectly competitive markets must do is to choose its level of output. And even that choice is mechanical: expand the rate of output produced per period of time up to, but not beyond, the rate at which marginal cost is made equal to the externally determined and fully known market price'.[64]

industries and make others vanish. See Schumpeter and Swedberg, *Capitalism, Socialism, and Democracy*, pp. 82–83.

61 Boudreaux, 'Schumpeter and Kirzner on Competition and Equilibrium', p. 54.

62 F. Hayek, *Individualism and Economic Order* (Chicago: University of Chicago Press, 1948), p. 45.

63 F. Hayek, 'The Use of Knowledge in Society', *American Economic Review*, 1945, vol. 35, no. 4, pp. 519–530.

64 Boudreaux, 'Antitrust and Competition from a Market-Process Perspective', p. 281.

16. Paul Romer revolutionised the discipline with his thesis of 'endogenous technological change', where he places the cause for novelty with 'the *intentional* actions taken by people who respond to market incentives'.[65] Romer contests the premise that inventions come from scientists outside the system, and highlights self-interested entrepreneurs as the drivers of innovation:

'The premise here is that market incentives nonetheless play an essential role in the process whereby new knowledge is translated into goods with practical value. Our initial understanding of electromagnetism arose from research conducted in academic institutions, but magnetic tape and home videocassette recorders resulted from attempts by private firms to earn a profit'.[66]

17. Romer perceives markets as discovery procedures, dynamic processes where knowledge accumulates via trial and error and experimentation.[67] He thus replaces the static model, whereby economic agents are trapped in endless cycles of the same behaviour, with a dynamic analysis, where knowledge disseminates and accumulates through learning. Importantly, his theory shows that creative knowledge is not a pure public good and that at least some of the benefits of science are excludable and thus appropriable.[68] Within the Romer-model, systems of property and exchange will partially overcome the predicted underinvestment in creative knowledge:

'Yet it is still the case that private, profit-maximising agents make investment in the creation of new knowledge and that they earn a return on these investments by charging a price for the resulting goods that is greater than the marginal cost of producing the goods'.[69]

18. Romer shows that science-based innovation will be engendered by markets. Entrepreneurs are intentional agents, and even if positive externalities are present, market pay-offs are sufficient for change to emerge from within the system. Interestingly, his model targets the high-end, technologically driven change, for which the initial investment costs are arguably the highest. So, his market process theory corrects the equilibrium analysis that simply omits *any change* coming from within the system. Now that Romer highlights 'intentional investment decisions made by profit-maximizing agents' as the basis for

---

65 P. Romer, 'Endogenous Technological Change', *The Journal of Political Economy*, 1990, vol. 98, no. 5, p. 72.

66 *Ibid.*

67 *Ibid.* ('The raw materials that we use have not changed, but as a result of trial and error, experimentation, refinement, and scientific investigation, the instructions that we follow for combining raw materials have become vastly more sophisticated').

68 To do so, his model assumes private property rights over specific products but not over research knowledge. Romer, 'Endogenous Technological Change', p. 84.

69 *Ibid.*, p. 89.

endogenous novelty, focusing on technological change; how can we get an image of how markets produce change, more generally?

19. To fully capture the dynamics of markets concerning innovation, we need an institutional framework. With this, we mean that we are looking for an economics that studies the patterns and long-term dynamics that are likely to arise under specific institutions and the rules that govern them. What is conceived as impersonal machinery is ultimately constituted by individuals, each one undertaking intentional actions. And these individuals, that are assumed to be fully informed according to equilibrium analysis, are in reality relatively uninformed. Entrepreneurs do not possess perfect knowledge of the cheapest technique to produce a product, nor are they in the know of what the preferences of each consumer are.[70] Consumers, too, do not always know which good will satisfy their preferences more, and often they are testing what these preferences contain.[71] Behind the universal forces, we find millions of persons with limited rationality pursuing their ends in the face of uncertainty and ignorance.[72] Building on this knowledge problem, institutional economists enriched the discipline by re-integrating the role of entrepreneurs.[73] Markets are never fixed states, but rather snapshots of imperfection within a movie that is in motion.[74] Innovation is driven by entrepreneurs who see an opportunity for profit – currently unnoticed by others.[75] The entrepreneurial initiative can take various forms, and it very often comes from people who do not necessarily think of themselves as entrepreneurs or label themselves as such. Within an entrepreneurial account, experiments within the production process emerge in

---

70 In other words, institutional economics starts the exercise with a market in disequilibrium, driven by asymmetry of information.

71 The knowledge problem is magnified once we realise that even consumers themselves do not know their own preferences. Consumers do not have fixed, predefined preferences; they are caught within a learning process where, over time, they test and revise their preferences. M. Dold, 'Back to Buchanan? Explorations of Welfare and Subjectivism in Behavioral Economics', *Journal of Economic Methodology*, 2018, vol. 25, no. 2, pp. 160–178.

72 See G. O'Driscoll and M. Rizzo, *Austrian Economics Re-Examined. The Economics of Time and Ignorance* (New York: Routledge, 2015), 302 p.

73 By underlying the role of the entrepreneur, Kirzner could solve the explanatory questions that haunted equilibrium analysis, such as the emergence of prices and the generation of knowledge within the market. See I. Kirzner, 'Entrepreneurial Discovery and the Competitive Market Process: An Austrian Approach', *Journal of Economic Literature*, 1997, vol. 35, no. 1, pp. 60–85.

74 See S. Metcalfe, 'Systems Failure and the Case for Innovation Policy', in P. Llerena and M. Matt, *Innovation Policy in a Knowledge-Based Economy* (Berlin, Heidelberg: Springer, 2005), p. 48.

75 I. Kirzner, *Competition and Entrepreneurship* (Chicago: University of Chicago Press, 2015), 256 p.; I. Kirzner, *Perception, Opportunity, and Profit: Studies in the Theory of Entrepreneurship* (Chicago: Chicago University Press, 1979), 246 p.; P. Boettke and F. Sautet (eds.), *Competition and Entrepreneurship (The Collected Works of Israel M. Kirzner)* (Indianapolis, Indiana: Liberty Fund, 2013), 224 p.

a fairly bottom-up and mundane way; that does not necessarily involve science and technology.[76]

20. For instance, when there is a discrepancy between a given price for a particular good and the underlying cost, this represents an opportunity for profit for the entrepreneur.[77] Entrepreneurs take on this role of acting against, or in disagreement with, the publicised market price of a particular good or service, and the given practices in the sector in which they are working.[78] It is the role of 'price-breakers', individual entrepreneurs that maximise revenue by lowering the price, that is one of the drivers behind the emergence of a price adjusted to the marginal buyer. It is the imperfection of the current price that creates opportunities for entrepreneurs to engage in alterations tomorrow.

21. Because of the incentive for profit, entrepreneurs are also trained in *alertness* regarding profitable modifications in the production process.[79] Such creativity arises from anyone trying out a new practice in a business environment in an attempt to be more competitive, whether that person is self-employed, an employee or an executive. Experiments within the production process happen continuously, resulting in alterations in a business organisation or production techniques.[80] For instance, a collaborator might discover a given resource can be purchased more cheaply elsewhere, or a sub-team discovers that fewer production hours make specialised workers that are actually more productive. A manager might discover that a product is more popular in another geographic region, or that workers perform better when they are not over-specialising. Because perfect knowledge is never given, producers are constantly experimenting with various components of the production process, making use of their understanding and perception. When the submitted alterations are

---

76 OECD and Eurostat, 'Oslo Manual 2018: Guidelines for Collecting, Reporting and Using Data on Innovation. The Measurement of Scientific, Technological and Innovation Activities' 2018, https://doi.org/10.1787/9789264304604-en.

77 Kirzner, 'Entrepreneurial Discovery and the Competitive Market Process: An Austrian Approach', pp. 60–85.

78 The essence of innovation is acting against a certain practice or price. See Metcalfe, 'Systems Failure and the Case for Innovation Policy', p. 52 (all innovations are based on disagreement, on a different reading of information much of which is currently available in the public domain.).

79 The concept of alertness is central to entrepreneurship theory, via the contributions of Israel Kirzner (Kirzner, *Competition and Entrepreneurship*, 256 p.; I. Kirzner, *Perception, Opportunity, and Profit: Studies in the Theory of Entrepreneurship* (Chicago: University of Chicago Press, 1979), 246 p.).

80 Indeed, innovations are often not technical but managerial, as businesses experiment with the organisational structure of a firm. See A. Chandler, *The Visible Hand: The Managerial Revolution in American Business* (Cambridge: Belknap Press of Harvard Univ. Press, 2002), 624 p.; T. Malone, *The Future of Work: How the New Order of Business Will Shape Your Organization, Your Management Style, and Your Life* (Boston: Harvard Business School Press, 2004), 240 p.

successful, they will generate profit and accumulate within the market process.[81] Indeed, within competitive conditions, the prospect of profit creates an incentive for entrepreneurs to see opportunities for reductions in cost, costs that others did not perceive. The presence of uncertainty regarding these opportunities systematically creates experiments and, when successful, results in alterations within the productive process, and the discovery of knowledge that was previously unknown.

22. Knowledge of the best price or the cheapest way to produce something is not externally given but is the very thing that a market generates. Once we drop the mechanistic view of producers, we can see entrepreneurs as 'discoverers' in a world of uncertainty.[82] The gradual or drastic alterations we witness within the market process are not confined to initiatives on price or production processes, but naturally – resonating Romer – also revolve around the products themselves. In their alertness for unexploited gain, entrepreneurs will test whether the current stock of goods is the one that maximally satisfies consumer preferences. They can bring modified or new products to the market that reveal the imperfections of previous states of affairs and turn them into private profit. They may enhance the quality by modifying the composition of the product (consider, for example, the improved albeit more expensive coffee machines now popular in homes and offices). Serving as 'product innovators', entrepreneurs help to cover previous gaps in the knowledge regarding people's preferences.

23. Where in the standard account, innovation is a methodological conundrum, the dynamic account of market processes explains the emergence of novelty and change. Romer shows that purposeful activities will engender new technologies and, consequently products and services, and reveals markets as dynamic; rather than as a closed system.[83] Institutional economists extend this dynamic image of markets. Entrepreneurial alertness for profit is omnipresent within markets and will lead to experimentation and thus innovation within the price structure, business organisation or production techniques. Innovation, broadly construed, once the Achilles heel of economic theory, is now simply the general tendency of markets when perceived as processes rather than states. Since the entrepreneur is bound by uncertainty, and no one knows the precise outcome of his endeavours, this process is one of 'discovery'.

---

81 The process of profit as driven by entrepreneurial discovery can be found in Kirzner, *Competition and Entrepreneurship*, 256 p.; Kirzner, *Perception, Opportunity, and Profit: Studies in the Theory of Entrepreneurship*, 246 p.; J. Buchanan and V. Vanberg, 'The Market as a Creative Process', *Economics and Philosophy*, 1991, vol. 7, no. 2, p. 167.

82 I. Kirzner, *Discovery and the Capitalist Process* (Chicago: University of Chicago Press, 1985), 183 p.; Kirzner, 'Entrepreneurial Discovery and the Competitive Market Process: An Austrian Approach', pp. 60–85.

83 Romer, 'Endogenous Technological Change', pp. 71–102.

3.2. INNOVATION: AN ENDOGENOUS AND UNPREDICTABLE PHENOMENON

24. Markets permit experimental interactions between individuals that can generally (but not always) lead to the discovery of better products and services. This spontaneous process is driven not by universal forces but rather by the experiments and personal knowledge of entrepreneurs and the subjective judgments of consumers.[84] Now that more dynamic models have delivered us an economic model to properly understand the endogenous manifestation of innovation; we can insist on another model of innovation.

The first element we can grasp is that innovation is something that occurs *endogenously*.[85] An economy is a dynamic and open system and entrepreneurial initiative is the internal dynamo of change. Every day there is a business trying a new product, a production technique, an organisational structure or a marketing technique.

Secondly, flowing from the previous, change is a phenomenon that is procedural, happening over time, and *continuous*.[86] Markets are constantly in motion. Because of the pressure for profit, an economy is never in stasis. There is always a firm trying a new business model, a company testing new advertising techniques or a developer adding alterations to the stock of goods.

The third element that stands out is that innovation is an *open concept*. Within entrepreneurship theory, innovation is nothing more than the successful exploitation of previously unseized opportunities.[87] This notion is thus procedural rather than substantial: something does not need to have a specific property (for instance being digital) to be 'innovative'.[88] As stressed in the literature, innovation does not always entail a new product, but sometimes the recombination of already existing elements.[89] Legal scholars have noted that innovation does not only stem from R&D, but that worker training, workplace designs, and organisational processes, are now considered to make

---

84 The variation in experiments partly arises from the fact that knowledge is in part subjective, and every entrepreneur 'perceives' things differently. See Metcalfe, 'Systems Failure and the Case for Innovation Policy', p. 52.

85 Koppl et al., 'Economics for a Creative World', pp. 1–31. ('[O]ur treatment locates novelty production within the process of evolution, rather than viewing it as exogenous or attributable primarily to individual creativity').

86 Hayek, 'The Use of Knowledge in Society', p. 523.

87 The term 'entrepreneur' is also not constrained to anyone labelling himself that way, but pertains to individuals who notice new opportunities in the system more generally. See Koppl et al., 'Economics for a Creative World', p. 24.

88 Harper also points at the fact that innovation rests in new combinations and need not involve new scientific-technological inventions per se. Harper, 'Innovation and Institutions from the Bottom Up', p. 977.

89 R. Nelson and S. Winter, *An Evolutionary Theory of Economic Change*, digitally reprinted (Cambridge, Mass.: The Belknap Press of Harvard Univ. Press, 1982), 437 p.

a commensurate contribution to innovation.[90] The market process account informs us that the source of innovation lies in the fact that an entrepreneur introduces an element in the price, production process or product that his competitors do not; and hereby gather success with consumers. If enough individuals are ready to turn away from digital products, the revival of mechanical products, for instance, LP-players, can be monetised and leads to altered consumption patterns.[91] Or the entrepreneur can use an existing resource for a different product, being inventive, but not necessarily an 'inventor'.[92]

Fourthly, on a market process account, it is *unpredictable* what the content of innovation will be.[93] First, entrepreneurs systematically come up with new combinations and creative insights that cannot be 'listed' a priori.[94] Furthermore, the selection mechanism that eventually decides whether these novelties will accumulate or disappear through an economy is the price mechanism. The price mechanism is the unintended consequence of subjective decisions of millions of people, and no one can predict the precise content.[95] Important for what follows, as neither the specific entrepreneurial initiatives nor the way consumers will respond to these is something predictable, is that the evolutionary pathways of an economy is not something we can forecast.[96] The last conclusion is that innovation is a *non-linear* concept. Innovation is part of a complex system, there is not just one sequence of interaction between the respective elements.[97] As now realised by economists, researchers are

90 Shay, Fleming and Peroni, 'R&D Tax Incentives: Growth Panacea or Budget Trojan Horse', p. 424.

91 Nelson and Winter, *An Evolutionary Theory of Economic Change,* 437 p.

92 Harper, 'Innovation and Institutions from the Bottom Up', p. 980.

93 *Ibid.*, p. 977. This also means that bringing up mathematical models does not raise our level of economic understanding. See Koppl et al., 'Economics for a Creative World', p. 4 ('If economic dynamics are 'creative' in some sense, then standard mathematical models cannot reliably predict the consequences of different policies, at least at the level of specificity such models often aim at').

94 There are an endless number of possible new and old elements, which are generated by the imagination and perception of the entrepreneur; hence, mathematical economics cannot model novelty. See id., Koppl, 'Economics for a Creative World', p. 15; Metcalfe, 'Systems Failure and the Case for Innovation Policy', pp. 49–50 ('Innovation is a question of dealing with the bounds on human decision making, it is to a substantial degree a matter of judgment, imagination and it is to a substantial degree a matter of judgment, imagination and guesswork, and the optimistic conjecturing of future possible economic worlds').

95 G. Stigler, *The Theory of Price*, 4th edn (New York, NY: Macmillan 1987), 371 p.; T. Sichelman, 'Commercializing Patents', *Stanford Law Review*, 2010, vol. 62, no. 2, pp. 341–412; M. Lemley, 'Reconceiving Patents in the Age of Venture Capital', *Journal of Small and Emerging Business Law*, 2000, vol. 4, no. 1, pp. 137–148.

96 Market process theorists are also called evolutionary economists because they draw upon models from evolutionary biology to better understand markets. See Nelson and Winter, *An Evolutionary Theory of Economic Change,* 437 p.

97 See Koppl et al., *Economics for a Creative World*, p. 5; Metcalfe, 'Systems Failure and the Case for Innovation Policy', p. 64 (discussing an intermediating role for companies and business organisations that will determine how individuals will respond to specific knowledge).

not necessarily the drivers of innovation.[98] A technician can discover a new application of an existing technique that leads to a new delivery method. Entrepreneurs themselves, without the help of labs or engineers, can have ideas to re-organise the organisational structure of a firm. Since knowledge is subjective and scattered within society, all the respective agents can deliver crucial inputs for the discovery process.

3.3. TAX INCENTIVES FOR INNOVATION: A CRITIQUE

25. The mainstream way of legal reasoning, so far, was to rest innovation policy on a static model of economic activity. Indeed, all OECD countries have used this model as the 'meta-rationale' for their innovation policy.[99] The static model is, of course, not a model *of innovation*. Once we acquired a more plausible model of economic activity, which enables us to properly characterise the nature of innovation, we are equipped to scrutinise the idea of tax incentives for innovation. The question is whether specific policy advice can survive once the methodological pillars on which it rests are taken away.[100] Importantly, I am not the first legal scholar to formulate informational concerns, as recently some tax scholars have written a critical piece on the matter.[101] Connected, we have highlighted the questionable empirical results for tax incentives for R&D. Armed with the market process account, we can now initiate a theoretic critique for tax incentives for innovation proposal. To execute this model, and design a tax incentive for innovation, implies both a qualitative and a quantitative task. The first concerns the goal to identify innovators, and specific expenditures worth supporting, the second regards the challenge of calculating the amount of benefits these recipients need to innovate.

3.3.1. Identifying Innovators

26. Which activities and associated expenditures are entitled to receive fiscal incentives? It is not an easy case to identify the operations that will be the drivers of innovation tomorrow. Once we are equipped with our enriched

---

98 Lewis, 'Technicians and Innovation'.

99 Harper, 'Innovation and Institutions from the Bottom Up', pp. 975–1001; OECD, 'The OECD Innovation Strategy', p. 88.

100 C. Delmotte, 'The Conception of Taxation: The Conventional versus the Constitutional Point of View', in D. Boudreaux, C. Coyne and B. Herzberg (eds.), *Interdisciplinary Studies of the Market Order: The Political Process and Political Order* (New York: Rowman and Littlefeld International Ltd, 2019), pp. 131–156 (applying a similar exercise to the Theory of Optimal Taxation).

101 Shay, Fleming, and Peroni, 'R&D Tax Incentives: Growth Panacea or Budget Trojan Horse', pp. 419–458.

understanding of innovation, we can understand the nature and scope of the epistemic challenges dawning upon governments when designing tax incentives for innovation. The reason it is difficult to forecast the type of expenditures that will alter the market structure is simply that when investments are made (and thus costs are deducted) the market process did not complete itself.[102] The idea that external observers can identify successful innovations, is influenced by equilibrium analysis, which is not descriptive for how policymakers act in the real world. As has been noted by other legal scholars, it is quite impossible to design tax incentives for innovation that encompass all input expenditures that contribute to innovation but that avoids the wastefulness of overbreadth.[103]

In other terms: any broad account of tax incentives will include activities that end up not being innovative and any narrow account will fail to properly identify all economic sources of innovation. Remember that the combined presence of the *variations* – experiments – that entrepreneurs raise in the system, and the continuous *selections* with which the price mechanism arbiters these novelties, lead to constant imputations of new economic phenomena in the system, i.e., innovation. The difficulty to tailor incentives to actual innovation that is also suggested by the empirical literature, is composed of two distinct information problems. To identify innovators, governments need to distinguish between market experiments and conformist activity, and between actual innovation and failing experiments, respectively. We reiterate that innovation is created by exploiting profitable opportunities so far neglected in the market process. It emerges against the backdrop of a knowledge problem: the cheapest way to produce something, the best advertising campaign, the optimal business model or the best-developed product is not objectively accessible knowledge. Being part of a discovery procedure, there is no way governments can make an exclusive list of experiments and effectively pick the winning initiatives from that list. Tax incentives, typically targeting specific investments, are interventions when the discovery is still ongoing and will, therefore, fail to be effective. Before consumers, the final arbiters in the discovery process, have assigned euros, no one, not even entrepreneurs themselves can forecast with certainty the result of the market process.

---

102 Compare *ibid.*, p. 424 ('[W]e question whether there is sufficient understanding of the process that leads from research to development to commercialisation to economic growth to be able to specify an appropriate (and appropriately narrow) target for government intervention that can be achieved with a cost-effective tax incentive').

103 *Ibid.*, p. 484; A. Mossoff, 'A Simple Conveyance Rule for Complex Innovation', *Tulsa Law Review*, 2010, vol. 44, no. 4, p. 731 (equalling the epistemic challenge to engage in institutional analysis of patent law and the discretion granted to judges). See also Shay, Fleming, and Peroni, 'R&D Tax Incentives: Growth Panacea or Budget Trojan Horse', p. 442.

3.3.2. *The Amount of the Tax Benefit*

27. The policy picture gets even sketchier when we bring in a second problem: the amount of subsidies to be allocated to specific projects. If we would know how much costumers value a new computer game more compared to an old one, or what the cheapest way to make new, more popular burgers, would be, we would not need a market that organises a competition between various producers of such goods. The question is how to decide on the amount of tax subsidies in the realistic scenario that we do *not* know the answer to these knowledge problems. The calibration of tax subsidies is of a similar difficulty to governments guessing what 'the price' of a good should be.[104] The question regarding how much funding respective projects receive gets even more difficult once we know that an invention concerns only the first step of innovation. The bulk of the costs of innovation are in commercialisation, the process by which novelty actually gets delivered to consumers.[105]

When it comes to prizes, scholars argue that 'it may be appropriate for rewards to be deferred until after there has been some time for commercialization' – since only then the true costs of commercialisation reveal themselves.[106] If ex-post rewards, such as prizes, need to be postponed as far as possible to deal with information problems, one can legitimately wonder whether tax subsidies, kicking in before the investment, can truly deal with information problems regarding the costs of inventions. Because of its 'ex-ante' nature, the knowledge problem that hinders the prize-proposal simply increases when it comes to tax subsidies. Apart from blackboard economics, knowledge of the cost for commercialisation, the value for the consumer, and the first-mover benefit, is not readily available, hence there is no way to know how much euros to transfer to all of the respective initiatives in society. Additionally, these values will differ for every single product, so that tailoring the tax benefit efficiently would demand differentiated solutions within every single case, which makes the policy even more complex.[107] Policies that grant rewards before the market process can never execute the theory on which they are based. The result is that often the wrong projects will receive subsidies (the previous problem), or that potentially successful experiments will receive too much or insufficient

---

104 In a way, it simply *is* the same task, since the point of tax subsidies is to level the market price to the theoretic equilibrium price. See *supra* section 2.2.

105 E. Kitch, 'The Nature and Function of the Patent System', *Journal of Law and Economics*, 1977, vol. 20, pp. 265–290; S. Kieff, 'Property Rights and Property Rules for Commercializing Inventions', *Minnesota Law Review*, vol. 85, pp. 697–754; J. Barnett, 'The Costs of Free: Commoditization, Bundling and Concentration', *Journal of Institutional Economics*, 2018, vol. 14, no. 6, p. 1114.

106 M. Abramovic, 'Perfecting Patent Prizes', *Vanderbilt Law Review*, 2003, vol. 115, p. 170.

107 This would also demand discretionary powers over the entire economy.

means.[108] This erratic stream of subsidies will distort the selection process that is performed by the price mechanism. Some goods or services will be presented at artificially low prices, whereas other projects will be over-subsidised.

3.4. INNOVATION POLICY: THE PROPERTARIAN APPROACH

28. Institutional economists underline the connection between the policy-proposals on innovation and the underlying philosophy of markets.[109] With the words of David Harper 'Our vision of the market economy affects how we define innovation problems and understand their various aspects and their interrelations, and how we think about alternative institutional and public-policy solutions to innovation problems. It shapes our thinking about the rationale, means, and limits of innovation policies'.[110] Koppl and others go further and contend that 'standard mechanistic models may have less to say about economic dynamics than their widespread use might suggest'.[111] The combined presence of the *variation* that entrepreneurs raise in the system, and the continuous *selections* with which the price mechanism arbiters these novelties lead to constant imputations of new economic phenomena in the system, i.e. innovation.[112] We cannot steer this evolutionary process in one way or another; as this would require knowledge on 1) all the possible variations in the system and 2) all the subjective preferences of consumers. The fact that we cannot orient the process in a specific substantive direction, and we cannot a priori support some experiments over others, does not mean we cannot facilitate the process that generates innovation. Now that we have shown the flaws of the meta-rationale for tax incentives for innovation and illustrated how this renders the specific policy epistemically unfeasible, we can, tentatively, raise some positive conclusions. Before we do so, two general points need to be made.

29. David Harper sees 'innovation as an open-ended, dynamic, endogenous process' hence, 'the focus of policy analysis is upon cultivating innovation by securing the appropriate institutional environment'.[113] From an institutional perspective, rather than deciding upon the outcome of the system, we can assist

---

108 Note here that we join the standard reasoning that assumes that there is a standard 'out there' to actually grant subsidies to some activities. Yet, even then, there is no way of knowing how much.

109 I. Kirzner, *How Markets Work: Disequilibrium, Entrepreneurship and Discovery*, (London: Inst. of Economic Affairs, 1997), 78 p.

110 Harper, 'Innovation and Institutions from the Bottom Up', p. 985.

111 Koppl et al., *Economics for a Creative World*, p. 2.

112 For an economy as a process of variation and selection, see Nelson and Winter, *An Evolutionary Theory of Economic Change*, pp. 14–17.

113 Harper, 'Innovation and Institutions from the Bottom Up', p. 991.

the process of change by strengthening the *background institutions* that set the system in motion.[114] Once we have identified innovation as part of a complex and self-organising system, intelligible policies are to be located at the level of the fundamental rules that shape the system itself; as distinct from specific interventions, intended to assist or prevent specific experiments or identifiable industries. In other terms, the desirability of innovation is something to bear in mind when constructing the 'rules of the game', and cannot be accomplished with measures oriented at specific players.[115] Leaning on institutional economics, jurists who wish to promote innovation need to identify basic rules that, as a general propensity, will promote the endogenous emergence of novelty from within the system.[116] This means that innovation will be promoted by legal institutions that facilitate entrepreneurship and smoothen the testing of their experiments within exchanges with consumers.

30. Secondly, from an institutional perspective, the task is not to identify an ideal benchmark, where all knowledge is perfectly given and can be appropriated in such a way that social value is maximised.[117] Once we have identified an economy as a world with imperfect information, where innovation emerges via trial-and-error mechanisms, intelligible policies are not those that promise perfection. The fundamental rules that we look for are rules that often (not always) and over time (not necessarily instantly) enable interplay between consumers and entrepreneurs create *better* social states, not perfect ones.[118]

31. From an institutional perspective, novelty emerges against the backdrop of legal rights that entrepreneurs and consumers use to exchange goods and services. The lure for profit that drives the experiments, requires a legal system

---

114 Metcalfe, 'Systems Failure and the Case for Innovation Policy', p. 68 ('The state is not promoting individual innovation events in this view; rather it is setting the framework conditions in which innovation systems can better self-organize across the range of activities in an economy').

115 G. Anderson, 'Behind the Veil: The Political Economy of Constitutional Change', in W.M. Crain and R.D. Tollison (eds.), *Predicting Politics: Essays in Empirical Economics* (Ann Harbor: University of Michigan Press, 1990), pp. 89–100; D. Harper, *Foundations of Entrepreneurship and Economic Development* (London: Routledge, 2003), p. 172.

116 Institutional economists warn us that no single rule is has an isolated effect, and that it will be the combination of sets of rules that will cause or hamper innovation.

117 This is the model used by Arrow.

118 As shown by Demsetz, what is efficient really depends on the 'ideal' with which one starts the economic exercise. Demsetz, 'Information and Efficiency: Another Viewpoint', pp. 1–22 ('To say that private enterprise is inefficient because indivisibilities and imperfect knowledge are part of life, or because people are susceptible to the human weaknesses subsumed in the term moral hazards, or because marketing commodity-options is not costless, or because persons are risk-averse, is to say little more than that the competitive equilibrium would be different if these were not the facts of life. But, if they are the facts of life, if, that is, they cannot be erased from life at zero cost, *then truly efficient institutions will yield different long-run equilibrium conditions* than those now used to describe the ideal norm.').

where profits are protected. Consumers are more likely to 'test and revise' their preferences when they know that firms are likely to keep their end of the deal and are enforced to deliver them the services they purchased. Most experiments require cooperative efforts, for which we should retain the traditional rules of contract law which enable us to do business with one another.[119] Novelty is a product of 'property and exchange', so legal systems that have relatively stable and secure property rights and contract law will facilitate more innovations than systems where one's possessions are insecure, or contracts are not enforced.[120] So we promote novelty by adopting the underpinning rules of the market process, such as the right to keep goods for yourself, modify them, manage them or exchange them for things we value more. It is in this regard that Harper and Endres suggest that the best innovation policy lies in support for general rules of property and contract.[121]

32. Our policy advice does not simply pertain to the kind of rights, *in casu* property rights, but also to the form they take. In an innovative society, entrepreneurs lack certainty over future successes. A legal system that cultivates secure and properly enforced rights will raise the amount of risk people are willing to take within the marketplace, by taking away any unnecessary uncertainty over the legal conditions that govern their experiments. That the need for secure legal institutions has a temporal element is noticed by Richard Epstein when he contends 'while I support innovation in technology and business, I think that *permanence and stability* are the cardinal virtues of the legal rules that make private innovation and public progress possible'.[122]

Indeed, when it comes to the legal structure, actors that deal with change and are engaged with experiments are likely to benefit from a set of rules that embraces continuity over time. Connected to this, entrepreneurs act within a world of limited knowledge, devoting their cognitive skills and creativity to experiments. The *simpler* and more transparent the legal rules will be, the easier the experiments will flow. Time and energy are scarce, and 'the fewer and the more accessible the inputs needed to make any legal decision', the more energy can be directed to experiments on the ground.[123] The last institutional lesson

---

119 R. Epstein, *Simple Rules for a Complex World* (Cambridge, MA: Harvard University Press, 1995), p. 327.

120 D. Harper and A. Endres, 'Innovation, Recombinant Capital and Public Policy', *Supreme Court Economic Review*, 2015, vol. 23, p. 211 ('The thrust of the argument is that government can cultivate innovation by providing an appropriate institutional scaffolding; government has a role in innovation only to the extent that it supports general rules of property and contract and other basic rules of the game that permit the participation of all potential entrepreneurs and entrepreneurial firms.').

121 D. Harper and A. Endres, 'Innovation, Recombinant Capital and Public Policy', *Supreme Court Economic Review*, 2015, vol. 23, no. 1, pp. 193–219.

122 Epstein, *Simple Rules for a Complex World*, p. xii.

123 This is how Epstein operationalises legal simplicity. See *ibid.*, p. 27.

that we can draw from our market process account is generality. Consonant with the earlier insight that innovation 'policy' is to be located at the level of the 'rules of the game', rules for innovation need to be sufficiently *general*. By this, we mean rules that intend to enhance innovation will apply over various sets of people and situations, irrespective of specific circumstances of time and place.[124] Since innovation is a serendipitous process, boiling up constantly from within the system, the law cannot foresee the circumstances that enable novel experiments, nor the kind of individuals that are suited to initiate novelty. Conversely, the point of innovation policy is to facilitate the use of unpredictable circumstances, subjective knowledge and suddenly appearing opportunities by people we do not know.[125] In order to maximise the range of action, and the use of knowledge, for these future entrepreneurs, we need a legal system that is open-ended and will apply to a wide range of unforeseeable circumstances. *Ceteris paribus*, this means that innovation-policy will favour general rules that apply indifferently to all market agents and situations, and rule-out regulatory commands and specific provisions for specific individuals or industries.[126]

With these institutional cues in mind, we can extend the defence for property rights to intellectual property rights. A patent is an exclusive right to market an invention for a fixed period.[127] The purpose of this chapter is not to render a full-blown defence of patents. However, we remark that the information problems for tax incentives are highly underestimated by policymakers and the legal literature.[128] As in many contributions, innovation is represented as a question of creating the proper incentive. Our more enriched, process-based model of economic activity nuances this perspective and posits that innovation policy is about how to deal with a knowledge problem. Once we depict innovation as an unpredictable phenomenon, part of a discovery process, we can tentatively suggest a preference for *ex-post* measures (like patents) and raise caution against *ex-ante* policies such as tax incentives. Within a comparative perspective, patent rights will promote entrepreneurial experiments, while being less vulnerable to the informational challenges that we uncovered.

---

124 See F. Hayek, *The Road to Serfdom* (London: Routledge, 2001), p. 78.

125 Hayek rests his case for general rules upon the unpredictability of the future. See, e.g., *ibid.*, p. 79 ('The state should confine itself to establishing rules applying to general types of situations and should allow the individuals freedom in everything which depends on the circumstances of time and place, because only the individuals concerned in each instance can fully know these circumstances and adapt their actions to them.').

126 V. Vanberg, *The Constitution of Markets: Essays in Political Economy* (London, New York: Routledge, 2001), 224 p.

127 Scotchmer, *Innovation and Incentives*, 357 p.

128 Hemel and Ouellette see an information problem for ex ante tax incentives but think these are circumstantial rather than categorical. See Hemel and Ouellette, 'Innovation Policy Pluralism', p. 557 ('Finally, refundable tax credits, like patents, are most effective when the government is at a disadvantage evaluating projects, but they may be more effective than patents when researchers face a high risk of failure and run up against binding capital constraints').

33. When following the precepts of generality, patent-rights are not required to favour *some experiments* or expenditures over others. Although some minor discretion cannot be avoided (e.g., within the drafting of patent law, within the process whereby patents are granted), the government is substantially less required to curate innovation by selecting the operations and expenditures as is the case with granting tax subsidies.[129] When the patent legislation is drafted in a general fashion, and the granted patent rights avoid the danger of being too broad or too long, numerous sets of experiments and types of entrepreneurs can rely upon patent-protection to try to monetise his experiment.[130] Whereas tax incentives prioritise knowledge on behalf of governments to pick experiments, well-designed patent legislation puts this competence (and risk) with entrepreneurs on the ground.

34. More importantly, patent rights prioritise consumer preferences in the production of creative knowledge and innovation. Contrary to a system where R&D support is derived through tax measures, under a patent-approach, income can be generated only in case of consumer consent to purchase the product or service. Respecting the sequence of the market process, patents will be rewarding only when proposed novelties gather success and accumulate within the economy. So, where patents structure the game, by rewarding *actual* (yet unknown) *discoveries*, crafting tax incentives involves gambling in a game of chance.

35. As an example, say there are thousands of technology firms in a market that all come up with different new applications every day. Some of these will be successful, others will need to be revised, and many will be commercial flops that disappear. Which legal rules facilitate the process of testing new applications in the marketplace? How do we make sure that those applications that satisfy consumer preferences disseminate within an economy? Under the patent approach, the government hands out property rights over inventions, meaning that once the patent is granted, that specific new product cannot be copied by competitors. A government can recognise property rights with respect to all new products without discrimination and does not need to valorise any of these new applications: the rewards are subsequently decided by consumers in the market. We can see patents as *permissions* we give to tech firms to enter the race with their new products. It is the race itself – i.e., consumers assigning euros – that decides the rewards that flow to these firms. Under a subsidy approach, on the other hand, the government gives financial support to specific investments

129 Tax incentives will generally be more specific and tailored than patent law, as the former directly grants tax subsidies.

130 It is crucial that the granted IP rights cover exactly the invented product, and are limited in time, if not, we risk overprotection and undermine the competition that drives innovation.

before products are brought to market. Not only will it need to identify novelty (which the patent process must also do), it finances only specific projects. So, if patents are permissions to join the race, subsidies are *rewards* – benefits that effectively increase corporate revenue. First, because the government transfers money, it must be more discriminating than under the patent approach: giving subsidies to all players would be a budgetary disaster. Second, to be efficient, the subsidy approach requires the government to know which of the new applications are for products that will be successful in the market. If it spends tax money on, say, a music application no one wants, this results in waste. If it transfers money to a new game on our phones that consumers dislike, this is inefficient. The same is not true of the property approach: if a patented product turns out to be unsuccessful, no tax money was pumped into a commercial flop. Patents do not require the government to valorise any project; they delegate this task to all consumers. The point of this chapter is that the subsidy approach only amplifies the knowledge problem to which innovation is already subject.

In conclusion, patents can be understood as relative basic rights, rules that structure the game, while tax incentives have more in common with specific interventions that wish to shape the outcome.[131] A system of patents that enables entrepreneurs and inventors to secure exclusive control over their findings, and that renders the value of these innovative creations subject to consumer assessment via market interactions, promotes experimental interactions between market agents while avoiding a priori evaluations over specific experiments and associated expenditures. We can tentatively argue that patents better deal with the knowledge problem to which the market process is a response.

4. CONCLUSION

36. This chapter examined the question of which legal rules are most conducive to the emergence of innovation in a market economy. The point was to show how different economic models of innovation will inspire different legal proposals to stimulate it. The neoclassical model perceives an economy as a static phenomenon about which we can easily gather information, and novelty as an exogenous shock. This justifies the creation of tax incentives, financial stimuli ex ante, at the time of investment. Contrary to the neoclassical model, and based on the work of Paul Romer and Israel Kirzner, I argued that innovation stems from the continuous stream of experiments that entrepreneurs insert into an economy, and consumers, via the price system, select among. This chapter outlines my belief that steering the market with tax breaks at the time of investment is an anachronistic exercise: we assume knowledge about the outcome of a process that only the process can produce. To make a comparison, it is like using biological

131 I admit that the difference is one of degree.

enhancement techniques today to optimise our adaptation to the environment ten thousand years from now. The information we need to efficiently interfere in the dynamic of innovation will reveal itself only during the process in which we try to intervene. This means we can stimulate innovation only indirectly, by securing the *background institutions* that drive the market process. This chapter highlights support for simple, stable, and general rules of property and contract as pivotal 'rules for innovation'. When following the precepts of generality, a patent system that grants entrepreneurs and inventors exclusive control over their findings, and that renders the value of these innovations subject to the voice of consumers in the marketplace, respects the sequence of the market process and is more consistent with the decentralised nature of knowledge than tax incentives are.

CHAPTER 3

SETTING THE SCENE: ON AI ETHICS AND REGULATION

Michiel Fierens*, Stephanie Rossello**
and Ellen Wauters***

1. INTRODUCTION

1. AI has the power to transform our societies and to have a profound impact across various societal domains. Consequently, it has sparked a debate about the principles and values that should guide its development and use. The concerns include loss of jobs, misuse, discrimination and so on. Against this background, we have in the past years witnessed an ever-richer debate on how AI *ought* and *ought not to be* (used). Participants in this debate rely not only (and some would say too little)[1] on the law, that what is (il-)legal, to provide an answer to this question.

In this chapter, we would like to provide the overarching ethical and legal framework underlying this debate by focusing on three aspects. To fully understand the impact of AI on the law (cf. subsequent chapters of this book), we present the main ethical challenges that AI raises and the principles that have been adopted to tackle them (part 2). We then touch upon a common feature of the policy documents and ethics guidelines on AI that have been published so far: there is a need for some form of regulation. Therefore, before we move on to form and substance of a possible regulation, we first answer some fundamental questions, namely: what is regulation and what, when and how exactly should we regulate (part 3)? Finally, we provide an overview of AI governance in some of the jurisdictions that have already taken policy actions on AI. As this domain is evolving fast, we do not aim to give a comprehensive overview. Rather, we intend to provide a bird's eye view of the direction in which the ethical and legal

* Ph.D. research, KU Leuven Centre for IT and IP Law.
** Legal researcher, KU Leuven Centre for IT and IP Law.
*** Legal researcher, KU Leuven Centre for IT and IP Law.

1 See: P. Nemitz, 'Constitutional democracy and technology in the age of artificial intelligence', SSRN, 2018, p. 12, https://ssrn.com/abstract=3234336.

framework on AI might evolve the coming years (part 4). We conclude with summarising the main findings (part 5).

2. ETHICS OF AI

2. Ethics, which can be described as the study of what is good and bad moral behaviour[2], has been relied on to the same extent as – and perhaps even more heavily than – the law in the debate on what AI ought (not) to be or do. Although this reliance on ethics has been criticised by some as 'ethics-washing'[3], approaching AI from both the perspective of ethics and the law has its merits. As remarked by Floridi, 'digital regulation indicates what the legal and illegal moves in the game are, so to speak, but it says nothing about what the good and best moves could be, among those that are legal, to win the game, that is, to have a better society'.[4] Ethics is hence ascribed the function of moral compass[5], steering the development, deployment and use of AI into a morally good direction.[6]

3. Ethics can contribute to 'making, shaping or changing the law' ('hard ethics')[7] or it can prescribe what 'ought and ought not to be done *over and above* the existing regulation' ('soft ethics').[8] Ethics may moreover be more flexible than the law and may hence more easily keep up with the pace of technological progress than the latter.[9]

2 E. Bietti, 'From ethics washing to ethics bashing: a view on tech ethics from within moral philosophy', SSRN (draft), 2020, title 2, https://papers.ssrn.com/sol3/papers.cfm?abstract_id=3513182.

3 E. Bietti, 'From ethics washing to ethics bashing'; B. Wagner, 'Ethics as an escape from regulation: from ethics-washing to ethics shopping?', in E. Bayamlioglu, I. Baraliuc, L. Janssens, M. Hildebrandt (eds.), *Being profiled. Cogitas ergo sum: 10 years of profiling the European citizen* (e-book: Amsterdam University Press, 2018), pp. 84–89.

4 L. Floridi, 'Soft ethics, the governance of the digital and the General Data Protection Regulation', *Philos. T. R. Soc. A 376*, 2018, vol. 376, no. 2133, p. 4.

5 P. Valcke and S. Rossello, 'The artificial lawyer', in VRG alumni (eds.), *Recht in beweging. 27ste VRG-Alumnidag* (Oud-Turnhout/'s-Hertogenbosch: Gompel & Svacina, 2020), p. 199.

6 It is important to make a distinction between ethics and codes of ethics. In the domain of business or professional activities, the latter can often be considered as public statements of values and business practices. These codes formalise a number of principles of action and 'minimum' standards. By issuing these codes of conducts, companies or professions commit themselves to adhere to these standards. For more information on this topic see: Y. Poullet, 'Ethique et droits de l'homme dans notre société du numérique', *Mémoire de l'académie royal de Belgique*, 2020, p. 14 and further.

7 Floridi, 'Soft ethics, the governance of the digital', p. 4.

8 *Ibid.*, p. 5.

9 P. Boddington, *Towards a code of ethics for artificial intelligence,* 1st edn (e-book: Springer, 2017), pp. 25.

4. Although there is no unanimously accepted definition of AI[10], we use the word in its broadest meaning, as a set of technologies (software, regardless of whether it is embedded in hardware) that intend to emulate the capacities of the human brain. We moreover mainly focus on AI systems implementing technologies such as ML, and its sub-fields deep learning and neural networks, which are fuelled by big data and represent the so-called 'second generation AI'.

It is crucial to understand that certain ethical challenges raised by these AI systems are similar to the ones raised by other rapidly evolving technologies relying on big data. First, this is the case for issues related to the (ab)use of data.[11] The collection and analysis of large datasets, often centralised in the hands of a few actors[12], may indeed lead to an increased capacity to re-identify individuals by, for instance, linking datasets or inferring new data from existing datasets.[13] Individuals may also be unaware of their data being collected or being used in another context than the one in which the data were originally collected.[14] Additionally, the collection and analysis of large datasets may infringe upon the so-called right to group privacy, which may occur when the identification of categories of individuals leads to 'serious ethical problems from group discrimination (e.g., ageism, ethnicism, sexism) to group-targeted forms of violence'.[15] A second issue common to many big data-driven technologies is that of data security and vulnerability to malicious cyberattacks.[16] A third challenge that is raised by AI is that, like other emerging digital technologies, it has an impact on work and may lead to unemployment.[17] AI therefore raises

10 One of the most recent definitions of AI has been offered by the High Level Expert Group on Artificial Intelligence appointed by the European Commission (hereinafter 'HLEGAI'): 'Artificial intelligence (AI) systems are software (and possibly also hardware) systems designed by humans that, given a complex goal, act in the physical or digital dimension by perceiving their environment through data acquisition, interpreting the collected structured or unstructured data, reasoning on the knowledge, or processing the information, derived from this data and deciding the best action(s) to take to achieve the given goal. AI systems can either use symbolic rules or learn a numeric model, and they can also adapt their behaviour by analysing how the environment is affected by their previous actions. As a scientific discipline, AI includes several approaches and techniques, such as machine learning (of which deep learning and reinforcement learning are specific examples), machine reasoning (which includes planning, scheduling, knowledge representation and reasoning, search, and optimization), and robotics (which includes control, perception, sensors and actuators, as well as the integration of all other techniques into cyber-physical systems', HLEGAI, 'A definition of Artificial Intelligence: main capabilities and scientific disciplines', 8 April 2019, p. 4, https://ec.europa.eu/digital-single-market/en/news/definition-artificial-intelligence-main-capabilities-and-scientific-disciplines.

11 Boddington, *Towards a code of ethics for artificial intelligence*, pp. 28–29.

12 Nemitz, 'Constitutional democracy', pp. 4–7.

13 L. Floridi and M. Taddeo, 'What is data ethics?', *Phil. Trans. R. Soc. A 374*, 2016, vol. 374, no. 2083, p. 3.

14 M. Coeckelbergh, 'The ethics of artificial intelligence', *Technology and Regulation*, 2019, p. 31.

15 Floridi and Taddeo, 'What is data ethics?', p. 3.

16 Coeckelbergh, 'The ethics of artificial intelligence', p. 31.

17 *Ibid.*, p. 32.

the question as to whether we have to restructure our labour market and social institutions.[18] Finally, AI-driven decisions may challenge the rule of law, as they may regulate human behaviour on the basis of unintelligible code (cf. *infra*), rather than on the basis of public rules enacted by democratically chosen representatives.[19]

Conversely, because of certain distinctive properties of AI systems, the latter also raise several distinctive ethical challenges. (Second-generation) AI systems are (albeit in varying degrees) autonomous and adaptable. With autonomous we mean that AI systems are capable of acting in complex environments without constant human intervention.[20] Adaptability refers to the AI systems' capacity to learn by themselves, on the basis of experience and interaction with the environment and to change their behaviour according to such experience.[21] AI also raises distinctive ethical questions because of its typical use to 'enhance or replace human decision making and human judgment'.[22] In particular, Mittelstadt and others[23] identify the following ethical challenges in relation to those decision-making algorithms that take actions that are difficult to predict or to understand for humans.

First, these algorithms produce statistically 'probable yet inevitably uncertain knowledge'[24] which may lead to output that cannot justifiably be acted upon. Second, there is a lack of knowledge on how these algorithms, based on a certain input A, produce a certain output B. This process may be inscrutable even for developers and designers of the algorithm.[25] This leads to opacity or, in other words, a lack of transparency in decision-making.[26] As pointed out by Zarsky, opacity may lead to the perception of algorithmic decision-making as arbitrary

18 *Ibid.*

19 The reader interested in the impact of data-driven decision-making on the rule of law is recommended to consult: E. Bayamlıoğlu and R. Leenes, 'The 'rule of law' implications of data-driven decision-making: a techno-regulatory perspective', *Law, Innovation and Technology*, 2018, vol. 10, no. 2, pp. 295–313.

20 Elements of AI, 'What is AI', https://course.elementsofai.com/1/1. See also: L. Floridi and J.W. Sanders, 'On the morality of artificial agents', *Minds and Machines*, 2004, no. 14, p. 357, which offer the following definition of autonomy in the context of artificial agents: 'Autonomy means that the agent is able to change state without direct response to interaction: it can perform internal transitions to change its state. So, an agent must have at least two states. This property imbues an agent with a certain degree of complexity and independence from its environment'.

21 Elements of AI, 'What is AI'. Floridi and Sanders, 'On the morality of artificial agents', p. 358, more specifically conceive of adaptability as a 'property [which] ensures that an agent might be viewed, at the given LoA, as learning its own mode of operation in a way which depends critically on its experience'.

22 Boddington, *Towards a code of ethics for artificial intelligence*, p. 29.

23 B. Mittelstadt, P. Allo, M. Taddeo, S. Wachter and L. Floridi, 'The ethics of algorithms: mapping the debate', *Big Data & Society*, 2016, vol. 3, no. 2, p. 3.

24 *Ibid.* p. 4.

25 *Ibid.*

26 *Ibid.* pp. 6–7. See also: Coeckelbergh, 'The ethics of artificial intelligence', p. 32.

and may hinder the affected person's capacity to understand and contest the outcome of the decision-making process.[27] This is especially the case for so-called 'black-box' AI systems. Third, AI systems may lead to biased decisions.[28] The bias may come from data, as the reliability and accuracy of the systems' output (also) depend on the quality of the data they have been fed with.[29] The bias can also come from the designer or developer, since the latter's values are inevitably reflected in the system's design and functionality.[30] A problem closely related to bias is that decision-making algorithms may lead to discrimination[31] against protected[32] (such as discrimination on the basis of race, religion or gender) and non-protected groups, thereby potentially introducing new forms of discrimination.[33] A frequently cited origin of discrimination is profiling, i.e. 'the construction or inference of patterns by means of data mining and [...] the application of the ensuing profiles to people whose data match with them'.[34] The technique of profiling (a type of grouping) is often at odds with the protection of the privacy of the resulting group (outcome or profile), as the designer or developer of the algorithm often pursues a different objective than the individual privacy or the collective privacy of the group. People are classified according to certain characteristics that are important for attaining that particular objective by the designer of the developer and may thus be negatively impacted if the classification in a particular group has certain negative practical consequences (e.g., creditworthiness of a particular group with certain characteristics).[35]

Additionally, AI algorithms used for decision-making can nudge human behaviour by filtering (so-called 'personalising') information: 'different content, information, prices etc. are offered to groups or classes of people within a population according to a particular attribute, e.g., ability to pay'.[36] This can result in the creation of so-called 'filter-bubbles'.[37] These could undermine

---

27 T. Zarsky, 'The trouble with algorithmic decisions: an analytic road map to examine efficiency and fairness in automated and opaque decision making', *Science Technology and Human Values*, 2016, vol. 41, no. 1, p. 129.

28 Mittelstadt et al., 'The ethics of algorithms', pp. 7–9. See also: Coeckelbergh, 'The ethics of artificial intelligence', p. 32.

29 Coeckelbergh, 'The ethics of artificial intelligence', p. 32.

30 Mittelstadt et al., 'The ethics of algorithms', p. 7.

31 *Ibid.* p. 8.

32 Zarsky, 'The trouble with algorithmic decisions', p. 126.

33 F. Zuiderveen Borgesius, 'Discrimination, artificial intelligence, and algorithmic decision-making', (study prepared for the Council of Europe) 2019, p. 35, https://rm.coe.int/discrimination-artificial-intelligence-and-algorithmic-decision-making/1680925d73.

34 M. Hildebrandt and B.J. Koops, 'The Challenges of Ambient Law and Legal Protection in the Profiling Era', *The Modern Law Review*, vol. 73, no. 3, 2010, p. 431, as quoted in Mittelstadt et al., 'The ethics of algorithms', p. 8.

35 L. Taylor, L. Floridi and B. van der Sloot, *Group Privacy: New Challenges of Data Technologies* (Cham: Springer International Publishing 2017), pp. 7–11.

36 Mittelstadt et al., 'The ethics of algorithms', p. 9.

37 This term was coined by the internet activist Eli Parisier: E. Parisier, *The Filter Bubble: What the Internet Is Hiding from You* (e-book: Penguin Books 2011).

human autonomy since they decrease information diversity[38], thereby limiting human choice.

Another frequently cited problem raised by AI algorithms is the one of accountability for AI actions/output.[39] To a certain extent, this is a problem that is common to many big data-driven technologies that rely on a complex web of interactions among different actors, which work on different elements of the system and at different levels of the supply chain.[40] However, as pointed out by Mittelstadt and others[41], this problem may be exacerbated by autonomous and self-learning decision-making algorithms. These may indeed display unpredictable behaviour because they do not follow a linear decision-making path.[42] In such an ecosystem it can be particularly challenging to establish *ex ante* duties of the AI systems evaluation and *ex post* responsibility (or, in legal terms, liability).

5. In response to the aforementioned challenges, we have over the past years witnessed the adoption of numerous ethical guidelines on AI by policymakers, academia, the private sector and civil society.[43] These guidelines contain principles that are close to those developed in bioethics, which is often seen as the field that most resembles digital ethics.[44] Poullet sees two reasons for this. The first is the nature of the internet, which requires an international dimension of the ethical principles. A global consensus must be found, not on their concrete translation, but setting out these principles. In bioethics, an international agreement was reached on common ethical values, based on human rights which, according to the Oviedo Convention[45], constitute the necessary foundation to ensure the primacy of the human being in technological change. These same requirements must be addressed in relation to the profound changes in the information society. The second reason is that the domain of bioethics can provide useful indication in the search of a common foundation. In both fields,

---

38 Mittelstadt et al., 'The ethics of algorithms', p. 9.

39 Boddington, *Towards a code of ethics for artificial intelligence*, p. 29.

40 Coeckelbergh, 'The ethics of artificial intelligence', p. 31.

41 Mittelstadt et al., 'The ethics of algorithms', p. 10–12.

42 *Ibid.* p. 10.

43 See for a mapping of existing ethical initiatives for example: Algorithm Watch, 'AI ethic guidelines: a global inventory'.

44 L. Floridi, J. Cowls, M. Beltrametti, R. Chatila, P. Chazerand, V. Dignum, C. Luetge, R. Madelin, U. Pagallo, F. Rossi, B. Schafer, P. Valcke and E. Vayena, 'AI4People – an ethical framework for a good AI society: opportunities, risks, principles, and recommendations', *Minds and Machines*, 2018, p. 696.

45 Article 2 Convention for the protection of Human Rights and Dignity of the Human Being with regard to the Application of Biology and Medicine: Convention on Human Rights and Biomedicine (ETS No. 164), 1 December 1999.

it is a question of human identity and of the position of individuals in relation to technologies.[46]

A recent review by Jobin, Ienca and Vayena of 84 documents containing ethical principles and guidelines on AI identified the following 11 'overarching ethical values and principles', mentioned in order of frequency with which they were cited in the reviewed documents: transparency, justice and fairness, non-maleficence, responsibility, privacy, beneficence, freedom and autonomy, trust, dignity, sustainability and solidarity.[47]

The OECD for instance published its Recommendation on AI in 2019 in which the following principles for responsible stewardship of trustworthy AI are expressed: inclusive growth, sustainable development and well-being; human-centred values and fairness; transparency and explainability; robustness, security and safety and accountability.[48] In addition the Recommendation provides five recommendations for policy-makers relating to national policies and international co-operation for trustworthy AI, namely: investing in AI research and development; fostering a digital ecosystem for AI; shaping an enabling policy environment for AI; building human capacity and preparing for labour market transformation and international co-operation for trustworthy AI.[49] In 2021, the United Nations Educational, Scientific and Cultural Organisation (UNESCO) adopted the Recommendation on the ethics of Artificial Intelligence.[50] One of the objectives is 'to provide a universal framework of values, principles and actions to guide States in the formulation of their legislation, policies or other instruments regarding AI, consistent with international law'. The Recommendation discerns values[51], which are motivating ideals in shaping policy measures and legal norms. These inspire desirable behaviour and represent the foundations of principles. Next to these values, there are also a set of principles[52] that unpack the values underlying them

---

46 Y. Poullet, 'Ethique et droits de l'homme dans notre société du numérique', (Bruxelles: Mémoire de l'académie royal de Belgique, 2020), p. 86.

47 A. Jobin, M. Ienca and E. Vayena, 'The global landscape of AI ethics', Nature Machine Intelligence, 2019, vol. 1, no. 9, p. 391. For other recent mappings of ethics guidelines see: J. Fjeld, N. Achten, H. Hilligoss, C.A Nagy and M. Srikumar, 'Principled Artificial Intelligence: mapping consensus in ethical and rights-based approaches to principles for AI', SSRN, 2020, pp. 1–71, https://papers.ssrn.com/sol3/papers.cfm?abstract_id=3518482; T. Hagendorff, 'The ethics of AI ethics: an evaluation of guidelines', Minds and Machines, 2020, no. 30, pp. 99–120.

48 OECD, Recommendation of the Council on Artificial Intelligence, OECD/LEGAL/0449, 2019, https://legalinstruments.oecd.org/en/instruments/OECD-LEGAL-0449.

49 *Ibid.*

50 UNESCO, Recommendation on the ethics of Artificial Intelligence, 2021, https://unesdoc.unesco.org/ark:/48223/pf0000377897.

51 The values are Respect, protection and promotion of human rights and fundamental freedoms and human dignity; Environment and ecosystem flourishing; Ensuring diversity and inclusiveness; Living in peaceful, just and interconnected societies.

52 The principles are Proportionality and Do No Harm; Safety and security; Fairness and non-discrimination; Sustainability; Right to Privacy, and Data Protection; Human oversight

more concretely so that the values can be more easily operationalised in policy statements and actions.[53] Below we provide a brief overview of how, according to the authors of the study, these principles are interpreted in the reviewed sources.

Transparency is said to 'comprise efforts to increase explainability, interpretability or other acts of communication and disclosure' and is often referred to in relation to data use, human-AI interaction, automated decisions.[54] Justice is often explained in terms of fairness and prevention of unwanted bias and discrimination[55], while non-maleficence refers to the general principle that AI should not cause any harm.[56] Moreover, references to responsibility and accountability include clarifying the attribution of responsibility and legal liability.[57] Privacy often encompasses data protection and security, while trust underlines (among others) the importance of trustworthy AI technology, research and development.[58] Sustainability includes protecting the environment, the planet's ecosystem, biodiversity, fair and equal societies and peace.[59] Finally, while beneficence (i.e. to promote good) and dignity are rarely defined in detail, solidarity is often mentioned in relation to the impact of AI on employment.[60] The report concludes that, while there is a growing convergence on the importance of certain principles[61], there is still substantial divergence on (among others) how these principles are interpreted and how they should be implemented in practice. Interestingly, these 11 principles suggest that there is a need to tackle both the challenges that AI poses to individual interests (as evidenced by, for instance, references to the principle of privacy) and collective interests (as evidenced by, for instance, references to the principle of sustainability). After all, various authors have held that current legal assessments mainly focus on the individual, whereas the challenges of an AI system also have a collective dimension, which may in future also express collective interests or give rise to group rights.[62] The inherent relationality of data, whereby the collection of data from a single individual can also be used to target another individual, ensures that possible harm can consist of different sums of harm,

and determination; Transparency and explainability; Responsibility and accountability; Awareness and literacy; Multi-stakeholder and adaptive governance and collaboration.

53 UNESCO, Recommendation on the ethics of artificial intelligence, 23 November 2021, https://unesdoc.unesco.org/ark:/48223/pf0000381137.

54 Jobin, Jenca and Vayena, 'The global landscape of AI ethics', p. 391.

55 *Ibid.*, p. 394.

56 *Ibid.*

57 *Ibid.*

58 *Ibid.*, p. 395.

59 *Ibid.*

60 *Ibid.*, pp. 395–396.

61 The principles are more specifically: transparency, justice and fairness, non-maleficence, responsibility and privacy. *Ibid.*, p. 391.

62 N. Smuha, 'Beyond the individual: governing AI's societal harm', *Internet Policy Review*, vol. 10, no. 3, 2021, p. 3; Taylor, Floridi and van der Sloot., *Group Privacy: New Challenges of Data Technologies*, pp. 233–235.

arising from multiple individual interests. Besides collective harm, account must also be taken of societal harm, which requires different measures than collective harm (sum of individuals).[63] At present, however, there is no suitable vocabulary to address these issues, and a concept of group privacy is not yet entirely workable due to, among other things, a lack of institutions that can represent the rights and obligations of such groups.[64]

6. Although this principled approach to AI helps laying a common ground for discussions on how to maximise the benefits and minimise the risks that AI poses, it is by itself insufficient to achieve this goal. First, as already noted by many, vague abstract principles such as the ones mentioned above need to be operationalised into more concrete guidelines.[65] This may, however, prove difficult given the absence of an established method in AI ethics to translate principles to practice.[66] Second, ethical principles are not legally binding and can hence not be enforced in a court of law. It is therefore questionable whether, absent any legal obligation to do so as well as a consistent enforcement of these obligations by the responsible authorities, the relevant actors would be sufficiently incentivised to abide by these principles *ex ante*, and potential victims of damage caused by AI would receive any form of redress *ex post*. Therefore, although we do not intend to engage in any form of 'ethics bashing', it is, in our view, of crucial importance to reflect on the concept of 'regulation', as we do in the following part.

3. REGULATION OF AI

7. Before looking into concrete regulatory solutions, it is fundamental that we define what regulation is. Although this seems an easy question, it is a hard one to answer. As is the case with AI (*infra*), there is no universally agreed-upon definition of this concept. Instead, there is a whole array of definitions, ranging from very narrow to very broad.[67] According to Black, there are three main definitions of regulation:

'In the first, regulation is the promulgation of rules by government accompanied by mechanisms for monitoring and enforcement, usually assumed

63 N. Smuha, 'Beyond the individual: governing AI's societal harm', pp. 5–12.

64 A.H. Vedder, 'Privatization, information technology and privacy: Reconsidering the social responsibilities of private organizations' in G. Moore (ed.), *Business ethics: Principles and practice* (Sunderland: Business Education Publishers, 1997) pp. 215–226; Taylor, Floridi and van der Sloot., *Group Privacy: New Challenges of Data Technologies*, pp. 233–235.

65 See for example: Coeckelbergh, 'The ethics of artificial intelligence', p. 33.

66 B. Mittelstadt, 'Principles alone cannot guarantee ethical AI', *Nature Machine Intelligence*, 2019, vol. 1, no. 11, p. 503.

67 E. Lievens, *Protecting Children in the digital era: the use of alternative regulatory instruments* (Leiden, Boston: Brill | Nijhoff 2010), p. 144.

to be performed through a specialist public agency. In the second, it is any form of direct state intervention in the economy, whatever form that intervention might take. In the third, regulation is all mechanisms of social control or influence affecting all aspects of behaviour from whatever source, whether they are intentional or not'.[68]

However, as Black was not convinced of these definitions, she developed one herself: 'regulation is a process involving the sustained and focused attempt to alter the behaviour of others with the intention of producing a broadly identified outcome or outcomes'.[69] This definition implies that the state is not the sole regulator and that other modalities of regulation can be envisaged.

Regulatory functions can be exercised primarily by one actor or be dispersed among several actors within a system. According to Black, whose research on regulation is relevant for our domain, a regulatory regime, system or network is a 'set of interrelated actors who are jointly attempting to address a particular set of problems to achieve a set of goals, its boundaries are defined by the definition of the problem being addressed, and it has some continuity over time'.[70] This line of reasoning is also followed by Gunningham and others, who introduced the concept of 'smart regulation', which refers to a form of regulatory pluralism that embraces flexible, imaginative and innovative forms of social control.[71] It encompasses self-regulation and co-regulation, whereby commercial interests and non-governmental organisations, for instance, can act as regulatory surrogates, in order to improve the effectiveness and efficiency of more conventional forms of direct government regulation. The underlying rationale is that, in most circumstances, the use of multiple, rather than single, policy instruments and a broader range of regulatory actors, will produce better regulation.[72]

8. In the next stage, the following questions will need to be answered: what should we regulate, when and how?[73]

Defining 'what' we should regulate when it comes to AI is not an easy task. AI is a catch-all term and at the moment, there is no universally accepted definition

---

68 J. Black, 'Critical reflections on regulation', *Australian Journal of Legal Philosophy*, 2002, 27, vol. 1, p. 35.

69 *Ibid.*, p. 35.

70 J. Black and A. Murray, 'Regulating AI and machine learning: setting the regulatory agenda', *Journal of Law and Technology*, 2019, 10, vol. 3, p. 10.

71 N. Gunningham and D. Sinclair, 'Smart Regulation', in P. Drahos (ed.), *Regulatory theory. Foundations and applications* (Canberra: Australian National University Press, 2017), p. 133.

72 *Ibid.*, p. 133. In this context, see for instance: Interinstitutional agreement on better law-making of the EU of 2003 (https://eur-lex.europa.eu/legal-content/EN/TXT/?uri=CELEX%3A32003Q1231%2801%29), which defines self - and co-regulation. However, this agreement was replaced in 2016 and the new version no longer includes a legal framework for the use of alternative methods of regulation (https://eur-lex.europa.eu/legal-content/EN/TXT/?uri=CELEX%3A32016Q0512%2801%29).

73 M. Fenwick, W.A. Kaal, E. Vermeulen, 'Regulation Tomorrow: What Happens When Technology is Faster than the Law?', *TILEC Discussion Paper*, 2016, No. 2016-024, p. 7.

(*supra*).[74] Moreover, AI poses different problems depending on who uses it, in what way and for what purpose.[75] For instance, AI in autonomous weapons does not pose the same challenges as AI used in high frequency trading, personalised advertising or autonomous cars.[76]

'When' we should regulate is about the timing of regulation. On the one hand, there is a concern that adopting regulation in the initial stages may hamper scientific advancement and prevent the development of potential advantages. Yet, paradoxically, if there is no reliable and secure legal environment, technological innovation can equally be burdened.[77] On the other hand, regulation cannot be adopted too late either, otherwise problems arise because of the absence of effective regulation.

Moreover, adopting regulation can take several years, while technology evolves quickly, thereby outpacing any attempt to regulate it. This is also known as the 'pacing problem', which can be defined as 'the gap between the introduction of a new technology and the establishment of laws, regulations, and oversight mechanisms for shaping its safe development'.[78] This problem is intensified by the 'Collingridge dilemma', which was defined by David Collingridge, who wrote about the challenges of governing emerging technologies in his book 'The Social Control of Technology'. He argues that 'the social consequences of a technology cannot be predicted early in the life of the technology', but '[b]y the time undesirable consequences are discovered, however, the technology is often so much part of the whole economics and social fabric that its control is extremely difficult'.[79] He called this the 'dilemma of control', and asserted that, '[w]hen change is easy, the need for it cannot be foreseen; when the need for change is apparent, change has become expensive, difficult and time-consuming'.[80]

A method to solve this gap between law and technology could be regulatory sandboxes in which a safe space is provided for testing innovative products and

---

74 Although the High-Level Expert Group on Artificial Intelligence has proposed such a definition, see: P. Boddington, *Towards a code of ethics for artificial intelligence*, p. 25.

75 A. Jabłonowska, M. Kuziemski, A.M. Nowak, H.-W. Micklitz, P. Pałka, G. Sartor, 'Consumer law and artificial intelligence: challenges to the EU consumer law and policy stemming from the business' use of artificial intelligence: final report of the ARTSY project, Working Paper, 2018, *EUI LAW*, 2018/11, p. 4.

76 *Ibid.*, p. 4.

77 R. Leenes, E. Palmerini, B.-J. Koops, A. Bertolini, P. Salvinic and F. Lucivero, 'Regulatory challenges of robotics: some guidelines for addressing legal and ethical issues', 2017, *Law, Innovation and technology*, vol. 9, no. 1, p. 22.

78 R. Hagemann, J. Huddleston and A. D. Thierer, 'Soft Law for Hard Problems: The Governance of Emerging Technologies in an Uncertain Future', *Colorado Technology Law Journal*, 2018, vol.3, p. 54.

79 E. Collingridge, *The Social Control of Technology* (London: Palgrave Macmillan, 1981), p. 11.

80 Collingridge, *The Social Control of Technology*, p. 11.

services without having to comply with the applicable regulations.[81] The concept first emerged in financial services where the financial regulatory body creates and supervises a framework in which organisations can experiment and test their products or services, in a live market with real consumers. In essence, it is a supervised 'safe haven'.[82] Both the European Parliament and the European Commission consider this to be an appropriate tool to cope with the regulatory challenges presented by AI.[83] Although the tool has potential benefits, it also creates some challenges, such as balancing the need for transparency, on the one hand, with the need to protect classified and commercially sensitive information and trade secrets, on the other hand.[84]

Finally, the how question deals with the form and substance of the regulation.[85] Related to this question is another important one that needs to be answered preliminarily: do we really need new regulation to cope with issues associated with new technologies, or are the classical instruments sufficient?[86]

The concern is that AI brings about new and unknown risks with which our current laws may not be able to cope. This is by no means a new question and the answer to it has already been much debated. Judge Frank Easterbrook already challenged the idea of a new cyberlaw in the 1990s. According to Easterbrook, there was no more a 'law of cyberspace' than there was a 'law of the horse'.[87] This was a reaction to the idea of Lawrence Lessig and others to introduce a new area of law, namely Cyberlaw. Easterbrook opined that 'the best way to learn the law applicable to specialised endeavours is to study general rules'[88], meaning that problems related to computers should be studied through traditional legal areas such as tort law, contract law and property law. In short, the general legal

81 M. Fenwick, W.A. Kaal and E. Vermeulen, 'Regulation Tomorrow: What Happens When Technology is Faster than the Law?', *TILEC Discussion Paper*, 2016, No. 2016–024, p. 25.

82 CIPL, Regulatory Sandboxes in Data Protection: Constructive Engagement and Innovative Regulation in Practice, 8 March 2019, https://www.informationpolicycentre.com/uploads/5/7/1/0/57104281/cipl_white_paper_on_regulatory_sandboxes_in_data_protection_-_constructive_engagement_and_innovative_regulation_in_practice__8_march_2019_.pdf.

83 European Parliament resolution of 12 February 2019 on a comprehensive European industrial policy on artificial intelligence and robotics (2018/2088(INI)). European Commission, Annex to the Communication from the Commission to the European Parliament, the European Council, the Council, the European Economic and Social Committee and the Committee of the Regions, Com(2018) 795 final.

84 FCA, Regulatory sandbox lessons learned report, October 2017, https://www.fca.org.uk/publication/research-and-data/regulatory-sandbox-lessons-learned-report.pdf; K. Yordanova, The Shifting Sands of Regulatory Sandboxes for AI, 18 July 2019, https://www.law.kuleuven.be/citip/blog/the-shifting-sands-of-regulatory-sandboxes-for-ai/.

85 M. Fenwick, W.A. Kaal and E. Vermeulen, 'Regulation Tomorrow: What Happens When Technology is Faster than the Law?', p. 7.

86 R. Leenes, 'Regulating New Technologies in Times of Change', in L. Reins (ed.) *Regulating New Technologies in Uncertain Times. Information Technology and Law Series*, vol 32. (The Hague: T.M.C. Asser Press, 2019), p. 6.

87 F.H. Easterbrook, 'Cyberspace and the Law of the Horse', *University of Chicago Legal Forum*, 1996, p. 207.

88 Easterbrook, 'Cyberspace and the Law of the Horse', p. 207.

concepts and mechanism are flexible enough to cope with new phenomena, such as AI, in a sufficient way.[89] Lawrence Lessig commented on this argument in the often-cited article 'The law of the horse: what cyberlaw might teach' and stated that by identifying the distinctive feature of cyberspace, one could find the key to regulating technology.[90] However, determining whether the existing legal frameworks are appropriate to deal with current technological developments without unintentionally hampering innovation[91], is not a minor task. Moreover, if we do find that certain laws or regulations are insufficient, how do we evaluate the necessary changes?

9. Black and Murray consider the experience of internet regulation from 1995 up until today as a warning which is applicable to all emerging technologies.[92] They state that 'by failing to take early steps to structurally regulate the internet and instead focusing on individual harms, governments failed to appreciate that they had left markets to control a communications technology which relies on network effects and can create system wide risks and impacts'.[93]

They identify two parallels between the internet regulation debate and the debate regarding the regulation of AI. First, there seem to be scarcity issues. While the internet is determined by bits, AI is about datasets, which seem limitless, scalable and more valuable as their accumulation grows. Second, in both cases, risks are being perceived as particular or individual rather than systemic or structural. Although there are already some clearly identified risks concerning bias, harms from data mining and profiling and copyright interests in AI generated works, these discussions remain gradual and grounded in specific rather than systemic risks of AI.[94]

They predict more or less the same phases in AI regulation as was the case for internet regulation. First there is AI Libertarianism: (1) the market will regulate; (2) there is not one government or regulator that has authority, or even the legitimacy to regulate; (3) the community is the source of legitimate authority to regulate. Over time, there will be AI Realism: (1) the market cannot control this; (2) key players will set the agenda and should be the focus of regulation; (3) regulation should focus on discrete risks and harms rather than processes or structures.

---

89 R. Leenes, 'Regulating New Technologies in Times of Change', p. 6.

90 L. Lessig, 'The law of the horse: what cyberlaw might teach', *Harvard Law Review*, 1999, vol. 113, p. 501; M.C. Buiten, 'Towards Intelligent Regulation of Artificial Intelligence', *European Journal of Risk Regulation*, March 2019, vol. 10, no. 1 (Symposium on Regulating the Risk of Disruptive Technology), p. 47.

91 See Chapter 2 in this book on innovation and law.

92 Black and Murray, 'Regulating AI and machine learning: setting the regulatory agenda', p. 10.

93 *Ibid.*

94 *Ibid.*

Subsequently, there is the possibility that the realisation dawns that governments did not act in a timely matter and a few large corporations have overtaken and have become self-governing 'within the sphere through contractualisation'. As the risks and harms are more clearly defined for AI than for the internet, they hope that governments will act faster this time. However, they indicate that this may not be the case and illustrate this with the example of the 'black box' issue. Although this has been much discussed in academic circles, there has been little development of answering how to best regulate these black boxes.[95]

10. For a long time, command and control regulation was considered the standard option for regulation. It is a centred form of regulation in which the state performs all regulatory tasks: creation, implementation, monitoring and enforcement. It is the state that has the capacity to command control, to be the only commander and controller and to potentially be effective in commanding and controlling. It is assumed to be unilateral in its approach (governments telling, others doing), to be based on simple cause-effect relations and to envisage a linear progression from policy information through to implementation.[96] However, the last years, it has become clear that this type of regulation suffers from several shortcomings. Black identifies the following: the instruments used are inappropriate and unsophisticated (instrument failure); governments have insufficient knowledge to be able to identify the causes of problems, design appropriate solutions, and identify non-compliance (information and knowledge failure); implementation of regulation is inadequate (implementation failure), those being regulated are insufficiently inclined to comply, and those regulating are insufficiently motivated to regulate in the public interest (motivation failure and capture theory).[97]

For these reasons, some alternative regulatory instruments have been developed. One of the well-known examples is self-regulation. As with many concepts, there does not seem to be one common definition. However, all definitions that have been reviewed contain the following two elements: first, a group of actors create, implement and enforce rules, and second, there is minimal involvement of the government.[98] Advantages that are often cited are flexibility, the capacity to adapt quickly to fast developing technologies, a higher degree of expertise and lower cost. Yet, there are also some disadvantages. One of the most frequently heard criticisms is the lack of effective enforcement. Self-regulation has also been known for having a low level of transparency and putting the private interest ahead of the public interest.[99]

---

95 *Ibid.*

96 Black, 'Critical reflections on regulation', p. 35.

97 *Ibid.*, p. 35.

98 Lievens, *Protecting Children in the digital era: the use of alternative regulatory instruments*, p. 193. Black, 'Critical reflections on regulation', p. 35.

99 Lievens, *Protecting Children in the digital era: the use of alternative regulatory instruments*, p. 193.

A tool that aims to find the middle ground between self-regulation and command and control regulation is co-regulation. Simply stated, co-regulation is a regulatory strategy which consists of elements of state regulation and elements of self-regulation.[100] According to CEPS[101], co-regulation couples the delegation of specific phases of the policy cycle to the private sector, with a legal backstop. CEPS proposes to use co-regulatory schemes whenever monitored self-regulation is ineffective in securing an adequate level of protection of users' rights, or any other lack of effectiveness in achieving policy objectives.[102]

Bottom-up (civil society-driven) options are also proposed as a slightly different set of alternatives to traditional self-regulatory initiatives by industrial actors. These alternatives could rely on third party regulatory schemes, privately developed by civil society organisations or NGOs, and use them as private standards. For instance, in the internet environment, an NGO (or public authority, when feasible) could define or adopt criteria for algorithmic accountability, transparency and non-discrimination, and translate them into an auditing and certification scheme, which leads to a trust-enhancing tool for end users. A specific logo/label could be used for those platforms whose algorithms have been checked and are constantly monitored by public authorities or NGOs, so that compliance is ensured over time.[103]

Other, more specific tools that have been suggested are:

- Phrasing statutes and guidelines in a technology-neutral way to ensure equal treatment and sustainable rules. For instance, the GDPR is conceived as technological neutral.
- Using multi-level legislation, especially by combining statutory rules with guidelines that can easily be adopted, evaluated, and amended by regulatory bodies and where self-assessment may also be subject to indirect *ex post* control by independent administrative authorities established under other laws such as DPOs who may include certain guidelines in their assessment (e.g. data protection by design or technical and organisational measures under the GDPR).
- Creating special environments for empirical testing and development in the form of a living lab or 'regulatory sandboxes' in which the regulator provides selected firms wishing to bring innovative products or services to the market with an opportunity to roll out and test them within a designated domain for a specified period, subject to monitoring and oversight by the relevant regulator but without being forced to comply with the applicable set of rules and regulations (cf. *supra*).[104]

---

100 *Ibid.*

101 The Centre for European Policy Studies, a think tank and forum for debate on EU affairs.

102 CEPS, Artificial Intelligence Ethics, governance and policy challenges, 2019, p. 77.

103 *Ibid.*, p. 76.

104 M. Ebers, 'Regulating AI and Robotics: Ethical and Legal Challenges', in M. Ebers and S. N. Navarro (eds.), *Algorithms and Law* (Cambridge: Cambridge University Press, 2019), p. 46.

4. CURRENT TRENDS IN AI GOVERNANCE

11. According to WIPO[105], companies from the United States and China currently dominate patenting activity regarding AI.[106] Apart from that, the European Union (EU) also has a significant share of the total world market[107] and wants to continue to shape[108] digital transformation by creating safe and trustworthy AI with a human-centric perspective. In this part we will focus on these three jurisdictions, which have already taken steps towards establishing a policy framework on AI and we will provide a brief overview of the key features of these policies. This will also allow us to get a more concrete idea of how countries exactly deal with the ethical and regulatory challenges posed by AI. Since facial recognition software and its possible misuse[109] has given rise to numerous discussions in these three jurisdictions, we will, by way of example, briefly touch upon specific regulatory initiatives concerning this topic.[110]

12. In the EU, the European Commission adopted a strategy on AI on 25 April 2018.[111] Ensuring an adequate ethical and legal framework on AI is identified as one of the core pillars of this strategy.[112] Compared to the Chinese (state-developed AI) and the American (company focused *laissez-faire*) approaches, the EU uses a so-called third way approach that is based on 'data ethics', 'human-centric AI' and the protection of consumer rights.[113] Therefore, in June 2018 the Commission set up the independent group of experts on AI, i.e. the HLEGAI[114],

---

105 World Intellectual Property Organization.

106 WIPO, 'WIPO Technology Trends 2019: Artificial Intelligence', https://www.wipo.int/edocs/pubdocs/en/wipo_pub_1055.pdf.

107 EUROPEAN COMMISSION, 'EU position in world trade', https://ec.europa.eu/trade/policy/eu-position-in-world-trade/#:~:text=The%20EU%20is%20the%20largest,of%20manufactured%20goods%20and%20services.

108 See for example: GDPR which already inspired Japan, Vietnam, Brazil, etc., C. Van De Wiel, 'Brussel had niet tot doel 'to rule the world' – maar doet dat wel', *NRC* 6 March 2020, https://www.nrc.nl/nieuws/2020/03/06/bedrijven-willen-juist-dat-de-strikte-europese-regels-de-standaard-worden-a3992944.

109 K. Hill, 'The Secretive Company That Might End Privacy as We Know It', *NY Times* 11 September 2020, https://www.nytimes.com/2020/01/18/technology/clearview-privacy-facial-recognition.html.

110 T. Klosowski, 'Facial Recognition Is Everywhere. Here's What We Can Do About It.', *NY Times* 15 July 2020, https://www.nytimes.com/wirecutter/blog/how-facial-recognition-works/.

111 Communication from the Commission to the European Parliament, the European Council, the Council, the European Economic and Social Committee and the Committee of the Regions on Artificial Intelligence for Europe, COM (2018) 237 final.

112 *Ibid.*, p. 16.

113 M. Boris, 'Legal tech in Europe: How will the EU's digital strategy impact legal tech', *LegalTech Weekly* 11 March 2020, https://contractbook.com/legaltechweekly/how-will-the-european-unions-digital-strategy-impact-legal-tech.

114 High Level Expert Group on Artificial Intelligence.

that has released two main deliverables: ethics guidelines on AI[115] and policy and investment recommendations on AI. The research service of the European Parliament also sheds some light on ethical rules for designing, developing, deploying and implementing or using AI products and services in the EU.[116]

The ethics guidelines on Trustworthy AI drafted by the HLEGAI define Trustworthy AI as AI that is 'lawful, ethical and robust'.[117] They take a human-centric approach to AI based on existing fundamental rights. Based on a report drafted by AI4People, these guidelines identify four ethical principles governing AI, namely: respect for human autonomy, prevention of harm, fairness and explicability. Subsequently, they translate these ethical principles into seven key requirements for Trustworthy AI, being: human agency and oversight, technical robustness and safety, privacy and data governance, transparency, diversity, non-discrimination and fairness, social and environmental wellbeing and accountability. Finally, the guidelines contain an assessment list intended to help developers and deployers of AI implement the aforementioned seven requirements in practice.

These ethics guidelines were endorsed by the Commission in its Communication of 8 April 2019 on building trust in human-centric artificial intelligence.[118] The Commission's ambition is to bring the EU's ethical approach to AI to the global stage and become a global leader on the matter.[119] The guidelines did, however, not remain immune from criticism, one of the most frequently voiced ones being that they did not explicitly ban the use of lethal autonomous weapons.[120] Two months after issuing these guidelines, the HLEGAI presented 33 policy and investment recommendations for EU institutions and Member States on how to realise Trustworthy AI.[121] The recommendations identified areas in which AI could have a beneficial impact and some enablers

---

115 The statement on AI, robotics and autonomous systems arguably served as one of the sources of inspiration for these guidelines, see European Group on Ethics in Science and New Technologies, 'Statement on Artificial Intelligence, Robotics and 'Autonomous Systems', ec.europa.eu/research/ege/pdf/ege_ai_statement_2018.pdf.

116 T. Madiega, 'EU guidelines on ethics in artificial intelligence: Context and implementation', *European Parliamentary Research Service (EPRS)*, https://www.europarl.europa.eu/RegData/etudes/BRIE/2019/640163/EPRS_BRI(2019)640163_EN.pdf.

117 HLEGAI, 'Ethics Guidelines for Trustworthy AI', 2019, p. 5.

118 Communication from the Commission to the European Parliament, the Council, the European Economic and Social Committee and the Committee of the Regions – Building Trust in Human Centric Artificial Intelligence, COM(2019) 168.

119 Communication from the Commission to the European Parliament, the European Council, the Council, The European Economic and Social Committee and the Committee of the Regions: Coordinated Plan on Artificial Intelligence, COM (2018), 795 final, p. 8.

120 European Parliament resolution of 12 September 2018 on autonomous weapon systems (2018/2752(RSP)); see also: T. Metzinger, 'Ethics washing made in Europe', *Tagesspiegel* 8 April 2019, https://www.tagesspiegel.de/politik/eu-guidelines-ethics-washing-made-in-europe/24195496.html.

121 European Commission's High-Level Expert Group on Artificial Intelligence: Policy and Investment Recommendations for Trustworthy AI, 8 April 2019.

that could facilitate such beneficial impact. In relation to the governance of AI, which is identified as an enabler of Trustworthy AI, the recommendations put forward, among others, a risk-based approach to regulation, and a precautionary principled-based approach for those AI applications that pose unacceptable risks.[122] Because of the general nature of these recommendations, the HLEGAI decided to explore their possible implementation with respect to a limited number of sectors. The report focuses on three sectors that are considered to be of crucial importance to the sustained well-being of society and Europe's sustainable growth: (i) the Public Sector; (ii) Healthcare; and (iii) Manufacturing and Internet of Things (IoT).[123]

After her election as President of the European Commission in the summer of 2019, Ursula Von Der Leyen pledged to put forward a legislative proposal on AI in her first 100 days of presidency.[124] This pledge resulted in a White Paper on AI: a European approach to excellence and trust, issued by the European Commission on 19 February 2020.[125] The European Commission sets out (among others) its vision on the regulation of AI. The White Paper proposes a risk-based approach to the regulation of AI, targeting only 'high-risk' applications of AI, which are identified based on the i) sector and ii) intended use.[126]

Besides, there may also be exceptional circumstances in which the use of AI is to be considered as high-risk.[127] The White Paper on AI, for example, mentions the use of AI for recruiting purposes and for the purposes of remote biometric identification.[128] However, it is still unclear which sectors (where AI systems can be applied) are considered to be high-risk and what circumstances, besides the ones mentioned above, are considered to be exceptional.[129] The White Paper highlights that prior assessments such as testing procedures or certification schemes can be of value, when dealing with high-risk AI systems.[130] Moreover, additional regulatory requirements including robustness, transparency, accuracy or the need to train data and keep records of the training process can also be

---

122 *Ibid.*, no. 26.1 and 26.2.

123 European Commission's High-Level Expert Group on Artificial Intelligence, 'Sectoral Considerations on the Policy and Investment Recommendations', 23 July 2020, https://futurium.ec.europa.eu/en/european-ai-alliance/document/ai-hleg-sectoral-considerations-policy-and-investment-recommendations-trustworthy-ai, p. 3.

124 Political guidelines of the Commission 2019–2024, pp. 13–14.

125 European Commission White Paper on Artificial Intelligence: A European approach to excellence and trust, 19 February 2020, COM(2020) 65 final.

126 White Paper on Artificial Intelligence, pp. 17–18.

127 White Paper on Artificial Intelligence, p. 18.

128 *Ibid.*, p. 18.

129 B. Benichou, T. Gils, J. De Bruyne and E. Wauters, 'Regulating AI in the European Union: Seven Key Takeaways', *Robotics & AI Law Society*, https://ai-laws.org/en/2020/02/regulating-ai-in-the-european-union-seven-key-takeaways/.

130 White Paper on Artificial Intelligence, pp. 23–24.

imposed on high-risk AI systems.[131] Additionally, the Commission pointed out that general legislation (data protection, product liability, consumer protection, etc.) may have to be modified in the future to deal with (the safety, robustness, transparency and accuracy of) AI systems.[132] The White Paper and the accompanying report on safety and liability also address liability issues of AI.[133] A draft report from the European Parliament's Committee on Legal Affairs also contained a possible set of concrete rules.[134] In the latest study requested by the European Parliament's Committee on Legal Affairs, Bertolini even suggested the use of *ad hoc* liability regimes for high-risk AI systems.[135] There is also the report from the Expert Group on Liability and New Technologies which compares various aspects of existing liability regimes.[136] Another report pleads for an extension of the former Product Liability Directive.[137]

Since the advent of facial recognition technology in the EU, there has also been a lively debate about its possible use (especially in public spaces).[138] Contrary to what was speculated before its release[139], the White Paper does not propose to (temporary) ban facial recognition. It introduces 'specific requirements for remote biometric identification systems'.[140] These biometric identification systems should only be deployed when such use is duly justified, proportionate and subject to adequate safeguards.[141]

---

131 *Ibid.*, pp. 18–22.

132 *Ibid.*, pp. 1316; The EC also stated in its Communication on Artificial Intelligence for Europe (25 April 2018) that the Product Liability Directive 85/374 may need to be reformed, Expert Group on Liability and New Technologies, Liability for Artificial Intelligence and other emerging digital technologies.

133 Report on the safety and liability implications of Artificial Intelligence, the Internet of Things and robotics, 19 February 2020, COM(2020) 64 final.

134 Draft report with recommendations to the Commission on a Civil Liability regime for artificial intelligence, 2020/2014(INL), https://www.europarl.europa.eu/doceo/document/JURI-PR-650556_EN.pdf.

135 A. Bertolini, 'Artificial Intelligence and Civil Liability', *European Parliament's Committee on Legal Affairs*, p. 110, https://www.europarl.europa.eu/RegData/etudes/STUD/2020/621926/IPOL_STU(2020)621926_EN.pdf.

136 The Expert Group on Liability and New Technologies – New Technologies Formation, 'Liability for Artificial Intelligence and other emerging digital technologies', 2019, https://www.europarl.europa.eu/meetdocs/2014_2019/plmrep/COMMITTEES/JURI/DV/2020/01-09/AI-report_EN.pdf.

137 European Law Institute, 'Guiding Principles for Updating the Product Liability Directive for the Digital Age', 2020, ELI_Guiding_Principles_for_Updating_the_PLD_for_the_Digital_Age.pdf (europeanlawinstitute.eu).

138 D. Sabbagh, 'Facial recognition technology scrapped at King's Cross site', *The Guardian* 2 September 2019, https://www.theguardian.com/technology/2019/sep/02/facial-recognition-technology-scrapped-at-kings-cross-development.

139 Draft structure for the White Paper on Artificial Intelligence – A European Approach, Draft as of 12/12, p. 15, https://www.euractiv.com/wp-content/uploads/sites/2/2020/01/AI-white-paper-EURACTIV.pdf.

140 White Paper on Artificial Intelligence, p. 21.

141 White Paper on Artificial Intelligence, pp. 21–22.

In reaction to the public consultation[142] on the Commission's White Paper, the EDPS[143] published its review of the White Paper.[144] The EDPS noted, for example, that the determination of high-risk sectors and applications should be more robust and nuanced, while reflecting the European Data Protection Board's Guidelines on Data Protection Impact Assessments.[145]

In April 2021, the Commission published its AI package, proposing new rules and actions to turn Europe into the global hub for trustworthy AI. The package consists of a Communication on Fostering a European Approach to Artificial Intelligence; the Coordinated Plan with Member States: 2021 update; a proposal for an AI Regulation laying down harmonised rules for the EU (Artificial Intelligence Act).[146] The proposed Regulation applies to providers that place AI systems on the market or put them into service in the EU, regardless of whether these providers are established within the EU or in a third country. It is also applicable to users of AI systems, both within the Union or outside, where the output produced by the system is used in the EU. This Regulation would not apply to AI systems developed or used exclusively for military purposes.[147]

The Commission adopts a risk-based approach, based on four different levels of risk: unacceptable risk, high risk, limited risk, and minimal risk. However, some AI systems would be prohibited because they could violate fundamental rights, such as the use of subliminal techniques, social scoring, AI systems that exploit any of the vulnerabilities of a specific group of persons due to their age, physical or mental disability and the use of 'real-time' remote biometric identification systems in publicly accessible spaces for the purpose of law enforcement. For the latter there are exceptions which are described in the proposal.[148] If an AI system is classified as high risk, it would need to comply with the requirements of Chapter 2 and the obligations of Chapter 3. The latter is applicable to both providers and users of high-risk AI systems. The proposed Regulation does not define the notion of 'high risk', but rather lists which

---

142 On 19 February 2020, the European Commission launched a Consultation on Artificial Intelligence. Citizens and stakeholders provided their feedback until 14 June 2020, https://ec.europa.eu/digital-single-market/en/news/white-paper-artificial-intelligence-european-approach-excellence-and-trust/.

143 European Data Protection Supervisor.

144 Opinion 4/2020: EDPS Opinion on the European Commission's White Paper on Artificial Intelligence – A European approach to excellence and trust, https://edps.europa.eu/sites/edp/files/publication/20-06-19_opinion_ai_white_paper_en.pdf.

145 *Ibid.*, pp. 16–17.

146 European Commission, 'A European approach to artificial intelligence', April 2021, https://digital-strategy.ec.europa.eu/en/policies/european-approach-artificial-intelligence.

147 Article 2, European Parliament & the Council, Proposal for a Regulation laying down harmonised rules on artificial intelligence (Artificial Intelligence Act) and amending certain Union legislative acts, COM/2021/206 final, 21 April 2021, https://eur-lex.europa.eu/legal-content/EN/TXT/HTML/?uri=CELEX:52021PC0206&from=EN.

148 Art. 5 Artificial Intelligence Act.

systems fall under this category.[149] In the proposal, an AI system is classified as high risk when is intended to be used as a safety component of a product, or is itself a product, covered by the Union harmonisation legislation listed in Annex II and is required to undergo a third-party conformity assessment with a view to the placing on the market or putting into service of that product pursuant to the Union harmonisation legislation listed in Annex II.[150] In addition, AI systems referred to in Annex III are also considered high risk.[151] Recital 32 considers these systems as stand-alone AI systems and it is appropriate to classify them as high risk if, in the light of their intended purpose, they pose a high risk of harm to the health and safety or the fundamental rights of persons, taking into account both the severity of the possible harm and its probability of occurrence and they are used in a number of specifically pre-defined areas specified in the Regulation.[152] The notion of high risk has sparked a lot of debate. Some are in favour of a more granular classification of risk, while others suggest an extension of the current 'list-based' approach with an approach based on broader risk-criteria.[153]

Like the GDPR, the proposed Regulation introduces a system of fines, which differ according to the type of infringement.[154]

At the time of writing this chapter (August 2022), the Slovenian, French and Czech presidency have proposed a compromise text. In addition, several committees of the European Parliament have submitted amendments to the Proposal.[155] The amount of amendments, several thousands, show that there is still a lot of work to be done before there will be an agreement on the final

---

149 N. Smuha, E. Ahmed-Rengers, A. Harkens, W. Li, J. MacLaren, R. Piselli and K. Yeung, 'How the EU can achieve legally trustworthy AI: A Response to the European Commission's Proposal for an Artificial Intelligence Act', 5 August 2021, http://dx.doi.org/10.2139/ssrn.3899991, p. 29.

150 Article 6 (1) Artificial Intelligence Act, Annex II contains products such as machinery, toys, lifts, equipment and protective systems intended for use in potentially explosive atmospheres, radio equipment, pressure equipment, recreational craft equipment, cableway installations, appliances burning gaseous fuels, medical devices, and in vitro diagnostic medical devices.

151 Article 6 (2) Artificial Intelligence Act.

152 Recital 32 Artificial Intelligence Act.

153 For commentaries on the proposal for the Artificial Intelligence Act, see for instance: N. Smuha, E. Ahmed-Rengers, A. Harkens, W. Li, J. MacLaren, R. Piselli and K. Yeung, 'How the EU can achieve legally trustworthy AI: A Response to the European Commission's Proposal for an Artificial Intelligence Act', 5 August 2021, http://dx.doi.org/10.2139/ssrn.3899991; M. Ebers, V.R.S. Hoch, F. Rosenkranz, H. Ruschemeier and B. Steinrötter, 'The European Commission's Proposal for an Artificial Intelligence Act – A Critical Assessment by Members of the Robotics and AI Law Society' (RAILS), *J – Multidisciplinary Scientific Journal*, 2021, vol. 4, no. 4; M. Veale & F. Zuiderveen Borgesius, 'Demystifying the Draft EU Artificial Intelligence Act', *Computer Law Review International*, 2021, no. 4, p. 106, https://arxiv.org/ftp/arxiv/papers/2107/2107.03721.pdf; Y. Poullet, 'Vers un droit européen de l'intelligence artificielle', *Journal de droit européen*, 2021, n° 284, pp. 454–463.

154 Article 71 Artificial Intelligence Act.

155 For a complete overview of all the documents, see: https://www.kaizenner.eu/post/aiact-part3.

text. For instance, the definition of AI is a controversial topic and each party advocates its own form of definition.[156] A major criticism of the Proposal was the lack of individual rights and it has been addressed in the amendments, albeit in different shapes. The notion of high risk is also contentious and several changes to the original text have been proposed.

In 2019 the Council of Europe set up an Ad Hoc Committee on Artificial Intelligence – CAHAI. The task of this Committee was to 'examine the feasibility and potential elements on the basis of broad multi-stakeholder consultations, of a legal framework for the development, design and application of artificial intelligence, based on Council of Europe's standards on human rights, democracy and the rule of law'.[157] The feasibility study was published in December 2020 and finds risks as well as opportunities of AI. It also maps instruments that are already applicable to AI, both (international) legal instruments and ethics guidelines. In addition, the study looked at the advantages, disadvantages and limitations of these instruments. Finally, the study sets out the main principles that are considered 'essential to respect in the context of AI systems including the concrete rights and obligations attached thereto, and that could be potentially considered for inclusion in a future Council of Europe legal instrument on AI'. These principles could be horizontally applied, but also be 'combined with a sector-specific approach that provides (more detailed) contextual requirements in the form of soft law instruments, such as sectoral guidelines or assessment lists'.[158] In 2021, the CAHAI conducted a multi-stakeholder consultation to gather the views of representative institutional actors.[159] In its final recommendations, the CAHAI states that an appropriate legal framework on AI based on the Council of Europe's standards on human rights, democracy and the rule of law, should take the form of a legally binding transversal instrument.[160]

13. Existing initiatives and views on AI regulation in the United States[161] must be seen against the traditional American *laissez-faire* approach, which is aimed at facilitating innovation. Indeed, the US government is nowadays still stressing the need to avoid regulatory overreach when dealing with AI.[162] The Executive

---

156 Although the High-Level Expert Group on Artificial Intelligence has proposed such a definition, see: P. Boddington, *Towards a code of ethics for artificial intelligence*, p. 25.

157 See: https://www.coe.int/en/web/artificial-intelligence/cahai.

158 CAHAI, Feasibility study, 17 December 2020, https://rm.coe.int/cahai-2020-23-final-eng-feasibility-study-/1680a0c6da.

159 See: https://www.coe.int/en/web/artificial-intelligence/cahai-multi-stakeholder-consultation.

160 See: https://search.coe.int/cm/Pages/result_details.aspx?ObjectId=0900001680a4e8a5.

161 See for a comprehensive overview: R. Girasa, *Artificial Intelligence as a Disruptive Technology* (Cham: Palgrave Macmillan, 2020), pp. 69–102.

162 J. Vincent, 'White House encourages hands-off approach to AI regulation', *The Verge*, https://www.theverge.com/2020/1/7/21054653/america-us-ai-regulation-principles-federal-agencies-ostp-principles.

Order 13859 of 11 February 2019 sketches the current US policy on AI and relies on five important pillars: AI R&D[163], unleash federal AI resources (e.g. enhance access to high-quality data)[164], remove barriers to AI innovation, empower the American worker with AI-focused education[165] and promote an international environment supportive of American AI innovation and its responsible use. The Executive Order is a call to action for federal agencies to start regulating AI around a set of general objectives.[166] The Order also tasks the NIST[167] with formulating a plan for federal engagement in developing technical standards for reliable, robust and trustworthy AI systems.[168] In this respect, it is also worth noting that the IEEE[169] is creating an Ethics Certification Program for Autonomous and Intelligent Systems.[170]

The White House also released a draft memorandum[171] together with the Executive Order, emphasising the importance of public trust in AI (reliable, robust, and trustworthy AI applications), information quality, fairness and non-discrimination, transparency, safety and security and so on.[172] According to this memorandum, governmental agencies should conduct a risk assessment and cost-benefit analysis before issuing any AI regulation. They should also pursue a performance-based and flexible approach that can adapt to rapid changes and updates to AI applications.[173] Shortly after the Executive Order, the House of Representatives also issued House Resolution 153 on Supporting the Development of Guidelines for Ethical Development of Artificial Intelligence.[174]

163 GrAITR Act, H.R.2202; Advancing Artificial Intelligence Research Act of 2020, S. 3891 (only introduced, not yet been adopted).

164 The US Congress issued an AI in Government Act establishing an AI Centre of Excellence that provides advice to the federal government when adopting or deploying an AI technology.

165 Innovation Corps Act of 2017, H.R.1576; AI Jobs Act of 2018, H.R.4829; see also: Pledge to America's workers, where Trump administration is asking companies to commit to keep reskilling American Workers, https://www.whitehouse.gov/ai/ai-american-worker/.

166 Y. Chae, 'U.S. Regulation Guide: Legislative Overview and Practical Considerations', *The Journal of Robotics, Artificial Intelligence & Law*, vol. 3, no. 1, pp. 19–20.

167 National Institute of Standards and Technology.

168 NIST, 'U.S. LEADERSHIP IN AI: A Plan for Federal Engagement in Developing Technical Standards and Related Tools', https://www.nist.gov/system/files/documents/2019/08/10/ai_standards_fedengagement_plan_9aug2019.pdf.

169 American Institute of Electrical and Electronics Engineers.

170 See: https://ethicsinaction.ieee.org/.

171 Memorandum for the heads of executive departments and agencies, https://www.whitehouse.gov/wp-content/uploads/2020/01/Draft-OMB-Memo-on-Regulation-of-AI-1-7-19.pdf.

172 K. Hao, 'The US just released 10 principles that it hopes will make AI safer', *MIT Technology Review* 7 January 2020, https://www.technologyreview.com/s/615015/ai-regulatory-principles-us-white-house-american-ai-initiatve/; AI Next Campaign, https://www.darpa.mil/work-with-us/ai-next-campaign.

173 Memorandum for the heads of executive departments and agencies, p. 5; see also: D. Shepardson, 'White House proposes regulatory principles to govern AI use', *Reuters* 7 January 2020, https://www.reuters.com/article/us-tech-ces-ai-white-house/white-house-proposes-regulatory-principles-to-govern-ai-use-idUSKBN1Z60GL.

174 Supporting the development of guidelines for ethical development of artificial intelligence, H. Res. 153.

While the Resolution has not yet been adopted, it contains similar principles concerning ethical and trustworthy AI to the ones mentioned in the draft memorandum.[175]

The National Initiative Act of 2020 (NAIIA) established the National Artificial Intelligence Initiative. 'The main purposes of the Initiative are to ensure continued U.S. leadership in AI research & development, lead the world in the development and use of trustworthy AI systems in public and private sectors, prepare the present and future US workforce for the integration of artificial intelligence systems across all sectors of the economy and society, and coordinate ongoing AI activities across all Federal agencies, to ensure that each informs the work of the others.'[176] The initiative provides an overarching framework to strengthen and coordinate AI research, development, demonstration, and education activities across all U.S. Departments and Agencies, in cooperation with academia, industry, non-profits, and civil society organizations.[177]

In June 2021, the Biden administration launched the National Artificial Intelligence (AI) Research Resource Task Force which will 'write the road map for expanding access to critical resources and educational tools that will spur AI innovation and economic prosperity nationwide.'[178] As stated in the NAIIA of 2020, the Task Force will serve as a Federal advisory committee to help create and implement a blueprint for the National AI Research Resource (NAIRR) – a shared research infrastructure providing AI researchers and students across all scientific disciplines with access to computational resources, high-quality data, educational tools, and user support.[179]

Next to these general initiatives, there were also more focused ones. For instance, the US Senate introduced the Algorithmic Accountability Act in 2019.[180] If the Act were to get enacted, it could have a serious impact considering its broad scope, obliging 'covered entities'[181] to fix any discrimination or bias they find when using algorithms. The GDPR has been a source of inspiration for the Act, as it contains similar provisions, albeit specifically designed for AI

---

175 Note that while legislation plays an important role in ensuring reliable, robust and trustworthy AI, much of the challenges posed by AI are tackled by DARPA in practice, see: M. Turek, 'Explainable Artificial Intelligence (XAI)', *DARPA,* https://www.darpa.mil/program/explainable-artificial-intelligence; NSF Program on Fairness in Artificial Intelligence (AI) in Collaboration with Amazon (FAI), https://www.nsf.gov/funding/pgm_summ.jsp?pims_id=505651.

176 See: https://www.ai.gov/legislation-and-executive-orders.

177 See: https://www.ai.gov/legislation-and-executive-orders.

178 See: https://www.whitehouse.gov/ostp/news-updates/2021/06/10/the-biden-administration-launches-the-national-artificial-intelligence-research-resource-task-force.

179 See: https://www.whitehouse.gov/ostp/news-updates/2021/06/10/the-biden-administration-launches-the-national-artificial-intelligence-research-resource-task-force.

180 Algorithmic Accountability Act of 2019, S.1108.

181 Any person, partnership or corporation subject to the jurisdiction of the FTC and generating more than fifty million per year or possessing or controlling information of at least one million people or on at least one million devices.

systems. The Act, for example, gives regulatory powers to the Federal Trade Commission[182], which can oblige covered entities to conduct an automated decision system impact assessment for any existing or new high-risk automated decision systems[183] and high-risk information systems[184] (thereby echoing the GDPR's data protection impact assessment obligation). These impact assessments ascertain whether the algorithms used pose threats to privacy or generate inaccurate, unfair or discriminatory decisions.[185] However, the Act has also been criticised for several reasons. There is, for example, no guidance on how to conduct impact assessments. Moreover, only large firms are targeted. Nevertheless, according to several critics, small firms may cause equal harm.[186] As the Act does not pre-empt any state law[187], several other States and cities have already tried to issue similar acts to regulate discrimination or bias in AI systems.[188] In February 2022, an update of the Algorithmic Accountability Act was introduced.[189] The new legislation has the same goals of the first bill, but 'includes numerous technical improvements, such as clarifying what types of algorithms and companies are covered, ensuring assessments put consumer impacts at the forefront, and providing more details about how reports should be structured'.[190]

It is moreover interesting to note that several States and cities also passed bills to improve AI's transparency. For instance, the State of Illinois adopted the Artificial Intelligence Video Interview Act[191], which requires employers to be transparent about using AI during job interviews. The State of California

182 Federal Trade Commission.

183 A computational process, including one derived from machine learning, statistics, or other data processing or artificial intelligence techniques, that makes a decision or facilitates human decision making, that impacts consumers.

184 A process, automated or not, that involves personal information, such as the collection, recording, organization, structuring, storage, etc. but does not qualify as an automated decision system.

185 K. Quezada, The Algorithmic Accountability Act: is the US about to apply EU standards to algorithmic governance?, *CiTiP Blog* 10 December 2019, https://www.law.kuleuven.be/citip/blog/the-algorithmic-accountability-act-is-the-us-about-to-apply-eu-standards-to-algorithmic-governance/.

186 J. New, 'How to Fix the Algorithmic Accountability Act', *Center for Data Innovation* 23 September 2019, https://www.datainnovation.org/2019/09/how-to-fix-the-algorithmic-accountability-act/.

187 See Section 4 Algorithmic Accountability Act.

188 See for example New Jersey Algorithmic Accountability Act, NJ A5430 (did not pass) and Washington SB 5527 and HB 1655 (to be adopted); Y. Chae, 'U.S. Regulation Guide: Legislative Overview and Practical Considerations', *The Journal of Robotics, Artificial Intelligence & Law*, 2020, vol. 3, no. 1, pp. 22–23.

189 See: https://www.wyden.senate.gov/news/press-releases/wyden-booker-and-clarke-introduce-algorithmic-accountability-act-of-2022-to-require-new-transparency-and-accountability-for-automated-decision-systems.

190 For a summary of the bill see: https://www.wyden.senate.gov/download/one-pager-bill-summary-of-the-algorithmic-accountability-act-of-2022.

191 Video Interview Act, HB2557.

passed a Bolstering Online Transparency Act[192] to protect users from automated bots. Bots are defined broadly and are required to identify themselves as non-human.[193] It also introduced an Anti-Eavesdropping Act[194], which, if enacted, could prohibit any recording that qualifies as personal information from being used for advertising purposes or being shared with third parties.[195]

Lastly, a well-known deployment of AI technology in the US is facial recognition software, which more US cities and States are banning. The Commercial Facial Recognition Privacy Act[196], for instance, obliged covered entities to obtain consent of end users *ex ante* and provide notice of the facial recognition software before deploying it. Covered entities are also prohibited to share the acquired data with third parties[197] (see also the California Consumer Privacy Act).[198] As a consequence, the Act mirrors certain aspects of the GDPR, just as the Algorithmic Accountability Act. In 2020, the Facial Recognition and Biometric Technology Moratorium Act was introduced in the Senate. If passed, the Act will impose limits on the use of biometric surveillance systems, such as facial recognition systems, by federal and state government entities.[199]

There also has been the introduction of several state bills to ban or delay the use of facial recognition technology by government agencies.[200] Moreover, the city of San Francisco banned the use of facial recognition software by police and other agencies.[201] Similarly, the State of Massachusetts also passed a bill, which

---

192 Bots: disclosure, SB-1001.

193 R. Diresta, 'A New Law Makes Bots Identify Themselves – That's the Problem', *Wired* 24 July 2019, https://www.wired.com/story/law-makes-bots-identify-themselves/.

194 Information privacy: other connected device with a voice recognition feature, A.B. 1395.

195 L. Ropek, 'California Proposal Would Curb Smart Speaker Snooping', *Government Technology* 2 May 2019, https://www.govtech.com/policy/California-Proposal-Would-Curb-Smart-Speaker-Snooping.html.

196 Commercial Facial Recognition Privacy Act of 2019, S.847.

197 T. Hatmaker, 'Bipartisan bill proposes oversight for commercial facial recognition', *Tech Crunch* 15 March 2019, https://techcrunch.com/2019/03/14/facial-recognition-bill-commercial-facial-recognition-privacy-act/.

198 The California Consumer Privacy Act has a broad scope and deals with consumer rights regarding personal information sales to third parties. One of the most important consumer rights in the CCPA is the right of deletion and opt-out. If information is transferred to a third party, consumers can still force those companies to delete personal information collected from them. However, deleting this data in practice is very difficult/nearly impossible when dealing with AI technologies; see: California Consumer Privacy Act of 2018; https://www.caprivacy.org/; J. Cowan and N. Singer, 'How California's New Privacy Law Affects You', *NY Times* 3 January 2020, https://www.nytimes.com/2020/01/03/us/ccpa-california-privacy-law.html.

199 S.4084 – Facial Recognition and Biometric Technology Moratorium Act of 2020, 116th Congress (2019–2020).

200 Y. Chae, 'U.S. Regulation Guide: Legislative Overview and Practical Considerations', p. 25. In March 2020, the Washington Engrossed Substitute Senate Bill 6280 was passed, regulating the use of facial recognition services by state or local authorities.

201 But not for airports or seaports which are run by federal agencies, see: K. Conger, R. Fausset and S. F. Kovalevski, 'San Francisco Bans Facial Recognition Technology', *NY Times* 14 May, https://www.nytimes.com/2019/05/14/us/facial-recognition-ban-san-francisco.html.

puts a moratorium on facial recognition and other remote biometric surveillance systems.[202] California's legislature did the same with facial recognition software (for police body cams) in September 2019.[203] As of January 2021, in Portland the use of facial recognition technology in public spaces by private entities is banned.[204]

14. China has on a national level been publishing several types of policy documents in which the Chinese government announces its intention to use AI in a multitude of sectors.[205] However, China does not consider these national policy documents as a tool to regulate AI on a central level. It considers these documents as instruments to coordinate innovation driven by the private sector and the local governments.[206] China has 'AI national champions' that are selected by the government to develop AI applications in specific sectors. These companies mostly agree to pursue certain strategic governmental aims in exchange for market share protection or easier access to financial resources. This phenomenon of national champions has led to the market domination of certain large companies in certain sectors.[207]

Although the Chinese government gives the impression to only coordinate innovation driven by the private sector[208] and the local governments[209], it also has the ambition to define ethical principles and standards for AI on a national level. The Chinese Association for Artificial Intelligence ('CAAI') for example

---

202 An Act establishing a moratorium on face recognition and other remote biometric surveillance systems, Bill S.1385.

203 R. Metz, 'California lawmakers ban facial-recognition software from police body cams', *CNN* 13 September 2019, https://edition.cnn.com/2019/09/12/tech/california-body-cam-facial-recognition-ban/index.html.

204 Press release, 'City Council approves ordinances banning use of face recognition technologies by City of Portland bureaus and by private entities in public spaces', 9 September 2020, https://www.portland.gov/smart-city-pdx/news/2020/9/9/city-council-approves-ordinances-banning-use-face-recognition.

205 G. Webster, R. Creemers, P. Triolo and E. Kania, 'Full Translation: China's 'New Generation Artificial Intelligence Development Plan', *New America* 1 August 2017, https://www.newamerica.org/cybersecurity-initiative/digichina/blog/full-translation-chinas-new-generation-artificial-intelligence-development-plan-2017/.

206 K.-F. Lee and M. Sheehan, 'China's Rise in Artificial Intelligence: Ingredients and Economic Implications', *Hoover Institution* 29 October 2018, Fall Series Issue 218, https://www.hoover.org/research/chinas-rise-artificial-intelligence-ingredients-and-economic-implications.

207 H. Roberts, J. Cowls, J. Morley, M. Taddeo, V. Wang and L. Floridi, 'The Chinese Approach to Artificial Intelligence: An Analysis of Policy and Regulation', SSRN 23 October 2019, pp. 4–5, https://papers.ssrn.com/sol3/papers.cfm?abstract_id=3469784.

208 Note that several private companies also pushed the government to develop ethical principles, see: Y. Yang, 'China's Tencent pitches vision of artificial intelligence', *Financial Times* 1 May 2019, https://www.ft.com/content/f92abc38-6bb8-11e9-80c7-60ee53e6681d; A. Hern, 'Chinese search firm Baidu joins global AI ethics body', *The Guardian* 17 October 2018, https://www.theguardian.com/technology/2018/oct/17/baidu-chinese-search-firm-joins-global-ai-ethics-body-google-apple-facebook.

209 Beijing for example established their own (ethical) AI principles, see: Beijing AI Principles, https://www.baai.ac.cn/blog/beijing-ai-principles.

established an AI ethics committee to draft ethics guidelines.[210] China is also planning to create supervision and evaluation systems to already monitor AI systems from the development phase. These evaluation systems would foresee sanctions for companies engaging in unethical activities.[211] With regard to standards, China has a national-level standardisation administration, in charge of the unified management, supervision and overall coordination of standardisation work in China.[212] However, it is important to keep in mind that in the past China frequently used standards to attain governmental policy aims.[213]

The Standardisation Administration issued a White Paper regarding standards for AI. This document states that AI standards should respect three main principles: human interest, accountability and transparency, consistency of rights and responsibilities.[214] China's Ministry of Science and Technology has also published 'Governance Principles for a New Generation of Artificial Intelligence: Develop Responsible Artificial Intelligence' on a national level.[215]

Finally, it is also noteworthy that China has become a world leader in the deployment of facial recognition software. Many (Chinese) companies offering facial recognition technology have benefited from this.[216] China has for example passed a law obliging all mobile phone users in China to submit to facial recognition scans when registering a new SIM card.

This law gives the Chinese government the ability to track mobile phone and internet users more easily in order to allegedly protect the legitimate rights

---

210 Xiaoxia, 'China Focus: China addresses building ethical AI', *Xinhua* 12 June 2019, www.xinhuanet.com/english/2019-06/12/c_138137273.htm.

211 G. Webster, R. Creemers, P. Triolo and E. Kania, 'Full Translation: China's 'New Generation Artificial Intelligence Development Plan', *New America* 1 August 2017, https://www.newamerica.org/cybersecurity-initiative/digichina/blog/full-translation-chinas-new-generation-artificial-intelligence-development-plan-2017/; E. Kania, D. Peterson, L. Laskai and G. Webster, 'Translation: Key Chinese Think Tank's 'AI Security White Paper' (Excerpts)', *New America* 21 February 2019, https://www.newamerica.org/cybersecurity-initiative/digichina/blog/translation-key-chinese-think-tanks-ai-security-white-paper-excerpts/.

212 Standardization Administration of the People's Republic of China, www.sac.gov.cn/sacen/.

213 S. Sacks and M. K. Li, 'How Chinese Cybersecurity Standards Impact Doing Business in China', *Center for strategic & international studies* 2 August 2018, https://www.csis.org/analysis/how-chinese-cybersecurity-standards-impact-doing-business-china.

214 J. Ding and P. Triolo, 'Translation: Excerpts from China's White Paper on Artificial Intelligence Standardization', *New America* 20 June 2018, https://www.newamerica.org/cybersecurity-initiative/digichina/blog/translation-excerpts-chinas-white-paper-artificial-intelligence-standardization/.

215 X., 'Governance Principles for the New Generation Artificial Intelligence – Developing Responsible Artificial Intelligence', *China Daily* 17 June 2019, https://www.chinadaily.com.cn/a/201906/17/WS5d07486ba3103dbf14328ab7.html.

216 T. Simonite, 'Behind the Rise of China's Facial-Recognition Giants', *Wired* 9 March 2019, https://www.wired.com/story/behind-rise-chinas-facial-recognition-giants/; Y. Yang and M. Murgia, 'Facial recognition: how China cornered the surveillance market', *Financial Times* 6 December 2019, https://www.ft.com/content/6f1a8f48-1813-11ea-9ee4-11f260415385.

and interests of citizens in cyberspace.[217] Furthermore, the city of Zhengzhou applied facial recognition technology to all of its metro check-in services.[218] Facial recognition technology was moreover reported to be used to track Uighurs (members of a predominantly Muslim minority) by keeping records of their whereabouts.[219] Nevertheless, more and more Chinese citizens seem to be wanting to curb the use of facial recognition technology.[220] The Chinese Ministry of Education even announced that it would restrict the use of facial recognition after some parents complained that facial recognition (to monitor attendance and focus of students) was used without their knowledge.[221] Notwithstanding this announcement, China still lacks precise regulation limiting facial recognition. On the first of August 2021, guidelines for the use of face-scanning technology and protection of people's identities and privacy, issued by the Supreme People's Court, came into force.[222]

These entail that private businesses need to acquire consent from customers before collecting and processing details about facial recognition. Individuals will have the right to refuse the use of facial recognition for identity verification and a reasonable alternative must be offered in the case of access to a building or service. Moreover, the consent must be explicit and independent, implying that it cannot be obtained by incorporating it in general terms of use or through bundled consent.[223] The new guidelines are not applicable to the government's nationwide surveillance system.

The National Governance Committee for the New Generation Artificial Intelligence published the 'Ethical Norms for the New Generation Artificial Intelligence' in September 2021. It contains six fundamental ethical principles: promoting human well-being; promoting fairness and justice, protecting personal privacy and security, ensuring reliability and controllability of AI

---

217 L. Kuo, 'China brings in mandatory facial recognition for mobile phone users', *The Guardian* 2 December 2019, https://www.theguardian.com/world/2019/dec/02/china-brings-in-mandatory-facial-recognition-for-mobile-phone-users.

218 W. Yamei, 'Chinese city fully launches face-scanning metro check-in service', *Xinhua* 3 December 2019, www.xinhuanet.com/english/2019-12/03/c_138602454.htm.

219 P. Mozur, 'One Month, 500,000 Face Scans: How China Is Using A.I. to Profile a Minority', *NY Times* 14 April 2019, https://www.nytimes.com/2019/04/14/technology/china-surveillance-artificial-intelligence-racial-profiling.html.

220 See for example: K. Allen, 'China facial recognition: Law professor sues wildlife park', *BBC* 8 November 2019, https://www.bbc.com/news/world-asia-china-50324342.

221 J. Feng, 'China To Curb Facial Recognition Technology in Schools', *Sup China* 5 September 2019, https://supchina.com/2019/09/05/china-to-curb-facial-recognition-technology-in-schools/.

222 The Supreme People's Court of the People's Republic of China, 'New rules to curb misuse of facial recognition tech', 29 July 2021, http://english.court.gov.cn/2021-07/29/content_37545967.htm.

223 A. Agrawal, 'China Supreme Court issues regulations against misuse of facial recognition technology', *Jurist. Legal News & Commentary* 1 August 2021, https://www.jurist.org/news/2021/08/china-supreme-court-issues-regulations-against-misuse-of-facial-recognition-technology/.

activities, strengthening accountability, and improving ethical literacy.[224] In addition, the code sets out eighteen specific requirements that will be applicable to all aspects of AI: AI management, research and development, supply, use and application.[225]

In March 2022, the Provisions on the Management of Algorithmic Recommendations in Internet Information Services came into force. This instrument is applicable to online services that use recommendations algorithms. Requirements are for instance, informing users of the use of algorithms, how they are used and what their purposes are, users must be able to opt-out and the algorithms may not be used to instigate overconsumption. In addition, the production and distribution of fake news is prohibited.[226]

5. CONCLUSION

15. There is much to say about ethics and regulation of AI. In this introductory chapter, we tried to sketch the main contours of the broad debate. Approaching AI from an exclusively ethical perspective or an exclusively legal perspective does not suffice. A combined approach is needed. Indeed, as explained above, although the function of ethics as a moral compass cannot be emphasised enough, we believe that legally binding rules that are enforced in a consistent way are indispensable for incentivising AI stakeholders to engage in AI solutions that maximise the benefits and minimise the harms of AI to individuals and society. We also believe that much existing legislation is potentially already applicable to AI systems (e.g. GDPR) and that more efforts should be invested into mapping the applicability of existing legal rules to AI, clarifying unambiguously how some concepts may apply to AI and, where necessary, highlighting the potential gaps. This should be the result of a collaborative and interdisciplinary effort of not only policymakers and other State authorities but also of AI developers and users, academia and civil society. It should moreover duly consider differences among AI systems based on the purpose for which they are used as well as the sector.

When we look at our analysis of jurisdictions, all of them aim at attaining some form of world leadership on AI technology. There is a common interest among them to regulate certain AI applications. Several countries, for example, want to 'curb and regulate' the use of facial recognition. Almost all stress (on

---

224 X., 'Ethics for AI', *China Business Law Journal* 17 June 2022, https://law.asia/ethics-for-ai.

225 K. Day, 'China unveils AI ethics code', *Global Government Forum* 8 October 2021, https://www.globalgovernmentforum.com/china-unveils-ai-ethics-code.

226 Provisions on the Management of Algorithmic Recommendations in Internet Information Services, https://www.chinalawtranslate.com/en/algorithms; J. Conrad & W. Knight, 'China Is About to Regulate AI – and the World Is Watching', *Wired*, https://www.wired.com/story/china-regulate-ai-world-watching.

paper) the use of AI ethics[227] and principles such as transparency, accountability and human involvement when dealing with AI technology. We notice the emergence of Advisory Councils as well. The regulatory approaches of several jurisdictions thus are converging. The 'race to AI' is now becoming a 'race to AI regulation'.[228]

Smuha believes that a model of regulatory competition that acknowledges the need for a combination of competition and cooperation can be appropriate in the future to avoid a regulatory race to the bottom.[229] The 'race to AI regulation' must eventually lead to a coherent regulatory framework for AI with strong and enforceable safeguards for fundamental rights, democracy and the rule of law.[230]

227 Contra: T. Chatfield, 'There's No Such Thing As 'Ethical A.I.', *Medium* 16 January 2020, https://onezero.medium.com/theres-no-such-thing-as-ethical-a-i-38891899261d.

228 N.A. Smuha, 'From a 'Race to AI' to a 'Race to AI Regulation' – Regulatory Competition for Artificial Intelligence', SSRN, 31 December 2019, pp. 15–22, https://papers.ssrn.com/sol3/papers.cfm?abstract_id=3501410.

229 *Ibid.*, pp. 22–26.

230 *Ibid.*, pp. 26–27.

CHAPTER 4

QUANTITATIVE LEGAL PREDICTION: THE FUTURE OF DISPUTE RESOLUTION?

Matthias Van Der Haegen*

1. INTRODUCTION

1. Civil procedure is not an area of law known for its innovative nature. The roots of civil procedural law for most of the European jurisdictions can be found in the Romano-canonical procedure. This common foundation has seen little profound change since.

Its long history, however, does not mean that civil procedure is insulated from innovation. On the contrary, its sometimes arcane and paper-driven methods and procedures leave much room for improvement, an endeavour in which recent legislative changes such as the 'Potpourri' legislation[1] in Belgium have only been incrementally successful. Such legislative change, however, stays within the boundaries of the existing paradigm. The dawn of AI within society and therefore also within the domain of civil procedure might break this status quo and provide a shock treatment to a legal field of which the framework has changed little in the last centuries.

Artificially intelligent civil procedure goes beyond the mere digitisation of existing procedures. It holds the promise of a transformed digitised justice in which the daily work of legal actors is to a large extent assisted by machines, changing the nature of human-centred judicial decision-making as we know it today. Litigants care little for lawyers, judges and the judicial process. They are

---

* Judicial trainee within the Belgian judiciary and invited professor of civil procedure at the Free University of Brussels. This text is written in a personal name. I am grateful to dr. Juan Gustavo Corvalán for his willingness to provide insight in Prometea, and to Caroline Calomme, dr. Rūta Liepiņa and Geneviève Vanderstichele for their helpful comments on an earlier version of this text.

1 See for an overview P. Taelman and B. Allemeersch (eds.), Het burgerlijk proces opnieuw hervormd (Antwerp: Intersentia, 2019), 284 p.

chiefly interested in a proper solution for their dispute. A transformation of the legal system should therefore be welcomed even when it does away with long held traditions, as long as it advances the fair and timely settlement of legal disputes.

2. The impact of AI on this issue of dispute resolution takes the form of algorithmic or quantitative legal prediction (henceforth QLP), colloquially known as predictive justice. Even though successfully operating applications in this field are still few and far between, their shape is already discernible. This is the focus of this chapter. As a book chapter of limited length does not lend itself to an in-depth study of this phenomenon, this chapter will only scrape the surface of some issues related to predictive justice. The interested reader will find more information in the referenced material. Even though this edited volume focuses on Belgium, this chapter will only briefly touch upon this jurisdiction given the general absence of Belgian initiatives in this field. Rather, some hurdles Belgium needs to overcome to facilitate the AI revolution in its legal system will be outlined in the final part of this text.

3. This chapter provides a brief introduction to legal analytics and QLP (part 2), followed by a short overview of some existing applications (part 3). Potential use cases and their advantages are highlighted (part 4), followed by a discussion of the challenges that QLP poses (part 5). I will then delve deeper into the Belgian situation with regards to QLP and discuss some of the reasons underlying the lack of any development in this jurisdiction (part 6). The main findings are briefly summarised in a conclusion (part 7).

2. LEGAL ANALYTICS

4. QLP belongs conceptually to two distinct fields. Firstly, QLP is part of a wider phenomenon called legal analytics, which can be described as the application of data mining techniques in the legal domain to gain substantively meaningful insight. Secondly, QLP is an application of the broader field of predictive analytics, which is the development of models to predict behaviour or future events based on a variety of analytical and statistical techniques.[2] Techniques that are central to this endeavour, such as ML and NLP, were examined in Chapter 1 of this book.

The legal domain is an area that lends itself well to predictive analytics. Law is built upon language-heavy, semi-structured data, be it legislation, case law, lawyers' briefs or doctrine. It underpins a multibillion-dollar industry characterised by work processes that have seen little profound change in the last

[2] H. Surden, 'Machine Learning and the Law', *Washington Law Review*, 2014, vol. 89, p. 90, p. 100.

decades or even centuries. Trials, the beating heart of civil procedure, operate moreover in a similar manner as algorithms: based on a given input, an output is reached by an impartial decision-maker following predetermined rules. This state of affairs invites efficiency-enhancing innovation through legal analytics.

5. QLP, just like other predictive models, detects patterns and correlations in existing (training) data, more specifically court decisions. The discovered patterns between the observed features and the outcome features are used to build a predictive model. In supervised ML, these features are manually labelled within the training data by domain experts. This model can then be used to make predictions by detecting the occurrence of these patterns in new data. Applied to the legal domain, predictive models generally look like this: a machine-learning algorithm identifies the patterns within the legal decisions used as training data and establishes which observed features are associated with particular outcomes. The patterns and correlations found in training data are then harnessed in order to predict what the outcome would be in a new, previously unseen factual scenario. Based on the relation of the features of the new case to the uncovered patterns, an outcome probability is generated by the predictive model.[3]

6. QLP automates a process that lies at the core of a lawyer's daily work: in order to advise clients on their legal situation or on the legality of their actions in their private or professional life, a lawyer predicts how the legal system would view the issue at hand.[4] In making these predictions, a lawyer draws on his or her schooling, experience and research. Fundamentally, a lawyer relies on what he or she has observed and tries to draw inferences from these observations, assuming the analysed data are representative for the underlying reality. The extent of the lawyer's experience thus determines the scope and accuracy of the legal assessment he or she makes. This endeavour is however limited by the lawyer's cognitive abilities: the amount of data the human mind can process and intelligently analyse is limited and moreover distorted by several biases.[5]

Computer-assisted or automated prediction is not burdened by these limitations. Its abilities are only dependent upon ever-increasing computing power[6], the availability of data and the scalability of data-processing techniques. It thus has an enormous potential to outperform the lawyer's prediction.[7] QLP

[3] Surden, 'Machine Learning and the Law', pp. 102–105.

[4] Cf. O. Wendell-Holmes Jr., 'The Path of the Law', *Harvard Law Review,* 1897, vol. 10, p. 457.

[5] See e.g., A. Tversky and D. Kahneman, 'Judgment Under Uncertainty: Heuristics and Biases', *Science,* 1974, vol. 185, pp. 1124–1131.

[6] Cf. Moore's law, the theorem that computing power (the transistor count in the world's leading central processing unit) doubles every two years since the 1960s.

[7] The recognition of this potential predates the possibility to act upon it. See L. Loevinger, 'Jurimetrics: Science and Prediction in the Field of Law', *Minnesota Law Review,* 1961, vol. 46, pp. 255–275; R. Lawlor, 'What Computers Can Do: Analysis and Prediction of Judicial

can thus outperform the limited cognitive ability of a lawyer's mind by the intelligent mining of a massive amount of legal data.

7. This evolution presents a paradigm shift on both a heuristic and a fundamental level. On a heuristic level, QLP changes the existing paradigm as it makes a multitude of data easily available to legal professionals. An algorithmic legal prediction complements the legal adviser or decision-maker by measuring the chance of success, estimating the amount of damages that could be obtained or highlighting those factors that impact outcomes but go unnoticed in traditional legal analysis.[8] In addition to their analysis based on experience, intuition and time-constrained legal research, lawyers have access to a wealth of information through QLP.

In many countries, supreme court decisions make up the bulk of the published and relied-upon case law. The advent of legal big data shifts attention to the more numerous decisions of lower courts, with possibly fundamental consequences for case law as a source of law.[9] This increased availability of legal information takes place through the prism of an algorithm, however. This evolution thus presents a paradox: the immensely larger amount of data paints a more accurate picture of the reality of legal life, which however needs to be simplified to a large extent to be accessible and insightful.[10] As such, QLP quantifies legal data and the legal process, whereas the legal profession has traditionally been an area of civil society insulated from statistics.[11] QLP therefore presents a profound cultural change to the world of legal practice.

The second dimension of the paradigm shift is more fundamental. Causation forms the backbone of many legal rules and institutions in both civil and criminal law.[12] Replacing human reasoning by algorithmic reasoning, however, means that correlation takes the place of causation.[13] As such, QLP debases the

---

Decisions', *American Bar Association Journal,* 1963, vol. 49, pp. 337–344; A. D'Amato, 'Can/Should Computers replace Judges?', *Georgia Law Review,* 1977, vol. 11, pp. 1277–1301.

8 Surden, 'Machine Learning and the Law', p. 107.

9 See L. Cadiet, *L'Open Data des décisions de justice. Mission d'étude et de préfiguration sur l'ouverture au public des décisions de justice,* 2017, https://www.justice.gouv.fr/publication/open_data_rapport.pdf, p. 189; P. Deumier, 'La justice prédictive et les sources du droit: la jurisprudence du fond', in R. Sève (ed.), *La justice prédictive* (Paris: Dalloz, 2018), pp. 53–60.

10 C. Devins et al., 'The Law and Big Data', *Cornell Journal of Law and Public Policy,* 2017, vol. 27, p. 385.

11 A. Van den Branden, *Les robots à l'assaut de la justice* (Brussels: Larcier, 2019), pp. 2–3.

12 See among others H. Hart and T. Honoré, *Causation in the law* (Oxford: Oxford University Press, 1985), Chapters VI-XV; M. Moore, *Causation and Responsibility: An Essay in Law, Morals and Metaphysics* (Oxford: Oxford University Press, 2009), 605 p.

13 H. Croze, 'La factualisation du droit', *La Semaine Juridique,* 2017, p. 101; A. Garapon, 'Les enjeux de la justice prédictive', *La Semaine Juridique,* 2017, doctr. 31, no. 14; Devins et al., 'The Law and Big Data', p. 364. Future advances in the field of argument retrieval could however counter the replacement of causation by correlation in legal analytics. See among others K. Ashley, *Artificial Intelligence and Legal Analytics* (Cambridge: Cambridge University Press, 2017), pp. 4–6, pp. 11–13.

value of legal rules: they are treated as mere factors in an algorithm and have the same value as e.g., the gender of the judge or the age of the (adult) defendant.[14] Such case features might be found to improve the accuracy of the predictive model and could thus be retained by it, even though they have little to no relevance in traditional conceptions of judicial decision-making.[15] This often overlooked aspect of predictive models in the legal domain again changes the nature of law and legal decision-making.

3. EXISTING APPLICATIONS

8. Recent advances in AI and computing power have made QLP a useful asset in (future) legal practice. Some QLP applications already exist, especially in the domain of criminal law, where predictive models are employed to assess the risk of recidivism a defendant poses. These applications have drawn considerable attention and profound criticism in recent years.[16] The examples in the criminal law domain provide insight into how QLP in civil law cases might be used in the (near) future. These existing applications therefore function as helpful examples to paint some of the challenges that predictive modelling brings to the legal domain. In this overview, only applications that are currently being used in practice will be discussed.[17] Some of these instruments were developed by for-profit companies who shield information on their inner workings, making

---

14 Garapon, 'Les enjeux de la justice prédictive', no. 14.

15 Research indicated for instance that the higher the arousal or excitement directed to a lawyer by a U.S. Supreme Court justice compared to his or her opponent, the less likely that lawyer was to win the justice's vote. The use of such a predictor would improve the accuracy of a predictive model but has no legal significance. See B. Dietrich et al., 'Emotional Arousal Predicts Voting on the U.S. Supreme Court', *Political Analysis,* 2019, vol. 27, pp. 237–243.

16 See e.g., for the Netherlands: G. van Dijck, 'Algoritmische risicotaxatie van recidive. Over de Oxford Risk of Recidivism tool (OXREC), ongelijke behandeling en discriminatie in strafzaken', *Nederlands Juristenblad,* 2020, vol. 95, pp. 1784–1790. The criticism on similar applications will be discussed in part 5.

17 QLP applications developed in academia will not be discussed, as it would lead our discussion too far. Examples of such research are e.g., N. Aletras et al., 'Predicting judicial decisions of the European Court of Human Rights: a Natural Language Processing perspective', *PeerJ Computer Science,* 2016, https://doi.org/10.7717/peerj-cs.93; D. Katz et al., 'A General Approach for Predicting the Behavior of the Supreme Court of the United States', *Plos One,* 2017, https://doi.org/10.1371/journal.pone.0174698; M. Medvedeva, M. Vols and M. Wieling, 'Using machine learning to predict decisions of the European Court of Human Right', *Artificial Intelligence and Law,* 2019, https://doi.org/10.1007/s10506-019-09255-y; M. Medvedeva, M. Vols and M. Wieling, 'JURI SAYS: An Automatic Judgement Prediction System for the European Court of Human Rights', in S. Villata, J. Harasta and P Kremen (eds.), *Legal Knowledge and Information Systems JURIX 2020* (Amsterdam: IOS Press 2020), pp. 270–280. See for a discussion of this and other research G. Vanderstichele, 'The Normative Value of Legal Analytics. Is There a Case for Statistical Precedent?', 2019, https://papers.ssrn.com/sol3/papers.cfm?abstract_id=3474878, pp. 27–45.

it rather difficult to describe their products.[18] This brief overview is only meant to sketch the outlines of some of the existing applications and is by no means exhaustive.[19]

3.1. COMPAS

9. COMPAS (Correctional Offender Management Profiling for Alternative Sanctions) is a decision support tool developed by Equivant (formerly Northpointe) that assesses the likelihood of recidivism in a criminal defendant. Several U.S. states make us of it. Defendants fill in a questionnaire containing 137 questions about their personal life. These answers are then coupled with socio-demographic data to arrive at a score between 1 and 10, with a higher number indicating a higher risk of recidivism. Even though COMPAS is strictly speaking not a QLP system in the sense of a machine-learning algorithm that predicts future behaviour based on data points from the past, it is relevant in the context of this chapter as it gave rise to fundamental issues with regards to the use of predictive algorithms within the administration of justice. Indeed, COMPAS has been met with fierce criticism. The company provides only few details on how the algorithm works, but vigorous research by ProPublica shed light on its inner workings and revealed the existence of biases in its operation. The different issues that were raised with regards to COMPAS will be discussed in part 5.

3.2. HART

10. HART (Harm Assessment Risk Tool) is in purpose similar to COMPAS but differs in its design as it employs a method called random forests, a form of ML. Developed by researchers from the University of Cambridge, it is currently being used by the Durham Constabulary in the United Kingdom. Based on a set of predictors, a score is calculated that indicates the risk of reoffending. Most predictors stem from the suspect's offending history, but others such as

---

18 Some companies even provide ample information on QLP on their website, giving the impression that their products benefit from predictive models. Scratching the surface of their products, however, reveals that they don't rely on ML and thus hardly qualify as QLP.

19 An unknown number of predictive models is currently being developed. Most often only scant information is available online, often presenting some early results of the model under development. With little to no information on their methodology, it is impossible to verify the claims put forward. An example can be found within the consultancy firm Deloitte, whose Dutch branch developed Tax-I, a predictive model within the tax law domain for internal and limited external use (see https://tax-i.deloitte.nl/). Deloitte claims Tax-I is able to predict the outcome of court cases.

age, gender and residential postcode are added (although the latter will change in the future).[20]

3.3. CASE LAW ANALYTICS

11. Case Law Analytics, a French legal tech company, built an application which presents and quantifies the different possible outcomes of a given case after analysing the existing case law. The model is powered by a highly supervised ML algorithm. According to its website, practitioners, judges and academics came together to identify the relevant criteria in different areas of legal decision-making. Users can select criteria that are relevant to their legal problem, which will then be used to identify the legal decisions relevant to the query. These decisions will then be fed to the probabilistic model in order to quantify the possible outcomes of the issue at hand. In 2020, the company partnered with French legal publisher Dalloz, a move which will probably help in expanding its database of legal decisions.

3.4. PROMETEA

12. Prometea is a multi-faceted legal case management tool developed in Argentina by the Public Prosecutor Office of Buenos Aires (*Ministerio Público de la Ciudad Autónoma de Buenos Aires*) in close cooperation with the Innovation and Artificial Intelligence Laboratory of the School of Law of the University of Buenos Aires. It comprises a virtual assistant and a QLP tool. As a virtual assistant, Prometea checks formal requirements of files, identifies procedural deadlines and automates document creation. It significantly improves efficiency for routine and mechanical operations, claiming for instance to reduce typing errors by 99%. The application is operated through voice command or via a chatbot.[21]

Prometea saw its first use within the Public Prosecutor's Office of Buenos Aires. In Argentina, public prosecutors draft judgements that the presiding judge either approves or amends. Prometea has been used since 2017 to automatically create such draft judgments in 'simple' cases in administrative law, tax law and misdemeanour cases. Trained on a dataset of more than 2.400 judgments and 1.400 legal opinions of the Public Prosecutor using topic classification[22],

---

20 M. Oswald et al., 'Algorithmic risk assessment policing models: lessons from the Durham HART model and 'Experimental' proportionality', *Information and Communication Technology Law,* 2018, vol. 27, pp. 228–229.

21 J. Corvalán, 'Inteligencia artificial: retos, desafíos y oportunidades – Prometea: la primera inteligencia artificial de Latinoamérica al servicio de la Justicia', *Revista de Investigações Constitucionais,* 2018, vol. 5, p. 303.

22 J. Corvalán, *Prometea: Artificial Intelligence to Transform Public Organisations* (Buenos Aires: Astrea, 2019), p. 51.

Prometea identifies the characteristics of the case at hand and searches for earlier cases with identical or similar characteristics within a knowledge base of 300.000 decisions. It does so with 96% accuracy.[23] Prometea retrieves the decision linked with the case with similar or identical characteristics, which is then used as a (editable) basis for the new draft judgment. Human actors can augment this draft by referencing new case law or crafting additional arguments.[24] In many cases in which Prometea has been used, the judge rubberstamped an automatically generated draft. By 2019, the predictions generated by the application had been followed by the court in 97 cases.[25]

Prometea is now being used by various other courts in Argentina, as well as by the Inter-American Court of Human Rights where it functions as a research platform – based on past judgments of the Court – and a decision-making support tool, generating notifications to the ambassadors and officials of the different member states in the four official languages of the Court. In the Constitutional Court of Colombia, Prometea is used to identify those appeals which have a high priority, an important task in a court with a high daily influx of new cases.[26]

4. POTENTIAL USE CASES AND THEIR ADVANTAGES

13. QLP has the potential to profoundly disrupt and innovate the administration of justice. The above-sketched applications are still relatively modest in their ambitions and moderate in their impact so far. This part examines three possible innovative use-cases and discusses the advantages they offer compared to the current state of affairs within the legal system.

4.1. POTENTIAL USE CASES

14. QLP can in the first place be used as an informational tool. By providing insight into a litigant's legal situation or chances of success if he or she chooses to litigate, QLP brings information that is otherwise readily nor freely available to litigants-in-person. This information suffers from a lack of nuance

---

23 Corvalán, *Prometea*, p. 16.

24 Corvalán, *Prometea*, p. 97.

25 Corvalán, *Prometea*, p. 52.

26 Interview with Juan Gustavo Corvalán: 'Prometea es el primer sistema de inteligencia artificial diseñado y desarrollado por el Ministerio Público Fiscal de la Ciudad Autónoma de Buenos Aires', *The Technolawgist*, 20 June 2019, https://www.thetechnolawgist.com/2019/06/20/entrevista-juan-gustavo-corvalan-buenos-aires-prometea-inteligencia-artificial/.

and contextual meaning, however, if not interpreted by a legal professional. Nonetheless, it could significantly increase access to justice by lowering the transaction costs of legal counsel, which can be a financial and psychological barrier to many. This effect could be even stronger if QLP as an informational tool would be coupled with online dispute resolution (ODR) systems, so that easily accessible online courts can settle conflicts efficiently.[27] Estonia's Ministry of Justice announced the development of such a tool in 2019, aiming to build a predictive model that would be used to decide small claims, i.e., those falling below a monetary threshold of 7.000 euros.[28]

15. Secondly, QLP can be used as decision support tool. The judiciary faces increasing budget constraints in many jurisdictions. At the same time, all too often, scarce resources have to be invested in sometimes unmeritorious cases.[29] QLP makes it possible to identify 'easy' cases, i.e., those of which the outcome can be predicted with a high accuracy. Junior members of the judiciary or at least a single judge (*unus judex*) could deal with those cases. QLP could, as Prometea exemplifies, detect cases with similar fact patterns as the case at hand, which could then be used as a basis for a new decision. QLP can assist judges in deciding 'hard' cases too, i.e., those that cannot be predicted with a high accuracy, by identifying relevant precedents. QLP systems could therefore be a helpful tool in the allocation of the judiciary's scarce resources.

16. Thirdly, law firms can make use of QLP in order to advise clients with higher efficiency and at a reduced cost. Legal technology is a game-changer in the legal services market that will likely drive prices down[30] and further democratise the industry[31] as low effort tasks will be increasingly automated.

---

27 Cf. G. Vanderstichele, 'Rechtspraak in een datagestuurde informatiemaatschappij', *Nieuw Juridisch Weekblad,* 2017, pp. 628–629. ODR could take the form of rule-based expert systems rather than data-driven machine-learning algorithms in areas of law with an emphasis on clear-cut rules and clearly defined concepts. Decision trees could also go a long way in providing easy understandable legal advice to litigants-in-person in cases that are more straightforward. See also M. Ebers, 'Automating due process – the promise and challenges of AI-based techniques in consumer online dispute resolution', in X. Kramer, J. Hoevenaars, B. Kas and E. Themeli (eds.), *Frontiers in Civil Justice: Privatisation, Monetisation and Digitisation* (Cheltenham: Edward Elgar Publishing 2022), pp. 142–168.

28 D. Cowan, 'Estonia: a robotically transformative nation', *The Robotics Law Journal,* 2019, https://www.roboticslawjournal.com/global/estonia-a-robotically-transformative-nation-28728942.

29 Cf. Vanderstichele, 'Rechtspraak in een datagestuurde informatiemaatschappij', p. 628.

30 D. Katz, 'Quantitative Legal Prediction – or – How I Learned to Stop Worrying and Start Preparing for the Data-driven Future of the Legal Services Industry', *Emory Law Journal,* 2013, vol. 62, pp. 910–912, pp. 928–936.

31 A. Yoon, 'The Post-Modern Lawyer: Technology and the Democratization of Legal Representation', *University of Toronto Law Journal,* 2016, vol. 66, pp. 469–471.

As an informational tool, it allows for more efficient legal research[32] and a better-informed litigation and negotiation strategy and risk management. As such, it also contributes to the out-of-court settlement of legal disputes. On a more fundamental level, QLP could contribute to an overhaul of the traditional practice of law. Law firms are increasingly pressured to drop their traditional hourly rates and accept payment per provided service or package.[33] QLP will likely fuel this evolution: offering access to and contextualisation of QLP-generated legal assessments, rather than to traditional legal research, will further commoditise the legal profession as the pricing power of lawyers would weaken.[34]

4.2. ADVANTAGES OF QLP

17. The advantages of QLP in these use-cases are easily visible. First of all, it broadens access to justice by making legal advice easier to obtain and at a lower cost.[35] Secondly, it improves the efficiency of legal actors and legal processes.[36] The use of Prometea in Argentina for instance has sped up the processing times within courts manifold: it originally took 174 days to process a thousand cases on housing rights; with Prometea this processing time dropped to 45 days.[37] More generally, legal analytics can to a certain extent automate many routine (clerical) tasks within the administration of justice. Thirdly, employed by judges as a support tool in decision-making, QLP furthers equality before the law, legal certainty and consistency between legal decisions[38] by informing decision makers on how previous judgments decided a specific legal question. Such an

---

32 Cf. the decision of the Superior Court of Justice of Ontario, where Mr. Justice Whitten decided on the question of the indemnity costs that 'if artificial intelligence sources were employed, no doubt counsel's preparation time would have been significantly reduced': Cass v. 1410088 Ontario Inc., 2018 ONSC 6959, at 34.

33 Katz, 'Quantitative Legal Prediction', pp. 929–932; P. Henry and P. Hoffströssler, *Rapport over de toekomst van de advocatuur,* 2018, pp. 249–252, https://justitie.belgium.be/sites/default/files/rapporttoekomstadvocatuurrapportavenirprofessiond_avocatfinal.pdf.

34 See also R. Susskind, *The End of Lawyers? Rethinking the Nature of Legal Services* (Oxford: Oxford University Press, 2010), p. 31.

35 B. Alarie et al., 'Law in the Future', *University of Toronto Law Journal,* 2016, vol. 66, pp. 426–427.

36 Surden, *Machine Learning and the Law,* p. 101; D. Chen, 'Judicial Analytics and the Great Transformation of American Law', *Artificial Intelligence and Law,* 2019, vol. 27, p. 15. See for an interesting law & economics study on the influence of QLP on legal actors' behaviour A. Casey and A. Niblett, 'Will Robot Judges Change Litigation and Settlement Outcomes? A First Look at the Algorithmic Replication of Prior Cases', 2020, https://papers.ssrn.com/sol3/papers.cfm?abstract_id=3633037.

37 Corvalán, *Prometea,* p. 44.

38 Chen, 'Judicial Analytics and the Great Transformation of American Law', p. 15; S.-M. Ferrié, 'Les algorithmes à l'épreuve du droit au procès équitable', *La Semaine Juridique,* 2018, doctr. 297, no. 10.

instrument would prove especially advantageous in issues where judges wield a higher degree of discretion, e.g., when deciding the amount of non-pecuniary losses to be compensated. Prometea illustrates this aspect yet again, as it identifies earlier judgments delivered in similar or identical fact patterns and uses those as the basis for a new decision. It is important to note, concluding, that the extent to which these possible advantages occur in practice depends on the way in which QLP is employed. A government-operated system is wholly different from an application developed by a law firm for internal use.

5. CHALLENGES

18. The use of AI within the realm of dispute resolution raises several challenges. Some of these challenges pertain to the application of predictive models to the legal domain, whereas other challenges are inherent to predictive models in general but are exacerbated within the field of civil procedure due to the fundamental rights of due process.

5.1. LIMITS OF PREDICTIVE MODELS WITHIN THE LEGAL DOMAIN

19. QLP informs its user on the outcome of a specific legal problem based on patterns found within case law. This operation is described as a prediction, but this term is misleading as it presumes the existence of predetermined and unchangeable rules whose application can be predicted within a margin of error, just like a weather forecast is an (often accurate) prediction based on well-known laws of nature. Legal forecasting threads however on much less secure ground, because legal rules are not (always) predetermined nor are they unchangeable. The parallel with scientific prediction carries with it however a risk of unjustly attaching a normative effect to QLP.

5.1.1. The Application of Law Does Not Adhere to Predetermined Rules

20. Neither law nor its application obeys to strict rules that can be determined in advance. The open-ended nature of many legal rules implies a dynamic ambiguity. Precedents that would *prima facie* determine the outcome of a dispute can be overruled. The influence of fundamental principles, the scopes of which are difficult to define, can unforeseeably render the application of a straightforward legal rule a capricious exercise.[39]

---

[39] See for example the decision by the French *Cour de cassation* of 4 December 2013, in which the Court discarded the application of a straightforward legal rule because its application

Simply put, law cannot be reduced to an equilibration and calculation of variables and factors with predetermined weights[40], at least not in the many areas of law that predominantly rely on principles and standards rather than clear-cut rules.[41] Moreover, the inability of QLP to capture the essence of legal rules, i.e. causation, relying instead on correlation as some sort of crude proxy, further debases the claim that QLP could predict case outcomes with any kind of statistical or mathematical certainty. This is even more the case if these correlations would be spurious.

21. These objections carry weight only to a certain extent, however. Indeed, neither legal rules nor their application can be reduced to a statistical problem. QLP, however, does not proclaim to apply legal rules. It claims to present a probable outcome if a case was brought to trial, based on how other disputes were decided by judges. This exercise does not necessitate interpreting or applying legal rules. It mimics the prediction a lawyer would give his client, but uses a completely different method, namely (supervised) ML, to arrive at this goal. To require that these algorithmic predictions be brought about in the same manner as a human prediction, only to then establish that the former fails where the latter succeeds, betrays a lack of understanding of AI. A valid comparison between the process of algorithmic and human legal prediction can only be made by comparing their outputs. If a human assessment of the outcome of a legal dispute is indistinguishable from an algorithmic prediction[42], the manner in which they came about is irrelevant. This does not mean, however, that we can safely ignore the methodology that lies behind these algorithmic predictions. The challenges in this regard are discussed in part 5.2.

5.1.2. Changeable Nature of Law

22. The changeable nature of law presents a possibly fatal flaw of QLP. The main premise of QLP is the stability of case law, so that correlations derived

---

would infringe on fundamental rights (Cass. (FR) 4 December 2013, no. 12-26.066, https://www.legifrance.gouv.fr). For a discussion of the influence of fundamental rights on private law, see H. Collins, 'The Challenges Presented by Fundamental Rights to Private Law', in K. Barker, K. Fairweather and R. Grantham (eds.), *Private Law in the 21st Century* (Oxford: Hart Publishing, 2017), pp. 213–235.

40 Devins et al., 'The Law and Big Data', p. 389.

41 Benjamin Alarie proclaims that the legal system will move away from principle-based system (applied post-hoc) towards a rule-based system. Although this might be possible in some areas of law, e.g., tax law as in Alarie's work, it is doubtful whether such an approach is at all feasible in other areas of law. Attempts at exhaustivity have been frustrated time and again in the history of codification. See B. Alarie, 'The Path of the Law: Toward Legal Singularity', *University of Toronto Law Journal*, 2016, vol. 66, pp. 446–451.

42 Cf. Alan Turing's Imitation game. A. Turing, 'Computing Machinery and Intelligence', *Mind*, 1950, vol. 59, pp. 433–460.

from past decisions remain applicable and valid in the future.[43] This assumption is false, but only to an extent. As the product of an ever on-going argumentative and discursive process[44], legal rules are neither set in stone nor scribbled in sand. Reversals in case law are – at least when considering supreme courts[45] – relatively rare. Legal change is an incremental process, slowly adapting legal rules to socio-economic evolutions. Legislative change takes place more frequently – both numerically and temporally – but dramatic legislative changes to traditional areas of substantive law, *viz.* civil and criminal law, are rare. Any changes that do take place often amount to a mere consolidation in legislation of an evolution brought about incrementally and iteratively through case law. Legislative change that introduces novel rules is more frequent in areas that fall under administrative or public law in its broadest of meanings, such as tax law, social security law, etc. In these areas, characterised by rules rather than standards, expert systems would indeed perhaps be a better fit than ML with legal data as a method to build a decision supporting or informative tool.[46] The ever-changing nature of legal rules is therefore not as fatal to QLP as one would think. In some areas, it may hamper legal prediction for the foreseeable future, whilst in others its impact is manageable, especially if QLP takes this characteristic into account by e.g., attaching greater weight to patterns found in more recent decisions.

5.1.3. Risk of a Normative Prediction

23. An important concern when introducing predictive models in the legal domain is the normative effect that legal actors might attach to QLP. The legal nature of these predictions is unregulated and thus uncertain. It is however clear that in civil law countries, where the latitude of a rule of binding precedent is at least officially severely restricted, legal culture would oppose attaching a

43 Surden, *Machine Learning and the Law*, p. 105.

44 Cf. J. Vranken, 'Keuzevrijheid en verantwoordingsplicht van de rechter in civiele zaken', in X (ed.), *Gemotiveerd gehuldigd. Opstellen aangeboden aan Mr. C.D. van Boeschoten* (Zwolle: Tjeenk Willink, 1993), p. 230.

45 For Belgium, see M. Van Der Haegen, 'Omgaan met omgaan. Een kwalitatief empirisch onderzoek naar de omkeringen in de cassatierechtspraak', *Tijdschrift voor Privaatrecht*, 2019, pp. 205–209.

46 In rule-based expert systems legal rules are programmed in the system, as opposed to data-centric systems such as QLP applications. On the basis of user input, an outcome is reached following the predetermined rules. In its simpler formats, expert systems operate through decision trees. See for a general overview of expert systems R. Susskind, 'Expert Systems in Law: A Jurisprudential Approach to Artificial Intelligence and Legal Reasoning', *Modern Law Review*, 1986, vol. 49, pp. 168–194; Ashley, *Artificial Intelligence and Legal Analytics*, pp. 8–11. See for some examples M. Sergot et al., 'The British Nationality Act as a Logic Program', *Communications of the ACM*, 1986, vol. 29, pp. 370–386; M. Araszkiewicz et al., 'Framing a knowledge base for a legal expert system dealing with indeterminate concepts', *The Scientific World Journal*, 2015, pp. 1–14. See also the Dutch website on demission cases (https://www.magontslag.nl).

binding effect to any prediction. Judges faced with an algorithmic prediction, be it generated within the judiciary or presented by a lawyer, cannot treat it as law or fact nor as a secondary source of law; its information would thus likely fall within a *sui generis* category in dispute resolution.[47]

24. The legal value of these predictions is however only one side of the coin; the psychological effect of an algorithmic prediction is another. Judicial decision-making might be influenced by predictions no matter the value they legally have, due to an implicit normative effect. Well-known biases, such as the automation bias or the McNamara or quantitative fallacy could influence the decision-making process.[48] The former implies that humans uncritically favour suggestions made by automatic decision-making systems and ignore contrary information, whereas the latter describes the propensity of humans to attach more weight to quantitative information than to qualitative observations. Scholars also warn for group conformism and herd effects: judges might flock to predicted outcomes that are based on how their colleagues decided similar cases in the past.[49] The occurrence of these biases could result in a performative effect of a prediction: the mere making of a prediction, whatever its validity or value, makes the actual occurrence of the predicted outcome more likely.[50]

The possible behavioural effects amount to a systemic risk for the legal domain. Earlier, the adaptability of the legal system was described as a serious but surmountable challenge for QLP. The potential for performativity could however pose a threat to this fundamental characteristic by reducing variance and heterogeneity within legal decisions.[51] As an algorithmic legal prediction is paradoxically inherently backward looking, it could result in sclerosis and ossification, stifling incremental evolution in legal rules.[52] Whether this risk materialises will depend on the way in which QLP is used and the critical interaction of legal actors with it. The latter presupposes that judges are digitally literate.[53]

---

47 Vanderstichele, 'The Normative Value of Legal Analytics', pp. 47–55. See also D. Cholet, 'La justice prédictive et les principes fondamentaux du procès civil, in R. Sève (ed.), *La justice prédictive* (Paris: Dalloz, 2018), pp. 229–230.

48 Vanderstichele, 'The Normative Value of Legal Analytics', p. 58.

49 Ferrié, 'Les algorithmes à l'épreuve du droit au procès équitable', no. 20.

50 Cadiet, *L'Open Data des décisions de justice*, p. 25.

51 Devins et al., 'The Law and Big Data', p. 360.

52 R. Re and A. Solow-Niederman, 'Developing Artificially Intelligent Justice', *Stanford Technology Law Review*, 2019, vol. 22, p. 268.

53 Vanderstichele, 'Rechtspraak in een datagestuurde informatiemaatschappij', pp. 632–633.

5.2. CHALLENGES INHERENT TO PREDICTIVE MODELS

25. Predictive analytics pose many different challenges, such as algorithmic bias, fairness and transparency. These challenges are present with any predictive model in every domain, but the dangers these challenges present are more pressing within the legal domain given the far-reaching consequences legal decisions can have for the lives and livelihoods of people. If it is to be used in practice, therefore, QLP must comply with the due process rights that lie at the core of civil and criminal procedure and are enshrined, for the member states of the Council of Europe, in Article 6 ECHR. The challenges that must be met are the eradication of biases, the transparency of an algorithm and trust building.

5.2.1. Bias Within Predictive Models

26. The presence of a bias of any kind renders the result of an algorithmic legal prediction invalid. Biases might be acceptable in other predictive analytics (e.g., user profiling in e-commerce), but the stakes are higher when such predictions take place within the legal domain. This is especially important as equality before the law is a core tenet of the administration of justice and, moreover, an aspect that QLP promises to reinforce. Biased outcomes thwart these ambitions and undermine the fundamentals of the legal system. Biases can occur in different constitutive elements of a predictive model: the training data might be biased, the data itself might be tainted by bias, and certain choices in the architecture of the algorithm may lead to a bias.

A. Biased Training Data

27. The choice of which data to include in the training dataset is important. In order to function well, a predictive model must be able to generalise the patterns inferred from the training data to unseen data. It will be unsuccessful in this endeavour if the training data is not sufficiently representative of the reality it aspires to model. The racial bias that was discovered in the blink detection feature present in many Nikon cameras offers a clear illustration of the importance of representative training data. This feature warned the camera's user when a person had blinked in the picture. Users were however regularly confronted with such warning messages when people with an Asian complexity were depicted, as the face detection algorithm was unable to distinguish a narrow eye from a half-closed one. Training data that predominantly consisted of Caucasian faces lied at the root of this problem.[54]

The requirement of representative training data also applies to ML within the legal domain. Training data that consists of decisions of just a few courts or

[54] K. Crawford, 'Intelligence's White Guy Problem', *New York Times*, 26 June 2016, p. 11.

single judges, or decisions that stem from disputes emblematic of metropolitan areas will most likely result in an 'overfitted' predictive model, i.e. a model that is too specifically tailored to the training data. As such, these models would not generalise well to unseen data, i.e. decisions from other judges.

B. Biased data

28. Biased data should be distinguished from a biased selection of the training data. This type of bias is perhaps more problematic than an unrepresentative training dataset, as the latter can be relatively easily overcome by making the training data more diverse. An undesirable bias found within the very phenomenon the algorithm wants to predict, is harder to tackle.

Any predictive exercise projects data from the past onto the future. As Mayson writes, 'the premise of prediction is that, absent intervention, history will repeat itself'.[55] This essential characteristic of predictions can be problematic when that past is – for some societal groups – troublesome. Discrimination based on race, gender or sexual orientation is prevalent within (recent) legal history and some of it persists to this day.[56] Algorithms used within the legal domain such as COMPAS faced severe criticism after intense scrutiny brought a racial bias to light. Even though COMPAS does not use race as a predictor, research by ProPublica revealed that a black defendant was twice as likely to be wrongly labelled as a future criminal than a white defendant, and white defendants were mislabelled as presenting a low risk more often than black defendants.[57] The company behind COMPAS refuted these accusations.[58] This disparity between black and white defendants likely followed from predictors functioning as a proxy to race. Having such predictors is problematic given the structural racial discrimination thought to be prevalent in the U.S. (criminal) justice system. For example, COMPAS takes prior arrests into account when assessing the recidivism risk, as well as the criminal record of parents.[59] Black defendants (and their parents) are perhaps more likely to have prior arrests, but biased policing and racial profiling – e.g., New York City's controversial stop-and-frisk

---

55 S. Mayson, 'Bias in, bias out', *Yale Law Journal*, 2019, vol. 128, p. 2251.

56 E.g., the prohibition for women to practice law (Brussel 12 december 1888, *Pasicrisie Appel*, 1888, p. 48), or more recently, the question whether differences in premiums based on gender are allowed with regards to car insurance (CJEU 1 March 2011, no. C-236/09, ECLI:EU:C:2011:100, *Association belge des Consommateurs Test-Achats ASBL and Others v. Conseil des Ministres*).

57 J. Angwin et al., 'Machine Bias', 2016, https://www.propublica.org/article/machine-bias-risk-assessments-in-criminal-sentencing.

58 W. Dieterich et al., 'COMPAS Risk Scales: Demonstrating Accuracy Equity and Predictive Parity', 2016, https://assets.documentcloud.org/documents/2998391/ProPublica-Commentary-Final-070616.pdf.

59 T. Brennan et al., 'Evaluating the Predictive Validity of the COMPAS Risk and Needs Assessment System', *Criminal Justice and Behavior*, 2009, vol. 36, p. 23.

policy – might explain these higher records to a large extent. Policing behaviour will determine who is put behind bars and who will thus be used for future comparison in a database.[60] Discrimination within society is therefore reflected in the data that fuels the algorithmic recidivism assessment. The same goes for HART: as indicated above, this algorithm relied on behavioural predictors in combination with age, gender, and residential postcodes to predict the chances of recidivism. The latter functions in a way as a proxy for socio-economic bias, as economically depraved communities will probably have more recorded police interventions and crimes compared to more affluent neighbourhoods.[61] Although this may represent reality and such a predictor may improve accuracy, it treats all inhabitants of a certain area in a blanketing and static way, thus perhaps even exacerbating the problem of inequality.

29. Even though the presence of biases is unintended, its implications and consequences can be far-reaching. They embed existing societal biases in algorithms and obfuscate them as such from scrutiny, barring intensive investigation such as ProPublica's probe into COMPAS. By doing so, existing biases can be entrenched and reinforced going forward. This is even more problematic when predictive models promise greater equality before the law by eliminating the biases that exist in human decision-making.

C. Biased Algorithms

30. Although data quality is essential to reach an unbiased and valid result, it is not enough. A common misconception is that algorithms are neutral.[62] This belief misconstrues the nature of algorithms. Algorithms process data, i.e. they combine and attach weights to data elements and establish rankings, which determines the eventual outcome.[63] These processes are tweaked to arrive at an – for the intended purposes – optimal outcome.

The choices made in building an algorithm are not neutral but reflect the intentions of the developers. Building an algorithm is no straightforward exercise. The public debate that arose in the summer of 2016 regarding COMPAS, on the alleged racial bias within the algorithm, boiled down to different conceptions of what constitutes fairness in algorithms: treating everyone the same, or giving everyone similar outcomes?[64]

---

60 A. Washington, 'How to Argue with an Algorithm: Lessons from the COMPAS – ProPublica Debate', *Colorado Technology Law Journal*, 2019, vol.17, p. 153.

61 Oswald et al., 'Algorithmic risk assessment policing models', pp. 234–235.

62 See e.g., B. Alarie, A. Niblett and A. Yoon, who hold that algorithms are devoid of bias. Alarie et al., 'Law in the Future', p. 423. Technology is never neutral. See M. Kranzberg, 'Technology and History: "Kranzberg's Laws"', *Technology and Culture*, 1986, vol. 27, pp. 545–548.

63 Washington, 'How to Argue with an Algorithm', p. 146.

64 See for an overview Washington, 'How to Argue with an Algorithm', pp. 150–151.

31. These questions highlight the fact that algorithm development requires a precursory theory building in light of its purpose. Such a theory decides which data needs to be gathered and why[65], informs the data processing decisions, justifies inferences[66] and forces developers to reflect on the choices they make from an ethical and legal perspective. Algorithms can then be assessed by judging their underlying theoretical choices. The requirement of an underlying theory, documenting and explaining all steps that were taken, leaves a paper trail that can be scrutinised to clarify the algorithm's behaviour. This requirement is especially relevant when algorithms are built with code copied from predictive algorithms in other domains. The assumptions and choices made for algorithms employed in e.g., the tourism industry are most likely not generalisable to the legal domain. A choice to do so nonetheless must therefore be substantiated and theoretically underpinned. Such requirements would hopefully lead to a 'responsibility-by-design' and as such influence systems' development by encouraging some options and dissuading others.[67]

An example of the importance of an underlying theory can once again be found in the COMPAS algorithm. Its developer admitted that the scoring mechanism included predictors that can be correlated with race, such as poverty, joblessness and social marginalization, but argued that without these predictors, accuracy would decrease.[68] Accuracy is however not the only criterion to which algorithms should be measured. For example, researchers showed that a simpler algorithm, with much less predictors and thus more explainable, provided the same level of accuracy as COMPAS' much more complex and hence less explainable algorithm.[69] Complexity is thus another relevant criterion, as is fairness.

5.2.2. Transparency

32. Another challenge to predictive models is the requirement of transparency. When applied within the legal domain, especially by judges as a basis for their judgments, algorithmic legal prediction needs to adhere to due process rights. This issue came to the fore in the case of State of Wisconsin v. Loomis. The defendant, Eric Loomis, was found driving a car that had been used in a drive-by-shooting. He denied taking part in the shooting but pleaded guilty to the charge of eluding an officer. The judge relied on his criminal record and a risk assessment using COMPAS to sentence him to six years of imprisonment.

---

65 Devins et al., 'The Law and Big Data', p. 374.

66 S. Wachter and B. Mittelstaddt, 'A Right to Reasonable Inferences: Re-Thinking Data Protection Law in the Age of Big Data and AI', *Colombia Business Law Review,* 2019, pp. 7–8.

67 F. Pasquale, 'Toward a Fourth Law of Robotics: Preserving Attribution, Responsibility, and Explainability in an Algorithmic Society', *Ohio State Law Journal,* 2017, vol. 78, pp. 1254–1255.

68 J. Angwin et al., 'Machine Bias', 2016, https://www.propublica.org/article/machine-bias-risk-assessments-in-criminal-sentencing.

69 See Washington, 'How to Argue with an Algorithm', p. 152.

Loomis applied for post-conviction relief, arguing that the court's reliance on COMPAS violated his due process rights. He argued *inter alia* that the use of COMPAS infringed his right to be sentenced on accurate information. In fact, Loomis had not been able to challenge the algorithm, as it is protected by trade secret. Nor was the judge, who was merely presented with the outcome of the risk assessment, in any position to scrutinise the algorithm or the prediction. The case was unsuccessfully appealed to the Wisconsin Supreme Court. In its decision, the Court argued that Loomis could have verified the accuracy of the risk assessment, as COMPAS uses only publicly available data and data provided by the defendant.[70] The U.S. Supreme Court denied a writ for certiorari.[71]

The Loomis case highlights a profoundly problematic issue of algorithmic legal prediction. The arguments of the Wisconsin Supreme Court do not hold water. Indeed, the way in which an algorithm processes data is just as important as the data it uses. Because of the proprietary nature of the COMPAS algorithm, Loomis was unable to verify the validity of its assessment. Protected by trade secret, opacity will likely be the norm for all QLP instruments developed by for-profit companies.[72]

33. Some arguments favour algorithmic opacity. A first argument, generalisable to all algorithms, states that opacity protects the proprietary nature of the algorithm. Transparency, without robust intellectual property or trade secret protection, would disincentivise further research and development in this area, leading to an overall poorer society. A second argument identifies a risk of rigging the algorithm: transparency would allow criminal defendants to game the system.[73] Assuming that the use of algorithmic risk assessment is beneficial to society, such behaviour would neutralise those benefits.

34. The counterarguments, infused by due process rights, should carry more weight however.[74] Algorithmic legal prediction might lead to substantially adverse decisions for litigants. Article 6 ECHR protects the right to an adversarial trial. This fundamental right implies that parties must have a meaningful opportunity to challenge all evidence brought before the court that aims to impact the decision.[75] This right has the same content in civil as in criminal

---

70 *Loomis*, 881 N.W.2d, 761–762 (Wis. 2016).

71 *Loomis v. Wisconsin*, 137 S.Ct. 2290 (2017).

72 Wachter and Mittelstadt, 'A Right to Reasonable Inferences', pp. 116–120.

73 See J. Kroll et al., 'Accountable Algorithms', *University of Pennsylvania Law Review*, 2017, vol. 165, p. 658; Vanderstichele, 'The Normative Value of Legal Analytics', p. 57.

74 Applying due process rights to predictive analytics in general, e.g., to credit ratings, has been suggested before. See D. Citron, 'Technological Due Process', *Washington University Law Review*, 2008, vol. 85, pp. 1301–1313; K. Crawford and J. Schultz, 'Big Data and Due Process: Toward a Framework to Redress Predictive Privacy Harms', *Boston College Law Review*, 2014, vol. 55, pp. 93–128.

75 ECtHR 28 Augustus 1991, no. 11170/84, *Brandstetter v Austria*, §67; ECtHR 4 April 2017, no. 2742/12, *Matanovic v Croatia*, §161.

matters.[76] Limits on this procedural right are only allowed in so far as they are absolutely necessary[77], i.e. to protect national security interests or the identity of a crucial witness who might face harm if identified.[78] The economic wellbeing of for-profit companies does not fall within these exemptions. In the member states of the ECHR, litigants should thus have an opportunity to challenge the results of an algorithmic legal prediction. Such an opportunity would be hollow without a certain degree of transparency[79] that developers should provide. Indeed, only few criminal defendants could incur the costs that ProPublica bore in uncovering biases present within COMPAS, in order to gain insight into a predictive algorithm.

35. The General Data Protection Regulation (GDPR)[80] contains a right to contest the result of automated individual decision-making (Article 22.3 GDPR). Some scholars have argued that this provision also contains a right to an explanation of algorithmic decision-making[81], but this claim is contested. The capacity of the GDPR to offer a meaningful right to transparency in this regard is debated.[82] Moreover, the GDPR is not applicable to algorithmic legal prediction instruments developed in and used by the judiciary.[83]

36. Pitching outright transparency against opacity presents us however with a false dilemma, since mere transparency does not satisfy the concerns that opacity raises. Providing full transparency would likely result in a transparency

---

76 ECtHR 24 November 1997, no. 21835/93, *Werner v Austria*, §66.

77 ECtHR 23 April 1997, no. 21363/93, *Van Mechelen v the Netherlands*, §58.

78 ECtHR 17 April 2018, no. 45597/09, *Paci v Belgium*, §85.

79 L. Edwards and M. Veale, 'Slave to the Algorithm? Why a 'Right to an Explanation' is probably not the remedy you are looking for', *Duke Law & Technology Review*, 2018, vol. 16, p. 40.

80 Regulation (EU) 2016/679 of the European Parliament and of the Council of 27 April 2016 on the protection of natural persons with regard to the processing of personal data and on the free movement of such data, and repealing Directive 95/46/EC, https://eur-lex.europa.eu/eli/reg/2016/679/oj.

81 B. Goodman and S. Flaxman, 'European Union regulations on algorithmic decision-making and a "right to explanation"', 2016, p. 2, https://arxiv.org/abs/1606.08813.

82 Edwards and Veale, 'Slave to the Algorithm?', pp. 44–51; Wachter and Mittelstadt, 'A Right to Reasonable Inferences', pp. 50–81; M. Ebers, 'Explainable AI in the European Union: An Overview of the Current Legal Framework(s)', in L. Colonna and S. Greenstein (eds.), *Nordic Yearbook of Law and Informatics 2020–2021: Law in the Era of Artificial Intelligence* (Stockholm: SJF 2022), pp. 111–114, available at irilaw.org/2022/02/16/new-publication-nordic-yearbook-of-law-and-informatics-2020–2021/..

83 See recital 20. The GDPR recommends however that a body within the judiciary should guarantee compliance of any instrument with the rules of the regulation. Other directives would apply to QLP systems developed by the judiciary, for instance the Directive (EU) 2016/680 of 27 April 2016 on the protection of natural persons with regard to the processing of personal data by competent authorities for the purposes of the prevention, investigation, detection or prosecution of criminal offences or the execution of criminal penalties, and on the free movement of such data.

fallacy[84]: litigants lack the time, resources and expertise for any meaningful interaction with an algorithm. It is cognitively impossible for litigants to conduct an effective, let alone, efficient review on an algorithm with possibly hundreds of parameters and millions of data points. In order to be effective, transparency must be directed.[85] If not, it would amount to inadvertent opacity, where large quantities of information create an information overload, making it nearly impossible to find the relevant information.[86] Under such conditions, transparency cannot lead to accountability.[87]

Transparency can only result in a meaningful review if done by a capable actor. Given the resources required and the concern of protecting trade secrets, state intervention seems to be a viable option. A certification process by a public agency could provide an alternative for algorithmic transparency, satisfying the right to an adversarial trial. Such oversight and review could ensure the fairness and accuracy of QLP through auditing, impact assessments and validation tests, making sure that these predictions adhere to a standard of technological due process.[88] Government intercession could also inspire trust by imposing standards and independent validation: research has established that there is little to no consistency in predictive validity measurement of risk assessment instruments, and that in one measurement in four the developers participated in it, thus undermining the independence of the review.[89] The possibility of a post hoc review, mirroring the judicial review of legislation or government acts, could complement ex ante certification.

5.2.3. Trust

37. Review by a public agency may satisfy due process requirements and might inspire trust towards the public at large, but perhaps less so for the litigants who are faced with the application of QLP in their case. Within the administration of justice, trust forms the bedrock of the judiciary's legitimacy. Experimental research suggests that litigants disapprove of algorithms within

84 Edwards and Veale, 'Slave to the Algorithm?', p. 67.

85 Cf. ECtHR 4 June 2019, no. 39757/15, *Sigurdur Einarsson v Iceland*, §90; ECtHR 25 July 2019, no. 1586/15, *Rook v Germany*, §67, §72.

86 C. Stohl et al., 'Managing Opacity: Information Visibility and the Paradox of Transparency in the Digital Age' *International Journal of Communication*, 2016, vol. 10, p. 133.

87 O. O'Neill, 'Transparency and the Ethics of Communication', in C. Hood and D. A. Heald (eds.), *Transparency: the Key to Better Governance?* (Oxford: Oxford University Press, 2006), pp. 75–90; M. Ananny and K. Crawford, 'Seeing without knowing: Limitations of the transparency ideal and its application to algorithmic accountability', *New Media and Society*, 2018, vol. 20, p. 984.

88 D. Citron and F. Pasquale, 'The Scored Society: Due Process for Automated Predictions', *Washington Law Review*, 2014, vol. 89, p. 19. Cadiet, *L'Open Data des décisions de justice*, p. 25.

89 J. Singh et al., 'Measurement of Predictive Validity in Violence Risk Assessment Studies: A Second-Order Systematic Review', *Behavioral Sciences & the Law*, 2013, vol. 31, pp. 55–73.

the administration of justice, even if their accuracy is high.[90] If this is indeed the case, the use of algorithms would undermine the perceived legitimacy of the administration of justice and the rule of law. The psychology, prior experience and digital literacy of a litigant, among others, influence to what extent he or she trusts an algorithm. Tellingly, algorithmic transparency does not inspire such trust, as was evidenced by experimental research.[91]

38. Trust is not a static measure but can be built up over time. The wish to build up trust underlies the explainable AI movement, which tries to provide an explanation for how an algorithm reached an outcome. It is indeed difficult to blindly trust a system without knowing its decision-making rationale. Different conceptions exist within this explainable AI movement, but, broadly speaking, this movement aims to relate properties of the input data to their output in order to make the algorithm interpretable or comprehensible.[92] For some predictive models, this goal is difficult to achieve, e.g., in neural networks where input features are transformed in non-linear ways.[93] Interpretable models differ from comprehensible models: interpretation provides the user insight into the mechanics underlying the algorithm (i.e., regression models, support vector machines, decision trees, etc.), whilst comprehension simplifies and visualises the algorithm's operation in a way non-expert users can understand.[94] Both models do not explain algorithms themselves, but enable explanation by experts.[95] These 'explanations' can differ in their form. Two approaches exist, a model-centric one or a subject-centric one.[96] The former provides information on the predictive model in general, e.g., the kind of model, its features, the training data, the performance metrics, etc. The latter is based on a specific input and tries to explain why a certain outcome was reached. A subject-centred explanation details among others how changes to the input data could have led to a different outcome, identifies which training data are similar to the input, or how difficult it was for the algorithm to decide on a specific input. The earlier-mentioned underlying theory can play a similar role as a model-centric algorithmic explanation. Such theory could partially cater to the need of an explanation, pending further development in the domain of explainable AI.

---

90 A. Wang, 'Procedural Justice and Risk-Assessment Algorithms', 2018, https://papers.ssrn.com/sol3/papers.cfm?abstract_id=3170136, pp. 5–13.

91 See Wang, 'Procedural Justice and Risk-Assessment Algorithms', pp. 13–16. This is contrary to the general trend within the judiciary, where more transparency heightens trust. See S. Grimmelikhhuijsen and A. Klijn, 'The effects of judicial transparency on public trust: evidence from a field experiment', *Public Administration*, 2015, vol. 93, pp. 995–1011.

92 D. Doran et al., 'What Does Explainable AI Really Mean? A New Conceptualization of Perspectives', 2017, https://arxiv.org/abs/1710.00794, pp. 4–5.

93 Doran et al., 'What Does Explainable AI Really Mean?', p. 4.

94 *Ibid.*, p. 5.

95 *Ibid.*, p. 7.

96 See Edwards and Veale, 'Slave to the Algorithm?', pp. 55–59.

39. We should heed, however, requiring a higher degree of explainability from predictive legal algorithms than from human judges. The latter operate as much as black boxes as some algorithms do, as they do not explain their behaviour. The reasoning contained in a judgement is a rationalisation of the outcome, not a walkthrough of the thought process through which the judge reached the verdict.[97] Legally irrelevant reasons sometimes play a role in the decision[98], but would not feature in the judgement itself. Judges thus provide a rationale for their decision, which is different from explaining why they reached a certain outcome. Just as with algorithms, judges' decision-making is sometimes clouded by biases.[99] Their educational, cultural and socio-economic background fulfils a similar function as training data does for a machine-learning algorithm.

6. THE CASE FOR BELGIUM

40. The above-sketched evolution has so far largely bypassed Belgium. Although the previous Minister of Justice, Koen Geens, hinted at the development of an algorithmic legal prediction instrument in Belgium in 2017[100], no steps seem to have been taken towards such an ambitious goal. The legal tech industry in Belgium equally seems to ignore this evolution[101], unlike the legal tech industry in its culturally close neighbour France.[102]

---

97 See for instance research that suggests that judges (unconsciously) hide biases in the reasoning of their decisions. J. Liu and X. Li, 'Legal Techniques for Rationalizing Biased Judicial Decisions: Evidence from Experiments with Real Judges', *Journal of Empirical Legal Studies*, 2019, vol. 16, pp. 630–670.

98 See among others H. Spamann and L. Klöhn, 'Justice is Less Blind, and Less Legalistic, than We Thought: Evidence from an Experiment with Real Judges', *Journal of Legal Studies*, 2016, vol. 45, pp. 255–280. See also Chen, 'Judicial Analytics and the Great Transformation of American Law', pp. 15–42.

99 E. Peer and E. Gamliel, 'Heuristics and Biases in Judicial Decisions', *Court Review*, 2013, vol. 49, pp. 114–118.

100 K. Geens, *Court of the Future*, 2017, https://www.koengeens.be/policy/court-of-the-future, p. 44.

101 A noticeable exception would be Wolters Kluwer's Legal Insights tool, which presents the likelihood of success for a legal problem given a query (within the area of dismissal) and directs its user towards relevant case law. The success ratio is likely based on the outcomes of the cases deemed relevant for the initial query, out of a total of 8.000 cases. This application makes use of advanced legal information retrieval tools to detect cases that are relevant to the user's query but does not rely on ML of any kind. For more information, see https://legalworld.wolterskluwer.be/nl/oplossingen/tools/legal-insights/.
A more advanced application exists in the Netherlands, where a rule-based algorithm assists employers (and employees) in challenging demission decisions (see https://www.magontslag.nl). Legidex, a new legal tech player appears to be developing a predictive tool as well, but they will probably be confronted – more so than publishing houses such as Wolters Kluwer – by the lack of published court decisions (see https://legidex.be/).

102 See paragraph 11.

What explains this lack of initiative? An essential prerequisite for algorithmic legal prediction instrument is the availability of data. The output of any algorithm depends on its input, so the quality and quantity of the data determine the algorithm's accuracy. With on average 1.3 million legal decisions a year[103], Belgium has arguably sufficient data to warrant a QLP application. The number of published legal decisions is however extremely low, making it nearly impossible to develop a reliable instrument with accurate results. Estimations of the publication ratio range between 1 and 2% of the total number of judgments[104], but even these low percentages are most likely inflated. In the latest EU Justice scoreboard, Belgium ranked 13th out of 27 member states (equalling with five other countries) when it comes to the online accessibility of published judgements for the general public, but this not unfavourable ranking is largely explained by the virtually complete publication of judgments from administrative courts.[105] The lack of government-sanctioned publication is not compensated by commercial publication by publishing houses. Recent legislative developments hold the promise of radically changing this state of affairs, however.

6.1. PUBLICATION OF CASE LAW BY THE JUDICIARY

41. The judiciary publishes its case law through the website JUPORTAL.[106] The direct predecessor of this online database, *Jure-Juridat*, finds its roots in the Law of 10 August 2005[107], which envisaged the development of an internal database – to contain all decisions of the judiciary, only accessible for its members – and a public database – to contain a selection of decisions aimed at the public at large. The internal database failed to materialise, the external database, *Jure-Juridat*, saw the light of day in 2007. The decisions that this latter database contained can now be accessed through JUPORAL.

Next to the decisions of the Court of Cassation, Belgium's supreme court in civil and criminal matters, there is not much case law to be found on *JUPORTAL*. No decisions from the Justices of the Peace (Belgium's small claims courts) or from the police tribunals have ever been uploaded to *Jure-Juridat*, even though

[103] H. Van Bossuyt, 'Toegang tot de rechtspraak en toegankelijke rechtspraak', in A. Bossuyt et al. (eds.), *Liber spei et amicitiae Ivan Verougstraete* (Brussel: Larcier, 2011), p. 109; P. Taelman, 'Potpourri en de burgerlijke rechtspleging', in W. Vanbiervliet (ed.), *De Potpourri-wetten: een eerste evaluatie van de waaiers aan quick wins, reparaties en grondslagen voor organisatorische vernieuwingen* (Brussel: Larcier, 2017), p. 4.

[104] M. Storme, 'Recht op recht', *Tijdschrift voor Privaatrecht,* 1993, p. x; M. Van Hoecke, 'Legal Doctrine: Which Method(s) for What Kind of Discipline?', in M. Van Hoecke (ed.), *Methodologies of legal research: which kind of method for what kind of discipline?* (Oxford: Hart Publishing, 2013), p. 12.

[105] EU Justice Scoreboard 2021, https://ec.europa.eu/info/sites/default/files/eu_justice_scoreboard_2021.pdf, p. 37.

[106] See www.juportal.be.

[107] Law of 10 August 2005 *tot oprichting van het informatiesysteem Phenix*, *BS* 1 September 2005.

their decisions constitute the largest share within the on average 1.3 million judgments rendered in Belgium every year. In JUPORTAL, these courts are not even listed under the judicial entities whose decisions can be found on the database. For those courts whose decisions have been published on JUPORTAL and its predecessor, the numbers of published judgments are dwindling in recent years: in 2015, 338 decisions of the courts of appeal were published on the database, in 2019 this number decreased to 78; 24 judgments of the courts of first instance were published on *Juridat* in 2015, but since 2017, only a handful judgments has been uploaded.[108] Overall, the number of decisions published on this freely available website has been extremely low.

It should be noted, however, that courts that fall outside the judicial branch *sensu stricto* – simply put those that hear disputes other than civil or criminal cases – tend to publish considerably more case law. The Constitutional Court publishes all its case law on its website, as do administrative courts such as the Council of State and the Flemish administrative tribunals.[109] The same goes e.g., for the Central Penitentiary Supervisory Board.[110]

42. The non-published judgments are not assembled on a central dataset but are largely stored by the courts on databases on local servers. This state of affairs was to be remedied through the development of VAJA (*Vonnissen en Arresten – Jugements et Arrêts*). This application, developed by the Antwerp Court of Appeals as a tool to facilitate the administrative handling of judgments, saves a digital copy of every rendered decision on a central database. It had been expanded to all (labour) courts of appeal and contained well over 100.000 decisions when the ministry of Justice cut its funding. The administrative function of VAJA will be taken over by MaCH (Mammouth at Central Hosting), a software program that was first introduced in the late 2000s, but it is unclear to what extent this software is capable of hosting a central database of all judgments and thus taking over the secondary role of VAJA as a central database of all judgments. MaCH will however only be a temporary solution, until the new Central Register of court decisions comes into existence (see below).

6.2. PUBLICATION OF CASE LAW BY PUBLISHERS

43. Most of the published case law in Belgium is to be found in legal journals and publisher houses' online libraries, such as *Jura*, *Jurisquare* and *Stradalex*.

---

108 Since the change from Jure-Juridat to JUPORTAL in 2020, it no longer seems possible to retrieve the total number of judgments per type of judicial entity for a given year.

109 See https://www.dbrc.be/dienst-van-de-bestuursrechtscolleges. The Flemish government also publishes a considerable number of decisions from the civil courts in cases concerning Flemish legislation. See https://arrestendatabank.be/index.php/.

110 Https://rechtspraak.ctrg.belgium.be/.

Whereas access to *JUPORTAL* is free of charge, these decisions are hidden behind a paywall. In general, the number of published decisions remains relatively low. The decisions published through these channels include considerably more judgments from the lower courts compared to *JUPORTAL*, but higher courts are numerically still over-represented. Even though this state of affairs is sensible viewed from the traditional legal information paradigm, where more weight is attached to decisions from higher courts, this policy inhibits predictive analytics due to a lack of representative decisions.

44. The lack of representative data is exacerbated by the fact that the peculiarity of a judgment is a factor in deciding whether to publish it.[111] Such a policy is detrimental to the application of ML, since the features of peculiar cases will most likely not be pertinent to the run-of-the-mill cases.[112]

6.3. GENERAL PUBLICATION OF CASE LAW IN THE NEAR FUTURE?

45. The lack of a large and representative dataset of Belgian case law makes the development of algorithmic legal prediction instruments virtually impossible. The training data is too limited, too idiosyncratic and thus not reflective enough of the underlying reality. This state of affairs might however change soon. Until recently, there was no obligation in Belgian law to publish judgments.[113] The Law of 5 May 2019[114] changed this, by imposing the online publication of all judgments in an anonymised way in a freely accessible database, whilst doing away with the existing obligation to pronounce every judgment in court.[115] This new obligation was to take effect on September 1st 2020, but its entry into force was postponed to September 1st 2021 shortly before the original date passed.[116] This date was again postponed by a year in the summer of 2021, despite the

111 Storme, 'Recht op recht', p. xi; Van Hoecke, 'Legal Doctrine', p. 12.

112 Surden, 'Machine Learning and the Law', p. 105.

113 Such obligation only existed for the case law of the Council of State and the Constitutional Court.

114 Law of 5 May 2019 *tot wijziging van het Wetboek van strafvordering en het Gerechtelijk Wetboek wat de bekendmaking van de vonnissen en arresten betreft*, *BS* 16 May 2019, which amended Article 782*bis* of the Code of Civil Procedure.

115 Similar legislation was passed in France in 2016 where the *loi pour une République numérique* mandates the publishing of every legal judgment (law no. 2016-1321 from 7 October 2016 *pour une République numérique*, *JORF* 8 October 2016). In 2019, the French legislator prohibited legal analytics on judges' names, e.g., in order to predict how a specific judge would rule on an issue. See Article 33 of Law no. 2019-222 of 23 March 2019 *de programmation 2018-2022 et de réforme pour la justice*, *JORF* 24 March 2019.

116 Article 73 of the Law of 31 July 2020 *houdende diverse dringende bepalingen inzake justitie*, *BS* 7 August 2020.

progress that had been made, due to the lack of an adequate legal framework for this intended database.[117]

This legal framework should however soon come into existence: in Spring 2022 a legislative bill was drafted by the government and introduced in Parliament that aimed to provide such framework and establish both a Central Register for Court Decisions, containing all judgements in original format, and a publicly accessible database of pseudonymised judgments.[118] At the same time, the government published a call of tender to develop, host and maintain this publicly accessible database which must include i.a. a pseudonymisation application, an indexing mechanism and an automated keyword extraction, and which must allow for extensions with business intelligence and ML applications. The call of tender stipulates that the project should be completed within 48 months, thrice extendable for twelve months. Thus within seven years at the latest, a publicly accessible database containing all pseudonymized legal decision should be fully operational and accessible. According to the Minister for Justice, however, the database should be operational already in 2023.[119] These recent developments raise the expectation that within the near future, all judgments pronounced in Belgium should be freely accessible, making an extensive amount of information available to ML algorithms.

7. CONCLUSION

46. This chapter discussed QLP as one possible evolution within the area of dispute resolution stemming from the advent of AI, highlighting its advantages such as heightened access to justice, an improved efficiency and an enforced consistency within legal decisions but also warning for the challenges inherent to any predictive model. A nascent technology, it is likely that for the foreseeable future QLP will only be able to be used in relatively simple, run-of-the-mill cases rather than hard cases. This can be explained by the fact that simple cases are far more common than hard cases, leading to a higher accuracy. An important step in the advancement of QLP would be the development of standards to which these algorithms must comply when it comes to training data, validity, accuracy and fairness. The lack thereof obfuscates their assessment and thus hinders their introduction in practice.

---

117 Law of 12 July 2021 *houdende dringende bepalingen inzake justitie*, *BS* 20 July 2021.

118 Wetsontwerp tot oprichting van het Centraal register voor de beslissingen van de rechterlijke orde en betreffende de bekendmaking van de vonnissen en arresten, *Parl.St.* Kamer 2021–22, nr. 2754. At the time of writing this chapter, the proposed legislative bill was amended but had not yet been adopted by Parliament. For his reason, I have refrained from detailing its content.

119 M. Verbergt, "Databank met alle vonnissen en arresten in 2023", *De Standaard* 31 March 2022, www.standaard.be/cnt/dmf20220330_97712372.

Even though criticism of QLP because of these challenges is often deserved, we should heed taking too critical a stance and remember that human judges can operate as much as black boxes as some algorithms do. A critical stance towards QLP is welcome and necessary, but using a double standard throws out the champagne with the cork.

47. Quantitative legal prediction, even though still a nascent technology, will change the traditional nature of the administration of justice, decreasing among others its central importance as a dispute resolution mechanism. Fears that human judicial decision-making will become a vestige of the past are however unfounded. Society's trust in the judiciary will remain of vital importance, necessitating a human-in-the-loop. Rather than replacing judges, machines will strengthen their functioning, the combination outperforming either operating in isolation and balancing out each other's potential prejudices and flaws. As long as legal singularity[120] remains the unattainable goal that it is today, robot-judges can have no place in the administration of justice. Whether such an evolution would be at all desirable, is of course a completely different discussion. As AI techniques become increasingly prevalent within society, it should be clear to all stakeholders that the legal system cannot and should not be insulated from these developments. If the COVID-19 pandemic has taught us one thing, it is that courts and the legal system can, if necessary, quickly adopt new technologies in response to changing circumstances.[121]

48. In this evolution, Belgium is left wanting. The lack of published case law inhibits the development of QLP applications. Recent legislative change promises to rectify this state of affairs. As its former Minister of Justice indicated[122], Belgium could profit from the law of the handicap of the head start. The recent evolutions in this regard will likely set the wheels in motion towards full publication of case law, which in turn would greatly facilitate the development of ML applications.

---

120 Legal singularity is a concept that refers to the achievement of total legal certainty due to a functionally complete law. Alarie, 'The Path of the Law: Toward Legal Singularity', p. 445.

121 For a study, see B. Krans and A. Nylund (eds.), *Civil Courts Coping with COVID-19* (Den Haag: Boom Juridische Uitgevers, 2021), 226 p.

122 Geens, *Court of the Future*, p. 33.

CHAPTER 5

AI ARBITRATORS ... 'DOES NOT COMPUTE'

Kevin Ongenae*

1. INTRODUCTION

1. Arbitration is a method of alternative dispute resolution in which parties give up their right to have a legal dispute decided by a state court. Instead, they agree to authorise a so-called arbitral tribunal (composed of 'private' arbitrators appointed by the parties) to decide their dispute by rendering a binding decision. The decisions of arbitral tribunals are called arbitral awards and can be enforced if necessary.[1]

2. One of the main selling points of arbitration is that it allows the parties to tailor the procedure to the specific needs of their dispute. More so than is the case for proceedings before state courts, the flexibility of arbitral procedure allows for the elimination of unnecessary procedural steps, saving both time and cost.[2]

Compared to the technological revolution of the last decades, however, arbitrations are still 'conducted in substantially the same way as they were 50 years ago'.[3] Of course, standard applications such as e-mail and telephone or video conferences are already routinely used.[4] Briefs are also usually created

---

* PhD Researcher (Ghent University) and Member of the Flemish Bar.

1 At the international level, the enforceability of arbitral awards is governed by the 1958 New York Convention.

2 G. Born, *International Commercial Arbitration*, 2nd edn (Alphen aan den Rijn: Kluwer Law International, 2014), pp. 84–89; N. Blackaby, C. Partasides, A. Redfern, and M. Hunter, *Redfern and Hunter on International Arbitration*, 6th edn (Oxford: Oxford University Press, 2015), p. 30.

3 S. Nappert and P. Cohen, 'Case Study: The Practitioner's Perspective', in M. Piers and C. Aschauer (eds), *Arbitration in the Digital Age* (Cambridge: Cambridge University Press, 2018), p. 126.

4 M. Piers and C. Aschauer, 'Survey on the Present Use of ICT in International Arbitration', in M. Piers and C. Aschauer (eds), *Arbitration in the Digital Age* (Cambridge: Cambridge University Press, 2018), p. 17.

and submitted electronically, and increasingly include hyperlink references to the file or hearing transcript. Even slightly more advanced processes (such as identification, collection and transmission of responsive documents for the purpose of document production) are now conducted electronically and sometimes even generate new questions (e.g., in relation to the metadata accompanying such 'electronically stored information' or 'ESI').[5] Generally speaking, however, this cannot be considered a true revolution.[6]

3. As far as revolutionary technologies go, the recent buzz surrounding artificial intelligence has left few areas of the law unaffected. International arbitration is no exception.

Indeed, AI-based applications can already provide support in many different ways throughout the course of a legal dispute.[7] They can, for instance, assist in the analysis[8] or even in the conclusion[9] of contracts; they can help the parties in making strategic decisions based on data-analytics (such as which arbitrator to appoint)[10]; they can help counsel in the analysis and the drafting of submissions[11]; and speedily process large amounts of data in electronic discovery.[12] The 2021 Queen Mary survey on International Arbitration shows that such applications are already used by arbitration practitioners, at least to some extent: 65% of the participating arbitration practitioners indicated that they already made use of AI-based applications in the context of their arbitration work.[13]

5 For an overview of technology that is already used in arbitration proceedings (and possible legal issues and case management techniques in relation thereto), see *ad gen.* ICC Commission on Arbitration and ADR, *Report on Information Technology in International Arbitration* (Paris: International Chamber of Commerce, 2017).

6 S. Brekoulakis, 'The Evolution and Future of International Arbitration', in S. Brekoulakis, J. Lew and L. Mistelis (eds), *The Evolution and Future of International Arbitration* (Alphen aan den Rijn: Kluwer Law International, 2016), p. 16.

7 M. Piers and C. Aschauer, 'Conclusion', in M. Piers and C. Aschauer (eds), *Arbitration in the Digital Age* (Cambridge: Cambridge University Press, 2018), p. 292.

8 A Google search for 'AI contract analysis' reveals that numerous companies are offering contract analysis software.

9 M. Wahab and E. Katsh, 'Revolutionizing Technologies and the Use of Technology in International Arbitration', in M. Piers and C. Aschauer (eds), *Arbitration in the Digital Age* (Cambridge: Cambridge University Press, 2018), pp. 46–47.

10 H. Snijders, 'Arbitrage en AI: van arbitrage naar robotrage en van menselijke arbiter naar robotarbiter?', *Tijdschrift voor Arbitrage*, 2019, no. 1, pp. 4–5.

11 Snijders, 'Arbitrage en AI: van arbitrage naar robotrage en van menselijke arbiter naar robotarbiter?', p. 5.

12 M. Scherer, 'Artificial Intelligence and Legal Decision-Making: The Wide Open?', *Journal of International Arbitration*, 2019, vol. 36, no. 5, p. 540.

13 Queen Mary University of London, *2021 International Arbitration Survey: Adapting Arbitration to a Changing World* (London: White & Case LLP, 2021) pp. 21–22 (and chart 13). The 2021 Survey reports an increase compared to the numbers of the 2018 Survey: 35% of respondents stated that they had never made use of AI applications;24% said they 'rarely' do so and 26% said they use it 'sometimes'. Only 13% indicated that they 'frequently' make use of AI, and the remaining 2%indicated that they 'always' make use of AI based tools. The

4. The most captivating form of AI use in arbitration, however, appears to be the rendering of a fully automated arbitral decision by an AI-based system.[14] In other words, a decision rendered by an AI arbitrator. The benefits of such a technology are clear. Provided it functions well, an AI arbitrator would revolutionise the practice of arbitration and would make it considerably cheaper and faster, and perhaps even better. Such fully automated AI arbitrators will be the topic of this chapter.[15] More specifically, this chapter will focus on the challenges that exist today and will address the following two key questions:

- First, which technical or data-related challenges would need to be overcome if we want to develop a well-functioning AI arbitrator (part 2)?
  This question will be addressed by looking into the requirements that need to be met in order to develop a well-functioning AI system, and by projecting those requirements onto the (data) realities of international arbitration practice.
- Secondly, would it be possible, from a legal perspective, to appoint an AI arbitrator under the current legal framework for (international) arbitration (part 3)?
  This question will be answered by identifying possible legal obstacles to the use of AI arbitrators in arbitration, and by applying the classic legal research method. This chapter will also rely on comparative insights where useful.

5. At this point in time, AI arbitrators (i.e., machines or algorithms that have a capacity for independent and highly complex legal problem solution through human-like reasoning) do not exist. This chapter will, therefore, not speculate as to whether an advanced AI arbitrator will ever be technically feasible. At the

---

subsequent interviews with participants of the survey showed that the vast majority of the measured AI use pertained to technology assisted document review.

14 The possibility of 'appointing' a fully automated 'AI arbitrator' is contemplated in a number of papers (both approval and criticism). See *inter alia* Wahab and Katsh, 'Revolutionizing Technologies and the Use of Technology in International Arbitration', pp. 48–50; Nappert and Cohen, 'Case Study: The Practitioner's Perspective', pp. 140–145; I. Ng and V. Benedetti del Rio, 'When the Tribunal is an Algorithm: Complexities of Enforcing Orders Determined by a Software under the New York Convention', in K. Fach Gomez and A. Lopez-Rodriguez (eds), *60 Years of the New York Convention: Key Issues and Future Challenges* (Alphen aan den Rijn: Kluwer Law International, 2019), pp. 121–134; C. Sim, 'Will Artificial Intelligence Take Over Arbitration?', *Asian International Arbitration Journal*, 2018, vol. 14, no. 1, pp. 1–13; J. Kwan, J. Ng and B. Kiu, 'The Use of Artificial Intelligence in International Arbitration: Where are we Right Now?', *International Arbitration Law Review*, 2019, vol. 22, no. 1, pp. 22–27; Snijders, 'Arbitrage en AI: van arbitrage naar robotrage en van menselijke arbiter naar robotarbiter?', pp. 1–8; J. Hope, 'Can a Robot be an Arbitrator?', in A. Calissendorff and P. Schöldstrom (eds), *Stockholm Arbitration Yearbook 2019* (Alphen aan den Rijn: Kluwer Law International, 2019), pp. 103–120; Piers and Aschauer, 'Conclusion', pp. 290–295; H. Eidenmüller and F. Varesis, 'What is an Arbitration? Artificial Intelligence and the Vanishing Human Arbitrator', *SSRN Electronic Journal*, 2020, pp. 1–50, https://ssrn.com/abstract=3629145.

15 This chapter will not deal with the hypothesis where an AI system plays a merely supporting role in the resolution of a dispute.

same time, I will also not advance any arguments against AI arbitrators along the lines that the 'jurisdictional act' of deciding factual and legal disputes is inherently human or requires inherently human faculties which AI will never be able to master. This chapter will focus on the here and now, and will mainly address the current technological, data, and legal challenges to appointing AI systems as arbitrators. Nevertheless, at the end of this chapter and on the basis of its findings, I will also consider more generally whether and how AI-based dispute resolution and arbitration might interact and evolve if AI arbitrators do become a real-life possibility (part 4).

Let us have a look at how an AI system would function in the arbitration context and how the technical aspects of AI affect its suitability for arbitral decision making.

2. THERE ARE CONSIDERABLE DATA-RELATED HURDLES TO AI-BASED ARBITRATORS

6. The fact that a computer would, in principle, be able to render a decision on a legal dispute, does not mean that we should let it. We would want our AI arbitrator to perform well, and to reach decisions that fall within the margin of arbitral appreciation.

In that respect, the way in which AI (currently) works, might pose a number of particular problems in relation to AI arbitration. They relate to the following four characteristics of AI:

- AI requires a vast amount of data.
- AI needs the data to follow recurrent patterns.
- AI works on the basis of data from the past.
- AI cannot fix the data.[16]

Each of these issues (and how they translate to arbitration) will be discussed below.

2.1. THE AMOUNT OF DATA NEEDED FOR PERFORMANT AI IS NOT AVAILABLE IN ARBITRATION

7. As mentioned in the introductory chapter to this book, any AI system that is based on machine learning needs vast amounts of data.[17] In fact, one of the

---

16 Scherer refers to these issues as the four V's: Volume, Variety, Velocity and Veracity (from the so-called five V's of big data). See Scherer, 'Artificial Intelligence and Legal Decision-Making: The Wide Open?', p. 554.

17 See also Chapter 1 of this book. A straightforward example of how data sets can be created and can be used to 'train' an AI system in a dispute resolution context can be found in F.

reasons – if not the main reason – for the recent surge in AI-applications, is the availability of so-called 'big data' as a result of the proliferation of data retention on the internet.[18]

8. At a very basic level (where even us lawyers can understand), the amount of data needed to train a particular AI system is determined by two variables. First, the amount of data required correlates with the complexity of the problem for which you are training the AI system (i.e., the system's goal or its so-called 'utility function'). Secondly, the amount of data will also directly affect the quality of the solutions provided by the AI system in question. Larger amounts of data lead to greater precision of the AI.[19]

9. Thus, nuanced solutions to complex problems require vast amounts of data. By way of comparison, Google Translate uses many millions of examples to train its Neural Machine Translation.[20] Despite the truly massive amount of data used, anyone familiar with Google Translate will know that it provides no more than a decent first draft for a translation. While free and very fast, it in no way matches the skill of a trained human translator (yet).

Obviously, if we ever were to employ AI systems in arbitration, they would need to be able to solve highly complex problems, and they would need to solve them well. This would require a vast amount of data – literally many millions of examples.

10. The problem is that arbitration simply does not produce sufficient data. The caseloads of major arbitration institutions usually do not exceed a thousand cases per year.[21] By way of illustration, the ICC's International Court of Arbitration (which was established in 1919 and is the world's leading arbitration institution), has recently announced its 25.000th case.[22] Considering the enormous diversity of those cases, it is very unlikely that this would be enough to (adequately) train an AI system to resolve arbitration cases.

Steffek and L. Bull, 'Paving the Way for Legal Artificial Intelligence – A Common Dataset for Case Outcome Predictions', in N. Aggarwal et al. (eds), *Autonomous Systems and the Law* (Munich: C.H. Beck, Hart Nomos, 2019), pp. 67–71.

18 J. Mueller and L. Massaron, *Artificial Intelligence for Dummies* (Hoboken (NJ): John Wiley & Sons, 2018), pp. 21–22.

19 See Mueller and Massaron, *Artificial Intelligence for Dummies*, p. 39 and J. Mueller and L. Massaron, *Machine Learning for Dummies* (Hoboken (NJ): John Wiley & Sons, 2016), p. 239. See also Scherer, 'Artificial Intelligence and Legal Decision-Making: The Wide Open?', p. 555.

20 M. Schuster, M. Johnson and N. Thorat, 'Zero-Shot Translation with Google's Multilingual Neural Machine Translation System', *Google AI Blog*, 22 November 2016.

21 See the overview of major arbitration institutions' caseloads in Born, *International Commercial Arbitration*, p. 94.

22 See the ICC's press release concerning its 25.000th case: https://iccwbo.org/media-wall/news-speeches/icc-celebrates-25000th-case-milestone-and-announces-record-figures-for-2019/.

A different issue is whether each of those 25.000 ICC cases would provide useful data points and/or would all count towards the same quantitative target. This will be addressed in part 2.2.

11. Secondly, even if such amounts of data would exist in relation to international arbitration, large parts of that data may not be available due to the confidentiality obligations that prevail in most arbitration procedures. While many awards are already published, and the (presumption of) confidentiality of arbitration has come under increasing pressure in recent years, most commercial cases are (to a large extent) still treated confidentially.[23] As will be discussed below (see paragraph 14), partial data is a problem in itself.

12. To circumvent the issue of insufficient data, it could of course be considered to include data from court litigations, in order to create a larger dataset. This would, however, not provide a solution for arbitration-specific issues. If, for instance, an AI system would be trained on the basis of litigation data relating to the validity of arbitration clauses, the result would almost certainly not reflect actual practice because it would not take into account the many disputes where arbitration clauses simply have their intended effect of having an arbitration to decide a dispute without state court intervention. Litigation data may also not adequately capture some of the most valued characteristics of arbitration, such as 'avoiding specific legal systems' and 'flexibility'.[24]

2.2. ARBITRATION DATA IS NOT SUITABLE FOR AI DEVELOPMENT

13. A comparable problem arises in relation to the type of data needed. Similar cases lead to similar outcomes, and for machine learning AI's such similarity is key. The strength of an AI system is that it can sift through enormous amounts of data in order to find trends and patterns. In doing so, it infers rules from the data, which it subsequently uses to make predictions about new data. In essence, an AI system measures different variables of a new case and projects those onto the existing cases in the dataset in order to make a similarity assessment. Once it has classified the new case on the basis of that comparison (in the relevant 'cluster' of the dataset), it will 'predict' (but in the case of an AI arbitrator 'decide') the outcome in the new case based on what happened in the cases of the database which it considers similar.[25]

---

23 Born, *International Commercial Arbitration*, pp. 89–90; Blackaby, Partasides, Redfern and Hunter, *Redfern and Hunter on International Arbitration*, p. 30.

24 Queen Mary University of London, *2018 International Arbitration Survey: The Evolution of International Arbitration* (London: White & Case LLP, 2018) p. 7 (chart 3).

25 Mueller and Massaron, *Machine Learning for Dummies*, pp. 237–241. Many AI systems will subsequently also add the new case to the existing dataset in order to expand it.

Hence, in order to be able to find such patterns, the dataset must not only be large (as discussed above). It is preferably also qualitative, complete, straightforward and coherent. Furthermore, it must contain a certain level of repetition from which similarity inferences can be made.[26]

14. The issue of completeness is related to dataset size and confidentiality. When you train an AI system, it learns to make predictions on the basis of the data which it has been fed. If it has been fed incomplete data, it may make imperfect predictions because it will be guided exclusively by the data it received. Therefore, if there is a difference between the data it received and relevant data it did not receive, that difference will not be reflected in the AI system's prediction. This would be a considerable flaw because the outcome will not reflect reality, which not only consists of the data fed to the AI, but also of the missing data.[27]

As we have discussed above, we simply do not have sufficient and reliable data in arbitration. In fact, we probably have more missing data (e.g., data from ad hoc arbitrations and confidential arbitrations) than available data. This would make an AI arbitrator particularly vulnerable to this issue. In arbitration, the existence of a publication bias has already been demonstrated in relation to enforcement decisions.[28] Because AI systems heavily rely on statistical methods, such biases are likely to be exacerbated by an AI arbitrator.

15. Similarly, if the dataset contains a lot of incoherent data, it will be difficult for the algorithm to derive the underlying pattern, because it will be confronted with conflicting information.[29]

Thus, data consistency is what would be needed. If there is no sufficient repetition in the dataset, it will be more challenging for the AI system to identify the underlying patterns. If all cases are unique, the algorithm will not be able to make predictions. It is obviously more difficult to infer the

---

26 Scherer, 'Artificial Intelligence and Legal Decision-Making: The Wide Open?', p. 556.

27 Mueller and Massaron, *Artificial Intelligence for Dummies*, p. 34.

28 Certain legal outcomes are more likely to be published in professional journals than others. See E. Cheng, 'Detection and Correction of Case-Publication Bias', *The Journal of Legal Studies*, 2018, vol. 48, no. 1, p. 151. This is certainly so in arbitration. In essence, the court decisions concerning arbitration that are published, are the problematic ones. First, the majority of arbitral awards is complied with voluntarily and will not ever appear before a court (see Blackaby, Partasides, Redfern and Hunter, *Redfern and Hunter on International Arbitration*, p. 607). Secondly, the majority of awards that are enforced through a court procedure, simply obtain the court's approval (A. J. Van den Berg, 'Why are some awards not enforceable?', in A. J. Van den Berg, *New Horizons in International Commercial Arbitration and Beyond* (Alphen aan den Rijn: Kluwer Law International, 2005), p. 291). Unless an interesting point of law arises, enforcement decisions are not reported because they are not newsworthy. Hence, only a small minority of a small minority gets published, and the decisions that are published are not at all representative of arbitral practice.

29 See also Scherer, 'Artificial Intelligence and Legal Decision-Making: The Wide Open?', p. 556.

underlying rule from three examples, than it is to infer the rule from 1.000 examples.[30]

16. While all legal disputes are evidently unique to some extent, it would presumably be considerably less difficult to identify a line in the abundant, repetitive and more numerical case law of, for instance, the Belgian bankruptcy courts. Many cases are decided every day and, while some outliers would obviously occur, the practice is likely to be relatively consistent. The fact that such cases inevitably end with a binary decision (i.e., 'bankrupt' or 'not bankrupt') makes them all the more suitable.

In that respect, an additional challenge for arbitration may lie in the fact that arbitration procedures take place under many different national laws and institutional rules and concern a wide variety of (often quite) complex disputes ranging across all economic sectors and areas of law. Such variety is intellectually stimulating for practitioners, but it is not particularly helpful for machine learning AI systems, which thrive in repetitive and straightforward environments.

17. For the development of our AI arbitrator, this means that not only would we need millions of data points; we would need millions of data points on each conceivable issue our robot arbitrator could be faced with. As Scherer puts it: 'While it is true that many legal questions of fact or law can be reduced to a 0/1 or yes/no binary task, the problem is that there will be a multitude of such binary tasks in each case, and determining all of them will be case specific. For an AI model to be able to extract the required patterns and algorithms from the input data, having one clear output question facilitates the model building process'.[31] Our fully functioning AI arbitrator, however, cannot be limited to just 'one clear output question'. Thus, our 25.000 ICC cases would not all count towards the same quantitative goal: some of them might count towards the quantitative goal for a security for costs algorithm; others might count towards an arbitrator challenge algorithm; etc.

2.3. AN AI ARBITRATOR MOST LIKELY COULD NOT COPE WITH NOVEL OR UNIQUE ISSUES

18. The dataset an AI uses to make its predictions necessarily consists of past cases. In order to be able to predict the outcome of a new case, some sort of similarity with previous cases needs to be established.[32]

---

30 Mueller and Massaron, *Machine Learning for Dummies*, p. 237: 'A rose is a rose. A tree is a tree. A car is a car. Even though you can make simple statements like this, one example of each kind of item doesn't suffice to identify all the items that fit into that classification. After all, many species of trees and many kinds of roses exist.'.

31 Scherer, 'Artificial Intelligence and Legal Decision-Making: The Wide Open?', p. 556.

32 Mueller and Massaron, *Machine Learning for Dummies*, pp. 240–241.

Consequently, it would be challenging for an AI arbitrator to deal with policy changes or novel (legal or factual) issues: if an issue is entirely new (e.g., due to societal changes or clever and creative argumentation from counsel) or if the existing policy has recently changed, the AI system would not be able to detect any similarities with the existing cases in its dataset.[33] It would be tempted to always trace the new issue back to what it does know, which would most likely result in a conservative solution. If 'law is a living thing', AI arbitrators might kill it.

19. The effect of policy changes is particularly strong when they are abrupt. The example provided by Maxi Scherer in her seminal paper on artificial intelligence and legal decision-making is illustrative: 'The decision of the Court of Justice of the European Union in Achmea has fundamentally changed the compatibility of investor-state arbitration with European law overnight'.[34] Indeed, after the Achmea case, any inferences or predictions made by an AI system concerning the compatibility of investor-state arbitration with EU law would instantly become wrong, because prior to the Achmea case, there were no compatibility issues with EU law. In addition, an algorithm could – in principle – not automatically incorporate this new information and adapt to it on the basis of the one new case which establishes the policy change. Statistically, the Achmea case would be irrelevant. Hence, it would somehow need to be hard coded into the algorithm that the policy change is, in fact, a policy change, and not a one-off outlier case.

20. Once again, this requirement also affects the availability and suitability of existing data in the first place. For instance, in our dataset of 25.000 ICC cases, a significant portion will have been decided under previous versions of the ICC Rules.[35] Insofar as the rules have not changed throughout time, the procedural decisions from the past could still be used to train the AI system to resolve current controversies arising out of the application of the ICC Rules. Decisions concerning provisions in the rules that have changed over time, however, will have little or no predictive value for new cases being conducted under today's rules.

---

33 See also Scherer, 'Artificial Intelligence and Legal Decision-Making: The Wide Open?', p. 557.

34 *Ibid.* In its *Achmea* decision, the ECJ outlawed arbitration as a method of dispute resolution for disputes between investors and EU member states arising out of intra-EU BIT's. Thus, the entire basis upon which intra-EU investment arbitration rested was drastically and immediately removed. See European Court of Justice, *Slowakische Republik v. Achmea BV*, case C-284/16 (6 March 2018), *b-Arbitra*, 2018, 107–123.

35 New ICC Rules were adopted in 1922, 1927, 1955, 1975, 1988, 1998, 2012 and 2017. For full text versions of historic ICC rules, see https://library.iccwbo.org/dr-rules.htm.

2.4. AN AI ARBITRATOR WOULD COPY MISTAKES IN PREVIOUS DATA

21. Finally, just like 'arbitration is only as good as the arbitrator'[36], an AI system is only as good as the underlying data.

It is a well-documented phenomenon that AI systems may copy or even exacerbate the (implicit) biases of the underlying data. Cases that have occurred in real life include a well-intended chatbot (based on Twitter data) quickly regressing into spouting racist and offensive messages[37], or Apple's Siri or Amazon's Alexa propagating sexualised gender stereotypes.[38]

Examples with serious real-life consequences include so-called criminal risk assessment algorithms, which predict the risk of recidivism in crime suspects. These tools have been used by law enforcement to assist in deciding whether a suspect should be set free on bail or imprisoned awaiting trial. Longitudinal research demonstrated that African American suspects were twice as likely to be wrongly placed in the high-risk category, whereas Caucasian suspects were also twice as likely to be wrongly placed in the low risk category.[39] A similar effect has been found in an AI system used by a tech company to screen job applicants. The system showed a bias against hiring women and unduly favoured male applicants.[40]

22. Considering that certain AI systems use their own output as a new and valid datapoint for their datasets (in order to 'learn' from new cases), their biases may become worse over time. With each undesirable decision, the overall dataset becomes more undesirable, and the AI system may evolve into something entirely undesirable. The abovementioned chatbot is an example of such a self-reinforcing regression.

23. In an arbitration context, it is not inconceivable that, for instance, certain parties are statistically more likely than others to be ordered to pay security for costs, or to be found to have committed bribery or fraud in an investment context.

---

36 See L. Levy and Y. Derains, *Is Arbitration Only as Good as the Arbitrator? Status, Powers and Role of the Arbitrator* (Alphen aan den Rijn: Kluwer Law International, 2011).

37 See E. Hunt, 'Tay, Microsoft's AI chatbot, gets a crash course in racism from Twitter', *The Guardian*, 24 March 2016.

38 See Y. Adegoke, 'Alexa, why does the brave new world of AI have all the sexism of the old one?', *The Guardian*, 22 May 2019: 'The new research also highlights how virtual assistants are programmed to respond to harassment with the deflecting, tight-grinned replies last heard from a Mad Men receptionist'.

39 J. Larson, S. Mattu, L. Kirchner and J. Angwin, 'How We Analyzed the COMPAS Recidivism Algorithm', *ProPublica*, 23 May 2016.

40 J. Dastin, 'Amazon scraps secret AI recruiting tool that showed bias against women', *Reuters*, 10 October 2018.

AI systems may turn those coincidental statistical correlations into biases, because they do not always make the distinction between variables that were truly determinative to the outcome, and irrelevant variables which happen to correlate to a certain outcome.[41]

24. Such biases are, furthermore, difficult to identify because of the so-called black box principle (which will be discussed further in part 3). As explained in the introductory chapter to this book, many of the currently used AI systems are a black box.[42] We know the data that these systems receive, and we know the data that comes out. We usually do not know, however, how the output was generated by the system, or which 'thought' processes it made. This makes it harder to detect potential biases in the model or in the data, because the AI system will not explain that it predicted X because Y. It will simply say 'X'.

At the same time, knowing the 'thought processes' of an AI system may also present certain problems. As Scherer points out, counsel that is aware of certain 'triggers' of the AI system in question might seek to exploit those triggers in an attempt to influence the system in favour of their client.[43]

2.5. CONCLUSION CONCERNING DATA-BASED FLAWS

25. Thus, from a purely technological point of view, considerable challenges still exist before we could train AI systems to act as arbitrators. Even if we had sufficient data of sufficient quality, an AI arbitrator would, in all likelihood, still not be able to deal with new situations and would copy or even exacerbate underlying biases in existing decisions.

These challenges also exist for other forms of dispute resolution, most notably for litigation before state courts. Nevertheless, the unavailability of data is particularly striking for international arbitration.

I would, therefore, expect that if an AI adjudicator would be possible in the future, it will be developed on the basis of litigation data, and not arbitration data.

This does not necessarily mean that such a litigation trained AI adjudicator could not be 'appointed' as an arbitrator. It would raise questions, however, concerning the added value of arbitrating with an AI adjudicator over conducting whatever other form of AI based dispute resolution.

---

41 K. Leetaru, 'A Reminder That Machine Learning Is About Correlations Not Causation', *Forbes*, 15 January 2019: 'Developers and data scientists increasingly treat their creations as silicon lifeforms 'learning' concrete facts about the world, rather than what they truly are: piles of numbers detached from what they represent, mere statistical patterns encoded into software. We must recognize that those patterns are merely correlations amongst vast reams of data, rather than causative truths or natural laws governing our world'.

42 See Chapter 1 of this book for more information.

43 Scherer, 'Artificial Intelligence and Legal Decision-Making: The Wide Open?', p. 561.

3. THE CURRENT LEGAL FRAMEWORK IS INHOSPITABLE TO AI ARBITRATORS

26. In this part, I will argue that even if technology could ensure that the abovementioned pitfalls are avoided, the existing legal framework of arbitration is not suitable for AI based adjudication of disputes.

Other technology related controversies have manifested themselves in the past:

- For a long time, there were doubts as to whether electronic arbitration agreements were an acceptable alternative to hard copy contracts with manuscript signatures or exchanges of letters, because the New York Convention (and other legal instruments) require an 'agreement in writing'.[44] Today, the controversy appears to be largely settled[45], and very few decisions have actually refused to recognise electronic arbitration agreements.[46] Nevertheless the issue is still raised from time to time, even in recent cases.[47] Sometimes to the detriment of the applicant.[48]

---

44 See, e.g., J. Arsić, 'International Commercial Arbitration on the Internet – Has the Future Come Too Early?', *Journal of International Arbitration*, 1997, vol. 14, no. 3, 215–217. See also R. Wolff, 'E-Arbitration Agreements and E-Awards: Arbitration Agreements Concluded in an Electronic Environment and Digital Arbitral Awards', in M. Piers and C. Aschauer (eds), *Arbitration in the Digital Age* (Cambridge: Cambridge University Press, 2018), p. 152.

45 See Born, *International Commercial Arbitration*, pp. 680–682, 687–689.

46 The one decision mentioned in each discussion of electronic arbitration agreements is Hålogaland Court of Appeal (Norway) 16 August 1999, *ICCA Yearbook Commercial Arbitration*, 2002, vol. 27, p. 519. The court refused the enforcement of an arbitral award because it considered that the exchange of emails which the claimant had submitted in support of its application was not 'the original agreement referred to in Article II NYC or a duly certified copy thereof'. Ironically, the underlying email correspondence between the brokers reads: 'Suppose it's first one of ours which have done via E-mail. Just imagine how much we saved on tlsx/faxes!!!'. For decisions upholding an electronic arbitration agreement, see, e.g., Bayerisches Oberstes Landesgericht (Germany) 12 December 2002, *ICCA Yearbook Commercial Arbitration*, 2004, vol. 29, p. 761; Corte di Cassazione (Italy) 14 June 2007, *ICCA Yearbook Commercial Arbitration*, 2009, vol. 34, p. 639; Tribunal Superior de Justicia de Catalunya (Spain) 15 March 2012, *ICCA Yearbook Commercial Arbitration*, 2013, vol. 38, p. 456; *Chloe Z Fishing Co. V. Odyssey Re (London) Ltd.*, 109 F. Supp. 2d 1236, p. 1250 (S.D. Cal. 2000). In Belgium, the courts have taken a pragmatic approach and have held that a written instrument was only required *ad probationem*. In other words, the writing requirement was not considered a substantive validity requirement (Ghent Court of Appeal 17 December 2002, *RDJP*, 2003, p. 227). See also G. Keutgen and G.-A. Dal, *L'arbitrage en droit belge et international* (Brussels: Bruylant, 2015), pp. 161–164.

47 See, e.g., Cairo Court of Appeal (Egypt) 7 February 2016, *ICCA Yearbook Commercial Arbitration*, 2020, vol. 45, case no. 7.

48 See, e.g., 's Hertogenbosch Court of Appeal (the Netherlands) 7 March 2019, *Tijdschrift voor Arbitrage*, 2019, no. 2, 78. The case concerned the recognition of an arbitral award, and the court (*sua sponte*) requested evidence that the e-mail exchanges evidencing the arbitration agreement were authentic (and had not been altered).

- Similarly, it was argued (unsuccessfully) in a number of cases that the conduct of witness examination or entire hearings by way of video conference was a violation of the parties' right to be heard.[49]
- The issue of whether electronic arbitral awards are allowed is still uncertain[50], and most arbitration institutions appear to endorse a 'better safe than sorry' policy in relation thereto.[51]
- etc.

27. If these simple forms of digitalisation already lead to controversy, it is likely that AI (which is obviously considerably more disruptive than e-mail and videoconferencing) will lead to much greater controversy. In that respect, it could be said that the adversarial nature of the arbitration process inhibits innovation: it is inherent to adversarial settings that an opposing party might seek to exploit any – even merely formal – violations of the applicable rules.

One should note, in that respect, that the entire regulatory landscape of arbitration is predicated on the assumption that an arbitrator is inevitably a natural person and must be able to produce 'human-like' reasoning. At all levels of regulation, arbitration treaties, laws and rules contain provisions which are (or could be interpreted as) incompatible with an AI arbitrator. There is no doubt that parties who are not satisfied with the outcome of their AI arbitrated case will argue that the decision generated by the AI arbitrator violates arbitration law, or is not an arbitral award at all and should therefore have no binding effect.

Below, I will discuss a number of issues that may arise.

---

49 See, e.g., US District Court for the Northern District of Illinois (Eastern Division) 12 August 2020, case no. 20C4700 (*Legaspy v. Financial Industry Regulatory Authority Inc.*); Austrian Supreme Court 23 July 2020, case no. 18 ONC 3/20S; Egyptian Court of Cassation 27 October 2020, case no. 18309; Amsterdam District Court (the Netherlands) 26 July 2012, *ITA Board of Reporters*, case no. 505950 / KG RK 11-3695; Ontario Superior Court of Justice (Canada) 29 December 2009, *ITA Board of Reporters*, case no. CV-09-376953; New South Wales District Registry Federal Court (Australia) 20 August 2014, *ITA Board of Reporters*, case no. VID 522.

50 Wolff, 'E-Arbitration Agreements and E-Awards: Arbitration Agreements Concluded in an Electronic Environment and Digital Arbitral Awards', pp. 174 et seq.

51 In its report on IT use in arbitration, the ICC Commission notes that 'other issues, such as the fully enforceable, fully electronic award, remain as barriers still to be conquered. Today, true digital copies of awards are sent to the parties in certain instances. A bitmap facsimile may not comply with the formal legal requirements concerning the recognition and enforcement of arbitral awards, however'. See ICC Commission on Arbitration and ADR, *Report on Information Technology in International Arbitration* (Paris: International Chamber of Commerce, 2017), p. 3.

3.1. ARBITRATION LAW IS BUILT AROUND THE ASSUMPTION OF A HUMAN ARBITRATOR

28. Several authors have pointed out that most arbitration laws and rules implicitly require a human arbitrator.[52] There are indeed a number of provisions that appear to be based on an assumption of humanity for arbitrators.

A first example is the fact that a large number of national laws refer to arbitrators as 'he' ('his') or as 'he/she' ('his/her') (e.g., Article 11 UNCITRAL Model Law; Section 7 of the Swedish Arbitration Act). The use of these gendered pronouns would, according to some authors, imply humanity, because gender is a characteristic of living organisms.[53]

A similar argument is made for provisions that deal with inherently human characteristics, such as an arbitrator's death (e.g., Article 26 of the English Arbitration Act), or which provide that a minor cannot be an arbitrator (Article 16 of the Egyptian Arbitration Act), or that a person cannot be excluded from sitting as an arbitrator on the basis of his nationality. The argument is that only living organisms can die, and that only humans can be minors.[54]

29. It is undisputed that the drafters of these provisions will have had a human arbitrator in mind. At the same time, however, it could be argued that none of these provisions would, strictly speaking, prevent an AI from being appointed as arbitrator:

- The use of gendered pronouns does not necessarily exclude AI arbitrators. In many languages, nouns have grammatical genders. Therefore, not every instance where the law refers to an arbitrator as 'he' should be construed as an implicit requirement of humanity (just like 'he' is not construed as an implicit requirement of masculinity). The word 'he' simply fulfils a grammatical function, i.e. referring to the word 'arbitrator'. In contrast, where the law uses 'he or she', as is the case in Sweden, it could perhaps be argued that this presents a binary choice that must be respected.
- The same goes for provisions relating to the death or the adulthood of an arbitrator. These provisions only prescribe what happens *if* an arbitrator were to decease pending an arbitration procedure. To argue that this unavoidably requires that an arbitrator must be mortal, is to stretch the meaning of the provision from merely hypothetical ('what if') to absolute ('must be able to'). Similarly, the rule that no minors can be appointed as arbitrators

---

52 Wahab and Katsh, 'Revolutionizing Technologies and the Use of Technology in International Arbitration', p. 49; Hope, 'Can a Robot be an Arbitrator?', pp. 104–111; Snijders, 'Arbitrage en AI: van arbitrage naar robotrage en van menselijke arbiter naar robotarbiter?', p. 5.

53 Wahab and Katsh, 'Revolutionizing Technologies and the Use of Technology in International Arbitration', p. 49.

54 *Ibid.*, p. 49.

> should be taken at face value. It provides that minors cannot be appointed as arbitrators. It in no way requires that an arbitrator must absolutely be capable of once having been a minor.

Thus, these requirements clearly imply humanity, but, interpreted very liberally, do not appear to require a human arbitrator in absolute terms.

30. A number of national laws go further, however, and leave no room for interpretation. They expressly provide that an arbitrator can only be a natural person.[55]

Thus, we read that Article 1450 of the French Code of Civil Procedure that 'The office of arbitrator may only be exercised by a natural person enjoying the full exercise of his rights'.[56]

Similarly, Article 1023 of the Dutch Code of Civil Procedure provides that 'every natural person with legal capacity can be appointed as an arbitrator'.[57]

Under English law, the question was recently answered in case law. The High Court decided in *Crowther v. Rayment* that 'only a natural person, not a legal person or a group of persons such as a firm, can be an arbitrator'.[58]

31. It is clear that such requirements do not – or at least not as a matter of course – permit an AI to function as an arbitrator under the current framework. It is also quite unlikely that the introduction of AI arbitrators would depend on creative or progressive interpretations of such provisions. If we would want an AI system to decide our disputes, and we would want that form of dispute resolution to qualify as arbitration, these provisions would most likely need to be amended. They could, for instance, provide that an arbitrator can also be a legal person (e.g., the company that is responsible for the operation of the AI arbitrator in question).

3.2. INDEPENDENCE AND IMPARTIALITY OF AN AI ARBITRATOR?

32. The possibility of appointing AI arbitrators via a legal person or with legal personality would presumably also have an impact on other requirements

---

55 *Ibid.*, p. 49; Hope, 'Can a Robot be an Arbitrator?', pp. 104–111; Snijders, 'Arbitrage en AI: van arbitrage naar robotrage en van menselijke arbiter naar robotarbiter?', p. 5.

56 Example quoted in Wahab and Katsh, 'Revolutionizing Technologies and the Use of Technology in International Arbitration', p. 49.

57 Example quoted in Snijders, 'Arbitrage en AI: van arbitrage naar robotrage en van menselijke arbiter naar robotarbiter?', p. 5.

58 *Crowther v. Rayment* [2015] EWHC 427 (Ch), paragraph 30. Example quoted in Hope, 'Can a Robot be an Arbitrator?', pp. 105–107.

in arbitration. In case AI arbitrators would become a reality, we would need to reassess a number of key concepts of arbitration law.[59] One of the more striking examples lies in the requirements of independence and impartiality for arbitrators. In relation to AI arbitrators, what constitutes an 'independent and impartial' arbitrator would probably depend on the data diet the AI system received. In that context, the developer of a particular AI system may be able to influence the decisions of the AI by tailoring the underlying dataset.

33. To give just one example: would we allow the provider of an AI-based dispute resolution mechanism for insurance disputes to be wholly or partially owned by insurance companies? Would the fact that an insurance dispute AI system was developed with capital from the insurance sector not create justifiable doubts as to the independence and impartiality of said AI system? It could certainly be argued that it would.

At the same time, it should also be considered that insurance companies are possibly the only realistic financiers, willing and able to invest in the development of an insurance dispute AI system. Preventing them from participating in the development of such an AI may unduly stifle technological development.

34. It could therefore be necessary to rethink the legal framework for conflicts of interest, which currently focuses on interests and relationships (between arbitrators, counsel, the parties and the dispute), and to shift towards more objective parameters for data (at least for AI arbitrators). In that respect, it could be considered to require some sort of certification that, indeed, this particular AI has been fed a data diet which can be considered neutral.[60]The EU Commission indeed appears to have moved in that direction. In April 2021, the Commission published a proposal for an EU Regulation concerning the use of artificial intelligence. The proposal contains a number of important requirements that would apply to so-called 'high risk' AI applications, such as the setting up and maintaining of a risk management system and data governance practices; having the necessary technical documentation; keeping records of the AI system's processes. Such AI systems would also be subject to transparency obligations; would require human oversight; and would need to be able to guarantee appropriate levels of accuracy, robustness and cybersecurity. In addition, a framework for regulatory oversight is created.[61]

---

59 See Piers and Aschauer, who argue that we should be prepared to rethink the fundamentals of arbitration. Piers and Aschauer, 'Conclusion', p. 295.

60 The idea of AI certification was already discussed in the EU Commission's ethics guidelines for AI. See EU High Level Expert Group on Artificial Intelligence, *Ethics Guidelines for trustworthy AI* (Brussels: European Commission, 2019), p. 23.

61 For more details on this EU initiative, see Chapter 3 of this book.

It is not clear whether a more advanced and entirely autonomous decision maker would be qualified as a high-risk AI system. According to Article 6(2) of the proposal, read in conjunction with Annex III, 'AI systems intended to assist a judicial authority in researching and interpreting facts and the law and in applying the law to a concrete set of facts' are considered 'High-Risk AI Systems'. For now, the proposal only envisages AI systems that 'assist' a judicial authority (Annex III, point 8, a).[62] It is unlikely, however, that robot arbitrators – should they ever emerge – would be subject to a more lenient legal regime.

3.3. FORMAL REQUIREMENTS FOR RENDERING AN ARBITRAL AWARD CURRENTLY EXCLUDE AN AI ARBITRATOR

35. Another potential issue relates to the fact that certain formal requirements in international arbitration can (*prima facie*) only be fulfilled by humans. The formalities relating to the rendering of an arbitral award provide a good example.

36. Under most national laws[63] and institutional rules[64], an arbitral award must be made in writing, must be signed by the arbitral tribunal, and must be delivered to the parties (sometimes in a specific manner, e.g., by registered mail or by courier). These requirements, to some extent, serve the overarching requirement of the New York Convention, pursuant to which a party needs to submit a 'duly authenticated original or duly certified copy' of an award in order to have it declared enforceable (Article IV (1) (a) New York Convention).[65]

Several authors have warned that (the combination of) these form requirements may complicate the use of electronic arbitral awards.[66] Arbitral institutions appear to heed those warnings and stick to the traditional hard copy

---

62 The Commission has the power to amend Annex III and to add new types of AI systems that relate to the administration of justice insofar as the AI systems in question pose a risk of adverse impact on fundamental rights that is equivalent to or greater than the risk of adverse impact posed by a judicial assistance AI system (Art. 7(1) and (2) of the Proposal). It is clear that a fully automated AI system poses a greater risk than an AI system that merely 'assists' a judicial authority.

63 See, e.g., Articles 1713, §8; 1720, §4 and 1721, §2 Belgian Judicial Code.

64 See, e.g., Article 35 ICC Rules (2017).

65 On the requirements of Article IV New York Convention, see, e.g., M. Scherer, 'Article IV: Formal Requirements for Recognition and Enforcement of Arbitral Awards', in R. Wolff (ed.), *New York Convention: Article by Article Commentary* (Oxford: Hart Publishing, 2019), pp. 213–230.

66 Wolff, 'E-Arbitration Agreements and E-Awards: Arbitration Agreements Concluded in an Electronic Environment and Digital Arbitral Awards', pp. 174–181. See also I. Amro, 'Enforcement of Cross-Border Online Arbitral Awards and Online Arbitration Agreements in National Courts', *Slovenska arbitražna praksa*, 2016, pp. 29–30.

originals with manuscript signatures, which they have used for decades, and which do not pose any formal validity issues.[67]

37. Regardless of whether these warnings in relation to electronic awards are well-founded[68], the issue of electronic awards would be further complicated if the arbitrator was an AI and not a human, because – for the time being – only humans have signatures and machines do not.[69]

While that is certainly true from a strictly factual point of view, the legal reality may soon turn out to be different. If the AI had legal personality[70], it would theoretically be capable of having and of contracting rights and obligations. How that would work in practice is not clear, but the same issue occurs with legal persons. It is, therefore, not inconceivable that an AI could be represented by the persons behind the legal entity (as is the case with corporations), or that it could acquire a personal digital 'stamp' or 'seal', which has the same value as a natural person's signature. This latter possibility is already foreseen in the EU eIDAS Regulation for corporate entities.[71] There is no apparent reason why this could, if necessary, not be extended to a legally personified AI. Once again, however, this would require active legislative intervention.

---

67 ICC Commission on Arbitration and ADR, *Report on Information Technology in International Arbitration* (Paris: International Chamber of Commerce, 2017) p. 3. See, however, the most recent version of the LCIA Rules, in which the possibility of electronically signed awards was expressly included (Article 26.2 LCIA Rules 2020). Several other arbitration institutions seem to follow suit (in the near future). See, e.g., Article 33.6 of the AIAC Rules 2021 and the NAI Rules 2022.

68 In my opinion, electronic awards are, in principle and in most cases, a viable alternative. An 'in writing' requirement can be satisfied by an electronic document, and a signature requirement can be met through electronic signature. An electronically signed document that offers the necessary guarantees of authenticity and integrity (e.g., those signed with a qualified electronic signature within the meaning of Article 25 (2) eIDAS Regulation), would (or should) be considered a 'duly authenticated original' or a 'duly certified copy'. The fact that a document can no longer be altered after it was signed electronically, makes any copy of that document a 'duly certified copy'. This does not mean that there are no difficulties in this respect. As a result of the multi-layered and international regulatory framework, different permutations may present themselves in practice, and issues of mutual recognition may arise. For more details, see K. Ongenae and M. Piers, 'Procedural Formalities in Arbitration: Towards a Technologically Neutral Legal Framework', *Journal of International Arbitration*, 2021, no. 1, pp. 21–31.

69 Ng and Benedetti del Rio, 'When the Tribunal is an Algorithm: Complexities of Enforcing Orders Determined by a Software under the New York Convention', pp. 124–128.

70 As Hope points out, such legal personality for AI's is already contemplated in European Parliament Resolution of 16 February 2017 with Recommendations to the Commission on Civil Law Rules on Robotics (2015/2103(INL)). See Hope, 'Can a Robot be an Arbitrator?', p. 111.

71 Concerning the legal framework for electronic seals in the EU, see Section 5 of the European eIDAS Regulation (Regulation (EU) No 910/2014 of the European Parliament and of the Council of 23 July 2014 on electronic identification and trust services for electronic transactions in the internal market and repealing Directive 1999/93/EC). Cons. 59 of the eIDAS Regulation explains that 'Electronic seals should serve as evidence that an electronic document was issued by a legal person, ensuring certainty of the document's origin and integrity'.

3.4. DUTY TO PROVIDE REASONS

38. Arbitrators must provide reasons for their decisions. In Belgium, for instance, providing reasons for a decision is considered a fundamental requirement for all jurisdictional acts.[72]

The duty to provide reasons serves different purposes in arbitration law. First of all, it legitimises the decision by explaining to the parties why certain decisions were taken, and it allows them to adapt their future behaviour accordingly. Secondly, reasons are deemed necessary to enable a subsequent tribunal (if an arbitral appeal mechanism is foreseen) or state court (in case of annulment or enforcement proceedings) to verify the legality (and, in case of arbitral appeal, factual accuracy) of the decision. It allows a subsequent tribunal or state court to adopt the reasoning of the decision, or to consciously deviate from it.[73]

In certain jurisdictions, parties are free to agree that their arbitrators do not need to provide reasons in their award.[74] Those jurisdictions are a minority, however. In Belgium, the duty to provide reasons is considered public policy.[75]

39. As mentioned previously, one of the characteristics of many machine learning AI systems is that they are a 'black box'. They receive input and provide output, but they do not give any justification for their output. An AI that provides no explanation at all for its decisions, would obviously be irreconcilable with the duty to provide reasons in arbitral awards.[76] We would either need to remove the requirement to provide reasons, or find a way to make the AI 'explainable'.

40. Making AI explainable is challenging because it does not 'think' like a human. An AI system does not say 'I consider facts X, Y and Z proven and will therefore apply rules A, B and C, leading to the conclusion that the claim should be dismissed'. An AI is essentially a similarity assessor that works out probabilities on the basis of similarities between the new case and the vast collection of cases in its dataset. On the basis of a number of parameters, it will place a new case in a cluster of existing cases in the dataset, and it will predict the outcome of the new case on the basis of the outcomes in the cases in the relevant cluster.[77]

---

72 Keutgen and Dal, *L'arbitrage en droit belge et international*, pp. 472–473.

73 *Ibid.*; Scherer, 'Artificial Intelligence and Legal Decision-Making: The Wide Open?', p. 562.

74 See, e.g., Section 52 (4) of the English Arbitration Act 1996: 'The award shall contain the reasons for the award unless it is an agreed award or the parties have agreed to dispense with reasons'.

75 Keutgen and Dal, *L'arbitrage en droit belge et international*, pp. 472–473.

76 This issue is discussed in Hope, 'Can a Robot be an Arbitrator?', pp. 112–114; Scherer, 'Artificial Intelligence and Legal Decision-Making: The Wide Open?', pp. 562–565; Kwan, Ng and Kiu, 'The Use of Artificial Intelligence in International Arbitration: Where are we Right Now?', pp. 24–25.

77 Mueller and Massaron, *Machine Learning for Dummies*, pp. 237–241.

The way AI researchers have sought to achieve explainable AI, is by using so-called counterfactual scenarios.[78] This entails that almost identical cases are inserted into the AI system, but with certain parameters (slightly) altered, to see whether the resulting outcome changes. If the result is indeed different, it can be concluded that the parameter that was altered played a role in the AI's 'decision'. This can lead to a list of relevant parameters, perhaps with an indication of the degree of relevance, but it still falls short of human explanation.

41. It is, therefore, unlikely that the minimal requirements of the duty to provide reasons could currently be met by AI systems. Even if the threshold is quite low, as is the case in Belgium[79], the reasons provided would still need to be complete, clear, precise and adequate. At the same time, the reasons provided in an arbitral award cannot be ambiguous or insufficient, and the award must not contain logical reasoning errors.[80]

Once again, these requirements presuppose a human kind of logical reasoning which, for now, cannot be provided by AI systems, which make use of approximative inference on the basis of similarity. Even if the AI system could explain its thought processes, it would not be sufficient to meet the applicable legal standards. As Scherer puts it, 'providing an explanation [...] that the likelihood of a claim to be dismissed is 86%, will not satisfy the losing party'.[81] Not even if such a probability statement would be supplemented with a list of parameters that played a role in the assessment.

3.5. CONCLUSION CONCERNING THE LEGAL FRAMEWORK

42. Thus, AI arbitrators are – at least legally speaking – not a natural fit for arbitration.[82]

As mentioned above, adversarial dispute resolution is not a fertile ground for such innovations. When confronted with an adverse AI-based arbitral award, it will always be tempting for the losing party to argue that, in fact, this is not arbitration at all, and that the – all in all – lenient annulment and recognition regime for arbitration should not apply to the AI arbitrator's award (so that a state court judge can decide the issues *de novo*).

---

78 Scherer, 'Artificial Intelligence and Legal Decision-Making: The Wide Open?', p. 563.

79 The duty to provide reasons is considered a formal and not a substantive requirement (Cour de Cassation (Belgium) 18 December 1972, *Pasicrisie*, 1973, I, p. 384).

80 Keutgen and Dal, *L'arbitrage en droit belge et international*, pp. 475–476, and the abundant case law references mentioned there.

81 Scherer, 'Artificial Intelligence and Legal Decision-Making: The Wide Open?', p. 565.

82 See Ng and Benedetti del Rio, 'When the Tribunal is an Algorithm: Complexities of Enforcing Orders Determined by a Software under the New York Convention', p. 133: 'It is suggested that laws or procedural amendments for the use of such technologies in arbitration should be made'.

43. Laws can be changed, however, and it could be considered to make the necessary amendments to make arbitration law more hospitable to AI. At some point in the future, if AI-based legal decision making becomes possible, we would indeed be faced with a binary regulatory choice: do we want to qualify this as arbitration or not? It is not simply a matter of reinterpreting existing legal norms.

44. From the arbitration regulator's perspective, that is not an easy choice. As Eidenmüller and Varesis point out, there are two conflicting policy considerations at play. First, there is a degree of regulatory competition: jurisdictions want to attract as much arbitration business as possible, and one of the things they may compete on is how permissive they are towards AI arbitration.[83] At the same time, however, it is not simply a question of enshrining AI arbitration into local arbitration laws. Because arbitration is, for the most part, an international phenomenon, it greatly depends on the recognition of awards in other jurisdictions. Therefore, local procedural liberalism is always limited by other states' (courts') willingness to accept the procedural liberalisation in question.[84] A country's arbitration laws cannot be too far ahead of the curve, or the awards rendered there might not be recognised elsewhere.

Thus, while AI arbitrators may not be fundamentally irreconcilable with the concept of arbitration[85], it is clear that regulatory intervention in favour of AI arbitration would be required. Actually making that decision is a delicate balancing exercise. As will be discussed below, this may considerably impede the evolution of fully automated AI arbitration.

4. CONCLUSION AND LOOK AHEAD

45. In this chapter, it has been argued that there are currently two large hurdles to fully automated AI arbitration.

The first is that we do not have enough data, and, in any event, not enough qualitative data relating in particular to arbitration to develop a performant AI arbitrator. Even if we did, the use of AI arbitrators could lead to a stagnation of the law. In terms of technology, we simply are not there yet.

The second is that international arbitration law and arbitration related regulatory instruments are – at least for now – not equipped to deal with AI arbitrators.

---

83 Eidenmüller and Varesis, 'What is an Arbitration? Artificial Intelligence and the Vanishing Human Arbitrator', pp. 43–45.

84 *Ibid.*, pp. 45–46.

85 *Ibid.*, p. 49.

46. Based on the two main observations of this chapter, a few predictions can be made about how the emergence of complex AI adjudication – if it ever happens – might interact with arbitration. The necessary disclaimers regarding predictions apply.

First, it is not unlikely that if fully automated dispute resolution by AI indeed emerges in the future, it will develop outside the (legal) framework of arbitration. This is because, as argued throughout this chapter, arbitration is not particularly suited for the development of AI from a data-technical point of view, and because the legal framework is not particularly hospitable to the idea of an AI arbitrator either.

Secondly, once a fully functional AI adjudicator would become available, arbitration would probably only adopt it very hesitantly (if at all). As we have seen, the laws and regulations of arbitration are not exactly accommodating to the idea of AI arbitrators, and active regulatory intervention would be required. The international nature of arbitration (where recognition is often sought abroad and is subject to local interpretations at the place of enforcement[86]) and the adversarial nature of binding dispute resolution in general, make it especially difficult to introduce novel phenomena with sufficient legal certainty when the legal framework is not neutral. Indeed, it would take a concerted effort from a large number of different jurisdictions and stakeholders to provide the necessary legal certainty which AI arbitration would most likely need in order to thrive. By the time such legal certainty is achieved, fully automated AI dispute resolution may have moved on to greener pastures (whatever those may be). It is, in my view, much more likely that AI adjudication will initially operate in a legal vacuum, as a form of non-binding ADR for small disputes, where parties accept the non-binding decision of the AI system simply because the cost of actually arbitrating or litigating the dispute exceeds the value at stake.

47. For these reasons, it is not certain at all that automated AI-based dispute adjudication will be fitted onto or into any of the existing methods of dispute resolution. True revolutions usually do not come from adaptations to the existing *modus operandi*. As Henry Ford famously said: 'If I had asked people what they wanted, they would have said faster horses'.[87]

Our idea of 'appointing' AI 'arbitrators' may therefore turn out to be a mirage that results from looking at AI adjudication through the paradigm of existing

86 As Van den Berg concluded in his treatise on the New York Convention: 'whilst international conventions are established to regulate a certain subject matter in a uniform manner, they are interpreted and applied differently by the courts in the States Party to them. [...] it appears that the New York Convention does not constitute an exception to this phenomenon'. See A. J. Van den Berg, *The New York Arbitration Convention of 1958* (The Hague: Asser Institute, 1981), p. 383.

87 The Henry Ford parable is taken from R. Susskind, *Online Courts and the Future of Justice* (Oxford, Oxford University Press, 2019), p. 185.

dispute resolution methods. However, once complex adjudication by an AI system would truly be possible, we may no longer look at it in terms of arbitration or litigation. AI adjudication will perhaps have some features in common with arbitration or litigation. But overall, it may evolve into something else entirely.

Whether there will still be a need or a demand for arbitration or litigation services in such a digitalised environment, is not clear. It is perfectly conceivable, however, that some disputes would be capable of AI adjudication and others would not (just like some disputes are arbitrable and others are not), or that people simply will not want certain disputes to be decided by an AI system. In that respect, the 'humanity' of arbitration and litigation may be its main selling point, so that human arbitrators and judges will, at most, be assisted by an AI system for questions requiring a more 'numerical' analysis.

CHAPTER 6

AI THROUGH A HUMAN RIGHTS LENS. THE ROLE OF HUMAN RIGHTS IN FULFILLING AI'S POTENTIAL

Charline DAELMAN* and Katerina YORDANOVA**

1. INTRODUCTION

1. AI, robotics and other forms of smart automation have the potential to bring great economic benefits – up to $15 trillion to global GDP by 2030 – causing a major shift in the global economy.[1] It is seen as a key driver and component of the Fourth Industrial Revolution. This Revolution is more transforming than any other industrial revolution we already experienced so far. It challenges our ideas about what it means to be 'human'.[2] The influence of AI can already be seen on the labour market (e.g., robotisation of work) as well as in public (e.g., facial recognition) and private spaces (e.g., virtual assistants at home). The integration of AI within our daily routines makes it hard to imagine life without it.

2. Many governments are also investing in AI. China is already a global leader in AI and will probably achieve its aspired $150 billion AI investment by 2030.[3] The United States (US) acknowledged that AI will be their second highest R&D priority after the security of the American people, investing up to $2 billion

---

* Social Sustainability Expert, Strategy & Innovation, amfori (PhD University of Leuven, LLM University of Essex).

** Lawyer and researcher at KU Leuven Centre for IT and IP Law.

1 PwC, 'Will robots really steal our jobs? An international analysis of the potential long term impact of automation', 2018, https://www.pwc.co.uk/economic-services/assets/international-impact-of-automation-feb-2018.pdf.

2 This development resulted in calls for adoption of tools mitigating the potential adversarial effects of the large-scaled adoption of AI technologies to humans and the environment. Such tools are for example contained in the concept and principles of Industry 5.0 formulated by Michael Rada in Industry 5.0 – from virtual to physical.

3 S. Srivastava, 'Top 10 countries leading the artificial intelligence race', *Analytics Insights*, 27 June 2019, https://www.analyticsinsight.net/top-10-countries-leading-the-artificial-intelli gence-race/.

between 2018–2023 for the advancement of AI. In Europe, primarily France and the United Kingdom (UK) are at the AI forefront, with France investing $1.5 billion and the UK $1.3 billion in AI-related research.[4] As a consequence, the geopolitical implications of AI should not be underestimated. This is even more so considering the relationship between many AI applications and automated warfare, providing any AI-investing country with a potential military advantage. The increased investments in AI research and development show the importance of AI and its potential ability to rebalance world power.

3. Considering that AI systems affect many aspects of our lives, it is necessary to question what the role of human rights will be in the AI and robotics era. To assess this role, a helicopter overview of the way in which selected internationally recognised human rights are or can be impacted by the commercialisation and use of AI is provided (part 2). Several issues addressed in this chapter are covered more thoroughly in other parts of this book. This chapter provides a more general and introductory overview on the relationship between human rights and AI systems. It is, therefore, somewhat different than the other chapters as it does not tackle a specific issue more extensively. However, the most significant way in which AI may affect human rights relates to possible intentional or unintentional discrimination. Non-discrimination is, therefore, taken as a case study. It will be demonstrated in more detail how AI applications contribute to bias and discrimination. We will also examine the different grounds on which such systems can discriminate (part 3). Finally, this chapter will turn the tables and explore the potential of using a human rights lens to govern future AI developments. This will contribute to human rights-sensitive AI design and user processes (part 4). We will briefly summarise the main findings in a conclusion (part 5).

2. THE IMPACT OF AI ON HUMAN RIGHTS: RISKS AND OPPORTUNITIES

4. The commercialisation of AI systems will pose several challenges from a legal and regulatory point of view. Given that human rights are interdependent and interrelated, AI affects nearly all of them. To understand the way in which AI is interacting with human rights, a helicopter overview is provided in this part. The structure follows the traditional way in which human rights are analysed, justified by the European Convention on Human Rights with the object of demonstrating how the risks created by AI systems may change the

[4] K. Walch, 'Why The Race for AI Dominance is More Global Than You Think', *Forbes*, 9 February 2020, https://www.forbes.com/sites/cognitiveworld/2020/02/09/why-the-race-for-ai-dominance-is-more-global-than-you-think/#2f0d7ffe121f.

approach of human rights law vis-à-vis certain rights such as right to privacy.[5] The potential benefits as well as risks of AI for human rights are highlighted. These benefits and risks are not (necessarily) unique to AI. Yet, AI has the potential to accelerate and expand their scale and scope.[6]

2.1. RIGHT TO LIFE, LIBERTY, SECURITY AND A FAIR TRIAL

5. A first category of human rights relates to the right to life,[7] to liberty and security[8] and to a fair trial.[9] One of the many applications of AI relates to the use of criminal risk-assessment software. This software supports the police and the judicial system when taking (detainments) decisions, ranging from assigning bail to imposing sentences.[10] Research conducted by *ProPublica* in 2016 investigated the risk scores of over 7000 arrested persons. It demonstrated that criminal risk-assessment software which is widely adopted in the US criminal justice system is consistently inaccurate in forecasting potential future crime and heavily biased against black defendants. They were falsely categorised as high risk and, as a result, given higher bail conditions, kept in pre-trial detention and sentenced to longer prison terms.[11] Facial recognition techniques deployed by law enforcement also show high error rates. These inaccuracies result in misidentification, thereby leading to increased wrongful arrests especially for non-white faces.[12]

By attributing a future level of potential guilt, the presumption of innocence required in a fair trial may be tainted.[13] The *ProPublica* study also showed that

---

5 A similar approach was proposed by Y. Poullet, *La vie privée à l'heure de la société du numérique*, Brussels, Larcier, 2019, 189 p.

6 Accessnow (lead author L. Andersen), 'Human Rights in the Age of Artificial Intelligence', November 2018, pp. 18–19, https://www.accessnow.org/cms/assets/uploads/2018/11/AI-and-Human-Rights.pdf.

7 Article 2 European Convention on Human Rights (ECHR), Article 3 Universal Declaration of Human Rights (UDHR).

8 Article 5 ECHR, Article 3 UDHR and Article 9 of the International Covenant on Civil and Political Rights (ICCPR).

9 Article 6 ECHR, Articles 6, 7, 8, and 10 UDHR and Article 14 ICCPR. See Chapter 4 on AI and procedural law and Chapter 5 on AI and arbitration. See for a more extensive discussion: A. Cowger, *The Threats of Algorithms and AI to Civil Rights, Legal Remedies, and American Jurisprudence: One Nation Under Algorithms* (Lanham: Rowman & Littlefield, 2020), 276 p.

10 C. McKay, 'Predicting risk in criminal procedure: actuarial tools, algorithms, AI and judicial decision-making', *Current Issues in Criminal Justice*, 2020, vol. 32, no. 1, pp. 22–39.

11 J. Larson and J. Angwin, 'Machine Bias', *ProPublica*, 23 May 2016, https://www.propublica.org/article/machine-bias-risk-assessments-in-criminal-sentencing.

12 Lauren Goode, 'Facial recognition software is biased towards white men, researcher finds', *The Verge*, 11 February 2018, https://www.theverge.com/2018/2/11/17001218/facial-recognition-software-accuracy-technology-mit-white-men-black-women-error.

13 Human Rights Committee, General Comment No. 32, 'Article 14: Right to equality before courts and tribunals and to a fair trial', U.N. Doc. CCPR/C/GC/32, July 2007.

many judges rely on the outcome of these risk-scoring systems even when not entirely understanding how they work. That is because judges are convinced that such systems are unbiased. Judicial and police functions are influenced by software systems developed by private companies using data analytics and design choices that are not shared publicly. Judicial and police systems using such criminal risk-assessment and facial recognition software may thus not be able to adequately motivate their decisions as they do not always know how certain scores were calculated, nor which identification techniques were used. Therefore, humans cannot always assess the validity of decisions taken by AI systems. As these risk-scoring systems are not prescribed by law and may use arbitrary inputs, judicial and police decisions based on these systems can be unlawful or arbitrary.[14]

Furthermore, using AI approaches such as machine learning for legal analytics is deemed to affect a broad range of principles and requirements that are relevant for the right to a fair trial. Examples are the requirement of equality of arms[15] or the party's ability to have knowledge of and be able to comment on relevant case materials when an AI-based tool is deployed during adversarial proceedings. As a result, these tendencies will contribute to the legal system becoming 'incomprehensible, alienating, disillusioning and data-based'.[16]

6. A specific application of AI that poses a potential threat to the right to life are fully autonomous weapon systems, more commonly referred to as lethal autonomous weapons (LAWs) or 'killer robots'. They are currently being developed in several countries.[17] Non-state actors can also have access to this AI technology, which raises concerns as they are not necessarily bound by the traditional laws of armed conflicts. Given their programmed nature, autonomous weapons may not be able to consider 'nuances' in a particular situation or react appropriately to unexpected circumstances. This may result in potential high error rates with fatal casualties, which a human operator could have been able to avoid.[18] Another way in which AI could potentially endanger

---

[14] J. Larson and J. Angwin, 'Machine Bias'; Accessnow, 'Human Rights in the Age of Artificial Intelligence', pp. 18–19. Also see: S. Gless, 'AI in the Courtroom: A Comparative Analysis of Machine Evidence in Criminal Trials', *Georgetown Journal of International Law*, 2020, vol. 51, no. 2, pp. 195–253.

[15] V.K. Steponenaite and P. Valcke, 'Judicial analytics on trial: An assessment of legal analytics in judicial systems in light of the right to a fair trial', *Maastricht Journal of European and Comparative Law*. 2020, vol. 27, no. 6, p. 767.

[16] R.M. Re and A. Solow-Niederman, 'Developing Artificially Intelligent Justice', *The Stanford Technology Law Review*, 2019, p. 242.

[17] An example of countries which are currently developing such killer robots are: China, Israel, South Korea, Russia, the United Kingdom and the United States. In addition, according to the UN Security Council's Panel of Experts on Libya's report in March 2020, Turkey deployed a STM Kargu-2 drone, being referred as the first officially recognised use of LAWs.

[18] Accessnow, 'Human Rights in the Age of Artificial Intelligence', p. 29. For a more detailed explanation on the specific topic of autonomous weapon systems, see Chapter 7. Also see:

and infringe the right to life is related to the increased use of cyber-physical systems. For example, AI has been a key element of the new infrastructure in various factories, which means that workers need to interact with autonomous robots on the shop floor. These physical interactions made people vulnerable to a variety of incidents or accidents which may have an adverse impact to their right to life.[19] Furthermore, the deployment of AI systems in medical devices that are necessary for the maintenance of vital bodily functions could also constitute a risk to the right to life, especially with more sophisticated methods for cyber-attacks being developed.[20] Finally, the right to life could be endangered by proxy through AI infringing other human rights such as the right to privacy or non-discrimination which is going to be further discussed in the following sections.

2.2. RIGHT TO PRIVACY

7. As we heavily rely on several technical applications to make our daily lives easier, we are not always aware of the trail of data (also called data exhaust) we leave behind. These aggregated data provide a very elaborated insight into various aspects of our (private) life.[21] All these data are and will increasingly be processed and analysed by AI systems, for example to create targeted advertising or improve public transportation. The data may also be processed to increase the governmental surveillance of citizens. Through access to and the analysis of big data sets, AI systems are continuously learning and improving themselves.[22]

8. The collection, processing and analysis of data may reveal private information of individuals (data subjects). This information is protected, even if it is extracted from big data sets consisting of publicly available information. For example, existing machine learning models use cell phone location data to predict a person's age, gender occupation and marital status. They can even estimate a person's future location via the location data of friends and past user history.[23] Other examples of how AI applications might interfere with the right

U.C. Jha, *Killer Robots: Lethal Autonomous Weapon Systems Legal, Ethical and Moral Challenges* (New Delhi: Vij Books India Pvt Ltd, 2016), 260 p.; L. Lauwaert, 'Killer robots: zegen of vloek?', Paper Kenniscentrum Data & Maatschappij, https://data-en-maatschappij.ai/publicaties/paper-killer-robots-zegen-of-vloek.

19 J. Allred, 'Robots, Automation, and Workplace Safety: 7 Common Hazards', Creative Safety Supply Blog, January 2020, https://blog.creativesafetysupply.com/robots-automation-and-workplace-safety-7-common-hazards/.

20 B. Schneier, 'The Coming AI Hackers', Belfer Center for Science and International Affairs Harvard Kennedy School, April 2021, https://www.schneier.com/academic/archives/2021/04/the-coming-ai-hackers.html.

21 See on the right to privacy: Article 8 of ECHR, Article 12 of UDHR, Article 17 of ICCPR.

22 Accessnow, 'Human Rights in the Age of Artificial Intelligence', p. 20.

23 S.M. Bellovin et al., 'When enough is enough: Location tracking, mosaic theory, and machine learning', *NYU Journal of Law and Liberty*, 2014, vol. 8, no. 2, pp. 555–628.

to privacy are: (i) the use of built-in sensors in consumer products that collect data from those in proximity without their knowledge or consent; (ii) the identification of persons that want to remain anonymous; (iii) the generating of sensitive information from non-sensitive data; and iv) the profiling of people.[24]

Many AI applications are based on algorithms that rely on datasets to gather answers, predictions and insights. As a result, in order to generate more powerful insights, AI systems are on a continuous basis hungry for vast quantities of data.[25] It is the fast, continuous and bulk gathering of data that makes it very invasive and difficult to control whether the collection and processing of data is done in a legitimate manner. Moreover, if the data-gathering systems are not sufficiently transparent regarding the way in which they will process such data or cannot be held accountable, they may violate the applicable data protection laws.[26] Lastly, besides the privacy issues in relation to training data and the gathering thereof, the insights generated can have severe consequences for an individual's right to privacy as well.[27]

The right to privacy has also been perceived as a 'gateway right' through which a myriad of other rights could be affected.[28] This led to initiatives such as the Human Rights, Big Data and Technology Project. It explores and promotes the utilisation of the precautionary principle being introduced as part of the companies' duty of care. By doing so, it goes beyond the requirements of the UN Guiding Principles on Business and Human Rights.[29] This established connection with preserving privacy, and through it other human rights including the right to life or freedom of expression, becomes more essential in

---

24 Privacy International and Article 19, 'Privacy and Freedom of Expression In the Age of Artificial Intelligence', April 2018, p. 17, https://www.article19.org/wp-content/uploaSocial Sustainability Expert, Strategy & Innovation, amfori (PhD University of Leuven, LLM University of Essex).ds/2018/04/Privacy-and-Freedom-of-Expression-In-the-Age-of-Artificial-Intelligence-1.pdf.

25 F.A. Raso, et. al, 'Artificial Intelligence & Human Rights: Opportunities & Risks', Berkman Klein Center for Internet & Society Research Publication, September 2018, pp. 18–19.

26 Accessnow, 'Human Rights in the Age of Artificial Intelligence', p. 20. For a more detailed explanation on AI and data protection, see Chapter 8. See for more information: T. Gils et al., 'Artificiële intelligentie en gegevensbescherming: een verkennende gids', Kenniscentrum Data & Maatschappij, June 2020, https://data-en-maatschappij.ai/publicaties/ai-en-gegevensbescherming-een-verkennende-gids; European Parliamentary Research Service, 'The impact of the General Data Protection Regulation (GDPR) on artificial intelligence', 25 June 2020, 100 p., https://www.europarl.europa.eu/RegData/etudes/STUD/2020/641530/EPRS_STU(2020)641530_EN.pdf.

27 F.A. Raso, et. al, 'Artificial Intelligence & Human Rights: Opportunities & Risks', p. 19.

28 A. Shaheed and B. Greenacre, 'Binary Threat: How Governments' Cyber Laws and Practice Undermine Human Rights in the MENA Region', *Middle East Political Science*, 2021, https://pomeps.org/binary-threat-how-governments-cyber-laws-and-practice-undermine-human-rights-in-the-mena-region.

29 Submission by the Human Rights, Big Data and Technology Project ('HRBDT') and the Essex Business and Human Rights Project ('EBHR') to the UN Working Group on Business and Human Rights ('UNWG') for the consultation process to inform its 2018 Report to the UN General Assembly from 30 May 2018.

the light of AI technologies, which pushes even the boundaries of personal data scope established in *Breyer v. Germany*.[30]

2.3. RIGHT TO FREEDOM OF THOUGHT, CONSCIENCE AND RELIGION, EXPRESSION AND ASSEMBLY/ ASSOCIATION

9. The freedom of thought, conscience and religion[31] as well as expression[32] and assembly or association[33] are fundamental rights as well. The European Court of Human Rights (ECtHR) recognises the important role of the internet in enhancing the public's access to news and facilitating the distribution of information in general. The internet provides an unprecedented platform for the exercise of freedom of expression.[34] Nonetheless, there are AI applications that interfere with the manner in which individuals access and disseminate information online. Search engines and social media platforms use AI applications to determine and control what information is made available and which is taken down. Search algorithms used by Facebook, for instance, determine a user's newsfeed and thus how broadly and to whom content is shared. Google's search engine uses such algorithms to determine what information comes out on top.[35] As a result, search algorithms may potentially undermine media pluralism and a

---

30 Case C-582/14, *Breyer v. Bundesrepublik Deutschland*, ECLI:EU:C:2016:779. The case concerns the question whether dynamic IP addresses could be considered personal data through the prisms of what is considered an 'identifiable' natural person. The court ruled that dynamic IP addresses are personal data 'where an online media services provider has legal means that enable them to identify natural persons', thus affirming that when determining if a person is identifiable, it is necessary to take into account 'all the means likely reasonably to be used either by the controller or by any other person to identify the said person' (Recital 26 Directive 95/46/EC of the European Parliament and of the Council of 24 October 1995 on the protection of individuals with regard to the processing of personal data and on the free movement of such data, *OJ* L 281 and Recital 26 Regulation 2016/679 of the European Parliament and of the Council of 27 April 2016 on the protection of natural persons with regard to the processing of personal data and on the free movement of such data, and repealing Directive 95/46/EC, *OJ* L 119).

31 Article 9 ECHR, Article 18 UDHR and Article 18 ICCPR.

32 Article 10 ECHR, Article 19 UDHR and Article 19 ICCPR.

33 Article 11 ECHR, Article 20 UDHR and Articles 21 and 22 ICCPR.

34 European Court of Human Rights (ECtHR), *Cengiz and Others v. Turkey*, Judgement of 1 December 2015, paras. 49 and 52.

35 In this regard, the 'New Deal for Consumers' initiative aims at strengthening enforcement of EU consumer law in light of a growing risk of EU-wide infringements and at modernising EU consumer protection rules in view of market developments. Before a consumer is bound by a distance contract, the online marketplace has to provide the main parameters determining the ranking of offers presented to the consumer as result of his search query on the online marketplace (Directive (EU) 2019/2161 of the European Parliament and of the Council of 27 November 2019 amending Council Directive 93/13/EEC and Directives 98/6/EC, 2005/29/ EC and 2011/83/EU of the European Parliament and of the Council as regards the better enforcement and modernisation of Union consumer protection rules, *OJ* L 328). See also Chapter 17 on the impact of AI on consumer protection.

wide diversity of views. They may even contribute to the spreading of 'fake news' influencing an individual's thoughts and views.[36]

AI-enabled censorship results in the restriction of freedom of religion when it is used to identify and take down religious content. It also threatens the freedom of association when it results in the removal of online groups, pages and content that facilitate the gathering of individuals.[37] This is of particular importance in the current COVID-19 crisis in which most of the human interaction and gathering is happening online. This may equally apply to the public sector and governments that apply AI to limit the availability of content online. There are many reasons to remove online content ranging from national security[38] to defamation, copyright, privacy and security, and others.[39] Besides the difficult balancing exercise between providing access to information while assuring other legitimate aims such as the protection of national security, government officials also overstep their gatekeeper mandate and actively adopt AI applications to distort online information.[40]

10. Another specific AI application with potentially serious consequences is AI-powered surveillance. The combination of the invasive and invisible nature of many AI applications and their ability to track and identify behaviour increasingly results in self-censorship and censorship of legitimate speech, changed behaviour in the public domain and even in private communications.[41] Self-censorship occurs when individuals have the feeling that their movements are being followed or that they lack anonymity, and consequently change their behaviour. As a result,

---

36 See also A.A.I. Vranaki, 'Social Networking Site Regulation: Facebook, Online Behavioral Advertising and Data Protection Laws', Queen Mary School of Law Legal Studies Research Paper No. 221/2016, 2016, 35 p.; J. Hendler and A.M. Mulvehill, *Social Machines: The Coming Collision of Artificial Intelligence, Social Networking, and Humanity* (Apress, 2016), 174 p.; C. Krönke, 'Artificial Intelligence and Social Media', in T. Wischmeyer and T. Rademacher (eds.), *Regulating Artificial Intelligence* (Ebook Springer, 2019), pp. 145–173; T.M. Massaro, M. Toni and H. Norton, 'Siri-Ously? Free Speech Rights and Artificial Intelligence', *Northwestern University Law Review*, 2016, vol. 110, no. 5, pp. 1169–1194.

37 Accessnow, 'Human Rights in the Age of Artificial Intelligence', p. 23, https://www.accessnow.org/cms/assets/uploads/2018/11/AI-and-Human-Rights.pdf.

38 See also the Draft EU Regulation on preventing the dissemination of terrorist content online, European Parliament Briefing, 'Terrorist content online – Tackling online terrorist propaganda', March 2020, https://www.europarl.europa.eu/RegData/etudes/BRIE/2020/649326/EPRS_BRI(2020)649326_EN.pdf.

39 See also the Google Transparency Report providing more details on government requests to remove online content, https://transparencyreport.google.com/government-removals/overview?hl=en.

40 See in general on the use of AI by governments: F. Finck, 'Automated Decision-Making and Administrative Law', Max Planck Institute for Innovation & Competition Research Paper No. 19–10, 2020, 25 p.; N.A. Smuha, 'Artificiële Intelligentie bij de overheid – Opportuniteiten en uitdagingen vanuit ethisch-juridisch perspectief', *Vlaams Tijdschrift voor Overheidsmanagement*, 2019, no. 4, pp. 43–64. See also *supra* nos. 12–13.

41 Privacy International and Article 19, 'Privacy and Freedom of Expression In the Age of Artificial Intelligence', p. 8.

the increased application by both public and private actors of AI surveillance techniques such as video surveillance, facial recognition and behaviour analysis may have a potential chilling effect on the freedom of expression, thought, religion, assembly and association.[42] A recent example was the revealed result of a multi-stakeholder investigation led by Forbidden Stories[43] and supported by Amnesty International against the Israeli company NSO. It was discovered that a certain highly sophisticated spyware, named Pegasus, was developed and used against thousands of devices including those of at least 180 journalists. The spyware provided NSO's customers, among which state governments, complete access to the infected devices including access to the GPS and recording of audio and video. The latest version of the spyware could be installed with just a missed call through WhatsApp.[44] Some of the targeted journalists had been constantly monitored for more than a year. One of the victims, Khadija Ismayilova, testified about the trauma she experienced as well as about the guilt and the chilling effect this spyware had on her.[45] Even through Pegasus is not an AI system as such, it is evident that using AI as a spyware or relying on it in combination with the latter could have a major impact on a number of human rights but especially on the freedom of expression through its immanent connection with the right to privacy in a digital context as discussed in paragraph 8.

2.4. PROHIBITION OF DISCRIMINATION

11. The risk of bias and discrimination is often raised in the AI and human rights debate.[46] As already mentioned,[47] AI applications may intentionally or unintentionally contribute to the discrimination on the basis of race. Google's image recognition algorithms, for example, accidentally categorised two black persons in a photo as gorillas.[48] AI systems can also discriminate on a plethora

---

42 Privacy International and Article 19, 'Privacy and Freedom of Expression In the Age of Artificial Intelligence', p. 8.

43 P. Rueckert, 'Pegasus: The New Global Weapon for Silencing Journalists', *Forbidden Stories*, 18 July 2021, https://forbiddenstories.org/pegasus-the-new-global-weapon-for-silencing-journalists/.

44 B. Gurijala, 'What Is Pegasus? A Cybersecurity Expert Explains How the Spyware Invades Phones and What It Does When It Gets In,' NextGov, 9 August 2021.

45 P. Rueckert, 'Pegasus: The New Global Weapon for Silencing Journalists,' 2021.

46 Article 14 ECHR, Article 7 UDHR and Articles 3, 26 and 27 ICCPR. See in general: K. Saslow and P. Lorenz, 'Artificial Intelligence Needs Human Rights: How the Focus on Ethical AI Fails to Address Privacy, Discrimination and Other Concerns', SSRN, 30 September 30 2019, 25 p., https://ssrn.com/abstract=3589473 or http://dx.doi.org/10.2139/ssrn.3589473; I. Cofone, 'Algorithmic Discrimination Is an Information Problem', *Hastings Law Journal*, 2019, vol. 70, no. 6, pp. 1389–1444; L. Naudts, 'AI en algoritmische categorisatie: gelijkheid en non-discriminatie', in: J. De Bruyne and N. Bouteca (eds.), *Artificiële intelligentie en maatschappij* (Turnhout: Gompel & Svacina, 2021), forthcoming.

47 See *supra* no. 5.

48 J. Vincent, 'Google 'fixed' its racist algorithm by removing gorillas from its image-labeling tech', *The Verge*, 12 January 2018.

of different other grounds such as ethnicity, age, financial means, gender, sexual orientation, religion, belief or political opinion. The algorithm used by Amazon when scanning cover letters appeared to discriminate against women.[49] It is also important to consider the emergence of new discrimination criteria on the basis of group's characteristics,[50] some of which are not even codified as a basis of discrimination. An additional problem associated with protecting an individual's rights through group's interests is the lack of *locus standi* of such groups under human rights treaties in a number of cases.[51] Furthermore, bias in the datasets has already demonstrated significant potential for discrimination in healthcare, leading to potential infringement of the right to health and right to life.[52] On the other hand, certain AI applications hold the potential to remedy human biases that have always existed. At the same time, however, AI systems could also exacerbate human and societal biases if not developed correctly and with respect for human rights.[53] A notorious example is the so called 'Dutch child-care benefits scandal' that affected more than 20.000 people who were labelled as fraudsters by an algorithm. A significant amount of the affected individuals had an immigration background.[54] The manner in which AI applications can discriminate and the potential implications thereof are addressed more thoroughly in several case studies below.

2.5. RIGHT TO POLITICAL PARTICIPATION AND PROHIBITION ON PROPAGANDA

12. As already mentioned, AI applications have the potential to taint the creation and spreading of and access to information. This is a crucial aspect when considering the fair character of elections and political participation.[55] AI-powered surveillance can undermine political participation if it is used

49 J. Dastin, 'Amazon scraps secret AI recruiting tool that showed bias against women', *Reuters*, 10 October 2018.

50 L. Floridi, 'Group Privacy: A Defence and an Interpretation', in: L. Taylor, L. Floridi and B. van der Sloot, *Group Privacy: New Challenges of Data Technologies* (Cham: Springer, 2017), pp. 83–100.

51 B. van der Sloot, 'Do Groups Have a Right to Protect Their Group Interest in Privacy and Should They? Peeling the Onion of Rights and Interests Protected Under Article 8 ECHR' Interpretation', in: L. Taylor, L. Floridi and B. van der Sloot *Group Privacy: New Challenges of Data Technologies* (Cham: Springer, 2017), pp. 197–224.

52 C. Novorol, 'How AI can develop biases and discriminate against patients,' *Artificial Intelligence in Medicine*, 10 January 2018.

53 J. Silberg and J Manyika, 'Tackling bias in AI (and in humans)', McKinsey Global Institute, June 2019, p. 1, https://www.mckinsey.com/~/media/mckinsey/featured%20insights/artificial%20intelligence/tackling%20bias%20in%20artificial%20intelligence%20and%20in%20humans/mgi-tackling-bias-in-ai-june-2019.pdf.

54 B. ten Seldam and A. Brenninkmeijer, 'The Dutch benefits scandal: a cautionary tale for algorithmic enforcement', 30 April 2021, https://eulawenforcement.com/?p=7941.

55 See Article 25 ICCPR.

to identify, discourage and limit certain groups in society from voting or to influence their voting behaviour. For example, the 2016 US presidential elections' outcome demonstrated how social media algorithms can be applied to enhance the distribution of incorrect information, thereby eventually influencing the voting behaviour. Some media reports even claim that Russian 'trolls' impacted the outcome of the US presidential elections by spreading pro-Trump and anti-Clinton messages.[56] If not addressed adequately, this could undermine the trust of voters in the legitimacy of elections and democratic political systems in the long-term. This in turn may jeopardise the right to effective political participation.[57]

13. AI applications can also be used to intentionally spread disinformation to incite discrimination, hostility, violence or even armed conflicts.[58] Some governments are increasingly making use of 'troll armies' to influence the spreading of information on the internet for political ends. In the recent conflict between Russia and Ukraine, Russian 'trolls' persistently spread disinformation vis-à-vis the ongoing war in Ukraine targeting not only the Russian web space, but countries all over the world with particular efforts towards states such as Bulgaria and Romania that are characterised by polarised opinions and low media culture. It is also alleged that Narendra Modi, the current Prime Minister of India, deployed 'social media volunteers' to control messages during the 2014 elections. This resulted in the spreading of unfavourable messages, which turned into violent hate speech against opponents of the political party of Narendra Modi.[59] Again, these practices need to be monitored and handled with care to make sure that AI applications do not increasingly contribute to the advocacy of hate, potentially violating the prohibition on propaganda.[60] Furthermore, it is important to consider that spreading disinformation on a large scale, which AI systems are able to do, could have a chilling effect on individuals and especially

56 C. Timberg, 'Russian propaganda effort helped spread 'fake news' during election, experts say', *Washington Post*, 24 November 2016; PropOrNot, *Black Friday Report: On Russian Propaganda Network Mapping*', 26 November 2016, 32 p.

57 Accessnow, 'Human Rights in the Age of Artificial Intelligence', p. 25. Also see: K.M. Manheim and L. Kaplan, 'Artificial Intelligence: Risks to Privacy and Democracy', *Yale Journal of Law & Technology*, 2019, vol. 21, pp. 106–188.

58 See Article 20 ICCPR.

59 M. Safi, 'India's ruling party ordered online abuse of opponents, claims book', *The Guardian*, 27 December 2016, https://www.theguardian.com/world/2016/dec/27/india-bjp-party-ordering-online-abuse-opponents-actors-modi-claims-book; M. White, 'How do you solve a problem like troll armies?', Accessnow, 21 April 2017, https://www.accessnow.org/solve-problem-like-troll-armies/.

60 Also see: K. Schoors, 'AI en digitale dictatuur', in J. De Bruyne and N. Bouteca (eds.), *Artificiële intelligentie en maatschappij* (Turnhout: Gompel & Svacina, 2021), forthcoming; European Parliamentary Research Service, 'Polarisation and the use of technology in political campaigns and communication', March 2019, 60 p.

on journalists,[61] violating both the freedom of expression and the principle of social justice.

2.6. RIGHT TO WORK AND TO AN ADEQUATE STANDARD OF LIVING

14. The right to work[62] and to an adequate standard of living[63] are relevant as well in an AI context.[64] AI, robotics and other forms of smart automation have the potential to bring great economic benefits, contributing up to $15 trillion to global GDP by 2030. This will generate the demand for additional jobs. However, there are also concerns that this evolution could displace existing jobs.[65] Today, 50% of work activities are technically automatable by adapting demonstrated technologies. Six out of ten jobs have more than 30% of activities that are technically automatable.[66] Fast Retailing – the parent company of Uniqlo – already replaced 90% of its workers by robots. It is even coming closer to a full automation of its flagship warehouse in Tokyo by creating a robot that is able to fold and box clothing.[67] Many professions are likely to disappear in the long term. In this regard, Professor Yuval Harari argues that AI will produce a 'useless class' of people that have no economic value to offer society.[68] A study conducted by PwC emphasised that the impact of automation on the

61 A. Baroni, L. d'Haenens and W. Han Lo, 'Protecting journalists from harassment. Comparing existing protection mechanisms and the effects on democracy', in: J. Trappel and T. Tomaz, *Success and failure in news media performance: Comparative analysis in the Media for Democracy Monitor 2021*, Gothenburg, Nordicom, University of Gothenburg, 2022, p. 59.

62 Article 23 UDHR and Articles 6 and 7 of the International Covenant for Economic, Social and Cultural Rights (ICESCR).

63 Articles 25 of the UDHR and Article 11 of the ICESCR. For a more detailed explanation on the specific topic of labour, social security and AI, see Chapters 11 and 12.

64 See for more information: M. Webb, 'The Impact of Artificial Intelligence on the Labor Market', SSRN,15 November 2019, Stanford University – Department of Economics, https://papers.ssrn.com/sol3/papers.cfm?abstract_id=3482150; C.B. Frey and M.A. Osborne, 'The future of employment: How susceptible are jobs to computerisation?', *Technological Forecasting and Social Change*, 2017, no.114, pp. 254–280; D. Acemoglu and P. Restrepo, 'Robots and Jobs: Evidence from US Labor Markets', MIT Department of Economics Working Paper No. 17-04, 2017, 88 p.

65 PWC, 'Sizing the prize – What's the real value of AI for your business and how can you capitalize?', 2017, https://www.pwc.com/gx/en/issues/analytics/assets/pwc-ai-analysis-sizing-the-prize-report.pdf.

66 C. Pissarides, 'Over half of the world's jobs are replaceable by a robot – is yours?', World Economic Forum, 16 December 2019, https://www.weforum.org/agenda/2019/12/automation-4ir-technology-robot-work-career/.

67 M. Hanbury, 'Uniqlo's robots have already replaced 90% of its human workers at its flagship warehouse, now they've cracked the difficult task of folding t-shirts', *Business Insider*, 24 December 2019, https://www.businessinsider.com/uniqlos-warehouse-robots-on-track-to-replace-human-workers-2019-12?r=US&IR=T.

68 Y.N. Harari, *Homo Deus. A Brief History of Tomorrow* (London: Random House, 2016),528 p. Also see: Y.N. Harari, *21 Lessons for the 21st Century* (New York: Random House, 2018), 432 p.

right to work should not be underestimated. By mid-2030s, 44% of jobs are at potential risk of replacement by automation. Financial services jobs could be relatively vulnerable to automation in the short term, while transport jobs are more vulnerable to automation in the long term. Especially female workers would be more affected by automation over the next decade. Male workers by contrast would be more at risk in the long term. In the short term, the impact of automation may be low for workers regardless of their educational background. In the long run, persons with lower education levels could be more vulnerable to being replaced by machines.[69]

15. The fear of humans to be replaced by robots persists because it is rooted in uncertainty regarding the creation of new jobs.[70] It is predicted that between 2020 and 2022 more than six million opportunities will be created from professions emerging from automation and other technological applications.[71] The true challenge will thus lie in re-skilling people to ensure that they will be able to work in these newly created positions, which are often very different from their current work environments. In this regard, AI4Belgium proposes a 'new learning deal' which would consist of a universal program to provide adults with the required digital skills.[72]

As the COVID-19 crisis shows, AI systems can also be deployed to the benefit of employees and the labour market in general, for instance by safeguarding productivity. AI systems based on deep learning, image classification and object recognition are used for prediction (e.g., calculating a person's probability of infection) and diagnosis (e.g., via pattern recognition using data related to symptoms).[73] However, some AI technologies that are predominantly designed for workers'/employees' benefits, for instance wearables that are supposed to promote healthy lifestyle through gamification of movement and improve productivity, possess risks to privacy and could have the opposite effect.[74] In any case, work as we know it today will be reshaped by AI systems. Future

69 PwC, 'Will robots really steal our jobs? An international analysis of the potential long term impact of automation'. See for more information: I. Tuomo et al., 'The Impact of Artificial Intelligence on Learning, Teaching, and Education', 2018, Publications Office of the European Union, https://publications.jrc.ec.europa.eu/repository/bitstream/JRC113226/jrc113226_jrcb4_the_impact_of_artificial_intelligence_on_learning_final_2.pdf.

70 Pissarides, 'Over half of the world's jobs are replaceable by a robot – is yours?'.

71 World Economic Forum, 'Jobs of Tomorrow – Mapping Opportunity in the New Economy', January 2020, www3.weforum.org/docs/WEF_Jobs_of_Tomorrow_2020.pdf.

72 See: AI4Belgium, 'Report', https://www.ai4belgium.be/wp-content/uploads/2019/04/rapport_nl.pdf. Also see: J. Weytjens and S. Baert, 'AI en de arbeidsmarkt', in J. De Bruyne and N. Bouteca (eds.), *Artificiële intelligentie en maatschappij* (Turnhout: Gompel & Svacina, 2021), forthcoming.

73 OECD, 'Using Artificial Intelligence to Help Combat COVID-19', 23 April 2020, https://read.oecd-ilibrary.org/view/?ref=130_130771-3jtyra9uoh&title=Using-artificial-intelligence-to-help-combat-COVID-19.

74 P.V. Moore et al., 'Data subjects, digital surveillance, AI and the future of work', Study for the European Parliament, Panel for the Future of Science and Technology, 2020.

collaboration opportunities between humans and machines will continue to unfold. Therefore, these developments and evolutions need to be closely monitored to ensure that they take a turn for the better and not for the worse.

2.7. RIGHT TO HEALTH

16. Healthcare is an area in which AI applications could have major benefits.[75] By providing insights into an individual's day-to-day patterns, AI applications may encourage healthier behaviour and support individuals to stay healthy.[76] AI is also used to detect diseases and to diagnose more accurately and timely. For instance, AI systems can review and translate mammograms 30 times faster than humans with 99% accuracy. This minimises the need for unnecessary biopsies.[77] IBM's Watson for Health is supporting healthcare institutions via cognitive technology to gather, connect and unlock vast amounts of health data. It reviews far more medical information than human beings (e.g., medical journals, symptoms and case studies), and does so exponentially faster. As its decisions are all evidence-based and free from potential cognitive bias or overconfidence, it enables more timely diagnosis while reducing misdiagnosis.[78] AI applications can also support hospitals in their disease management and care plan installation, but also patients in managing and complying with their treatment programs. Robots can be deployed for various applications ranging from simple laboratory robots to highly complex surgical robots that support surgeons. Some of them can even execute operations on their own.[79] A more recent AI application in healthcare relates to drug research and discovery. As the

---

75 Article 12 ICESCR. For a more detailed explanation on the specific topic of health and AI, see Chapter 18.

76 PwC, 'What doctor? Why AI and robotics will define New Health', June 2017, pp. 4–5, https://www.pwc.com/gx/en/industries/healthcare/publications/ai-robotics-new-health/ai-robotics-new-health.pdf. See for more information: A. Bohr and K. Memarzadeh, *Artificial Intelligence in Healthcare* (Cambridge: Academic Press, 2020), 378 p.; T. Davenport and R. Kalakota, 'The potential for artificial intelligence in healthcare', *Future healthcare journal*, 2019, no. 2, pp. 94–98.

77 S. Griffiths, 'This AI software can tell if you're at risk from cancer before symptoms appear', 26 August 2016, https://www.wired.co.uk/article/cancer-risk-ai-mammograms (last accessed 31 October 2020).

78 More information on IBM Watsom Health: https://www.ibm.com/watson/uk-en/health/#:~:text=IBM%20Watson%20Health%20applies%20data,efficiencies%2C%20and%20improve%20population%20health.; PwC, 'What doctor? Why AI and robotics will define New Health', p. 6.

79 PwC, 'What doctor? Why AI and robotics will define New Health', pp. 9–10. See more in general: E. Fosch-Villaronga, *Robots, Healthcare, and the Law: Regulating Automation in Personal Care* (London: Routledge, 2019), 256 p.

development of new drugs is often a long and costly process,[80] AI can contribute to the streamlining of drug discovery and drug repurposing processes.[81]

Although many AI applications can positively contribute to the realisation of the right to health, some caution is warranted as well. AI applications may potentially result in discrimination or may be developed and used for other goals than a patient's well-being (e.g., cost-reduction). AI applications may be programmed in such a manner that the different treatment recommendations are made dependent on the insurance status of patients or on their income. This could eventually result in (further) limiting the access to healthcare for population groups that may already be marginalised.[82] Moreover, medical staff should not solely rely on AI applications. Instead, AI systems in healthcare should (still) be combined with human judgement (cf. *human oversight*). For certain medical conditions such as extreme premature birth or severe brain injuries, machine learning-based systems may for instance recommend not to treat a patient as these conditions are almost always fatal. Yet, there may be examples where treatment can be effective.[83] We also need to realise that, although AI systems are continuously learning and improving themselves, they are still prone to error. Therefore, moving forward it will be necessary to consider to what extent certain health processes should be automated. It will also be required to determine how and when human intervention will remain necessary.[84] In order for this to be possible, however, there is a serious need for a proper debate on the notion of explainability,[85] between others, which may greatly differ from one person to another. For example, the reasoning behind a certain diagnose proposed by an AI tool may be explainable for a computer scientist working in the field of machine learning but it may not be explainable for the doctor who will eventually need to communicate it to the patient, and potentially exercise human oversight.

---

80 According to the California Biomedial Research Association, it takes an average of 12 years for a drug development process. On average it will cost a company $ 359 million to develop a new drug.

81 PwC, 'What doctor? Why AI and robotics will define New Health', pp. 13–14; O. Gurgula, 'AI-Assisted Inventions in the Field of Drug Discovery: Readjusting the Inventive Step Analysis', *International Journal of Social Science and Public Policy*, 2020 (forthcoming), https://papers.ssrn.com/sol3/papers.cfm?abstract_id=3683127.

82 Accessnow, 'Human Rights in the Age of Artificial Intelligence', p. 27.

83 P. Hannon, 'Researchers say use of artificial intelligence in medicine raises ethical questions', *Stanford Medicine News Center*, 14 March 2018, https://med.stanford.edu/news/all-news/2018/03/researchers-say-use-of-ai-in-medicine-raises-ethical-questions.html (last accessed 31 October 2020).

84 Accessnow, 'Human Rights in the Age of Artificial Intelligence', p. 27. Also see: A. van Wynsberghe, *Healthcare Robots: Ethics, Design and Implementation* (London: Routledge, 2016), 166 p.

85 M. Graziani, L. Dutkiewicz, D. Calvaresi et al., 'A global taxonomy of interpretable AI: unifying the terminology for the technical and social sciences', *Artificial Intelligence Review*, 2022, https://link.springer.com/content/pdf/10.1007/s10462-022-10256-8.pdf.

2.8. RIGHT TO EDUCATION

17. In addition to what has already been mentioned, AI applications could also influence the right to education.[86] It has been reported that US universities already apply algorithmic systems to define their admission process. These systems are often tailor-made to the needs and preferences of universities. There is thus a risk that they can intentionally or unintentionally lead to discrimination. For example, the models of these algorithmic systems are developed and trained inter alia by data of previously admitted students. Knowing that many of the top US universities have traditionally been attended by white males, it is apparent that algorithmic systems using those data sets risk repeating past trends, hinder the access to education for women and men with diverse ethnic and racial backgrounds.[87]

18. At the same time, however, the introduction of AI also creates opportunities to transform education for the better. First, AI applications can enhance education processes in the classroom, but also at a governance level. AI can accelerate personalised learning allowing students to master subjects at their own pace.[88] This was already demonstrated in the *Teach to One* math programs, which provide instructions that are adapted to learners' abilities by assessing their skill level on a daily basis and using algorithms to distribute instructions based on the students' skill level.[89] AI applications can also increasingly be relied upon to support students with special needs.[90] Wearables using AI can support visually impaired students with reading and recognising faces. Technologies such as augmented and virtual reality (AR/VR) also contribute to the engagement of students with (mental) health impairments.[91] At a governance level, predictive analysis enables schools to use existing data to identify potential dropout profiles and intervene in a preventative manner, thereby reducing the overall dropout rates. AI applications also allow educational institutions to reorganise standardised assessments in such a manner that they go beyond mere knowledge content and instead also include more complex skill sets (e.g.,

---

86 Article 13 ICESCR. See for a more thorough analysis: B. Berendt et al., 'AI in education: learner choice and fundamental rights', *Learning, Media and Technology*, 2020, vol. 45, no. 3, pp. 312–324; A. Flogie and B. Aberšek, *The Impact of Innovative ICT Education and AI on the Pedagogical Paradigm* (Newcastle upon Tyne: Cambridge Scholars Publishing, 2019), 171 p.

87 Accessnow, 'Human Rights in the Age of Artificial Intelligence', p. 28.

88 OECD Directorate for Education and Skills, 'Trustworthy artificial intelligence (AI) in education: promises and challenges', 6 April 2020, pp. 7–8, www.oecd.org/officialdocuments/publicdisplaydocumentpdf/?cote=EDU/WKP(2020)6&docLanguage=En. See also I. Tuomi, 'The Impact of Artificial Intelligence on Learning, Teaching, and Education', November 2018, p. 29, https://publications.jrc.ec.europa.eu/repository/bitstream/JRC113226/jrc113226_jrcb4_the_impact_of_artificial_intelligence_on_learning_final_2.pdf.

89 For more information: https://teachtoone.org/.

90 Tuomi, 'The Impact of Artificial Intelligence on Learning, Teaching, and Education', p. 27.

91 OECD Directorate for Education and Skills, 'Trustworthy artificial intelligence (AI) in education: promises and challenges', pp. 8–9.

problem solving, collaboration, social and emotional skills).[92] Second, current education programs will have to include and offer new skills that are required in increasingly automated societies.[93] Skills that are less easy to automate will become very important. There may be more need for higher cognitive skills such as creativity and critical thinking. As AI applications are increasingly becoming part of our daily life, a good understanding of AI and its opportunities and challenges needs to be embedded in our education programs.[94] It has also been suggested that due to the special nature of education as a societal function and the vulnerability of subjects, being predominantly children, a solid human rights preserving approach should be adopted as a first step towards mass deployment of AI technologies in education.[95]

2.9. THE PROTECTION OF INTELLECTUAL PROPERTY

19. As a new technology, AI and its applications interact with the protection of intellectual property (IP) in various manners.[96] The overlap between AI and IP can be divided in three main categories. First, AI is a technology that can support the management of IP rights. As such AI is increasingly adopted in the administration of IP protection applications. For example, AI systems are used by WIPO Translate and WIPO Brand Image Search for automated translation and image recognition. Other AI applications are (currently) being discussed and considered.[97] Second, IP provides a legal system that protects the development of AI applications contributing to the encouragement of innovation and creativity in the AI arena. Third, IP rights can also undermine the need for more transparency and accountability regarding AI systems and programs.[98]

---

92 *Ibid.*, pp. 9–11.

93 See also *infra* nos. 14–15.

94 OECD Directorate for Education and Skills, 'Trustworthy artificial intelligence (AI) in education: promises and challenges', pp. 11–12. See in this regard also: https://www.aiopschool.be/. See general on data literacy: A. Wolff et al., 'Creating an Understanding of Data Literacy for a Data-driven Society', *The Journal of Community Informatics*, 2016, no.3, pp. 9–26; E.S. Deahl, *Better the data you know: Developing youth Data Literacy in schools and informal learning environments* (Yale: Yale University Press, 2014), 119 p.

95 B. Berendt, A. Littlejohn and M. Blakemore, 'AI in education: learner choice and fundamental rights', *Learning, Media and Technology*, 2020, vol. 45, no. 3, pp. 312–324.

96 Article 27 UDHR and Article 15 ICESCR. Also see Chapter 9 of this book.

97 See WIPO, 'Conversation on Intellectual Property (IP) and Artificial Intelligence (AI): Revised Issues Paper on Intellectual Property Policy and Artificial Intelligence', 21 May 2020, https://www.wipo.int/edocs/mdocs/mdocs/en/wipo_ip_ai_2_ge_20/wipo_ip_ai_2_ge_20_1_rev.pdf.

98 C. Castets-Renard, 'The Intersection between AI and IP: Conflict or Complementarity?', *International Review of Intellectual Property and Competition Law,* 2020, vol. 51, pp. 141–143; F. Vehar and T. Gils, 'I'm sorry AI, I'm afraid you can't be an author (for now)', *Journal of Intellectual Property Law & Practice*, 2020, vol. 15, no. 9, pp. 718–726; F. Gotzen and M.-C. Janssens, 'Kunstmatige Kunst. Bedenkingen Bij de Toepassing van Het Auteursrecht Op Artificiële Intelligentie', *AM*, 2018–2019, pp. 335–341.

2.10. THE RIGHT TO A CLEAN, HEALTHY AND SUSTAINABLE ENVIRONMENT

20. On 8 October 2021, the UN Human Rights Council adopted Resolution 48/13 which internationally recognised the human right to a clean, healthy and sustainable environment. Additionally, Resolution 48/14 appointed a Special Rapporteur on the human rights impact of climate change. These international actions correspond with the developments at the EU level where the adoption of the 'Green Deal'[99] mapped the EU's twin transitions to a green and digital economy. These two transitions are not parallel but rather intertwined due to the evident effect of technologies and in particular AI to the environment,[100] and consequently the human right to a clean, healthy and sustainable environment.

21. On the positive side, AI alone and in combination with other technologies such as the Internet of Things have the potential to collect and analyse tremendous amounts of data. This allows us to gather greater insights on the environmental impacts and design strategies to mitigate their effect on human rights or better respond to adversarial events such as natural disasters.[101] Furthermore, AI is able to optimise current processes and supply chains,[102] making them energy efficient, preventing waste,[103] or improving the planning of transport systems.[104] On the negative side, however, AI itself is a very energy consuming technology through its whole life cycle. It also requires the necessary infrastructure such as data centres, which leads to an increase in the use of raw materials and energy.[105] Moreover, AI systems controlling critical infrastructure such as power grids increase the attack surface leading to potential cyber-attacks causing actual physical damage to the environment, for example a fire. The balance between the positive and negative impact of AI on the environment and subsequently to the human right to a clean, healthy and sustainable environment is yet to be examined in depth. Nevertheless, there has been support for concrete

---

99 Communication from the Commission to the European Parliament the European Council, the Council, the European Economic and Social Committee and the Committee of the Regions, 'The European Green Deal', COM(2019) 640 final, 11 December 2019.

100 P.H. Gailhofer et al., 'The role of Artificial Intelligence in the European Green Deal Study', European Parliament, 2021.

101 UNESCO, First draft of the recommendation on the ethics of artificial intelligence, SHS/BIO/AHEGAI/2020/4 REV.2, 2020.

102 B. Gesing et al., 'Artificial intelligence in logistics – a collaborative report by DHL and IBM on implications and use cases for the logistics industry', DHL Customer Solutions & Innovation, 2018.

103 I. Seifert et al., 'Potential of Artificial Intelligence in Germany's Producing Sector', 2018, https://www.digitaletechnologien.de/DT/Redaktion/DE/Downloads/Publikation/PAiCE_AI_Study.pdf?__blob=publicationFile&v=5.

104 L. Kaack et al., 'Truck traffic monitoring with satellite images', *Deep AI*, 2019, https://arxiv.org/abs/1907.07660.

105 See *supra* fn. 93.

actions to fill this gap in the existing state of the art, such as conducting a mandatory environmental impact assessment for AI technologies.[106]

3. THE RECURRING ISSUE: DISCRIMINATION AND BIAS

22. The overview given in the previous part indicated which risks or opportunities AI applications may pose to human rights. The use of AI systems can affect the values on which the EU is founded and lead to breaches of fundamental rights including the rights to freedom of expression, freedom of assembly, human dignity, protection of personal data and private life and the right to an effective judicial remedy and a fair trial. The impact on human rights caused by AI applications such as facial recognition and risk-assessment tools can also result in intentional or unintentional discrimination based on sex, racial or ethnic origin, religion or belief, disability, age or sexual orientation.[107] The potential risk of discrimination and bias is a recurring issue in several policy documents and is explicitly addressed in the EU White Paper on AI as well as in the Ethics Guidelines on Trustworthy AI issued by the High Level Expert Group on AI (AI HLEG). The latter stipulate that inclusion and diversity throughout the entire AI system's life cycle should be ensured to achieve trustworthy AI. Data sets used by AI systems (both for training and operation) may suffer from the inclusion of inadvertent historic bias, incompleteness and bad governance models. The continuation of such biases could lead to unintended (in)direct prejudice and discrimination against certain groups or people. This could potentially exacerbate prejudice and marginalisation.[108] The following paragraphs will, therefore, take discrimination in an AI-context as a case-study.[109]

3.1. DISCRIMINATION CAUSED BY AI SYSTEMS

23. To better understand how the development of AI systems can contribute to discrimination, Martin Ebers makes a distinction between discrimination at the

---

106 D. Rejeski, 'When Software Rules: Rule of Law in the Age of Artificial Intelligence,' 2018.

107 European Commission, 'White Paper On Artificial Intelligence – A European approach to excellence and trust', 19 February 2020, COM(2020) 65 final, p. 11.

108 High-Level Expert Group on Artificial Intelligence – European Commission, 'Ethics Guidelines for Trustworthy AI', 8 April 2019, p. 18, https://ec.europa.eu/digital-single-market/en/news/ethics-guidelines-trustworthy-ai.

109 See more thoroughly: R. Xenidis and L. Senden, 'EU non-discrimination law in the era of artificial intelligence: Mapping the challenges of algorithmic discrimination', in U. Bernitz et al. (eds.), *General Principles of EU law and the EU Digital Order* (Alphen aan den Rijn: Kluwer Law International, 2020), pp. 151–182.

process level and at the classification level.[110] I will illustrate the importance of each level with additional examples where necessary.

3.1.1. *Discrimination at the Process Level*

24. The process level refers to the different steps an AI system has gone through to make an autonomous decision. This usually begins with the data-acquisition phase, followed by data pre-processing, the selection of features, the training and application of the AI model and the post-processing phase. In this last stage, steps are taken to improve and revise the output of the model.[111] Discrimination at this process level occurs when the algorithmic model is fed with biased training data. In this regard, two forms of bias with training data can occur.[112]

25. On the one hand, errors in data collection may result in inaccurate depictions of reality due to improper measurement methodologies. This is especially the case when conclusions are deducted from incorrect or nonrepresentative data. This type of bias can be remedied by cleaning the data or improving the data-collection process.[113]

Bias can, on the other hand, also occur when the underlying process relies on information that is inextricably linked to structural discrimination, exhibiting long-standing inequality. This type of bias is more problematic.[114] AI applications continuously learn from data. When designing an image-recognition algorithm that can recognise dogs, the algorithm needs to learn to comprehend a dog's appearance. As a result, a large amount of dog photos will be shown to train the algorithm. The algorithm will subsequently start to establish relationships and identify patterns in dog pictures, thereby grasping a dog's image. The data that is used to train AI applications to recognise and consequently act upon is defined as 'training data'. As the input determines the output, the quality and quantity of training data is crucial to create adequate AI applications. If the 'training data' is

---

110 M. Ebers, 'Regulating AI and Robotics: Ethical and Legal Challenges', in M. Ebers and S. Navas (eds.), Algorithms and Law (Cambridge: Cambridge University Press, 2020), pp. 76–78 referring to S. Barocas and A.D. Selbst, 'Big Data's Disparate Impact', *California Law Review*, 2016, vol. 104, p. 680; J.A. Kroll et al., 'Accountable Algorithms', *University of Pennsylvania Law Review*, 2016, vol. 165, p. 680 and further. Also see: F.Z. Borgesius, 'Discrimination, artificial intelligence, and algorithmic decision-making', Council of Europe, 2018, pp. 10–14, https://rm.coe.int/discrimination-artificial-intelligence-and-algorithmic-decision-making/1680925d73.

111 Ebers, 'Regulating AI and Robotics: Ethical and Legal Challenges', p. 49. Also see Chapter 1 for an extensive discussion.

112 *Ibid.*, p. 77.

113 *Ibid.*

114 *Ibid.*

somehow tainted, this could have far-reaching consequences and potentially lead to discrimination. First, AI applications will be trained on biased data. Second, AI applications will learn from a biased sample and replicate that bias or even potentially scale it.[115]

26. Several case studies demonstrate how (problematic) training data in AI applications can contribute to bias and discrimination. The algorithm that was used by Amazon to scan cover letters appeared to discriminate against women is an example. Amazon's computer models were trained to examine applicants by observing patterns in resumes submitted to the company over a 10-year period. Most of these resumes came from men. The algorithm penalised resumes that included the word 'women' and downgraded graduates of two all-women's colleges.[116] Another example occurred when a university in the UK relied on a computer program to process student applications. The training data was based on previous admissions disfavouring eligible women and applications from racial minorities. This biased training data was eventually included in the computer program and continued to discriminate against qualified women and members of racial minorities. In this specific case, it was thus not a new bias but an extension of existing biased training data (cf. historical bias).[117] A 2012 FBI-co-authored study reviewed three commercial algorithms on mug shots.[118] All three algorithms were consistently 5 to 10% less accurate on African Americans. This was caused by underrepresentation in the training data. As a result, African Americans were less likely to be identified correctly in comparison to other racial groups. The same issues were identified for females when compared to males and for younger persons compared to older persons.[119] Depending on how the AI system is configured, this could result in a higher probability of misidentification and investigation of a wrong person if that person is African American, female or of a young age.[120]

27. Proper training data is thus crucial for the functioning of AI applications. The way in which data collection is generated has far-reaching consequences

[115] Borgesius, 'Discrimination, artificial intelligence, and algorithmic decision-making', p. 11. Also see Chapter 1 for more information.

[116] J. Dastin, 'Amazon scraps secret AI recruiting tool that showed bias against women', *Reuters*, 10 October 2018.

[117] Barocas and Selbst, 'Big Data's Disparate Impact', pp. 681–684.

[118] B.F. Klare et al., 'Face Recognition Performance: Role of Demographic Information', *IEEE Transactions on Information Forensics and Security*, 2012, vol. 7, no. 6, p. 1789, https://www.mitre.org/sites/default/files/pdf/11_4962.pdf.

[119] *Ibid.*, pp. 1797–1798.

[120] C. Garvie, A.M. Bedoya and J. Frankle, 'The Perpetual Line-Up: Unregulated Police Face Recognition in America', Georgetown Law Center on Privacy & Technology, 18 October 2016, https://www.perpetuallineup.org/.

for the output of AI applications. In other words, if the sampling procedure is biased, discrimination may be the result. When looking at today's society, data is not necessarily collected and processed in the same manner for all categories of persons. In general, there may be less available data of minorities. There is also a risk that existing data may be (more) tainted. Several reasons have been acknowledged explaining why there is a lack of or tainted information of certain minorities (e.g., less access to technology or more limited in creating data). As a result, some groups of people may become less valuable data subjects, eventually resulting in underrepresentation. If the training data is incorrect, partial or nonrepresentative, AI applications may thus perpetuate, continue and enforce a discriminatory practice in the future.[121]

At the same time, focusing on one specific group when gathering data could also lead to discrimination. For example, when generating data relating to crime, it is possible that the police arrests more people with an immigrant background or focuses more on specific 'problematic' neighbourhoods. Such practices may result in police records that systematically overrepresent those groups and neighbourhoods. If a system is subsequently trained by using this biased data, it will draw the conclusion that immigrants are more likely to commit crime.[122] The overrepresentation could also lead to other undesired consequences such as police focusing on a specific group that is identified as committing more crime or on an area as a crime hotspot leading to even more controls.[123]

3.1.2. Discrimination at the Classification Level

28. Discrimination can also occur at the classification level. This level provides information regarding the attributes (e.g., gender, race, age, sexual orientation or salary) that are used in the model and the weight attributed to each of them.[124] AI applications can be used to find solutions to complex issues. However, capturing every angle of a problem can be very demanding. As AI applications attempt to predict outcomes automatically, the world as such needs to be 'simplified' allowing it to be captured in data (points).[125] Therefore, developers of AI systems decide to simplify the scenario and eliminate dimensions by selecting those (relevant) features they think will represent the issue. This process is called 'feature selection' and means that

121 Ebers, 'Regulating AI and Robotics: Ethical and Legal Challenges', p. 77.

122 K. Lum and W. Isaac, 'To predict and serve?', *Significance*, 2016, vol. 13, no. 5, p. 15.

123 Borgesius, 'Discrimination, artificial intelligence, and algorithmic decision-making', pp. 11–12.

124 Ebers, 'Regulating AI and Robotics: Ethical and Legal Challenges', p. 49.

125 Barocas and Selbst, 'Big Data's Disparate Impact', p. 688.

relevant data is identified and more irrelevant data removed.[126] When selecting features, bias can occur towards certain groups. Employers may, for example, give prevalence to employees that studied at prestigious universities. Admission to those universities might be difficult for certain racial groups or women. As a result, discrimination can result from the features selection process that AI applications adopt for predicting outcomes.[127]

29. Discrimination at the classification level can also be caused by relying on factors that happen to serve as proxies for protected characteristics.[128] AI systems need training data that may include sensitive personal data such as race, ethnicity and political preference. The applicable legislation – e.g., the GDPR – imposes special procedures to process such information as it can affect human rights.[129] As a response, developers may decide to remove sensitive personal data from the training data, thereby striving for 'fairness through unawareness'.[130] However, 'redundant encodings' might undermine this attempt. These entail the inclusion of one variable that can be a proxy for another variable, which you actually do not want to include in a model.[131]

30. This can be illustrated with a simple example. A bank relies on an AI system to predict which loan applicants will have problems repaying the loan. The model is trained on data covering the last twenty years based on a certain postal code. This data does not contain information about protected characteristics such as skin colour, race or gender. The model may learn that people from a certain postcode had a higher chance to default on their loans and subsequently use that correlation to predict failure to pay. In other words, the system relies on a rather neutral criterion (postcode) to predict defaulting on loans. Suppose now that the postcode correlates with racial origin (i.e., people of a certain origin live in that particular postcode). If the bank acted on the basis of this prediction and denied loans to the people in that postcode, the practice would thus harm people from a certain racial origin.[132]

---

126 V. Kumar and S. Minz,'Feature Selection: A literature Review', *Smart Computing Review*, 2014, vol. 3, no. 2, pp. 214–229.

127 Borgesius, 'Discrimination, artificial intelligence, and algorithmic decision-making', p. 12 with further references.

128 Ebers, 'Regulating AI and Robotics: Ethical and Legal Challenges', p. 78; Barocas and Selbst, 'Big Data's Disparate Impact', p. 692; Borgesius, 'Discrimination, artificial intelligence, and algorithmic decision-making', p. 13 with further references.

129 See Chapter 8 for more information.

130 M. Hardt, 'Equality of Opportunity in Machine Learning', *Google AI Blog*, 7 October 2016, https://ai.googleblog.com/2016/10/equality-of-opportunity-in-machine.html.

131 B. Purcell, 'The Ethics Of AI: How To Avoid Harmful Bias And Discrimination Build Machine Learning Models That Are Fundamentally Sound, Assessable, Inclusive, And Reversible', IBM, 27 February 2018, https://www.ibm.com/downloads/cas/6ZYRPXRJ.

132 As discussed in Borgesius, 'Discrimination, artificial intelligence, and algorithmic decision-making', p. 13.

3.2. DISCRIMINATION GROUNDS

3.2.1. Discrimination Based on Ethnicity: Uyghur Muslim in China

31. Uyghurs are a minority residing in China that speak their own language, Uyghur, and practice their own religion, the Sunni Islam. In China, they are regarded as an ethno-nationalist threat. As a consequence, they are heavily discriminated against. They are the victim of political indoctrination, arbitrary mass detention, religious oppression and restrictions on movement. Human Rights Watch estimates that approximately one million Uyghurs are held captive in so-called political education camps.[133] Different AI applications, especially facial recognition, are used to increasingly gain social control over the Uyghur minority by facilitating their identification, tracking and targeting.[134]

32. The Integrated Joint Operations Platform plays a crucial role in the systematic oppression and discrimination of the Uyghur people. It supports the information collection from a wide variety of sources such as smartphones, wi-fi sniffers, online and offline surveillance, voice recording, etc. That data is then used to predict potential terrorists and profile the Uyghur minority. Law enforcement in the Xinjiang province applies facial recognition systems to identify, track and target labelled individuals in every aspect of their daily life: checkpoints, schools, shopping malls, mosques, hospitals and resident areas. Teaching Islam to their children, praying and having relatives abroad are considered suspicious and might amount to a forced deportation to a political education camp. Allegedly, torture, cruel, inhuman and degrading treatment are common practices in these camps.[135] Given the failing rule of law in the Xinjiang province, the Uyghur minority is subjected to severe human rights violations that are made possible through different AI applications. This particular case-study demonstrates how different AI applications can form a very intrusive combination and have severe destructive consequences if they fall in the wrong hands and are adopted with malintent.

---

133 Human Rights Watch, 'China's Algorithms of Repression Reverse Engineering a Xinjiang Police Mass Surveillance App ', 1 May 2019, p. 1, https://www.hrw.org/sites/default/files/report_pdf/china0519_web5.pdf.

134 Human Rights Watch, 'Eradicating Ideological Viruses' China's Campaign of Repression Against Xinjiang's Muslims', 9 September 2018, pp. 15, 17, 75–76, https://www.hrw.org/sites/default/files/report_pdf/china0918_web2.pdf.

135 B. Darren, 'China's hi-tech war on its Muslim minority', *Guardian*, 11 April 2019, https://www.theguardian.com/news/2019/apr/11/china-hi-tech-war-on-muslim-minority-xinjiang-uighurs-surveillance-face-recognition; Human Rights Watch, 'China's Algorithms of Repression Reverse Engineering a Xinjiang Police Mass Surveillance App', pp. 13–28.

3.2.2. Discrimination Based on Gender: Online Job Advertisements

33. A majority of job advertisements these days are shared and spread online. Search engines such as Google play a key role in providing access to job vacancies. Interestingly, as the algorithms of search engines learn from user behaviour, they tend to show targeted advertisements for coaching services regarding high paid positions more to men than to women. This could result in male candidates getting more encouragement and support to apply for high-paying jobs than women. This can contribute to gender pay gaps.[136]

3.2.3. Discrimination Based on Religion, Belief and Political Opinion: Facebook

34. It is hard to imagine our daily lives without social media. Facebook is the most widely used social media platform. It holds big amounts of personal data. Researchers developed an algorithm that uses 'Facebook likes' to predict a wide variety of features such as gender, sexual orientation, ethnic origin, political opinion and religious belief. The accuracy of the algorithm was impressive. It was able to make a distinction between a Caucasian and an African American with a 95% accuracy rate, to distinguish male from female persons with a 93% accuracy rate and to differentiate between Democrats and Republicans with 85% accuracy. The system was also able to identify gay men with a 88% accuracy rate and lesbians with a 75% accuracy rate. It was able to separate Christians from Muslims with a 82% accuracy rate.[137] Such precise algorithm could contribute to far-reaching profiling activities. Another related issue are the (weak) data protection policies of social media. The Cambridge Analytica Scandal demonstrated how third parties can capture Facebook users' data regardless of their consent. This harvested data in combination with very precise algorithms may result in AI applications that make (intentional) discrimination possible.[138]

3.2.4. Discrimination Based on Race: Gerrymandering

35. The term 'gerrymandering' is usually used to describe the manipulation process of electoral district boundaries allowing a political party or candidate

---

136 D. Amit, D. Anupam, 'Automated Experiments on Ad Privacy Settings A Tale of Opacity, Choice, and Discrimination', *Proceedings on Privacy Enhancing Technologies*, 2015, pp. 105–106. Also see: K. Yordanova, 'AI is a Girl's Best Friend? A Gender-Based Analysis of the Legal and Ethical Challenges of AI systems', *Global Wo.Men Hub Blog*, 2020-11, https://gwmh.org/ai-is-a-girls-best-friend-a-gender-based-analysis-of-the-legal-and-ethical-challenges-of-ai-systems/ and the references *supra* in part 2.7.

137 M. Kosinski, T. Graepel and D. Stillwell, 'Private traits and attributes are predictable from digital records of human behavior', *Proceedings of the National Academy of Sciences*, 2013, vol. 110, no. 15, pp. 5802–5805.

138 Yavuz, 'Machine Bias: Artificial Intelligence and Discrimination', pp. 37–38. Also see: N. Smuha, 'Artificiële Intelligentie, Sociale Media en Democratie: Reflecties & Aanbevelingen voor de Belgische Kamer van volksvertegenwoordigers', Reflecties & Aanbevelingen, 23 June 2020, https://hiw.kuleuven.be/wgpt/policy-paper-ai-hoorzitting/.

to gain advantages during the elections.[139] Many countries are confronted with this process, especially the US where political gerrymandering (i.e. shaping electoral district boundaries to contribute to a political party's success) is allowed,[140] but racial gerrymandering (i.e. manipulating electoral district boundaries to underrepresent racial minorities) is prohibited.[141] Gerrymandering relies on processing high volumes of data, profiling and calculation of probabilities. It is, therefore, no surprise that AI applications have taken gerrymandering to a whole new level.[142] Although racial gerrymandering is prohibited, we already showed that AI applications can easily bypass that prohibition by using the political affiliation as a proxy for race. The establishment of this correlation could result in proxy discrimination, which was already addressed.[143]

3.3. SILVER LININGS

36. Several AI applications can contribute to discrimination as well as to the embedding and scaling of bias. Nonetheless, as 'general' AI is still an utopia, it is important to also stress the human influence and impact on the development or use of AI. First, AI systems may discriminate because they were trained on data generated by human discriminatory behaviour. Second, AI applications may discriminate when being created with the intention to do so (cf. intentional discrimination) or because of human bias when using the AI applications. For example, employers may process future employees' credit history in such a manner that it disadvantages certain minority groups even when a clear link between credit history and professional performance was not confirmed.[144] This bias can be conscious or unconscious depending on whether a person is aware of the factors that may influence his/her thinking.[145]

---

139 P. Andrew, 'Gerrymandering, explained', *Vox*, 9 May 2019, https://www.vox.com/2014/8/5/17991934/gerrymandering-explained.

140 *Gill v. Whitford*, Supreme Court of the United States, 18 June 2018.

141 *Cooper v. Harris*, Supreme Court of the United States, 22 May 2017.

142 E. Jordan, 'How Computers Turned Gerrymandering Into a Science', *New York Times*, 6 October 2017, https://www.nytimes.com/2017/10/06/opinion/sunday/computers-gerrymandering-wisconsin.html.

143 See *supra* part 3.1. Also see: C. Yavuz, 'Machine Bias Artificial Intelligence and Discrimination', Lund University Law Faculty, SSRN, 19 August 2019, https://papers.ssrn.com/sol3/papers.cfm?abstract_id=3439702.

144 B. Kiviat, 'The art of deciding with data: Evidence from how employers translate credit reports into hiring decisions', *Socio-Economic Review*, 2017, vol. 17, no. 2, pp. 283–309; See also R.L. O'Brien and B. Kiviat, 'Disparate impact? Race, sex, and credit reports in hiring', *Socius*, 2018, vol. 4, pp. 1–20.

145 J. Kleinberg et al., 'Discrimination in the age of algorithms', SSRN, 5 February 2019, p. 2, https://papers.ssrn.com/sol3/papers.cfm?abstract_id=3329669.

Third, AI applications can result in discrimination because they are designed with certain flaws contributing to discrimination.[146] These design flaws can be grouped in two categories: (i) the data used as inputs; and (ii) the working of the algorithm itself. Within the first category, the poor selection of data, the decision to use incomplete, incorrect or outdated data or the presence of selection bias can result in discriminatory practices.[147] When it comes to the second category, there are other flaws that may contribute to discriminatory behaviour. Examples are the implementation of decision-making systems that assume that correlation implies causation, the use of datasets that lack information or disproportionately represent certain population groups or poorly designed matching systems.[148]

37. Understanding the human contribution to discrimination by AI systems also highlights the potential to do good. By continuously improving AI applications, they can support the discovery of discrimination, decrease the effect of human bias and potentially reduce inequality.[149] To accomplish these goals, fairness and ethics will need to be a core part of the original AI applications' design process. This will guarantee that AI systems adequately tackle implicit or explicit bias.[150] As a result, further collaborations between different disciplines (and institutions) will be required to adopt a proper ethical framework governing the creation of AI applications. Such interdisciplinary cooperation will ensure the alignment between core human values and AI systems.[151]

---

146 Borgesius, 'Discrimination, artificial intelligence, and algorithmic decision-making', p. 18.

147 C. Munoz, M. Smith and D.J. Patil, 'Big data: A report on algorithmic systems, opportunity, and civil rights', Executive Office of the President, 2016, pp. 7–8, https://obamawhitehouse.archives.gov/sites/default/files/microsites/ostp/2016_0504_data_discrimination.pdf.

148 *Ibid.*, pp. 8–9.

149 Silberg and Manyika, 'Notes from the AI frontier: Tackling bias in AI (and in humans)', p. 1.

150 The Federal Trade Commission,'Big Data: A Tool for Inclusion or Exclusion? Understanding the Issues', January 2016, p. v, https://www.ftc.gov/reports/big-data-tool-inclusion-or-exclusion-understanding-issues-ftc-report.

151 M. Risse, 'Human Rights and Artificial Intelligence: An Urgently Needed Agenda', HKS Working Paper No. RWP18-015, May 2018, p. 8, https://www.hks.harvard.edu/publications/human-rights-and-artificial-intelligence-urgently-needed-agenda. See in this regard also the Flemish AI Action Plan which created the Knowledge Centre for Data & Society (see https://www.ewi-vlaanderen.be/nieuws/vlaams-actieplan-artificiele-intelligentie-gelanceerd). This Centre focuses on the interplay between data, AI and society. It enables the socially responsible, ethical and legally appropriate implementation of AI in Flanders. The Centre aims to enable Flemish companies, policymakers, regulators and citizens to achieve the greatest social and/or economic benefits of AI. To that end, it brings together diverse stakeholder representative organisations and facilitates the creation of tools, advice and recommendations (see https://data-en-maatschappij.ai/en/about-us).

4. BENDING THREATS INTO OPPORTUNITIES: HUMAN RIGHTS AS THE ETHICAL FRAMEWORK TO ENSURE AI'S POTENTIAL

38. Besides the potential risks for human rights, AI applications can also support future generations in reducing their environmental and social impact. This can be achieved via the improvement of efficiency and the development of new products and services.[152] As AI applications are gaining ground and becoming an institutional part of our daily lives, there is a growing understanding that they need to be designed, developed and applied in an adequate and fair manner in order to make the most of their potential. However, the previous analysis showed that danger lurks around the corner if AI applications cause harm, either intentionally or unintentionally. The case of discrimination was further elaborated upon.

Being aware of the potential negative impact of AI systems, Stephen Hawking, Elon Musk and Steve Wozniak signed the Future of Life Institute 2015 open letter. This letter warns for the risks that AI may entail and calls for a ban on offensive autonomous weapons.[153] In 2018, a coalition of human rights and technology groups adopted the Toronto Declaration on Machine Learning Standards, calling on both governments and tech companies to ensure that algorithms respect basic principles of equality and non-discrimination.[154] More importantly, the High-Level Expert Group on AI also presented the 'Ethics Guidelines for Trustworthy Artificial Intelligence' in April 2019. The Guidelines put forward a human-centric approach to AI. Trustworthy AI has three components that have to be met throughout the AI system's entire life cycle. First, it should be lawful, which means that it must comply with all applicable laws and regulations. Second, AI systems must be ethical, thus ensuring adherence to ethical principles and values. Third, the AI system should be robust both from a technical and social perspective. Each component in itself is necessary but not sufficient for the achievement of trustworthy AI. Ideally, all three components work in harmony and overlap in their application.[155] Based on fundamental rights and these ethical principles, the Guidelines subsequently list seven key requirements that AI systems should meet to be trustworthy:

---

[152] C. Herweijer, '8 ways AI can help save the planet', World Economic Forum, 24 January 2018, https://www.weforum.org/agenda/2018/01/8-ways-ai-can-help-save-the-planet.

[153] Future of Life, 'Autonomous Weapons: An Open Letter from AI & Robotics Researchers', 28 July 2015, https://futureoflife.org/open-letter-autonomous-weapons/; E. Mack, 'Hawking, Musk, Wozniack Warn about Artificial Intelligence's Trigger Finger', *Forbes*, 27 July 2015.

[154] Accessnow, 'The Toronto Declaration: Protecting the rights to equality and non-discrimination in machine learning systems', 16 May 2018, https://www.accessnow.org/cms/assets/uploads/2018/08/The-Toronto-Declaration_ENG_08-2018.pdf.

[155] High-Level Expert Group on Artificial Intelligence – European Commission, 'Ethics Guidelines for Trustworthy AI', pp. 6–7.

(1) human agency and oversight; (2) technical robustness and safety; (3) privacy and data governance; (4) transparency; (5) diversity, non-discrimination and fairness; (6) societal and environmental well-being; and (7) accountability.[156] The requirements are applicable to the different stakeholders taking part in the life cycle of AI systems. After a piloting process, the AI HLEG presented its final Assessment List for Trustworthy Artificial Intelligence (ALTAI) on 17 July 2020. Through ALTAI, AI principles are translated into an accessible and dynamic checklist that guides developers and deployers of AI systems when implementing such principles in practice. By indicating a set of concrete steps for self-assessment, ALTAI will help to ensure that users benefit from AI without being exposed to unnecessary risks.[157]

The latest set of policy guidelines is the OECD Recommendation on AI that promotes five principles for the responsible development of trustworthy AI. It also provides complementary strategies for developing national policy and international cooperation. When further developing AI, one should consider the following values: (i) inclusive growth, sustainable development and well-being; (ii) human-centred values and fairness; (iii) transparency and explainability; (iv) robustness, security and safety; and (v) accountability.[158]

39. The many ethical initiatives contribute to raising awareness regarding AI applications and their potential risks. Yet, they do not necessarily provide a comprehensive ethical framework to govern those risks, nor can they claim to have universal acceptance. Furthermore, the principles may be defined differently depending on the stakeholder(s) involved. Similar to companies adopting different policies on ethical AI,[159] countries can also, inspired by their own AI development roles, have divergent ideas regarding which 'ethics' principles need to be protected.[160] Self-regulation that comes with ethical principles may also be too weak to accommodate the increasing implications

---

156 *Ibid.*, pp. 14–23. N.A. Smuha, 'The EU Approach to Ethics Guidelines for Trustworthy Artificial Intelligence', *Computer Law Review International*, 2019, vol. 20, no. 4, pp. 97–106.

157 High Level Expert Group on AI, 'Assessment List for Trustworthy Artificial Intelligence (ALTAI) for self-assessment', 17 July 2020, https://ec.europa.eu/digital-single-market/en/news/assessment-list-trustworthy-artificial-intelligence-altai-self-assessment.

158 OECD, 'Recommendation of the Council on Artificial Intelligence', 5 May 2019, https://legalinstruments.oecd.org/en/instruments/OECD-LEGAL-0449. Also see Chapter 3 for an extensive discussion.

159 See in this regard for example: K. Yordanova and I. Emanuilov, 'Do You Believe in FAIR-y-tales? An Overview of Microsoft's New Toolkit for Assessing and Improving Fairness of Algorithms', *KU Leuven CiTiP Blog*, 14 July 2020, https://www.law.kuleuven.be/citip/blog/do-you-believe-in-fair-y-tales-an-overview-of-microsofts-new-toolkit-for-assessing-and-improving-fairness-of-algorithms/.

160 K. Saslow, and P. Lorenz, 'Artifical Intelligence Needs Human Rights: How the focus on ethical AI fails to address privacy, discrimination and other concerns', SSRN, September 2019, p. 2, https://papers.ssrn.com/sol3/papers.cfm?abstract_id=3589473.

that AI technologies have due to the lack of clear enforcement capabilities.[161] All of this becomes even more challenging as research illustrated that the problem of algorithmic discrimination has been insufficiently addressed in the EU and in the US. Anti-discrimination law in the EU, for instance, does not (yet) provide adequate protection against algorithmic discrimination.[162]

40. As a result, a common global framework will be needed to assure that AI applications are developed and applied in a manner that respects human dignity and democratic accountability in addition to regional instruments which are designed to reflect the economic and social specificities. This was clearly demonstrated by the UN on a number of occasions, for example, through the mandate of the UN Special Rapporteur on the right to privacy to draft the Data Privacy Guidelines for the development and operation of Artificial Intelligence solutions[163] or the adoption of the Report of the Special Rapporteur on the promotion and protection of the right to freedom of opinion and expression[164] exploring the implications of artificial intelligence technologies for human rights in the information environment. These reports culminated with the adoption of the UNESCO's Recommendations on the Ethics of AI on the 24th of November 2021 becoming the 'first global standard-setting instrument on the ethics of artificial intelligence'.[165]

At the European level, there are currently two regional legislative initiatives that are of paramount importance for the development in the field, one coming from the Council of Europe and one from the EU. The former, through its Ad hoc Committee on AI (CAHAI), conducted extensive multi-stakeholder consultations in order to examine the feasibility and determine the potential elements of a legal framework for the development, design and application of AI. Their work is based on the Council of Europe's standards on human rights, democracy and the rule of law[166] and resulted in the establishment of the

---

161 *Ibid.*, p. 3.

162 Ebers, 'Regulating AI and Robotics: Ethical and Legal Challenges', pp. 78–79; P. Hacker, 'Teaching Fairness to Artificial Intelligence: Existing and Novel Strategies Against Algorithmic Discrimination Under EU Law', *Common Market Law Review*, 2018, no. 4, pp. 1143–1185; Borgesius, 'Discrimination, Artificial Intelligence and Algorithmic Decision-Making', pp. 35–38.

163 Draft for Consultation, UN Special Rapporteur on the Right to Privacy Data Privacy Guidelines for the development and operation of Artificial Intelligence solutions, 2 November 2020, https://www.ohchr.org/sites/default/files/Documents/Issues/Privacy/SR_Privacy/2020_Sept_draft_data_Privacy_guidelines.pdf

164 Report of the Special Rapporteur on the promotion and protection of the right to freedom of opinion and expression, UNGA, Seventy-third session, A/73/348, 29 August 2018, https://freedex.org/wp-content/blogs.dir/2015/files/2018/10/AI-and-FOE-GA.pdf

165 UNESCO, 'Recommendation on the Ethics of Artificial Intelligence,' SHS/IGM-AIETHICS/2021/JUN/INF.2, 24 November 2021.

166 I. Ben-Israel et al., 'Towards Regulation of AI systems. Compilation of contributions', Council of Europe, December 2020, https://rm.coe.int/prems-107320-gbr-2018-compli-cahai-couv-texte-a4-bat-web/1680a0c17a.

Committee on AI (CAI) responsible for the negotiation, drafting and adoption of the Council of Europe AI Treaty.

The EU initiative was conducted through the Commission's proposal for a Regulation on AI (the AI Act).[167] The instrument steps on the work of the AI HLEG, although it alternates some of the key elements due to the scope of the proposed Regulation. The most notable feature of the draft Regulation is the division of AI systems into categories, requiring different standards of care, based on the risk they pose for the health, safety and fundamental rights of persons. Although this approach is sound on paper, there are some implementation issues. For example, in the AI HLEG Guidelines, explainability is part of transparency and adapted to the expertise of the concerned stakeholder. In the AI Act, however, the transparency obligation is directed towards 'users' (cf. Art. 13) including 'any natural or legal person, public authority, agency or other body using an AI system under its authority, except where the AI system is used in the course of a personal non-professional activity' (cf. Art. 3).[168] This discrepancy between the AI Act and the AI HLEG Guidelines creates a gap between ethics and law, and undermines the rights of the individuals who are de facto excluded from the personal scope of the AI Act as they may not be qualified as 'users' and 'providers'. The introduction of these 'intermediary actors' in the AI Act combined with the lack of effective remedy for individuals to enforce their legal rights under the regulation leaves much leeway and discretion to future regulation(s) in terms of effectively protecting human rights.[169]

Even though the aim of the draft Regulation remains closely connected to human rights protection through the notion of 'trustworthy AI'[170] and the seven requirements are being reflected in its text, there is a number of persistent problems that remain in the current version. These are being debated by the European Parliament and the Council of the EU. One of the most fundamental issues concerns the material scope of the Regulation, namely the definition of AI. The most recent proposals coming from certain members of the European Parliament suggest further limiting AI to solely machine learning models which put human rights in danger since companies could just avoid using ML models

167 European Commission, 'Proposal for a Regulation of the European Parliament and of the Council Laying down Harmonised Rules on Artificial Intelligence (Artificial Intelligence Act) and Amending Certain Union Legislative Acts', COM(2021) 206 Final.

168 *Supra* 85, Section 4.7.

169 N. Smuha, E. Ahmed-Rengers, A. Harkens, W. Li, J. MacLaren, R. Piselli, and K. Yeung 'How the EU Can Achieve Legally Trustworthy AI: A Response to the European Commission's Proposal for an Artificial Intelligence Act', 5 August 2021, https://ssrn.com/abstract=3899991.

170 The HLEG describes trustworthy AI as being lawful, ethical, and robust which is complemented by seven requirements for trustworthy AI: robustness and safety, privacy and data governance, transparency, diversity, non-discrimination and fairness, societal and environmental well-being, accountability, and human agency and oversight.

all together and develop rule-based systems or decision trees.[171] Second, some of the requirements for high-risk AI systems, which are supposedly posing the highest risk to human rights, are just not serving their intended purpose in the way they are currently regulated by the proposal for the AI Act. For example, human oversight might be completely useless in certain cases of complicated models, especially because it is not determined where in the process the 'human-in-the-loop' should be established. Furthermore, explainable models could also mean compromised security,[172] which could further affect a number of rights ranging from privacy to the right to life.

41. The short overview of the current legislative initiatives demonstrates that a human rights-based approach to the design and governance of AI makes up for the weaknesses of current (ethical) frameworks and can enhance the opportunities that AI offers. There are four features of the human rights framework that show its potential as the leading normative framework to govern AI. First, it places the human being at the core of any AI impact assessment implying that the assessment of AI applications must be based on what influence they (will) have on people and their inherent rights. Second, it directly addresses the most pressing societal concerns regarding AI as it includes a broad spectrum of substantive and procedural rights. Third, the current human rights framework prescribes the roles and responsibilities of two crucial actors, being governments and companies, in protecting and respecting human rights and remedying violations of those obligations. Finally, the human rights framework is a universal framework that is globally recognised and (even) enjoys an international law status.[173] While AI poses many risks to human rights, there are also great opportunities. By applying a human rights framework to AI design and governance processes, we will be able to assure that human rights risks are minimalised while fully developing AI's potential.

5. CONCLUSION

42. Given that many AI applications are increasingly integrated in our daily life, it does not come as a surprise that a wide variety of human rights are or can be affected by AI. The general overview showed that AI can indeed have a negative impact on several fundamental rights. Yet, the influence can be

171 J. Bryson, 'Europe Is in Danger of Using the Wrong Definition of AI', *Wired*, 2 March 2022, https://www.wired.com/story/artificial-intelligence-regulation-european-union.

172 *Supra* 20.

173 E. Donahoe and M.M. Metzger, 'Artificial Intelligence and Human Rights', *Journal of Democracy*, 2019, vol. 30, no. 2, 2019, pp. 119–122. See also N.A. Smuha, 'Beyond a Human Rights-based approach to AI Governance: Promise, Pitfalls, Plea', February 2020, https://ssrn.com/abstract=3543112 or http://dx.doi.org/10.2139/ssrn.3543112.

beneficial as well if the development of AI applications is addressed accordingly and aligned with human values. The majority of the applications developed through AI techniques such as facial recognition, search engine algorithms and risk assessment methodologies may contribute to the discrimination of minority groups in society. Therefore, discrimination was scrutinised into more detail. Real life examples were provided to demonstrate how AI applications contribute to discrimination on the basis of traditional attributes such as ethnicity, gender, religion, belief, political opinion and race, as well as some novel ones arising from group privacy.

43. An important element to consider in the discussion of AI and human rights is the role of human beings. The examples provided in the case studies showed that AI applications may discriminate when the training data is biased, for instance because of discriminatory human behaviour. Consequently, AI systems can continue to enforce and scale a discriminatory practice. The analysis also illustrated the human influence when developing AI systems. AI applications should not be completely discarded in the future, but the human hand in (reducing) the potential negative impact should be kept in mind. Core principles such 'human in the loop, human on the loop and human in command' need to be implemented with precision in order to fulfil their purpose without compromising other important guarantees of human rights protection such as (cyber)security. In addition, it is important to ensure that the socio-technical guarantees provided by future AI legislation such as accountability or transparency are to be applied during the whole lifecycle of a system and through the entire supply and value chain. Nevertheless, and regardless of the quality of AI regulations around the world, the most important point remains that it is just a tool that we can use for various purposes but at the end of the day humans remain accountable for their actions.

CHAPTER 7

'LAWS' AND THE LAW: REGULATING LETHAL AUTONOMOUS WEAPONS

Sebastiaan VAN SEVEREN* and Carl VANDER MAELEN**

1. INTRODUCTION

1. According to Isaac Asimov's 1942 sci-fi story Runaround,[1] the 'First Law of Robotics' prescribes that 'a robot may not injure a human being or, through inaction, allow a human being to come to harm'. The Second law states that 'a robot must obey the orders given it by human beings except where such orders would conflict with the First Law'. Technology has come a long way since the heyday of sci-fi books and films about robot overlords and robotised weaponry. And while science-fiction literature and Hollywood have surely fuelled the imagination of the general audience, our civilisation is nowhere near robot domination yet. Nevertheless, technological developments in the methods and means of warfare brew at the horizon like an ever more ominous cloud, and the question of whether humanity needs its own Laws of Robotics becomes increasingly prominent.

2. As this book amply shows, the potential of robots and AI in law is tremendous. It certainly seems that in many fields of human activity, this great potential is of a largely beneficial kind. Efficiency, autonomy, and an unmatched computational power promise sizeable gains in an array of legal domains. In international law, and more particularly in the realm of the conduct of hostilities, there is not as much space for unbridled optimism since the introduction of more advanced technology now means that lethal autonomous weapons (LAWs) are being introduced on the battlefield. This chapter will attempt to evaluate whether LAWs fit into the current international legal framework regarding the *jus ad*

* Academic assistant in Public International Law at Ghent University, Faculty of Law and Criminology.

** Academic assistant in Law & Technology at Ghent University, Faculty of Law and Criminology.

1 I. Asimov, 'Runaround', *Astounding Science Fiction*, 1942, vol. 29, no. 1.

bellum and *jus in bello*, in particular by investigating whether the principles of these legal systems can be successfully applied to LAWs. First, the reader is introduced to the basic concepts of international humanitarian law and several *prima facie* concerns regarding their relationship to LAWs, in particular the principles of distinction and the prohibition of superfluous injury or unnecessary suffering (part 2). We then explore the legal aspects of LAWs relating to two themes: the authority awarded to machines and automated decision-making processes on wounding and/or killing humans in an armed conflict, as well as the processes and procedural safeguards behind targeting and engagement choices (part 3). This is followed by a briefing on current applications of LAWs and their foreseeable developments, with a particular focus on the US and China as the two military actors most advanced in developing such technology (part 4). State actor views on the necessity of a legal framework to regulate LAWs are also discussed (part 5). A brief conclusion that summarises the main points ends the chapter's investigation into the lawful use of LAWs (part 6).

3. For the purpose of this chapter, the snappy term 'killer robots' will be avoided in favour of 'lethal autonomous weapons' or LAWs – a sacrifice we must make in the name of academic accuracy and objectivity. Furthermore, to subdue the length and improve the depth of this contribution, we limit ourselves to discussing LAWs from the perspective of *jus ad bellum* and *jus in bello*. For discussions on the potential human rights issues involved in the use of LAWs[2] or the use of LAWs in domestic law enforcement,[3] we would like to refer to the work of other authors.

2. INTERNATIONAL HUMANITARIAN LAW

4. In legal discussions on lethal autonomous weapons, considerable attention is devoted to a number of concepts in international humanitarian law (IHL), the branch of international law dealing with the rules of conduct during armed conflict, either international or non-international. Bearing in mind that this book is meant for a wider audience, a short deliberation of some of those central concepts is in order, after which a more detailed assessment of their application to the issue of lethal autonomous weapons will follow.

---

2 See, for example: P. Asaro, 'On Banning Autonomous Weapon Systems: Human Rights, Automation, and the Dehumanization of Lethal Decision-Making', *International Review of the Red Cross*, June 2012, vol. 94, no. 886, pp. 687–709.

3 A. Spagnolo, 'Human Rights Implications of Autonomous Weapon Systems in Domestic Law Enforcement: Sci-Fi Reflections on a Lo-Fi Reality', *Questions of International Law*, 31 October 2017, vol. 43, pp. 33–58.

5. At its core, IHL regulates the conduct of hostilities by balancing considerations of humanity with those of military necessity. From these considerations flow the closely linked principles of distinction, proportionality, precautions, and the prohibition of superfluous injury or unnecessary suffering. Firstly, the principle of distinction prescribes that parties to a conflict must distinguish between military and civilian objects, and thus between combatants and non-combatants. During armed conflict, military goals may be vigorously pursued, but non-combatants are to be protected from harm.[4] The principle of distinction primarily entails a prohibition of attacks on civilians and civilian targets,[5] but any attack that is by its nature indiscriminate is prohibited. Secondly, the principle of 'Precautions in Attack' dictates that 'constant care must be taken to spare the civilian population, civilians and civilian objects' and that '[a]ll feasible precautions must be taken to avoid, and in any event to minimise, incidental loss of civilian life, injury to civilians and damage to civilian objects.'[6] It is enshrined in Article 57(1) AP I. Thirdly, the rule of Proportionality prohibits reckless attacks, in which civilians are likely to suffer excessive losses, compared to anticipated military advantages, are not permitted.[7] Accordingly, an attacker must ensure that, even if civilian objects and civilians are to be impacted by an attack, the consequences of the attack must be proportional to the anticipated military goal: the anticipated military advantage must be weighed against the expected harm to civilians. In short, participants must take precautionary measures and assess the proportionality of their actions. In the context of this chapter, the implication is that LAWs must make – and, perhaps, more crucially, must *be able* to make – the distinction between combatants and non-combatants, as well as the analyses associated with this distinction, if they are to comply with international law.

6. The final principle of IHL to take into account is the prohibition of superfluous injury or unnecessary suffering.[8] Throughout history, attempts to curb the worst excesses of warfare – at least to an extent – have emerged as religious, customary or treaty-based rules. Around the turn of the twentieth century, rules concerning the limits on weapons during the conduct of hostilities

---

4 Protocol Additional to the Geneva Conventions of 12 August 1949, and relating to the Protection of Victims of International Armed Conflicts (AP I), 8 June 1977, 1125 UNTS 3, Art. 48; ICRC, *Customary International Humanitarian Law Volume I: Rules* (Cambridge: Cambridge University Press, 2005), Rule 1.

5 I. Henderson, *The Contemporary Law of Targeting: Military Objectives, Proportionality and Precautions in Attack under Additional Protocol I*, International Humanitarian Law Series (Leiden, Boston: Martinus Nijhoff Publishers, 2009), p. 44.

6 ICRC, *Customary International Humanitarian Law Volume I: Rules* (Cambridge: Cambridge University Press, 2005), Rule 15.

7 Art. 51(5)(b) AP I; ICRC, *Customary Law Study*, Rule 14.

8 Art. 35(2) AP I; ICRC, *Customary Law Study*, Rule 70.

were central to what was colloquially called Hague Law.[9] While the goal of armed conflict is the weakening of the enemy, human suffering is to be limited wherever it is superfluous in light of that goal. The rules that flow from the prohibition of unnecessary suffering apply equally to all conventional and non-conventional weaponry. This means that newly developed weapons must comply with the same obligations as any other weapon. As LAWs are developed in a number of countries around the world at an increasing rate, this rule, enshrined in Article 36 AP I, is of particular interest to the subject at hand.[10] It stresses the need for considerations of international humanitarian law in the development of autonomous weapons *ab initio*.

7. To conclude this introduction, another principle merits some preliminary attention. The so-called 'Martens Clause' is a formula that originated in the preamble to Hague Convention (II) of 1899 and Hague Convention (IV) of 1907 Respecting the Laws and Customs of War on Land.[11] The Martens Clause, named after its 'inventor', the Russian diplomat Fyodor Martens, has been included in several international documents,[12] among which Article 1(2) AP I:

> *'In cases not covered by this Protocol or by other international agreements, civilians and combatants remain under the protection and authority of the principles of international law derived from established custom, from the principles of humanity and from the dictates of public conscience.'*

It may serve as a subsidiary means of interpreting the laws of armed conflict.[13] Central to understanding this clause is its reference to 'the principles of humanity' and to 'the dictates of public conscience'. The ICJ has stated in its Advisory Opinion on Nuclear Weapons that the 'continuing existence and applicability' of the Martens Clause 'is not to be doubted'.[14] And while its status

---

9 For example, Regulation 22 annexed to Hague Convention (II) of 1899 and Hague Convention (IV) of 1907 reads as follows: 'The right of belligerents to adopt means of injuring the enemy is not unlimited'.

10 Article 36 AP I: 'In the study, development, acquisition or adoption of a new weapon, means or method of warfare, a High Contracting Party is under an obligation to determine whether its employment would, in some or all circumstances, be prohibited by this Protocol or by any other rule of international law applicable to the High Contracting Party'.

11 Hague Convention (IV) Respecting the Laws and Customs of War on Land and Its Annex: Regulations Concerning the Laws and Customs of War on Land, 18 October 1907.

12 See, for example, the United Nations Convention on Prohibitions or Restrictions on the Use of Certain Conventional Weapons Which May be Deemed to be Excessively Injurious or to Have Indiscriminate Effects (and Protocols) (As Amended on 21 December 2001), 10 October 1980, 1342 UNTS 137.

13 A. Cassese, 'The Martens Clause: Half a Loaf or Simply Pie in the Sky?', *European Journal of International Law*, 2000, vol. 11, no. 1, pp. 187–216.

14 International Court of Justice (ICJ), 'Advisory Opinion on the Legality of the Threat or Use of Nuclear Weapons', ICJ Reports 1996, p. 226, para. 87.

as an autonomous source of law is heavily debated,[15] its appeals to humanity and ethics seem fitting in a debate that originates in the uncoupling of humans and combat.

8. The debate concerning LAWs is subject to an important consideration: some of the most vocal State opponents of a treaty regarding the possible prohibition of LAWs have not ratified Additional Protocol I to the Geneva Conventions.[16] In this context, the applicability of the norms surrounding the means of warfare and their development cannot be based in treaty law, but must depend on their status as customary international law. Scholars and the International Committee of the Red Cross (ICRC) agree on the customary nature of the rules on distinction, of the rules prohibiting weapons that cause superfluous injury or unnecessary suffering, and of the prohibition of weapons that are by their nature indiscriminate.[17] Article 35 AP I is therefore equally applicable for States that have not ratified the Additional Protocol. This unanimity on customary status, however, does not presently exist concerning Article 36 AP I. Nevertheless, some manuals state that, even if not a signatory to the Additional Protocols, 'States are obligated to assess the legality of weapons before fielding them.'[18] Boothby[19] and Copeland[20] similarly argue for a wider duty to *ex ante* investigate the legality of new weapons, based on the Martens principle, and its analogous provisions in the general IHL treaties. For the purpose of this chapter, the rules concerning the prohibition of certain weapons (Article 35 AP I) and the development of new weapons (Article 36 AP I) will therefore be considered to apply to the entire international community, regardless of their ratification by states as part of AP I.

3. APPLYING THE CURRENT LEGAL FRAMEWORK TO LAWS

9. Although a substantial amount of literature exists by now on lethal autonomous weapons (LAWs), there is currently no framework on the international level to govern their development and/or deployment. Instead, our understanding of the legal aspects of LAWs must be formed through other

---

15 Cassese, 'The Martens Clause: Half a Loaf or Simply Pie in the Sky?', pp. 187–216.

16 E.g., the United States of America, Israel and Turkey.

17 ICRC, *Customary Law Study*, Rule 1, 7, 11, 70 and 71.

18 Harvard School of Public Health et al., *HPCR Manual on International Law Applicable to Air and Missile Warfare*.

19 B. Boothby, 'How Will Weapons Reviews Address the Challenges Posed by New Technologies?', *Military Law and Law of War Review*, 2013, vol. 52, no. 1, p. 41.

20 D.P. Copeland, 'Legal Review of New Technology Weapons', in: H. Nasu and R. McLaughlin (eds.), *New Technologies and the Law of Armed Conflict* (The Hague: T.M.C. Asser Press, 2014), p. 44.

sources: the general IHL treaties, customary international law, non-binding reports by international organisations, national state policies, reports by NGOs and legal doctrine. Although much scholarly work has been carried out on related topics such as the programmability of moral decision-making abilities,[21] this chapter will focus exclusively on the legal aspects related to LAWs.

10. Before discussing any legal repercussions that automated weaponry can have on international law and vice versa, it is important to understand what exactly LAWs are. An all-round definition given by the United States Congressional Research Service in a March 2019 report defines LAWs as 'a special class of weapon systems that use sensor suites and computer algorithms to independently identify a target and employ an onboard weapon system to engage and destroy the target without manual human control of the system'.[22] This is also in line with Singer's description of LAWs, considering them to consist of 'sensors that give them a degree of situational awareness; processors or artificial intelligence that 'decides' how to respond to a given stimulus; and effectors that carry out those 'decisions''.[23]

11. Importantly, the United States' leading policy document 'Department of Defense Directive 3000.09: Autonomy in Weapon Systems'[24] makes a distinction between three different categories of autonomous weapons systems according to the role played by human operators (or the lack thereof) in target selection and engagement. The first category is 'fully autonomous weapon systems' (also dubbed 'human out of the loop'). Once such systems are activated, they select and engage targets without the further intervention of human operators.[25] These fully autonomous weapons represent the most advanced manifestation of LAWs. The second category are 'human-supervised autonomous weapon systems' (also dubbed 'human on the loop'), designed to allow human operators to intervene and terminate engagements, including if a weapon systems failure would occur.[26] The final category is that of 'semi-autonomous weapon systems'. These systems are only intended to engage individual targets or specific target groups selected

21 W. Wallach, C. Allen and I. Smit, 'Machine Morality: Bottom-up and Top-down Approaches for Modelling Human Moral Faculties', *AI & Society*, 2008, vol. 22, no. 4, pp. 565–82; A.M. DeBaets, 'Can a Robot Pursue the Good? Exploring Artificial Moral Agency', *Journal of Evolution and Technology*, 2014, vol. 24, no. 3, pp. 76–86.

22 US Congressional Research Service, 'Defense Primer: U.S. Policy on Lethal Autonomous Weapon Systems', 27 March 2019.

23 P.W. Singer, *Wired for War: The Robotics Revolution and Conflict in the Twenty-First Century* (New York: Penguin Press, 2009), p. 67.

24 US Department of Defense, 'Directive 3000.09 – Autonomy in Weapon Systems', 21 November 2012, pp. 13–14; However, it must be noted that the US has clarified or nuanced some of the Directive's contents in later documents.

25 *Ibid.*, p. 13.

26 *Ibid.*, p. 14.

by a human operator ('human in the loop').[27] To avoid conflation with other military weapons or technologies that might not need human intervention, the Directive excludes from those three categories 'autonomous or semi-autonomous cyberspace systems for cyberspace operations; unarmed, unmanned platforms; unguided munitions; munitions manually guided by the operator (e.g., laser- or wire-guided munitions); mines; [and] unexploded explosive ordnance'.[28]

12. The distinction employed in the Directive has been endorsed by a wide array of actors, such as the former UN Special Rapporteur on extrajudicial, summary or arbitrary executions, Christof Heyns,[29] and the NGO Human Rights Watch.[30] Heyns has conducted valuable theoretical work on LAWs and considers the abovementioned threefold distinction not to consist of sharp cut-off points, but rather to be 'a continuum with significant human involvement on one side, as with UCAVs (unmanned combat aerial vehicles) where there is 'a human in the loop', and full autonomy on the other, as with [lethal autonomous robotics] where human beings are 'out of the loop''.[31] Not only does such fluidity in legal classification help mitigate the situation whereby state actors would attempt to circumvent rules by claiming that their weapons do not fit into existing legal frameworks, it also helps to highlight that the legal questions and ramifications discussed in this chapter are applicable to more tools than merely the first category of fully autonomous, human-out-of-the-loop weapons. Additionally, it is worth noting that the 'autonomous' characteristic of LAWs describes that a system is 'pre-programmed to function independent of human control or supervision'.[32] That does not necessarily mean that the weapon operates on the basis of AI, which goes a step further than mere pre-programmed behaviour by indicating – as an umbrella term – technology that possesses a certain autonomy to achieve specific goals *through* the mimicking of intelligent behaviour.[33] Nonetheless, the ability for AI-driven systems to decipher complex problems and even learn through machine learning techniques, means that it is

---

27 *Ibid.*

28 *Ibid.*, p. 2.

29 UN Human Rights Council, 'Report of the Special Rapporteur on Extrajudicial, Summary or Arbitrary Executions, Christof Heyns', 9 April 2013, UN Doc. A/HRC/23/47, p. 8.

30 Human Rights Watch, 'Losing Humanity: The Case against Killer Robots', 19 November 2012, p. 2; Human Rights Watch, 'Mind The Gap: The Lack of Accountability for Killer Robots', April 2015, p. 6.

31 UN Doc. A/HRC/23/47, p. 8.

32 S. Umbrello, P. Torres and A.F. De Bellis, 'The Future of War: Could Lethal Autonomous Weapons Make Conflict More Ethical?', *AI & Society*, 2020, vol. 35, pp. 273–282.

33 High-Level Expert Group on Artificial Intelligence, 'A Definition of Artificial Intelligence: Main Capabilities and Scientific Disciplines' (European Commission, 2018), https://ec.europa.eu/digital-single-market/en/news/definition-artificial-intelligence-main-capabilities-and-scientific-disciplines. See also: N.J Nilsson, *The Quest for Artificial Intelligence* (New York: Cambridge University Press, 2009), 580 p. Also see Chapter 1 of this book.

nearly inevitable that LAWs are designed to operate on the basis of AI to tackle the complex issues raised by combat situations on the battlefield.

13. The main questions that have been and are still being discussed surrounding LAWs are mainly focused on two themes: first, the principal proposition that machines and automated decision-making processes would be granted the sole authority to decide on whether or not to wound and/or kill humans in an armed conflict. Such discussions are not merely of a legal nature but inherently also involve ethical questions. The second important theme revolves around the technical processes and procedural safeguards behind targeting and engagement choices, which lean heavily into ongoing scholarly debates in law and computer science on the use of sensors, facial recognition technology, algorithms and machine learning to automate decision-making. Although these two themes can be treated separately to a certain extent, they are inherently intertwined. After all, the wounding or killing of combatants is a direct result of decision-making procedures regarding targeting and engagement.

14. In this regard, some scholars are optimistic and believe that the algorithm-based decision-making processes by which LAWs operate guarantee more objective decision-making procedures regarding the targeting and engagement of enemy targets compared to the high-stress, psychologically-demanding situations and fatigue that human combatants on the battlefield undergo and which can drive them to excessively violent reactions.[34] Furthermore, autonomous weapons systems react significantly faster than humans. This would prove relevant in situations where a large number of parallel attacks were to be analysed at the same time. It could also be argued that complete automation of targeting would be better than hybrid systems that target automatically but still leave the ultimate execution to humans since this could result in a far-reaching detachment and desensitising from decisions to kill.[35] If an automated, non-emotive and objective approach to warfare is coupled with precise targeting parameters, authors claim it could lead to more ethical battlefield behaviour that could greatly reduce war crimes and unnecessary violence, resulting in an overall reduction of casualties and less harm to civilians during conflicts.[36] The United States' policy echoes this viewpoint by saying that '[a]utomated target

---

34 Umbrello, Torres and De Bellis, 'The Future of War: Could Lethal Autonomous Weapons Make Conflict More Ethical', pp. 273–282.

35 UN Doc. A/HRC/23/47, p. 5.

36 R.C. Arkin, 'The Case for Ethical Autonomy in Unmanned Systems', *Journal of Military Ethics*, 2010, vol. 9, no. 4, pp. 332–341; M. Klincewicz, 'Autonomous Weapons Systems, the Frame Problem and Computer Security', *Journal of Military Ethics*, 2015, vol. 14, no. 2, pp. 162–176; S. Umbrello, 'Lethal Autonomous Weapons: Designing War Machines with Values', *Delphi – Interdisciplinary Review of Emerging Technologies*, 2019, no. 2, pp. 30–34.

identification, tracking, selection, and engagement functions can allow weapons to strike military objectives more accurately and with less risk of collateral damage'.[37]

15. The tactics of deception that are so commonplace in asymmetric conflicts raise many concerns with regard to the autonomous targeting capacities of LAWs and their proficiency to take into account the international law obligation to distinguish between combatants and civilians. This is crucial, because the difference between both entails unique obligations: it is prohibited to engage civilians 'unless and for such time as they take a direct part in hostilities' (Article 51(3) AP I) while lawful combatants may be attacked, unless they are wounded – after which they enjoy the protection of potentially becoming prisoners of war who may not be punished for directly participating in hostilities. The question then arises whether sensors and algorithm-based decision-making processes can truly make distinctions between these categories and successfully act on the differing obligations that they require. Deciding when civilians take a *direct* part in hostilities is an endlessly complex discussion, since 'combative behaviour' might not be overt; additionally, combatants often conceal their identities, and distinctions must be made between active, injured and surrendering combatants, and combatants preparing ambushes by acting injured or falsely claiming surrender. Are machines truly able to deduce human intentions through subtle body language or tone of voice to adequately identify combatants?[38]

16. Further complicating targeting measures is the rule of proportionality, which has been explained earlier as the weighing of an anticipated military advantage against the expected harm to civilians. The Commentary on the Additional Protocols of 8 June 1977 to the Geneva Conventions of 12 August 1949 states that discussions regarding proportionality are 'a question of common sense and good faith for military commanders',[39] with the ultimate decision being whether or not a 'reasonable military commander' would have engaged

---

37 United States of America, 'Humanitarian Benefits of Emerging Technologies in the Area of Lethal Autonomous Weapon Systems (Submitted by the United States to the Group of Governmental Experts of the High Contracting Parties to the Convention on Prohibitions or Restrictions on the Use of Certain Conventional Weapons Which May Be Deemed to Be Excessively Injurious or to Have Indiscriminate Effects) (UN Doc. CCW/GGE.1/2018/WP.4)', 28 March 2018, para. 26.

38 UN Human Rights Council, *Report of the Special Rapporteur on Extrajudicial, Summary or Arbitrary Executions, Christof Heyns*, p. 13; Human Rights Watch, 'Mind The Gap: The Lack of Accountability for Killer Robots', p. 8; For an optimistic author who believes that recognition technology can improve on human performance, see: Arkin, 'The Case for Ethical Autonomy in Unmanned Systems', pp. 332–341.

39 B. Zimmermann et al., *Commentary on the Additional Protocols of 8 June 1977 to the Geneva Conventions of 12 August 1949* (Leiden: Brill Nijhoff, 1987), p. 682.

the target under the same circumstances.[40] Such a thought exercise is ultimately the result of 'subjective estimates of value and context-specificity' that must be assessed on a case-by-case basis with consideration for all circumstances.[41] Some authors believe that no algorithm can ever truly estimate the value and context of military targets in a sufficiently adequate way to justify a proportionality exercise.[42]

17. The aggregation of these rules leads to an extremely complex and nuanced system for on-the-ground engagements. While the capability of automated decision-making processes to take into account enormous swathes of input data might theoretically help lift the 'fog of war' (i.e. the situational uncertainty experienced by combatants during military operations that might drive them to act 'irrationally') and make objectively 'better' decisions[43] or more ethical decisions (if one follows certain of the aforementioned schools of thought[44]), automated decision-making processes have the major downside of often proving 'inexplicable'. This term is meant to indicate that the end result of an automated decision-making process might be incapable of investigation, correction and reparation since the inferences drawn by the algorithmic process are based on such an enormous quantity of data that they are nearly impossible to track or understand for the human mind.[45] Such *ex ante* and *ex post* inexplicability is simply unacceptable where decisions on human life are concerned. The implication for IHL is that the incomprehensibility renders judgements on compliance and accountability more difficult. If one is incapable of reconstructing the decision process, how does one determine whether or not a violation of humanitarian law has been committed?

18. Another well-known concern regarding the use of AI for decision-making might rear its ugly head in military operations: the algorithms that drive AI are of human design and can therefore contain biases and other flaws that characterise human judgment,[46] while machine learning tools might build their analytical model from data that contains historically discriminatory

---

40 International Criminal Tribunal for the Former Yugoslavia, 'Final Report to the Prosecutor by the Committee Established to Review the NATO Bombing Campaign Against the Federal Republic of Yugoslavia', International Criminal Tribunal for the Former Yugoslavia, 8 June 2000, para. 50.

41 UN Doc. A/HRC/23/47, p. 13.

42 G. de Boisboissel, 'Uses of Lethal Autonomous Weapon Systems', International Conference on Military Technologies (ICMT) 2015, 2015, pp. 1–6.

43 Singer, *Wired for War*, p. 398.

44 Arkin, 'The Case for Ethical Autonomy in Unmanned Systems', pp. 332–341; Umbrello, 'Lethal Autonomous Weapons: Designing War Machines with Values', pp. 30–34.

45 R. Clarke, 'Responsible AI – Part 1: Why the World Wants Controls over Artificial Intelligence', *Roger Clarke* (blog), 24 April 2019, www.rogerclarke.com/EC/AII.html.

46 J. Angwin and others, 'Machine Bias', *ProPublica*, 2016, https://www.propublica.org/article/machine-bias-risk-assessments-in-criminal-sentencing.

patterns, leading to a continuation or exacerbation of existing discriminatory patterns.[47] Coupled with the finding that facial recognition technology – which will inevitably be heavily used by LAWs to identify combatants – is much more accurate in identifying white males than any other race-gender group,[48] this clearly raises questions regarding the accuracy of automated targeting. When taking into account that the hotbeds of military operations are currently mostly situated in the Middle East and Africa and this naturally includes combatants from these regions, these racial biases become deeply problematic for use in the context of an armed conflict.

19. As stated before, Article 36 AP I dictates that states must determine whether the employment of a newly developed weapon would be prohibited by IHL. The UK explicitly recognises this obligation and notes that:

> '[u]nmanned ... aircraft (although a platform rather than a weapon) are subject to multiple legal reviews under Article 36 ... before entering service and operate under the same political authority, command chain supervision, international humanitarian law and rules of engagement as manned aircraft'.[49]

20. More extensive hesitation on placing LAWs outside of human supervision can be found – once again – in the policy of the United States. Its 'Department of Defense Directive 3000.09' states that the design of all autonomous systems, including fully autonomous weapons systems, should 'allow commanders and operators to exercise appropriate levels of human judgment over the use of force'.[50] Two terms in this statement deserve further elucidation: 'appropriate' and 'human judgment over the use of force'. Regarding the latter, the US explained in its 2018 submission to the Group of Governmental Experts of the High Contracting Parties to the Convention on Certain Conventional Weapons (CCW) that 'human judgment over the use of force' should not be conflated with physical control over a weapon, but rather must be understood as the assessment as to how, when, where, and why weapons should be employed.[51] Additionally, it views 'appropriate' as a:

---

47 S. Buranyi, 'Rise of the Racist Robots – How AI Is Learning All Our Worst Impulses', *The Guardian*, 8 August 2017, sec. Inequality, https://www.theguardian.com/inequality/2017/aug/08/rise-of-the-racist-robots-how-ai-is-learning-all-our-worst-impulses; J. Podesta et al., 'Big Data: Seizing Opportunities, Preserving Values' (Executive Office of the US President, May 2014).

48 J. Buolamwini and T. Gebru, 'Gender Shades: Intersectional Accuracy Disparities in Commercial Gender Classification', *Conference on Fairness, Accountability and Transparency*, 2018, http://proceedings.mlr.press/v81/buolamwini18a.html.

49 United Kingdom Ministry of Defence, 'Unmanned Aircraft Systems (Joint Doctrine Publication 0-30.2)', p. 5.

50 US Department of Defense, 'Directive 3000.09 – Autonomy in Weapon Systems', p. 2.

51 *Ibid.* Also see: US Congressional Research Service, *Defense Primer: U.S. Policy on Lethal Autonomous Weapon Systems* (2019).

> 'flexible term that reflects the fact that there is not a fixed, one-size-fits-all level of human judgment that should be applied to every context. What is 'appropriate' can differ across weapon systems, domains of warfare, types of warfare, operational contexts, and even across different functions in a weapon system'.[52]

21. Such a statement implicitly refers to the 'responsibility gap': when engaging in 'technologically mediated warfare' (i.e. whereby machines are used as intermediary tools to engage enemy combatants, or where they act as fully autonomous agents) it becomes increasingly difficult to identify the locus of responsibility for military crimes since LAWs blur the basic distinction between weapons and combatants.[53] How would one even condemn or punish a LAW for committing a war crime? To fill this gap in responsibility, authors such as Galliot suggest applying responsibility in a functional sense: by holding the institutions or those who engineered and deployed the technology in question responsible, the responsibility gap can be closed to an important degree.[54] It remains to be seen whether such a technique would discourage developers from intentionally programming to commit war crimes in a bid to intimidate enemy troops or the civilian population, let alone whether such a system of vicarious responsibility based on the acts of an autonomous weapon would hold up in court.

22. Finally, it is worth noting that LAWs are a striking example of the 'dilemma of control' as posited by Collingridge: it is difficult to exert meaningful regulatory control over emerging technologies due to the lack of knowledge on potentially harmful consequences, yet by the time these adverse effects manifest themselves regulation has become equally difficult due to the proliferation of the technologies in question and the vested interests that have taken shape.[55] One way to possibly address or at the very least anticipate such problems before a technology is implemented into society, is by conducting constructive technology assessments (CTA) when developing LAWs. The goal of CTAs is to bridge the separation between the isolated development of a new technology and its societal uptake through a reflexive process.[56] This is done by way of workshops that gather a variety of actors external to the development of the

---

52 United States of America, 'Human-Machine Interaction in the Development, Deployment and Use of Emerging Technologies in the Area of Lethal Autonomous Weapons Systems (Submitted by the United States to the Group of Governmental Experts of the High Contracting Parties to the Convention on Prohibitions or Restrictions on the Use of Certain Conventional Weapons Which May Be Deemed to Be Excessively Injurious or to Have Indiscriminate Effects) (UN Doc CCW/GGE.2/2018/WP.4)', p. 2.

53 UN Doc A/HRC/23/47, p. 6.

54 J. Galliott, *Military Robots: Mapping the Moral Landscape* (London: Routledge, 2016), pp. 211–232.

55 D. Collingridge, *The Social Control of Technology* (London: Frances Pinter, 1980), p. 19.

56 A. Rip, 'Co-Evolution of Science, Technology and Society (Expert Review for the Bundesministerium Bildung and Forschung, Forderinitiative: Politik, Wissenschaft Und Gesellschaft (Science Policy Studies))' (Berlin: Brandenburgische Akademie der

technology, in addition to the developers of the technology themselves.[57] This allows risks and consequences to be identified that the development team might not have foreseen, or might have chosen to bypass (a phenomenon known as the 'enactment frame', i.e. the perception by developers that society poses a 'challenge' that the technology in question must overcome at all costs).[58] Interestingly, the US Defense Innovation Unit – the branch that awards contracts to private enterprises for the US Department of Defense – issued its so-called 'Responsible AI Guidelines In Practice' document in November 2021 to provide all those involved in defense contracting work with 'specific questions that should be addressed at each phase in the AI lifecycle ... to ensure AI programs align with the DoD's Ethical Principles for AI and ensure that fairness, accountability, and transparency are considered at each step in the development cycle'.[59] The broad scope of the guidelines means their applicability would not just be limited to weaponry, but also to other services built for the military such as HR programs.[60]

23. As a final remark, the inherent expendability and relatively low cost of LAWs compared to human combatants[61] have the repercussion that LAWs could result in a 'normalisation' of armed conflicts, which in turn might reduce the threshold for states to resort to lethal force on the global stage and might cause a reconsideration of armed conflict as being a measure of last resort.[62] The UK, for its part, vehemently rejects this, stating that there is no evidence that the threshold for initiating armed conflicts has been lowered by the use of unmanned weapons.[63] Nonetheless, it is remarkable that the United States

Wissenschaften, 2002); A. Rip, *Futures of Science and Technology in Society* (Enschede: Springer, 2018), p. 100, https://www.springer.com/gp/book/9783658217532.

57 J. Schot and A. Rip, 'The Past and Future of Constructive Technology Assessment', *Technological Forecasting and Social Change*, Technology Assessment: The End of OTA, 54, no. 2, 1 February 1997, pp. 251–268.

58 R. Garud and D. Ahlstrom, 'Technology Assessment: A Socio-Cognitive Perspective', *Journal of Engineering and Technology Management*, 1997, vol. 14, no. 1, pp. 25–48.

59 J. Dunnmon et al., 'Responsible AI Guidelines In Practice', *US Defense Innovation Unit*, November 2021, p. 4.

60 W.D. Heaven, 'The Department of Defense is issuing AI ethics guidelines for tech contractors', *MIT Technology Review*, 16 November 2016, https://www.technologyreview.com/2021/11/16/1040190/department-of-defense-government-ai-ethics-military-project-maven.

61 W. McLean, 'Drones Are Cheap, Soldiers Are Not: A Cost-Benefit Analysis of War', *The Conversation*, 26 June 2014, http://theconversation.com/drones-are-cheap-soldiers-are-not-a-cost-benefit-analysis-of-war-27924.

62 P. Asaro, 'How Just Could a Robot War Be?' in P. Brey, A. Briggle and K. Waelbers (eds), *Current Issues in Computing and Philosophy* (Amsterdam: Ios Press, 2008); A. Krishnan, *Killer Robots: Legality and Ethicality of Autonomous Weapons* (London: Routledge, 2016), p. 150.

63 United Kingdom Ministry of Defence, 'Unmanned Aircraft Systems (Joint Doctrine Publication 0-30.2)', August 2017, p. 5.

(arguably the most powerful military actor in the world with its strong focus on constant research and development to maintain a leading role on the global stage) has indicated hesitation to use LAWs since it fears this might trigger adversaries to also deploy them. On the level of non-state actors, the main concern is that terrorist groups would seize or reverse engineer LAWs to carry out domestic attacks. On the state actor level, one could argue that LAWs might (or already) replace nuclear weapons as the leading deterrence instrument.[64] Of course, deterrence theory presupposes that all rivalling factions possess (more or less) the same destructive power. If the situation would arise, however, whereby one party in a conflict possesses LAWs while the other does not, scholars have noted that the use of unmanned systems possibly creates a morally problematic 'radical asymmetry' that renders it difficult to interpret and apply just war theory.[65] LAWs could thereby exacerbate the existing tendency for modern conflicts to be asymmetrical.

4. CURRENT APPLICATIONS AND FORESEEABLE DEVELOPMENTS

24. Offensive lethal autonomous weapons are currently not widely used on battlefields; in fact, according to the United States, they 'generally do not yet exist'.[66] The most advanced currently used weapons systems could be labelled as 'automatic' weapon systems that focus on defensive posture. Examples thereof are the US Navy Phalanx Close-In Weapon System and Israel's Iron Dome air defence system. Both weapon systems are stationary 'and operate only within tightly set parameters and time frames in comparably structured and controlled environments'[67] while human operators are always on standby, so that they should be distinguished from LAWs. Nonetheless, there are indications that the very 'first' alleged attack by a LAW was carried out in Libya, in the context of Operation 'Peace Storm'. The armed forces associated with the Libyan Government of National Accord (the GNA-AF) launched an assault

64 Umbrello, Torres and De Bellis, 'The Future of War', p. 3.

65 J. Galliott, 'The Asymmetry Objection', in *Military Robots: Mapping the Moral Landscape* (London: Routledge, 2016), pp. 165–186. Just war theory studies the justification of using war in relations between states. For an excellent and extensive discussion, see: R. Lesaffer, 'Too Much History: From War as Sanction to the Sanctioning of War', in M. Weller, *The Oxford Handbook of the Use of Force in International Law* (Oxford: Oxford University Press, 2015), p. 35.

66 US Congressional Research Service, 'Defense Primer: U.S. Policy on Lethal Autonomous Weapon Systems'.

67 F. Sauer, 'Stopping "Killer Robots": Why Now Is the Time to Ban Autonomous Weapons Systems', *Arms Control Association*, https://www.armscontrol.org/act/2016-09/features/stopping-%E2%80%98killer-robots%E2%80%99-why-now-time-ban-autonomous-weapons-systems.

on the Libyan National Army (HAF) along the coast. A United Nations report notes that retreating HAF forces were remotely engaged by 'lethal autonomous weapons systems such as the STM Kargu-2 and other loitering munitions. The lethal autonomous weapons systems were programmed to attack targets without requiring data connectivity between the operator and the munition: in effect, a true "fire, forget and find" capability'.[68] The STM Kargu-2 is described in the report as a rotary wing loitering munition.[69]

25. A 2019 policy primer by the US Congressional Research Service remarkably states that the US is currently not developing LAWs.[70] This comes as something of a surprise, since US state policy does not prohibit the development and/or deployment of LAWs[71] and budget reports disclose that the unclassified expenditures of the US Department of Defense regarding AI contracts amounted to over 600 million dollars in fiscal year 2016 and increased to over 800 million dollars for fiscal year 2017.[72] Moreover, the 2018 national defence strategy of the US noted that '[t]he Department will invest broadly in military application of autonomy, artificial intelligence, and machine learning, including rapid application of commercial breakthroughs, to gain competitive military advantages'[73] and a total budget of 927 million dollars was requested by the Pentagon to carry out further AI investments in fiscal year 2020.[74] In spite of this focus on employing AI to gain strategic military advantages by the Pentagon, audits have nonetheless demonstrated that the internal procedures and infrastructure at the DOD are severely lacking to reach the lofty goals set forward.[75]

26. In what can be seen as a reprise of the arms race that characterised the Cold War, the world's superpowers are clearly engaged in what former US

68 'Final report of the Panel of Experts on Libya established pursuant to Security Council resolution 1973 (2011)', *United Nations Security Council*, 8 March 2021 (UN Doc S/2021/229), https://documents-dds-ny.un.org/doc/UNDOC/GEN/N21/037/72/PDF/N2103772.pdf?Open Element, 17.

69 *Ibid.*, p. 148.

70 US Congressional Research Service, 'Defense Primer: U.S. Policy on Lethal Autonomous Weapon Systems'.

71 *Ibid.*

72 Department of Defense, 'Artificial Intelligence, Big Data, and Cloud Taxonomy', *Govini*, December 2017, p. 9; US Congressional Research Service, 'Artificial Intelligence and National Security', 30 January 2019.

73 United States Department of Defense, 'Summary of the 2018 National Defense Strategy of the United States of America – Sharpening the American Military's Competitive Edge', 2018, p. 7.

74 US Department of Defense, 'DOD Releases Fiscal Year 2020 Budget Proposal', *US Department of Defence* (blog), 12 March 2019.

75 D.C. Tarraf et al., 'The Department of Defense Posture for Artificial Intelligence: Assessment and Recommendations', Product Page (RAND Corporation, 2019), 187 p.

military official and ex-CIA Director David Petraeus calls a 'tech cold war'[76] to acquire the quickest advances in technology to apply them in a military context, with AI being seen as the most valuable technology. Interest groups too note the steady advances towards increased automated decision-making in military applications and the use of political euphemisms to describe these evolutions.[77] Such a general movement towards the higher accuracy that technology can achieve is consistent with the trend to increasingly high-precision weaponry instead of large-scale destructive weapons.[78] Military strategists themselves have acknowledged such a shift towards 'unmanned, intangible, silent warfare'.[79]

27. The United States established the Joint Artificial Intelligence Center in 2018 with the goal of establishing AI 'standards... tools, shared data, reusable technology, processes, and expertise' for the whole US Department of Defense.[80] China too has invested heavily in developing AI for military applications in a bid to solidify its standing on the global stage,[81] establishing the Intelligent Unmanned Systems and Systems of Systems Science and Technology Domain Expert Group within the framework of its People's Liberation Army (PLA). Not only have PLA officials openly conveyed their belief that AI will disruptively change the dynamics of military operations such as joint operations command systems, they have already experimented with an integration of AI into a command and decision-making structure.[82] Nonetheless, China's policy on autonomous weapons is ambiguous: the country has expressed support for prohibiting the use of fully autonomous weapons on the battlefield but does not oppose their development nor production.[83]

28. Additionally, China's research and development (R&D) policy is particularly noteworthy since it employs a national strategy of civil-military integration whereby 'nominally civilian technological capabilities will eventually be utilized

---

76 Interview with CNBC, 'David Petraeus: "We Are in the Early Stages of a Tech Cold War"' (23 July 2019), https://www.cnbc.com/video/2019/07/23/david-petraeus-we-are-in-the-early-stages-of-a-tech-cold-war.html.

77 M.K. Chan, 'Could China Develop Killer Robots in the Near Future? Experts Fear So', *Time*, 13 September 2019, https://time.com/5673240/china-killer-robots-weapons/.

78 Umbrello, 'Lethal Autonomous Weapons: Designing War Machines with Values', p. 32.

79 E. Kania, 'China May Soon Surpass America on the Artificial Intelligence Battlefield', *The National Interest*, 21 February 2017, https://nationalinterest.org/feature/china-may-soon-surpass-america-the-artificial-intelligence-19524.

80 A. Egozi, 'Joint Artificial Intelligence Center Created Under DoD CIO', *Breaking Defense*, https://breakingdefense.com/2018/06/joint-artificial-intelligence-center-created-under-dod-cio/.

81 Kania, 'China May Soon Surpass America on the Artificial Intelligence Battlefield'; P. Robles, 'China Plans to Be a World Leader in Artificial Intelligence by 2030', *South China Morning Post*, https://multimedia.scmp.com/news/china/article/2166148/china-2025-artificial-intelligence/index.html.

82 Kania, 'China May Soon Surpass America on the Artificial Intelligence Battlefield'.

83 Campaign to Stop Killer Robots, 'Country Views on Killer Robots', 22 November 2018.

in a military context'.[84] By relying on the technological prowess of Chinese corporate behemoths such as Alibaba Group, Tencent Holding Ltd., SenseTime and Yitu, as well as new tech start-ups, China is successfully at the top of the field regarding research on AI. Although the US also employs such a strategy to a certain extent, the employees of the private companies in question often protest, leading to a cancellation of public-private partnerships. See, for example, Google's withdrawal from Project MAVEN[85] and the outspoken protest by Microsoft employees regarding the Joint Enterprise Defense Infrastructure (JEDI).[86]

29. LAWs can physically manifest themselves in a number of different ways. Regarding aerial military operations, unmanned aerial vehicles (UAVs) are becoming increasingly autonomous through the use of AI. The most advanced example thereof is perhaps Israel's Harpy drone, which as a 'loitering munition' patrols in one area until a suitable target (i.e. enemy radars) emerges and then proceeds to attack.[87] Scholars argue that the Chinese Army is also planning on using steadily more autonomous UAVs to enhance its 'anti-access/area-denial' (A2/AD) counter-intervention capabilities and carry out more accurate intelligence, surveillance, and reconnaissance (ISR).[88]

30. Additionally, the country is perfecting its tactic of 'swarm warfare' (sometimes also called 'wolfpacks') based on swarm intelligence research, whereby advanced visual and communications technology allows vast amounts of UAVs (but potentially also satellites, combat aircraft or ground vehicles) to group together in hard-to-destroy formations to conduct asymmetric assaults against large weapons platforms (e.g., aircraft carriers).[89] The Blowfish A2 drone by manufacturer Ziyan displays several of those characteristics. A swarm is not centrally controlled and can continue operating, even if it loses numerous units. In 2021, the Pentagon conducted swarm experiments, prompting questions whether 'it is within a human's ability to pick out which ones have to

---

84 Kania, 'China May Soon Surpass America on the Artificial Intelligence Battlefield'.

85 D. Harwell, 'Google to Drop Pentagon AI Contract after Employee Objections to the "Business of War"', *Washington Post*, 2 June 2018, https://www.washingtonpost.com/news/the-switch/wp/2018/06/01/google-to-drop-pentagon-ai-contract-after-employees-called-it-the-business-of-war.

86 M. Murphy, 'Microsoft Workers Protest Bid to Build Pentagon's $10bn AI Warfare System' *The Telegraph*, 13 October 2018, https://www.telegraph.co.uk/technology/2018/10/13/microsoft-workers-protest-bid-build-pentagons-10bn-ai-warfare.

87 See: P. Scharre, *Army of None: Autonomous Weapons and the Future of War*, 1st edition (New York; London: W.W. Norton & Company, 2018), 384 p.

88 E. Kania, 'China's Employment of Unmanned Systems: Across the Spectrum from Peacetime to Wartime', *Lawfare*, 22 May 2017, https://www.lawfareblog.com/chinas-employment-unmanned-systems-across-spectrum-peacetime-wartime.

89 L. Yang, 'Drone Swarming Technique May Change Combat Strategies: Expert', *Global Times*, 13 February 2017, www.globaltimes.cn/content/1032741.shtml; Kania, 'China May Soon Surpass America on the Artificial Intelligence Battlefield'.

be engaged' and whether 'it [is] even necessary to have a human in the loop?'.[90] Notably, the first question must not logically lead to the second. If no human *or* artificial intelligence is able to make the necessary distinction, the weapon cannot comply with international humanitarian law. The United Nations has also employed UAVs during peacekeeping operations, but while former Under-Secretary-General for Peacekeeping Operations Hervé Ladsous endorsed their increasing autonomy, he also explicitly stated that he would only allow their use for surveillance purposes, preferring the use of manned attack helicopters 'under the direct control of the force commander'.[91] In May 2021, Israel became the first country to deploy drone swarms in combat to find and eliminate militants that used highly mobile rocket launchers.[92] Although exact technical details remain scarce, some drones in the swarm would be multi-sensory and the swarm architecture can be integrated with other technologies so that it could communicate data to other weapons or engage targets autonomously.[93] Finally, on aerial combat, the US Air Force published a brief 2019 annex to the Department of Defense AI Strategy wherein it sets out its dedication to wielding AI,[94] and it has been reported to be developing a pilotless version of the F16 fighter as part of the creatively-named 'SkyBorg' program.[95]

31. Another current application is that of 'unmanned maritime systems'. This term indicates two types of vehicles. First, there are unmanned surface vehicles (USVs). These are 'water craft that are either autonomous or remotely navigated and may be launched from the surface, subsurface, air, or land' and are seen as force multipliers due to their anticipated capabilities in stealth, mobility, flexible employment and network usage.[96] One such technology is Sea Mob, a US Marine Corps program that saw a successful demonstration in October 2018.[97] Sea Mob essentially is 'a group of USVs capable of cooperative swarming behaviors'.[98]

---

90 Knight, 'The Pentagon Inches Toward Letting AI Control Weapons'.

91 H. Ladsous, 'Unmanned aerial vehicles are effective in protecting civilians', n.d., https://www.un.org/africarenewal/web-features/unmanned-aerial-vehicles-are-effective-protecting-civilians%E2%80%94herv%C3%A9-ladsous.

92 D. Hambling, 'Israel's Combat-Proven Drone Swarm May Be Start Of A New Kind Of Warfare', *Forbes*, 21 July 2021, https://www.forbes.com/sites/davidhambling/2021/07/21/israels-combat-proven-drone-swarm-is-more-than-just-a-drone-swarm.

93 *Ibid.*

94 US Air Force, 'Artificial Intelligence Annex to The Department of Defense Artificial Intelligence Strategy', 12 September 2019.

95 H. Lye, 'Skyborg: the US Air Force's future AI fleet', *Airforce Technology*, 28 August 2019, https://www.airforce-technology.com/features/skyborg-the-us-air-forces-future-ai-fleet/.

96 United States Navy, *The Commander's Handbook on the Law of Naval Operations August 2017 Edition NWP 1-14M MCTP 11-10B COMDTPUB P5800.7A*, 2017, para. 2.3.4.

97 Fryer-Biggs, 'Coming Soon to the Battlefield', *The Atlantic*, https://www.theatlantic.com/technology/archive/2019/09/killer-robots-and-new-era-machine-driven-warfare/597130/.

98 J. Katz, 'Marine Corps aiming to fully field LRUSV between FY-25 and FY-27', *Inside Defense*, https://www.insidedefense.com/insider/marine-corps-aiming-fully-field-lrusv-between-fy-25-and-fy-27.

Second, the category of unmanned undersea vehicles (UUVs) is different, in that they are 'underwater craft that are either autonomous or remotely navigated and may be launched from the surface, subsurface, air, or land' with employment for – among others – ISR, payload delivery, information operations (IO), and barrier patrol (homeland defence, antiterrorism/force protection (AT/FP)).[99] Their regulation under international law is highly unclear: their status as 'ships' under the United Nations Convention on the Law of the Sea (UNCLOS) is ambiguous, while their classification as warships seems very unlikely; yet, neither the law prevailing in peacetime nor the law of armed conflict seems to preclude their lawful use.[100] Additionally, the status of USVs and UUVs is not dependent on the status of their launch platforms.[101] Differences in human control versus autonomous behaviour or systems being manned or unmanned have not yet been recognised as defining characteristics of what constitutes a 'vessel' or 'ship' under international maritime law.[102] China's development of such vehicles is currently underway through the classified program 912 Project.[103] While the United States Navy has long-since had the Navy Center for Applied Research in Artificial Intelligence (NCARAI), its diminishing output in publications in recent years seems to indicate slow progress in implementing AI into its projects. Nonetheless, in cooperation with the US Defense Advanced Research Projects Agency (DARPA), the 'Sea Hunter' was debuted in 2019. Formerly titled Anti-Submarine Warfare Continuous Trail Unmanned Vehicle (ACTUV), this autonomous submarine scans the ocean and reports the locations of enemy submarines.[104]

32. Finally, autonomous ground vehicles are also in development. In China, the unmanned Cavalry vehicle by Norinco possesses near-autonomy while also being equipped with a machine gun and heavy ordnance such as rocket launchers.[105] The US Army is still conducting tests on the operational readiness of its Squad Multipurpose Equipment Transport (SMET) and is also developing

99 United States Navy, *The Commander's Handbook on the Law of Naval Operations August 2017 Edition NWP 1-14M MCTP 11-10B COMDTPUB P5800.7A*, para. 2.3.5.

100 M.N. Schmitt and D.S. Goddard, 'International Law and the Military Use of Unmanned Maritime Systems', *International Review of the Red Cross* 98, August 2016, no. 902, pp. 567–592.

101 United States Navy, *The Commander's Handbook on the Law of Naval Operations August 2017 Edition NWP 1-14M MCTP 11-10B COMDTPUB P5800.7A*, para. 2.3.6.

102 J. Kraska and R. Pedrozo, 'China's Capture of U.S. Underwater Drone Violates Law of the Sea', *Lawfare*, 16 December 2016, https://www.lawfareblog.com/chinas-capture-us-underwater-drone-violates-law-sea.

103 Chan, 'Could China Develop Killer Robots in the Near Future?'

104 M.T. Klare, 'Autonomous Weapons Systems and the Laws of War', *Arms Control Association*, March 2019, https://www.armscontrol.org/act/2019-03/features/autonomous-weapons-systems-laws-war.

105 Chan, 'Could China Develop Killer Robots in the Near Future?'

its so-called Robotic Combat Vehicle (RCV).[106] In a 2017 document, it moreover explained that it takes a progressive approach to robotic and autonomous systems (RAS) 'that begins with tethered systems, followed by wireless remote control, teleoperation, semi-autonomous functions, and then fully autonomous systems'.[107]

5. NECESSITY OF A LEGAL FRAMEWORK

33. A truly autonomous lethal weapon might not exist just yet, but as the previous part shows, that development looms prominently on the horizon. It is therefore not unreasonable to anticipate actual LAWs with a separate legal framework governing their development and/or deployment. In the debate on the regulation of LAWs, the main positions staked out over the past few years have existed along a continuum that ranges from the most restrictive, namely a pre-emptive ban on all fully autonomous lethal weapons *per se*, to the principled assertion that IHL as it exists today provides sufficient rules to forego any regulatory initiative. However, between these two poles, plenty of nuanced positions have been taken, usually involving a separate legal framework for LAWs, such as a treaty. For example, there have been debates within the UN's 1980 Convention on Certain Conventional Weapons (CCW) to respond to the challenges relating to the potential development of lethal autonomous weapons system, most recently in November 2019.[108]

34. In determining whether a new regulatory framework is necessary, the positions taken largely correspond with how stakeholders and policy makers assess the application of existing rules of international humanitarian law. According to the NGO coalition 'Campaign to Stop Killer Robots' (CSKR), 'fully autonomous weapons would lack the inherently human characteristics such as compassion that are necessary to make complex ethical choices',[109] implying that LAWs are by their nature unable to comply with the core principles of distinction and the prohibition of unnecessary suffering. To stress this point, CSKR argues that LAWs 'would lack the human judgment necessary to evaluate the proportionality of an attack, distinguish civilian

---

106 Klare, 'Autonomous Weapons Systems and the Laws of War'.

107 U.S. Army Training and Doctrine Command, 'The U.S. Army Robotic and Autonomous Systems Strategy', March 2017, p. 3.

108 CCW, Meeting of the High Contracting Parties to the Convention on Prohibitions or Restrictions on the Use of Certain Conventional Weapons Which May Be Deemed to Be Excessively Injurious or to Have Indiscriminate Effects, 15 November 2019, UN Doc. CCW/MSP/2019/CRP.2/Rev.1.

109 Campaign to Stop Killer Robots, https://www.stopkillerrobots.org/learn.

from combatant, and abide by other core principles of the laws of war'.[110] At least 30 states have expressed their support for a ban on LAWs.[111] According to CKSR, a treaty on fully autonomous weapons should entail three core obligations: (1) a general obligation to maintain meaningful human control over the use of force; (2) prohibitions on weapons systems that select and engage targets and by their nature pose fundamental moral or legal problems; (3) specific positive obligations to help ensure that meaningful human control is maintained in the use of all other systems that select and engage targets.[112]

35. On the other hand, states with a more permissive stance on LAWs generally agree that international humanitarian law as it exists suffices. It is significant in this context that, with the exception of China, the four other Permanent Members of the United Nations Security Council oppose prohibition.[113] Other notable opponents of a treaty on fully autonomous weapons are Australia, Israel, South Korea and Turkey. In general, these states argue that LAWs do not necessarily violate the IHL rule that weapons cannot be indiscriminate by their nature. The argument against a blanket prohibition can be summarised as the stance that the autonomous character of a weapon does not render it illegal *per se*.

It is primarily argued that LAWs are not *by their nature* indiscriminate, and thus do not violate Article 51(4)(b) AP I. Any weapon can be deemed indiscriminate when not applied in its intended battlefield condition. For instance, an anti-aircraft gun aimed at a village cannot discriminate between military and non-military objectives. Furthermore, regarding the prohibition of unnecessary suffering or superfluous injury, opponents of a ban on LAWs stress that LAWs are not necessarily any different from regular weapons in this context. In that sense, they would not violate Article 35 AP I. States opposed to a treaty will therefore argue that the phrase 'of a nature' in Article 35(2) AP I should be read in the light of the situation in which the weapon is deployed.[114] Finally, opponents of a prohibition argue that Article 36 AP I provides a strong safeguard, as it entails the duty to assess IHL compliance during the development

---

110 *Ibid.*

111 CSKR, *Country Views on Killer Robots*: the states in favor of a ban are Algeria, Argentina, Austria, Bolivia, Brazil, Chile, China, Colombia, Costa Rica, Cuba, Djibouti, Ecuador, Egypt, El Salvador, Ghana, Guatemala, Holy See, Iraq, Jordan, Mexico, Morocco, Namibia, Nicaragua, Pakistan, Panama, Peru, State of Palestine, Uganda, Venezuela, Zimbabwe, https://www.stopkillerrobots.org/wp-content/uploads/2019/10/KRC_CountryViews_25Oct2019rev.pdf.

112 CSKR, 'Key elements of a Treaty on Fully Autonomous Weapons', November 2019, https://www.stopkillerrobots.org/wp-content/uploads/2020/04/Key-Elements-of-a-Treaty-on-Fully-Autonomous-WeaponsvAccessible.pdf.

113 I.e. France, the Russian Federation, the United States of America and the United Kingdom.

114 K. Anderson, D. Reisner and M. Waxman, 'Adapting the Law of Armed Conflict to Autonomous Weapon Systems', *International Law Studies*, 2014, vol. 90, pp. 386–411.

and acquisition of new weapons. One must, however, wonder how comforting it is to rely on this process when it is largely conducted behind closed doors.

36. Efforts have been made to debate the regulation of LAWs within UN mechanisms. The High Contracting Parties to the CCW decided in December 2016 to establish an open-ended Group of Governmental Experts (GGE) related to emerging technologies in the area of lethal autonomous weapon systems.[115] The Group held its first session from 13 to 17 November 2017 in Geneva. Since then, it has regularly met to discuss regulation of lethal autonomous weapons. These debates do not solely concern IHL aspects of LAWs, but also cover ethics, technology and political issues, with room for states and non-state entities to voice their opinions and share their expertise. The International Committee of the Red Cross has argued in these debates that a minimal level of human control must be maintained over weapon systems to ensure compliance with international law.[116] UN Secretary-General António Guterres stated his opposition to fully autonomous lethal weapons in a message to the GGE on 25 March 2019: 'machines with the power and discretion to take lives without human involvement are politically unacceptable, morally repugnant and should be prohibited by international law'.[117] The UN Secretary General's May 2020 report on the Protection of Civilians in Armed Conflict acknowledged the divergent views among nations with regards to the need for a treaty, but noted that 'all sides appear to be in agreement that, at a minimum, retention of human control or judgment about the use of force is necessary'.[118]

37. The arguments brought forward by the states opposing a treaty may sound altogether convincing when assessed from a world in which the march of technological progress is as unstoppable as it is unpredictable, and where growing rifts between global factions complicate international negotiations over treaties. When applied correctly, a limited number of clearly worded principles provide more legal certainty, whatever the future brings, than a proliferation of detailed legal instruments that enjoy less-than-overwhelming support. Nevertheless, it must be noted that the proponents of the principled hands-off approach to this question of international law have undeniable economic and military interests

---

115 CCW, Decision 1, UN Doc. CCW/CONF.V/10.

116 ICRC, 'Ethics and autonomous weapon systems: An ethical basis for human control?', 29 March 2018, UN Doc. CCW/GGE.1/2018/WP.5.

117 UN, 'Secretary-General's message to Meeting of the Group of Governmental Experts on Emerging Technologies in the Area of Lethal Autonomous Weapons Systems', 25 March 2019, press release, https://www.un.org/sg/en/content/sg/statement/2019-03-25/secretary-generals-message-meeting-of-the-group-of-governmental-experts-emerging-technologies-the-area-of-lethal-autonomous-weapons-systems.

118 UN Secretary-General, 'Protection of civilians in armed conflict', 6 May 2020, UN Doc. S/2020/366, p. 9.

in the development, manufacture and sale of lethal autonomous weapons. It is therefore unsurprising that a rising number of states are opposed to the existing body of IHL being the only form of regulation of LAWs. Put more forcefully, the odds of ratifying new instruments by States that develop, sell, or deploy LAWs are very slim.

38. The prospect of reaching global consensus on the regulation of LAWs seems more unlikely than ever, with experts noting that Russia's invasion of Ukraine has further exacerbated existing fault lines within the GGE. There have always been strong disagreements between states on a common definition, on the required degree of human control, and on the possibility of LAWs giving any state a decisive military advantage. However, Russia now takes the position that 'meaningful human control' over LAWs is indispensable while also opposing any expansion of existing international legal frameworks – raising the question of whether different forums than the GGE should be pursued to negotiate on the regulation of LAWs.[119]

6. CONCLUSION

39. Autonomous 'killer robots', as such, do not yet exist. However, their realisation is on the horizon. Accordingly, it is prudent to assess what the applicable body of law would be to regulate fully autonomous lethal weapons. As the means of warfare available to parties in an armed conflict are not unlimited, any lethal autonomous weapon would have to comply with international humanitarian law, and more specifically with its cardinal principles; the principle of distinction, proportionality, precaution, the prohibition of unnecessary or superfluous suffering, and the rules that derive from these principles. Moreover, parties to an armed conflict are restrained by the principles of humanity and dictates of public conscience, wherever existing IHL instruments do not provide adequate regulation.

40. Opinions differ as to whether LAWs are ultimately capable of complying with these principles. Ethical and moral arguments, as well as economic ones, feature prominently in the debate over the degree of autonomy that ought to be entrusted to weapon systems. In any case, research and development of LAWs is racing ahead. A rising number of states appeal for a treaty to either regulate or ban LAWs on moral grounds. Some very powerful actors, chiefly states

---

[119] E. Hoffberger-Pippan, V. Vohs and P. Köhler, 'Autonomous Weapons Systems: UN Expert Talks Facing Failure', *Stiftung Wissenschaft und Politik*, 5 July 2022, https://www.swp-berlin.org/en/publication/autonomous-weapons-systems-un-expert-talks-facing-failuretime-to-consider-alternative-formats.

involved in the development of LAWs oppose a separate treaty and argue that the current body of IHL suffices. As UN talks move forward, an international legal instrument inches closer.

CHAPTER 8

AI IN THE HOME: DATA PROTECTION REQUIREMENTS FOR SMART HOME ASSISTANTS

Carl VANDER MAELEN*, Eva LIEVENS**, Ingrida MILKAITE*** and Judith VERMEULEN****

1. INTRODUCTION

1. More and more appliances that are connected to the internet – also known as the 'internet of things' or IoT – are entering the home. Such domestic appliances offer convenience to the user, but also collect information about the environment in which they are placed. The information collected can range from objective facts, such as the ambient temperature, to very personal data concerning its user. This contribution focuses on one specific application of AI in a domestic IoT setting: smart home assistants (SHAs).

2. This contribution chooses to investigate the currently most widely used SHAs: the combination of a smart speaker with a virtual personal assistant (VPA). In 2021, it was estimated that 94 million people in the United States own at least one smart speaker; of that group, 24% owns Amazon Echo devices and 13% owns Google devices.[1] In Australia, 26% of the population was estimated to own a smart speaker, with the majority owning Google devices (24%, compared to 3% Amazon speakers).[2] A 2020 UK survey revealed that 22% of

* Academic assistant, research group Law & Technology, Faculty of Law and Criminology, Ghent University.
** Professor Law & Technology, research group Law & Technology, Faculty of Law and Criminology, Ghent University.
*** Postdoctoral researcher, research group Law & Technology, Faculty of Law and Criminology, Ghent University.
**** Voluntary postdoctoral researcher, research group Law & Technology, Faculty of Law and Criminology, Ghent University.

1 X, 'The Infinite Dial 2021', *Edison Research*, March 2021, 8–10.

2 X, 'The Smart Audio Report Australia 2021', *Edison Research*, July 2021, 3–6.

those interviewed owned such a device.[3] In the Netherlands, around 19% of the population is estimated to have a smart speaker in their household.[4] For Belgium, no numbers were found.

3. A smart speaker can be defined as '[a] wireless speaker that includes other functions'[5] and is produced by a range of companies, including audio technology companies such as Sonos. VPAs are communicative programs that operate on the basis of AI.[6] They accept the voice of users as input, identify commands or questions in the voice input, and then produce a response.[7] The European Data Protection Board (EDPB) calls them 'virtual voice assistants' and defines them as 'a software application that provides capabilities for oral dialogue with a user in natural language'.[8] The most well-known example is perhaps Apple's Siri: a disembodied voice present on all recent mobile Apple devices that helps users look up information and control their device through voice commands. Other tech companies have also developed their own VPAs, such as Amazon's Alexa, Microsoft's Cortana and Samsung's Bixby.

4. The combination of a VPA and smart speaker usually takes the form of a small sphere (the smart speaker) placed in a central location or possibly several rooms in the house. The device remains on stand-by mode while waiting for owners to activate it through a 'wake-up word' (generally the name of the VPA, such as 'Alexa'). This is usually followed up by a request to look up information, send messages, call someone, make a note, set a reminder or an alarm, provide entertainment such as music, or manipulate living conditions in the house through interactions with individual connected smart devices,[9] such as changing the temperature through smart thermostats[10] or the lighting through smart

[3] Shankar and others, 'Taking New Steps into the Smart Home', p. 4.

[4] X, 'Smart home monitor', *Multiscope*, 2020, www.multiscope.nl/persberichten/slimme-speaker-verovert-huiskamer-consument.

[5] X, 'Definition of Smart Speaker', *PCMag*, https://www.pcmag.com/encyclopedia/term/smart-speaker.

[6] N. Ni Loideain and R. Adams, 'From Alexa to Siri and the GDPR: The Gendering of Virtual Personal Assistants and the Role of Data Protection Impact Assessments', *Computer Law & Security Review*, 2020, vol. 36, article 105366, pp. 1–14.

[7] X, 'TechDispatch #1 Smart Speakers and Virtual Assistants', *European Data Protection Supervisor*, https://edps.europa.eu/data-protection/our-work/publications/techdispatch/techdispatch-1-smart-speakers-and-virtual_en.

[8] European Data Protection Board (EDPB), 'Guidelines 02/2021 on virtual voice assistants – Version 2.0', 7 July 2021, 8.

[9] M. Simon, 'Google Assistant Works with over 5,000 Smart Devices, but Alexa Is Far in the Lead with 12,000', *Tech Hive*, 3 May 2018, https://www.techhive.com/article/3269825/google-assistant-5000-smart-devices.html.

[10] X, 'Alexa.ThermostatController Interface', *Alexa Skills Kit*, https://developer.amazon.com/en-US/docs/alexa/device-apis/alexa-thermostatcontroller.html.

lights and switches.[11] Those domestic tasks are presented as the main application for the combination of VPAs and smart speakers,[12] justifying our choice for the term 'smart home assistants'.

5. It must be noted that a new trend is emerging whereby SHAs forgo the need for a wake-up word and instead proactively offer services. The Google Nest Hub can automatically track sleep patterns (after the initial set-up has been completed) and enlarge information on the screen when users are further away.[13] When the Amazon Echo Show 10 has been activated, its screen will rotate automatically to face the user and will continue to do so as they move around.[14] The underlying reasoning behind such functionalities is to reduce 'the burden or cognitive load on a customer' and guide them towards device features that they may otherwise not use.[15]

6. SHAs provide an ideal case study for this chapter due to their reliance on AI, their high consumer uptake,[16] the fact that they engage in extensive and sensitive data collection due to their placement in a domestic setting, and the low awareness among users of the data protection concerns associated with them.[17] The issues and questions surrounding them strike at the core of data protection and privacy concerns. It was found, for instance, that the devices can be inadvertently activated due to the smart speaker mistakenly recognising its wake-up word.[18] This is highly problematic when taking into account revelations by whistle-blowers that many tech companies share recordings with contractors 'tasked with grading the responses on a variety of factors, including whether the activation of the voice assistant was deliberate or accidental, whether the query was something [the VPA] could be expected to help with and whether

---

11 X, 'Alexa Smart Lighting & Switches', *Alexa Skills Kit*, https://developer.amazon.com/en-US/alexa/devices/lighting-switches-plugs.

12 EDPB, 'Guidelines 02/2021 on virtual voice assistants – Version 2.0', p. 7.

13 A-M. Alcántara, 'Smart Speakers Go Beyond Waiting to Be Asked', *The Wall Street Journal*, 10 May 2021, https://www.wsj.com/articles/smart-speakers-go-beyond-waiting-to-be-asked-11620640802?mc_cid=286f9a7bcb&mc_eid=124d5bb316.

14 W. Greenwald, 'Amazon Echo Show 10 (3rd Gen) Review', *PCMag*, 9 June 2021, https://www.pcmag.com/reviews/amazon-echo-show-10–3rd-generation.

15 Alcántara, 'Smart Speakers Go Beyond Waiting to Be Asked'.

16 A. Al-Heeti, 'Amazon Has Sold More than 100 Million Alexa Devices', *CNET*, 4 January 2019, https://www.cnet.com/news/amazon-has-sold-more-than-100-million-alexa-devices; K. Bitterly, '1 in 4 Americans Own a Smart Speaker. What Does That Mean for News?', *Medium*, 23 August 2019, https://open.nytimes.com/how-might-the-new-york-times-sound-on-smart-speakers-3b59a6a78ae3.

17 J. Lau, B. Zimmerman and F. Schaub, 'Alexa, Are You Listening? Privacy Perceptions, Concerns and Privacy-Seeking Behaviors with Smart Speakers', *Proceedings of the ACM on Human-Computer Interaction*, 2018, vol. 2, Article 102.

18 D.J. Dubois and others, 'Smart Speakers Study – When Speakers Are All Ears: Understanding When Smart Speakers Mistakenly Record Conversations', *Mon(IoT)r Research Group*, 2020, https://moniotrlab.ccis.neu.edu/smart-speakers-study.

[the VPA's] response was appropriate'.[19] In the course of doing so, contractors have reported hearing highly private information, such as a doctor-patient discussion and individuals having sex.[20] Since the whistle-blowers also report that '[t]hese recordings are accompanied by user data showing location, contact details, and app data [...] it wouldn't be hard to identify [the individuals on the recordings]'.[21]

7. Yet, the right to personal data protection is a fundamental right encapsulated in Article 8 of the Charter of Fundamental Rights of the European Union (EU).[22] The Article states that everyone does not merely have 'the right to the protection of personal data concerning him or her', but also stipulates that

> '[s]uch data must be processed fairly for specified purposes and on the basis of the consent of the person concerned or some other legitimate basis laid down by law. Everyone has the right of access to data which has been collected concerning him or her, and the right to have it rectified.'

8. In the EU, the main legislative instrument that aims to guarantee the right to protection of personal data is the General Data Protection Regulation (GDPR). This instrument became applicable in May 2018 and updated the EU's personal data protection framework – previously established in the 1995 Data Protection Directive – to better take into account the technological developments of the past decades.

9. The research aim of this contribution is to study SHAs through the lens of the data protection framework and the GDPR in particular. As a result, the central research question aims to uncover which data protection issues arise due to the specific characteristics of SHAs. In order to sketch a comprehensive answer to this question, the contribution also investigates which obligations data controllers and processors need to fulfil, which rights data subjects – i.e., the individuals whose data is processed – have, which remedies the latter can rely on and whether enforcement actions have already been undertaken in relation to SHAs' data protection issues.

---

19 A. Hern, 'Apple Contractors 'regularly Hear Confidential Details' on Siri Recordings', *The Guardian*, 26 July 2019, https://www.theguardian.com/technology/2019/jul/26/apple-contractors-regularly-hear-confidential-details-on-siri-recordings; G. Corera, 'Smart Speaker Recordings Reviewed by Humans', *BBC News*, 11 April 2019, https://www.bbc.com/news/technology-47893082.

20 Hern, 'Apple Contractors 'regularly Hear Confidential Details' on Siri Recordings'.

21 *Ibid.*

22 The right to personal data protection must be distinguished from the right to privacy, which features in Article 7 of the Charter.

10. These research questions are discussed at length in the next part, which is structured parallel to, and in the same order as the GDPR (part 2). It first investigates the complicated relationship between SHAs and the principle of lawfulness (Articles 5–7 GDPR). We also shed light on the rights of children as a category of data subjects who not only merit extra protection but are often 'invisibly' present in the settings where SHAs are located[23] (recital 38 and Article 8 GDPR), and on the processing of special categories of personal data by SHAs (Article 9 GDPR). The next section sets out the transparency requirements of the GDPR, which are especially challenging for SHAs to fulfil (Articles 12, 13 and 14 GDPR). Other rights bestowed to data subjects, such as the rights to erasure, restriction, portability and objection (Articles 15–21 GDPR), are addressed as well. The chapter then casts light on automated decision making and SHAs, which forms a particular cause for concern (Article 22 GDPR). We also look at the main obligations for data controllers and processors and emphasise in particular the usefulness of data protection impact assessments (Articles 24–35 GDPR). We subsequently discuss the limited enforcement action that has been taken regarding potential GDPR violations in the context of SHAs (Articles 66 and 77–80 GDPR). The last part of this chapter draws brief conclusions on how a shift towards data protection compliant SHAs could be endeavoured in the near future (part 3).

11. This chapter employs traditional legal doctrinal research methods. We interpret and analyse the rules laid down in the GDPR within the context of the use of SHAs as an increasingly widespread new phenomenon in our society.[24] The rules governing the field of personal data protection are systematically exposed and applied to SHAs, while also analysing the relationship between applicable rules, areas of concern and future developments.[25] By using a legislative instrument as a starting point and examining how the rules are applied to this specific technology, we employ a method of deductive and explanatory legal reasoning.[26]

12. This contribution does not represent an exhaustive and definitive study on SHAs. Certain considerations in that respect are relevant. First, SHAs are made by a broad range of manufacturers who have very different compliance policies and technical approaches. Although we oftentimes know about differences regarding the former (such as through publicly disclosed statements

---

23 Recital 38 GDPR.

24 T. Hutchinson and N. Duncan, 'Defining and Describing What We Do: Doctrinal Legal Research', *Deakin Law Review*, 2012, vol. 17, no. 1, p. 110.

25 T. Hutchinson, *Researching and Writing in Law* (Pyrmont: Thomson Reuters/Lawbook Company, 2010), p. 7.

26 J. Hynes Farrar, *Legal Reasoning* (Pyrmont: Thomson Reuters/Lawbook Company, 2010), p. 91; Hutchinson and Duncan, 'Defining and Describing What We Do', p. 111.

on companies' policy regarding the erasure of recordings), the latter frequently remains opaque since developers often choose to not publicly share how the algorithms driving their AI assistants function. Much more research into the different approaches taken by these companies is still necessary, and it should furthermore be interdisciplinary in nature, involving in particular computer scientists and experts in natural language processing to paint a complete picture. Second, the use of SHAs also raises important ethical questions, about which valuable research regarding smart technologies in the domestic sphere has already been conducted.[27] Even though there might be overlapping considerations from an ethical and a legal perspective, this contribution solely focuses on the latter, and particularly on specific data protection issues. Finally, as has been noted extensively in scholarly work, the development of modern technological innovation is occurring at an unprecedented pace.[28] In combination with the fact that producers of SHAs regularly amend their policies or the functionalities of these devices as a result of internal or external factors (for instance, leaked information)[29] we concede that certain practices that are included in this chapter might cease to exist or might change in the near future. The chapter includes developments up to December 2021.

13. Other delineations of the scope of this chapter relate to the legislative instruments that guide the analysis. As a regulation, the GDPR is directly applicable in all EU Member States. Although some of its clauses are 'open' and Member States thus have a choice in how to implement them (for example regarding the age of consent for the processing of children's personal data in the context of information society services), the majority of the provisions does not allow for derogations. Therefore, the Belgian federal law '*Wet betreffende de bescherming van natuurlijke personen met betrekking tot de verwerking van persoonsgegevens*' of 30 July 2018 which implements (a.o.) certain provisions of the GDPR will not feature extensively in this contribution. The future ePrivacy Regulation has also been excluded from the scope of this contribution. Designed as a replacement for the ePrivacy Directive (Directive 2002/58/EC), it will act as *lex specialis* to the GDPR by specifying and complementing the GDPR regarding

---

27 F. Allhoff and A. Henschke, 'The Internet of Things: Foundational Ethical Issues', *Internet of Things*, 2018, vol. 1–2, pp. 55–66; See also specifically regarding smart home health technologies: G. Birchley et al., 'Smart Homes, Private Homes? An Empirical Study of Technology Researchers' Perceptions of Ethical Issues in Developing Smart-Home Health Technologies', *BMC Medical Ethics*, 2017, vol. 18, Article 23; V. Gabriela Sánchez, I. Taylor and P. Cecilie Bing-Jonsson, 'Ethics of Smart House Welfare Technology for Older Adults: A Systematic Literature Review', *International Journal of Technology Assessment in Health Care*, 2017, vol. 33, pp. 691–699.

28 N. Cortez, 'Regulating Disruptive Innovation', *Berkeley Technology Law Journal*, 2014, vol. 29, p. 175; S. Ranchordás, 'Does Sharing Mean Caring: Regulating Innovation in the Sharing Economy', *Minnesota Journal of Law Science & Technology*, 2015, vol. 16, pp. 413–475.

29 See, for example, part 2.5.

the provision and use of electronic communications services.[30] Negotiations regarding this instrument are still underway at the time of writing (in fact, several rounds of negotiations between the Member States resulted in a failure to find consensus up until the middle of 2022).

2. SHAS AND THE GENERAL DATA PROTECTION REGULATION

14. In 2018, the GDPR became applicable throughout the EU. It is a common misconception that the GDPR is a trailblazing instrument that creates a framework for data protection where formerly there was none, when in fact it updates and builds upon the provisions of the Data Protection Directive dating from 1995.[31] The GDPR thus did not create an EU personal data protection framework, but rather modernised the existing legislative framework to keep pace with rapid technological evolutions.

2.1. SCOPE OF THE GDPR

15. A crucial aspect for this chapter is the applicability of the GDPR's provisions to SHAs. As determined by the definitions set out in Article 4 GDPR, the regulation is applicable insofar as personal data is processed. Both the concepts of 'personal data' and 'processing' deserve further elucidation.

16. Personal data refers to 'any information relating to an identified or identifiable natural person' (Article 4 (1) GDPR). The EDPB notes that any interaction that a data subject has with a VPA can be brought under this definition and that the initial input of personal data will generate subsequent personal data such as 'primary data (e.g., account data, voice recordings, requests history), observed data (e.g., device data that relates to a data subject, activity logs, online activities), as well as inferred or derived data (e.g., user profiling)'.[32] The processing of these different types of data can have distinct repercussions.

---

[30] Notably, the EDPB has emphasised the importance of the application of the ePrivacy Directive in its Guidelines on virtual voice assistants.
For more information on the interplay between the currently applicable ePrivacy Directive and the GDPR, please refer to the EDPB Opinion 5/2019 on the interplay between the ePrivacy Directive and the GDPR, in particular regarding the competence, tasks and powers of supervisory authorities (adopted on 12 March 2019).

[31] In turn, the Data Protection Directive was inspired by the Council of Europe Convention for the Protection of Individuals with regard to Automatic Processing of Personal Data of 1981; https://www.coe.int/en/web/conventions/full-list/-/conventions/treaty/108.

[32] EDPB, 'Guidelines 02/2021 on virtual voice assistants – Version 2.0', 14.

This will be further discussed in the next sub-sections in this chapter (see sections 2.1, 2.3 and 2.6).

17. Many devices, such as laptops and phones, generally only have one user. The information produced during the device's lifespan is therefore linked to this individual. This is quite different for SHAs in domestic settings. Where individuals live together under one roof, different probable data subjects emerge. In case of families, for instance, one parent might be the buyer of the device, the other could be the account holder, there might be children in the household, and occasionally guests could visit. The multitude of natural persons and information relating to them is one of the specific characteristics of SHAs and therefore it is useful to make distinctions based on design space literature.[33] *Primary* users are those who connect the SHA to their personal account; *secondary* users – often household members – are users of the SHA who do not have an account linked to a SHA (and who, hence, have potentially less control over the system and may not be informed on data collection and processing practices); and *incidental* users – such as guests in the home – are present in the setting where the SHA is functioning but may not be aware of the collection and processing of their personal information or may only interact with the SHA on an incidental basis.[34]

18. This raises important questions regarding the ability of SHAs to distinguish between individual users. Such a distinction is vital in the context of the GDPR, since the identification of an individual whose data is processed as a data subject has important implications for the observance of the principles and obligations laid down in the regulation. On the basis of information that is shared by SHAs it seems that (at least some) SHAs are able to differentiate between user voices.[35] The creation of acoustic models of voice characteristics not only allow SHAs to make *prima facie* assessments about different individuals speaking to it, but by aggregating this with additional data such as metadata (e.g., the individual's location[36]) and input data (such as the questions asked by the individual) a detailed profile of a user can be constructed.[37]

---

33 F. Schaub and others, 'A Design Space for Effective Privacy Notices', *SOUPS '15: Proceedings of the Eleventh USENIX Conference on Usable Privacy and Security*, 2015, pp. 1–17.

34 J. De Meyer, *The Domestication of Smart Home Assistants: Recommendations for Data Controllers on How to Protect Children's Personal Data in Accordance with the GDPR – A Case Study of Amazon Alexa, Google Assistant and Apple Siri*, Master's dissertation law Ghent University, 2020; Schaub and others, 'A Design Space for Effective Privacy Notices', p. 4.

35 See for instance X, 'Alexa and Alexa Device FAQs', *Amazon Inc.*, https://www.amazon.com/gp/help/customer/display.html/ref=hp_left_v4_sib?ie=UTF8&nodeId=201602230: 'Alexa can automatically recognize the voices of users in your household over time to improve personalization of certain Alexa features. You can also create a voice profile, so Alexa can call you by name and do more to personalize your experience.'

36 X, 'Alexa Terms of Use', *Amazon Inc.*, 30 June 2020, https://www.amazon.com/gp/help/customer/display.html?nodeId=201809740.

37 X, 'Alexa and Alexa Device FAQs'.

19. The next part will explore the implications of the fact that primary, secondary and incidental users interact with a SHA for the lawfulness of processing. Additionally, the creation of profiles and the use thereof will be further scrutinised in part 2.6.

20. Processing is defined by the GDPR as:

> 'any operation or set of operations which is performed on personal data or on sets of personal data, whether or not by automated means, such as collection, recording, organisation, structuring, storage, adaptation or alteration, retrieval, consultation, use, disclosure by transmission, dissemination or otherwise making available, alignment or combination, restriction, erasure or destruction' (Article 4 (2) GDPR).

21. When a SHA, for instance an Amazon/Alexa device, is in stand-by mode (i.e. it has not been activated by the wake-up word) it records several seconds of sound that are 'continuously overwriting the contents of the small internal audio buffer' without local records of audio being kept.[38] The device does not transmit audio and remains in this dedicated operation of detecting a wake-up word.[39] However, when the wake-up word is said, the smart speaker begins recording audio and this is streamed to the data controller's processing servers.[40] Here, the audio is transcribed into text through automatic speech recognition technologies, such as natural language processing. All of these acts fall within the notion of 'processing' (Article 4 (2) GDPR). What is being processed predominantly falls within the scope of the notion of 'personal data' (Article 4 (1) GDPR). Besides the content of the user's command or questions, elements such as the user's location are also processed.[41] Additionally, the user's voice is analysed acoustically,[42] which, according to the EDPB, entails the processing of biometric data (see below).

22. The input audio is not only processed to allow users' questions to be answered as correctly as possible, but also with the long-term goal of improving the functioning of the speech recognition technology.[43] In this way, the

---

38 X, 'Alexa Privacy and Data Handling Overview', *Amazon Web Services Inc.*, July 2018, p. 2 https://d1.awsstatic.com/product-marketing/A4B/White%20Paper%20-%20Alexa%20Privacy%20and%20Data%20Handling%20Overview.pdf.

39 EDPB, 'Guidelines 02/2021 on virtual voice assistants – Version 2.0', p. 10.

40 Amazon has indicated that it will move to voice processing via the device itself, bypassing the need for streaming to servers. See: Larry Hardesty, 'Alexa's new speech recognition abilities showcased at Interspeech', *Amazon Science*, 22 October 2020, https://www.amazon.science/blog/alexas-new-speech-recognition-abilities-showcased-at-interspeech.

41 X, 'Alexa Terms of Use'.

42 X, 'Alexa and Alexa Device FAQs'.

43 M. Kelly and N. Statt, 'Amazon Confirms It Holds on to Alexa Data Even If You Delete Audio Files', *The Verge*, 3 July 2019, https://www.theverge.com/2019/7/3/20681423/amazon-alexa-echo-chris-coons-data-transcripts-recording-privacy.

technology is taught how to deal with different accents and dialects,[44] new vocabulary and challenging acoustic environments.[45] A related goal is to personalise the user's experience. By building up a profile of the user, the SHA can offer more relevant answers and also lead the user to relevant commercial products (see for instance Amazon's example that Alexa can recommend purchasing music that matches the user's taste).[46]

23. A variety of actors is inevitably involved in the entire life cycle of a SHA. The EDPB discerns five main categories: the provider or designer of the VPA; developers of applications for the VPA; the integrator (the entity that manufactures connected objects (such as a smart speaker) and wishes to equip them with a VPA); the owner (in charge of physical spaces receiving people); and the user.[47] Because of the many actors involved in this ecosphere, it is essential to establish which actors can be classified as 'data controllers' and which other actors would be 'data processors'. The former refers to 'the natural or legal person, public authority, agency or other body which, alone or jointly with others, determines the purposes and means of the processing of personal data' (Article 4 (7) GDPR) while the latter is 'a natural or legal person, public authority, agency or other body which processes personal data on behalf of the controller' (Article 4 (8) GDPR). Such distinctions are crucial, since the controller ultimately carries the main responsibility for the handling of personal data and is responsible for implementing 'appropriate technical and organisational measures to ensure and to be able to demonstrate that processing is performed in accordance with [the GDPR]' (Article 24 GDPR).

24. The EDPB has clarified that the qualifications of the different actors should be established on a case-by-case basis and that a single actor can take on different qualifications depending on the situation.[48] As an example, a company such as Amazon would be considered the data controller if it determines the purposes and means of a processing operation with an Amazon Alexa device. However, if the data subject is using an application built by a third-party developer, Amazon would act in the role of data processor since it processes personal data on behalf of the application developer, and the application developer would be the data controller. The EDPB also states that the designer, the integrator and

---

44 D. Monsees, 'More Information about Our Processes to Safeguard Speech Data', *Google*, 11 July 2019, https://blog.google/products/assistant/more-information-about-our-processes-safeguard-speech-data.

45 X, 'Alexa and Alexa Device FAQs'.

46 *Ibid.*

47 EDPB, 'Guidelines 02/2021 on virtual voice assistants – Version 2.0', p. 9.

48 EDPB, 'Guidelines 02/2021 on virtual voice assistants – Version 2.0', p. 16.

the developer could be 'grouped into a single body acting as a unique data controller'.[49]

25. Moreover, where two or more controllers jointly determine the purposes and means of processing, they are joint controllers who need to determine their respective responsibilities to comply with the GDPR (Article 26 GDPR). The EDPB notes that such a distribution of compliance responsibilities is not limited to the topics found in Article 26 (1) GDPR, but that the joint controllers must ensure the compliance of the whole joint processing with the GDPR.[50] In this context, the question has been raised whether the owner of SHA could be considered such a 'joint controller' (together with the provider of the SHA), for instance when voices of guests or incidental users are recorded.[51] In order to answer this question, the actual control that an owner has over the processing and whether this control relates to the purposes and means needs to be examined.[52] While this assessment should be carried out on a case-by-case basis, authors such as De Conca have warned against an extensive interpretation of the notion of 'joint controller' in this context in light of the rationale and purposes of the GDPR, as well as the large power asymmetry that exists between individual owners and the producers of the devices (such as Apple, Google and Amazon).[53]

26. Another question relates to the territorial scope of the GDPR, as many companies developing SHAs are established outside the EU, e.g., in the United States. The GDPR's territorial scope, however, has been designed in such a way as to encapsulate actors that do not necessarily have a physical presence in the Union. This territorial scope can be found in Article 3 GDPR and determines the following:

> '1. This Regulation applies to the processing of personal data in the context of the activities of an establishment of a controller or a processor in the Union, regardless of whether the processing takes place in the Union or not.
> 2. This Regulation applies to the processing of personal data of data subjects who are in the Union by a controller or processor not established in the Union, where the processing activities are related to:
> - the offering of goods or services, irrespective of whether a payment of the data subject is required, to such data subjects in the Union; or

---

49 EDPB, 'Guidelines 02/2021 on virtual voice assistants – Version 2.0', p. 16.

50 EDPB, 'Guidelines 07/2020 on the concepts of controller and processor in the GDPR – Version 2.0', 7 July 2021, p. 44.

51 S. De Conca, 'Between a Rock and a Hard Place: Owners of Smart Speakers and Joint Control', *SCRIPTed*, 2020, vol. 17, no. 2, pp. 238–268. See also S. De Conca, 'The Enchanted House – an analysis of the interaction of intelligent personal assistants (IPHAs) with the private sphere and its legal protection', PhD thesis (Tilburg University), 2021.

52 *Ibid.*

53 *Ibid.*

- the monitoring of their behaviour as far as their behaviour takes place within the Union.'

27. Whereas Article 3 (1) GDPR is rather straightforward, Article 3 (2) GDPR deserves explanation. First, the phrasing 'data subjects who are in the Union' indicates that not only EU nationals, but rather anyone who is physically in the EU is covered by this scope. Secondly, both (a) and (b) take into account the reality that data and data flows are inherently borderless by determining that the application of the regulation is not dependent on whether or not actors have a physical presence in the Union, but rather on whether actors consciously process the personal data of individuals in the EU.[54]

28. Clarifying (a)'s 'offering of goods or services [...] to such data subjects', recital 23 GDPR states that it should be ascertained whether it is the intention of the company in question to offer services in one or more EU Member States by taking factors into account such as 'the use of a language or a currency generally used in one or more Member States with the possibility of ordering goods and services in that other language, or the mentioning of customers or users who are in the Union'.

29. Regarding (b), recital 24 GDPR specifies that 'it should be ascertained whether natural persons are tracked on the internet including potential subsequent use of personal data processing techniques which consist of profiling a natural person, particularly in order to take decisions concerning her or him or for analysing or predicting her or his personal preferences, behaviours and attitudes'. Profiling is defined by the GDPR as 'any form of automated processing of personal data consisting of the use of personal data to evaluate certain personal aspects relating to a natural person, in particular to analyse or predict aspects concerning that natural person's performance at work, economic situation, health, personal preferences, interests, reliability, behaviour, location or movements'.[55] The clearest targets of Article 3 (2) (b) GDPR are behavioural targeting companies that track online browsing behaviour,[56] and they will fall within the ambit of the regulation, even if they have no establishment in the EU, as soon as they track individuals present within the Union.

30. Almost all large tech companies have establishments in the Union so that the regulation will apply on the basis of Article 3 (1) GDPR. Even if these

---

54 C. Jay Hoofnagle, B. van der Sloot and F. Zuiderveen Borgesius, 'The European Union General Data Protection Regulation: What It Is and What It Means', *Information & Communications Technology Law*, 2019, vol. 28, p. 74.

55 Article 4 (4) GDPR.

56 Hoofnagle, van der Sloot and Zuiderveen Borgesius, 'The European Union General Data Protection Regulation', p. 74.

companies would not have establishments in the Union (or if a new market entrant appears that does not want to establish itself in the Union) the regulation will apply via Article 3 (2) (a) GDPR if these companies gear their products towards consumers in Member States (for example by offering goods or services in the language of a specific Member State).

31. A final question regarding the scope of the GDPR, is whether SHAs could perhaps fall under the so-called 'household exemption'. Article 2 (2) (c) GDPR stipulates that the Regulation does not apply to personal data processing by a natural person in the course of a purely personal or household activity. Although such products are indeed used in the context of domestic or personal activities, the SHA providers in question offer a means (e.g., Siri or Alexa) to process personal data for their own goals.[57] Thus, they cannot rely on the household exemption to escape the provisions of the GDPR.

2.2. SHAS AND THE LAWFUL PROCESSING OF DATA: 'IT'S COMPLICATED'

32. One of the bedrocks of the GDPR is that data must be processed lawfully, fairly and in a transparent manner (the principle of 'lawfulness, fairness and transparency', found in Article 5 (1) (a) GDPR). For the processing of personal data to be considered lawful, at least one of the six conditions in Article 6 (1) GDPR must be fulfilled. Legally, there is no hierarchy between any of the different grounds,[58] but the controller must make a predetermined choice regarding the basis of the processing since the lawfulness of a processing activity cannot be retrospectively based on a different ground.[59] Should any changes take place regarding the lawful basis for processing, data subjects are to be notified thereof in accordance with the general principles of fairness and transparency and the information requirements of Articles 13 and 14 GDPR.[60]

33. In the context of SHAs, depending on the specific purpose of each distinctive processing activity, four main grounds for lawful processing appear to be relevant. First and foremost, the data subject's consent to the processing of personal data for one or more specific purposes (Article 6 (1) (a) GDPR). Second, the necessity of the processing for the performance of a contract to which the data subject is party (Article 6 (1) (b) GDPR). Third, the necessity

[57] X, 'Artificiële Intelligentie en Gegevensbescherming: Een Verkennende Gids', *Kenniscentrum Data & Maatschappij*, June 2020, p. 26.

[58] EDPB, 'Opinion 15/2011 of the Article 29 Data Protection Working Party on the Definition of Consent (WP187)', 13 July 2011.

[59] EDPB, 'Guidelines 05/2020 on consent under Regulation 2016/679', p. 25.

[60] EDPB, 'Guidelines 05/2020 on consent under Regulation 2016/679', p. 25.

of the processing for the purposes of the legitimate interests pursued by the controller or by a third party (Article 6 (1) (f) GDPR).[61] Fourth, the necessity of the processing 'for compliance with a legal obligation to which the controller is subject' (Article 6 (1) (c) GDPR). This is particularly relevant in cases of access to evidence by the law enforcement authorities.[62]

34. The EDPB considers the performance of a contract to be the most appropriate legal basis for SHAs to process personal data – at least in the context of executing requests that the (registered) user has directed to the SHA.[63] Its reasoning is that the creation of an account to activate the device leads to a contractual relationship between the user and the SHA provider, with the core purpose of the contract being the execution of user requests through the device.[64] It therefore considers that '[a]ny personal data processing that is necessary to execute the user's request can therefore rely on the legal basis of the performance of the contract'.[65] Such processing encompasses audio capture of the request, its transcription into text, the interpretation thereof, preparation of the reply through interaction with knowledge sources, and the transcript to a vocal reply to the user.[66] The EDPB also notes that the use of machine learning to process personal data can use the performance of a contract as a legal basis, but only if this is necessary for the provision of the service (i.e. executing user requests); other purposes such as improving services or developing new functions cannot rely on the performance of the contract as a legal basis.[67]

35. 'Consent' remains an important legal basis for additional aspects, such as features like user identification on the basis of voice data. Article 4 (11) GDPR defines 'consent' as any (1) free, (2) specific, (3) informed and (4) unambiguous expression of will by which the data subject accepts the processing of personal data concerning him or her, either through a declaration or an unambiguous active act. The Article 29 Data Protection Working Party (A29WP)[68] and the

---

61 A legitimate interest of a data controller could, for instance, be the improvement of the service: EDPB, 'Guidelines 2/2019 on the Processing of Personal Data under Article 6(1)(b) GDPR in the Context of the Provision of Online Services to Data Subjects', 8 October 2019, p. 12.

62 X, 'Amazon Asked to Share Echo Data in US Murder Case', *BBC News*, 12 November 2018, https://www.bbc.com/news/technology-46181800; EDPB, 'Guidelines 02/2021 on virtual voice assistants – Version 2.0', p. 29.

63 EDPB, 'Guidelines 02/2021 on virtual voice assistants – Version 2.0', p. 22.

64 EDPB, 'Guidelines 02/2021 on virtual voice assistants – Version 2.0', p. 22.

65 EDPB, 'Guidelines 02/2021 on virtual voice assistants – Version 2.0', p. 22.

66 EDPB, 'Guidelines 02/2021 on virtual voice assistants – Version 2.0', p. 22.

67 EDPB, 'Guidelines 02/2021 on virtual voice assistants – Version 2.0', p. 23.

68 The Article 29 Data Protection Working Party (A29WP) was the independent European working group which consisted of all European supervisory authorities and dealt with issues relating to the protection of privacy and personal data in the European Union. It was replaced by the European Data Protection Board (EDPB) on 25 May 2018 but (most of) its guidance

European Data Protection Board[69] – bodies entrusted with the task of ensuring the consistent application of the EU data protection law – have further elaborated on all four of those elements.

36. 'Free' consent implies that those involved have a real choice and control. Recital 42 GDPR explores this further by stating that '[c]onsent should not be regarded as freely given if the data subject has no genuine or free choice or is unable to refuse or withdraw consent without detriment'. Additionally, recital 43 GDPR requires a certain 'granularity' whereby 'separate consent [is] to be given to different personal data processing operations' instead of forcing data subjects to consent to a bundle of processing purposes.[70]

37. The fact that consent should be 'specific' aims to ensure user control and transparency and as a result also necessitates granularity. In particular, the EDPB is of the view that if data processing is based on consent and the controller wishes to process that same data for another purpose, additional consent must be sought for the other purpose (unless a different lawful basis better reflects the situation).[71] Moreover, the underlying goal of a specification of purposes is intended to 'safeguard against the gradual widening or blurring of purposes for which data is processed, after a data subject has agreed to the initial collection of the data' (function creep).[72]

38. Consent must also be 'informed' and in this respect the following information is necessary: the identity of the controller; the purpose of each of the processing operations for which consent is sought; the (type of) data that are collected and used; the existence of the right to withdraw consent; information on the use of the data for automated decision making in accordance with Article 22 (2) (c) GDPR, where applicable.[73]

39. Finally, the requirement of an 'unambiguous indication of wishes' necessitates an 'intentional' act or statement in connection with a specific processing operation. The use of pre-ticked opt-in boxes will not lead to valid consent, nor will silence or inactivity from the side of the data subject.[74] In

---

remains applicable. In 2017 and 2018, it adopted and revised its 'Guidelines on consent under Regulation 2016/679' which have since been replaced by the EDPB Guidelines on consent adopted in May 2020.

69 EDPB, 'Guidelines 05/2020 on consent under Regulation 2016/679', Version 1.1, adopted on 4 May 2020.

70 EDPB, 'Guidelines 05/2020 on consent under Regulation 2016/679', p. 10.

71 *Ibid.*, p. 12.

72 *Ibid.*

73 It must be noted that these criteria should also be combined with the transparency requirements set out in Articles 12–14 GDPR, which are even more extensive.

74 EDPB, 'Guidelines 05/2020 on consent under Regulation 2016/679', p. 18.

certain situations, when a data subject should have a high level of individual control over personal data, explicit consent is required. This is particularly the case for the processing of special categories of personal data (Article 9 GDPR; see below) and in the context of automated individual decision-making, including profiling (Article 22 (2) (c) GDPR; see below). Examples of explicit consent include a signed written statement, an explicit confirmation via telephone call, the filling in of an electronic form, sending an email, uploading a scanned document carrying the signature of the data subject, or using an electronic signature.[75]

40. Moreover, even if consent has been acquired, the data subject is empowered by Article 7 (3) GDPR to withdraw consent at any time. This withdrawal of consent must be as easy as the procedure through which consent was given, and data subjects must be informed that revocation does not affect the lawfulness of the processing based on consent prior to withdrawal. If no other lawful basis justifying the processing (e.g., further storage) of the data has been determined, the data in question should be deleted by the controller.[76]

41. The presence of secondary and incidental users with regard to SHAs remains a tricky legal point when it comes to the legal basis for processing. As they do not have a contractual relationship with the data controller, data controllers will not be able to rely on Article 6 (1) b GDPR for processing their data. The EDPB's 'Guidelines 02/2021 on Virtual Voice Assistants' do not offer a clear solution on how SHA providers should best deal with this issue. It is implied in the guidelines that consent is the most suitable basis to process the data of such secondary and incidental users. Importantly, consent should be attributed to specific users,[77] and, as noted before, it is important that the consent is 'informed'. The Board notes that not only the user setting up the SHA should be informed,[78] but that all categories of users should be properly informed at the earliest time possible and at the latest, at the time of the processing[79] while taking into account the specificities of each category.[80] These secondary and incidental users should also be able to exercise their data subject rights,[81] and this should occur without prejudice to the rights of other users.[82] This is particularly important when an SHA has a user identification feature; after all, the voices of incidental users in the vicinity will also have to be processed to identify the

75 *Ibid.*, pp. 20–21.
76 *Ibid.*, p. 24. Also, see Article 17(1)(b) and (3) GDPR.
77 EDPB, 'Guidelines 02/2021 on virtual voice assistants – Version 2.0', p. 13.
78 EDPB, 'Guidelines 02/2021 on virtual voice assistants – Version 2.0', p. 17.
79 EDPB, 'Guidelines 02/2021 on virtual voice assistants – Version 2.0', pp. 19–20.
80 EDPB, 'Guidelines 02/2021 on virtual voice assistants – Version 2.0', p. 15.
81 EDPB, 'Guidelines 02/2021 on virtual voice assistants – Version 2.0', p. 33.
82 EDPB, 'Guidelines 02/2021 on virtual voice assistants – Version 2.0', p. 34.

'right' speaker.[83] In practice, however, obtaining consent from secondary and incidental users is challenging and will need to be carefully considered.

42. Data controllers could also choose another lawful basis to streamline dealing with secondary and incidental users, such as 'legitimate interests' (Article 6 (1) (f) GDPR). The EDPB, however, states in its Guidelines that 'reliance on legitimate interest could in certain cases, risk undermining the additional level of protection provided by Article 5(3) of the e-Privacy directive', which requires consent for the storing or gaining of access to information.[84] In any case, the use of this ground does require a 'sufficiently detailed and transparent' explanation by the data controller of the purpose and necessity of the processing, as well as how its interests are balanced against the interests or fundamental rights and freedoms of the data subject.[85] At the moment, however, many SHA operators seem to be falling short of this requirement.[86]

43. The grounds for lawful processing as well as the other principles found in Article 5 GDPR demonstrate the tension that inherently exists between the objectives of the GDPR and certain goals of companies developing SHAs. The strictly-worded grounds for processing must be read alongside the Regulation's requirements that personal data shall be 'collected for specified, explicit and legitimate purposes and not further processed in a manner that is incompatible with those purposes' (Article 5 (1) (b) GDPR; the purpose limitation principle); that the collected personal data must be 'adequate, relevant and limited to what is necessary in relation to the purposes for which they are processed' (Article 5 (1) (c) GDPR; the data minimisation principle); and that personal data shall be 'kept in a form which permits identification of data subjects for no longer than is necessary for the purposes for which the personal data are processed' (Article 5 (1) (e) GDPR; the storage limitation principle). The over-arching goal is to protect data subjects against excessive and overly long data processing practices. Certain principles, for instance the data minimisation principle, appear to stand in contrast to the practices of the companies developing SHAs, who seek to garner as much and as detailed information as possible to make the responses of their AI more accurate, dynamic and tailored, while also keeping such information for longer periods

83 EDPB, 'Guidelines 02/2021 on virtual voice assistants – Version 2.0', p. 31.

84 EDPB, 'Guidelines 02/2021 on virtual voice assistants – Version 2.0', p. 24. Another implicit reference to 'legitimate interests' can be found in para. 164.

85 A29WP, 'Opinion 06/2014 on the Notion of Legitimate Interests of the Data Controller under Article 7 of Directive 95/46/EC (WP217)', 9 April 2014, p. 25.

86 De Meyer, 'The Domestication of Smart Home Assistants', p. 105.

of time to better understand consumer behaviour and make more accurate purchasing recommendations.[87]

44. This can be observed in the behaviour of Amazon, for example. Only in mid-July of 2019 did the company introduce very limited erasure tools for its SHA,[88] later followed by a 'no human review' opt-out option in the Alexa settings.[89] A few weeks later it was revealed that Amazon held on to some data gathered by Alexa, regardless of whether the user had selected to make use of the erasure function.[90] It is clear that the companies behind SHAs should critically evaluate their policies regarding the saving and storing of audio recordings – whether that be locally or in the cloud.[91] In this context, the EDPB recommends that personal data should be erased when a query has been answered or a command executed, unless the data controller can rely on a valid lawful ground to retain the data for a specific purpose.[92] Moreover, default settings should be set to the minimum required amount of personal data needed to provide the service and an absolute minimum of stored user information.[93]

2.2 CHILDREN AND SHAS: PRESENT BUT 'INVISIBLE' DATA SUBJECTS[94]

45. Due to their user-friendliness and accessibility, SHAs may offer positive opportunities for children, such as easy access to entertainment, flexible learning tools that could result in an educational advantage or future professional success, and ways to engage in identity development.[95] While initially SHAs were predominantly aimed at adults, children have become a new target audience. In

---

87 J. Vlahos, 'Smart Talking: Are Our Devices Threatening Our Privacy?', *The Guardian*, 26 March 2019, https://www.theguardian.com/technology/2019/mar/26/smart-talking-are-our-devices-threatening-our-privacy.

88 J. Kastrenakes, 'Amazon Now Lets You Tell Alexa to Delete Your Voice Recordings', *The Verge*, 29 May 2019, https://www.theverge.com/2019/5/29/18644027/amazon-alexa-delete-voice-recordings-command-privacy-hub.

89 N. Lomas, 'Amazon Quietly Adds 'No Human Review' Option to Alexa Settings as Voice AIs Face Privacy Scrutiny', *Tech Crunch*, 3 August 2019, https://social.techcrunch.com/2019/08/03/amazon-quietly-adds-no-human-review-option-to-alexa-as-voice-ais-face-privacy-scrutiny.

90 Kelly and Statt, 'Amazon Confirms It Holds on to Alexa Data Even If You Delete Audio Files'.

91 Milkaite and Lievens, 'The Internet of Toys', pp. 780–794.

92 EDPB, 'Guidelines 02/2021 on virtual voice assistants – Version 2.0', p. 27.

93 EDPB, 'Guidelines 02/2021 on virtual voice assistants – Version 2.0', p. 27 and 32.

94 Parts of this section have been inspired by I. Milkaite and E. Lievens, 'The Internet of Toys: Playing Games with Children's Data?'.

95 Milkaite and Lievens, 'The Internet of Toys', pp. 780–794; D. Lupton and B. Williamson, 'The Datafied Child: The Dataveillance of Children and Implications for Their Rights', *New Media & Society*, 2017, vol. 19, pp. 780–794; D. Holloway and L. Green, 'The Internet of Toys', *Communication Research and Practice*, 2016, vol. 2, pp. 506–519.

2018, Amazon released the first voice assistant specifically tailored for children – Amazon Echo Dot Kids – which is currently available in the United States but not in the EU. In addition, a significant increase in the use of voice recognition devices has occurred during the COVID-19 pandemic which has evidenced reliance on voice assistance technology by children, families and educators.[96] The EDPB also acknowledged in its Guidelines that children interact with SHAs and that some of the virtual voice assistants 'are embedded in devices which are specifically aimed at children.'[97] There are academics, technology and market experts who predict that by 2025, most children will have voice assistants in their bedrooms from birth.[98] In January 2021, the UN Special Rapporteur on the right to privacy stressed that

> '[Y]oung people's immersion in the ever-expanding range of digital technologies produces an ongoing stream of data, collected and enhanced by artificial intelligence, machine-learning applications and facial and speech recognition technologies. Children and their data fuel the business of the digital world.'[99]

46. Given the commercial potential, it is thus not surprising that tech companies are increasingly emphasising the role of SHAs within a family-with-children context or target SHAs towards children explicitly.[100] This is evident, for example, in advertisements where a young boy is talking to the Google Home device, while his sister uses it to get help with her schoolwork; or commercial messages in which the virtual assistant Siri is advertised by not only showing a young girl interacting with it but also features the Cookie Monster from Sesame Street. More recently, Apple's intelligent assistant HomePod mini was also advertised as a family friendly device which can help children with their homework.

47. These as well as other developments have directed regional and international policymakers' attention[101] towards internet-connected technologies surrounding

---

96 L. Hall, 'Living the Future: The Technological Family and the Connected Home', 2020, https://www.internetmatters.org/wp-content/uploads/2020/10/Internet-Matters-Living-For-The-Future-Report.pdf; J. Tapper, 'Alexa, Siri… Elsa? Children Drive Boom in Smart Speakers', *The Guardian*, 18 October 2020, www.theguardian.com/technology/2020/oct/18/alexa-siri-elsa-children-drive-boom-in-smart-speakers.

97 EDPB, 'Guidelines 02/2021 on virtual voice assistants – Version 2.0', p. 91.

98 L. Hall, 'Living the Future: The Technological Family and the Connected Home'.

99 Special Rapporteur on the right to privacy, J.A. Cannataci, 'Artificial Intelligence and Privacy, and Children's Privacy (A/HRC/46/37)', 2021, paras 86, 90, https://documents-dds-ny.un.org/doc/UNDOC/GEN/G21/015/65/PDF/G2101565.pdf?OpenElement.

100 Milkaite and Lievens, 'The Internet of Toys', pp. 780–794.

101 Other relevant documents in this context are UNICEF, 'Policy Guidance on AI for Children (Draft 1.0)', September 2020, https://www.unicef.org/globalinsight/media/1171/file/UNICEF-Global-Insight-policy-guidance-AI-children-draft-1.0–2020.pdf> and UNICEF, 'The Case for Better Governance of Children's Data: A Manifesto', UNICEF, https://www.unicef.org/globalinsight/reports/better-governance-childrens-data-manifesto.

children as they grow up. First, the Council of Europe 'Recommendation CM/Rec(2018)7 of the Committee of Ministers to member States on Guidelines to respect, protect and fulfil the rights of the child in the digital environment' adopted in July 2018 states that with respect to 'connected or smart devices, including those incorporated in toys and clothes, States should take particular care to ensure that data-protection principles, rules and rights are also respected when such products are directed principally at children or are likely to be regularly used by or in physical proximity to children.'[102] In March 2021, the UN Committee on the Rights of the Child adopted its 'General Comment No. 25 (2021) on children's rights in relation to the digital environment', which recommends that 'States parties should ensure that the products and services that contribute to ['connected'] environments are subject to robust data protection and other privacy regulations and standards'.[103]

48. The increasing presence of SHAs in domestic settings where children are present warrants a closer inspection as to how their data is protected. At the EU level, the right to the protection of personal data under Article 8 of the EU Charter of Fundamental Rights should be read in conjunction with Article 24 of the Charter of Fundamental Rights, which acknowledges children's right to such protection and care as is necessary for their well-being and their right to be heard. Additionally, it emphasises that in all actions that concern them, whether taken by public authorities or private institutions, the child's best interests must be a primary consideration. The latter provision reflects Article 3 (1) of the United Nations Convention on the Rights of the Child (UN CRC).

49. The acknowledgement in the GDPR that children's data merit specific protection is an important innovation compared to the 1995 Data Protection Directive, which contained no explicit provisions regarding the protection of children's data. Recital 38 GDPR argues that this specific protection is warranted, as children may be less aware of the risks, consequences, safeguards and rights in relation to the processing of their personal data, in particular in relation to marketing or creating personality or user profiles. Yet, (most) SHAs record and store voice recordings and process the personal data associated therewith,[104] irrespective of whether the voice belongs to a household member

---

[102] Council of Europe, 'Recommendation CM/Rec(2018)7 of the Committee of Ministers to Member States on Guidelines to Respect, Protect and Fulfil the Rights of the Child in the Digital Environment', 4 July 2018, para 36, https://rm.coe.int/guidelines-to-respect-protect-and-fulfil-the-rights-of-the-child-in-th/16808d881a.

[103] UN Committee on the Rights of the Child, 'General Comment No. 25 (2021) on Children's Rights in Relation to the Digital Environment', para 74.

[104] M. Harris, 'Virtual Assistants Such as Amazon's Echo Break US Child Privacy Law, Experts Say', *The Guardian*, 26 May 2016, https://www.theguardian.com/technology/2016/may/26/amazon-echo-virtual-assistant-child-privacy-law.

or a guest, an adult or a child. This issue is also alluded to by the EDPB in their Guidelines on virtual voice assistants where the Board considers the 'plurality of users and the presence among them of vulnerable categories of individuals, such as children, elderly people or users with audio-visual disabilities'.[105] The question thus remains how specific protection is or should be offered in respect of children's data in the context of SHAs.

50. With regard to the lawfulness of processing of children's personal data, Article 8 GDPR provides for specific conditions applicable to consent in relation to information society services being offered directly to children.[106] Article 8 GDPR states that when consent is the ground for data processing in the context of information society services offered directly to a child, data processing shall be lawful when the data subject is at least 16 years old. In situations where the child is younger than 16 years old, consent must be given by the holder of parental responsibility in order for data processing to be lawful. According to paragraph 2, controllers must undertake reasonable efforts to verify that consent is given or authorised by the holder of parental responsibility over the child. That being said, EU Member States do have the opportunity to derogate and choose a lower age than 16, provided it is not below 13 years. It means that the 27 EU Member States had to decide whether or not to lower the age threshold to 15, 14 or 13. Research into the implementation across the EU demonstrates that Member States have used their margin of discretion, leading to a fragmented landscape of 'digital ages of consent',[107] which may have significant practical and enforcement implications for children and data controllers who are active throughout the EU.

51. The EDPB has clearly acknowledged that 'VVAs may process data of multiple data subjects'.[108] Consequently, the processing of the personal data of each data subject by the SHA providers needs to be based on a separate lawful ground for data processing (such as consent or contract), including for children. However, despite special legal provisions enabling children of different ages to consent to information society services being directly offered to them, it is questionable whether children actually have a meaningful opportunity to provide such consent in practice. According to the EDPB, it is more difficult to comply with the GDPR transparency requirements when multiple users

---

105 EDPB, 'Guidelines 02/2021 on virtual voice assistants – Version 2.0', p. 52.

106 Information society services are services normally provided (1) for remuneration, (2) at a distance, (3) by electronic means and (4) at the individual request of a recipient. See: 'Directive (EU) 2015/1535 of the European Parliament and Council, 9 September 2015 Laying down a Procedure for the Provision of Information in the Field of Technical Regulations and of Rules on Information Society Services (Codification)' Article 1(1)(b).

107 I. Milkaite and E. Lievens, 'Status quo regarding the child's Article 8 GDPR age of consent for data processing across the EU', *Better Internet for Kids*, December 2019, https://www.betterinternetforkids.eu/nl/web/portal/practice/awareness/detail?articleId=3017751.

108 EDPB, 'Guidelines 02/2021 on virtual voice assistants – Version 2.0', p. 4.

interact with a SHA, as opposed to situations when the device is only used by one person – the owner. Therefore, the designers of SHAs 'must consider how to properly inform non-registered and accidental users when their personal data is processed. When consent is the legal basis for processing users' data, users must be properly informed for the consent to be valid'.[109]

52. In its recent Guidelines on virtual voice assistants, the EDPB has provided very limited attention to the processing of children's personal data and their best interests in the context of SHAs. While the document does have a dedicated section on the processing of children's data, the section only contains four short paragraphs. With regard to lawfulness, the Board states that when the contractual legal ground for data processing is applicable, the conditions for the processing of children's personal data 'will depend on national contract laws'.[110] It also refers to Article 8 GDPR and provides that 'when consent is the legal basis [for the processing of children's personal data], explicit permission should be sought from parents or guardians to collect, process, and store children's data (voice, transcripts, etc.).'[111] No further explanation is provided in this regard, and it is not clear what exactly the EDPB means when it refers to 'explicit permission' rather than parental consent or authorisation as provided by the GDPR. Finally, the EDPB focuses on parental controls and acknowledges that they are 'available to a certain degree but in their current form they are not user friendly (e.g., it is necessary to sign in a new service) or have limited capacities.'[112] In addition to this, the Board encourages data controllers to 'invest in developing means for parents or guardians to control children's use of VVAs'.[113] It is unfortunate that the EDPB did not adopt a children's rights perspective and elaborate on the potential impact of SHAs on children's rights, their best interests and the general fairness of the processing of children's personal data through SHAs.[114]

53. Furthermore, if children's data collected through SHAs are processed for marketing and profiling purposes (for an in-depth discussion, see below at 2.6)

109 *Ibid.*, p. 19.
110 *Ibid.*, p. 92.
111 *Ibid.*, p. 93.
112 *Ibid.*, p. 94.
113 *Ibid.*
114 With regard to the fairness of child data processing, the A29WP has previously stated that the 'duty to process personal data in accordance with the principle of fairness [...] must be interpreted strictly when it concerns a child. As a child is not yet completely mature, controllers must be aware of this, and act with the utmost good faith when processing their data' (A29WP, 'Opinion 2/2009 on the Protection of Children's Personal Data (General Guidelines and the Special Case of Schools) (WP 160)', 11 February 2008, p. 7, https://ec.europa.eu/justice/article-29/documentation/opinion-recommendation/files/2009/wp160_en.pdf.

specific protection should be afforded to children.[115] Although the Article 29 Working Party does not believe Article 22 GDPR prohibits the profiling of children in general,[116] data controllers should nonetheless refrain from intrusive profiling and behavioural advertising practices regarding children.[117] Since the adoption of the GDPR, a few important developments occurred with respect to the profiling of children. First, the abovementioned CoE 'Recommendation on Guidelines to respect, protect and fulfil the rights of the child in the digital environment' provides that '[p]rofiling of children, which is any form of automated processing of personal data which consists of applying a "profile" to a child, particularly in order to take decisions concerning the child or to analyse or predict his or her personal preferences, behaviour and attitudes, should be prohibited by law.'[118] In the same vein, the UN 'General Comment No. 25 (2021) on children's rights in relation to the digital environment' recommended that 'States parties should prohibit by law the profiling or targeting of children of any age for commercial purposes on the basis of a digital record of their actual or inferred characteristics, including group or collective data, targeting by association or affinity profiling.'[119] According to the UN Special Rapporteur on the right to privacy, '[p]rofiling children limits their potential self-development in childhood, adolescence and possibly adulthood, as behavioural predictions and nudging techniques can predetermine options and choices.'[120] In that context, the Special Rapporteur recommends that 'States prohibit automated processing of personal data that profiles children for decision-making concerning the child or to analyse or predict personal preferences, behaviour and attitudes, with exemption only in exceptional circumstances in the best interests of the child or an overriding public interest, with appropriate legal safeguards'.[121] On a national level, the ICO – the UK's supervisory authority (SA) – has recently

---

115 E. Lievens and V. Verdoodt, 'Looking for Needles in a Haystack: Key Issues Affecting Children's Rights in the General Data Protection Regulation', *Computer Law & Security Review*, 2017, vol. 34, pp. 269–278.

116 A29WP, 'Guidelines on Automated Individual Decision-Making and Profiling for the Purposes of Regulation 2016/679 (WP251 Rev.01)', 6 February 2018, p. 28.

117 *Ibid.*, p. 29.

118 Council of Europe, 'Recommendation CM/Rec(2018)7 of the Committee of Ministers to Member States on Guidelines to Respect, Protect and Fulfil the Rights of the Child in the Digital Environment' (4 July 2018) para 37 <https://rm.coe.int/guidelines-to-respect-protect-and-fulfil-the-rights-of-the-child-in-th/16808d881a> accessed 11 July 2018.

119 UN Committee on the Rights of the Child, 'General Comment No. 25 (2021) on Children's Rights in Relation to the Digital Environment', 2 March 2021, para 42, https://tbinternet.ohchr.org/_layouts/15/treatybodyexternal/Download.aspx?symbolno=CRC%2fC%2fGC%2f25&Lang=en.

120 Special Rapporteur on the right to privacy, Joseph A. Cannataci, 'Artificial Intelligence and Privacy, and Children's Privacy (A/HRC/46/37),' 2021, para 92, https://documents-dds-ny.un.org/doc/UNDOC/GEN/G21/015/65/PDF/G2101565.pdf?OpenElement.

121 Special Rapporteur on the right to privacy, J.A. Cannataci, 'Artificial Intelligence and Privacy, and Children's Privacy (A/HRC/46/37)', para 127.

adopted its Children's Code as part of the national Data Protection Act.[122] In this document, the ICO also recommends that data controllers 'switch options which use profiling 'off' by default (unless [they] can demonstrate a compelling reason for profiling to be on by default, taking account of the best interests of the child).'[123] According to the SA, children's profiling should only be allowed if data controllers 'have appropriate measures in place to protect the child from any harmful effects (in particular, being fed content that is detrimental to their health or wellbeing)'.[124] Assuming that the voice recognition technology embedded in SHAs could technically accurately differentiate between different people as well as between adults and children,[125] child voice recordings should not be used for such (often commercial) practices. In fact, they should be immediately deleted and not stored, transferred and processed further after their voice inquiry is fulfilled.

54. In terms of the enforcement initiatives by the national authorities, the attention to the legal effects of (children's) voice data processing is emerging in the United States, but few developments have occurred in the EU. In 2019, two class action lawsuits against Amazon were filed in Los Angeles and Seattle. They allege routine voice recording and the creation of millions of children's voiceprints without children's or parental consent.[126] In the EU, recently, the SAs in Hamburg and Luxembourg investigated legal questions linked with voice assistants, (see below) but those investigations did not focus on children's (voice) data processing.[127] Similarly, in December 2020, CNIL – the French supervisory authority – adopted their white paper 'On the record: Exploring the ethical, technical and legal issues of voice assistants',[128] yet children's voice data processing is barely mentioned in the document. These developments demonstrate that the discussion on children's voice data processing, its legal

---

122 ICO, 'Age Appropriate Design: A Code of Practice for Online Services (the Final Version)', 2 September 2020, https://ico.org.uk/for-organisations/guide-to-data-protection/key-data-protection-themes/age-appropriate-design-a-code-of-practice-for-online-services.

123 ICO, 'Age Appropriate Design: A Code of Practice for Online Services (the Final Version)', p. 64.

124 *Ibid.*, p. 64.

125 See: C. Vander Maelen, 'The Coming-of-Age of Technology', *Delphi – Interdisciplinary Review of Emerging Technologies*, 2019, vol. 2, pp. 115–121.

126 B. Romano, 'Suits Allege Amazon's Alexa Violates Laws by Recording Children's Voices without Consent', *The Seattle Times*, 12 June 2019, https://www.seattletimes.com/business/amazon/suit-alleges-amazons-alexa-violates-laws-by-recording-childrens-voices-without-consent.

127 Hamburg Commissioner, 'Sprachassistenzsysteme Auf Dem Prüfstand – Datenschutzbehörde Eröffnet Verwaltungsverfahren Gegen Google', 2019, https://datenschutz-hamburg.de/pressemitteilungen/2019/08/2019-08-01-google-assistant; L. Kelion, 'Amazon Alexa: Luxembourg Watchdog in Discussions about Recordings', *BBC News*, 6 August 2019, https://www.bbc.com/news/technology-49252503.

128 CNIL, 'On the Record: Exploring the Ethical, Technical and Legal Issues of Voice Assistants', 2020, https://www.cnil.fr/en/record-cnil-publishes-white-paper-voice-assistants.

consequences under the EU data protection framework and its effects on children's rights is only just starting.

2.3. SPECIAL CATEGORIES OF PERSONAL DATA: BIOMETRICS AND VERY PRIVATE INFORMATION

55. In the context of SHAs and the voice recordings that are central to their functioning, Article 9 GDPR is especially relevant. This provision sets out the rules regarding 'special categories of personal data', which are 'personal data revealing racial or ethnic origin, political opinions, religious or philosophical beliefs, or trade union membership, and the processing of genetic data, biometric data for the purpose of uniquely identifying a natural person, data concerning health or data concerning a natural person's sex life or sexual orientation'. It is possible – and even likely – that since SHAs are present in the home setting, where individuals share, disclose or formulate inquiries regarding private issues such as their beliefs and health, that such data will be processed. Moreover, since the processing of voice recordings by SHAs could be considered the result of 'a specific technical processing', they could fall under the definition of biometric data (recital 51 GDPR, Article 4 (14) GDPR).[129] In that regard, the EDPB has now also explicitly stated that 'voice data is inherently biometric personal data'.[130] Since SHAs are increasingly making use of 'voice model recognition' technologies to associate specific voices with specific individuals, the biometric data can be used to uniquely identify natural persons – at least the primary users, but possibly also the secondary and incidental users.[131] When this happens, these biometric data will be classified as special categories of data.[132] Without prejudice to Article 6 (1) GDPR, this entails that Article 9

[129] E.J. Kindt, 'Having Yes, Using No? About the New Legal Regime for Biometric Data', *Computer Law & Security Review*, 2018, vol. 34, no. 3, pp. 523–538.

[130] EDPB, 'Guidelines 02/2021 on virtual voice assistants – Version 2.0', p. 13. At the same time, the EDPB also stated that the 'use of voice data for user identification implies the processing of biometric data as defined in Article 4.14 of the GDPR.' EDPB, 'Guidelines 02/2021 on virtual voice assistants – Version 2.0', p. 23. Article 4 (14) GDPR defines biometric data as 'personal data resulting from specific technical processing relating to the physical, physiological or behavioural characteristics of a natural person, which allow or confirm the unique identification of that natural person, such as facial images or dactyloscopic data'.

[131] According to the EDPB, '[s]ome VVA have the capability of uniquely identifying their users merely based on their voice.' EDPB, 'Guidelines 02/2021 on virtual voice assistants – Version 2.0', p. 30. Reports appear to indicate that in 2015, Amazon enabled Alexa to distinguish between its different users through Voice ID, with Google following suit in 2017: L. Eadicicco, 'Amazon Developing Advanced Voice-Recognition for Alexa', *Time*, 27 February 2017, http://time.com/4683981/amazon-echo-voice-id-feature-2017/; C. Welch, 'Google Home Now Supports Multiple Users, but Still Can't Separate Work and Personal Accounts', *The Verge*, 20 April 2017, https://www.theverge.com/circuitbreaker/2017/4/20/15364960/google-home-speaker-multi-user-new-feature.

[132] EDPB, 'Guidelines 02/2021 on virtual voice assistants – Version 2.0', p. 30.

GDPR will apply, meaning that the processing of such data is in principle prohibited.[133]

56. Nonetheless, Article 9 (2) (a) to (j) GDPR does foresee certain conditions that allow the processing of special categories of personal data. In the context of SHAs, explicit consent is especially pertinent. Under (a), it is allowed to process special categories of data if explicit consent (*supra*) has been given by the data subject 'to the processing of those personal data for one or more specified purposes'. The EDPB has stated that for user identification in particular explicit consent is the only applicable exemption.[134]

57. To avoid that in the process of improving voice recognition technology human contractors encounter sensitive data, it has been suggested that tech companies should take inspiration from medical research whereby systems are tested in a controlled environment, with test subjects who willingly and knowingly share sensitive information.[135] The EDPB, for its part, recommends only using pseudonymised data and limiting the amount of processed data to what is 'strictly necessary'.[136] Moreover, due to the inevitably sensitive nature of much of the data that will be processed, it is crucial that SHA actors use advanced data security practices.[137] Strong encryption standards are crucial, as well as technical standards that can prevent unauthorised devices from communicating with the smart speaker.[138] A focus on data-protection-by-design and data-protection-by-default[139] (see below) is essential to achieve such goals.

---

133 According to the EDPB, 'when such data is processed for the purpose of uniquely identifying a natural person or is inherently or determined to be special category personal data, the processing must have a valid legal basis in Article 6 and be accompanied by a derogation from Article 9 GDPR (EDPB, 'Guidelines 02/2021 on virtual voice assistants – Version 2.0', p. 28).

134 EDPB, 'Guidelines 02/2021 on virtual voice assistants – Version 2.0', p. 23.

135 T. Verheyden, 'Het valt niet te verdedigen dat Google meeluistert naar mijn intiemste momenten', *VRT NWS*, 10 July 2019, https://www.vrt.be/vrtnws/nl/2019/07/09/de-analyse-van-onze-stem-door-google-valt-perfect-te-verdedigen.

136 EDPB, 'Guidelines 02/2021 on virtual voice assistants – Version 2.0', p. 29.

137 Article 32 GDPR.

138 To address such security concerns, European Commission President Ursula von der Leyen announced in September 2021 that the Commission would develop a proposal for a Cyber Resilience Act. One of the purposes of such an act is to set common European cyber security standards for connected devices. See also: T. Breton, 'How a European Cyber Resilience Act will help protect Europe', https://ec.europa.eu/commission/commissioners/2019–2024/breton/blog/how-european-cyber-resilience-act-will-help-protect-europe_en.

139 Article 25 GDPR.

2.4. TRANSPARENCY: INNOVATIVE AND EFFECTIVE INFORMATION FORMATS NEEDED

58. The data subject has the right to receive information about the processing of his or her personal data. Articles 12, 13 and 14 GDPR determine that data controllers should inform data subjects about the processing of their data in a concise, transparent, comprehensible and easily accessible form and in clear and simple language. A broad range of information must be communicated. Article 13 GDPR provides a list of different pieces of information which is to be provided when personal data are collected from data subjects themselves while Article 14 GDPR lists the information to be provided when personal data have *not* been obtained from the data subject. Data subjects should for instance be informed of the identity and contact details of the controller, the purposes of the processing and the legal basis for the processing, the legitimate interests of the controller or of a third party, the recipients or categories of recipients of the personal data, the period for which the personal data will be stored and the rights of the data subject. The EDPB states very clearly that *all* users – primary, secondary and incidental – must be informed, and acknowledges that this may be difficult in practice.[140]

59. Articles 5 (1) (a) and 12 GDPR require that information and communication towards the data subject should occur in a 'concise, transparent, intelligible and easily accessible form, using clear and plain language', and this is particularly so when a child is being addressed. Regarding online services, the A29WP has recommended providing a 'layered' privacy notice to comply with the obligations of being 'concise and transparent' and aiming at language that is understandable to 'an average member of the intended audience' ('intelligible').[141] When children interact with SHAs, controllers should think of creative and age-appropriate audio-visual notifications that inform children as well as parents. The A29WP has offered plenty of inspiration in that regard, mentioning among others:

> 'icons, QR codes, voice alerts, written details incorporated into paper set-up instructions, videos incorporated into digital set-up instructions, written information on the smart device, messages sent by SMS or email, [...] or public information campaigns'.[142]

Voice alerts, in particular, seem to be especially relevant in the context of SHAs, as well as clear information in an instruction manual or QR codes on the box of the device. If SHAs would use audio to inform data subjects, the EDPB states

140 EDPB, 'Guidelines 02/2021 on virtual voice assistants – Version 2.0', pp. 17–18.

141 A29WP, 'Guidelines on Transparency under Regulation 2016/679 (WP260 Rev.01)', 11 April 2018, p. 7.

142 *Ibid.*, p. 21.

that the information should be communicated concisely and clearly, as well as that there should be a way to re-listen to the information.[143] In any event, the information mandated to be provided per Article 13 GDPR should be provided to consumers 'at the commencement phase of the processing cycle'.[144] During the lifespan of the product too, controllers should facilitate data subjects to have continuous and easy access to the information to re-acquaint themselves with the scope of the data processing.[145]

60. Tech companies offering SHAs should especially be much more transparent on whether recorded data is sent to other actors and what the purpose would be of such a transmission. After all, if the user of an SHA issues a command involving a functionality provided by a third party through a specific app, the provider communicates the intentions and informational variables (so-called 'slots') to the app developer.[146] Studies are also creating a picture of how often and through which sounds SHAs accidentally 'wake up' and start recording. This has in fact become such an issue that new products blocking near constant listening and recording by 'stand-by' SHAs are emerging on the market.[147] Since this differs drastically from device to device,[148] it should be mentioned explicitly for each device what the 'wake-up rate' is on average, what words could act as a trigger for involuntary activation and whether and to whom such recordings are disclosed.

2.5. DATA SUBJECT RIGHTS: RECTIFICATION, ERASURE, RESTRICTION, PORTABILITY AND OBJECTION

61. Article 15 GDPR sets out the right of access by data subjects, entailing that the data subject has the right to ask data controllers whether they have processed personal data relating to him or her and, if so, to obtain access to those data and information about the processing. This right is essential as it also serves as a steppingstone that enables data subjects to exercise the other rights available to them.[149] In practice, the information about and access to the information will

---

143 EDPB, 'Guidelines 02/2021 on virtual voice assistants – Version 2.0', p. 19.

144 *Ibid.*, p. 14.

145 *Ibid.*, p. 18.

146 EDPB, 'Guidelines 02/2021 on virtual voice assistants – Version 2.0', p. 10.

147 A. Bradford, 'Paranoid Prevents Smart Speakers from Eavesdropping', *Digital Trends*, 2 April 2020, https://www.digitaltrends.com/home/paranoid-prevents-smart-speakers-from-eavesdropping; X, 'Our Smart Speaker Privacy Devices', *Paranoid.com*, 2020, https://paranoid.com/products.

148 Dubois and others, 'Smart Speakers Study'.

149 J. Ausloos and P. Dewitte, 'Shattering One-Way Mirrors – Data Subject Access Rights in Practice', *International Data Privacy Law*, 2018, vol. 8, no. 1, pp. 4–28.

need to be meaningful and provided in a format that is easily consultable by the data subject (for example, through a dashboard or export feature).

62. A natural consequence of a data subject acquiring access to the data collected about them, is that incorrect or incomplete data may be discovered. For that reason, Article 16 GDPR grants data subjects the right to rectification: a data subject may ask that incorrect data is corrected and that incomplete data is completed. In specific cases, the data subject has the right to ask for certain personal data to be deleted (Article 17 GDPR), in particular where (a) the personal data are no longer necessary for the purposes for which they were collected or otherwise processed; (b) the data subject withdraws the consent on which the processing is based and there is no other legal basis for the processing; (c) the data subject objects to the processing in accordance with Article 21 (1) GDPR and there are no overriding compelling legitimate grounds for processing, or the data subject objects to the processing in accordance with Article 21 (2) GDPR; (d) the personal data have been unlawfully processed; (e) the personal data must be erased in order to comply with a legal obligation incumbent on the controller laid down in Union or Member State law; (f) the personal data have been collected in connection with an information society services offer as referred to in Article 8 (1) GDPR.

63. Article 17 (3) GDPR does, however, determine that the right to erasure is not absolute. In specific circumstances, such as when the processing is necessary to exercise the right to freedom of expression and information, or to institute, exercise or substantiate legal proceedings, the data controller will not have to erase the data. The SHA provider will need to consider a request for erasure on a case-by-case basis. Nevertheless, the Article 29 Working Party has stated that inactivity by a user for a 'defined period of time' should result in the profile being marked as 'inactive' and that the profile should be outright deleted '[a]fter another period of time' of inactivity.[150] Amazon seems to have considered this requirement by stipulating in the Alexa FAQ page that if a user's voice 'is not recognised for three years, we will automatically delete the acoustic model for their voice',[151] although it could be argued that three years might be a(n excessively) long period. In addition to the abovementioned rights, data subjects also have the right to restrict the processing on the basis of Article 18 GDPR, and the right to object to the processing of personal data, for instance for direct marketing purposes (Article 21 GDPR).

64. Data subjects also have the right to transfer their data to another controller (the right to data portability). As determined by Article 20 GDPR, the data

150 A29WP, 'Opinion 8/2014 on the Recent Developments on the Internet of Things (WP 223)', 16 September 2014, p. 17.

151 X, 'Alexa and Alexa Device FAQs'.

subject has the right to obtain the personal data relating to him or her 'which he or she has transmitted to a controller, in a structured, standard and machine-readable form, and he or she shall have the right to transfer those data to another controller, without prejudice to the controller to whom the personal data were transmitted'. In the context of SHAs, the right to data portability could be relevant when an individual purchases a new smart speaker or switches to a different SHA, yet would wish to transfer certain data such as personal preferences. In general, the exercise of this right aims to grant data subjects more control over their personal data, while on a macro-level it facilitates the free flow of personal data within the EU, fosters competition between controllers, prevents lock-in effects[152] and hence encourages the development of new services in the context of the Digital Single Market Strategy.[153] In that regard, the EDPB states that users should gain extensive control over data concerning them, including 'data that [they have] communicated by means of [their] voice (e.g., the history of voice interactions) and within the framework of the creation of [their] user account (e.g., name and first name)'.[154] The EDPB also believes the user should receive 'means that contribute to answer data portability requests (such as download tools and Application Programming Interfaces)'.[155]

2.6. AUTOMATED DECISION-MAKING: CAUSE FOR CONCERN

65. Importantly, Article 22 GDPR prohibits decision-making solely based on automated processing – that is, without human intervention –, including profiling, which produces legal effects concerning a data subject or similarly significantly affects.[156] An example of the latter condition is a decision that affects an individual's financial situation, e.g., setting a higher insurance premium.[157]

66. In this context, it is particularly relevant to consider the decision-making process involved in the SHAs formulation of a 'reply' in response to a 'request' by the user. As indicated above, to provide a reply, a SHA processes not only the request itself, but can also take into account the data subject's 'profile characteristics' – which it continuously learns about by interacting with an

[152] X, 'Protecting European Consumers with Connected and Automated Cars – Position Paper', *The European Consumer Organisation (BEUC)*, 2017, https://www.beuc.eu/publications/beuc-x-2017-138_dve_beuc_connected_autonomous_cars.pdf.

[153] A29WP, 'Guidelines on the Right to Data Portability (WP 242 Rev.01)', 5 April 2017, p. 3.

[154] EDPB, 'Guidelines 02/2021 on virtual voice assistants – Version 2.0', p. 37.

[155] *Ibid.*, pp. 36–37.

[156] A29WP, 'Guidelines on Automated Individual Decision-Making and Profiling for the Purposes of Regulation 2016/679 (WP251 Rev.01)', pp. 23–24.

[157] *Ibid.*, p. 26.

individual ('profiling').[158] The EDPB, in its guidelines 02/2021, explains in that regard that SHAs 'have access to the content of all voice commands even when they are aimed at services provided by third parties'.[159] According to the Board, '[t]his access would enable the [SHA] designer to construct *very accurate* user profiles that could be used to offer personalised services or advertisements' (emphasis added).[160] Amazon's Alexa, for example, constructs a personal profile of individual users and gradually adapts to their speech pattern, vocabulary and personal preferences.[161] Google Assistant has had a similar function for a while now,[162] only providing content (such as emails, reminders and also music and news) that is related to the profile of the one addressing the device.[163] Surprisingly, the EDPB does not link profiling and the personalisation of SHA replies to Article 22 GDPR, as the guidelines make no mention of this provision. Yet, the Article 29 Working Party and the EDPB have previously held that personalisation and targeting, for instance of advertising but also of other information, can come within the ambit of Article 22 GDPR, depending upon the particular characteristics of the case, including 'the *intrusiveness* of the profiling process' (emphasis added).[164]

67. A relevant question in that regard is thus whether the construction and use of distinctive profiles of different household members on the basis of which a reply is offered, being the result of a *fully automated process*, produce *legal* or *similarly significant legal effects* in respect of the data subjects concerned. Arguably, this could, for instance, be the case when the information provided would, when being (partly) based on one's inferred profile characteristics, minimise access and exposure to (diverse) content (e.g., news).[165] Specifically, the systematic personalisation of SHA replies may interfere with both the right to receive information as well as the freedom to form opinions without undue influence.[166] If those practices in fact do violate fundamental rights, they are to

---

158 Article 4 (4) GDPR.

159 EDPB, 'Guidelines 02/2021 on virtual voice assistants – Version 2.0', p. 23.

160 *Ibid.*, pp. 23–24.

161 X, 'Alexa Privacy and Data Handling Overview'.

162 For more information, see https://support.google.com/assistant/answer/9071681?hl=en-GB&co=GENIE.Platform%3DAndroid.

163 S. De Conca, 'Between a Rock and a Hard Place', p. 244.

164 A29WP, 'Guidelines on Automated Individual Decision-Making and Profiling for the Purposes of Regulation 2016/679 (WP251 Rev.01)', p. 22; EDPB, 'Guidelines 8/2020 on the targeting of social media users', p. 24.

165 D. Kaye, 'Report on Artificial Intelligence Technologies and Implications for the Information Environment (UN Doc A/73/348)', *United Nations General Assembly – Special Rapporteur on the promotion and protection of the right to freedom of opinion and expression*, 29 August 2018, point 10.

166 European Convention for the Protection of Human Rights and Fundamental Freedoms (ETS No 005 1950) Article 10 (1); J. Vermeulen, 'Recommended for You: 'You Don't Need No Thought Control'. An Analysis of News Personalisation in Light of Article 22 GDPR', in M. Friedewald and others (eds), *Privacy and Identity Management. Data for Better Living: AI*

be considered to affect a person's legal rights, thus breaching the prohibition laid down in Article 22 (1) GDPR.[167] Another example relates to circumstances where the profiling of individuals is based on big data sets in which a systemic bias is engrained (for instance, on the basis of gender or ethnicity). This may result in poor predictions and discriminatory replies, possibly entailing a violation of the prohibition of non-discrimination.[168]

68. Article 22 (2) GDPR contains a number of exceptions to the prohibition of automated individual decision-making having legal or significantly similar effects: (a) where the decision is necessary for the conclusion or performance of a contract between the data subject and a data controller, (b) where the decision is permitted by a provision of European Union or national law applicable to the controller which also provides for appropriate measures to protect the rights and freedoms and legitimate interests of the data subject or (c) where the data subject has given his or her explicit consent.[169] In the context of automated individual decision-making with a view to personalising SHA replies, firstly, the condition of 'explicit consent' is relevant. Secondly, such processing of personal data could possibly be considered 'necessary for the [...] performance of a contract'. In its Guidelines 02/2021, the EDPB notes that the personalisation of content may constitute an intrinsic and expected element of the service provided by SHAs.[170] According to the Board, the SHA provider can therefore use Article 6(1)(b) GDPR as a legal basis for the personalisation, provided that such processing takes place in the context of a contractual relationship, it is limited to what is necessary to provide the service, and the end-user has explicitly requested the service.[171] As Article 6(1)(b) and Article 22(2)(a) are very similar in wording, the EDPB's reasoning in relation to the former 6(1)(b) seems applicable also in respect of the latter.

---

and Privacy (Cham: Springer, 2020), pp. 193–198. See also EDPB, 'Guidelines 8/2020 on the targeting of social media users', p. 6: 'the use of algorithms to determine which information is displayed to which individuals may adversely affect the likelihood of access to diversified sources of information in relation to a particular subject matter'.

167 A29WP, 'Guidelines on Automated Individual Decision-Making and Profiling for the Purposes of Regulation 2016/679 (WP251 Rev.01)', p. 21.

168 *Fundamental Rights Agency*, '#BigData: Discrimination in Data-Supported Decision Making', 2018, https://fra.europa.eu/sites/default/files/fra_uploads/fra-2018-focus-big-data_en.pdf; European Convention for the Protection of Human Rights and Fundamental Freedoms (ETS No 005 1950) Article 14; A29WP, 'Guidelines on Automated Individual Decision-Making and Profiling for the Purposes of Regulation 2016/679 (WP251 Rev.01)', p. 21.

169 A29WP, 'Guidelines on Automated Individual Decision-Making and Profiling for the Purposes of Regulation 2016/679 (WP251 Rev.01)', p. 23.

170 For this assessment, the Board refers to: EDPB, 'Guidelines 2/2019 on the processing of personal data under Article 6(1)(b) GDPR in the context of the provision of online services to data subjects – version 2.0', 8 October 2021, p. 15.

171 EDPB, 'Guidelines 02/2021 on virtual voice assistants – Version 2.0', 24. Note that the EDPB states that user profiling for advertisement is never considered as a service explicitly requested by the end-user.

69. If (a) or (c) is relied upon, Article 22 (3) GDPR determines that the data controller must implement suitable measures to safeguard the data subject's rights and freedoms and legitimate interests, at least the right to obtain human intervention on the part of the controller, to express their point of view and to contest the decision. In addition, 'the controller must also provide the data subject with information on the data collected, the existence of automated decision making, the underlying logic and the importance and expected consequences of such processing'. Lastly, the decisions mentioned in Article 22 (2) GDPR cannot be based on special categories of personal data unless suitable measures to safeguard the data subject's rights and freedoms and legitimate interests are in place and one of two conditions are fulfilled (Article 22 (4) GDPR).

2.7. MAIN DATA CONTROLLER AND PROCESSOR OBLIGATIONS: THE IMPORTANCE OF DATA PROTECTION IMPACT ASSESSMENTS AND CODES OF CONDUCT

70. Article 25 GDPR contains the principles of data protection by design and by default. This provides that the controller, when setting up their processing activities, must take appropriate technical and organisational measures to protect the persons who will be affected. The assessment of which measures create an appropriate level of protection and security should be made on a case-by-case basis, taking into account, *inter alia*, the nature, scope and context of the processing (recital 83 GDPR). The EDPB has emphasised in its Guidelines on Article 25 GDPR that consideration of data protection by design should be evaluated as early as possible in the planning process of a new processing operation.[172] SHA providers should thus from the earliest conception of the devices and processing activities take the principles and obligations imposed by the GDPR into account. Examples of data protection by design in the context of SHAs are the lighting up of the smart speaker when it is recording, or the automatic deletion of voice recordings once an inquiry has been fulfilled. The EDPB adds in its Guidelines on Virtual Voice Assistants that a '[a] privacy and data protection friendly default VVA would only process users' data for executing users' requests and would store neither voice data nor a register of executed commands'.[173]

---

172 EDPB, 'Guidelines 4/2019 on Article 25: Data Protection by Design and by Default', 13 November 2019, p. 4.

173 EDPB, 'Guidelines 02/2021 on virtual voice assistants – Version 2.0', p. 33.

71. Article 30 GDPR imposes an obligation on controllers to keep a register of the processing activities that take place under their responsibility. The register must contain a number of elements, such as the name and contact details of the controller, the purposes of the processing, a description of the categories of data subjects and of the categories of personal data, the envisaged time limits for erasure of the different categories of data and a description of the technical and organisational security measures.

72. Article 32 GDPR obliges controllers and processors to implement appropriate technical and organisational measures to ensure a level of security appropriate to the risk presented, taking into account the state of the art and the cost of their implementation, as well as the nature, scale, context and purposes of the processing operations and the varying degrees of probability and seriousness of the risks to the rights and freedoms of individuals. Such measures may concern, for example, the pseudonymisation and encryption of personal data, as well as secure state-of-the-art authentication procedures for users.[174] Given the fact that IoT devices in general, and SHAs in particular have been claimed to suffer from security issues,[175] this is an obligation that must be seriously considered by data controllers.

73. In the case of a personal data breach, the controller must, without undue delay and, where feasible, not later than 72 hours after having become aware of it, notify the personal data breach to the competent supervisory authority, unless the personal data breach is unlikely to result in a risk to the rights and freedoms of natural persons.[176] If no notification occurs within 72 hours, the reasons for the delay must be communicated.

74. Article 35 GDPR sets out the obligation for data controllers to carry out a data protection impact assessment (DPIA) in certain circumstances. In particular, recitals 89 and 90 GDPR set out that a DPIA is meant for processing operations which are likely to result in a high risk to the rights and freedoms of natural persons by virtue of their nature, scope, context and purposes. The A29WP describes a DPIA as 'a process designed to describe the processing, assess its necessity and proportionality and help manage the risks to the rights and freedoms of natural persons resulting from the processing of personal data by assessing them and determining the measures to address them'.[177]

---

174 EDPB, 'Guidelines 02/2021 on virtual voice assistants – Version 2.0', p. 29.

175 N. Perlroth, 'With a Laser, Researchers Say They Can Hack Alexa, Google Home or Siri', *The New York Times*, 4 November 2019, https://www.nytimes.com/2019/11/04/technology/digital-assistant-laser-hack.html.

176 Article 33 GDPR.

177 A29WP, 'Guidelines on Data Protection Impact Assessment (DPIA) and Determining Whether Processing Is 'Likely to Result in a High Risk' for the Purposes of Regulation 2016/679 (WP248 rev.01)', 4 October 2017, p. 4.

75. To help determine when exactly a processing operation would be 'likely to result in a high risk to the rights and freedoms of natural persons', the A29WP has developed criteria. Meeting two of these criteria requires an actor to carry out a DPIA; the more additional criteria are met, the more an impact assessment is required. The criteria are: (1) conducting evaluation and scoring, (2) automated decision making with legal effect or comparable substantial effect, (3) systematic monitoring, (4) sensitive data or data of a highly personal nature, (5) data processed on a large scale, (6) matching or combining datasets, (7) data concerning vulnerable data subjects, including children, (8) innovative use or applying new technological or organisational solutions, and (9) when the processing in itself 'prevents data subjects from exercising a right or using a service or a contract'.[178]

76. One could certainly claim that the processing in the context of SHAs potentially entails the processing of sensitive data or data of a highly personal nature (criterion 4) due to its placement in a domestic setting. Furthermore, data concerning vulnerable data subjects (criterion 7) could also be processed. Recital 75 GDPR refers explicitly to children as a group of particularly vulnerable persons and when we consider that SHAs are aimed at families and are specifically starting to target children,[179] this criterion is relevant as well. The last potentially applicable criterion is the innovative use or application of new technological or organisational solutions (criterion 8). The Working Party has stated specifically that relying on a new technology in particular compels an actor to conduct a DPIA,[180] since this can 'involve novel forms of data collection and usage [... with] the personal and social consequences' as of yet unknown.[181] IoT devices are listed as a specific example since 'certain Internet of Things applications could have a significant impact on individuals' daily lives and privacy and therefore require a DPIA'.[182] The VPAs present in SHAs also operate on the basis of AI, further reinforcing the applicability of this criterion. Hence, a DPIA seems to be a prerequisite for the data controllers behind the SHAs. Publishing at least a summary of the outcome of such a DPIA should be considered, according to the Article 29 Working Party, as this could 'help foster trust in the controller's processing operations, and demonstrate accountability and transparency'.[183]

---

178 *Ibid.*, pp. 9–11.

179 Milkaite and Lievens, 'The Internet of Toys'; Harris, 'Virtual Assistants Such as Amazon's Echo Break US Child Privacy Law, Experts Say'.

180 A29WP, 'Guidelines on Data Protection Impact Assessment (DPIA) and Determining Whether Processing Is 'Likely to Result in a High Risk' for the Purposes of Regulation 2016/679 (WP248 rev.01)', p. 8.

181 *Ibid*, p. 10.

182 A29WP, 'Guidelines on Data Protection Impact Assessment (DPIA) and Determining Whether Processing Is 'Likely to Result in a High Risk' for the Purposes of Regulation 2016/679 (WP248 rev.01)', p. 9.

183 *Ibid.*, p. 17.

77. In order to implement the obligations imposed on data controllers, industry actors can develop and adhere to codes of conduct (Articles 40 and 41 GDPR). These are sector-level tools that are developed in close cooperation with national supervisory authorities and the European Data Protection Board (for codes on the EU-level), allowing for practical guidelines to the more abstract principles of the GDPR. In May 2021, the 'EU Data Protection Code of Conduct for Cloud Service Providers' was approved as the first transnational GDPR code of conduct by the EDPB and the Belgian Supervisory Authority (as the leading supervisory authority for the code).[184] SHAs could benefit from the additional legal certainty granted by such codes due to SHAs' close links with new technologies such as AI and the IoT. After all, adherence to an approved code can result in lower fines for violating the GDPR and they can furthermore specify how transfer mechanisms should be implemented in practice.[185] Finally, industry actors should also consider the development of certification seals, as set out in Articles 42 and 43 GDPR. Such labels can stimulate sectorial uniformity in how to approach data protection concerns and thereby raise standards. Additionally, such seals should be easy-to-understand, making them consumer-friendly.[186]

2.8. ENFORCEMENT: SLOWLY BUT SURELY SUPERVISORY AUTHORITIES TAKE ACTION

78. If data subjects considers that the processing of personal data relating to them infringes the GDPR, a complaint can be filed with the national supervisory authority (SA) (Article 77 GDPR). The data subject also has the right to an effective judicial remedy against a legally binding decision of a supervisory authority concerning them (Article 78 GDPR) or against a data controller or processor (Article 79 GDPR). Interestingly, the Regulation attempts to lower the threshold for data subjects to undertake action by allowing them to mandate a non-profit organisation to lodge a complaint on their behalf. However, this body must be properly constituted in accordance with the law of a Member State, must have statutory objectives which are in the public interest, and has to be active in

184 EDPB, 'Opinion 16/2021 on the Draft Decision of the Belgian Supervisory Authority Regarding the "EU Data Protection Code of Conduct for Cloud Service Providers" Submitted by Scope Europe'; Belgian Data Protection Authority (Autoritée de protection des données, Gegevensbeschermingsautoriteit), 'Decision N° 05/2021 – Subject: Approval Decision of the "Eu Data Protection Code of Conduct for Cloud Service Providers" by the General Secretariat of the Belgian Data Protection Authority (AH-2018–0084)'.

185 'Communication (European Commission) Data Protection as a Pillar of Citizens' Empowerment and the EU's Approach to the Digital Transition – Two Years of Application of the General Data Protection Regulation', 24 June 2020, pp. 11–12.

186 Holloway and Green, 'The Internet of Toys'.

the field of the protection of data subjects' rights and freedoms with regard to the protection of their personal data (Article 80 GDPR).

79. At the time of writing, to the best of our knowledge, there are seemingly no complaints or court cases pending within the EU initiated by data subjects that claim violations of the GDPR by SHAs specifically.[187] However, the summer of 2019 saw several national supervisory authorities (SAs) expressing unease and sometimes taking action with regard to SHAs, after whistle-blowers and investigative journalists revealed that the devices not only often captured intimidate details, but that they were also reviewed by human contractors.[188]

80. When learning of a data leak by Google Assistant, the SA of the German Bundesland Hamburg used its power under Article 66 of the GDPR to begin an 'urgency procedure' that allows it to 'immediately adopt provisional measures intended to produce legal effects on its own territory with a specified period of validity which shall not exceed three months' with the goal of protecting the rights and freedoms of data subjects. Noting that 'automatic speech assistants' form a high risk to the private and intimate sphere of data subjects[189] and calling on other national SAs to perform checks of this technology, the Hamburg SA used Article 66 GDPR to prohibit Google from carrying out reviews of audio recordings by both employees and third parties.[190] In response, Google suspended audio reviews of Google Assistant in the entirety of Europe.[191]

---

187 Notably, a homicide case in Germany relied on the use of audio recordings made by Amazon Alexa as court evidence. See: W. Kummer, 'German Court Calls Alexa to the Stand', Datenschutz Notizen, 12 February 2021, https://www.datenschutz-notizen.de/german-court-calls-alexa-to-the-stand-2028997/. However, since this concerns criminal law it falls outside the ambit of this chapter.

188 Hern, 'Apple Contractors 'regularly Hear Confidential Details' on Siri Recordings'; T. Verheyden et al., 'Google Employees Are Eavesdropping, Even in Your Living Room, VRT NWS Has Discovered', *VRT NWS*, 10 July 2019, https://www.vrt.be/vrtnws/en/2019/07/10/google-employees-are-eavesdropping-even-in-flemish-living-rooms; X, 'The DPC's Take on Digital Assistants', *Data Protection Commission (Ireland)*, 2 December 2019, https://www.dataprotection.ie/news-media/blogs/dpcs-take-digital-assistants.

189 Interestingly, the Hamburg SA also opened an investigation into voice transcriptions by Facebook through its Messenger service. See: A. White and N. Drozdiak, 'Facebook Gets German Data Probe Into Voice Transcriptions', *Bloomberg*, 26 August 2019, https://www.bloomberg.com/news/articles/2019-08-26/facebook-gets-german-data-probe-into-voice-transcriptions.

190 X, 'Sprachassistenzsysteme Auf Dem Prüfstand – Datenschutzbehörde Eröffnet Verwaltungsverfahren Gegen Google', *Der Hamburgische Beauftragte für Datenschutz und Informationsfreiheit*, 1 August 2019, https://datenschutz-hamburg.de/pressemitteilungen/2019/08/2019-08-01-google-assistant.

191 N. Lomas, 'Google Ordered to Halt Human Review of Voice AI Recordings over Privacy Risks', *Tech Crunch*, 2 August 2019, https://social.techcrunch.com/2019/08/02/google-ordered-to-halt-human-review-of-voice-ai-recordings-over-privacy-risks.

81. Due to the affair, Google also filed a breach notification with the Irish SA (which is the lead supervisory authority since Google's main European establishment is in Ireland) under Article 33 GDPR. As stated by the Irish SA: 'We note that as of 10 July [2019] Google Ireland ceased the processing in question and that they have committed to the continued suspension of processing for a period of at least three months starting today (1 August). In the meantime, we are currently examining the matter'.[192] As of November 2021, no additional public information on the matter could be found.

82. Around the same period as the Hamburg SA, the Luxembourg SA (Commission Nationale pour la Protection des Données (CNPD)) as the lead SA of Amazon began interviewing the company over its data collection and audio review practices of Alexa.[193] The CNPD did not take action, however, and instead stated that the members of the EDPB 'should work out a common position in line with the consistency mechanism to apply data protection rules in a harmonised way for this type of treatment'.[194] Since then, this common position was voiced in the EDPB Guidelines on Virtual Voice Assistants.

3. CONCLUSION: TOWARDS DATA PROTECTION COMPLIANT SHAS

83. SHAs could yield significant advantages to individuals and to society in general. Voice-driven technology could, for instance, be especially helpful for older demographics who might not feel comfortable operating technology or who have become isolated and for whom the presence of a voice (albeit one driven by AI) might bring comfort. Similarly, SHAs allow individuals with physical disabilities – such as blindness[195] – to meaningfully interact with their household and information available on the internet.

84. Despite the ways in which SHAs offer convenience, efficiency and entertainment, the ongoing increases in data collection through the IoT diminishes the meaning of private spaces and might negatively impact our bodily, emotional and informational privacy.[196] Additionally, the feeling of

---

192 *Ibid.*

193 L. Kelion, 'Amazon Alexa: Luxembourg Watchdog in Discussions about Recordings', *BBC News*, 6 August 2019, https://www.bbc.com/news/technology-49252503.

194 S. Bodoni, 'Amazon's Snooping on Alexa Chats Spurs EU Privacy Response', *Bloomberg*, 17 January 2020, https://www.bloomberg.com/news/articles/2020-01-17/amazon-s-snooping-on-alexa-chats-spurs-eu-wide-privacy-response.

195 Siddique, 'NHS Teams up with Amazon to Bring Alexa to Patients'.

196 G. Rosner and E. Kenneally, 'Privacy and the Internet of Things: Emerging Frameworks for Policy and Design', *UC Berkeley – Center for Long-Term Cybersecurity*, https://cltc.berkeley.edu/iotprivacy.

corporate surveillance in a domestic setting might have a chilling effect on the freedom of expression within private homes.[197] As has been stressed repeatedly throughout this chapter, the gathering of (often sensitive) data from individuals' homes is also deeply problematic when it is used for profiling purposes. If medical data, religious and political beliefs and sexual preferences are recorded, stored, processed and transferred, the detailed profiles that would be constructed could very easily result in discriminatory practices, especially when important decisions are made on the basis of such profiles. The impact thereof might even be larger on children, affecting their best interests and the right to development (Articles 3 and 6 UN CRC).

85. In addition, the automated and profiling-based generation of SHA replies to information requests by a data subject could potentially violate one's right to receive information, one's freedom to form opinions without undue influence and/or the prohibition of non-discrimination. If so, such processing of personal data would be prohibited on the basis of Article 22 (1) GDPR, unless one of the exceptions in the second paragraph of that provision applies.

86. Actors in the SHAs 'chain', who are data controllers, need to consider their data collection and processing practices carefully, with the principles, rights and obligations imposed by the GDPR in mind. Key concerns and complex questions regarding lawfulness (consent in particular), transparency, and profiling need to be taken seriously and measures to address these concerns should be integrated in the design and operation of SHAs, at their very conception and – importantly – throughout their lifecycle. Users – both adults and children – should be consulted in order to test certain assumptions, mechanisms or information that are central to the company policies.

87. Additionally, enhancing the digital (or AI) literacy skills of citizens (both adults and children) is important to improve their understanding of data processing practices and the rights they have as data subjects. Increasing the digital literacy of parents should focus specifically on how they use or allow technology to interact with their children, without putting a too heavy burden on their shoulders and expecting them to assess the extent to which SHAs comply with the obligations that are imposed on them by the GDPR.[198] In that

---

197 M.E. Kaminski, 'Robots in the Home: What Will We Have Agreed To?', *Idaho Law Review*, 2015, vol. 51, pp. 661–677; M.E. Kaminski and S. Witnov, 'The Conforming Effect: First Amendment Implications of Surveillance, Beyond Chilling Speech', *University of Richmond Law Review*, 2015, vol. 49, pp. 465–518.

198 E. McReynolds et al., 'Toys That Listen: A Study of Parents, Children, and Internet-Connected Toys', *Proceedings of the 2017 CHI Conference on Human Factors in Computing Systems* (Association for Computing Machinery), 2017, pp. 5197–5207.

regard, SAs have an essential role to play. SAs should take into account evidence-based research (including technical research into the actual data processing by SHAs), the valuable insights of non-governmental organisations, and consumer experiences to underpin their handling of complaints and the guidance they issue. As SHAs become a 'member' of a household, blending in very private spaces, close scrutiny is warranted.

CHAPTER 9

AI AND IP: GREAT EXPECTATIONS

Jozefien VANHERPE*

1. INTRODUCTION

1. The novel that lends its name to this chapter tells us a tumultuous and multi-faceted coming-of-age story, not unlike the rocky road faced by the relationship between AI and intellectual property (IP) law over the past few years.[1] The interface between AI and IP is readily apparent and the possible topics of this chapter are manifold.[2] The recent explosion of relevant legal doctrine, case law and even impending legislation at the EU level makes it hard to see the forest for the trees. This chapter takes a step back from the multitude of available sources and provides a bird's-eye view of the current status of research into some of the relevant legal issues from a primarily EU, civil law perspective.[3] It contrasts the position of optimistic commentators who have great expectations for the application of IP law in the AI realm with the perspective of scholars who take a more reserved stance.

The present extensive introduction further delineates the topic (part 1). It includes a brief analysis of the possible uses of AI as a tool in the IP sector as well a detour along the essentials of IP law. The two-pronged substantive body of the chapter analyses the main legal challenges raised by AI – primarily machine

* Assistant Professor, KU Leuven Centre for IT and IP Law (CiTiP).

1 For the sake of clarity: the title of the chapter included in the first edition of this book ('A Tale of Two Acronyms') referred to another Dickens novel, namely *A Tale of Two Cities* (1859).

2 See for an overview of issues: WIPO Secretariat, 'Revised Issues Paper on Intellectual Property Policy and Artificial Intelligence' (WIPO Conversation on IP and AI, 21 May 2020), 15 p.; R. Hilty, J.-A. Lee, and K.-C. Liu, *Artificial Intelligence and Intellectual Property* (Oxford: Oxford University Press, 2021), 464 p.

3 See in relation to common law extensively (i) primarily from the perspective of United States (US) law: US Patent and Trademark Office (USPTO), 'Public Views on Artificial Intelligence and Intellectual Property Policy' (2020), 45 p., https://bit.ly/3wlNmQL; and (ii) primarily from the perspective of the law of the United Kingdom (UK): UK Intellectual Property Office (UKIPO), 'Consultation outcome. Artificial Intelligence and Intellectual Property: Call for Views' (2020, updated 2021), https://bit.ly/3HPITuY and UKIPO, 'Open Consultation. Artificial Intelligence and IP: Copyright and Patents' (2021), https://bit.ly/3cHmzFl.

learning[4] AI – in an IP context. First, focus lies with the IP protection of AI technology under patent law and copyright law (part 2). Subsequently, attention shifts to the IP protection of output generated through or by an AI system (part 3). Could such output be susceptible to IP protection under copyright and/or patent law? If this is not the case, should it, and, if so, who could or should own the rights, and what should the modalities of protection be? While the confines of this chapter do not allow for a final or even full answer to these questions, its conclusions (part 4) caution against unreservedly tearing down the foundations of IP protection for the mere sake of additional incentive creation.

2. AI is a multidimensional, evolving concept with different possible definitions, as explained in Chapter 1, part 2 of this book. This chapter looks at AI as the science and engineering of 'making intelligent machines', of 'making computers do things that require intelligence when done by humans'.[5] However, AI algorithms do not function in the same way as the human brain does – in other words, computers do not 'think' as we humans do.[6] This is in part due to the fact that we have until now been unable to fully describe how exactly the human thought process works. Until we have figured out exactly how the human brain functions and how to formulate this as a series of steps to be followed, genuinely 'thinking' computers are not on the horizon. It has moreover been argued that machines will never be able to think as humans since they lack the requisite free will and the possibility to feel emotions.[7]

A final technical AI-related aspect worth repeating in the context of this chapter is the so-called 'black box' nature of much AI technology (especially in relation to deep learning[8]). This refers to a situation where we know which data were provided to the system (input A) and which result is eventually reached (output B), but where it is unclear what exactly makes the AI system go from A to B; in other words, how the AI 'works'.

---

4 See in relation to this concept Chapter 1, part 3.3 of this book.

5 See respectively J. McCarthy (2001), https://bit.ly/3lqijz9 and R. Kurzweil (1990), as quoted by M.-C. Janssens, 'The Challenges of Artificial Intelligence – Setting the Scene' (European Copyright Society, Brussels, 25 May 2018).

6 As indicated in Chapter 1, research shows that a very high percentage of AI experts believe that high-level machine intelligence will be developed by 2075 and that so-called 'superintelligent' computers may come into existence around the turn of the 22nd century, see V.C. Müller and N. Bostrom, 'Future Progress in Artificial Intelligence: A Survey of Expert Opinion' in *Fundamental Issues of Artificial Intelligence* (Synthese Library – Studies in Epistemology, Logic, Methodology, and Philosophy of Science; vol. 376) (Cham: Springer, 2016), 572 p. See also D. Gervais, 'The Human Cause', in R. Abbott (ed.), *Research Handbook on Intellectual Property and Artificial Intelligence* (Cheltenham: Edward Elgar Publishing, 2022), draft available at https://bit.ly/3xnTTL2.

7 See for an overview of the main arguments in this regard https://stanford.io/3CRdnsO. The interested reader is referred to J. Searle, 'Minds, Brains and Programs', *Behavioural and Brain Sciences*, 1980, p. 417. While this debate is quite fascinating in itself, the scope of this chapter does not allow any further elaboration on this topic.

8 See for a definition of this concept Chapter 1, part 3.4 of this book.

3. The buzz surrounding AI technology is omnipresent and ever-growing. Innovation in the AI field has been increasing exponentially over the past few years and possible practical applications of this technology are raising keen interest on a global scale. The legal world, typically rather slow to respond to societal and technological developments, has now also woken up to the opportunities AI has to offer. With the scrutiny of legal minds, however, also comes the unveiling of certain fundamental theoretical and practical challenges, many of which are the subject of discussion in the second edition of this book.

4. This chapter is no different. In particular, it reflects on the interaction between AI and IP rights. Simply put, IP rights are exclusive rights vested in intangible, immaterial assets that grant their owner a temporary monopoly in relation to the use thereof in a given territory.[9] IP rights may be divided into industrial property on the one hand and literary and artistic property on the other.

Industrial property rights protect creations that play a largely economic role and primarily include patents, trademarks and design rights. These rights may be categorised on the basis of the type of immaterial creation they seek to protect. Patents are granted for technological improvements, while trademarks aim to protect distinctive brand signs and design rights relate to the appearance of products.[10] In most cases, industrial property rights are subject to a registration requirement.[11]

The concept of literary and artistic property rights refers to copyright and neighbouring rights. These rights are generated automatically upon the creation of the work at issue. Copyright offers the author(s) protection for 'literary and artistic works',[12] a broad concept that may include music, paintings and photographs, but also less obvious categories such as databases and software.[13]

---

9 See re intellectual property rights in general e.g., L. Bently, B. Sherman, D. Gangjee and P. Johnson, *Intellectual Property Law*, 5th edn (Oxford: Oxford University Press, 2018), 1520 p.; R. Dreyfuss and J. Pila (eds), *The Oxford Handbook of Intellectual Property Law* (Oxford: Oxford University Press, 2018), 1010 p.; J. Pila and P. Torremans, *European Intellectual Property Law*, 2nd edn (Oxford: Oxford University Press, 2019), 712 p.

10 Bently et al., *Intellectual Property Law*, pp. 1–4; W. Cornish, D. Llewelyn and T. Aplin, *Intellectual Property: Patents, Copyright, Trade Marks and Allied Rights*, 8th edn (London: Sweet & Maxwell, 2013), pp. 6–10.

11 Unregistered Community designs are an exception to this rule, see Articles 11 and 19(2) Council Reg. (EC) no. 6/2002 of 12 December 2001 on Community designs, *OJ L* 5 January 2002, no. 3, 1.

12 Article 2(1) Berne Convention for the Protection of Literary and Artistic Works (9 September 1886, as amended), *Belgian Official Gazette* 11 December 1999, 41901 ('Berne Convention', the main international copyright convention).

13 See at the EU level e.g., Dir. 96/9/EC of the European Parliament and of the Council of 11 March 1996 on the legal protection of databases, *OJ L* 27 March 1997, no. 77, 20, with consolidated version published in *OJ L* 6 June 2019; Dir. 2009/24/EC of the European Parliament and of the Council of 23 April 2009 on the legal protection of computer programs, *OJ L* 5 May 2009, no. 111, 16.

The three main neighbouring rights relate to performances, phonograms and broadcasts and are granted to performing artists, producers and broadcasting organisations.

Without seeking to turn this chapter into a fully-fledged introduction to IP law, a final notable point is that the economic aspects of intellectual property rights may be transferred to a third party, be it a natural person or a legal entity.[14] The identity of the rights owner(s) may therefore – and often does – differ from the initial holder of the IP right at issue.

5. Before we dive deep into the substantive legal challenges raised by AI systems in an IP context, it is interesting to note the increased (and still increasing) use of AI systems as a tool in the IP sector. The ability of AI systems to process and analyse vast amounts of data quickly and efficiently offers various opportunities in a sector that has traditionally been characterised by large amounts of paper, laborious manual searches and often inefficient, error-prone administration. First, the opportunities for IP offices are significant, as proven by the pioneering efforts of the World Intellectual Property Organization (WIPO). WIPO has been actively mining the possibilities offered by AI solutions with regard to the automatic categorisation of patents and trademarks as well as prior art searches, machine translations and formality checks.[15] IP offices across the globe are following suit.[16] Second, AI technology may be applied to the benefit of prospective IP registrants in optimising the application and renewal process, both on a formal and substantive level. As to the former, among other things, AI technology may be used to suggest relevant classes of goods and services for trademarks and/or designs at the application stage. As to the latter, on a substantive level, AI technology may be used to aid in patent drafting and to screen IP registers for existing registrations to minimise risk. Indeed, AI technology may assist in determining the similarity of existing trademarks and/or designs and even in evaluating prior art relating to patents.[17] In addition, AI-based IP analytics and

14 By contrast, the moral aspects of copyright are unalienable (although the exercise thereof may be modulated by contract), see, e.g., Article XI.165(2) Belgian Code on Economic Law (BCEL).

15 See, e.g., https://bit.ly/3p2VqTo. See regarding automatic categorisation in particular P. Fiévet, 'Artificial Intelligence Applied to IPC and Nice Classifications' (WIPO, Geneva, 25 May 2018) and WIPO's Vienna Classification Assistant, https://bit.ly/3CRod1Q.

16 See e.g. (i) as to the European Union Intellectual Property Office (EUIPO): https://bit.ly/30XlRRJ; and (ii) as to the UKIPO: https://bit.ly/3DOiNWX.

17 Re trademarks, see, e.g., Brandstock (website: https://bit.ly/30Voofc); CompuMark (website: https://clarivate.com/compumark); Rocketeer (website: https://bit.ly/31leuZX); TrademarkNow (website: https://www.trademarknow.com and https://corsearch.com). Re patents, see e.g. Rowan Patents (website: https://rowanpatents.com). See extensively on the possible role of AI in prior art searches A.K. Rai, 'Machine Learning at the Patent Office: Lessons for Patents and Administrative Law', *Iowa L Rev*, 2019, p. 102.

management software is available.[18] Finally, AI-powered applications are used as a tool in the fight against counterfeit products.[19] Given the fast pace of technological innovation in this field and the significant margin for improvement in relation to the enforcement and management of IP on a global scale, close monitoring of future evolutions in this context will undoubtedly be both interesting and useful. In view of the high value of immaterial assets for companies today, the stakes are undeniably high, as is the market potential of a fully-fledged, trustworthy, AI-based IP portfolio tool.

6. The exponentially increasing amount of technological innovation in the field of AI provides the starting point for the first substantive part of this chapter, which treats the avenues open to innovators who seek to protect AI technology developed by themselves or by their employees. The subsequent part focuses on the possibility of IP protection for 'things' produced by an AI system, in particular under copyright and patent law.[20] This part examines whether AI systems may be a source of artistry and innovation. The analysis is largely limited to the legal framework as applicable in the EU, referring to national (Belgian) law where useful and relevant.

7. Before analysing the thorny questions indicated above, however, we go back to the foundational theories of IP law.[21] Simply put, the primary justifications for IP protection are either moral-ethical or utilitarian in nature. The first strain of thought is the prevailing view under continental EU IP law. Subsequent to John

---

18 See, e.g., Cipher (website: https://cipher.ai), elementary IP (website: https://elementaryip.com), IP Check-Up (press release: https://bit.ly/3E3Dxdr); Octimine (website: https://www.octimine.com) and SHIP Global IP (website: https://shipglobalip.com). Re IP analytics, see L. Aristodemou and F. Tietze, 'The state-of-the-art on Intellectual Property Analytics (IPA): A literature review on artificial intelligence, machine learning and deep learning methods for analysing intellectual property (IP) data', *World Patent Information*, 2018, p. 37.

19 See, e.g., Visual-AI (website: https://bit.ly/3HQtt9B).

20 There are also several interesting questions regarding the interface of AI and trademark law, such as how the increased intervention of AI in the online product suggestion and purchasing process may be reconciled with the anthropocentric conception of trademark law as apparent from the use of criteria such as the 'average consumer', 'confusion', 'imperfect recollection' – all criteria with a built-in margin for *human* error. Regrettably, the scope of this chapter does not allow for substantive analysis in this regard. See however B. Clark in Legal Services Board, 'How Can Legal Services Regulation Support Responsible Technological Innovation that Improves Access to Justice?', *Perspectives on Lawtech and Regulation*, April 2020, pp. 19–21; M. Grynberg, 'AI and the "Death of Trademark" ', *Ky L J*, 2019–2020, pp. 199–238; WIPO Secretariat, 'Revised Issues Paper', p. 12; A. Moerland and C. Freitas, 'Artificial Intelligence and Trademark Assessment' in R. Hilty, J.-A. Lee, and K.-C. Liu (eds), *Artificial Intelligence and Intellectual Property* (Oxford: Oxford University Press, 2021), pp. 266–291; M.-C. Janssens and V.K. Dessers, 'The Artificially Intelligent Consumer in EU Trademark Law' in V. Fischer, G. Nolte, M. Senftleben and L. Specht-Riemenschneider, *Gestaltung der Informationsordnung. Festschrift Commemorating the 65th Anniversary of Professor Thomas Dreier* (Baden-Baden: Nomos-Verlag, 2022), pp. 143–160.

21 Cf. J.P. Osha et al., 'AIPPI Summary Report on Copyright in Artificially Generated Works', 2019, p. 1 in *AIPPI Yearbook 2019 / I*, https://bit.ly/3l4Ekmz.

Locke's natural rights paradigm, it considers creators to have a natural or human right to their creations, which are considered to be the 'fruits of their labour'.[22] This view may be contrasted with the traditional common law tradition, which favours the utilitarian, economic idea of IP as adding 'the fuel of interest to the fire of genius'[23] by providing an incentive for creative and/or innovative activity.[24] As always, the truth lies somewhere in the middle: both incentive creation and protection of creators are essential, interlinking objectives of IP law.

The essentially anthropocentric natural rights paradigm is much less conducive to the protection of AI and AI-generated output than the economic utilitarian theory.[25] Indeed, granting IP rights to such output could, in accordance with the latter, stimulate investment in AI and thus provide an (albeit indirect) incentive to create and/or innovate.[26] It is useful to bear this in mind throughout the entire chapter. In addition, the reader is reminded of the importance of achieving the notoriously tricky appropriate balance between the goals of securing proportionate protection for IP right holders on the one hand, and legal certainty as well as the requisite freedom for third parties (to create and/or innovate) on the other.[27]

8. A final introductory remark is that this chapter focuses on IP *protection*. When we flip this coin, another issue is unveiled, namely the question of liability in case of IP *infringement*. AI systems may find themselves on the wrong side of the law, by infringing the rights of third parties in works protected by copyright, patents, trademarks and/or designs. Who is responsible in such a situation and who should bear the costs? These questions are not purely hypothetical. By way of example, an AI program could create a song containing original elements of a pre-existing work, thus infringing the reproduction right of the owner of the copyright in the musical work at issue. Neither may it be excluded that an

---

22 Bently et al., *Intellectual Property Law*, pp. 5, 35–36, 41–42; Pila and Torremans, *European Intellectual Property Law*, pp. 78–81.

23 A. Lincoln, 'Discoveries and Inventions' (1859), excerpt of speech available at https://bit.ly/3CRny1d.

24 Bently et al., *Intellectual Property Law*, pp. 5–6; Pila and Torremans, *European Intellectual Property Law*, pp. 85–88; S. Yanisky-Ravid and X. Liu, 'When Artificial Intelligence Systems Produce Inventions: An Alternative Model for Patent Law at the 3A Era', *Cardozo L Rev*, 2018, pp. 2215, 2237–2240.

25 M. de Cock Buning, 'Autonomous Intelligent Systems as Creative Agents under the EU Framework for Intellectual Property', *Eur J Risk Regul*, 2016, pp. 310, 319–20; M.E. Kaminski, 'Authorship, Disrupted: AI Authors in Copyright and First Amendment Law', *UCD L Rev*, 2017, pp. 589, 599; Yanisky-Ravid and Liu, 'When Artificial Intelligence Systems Produce Inventions', pp. 2243–2246.

26 P. Blok, 'The Inventor's New Tool: Artificial Intelligence – How Does It Fit in the European Patent System?', *EIPR*, 2017, pp. 69, 72.

27 European Commission Communication to the European Parliament, the European Council, the Council, the European Economic and Social Committee and the Committee of the Regions of 25 April 2018 on Artificial Intelligence for Europe, COM(2018) 237 final, 15; Yanisky-Ravid and Liu, 'When Artificial Intelligence Systems Produce Inventions', p. 2221.

inventive machine was to develop a process and/or product that infringes a patent, or devise a sign that is confusingly similar to a registered trademark, or a product that falls within the scope of a protected (un)registered design. This in turn leads to further contentious matters, such as whether or not relevant exceptions and/or limitations (should) apply and whether fundamental rights such as freedom of expression may still play a role in such a case.[28]

Another aspect of this issue is that, in order to train an AI algorithm, more often than not a significant amount of data (even so-called 'big data') is required. If (part of) the relevant training data is subject to copyright and/or database protection, the use of such data – even for training purposes – is in principle subject to the prior authorisation of the copyright owner. This explains the relevance of a workable and balanced text and data mining (TDM) exception that allows access to as well as subsequent use and disclosure of relevant input data for research purposes, at least to a certain extent. While the Digital Single Market Directive presented itself as a choice opportunity to quell concerns of AI innovators in this regard, the limited scope of its provisions on TDM has offered several distinguished commentators ample food for criticism.[29]

The scope of this chapter does not allow for an in-depth discussion of issues of infringement or liability. By way of a (very) brief summary: there is quite a lot of uncertainty, which is why contractual solutions to mitigate risks are

---

28 Osha et al., 'AIPPI Summary Report on Copyright', p. 1. See in detail A. Škiljić, 'When Art Meets Technology or Vice Versa: Key Challenges at the Crossroads of AI-Generated Artworks and Copyright Law', *IIC*, 2021, ss. 4–5.

29 Articles 3–4 Dir. (EU) 2019/790 of the European Parliament and of the Council of 17 April 2019 on copyright and related rights in the Digital Single Market and amending Directives 96/9/EC and 2001/29/EC, *OJ L* 17 May 2019, no. 130, 92. In particular, the material and personal scope of these provisions is limited. See on this topic in detail e.g., C. Geiger, G. Frosio and O. Bulayenko, 'Text and Data Mining in the Proposed Copyright Reform: Making the EU Ready for an Age of Big Data?: Legal Analysis and Policy Recommendations', *IIC*, 2018, pp. 814–844; R. Ducato and A. Strowel, 'Limitations to Text and Data Mining and Consumer Empowerment: Making the Case for a Right to "Machine Legibility"', *IIC*, 2019, p. 649; E. Rosati, 'Copyright as an Obstacle or an Enabler? A European Perspective on Text and Data Mining and Its Role in the Development of AI Creativity', *Asia Pac Law Rev*, 2019, p. 217; P.B. Hugenholtz, 'The New Copyright Directive: Text and Data Mining (Articles 3 and 4)', *Kluwer Copyright Blog*, 24 July 2019, https://bit.ly/3kcuWx3; S. Flynn et al., 'Implementing User Rights for Research in the Field of Artificial Intelligence: A Call for International Action', *EIPR*, 2020, pp. 393–398; C. Geiger, 'The Missing Goal-Scorers in the Artificial Intelligence Team: Of Big Data, the Fundamental Right to Research and the failed Text and Data Mining limitations in the CSDM Directive' (Joint PIJIP/TLS Research Paper Series, 2021), 11 p.; M. Senftleben et al., 'Ensuring the Visibility and Accessibility of European Creative Content on the World Market – the Need for Copyright Data Improvement in the Light of New Technologies and the Opportunity Arising from Article 17 of the CDSM Directive', *JIPITEC*, 2002, 67-86, s. 2. See also T. Chiou, 'Copyright Law and Algorithmic Creativity: Monopolizing Inspiration?' in T.-E. Synodinou et al., *EU Internet Law in the Digital Single Market* (Cham: Springer, 2021), pp. 273–288.

desirable.[30] For a thorough analysis of the interface between AI and liability law, the reader is directed to Chapter 14 of this book.[31]

2. IP PROTECTION FOR AI TECHNOLOGY

2.1. OVERVIEW

9. First, the question arises what options are available to companies who seek to protect innovation relating to AI technology. Trademark and/or design law appear to be rather unsuitable for this purpose, with the words 'AI' or 'artificial intelligence' lacking distinctive character as such[32] (thus falling at the first hurdle of trademark protection) and with (hardly) no AI algorithm having a new product appearance with an individual character as its direct consequence.[33] A more viable option is to seek patent protection, the first step of which is to file a patent application. Another strategy opted for by innovators is to keep AI-related inventions a secret and avoid the requirement of disclosure that a patent application inevitably entails.[34] A final avenue is provided by the protection granted under copyright law.

2.2. PROTECTION UNDER PATENT LAW

10. Patent law aims to reward investment into research and development in order to spur future innovation. It does so by providing patentees with an exclusive right to exclude others from using a certain 'invention', a technological

---

30 See in relation to liability for IP infringement in an AI context in particular C. Vermosen, 'Copyright, Liability and Artificial Intelligence: Who is Responsible When an Artificial Intelligence System Infringes Copyright in the Context of the EU?' (Leuven: KU Leuven, 2017); B. Watson, 'A Mind of Its Own – Direct Infringement by Users of Artificial Intelligence Systems', *IDEA*, 2017, p. 31.

31 See also in relation to liability for IP infringement in particular F. Gotzen and M.-C. Janssens, 'Kunstmatige Kunst. Bedenkingen Bij de Toepassing van Het Auteursrecht Op Artificiële Intelligentie', *AM*, 2018–2019, pp. 335–341.

32 Although it is noted that, already over a decade ago, a EU word mark 'ARTIFICIAL INTELLIGENCE' (still in force at the time of writing) was registered for, among other things, synthetic rugs and artificial grass. This implies that this term may serve as an indication for origin for certain goods and/or services and thus constitute a valid trademark in certain cases.

33 See respectively Articles 4 and 7 Reg. (EU) 2017/1001 of the European Parliament and of the Council of 14 June 2017 on the European Union trademark, *OJ L* 16 June 2017, no. 154, 1; Articles 3–6 Council Reg. (EC) no. 6/2002 of 12 December 2001 on Community designs, *OJ L* 5 January 2002, no. 3, 1.

34 See the current EU framework on trade secret protection Dir. (EU) 2016/943 of the European Parliament and of the Council of 8 June 2016 on the protection of undisclosed know-how and business information (trade secrets) against their unlawful acquisition, use and disclosure, *OJ L* 15 June 2016, no. 157, 1.

improvement that takes the form of a product or a process (or both). This monopoly right is limited in time (i.e. 20 years following the patent application, subject to payment of the applicable annual fees) as well as in scope: while patentees can bring both direct and indirect infringements of their patent(s) to an end, they must accept certain exceptions as a defence to their claims, including use for experimental purposes and non-commercial use.[35] In order to be eligible for a patent, the invention must satisfy a number of conditions. First, there are certain exclusions to patent protection based on the claimed subject matter. The list of excluded subject matter under the European Patent Convention (EPC) includes inventions that are contrary to public order, but also ideas that are deemed too abstract to qualify for patent protection, such as computer programs as such, mere presentations of information, discoveries, methods for performing mental acts and mathematical methods (such as pure algorithms).[36]

This clearly constitutes a first obstacle for innovators seeking to obtain patent protection for AI-related technology. Indeed, abstract and thus patent-ineligible algorithms are essential to AI systems. Moreover, the 'Guidelines for Examination' of the European Patent Office (EPO) explicitly confirm that the EPO considers AI to be a kind of mathematical method, thus excluding its patentability *as such* in accordance with Article 52 EPC – the same exclusion that applies to, among other things, software.[37] However, this does not mean that the curtain falls completely on patent protection for computer-implemented inventions such as technology related to AI algorithms. This rings especially true given the rather lenient interpretation of the 'as such' proviso in practice, as evidenced by case law on software patents in particular. Indeed, if the invention is claimed in the context of a technical system, if it is proven that the invention at issue has a technical character, patentability may yet arise.[38] According to the EPO Guidelines, this will for example be the case for a neural network used 'in a heart-monitoring apparatus for the purpose of identifying irregular heartbeats', as well as – in certain circumstances – methods for training AI systems.[39]

35 The definition of 'infringement' is left to national law, see Article 64(3) EPC. The relevant provisions of Belgian law are Articles XI.29-XI.46 BCEL.

36 Articles 52–53 EPC.

37 European Patent Office (EPO), 'Guidelines for Examination, Part G, Chapter II, 3.3.1', 2018, https://bit.ly/3BQb8W9; J.-M. Deltorn et al., 'The Examination of Computer-Implemented Inventions and Artificial Intelligence Inventions at the European Patent Office' (European Patent Office, 2019), 7 p.; M. Iglesias et al., 'Intellectual Property and Artificial Intelligence: A Literature Review' (European Commission Joint Research Centre, 2019), pp. 6–8; K. Foss-Solbrekk, 'Three Routes to Protecting AI Systems and their Algorithms under IP Law: the Good, the Bad and the Ugly', *JIPLP*, 2021, pp. 253–256.

38 M. Hashiguchi, 'The Global Artificial Intelligence Revolution Challenges Patent Eligibility Laws', *J Bus & Tech L*, 2017, pp. 1, 16–19, 23; M. Hashiguchi, 'Artificial Intelligence and the Jurisprudence of Patent Eligibility in the United States, Europe, and Japan', *Intell Prop & Tech LJ*, 2017, pp. 3, 6–7.

39 See for another example B. Gallagher, 'The Singularity is Near: Implications for Patent and Copyright Law in the Age of Whole Brain Emulation', *Fed Cir BJ*, 2016, pp. 1, 21–25.

Despite these specifications, the EPO Guidelines leave an undeniable margin for interpretation as to the patentability of AI-related innovation in practice, in particular as to simulations. The decision of the Enlarged Board of Appeal (EBA) at the EPO in the *Pedestrian simulation* case was therefore eagerly awaited by many. This case concerns an invention whereby the movement of a pedestrian crowd is simulated so as to inform the architectural design of venues such as railway stations or stadia. In March 2021, the EBA held that the principles applicable to computer-implemented inventions (CIIs) also apply to simulations and that the requisite technical character of a simulation is established if it produces a technical effect beyond its implementation on a computer – in other words: a connection to a material object in the 'real' world.[40] In this context, the mere (partial or full) foundation of the simulation on technical principles that underly the simulated system or process is deemed neither necessary nor sufficient.[41] Subsequent to the EBA decision, the underlying patent application was referred back to the Technical Boards of Appeal (TBA), where it is still pending at the time of writing – over 19 years after its filing date.

11. Further, a patentable invention must satisfy a number of substantive conditions: it must be novel and inventive as well as industrially applicable.[42] The novelty requirement implies that the invention may not form part of the state of the art (i.e. what has been made available to the public) at the date of filing of the patent application, while the condition of inventive step requires the invention to not have been obvious to a theoretical person skilled in the art (PSA) on the basis of this state of the art.[43] Finally, the invention must be susceptible to use in an industrial context.[44] Both the novelty and industrial applicability requirements do not appear to pose any challenges specific to AI-related innovation.[45] Conversely, the requirement of inventive step is assessed on the basis of the features that contribute to the 'technical character' of the invention. This again highlights the importance of the EBA's findings in the *Pedestrian*

40 EBA Decision 10 March 2021 re patent application 03793825.5, G 0001/19, https://bit.ly/31o8x9g. See T. Minssen and M. Aboy, 'The Patentability of Computer-Implemented Simulations and Implications for Computer-Implemented Inventions (CIIs)', *JIPLP*, 2020, pp. 633–635.

41 EBA Decision 10 March 2021 re patent application 03793825.5, G 0001/19, https://bit.ly/31o8x9g, para. 142.

42 Articles 52 *juncto* 54–57 EPC.

43 Respectively Articles 54–55 EPC and Article 56 EPC. In determining whether a certain invention involves an inventive step (and is therefore not 'obvious'), the EPO as well as the Belgian courts apply the so-called 'problem-solution approach'. This approach involves (i) determining the so-called 'closest prior art', (ii) establishing the 'objective technical problem' in the state of the art, and (iii) considering whether or not the claimed invention, starting from the closest prior art and the objective technical problem, would have been obvious to the skilled person ('could-would approach', see in more detail EPO, 'Guidelines for Examination, Part G, Chapter VII.5', https://bit.ly/3GQL5ln). See also *infra* para. 32.

44 Article 57 EPC.

45 See however in relation to patent protection of AI-generated output *infra* paras 26 et seq.

Simulation case. In particular, the EBA ruled that the traditional 'COMVIK approach' established in the context of CIIs applies to computer-implemented simulations.[46] This means that the inventiveness analysis only takes account of the patent claim features that contribute to the solution of a technical problem, whereas the non-technical features are removed from the equation.[47]

12. There may be yet another obstacle for innovators seeking to patent AI-related innovation. This relates to the so-called 'patent bargain' between patentee and issuing government. This concept is essential to patent law. It implies that a prospective patentee must disclose their invention in a way that is 'sufficiently clear and complete for it to be carried out by a person skilled in the art', in return for the temporary monopoly right granted by a patent.[48] This requirement of disclosure may be at odds with the apparent 'black box' nature of many forms of AI technology – in particular in a deep learning context –, which makes it impossible to know precisely why an AI algorithm arrived at a certain conclusion in a specific case.[49] Arguably, such AI-related inventions can therefore not be explained in a 'sufficiently clear and complete' manner, rendering the procurement of a patent for such an invention impossible. As of yet, however, the scope of the disclosure requirement in AI-related inventions is not crystal-clear. While explaining why an AI system made (or did not make) a specific decision may not be possible in some cases, experts will generally be able to disclose the AI system's structure, the applicable parameters and the basic principles to which the AI system adheres.[50] It is quite plausible that patent offices will deem this to be sufficient for patenting purposes. The risk of being excluded from patent protection constitutes an additional incentive for AI innovators to invest in so-called 'explainable' and transparent AI.[51] Simultaneously, however,

---

46 EBA Decision 10 March 2021 re patent application 03793825.5, G 0001/19, https://bit.ly/3lo8x9g, in particular paras 106–138. See Minssen and Aboy, 'The Patentability of Computer-Implemented Simulations and Implications for Computer-Implemented Inventions (CIIs)', pp. 633–635.

47 TBA Decision 26 September 2002 re patent application 92907791.5, T 0641/00, https://bit.ly/3CNSHmj. See also EPO, 'Case Law of the Boards of Appeal', Part I, D 9.1.3 b), https://bit.ly/2YjYMbd.

48 Article 83 EPC. See also B. Higgins, 'The Role of Explainable Artificial Intelligence in Patent Law', *Intell Prop & Tech LJ*, 2019, pp. 3–4.

49 Hashiguchi, 'The Global Artificial Intelligence Revolution Challenges Patent Eligibility Laws', pp. 29–30. The 2021 AIPPI World Congress expressly treated this issue in one of its Study Questions. See in detail A.M. Verschuur et al., 'Summary Report on Inventiveness and Sufficiency of Disclosure in AI Inventions', 2021, 34 p., https://bit.ly/3DSH6D0. The national reports are available at https://aippi.org. The ensuing AIPPI Resolution of 22 October 2021 on Inventiveness and Sufficiency of Disclosure in AI Inventions is available at https://bit.ly/3rb3vYG. See on sufficiency of disclosure in particular paras. 6–7.

50 Higgins, 'The Role of Explainable Artificial Intelligence in Patent Law', p. 7.

51 See, e.g., Higgins, 'The Role of Explainable Artificial Intelligence in Patent Law'; W. Samek et al. (eds), *Explainable AI: Interpreting, Explaining and Visualizing Deep Learning*, Lecture Notes in Computer Science Vol 11700 (Cham: Springer International Publishing, 2019), 439 p.

an overly strict assessment of the requirement of disclosure may push innovators towards recourse to trade secrets as an alternative way to protect AI-related innovation.[52]

13. The above questions relating to the patentability of AI-related innovation remain quite contentious. As a result, it is often difficult to predict the outcome of the patenting process in a particular case. However, this uncertainty does not seem to deter prospective patentees, as evidenced by the steeply rising number of AI-related patent applications filed annually – an increase that is much higher than in other fields of technology.[53] Since the 1950s, over 300.000 AI-related patent applications have been filed worldwide, with a significant spike in identified AI-related inventions in the past decade.[54] Interestingly, the degree of AI-related innovation differs starkly per sector, with the telecom, transport and health care sectors in particular being seemingly AI-intensive industries.[55]

2.3. PROTECTION UNDER COPYRIGHT LAW

14. As mentioned above, not all intellectual property rights are subject to a requirement of registration.[56] In particular, copyright protection is generated automatically upon creation of an original work. The question therefore arises whether AI-related innovation could be susceptible to copyright protection.

Copyright protection is available to literary and artistic works that constitute a concrete and original expression by the author(s). The requirement of concrete form is linked to the so-called 'idea-expression dichotomy', which entails that copyright protection is not available to mere abstract ideas and principles – that these must be expressed in a concrete way.[57] In accordance with established case law of the Court of Justice of the European Union (CJEU), the condition of originality implies that the work must be an intellectual creation of the author(s), reflecting their personality and expressing free and creative choices.[58] If the conditions for copyright protection are fulfilled, it applies automatically, without the need for registration. Applied to AI-related works in particular, it

52 Cf. Foss-Solbrekk, 'Three Routes to Protecting AI Systems and their Algorithms under IP Law', pp. 256–258.
53 Higgins, 'The Role of Explainable Artificial Intelligence in Patent Law', p. 7; WIPO Technology Trends 2019 – Artificial Intelligence (WIPO 2019), p. 14, https://bit.ly/3wlRQH5.
54 WIPO Technology Trends 2019, p. 13; WIPO Technology Trends 2021, Assistive Technology, https://bit.ly/3EO8T7z.
55 WIPO Technology Trends 2019, pp. 14–15.
56 See *supra* para. 4.
57 Article 9(2) TRIPS Agreement. See also Pila and Torremans, *European Intellectual Property Law*, pp. 282–283.
58 CJEU 16 July 2009, no. C-5/08, ECLI:EU:C:2009:465, *Infopaq/Danske Dagblades Forening*; CJEU 22 December 2010, no. C-393/09, ECLI:EU:C:2010:816, *BSA/Ministerstvo kultury*; CJEU 1 December 2011, no. C-145/10, ECLI:EU:C:2011:798, *Painer/Standard*.

is fair to say that the abstract idea, the functional algorithm in its purest sense, does not satisfy the first condition and is therefore not susceptible to copyright protection.[59] However, the object and source code of the computer program expressing this idea will be considered sufficiently concrete, allowing for copyright protection once the condition of originality is fulfilled.[60] Given the traditionally low threshold set for originality in practice, it is likely that software that implements AI technology will receive automatic protection as a computer program under copyright law upon its creation.[61] Even so, the multiplicity of authors in a software programming context, combined with the prevalence of open source software (the essence of which is its public accessibility[62]), may lead to difficulties relating to the application of copyright protection in practice.

15. All in all, innovators seeking intellectual property protection for AI-related technology are still confronted with a number of obstacles. While copyright law offers a relatively clear avenue for protection, any lingering uncertainty regarding the patentability of CIIs is undesirable. It goes without saying that a clear, harmonised solution is warranted on both fronts. While investment in AI-related innovation must be encouraged,[63] overprotection and the ensuing 'tragedy of the anti-commons'[64] always loom around the corner. A workable balance must therefore be attained, focusing on explainable AI and keeping the requisite technical character of an invention in mind.

3. IP PROTECTION FOR AI-GENERATED OUTPUT

16. Second, the rapid evolution of AI systems raises questions regarding the possibility as well as the desirability of IP protection for 'things' (in the broadest sense) created by or through the intervention of artificially intelligent systems. Not only must we think about whether creative and/or inventive AI systems have a place within IP law or whether IP law could be adjusted to take account thereof, but also about whether such steps *should* be taken.

---

59 Article 1(2) Dir. 2009/24/EC of the European Parliament and of the Council of 23 April 2009 on the legal protection of computer programs, *OJ L* 5 May 2009, no. 111, 16; CJEU 2 May 2012, no. C-406/10, ECLI:EU:C:2012:259, *SAS Institute/World Programming*, paras 39–40 and 46.

60 CJEU 22 December 2010, no. C-393/09, ECLI:EU:C:2010:816, *BSA/Ministerstvo kultury*, paras 33–35.

61 See in more detail Foss-Solbrekk, 'Three Routes to Protecting AI Systems and their Algorithms under IP Law', pp. 249–253; B.G. Otero, 'Machine Learning Models Under the Copyright Microscope: Is EU Copyright Fit for Purpose?', *GRUR International*, 2021, pp. 1–13.

62 See more on this topic online at https://red.ht/3BQlrtp.

63 Osha et al., 'AIPPI Summary Report on Copyright', p. 2.

64 See M. Heller, *The Gridlock Economy: How Too Much Ownership Wrecks Markets, Stops Innovation, and Costs Lives* (New York, NY: Basic Books, 2008), 304 p.

This part consists of three sections. The first two sections treat the question whether AI systems could (and, if not, should) claim authorship and/or inventorship in relation to output that is produced through or by AI systems.[65] The third section of this part brings the fields of copyright and patent law together and centres around the broader issue of IP ownership.

3.1. AI AUTHORSHIP OF AI-GENERATED WORKS

17. The first issue under review here is whether AI systems may claim authorship of AI-generated output. This topic is divided into several sub-questions. First, it may be asked whether certain AI-generated output available today would enjoy copyright protection if it had been solely created by a human, as well as what the exact role is for the AI system in such cases: is it merely a tool to enhance human facilities or do creative machines actually already exist? In addition, this part discusses whether an AI system can be considered an author and, if not, whether it should be.

18. Certain AI systems available today can create – or can be used as a tool to create – works that would satisfy the conditions for copyright protection set out above if they had been solely created by humans.[66] Interestingly, the use of computers in the creation process is not novel. In this regard, the reader is referred to the 'Datatron' digital computer that was already programmed to compose songs in 1956,[67] as well as 'AARON', the AI system that creates visual art on the basis of code that was written as far back as 1973.[68] Many striking instances of works created through or by AI systems over the past few years

---

65 Analogous considerations may be made in relation to the identity of the designer under the law of designs. See extensively: H. Yılmaztekin, *Artificial Intelligence, Design Law and Fashion* (London: Routledge, 2023), 248 p.

66 See *supra* para. 14. See for other examples among others J. McCutcheon, 'The Vanishing Author in Computer-Generated Works: A Critical Analysis of Recent Australian Case Law', *Melb U L Rev*, 2013, pp. 915, 929–931; A. Guadamuz, 'Do Androids Dream of Electric Copyright? Comparative Analysis of Originality in Artificial Intelligence Generated Works', *IPQ*, 2017, pp. 169, 170–174; Hashiguchi, 'The Global Artificial Intelligence Revolution Challenges Patent Eligibility Laws', p. 3; N.I. Brown, 'Artificial Authors: A Case for Copyright in Computer-Generated Works', *Colum Sci & Tech L Rev*, 2018, pp. 1, 2–4, 9–14; E. Bonadio and L. McDonagh, 'Artificial Intelligence as Producer and Consumer of Copyright Works: Evaluating the Consequences of Algorithmic Creativity', *IPQ*, 2020, pp. 112–13; D. Gervais, 'The Machine as Author', *Iowa L Rev*, 2020, pp. 2053–2057; P. Mezei, 'From Leonardo to the Next Rembrandt – The Need for AI-Pessimism in the Age of Algorithms', *UFITA*, 2020, pp. 6–9 of draft, https://ssrn.com/abstract=3592187.

67 Referred to in A. Bridy, 'The Evolution of Authorship: Work Made by Code', *Colum JL & Arts* 2016, pp. 395–396; S.F. Hedrick, 'I "Think," Therefore I Create: Claiming Copyright in the Outputs of Algorithms', *NYU Journal of Intell Prop & Ent Law*, 2019, p. 330.

68 Referred to in Bridy, 'The Evolution of Authorship', pp. 397–98. See also extensively https://bit.ly/3bGQe1b.

can be found in the music sector.[69] By way of example, you may be reading this chapter with AI-generated music playing in the background, such as the Spotify playlist 'AI-composed music',[70] piano music composed and performed by Google's 'DeepMind' AI,[71] the latest album released by the 'Auxuman'[72] algorithm, one of the 600 soundscapes created by the 'Endel'[73] app or one of the unfinished symphonies of either Franz Schubert or Ludwig van Beethoven as completed with the aid of an AI system.[74] If you would rather create your own music for this purpose, Sony's 'Flow Machines' project may offer assistance by augmenting your own creativity through its AI algorithm.[75] On another note, if you are bored with the present text, which was written (solely) by a human author, you may find solace in a short story,[76] a novel[77] or even a sonnet[78] drafted by an AI algorithm – or translate it using 'DeepL',[79] the artificially intelligent translation app. Software adepts may enhance their abilities using GitHub's virtual coding assistant.[80] If, instead, you are more visually inclined, AI-generated artworks are also available.[81] Most famously, all of Dutch artist Rembrandt van Rijn's paintings were fed to an AI algorithm that went on to create a 3D-printed painting in Rembrandt's style on this basis in 2016.[82] Since then, the use of AI in the course of artists' creation processes has skyrocketed, resulting in several high-profile auctions of AI art over the years as well as the establishment of communities such as 'AIArtists.org'.[83]

---

69 See on this topic in detail O. Bulayenko, J. Quintais, D. Gervais and J. Poort, 'AI Music Outputs: Challenges to the Copyright Legal Framework', 2022, https://ssrn.com/abstract=4072806.

70 Playlist available at https://spoti.fi/31pPGe0.

71 Video available at youtu.be/Y8UawLT4it0.

72 See website: https://www.auxuman.space.

73 See website: https://endel.io.

74 See respectively https://bit.ly/3whiQHy and https://bit.ly/3wrGrFO. See also the collaborative platform 'Mubert' (website: https://mubert.com); and 'From the Future World', a piece composed by an AI system on the basis of a musical sketch drafted by Czech composer Antonin Dvořák (1841–1904), as described in R. Johnston, 'A Rediscovered Dvořák Score, Completed by Artificial Intelligence, Premieres in Prague', 9 November 2019, https://bit.ly/3GWH8eU.. See also J.-M. Deltorn and F. Macrez, 'Authorship in the Age of Machine Learning and Artificial Intelligence' in S. O'Connor (ed.), *The Oxford Handbook of Music Law and Policy* (Oxford: Oxford University Press, 2019).

75 See website: https://www.flow-machines.com.

76 See, e.g., S. Bringsjord and D.A. Ferrucci, *Artificial Intelligence and Literary Creativity: Inside the Mind of BRUTUS, a Storytelling Machine* (London: Routledge, 1999), 262 p.

77 See, e.g., T. Hornigold, 'The First Novel Written by AI Is Here – and It's as Weird as You'd Expect It to Be', 25 October 2018, https://bit.ly/3mOs4rP. See however for a (convincing) sceptical perspective G. Smith, 'The Great American Novel Will Not Be Written by a Computer', 30 June 2021, https://bit.ly/3HOUQRy.

78 See, e.g., J.H. Lau et al., 'Deep-speare: a Joint Neural Model of Poetic Language, Meter and Rhyme', 2018, https://arxiv.org/pdf/1807.03491.pdf.

79 See website: https://www.deepl.com.

80 See website: https://copilot.github.com.

81 See for a detailed timeline of AI artworks: https://aiartists.org/ai-timeline-art.

82 See website: https://www.nextrembrandt.com.

83 See, e.g., 'Is Artificial Intelligence Set to Become Art's Next Medium?', 12 December 2018, https://bit.ly/2Yk2OAl; J. Vincent, 'A Never-Ending Stream of AI Art Goes Up for Auction',

19. A feature common to many of these examples is that there is still some form of human intervention, be it by a programmer, by a person training the AI system through data input or by somebody who modifies and/or selects certain specific output deemed 'worthy' to disclose to the public.[84] If such human(s) were to have created the work(s) at issue without the assistance of any AI system, there would be little to no doubt that copyright protection would be available to them. Indeed, music, novels, paintings and the like all fall within the broad category of 'literary and artistic works'. Subsequently, provided that the works at issue constitute a concrete, original expression of the author(s), copyright would apply.[85] However, given the intervention of AI in these (and other) cases, the matter is less straightforward.[86]

20. The main challenge in this regard is that copyright law requires the work at issue to show *authorship,* i.e. the personal stamp of the author. This author is a being that is traditionally considered to be a physical person, especially in the civil law '*droit d'auteur*' tradition, where copyright protection is viewed as a natural right, granted to the author to protect emanations of their personality.[87] As the name suggests, the '*droit d'auteur*' tradition (in Dutch '*auteursrecht*' and in German '*Urheberrecht*') places the idea of the romantic author squarely in its centre. Creativity is hereby viewed as a quintessentially human faculty, whereby a sentient being expresses its personality by making free, deliberate choices.[88] From a societal perspective, the essentially human nature of authorship is linked to our equally essential thirst for human communication; for the social practice that makes us feel alive.[89]

5 March 2019, https://bit.ly/3wgv3wk; 'Artificial Intelligence-Created Paintings to Be Put on Sale by Sotheby's in New York', 13 November 2019, https://bit.ly/2ZV2R5Y. See for relevant examples, e.g., https://aiartists.org; https://www.artaigallery.com; https://deepart.io; https://bit.ly/3BLx7NT; https://bit.ly/3ESz1OR; https://bit.ly/3wlNVd7; https://bit.ly/2ZZzGis.

84 By way of example, users provide the DeepL translation app with relevant input and may manually modify the translated text.

85 CJEU 16 July 2009, no. C-5/08, ECLI:EU:C:2009:465, *Infopaq/Danske Dagblades Forening*; CJEU 22 December 2010, no. C-393/09, ECLI:EU:C:2010:816, *BSA/Ministerstvo kultury*; CJEU 1 December 2011, no. C-145/10, ECLI:EU:C:2011:798, *Painer/Standard*.

86 Interestingly, legal scholarship regarding the question of computer authorship already spans several decades. See, e.g., K.F. Jr. Milde, 'Can a Computer Be an Author or an Inventor', *J Pat Off Soc'y*, 1969, pp. 378–405; T.L. Butler, 'Can a Computer Be an Author? Copyright Aspects of Artificial Intelligence', *Comm/Ent LS*, 1981, p. 707; P. Samuelson, 'Allocating Ownership Rights in Computer-Generated Works', *U Pitt L Rev*, 1986, pp. 1185–1228; US Congress, Office of Technology Assessment, 'Intellectual Property Rights in an Age of Electronics and Information', April 1986.

87 See also *supra* para. 7.

88 Cf. Bridy, 'Coding Creativity', p. 4; E. Treppoz et al., 'AIPPI Study Question – Copyright in Artificially Generated Works – France', 24 May 2019, p. 10.

89 J. Grimmelmann, 'Copyright for Literate Robots', *Iowa L Rev*, 2016, pp. 657, 660; C.J. Craig and I.R. Kerr, 'The Death of the AI Author', 2019, p. 42.

The need for human intellectual authorship is ingrained in our system.[90] The pivotal role of the author as a (sometimes starving) artist whose interests deserve to be protected, pervades all aspects of copyright law. First and foremost, copyright laws grant first ownership of copyright in a certain work to its author.[91] Further, the term of protection is calculated from the death of the author.[92] In addition, provisions apply that expressly seek to protect the author, such as those included in copyright contract law as well as the resale right applicable to original works of art.[93] Moreover, certain copyright exceptions only apply if the author is acknowledged and/or if an equitable remuneration is paid to such author.[94] The focus on the human author also explains the importance placed on moral rights protection, translated into the author's right to disclosure, integrity and attribution.[95]

21. Such a system simply leaves no room for authorship on the part of a non-human entity.[96] As succinctly formulated by Advocate General Maciej Szpunar, 'the origin of and justification for copyright, in the form of both moral and property rights, lies in the special relationship between the author and his work. Thus, where there is no author, there is no copyright, in the form of either moral or property rights.'[97] If there is insufficient human input, if the AI crosses a certain threshold of autonomy, copyright protection will be unavailable.[98] This anthropocentric view is unsurprising, since intellectual property laws were largely drafted at a time when the concept of non-human 'creators' belonged squarely in the realm of fiction.

22. Another reason to exclude AI authorship as the law currently stands, is that initial copyright in a work is granted to its author. An AI system *as such* is not a legal entity, which implies that it cannot be endowed with rights of any kind,

---

90 De Cock Buning, 'Autonomous Intelligent Systems as Creative Agents', pp. 314–16; Osha et al., 'AIPPI Summary Report on Copyright', pp. 1, 18; Gervais, 'The Machine as Author', pp. 2072–2085.

91 See, e.g., Article 2(6) Berne Convention, where copyright is conceptualised as a form of protection for the *author* and their successors in title. See under Belgian law Article XI.167(1) BCEL.

92 See under Belgian law Article XI.166 BCEL.

93 See under Belgian law Articles XI.167 through XI.167/6 BCEL and XI.175 BCEL.

94 See under Belgian law Articles XI.190(1), and XI.191/1(5) BCEL.

95 Bridy, 'The Evolution of Authorship', p. 401; Mezei, 'From Leonardo to the Next Rembrandt', pp. 19–20 of draft.

96 See, e.g., Guadamuz, 'Do Androids Dream of Electric Copyright?', pp. 173–74; Osha et al., 'AIPPI Summary Report on Copyright', p. 1; Mezei, 'From Leonardo to the Next Rembrandt', pp. 11–16 of draft.

97 Opinion AG Szpunar 25 October 2018, no. C-469/17, ECLI:EU:C:2018:870, Funke Medien/Bundesrepublik Deutschland, para. 60. Cf. Hedrick, 'I "Think," Therefore I Create', p. 375.

98 Gervais, 'The Machine as Author', pp. 2062, 2098–2101, 2106. See regarding the requisite degree of human input among others Osha et al., 'AIPPI Summary Report on Copyright'.

including ownership rights.[99] This begs the question whether AI systems should be able to obtain legal personality. While being mindful of the can of worms that such a question might open – a 'box of Pandora' that would be impossible to contain in the context of this chapter – it is submitted that it should be answered in the negative, for the reasons set out in the open letter addressed to the European Commission on AI and Robotics, signed by a significant number of experts in the field.[100]

23. However, this does not solve the conceptual core of the issue, which is whether the abstract idea of originality *should* be held to include the creating behaviour of an AI system. In this context, account must be taken of the broad range of potential AI activity and the ensuing distinction between AI-assisted and truly AI-generated content.

At the one end of the spectrum, we may find AI systems that function as a tool to assist and/or enhance human creativity. In such a context, the AI itself is not fully autonomous. Instead, it acts as a mere executer that lacks creative capabilities and thus cannot reasonably claim authorship.[101] We can compare this to the quill used by William Shakespeare, the paintbrush wielded by William Turner or the Sibelius music notation software used by contemporary composers.[102] Further down the line, there are many forms of AI-exhibited creativity that still result from creative choices made by a human, where the output flows directly from the parameters set by the AI system's programmer

---

99 N. Nevejans, 'Study on European Civil Law Rules in Robotics', 2016, pp. 14–16. Notably, continental EU law does not have a rule similar to the 'work-made-for-hire' doctrine that applies in the United States, which allows employers to be 'treated *ab initio* as the author of a work created by its human employee', see Bridy, 'The Evolution of Authorship', p. 400. For an argument in favour of applying the made-for-hire doctrine to AI-generated works, see K. Hristov, 'Artificial Intelligence and the Copyright Dilemma', *IDEA*, 2017, p. 431; S. Yanisky-Ravid, 'Generating Rembrandt: Artificial Intelligence, Copyright, and Accountability in the 3A Era – the Human-Like Authors Are Already Here – A New Model', *Mich St L Rev*, 2017, pp. 660–726. See for a less enthusiastic stance Y.J. Liebesman, 'The Wisdom of Legislating for Anticipated Technological Advancements', *J Marshall Rev Intell Prop L*, 2010, pp. 170–177; Bonadio and McDonagh, 'Artificial Intelligence as Producer and Consumer of Copyright Works', pp. 118–119; Gervais, 'The Machine as Author', pp. 2094–96.

100 See for the full text of this letter https://bit.ly/3mK3EzI. Cf. also C.R. Davies, 'An Evolutionary Step in Intellectual Property Rights – Artificial Intelligence and Intellectual Property', *CLSR*, 2011, pp. 601, 617–18; N. Shemtov, 'A Study on Inventorship in Inventions Involving AI Activity', European Patent Office, 2019, p. 25. See for an interesting argument on the requisite link between rights and responsibilities (incl. liability) Gervais, 'The Machine as Author', pp. 2085–88. See also Chapter 13, part 3 of this book.

101 J. Grimmelmann, 'There's No Such Thing as a Computer-Authored Work – And It's a Good Thing, Too', *Colum JL & Arts*, 2016, pp. 403, 406–08; E. Fraser, 'Computers as Inventors – Legal and Policy Implications of Artificial Intelligence on Patent Law', *SCRIPTed*, 2016, pp. 305, 306; Gotzen and Janssens, 'Kunstmatige Kunst', pp. 329–330; Hedrick, 'I "Think," Therefore I Create', p. 329; Gervais, 'The Machine as Author', p. 2069.

102 Cf. Kaminski, 'Authorship, Disrupted', p. 595.

or user.[103] Such AI activity may still be viewed as pure execution and should thus in any case fall outside the scope of 'true' creativity and ensuing copyright protection on the part of the AI system. In such cases, copyright is and should be reserved to the human actor behind the machine. At the far end of the spectrum, finally, we could find a hypothetical, more autonomous AI, having transcended its role as an instrumentality and having independently created a work that exhibits the requisite creativity, which experts and non-experts alike cannot distinguish from a work generated by a human.[104] If this occurs – and some argue that it already has occurred or that it will soon[105] – our current copyright framework will come under even more vigorous attack, since the supposedly 'creative' AI only really comes to the fore in such cases.[106] Even so, given that every piece of AI-generated output is, in one way or another, the result of prior input, it may be argued that there is no real act of 'conception' in the AI system (and that there will never be).[107] Arguably, precisely this act, the *process* of creation, is the essence of creativity – not the eventual, possibly creative end result. As long as the human thought process cannot be formulated as an algorithm that may be implemented by a computer, this process is and will remain quintessentially human. This would exclude the possibility of 'creativity' and, thus, authorship, on the part of an AI system. Then again, the 'prior input' argument also applies *mutatis mutandis* to humans, who create literary and artistic works while 'standing on the shoulders of giants'.[108] Given the ever-expanding corpus of works, it might even be questioned whether anybody can ever be fully original.[109] This could render the 'act of conception' argument against AI authorship moot, as could choosing the end result and thus the originality of the output as a (functionalist) focal point instead of the creative process.[110]

The main argument in favour of granting copyright protection to such (quasi-)independently created works is that it may stimulate further creative

---

103 Hedrick, 'I "Think," Therefore I Create', pp. 353, 358–60.

104 Today, such a distinction by experts is often still possible. By way of example: for the trained ear, DeepMind's piano music mentioned *supra* (para. 18) sounds wholly artificial and quite contrived.

105 Hedrick, 'I "Think," Therefore I Create', p. 328.

106 Milde, 'Can a Computer Be an Author or an Inventor', pp. 378, 403–404; Bridy, 'The Evolution of Authorship', pp. 398–399; Grimmelmann, 'Copyright for Literate Robots', pp. 680–681.

107 See in relation to patent law *infra* para. 30. See also Shemtov, 'A Study on Inventorship in Inventions Involving AI Activity', pp. 6, 20, 35.

108 'If I have seen further, it is by standing upon the shoulders of Giants.' – Sir I. Newton in a letter to his rival R. Hook (1675).

109 Cf. J. Vanherpe, 'Stealing Good Steals – A Plea for Realism in Music Copyright' in KU Leuven Centre for IT & IP Law (ed.), *Rethinking IT and IP law. Celebrating 30 Years CiTiP* (Antwerp/Cambridge: Intersentia, 2019) pp. 153–158.

110 Cf. in relation to patent law Shemtov, 'A Study on Inventorship in Inventions Involving AI Activity', pp. 28–29; R. Abbott, 'I Think, Therefore I Invent: Creative Computers and the Future of Patent Law', *BC L Rev*, 2016, pp. 1082, 1099, 1108–1111.

efforts on the part of AI systems. This appears to be in line with the economic, utilitarian rationale of copyright.[111] However, copyright seeks to incentivise human creators, not AI systems, as prescribed by the anthropocentric paradigm of natural justice that underlies continental EU copyright law.[112] Moreover, it is difficult if not impossible to see how AI systems may respond to incentives in the absence of human consciousness.[113] Without convincing economic evidence in this regard, caution is advised against tearing down one of the fundamental principles of copyright law.[114] The mere fact that we can create certain incentives does not in itself imply that we should. Further, if we were to allow AI authorship, we must be prepared for an upsurge in algorithmic creations and even 'a saturation of the range of possible creations' in case artificial superintelligence (ASI)[115] were to be attained.[116] This could have drastic and unforeseen effects on the freedom to create on the part of humans, both with regard to the standard of protection and copyright infringement. Indeed, such a proliferation in AI-generated works might not only aggravate the risk of copyright infringement by humans, but could also make it more difficult for them to attain the requisite standard of originality. Put somewhat provocatively, this leads to the following (as of yet unanswered) question: if we grant authorship to AI systems, will human authors still be able to compete?[117] All things considered, it is submitted that AI authorship would be a bridge too far.

24. The risk of extending authorship to AI systems could be mitigated by instead establishing either a neighbouring or *sui generis* right to AI-generated works and thus provide a limited degree of exclusivity in order to protect investments and incentivise research in this area. Such a right could be modelled in a similar way to the *sui generis* database right established by the EU in 1996, e.g., requiring a substantial investment for protection to be available.[118] Arguably,

---

111 See, e.g., McCutcheon, 'The Vanishing Author in Computer-Generated Works', p. 954.

112 Kaminski, 'Authorship, Disrupted', p. 598; L. Bently, 'The UK's Provisions on Computer-Generated Works: A Solution for AI Creations?' (European Copyright Society, Brussels, 25 May 2018); Gotzen and Janssens, 'Kunstmatige Kunst', p. 332.

113 Samuelson, 'Allocating Ownership Rights in Computer-Generated Works', pp. 1185, 1199; Hedrick, 'I "Think," Therefore I Create', pp. 334–336; Yanisky-Ravid and Liu, 'When Artificial Intelligence Systems Produce Inventions', pp. 2239–41; G.A. Gabison, 'Who Holds the Right to Exclude for Machine Work Products?', *IPQ*, 2020, pp. 20, 37.

114 Cf. Gotzen and Janssens, 'Kunstmatige Kunst', p. 332; P. Mezei, ' "You AIn't Seen Nothing yet" – Arguments against the Protectability of AI-Generated Outputs by Copyright Law', in M. Borghi and R. Brownsword (eds), Law, *Regulation and Governance in the Information Society: Informational Rights and Informational Wrongs* (London: Routledge, forthcoming in 2023).

115 See in this regard Chapter 1 of this book.

116 Treppoz et al., 'AIPPI Study Question', p. 11.

117 Cf. Bently, 'The UK's Provisions on Computer-Generated Works'; Gervais, 'The Machine as Author', pp. 2060–2061.

118 See Database Directive. See extensively on what form such a *sui generis* right could take S. Blair et al., 'AIPPI Study Question – Copyright in Artificially Generated Works – United Kingdom', 11 June 2019, pp. 9–13.

however, such a right would suffer similar defects in practice as an extended authorship concept would: granting additional IP rights in AI-generated output would inevitably entail an even steeper increase in AI-generated output. This could in turn be unfortunate for human authors.[119] The creation of a new right, even if limited in scope, would moreover lead to further and arguably undesirable fragmentation of IP law.[120] In addition, it is questionable whether the scope of IP protection should be further increased, not only in view of the crisis in public opinion IP has had to face over the past few decades, but also in view of economic considerations.[121] Before establishing yet another IP right, we should ask ourselves whether such a right would actually overcome a market failure – in other words, whether an additional property incentive to R&D in the field of AI is actually necessary.[122]

25. By way of interim conclusion, it may be said that, while the discussion on the copyrightability of AI-generated output has been ongoing for a long time, the final word on this topic has not yet been spoken. The first steps towards a harmonised solution were taken at the World Congress of AIPPI[123] in 2019. The Study Question on this topic garnered 30 extensive reports,[124] culminating in a summary overview[125] and a Resolution[126] that gives an outline of the state of play on this topic.[127] First, it is resolved that copyright protection should only be granted to AI-generated output if the traditional conditions of concrete form and originality are fulfilled. Moreover, copyright protection should only be available in the event of 'sufficient' human intervention during the creative process – a rather vague concept that could use further concretisation.[128] In case these conditions are fulfilled, the modalities[129] of protection should be the same as for purely human-generated output. Finally, AIPPI found that it was too early to tell at the time whether evolutions in the field of AI technology require additional legislative action, such as the creation of a new *sui generis* right.

---

119 See *supra* para. 23.

120 Cf. Gotzen and Janssens, 'Kunstmatige Kunst', pp. 333–334.

121 Treppoz et al., 'AIPPI Study Question', p. 11.

122 See re the (limited) economic impact of the Database Directive among others 'Study in support of the evaluation of Directive 96/9/EC on the legal protection of databases', 2018, https://bit.ly/2ZZB1pD.

123 An acronym for 'Association Internationale pour la Protection de la Propriété Intellectuelle', in English 'International Association for the Protection of Intellectual Property'.

124 Available at aippi.org.

125 Osha et al., 'AIPPI Summary Report on Copyright'.

126 AIPPI Resolution of 18 September 2019 on Copyright in Artificially Generated Works, https://bit.ly/3BQm9GO.

127 Notably, for the 2020 AIPPI World Congress, which took place online, this study was repeated with regard to AI *inventorship. See below, para. 31.*

128 The issue of what exactly constitutes 'sufficient' human intervention is treated in more detail in paras 35–37 below.

129 This refers to economic rights, moral rights, term of protection, exceptions and limitations and initial ownership.

The AIPPI Resolution is quite general and leaves the informed reader wanting for more. However, it seems that we must accept a degree of uncertainty as we wait for (regionally or even globally) harmonised, clear solutions to some of the questions outlined above. In this regard, the role of WIPO as a key interlocutor on AI and IP is paramount. The WIPO consultation process on this topic garnered over 250 substantive submissions, while the virtual WIPO seminars on AI and IP that WIPO organised between 2019 and 2021 attracted over 2000 participants from all over the world.[130] The issues up for discussion in this context not only include copyright law, but also questions relating to the patent law regime, which is the subject of the next section.

3.2. AI INVENTORSHIP OF AI-GENERATED INVENTIONS

26. Before delving into the theoretical interface between patent law and AI, it is relevant to establish whether such an interface also exists in practice today. In other words, we should first treat the question whether there are already 'inventive machines': AI systems that generate technical advancements that would be patentable if invented by humans. Interestingly, such systems appear to be much more scarce than AI systems engaged in the creation of artistic and literary works. It could even be argued that, as of yet, no 'real' AI-generated inventions exist, given the essentially deterministic nature of AI systems, the prevalence of 'trial and error' AI processes and the ensuing absence of genuinely 'thinking' computers (to date).[131]

27. However, progress on this particular front is undeniable.[132] A first notable innovator is computer science pioneer Dr John Koza, who already claimed to have built an 'invention machine' relying on so-called 'genetic programming' in the '80s.[133] The AI sector's other allegedly inventive champion is 'DABUS',[134] a more recent creation labelled the 'Creativity Machine' by its inventor, physicist

---

130 The submissions to the consultation process are available online at https://bit.ly/3GU9M09. More information is available online at https://bit.ly/3GNV7DX.

131 Cf. M. Summerfield, 'The Impact of Machine Learning on Patent Law, Part 1: Can a Computer "Invent"?', *Patentology,* 13 January 2018, https://bit.ly/3xlhtZ5. See in detail D. Burk, 'AI Patents and the Self-Assembling Machine', *Minn Law Rev Headnotes*, 2021, pp. 301–322; D. Kim et al., 'Ten Assumptions about Artificial Intelligence that Can Mislead Patent Law Analysis. Max Planck Institute for Innovation and Competition Research Paper No. 21-18' (2021), 76 p.

132 See, e.g., R. Plotkin, *The Genie in the Machine; How Computer-Automated Inventing is Revolutionizing Law and Business* (Stanford: Stanford University Press, 2009), 270 p.

133 See J. Keats, 'John Koza Has Built an Invention Machine', *Popular Science*, 19 April 2006, https://bit.ly/2ZVhYNm. See also https://bit.ly/3wxCRdn and https://bit.ly/3kuHwIf. See also Abbott, 'I Think, Therefore I Invent', pp. 1079, 1086–88.

134 An acronym for 'Device for the Autonomous Bootstrapping of Unified Sentience'.

Dr Stephen Thaler.[135] DABUS is a neural network-based system meant to generate 'useful information' autonomously, thereby 'simulating human creativity'.[136]

In the autumn of 2018, a number of patent applications were filed for two of DABUS' inventions. The first invention concerns a food container that uses fractal designs to create pits and bulges in its sides, thus enabling the containers to interlock and improving grip as well as heat transfer.[137] Second, a number of patent applications were filed for a 'neural flame'. This invention relates to a light designed to flicker in a rhythm that mimics a human brain's 'speed of thought', thereby attracting enhanced attention.[138] The prosecution file for both patent applications indicates DABUS as the alleged inventor and clarifies that Dr Thaler obtained the right to the inventions as a successor in title – being the employer and/or the owner of the machine.[139] These patent applications offer a very interesting test case for the following two-pronged question: assuming that these 'inventions' sprung from the 'mind' of an AI system, would the patents ultimately be granted and, perhaps more pressingly, should they be?

28. In other words, we must ask whether patent law requires inventors to be human or whether it instead leaves room for an artificial inventor. While relevant provisions of patent legislation do not really contain any explicit requirement in this sense, there are several indications that the inventor's need for physical personhood is implied in the law.[140] Indeed, while the focus on the human inventor is much less pronounced than it is on the human author,

---

135 See websites: https://bit.ly/3qgbWSd; https://bit.ly/3CQNf26.

136 Dr Thaler has obtained several patents in relation to the technology behind DABUS. The patents embodying the initial invention (EP 0 786 106 B1 and US 5,659,666) were originally filed in 1995 and 1994 respectively and have expired. Patents relating to a number of follow-on innovations are still in force at the time of writing (see US 7,454,388 and, most recently, US 10,423,875). The EP application equivalents of these patents have not yet been granted: the application with number 11002179.7 (EP 2 360 629 A2) was ultimately abandoned, while the application with number 15734978.8 (EP 3 092 590 A4) was refused by the EPO in March 2021. A divisional application having the same title, with number 21151608.3 (EP 3 848 828 A1), was published in July 2021. See also Abbott, 'I Think, Therefore I Invent', pp. 1083–1086.

137 EP application with number 18275163.6 (EP 3 564 144 A1), filed on 17 October 2018. See also the UK patent application GB1816909.4. The substantively equivalent US patent application is available at https://bit.ly/3EEUkDo.

138 EP application with number 18275174.3 (EP 3 563 896 A1), filed on 7 November 2018. See also the UK patent application GB1818161.0. The substantively equivalent US patent application is available at https://bit.ly/2ZSoOmc.

139 See Legal Board of Appeal Decision 21 December 2021 re EP applications 18275163.6 and 18275174.3, J 0008/20, paras I–III, https://bit.ly/3RpeyZ3. See also, at first instance, EPO Decisions 27 January 2020, paras 1–5, https://bit.ly/31AzVRF.

140 See, e.g., with regard to the priority right to a patent Article 4(A) Paris Convention for the Protection of Industrial Property, 20 March 1883, as amended. This is the oldest international convention on industrial property rights. See also Yanisky-Ravid and Liu, 'When Artificial Intelligence Systems Produce Inventions', p. 2230; E. Stanková, 'Human Inventorship in European Patent Law', *Cambridge Law Journal*, 2021, pp. 338–365.

a number of provisions of patent law would simply make no sense if we were to accept AI inventorship.

First, many patent laws stipulate that, in principle and in similar vein as under copyright law, the 'inventor' is the first owner of an invention, except in an employment context, where (under the laws of some countries) the employer may be deemed to be the first owner.[141] Since AI systems do not have legal personality (as of yet), they arguably cannot be the bearer of ownership rights, nor can they be an employee as such.[142] Given that those are the only two available options, such systems cannot be considered 'inventors' under patent law as it currently stands.[143]

Another argument against AI inventorship may be drawn from the inventor's right of attribution. Indeed, every inventor has the right to be mentioned as such and all patent applications must designate the inventor.[144] This moral right, which is meant to incentivise the inventor to innovate further, may become meaningless when the application of the concept of inventorship is extended to AI systems.[145]

29. In view of the above, patent law currently does not allow for AI systems to be considered as inventors for patenting purposes. This is also the stance taken by the EPO Boards of Appeal, which refused to grant the two EP applications for inventions that sprung from the 'mind' of DABUS, the so-called 'Creativity Machine' mentioned above.[146] The EPO holds that the formal requirement for

---

141 See Article 60 EPC. The corresponding provision under Belgian law is Article XI.9 BCEL. See regarding employee output under Belgian law Articles XI.187 and XI.296 BCEL.

142 Shemtov, 'A Study on Inventorship in Inventions Involving AI Activity', pp. 10–11, 20; Blok, 'The Inventor's New Tool', pp. 71–72.

143 A counterargument advanced by Dr. Thaler is that the attribution of inventorship should take place *before* any rights are determined.

144 See Article 4*ter* Paris Convention. See also respectively Articles 62 and 81 *jo.* 90 and Rule 19.1 EPC. The corresponding provisions under Belgian law are Articles XI.13 and XI.16(1), 7° BCEL. See also Shemtov, 'A Study on Inventorship in Inventions Involving AI Activity', p. 8.

145 Shemtov, 'A Study on Inventorship in Inventions Involving AI Activity', pp. 5, 23–25, 27; J.P. Osha et al., 'AIPPI Summary Report on Inventorship of Inventions Made Using Artificial Intelligence', 2021, pp. 5–6, https://bit.ly/30Vmg7U.

146 See *supra* para. 27. This conclusion also applies under UK law, as confirmed by (i) the UK Intellectual Property Office (IPO): UKIPO Decision 4 December 2019, BL O/741/19, https://bit.ly/3BNVACi; see also *UKIPO Formalities Manual,* online version of 4 January 2021, para. 3.05, https://bit.ly/3CKy4ay; and (ii) the UK courts, see England and Wales High Court (Patents Court) 21 September 2020, EWHC 2412 (Pat), https://bit.ly/3COgeDF, and, on appeal, England and Wales Court of Appeal (Civil Division) 21 September 2021, EWCA Civ 1374, https://bit.ly/3mP5vn0. At the time of writing, the appeal proceedings before the UK Supreme Court are pending. In the US, AI inventorship was rejected in (i) USPTO Decision 22 April 2020, 50567-3-01-US, https://bit.ly/2ZSfbE3 and (ii) US District Court, Eastern District of Virginia 2 September 2021, 1:20-cv-903(LMB/TCB), https://bit.ly/3mKMQZq. In Australia, the initial decision by Justice Beach of the Federal Court of Australia (FCA) (Thaler v Commissioner of Patents [2021] FCA 879) that accepted artificial inventorship was overturned by the Full Court of the Federal Court in Commissioner of Patents v Thaler [2022]

patent applications to designate the inventor(s) as set by the EPC (Article 81 *jo* Rule 19.1) refers to a human being, not a machine.[147] Since the patent applications filed for DABUS' inventions designate DABUS as the inventor, both applications are tainted by a formal deficiency and the patents must therefore be refused – even before the analysis of the substantive requirements for patentability (novelty, inventive step and industrial applicability) may take place.[148]

30. However, this should not be the end of our analysis. We must keep an open mind and assess the arguments in favour as well as against possible changes to the patent law regime on this particular point.

The main argument made in favour of AI inventorship is that it would incentivise research and development in the field of AI.[149] This would be in line with the EU's long-term plans to stimulate investment in this sector.[150] However, in the absence of compelling empirical evidence, the incentive argument does not appear to be wholly convincing, especially since AI systems as such are not susceptible to incentives and the cost of AI invention will likely decrease over time.[151]

Another reason to accept AI inventorship would be to avoid humans incorrectly claiming inventorship to the work of an AI system. Yet, AI systems are primarily (arguably even solely) used as a tool that may assist humans in the conception process of an invention, which renders this point moot at present.[152] This as of yet purely instrumental nature of AI systems provides a strong argument against endowing AI systems with inventorship rights. Indeed, it may be questioned whether the actual contribution of AI systems to the inventive process (at least today) is sufficiently intellectual, creative and concrete for actual inventorship to arise.[153]

Further and as already explained above in the context of copyright law, there is no AI-generated output without some form of prior input.[154] As is the case

FCAFC 62, https://bit.ly/3Uz5rG9. Thaler's appeal to the Australian High Court was declined in November 2022.

147 Legal Board of Appeal Decision 21 December 2021 re patent applications 18275163.6 and 18275174.3, sections 4.1–4.4. See also EPO Decisions 27 January 2020, paras 23–30.

148 Legal Board of Appeal Decision 21 December 2021 re patent applications 18275163.6 and 18275174.3, sections 4.1–4.4. See also EPO Decisions 27 January 2020, paras 35–37.

149 Abbott, 'I Think, Therefore I Invent', pp. 1081–82, 1098–99, 1104; S. Cattoor et al., 'Inventorship of AI Made Inventions', *IRDI*, 2020, pp. 9–10, 13–14. See also EPO Decisions 27 January 2020 re patent applications 18275163.6 and 18275174.3, paras 5, 13.

150 Commission Communication, 'Artificial Intelligence for Europe', pp. 5–10; White Paper of 19 February 2020 on Artificial Intelligence – A European approach to excellence and trust, COM(2020) 65 final, pp. 1–9, 25.

151 W.M. Schuster, 'Artificial Intelligence and Patent Ownership', *Wash & Lee L Rev*, 2018, pp. 1945, 2002; Yanisky-Ravid and Liu, 'When Artificial Intelligence Systems Produce Inventions', p. 2239. See also *supra* para. 23.

152 Abbott, 'I Think, Therefore I Invent', p. 1093; Blok, 'The Inventor's New Tool', p. 73.

153 Shemtov, 'A Study on Inventorship in Inventions Involving AI Activity', pp. 5, 17, 19.

154 See in relation to copyright law *supra* para. 23.

for authorship, it may therefore be argued that the resulting absence of an act of 'conception', of the *process* of invention, excludes any extension of the scope of inventorship to non-human actors such as AI systems.[155] Again, however, the 'prior input' argument also applies *mutatis mutandis* to humans, whose insights are invariably at least partially prompted by prior knowledge; by the state of the art and what may be learnt from this. Also, in the realm of patent law, therefore, the 'act of conception' argument against AI inventorship is susceptible to counterarguments.[156]

A final aspect that should be borne in mind resembles the risk of creativity saturation in copyright mentioned above, namely that allowing AI inventorship would entail an increased risk of patent thickets as well as non-practicing entities (so-called 'patent trolls') – a risk that we would be wise to avoid if at all possible.[157] On a more optimistic note, AI technology could be used to separate the wheat from the chaff in this regard.

31. In summary: while the EPO's firm stance against AI inventorship explained above has the benefit of clarity, further substantive debate on this topic is merited. There are many arguments of varying degrees of persuasiveness on both sides of the discussion. The express focus of one of the Study Questions of the 2020 World Congress of AIPPI on this issue was therefore clearly warranted. 37 group reports[158] were submitted and summarised in an overarching report.[159] This ultimately led to a Resolution that highlights the desirability of harmonisation in this context.[160] Further policy action at the international level, such as through the WIPO consultation process, is yet to be awaited. In the meantime, we are still quite a long way from full clarity and ensuing legal certainty.

32. Finally and perhaps even more fundamentally, the (as of yet hypothetical) advent of ASI could have major implications for the inventiveness standard under patent law.[161] The analysis of inventive step is clearly tailored to humans. It centres around the so-called 'person skilled in the art' (PSA), a hypothetical person (or team) whose level of knowledge and skill depend on the relevant field

155 Summerfield, 'The Impact of Machine Learning on Patent Law, Part 1'; Shemtov, 'A Study on Inventorship in Inventions Involving AI Activity', pp. 6, 20, 35.

156 Cf. Shemtov, 'A Study on Inventorship in Inventions Involving AI Activity', pp. 28–29; Abbott, 'I Think, Therefore I Invent', pp. 1082, 1099, 1108–11.

157 Cf. *supra* para. 23. See Blok, 'The Inventor's New Tool', p. 73; Schuster, 'Artificial Intelligence and Patent Ownership', pp. 1995–1990.

158 Available at aippi.org.

159 Osha et al., 'AIPPI Summary Report on Inventorship'.

160 AIPPI Resolution of 14 October 2020 on Inventorship of Inventions Made Using Artificial Intelligence, https://bit.ly/3DRMOoN.

161 See in detail T. Dornis, 'Artificial Intelligence and Innovation: The End of Patent Law As We Know It', *Yale J L & Tech*, 2020, pp. 104, 124–134; D. Fabris, 'From the PHOSITA to the MOSITA: Will "Secondary Considerations" Save Pharmaceutical Patents from Artificial Intelligence?', *IIC*, 2020, pp. 685–708.

of technology.[162] If it is found that the PSA would have arrived at the invention on the basis of the state of the art, the invention will be deemed obvious and, therefore, not patentable. The hypothetical knowledge and skill of the PSA are pivotal to the functioning of patent law. If, at some point in the future, the use of inventive machines becomes commonplace in certain (or even all) sectors of technology, the PSA standard will evolve into a PSA using such an inventive machine – and eventually maybe even an inventive machine as such.[163] This would greatly raise the bar for inventive step and ensuing patentability, since such a machine would (again, hypothetically) be able to innovate based on the entirety of available prior art.[164] Taken to its logical extreme, this argument could shake the very foundations of our patent system. Indeed, if the 'artificially superintelligent' PSA is capable of inventive step, everything becomes obvious, leaving no more room for patentable inventions.[165] This conclusion may seem quite drastic, because it is. We therefore need to start thinking about alternatives and/or supplements to the current non-obviousness analysis – and maybe even to the patent regime as such as a way to provide incentives to innovation.[166]

Then again, we are still a long way from ASI computers providing us with the answer to 'life, the universe, and everything'.[167] As of yet and for the foreseeable future, AI is used by humans as a tool, an instrument to innovate in specific situations. While thinking out of the box on these topics is certainly a laudable and even a necessary venture, the proverbial patent-doomsday-thinking is as of yet rather premature.

3.3. OWNERSHIP OF AI-GENERATED OUTPUT

33. Under the hypothesis that works/inventions generated by an AI system could be susceptible to copyright and/or patent protection – which is in itself not

162 See in more detail EPO, 'Guidelines for Examination, Part G, Chapter VII.3', https://bit.ly/3xBzu5H.

163 W. Samore, 'Artificial Intelligence and the Patent System: Can a New Tool Render a Once Patentable Idea Obvious?', *Syracuse Sci & Tech L Rep*, 2013, pp. 113, 128–37; Blok, 'The Inventor's New Tool', p. 72; R. Abbott, 'Everything is Obvious', *UCLA L Rev*, 2018, pp. 2, 5–6, 17, 34–37; Gabison, 'Who Holds the Right to Exclude for Machine Work Products?', pp. 28, 43. The 2021 AIPPI World Congress expressly treated this issue in one of its Study Questions. See in detail Verschuur et al., 'Summary Report on Inventiveness and Sufficiency of Disclosure in AI Inventions'. The national reports are available at https://aippi.org. The ensuing AIPPI Resolution of 22 October 2021 on Inventiveness and Sufficiency of Disclosure in AI Inventions is available at https://bit.ly/3rb3vYG. See on the standard of inventive step in particular paras. 1–5.

164 Abbott, 'Everything is Obvious', pp. 8, 34; Yanisky-Ravid and Liu, 'When Artificial Intelligence Systems Produce Inventions', pp. 2248–49.

165 Abbott, 'Everything is Obvious', pp. 8–9, 31, 34, 37–38.

166 Abbott, 'Everything is Obvious', pp. 48–50, 52.

167 D. Adams, *The Hitchhiker's Guide to the Galaxy* (New York, NY: Pocket Books, 1979), pp. 176–180.

self-evident –, the next question is how ownership rights in such creations should be allocated.[168] In other words: who, if anybody, should own AI-generated output? This question has garnered a substantial amount of research in recent years, with various authors arguing for (and against) a wide range of possible answers, including the programmer, the user, the owner of the data and/or some form of joint ownership between these actors.[169] Alternatively, it could be argued that AI-generated output should not accrue to any entity and should thus automatically fall into the public domain.[170]

34. As explained above, intellectual property law as it currently stands in principle does not allow for AI systems to be recognised as either an author or an inventor, due to their lack of both physical and legal personhood as well as their (currently) largely instrumental nature.[171] Even if an AI system were to transcend its status as a tool and create or innovate in a more autonomous way, it could be argued that an AI system – being a machine – does not need any incentive to do so and that, thus, allocating any IP rights to it would be devoid of any real purpose.[172]

Yet another complicating factor arises if the creative/inventive AI system at issue is built on open-source software.[173] Indeed, the essence of open source is that users have the right to study, change, and distribute the software at issue to anyone and for any purpose, a principle that is sheer irreconcilable with the idea of exclusive ownership.

35. The next question is whether the intervention of a creative and/or inventive AI excludes *any* kind of human authorship or inventorship (and thus ownership) in relation to the output at issue. It is submitted that it does not, as long as there is a physical person who commands the AI and maintains the requisite level of control over its output.[174] In such a case, IP rights may fulfil their role of protecting the interests of creators as well as provide an indirect incentive for

---

168 IP ownership is (as of yet) primarily a matter of national law.

169 See *infra* paras 38–43.

170 See *infra* paras 44.

171 See *supra* paras 22–23 and 28–29. The Committee on Legal Affairs of the European Parliament deems it not appropriate to impart legal personality on AI systems for this purpose, see Report of 2 October 2020 on Intellectual Property Rights for the Development of Artificial Intelligence Technologies, 2020/2015(INI), p. 9, para. 14, https://bit.ly/3xrHDJB.

172 See *supra* paras 23 and 29.

173 See, e.g., https://github.com/openai. See as to open source AI in detail A. Theben, 'Challenges and limits of an open source approach to Artificial Intelligence. Study Requested by the AIDA Committee, PE 662.908' (European Parliament, 2021), 47 p.

174 Cf. Bridy, 'Coding Creativity', p. 20; Shemtov, 'A Study on Inventorship in Inventions Involving AI Activity', pp. 12–13, 19–20; Hedrick, 'I "Think," Therefore I Create', pp. 328–29, 332, 352. See however extensively T. Dornis, 'Of 'Authorless Works' and "Inventions without Inventor" – The Muddy Waters of 'AI Autonomy' in Intellectual Property Doctrine', *EIPR*, 2021, pp. 570–585.

future creation and/or innovation.[175] However, if there is no sufficient causal relationship between the (in)actions of a creative and/or inventive human and the end result – in other words, if the AI system becomes more than an assisting tool wielded by a human –, the argument in favour of a human author and/or inventor becomes simply untenable. Then again, what exactly constitutes 'sufficient' control is particularly tough to establish, given the wide spectrum that exists between different types of AI systems, between output that is merely AI-assisted and output that is purely AI-generated.[176]

36. A further layer of complexity is added by the black box nature of some AI systems: how can we determine whether a sufficiently strong causal link exists between the human 'mastermind' and the AI system's output if this output is inherently unpredictable and if it is impossible to find out exactly why it was reached?[177] However, both copyright and patent protection may be available to works and/or inventions that result from coincidence or even dumb luck.[178] The analogy between the intervention of AI systems and serendipity may be strenuous at first sight, but, if we take a step back, both may be considered as a factor outside the scope of human control, as an unknown and even unknowable actor in the creative/inventive process. Given that Jackson Pollock may claim copyright protection in his action paintings and given the significant and inherent role that chance plays in Pollock's creation process, can we really deny such protection to the person (or team of persons) behind 'the next Rembrandt'?[179]

37. In copyright jargon, we could say that for a human to be able to claim copyright in a work created through the intervention of AI, their 'personal stamp' must be discernible in the end result. If we continue the above analogy, Pollock's paintings clearly reflect his personal choices as an artist, regardless of the aspects of randomness that they are imbued with. In patent law terms, human inventorship may arise in case of a contribution that transcends the purely financial, abstract or administrative and that is aimed at conceiving the claimed invention.[180] In this context, the abovementioned 2020 AIPPI Resolution stressed the need for an 'intellectual contribution to the inventive

---

175 Brown, 'Artificial Authors', pp. 20–22; Hedrick, 'I "Think," Therefore I Create', pp. 337, 440.

176 Gotzen and Janssens, 'Kunstmatige Kunst', pp. 327–8.

177 Cf. Hedrick, 'I "Think," Therefore I Create', pp. 367, 371–374.

178 Grimmelmann, 'There's No Such Thing as a Computer-Authored Work', p. 413; Blok, 'The Inventor's New Tool', p. 73; M. Summerfield, 'The Impact of Machine Learning on Patent Law, Part 2: "Machine-Assisted Inventing"', *Patentology,* 21 January 2018, https://bit.ly/3r4FK4y; Hedrick, 'I "Think," Therefore I Create', pp. 354, 365; Shemtov, 'A Study on Inventorship in Inventions Involving AI Activity', p. 20. It is noted that patent protection is not available to 'discoveries' as such (Article 52 EPC).

179 See *supra* para. 18.

180 Shemtov, 'A Study on Inventorship in Inventions Involving AI Activity', pp. 19–21.

concept' – be it through input or output selection, algorithm design, or otherwise – for (co-)inventorship to arise on the part of a natural person.[181] In practice, drawing a line in the sand regarding what level of human intervention is required for a sufficient personal stamp and/or an inventive contribution to arise, will be particularly tricky and will most likely require a case-by-case analysis.[182] Different categories of people involved in AI systems may stake a claim in this regard.

38. First in line are the initial programmer(s),[183] designer(s)[184] and/or producer(s) of the AI system – or, in many cases, the legal entity that employs them (hereinafter collectively referred to as 'AI creators'). By creating the AI system itself, these actors play an undeniably substantive role in the production of AI-generated output.[185] Put simply: without them, no AI system and without AI system, no AI-generated output.

The argument in favour of granting ownership rights to the AI creators has the advantage of precedent, at least in the field of copyright law. Already in the '80s, the UK legislator included a provision in its IP act designed to cater for works generated by a computer and without a human author – so-called 'computer-generated works'.[186] In such a case, the author of the work (for copyright purposes) would be deemed to be 'the person by whom the arrangements necessary for the creation of the work are undertaken'.[187] Several authors argue in favour of applying this criterion to AI output, leaving the AI creator as the logical choice.[188] However, the UK provision regarding computer-generated works entirely delinks copyright ownership from the creative process.[189] It does not matter whether any human creativity is exhibited

---

181 AIPPI Resolution of 14 October 2020 on Inventorship of Inventions Made Using Artificial Intelligence, https://bit.ly/3DRMOoN.

182 Shemtov, 'A Study on Inventorship in Inventions Involving AI Activity', p. 31.

183 See regarding a Chinese court decision in favour of this solution P. Sawers, 'Chinese court rules AI-written article is protected by copyright', 10 January 2020, https://bit.ly/3DW5SlD.

184 See in favour M. Summerfield, 'The Impact of Machine Learning on Patent Law, Part 3: Who is the Inventor of a Machine-Assisted Invention?', 4 February 2018, https://bit.ly/3xlHNlM.

185 Samuelson, 'Allocating Ownership Rights in Computer-Generated Works', p. 1205; Shemtov, 'A Study on Inventorship in Inventions Involving AI Activity', p. 22; Gabison, 'Who Holds the Right to Exclude for Machine Work Products?', p. 23.

186 See Article 178 Copyright, Designs and Patents Act 1988 (hereinafter: UK CDPA). See on this topic Bently, 'The UK's Provisions on Computer-Generated Works'; P.B. Hugenholtz and J. Quintais, 'Copyright and Artificial Creation: Does EU Copyright Law Protect AI-Assisted Output?', *IIC*, 2021, pp. 1190–1216, s. 4.3.

187 Article 9(3) UK CDPA. Such a work is protected for a shorter period of 50 years (Article 12(7) UK CDPA). No moral right protection applies (Articles 79, 81 UK CDPA regarding right to paternity and integrity respectively). See also Bonadio and McDonagh, 'Artificial Intelligence as Producer and Consumer of Copyright Works', pp. 119–122.

188 See, e.g., McCutcheon, 'The Vanishing Author in Computer-Generated Works', pp. 958–964; Guadamuz, 'Do Androids Dream of Electric Copyright?'.

189 Guadamuz, 'Do Androids Dream of Electric Copyright?', p. 176.

at any stage: what matters is who made the creation possible. This approach is difficult to reconcile with continental copyright's traditional focus on the act of conception and the author's creative effort.

39. Further and regardless of the analogy with chance creations/innovations, the allocation of ownership rights to the creator sits uneasily (at least to a certain extent) with the unpredictable nature of AI-generated output.[190] Indeed, it could be argued that the AI's intervention cuts the requisite direct link between the programmer's actions and the AI-generated output. While the AI creator's choices and parameters define the AI system, they do not define the 'final form of the work' as such.[191] This argument gains in strength the more autonomous the AI algorithm becomes.[192] Then again, a programmer who is somehow dissatisfied with the AI's initial output may tweak the AI's algorithm at a later stage, thus manipulating and shaping further output, as well as curate the AI output based on their own, personal (perhaps creative and/or innovative) choices. Could these be the steps necessary for a programmer to rightfully claim control over and, thus, ownership of the AI's output?[193] A generalised answer to this question is, at present, impossible to give.[194]

40. In any case, a rather strong economic argument against granting the creator ownership rights in AI-generated output is that this may lead to 'double-dipping'.[195] For example, this would be the case if the creator also holds ownership rights in a patent or multiple patents granted in relation to the AI system or the copyright therein, or if the AI system is acquired by a third party for a (presumably rather significant) fee and the original and/or inventive output at issue postdates this transfer.[196] In both cases, the creator would obtain two separate sources of income for essentially the same thing. This would arguably be an unfavourable outcome. In addition, we must consider the user's right to data protection, as well as practical aspects, such as issues of enforceability. Enforcing ownership rights on the part of the AI creator would be problematic if the AI system generates the output at issue after a third party has started using it. Indeed, knowing that ownership rights would be allocated to the creator, the subsequent user would have strong incentives not to report back on the

190 Samuelson, 'Allocating Ownership Rights in Computer-Generated Works', p. 1209; Yanisky-Ravid and Liu, 'When Artificial Intelligence Systems Produce Inventions', pp. 2231–2232.
191 Bridy, 'Coding Creativity', p. 25.
192 Hedrick, 'I "Think," Therefore I Create', pp. 354, 362.
193 Cf. Hedrick, 'I "Think," Therefore I Create', pp. 338–339, 343, 354.
194 See on this topic Osha et al., 'AIPPI Summary Report on Inventorship', pp. 9–13.
195 See contra Brown, 'Artificial Authors', pp. 22–24.
196 Samuelson, 'Allocating Ownership Rights in Computer-Generated Works', pp. 1207–1208, 1225; Yanisky-Ravid and Liu, 'When Artificial Intelligence Systems Produce Inventions', p. 2233; Shemtov, 'A Study on Inventorship in Inventions Involving AI Activity', p. 31.

(modalities of) creation of protectable output.[197] Effective enforcement of such rights would moreover risk negatively impacting potential users' incentives to purchase AI-driven systems.[198]

41. A similar claim to the AI system's creator (especially the programmer who alters the algorithm in a way that influences future output) may be made by the AI's trainer who feeds input to the AI system with the aim of achieving a certain result.[199] Alternatively, also the user who has contributed substantially to the original elements of the AI system's output at issue may claim ownership.[200] An economic argument in favour of the latter solution is that this would incentivise the user to further distribute the output.[201] Again, however, it is unclear how much input (and ensuing influence on output) exactly would be required for them to be able to validly stake a claim in the output. Merely pressing the 'on'-button that brings the AI system into action would definitely be insufficient, while translating the AI system's discoveries to a patentable technical teaching would arguably be enough, as well as making creative choices in the selection and editing of the AI system's output.[202] Then again, it might be near impossible to properly distinguish button-pushers from genuine user-authors/inventors in practice.[203]

42. The list of stakeholders continues with the investor,[204] the owner of the AI system and/or the data used to train the algorithm, the publisher of the work,[205] the general public and even the government.[206] Moreover, some form

---

197 Samuelson, 'Allocating Ownership Rights in Computer-Generated Works', p. 1208.

198 Gabison, 'Who Holds the Right to Exclude for Machine Work Products?', pp. 25, 34, 41.

199 Shemtov, 'A Study on Inventorship in Inventions Involving AI Activity', p. 31.

200 Samuelson, 'Allocating Ownership Rights in Computer-Generated Works', pp. 1201–04; Brown, 'Artificial Authors', pp. 37–39; Schuster, 'Artificial Intelligence and Patent Ownership', pp. 1950, 1988–1991; Hedrick, 'I "Think," Therefore I Create', p. 344; Gabison, 'Who Holds the Right to Exclude for Machine Work Products?', p. 35. See in detail L. Buijtelaar and M. Senftleben, 'Auteursrecht op robotcreaties? Een analyse op basis van de incentivetheorie', *AMI*, 2020, pp. 77–93; Dornis, 'Artificial Intelligence and Innovation', pp. 154–157.

201 Samuelson, 'Allocating Ownership Rights in Computer-Generated Works', p. 1226; Hedrick, 'I "Think," Therefore I Create', pp. 345–346.

202 See regarding the possible originality of a selection process CJEU 16 July 2009, no. C-5/08, ECLI:EU:C:2009:465, *Infopaq/Danske Dagblades Forening*, para. 45. See also Samuelson, 'Allocating Ownership Rights in Computer-Generated Works', p. 1201; Blok, 'The Inventor's New Tool', p. 73; Hedrick, 'I "Think," Therefore I Create', p. 346; Shemtov, 'A Study on Inventorship in Inventions Involving AI Activity', p. 22.

203 Cf. Grimmelmann, 'There's No Such Thing as a Computer-Authored Work', pp. 410–11.

204 Cf. Bonadio and McDonagh, 'Artificial Intelligence as Producer and Consumer of Copyright Works', pp. 124–5.

205 See, e.g., European Parliament Report, p. 13, which proposes to undertake an assessment 'of the advisability of granting copyright to such a "creative work" to the natural person who prepares and publishes it lawfully, provided that the designer(s) of the underlying technology has/have not opposed such use'.

206 See, e.g., Yanisky-Ravid and Liu, 'When Artificial Intelligence Systems Produce Inventions', pp. 2232–33. See also EPO Decisions 27 January 2020 re patent applications 18275163.6 and 18275174.3, para. 13 and in particular para. 33: '(...) The owner of an AI system may (...)

of co-ownership may be envisaged between two or more of the actors mentioned above, such as the user and the creator of the AI.[207] However, this would entail other theoretical and practical issues, such as (respectively) an unnecessary fragmentation of ownership rights and difficulties in proving (the extent of) the claims of wannabe right holders.[208] It could even be argued that, in view of the ever-rising number of players involved, no individual entity can rightfully claim to have made a significant contribution 'worthy' of IP ownership.[209]

43. As of yet, therefore, no solution to the ownership conundrum appears to be wholly satisfactory. Moreover, it is unlikely that this question will be definitively resolved any time soon.[210] It could even be argued that a catch-all solution would be both impossible and undesirable and that a case-by-case assessment of ownership claims will remain warranted.[211] The void left by this lingering uncertainty will likely be filled with contractual solutions between the relevant parties.[212] As a result of unequal bargaining power, Coasean bargaining[213] may be prevented and instances of unfair ownership and licensing arrangements are to be expected.[214]

44. A more preferable solution could be to not allocate ownership in AI-generated output to anyone at all and instead allot such output to the public domain.[215] Indeed, without a human author and/or inventor, how can any human actually be motivated to create and what would the point of granting any IP right be?[216] Arguably, the relevant stakeholders could sufficiently protect their investment in AI-related innovation by relying on patent protection for

own the output of that system, just as an owner of any machine may own the output of that machine. However, the question of ownership must be distinguished from the question of inventorship and from the rights connected herewith.'

207 Kaminski, 'Authorship, Disrupted', p. 597; Shemtov, 'A Study on Inventorship in Inventions Involving AI Activity', pp. 6, 30; Bonadio and McDonagh, 'Artificial Intelligence as Producer and Consumer of Copyright Works', p. 124.

208 Samuelson, 'Allocating Ownership Rights in Computer-Generated Works', pp. 1221–24; McCutcheon, 'The Vanishing Author in Computer-Generated Works', p. 949; Brown, 'Artificial Authors', pp. 34–35; Hedrick, 'I "Think," Therefore I Create', p. 348.

209 Cf. Yanisky-Ravid and Liu, 'When Artificial Intelligence Systems Produce Inventions', p. 2235.

210 Hedrick, 'I "Think," Therefore I Create', p. 362.

211 Hedrick, 'I "Think," Therefore I Create', pp. 347–348.

212 Hedrick, 'I "Think," Therefore I Create', p. 348.

213 See extensively Schuster, 'Artificial Intelligence and Patent Ownership', pp. 1951–1952, 1967–1982.

214 Cf. Abbott, 'I Think, Therefore I Invent', p. 1117; Hedrick, 'I "Think," Therefore I Create', p. 347.

215 See in this sense A.H. Khoury, 'Intellectual Property Rights for Hubots: On the Legal Implications of Human-like Robots as Innovators and Creators', *Cardozo Arts & Ent LJ*, 2017, p. 635; Gotzen and Janssens, 'Kunstmatige Kunst', pp. 334–5; Gabison, 'Who Holds the Right to Exclude for Machine Work Products?', pp. 22 and 41–43.

216 Samuelson, 'Allocating Ownership Rights in Computer-Generated Works', pp. 1224–1225.

the AI system itself,[217] first-mover advantage, trade secret law, contractual arrangements and technological protection measures as well as general civil liability and the law of unfair competition.[218] While proponents of additional IP protection will undoubtedly argue that additional protection is needed to incentivise R&D, no empirical evidence backing up this claim appears to be available to date. Therefore, it is submitted that granting IP protection to purely AI-generated output would be excessive.

As of yet, however, there is a very pragmatic reason not to ban AI-generated output to the public domain, namely that it is increasingly difficult to distinguish output in the creation of which AI played a certain role from creations that were made solely by a human author.[219] While this issue could in theory be remedied by requiring aspiring IP owners to disclose AI intervention in the creation and/or innovation process, the practical application of such a requirement would be problematic, to say the very least.[220] Indeed, the prospect having a work be banished to the public domain would provide stakeholders seeking a return on investment with strong incentives to keep quiet on this point. Thus, this could invite misleading statements on authorship and/or inventorship of AI-generated output in the future.[221] This is the crux of the matter: IP protection is (and, arguably, should only be) available if the creator is human, but disproving a claim for human authorship in relation to AI-generated output *with certainty* is, as of yet, impossible. Therefore, as long as it is impossible to prove whether or not AI technology was used in the production of certain output, blindly refusing protection to AI-generated output may lead to unfair situations in practice. Transparency obligations such as those proposed in the draft AI Act regarding, for example, chatbots, may bring us closer to a solution in this regard.[222]

---

217 See *supra* paras 10–13.

218 Yanisky-Ravid and Liu, 'When Artificial Intelligence Systems Produce Inventions', pp. 2222, 2252–2256; Shemtov, 'A Study on Inventorship in Inventions Involving AI Activity', p. 24; Gabison, 'Who Holds the Right to Exclude for Machine Work Products?', pp. 32–33, 39; Gervais, 'The Machine as Author', p. 2060; Hugenholtz and J. Quintais, 'Copyright and Artificial Creation', s. 5.

219 See, e.g., McCutcheon, 'The Vanishing Author in Computer-Generated Works', p. 950.

220 Higgins, 'The Role of Explainable Artificial Intelligence in Patent Law', pp. 6, 34–35.

221 Abbott, 'I Think, Therefore I Invent', pp. 1097–98; A. Brandi-Dohm et al., 'AIPPI Study Question – Copyright in Artificially Generated Works – Germany', 7 June 2019, p. 13; Higgins, 'The Role of Explainable Artificial Intelligence in Patent Law', p. 29.

222 Commission Proposal of 21 April 2021 for a Regulation of the European Parliament and of the Council Laying Down Harmonised Rules on Artificial Intelligence (Artificial Intelligence Act) and Amending Certain Union Legislative Acts, COM/2021/206 final, https://bit.ly/2ZZUM08. See the compromise text by the Council of the European Union dating from 3 November 2022 at https://bit.ly/3tufQqU.

4. CONCLUSIONS

45. The above analysis of the interface between AI and IP reveals a field of law and technology of increasing intricacy. The opportunities offered by AI in relation to IP management are readily apparent and rapidly evolving. On a substantive level, challenges abound relating to the IP protection available to both AI technology itself and AI-generated output. Given the wide array of issues dealt with in this chapter, it is likely to have raised more questions than it could answer. However and as the reader will (hopefully) agree, raising the right questions is a crucial step to finding a satisfactory answer.

46. As the term itself suggests, 'intellectual' property law has traditionally catered for creations of the conscious, human mind. Technological evolutions in the field of AI have prompted challenges to this essentially anthropocentric view to creation as well as fundamental questions regarding the role of IP in our society's innovation paradigm. The most contentious questions in this regard are whether core IP law concepts such as authorship and inventorship should be extended to AI systems and who, if anybody, should acquire IP ownership in relation to AI-generated content.

47. While valid points may be raised on all sides of the argument, we should not unreservedly start tearing down the foundations of IP law purely for the sake of additional – and moreover in reality merely indirect – incentive creation. Further, at this point in time and for the foreseeable future, AI systems are a tool wielded by humans in the creative and/or innovative process. While many commentators appear to expect great things of the future of AI-related technology, the thinking computer imbued with ASI does not yet appear to be on the horizon.[223] Moreover, upon its advent, the appropriate protection of such an ASI system's creative and/or inventive output may well be the very least of our concerns.

In any case, regardless of the eventual (legislative) outcome, the cross-border exploitation of AI-assisted or -generated output and the pressing need for transparency of the legal framework require a harmonised solution based on a multi-stakeholder conversation, preferably on a global scale.[224] Several on-going initiatives under the auspices of WIPO as well as at the EU level offer promise in this regard. Who knows, maybe one day an ASI supercomputer will be able to find this solution in our stead.[225]

---

223 Summerfield, 'The Impact of Machine Learning on Patent Law, Part 3'.

224 Cf. Osha et al., 'AIPPI Summary Report on Copyright', pp. 6, 18.

225 Yanisky-Ravid and Liu, 'When Artificial Intelligence Systems Produce Inventions', pp. 2261–2262.

CHAPTER 10
TAX AND ROBOTS

Dina SCORNOS*

1. INTRODUCTION

1. It is unthinkable to imagine a world without computers and the Internet. Pretty soon, it will be unimaginable to live in a world without robots and AI. Increased automation is currently becoming part of our lives and is not only limited to the industry sector. It has also penetrated the services sector and soon it will become prominent in our everyday lives.[1] As it appears from different chapters in this book, increased automation presents many opportunities to different elements of our society but also many challenges. This is not different in the framework of taxation.

2. In the current state of play, a specific tax on robots does not exist in Belgium. Rather, the profits of corporations generated by robots are subject to tax according to the general corporate income tax (CIT) rules. In this respect, most states treat robots owned by corporations as assets similar to machines or computers which form part of the process of the production of goods or the performance of services.[2] However, there are some governments that have issued proposals or implemented legislation aiming at taxing automation because it is perceived as presenting a threat to the labour market. For example, South Korea has reduced tax incentives for corporations using robots[3] and New York City mayor Bill de Blasio has proposed a specific tax on large corporations that use robots to the

* Tax Lawyer at Deloitte Legal and voluntary researcher at the KU Leuven.

1 See for example X. Oberson, 'Taxing Robots? From the Emergence of an Electronic Ability to Pay to a Tax on Robots or the Use of Robots', *World Tax Journal*, 2017, p. 248; See also on how the Internet of Things might penetrate our daily lives: PYMNTS, 'Samsung Reinvents the 'Family Hub' With Smart Fridge', *PYMNTS*, 21 June 2017, https://www.pymnts.com/internet-of-things/2017/samsung-reinvents-the-family-hub-with-iot-smart-fridge/.

2 X. Oberson, *Taxing Robots – Helping the Economy Adapt to the Use of Artificial Intelligence*, 1st edn (Northampton: Edward Elgar Publishing, 2019), p. 45.

3 See for more information e.g., R. Kovacev, 'A Taxing Dilemma: Robot Taxes and the Challenges of Effective Taxation of AI, Automation and Robotics in the Fourth Industrial Revolution', *The Contemporary Tax Journal*, 2020, pp. 38–40.

detriment of labour forces.[4] In this regard, it should be observed that, even in the few cases in which a tax on automation has been proposed/implemented, there is not yet a comprehensive and generally agreed system of taxation of robots amongst countries.[5] In Belgium, the profits derived by robots are taxed together with the other profits of a corporation according to the general CIT rules. However, certain tax incentives apply for companies investing in robots/AI.

3. Although robots are as such not yet being taxed, governments have recognised that the use of robots/AI (and the digitalisation of the economy in general) has changed business models in such a way that corporations can scale up without mass and as such do no longer need the presence of premises or personnel in a particular country in order to conduct their business there. For example, in the context of AI, a service provider can offer a service entirely through an electronic network (e.g., a chatbot function). As such, it does not need to have personnel present at the location of the users to provide the service. This evolution has led to the loss of tax revenues for countries with a large consumer/user base. On an international level, taxation of a corporation in a country where there are only consumers/users present (without any premises or personnel) is not yet possible. This issue is currently heavily being discussed by governments all over the world and the Organisation for Economic Co-operation and Development (OECD) has been mandated by the G20 to come with a final solution initially by the end of 2020. However, this task has proven to be very difficult and the OECD has yet to come with a final solution to date.

4. Finally, although the use of increased automation presents many tax challenges, it also presents opportunities for tax authorities, tax practitioners and corporations to become more efficient. As such, robots and AI can be used to identify tax fraud or to facilitate and increase tax compliance. They can also be used for the performance of time-consuming or low-level tasks and for identifying opportunities for tax incentives. For example, AI can review specific licensing arrangements to establish whether the parties involved in R&D qualify for R&D tax credits or other government incentives. If this process would be done manually, it would be prone to error and be very laborious.[6]

5. Bearing the above in mind, the main research question of this chapter can be described as follows: 'What are the main tax challenges and opportunities

---

4 See for more information: V. Chand, S. Kostic and A. Reis, 'Taxing artificial Intelligence and Robots: Critical Assessment of Potential Policy Solutions, and Recommendation for Alternative Approaches – Sovereign Measure: Education Taxes/Global Measure: Global Education Tax or Planetary Tax', *World Tax Journal*, 2020, p. 730. For other similar developments in the US, see e.g., Kovacev, 'A Taxing Dilemma', pp. 29–30.

5 Oberson, *Taxing Robots*, p. 44; Kovacev, 'A Taxing Dilemma', pp. 38–46.

6 Deloitte, 'Artificial Intelligence – Entering the world of tax', *Deloitte*, October 2019, p. 6, https://www2.deloitte.com/global/en/pages/tax/articles/artificial-intelligence-in-tax.html.

presented by smart robots and/or AI from a domestic and international perspective?'. To answer this question, the following sub-questions will be analysed: 'How does Belgian legislation currently tax corporations that use smart robots or AI?';[7] 'To what extent should smart robots and/or AI be taxed separately?'; 'What are the main tax challenges presented by smart robots and/or AI from an international perspective?' and 'What are the opportunities presented by smart robots and/or AI for tax authorities, tax practitioners and corporations?'.

6. In this context, this chapter will first provide a brief overview of how Belgium currently treats (smart) robots and AI for taxation purposes (part 2). It will then move into the controversial discussion on the taxation of smart robots and/or AI (part 3), continue with the impact of the use of smart robots and/or AI on international tax rules (part 4) and conclude with the opportunities that smart robots and/or AI create for tax authorities, tax practitioners and corporations (part 5). A general conclusion will also be provided at the end (part 6).

7. For purposes of this chapter, the term 'smart robot' will be used to indicate a machine that contains AI.

2. RELEVANT BELGIAN TAX RULES FOR CORPORATIONS USING SMART ROBOTS AND/OR AI

8. There is currently no separate robot/AI tax in Belgium. Robots/AI are considered to be assets and not people or corporations.[8] Consequently, they are not subject to personal income tax (PIT) or CIT in Belgium. However, since robots/AI create value for enterprises, the profits derived from the use of such robots/AI are taxable together with the other profits of the enterprise according to the general CIT rules. This being said, the federal and regional governments of Belgium have introduced some tax incentives in order to promote innovation, which can lower the overall tax burden of (some) corporations. Those incentives are generally for companies either investing in robots and/or AI or developing new technologies (such as robots/AI) and include:

[7] In this respect, it should be noted that this chapter will not focus on enterprises other than corporations for simplification purposes.

[8] Since AI is a computer programme and therefore software, see Article 3:82, II Belgian Companies and Associations Code (BCAC) and Commission for Accounting Norms, *CBN-advies 138/5 – Software*, *Bull. CBN* no. 35, 1 October 1995; Regarding robots (which are machines) see Article 3:82, III BCAC.

- the investment deduction;
- the innovation income deduction; and
- the exemption of the regional real estate tax on equipment, machines and installations.

These incentives will be discussed in more detail below.

2.1. THE INVESTMENT DEDUCTION

9. In certain circumstances, the profits of an enterprise can be reduced with an amount equal to a percentage of the acquisition or investment value of a newly acquired or achieved fixed asset (the 'investment deduction'). The amount of the deduction is applied to the profits of the tax period in which the investment was made. In case there are no profits from which this deduction can be made, it can be carried forward to subsequent years.[9]

10. Companies that are categorised as 'small' according to the Belgian Companies and Associations Code[10] are generally entitled to a deduction of 8%[11] when they invest in new depreciable tangible or intangible fixed assets to the extent those assets are directly related to the existing or future activities of the company.[12] In addition, small companies are entitled to an increased deduction of 13,5% for investments in digital assets (such as software) that are used for electronic payment and invoicing systems or for the security of information and communication technology.[13]

The criterion of 'new' needs to be applied strictly. Regarding tangible assets, second-hand goods or goods used for demonstrations do not qualify for the investment deduction. Regarding intangible assets, they are considered as 'new' when they have not previously been used by another company and when they have not yet been used by another company in Belgium for its business activity.[14]

---

9 Article 72 Belgian Income Tax Code 1992 (BITC 1992); The amount of the deduction that can be carried forward is however capped; FOD Financiën, Commentary on the Belgian Income Tax Code on Article 199, Number 199/120.

10 See Article 1:24 BCAC for what constitutes a small enterprise.

11 Article 201, §1, 1° BITC 1992; For completeness' sake, the percentage is 20% for investments made between 1 January 2018 and 31 December 2019.

12 Articles 68, 69, 201, §1, 1° and *a contrario* 75, 4° BITC 1992; FOD Financiën, Commentary on the Belgian Income Tax Code on Article 68, Numbers 68/18 and 68/19; C. Chevalier, *Vademecum Vennootschapsbelasting*, 19th edn (Brussel: Larcier, 2019), p. 1169.

13 Article 69, §1, 2° f) BITC 1992.

14 FOD Financiën, Commentary on the Belgian Income Tax Code on Article 68, Numbers 68/15, 68/16 and 68/16.1.

11. With regard to robots which are essentially machines, it is clear that small companies are entitled to use the investment deduction regarding the acquisition of such assets when the abovementioned conditions are complied with. The same reasoning applies to computers which are also considered as tangible fixed assets.[15] The situation is, however, less straightforward with respect to the acquisition of AI as such.

12. According to Belgian accounting law, two types of software need to be distinguished: (i) operations software and (ii) applications software. Operations software such as Windows or Linux is to be characterised as a tangible fixed asset because it is embedded in hardware. On the contrary, applications software is to be considered as an intangible fixed asset. Applications software is depreciable when it is used for the performance of the company's activities and it is expected to have future economic benefits.[16]

If AI is to be categorised as a form of applications software, this would lead to the conclusion that it should also be considered as an intangible fixed asset. Since intangible fixed assets can be depreciated over time (i.e., in a linear way with a minimum of 5 years[17]), investments in AI could potentially be subject to the investment deduction. However, from a tax perspective, assets are only depreciable when a reduction in value has effectively occurred in a given year.[18] One can ask in this respect, whether AI, especially strong AI such as ML, in contrast with regular software, can be said to decrease in value over time. There are in fact arguments to be made that the reverse occurs. Since computers with strong AI become smarter over time, these assets could be expected to increase in value rather than decrease.[19] It seems as though current Belgian legislation does not (yet) take this into account, which makes the application of the investment deduction on AI less straightforward.

Assuming that investments in AI are potentially subject to the investment deduction, they should also be categorised as 'new' for that deduction to apply. Standard software will not be subject to the investment deduction because it cannot be considered as 'new'.[20] On the contrary, applications software made on

---

15 Commission for Accounting Norms, *CBN-advies 138/5 – Software*, *Bull. CBN* no. 35, 1 October 1995, introduction.

16 Commission for Accounting Norms, *CBN-advies 138/5 – Software*, *Bull. CBN* no. 35, 1 October 1995, section I.; E. Lesage, 'ICT-Investeringen en afschrijvingen', Genius repertorium, p. 1, https://www.monkey.be.

17 Article 63 BITC 1992. For completeness' sake, investments in R&D are depreciable in a linear way with a minimum of 3 years.

18 Article 61 BITC 1992; Cass. 21 March 1961, *Pas.* 1961, I, p. 799; Cass. 9 December 1958, *Bull. Bel.* no. 351, p. 112; Cass. 22 March 1991, *FJF* no. 91/130; Chevalier, *Vademecum Vennootschapsbelasting*, p. 389.

19 S. Kirk, 'Artificial Intelligence could yet upend the laws of finance', *Financial Times*, 22 January 2018, https://www.ft.com.

20 Chevalier, *Vademecum Vennootschapsbelasting*, p. 1169.

demand or self-made applications software for internal use could qualify for the investment deduction if certain conditions are met.[21]

13. Regarding the acquisition of smart robots, it is likely that on the basis of analogical reasoning a similar distinction would be made as for a computer with regular software. The robot (i.e., the machine) would be considered as a tangible fixed asset whereas the AI embedded in the robot would be considered as an intangible fixed asset, presenting the same issues as described above.

14. In contrast to small companies, large companies are not entitled to the general investment deduction as described above but they could qualify for a specific investment deduction of 13,5% if they invest in fixed assets used to encourage R&D of new environmental-friendly products and future-oriented technologies.[22] In this respect, such companies could apply an investment deduction on the acquisition of robots that are used to develop said products or technologies. It should be noted in this respect, that robots that are used in performing routine or recurrent functions (e.g., quality control) cannot be subject to the investment deduction.[23] Regarding AI (or the AI part of smart robots), the same issues as for small companies present themselves. AI could be considered as an intangible fixed asset which is depreciable over time. However, whether AI effectively decreases in value over time is debatable and makes the application of the investment deduction less certain.

2.2. THE INNOVATION INCOME DEDUCTION

15. Belgian companies and Belgian establishments of foreign companies are allowed to deduct, from their taxable profits, 85% of the net qualifying income they derive from newly developed intellectual property (IP)[24] when certain conditions are complied with (the 'innovation income deduction').[25] The net

21 See for more information: Chevalier, *Vademecum Vennootschapsbelasting*, pp. 417–418.

22 Article 69, §1, 2°, b) BITC 1992; The 13,5% applies for tax year 2019: see Circulaire 2018/C/108 over de investeringsaftrek, *FOD Financiën*, 6 September 2018, section III.A. For completeness' sake, companies can also opt to apply a tax credit for the same type of investments. However, the tax credit and the investment deduction cannot be applied at the same time. A detailed analysis of the tax credit falls outside the scope of this chapter. See for the basis of this regime: Articles 289*quater* – 289*novies* BITC 1992.

23 Article 48, §1, A. b) Royal Decree on the Belgian Income Tax Code (RD/BITC).

24 The company should be the full owner, co-owner, usufructuary, licensor or rights holder of the IP. See also Article 205/1, §2, 1° BITC 1992; Chevalier, *Vademecum Vennootschapsbelasting*, p. 1156; For more detailed information on when a company is considered to be the owner of a computer programme see for example: B. Springael, 'Hoofdstuk I – De aftrek voor innovatie-inkomsten', in B. Springael (ed.), *Aftrek voor innovatie-inkomsten* (Gent: Larcier, 2019), pp. 96–97, para. 257.

25 Article 205/1, §1 BITC 1992.

income implies that professional R&D expenses need to be deducted from the IP income before applying the deduction.[26] In case there are no profits from which this deduction can be made, it can be carried forward to subsequent years.[27]

16. The IP in scope, and potentially relevant for AI (robots as such, not being IP, are not targeted by this deduction), are:[28]

1. patents and supplementary protection certificates;
2. copyright protected software provided that the software results from a R&D project or programme

The following IP income is considered as qualifying income:[29]

- revenues from licenses;
- innovation income included in the sales price of products and services (so-called embedded royalties);
- innovation income embedded in the application of production processes;
- damages from IP infringement (court decision, amicable settlement or insurance settlement);
- capital gains realised by selling IP rights (subject to a re-investment condition).

In principle, the determination of the qualifying IP income should be performed separately for each IP right.[30] However, if the company can demonstrate that, from a practical perspective, it is not possible to identify the income per IP right separately, the qualifying IP income can be determined per type of product or service or group of products or services.[31]

17. The innovation income deduction is potentially applicable for companies developing AI. Article XI.294 of the Belgian Code of Economic Law provides that a computer programme is, in principle, protected by copyright.[32] According to Article XI.295 of the same code, the protection shall apply to

---

26 Article 205/1, §2, 3° BITC 1992.

27 Article 205/1, §1 BITC 1992; Chevalier, *Vademecum Vennootschapsbelasting*, p. 1155.

28 Article 205/1, §2, 1° BITC 1992; See also S. Loosvelt, 'De nieuwe aftrek voor innovatie-inkomsten doorgelicht', *Fiscale Wenken*, 2017, p. 2.

29 Article 205/1, §2, 2° BITC 1992; See for more information Loosvelt, 'De nieuwe aftrek voor innovatie-inkomsten doorgelicht', p. 3; C. Borgers, 'De nieuwe aftrek voor innovatie-inkomsten', *Algemeen Fiscaal Tijdschrift*, 2017, pp. 10–12 and Springael, 'Aftrek voor Innovatie-inkomsten', pp. 107–115, paras. 281–305.

30 Article 205/2, §1 BITC 1992.

31 Article 205/4, §1 BITC 1992.

32 Even if the computer programme has not been registered and as of its creation.

'the expression, in any form, of a computer programme'.[33] Whether AI could be protected by copyright depends on how AI is viewed. AI can be seen as a combination of algorithms, which are abstract ideas (not necessarily expressed in source code which constitutes a computer programme). The algorithms as such are not susceptible to copyright protection.[34] However, AI can also be seen as a computer programme (i.e., source code), which, as opposed to algorithms, is susceptible to copyright protection.[35] From a tax perspective, assuming that AI would be copyright-protected, the revenues derived from it would qualify as qualifying income in the application of the innovation income deduction.[36]

18. A question as to the patentability of AI could also be formulated. Regarding AI, although it is a difficult analysis to make, it would seem that AI, as such, would not qualify for patent protection whether one views it as a computer programme or a combination of algorithms. Computer programmes and mathematical methods (such as pure algorithms) as such are not patentable since they are too abstract.[37] Consequently, from a tax perspective, it would seem that AI as such would not be able to produce patent income eligible for the innovation income deduction.

19. The situation for smart robots is slightly more complicated because they are a combination of machines and AI. Some parts of the robot could potentially be subject to copyright protection and, as mentioned above, the source code of AI could also be copyright-protected. Regarding patentability, AI as such cannot be patented. However, even if it contains software, a machine operated by a computer programme (and therefore containing AI) is patentable provided that the general conditions for obtaining a patent are complied with.[38]

---

33 Authors' translation. The original text is as follows: 'De bescherming overeenkomstig deze titel wordt verleend aan de uitdrukkingswijze, in welke vorm ook, van een computerprogramma'.

34 Article XI.295, (2) Belgian Code of Economic Law (BCEL).

35 Article XI. 295 (1) BCEL; See however for a more detailed analysis and a more nuanced perspective: J. Vanherpe, 'AI and IP – a Tale of Two Acronyms' in this book; Borgers, 'De nieuwe aftrek voor innovatie-inkomsten', p. 7 and Springael, *Aftrek voor innovatie-inkomsten*, pp. 97–98, para. 258.

36 The Belgian Ruling Commission has issued many rulings on the applicability of the innovation income deduction and copyright protected software. See for example: Belgian Ruling Commission, 19 March 2019, no. 2019.0161, https://www.fisconet.fgov.be; Belgian Ruling Commission, 19 March 2019, no. 2019.0162, https://www.fisconet.fgov.be; Belgian Ruling Commission, 5 February 2019, no. 2018.1213, https://www.fisconet.fgov.be; Belgian Ruling Commission, 20 March 2018, no. 2018.0148, https://www.fisconet.fgov.be.

37 Regarding the non-patentability of computer programmes see: Article XI. 4, 3) BCEL; Regarding the non-patentability of pure algorithms see for a more detailed analysis: Vanherpe, 'AI and IP – a Tale of Two Acronyms' in this book; Article 52 (2) European Patent Convention (EPC).

38 Article XI.4, §2. BCEL; FOD Economie, 'Door welke rechten kunnen computerprogramma's worden beschermd?', 21 October 2020, https://economie.fgov.be/nl/themas/intellectuele-

Consequently, when smart robots are effectively patented or subject to copyright protection, qualifying income from such patents/copyright could be subject to the innovation income deduction.

20. From the brief analysis above, it is apparent that the application of patent law and/or copyright protection on AI and smart robots is not a straightforward exercise. Taking this into account, it is likely that a company is not able to distinguish the qualifying income derived per IP right (as the law originally requires). Fortunately, as mentioned above, the Belgian Income Tax Code provides that, in that case, the qualifying income can be determined based on the type of product or the group of products for which IP rights are obtained. In the context of AI and smart robots, it is likely that companies will rather make use of this provision if they wish to apply the innovation income deduction.[39]

Finally, even if it is established in a specific case that the innovation income deduction is applicable to newly developed AI or smart robots, it will not be easy to determine the income on which the deduction should be applied. The Belgian Ruling Commission has accepted different methods to calculate the income which as a principle should be in conformity with market prices (i.e., at arm's length).[40] Regarding software licences, one could ask whether the entire licence income should qualify for the innovation income deduction. If you consider software-as-a-service[41] for example, one could argue that the innovation income deduction is only applicable to the pure licence income and not to the income received for the provision of services.[42] It is not unthinkable that such discussions could also arise in the context of AI since many cloud services are provided using AI[43] and AI has more autonomous capabilities than a standard software application.

---

eigendom/intellectuele-eigendom-op/creatie-van-een/door-welke-rechten-kunnen; See also for more information on these so-called computer-implemented inventions: J-K. Pinxten, 'De bescherming van software: auteursrecht en/of octrooirecht?', *Jura Falconis,* 2009–2010, pp. 654–657; However, it should be noted that even in this case there could be obstacles for patent protection: See for a more detailed analysis the chapter on intellectual property in this book by J. Vanherpe.

39 See also Chevalier, *Vademecum Vennootschapsbelasting*, p. 1160.

40 See fn. 36.

41 Software-as-a-service allows you to access and use an application via an internet browser. See for more information for example: B. Turner, 'What is Saas? Everything you need to know', *Tech Radar,* 15 December 2019, https://www.techradar.com/news/what-is-saas.

42 Springael, *Aftrek voor innovatie-inkomsten*, p. 135, para. 354.

43 See for example the services provided by Amazon: Amazon, 'Easily Add Intelligence to Applications – No Machine Learning Skills Required', https://aws.amazon.com/machine-learning/ai-services/.

2.3. THE EXEMPTION OF THE REGIONAL REAL ESTATE TAX ON EQUIPMENT, MACHINES AND OTHER INSTALLATIONS

21. The three Belgian regions[44] in principle impose a real estate tax on equipment, machines or other installations used for industry, commercial or crafts companies. This equipment and the machines or installations have the character of immovable property when they are intended to be used permanently for the company's activities and when they are not intended to be moved to another location.[45]

To date, Flanders and Brussels exempt this real estate tax on new equipment, machines or installations to promote innovation.[46] This exemption needs to be specifically requested and does not apply automatically. In contrast, the Walloon region used to have an exemption as well, but this was abolished as of 1 January 2017.[47]

This particular incentive is only applicable to robots as AI, as such, does not qualify as equipment, a machine or other installation.[48] It is not clear how the real estate tax and the exemption should be applied to smart robots. Presumably, it will only be relevant for the robot-part (i.e., physical embodiment) of the smart robot since AI is an intangible asset.

3. TO TAX OR NOT TO TAX ROBOTS?

3.1. DISCUSSIONS TO INTRODUCE A ROBOT TAX IN BELGIUM

22. As can be derived from the previous sections, Belgium is generally still in favour of stimulating innovation (especially Flanders) with the provision of tax incentives for corporations. However, this does not mean that discussions to introduce a 'robot tax' have not yet emerged. Throughout this chapter, a 'robot tax' is intended to mean a tax on any form of automation (e.g., AI/smart robots) that has the potential to have a disruptive effect on the labour market (see also *infra* part 3.3.1. for a more detailed discussion on the scope of a robot tax).

---

44 I.e., Flanders, Brussels and the Walloon Region.

45 Article 471, §3, (2) BITC 1992.

46 Article 2.1.6.0.1., 4°- 6° Flemish Tax Code; Article 255(5) BITC 1992 (Brussels Region).

47 Articles 60 and 64 of the Walloon Decree-programme on diverse measures concerning the budget.

48 AI is likely to be categorised as an intangible asset since it is in essence a computer programme. See part 2.1. in this chapter.

23. The term 'robot tax' has first made its entrance in Belgium in 1982. This tax was proposed as a potential solution to uphold the Belgian social security system. This discussion was triggered at that time because of a large increase of unemployment in Belgium and a fear that the payroll taxes would no longer cover the costs of unemployment benefits.[49] A specific proposal for a robot tax from the Walloon socialist party only came several years later in 2005. However, this proposal was dismissed by the Flemish politicians and was, therefore, not further explored.[50] In 2016 the Minister of Budget of the Walloon region tried to put the proposal for a robot tax back on the table. The idea was to impose a tax on companies if they substitute people for machines. This proposal also received much criticism as it would penalise companies wanting to modernise.[51]

24. Because there currently does not seem to be a consensus amongst politicians in Belgium regarding the need for a robot tax, it is unlikely that such a tax will be designed and implemented in the near future. In addition, the introduction of a robot tax is likely to require a significant shift in tax policy. It is the author's opinion that it does not make sense from a policy perspective to implement a robot tax while at the same time keeping the existing tax incentives (i.e., the investment deduction/the innovation income deduction). Keeping these incentives (at least as they are currently applied) together with a robot tax would send a mixed message to corporations.[52] In addition, the Flemish region itself is currently continuously investing in new technologies and automation in different sectors. One example is the smart shipping program in Flanders relating to fully automated vessels for the inland waterways.[53] Perhaps it would be somewhat controversial, from a policy perspective, to impose a robot tax on corporations because labour forces are lost when the government itself is substituting labour forces with robots or AI.

---

[49] J. Wetz, 'Belgique: Le poids des inactifs', *Le Monde*, 7 December 1982, https://www.lemonde.fr/archives/article/1982/12/07/belgique-le-poids-des-inactifs_2907288_1819218.html.

[50] Mines-ParisTech, 'Taxer les Robots? – Débats au Parlement Européen', *Mines Paristech*, 2017, https://controverses.mines-paristech.fr/public/promo17/promo17_G14/www.controverses-minesparistech.fr/groupe14/debats-au-parlement-europeen/index.html.

[51] P. Lawson and F-X. Lefèvre, 'A peine proposée, la taxe automatisation en Wallonie est déjà contestée', *L'Echo*, 21 October 2016, https://www.lecho.be/economie-politique/belgique/wallonie/a-peine-proposee-la-taxe-automatisation-en-wallonie-est-deja-contestee/9822233.html.

[52] See also O. Mazur, 'Taxing the Robots', *Pepperdine Law Review*, 2019, p. 280, who argues that a robot tax is essentially a tax on innovation.

[53] De Vlaamse Waterweg, 'Smart Shipping', *De Vlaamse Waterweg*, https://www.vlaamsewaterweg.be/smart-shipping-english-version (accessed 28 October 2020). See also an informative article by PwC related to the international study that they performed on Flanders' competitive position in AI: G. Bergen and P. Nys, 'AI: Taking a look at Flanders', *PwC*, 2016, https://www.pwc.be/en/news-publications/client-case-studies/ai-taking-a-look-at-flanders.html.

3.2. TAX POLICY CONSIDERATIONS

3.2.1. Is There a Need for a Robot Tax?

25. There is a general perception that all sectors of the economy are likely to be affected by robotics and AI. Robots are no longer only used in the industry sector but also in the service economy.[54] For example, robots in the medical industry help patients move or walk, whereas robots in the legal sector can help lawyers with their research.[55]

Whether this development is problematic is assessed very differently among scholars. There are different views that can be summarised in two broad categories: the optimists and the pessimists.[56] The optimists argue that smart robots and AI will lower production costs, improve productivity and create more jobs than they will destroy.[57] On the contrary, the pessimists argue that most if not all jobs would disappear if smart robots are introduced.[58] In the long term, the truth is likely to lie somewhere in the middle but there seems to be a general consensus (at least amongst economic scholars[59]) that in the short term, automation will significantly disrupt the labour market.[60]

---

54 Oberson, *Taxing Robots*, p. 7; Mazur, 'Taxing the Robots', p. 285 and the economic literature cited by this author, among others: M. Ford, *Rise of the Robots: Technology and the Threat of a Jobless Future*, 1st edn (New York: Basic Books, 2016), pp. 33–51, 58–61.

55 Oberson, *Taxing Robots*, p. 7; Mazur, 'Taxing the Robots', p. 279.

56 R. Abbott and B. Bogenschneider, 'Should Robots Pay Taxes: Tax Policy in the Age of Automation', *Harvard Law & Policy Review*, 2018, p. 158.

57 Mazur, 'Taxing the Robots', p. 285; and the economic studies cited by this author, among others: J. Manyika (ed.), *Jobs lost, jobs gained: workforce transitions in a time of automation*, 1st edn (San Francisco: Mc Kinsey Global Institute, 2017), pp. 11–12.

58 Oberson, *Taxing Robots*, pp. 9–10; Mazur, 'Taxing the Robots', p. 285 and the economic studies cited by these authors, among others: C.B. Frey and M.A. Osborne, 'The Future of Employment: How Susceptible are Jobs to Computerisation?', *Technological Forecasting & Social Change*, 2017, pp. 265–269; World Economic Forum, 'The Future of Jobs: Employment, Skills and Workforce Strategy for the Fourth Industrial Revolution 3–4', *World Economic Forum*, 2016, p. 13, https://www3.weforum.org/docs/WEF_Future_of_Jobs.pdf; M. Ford, *The Lights in the Tunnel: Automation, Accelerating, Technology and the Economy of the Future*, 1st edn (US: Acculant Publishing, 2009), pp. 131–138.

59 See however for a more nuanced view from a labour law perspective the chapter of S. Taes in this book.

60 J. Englisch, 'Digitalisation and the Future of National Tax Systems: Taxing Robots?', 1 December 2018, p. 2, https://papers.ssrn.com/sol3/papers.cfm?abstract_id=3244670; Mazur, 'Taxing the Robots', p. 287 and the economic literature cited by that author, among others Manyika, *Jobs lost, jobs gained*, pp. 12, 33, 48; OECD, 'Automation and Independent Work in a Digital Economy', *OECD*, May 2016, https://www.oecd.org/employment/Policy%20brief%20-%20Automation%20and%20Independent%20Work%20in%20a%20Digital%20Economy.pdf; Abbott and Bogenschneider, 'Should Robots Pay Taxes', pp. 147, 159. There are also authors who believe that worker displacement is likely to occur in the short term only in some particular sectors and job classes (e.g., truck drivers replaced by self-driving trucks) where the replaced people do not necessarily possess other skills that can be used in alternative jobs. See V. Ooi and G. Goh, 'Taxation of Automation and Artificial Intelligence as a Tool of Labour Policy', *SMU Centre for AI and Data Governance*, 1 November 2018, pp. 6–7, http://

26. From a tax perspective, the implications that automation will have on labour are important. If human labour forces are going to significantly decrease, the state will suffer considerable losses of PIT and social security contributions.[61] Even if the profits of corporations would increase by the use of AI or robots, the taxes collected from the CIT would not compensate the loss incurred in PIT and social security contributions. CIT rates are usually lower than PIT rates and, as mentioned above in part 1, when investing in automation corporations can often apply tax incentives which lowers their taxable base and consequently their taxes.[62] Based on this argument, rapporteur Mady Delvaux proposed the examination of a robot tax to the European Parliament in 2017.[63] The European Parliament, however, did not further elaborate on this point in its resolution for the European Commission.[64]

In addition, with the loss of jobs, inequality of income would increase among people. As Oberson argues, corporations are compelled to substitute labour for capital which would enrich those who already have a certain amount of capital and reduce the wealth of people who depend on their labour.[65] Furthermore, Mazur argues in this regard that wage shifts are likely to occur. Increased automation is likely to put downward pressure on low-skilled jobs relative to high-skilled jobs.[66]

---

dx.doi.org/10.2139/ssrn.3322306. However, for a more detailed analysis on the long term effects, see the chapter by S. Taes in this book and Chand, Kostic and Reis, 'Taxing artificial Intelligence and Robots', pp. 718–723.

61 For example in the EU, on average 50% of income from taxes comes from taxes on labour. See the most recent report: European Commission, 'Taxation Trends in the European Union', June 2021, p. 23, https://op.europa.eu/en/publication-detail/-/publication/d5b94e4e-d4f1-11eb-895a-01aa75ed71a1/language-en. For recent figures published by the OECD: C. Enache, 'Sources of Government Revenue in the OECD', *Tax Foundation Fiscal Fact No.748*, February 2021, p. 3, https://files.taxfoundation.org/20210210172143/Sources-of-Government-Revenue-in-the-OECD-2021.pdf. (relating to individual taxes and social insurance taxes). See also Oberson, *Taxing Robots*, p. 112; Mazur, 'Taxing the Robots', pp. 290–295, 305; Abbott and Bogenschneider, 'Should Robots Pay Taxes', p. 150. Some authors point out that losses in VAT income could also occur since robots do not consume as human beings do (Chand, Kostic and Reis, 'Taxing artificial Intelligence and Robots', p. 714).

62 Mazur, 'Taxing the Robots', p. 293; See also Oberson, *Taxing Robots*, pp. 116–120.

63 M. Delvaux, 'Report with Recommendations to the Commission on Civil Law Rules on Robotics', *European Parliament*, 21 January 2017, p. 4, (K), https://www.europarl.europa.eu/doceo/document/A-8-2017-0005_EN.pdf.

64 European Parliament, 'European Parliament Resolution of 16 February 2017 with recommendations to the Commission on Civil Law Rules on Robotics (2015/2103(INL))', https://www.europarl.europa.eu/doceo/document/TA-8-2017-0051_EN.pdf. The resolution no longer mentions the need for a robot tax but only retained the recommendation to introduce a legal personality for robots for civil liability purposes. See part 3.3.3.

65 Oberson, *Taxing Robots*, pp. 11–12, 112–113; See also Mazur, 'Taxing the Robots', pp. 282, 287; Abbott and Bogenschneider, 'Should Robots Pay Taxes', p. 155; A. Rathi, 'Stephen Hawking: Robots aren't just taking our jobs, they're making society more unequal', *Quartz*, 9 October 2015, https://qz.com/520907/stephen-hawking-robots-arent-just-taking-our-jobs-theyre-making-society-more-unequal/.

66 Mazur, 'Taxing the Robots', pp. 287–289. The concerns of decreasing tax revenues and inequality of income were also shared by rapporteur Mady Delvaux in the European Parliament in 2017. In her draft report, she proposed that the implementation of a robot tax

27. How these issues need to be resolved from a tax perspective is not an easy question to answer. Any tax on automation would likely increase costs for companies, which could also have economic implications. In order to prevent distortions, a tax on automation should in principle be neutral. This means that a corporation should only replace humans by smart robots for economic efficiency reasons and not tax reasons.[67] Ideally, this means that smart robots that replace humans should be taxed in the same way as the humans they replace.[68] However, even in that case, it is the author's opinion that the achievement of tax neutrality in a purely domestic context would not be sufficient to mitigate job losses. If other countries do not impose such a tax, this may perhaps lead the corporation to relocate. As a consequence, labour forces will also decrease in the original country (this is exactly what we would want to avoid with a robot tax).[69] In addition, the reality is likely to be more complex. Corporations investing in robots will not necessary fire existing human employees. Conversely, they may fire low-skilled employees but replace them with high-skilled employees that are able to work with the robot resulting in a break-even from the perspective of total number of employees.[70] These considerations are likely to complicate the debate with respect to the requirement of neutral treatment.[71]

Despite this fact, Oberson argues that the introduction of a tax on automation could nevertheless be interesting in the short term. The purpose of the tax would

---

should be examined: See Delvaux, 'Report on Civil Law Rules on Robotics', p. 4, (K). However, this proposal was subsequently dismissed by the European Parliament: see for example: Tech. News, 'European Parliament Calls For Robot Law, Rejects Robot Tax', *Reuters,* 16 February 2017, https://www.reuters.com/article/us-europe-robots-lawmaking/european-parliament-calls-for-robot-law-rejects-robot-tax-idUSKBN15V2KM.

67 Abbott and Bogenschneider, 'Should Robots Pay Taxes', p. 151. Some argue that the current tax code in the US even has the effect of providing an incentive for enterprises to invest in automation to the detriment of human workers: R. Kovacev, 'A Taxing Dilemma', p. 26.

68 Although it should be noted that, in practice, in such a case the robot tax would need to be quite high and it should be analysed whether this would be a realistic scenario. The choice of a company for a robot or a person will not be affected by taxation if the cost to employ a person is the same or similar to the cost of using a robot. In order to compensate personnel costs, the robot tax would need to be quite high since the costs to employ a person is composed of his salary but also of taxes and social security contributions, whereas the cost of a robot only comprises the cost of the machine.

69 See e.g. Englisch, 'Digitalisation and the Future of National Tax Systems: Taxing Robots?', pp. 12–13; Kovacev, 'A Taxing Dilemma', p. 37; Mazur, 'Taxing the Robots', pp. 300–301; Abbott and Bogenschneider, 'Should Robots Pay Taxes', pp. 168–169. Corporations have relocated their activities in the past from countries with high labour costs to countries with low labour costs. See for example: N. Bottini, C. Ernst and M. Luebker, 'Offshoring and the labour market: what are the issues?', *Economic and Labour Market Paper,* 2007, pp. 7–8, https://ilo.org/wcmsp5/groups/public/---ed_emp/---emp_elm/---analysis/documents/publication/wcms_113922.pdf. Perhaps a similar trend will occur in case of high robot costs.

70 Kovacev, 'A Taxing Dilemma', pp. 34–35.

71 Some authors also argue that robots (no matter how smart) and humans are simply not comparable and, therefore, dismiss any type of proposal that is rooted in the requirement of neutrality. See Chand, Kostic and Reis, 'Taxing artificial Intelligence and Robots', pp. 733–734.

be to limit automation but only for a certain period allowing the economy to adapt. The idea is not to stop the progress of automation but rather to protect workers from losing their jobs and allowing them time to re-educate to obtain new skills.[72] Perhaps, if this tax is only implemented as a temporary measure, this would not lead to adverse effects (such as the relocation of corporations to other countries). However, in this context, it is interesting to note that a survey performed by O'Reilly has indicated that many businesses already slow down the implementation of AI because of the lack of data and skilled people.[73] If this is the case, the fear that, even in the short term, labour forces will be replaced by AI might also be unfounded. A thorough analysis of this trend, however, is not the purpose of this chapter and for the remainder of this chapter, the hypothesis will be used that there is indeed a need for a robot tax.

3.2.2. Hypothesis: It Is Established That There Is a Need for a Robot Tax

28. Assuming that it is generally agreed that a robot tax should be implemented, there are still other questions that need to be answered. If the idea is to protect the labour market, should this tax also apply to people (as opposed to corporations) who substitute household help with robots?[74] If not, and the tax thus only applies to corporations, should it be limited to multinationals exceeding a certain income threshold or should it apply to all corporations? An income threshold may be useful since imposing a robot tax on small corporations or start-ups might significantly impact their ability to grow, which is probably not intended since it would also have a negative impact on labour.[75]

29. It should also not be forgotten that innovation and automation do not only have a negative impact on labour. New technologies can also benefit workers on different levels.[76] For example, the use of cobots is helpful for workers since

---

72 Oberson, *Taxing Robots*, p. 126. See for a similar view from Bill Gates: K.J. Delaney, 'The robot that takes your job should pay taxes, says Bill Gates', *Quartz*, 17 February 2017, https://qz.com/911968/bill-gates-the-robot-that-takes-your-job-should-pay-taxes/. Regarding the re-education of employees see also: Abbott and Bogenschneider, 'Should Robots Pay Taxes', p. 160.

73 B. Lorica and P. Nathan (eds.), *AI Adoption in the Enterprise – How Companies Are Planning and Prioritizing AI Projects in Practice*, 1st edn (California: O'Reilly Media Inc., 2019), pp. 9–10.

74 For more information on this subject, see, e.g., Englisch, 'Digitalisation and the Future of National Tax Systems: Taxing Robots?', pp. 8–9.

75 In the case of start-ups, one could also argue that there is no labour disruption as such since the company did not exist and did not have any employees to begin with. Maus, however, argues that this could be a discrimination between start-ups and pre-existing companies: M. Maus, 'Moeten Robots Belasting Betalen?', in M. Maus (ed.), *Homo Roboticus* (Brussel: VUBpress, 2019), p. 239. It is the author's opinion that this discrimination would be justified taking into account the objective of the robot tax (i.e., the mitigation of labour disruption).

76 See for a more detailed analysis the chapter by S. Taes in this book; Chand, Kostic and Reis, 'Taxing artificial Intelligence and Robots', p. 713.

they can perform dirty or unsafe tasks, while the employees can focus on other more meaningful tasks.[77] Consequently, one needs to consider, from a policy perspective, whether imposing a tax that would also eliminate the positive impact of automation would be desirable.

3.3. CHALLENGES IN THE DESIGN AND IMPLEMENTATION OF A ROBOT TAX

30. Assuming that a robot tax would need to be designed and implemented, several challenges would present themselves. In a first instance, the object of the tax (i.e., what is a 'robot'?) would need to be determined. In addition, it will be important to establish the taxable subject. Are corporations going to pay the tax or will robots themselves be subjected to the tax?

3.3.1. How to Define Robots for Tax Purposes

31. The notion of a 'robot' would need to be adequately defined and any definition should, as Mazur points out, be clear, practicable and justifiable. This, however, is not an easy task since automation can take many forms. Should the tax apply to any machine that replaces a human job? Or should it only apply to a machine with AI? In addition, is it required for a robot to have physical qualities or can it include software or algorithms that allow a computer to perform human tasks?[78]

According to the Cambridge dictionary, a 'robot' is 'a machine controlled by a computer that is used to perform jobs automatically'.[79] This definition is very broad and could encompass almost all technology, such as a vending machine or even widely-used software such as Excel.[80] Therefore, it does not seem fit for tax purposes. If such a broad definition would be used, the tax would not only have a discouraging effect on labour-disrupting technologies but also on labour-enhancing technologies, which is not desirable from a tax policy perspective.[81] Indeed, Excel, for example, can also be considered as having the ability to perform tasks that were previously done by hand in an automated way.[82]

---

77 See for example: Bax and Company, 'Are Cobots the Answer to Technological Unemployment?', *Bax and Company*, https://baxcompany.com/insights/are-cobots-the-answer-to-technological-unemployment/.

78 Mazur, 'Taxing the Robots', p. 298. Also see: Kovacev, 'A Taxing Dilemma', p. 33.

79 Cambridge Dictionary, https://dictionary.cambridge.org/dictionary/english/robot.

80 Lewis Silkin LLP, 'Robot tax: The pros and cons of taxing robotic technology in the workplace', *Future of work hub*, 4 December 2019, https://www.futureofworkhub.info/comment/2019/12/4/robot-tax-the-pros-and-cons-of-taxing-robotic-technology-in-the-workplace.

81 Oberson, *Taxing Robots*, p. 26; Mazur, 'Taxing the Robots', p. 298.

82 M. Baxter, 'Is a robot tax, or even an AI tax, really a good idea?', *Information Age*, 18 September 2019, https://www.information-age.com/robot-tax-ai-tax-debate-123485375/.

However, most people would agree that imposing a robot tax on each company using Excel would go beyond its current purpose.

32. The scope of the definition of a 'robot' should, therefore, be narrowed. According to Oberson, the definition of a robot for tax purposes should be driven by the purpose of a robot tax, namely to minimise the disruption of labour caused by AI.[83] As such, a 'robot' should be a machine that specifically has 'the ability to process, plan and act on its own'. It should be form-neutral, meaning that it does not matter whether a robot has any physical support. Indeed, the form does not matter since both a robot in a physical support and AI software in a computer are capable of performing human activities that will have an impact on the labour market.[84] These characteristics of a robot make sense taking into account the objective of the tax. Since the objective is to create a level-playing field between humans and robots, it would be logical to include only those robots that express human-like behaviours and are fully capable of replacing a human being.

However, it is unclear whether this definition is intended to also include cobots, which can be considered as labour-enhancing robots working alongside humans.[85] According to Oberson, 'robots are defined broadly, as the implementation of AI in the market. In a way, AI is the "brain" and the robots are the material implementation and effects of the algorithm designed for the robots to act'.[86] Based on this statement, a cobot could easily fall within the category of a robot although it is not conclusive that such robots would disrupt the labour market. Therefore, it can be debated whether the use of such robots should be taxed. Perhaps the definition of a robot should not focus on whether the robot has 'the ability' to process, plan and act on its own but rather on whether it effectively does so to the detriment of a human worker. Alternatively, if in practice cobots cannot easily be distinguished from job-displacing robots[87] and the difference cannot be captured in a definition, perhaps it could be envisaged to apply a robot tax only when it is established that an increase in robots is accompanied by a decrease in labour forces in a company.[88]

---

83 See also Oberson, *Taxing Robots*, pp. 26–27.

84 Oberson, *Taxing Robots*, pp. 15–16.

85 Although Oberson reiterates that we should focus on the impact of AI, implemented by robots, on the labour market. See Oberson, *Taxing Robots*, pp. 26–27.

86 Oberson, *Taxing Robots*, p. 16.

87 A job-displacing robot is a robot that replaces a human being in the workplace. On the other hand, a job-enhancing robot is a robot that works together with a human being and makes the job in general more efficient. See also for example Mazur, 'Taxing the Robots', p. 302 and fn. 153.

88 However, this system will also have its challenges in practice. See Ooi and Goh, 'Taxation of Automation and Artificial Intelligence as a Tool of Labour Policy', pp. 16–17. Ooi and Goh instead propose to impact a corporation's tax liability by influencing the amount of deductibility of capital investments. In this sense, corporations that adopt a certain level of automation for complementary purposes (without a significant amount of human

3.3.2. *A Tax on the Use of Robots?*

33. In case one would design a tax on the use of robots, the taxpayer would be the corporation who owns the robots. In order to compensate for the loss in PIT, the taxable base could be an 'imputed income'. This imputed income could be determined on the basis of the same activities performed by human beings.[89] A San Francisco politician, for example, has made such a proposal after Bill Gates made a statement to introduce a robot tax.[90]

A system of imputed income for tax purposes is not new. This already exists in the framework of real estate in several countries such as Belgium. Owners of real estate in Belgium are taxed on an imputed income equal to the rental income they would have received if their house was rented to third parties. This income is an 'imputed' income because the real estate owners do not really receive it (but they are taxed on it nonetheless).[91]

34. Mazur believes that determining an imputed income for robots is virtually impossible.[92] According to her, even if an imputed salary were to be calculated, it is not clear how this would need to be adjusted the following years. In addition, it is not clear how this salary would need to evolve if the robot is taking over new functions over time. Finally, robots often complement human workers and it will not be easy to differentiate between job-enhancing and job-displacing robots.[93]

35. Oberson, on the other hand, believes that the determination of an imputed salary for robots is not impossible. Mazur's concerns relating to a robot performing different functions could be solved by the performance of a functional analysis in order to determine the correct imputed salary. Another

---

replacement) would be able to deduct higher amounts than corporations that cause more replacement of humans. See Ooi and Goh, 'Taxation of Automation and Artificial Intelligence as a Tool of Labour Policy', p. 20. See also further section 3.4., no. 46, concerning a proposal made by Abbott and Bogenschneider.

89 Oberson, *Taxing Robots*, p. 114.

90 T. Gillies, 'What would Skynet do? One San Francisco official is pushing for a 'robot tax', *CNBC*, 8 October 2017, https://www.cnbc.com/2017/10/08/san-franciso-official-pushes-for-taxes-on-robots.html; This proposal was launched following a statement made by Bill Gates that robots should be subject to tax, see for example: Delaney, 'The robot that takes your job should pay taxes, says Bill Gates'.

91 The imputed income in Belgium is called 'kadastraal inkomen' (Dutch) / 'revenu cadastral' (French). See also on a system of imputed income in Switzerland: Oberson, *Taxing Robots*, p. 114.

92 For a similar view also see Chand, Kostic and Reis, 'Taxing artificial Intelligence and Robots', p. 740.

93 Mazur, 'Taxing the Robots', p. 302 and fn. 153.

solution would be to use a lump-sum amount based on an approximation of an adequate remuneration or average estimates of the value of theoretical work.[94]

36. Regarding Mazur's last concern with respect to the difficult differentiation between job-enhancing and job-displacing robots, the robot tax could perhaps be designed in such a way that it would only apply to a company if the increase in robots was accompanied by a decrease in labour (to be assessed each year).[95] If the increase in robots does not coincide with a decrease in human labourers, this would rather point to an investment in job-enhancing robots and the company would not be subject to the robot tax. On the contrary, if the use of robots increases while the amount of human workers decreases over time, this would rather indicate the use of job-displacing robots and taxation on robots would take place. However, this solution would also be far from perfect as it would increase the CIT effective rate for many companies and make the tax system more complex. This is likely to play a negative role in terms of international tax competition.[96]

3.3.3. A Tax on Robots Themselves?

37. If the tax is designed in such a way that it applies to robots themselves, this would imply the allocation of some form of legal personality to robots. A robot would need to be responsible to pay the tax and be able to pay the tax itself. This idea is quite controversial and leads to many difficulties.

The idea of a legal personality for robots has already been introduced in 2017. For civil liability purposes, in a report to the European Parliament, Mady Delvaux proposed the granting of legal personality to robots.[97] Following this report, the European Parliament issued a resolution containing a recommendation for attributing legal personality to robots to the European Commission.[98] The resolution proposed that robots should obtain the specific status of electronic persons responsible for purposes of damage claims and possibly for cases where robots make autonomous decisions.[99] However, the European Commission did not follow this recommendation.[100]

---

94 Oberson, *Taxing Robots*, p. 115; Reiterated and further elaborated upon in X. Oberson, 'Robot Taxes: The Rise of a New Taxpayer', *Bulletin for International Taxation*, 2021, p. 373.

95 See also Abbott and Bogenschneider, 'Should Robots Pay Taxes', p. 170.

96 Abbott and Bogenschneider, 'Should Robots Pay Taxes', pp. 170–171.

97 Delvaux, 'Report on Civil Law Rules on Robotics', p. 18.

98 European Parliament, 'Resolution with Recommendations on Civil Law Rules on Robotics', para. 59 f).

99 European Parliament, 'Resolution with Recommendations on Civil Law Rules on Robotics', para. 59 f).

100 See Oberson, *Taxing Robots*, p. 20. See also for more information on the legal personality of robots in general: J. De Bruyne, E. Van Gool and T. Gils, 'Tort Law and Damage Caused by AI', in this book.

38. The fact that no legal personality is granted to a robot from a civil law point of view does not preclude the tax legislator from considering a robot as a taxable entity. There are already examples where entities, not regarded as legal entities from a civil law point of view, are treated as separate taxpayers.[101] However, if legal personality were to be allocated to robots, this would need to be justified for tax purposes. According to Oberson, this implies that a robot would have an economic ability to pay, i.e., they should have access to sufficient funds in order to be able to pay the tax. Although he acknowledges that recognising a tax capacity of robots at this stage would raise many legal and technical issues (e.g., how will the robot pay the tax?), he also believes that these issues could be solved by AI in the nearest future. AI could be designed in such a way that it includes a tax component to a robot transaction occurring electronically.[102]

39. Provided that the technical and legal issues related to the attribution of a tax capacity to robots are solved, one could ask what type of tax should be imposed on robots. This question is particularly difficult to answer since robots are neither human beings nor corporations. According to Oberson, one solution would be to introduce a 'robot income or revenue tax'. However, this approach would raise several issues. If the tax is designed as a profit tax (similar to corporations), robots would be able to use these profits for future investments or distribute it to their owners.[103] It is the author's opinion that such a possibility is likely to overcomplicate the tax system and is therefore not desirable. In a cross-border scenario, considering a robot as a corporation would lead to economic double taxation when the owner of the robot is also taxed on the same income.[104] In addition, one would also need to take into account spill-over effects, such as potential profit distribution of a robot to its owners and the taxation thereof.[105] On the other hand, if the tax is designed as an income tax, different other factors would need to be taken into account. Robots are not entirely similar to people and are in principle not exposed to costs. It is, therefore, possible that the tax for robots should rather be designed on gross revenues rather than net income.[106]

---

101 Oberson, *Taxing Robots*, p. 23.

102 See for more information: Oberson, *Taxing Robots*, p. 132; Kovacev on the other hand argues that even if legal personality were to be attributed to a robot, this would not change the analysis of who pays the tax since the money comes in essence from a human actor (Kovacev, 'A Taxing Dilemma', pp. 33–34).

103 Oberson, *Taxing Robots*, p. 133. See also Oberson, 'Robot Taxes: The Rise of a New Taxpayer', p. 378.

104 This could for example be the case for a corporation, resident in state A having an autonomous vehicle in state B that offers rides to customers. See Chand, Kostic and Reis, 'Taxing artificial Intelligence and Robots', p. 738.

105 Should the distribution of ownership to the owners be assimilated with dividends subject to withholding tax? See also part 4.4.

106 Oberson, *Taxing Robots*, p. 133. However, see for a different view Chand, Kostic and Reis, 'Taxing artificial Intelligence and Robots', p. 738.

Another solution proposed by Oberson would be the introduction of a 'robot capital tax' instead of an income tax. In this case, the robot would be taxed on the net value of assets owned or controlled by the robot.[107] In this scenario, but also in the case of an income or revenue tax, it is not clear how the robot would be entitled to such income/assets. In reality, the corporation for which the robot is working (considering the robot is comparable to an employee) is not likely to pay the robot for its activities. How will the robot obtain funds on which it would need to pay tax? In addition, a capital tax presupposes that a robot would to a certain extent be able to acquire assets or capital. However, it is not clear in which situations this would be realistic as it presupposes that AI would have the capability to make this type of decisions on its own.[108] Although this would theoretically be possible, it is not clear why a company would invest in such type of AI as it does not serve the purposes of the company.

However, Oberson recently made an interesting observation if one considers that robots are capable of performing management functions rather than only employee's functions. In this respect, it is not unconceivable that a robot could gain control of a limited liability company (LLC), allowing it to exercise rights in the LLC which would result in the robot owning wealth and entering in commercial transactions.[109] If robots are not taxed, this could lead to massive tax evasion since the LLC could be situated in a low-tax jurisdiction and the robot would not be subject to tax at all. A (profit) tax on the robot itself could make more sense and therefore be justifiable in such a context.[110]

40. Finally, in the implementation of a robot tax, one should also consider how this tax would need to be enforced. If a robot is a taxable person but does not have a legal personality for civil law purposes, will the state be able to sue a robot if it does not pay the tax? This would also need to be clarified before introducing a robot tax on robots as such.[111]

41. It follows from the above that considering a robot as a taxable entity is a complicated exercise, prone to many issues. However, this discussion might be overcome by first answering more ethical questions relating to the acceptable capability of AI. Is it our wish to have smart robots with a mind of their own simply because we can develop them from a technical perspective? Or should we impose limits to their development and only allow AI to be developed as a tool

---

107 Oberson, *Taxing Robots*, p. 153; According to Oberson, a robot would need to hold or control some financial means, in forms of equity or access to a fund.

108 See also Englisch, 'Digitalisation and the Future of National Tax Systems: Taxing Robots?', pp. 4–5.

109 Oberson, 'Robot Taxes: The Rise of a New Taxpayer', p. 377.

110 *Ibid.*, pp. 376–378. However, not all authors believe that this scenario is realistic (see, e.g., Chand, Kostic and Reis, 'Taxing artificial Intelligence and Robots', p. 736).

111 See also in a more general way Kovacev, 'A Taxing Dilemma', p. 34 who argues that there are difficulties in holding a robot accountable for its actions.

to facilitate people's lives or corporations' businesses? Although these are serious questions that cannot be addressed in a few lines, it is the author's opinion that if AI is only used as a tool, a tax on robots themselves would make less sense and a tax on the use of robots would seem more appropriate.

3.4. ALTERNATIVES TO A ROBOT TAX

42. Since there are many challenges associated with the introduction of a robot tax in general (whether it is a tax on the use of robots or a tax on robots themselves), it may be interesting to briefly analyse some alternatives for addressing the issues brought forward by increased automation.[112]

43. According to Mazur, many of the concerns expressed are symptoms of a larger problem, namely the fact that capital income is undertaxed while labour income is overtaxed.[113] Currently, the investment in robots is often incentivised from a tax perspective. Consequently, investing in robots might become efficient in certain circumstances, not solely based on economic factors but also on tax factors.[114] In this case, taxation is a distortive factor that can potentially exacerbate any disruption of the labour market.[115]

Consequently, in order to mitigate labour displacement and achieve tax neutrality, it could, as a preliminary step, be considered to abolish tax incentives applicable to investments in smart robots.[116] South Korea for example has followed such an approach.[117] Companies had a tax deduction of 3% to 7% of their corporate tax when they invested in automated machines. The government has reduced this rate with two percentage points.[118] According to Abbott and Bogenschneider, the disallowance of tax deductions for capital investments could also be designed in such a way that they do not apply in general but they are made subject to a reported level of automation. Companies with a high level of automation could have their tax deduction reduced beyond a certain threshold.[119]

---

112 It is not the objective of this chapter to give an exhaustive overview of the alternatives. Consequently, only certain proposals have briefly been discussed. For a more comprehensive list see for example Oberson, *Taxing Robots*, pp. 120–131; Chand, Kostic and Reis, 'Taxing artificial Intelligence and Robots', pp. 729–733.

113 Mazur, 'Taxing the Robots', p. 281.

114 See for an example: Abbott and Bogenschneider, 'Should Robots Pay Taxes', p. 163; Mazur, 'Taxing the Robots', p. 306.

115 Mazur, 'Taxing the Robots', p. 306; Maus, 'Moeten Robots Belasting Betalen?', p. 240.

116 Abbott and Bogenschneider, 'Should Robots Pay Taxes', p. 169; See also Oberson, *Taxing Robots*, pp. 124–125.

117 Mazur, 'Taxing the Robots', p. 297.

118 Kovacev, 'A Taxing Dilemma', pp. 38–39; Chand, Kostic and Reis, 'Taxing artificial Intelligence and Robots', p. 731.

119 Abbott and Bogenschneider, 'Should Robots Pay Taxes', p. 169; See also Ooi and Goh, 'Taxation of Automation and Artificial Intelligence as a Tool of Labour Policy', p. 20.

44. However, eliminating tax incentives for smart robots is not likely to be sufficient.[120] In this context, according to Mazur, a more general tax reform that promotes labour, improves economic equity but also encourages the development of technology is needed.[121] According to the same author, such a tax reform could be the introduction of a tax on capital income which would target capital in general and not only robots. However, the taxation of capital is a controversial and heavily debated subject and, therefore, falls outside the scope of this chapter.[122] Given the controversy, it is safe to state that it is not likely to be implemented in the near future.[123]

45. Another proposal that has been made by Abbott and Bogenschneider to target capital rather than labour is to significantly increase the CIT rate. However, they also acknowledge that this proposal is unlikely to be implemented since it is politically unfeasible. Higher taxes could have negative psychological effects on capital investment. They will target all companies even those not investing in automation and companies may be inclined to shift the tax incidence to workers or consumers.[124]

46. These authors also alternatively propose to introduce a 'corporate self-employment tax'. The idea of this tax is that it would be calculated as a substitute for what employment taxes would have been if the human worker had not been replaced by a machine. More specifically, the corporate self-employment tax could be calculated based on a ratio of a company's profits to its number of employees and only apply when a certain threshold has been exceeded.[125] According to Oberson, such a tax would be far from ideal as it could have a different impact depending on the industry, which could breach the principle of equality of treatment.[126]

---

120 *Ibid.*, p. 170.

121 Mazur, 'Taxing the Robots', p. 304.

122 For a more detailed discussion on the subject See: Mazur, 'Taxing the Robots', pp. 313–328. Mazur also argues in this respect that tax policy alone (e.g., introducing a tax on capital) will not be able to solve the disruption on the labour market or the growing inequality gap. She states: 'tax policy needs to be taken into account together with government regulation and targeted government spending to better address some of these concerns'. In addition, she believes that measures should also be taken to keep promoting innovation although these may not necessarily come from a tax policy perspective (but rather from other governmental actions).

123 See for other counterarguments Oberson, *Taxing Robots*, p. 141.

124 Abbott and Bogenschneider, 'Should Robots Pay Taxes', pp. 172–173; See also Oberson, *Taxing Robots*, p. 139.

125 *Ibid.*, pp. 171–172. This idea was originally proposed by William Meisel. However, this author proposed a ratio based on sales rather than profits because he believes that profits can easily be manipulated. See also Oberson, *Taxing Robots*, p. 121.This type of tax is usually referred to as an automation tax. Different variations of automation taxes have been proposed. See e.g. Chand, Kostic and Reis, 'Taxing artificial Intelligence and Robots', pp. 732–733.

126 For a more detailed analysis see *ibid.*, pp. 121–122; However, the author also believes that, even though this system is not perfect, it could be used as a transitory compromise. See Oberson, 'Robot Taxes: The Rise of a New Taxpayer', pp. 373–374.

47. Finally, Chand, Kostic and Reis favour an earmarked educations tax as a possible measure to combat the disruptive effect of robots on labour. This tax would be borne by all corporations and wealthy individuals. The proceeds of the tax would exclusively be used to fund re-education programmes for employees.[127] These authors view this issue as a societal problem that requires solidarity from almost all people (excluding the middle-class) and believe that an earmarked solution has the benefit of increasing compliance since people are aware of the exact purpose of the tax. In addition, it would be easy to implement and the difficulties associated with a classic robot tax (e.g. definition) would be avoided.[128]

3.5. CONCLUSION

48. The question of whether or not a robot tax should be introduced is a complicated one for which there is currently no clear answer. There is no consensus on the introduction of such a tax yet. Furthermore, even if there were a consensus, many questions remain unresolved regarding its concrete design (e.g. what is the definition of a robot?; who is liable to pay the tax? etc.). Alternatives to a robot tax have also been made but, so far, a perfect solution is far from being found.

4. SMART ROBOTS AND INTERNATIONAL TAX RULES

49. The use of robots has also posed challenges for the application of international tax rules. Traditionally, international tax rules were designed when technology was almost inexistent. In the 1920s, it was decided that, from a policy perspective, enterprises could only be taxed by their country of residence unless they were significantly involved in the economy of another jurisdiction as well. In that case, the other jurisdiction is also allowed to tax a part of the enterprise's profits. The significant involvement in the economy of another jurisdiction was assessed based on physical factors such as the location of premises or personnel in that jurisdiction.[129] However, technology has changed the way in which businesses operate and companies do no longer need premises and/or personnel

---

127 Chand, Kostic and Reis, 'Taxing artificial Intelligence and Robots', pp. 745–754.

128 Chand, Kostic and Reis, 'Taxing artificial Intelligence and Robots', pp. 750–754. It should be noted, however, that these authors do not in first instance believe that there is a need for a robot tax. In addition, they also state that a better solution than the earmarked educations tax would be global (intercontinental) fiscal redistribution. See Chand, Kostic and Reis, 'Taxing artificial Intelligence and Robots', pp. 745, 756–760.

129 See also OECD, *Are the Current Treaty Rules for Taxing Business Profits Appropriate for E-Commerce? Final Report*, (Paris: OECD Publishing, 2004), p. 15, para. 49.

in order to conduct significant business activities in a non-resident jurisdiction. Therefore, it is currently being debated whether the significant involvement in a jurisdiction's economy can only be adequately determined based on physical factors or whether certain digital factors could also be taken into account.

50. This being said, it should be noted that the discussion on an international level concerns the consequences brought forward by the digitalised economy in general and does not target smart robots/AI separately. The current rules and reforms that will be discussed in this part therefore only indirectly target smart robots/AI to the extent they entail consequences for the allocation of taxing powers amongst countries.[130]

4.1. OVERVIEW OF CURRENT INTERNATIONAL TAX RULES AND THEIR (NON?) APPLICABILITY TO SMART ROBOTS/AI

51. Taxing powers between states are traditionally allocated by virtue of rules determined in double tax treaties (DTT). The OECD has developed a model convention (MC) and Commentaries on which many of the existing DTTs are based. The provisions of the OECD MC will be discussed as a general guideline.[131]

52. In the case of business profits, the right of a state to tax those profits is determined by the concept of a permanent establishment (PE). Accordingly, a PE is generally considered to exist in the following two scenarios:[132]

i. there is a 'fixed place of business' in the non-resident state from which the business is wholly or partially carried on (further the 'fixed place of business PE'); or
ii. there is a dependent agent in the non-resident state that has the ability to negotiate/conclude contracts on behalf of and in the name of the non-resident enterprise (further the 'agency PE');

53. In order to assess the applicability of those rules to enterprises using smart robots/AI, the following simplified case study will be used:[133]

---

130 Oberson, *Taxing Robots*, pp. 85–86, 141–142.

131 OECD, *Model Tax Convention on Income and on Capital (21 November 2017),* (Paris: OECD Publishing, 2017); The provisions of the UN Model Convention or other specific DTTs fall outside the scope of this chapter.

132 OECD, *Model Tax Convention,* Article 5.

133 This case study is entirely fictional and perhaps somewhat extreme but only serves to illustrate the potential application of the international tax rules in a more comprehensive way.

ACo is a company resident in state A and is active in the pharmaceutical/health care business. ACo provides different AI services to customers in State D. For example, customers can receive tailored information on medication based on their needs, they can ask a chatbot different questions on ACo's products and they can receive relevant statistics and recommendations on new products. Based on the input provided by the customers on patients, AI can also prepare studies and compare them with other studies on the market. The AI used for the provision of services is located in servers in state C and D. Those servers are owned by ACo and operated by ACo's personnel in country A. Customers in state D do not interact with ACo's personnel in state A.

In addition to the AI services provided, ACo also runs a shop in state B which is fully automated and sells orthopaedic material. The building in which the shop is located is rented by ACo. Customers can enter the shop by using a bar code, do their shopping and make use of automated cashiers. The orthopaedic material is transported from ACo to the shop by a third party. Smart robots in state B are responsible for the adequate organisation of the material in the shop. Customers in state B do not interact with ACo's personnel in state A. ACo's personnel have access to the building where the shop is located should the need arise.

The above scenario can be summarised as follows:

4.1.1. Fixed Place of Business PE

A. Existence of a PE

54. In the case of ACo, the question that needs to be answered is whether the smart robots in country B and the servers in countries C and D could qualify as

fixed places of business through which the business of ACo is wholly or partly carried on.

As a general rule, a PE is said to exist when a non-resident enterprise has (i) a place of business in the non-resident state, (ii) the place of business is fixed and (iii) the enterprise conducts business in the non-resident state through that fixed place of business.[134] However, even in that case, a fixed place of business will not be considered to be a PE when the activities conducted by it are of an auxiliary or preparatory nature.[135]

55. In a first scenario, a place of business can be said to exist when the non-resident enterprise has premises, facilities or installations at its disposal in the other country. According to the OECD, an enterprise has a place of business at its disposal when it has the effective power to use that location. In this respect, whether the place of business is owned or rented by the enterprise is therefore not relevant.[136] In the case at hand, ACo rents a building in country B in which it makes use of smart robots to perform its activity. Considering that the smart robots are owned and programmed by ACo in its own interest and ACo's personnel have access to the building should it be necessary, it can be concluded that ACo has the building in country B at its disposal and it will therefore have a place of business in country B. This place of business can also said to be fixed since a building is immovable property.[137]

56. Whether ACo is conducting business in the non-resident state through that fixed place of business is more difficult to assess. Generally speaking, business is conducted through the use of personnel that receive instructions from the enterprise.[138] However, the OECD acknowledges that exceptionally, when the business is carried on through automated equipment (such as computer equipment) 'the presence of personnel is not necessary to consider that an enterprise wholly or partly carries on its business at a location when no personnel are in fact required to carry on business activities at that location'.[139] However, even in this case, the OECD only concludes to a PE when there is personnel performing other activities besides the mere setting up of the machines in the place of business. For example, there could be a PE when the personnel are also responsible for the operation and the maintenance of the machines for their own account in the other state.[140]

---

134 OECD, *Model Tax Convention,* Article 5, §1; OECD, *Model Tax Convention,* Commentary on Article 5, para. 6.

135 OECD, *Model Tax Convention,* Article 5, para. 4; OECD, *Model Tax Convention,* Commentary on Article 5, para. 58.

136 OECD, *Model Tax Convention,* Commentary on Article 5, paras 10–12.

137 See for more information on the 'fixed' requirement: *ibid.*, paras 6, 21–34.

138 *Ibid.*, para. 39.

139 *Ibid.*, para. 127.

140 *Ibid.*, para. 41.

57. In the case at hand, ACo's personnel are unlikely to operate the machines in country B since smart robots are perfectly capable of operating on their own. In addition, because of their smart capabilities they are less likely to require (regular) maintenance and any update to the system is likely to be performed from a distance. Consequently, ACo should not have a PE in country B. However, ACo's tax position in country B will in reality be less certain as there is local case law that is less strict and concludes to a PE in the mere presence of automatic equipment in the non-resident jurisdiction that is used for the business even if all operations of the equipment occur abroad.[141] Consequently, and since the activities performed by ACo in country B cannot be considered to be preparatory or auxiliary (i.e. ACo is performing its core activities in that country (i.e. the sale of pharmaceutical products)), it is further assumed for this exercise that ACo has a PE in country B.

58. When assessing the PE exposure of ACo in countries C and D, one should determine whether the presence of the servers or AI on those servers in those countries can constitute a PE. In this regard, the OECD discusses the situation of a server containing a website through which the company is conducting its activities. According to the OECD, a server, being tangible property, can possibly constitute a PE. On the contrary, a website by itself (which is a combination of software and electronic data) cannot constitute a PE because it cannot be considered as a place of business. Since a website is intangible property, it cannot have a 'location' that by itself can constitute a place of business.[142]

In order for a server to effectively constitute a PE, however, it should be at the disposal of the enterprise that carries on business through a website located on that server. This would, for example, be the case when the enterprise owns or leases a server on which its website is stored and operates that server.[143] However, when server capacity is merely leased to an enterprise (without that enterprise operating the server), the server would not be considered to be at the disposal of that enterprise.[144] The server should also be fixed. Regarding this criterion, the OECD mentions that, for a server, it is sufficient to assess whether the server is actually moved (rather than if it has the capacity to be moved).[145]

Although the OECD does not specifically deal with AI stored in servers, it can by analogy be derived from the above that, like a website, AI is unlikely to constitute a PE by itself. After all, AI can also be considered as intangible

141 See for example a German pipeline case explained in: K. Eicker, 'Transfer Pricing Aspects of Electronic Commerce', *International Transfer Pricing Journal*, 2001, pp. 12–13.

142 OECD, *Model Tax Convention,* Commentary on Article 5, para. 123.

143 *Ibid.*, para. 124.

144 OECD, *OECD Model Tax Convention: Revised Proposals Concerning the Interpretation and Application of Article 5 (Permanent Establishment),* (Paris: OECD Publishing, 2013), para. 132.

145 See OECD, *Model Tax Convention,* Commentary on Article 5, para. 125.

property and as a combination of software and electronic data. On the contrary, in the case at hand, the servers on which AI is stored in countries C and D are likely to constitute a PE since ACo has the servers at its disposal (i.e. ACo owns and operates the servers) and the servers are fixed as they are not intended to be moved.[146] Finally, the AI services provided through the servers cannot be said to be of a preparatory or auxiliary nature.

B. Profit Allocation to the PE

59. The existing profit allocation rules for PEs are based on the determination of functions, assets and risks. Each PE should be remunerated according to the functions its performs, the assets it has and the risks it takes.[147] These rules were created with the policy and economic objective that profits should be taxed where economic value is created (also referred to later as 'the principle of value creation').[148]

In order to determine which functions and risks the PE is performing/ assuming, the OECD puts an emphasis on the concept of 'significant people functions'. In other words, profits should be attributed to a PE based on the significant functions performed by *people* present in the PE and risks and assets should be attributed to the PE based on those functions.[149]

60. Regarding server PEs, there has been a debate as to whether this concept of significant people functions adequately takes the increased use of automation by businesses into account. In 2001, a Technical Advisory Group (TAG) at the OECD[150] issued a discussion paper that explored the applicability of the current profit allocation rules to PEs on a PE performing e-tailing activities.[151] An 'e-tailer' can be described as an enterprise that sells its products (both tangible and intangible) through a website on the internet.[152] In this report, the TAG

146 See also Oberson, *Taxing Robots*, p. 52.

147 See for more information D. Scornos, 'Cloud Computing: Difficulties in Applying Current and Proposed Nexus and Profit Allocation Rules in a Cross-Border Scenario', *Bulletin for International Taxation*, 2020, p. 5; OECD, *2010 report on the Attribution of Profits to Permanent Establishments*, (Paris: OECD Publishing, 2010).

148 Originally determined for transfer pricing purposes: see for example: OECD, *Are the Current Treaty Rules for Taxing Business Profits Appropriate for E-Commerce?*, pp. 16–17, para. 55; See also OECD, *Tax Challenges Arising from Digitalisation – Interim Report 2018: Inclusive Framework on BEPS*, (Paris: OECD Publishing, 2018), p. 167, para. 376.

149 OECD, *2010 report on the Attribution of Profits*, para. 62.

150 The Technical Advisory Group on Monitoring the Application of Existing Treaty Norms for the Taxation of Business Profits.

151 OECD, *Attribution of Profit to A Permanent Establishment Involved in Electronic Commerce Transactions – A Discussion Paper from the Technical Advisory Group on Monitoring the Application of Existing Treaty Norms for the Taxation of Business Profits*, (Paris: OECD Publishing, 2001).

152 OECD, *Discussion Paper from the Technical Advisory Group*, p. 11, paras 41–42.

came to the conclusion that a server PE of an e-tailer will most likely not be attributed a large amount of profit. The TAG came to this conclusion because of the absence of people or AI in the PE.[153] Consequently, although not explicitly mentioned, the TAG seemed to consider that the presence of AI in the PE (and not only people) might be an important consideration in determining the profits to be attributed to the PE. When AI would be present in the PE, perhaps one could come to a different conclusion.

However, this report was not further developed and when the OECD issued its final report in 2010 on the attribution of profits to PEs in general, it clearly stated that the general rules also applied to server PEs – i.e., based on significant people functions. Consequently, when the server only performs automated functions and in the absence of personnel, the assets or risks attributed to the PE are only likely to be those directly associated with the server hardware. Due to the lack of significant people functions, no significant profit would be allocated to the server PE.[154] The 2010 report no longer takes the presence or absence of AI in the PE into consideration. By taking this position, the OECD has implicitly decided that significant economic value (and consequently the realisation of profits) will always be the result of human activity.

61. Based on the latest OECD guidance, one can therefore conclude that no significant amount of income (if any) will be attributed to ACo's PEs as ACo does not employ any personnel in countries B, C or D.

4.1.2. Agency PE

62. When no fixed place of business exists, a non-resident enterprise can still have a PE in a country when there are dependent agents conducting certain activities in that country. The agents need to have the capacity to conclude contracts in the name of and on behalf of the enterprise or must be able to negotiate the most important elements of a contract.[155] In addition, like with the fixed place of business PE, the activities conducted by the agents cannot be characterised as preparatory or auxiliary in order for a PE to exist.[156]

63. In the case at hand, one should determine whether ACo could be considered to have agency PEs in countries B, C and/or D. In this respect, the OECD clarifies that the persons whose activities may create a PE may either

---

153 *Ibid.*, p. 17, para. 63.

154 OECD, *2010 report on the Attribution of Profits*, para. 66. There is criticism in the literature on this point of view with respect to functions performed by smart robots. See, e.g., Englisch, 'Digitalisation and the Future of National Tax Systems: Taxing Robots?', p. 20.

155 OECD, *Model Tax Convention*, Commentary on Article 5, para. 84.

156 *Ibid.*, para. 85.

be 'individuals or companies'.[157] In the situation of an e-tailer, the OECD has specifically stated that a website (which as previously mentioned is in essence software and electronic data) through which the activity is carried on is not in itself a 'person'. An agency PE cannot be deemed to exist by virtue of a website, acting as an agent of the enterprise.[158] Based on this reasoning, AI (also being in essence software and electronic data) will also not qualify as a person and there will be no agency PE in countries C or D.

In addition, based on a similar reasoning, ACo will not have an agency PE in country B. Even though smart robots are responsible for selling orthopaedic material to customers, they are not likely to qualify as 'persons'. As mentioned above, AI is not by itself a person and the robot without the AI is likely to be considered as mere equipment.

4.2. NECESSITY TO ADAPT THE INTERNATIONAL TAX RULES FROM A POLICY PERSPECTIVE

64. From the case study described above, it became apparent that the current international tax rules can no longer be applied in the way they were intended to. Businesses that are significantly involved in the economy of a non-resident country escape taxation in that country if they only have servers with AI or robots in that country. From a policy perspective, it has therefore been argued that the current international tax rules no longer attribute profits amongst jurisdictions based on the principle of value creation.[159]

This issue is not novel and has to a certain extent been subject to discussion since the development of the Internet.[160] However, it only received urgent international attention by governments as of the 2015 final report of the OECD: '*Addressing the Tax Challenges of the Digital Economy, Action 1*' when certain governments realised they were missing out on significant amounts of tax revenues. Following this report, the G20 mandated the OECD to come up with a global and final solution.[161] In this respect, after a series of other

157 *Ibid.*, para. 83.
158 *Ibid.*, para. 131.
159 The author is aware of the discussions among legal scholars on this principle and recognises that there are also other principles that drive the reform of the current international tax rules. However, a discussion on these legal principles would go too far for the purpose of this chapter and therefore falls outside its scope.
160 See for example: F. Horner and J. Owens, 'Tax and the Web: New Technology, Old Problems', *Bulletin for International Fiscal Documentation,* 1996, pp. 516–523; D. Tillinghast, 'The Impact of the Internet on the Taxation of International Transactions', *Bulletin for International Fiscal Documentation,* 1996, pp. 524–526; R. Avi-Yonah, 'International taxation of Electronic Commerce', *Tax Law Review,* 1997, pp. 507–556.
161 It should be noted that the EU Commission has also taken initiatives on this subject. In 2018 it introduced two proposals for a Directive containing, on the one hand, a proposal to introduce a digital services tax and, on the other hand, a proposal to introduce a significant digital

reports and drafts discussing possible solutions, the Secretariat of the OECD issued a final proposal: '*Secretariat Proposal for a "Unified Approach" under Pillar One*' which is the subject of further work. The OECD then came with a public consultation document '*Tax Challenges Arising from Digitalisation – Report on Pillar One Blueprint*', issued on 14 October 2020 (hereafter the 'Pillar One Blueprint').[162] This proposal was open for public comments until 14 December 2020 and was followed by a public consultation mid-January 2021.[163] Since then, the OECD has continued its extensive work on the Pillar One project issuing several draft reports on a fairly regular basis. However, to date, political consensus on the contents of the Pillar One project is yet to be achieved.[164]

65. For the sake of the exercise, the next part will discuss the Pillar One Blueprint and its potential application to corporations such as ACo exclusively using AI or robots in performing their services or selling their goods. Considering that the proposal is quite extensive, the analysis will only focus on the aspects of the proposal that are most relevant for the case study. In addition, this chapter will not discuss the new rules embedded in the proposal applicable to related party distributors performing baseline marketing and distribution activities. Although these are likely to be relevant for the case study at hand, these rules aim to standardise the remuneration of those distributors for simplicity reasons rather than to mitigate the international tax challenges posed by the use of AI and robots.

---

presence (i.e., a digital PE). See: European Commission, 'Proposal for a Council Directive laying down rules relating to the corporate taxation of a significant digital presence', 21 March 2018, https://eur-lex.europa.eu/legal-content/en/TXT/?uri=CELEX%3A52018PC0147 and European Commission, 'Proposal for a Council Directive on the common system of a digital services tax on revenues resulting from the provision of certain digital services', 21 March 2018, https://eur-lex.europa.eu/legal-content/EN/TXT/?uri=COM%3A2018%3A148%3AFIN. A detailed analysis of the EU initiatives, however, falls outside the scope of this chapter. See for that purpose for example: D. Scornos, 'Cloud Computing', pp. 92–94; D. Scornos and N. Bammens, 'Chapter 1. International Corporate Taxation of Digital Platforms', in B. Devolder (ed.), *The Platform Economy* (Mortsel: Intersentia, 2018), pp. 335–357.

162 OECD, *Tax Challenges Arising from Digitalisation – Report on Pillar One Blueprint*, (Paris: OECD Publishing, 2020), p. 234.

163 OECD, 'OECD/G20 Inclusive Framework on BEPS invites Public Input on the Reports on Pillar One and Pillar Two', *OECD*, 12 October 2020, https://www.oecd.org/tax/beps/oecd-g20-inclusive-framework-on-beps-invites-public-input-on-the-reports-on-pillar-one-and-pillar-two-blueprints.htm.

164 OECD, *Pillar One Blueprint*, pp. 12–13, paras 8–9. Since the contents of the most recent Pillar One draft reports have not yet been politically validated, the author has chosen, for the time being, to conduct an analysis based on the Pillar One Blueprint Report. This section will be updated accordingly once the Pillar One project will be finalised.

4.3. THE PILLAR ONE BLUEPRINT

4.3.1. Activities and Businesses Targeted by the Proposal[165]

66. The aim of the proposal is that the new rules would be applied to a broad range of businesses that generate profits through active and sustained engagement in market jurisdictions (whether or not they have physical presence there).[166] In this context, the proposal is meant to apply to two types of businesses/activities: (i) automated digital services (ADS) and (ii) consumer-facing businesses (CFB).

A. Automated Digital Services

67. Regarding ADS, the definition is comprised of three elements:[167]
- a positive list;
- a negative list; and
- a general definition

When businesses want to determine whether their activities fall within the scope of ADS, they should first identify whether their activity is listed on the positive list. If it is on the positive list, the conclusion is simple and their activity qualifies as an ADS. If on the other hand, their activity is on the negative list, the conclusion is equally simple and their activity will not be qualified as an ADS. The businesses should only consider the general definition if their activity is not listed on either the positive or the negative list.[168] The OECD introduced those lists in order to provide certainty to taxpayers for business models that are currently known. As new business models evolve and governments gain experience with these rules, the lists can be updated with new business models in order to ensure that the lists will continue to provide certainty over time.[169]

The general definition (provided the activity is not on either one of the two lists mentioned above) is described as follows: 'An automated digital service is one where:

---

165 According to the most recent OECD draft reports, the new proposed legislation will no longer differentiate between automated digital services and consumer-facing businesses. In-scope companies will simply be multinational entities with a global turnover above 20 billion euros and a profitability above 10%. See a.o., OECD, 'Statement on a Two-Pillar Solution to Address the Tax Challenges Arising from the Digitalisation of the Economy', *OECD*, 1 July 2021, p. 1.

166 *Ibid.*, p. 60, para. 165; The term 'market jurisdiction' is considered to be a jurisdiction 'where a MNE group sells its products or services or, in the case of highly digitalised businesses, provides services to users or solicits and collects data or content contribution from them'. See OECD, *Pillar One Blueprint*, p. 11, para. 6, fn. 6.

167 OECD, *Pillar One Blueprint*, p. 19–20, para. 25.

168 OECD, *Pillar One Blueprint*, p. 20, para. 25.

169 *Ibid.*, p. 23, para. 41.

- The service is
  - automated (i.e., once the system is set up the provision of the service to a particular user[170] requires minimal human involvement on the part of the service provider); and
  - digital (i.e., provided over the internet or an electronic network).'[171]

Regarding the requirement that the service has to be 'automated', the proposal further clarifies that in order to determine whether a service is provided with minimal human intervention, one should only look at the supplier of the service, without taking into account any human intervention from the side of the user (e.g. where the user may input certain information into an automated system to obtain a customised result). In addition, the definition focuses on the human involvement in the provision of the service itself and not on the human involvement necessary to create, support or update the system.[172] Finally and most importantly, in order to determine whether a service is 'automated', the test looks at whether there is an ability to scale up and provide the same type of service to new users with minimal human intervention. If the marginal cost in terms of additional human involvement of providing the same services to additional users is (almost) zero, the service will qualify as an ADS.[173]

Regarding the requirement that the service has to be 'digital', the proposal simply states that it does not distinguish between different internet or electronic network transmissions and it is also irrelevant whether or not the service provider owns, leases or otherwise controls the transmission equipment.[174]

68. In order to determine whether the AI services provided by ACo in our example fall within the category of ADS, it should first be determined whether the provided activities are included in the positive or negative list.[175] Since this does not appear to be the case, the general definition should be analysed. Based on this definition, the AI services provided by ACo are likely to fall within the category of ADS. In the first place, it is clear that the chatbot function does not

---

170 A 'user' is defined as: 'any individual or business accessing a service, but does not include the provider, or member of the same MNE group as the provider, of that service'. See OECD, *Pillar One Blueprint*, p. 38, para. 51.

171 OECD, *Pillar One Blueprint*, p. 23, para. 43.

172 *Ibid.*, p. 20, para. 27.

173 *Ibid*, p. 24, para. 43.

174 *Ibid.*, p. 25, para. 43.

175 The categories of services that are on the positive list are currently: (i) Online advertising services, (ii) Sale or other alienation of user data; (iii) Online search engines, (iv) Social media platforms; (v) Online intermediation platforms, (vi) Digital content services (vii) Online gaming, (viii) Standardised online teaching service; and (ix) Cloud computing services. The categories of services that are on the negative list are currently: (i) Customised professional services, (ii) Customised online teaching services, (iii) Online sale of goods and services other than ADS, (iv) Revenue from the sale of a physical good, irrespective of network connectivity ('Internet of Things'); and (v) Services providing access to the Internet or another electronic network. See OECD, *Pillar One Blueprint*, p. 25, para. 44 and p. 33, para. 46.

require any further human intervention besides setting up and updating the system. It can also be used simultaneously by different users with little marginal cost. In addition, it is clear that the service is provided through the internet and can therefore qualify as a digital service.

Regarding the other AI function (i.e. the preparation of customised reports based on input provided by the users), further analysis of the facts should be made. If the AI is capable of performing the function entirely on its own and can be deployed by another user with no or almost no marginal cost, it would likely qualify as an ADS. However, if significant human involvement is necessary to perform the function, the service will likely not qualify as an ADS.[176] For purposes of the exercise, however, it will be further assumed that all AI services provided by ACo qualify as ADS.

B. Consumer-facing Businesses (CFB)

69. A CFB is defined as follows:

> 'A business that supplies goods or services, directly or indirectly, that are of a type commonly sold to consumers, and/or licenses or otherwise exploits intangible property that is connected to the supply of such goods or services.'[177]

In this respect, a 'consumer' means 'an individual (whether or not the direct purchaser) who acquires a good or service for personal purposes, rather than for commercial or professional purposes'.[178] In addition, a good or service is considered as 'of a type commonly sold to consumers' when 'it is made available in ways capable of being for personal consumption'.[179] In this respect, it important to note that it suffices that a good or service is of a type commonly sold to consumers. Whether or not the good or service is actually sold to consumers or to businesses is irrelevant and both sales would be in scope.[180] It should also be noted that a service which is considered an ADS is excluded from the definition of a CFB.[181]

70. Based on the above, it is likely that ACo will be considered as a CFB with respect to its activities in country B since ACo owns a shop in the country where consumer products (e.g., orthopaedic material) are being sold.[182] The fact

---

176 See also comments made by the OECD on the performance of customised professional services: OECD, *Pillar One Blueprint*, pp. 33–34, para. 47.

177 OECD, *Pillar One Blueprint*, p. 39, para. 53.

178 *Ibid.*, p. 39, para. 53.

179 *Ibid.*, p. 39, para. 53.

180 *Ibid.*, p. 48, para. 98.

181 *Ibid.*, p. 39, para. 53.

182 The proposal considers specifically the case of pharmaceuticals. In this respect, it states that 'to the extent that medical devices are products of a type commonly sold to consumers, these will be in scope'. See OECD, *Pillar One Blueprint*, p. 40, para. 57.

that there is no personnel of ACo working in country B should not alter this conclusion since the presence of personnel does not appear to be a requirement under the definition of a CFB according to the proposal.

4.3.2. Quantitative Thresholds

71. In order to minimise compliance and administrative costs, the proposal states that the new rules should only apply to large MNEs that exceed certain thresholds even if their activities are within the scope of the proposal.[183]

In this regard, two tests need to be performed: (i) a global revenue test and (ii) a *de minimis* foreign in-scope revenue test.[184] Regarding the global revenue test, the threshold to be applied is not yet definitive but the proposal is likely to only target MNE's with an annual group consolidated gross revenue exceeding EUR 750M.[185] The *de minimis* foreign in-scope revenue test would only apply if the global revenue threshold is exceeded. This second test would have two steps. First, an MNE should determine whether the in-scope revenues (i.e., the revenues generated from ADS and CFB) exceed the threshold. Second, if their in-scope revenues exceed the threshold, the MNE would need to determine whether it earned more than the *de minimis* threshold from 'foreign' in-scope activities. How the concept of 'foreign' should be determined requires further work but the proposal favours the use of a standardised definition such as the country where the group is headquartered or the country in which the ultimate parent entity is a tax resident.[186] The amount of the *de minimis* foreign in-scope revenue threshold still needs to be agreed upon and is not mentioned in the proposal.[187]

72. For the exercise's sake, it is assumed in this chapter's case study that for ACo, both quantitative thresholds are exceeded.

4.3.3. Determination of Taxing Rights of the Market Jurisdiction[188]

73. A market jurisdiction will only have taxing rights on the profits of a non-resident enterprise when certain conditions are met (also referred to as 'nexus' or 'nexus requirements'). With respect to dividing the in-scope revenues among

[183] OECD, *Pillar One Blueprint*, p. 61, para. 171.

[184] *Ibid.*, p. 61, para. 174.

[185] *Ibid.*, pp. 61–62, paras 175–178; In this respect, it should be noted that the proposal also mentions that the threshold needs to ensure that it does not exclude a material part of residual profits otherwise in scope. How this will need to be addressed, will be the subject of further work: OECD, *Pillar One Blueprint*, p. 62, para. 180.

[186] *Ibid.*, pp. 63–64, paras 182–184.

[187] *Ibid.*, p. 64, para. 185.

[188] According to the most recent OECD draft reports, this system will be replaced by a special purpose nexus rule that would allocate Amount A (see point 4.3.4) to a market jurisdiction when the in-scope multinational enterprise derives at least 1 million euros in revenue from that jurisdiction. For smaller jurisdictions, the nexus will be set at 250 000 euros. Revenue

various jurisdictions, different criteria will be used depending on whether the situation concerns ADS or CFB:

- ADS: in this case, a market jurisdiction will have taxing rights on the profits of a non-resident enterprise when that enterprise has generated in-scope revenues of a particular amount (that is still to be determined) in that jurisdiction.[189] In-scope revenues for AI services are likely to be sourced to a particular jurisdiction when the users of that service have their ordinary residence there.[190] According to the OECD, for those businesses, an amount of revenues generated in the market jurisdiction is sufficient evidence of a significant and sustained engagement in that jurisdiction.[191]
- CFB: for these types of businesses, the OECD states that an amount of in-scope revenues generated in a jurisdiction will be relevant to confer taxing rights to that jurisdiction but it cannot be used as sole criterion.[192] Consequently, other factors (called 'plus factors') will also need to be taken into account to indicate a significant and sustained engagement with the market jurisdiction. At this time, these additional factors have not yet been determined. These could however be: the existence of physical presence in the jurisdiction in the form of a PE or other factors not related to physical presence.[193] When consumer-facing goods are sold directly to the consumer, in-scope revenue of CFB is sourced in principle to the jurisdiction of the retail storefront directly selling to consumers; or if not applicable, the jurisdiction of the final delivery address of the goods to the consumer.[194]

It should be noted that for the existence of physical presence for CFB as a plus factor, the proposal favours the application of a new standalone group-PE provision in order to ensure equality in the application of the new rules. The new standalone provision would make sure the new rules would be applied in an equal manner and would not depend on domestic PE thresholds or PE definitions that vary among DTTs.[195] The proposal further explains that the group-PE test is likely to be designed based on the basic PE principle shared between the OECD and UN MC (i.e. applied to CFB: a fixed place of business through which an in-scope CFB is wholly or partly carried on and applied to

will be sourced where goods or services are used or consumed. See a.o., OECD, 'Statement on a Two-Pillar Solution', pp.1–2.

189 *Ibid.*, p. 67, para. 201.

190 It is the author's opinion that the sourcing rule for digital content services would apply in a similar way to AI service providers: OECD, *Pillar One Blueprint*, p. 79, para. 267. In addition, it should be noted that if the ordinary residence of the user cannot be found or is unreliable, the enterprise in question can use other indicators that apply in a particular hierarchical order. For more information see: OECD, *Pillar One Blueprint*, p. 79, para. 268.

191 OECD, *Pillar One Blueprint*, p. 65, para. 190.

192 *Ibid.*, p. 65, para. 191.

193 *Ibid.*, p. 66, para. 192.

194 *Ibid.*, p. 81, paras 277–278.

195 *Ibid.*, p. 68, paras 207–209.

the MNE group). The proposal recognises that further work needs to be done with respect to other PE aspects such as the agency PE and the exclusion of preparatory or auxiliary activities.[196]

74. Interestingly, the OECD reiterates that these new nexus rules, including the group-PE provision, are not intended to affect the application of the existing PE rules for tax purposes other than the allocation of income based on the new rules. According to the OECD, the existing PE rules 'will continue to operate as at present'.[197]

75. When looking at ACo's situation, the applicability of the new rules should be assessed jurisdiction by jurisdiction. Regarding country D, it seems that ACo will have a taxable presence there when the threshold of revenues generated by the provision of AI services to users resident in that country is exceeded. On the other hand, ACo is unlikely to have a taxable presence in country C based on the new rules because it does not generate any revenues in that country (i.e., there are no users resident there). However, since the new rules do not override the existing PE rules, Aco could still have PE exposure in country C because of the existence of its server in that country (cf. *supra* part 4.1.1.). Finally, regarding country B, it is not yet clear from the proposal whether Aco will have a taxable presence there. It will depend on the additional factors that still need to be determined and on how the new group-PE test will further be designed once adopted. However, if the group-PE test is to be designed based on the basic principles of the existing PE definition, Aco could also have a taxable presence in country B (cf. *supra* part 4.1.1.) according to the new rules.[198]

4.3.4. Profit Allocation to the Non-Resident Country

76. Once it has been determined that a jurisdiction has a right to tax profits of the non-resident enterprise, it will be important to determine how much of the profits it will be able to tax. The new rules developed in this context by the OECD significantly deviate from current existing tax rules (i.e., the arm's length principle) and the profits that need to be allocated to a particular jurisdiction should be determined based on the following three steps:[199]

- In the first place the group profit of a multinational, i.e., the profit before tax as derived from the consolidated financial accounts,[200] should be divided

196 *Ibid.*, p. 69, para. 211.

197 *Ibid.*, p. 66, para. 194 and p. 69, para. 210.

198 Assuming of course that the quantitative threshold of in-scope revenue is exceeded in country B.

199 This chapter only outlines the general principles upon which the profit allocation rules are based. For further detailed information see OECD, *Pillar One Blueprint*, pp. 123–138.

200 For further details on the tax base (including the processing of tax losses) see OECD, *Pillar One Blueprint*, pp. 100–109.

into two pools, i.e. the routine profit and the residual profit. The split should be done by using a fixed percentage (that is yet to be determined).
- Once the residual profit has been established, it is then necessary to determine the split of those profits between the portion that is allocable to market jurisdictions and the portion that is allocable to other factors (e.g., trade intangibles). This calculation will be based on a fixed percentage (that is yet to be determined). The portion that is allocable to the market jurisdictions is called Amount A.
- The attribution of Amount A between the different market jurisdictions should occur based on an agreed allocation key. This allocation key would be based on in-scope revenue derived from each eligible market jurisdiction.

77. Assuming that ACo has both a taxable presence in countries B and D according to the new rules, an Amount A would need to be determined based on ACo's group profit, which would then need to be allocated to each country based on an allocation key. No part of Amount A will be allocated to country C since ACo would not have a taxable presence there according to the new rules.

4.3.5. The Issue of Double Counting[201]

78. Since the application of the new rules does not exclude the application of the existing income tax rules, an overlap between Amount A and existing arm's length based profit allocation could occur in the same jurisdiction.[202] In order to mitigate this issue, the proposal suggests amongst others the introduction of a 'marketing and distribution profits safe harbour'. This safe harbour would consider the profit already subject to tax in the market jurisdiction under existing tax rules and the allocation of the residual profit to the same jurisdiction based on the new rules (i.e., called the 'safe harbour return'). If there is an amount of residual profit already taxed in the market jurisdiction based on the existing tax rules, Amount A would be limited to the amount of residual profit that is not captured by the existing rules (i.e., equal to the safe harbour return minus profit already taxed).[203]

79. This safe harbour rule will potentially be relevant for ACo's business in country B since it sells orthopaedic material to consumers located there. In order to avoid double counting, the profits that need to be attributed based on the new rules will be limited to the safe harbour return minus the profits already subject to tax in country B. However, as mentioned above, since ACo's shop in country

[201] It follows from the OECD's most recent work that a safe harbour rule will be kept. Further details still need to be published. See a.o., OECD, 'Statement on a Two-Pillar Solution', p. 2.

[202] OECD, *Pillar One Blueprint*, p. 132, para. 528.

[203] *Ibid.*, p. 133, para. 533. For the exact details of this safe harbour rule see OECD, *Pillar One Blueprint*, pp. 134–135, paras 535–540.

B is solely operated by smart robots and there is an absence of significant people functions, the profits taxable in country B based on the existing tax rules are likely to be low (see *supra* part 4.1.1.) and the overlap between the profits attributed based on the existing rules and the new rules will likely be limited.

4.3.6. Conclusion

80. The OECD's work on mitigating the issues posed by AI has been commendable so far. The proposal clearly includes services provided by AI (under ADS) and the positive and negative lists (that are to be updated from time to time) may provide for more tax certainty. However, the application of the proposed rules on the use of smart robots is less clear as it does not (yet?) envisage a scenario in which smart robots are capable of fully replacing humans in certain circumstances.

81. Regarding the sourcing rules and profit allocation rules, the OECD has undertaken substantial work in the design and application thereof. However, the new rules still lack a uniform policy objective or at least multiple coherent policy objectives. On the one hand, more tax revenues (i.e., Amount A) are allocated to market jurisdictions based on rules that completely depart from the arm's length principle while, on the other hand, the new proposed rules are still intended to coexist in some manner with existing PE rules, which on their turn are entirely based on the arm's length principle. In addition, the coexistence of those rules currently seems quite complex and although the OECD has put much effort in designing methods to eliminate double taxation, it is debatable whether the application of both rules will eventually achieve the desired result of simplicity and tax certainty.

4.4. IMPLICATIONS OF ALLOCATING LEGAL PERSONALITY TO ROBOTS ON THE APPLICABILITY OF INTERNATIONAL TAX RULES

82. Assuming that smart robots should be allocated legal personality (see *supra* part 3.3.3.), this would also have many implications in an international context.

83. Looking at ACo, the question whether it would have a PE in country B will not be easy to answer. If legal personality is attributed to smart robots, there could be an issue with the criterion 'at the disposal of' required to conclude to a PE. If smart robots become more autonomous, can it be said that they are still under control of ACo and therefore at its disposal? In principle, a legal entity should not be considered as a PE, unless it remains under the control of another entity, which uses its infrastructure in order to carry on its activities.[204]

[204] Oberson, *Taxing Robots*, p. 53.

It should, however, be noted that this issue will be mitigated by the new rules proposed by the Pillar One Blueprint. This proposal focuses on the type of activities that an enterprise performs rather than on the way in which those activities are conducted (e.g., PE, subsidiary or even no physical presence).

84. The allocation of legal personality to robots could potentially also have implications for the agency PE rule. Although the OECD strictly indicates that the agency PE can only apply to persons, it could be argued that there would be a thin line between a person and a smart robot for which the agency PE rule could, nevertheless, apply.[205] Such an idea is not new and has been discussed in the past by different authors in the context of a software agent.[206] A software agent is a software programme that operates on a website and which is used to conduct sales.[207]

85. Finally, allocating legal personality to robots could raise a myriad of other questions as well.[208] Is that smart robot to be considered as a resident of the country in which it is located?[209] If so, would it be subject to PIT in that country? If this would be the case, the company would not only incur an additional compliance burden in the filing of payroll tax returns but also in the calculation of potential imputed income in another country. In addition, it would need to be determined whether the smart robot would obtain legal personality comparable to a person or to a corporation. This distinction is important because it could lead to absurd situations if a smart robot would be considered to have legal personality similar to a corporation. In case a company employs 50 robots in a particular country, it would legally have 50 subsidiaries in that country which does not make any sense. In addition, the distribution of profits of the robot to its owner(s) would potentially trigger withholding tax on dividends, which is also an unintended side effect.

5. OPPORTUNITIES CREATED BY AI AND ROBOTS

86. While AI and smart robots present many issues from a tax perspective, they also present opportunities for tax authorities, tax practitioners and corporations to become more efficient.

---

205 Oberson, *Taxing Robots*, pp. 53–54.

206 See for example: A. Cockfield, W. Hellerstein, R. Millar and C. Waerzeggers, *Taxing the global digital commerce*, 3rd edn (Alphen aan den Rijn: Kluwer Law International, 2013), pp. 122–123; B. Schaefer, 'International Taxation of Electronic Commerce Income: A Proposal to Utilize Software Agents for Source-Based Taxation', *Santa Clara Computer & High Technology Law Journal*, 2000, pp. 111–140.

207 Schaefer, 'International Taxation of Electronic Commerce Income', p. 130.

208 See also e.g., Chand, Kostic and Reis, 'Taxing artificial Intelligence and Robots', pp. 738–739.

209 See for example the analysis made by Oberson: Oberson, *Taxing Robots*, pp. 150–152.

5.1. OPPORTUNITIES FOR TAX AUTHORITIES

87. AI presents opportunities for tax authorities in a variety of ways. Firstly, it can identify potential tax fraud in even the most difficult cases.[210] AI is able to analyse large amounts of data and efficiently find patterns in those data that would otherwise remain obscured.[211] In this context, AI can also be used to scan social media profiles to identify tax fraud or other unlawful practices.[212] The IRS in the US has already purchased such AI and France has equally announced plans to do so.[213]

88. Aside from fraud, tax authorities are looking to implement AI for other purposes as well. AI could be used to protect their databases, which contain a significant amount of information on different taxpayers.[214] It could also be used to provide better services to taxpayers. For example, the Australian Tax Office (ATO) has integrated a chatbot called Alex which answers basic questions from taxpayers. The more complex questions are redirected to personnel.[215] In Belgium, such a chatbot, called Finny, is also relied on to answer questions on the MyRent application (i.e., an application that can be used to register a rental agreement).[216]

89. Finally, AI can also offer solutions for tax authorities that want to ensure real-time tax compliance and collection. In Hungary, for example, an increase

---

210 B. Van Volkenburgh, 'Artificial Intelligence and Taxes: 8 Ways it's Being Used', *Crowdreason*, 11 September 2019, point 5, https://www.crowdreason.com/blog/artificial-intelligence-tax.

211 D. Pianko, 'Machine-Learning Technology can serve as a valuable tool for tax auditors, but what is the best Technique?', *Nextgov*, 27 April 2018, https://www.nextgov.com/ideas/2018/04/using-artificial-intelligence-reduce-tax-fraud/147807/. This article also provides for different techniques tax authorities could use to detect fraud.

212 A. Kovacevic, 'AI is Changing How We Pay Taxes, and How They're Collected Too', *Readwrite*, 22 March 2019, https://readwrite.com/2019/03/22/ai-is-changing-how-we-pay-taxes-and-how-theyre-collected-too/; J. Rohrlich, 'The IRS wants to use social media to catch tax cheats', *Quartz*, 26 December 2018, https://qz.com/1507962/the-irs-wants-to-use-facebook-and-instagram-to-catch-tax-evaders/.

213 M. Leonardis, 'Artifical Inteligence to Help Resource-Strapped IRS More Efficiently Identify Tax Crimes', *aronsonllc*, 26 April 2019, https://aronsonllc.com/artificial-intelligence-to-help-resource-strapped-irs-more-efficiently-identify-tax-crimes/#:~:text=The%20IRS%20is%20now%20using,identity%20theft%2C%20and%20other%20noncompliance.&text=The%20IRS%20plans%20to%20mine,and%20even%20social%20media%20accounts; Angelique Chrisafis, 'French Plan to Scan Social Media for Tax Fraud Causes Alarm', *The Guardian*, 1 October 2019, https://www.theguardian.com/world/2019/oct/01/french-plan-to-scan-social-media-for-tax-causes-alarm.

214 Kovacevic, 'AI is Changing How We Pay Taxes'.

215 TPA Global, 'Tax Authorities Are Powering Processes With Artificial Intelligence (AI)', *TPA Global*, 16 September 2019, https://www.tpa-global.com/nieuws/2019-09-16/tax-authorities-are-powering-processes-with-artificial-intelligence-ai.

216 The following link provides direct access to the chatbot: https://financien.belgium.be/sites/default/files/chatbot/chatbot_NL.html.

of 10%-23% of VAT revenue was obtained in certain sectors through the use of online cash registers and special software implemented by the National Tax and Customs Administration (NTCA).[217]

5.2. OPPORTUNITIES FOR TAX PRACTITIONERS

90. AI can also present many opportunities for tax practitioners. For example, one advantage of using AI is that it could be designed in such a way to analyse raw data received from a client. Clients would not need to adapt the available data (e.g., expenses, general ledger, accounts payable, etc.) for tax purposes considering that AI would be able to analyse this data without prior adjustments.[218] In addition, AI can be used to perform other time-consuming tasks such as benchmarking studies for transfer pricing purposes. Instead of having people manually screen databases for companies that are similar and perform similar activities, AI can perform those tasks more efficiently and autonomously.[219]

However, there remains some scepticism regarding the use of AI in tax practice, both from tax professionals and their clients. In the first place, there is a perception that the outcome produced by AI may not be entirely reliable and some clients might need reassurance that a human specialist has reviewed and confirmed the results. In addition, some practitioners may fear that they will no longer have any added value when implementing AI. However, according to Deloitte, AI will not replace tax advisors, but it will most likely be used as a tool that can assist tax advisors in their jobs. Tax issues are often complex and are characterised by a unique fact pattern, which makes them almost impossible to efficiently solve by only using AI. In this regard, AI would rather be used to efficiently solve certain aspects of a larger problem (e.g., low-level tasks) allowing the tax professionals to focus on the more challenging parts. In this respect, AI should rather be seen as part of the team.[220]

---

217 TPA Global, 'Tax Administrations Raise The Playing Field With Technological Solutions', *TPA Global,* 2018, https://www.tpa-global.com/nieuws/2018-07-18/tax-administrations-raise-the-playing-field-with-technological-solutions.

218 Deloitte, 'Artificial Intelligence – Entering the world of tax', p. 5; See also on the use of automated ledger review tools: EY, 'How AI looks to upend the tax function's 80/20 rule', *EY,* 17 April 2019, https://www.ey.com/en_gl/tax/how-ai-looks-to-upend-the-tax-function-s-80-20-rule.

219 Van Volkenburgh, 'Artificial Intelligence and Taxes', point 7; See for more information: Deloitte, '16 Artificial Intelligence projects from Deloitte – Practical cases of applied AI', *Deloitte,* 2018, pp. 12–13, https://www2.deloitte.com/content/dam/Deloitte/nl/Documents/innovatie/deloitte-nl-innovatie-artificial-intelligence-16-practical-cases.pdf; For even more applications of AI for tax practitioners see also: PwC, 'How Tax is Leveraging AI – Including Machine Learning – In 2019', *PwC,* 2019, https://www.pwc.com/cb/en/services/pdf/how-tax-leveraging-ai-machine-learning-2019.pdf.

220 Deloitte, 'Artificial Intelligence – Entering the world of tax', pp. 4–5.

5.3. OPPORTUNITIES FOR CORPORATIONS

91. Finally, AI presents many opportunities for corporations operating in the tax sector. It can address accounting needs and support decisions with information that was previously not available. In addition, it can extract relevant information from all types of raw data making the filling in of the corporate tax return easier, faster and more efficient.[221] Furthermore, AI can be used by corporations to identify areas in which they can use tax incentives and deductions.[222] Nowadays, AI is even able to calculate the probability of being audited based on potential sales and expanses in the upcoming year by analysing internal tax data and comparing it to available information on the broader economy. As futuristic as it may sound, AI is even capable of analysing the effect of the likely outcome of a local or national election on a business tax risk.[223]

6. CONCLUSION

92. The opportunities presented by AI and smart robots in the tax world are countless. All relevant actors, in particular tax authorities, corporations and tax practitioners, can benefit from AI as it makes their business more efficient, reducing the need to have low-level tasks performed by people and gaining significant time in fulfilling their functions. However, although there are many benefits of AI, significant tax challenges arise both at a national and an international level.

93. On a national level, there are concerns from certain economic scholars that AI and smart robots will significantly disrupt the labour market at least in the short term and will create inequality of income. Consequently, those scholars propose to design and introduce a tax on AI and smart robots (so-called 'robot tax'). Even if a general consensus that such a robot tax should be implemented can be reached, there remain many challenges with regard to its design. An adequate definition of a 'robot' would need to be established and the taxpayer (i.e., the corporation or the robot itself?) should be determined. It is the author's opinion that a tax on robots presents too many challenges and that a solution should, therefore, rather be sought in alternatives such as a tax on capital, although the introduction of such a tax can also be questioned. It should also be noted that there are currently no plans in Belgium to introduce a robot tax

221 See for example the solutions provided by Dlabs: P. Majewski, '3 A.I. solutions for tax and accounting that will help you keep your business alive', *Dlabs*, 13 August 2018, https://medium.com/dlabs-pl/3-a-i-solutions-for-tax-and-accounting-that-will-help-you-keep-your-business-alive-e76627cb6ece.

222 Van Volkenburgh, 'Artificial Intelligence and Taxes', point 6.

223 Majewski, '3 A.I. solutions for tax and accounting'.

although there have been proposals from the Walloon Region in the past. The use of AI and smart robots in Belgium, especially in Flanders, seems to be rather incentivised than penalised.

94. Finally, there are also challenges on an international level. By using AI and smart robots, corporations are able to perform their activities abroad without the need of establishing any physical presence in those countries. Since our current international tax system is built upon the requirement of a physical presence, many countries in which businesses perform their activities are no longer able to tax those activities. This leads to a sense of inequality in the division of the tax base amongst different countries. In order to mitigate this issue, the OECD has been mandated to design a new international tax system that would restore equality amongst jurisdictions. In the Pillar One Blueprint, the OECD has already made significant progress. However, this proposal will significantly change in the near future (following from a Statement made on 1 July 2021 and more recent draft reports). At the moment of writing, the final rules have yet to be determined and it is therefore still unclear whether the principles of tax certainty and simplicity will be achieved.

CHAPTER 11

ROBOTISATION AND LABOUR LAW

The Dark Factory: the Dark Side of Work?

Simon Taes*

1. INTRODUCTION

1. At the shareholders meeting in 2016, Elon Musk presented the Tesla factory as 'the machine that makes the machine'. He referred to this machine-making machine in the context of Tesla's manufacturing plant that would not need much human involvement. The goal was to produce cars by using smart robots and with as few employees as possible on the assembly line. However, the production of these cars incurred serious delays. In 2018, Elon Musk had to admit that he had relied too much on the capabilities of robots and that 'humans are underrated'.[1] Another example of underestimating human input in robotised work environments is the robotic production of Adidas shoes. The company had to shut down these factories after two years because the robots could not adjust to the flexible production rate. It was more difficult to readjust these robots than to rely on human workers instead.

2. These examples express the idea of the so-called 'Dark Factory', which refers to manufacturing plants using intelligent machines and systems that require hardly any involvement of human operators.[2] The concept appeals to the image of a factory that operates in the dark without any lights. However, the examples mentioned above show that human workers are still needed in these robotised work environments. This is taken as guiding principle throughout this entire chapter. When it comes to robots that replace human workers, this chapter argues that fully automated working environments cannot be created

---

* Doctoral researcher labour law, KU Leuven Institute for Labour Law.

1 M. Ruskowski, T. Legler, M. Beetz and G. Bartels, 'Editorial Special Issue on Smart Production', *Künstliche Intelligenz*, 2019, vol. 33, no. 2, p. 111.

2 E. Ozlemel, 'Intelligent Manufacturing Systems, Smart Factories and Industry 4.0: A General Overview', in K. Kumar, D. Zindani and J. P. Davim (eds.), *Digital Manufacturing and Assembly Systems in Industry 4.0* (Boca Raton: Taylor & Francis Group, 2019), p. 21.

with the current technological capabilities of robots. On the contrary, robots will perform only a part of the tasks of human workers. Therefore, human workers and robots will have to work more closely together. This will have an impact on the relationship between them. As will be discussed below, this evolving human-robot relationship will change the working conditions for workers and will affect the employment relationship.

3. This chapter does not disregard the fact that robots have been part of manufacturing plants for several decades. Nevertheless, it will be argued that the view of the robot in the workplace as a huge robot arm in the assembly line will soon become outdated or might already be outdated. New types of robots will increasingly be introduced in the workplace, and they will be used in several sectors. Social robots could support medical staff in hospitals and health services or exoskeletons could provide more strength to construction workers. As a consequence of the COVID-19 pandemic, mobile robots are increasingly being implemented in hospitals, for instance to transport medicines and food or to sterilise rooms in order to prevent infections and contact between people.[3] This new generation of robots will show an improved flexibility and mobility by using enhanced artificial intelligent systems, which will lead to more autonomous or smarter robots than the current robots in the workplace. This changing worker-robot interaction will entail some opportunities but also new risks.

The aim of this chapter is to provide a brief overview of the opportunities of and concerns about these autonomous robots from the perspective of labour law. More precisely, this chapter explains the social consequences of these robots in working environments. This chapter considers social consequences as the implications for workers and, more in general, for employment in the robot age. In order to achieve this objective, doctrinal views in labour law on the implications of intelligent technologies and robots in the workplace are examined and summarised in this chapter. From a labour law perspective, scholarship is mainly focused on the impact of autonomous robots on employment, working conditions (such as health and safety and responsibility) and the protection of fundamental rights of workers (e.g., right to privacy and equal treatment).

Because of the complex and diverse nature of these implications, this chapter starts by positioning technological innovations within the broader framework of the fourth industrial revolution and by clarifying the concept of robotisation (part 2). This is followed by an explanation of the consequences of introducing intelligent robots in the workplace in terms of employment (part 3) and the employment relationship (part 4). These consequences are also applied to Belgian labour law and some recommendations for Belgian labour law are mentioned. Therefore, these recommendations aim at enlightening the dark factory and bringing Rifkin's 'techno-paradise' to the robotised workplace. Finally, this

[3] M. Cardona, F. Cortez, A. Palacios and K. Cerros, 'Mobile Robots Application Against Covid-19 Pandemic', *IEEE ANDESCON* 2020, p. 1.

chapter concludes with the role of labour law in robotised workplaces from the perspective of a human-centred agenda (part 5).

2. THE APPEARANCE OF ROBOTISATION

2.1. TOWARDS A FOURTH INDUSTRIAL REVOLUTION

4. Scholarship in labour law woke up from its AI winter sleep by the call of Klaus Schwab in 2016. He introduced the German paradigm of Industry 4.0 at the World Economic Forum. According to Schwab, this 'fourth industrial revolution' is characterised by 'much more ubiquitous and mobile internet, by smaller and more powerful sensors that have become cheaper, and by artificial intelligence and machine learning'.[4] The scope of Industry 4.0 is much wider than only smart and connected machines. It is also about breakthroughs in the fields of nanotechnologies and quantum computing, e.g., 3D printing, AI, the internet of things, nanotechnology, biotechnology, materials science, energy storage.[5] The core aspect of the fourth industrial revolution is the fusion and interaction of technologies across the physical, digital and biological domains.[6] According to a report, published by the European Commission, this industry 4.0 framework should be complemented by an Industry 5.0 approach in order to achieve societal goals, such as the well-being of workers and the respect for the boundaries of our planet. Industry 5.0 highlights, in this respect, the importance to support industry 'in its long-term service to humanity within planetary boundaries' and emphasises the need to adopt a human-centric approach.[7]

Schwab argues that this will lead to a 'profound and systemic change' in society, which explains why he refers to a new 'revolution'. These societal changes are of an economic, social and cultural nature. With regard to the topic of labour law, two societal changes are primarily relevant: the impact of new technologies on the labour market and the changes in the nature of work by technological innovations.[8] Both societal changes are examined in this chapter. This dichotomy, as highlighted by Schwab, is used to structure the possible influences of AI, robots and other new technologies on labour law and to explain which challenges labour law will have to meet in the robotisation age.

---

4 K. Schwab, *The Fourth Industrial Revolution* (Geneva: World Economic Forum, 2016), p. 12.

5 L. Soete, 'Destructive creation: Explaining the productivity paradox in the digital age', in M. Neufeind, J. O'Reilly and F. Ranft (eds.), *Work in the digital age: Challenges of the Fourth Industrial Revolution* (London-New York: Rowman & Littlefield, 2018), p. 30.

6 Schwab, *The Fourth Industrial Revolution*, p. 12.

7 M. Breque L. De Nul and A. Petridis, *Industry 5.0 Towards a sustainable, human-centric and resilient European industry*, (Luxemburg: Publications Office of the European Union, 2021), p. 8 and 15.

8 Schwab, The Fourth Industrial Revolution, p. 49.

2.2. ROBOTISATION: THE NEXT STAGE IN THE DIVISION OF LABOUR

5. This broader debate on the fourth industrial revolution shows the relevance of the interaction between technology and labour. It also shows that this revolution will affect the quantity (employment) as well as the quality (nature) of jobs. When describing the effect of technologies on jobs, the use of the term 'automation' or 'robotisation' is more common than Industry 4.0. That is the reason why this chapter will refer to these concepts to identify the impact of new technologies on labour law.

These concepts can be situated in the context of the division of labour between humans and machines. Division of labour, in general terms, refers to the separation and allocation of tasks to different persons cooperating in an economic process.[9] This has a technical as well as a social attribute of economic activity.[10] It aims at the coordination of workers as social beings and it allows to improve efficiency of labour input.[11] Therefore, a trade-off between technological change and a division of labour can be identified. Technological change has an impact on the evolution of the division of labour because it changes the production process and the required types of labour input directly. At the same time, the division of labour could also be considered as a key enabler of technological change by breaking down production processes and identifying problems and potential technological solutions.[12] It is possible to identify four different phases within this process. These phases show some overlap with the four industrial revolutions, but they are situated in different time periods.

6. The first phase concerns 'mechanisation' in which steam engines were introduced in manufacturing plants at the end of the 18th century. This is followed by the 'automation' period, situated in the second half of the 20th century. Automation processes are characterised by the introduction of 'automatic machines'. The major difference with machines from the first phase is that automatic machines can execute tasks independently from their human operator. However, the movements of automatic machines are still preprogramed by the use of software codes and run through a sequence of actions.[13]

7. The next phase, 'digitalisation', refers to the 'conversion of an analogue signal containing information (e.g., sound, image, text, etc.) into binary bits'

---

9 E. Fernandez-Macias, *Automation, digitalization and platforms: Implications for work and employment* (Luxembourg: Publications Office of the European Union, 2018), p. 5.

10 *Ibid.*

11 *Ibid.*

12 *Ibid.*, p. 6.

13 A. Winfield, *Robotics: A Very Short Introduction* (Oxford: Oxford University Press, 2012), p. 12.

by the use of information and communication technologies.[14] Through this digitalisation process, cognitive tasks of human workers could be conducted by machines (i.e., computers and software) for the first time. In addition, these ICT-technologies enable and reinforce many other technologies, which can be situated in the fourth phase. This fourth phase is characterised by the fusion of several new technologies and the incorporation of these technologies into physical objects. This convergence of the physical and virtual world will increasingly lead to machines that are connected with each other within a network, yet are able to act autonomously. This will lead to a new redistribution of labour between humans and machines because these 'smart' robots could replace cognitive skills as well as muscular strength of human workers.[15] Through this incorporation of 'smart technologies', these systems represent the physical embodiment of artificial intelligence.[16] As artificial intelligence will be integrated in physical devices, 'robotisation' is the most appropriate term for this fourth phase in the division of labour. When examining the characteristics of robots, artificial intelligence is considered as one of the aspects of a robot. Scholarship traditionally distinguishes three characteristics of robots: sensors, artificial intelligence and a physical component (actuators).[17] Indeed, the behaviour of robots has to be derived equally from both their morphology and AI.[18] Moreover, these characteristics are clearly mentioned in the Resolution on Civil Law Rules on Robotics of the European Parliament (hereinafter: 'Robot Resolution'): '(1) the capacity to acquire autonomy through sensors and/or by exchanging data with its environment (inter-connectivity) and the analysis of those data; (2) the capacity to learn through experience and interaction; (3) the form of the robot's physical support; (4) the capacity to adapt its behaviour and actions to the environment'.[19]

8. To explain the relationship between these four phases, an automation continuum could be proposed. This continuum represents a timeline with the four mentioned phases in the division of labour. Robotisation could then be considered as the final section of AI-enabled automation processes. Robotisation is described as 'the application in the operational process of a set of physical machines with 'senses' (sensors, such as cameras) and limbs (actuators, such as moving arms and grippers), driven by (potentially self-learning) software to

---

14 SERV, *Vision statement: the transition to a digital society,* p. 10, https://cutt.ly/rymnzBa.

15 *Ibid.*, p. 11.

16 I. Revolidis and A. Dahi, 'The Peculiar Case of the Mushroom Picking Robot: Extra-contractual Liability in Robotics', in M. Corrales, M. Fenwick and N. Forgo (eds.), *Robotics, AI and the Future of Law* (Singapore: Springer Nature Singapore, 2018), p. 60.

17 R. Murphy, *Introduction to AI robotics* (London: MIT Press, 2000), p. 5.

18 Winfield, *Robotics: A Very Short Introduction,* p. 11.

19 Annex, Resolution European Parliament no. A8-0005/2017, 16 February 2017 with recommendations to the Commission on Civil Law Rules on Robotics, *OJ. C.* 18 July 2018, no. 252, p. 252.

perform a range of actions that were previously performed by human workers'.[20] This definition of robotisation allows to make a distinction with automation processes of the seventies. Automation is a process that is repeated by a machine, whereas robotisation is accomplished by means of robots that act autonomously in the sense of making autonomous choices even if they interact with a human in taking that decision.[21]

9. However, robots which operate completely autonomously do not feature in present robotisation processes. Therefore, it remains difficult to estimate where technological innovations will take robotisation. There are certain engineering bottlenecks that currently prevent robots from operating with full autonomy. Two well-known paradoxes are often cited in this context, namely Polanyi's paradox (humans know more than they can tell) and Moravec's paradox (computers easily learn complex intelligent or cognitive tasks but it is difficult or impossible to give them the sensory-motor capabilities of a one-year-old[22]). Therefore, humans can still learn faster than robots in certain areas, as it is hard for robots to continuously learn new tasks for short periods of time. That is why robots are less flexible than humans when it comes to learning new skills and adapting to new and unstructured environments. Thus, human labour will remain necessary and essential during the robotisation era. This assumption is confirmed by the 'robot'-factories of Tesla and Adidas and also by a Japanese hotel that relied solely on robot personnel. It had to hire human workers after one year. Robotisation is not just about replacing human labour, it is just as much about the increased cooperation between man and robot. Hence, the growing autonomy of the robot does not necessarily lead to the replacement of human labour, but it will rather lead to complementing human labour.

Therefore, the question remains how this autonomy of robots will be reached and to what extent they will really be independent from human operators. Several technological innovations of the last decade(s) might facilitate the development of these autonomous robots. Most of these innovations contribute to the artificial intelligence aspect of a robot. They allow the robot to independently process the received data. Examples are advances in machine-learning, data mining and internet of things. These technologies give meaning to the signals that are captured by the sensors of the robots. These sensors will be able to capture more data and to capture them more accurately. Cameras, microphones and lasers will be capable of receiving signals in better quality. Other sensors will support a real-time transfer of the received data and communication with other robots or systems, e.g., better connection to WiFi or mobile internet (5G-network). With regard to the physical appearance of the robot, more flexibility could be reached

20 C. Freese and R. Dekker, *Samen werken met robots* (Amsterdam: De Burcht, 2018), p. 12.
21 J. Turner, *Robot Rules* (Cham: Palgrave Macmillan, 2019), p. 17.
22 H. Moravec, *Mind Children* (Cambridge – London: Harvard University Press, 1988), p. 15.

by the use of 3D-printing and new materials. This will lead to robots that are lighter and more mobile.

Hence, the representation of the static robot next to the manufacturing line will become outdated. The robots in the robotisation era will work amongst human workers. This will change the interaction between a human worker and a robot in a profound way. Within this context, it could be more appropriate to refer to 'cobots' or collaborative robots when humans work together with robots to complete specific tasks.

3. SOCIAL IMPLICATIONS OF ROBOTISATION

10. These autonomous robots will present opportunities and risks for employees and employers when they will be introduced in the workplace. This will create new questions and challenges for labour law to deal with these risks. The next parts will explain the effects of the application of data-analytic technologies, such as machine learning and data mining, in the workplace. This leads to a shift from traditional management approaches to the so-called data or algorithmic management.[23] However, the essential issue of robotisation is the shift from systems running on a sequence of pre-programmed steps to systems that act on the basis of data and experiences. It emphasises the premise that physical systems will no longer follow clearly defined instructions (e.g., software codes). This part will discuss the social implications of robotisation and how this technological shift could affect the employment relationship between workers and their employers. Two categories of implications of robotisation can be distinguished: the impact on employment and on working conditions. Both implications are also mentioned in the Robot Resolution.

3.1. THE 'ROBOTISED' LABOUR MARKET: THREE HYPOTHESES

11. There exists a lot of scholarship concerning the impact of technological innovations on employment. Hammershøj analysed this literature and distinguished three scenarios for future employment in the context of the division of labour between humans and machines.

The first scenario represents the hypothesis of job reduction in which technological innovations will have a negative impact on employment. It is based on the idea that the pace at which robotics replace jobs is higher than the

[23] A.R. Barzilay, 'Data analytics at work: a view from Israel on employee privacy and equality in the age of datadriven employment management', *Comparative Labor Law and Policy Journal*, 2019, vol. 40, no. 3, pp. 421–422.

pace at which humans can develop new skills. In this scenario, the application of robotics would eventually lead to mass unemployment.[24] This scenario could be considered as perhaps the oldest one. In the 1930's, economist John Maynard Keynes already proposed the concept of technological unemployment. This is 'the unemployment due to our discovery of means of economising the use of labour outrunning the pace at which we can find new uses for labour'.[25] According to Keynes, technological unemployment is only a temporary phase of maladjustment between new production methods and the use of human labour. This fear of mass unemployment already occurred in the context of the first Industrial Revolution, causing the so-called Luddite riots.[26] As robots replace human workers, they could be considered as a new method to organise businesses and workplaces. Therefore, this pessimistic scenario seems possible in the context of robotisation. Economists found evidence that the application of industrial robots led to less employment of low-skilled workers and to a lesser extent middle-skilled workers between 1993 and 2007.[27] While technological innovation leads to greater productivity in this hypothesis, technology will, nevertheless, replace human labour on a large scale, which means that technological innovation leads to less work and an imbalanced distribution of prosperity. This in turn results in lower purchasing power and consumption, and hence dwindling profits and markets.[28]

The second scenario represents a positive hypothesis in which robotics and artificial intelligence will create more jobs and mass employment in a digitalised and creative society.[29] A study, commissioned by Cedefop, also highlights the positive impact of digitalisation and robotisation. It states that initial labour-saving effects tend to be substituted by price or income effects, such as lower prices of goods and the development of new goods. It reiterates that the spread of ICT-technologies created many new jobs, such as ICT professionals and technicians. Regardless of their contested status in terms of labour protection, digitalisation processes also led to new online forms of work or crowd work in the so-called collaborative economy.[30] This optimistic hypothesis could

24 L.G. Hammershøj, 'The new division of labor between human and machine and its educational implications', *Technology in Society,* 2019, vol. 59, no. 101142, p. 5.

25 J.M. Keynes, *Essays in Persuasion* (New York: Harcourt Brace, 1932), p. 360.

26 C.B. Frey and M.A. Osborne, 'The future of employment: How susceptible are jobs to computerisation?', *Technological Forecasting & Social Change,* 2017, vol. 114, p. 255.

27 G. Graetz and G. Michaels, 'Robots at work', CEP Discussion paper, no. 1335, 2015, p. 21n http://cep.lse.ac.uk/pubs/download/dp1335.pdf.

28 L. Kool, R. van Est, I. van Keulen and A. van Waes, 'Introduction', in R. van Est and L. Kool (eds.), *Working on the robot society* (The Hague: Rathenau Instituut, 2015), pp. 28–29.

29 Hammershøj, 'The new division of labor between human and machine and its educational implications', p. 5.

30 Cedefop, *Insights into skill shortages and skill mismatch: learning from Cedefop's European skills and jobs survey* (Luxembourg: Publications Office, 2018), p. 20, https://www.cedefop.europa.eu/files/3075_en.pdf. Collaborative economy is described 'as to business models where activities are facilitated by collaborative platforms that create an open marketplace for the

be achieved by technological innovations leading to greater productivity and cheaper products, which in turn brings higher consumption and growth on the market and eventually more jobs.[31]

The third scenario is the hypothesis of polarisation of the labour market. This means that new technologies and artificial intelligence will replace mostly white-collar jobs and will hollow out the so-called middle class.[32] This scenario of job polarisation is mentioned in the well-known article of Frey and Osborn. These authors estimated the probability of automation for more than 700 occupations. For this purpose, they looked into the key features of occupations and the variety of tasks involved. The authors then assessed to what extent the tasks could be subject to automation. Their results confirm the labour market polarisation hypothesis because they estimate growing employment in high and low-wage occupations and declining employment in middle-income jobs.[33] In addition, these results are in line with older studies that showed evidence of job polarisation in the last decades of the 20th century due to the replacement of human labour by technology.[34] This scenario could, therefore, lead to larger gaps between the incomes of workers and more inequality on the labour market.[35] In this regard, there is still an ongoing debate questioning why job polarisation occurs.[36] Some authors argue that technology may generate demand for high-skilled workers, but it will not replace jobs with non-routine and location-specific tasks even if they are low paid.[37] Other authors argue that a distinction between automatable and non-automatable jobs is now more appropriate because recent technologies (e.g., machine learning and big data) will also replace non-routine tasks through advanced robots with enhanced sensors and manipulators.[38]

---

temporary usage of goods or services often provided by private individuals' (e.g., Deliveroo and Uber). See also Communication from the Commission to the European Parliament, the Council, the European Economic and Social Committee and the Committee of the Regions, A European Agenda for the Collaborative Economy, COM/2016/0356 final. V. De Stefano and A. Aloisi, *European legal framework for digital labour platforms* (Luxembourg: European Commission, 2018), p. 7, https://bit.ly/3j2WVeV.

31 Kool et al., 'Introduction', p. 28.

32 Hammershøj, 'The new division of labor between human and machine and its educational implications', p. 5.

33 C.B. Frey and M.A. Osborne, The future of employment: How susceptible are jobs to computerisation?, p. 267.

34 M. Goos and A. Manning, 'Lousy and Lovely Jobs: The Rising Polarization of Work in Britain', *The Review of Economics and Statistics*, 2007, vol. 89, no. 1, p. 126.

35 *Ibid.*, p. 129.

36 *Ibid.*, p. 118.

37 Goos and Manning, 'Lousy and Lovely Jobs: The Rising Polarization of Work in Britain', p. 118; J. Berg, 'Labour market institutions: the building blocks of just societies', in J. Berg (ed.), *Labour Markets, Institutions and Inequality: Building Just Societies in the 21st Century* (Cheltenham: Edward Elgar Publishing, 2015), p. 47.

38 Frey and Osborne, The future of employment: How susceptible are jobs to computerisation?, pp. 260–262; G. Lordan, *Robots at work A report on automatable and non-automatable employment shares in Europe*, Luxembourg: Publications Office of the European Union, 2018, p. 9.

12. Taking these three scenarios together, it is clear that there is no consensus on the exact outcomes of robotisation on the labour market. In addition, these scenarios do not take into account changes over time. According to the research institute Rathenau, there is consensus among economists that, in the short term, automation and robotisation come at the expense of jobs, but that they provide new jobs in the longer term.[39] This report also states that high-skilled and low-skilled jobs are not 'immune' to automation by means of ICT. This can affect all levels of education and training.[40] This more nuanced view of the effect of robotisation on employment could lead to a more realistic estimation of the possible outcomes. Indeed, several jobs that exist today rely on technological aspects. New jobs have been created by the introduction of new technologies in the workplace, for instance software developers or computer operators. In addition, a report of OECD on middle-skill workers found that most of these workers work in manufacturing and that male middle-skill workers are most likely to be machinery mechanics and repairers.[41] Based on this result, the following hypothesis could be proposed. Middle-skill jobs are more easily created by the introduction of technology, but they are also more easily destructed by new technological innovations than low-skill or high-skill jobs. In this sense, technological innovations facilitate both the creation and destruction of middle-skill employment to a larger extent than low-skill and high-skill jobs. This hypothesis also better fits into the dynamic effects of technology on employment than the static view of job polarisation. This means that it could be expected that even if robotisation will destruct more existing middle-skill jobs, it will also create more new types of middle-skill jobs than low-skill and high-skill jobs. This means that middle-skill jobs could be considered as more dynamic than low-skill or high-skill jobs. According to this hypothesis, the mass unemployment in middle-skill as well as in low-skill and high-skill jobs might be overestimated. It should be taken into account that new jobs will be created. Jobs using data mining technologies (data-analysts or data-managers), for instance, could appear more frequently in the near future. The European Parliament confirms this hypothesis. It notes that on the one hand some jobs will be replaced due to automation but that on the other hand these technologies have the potential to create new jobs as well.[42]

---

39 R. van Est, L. Kool and F. Brom, 'The robot society as a mobilizing perspective', in R. van Est and L. Kool (eds.), *Working on the robot society* (The Hague: Rathenau Instituut, 2015), p. 158.

40 *Ibid.*

41 A. Green, 'What is happening to middle skill workers', *OECD Social, Employment and Migration Working Papers*, no. 230, pp. 22 and 24, https://dx.doi.org/10.1787/a934f8fa-en.

42 Recital 1 Resolution European Parliament no. P8_TA(2019)0081, 12 February 2019, A comprehensive European industrial policy on artificial intelligence and robotics, *OJ. C.* 23 December 2020, no. 449, p. 40. (hereinafter: Resolution European industrial policy on AI).

3.2. CONSEQUENCES FOR LABOUR MARKET POLICY

13. Given the uncertain implications of robotisation on employment rates, the following part will focus on the consequences of the implications rather than on the implications themselves. Two underlying consequences can be identified.

Regardless of the scenario of job creation, reduction or polarisation, it is noticeable that existing skills of workers might be insufficient for the requirements of the jobs in the robotisation age. This undesirable outcome is also known as the phenomenon 'skill mismatch' in which employers are unable to find the right talent and face skill shortages. It also occurs when workers have to take jobs that do not match their qualifications and results in over- or underqualification. Hence, skill mismatch occurs if skill gaps appear because the required skills are unavailable in the workforce, for example, due to technological advances.[43] Indeed, it is likely that robotisation will create new forms of employment and new types of jobs that will require new sets of skills. In its Robot Resolution, the European Parliament also calls to support the development of digital abilities and to align labour market shortages and demand better.[44] Moreover, the European Parliament considers digital literacy as one of the most important factors for future AI development and calls on the Member States to pursue digital skills training and retraining strategies.[45]

Another consequence is the increase of inequality on the labour market. Studies show that the increase of wages of workers in low-skilled and middle-skilled occupations is already lower than the increase in high-skilled jobs in the last decades.[46] Computer technology in particular raised the demand for high-skilled workers and led to widening wage gaps between low- and high-skilled workers.[47] This inequality will increase even more due to technological innovations, for instance, if more jobs become available in low-skilled occupations with less wage growth opportunities than high-skilled occupations.[48] Hence, it could be assumed that technological advancement affects the growing inequality on labour markets and that this ongoing phenomenon will be facilitated by robotisation processes.

---

43 Cedefop, *Insights into skill shortages and skill mismatch*, p. 3.

44 Recital 41 Robot Resolution.

45 Recital 7 Resolution European industrial policy on AI.

46 Berg, 'Labour market institutions: the building blocks of just societies', p. 4.

47 S. Hayter, 'Unions and collective bargaining', in J. Berg (ed.), *Labour Markets, Institutions and Inequality: Building Just Societies in the 21st Century* (Cheltenham: Edward Elgar Publishing, 2015), p. 113.

48 F. Hendrickx, 'From digits to robots: the privacy-autonomy nexus in new labor law machinery', *Comp. Labor Law & Policy Journal*, 2019, vol. 40, no.3, p. 366.

3.3. RECOMMENDATIONS FOR BELGIAN LABOUR MARKET POLICY

3.3.1. *Matching Skills on the 'Robotised' Labour Market*

14. Considering the abovementioned consequences of robotisation on employment, the question is how labour market policy should deal with the increasing skill mismatch and inequality on the labour market. Active labour market policy aims at structuring both the demand-side and supply-side of the labour market to a maximum extent.[49] This means that labour market policies should aim at aligning the needs of employers to find the employees they require and the needs of employees to find a job in line with their talents and employability.[50] Not only labour market policies should align the skills of the employees with the requirements of the employers, but well-regulated labour markets should also imply concerns on the equality between groups, wages and household incomes.[51] Therefore, active labour market policy has a major role to play with regard to both aforementioned consequences of robotisation. However, it is important not to neglect the impact of other legal disciplines (e.g., social security or tax law) on these consequences. These are examined in other chapters of this book.

15. Many recommendations have already been proposed to deal with these consequences for labour markets. However, for the purpose of this book only recommendations relevant to Belgian labour market policy will be mentioned. The Belgian work landscape has been confronted with the consequences of digitalisation. In the last few years major restructurings were notable in some of the largest companies from different sectors (e.g., telecommunications, bank and supermarket sectors) due to the introduction of new technologies and digital processes.[52] Media focused to a large extent on the negative impact of these digitalisation processes and the subsequent job loss within these companies. In addition, the employment challenges associated with robotisation have already been present in Belgium for years. Evidence of this can be found in the country-specific recommendations of the European Semester, in which the Council of the European Union has been warning Belgium for its labour market policies for several years.

Since 2012, the country-specific recommendations warned that fundamental and consistent skill shortages, skill mismatches, skill gaps and the lack of

49 S. Deakin and F. Wilkinson, *The Law of the Labour Market: Industrialization, Employment, and Legal Evolution* (Oxford: Oxford University Press, 2005), p. 285.

50 R. Blanpain, *Arbeidsmarktrecht* (Bruges: die Keure, 2012), p. 21.

51 Berg, 'Labour market institutions: the building blocks of just societies', p. 1.

52 E.g., Telecommunications sector: Proximus, bank sector: BNP Paribas, supermarket sector: Carrefour.

lifelong learning are prominent on the Belgian labour market.[53] In 2019, the Council recognised the country's progress in terms of educational reforms. Nevertheless, it still stressed the issue of labour shortages, pointing out that the workforce needs to be re-skilled in several sectors, in particular in information and communication technologies.[54] In short, these recommendations mention two major deficits on the Belgian labour market: low job mobility and skill mismatches. It is noticeable that during the last decade some reforms in Belgian labour law could be characterised as measures to make its labour market more flexible, which concern, amongst others, employment protection laws, restrictions on working time and wage policies.[55] In Belgium, there have been reforms to introduce time and place independent working arrangements[56] and a flexible working arrangement (e.g., so-called flexi-jobs) and to reduce the dismissal protection for white-collar workers.[57] There have also been some measures focusing on the education of workers, but as the Council of the European Union recommends, more measures could be taken to reduce skill mismatches and skill shortages on the Belgian labour market.

16. There are several possible policy approaches to deal with skill matching.[58] For instance, lifelong learning has been put forward by policymakers in the context of skill match caused by technological innovations. The Robot Resolution of the European parliament also emphasises that more flexible training and education systems will be required to ensure a match between skill strategies and the needs of the robot economy.[59]

Based on the first principle of the European Pillar of Social Rights (the right to quality and inclusive education, training and lifelong learning), the Council of the European Union adopted a recommendation on key competences for lifelong learning in 2018.[60] The Council recognises that the 'competence requirements have changed with more jobs being subject to automation'.[61] That is why the

[53] Council Recommendation of 10 July 2012 on the National Reform Programme 2012 of Belgium and delivering a Council opinion on the Stability Programme of Belgium, 2012–2015, *OJ C.* 24 July 2012, no. 219, p. 5, consid. 13 and 14; Council Recommendation of 13 July 2018 on the 2018 National Reform Programme of Belgium and delivering a Council opinion on the 2018 Stability Programme of Belgium, *OJ C.* 10 September 2018, no. 320, p. 4, consid. 18.

[54] Council Recommendation of 9 July 2019 on the 2019 National Reform Programme of Belgium and delivering a Council Opinion on the 2019 Stability Programme of Belgium, *OJ C.* 5 September 2017, no. 301, p. 5, consid. 16.

[55] Berg, 'Labour market institutions: the building blocks of just societies', pp. 8–9.

[56] Act of 5 March 2017 concerning workable and flexible work, *BS* 15 March 2017.

[57] Act of 26 December 2013 concerning the introduction of the unified status between blue collar and white collar workers regarding the notice periods, first day of unpaid sick leave and accompanying measures, *BS* 31 December 2013.

[58] Cedefop, *Insights into skill shortages and skill mismatch*, p. 16.

[59] Recital 41 Robot Resolution.

[60] Council Recommendation of 22 May 2018 on key competences for lifelong learning, *OJ C.* 4 June 2018, no. 189, p. 1, consid. 1.

[61] *Ibid.*, consid. 4.

Council recommended to make use of good practices in order to support the development of these key competences, in particular by promoting a variety of learning approaches and environments. This includes the adequate use of digital technologies in education, training and learning settings.[62] All individuals need these key competences for their personal fulfilment, development and employability.[63] The Council puts forward eight key competences, which will be hard to automate (e.g., literacy competence, digital competence, personal, social and learning to learn competence and entrepreneurship competence).[64]

17. The Global Commission on the future of work of the International Labour Organization also calls for lifelong learning for all workers in this context. By referring to Article 26 of the Universal Declaration of Human Rights as legal basis, lifelong learning will be key for people to benefit from new technologies and the new work tasks that will follow.[65] This expert committee proposes skills development policies, employment services and training systems to provide workers with the time and financial support they need to learn. Social partners should also have an active role with regard to lifelong learning. However, the Global Commission is eager to put the emphasis on the role of governments, by proposing a system of 'employment insurance' or 'social funds' that would allow workers to take paid time off to engage in training. They also propose to establish institutions, managed by tripartite boards, to provide workers access to education and training, with a special focus on vocational skills.[66] In this regard, it should be noted that vocational learning is also a fundamental right at European level and that Member States of the European Union have the positive obligation to provide access to vocation learning, according to the case law of the European Court of Justice.[67]

18. Based on the abovementioned approaches that deal with skill mismatch, it could be argued that the most important challenge for the Belgian labour market will be to further develop educational systems for workers. Belgian labour law already contains some provisions on education of employees, e.g., the possibility to include an educational clause in employment agreements, educational leave, educational vouchers and outplacement services for dismissed employees.[68]

---

62 *Ibid.*, recommendation 3.1.

63 *Ibid.*, p. 7, Annex.

64 *Ibid.*

65 Global Commission on the Future of Work, *Work for a brighter future* (Geneva: International Labour Office, 2019), p. 30.

66 *Ibid.*

67 Article 14 Charter of fundamental rights of the European Union, *OJ C*. 26 October 2012, no. 326, p. 398; CJEU 13 February 1985, C-293–83, *Françoise Gravier v. City of Liège*; H. Ertl, 'European Union policies in education and training: the Lisbon agenda as a turning point?', *Comparative Education*, 2006, vol. 42, no. 1, p. 7.

68 Article 22*bis* Act of 3 July 1978 concerning employment contract, *BS* 22 August 1978; Article 111 Amending act of 22 January 1985 on social measures, *BS* 24 January 1985;

However, as stated by the Council of the European Union, there is a need for educational systems to facilitate adult vocational learning on a formal and informal basis. This workplace learning is important to acquire work-relevant skills and to improve overall employment prospects.[69] Since 2017, there are some legal provisions in Belgium on vocational formal and informal learning, but the application of these learning systems should be facilitated.[70] With one of the highest participation rates in job-related learning activities, Finland could be used as an example to promote vocational learning systems.[71] Attention should be paid to the accessibility to information, public funding of non-formal training and the involvement of employers and social partners.[72]

3.3.2. Closing the Social Inequality Gap

19. Although it is one of its fundamental goals, less research could be found on the role of active labour market policy to reduce social inequality in the context of robotisation. This will become more important as labour markets will have to deal with robotisation. As labour markets become more flexible, social inequality could increase. Studies show that the increased use of non-standard employment contracts (e.g., temporary contracts and part-time work) could be a source of inequality depending on how they are regulated in national labour markets.[73] If robotisation requires a flexible labour market, regulators should therefore be aware of the risk of this increasing social inequality.

Several approaches exist to counteract social inequality, such as regulation on minimum wages, fiscal policies and non-discrimination.[74] From a labour law perspective, the role of collective bargaining and social partners could be highly relevant for combatting social inequality in the context of robotisation. The European Parliament also noted that implementing AI in industry should be made with broad consultation of social partners.[75] A study showed that trade unions' loss of power resulted in a decline of wages and working conditions for less skilled workers and that highly skilled workers benefited most from the rising share of capital over the past decades.[76] Therefore, collective bargaining could reduce inequality on labour markets by influencing wage distribution in broader

---

Article 11/4 Act of 5 September 2001 on the improvement of employment of workers, *BS* 15 September 2001.

69 Cedefop, *Insights into skill shortages and skill mismatch*, p. 34.

70 Article 9 a) and b) Act of 5 March 2017 concerning workable and agile work, *BS* 15 March 2017.

71 OECD, *Continuous Learning in Working Life in Finland* (Paris: OECD Publishing, 2020), p. 10.

72 Cedefop, *Matching skills and jobs in Europe*, p. 32; A. Green, 'What is happening to middle skill workers', p. 43; OECD, Continuous Learning in Working Life in Finland, p. 59.

73 Berg, 'Labour market institutions: the building blocks of just societies', p. 22.

74 *Ibid.*, pp. 21, 23 and 28.

75 Recital 5 Resolution European industrial policy on AI.

76 *Ibid.*, p. 31.

economic and social policy and by negotiating agreements at company or sectoral level.[77] Based on this approach, the involvement of unions and social dialogue should be promoted to counter inequality on labour markets due to technological innovations. In Belgium, there already exists a collective bargaining agreement on the implementation of new technologies in the workplace.[78] This agreement has been adopted in the eighties but is rarely applied in practice. However, its importance cannot be underestimated. It obliges employers to involve workers representatives and inform workers when they decide to introduce new technologies, regardless of whether these technologies lead to a collective dismissal. In order to promote collective bargaining in the context of robotisation, the government should examine how the application of this collective bargaining agreement could be enforced more efficiently. This could not only reduce social inequality but also lead to a higher success rate of robotisation processes. Workers could then share their expertise and experience in the allocation of the required tasks of their jobs. This expertise could give employers a better understanding of how robots should be implemented in the workplace.

4. LABOUR LAW IN THE 'ROBOTISED' WORK ENVIRONMENT

20. In addition to the impact on employment, attention has been paid to the qualitative side of work in the context of robotisation. As demonstrated by the discussion in this paragraph, several labour law scholars have been concerned with the impact of new technologies, artificial intelligence and robotics on several aspects of work and the employment relationship.[79] These concerns on the quality of work derive from the nature of workplaces as material 'spaces' where human beings are subject to managerial powers of control and instructions of other people.[80] This part summarises the most mentioned issues in this regard and discusses them by applying a taxonomy.

This taxonomy consists of a classification model with two overarching categories. The first category concerns the evolving human-robot interaction. As robots become more autonomous and appear in more sectors, employees will have to cooperate with robots in different ways. The image of a robot as a working tool will become outdated and they will have to be considered as

[77] *Ibid.*, p. 20.

[78] Collective Bargaining Agreement no. 39 of 13 December 1983 concerning the information and consultation on the social impact of the introduction of new technologies.

[79] M. Servoz, 'The future of work? Work of the future!', AI Report European Commission (Luxembourg: Publications Office of the European Union, 2019), p. 98, https://ec.europa.eu/digital-single-market/en/news/future-work-work-future.

[80] V. De Stefano, '"Negotiating the algorithm": Automation, artificial intelligence and labour protection', *ILO Employment Working Paper*, no. 246, p. 5, https://bit.ly/3dBx0ca.

'colleagues'. This will change the way human workers interact and communicate with these machines when fulfilling their tasks. Therefore, the autonomy of the robot will have an impact on the interaction with human workers. Perhaps this is also the reason why labour law is an interesting legal domain to examine the societal effects of new technology. Not only are humans in close contact with autonomous robots in the workplace, they also have to cooperate with them which means that they are partially dependent on their robot colleagues. The second overarching category is related to the employment relationship between employers and employees. This relationship is characterised by subordination of the employee to the employer. This means that an employee has to obey the instructions of the employer and that the employer may be authorised to monitor employees. This relationship of subordination results in a human being who is obligated to work with artificial intelligence and robots. These new technologies lead to new possibilities to monitor employees and could redefine the interaction between employers and employees. For this reason, robotisation could cause changes in the employment relationship. However, this category shows that issues regarding robotisation are complex when it comes to an approach from labour law.

4.1. THE EVOLVING HUMAN-ROBOT RELATIONSHIP

21. The first category of the framework consists of issues arising from the evolving human-robot interaction. According to the European Agency for Safety and Health at Work (EU-OSHA), cobots and smart robots will appear more often in the workplace as highly developed sensors make it possible for employees and robots to work together.[81] This means that employees will have to increasingly rely on robots when they perform their job and will be in close contact with them. This evolving human-robot interaction creates several new opportunities and risks. Issues mentioned in this regard are mostly concerned with the physical safety, mental health and responsibility of employees.

4.1.1. Guaranteeing Physical Safety and Mental Health

22. In terms of the physical safety of employees, authors expect a rather positive impact of robotisation. Robots allow people to be removed from dangerous physical work and environments with chemical and ergonomic hazards and, therefore, reduce safety risks for workers.[82] However, these robots

---

81 EU-OSHA, *Digitalisation and occupational safety and health – An EU-OSHA research programme*, p. 7, https://bit.ly/3czkqtY.

82 P.V. Moore, 'OSH and the Future of Work: benefits and risks of artificial intelligence tools in workplaces', *EU-OSHA Discussion paper*, p. 5, https://bit.ly/2YYo78x.

could create new risks because their increased flexibility allows them to move and to work among human workers.[83] These new risks will demand new safety obligations to guarantee the physical safety of employees. The Robot Resolution of the European Parliament confirms this view. It notes that a number of hazardous and harmful tasks could be transferred from humans to robots, but they also have the potential to create a set of new risks. There is, therefore, a need to adopt strict and forward-looking rules for human-robot interactions in order to guarantee health and safety in the workplace.[84] Examples of new safety obligations for such human-robot collisions are the use of new (softer) materials and 'virtual' cages in which robots can distinguish humans from the other objects by using their sensors or machine vision technologies. In the context of human safety and robotics, three types of hazardous interactions in a human-cobot-environment can be distinguished: '1. robot-human collision risks, in which machine learning can lead to unpredictable robot behaviour; 2. security risks, in which robots' internet links can affect the integrity of software programming, leading to vulnerabilities in security; and 3. environmental risks, in which sensor degradation and unexpected human action in unstructured environments can lead to risks to the environment'.[85] Especially cybersecurity is considered to be an important aspect of AI and the development of safe robotic systems. The European Parliament emphasises, in this regard, the requirements for transparency and accountability.[86]

The regulation on the safety of workers is unadjusted to robotisation because a lot of provisions are designed for manufacturing robots behind physical cages with programmed movements. The essential health and safety requirements with regard to robotics fit into the framework of Directive 2006/42, the so-called Machine Directive.[87] The principles of the ISO standards also have to be taken into account to guarantee the health and safety of workers, for instance the prevention of physical damage due to human-robot collision or the role of technological evolution in determining the application of the standards.[88] However, a lot of these safety requirements will have to be modified to deal with the new risks due to the implementation of smart robotics in the workplace. The European Commission also suggests in the proposal for a regulation on machinery products that the Machine Directive does not sufficiently address the new risks related to the direct human-robot collaboration, the connected machinery, the software affecting the behaviour of machinery and the increase

[83] J.M. Uguina and A.M. Ruiz, 'Robotics and Health and Safety at Work', *International Journal of Swarm Intelligence and Evolutionary Computation*, 2019, vol. 8, no. 1, p. 2.

[84] Recital 46 Robot Resolution.

[85] Moore, 'OSH and the Future of Work: benefits and risks of artificial intelligence tools in workplaces', p. 6.

[86] Recital 100 Resolution European industrial policy on AI.

[87] Uguina and Ruiz, 'Robotics and Health and Safety at Work', p. 4.

[88] *Ibid.*

of autonomous machines and remote supervisory stations.[89] Risk assessment of human-cobot interaction should, therefore, consider the totality of the cooperative task and the workplace, and should take into account several aspects of this interaction. Examples are the characteristics of the robot, the dangers of the piece of work (for example sharp edges), the scheme of the robot system and the location of the operating criteria of the associated safety functions.[90] Due to the specific risks of each human-robot interaction, it is recommended that workers participate in this process of risk assessment.[91] Risk assessment of the safety of the worker should aim at (1) identifying the conditions in which contact would occur, (2) assessing the potential risk of contacts, (3) specifying the robot system and the collaborative space so that contact is infrequent and avoidable and (4) applying risk-reduction measures that maintain contact situations below the limit values.[92] As mentioned above, the legal basis of this need for new measures lies in the assumption that the distance between robots and humans will reduce and that physical contact will occur. In traditional robot settings, human safety was guaranteed through separation of the operator from the robot system. In the context of collaborative operation between human and robot, risk reduction will have to be achieved through the design of the robot system and of the workplace.[93]

23. Smart robots will also affect the mental health of human workers in a positive and negative way. A lot depends on how these robots will be incorporated at company level because they could either reduce stress or intensify it.[94] The positive effect is that robots could allow employees to obtain more autonomy and flexibility and could facilitate the access to the labour market for disabled people or ageing workers.[95] When implemented appropriately, cobots could reduce health risks because they can carry out more routine tasks associated with stress, overwork and boredom. However, in terms of its negative effects, the autonomy of robots could increase the work rate for human employees. When robots are not introduced appropriately, they could entail psychosocial risk factors if humans have to work at the cobots' pace, if they have to look after these cobots by receiving notifications on their personal devices and if collisions between cobots and people occur. This could lead, once again, to overwork and disruption

89 Proposal for a Regulation of the European Parliament and of the Council on machinery products, 21 April 2021, COM(2021) 202 final 2021/0105 (COD), p. 2.

90 Uguina and Ruiz, 'Robotics and Health and Safety at Work', p. 6.

91 *Ibid.*

92 *Ibid.*, p. 7.

93 *Ibid.*, p. 6.

94 T. Klebe and M. Weiss, 'Workers' participation 4.0 – digital and global?', *Comparative Labor Law & Policy Journal,* 2019, vol. 40, no. 2, p. 277.

95 EU-OSHA, 'Digitalisation and occupational safety and health – An EU-OSHA research programme', p. 17.

of the work-life balance.[96] This increase of stress, working time duration and fear of accidents in the workplace could result in an increased prevalence of psychological illnesses.[97] As these technologies could alleviate physical burdens, it must also be ensured that the remaining tasks are not monotonous.

These risks for the mental health of employees should be situated in the context of technostress. Technostress is 'any negative impact on attitudes, thoughts, behaviours, or body physiology that is caused either directly or indirectly by technology'.[98] More specifically, technology could lead to an overwhelming amount of information, a higher work rate, a feeling of incompetence due to its complexity and continuous changes, job insecurity and an increase in demands placed on the worker during and outside his working hours.[99] This kind of stress is not new and already occurred due to the increased use of ICT (computers) and internet in the workplace. However, these risks for the mental health of employees and, more broadly, technostress could be amplified by the introduction of autonomous robots in the workplace. These robots will be more complex, will demand more time of workers and will provide more information than existing robots. Therefore, it could be estimated that this type of psychosocial risks will become more prevalent in the future.

24. In light of the increased use of ICT in the workplace and the related technostress, legal initiatives have been taken by some European Member States. These legal initiatives aim at establishing the so-called right to disconnect. Among these countries, Belgium had developed a right to disconnect in 2018. However, this right did not give an employee an actual right to be disconnected from work at certain times. It only gave employees' representatives the right to request a consultation at scheduled intervals on the disconnection of work and the use of digital means of communication.[100] In the explanatory memorandum, the government argued that no strict obligations have been adopted because every company has its own economic needs and work structure/organisation.[101] This provision was contested in Belgian scholarship, and eventually resulted in the adoption of an actual right to disconnect in 2022. This regulation modifies the former legal basis of this right. It provides that a collective bargaining agreement

96 Moore, 'OSH and the Future of Work: benefits and risks of artificial intelligence tools in workplaces', p. 6; Uguina and Ruiz, 'Robotics and Health and Safety at Work', p. 2.

97 Klebe and Weiss, 'Workers' participation 4.0 – digital and global?', pp. 277–278.

98 B. Tombeur, *De smartphone en technostress* (Mechelen: Wolters Kluwer, 2018), p. 10; J. Popma, *The Janus face of the 'New Ways of Work': Rise, risks and regulation of nomadic work, ETUI Working paper*, no. 2013.07 (Brussels: European Trade Union Institute), p. 10.

99 K. Wang, Q. Shu and Q. Tu, 'Technostress under different organizational environments: An empirical investigation', *Computers in Human Behavior*, 2008, vol. 24, p. 3004.

100 Article 16 Act of 26 March 2018 concerning the strengthening of the economic growth and the social cohesion, *BS* 30 March 2018.

101 Memorandum act concerning economic reliance and strengthening of the social cohesion, *Parl. Doc.* Chamber 2017–18, no. 2839/001, p. 138.

on a company or sectoral level has to elaborate on the right to disconnect in terms of the right not to be reached outside the working hours, on guidelines regarding the use of digital means with respect to the work life balance and on measures to educate employees on the appropriate use of digital means.[102] Still, it may be questioned whether the right to disconnect is able to address the risks for mental health related to the use of ICT in the workplace. As emphasised by Reyniers, this right might turn into an obligation to disconnect for employees, which potentially leads to a tsunami of information when employees are allowed to reconnect after an obliged period of disconnection.[103] Another critical view states that the right to disconnect only aims to ensure minimum rest periods of workers and respect for private life.[104] This is only one aspect of technostress. That is why a right to disconnect will not be sufficient to deal with other aspects of technostress in the context of robotisation. For instance, due to the complexity and rapid successive changes of robots, workers could feel insecure and incompetent. Therefore, it could be argued that new regulation, other rights or obligations will be required to deal with these issues for the mental health of employees in light of the robotisation era.

In this respect, not only preventive measures for physical human-robot collision are needed, but also a multidisciplinary approach to take ergonomic principles and psychosocial aspects into consideration will have to be adopted.[105] Psychosocial risks will appear more frequently due to the imposed work rhythms of the robot on human workers and the mental load caused by the fear of contact with the robot. Human workers could also feel more isolated because of the decreased presence of human workers and the increased, even non-stop, monitoring by their robotic co-worker.[106] Therefore, scholarship calls for a proactive approach in which risks associated with the presence of robots in the workplace are assessed and managed in relation to training opportunities and technical skills of workers.[107]

4.1.2. Workers' Responsibility for Robot Colleagues

25. The reference to training opportunities alluded to at the end of the previous part is also relevant for the debate of workers' responsibility when they carry out tasks together with and interact with autonomous robots. In this regard, the European Robot Resolution calls for more efficiency, transparency

[102] Articles 29 and 30 Memorandum Act of 7 juli 2022 concerning various provisions on labour, *Parl. Doc.* Chamber 2021–22, no. 2810/001, pp. 48–49.

[103] Reyniers, 'Een recht op deconnectie, of hoe omgaan met technostress?', *TSR*, 2019, no. 1, p. 109.

[104] Tombeur, *De smartphone en technostress*, p. 10.

[105] Uguina and Ruiz, 'Robotics and Health and Safety at Work', p. 5.

[106] *Ibid.*

[107] *Ibid.*

and consistency to achieve legal certainty in civil liability for damage caused by robots.[108] Especially to enable smooth human-robot joint activity, these interdependent relationships should be based on principles of predictability and directability to determine what information needs to be shared between humans and robots.[109] This also calls for a proactive approach to assess the responsibility of the workers because there are no obvious solutions in terms of liability in the context of the robot's unpredictable behaviour and collisions between cobots and human workers.[110] In other words, current legislation cannot provide a clear answer as to whether the manufacturer, designer, manager or worker should be held liable when the cooperation between autonomous robots and workers causes damage. In order to deal with this legal uncertainty, the European Parliament proposes to draw up a regulation on liability for the operation of artificial intelligence systems, either software-based or embedded in hardware devices. This proposal holds operators of high-risk AI systems strictly liable for any harm or damage. This would mean that if a worker would be considered as an operator of this kind of AI-system, this person would have a high level of responsibility when exercising control over its operation and functioning. However, it is rather unclear whether a worker could be considered as an operator because, according to the proposal, this person not only exercises a degree of control but also benefits from its operation.[111] One may argue that the person who has really control over and benefits from its operation is in fact the employer. Therefore, this regulation should clarify the responsibility of workers and employers in case autonomous robots and other AI systems are implemented in workplaces. This paragraph examines only the responsibility of the worker from a Belgian liability law perspective. The responsibility of the employer is addressed in the next part.

26. Under Belgian liability law, employees are granted partial immunity in terms of their liability because they are only liable in cases of fraud, serious faults or reoccurring minor faults.[112] This implies that they are only held liable if the damage is foreseeable. This requires that employees know or should have known that their acts would cause damage. Based on this criterion, if an employee has to work together with an autonomous robot, it could be difficult to predict or to foresee the damage caused by the robot due to its unpredictable movements.[113] Therefore, in most cases the employee should not be liable for the damage

108 Recital 49 Robot Resolution.

109 Recital 50 Robot Resolution.

110 Uguina and Ruiz, 'Robotics and Health and Safety at Work', p. 5; P.V. Moore, 'The Mirror for (Artificial) Intelligence: In Whose Reflection?', *Comparative Labor Law & Policy Journal*, 2020, vol. 41, no. 1, p. 55.

111 Article 3, e European Parliament resolution of 20 October 2020 with recommendations to the Commission on a civil liability regime for artificial intelligence.

112 Article 18 Act of 3 July 1978 concerning employment contract, *BS* 22 August 1978.

113 S. Taes en F. Hendrickx, 'Robots en arbeidsrecht: vragen voor het arbeidsrecht 4.0', in VRG-Alumni (red.), *Recht in beweging: 26ste VRG-Alumnidag 2019* (Oud-Turnhout: Gompel&Svacina, 2019), p. 13.

caused by the robotic co-worker. However, the injured party could argue that the employee has sufficient experience to work with this robot or that he should have known that the acts of the robot can cause damage. Under Belgian liability law, there is no clear answer to this point. It will probably depend on the context in which the damage occurred. Considering the high risk of accidents between workers and robots, clear regulatory principles are still needed to determine the responsibility of workers.

4.1.3. Recommendations for the Evolving Human-Robot Relationship

27. These issues, caused by this evolving human-robot interaction, ask for new regulation to guarantee the physical safety and mental health of workers in a robotisation era. EU-OSHA, in particular, proposes several recommendations to address these challenges: '1) the development of an ethical framework for digitalisation, codes of conduct and proper governance; 2) a strong 'prevention through design' approach that integrates human factors and worker-centred design; 3) the involvement of workers in the design and implementation of any digitalisation strategies; 4) collaboration between academics, industry, social partners and governments on research and innovation in digital technologies to properly take account of the human aspects; 5) a regulatory framework to clarify OSH liabilities and responsibilities in relation to new systems and new ways of working; 6) an adapted education system and training for workers; 7) the provision of effective OSH services to all workers of the digital world of work'.[114] Based on these recommendations, the evolving human-robot interaction calls for a European and/or national legal framework, created with the involvement of workers and based on dialogue between social partners, that clarifies the risks and responsibilities regarding the close cooperation with robots in the workplace. As the fourth recommendation of EU-OSHA states, the role of social partners cannot be underestimated when drafting this legal framework.

4.2. IMPACT OF ROBOTS ON THE EMPLOYMENT RELATIONSHIP

28. The second category of the aforementioned taxonomy comprises the issues related to the impact of the robotisation process on the employment relationship. With regard to artificial intelligent systems, some scholars argue that an increased possibility to monitor employees allows the employer to extend his authority on employees.[115] This phenomenon is referred to as 'management by algorithm'. Its importance cannot be underestimated in the robotisation age

[114] EU-OSHA, *Digitalisation and occupational safety and health – An EU-OSHA research programme*, p. 19.

[115] Hendrickx, 'From digits to robots', p. 366.

because autonomous robots could amplify these monitoring techniques. These robots can collect a lot of personal data of employees, both online and offline. Their improved sensors will be able to gather several new kinds of data in the physical world (behaviour, location tracing, psychometric and biometric data of employees). Robots could then combine this data with personal data in the virtual world. With this new information, they are capable of decision-making in a structured way. From the perspective of the employment relationship, autonomous robots should therefore be considered as robotic co-workers instead of working tools. This raises questions, amongst others, about the privacy of employees, discriminatory decisions taken by the employer and the distribution of responsibility between employers and employees.

4.2.1. Robotic Decision-Making and Privacy

29. The protection of privacy in the robot age is one of the most discussed issues in labour law. This issue requires to strike a balance between the data that the robot has to capture in order to work properly and the protection of the personal data of workers. More specifically, autonomous robots base their actions on the collection and the processing of data in their environment. This means that if workers are in the vicinity of these robots, their personal data will be part of this autonomous data collection and processing. It will thus be necessary to gather information about human co-workers in order to establish a good-functioning human-robot interaction. This will be achieved by the use of advanced sensors and connectivity to the internet and other machines which enable the collection of more (kinds) of personal data of workers. In addition, through their improved learning capabilities robots will analyse this collected data better and more efficiently. As this information will be stored and communicated by machines owned by employers, the latter will gain access to more information of their employees and will monitor them more closely than ever before. Considering these data processing capabilities of robots, the European Parliament highlights the importance of ensuring a high level of privacy with respect to data used for communication between people and robots and of adopting sufficient guarantees in light of the personal data protection principles.[116]

However, the debate on the implications of new technologies on the right to privacy for employees is not new and many concerns already exist on the processing of data by technology in general. In his historical overview, Hendrickx explains that technology in the workplace always has implications for the privacy of employees. An example is the importance of data protection in the context of technology as a monitoring tool, as the flow of information increased through the intensified connection between computers and other

[116] Recitals 125 and 128 Resolution European industrial policy on AI.

devices.[117] The next step is the use of AI and smart robots to make automated decisions on employees and to manage them without human involvement. They could, for example, be applied for recruiting or dismissing employees. For this reason, it could be expected that new measures will be needed to guarantee a fair use of the technological opportunities in the robotisation era. Within this context, the proposals for an 'Artificial Intelligence Act' and a directive on improving working conditions in platform work (hereinafter: Platform Work Directive), published by the European Commission, are worth mentioning as useful starting points for these new measures. However, the expected impact of the proposed Artificial Intelligence Act on labour law is rather limited because it explicitly states that employees are not considered as users within the meaning of the regulation.[118] Furthermore, legal scholars criticized that this proposed act imposes rather weak mandatory requirements regarding the protection of employees' rights and interests in the context of the introduction of AI systems in the workplace.[119] The proposed regulation is still relevant because it classifies AI systems applied in an employment context as high-risk AI systems. This classification entails that AI systems 'intended to be used for recruitment or selection of natural persons, notably for advertising vacancies, screening or filtering applications, evaluating candidates in the course of interviews or tests' or 'intended to be used for making decisions on promotion and termination of work-related contractual relationships, for task allocation and for monitoring and evaluating performance and behaviour of persons in such relationships' would have to comply with several specific requirements regarding, amongst others, risk management, training of data models, documentation and transparency.[120] With regard to systems that evaluate work performance or affect working conditions (for example in terms of access to work assignments, earnings or promotion), the proposed Platform Work Directive also provides additional safeguards to platform workers. This proposed directive obliges digital labour platforms to inform platform workers and their representatives on, amongst others, the categories of decisions that are taken or supported by these automated decision-making systems, the parameters that these systems

117 F. Hendrickx, 'Privacy 4.0 at Work: Regulating Employment, Technology and Automation', *Comparative Labor Law & Policy Journal*, 2020, vol. 41, no. 1, pp. 156–162.

118 Recital 36 Proposal for a Regulation of the European Parliament and of the Council laying down harmonised rules on artificial intelligence (artificial intelligence act) and amending certain union legislative acts, 21 April 2021, COM(2021)206 final 2021/0106(COD) (hereinafter: Proposal AI-Regulation).

119 A. Ponce Del Castillo, 'The AI Regulation: entering an AI regulatory winter? Why an ad hoc directive on AI in employment is required', *ETUI foresight Brief*, 2021, no. 7, pp. 5–6; V. De Stefano and S. Taes, 'Algorithmic management and collective bargaining', *ETUI foresight Brief*, 2021, no. 10, pp. 10–11; J. Adams-Prassl, 'Regulating algorithms at work: Lessons for a 'European approach to artificial intelligence'', *European Labour Law Journal*, 2022, no. 1, pp. 48–49; V. De Stefano, 'The EU Commission's proposal for a Directive on Platform: an overview', *Italian Labour Law e-Journal*, 2022, no. 1, p. 115.

120 Articles 8–13 and Annex III Proposal AI-Regulation.

take into account and the grounds for decisions to suspend or terminate the platform workers' accounts and to refuse their remuneration.[121] In addition, the proposed directive requires that these platforms regularly monitor and evaluate the impact of these decisions (human monitoring) and that platform workers have the right to obtain an explanation from these platforms for any of these decisions (human review).[122] Although this directive does not relate directly to the application of robots and AI systems in the 'conventional' workplaces, these requirements and obligations may provide some guidance to establish a fair use of the technological opportunities in the robotisation era. Besides these recent proposals, legal scholarship also pays a lot of attention to the provisions of the GDPR as this instrument contains a set of new measures to protect the privacy of people in the processing of their personal data.

30. Many of these provisions show potential to cope with the privacy issues associated with robotisation. One of the key provisions of the GDPR in light of robotisation is Article 22 on automated decision-making and profiling. This article gives the data subject, in this case the employee, the right not to be subject to a decision based solely on automated processing, including profiling, which produces legal effects concerning him or her or similarly significantly affects him or her. According to the Article 29 Working Party (WP29), this Article establishes a general prohibition for decision-making systems falling within its scope of application.[123] Therefore, this article becomes relevant when decisions in the employment relationship are based on the processing of (personal) data of workers by autonomous robots. As this relationship between an employer and an employee heavily relies on the processing of personal data, this article could have large implications on the use of robots in the workplace.[124] With regard to the profiling of employees, robots could affect decisions in, for instance, recruiting, assessment of employees or selection for dismissals.[125]

Article 22 could offer strong protection for the privacy of the employees, but at the moment it is not clear how this provision should be applied in the context of the employment relationship.[126] Firstly, there are questions regarding the scope of this article because it is not clear for which specific decisions the

---

121 Articles 6 and 9 Proposal for a Directive of the European Parliament and of the Council on improving working conditions in platform work, 9 December 2021, COM(2021) 762 final 2021/0414 (COD) (hereinafter: Proposal Platform Work Directive).

122 Articles 7 and 8 Proposal Platform Work Directive.

123 Article 29 Data Protection Working Party (WP29), 'Guidelines on Automated individual decision-making and Profiling for the purposes of Regulation 2016/679', 6 February 2018, no. WP251rev.01, p. 19.

124 F. Hendrickx, 'Privacy 4.0 at work: regulating employment, technology and automation', *Regulation for Globalization*, 23 September 2019.

125 *Ibid.*

126 A. Aloisi and E. Gramano, 'Artificial Intelligence Is Watching You at Work'. Digital Surveillance, Employee Monitoring and Regulatory Issues in the EU Context', *Comparative Labor Law & Policy Journal*, 2020, vol. 41, no. 1, p. 106.

employee has the right to contest the decision. Another question relates to what it means for processing to be 'solely' automated. It is rather unclear whether and to what extent this article will apply if employers partially base their decisions on the profiling and processing by the robot. Secondly, if this article applies, it is not clear whether the worker will be able to review the decision-making process of a robot.[127] It could be very complex to understand the information and techniques that led to the decision of the robot. Thirdly, this article gives the data subject the right to obtain a human intervention to review the decision based on the automated data processing. However, it is not clear whether the person who has to review the decision has to be the same as the person who took the decision in the first place.[128] The WP29 states that to qualify as human involvement, the oversight of the decision should be carried out by someone who has the authority and competence to change the decision.[129] Finally, there are exceptions to which Article 22 does not apply, for instance if the decision is necessary for entering into or performing a contract. It is not clear whether or to what extent the employer, as data controller, can argue that these automated decisions are necessary for the performance of the employment contract. The WP29 considers that this automated decision-making may be necessary to make a shortlist of possible candidates in the context of recruitment.[130] Another exception also raises questions when applied in the employment relationship. According to Article 22, a data subject could give his consent to this kind of decisions. However, the consent of employees with regard to their privacy is highly questionable. The WP29 argues that an employee as data subject cannot freely give his consent in a relationship characterised by an imbalance of power, which refers to the authority of the employer. The WP29 therefore states that consent of employees cannot offer a lawful basis for data processing at work.[131] This perspective raises questions whether this exception in Article 22 can ever be applied in the context of an employment relationship.

These questions on the relationship between Article 22 and technologies applied in employment context also appear in the debate on algorithmic management. This ongoing debate refers to the application of algorithms to direct employees, to assess their performance in the workplace and to discipline them by imposing sanctions in case of misconduct or failure to achieve the algorithms' objectives.[132] In this regard, scholars express concerns that these

---

127 *Ibid.*, p. 14.

128 *Ibid.*

129 WP29, 'Guidelines on Automated individual decision-making and Profiling for the purposes of Regulation 2016/679', 6 February 2018, no. WP251rev.01, p. 21.

130 *Ibid.*, p. 23.

131 WP29, 'Guidelines on consent under Regulation 2016/679', 10 April 2018, no. WP259rev.01, p. 6.

132 K. Kellogg, M. Valentine and A. Christin, 'Algorithms at Work: The New Contested Terrain of Control', *Academy of Management Annals*, 2020, no. 1, pp. 368–369 and 378–380; A. Wood,

uses of algorithms may entail systems that make decisions on employees and affect their working conditions without human oversight.[133] For this reason, they question whether Article 22 may offer a safe harbour for employees who are subject to algorithmic management systems and may restrict excessive monitoring of employees by means of these systems.[134] In this regard, the Platform Work Directive emphasises that employees face limitations and difficulties when aiming to assert their data protection rights in context of algorithmic management.[135] This is demonstrated, for instance, in three judgments of the District Court of Amsterdam on 11 March 2021.[136] These cases concerned the claim of drivers to gain access to information on automated decision-making systems applied by two digital labour platforms, Uber and Ola Cabs. In essence, the Court ruled that Article 22 does not apply to most of these systems. On the one hand, the Court particularly found that systems to allocate rides to drivers and to assess their performance in order to grant bonuses do not produce legal effects or similarly significantly affect drivers. On the other hand, Uber demonstrated, in the Court's opinion, that staff members meaningfully intervened in the decision-making process of the system to discipline drivers. In this regard, Uber elaborated the procedure that staff members have to follow when the system notices fraudulent behaviour that could lead to the permanent deactivation of the drivers' accounts on the platform. The Court held that Article 22 is applicable on only one system of Ola Cabs which imposes, without any meaningful human intervention, penalties and deductions to drivers when detecting an invalid ride. Therefore, these judgments of the District Court may imply that Article 22 of the GDPR does not apply on every tool and system that makes decisions on employees or has an impact on their working conditions. De Stefano and Wouters concluded, in light of these judgments, that although the GDPR may impose many theoretical restrictions, employees may not manage to

---

'Algorithmic Management: Consequences for Work Organisation and Working Conditions', *JRC Working Papers Series on Labour, Education and Technology*, 2021, no. 7, p. 1.

133 De Stefano and Taes, 'Algorithmic management and collective bargaining', pp. 7–8; E. Klengel and J. Wenckebach, 'Artificial intelligence, work, power imbalance and democracy – why co-determination is essential', *Italian Labour Law e-Journal*, 2021, no. 2, pp. 158–159; A. Todoli-Signes, 'Algorithms, artificial intelligence and automated decisions concerning workers and the risks of discrimination: the necessary collective governance of data protection', *Transfer*, 2021, no. 4, pp. 469–470.

134 Todoli-Signes, 'Algorithms, artificial intelligence and automated decisions concerning workers and the risks of discrimination: the necessary collective governance of data protection', pp. 469–470; J. Adams-Prassl, 'Regulating algorithms at work: Lessons for a 'European approach to artificial intelligence'', p. 42; H. Parviainen, 'Can algorithmic recruitment systems lawfully utilise automated decision-making in the EU?', *European Labour Law Journal*, 2022, no. 2, p. 226.

135 Proposal Platform Work Directive, p. 7.

136 District Court Amsterdam (NL) 11 March 2021, no. C/13/687315 / HA RK 20-207, https://wwww.rechtspraak.nl; District Court Amsterdam (NL) 11 March 2021, no. C/13/692003 / HA RK 20-302, https://wwww.rechtspraak.nl; District Court Amsterdam (NL) 11 March 2021, no. C/13/689705 / HA RK 20-258, https://wwww.rechtspraak.nl.

fully rely on the safeguards to protect their personal data.[137] Hence, with regard to the application of robots or wearables that give instructions to employees or grant them bonuses or job opportunities, the protection of Article 22 may not always offer a safe harbour for those who experience an impact on their wellbeing or remuneration by these technologies.

Furthermore, Article 22 of the GDPR is only one of the provisions that will gain relevance in the context of robotisation. For instance, Article 25 provides a so-called data protection by design and by default. This implies that the data controller has to implement appropriate technical and organisational measures and has to integrate the necessary safeguards in order to meet the requirements of the GDPR. The article states that measures should be implemented for ensuring that only personal data which are necessary for a specific purpose are processed. This will also raise questions on how this provision has to be applied in the workplace. It is thus rather unclear to what extent this article entails a duty for the employer, as data controller, to limit the collection and processing of personal data by robots. In addition, it should be noticed that the European Robot Resolution pays close attention to these principles of the GDPR. Therefore, the Resolution asks for clarification when implementing this framework of the GDPR and for the development of criteria regarding the use of cameras and sensors in robots. The Resolution also emphasises the need for a high level of security to prevent potential security breaches in networks of interconnected robots.[138]

31. These concerns show that the provisions of the GDPR might not be sufficient to guarantee the protection of the worker's privacy in the robotisation age. Therefore, several scholars advocate in favour of additional protection measures, as technology will evolve and will entail new risks of processing personal data. Some authors call for the creation of an additional procedural layer to the right to privacy throughout the entire employment period. This will lead to an obligation to create clear rules in the workplace regarding the privacy of workers.[139] These rules should be created together with the workers' representatives, which implies an information procedure to involve employees. This information procedure could be considered as another example of additional protection as it could reduce the imbalance between workers who may not be aware of the characteristics of this complex data processing and the employers

137 V. De Stefano and M. Wouters, 'AI and digital tools in workplace management and evaluation An assessment of the EU's legal framework', *STUDY Panel for the Future of Science and Technology EPRS | European Parliamentary Research Service, Scientific Foresight Unit (STOA)*, 2022, no. PE 729.516, p. 22.

138 Recitals 20–21 Robot Resolution.

139 T. Katsabian, 'Employees' privacy in the Internet Age: Towards a New Procedural Approach', *Berkeley Journal of Employment and Labor Law*, 2019, vol. 40, no. 2, p. 207.

who use the results of this data processing in their decision-making.[140] As the artificial decision-making becomes increasingly incomprehensible, an obligation to provide transparent information will indeed be more necessary.[141] This also requires the further development of the application of Article 12 of the GDPR in the workplace. Finally, other authors suggest to safeguard workers' privacy on a more fundamental level. As artificial intelligent technologies have an impact on the freedom or autonomy of workers due to increasing monitoring possibilities, it might be necessary to construe new kinds of rights from the perspective of privacy.[142] The questions relating to the right to human intervention in Article 22 could give rise to 'a right of humanisation of the workplace', which would form a fundamental guarantee, for instance, in relation to the protection of workers' right to privacy.[143] Intelligent machines could indeed entail risks to a deepening dehumanisation of labour. Space for freedom, creativity and sympathy should, therefore, be ensured in the robotisation age and a re-humanisation of labour should be achieved.[144]

4.2.2. Robotic Decision-Making and Discrimination

32. Not only the privacy of workers is at risk in light of these automated decisions by autonomous robots. These decisions could also be biased by the use of an algorithm that applies discriminatory parameters. This risk of discriminatory decisions has already been demonstrated in the context of recruiting employees. In 2014, Amazon introduced an automated recruiting tool by means of machine learning and natural language processing. This tool rated applicants that would fit in the job profile. One year later, Amazon had to abandon this tool because they noticed that for technical job titles such as software developers, the tool only suggested male applicants. The explanation is that the tool reflected the male dominance in the tech industry and it therefore downgraded resumes that included words like 'women'.[145] Although engineers did not program gender-biased criteria into this system, it generated a discriminatory parameter in the algorithm by its learning capabilities.

This example shows the risk of AI decision-making in the workplace. But this risk of discrimination by technology could have even worse outcomes

---

140 E. Dagnino and I. Armaroli, 'A Seat at the Table: Negotiating Data Processing in the Workplace. A National Case Study and Comparative Insights', *Comparative Labor Law & Policy Journal*, 2020, vol. 41, no. 1, p. 175.

141 Aloisi and Gramano, 'Artificial Intelligence Is Watching You at Work', p. 99.

142 Aloisi and Gramano, 'Artificial Intelligence Is Watching You at Work', p. 99; Hendrickx, 'From digits to robots', p. 366.

143 Hendrickx, 'From digits to robot's, p. 385.

144 A. Supiot, 'The tasks ahead of the ILO at its centenary', *International Labour Review*, 2020, vol. 159, no. 1, p. 119.

145 A. Kodiyan, 'An overview of ethical issues in using AI systems in hiring with a case study of Amazon's AI based hiring tool', *Researchgate* 12 November 2019, https://bit.ly/2T4oWbQ.

when smart robots with access to a lot of data are allowed to take decisions on the employees' professional life. For example, if robots have the ability to rate the productivity of employees and the decision of the employer is based on this rating. Even though this is not a fully automated decision, it entails the risk of a discriminatory treatment of workers if the employer is not aware of the parameters that the robot applies in this rating procedure. Therefore, there is not only a need for transparency in case of automated decisions to protect the privacy of the employee but also to avoid discriminatory decision-making. The European Parliament also emphasises the difficulty and complexity of predicting the future behaviours of AI systems and calls 'for people to have a right to know, a right of appeal and a right to redress when AI is used for decisions affecting individuals which carry a significant risk to an individual's rights or freedom or may cause them harm'.[146] As EU-OSHA demonstrates, there are a lot of AI-enabled tools based on the use of individualised data about workers to support employers when making decisions about recruitment, performance appraisals, promotion considerations, dismissal and management positions.[147] These decisions may significantly affect individuals, especially in case they are deprived of job opportunities. Therefore, the importance of a transparent decision-making process cannot be underestimated in the context of robotisation. Through the complexity of these systems, it is possible that the employer is not aware that his decisions are based on discriminatory criteria.

33. Belgian discrimination law protects workers against employers who treat them different directly or indirectly on the basis of protected criteria. This direct or indirect discrimination is only allowed if the different treatment is objectively justified by a legitimate aim and the means of achieving that aim are appropriate and necessary. Direct discrimination on the basis of age, gender, religion or disability can only be justified for 'genuine and determining occupational requirements'.[148] AI and robots could challenge these provisions because the type of discrimination can remain hidden or could even fall outside the scope of discrimination law.[149]

---

146 Recitals 153 Resolution European industrial policy on AI.

147 Moore, 'OSH and the Future of Work: benefits and risks of artificial intelligence tools in workplaces', p. 3.

148 Articles 7 and 8 Act of 10 May 2007 combating certain forms of discrimination, *BS* 30 May 2007.

149 F. Zuiderveen Borgesius, *Discrimination, artificial intelligence, and algorithmic decision-making* (Strasbourg: Council of Europe, 2018), p. 20, https://rm.coe.int/discrimination-artificial-intelligence-and-algorithmic-decision-making/1680925d73.

4.2.3. *Sharing Responsibility in the 'Robotised' Employment Relationship*

34. A lot of questions also arise in terms of responsibility between employers and workers. Indeed, robots have an impact on human-to-human interaction in the fields of contractual and extra-contractual liability.[150] They could affect the way humans negotiate, enter into contracts or establish rights and obligations. However, the employment relationship between an employer and worker has an extraordinary nature. It is based on the idea of control and/or subordination.[151] As mentioned above, this means that the worker has to obey the instructions of the employer and the employer may control the workers. Because of this extraordinary nature, many countries, Belgium included, have a vicarious liability system. This means that the employer could be held liable for faults of the worker when causing damage to a third party. This extraordinary relationship also involves a duty to take care of employees and to protect them from possible risks associated with their work. Therefore, the employer is responsible for the conditions in which employees have to work. When autonomous robots are introduced in the workplace, they will intervene in the employment relationship and will affect how rights and obligations in this relationship are realised. The responsibility between employer and employee is perhaps the most essential issue of the robotisation age, because it affects the outcomes of other issues such as the necessary measures to guarantee the health, safety and privacy of workers.[152] The core aspect of this responsibility issue is the impact of a physical object, acting autonomously and unpredictably, on the relationship between the employer and employee. From the perspective of the employment relationship, the autonomous robot should be considered as an independent third party rather than a working tool.

At the moment, most issues in terms of liability are associated with the use of AI systems in the workplace. These concerns relate to the fundamental question of who is responsible for defects in data technologies in the workplace: employers, designers of the software, providers of training data or employees?[153] This question is partially caused by the so-called AI black box decision-making. This refers to the fact that it might not be possible to trace back why certain decisions were taken by an AI system. This creates a liability minefield because it is nearly impossible to explain the actions of an AI system when it causes

---

150 U. Pagallo, 'Robotrust and Legal Responsibility', *Knowledge, Technology & Policy,* 2010, vol. 23, no. 3–4, p. 368.

151 J. Prassl, 'What if your boss was an algorithm? Economic incentives, legal challenges, and the rise of artificial intelligence at work', *Comparative Labor Law & Policy Journal*, 2020, vol. 41, no. 1, p. 141.

152 Moore, 'OSH and the Future of Work: benefits and risks of artificial intelligence tools in workplaces', p. 10.

153 Prassl, 'What if your boss was an algorithm?', p. 141; Moore, The Mirror for (Artificial) Intelligence: In Whose Reflection?, p. 56.

damage. These AI systems only have a virtual nature. Thus, the damages they cause are in principle of a virtual nature. However, they could still harm their physical environment indirectly. This is a major difference with autonomous robots that could also perform physical acts and could cause damages directly in their physical environment. Not only the software of robots could be faulty and unstable, but also their sensors or connectivity.[154] Therefore, the black box decision-making of robots could lead to even more complex questions than AI systems. This black box decision-making causes also another uncertainty in the field of liability legislation because the liability of a person often requires that this person could foresee that his acts would cause damage. As demonstrated above, this requirement of foreseeability in current legislation is difficult to reconcile with autonomous robots. Based on their autonomous data-processing and decision-making, their physical acts could be unpredictable.[155] If a robot causes damage to a human co-worker, then an employer could argue that, based on this principle, he could not foresee that the robot would perform these movements.

35. Several suggestions have already been proposed to deal with these challenges for current liability legislation. Some authors suggest to adopt a compulsory insurance system when using autonomous robots.[156] Other researchers state that new models of accountability and liability may be required to approach the relationship between humans and smart robots.[157] Finally, there are also authors that propose to treat a robot as an employee in terms of the liability of employers. In this regard, assigning electronic personality to robots could indeed allow to shed responsibility of different parties in the workplace. However, this does not necessarily have to lead to assigning robots the same legal rights and obligations as human beings.[158]

At the moment, there is no clarity on the distribution of responsibility in the context of working with autonomous robots.[159] Thus, more research is needed to explore the most feasible liability distribution between employers and employees when it comes to the use of robots in the workplace. The Belgian vicarious liability system also needs to be examined if autonomous robots would be applied in the workplace. As this chapter has shown, the risks of using robots in the workplace cannot be underestimated. It should be made clear whether the employer, employee or a third party is responsible for the acts of an autonomous

---

154 Moore, 'OSH and the Future of Work: benefits and risks of artificial intelligence tools in workplaces', p. 6.

155 E. Tjong Tjin Tai, 'Aansprakelijkheid voor robots en algoritmes', *Nederlands Tijdschrift voor Handelsrecht*, 2017, no. 3, p. 126.

156 Pagallo, 'Robotrust and Legal Responsibility', p. 376.

157 The royal society, *Machine learning: the power and promise of computers that learn by example* (London: The Royal Society, 2017), p. 96, royalsociety.org/machine-learning.

158 De Stefano, '"Negotiating the algorithm": Automation, artificial intelligence and labour protection', p. 4.

159 Moore, 'The Mirror for (Artificial) Intelligence: In Whose Reflection?', p. 11.

robot in the workplace. To determine the boundaries of this distribution, the fundamental functions of liability law should not be forgotten. Liability law aims at providing an incentive for the 'responsible' person to take adequate measures to prevent the occurrence of damage and at providing protection for victims in terms of compensation.[160] This means that, in principle, the employer, who has the authority over and a duty of care towards employees, should guarantee their safety and should take adequate measures to prevent risks of working with autonomous robots.

5. HUMANISATION IN CONTEXT OF ROBOTISATION

36. Robots have already been part of the workplace for a long time. Nevertheless, awareness should be created for the second generation of robots that will invade the workplace. These robots will no longer be limited to the classic robot arms next to the production lines, but they will instead take many forms. Social robots and cobots will increasingly be used in many sectors to support workers in their tasks. Through the use of technologies that enable robots to act autonomously (e.g., through data analysis or self-learning technologies), robots will be able to move much more flexible and become (more) mobile. The workplace will, therefore, transform from a workplace in which robots and workers are separated from each other to a single common workplace in which workers and robots move around each other and work together. This will bring fundamental changes to the way people and robots interact, but also to the employment relationship between workers and employers. Indeed, the robot can no longer be seen as a working tool but rather as a robotic colleague of the employees. These fundamental changes can be considered as part of the fourth industrial revolution and also as the next phase in the division of labour between man and machine: robotisation.

37. As this chapter has shown, the consequences of robotisation are very diverse. They demonstrate once again that technology in the workplace has both positive and negative sides. Rifkin calls this the two faces of technology, which lead either to the end of work or to techno-paradise. Robots can lead to techno-paradise if they promote recruitment and create new jobs and protect workers' social rights more efficiently by guaranteeing their privacy, ensuring their health

[160] E. Palmerini, F. Azzarri, F. Battaglia, A. Bertolini, A. Carnevale, J. Carpaneto, F. Cavallo, A. Di Carlo, M. Cempini, M. Controzzi, B.-J. Koops, F. Lucivero, N. Mukerji, L. Nocco, A. Pirni, H. Shah, P. Salvini, M. Schellekens and K. Warwick, *D6.2 Guidelines on Regulating Robotics*, p. 55, https://www.robolaw.eu/RoboLaw_files/documents/robolaw_d6.2_guidelinesregulatingrobotics_20140922.pdf.

and safety, making more objective decisions and sharing responsibility more equitably. On the contrary, robotisation can also lead to a scenario of the end of work in which fewer jobs remain for human workers and labour protection is reduced by robots that, for example, continuously monitor workers, take decisions on employees on the basis of discriminatory criteria, increase work pressure and stress, and cause an ambiguous division of responsibilities due to the complexity of their functioning. Which of the two faces robotisation will obtain depends a lot on the way in which robots will be implemented and used in the workplace.

38. The role of labour law in this regard is to lead the world of work to techno-paradise. To achieve this goal, traditional principles of labour law might have to be redefined due to the changing human-robot relationship and employment relationship. For instance, the traditional legal interpretation of the employer's authority is already contested but this might be questioned even more because of the changing employment relationship. The Global Commission on the future of work argues that one principle of labour law should continue to be applied, namely 'labour is not a commodity'. However, the Commission immediately adds 'nor [is] it a robot'.[161] When redefining principles of labour law, the human-centred agenda, as proposed in the Centenary Declaration of the ILO, can be used as a guiding principle. The human-in-command approach, derived from the human-centred agenda, is an important starting point when dealing with autonomous robots in the workplace. The importance of human oversight for high-risk AI systems is also recognised in the proposed AI-Regulation. This regulation requires that the individual to whom the oversight is assigned, fully understands the capacities of the AI system and is able to correctly interpret its output, to override its decisions and to intervene in its operation.[162] Based on these legal developments, it may be expected that the humanisation of the workplace will again become relevant during the robotisation era and should be considered as the ultimate goal of adapting the workplace to the challenges of robotisation. In light of the humanisation of the workplace, this chapter showed the importance of the dialogue between social partners, the involvement and education of workers, the respect for their social rights and the establishment of a clear legal framework with applicable rights and obligations in the 'robotised' employment relationship.

---

161 Global Commission on the Future of Work, *Work for a brighter future*, p. 43.

162 Article 14 Proposal AI-Regulation.

CHAPTER 12
THE HYPOTHESIS OF TECHNOLOGICAL UNEMPLOYMENT CAUSED BY AI-DRIVEN AUTOMATION AND ITS IMPACT ON SOCIAL SECURITY LAW

Jakob Markus WERBROUCK*

1. INTRODUCTION

1. In this chapter we will examine the hypothesis of AI-driven automation, and the resulting technological unemployment and its impact on social security law. After briefly explaining, by way of several examples, what AI-driven automation entails (part 1), this chapter introduces the hypothesis of technological unemployment as a starting point for the analysis (part 2). Assuming this hypothesis is valid, this chapter then discusses its impact on social security law (part 3). In doing so, a distinction is made between employment as a structural feature of the design of social security legislation, and employment as the legitimation for the rights-based character of social security entitlements. Finally, this chapter concludes with the key message that this technological unemployment hypothesis demonstrates the vulnerability of our social security system to radical societal changes caused by technological advancement (part 4).

2. At the 2018 Google I/O conference Google CEO Sundar Pichai revealed Duplex, which is an extension of the Google Assistant application. It allows for the automation of conversations, with the presentation showcasing how the virtual assistant can autonomously complete calls such as booking a hairdresser's appointment or making reservations for a restaurant. It did so with notable ease, even if, when making reservations, the human on the other end of the line adds a

* Policy advisor for the Belgian minister for pensions and voluntary scientific collaborator at KU Leuven.

factor of complexity by misunderstanding what is said. Remarkably, this virtual assistant makes the calls in a surprisingly human-like manner, incorporating several elements in its speech that make it difficult to distinguish from a real human, such as using filler words ('um' or 'hmm'), adopting a human-like intonation, and introducing more response latency to make the conversation feel more natural.[1] Google Duplex is but one of several examples of the recent popularisation of new technologies that involve natural language understanding, others being Amazon's Lex, IBM's Watson, or Apple's Siri. The commercial interest in these technologies is considerable, since they mean a new leap forward in automating tasks such as translation, content analysis, or reasoning. Customer service, an integral part of any organisation's operation, for example, represents a commercial area in which substantial efficiency gains could be made through the existence of intelligent chat bots that never tire, forget, or make errors, and are considerably cheaper than their human counterparts.

3. The progress made in developing technology for natural language processing is paradigmatic of the wider promise of automation that the fourth industrial revolution brings. Cars that drive themselves, farms that grow crops autonomously, and robots that perform surgeries more accurately than specialist doctors can, are several other examples.[2] While AI-driven automation can undoubtedly yield great benefits for society as a whole, this chapter explores the extent to which it might challenge us to rethink the status quo, from the perspective of social security law. It is the central thesis of this chapter that should the fourth industrial revolution bring about fundamental, long-lasting changes in labour markets, this will force us to reconsider the legal foundations upon which social security law in Belgium is built. How will our social security, premised on the idea that rights to benefits must be 'earned', be reoriented when faced with a structural mass unemployment caused by far-reaching levels of automation? We will first consider the validity of the hypothesis that AI-driven automation will greatly impact labour markets and lead to technological unemployment, to then explore the challenges social security law would face in this new context.

---

1 'Google Duplex: An AI System for Accomplishing Real-World Tasks Over the Phone', Google AI Blog, 2018, https://ai.googleblog.com/2018/05/duplex-ai-system-for-natural-conversation.html.

2 T. O'Reilly, *De nieuwe economie: hoe gaat technologie de wereld veranderen en wat betekent dit voor ons?* (Uithoorn: Karakter Uitgevers, 2018), p. 18; M. Frank, B. Pring and P. Roehrig, *What to Do When Machines Do Everything: Five Ways Your Business Can Thrive in an Economy of Bots, AI, and Data* (Hoboken: John Wiley & Sons, 2017), p. 2.

2. THE TECHNOLOGICAL UNEMPLOYMENT HYPOTHESIS

4. This chapter's central thesis is that the increasing prevalence of robots and AI-driven automation will force us to reconsider the premises upon which social security is built. In order to formulate this conclusion, however, it makes the assumption that AI-driven automation will bring about fundamental changes in labour markets. More specifically, it assumes that automation will result in *at least* a transitional period characterised by structurally high levels of technological unemployment. In this regard, the British economist Keynes defines technological unemployment as 'unemployment due to our discovery of means of economising the use of labour outrunning the pace at which we can find new uses for labour'.[3]

5. However, it is important to note that not everyone will readily accept this hypothesis of significant and structural unemployment caused by the technological progress associated with the fourth industrial revolution. The debate whether or not the further development and integration of AI and robots will indeed lead to mass structural unemployment is a contested one.[4] There are those who maintain that it is unlikely that, given for example the right government interventions and other measures, the advances of the fourth industrial revolution will lead to a lasting prevalence of technological unemployment.[5] Their argument is – at least in part – based on the experience of previous industrial revolutions.

6. Ever since the first industrial revolution introduced machines in the workplace, the fear that an increasing proportion of the labour market would be threatened by technological progress has been a recurring theme. In 19th century England, *luddism* was born, a social movement that fought for better working conditions in the textile industry. People, however, mainly remember this movement because of protests that involved the destruction of weaving machines. In this way, it serves as the historical symbol of the

3 J.M. Keynes, *Essays in Persuasion* (New York: W.W. Norton & Company, 1963), pp. 358–373.

4 In this regard, it is interesting to note the study performed by Walsh, who discovered that while both experts and non-experts in the fields of AI and robotics predict a large fraction of occupations to be at risk due to automation in the next couple of decades, the experts were significantly more cautious in their predictions than non-experts. See T. Walsh, 'Expert and non-expert opinion about technological unemployment', *International Journal of Automation and Computing*, 2018, vol. 15, no. 5, pp. 641–642; H. Adachi, K. Inagaki, T. Nakamura and Y. Osumi, *Technological progress, income distribution, and unemployment: theory and empirics* (Singapore: Springer, 2019), p. 48; J. Øvretveit, 'Impact of digitalization on employment and working conditions', in A. Larsson and R. Teigland (eds.), *The Digital Transformation of Labor* (London-New York: Routledge, 2020), pp. 334–335.

5 See for example Y.J. Kim, K. Kim and S. Lee, 'The rise of technological unemployment and its implications on the future macroeconomic landscape', *Futures*, 2017, vol. 87, pp. 8–9.

tension between technological progress and employment.[6] The last two centuries, from the first industrial revolution to the present day, have not set a convincing historical precedent that gives substance to this fear of technological unemployment.[7] Although technological progress has on several occasions caused certain workers to lose their place because their tasks could now be performed by machines, the net effect has remained positive. Today, compared to the era of the first industrial revolution, we earn more, work less, and have a higher standard of living. Economists describe pointing to the opposite, namely that automation would lead to large-scale and systemic unemployment, as the 'fallacy of the luddites': new technology does not destroy jobs, it merely changes the composition of jobs in the economy.[8] Past industrial revolutions have all seen radical changes in labour market composition, yet with a net positive effect as the outcome. For example, whereas pre-industrial Belgium could still be characterised as an agricultural society, with one in three Belgians working in agriculture, the transition towards an industrial society has resulted in an ever smaller proportion of the working population employed in agriculture, coming in at only one in eighty nowadays.[9] Likewise, the shift from an industrial to a post-industrial society has meant a steady decline in the number of those working in manufacturing, dropping from nearly 45% of the population in the 1950s to under 25% half a century later.[10] However, this shift away from employment in agriculture and manufacturing has not lead to food shortages, shortages of manufactured goods, nor mass structural unemployment. The same line of reasoning is used to argue that, while AI-driven automation might lead to the gradual disappearance of middle-skill jobs, resulting in a likely more polarised labour market with an increased demand for either low-skilled or high-skilled jobs,[11] the net effect remains positive or neutral.

7. On the other side of the argument, the assumption that AI-driven automation will fundamentally alter labour markets is based on the idea that, under the influence of the fourth industrial revolution, the labour landscape, affected by labour-saving innovation, will change so radically in such a relatively short period of time that – *at least* for a significant transitional period – a

---

6 M.A. Cherry, 'The Future Encyclopedia of Luddism', in W. Davies, *Economic Science Fictions* (London: Goldsmiths Press, 2018), pp. 327–341.

7 E. Brynjolfsson and A. McAfee, *The Second Machine Age – Work, Progress, and Prosperity in a Time of Brilliant Technologies* (New York-London: W.W. Norton & Company, 2014), pp. 99–101.

8 M.R. Ford, *The Lights in the Tunnel: Automation, Accelerating Technology and the Economy of the Future* (United States: Acculant Publishing, 2009), pp. 95–96.

9 FOD Economie, 'Kerncijfers landbouw' [Core figures agriculture], *Algemene Directie Statistiek*, 2016, p. 9.

10 P. De Grauwe, 'De toekomst van de industrie in België', *Leuvense economische standpunten*, 2003, vol. 102, p. 2.

11 D.H. Autor, 'Polanyi's paradox and the shape of employment growth', *NBER Working Paper*, 2014, no. 20485, pp. 10–12.

structural form of unemployment will occur.[12] There are reasons to believe that the advent of AI and robots will indeed shake up the labour market in ways unlike the past. In the past, automation mainly affected tasks that the unskilled could perform. In this new reality, however, the scope of automation is predicted to be much broader, affecting middle-skill jobs more than low-skill ones, and even including tasks traditionally associated with highly skilled people.[13] Artificial intelligence and robotisation have opened up avenues for automation that go beyond what used to be thought possible. For example, software with artificial intelligence is already being used to interpret mammography data, thirty times faster than specialised doctors and with significantly greater accuracy.[14] Whereas newspaper editors used to need experienced journalists to fact-check and synthesise information from different sources into a single newspaper article, creative software can now already automate certain standard news reporting, such as sports coverage or weather forecasting.[15] This capacity for automation will affect a large percentage of the professionally active population. In 2017, McKinsey Global Institute performed a study of 46 countries, accounting for 80% of the global labour market, and concluded that almost half of all labour can be automated already using available technology.[16] Although few occupations today can be fully automated, 60% of all occupations have at least 30% technically automated activities.[17]

8. The level of automation that is technologically feasible thus raises important questions. Brynjolfsson and MacAfee for example wonder what will happen if future societies have robots at their disposal that can perform every task a human worker can, including building more robots, and do so all day long at a significantly lower cost.[18] If a substantial part of the population is made technologically unemployed, so that unemployment is no longer a contingent social risk but a structural necessity of future society, how would we reorient our social security principles that revolve around earning one's rights to social benefits? It is this hypothesis of technological unemployment that this chapter takes as a starting point for further analysis.

---

12 Adachi, Inagaki, Nakamura and Osumi, *Technological progress, income distribution, and unemployment: theory and empirics*, pp. 48, 86.

13 McKinsey Global Institute, *Harnessing Automation for a Future that Works* (New York: McKinsey Global Institute, 2017), pp. 30–31; M. Loi, 'Technological unemployment and human disenhancement', *Ethics Inf Technol*, 2015, vol. 17, p. 208.

14 Frank, Pring and Roehrig, *What to Do When Machines Do Everything: Five Ways Your Business Can Thrive in an Economy of Bots, AI, and Data*, p. 2.

15 *Ibid.*, pp. 97–100.

16 McKinsey Global Institute, *Harnessing Automation for a Future that Works*, pp. 39–60.

17 *Ibid.*, p. 15.

18 Brynjolfsson and McAfee, *The Second Machine Age – Work, Progress, and Prosperity in a Time of Brilliant Technologies*, pp. 101–103.

3. THE POTENTIAL IMPACT OF TECHNOLOGICAL UNEMPLOYMENT ON SOCIAL SECURITY

9. Taking the hypothesis of technological unemployment as a starting point, this part explores the legal questions that may be raised when modern social security systems are confronted with significant and structural unemployment.[19] This analysis focuses on the Belgian context but presents insights that can be generalised to social security systems with similar characteristics. We will be discussing two important ways in which technological unemployment could make us question some of the premises underlying modern social security systems. On the one hand, we will discuss how employment functions as an essential variable in social security legislation. On the other hand, we will explore how employment has been key in anchoring rights-based entitlement to social security benefits.

3.1. EMPLOYMENT AS AN ESSENTIAL VARIABLE IN SOCIAL SECURITY LEGISLATION

10. The first important question that the technological unemployment hypothesis raises, is that of the how social security legislation is to be conceived. Past or present employment status is a necessary structural feature of the design of several social security systems around the world, as it is used to define *inter alia* scope of application, benefit levels, and benefit conditionality.[20] The reason for this is that several social security systems around the world have been deliberately constructed or have organically evolved with the purpose of providing social benefits *by and for workers* – which necessarily presumes some form of employment status.[21] These are what are traditionally called *Bismarckian* social security systems.[22] Indeed, an analysis of the historical context in which the Belgian welfare state came to be explains why the variable of employment and the design of social security systems are inextricably linked.

---

19 The analysis made in this chapter is in part based on an analysis made earlier on the concept of work history. See in greater detail J. Werbrouck, 'Understanding Bismarck's Legacy: The concept of work history in Belgian social security law', *European Journal of Social Security*, 2019, vol. 21, no. 4, pp. 326–350.

20 Another important dimension is how employment serves as the basis for the mode of financing of social security systems, as social security contributions may be levied as a payroll tax. However, discussing a complex matter such as the financing of social security systems would take us too far for the purposes of this chapter. We will thus be limiting our analysis to a strictly legal perspective.

21 It can also presume linking benefits to wages, however, again, we will be restricting our analysis to a purely legal one.

22 B. Scheubel, *Bismarck's Institutions: A Historical Perspective on the Social Security Hypothesis* (Tübingen: Mohr Siebeck, 2013), pp. 93–94.

3.1.1. *Historical Significance of Employment in the Design of the Belgian Welfare State*

11. In Belgium, the so-called 'Social Pact',[23] secretly negotiated between social partners during World War II, is generally regarded as the foundation of the modern welfare state that would rise from the rubble. The Pact entailed a mutual recognition of interests between both employers and workers and the institutionalisation of dialogue between them, with the intention of putting a halt to social unrest and allowing for the achievement of common socio-economic goals.[24] While the pivotal nature of the Social Pact has been subject to some debate,[25] its materialisation is widely viewed as the birth of a consolidated and comprehensive system of social security.[26] By making social security coverage compulsory and integrating existing schemes, the Social Pact marked the transition from a collection of different social insurance schemes in to one consolidated welfare system.[27]

12. Crucial to a full understanding of the potential impact of technological unemployment on modern Belgian social security is to take into account the theoretical framework upon which the Social Pact was built. While this 'contract of social solidarity' unmistakably served as the catalyst for implementing a comprehensive system of social protection that would ultimately encompass nearly all citizens, its originally intended field of application was decidedly narrower. As the name itself suggests, the Social Pact was above all a compromise between workers' organisations and industrialists. It was the result of numerous meetings concerning the 'profound study of the worker's questions'.[28] Its goal was to 'take urgent measures' in order to 'combat the misery suffered by the majority of workers during the occupation and thereby pave the way for new societal progress', which above all meant an absence of further labour conflicts.[29]

---

23 The *Ontwerp van overeenkomst tot sociale solidariteit* [Draft of agreement of social solidarity] is colloquially referred to as the Social Pact. The proposals put forward in the Pact were materialised by the decree-law of 28 December 1944 (*B.S.* 30 December 1944). See 'Ontwerp van overeenkomst tot sociale solidariteit', *Arbeidsblad*, LXVI(1945), pp. 9–19.

24 I. Cassiers and L. Denayer, 'Sociaal overleg en sociaal-economische veranderingen in België van 1944 tot heden', *UCL Discussion Paper*, 2009, pp. 23–24.

25 Some authors have pointed to pivotal events that took place both before and after the Social Pact to provide nuance to the idea that the Social Pact was a radical breaking point with the past. See notably D. Luyten and G. Vanthemsche (eds.), *Het Sociaal Pact van 1944. Oorsprong, betekenis en gevolgen* (Brussels: VUBPress, 1995), pp. 9–15.

26 K. Vleminckx, 'Van de redactie', *Belgisch Tijdschrift voor Sociale Zekerheid*, 2014, vol. 4, pp. 385–388.

27 A. Hemerijck and I. Marx, 'Continental Welfare at a Crossroads: The Choice between Activation and Minimum Income Protection in Belgium and the Netherlands', in B. Palier (ed.), *A Long Goodbye to Bismarck? The Politics of Welfare Reform in Continental Europe* (Amsterdam: Amsterdam University Press, 2010), p. 139.

28 'Ontwerp van overeenkomst tot sociale solidariteit', *Arbeidsblad*, LXVI(1945), p. 9.

29 *Ibid.*

Included in these urgent measures was the establishment of a 'complete system of social security for employees', which implied the levying of social contributions from workers' wages in order to finance their own social protection.[30] This social protection consisted of pensions, unemployment benefits, sickness and invalidity benefits, child benefits, and paid holidays. All these benefits were directly linked to the benefit seeker's (former) professional status.

13. The underlying idea behind this contributory model of social security by and for workers clearly resonated with the words of Otto von Bismarck. When Bismarck implemented reforms that led to the first welfare state in Europe, he likewise proclaimed the need to find a solution for 'the real grievance of the worker', i.e. the 'insecurity of his existence'.[31] The social issues that stemmed from the rapid growth in population and urbanisation associated with the 19th century industrial revolution put the question of the workers' insecurity of existence on the forefront of the political agenda.[32] Consequently, the historical context that incited Bismarck to create his workers' insurance was similar to that of the Social Pact, in that it is characterised by a desire to prevent social conflict by answering the demands of workers' movements.[33] It was an integral part of the chancellor's *Realpolitik* to enact profound social reforms in order to curtail the political impact of these movements.[34] A highly visible system of state-led social security appealed to Bismarck, as it would enable him to secure both workers' votes and loyalty.[35] Bismarck's focus on providing protection for workers consequently led to a conception of social security, which builds upon the idea that entitlements should be associated with employment status, aiming at providing a *social insurance* for salaried workers who have paid contributions.[36] As a result of these similarities, as well as those in administrative organisation, financing, and benefit structure, it has been widely accepted that the Belgian

---

30 *Ibid.*, 12–16.

31 F. Hollyday, *Bismarck* (Englewood Cliffs: Prentice-Hall, 1970), p. 65.

32 M. Stolleis, *Origins of the German Welfare State: Social Policy in Germany to 1945* (Berlin-Heidelberg: Springer, 2013), p. 5.

33 M. Van Meerhaeghe, 'Bismarck and the social question', *Journal of Economic Studies*, 2006, vol. 33, no. 4, p. 295.

34 Bismarck was open about his intentions, even later stating that his idea was to 'bribe the working class' to regard the state as a social institution existing for their sake and interested in their welfare. See P. Paur, 'The Corporatist Character of Bismarck's Social Policy', *European History Quarterly*, 1981, vol. 11, no. 4, p. 445; Stolleis, *Origins of the German Welfare State: Social Policy in Germany to 1945*, pp. 54–55.

35 O. Pflanze, *Bismarck and the Development of Germany, Volume III: The Period of Fortification 1880–1898* (Princeton: Princeton University Press, 1990), pp. 154–155.

36 B. Palier, 'Ordering change: Understanding the 'Bismarckian' Welfare Reform Trajectory', in B. Palier (ed.), *A Long Goodbye to Bismarck? The Politics of Welfare Reform in Continental Europe* (Amsterdam: Amsterdam University Press, 2010), p. 24.

social security system created by the Social Pact follows the Bismarckian tradition of welfare systems.[37]

14. It is this resonance with Bismarck's idea on social security that explains why employment – or lack thereof – can have such an impact on the Belgian system. In both cases, the creation of a system of social security was a response to a specific political, sociological, and economic context.[38] Bismarck was confronted with the effects of rapid industrialisation, while the Belgian population sought relief after the damage inflicted by two world wars with a global economic meltdown in-between.[39] In attempting to prevent the escalation of social conflict driven by the demands of the workers' movement, both Bismarck and the Belgian government adopted legislative reforms that created a comprehensive system of social protection *for workers*. Since the primary target of these social reforms were workers, it logically follows that past or present employment status is structurally at the centre of this system. Past or present employment allows the legislator to clearly delineate the circle of solidarity to which the system of social protection extends. In accordance with Bismarck's underlying goals, his conception of social security intrinsically offers income security only to those who have contributed through work.[40] In this way, the contributory principle serves as an answer to both the question of defining the relevant scope of application as well as the funding source of social security.

3.1.2. Resulting Impact of this Genesis on Social Security Legislation

15. As a result of the historical context in which the fundamental pieces of social security legislation were drafted in Belgium, the hypothesis that at least a majority of the population would become unemployed is problematic from a systemic legislative standpoint. An individual's past or present employment status fulfils a specific functional role within Bismarckian social security systems such as that of Belgium. Employment is an imperative that is anchored in the legal framework of social security in three important ways: it defines access to benefits, benefit levels, as well as the conditionality for continuing to receive benefits. In other words, an individual's past or present employment is a variable in the equation of social security which represents a certain number of days or years, which, by virtue of that number alone, can impact their social security

37 Important to note is that this typology as being Bismarckian (or Beveridgean) is not to be thought of in terms of absolutes. As for example Palier argues, one could also classify countries within the Bismarckian tradition as being conservative-corporatist under Esping-Andersen's typology of welfare systems. See B. Palier, 'Ordering change: Understanding the 'Bismarckian' Welfare Reform Trajectory', pp. 21–25.

38 Stolleis, *Origins of the German Welfare State: Social Policy in Germany to 1945*, p. 55.

39 Vleminckx, 'Van de redactie', p. 387.

40 W. Scholz, 'Financing social security out of contributions: About origins, present discussions and prospects of a success story', *International Social Security Review*, 2015, vol. 68, no. 4, p. 3.

status in three ways: it can open up a right to certain benefits, alter the level of the benefit in question, or decide on the continuing entitlement to benefits.[41]

16. Firstly, we can see this inextricable link between employment and the design of social security systems manifested in the admissibility criteria of social security benefits. Given how the original goal of the Belgian welfare state was to provide protection for *workers*, the concept of work history is a logical accessory to accomplishing this goal: it enables the legislator to *identify who is a worker*. Only those that pass a certain threshold of occupational activity can be considered as such for the purposes of social security legislation. Employment history thus translates the status of being a worker into a specific numerical requirement, which is then used to form cut-off points in benefit entitlement.

17. For sickness and invalidity benefits, this is materialised in the 'waiting time' requirement. Prior to being able to claim entitlement to sickness benefits, the benefit seeker must have gone through a waiting period of 12 months, in which a record of at least 180 days worked must have been established.[42] A similar requirement is made for the unemployment benefit, which demands that a certain amount of days must have been worked during a reference period. Both the amount of days worked and the length of the reference period depend on the age of the benefit seeker.[43] In pension legislation, the admissibility criterion based on work history is found in the early retirement scheme, which allows for a lower minimum pensionable age when a certain amount of years worked is reached. As of 2019 for example, it is possible to retire at the earliest at age 63 when a career of at least 42 years has been established.[44]

18. Secondly, employment is also relevant for the calculation of benefit levels. Whereas its primary function is arguably to identify those admitted to the circle

---

41 Furthermore, due to the levying of social security contributions as a payroll tax, directly linked to employment is contribution history, with the level of contributions having a significant impact on benefit levels as well. Since wages serve as the basis for calculating social security contributions, the difference between low and high wages, and corresponding contribution levels, can result in significant differences in benefits ultimately received. This is however a more complex matter, as legislative trends over the past few decades have limited the proportionality between wage contributions and social benefit. As a result, the fact that one has worked is in general in and of itself sufficient. The *de minima* and *de maxima* limits, and the sometimes small spread between the two, make that employment, and not income contributions, is the primordial condition that opens a right to social benefits.

42 Article 116/1 Wet van 14 juli 1994 betreffende de verplichte verzekering voor geneeskundige verzorging en uitkeringen [Law concerning mandatory health insurance].

43 Article 30 Koninklijk Besluit van 25 november 1991 houdende de werkloosheidsreglementering [Royal decree concerning unemployment regulation].

44 Article 4 Koninklijk Besluit van 23 december 1996 tot uitvoering van de artikelen 15, 16 en 17 van de wet van 26 juli 1996 tot modernisering van de sociale zekerheid en vrijwaring van de leefbaarheid van de wettelijke pensioenen [Royal decree that gives execution to the law of 26 July 1996 on the modernisation of social security and the safeguarding of the financial viability of statutory pensions].

of solidarity, not everyone admitted can present a similarly strong claim. Inside this large circle, a smaller circle is drawn where the number of contributing days or years is used as a tool to differentiate those that have earned the right to 'more' solidarity. In this way, a qualified record of work history legitimises higher benefit levels. The Belgian unemployment benefit for example is regressive in nature, meaning that benefit levels go down as time spent under the scheme progresses. This regression is spread out over three time periods, each divided into multiple phases, with each time period and each phase signifying a lower level of unemployment benefit.[45] The first time period lasts one year for all benefit recipients, but the duration of the second time period is entirely dependent on the work history of the benefit recipient. A limited work history means that the benefit recipient will end up in the third period shortly after completing the first time period. Depending on the family situation, this can have a significant financial impact, as the third period is a fixed amount in nature and closely resembles social assistance benefit levels, whereas the second period maintains a higher benefit level.

19. In addition, we can find two examples of the impact of a qualified employment record on the benefit levels in pension legislation as well. First, Belgian pension legislation has two minimum pension schemes. For every year in one's career, an amount which is representative of that year, calculated as a percentage of the annual wage, is added until a full career is reached. One minimum scheme ensures a minimum for every yearly amount should it fall below a certain threshold, while the other minimum scheme reviews the ultimate pension and tops that up if necessary. Both minimum schemes are reserved for those who can establish a qualified work history. The first minimum scheme requires at least 15 years of prior occupational activity with a minimum of 104 full-time equivalent days worked per year.[46] The second minimum scheme demands at least two thirds of a 'full career', meaning at least 30 years of work history.[47] The recent 2022 pension reform added another condition to this: that of a record of "actual work".[48] A day of "actual work" is to be understood as a day on which the individual concerned performs labour for which social security contributions are paid, to the exclusion of periods which do not involve any labour but are assimilated as such, e.g., unemployment, statutory holidays,

45 Articles 114–115 Koninklijk Besluit van 25 november 1991 houdende de werkloosheidsreglementering [Royal decree concerning unemployment regulation].

46 Article 8 Koninklijk Besluit van 23 december 1996 tot uitvoering van de artikelen 15, 16 en 17 van de wet van 26 juli 1996 tot modernisering van de sociale zekerheid en vrijwaring van de leefbaarheid van de wettelijke pensioenen [Royal decree that gives execution to the law of 26 July 1996 on the modernisation of social security and the safeguarding of the financial viability of statutory pensions].

47 Article 152 Wet 8 augustus 1980 betreffende de budgettaire voorstellen 1979–1980 [Law concerning the budgetary proposals for 1979–1980].

48 Belgian government, 2022 Pension reform agreement, 19 July 2022.

sickness and invalidity, etc. Exceptions are made for leaves due to maternity, breastfeeding, and palliative care, as well as any period of inactivity due to a recognised disability. These periods of inactivity are still assimilated, even under the "actual work" condition. The benefit claimant must prove either 20*250 days (strict criterion) or 20*156 days (flexible criterion, for part-time workers) of actual work over the course of his career to gain access to the minimum pension. This new condition is expected to significantly restrict the possibility of individuals accessing minimum pension benefits with a limited track record of actual work, as they can no longer rely on assimilated periods to meet the work history conditions of the minimum pension. Second, pensioners with a qualified work history are allowed to deviate from the general principle that pensions cannot be cumulated with a wage without a proportional deduction. If the pension recipient can showcase a work history of at least 42 years, he is allowed to cumulate the pension with a wage without deduction. This rule, however, only applies to those younger than 65, as cumulation is allowed in any case when the age of 65 is reached.[49]

20. Thirdly and lastly, employment can serve as a necessary ground for continuing to receive benefits. Since the 1970s, the doctrine of activation has steadily been gaining ground in social policy. The essence of this doctrine is an attempt to connect social rights to conditions, by for example obligating benefit recipients to participate in work activities.[50] In other words, benefit recipients must do everything reasonably possible to reduce their financial dependence on the relevant social benefit, so as to promote economic self-reliance.[51] Those who cannot refute their suitability to provide services on the labour market, whether due to incapacity to work or old age, are legally obliged to look for work in order to (be able to) obtain benefits. The refusal to participate in the employment process may result, among other things, in the loss of benefits for the person concerned. This activation logic is perhaps most clearly manifested in the social assistance scheme: before the age of 25, people no longer have an absolute right to any social benefits, but only to integration in a working environment.[52] It is

---

49 Article 2 Koninklijk Besluit van 28 mei 2013 tot wijziging van diverse reglementaire bepalingen betreffende de cumulatie van een pensioen in de werknemersregeling met beroepsinkomsten of met sociale vergoedingen [Royal decree amending diverse regulatory clauses concerning the cumulation of an employee pension with a professional income or with social benefits].

50 J.T. Jessen and P.A. Tufte, 'Discretionary decision-making in a changing context of activation policies and welfare reforms', *Jnl. Soc. Pol.*, 2014, vol. 43, no. 2, pp. 272–273.

51 A. Molander and G. Torsvik, 'Getting people into work: what (if anything) can justify mandatory activation of welfare recipients?', *Journal of Applied Philosophy*, 2015, vol. 32, no. 4, p. 373.

52 P. Reman and P. Pochet, 'Transformations du système belge de sécurité sociale', in P. Vielle, P. Pochet and I. Cassiers (eds.), *L'Etat social actif. Vers un changement de paradigme?* (Brussel: Peter Lang, 2005), p. 141.

also clearly discernible in the legislation on unemployment, which requires that the benefit seeker is to be unemployed 'due to circumstances independent of one's own volition'[53] and that he or she must remain 'available for the labour market'.[54]

21. As a result, a future in which a significant part of society is structurally unemployed due to technological advances would force us to reconsider the way in which employment features so centrally in our social security legislation. A serious question to consider is: if social security rights become *de facto* unattainable for a significant part of the population, and social security is thus arguably no longer 'social' nor offering security, would the reliance on employment as a distinguishing factor for access to benefits, benefit levels, and continuing entitlement still be sustainable from a social policy standpoint?

3.2. EMPLOYMENT AS A LEGITIMATION FOR THE RIGHTS-BASED CHARACTER OF SOCIAL SECURITY ENTITLEMENTS

22. Secondly, employment may not only be essential to the way social security legislation is conceived but can also be a *legitimating factor in the rights-based character of social security entitlements*. While the majority of social security benefits require the benefit seeker to demonstrate a particular employment history, or at least a willingness to work, this premise can also be regarded in a *normative sense*, as arguably many would opine that employment history or willingness to work *should be considered* the '*raison d'être*' of someone's right to social protection. Without this element of work, and its logical accessory, social security contributions, it is difficult to imagine that someone could assert full rights to social protection. This should in and of itself not be surprising: historically, society had to count on a working population in order to survive, and so redistributing valuable resources without any contributions or a commitment to get back to contributing as soon as possible, would not only have displayed a lack of solidarity with the rest of the population, but also would have likely meant, from a financial standpoint, the end of collective social protection. In this way, the contributory principle found in social insurance serves as an answer to the collective action problem posed by the mass poverty that was acutely present in post-war Belgium.[55] Consequently, from the perspective of the individual benefit seeker, the link with employment *ensures the legitimacy* of any claim to

53 Article 44 Koninklijk Besluit van 25 november 1991 houdende de werkloosheids-reglementering [Royal decree concerning unemployment regulation].

54 Article 56 Koninklijk Besluit van 25 november 1991 houdende de werkloosheids-reglementering [Royal decree concerning unemployment regulation].

55 A. De Swaan, 'The sociogenesis of the welfare state: By way of introduction', *Sociologisch Tijdschrift*, 1987, vol. 13, no. 4, pp. 581–582.

social security benefits, by presenting an objectively measurable justification in the form of days or years worked, or a demonstrable willingness to work.

23. Furthermore, from the perspective of the relation between citizens and government, linking employment to social security rights also provides an alternative to the more arbitrary way of granting rights through merit, by making it possible to objectively 'earn' one's own entitlement. As U.S. president Franklin Delano Roosevelt famously retorted to the remark that it would have made more economic sense to fund social security through general revenues instead of a payroll tax: 'We put those payroll contributions there so as to give the contributors a legal, moral, and political right to collect their pensions and their unemployment benefits. With those taxes in there, no damn politician can ever scrap my social security program. Those taxes aren't a matter of economics, they're straight politics'.[56] In the past, alternative principles such as individual merit or citizenship were used in making the decision whether or not to grant social benefits. For example, the first comprehensive piece of social protection legislation in Belgium, which implemented a state pension scheme for civil servants, demanded a work history of at least 30 years of civil service in order to grant access to the pension.[57] However, establishing such a record of service was in and of itself *not sufficient* to obtain a pension. The government 'could' award a pension to a civil servant who 'has dedicated his life to providing services to the state', but had no legal obligation to do so.[58] The government thus retained the right to decide when to grant pension rights, interpreting a civil servant's work history as neither an 'imperative, nor absolute' reason to do so.[59] Viewed from this historical perspective, arguably one of the most enduring legacies of Bismarck's idea of linking social security to employment is the widespread acceptance that it is both a necessary and sufficient condition for access to social security rights. Implementing a social security scheme that would give the government the right to arbitrarily decide whether or not one has sufficiently

---

56 A. Meier Schlesinger, *The coming of the new deal, 1933–1935* (Boston: Houghton Mifflin Harcourt, 2003), pp. 308–309.

57 Article 1 Algemene wet van 21 juli 1844 op de burgerlijke en kerkelijke pensioenen [Law concerning ecclesiastical and civil pensions].

58 In the words of then Minister for Public Works Rolin, a pension could not be thought of as a legally enforcable right: 'La pension que l'État paye à des fonctionnaires d'un âge avancé, qui l'ont servi pendant de longues annés, est une dette, il est vrai, mais une dette dont le principe n'est pas de la même nature que celui d'une dette civile. C'est une dette d'équité, de reconnaissance [...]" [The pension that the State pays to civil servants of an advanced age, who have served for many years, is a debt, it is true, but a debt of which the principle is not of the same nature as that of a debt under private law. It is a debt of equity, of gratitude (...)]. See *Parl. Hand.* Kamer 18 januari 1849, 480 [Parliamentary acts Belgian Chamber of Representatives].

59 Zitting van de Kamer van 14 maart 1844, *BS* 15 maart 1844 [Session of the Belgian Chamber of Representatives]; zitting van de Senaat van 11 juli 1844, *BS* 12 juli 1844 [Session of the Belgian Senate].

'merited' social protection, with one's work history being merely indicative, seems hardly imaginable nowadays.[60]

24. It must be noted, however, that the question has arisen whether or not the idea that social security must necessarily be 'earned' still stands today. It is indeed true that the years after World War II have seen a gradual incorporation of elements outside of the logic of a social security *by and for* workers propagated by Bismarck, making some express doubts as to the accuracy of the classification of present-day Belgian social security as still being Bismarckian.[61] While the 19th century context allowed for a unitary logic, narrowing down the scope of application of social protection to the generally poor working class, the past decades have demanded a different approach, since workers are no longer necessarily poor nor are the poor typically workers.[62] One of the most visible departures from this logic arguably is the weakening of the contributory principle, through adding a multitude of exceptions to the general rule that benefits should be awarded to the extent that contributions are paid.[63] The introduction of certain minimum protection measures, reducing or even removing the duty to pay contributions, forms an apt illustration of this weakening bond.[64] Another well-known example is the incorporation of a universalist and means-tested logic into the child benefit scheme by creating a residual 'guaranteed child benefit' for those children that cannot rely on the professional status of their parents to obtain a right to social security, but

60 However, even though linking employment to social security rights thus presents itself as the objective and neutral alternative to establishing social security rights based on other principles, this does not mean it is entirely value-free itself. Concepts such as work history, which measures past employment in terms of years and days worked, is not a purely mathematical notion, but contains a number of minimal qualitative characteristics required to make it function within a legal framework. These minimal qualitative characteristics include how to define a working day, by requiring a certain number of hours worked, or how to define work itself, by distinguishing between formal and informal employment. These unstated value judgments that were involved in designing the quantitative dimension of work history surface when confronted with certain cases that sit uneasy with the current legislative framework of social security, such as gender equality, given how women more often work part-time and have a more difficult time accumulating the necessary amount of days worked. See in greater detail Werbrouck, 'Understanding Bismarck's Legacy: The concept of work history in Belgian social security law', pp. 326–350.

61 J.J. Dupeyroux, *Ontwikkeling en tendenties van de stelsels van sociale zekerheid der lid-staten van de Europese Gemeenschappen en Groot-Brittannië* (Luxemburg: E.G.K.S., 1966), pp. 70 & 184–185; D. Pieters, *Onze sociale zekerheid: anders en beter* (Kapellen: Pelckmans, 2009) pp. 21–25; J. Van Langendonck, A. Van Regenmortel and Y. Stevens, *Handboek Socialezekerheidsrecht* (Antwerp-Cambridge: Intersentia, 2015), p. 36.

62 J. Van Langendonck, 'Een rechtmatige financiering van de sociale zekerheid' [A just financing of social security], *Tijdschrift voor Sociaal Recht*, 2005, p. 223.

63 J. Van Langendonck, 'Einde van het tijdperk van de werkgeversbijdrage?' [The end of the era for employer contributions?], *Tijdschrift voor Sociaal Recht*, 2018, p. 103.

64 G. Gieselink, H. Peeters, V. Van Gestel, J. Berghman and B. Van Buggenhout, *Onzichtbare pensioenen in België* (Leuven: KU Leuven Departement sociologie, 2002), pp. 85–86.

are needy. This has resulted in virtually every child in Belgium being socially insured.[65]

25. However, even if we accept the steady integration of elements extraneous to the contributory logic of social insurance, it is hard to deny the enduring legacy of Bismarck in the way we think about social security. While certain rights can nowadays exist independently from contributions, the *idea of social security* itself still relies on the Bismarckian notion that work and entitlement to social security benefits are inextricably linked. For example, the coalition agreement that led to the formation of the Michel I government in 2014 typified the Belgian social security system as a careful balancing act between 'the principle of solidarity and the principle of insurance'.[66] It proclaimed that as a *quid pro quo* for the broadest shoulders bearing the biggest burden, the poorest who enjoy social security benefits 'should as much as possible be guided towards finding employment so that they too can contribute to the financing of the social security system'.[67] The same idea can be found in the coalition agreement of the subsequent De Croo government, which states that 'a strong and effective social security system relies on a healthy mix of solidarity and insurance'.[68] Indeed, the idea that social security rights must be earned through work is still firmly accepted in Belgian popular opinion.[69]

26. These words illustrate what can be described as the two essential elements of contributory social security systems: the need for social insurance and the fact that one needs to *earn access* to this social insurance scheme.[70] Even if newer legislation progressively dismantles the once strict relationship between contribution and social protection, the idea that the legitimacy of one's claims to social security benefits comes from having earned them through employment, one of the essential characteristics of the Bismarckian theoretical framework, still stands firm. An individual's past or present employment thus remains one

65 T. Hufkens, D. Vandelannoote, W. Van Lancker and G. Verbist, *Hervorming van de Vlaamse kinderbijslag en armoedebestrijding: een simulatie van alternatieven* (Antwerp: Universiteit Antwerpen – Centrum voor Sociaal Beleid Herman Deleeck, 2013), pp. 4–5.

66 Coalition agreement Belgian government 10 October 2014, p. 43.

67 *Ibid.*

68 Coalition agreement Belgian government 30 September 2020, p. 47.

69 A survey performed in 2012 revealed that nearly 75% of the population agrees with the statement that contributing to social security should always be obligatory. According to Elchardus and Spruyt, this confirms that the 'the core idea of social security as based on social insurance is still supported by an overwhelming majority'. See M. Elchardus and B. Spruyt, *Bevolkingsonderzoek solidariteit. Deelrapport 1: Het draagvlak van de verzorgingsstaat* (Bond Moyson, 2014), pp. 10–11.

70 D. S. Kaplan and S. Levy, 'The Evolution of Social Security Systems in Latin America', in M. Frolich, D.S. Kaplan, C. Pages, J. Rigolini and D. Robalino (eds.), *Social Insurance, Informality and Labor Markets. How to Protect Workers while Creating Good Jobs* (Oxford: Oxford University Press, 2014), p. 37.

of the quintessential characteristics of modern-day Belgian social security. It is precisely in this context that we must consider the impact of technological unemployment on social security. The exceptions to the logic of social insurance still imply that the normal state of being in a welfare state is full employment. Credits are considered periods of fictitious employment, derived entitlements are still connected to a worker's professional status, and even though minimum and maximum benefit levels are in place, they still require a previous professional past. In the event that an individual's past employment is not taken into account, for instance in the case of social assistance schemes, the benefit seeker is faced with more restrictive conditions for access to benefits, such as means testing, as well as with benefits being considerably lower. This demonstrates that social assistance is viewed above all as a secondary track or 'safety net'. Only if one has not independently earned one's own social security through employment, does one end up in a parallel protection track with more conditions and lower benefit levels.

27. As a result, the hypothesis of technological unemployment would be problematic given the enduring emphasis on 'earning' social security rights and the way in which this idea is still present in popular and political opinion. Accepting that a significant part of the population is structurally unable to find employment would force us to think of ways on how to separate this underlying idea from the way in which we conceive social security legislation.

4. CONCLUSION: A DUTY TO RETHINK THE STATUS QUO?

28. Taking the hypothesis of technological unemployment as a starting point, this chapter has attempted to spark a debate on the potentially transformative impact of AI-driven automation and robotisation on social security law. As things stand in the year 2022, our social security systems seem ill-prepared for the hypothesis of a mass technological unemployment caused by the technological advances associated with the fourth industrial revolution. The theoretical groundwork of any social security system that is primarily based on employment and underpinned by a contributory logic can conceivably be exposed by a far-reaching automation and robotisation that renders a significant part of the population structurally unemployed. The question therefore arises whether we can still view social protection in terms of contributory social insurance if an increasing proportion of the population in unable to pay contributions. As in arguably all fields of law, legal relevance should follow societal relevance: as the meaning of work and employment shifts, it is up to social security, as the primordial collective expression of humanity, to follow this change.

29. As a result, we not only need to think of a way in which we, from a technical legal standpoint, would draft social security legislation that is able to function independently of the concept of employment. Above all, in order to find sufficient societal support for social security in the hypothesis of technological unemployment, we would need a true Copernican revolution of the moral compass that serves as the basis of our idea on social protection, letting go of the notion that we must 'earn' social security rights through employment and contributions. Under the current status quo, those unable to find employment due to the efficiency and lower cost of automation processes, will not be entitled to protection. A possible solution to this is to envisage social protection as a citizenship right: merely being a citizen opens up a right to social security. As a result, it is not inconceivable that, as a result of large-scale and far-reaching automation, we will evolve into a universal assistance system, or even towards an unconditional basic income.

CHAPTER 13

AI IN BELGIAN CONTRACT LAW: DISRUPTIVE CHALLENGE OR BUSINESS AS USUAL?

Alexander APPELMANS*, Maarten HERBOSCH**
and Benjamin VERHEYE***

1. INTRODUCTION

1. Imagine that for your next holiday you are interested in flying from Brussels to Windhoek, Namibia, because you want to go on a safari in the much-praised Etosha Park. On social media you read about a small start-up in London which developed a new AI tool that can help you book air travel. Instead of having to manually compare countless possible flights on a myriad of booking websites, this new tool autonomously makes a comprehensive analysis of all possibilities. Based on some pre-specified variables, the AI system books the best flight on offer. You are, for instance, happy to pay any price below € 1.000 for a return ticket to Windhoek, but of course you are aiming for 'as cheap as possible'. You only want a direct flight, if possible, in the morning. Based on these preferences, the AI tool will book a seat and, in doing so, conclude a contract that binds both you and the airline.[71]

While this example sounds straightforward, and is technically not far-fetched, it stands in sharp contrast with current Belgian contract law, which is by no means ready to deal with an AI tool, even such a simple one. What happens, for instance, if the AI tool makes a mistake and books you a flight to Cape Town instead? Or what happens if you refuse to pay the ticket price because you just found a cheaper ticket anyway? These are typical contractual issues, but here the problem pertains to an intermediary and autonomous system which is not

* PhD researcher at the Institute for Property Law (KU Leuven).
** PhD researcher at the Centre for Methodology of Law (KU Leuven) and research fellow at FWO Flanders.
*** Post-doctoral researcher, Institute for Property Law, Leuven University; notarial intern.

behaving as expected, something any AI tool is statistically bound to do in a certain percentage of cases.[1]

2. We believe it is important to have a contractual framework that is adapted to AI because the use of this technology brings about many advantages. As a digital tool, it allows for faster decision-making, which in turn may help in cost-cutting, e.g., via supply chains based on just-in-time principles.[2] Furthermore, decisions made by AI systems are generally more accurate and less biased than those made by humans.[3] On top of that, the use of automated systems helps to eliminate clerical errors.[4] As such, it is clear that the use of AI systems can offer significant improvements to many contractual relationships. We should thus opt for a contractual environment that allows for the equitable use of AI.

3. The above-discussed example of a booking tool raises some interesting contract law issues. These stem primarily from the fact that Belgian contract law is rooted in an idealised model of direct communication between two equal natural persons. The fact that current research opens the possibility of AI thinking and deciding independently creates a persistent theoretical problem.

Autonomy, freedom of contract and the binding force of a contract are fundamental building blocks of Belgian contract law.[5] Over the years, these notions have evolved under the influence of societal changes. Freedom of contract, for instance, was heavily impacted by the emergence of consumer protection law. Likewise, we anticipate that the rise of AI will be a potential key driver in forthcoming legal change. There is no doubt that the so-called 'disruptive technologies', including AI, distributed ledger technology (DLT), the Internet of Things (IoT), and big data, will significantly influence contract law. The question then shifts from 'if' to 'how' and 'to what extent'. This chapter offers a first analysis of the different possible directions in which the Belgian contractual framework could evolve.

---

1 See also, e.g., T. Balke and T. Eymann, 'The conclusion of contracts by software agents in the eyes of the law', in *Proceedings of the 7th international joint conference on Autonomous agents and multiagent systems – Volume 2* (International Foundation for Autonomous Agents and Multiagent Systems, 2008), p. 771.

2 See also: T. Allen and R. Widdison, 'Can Computers Make Contracts?', *Harvard Journal of Law & Technology*, 1996, vol. 9, no. 1, p. 26.

3 See also: R. Calo, 'Symposium: Singularity: AI and the Law', *Seattle University Law Review*, 2018, p. 1124; T. Matsuzaki, 'Ethical Issues of Artificial Intelligence in Medicine', *Californian Western Law Review*, 2018, pp. 255–256; M. Fierens, E. Van Gool and J. De Bruyne, 'De regulering van artificiële intelligentie (deel 1) – Een algemene stand van zaken en een analyse van enkele vraagstukken inzake consumentenbescherming', *RW*, 2020–21, p. 964.

4 See also: Allen and Widdison, 'Can Computers Make Contracts?', p. 29.

5 For a general introduction on these principles in Belgian law: L. Cornelis, 'De achtereenkomst', in R. Feltkamp and R. Vanbossele (eds.), *Wilsautonomie, contractvrijheid en ondernemingscontracten* (Antwerp: Intersentia, 2011), pp. 26–28; W. Van Gerven and A. Van Oevelen, *Verbintenissenrecht* (Leuven: Acco, 2015), pp. 71–72.

4. Today, most legal discussions in AI scholarship focus on the question of whether it is justified – or even required[6] – to grant legal personality to AI systems.[7] The answer to this question makes a crucial difference in contract law.[8]

If a jurisdiction refuses to grant legal personality to an AI system, it can only be considered a mere 'communication tool' between parties. In the context of contract law, the system is then comparable to a sheet of paper, a telephone, or an e-mail. As such, any agreement the tool makes will be attributed to the person using the AI, who we refer to in this chapter as the principal (cf. *infra*, para. 6).

If, however, AI systems are granted legal personality, different legal rules become applicable. If an AI system can conclude contracts on its own, it becomes subject to legal rights and duties (cf. *infra*, para. 16). When does, for example, the 'meeting of the minds' – which is often presented as an essential condition in Belgian contract law (Article 1108 CC; new Article 5.27 CC) – happen?

5. This chapter consists of three parts. In the first, the hypothesis of an AI system as a mere tool is analysed (part 2). In the second, the hypothesis of an AI system being a separate legal person is discussed (part 3). In the third part, we suggest a short thought experiment to come up with an alternative and more granular solution (part 4). Finally, we end with a general conclusion (part 5).

2. AI AS A COMMUNICATION TOOL

2.1. INTRODUCTION

6. The central issue of this chapter is the following: what happens when an AI-concluded contract is not aligned with the reasonable expectations of a principal? In the following paragraphs, we discuss this contractual mismatch in the hypothesis where an AI system acts purely as a communication tool.[9] In doing so, we have to ignore its autonomous nature.[10] Such a 'mere tool'

---

6 Although some recent studies also indicate that the granting of legal personality may not be required, e.g., from a liability perspective, see Expert Group on Liability and New Technologies – New Technologies Formation, 'Report on liability for Artificial Intelligence and other emerging technologies' 2019, https://www.europarl.europa.eu/meetdocs/2014_2019/plmrep/COMMITTEES/JURI/DV/2020/01-09/AI-report_EN.pdf (last consulted on July 27, 2022), pp. 37–39.

7 Balke and Eymann, 'The conclusion of contracts by software agents in the eyes of the law', p. 772.

8 See for a similar approach: Balke and Eymann, 'The conclusion of contracts by software agents in the eyes of the law', p. 772.

9 Also see Poullet, 'La conclusion du contrat par un agent elecontrique', *CRID* 2000, pp. 140–141.

10 See also, e.g.: Balke and Eymann, 'The conclusion of contracts by software agents in the eyes of the law', p. 773. See *a contrario*: J. Grapetin, 'Die Erosion der Vertragsgestaltungsmacht durch das Internet und den Einsatz Künstlicher Intelligenz', *NJW*, 2019, p. 185.

approach is appealing for its simplicity. It makes fitting AI into our existing legal framework rather straightforward and does not seem to require a statutory reform.[11]

7. In what follows, we discuss two traditional contract law issues that shed a light on our theoretical conundrum: how can a (human) statement of intent be the basis of a contract, when this intent was never expressed? To this end, we consider how Belgian law handles conflicts between the expressed will (in our example: the will expressed of the AI tool) and the actual will (in our example: the will of the person wanting to fly to Namibia). Subsequently, we consider the Belgian contractual validity requirements.[12] In particular, we examine error as a defect of consent in an AI context.

2.2. CONFLICT BETWEEN THE EXPRESSED WILL AND THE ACTUAL WILL

8. The easiest way to study the impact of the Belgian regime on conflicts between the expressed will and the actual will, is by considering the following example. Imagine that the AI system books an economy class plane ticket to Windhoek for € 100.000, while it was supposed to book a ticket for less than € 1.000. Will the principal be bound by this action, although any reasonable person could have known this was a mistake?[13] Or does the Belgian legal system allocate the risk of a discrepancy between the expressed will and the actual will to the counterparty, by holding that there is no contract in this case?

In Belgium, such conflicts are resolved by the theory of confidence (*vertrouwensleer, théorie d'apparence*) regarding the binding force of the contract (Article 1134 CC; new Article 5.69 CC). To fully grasp this theory, it is useful to look at the alternatives in this situation: on the one hand there is

---

11 CoJ 12 November 2015, ECLI: EU:C:2015:750, *RABG*, 2016, p. 1453 (European copyright law); Balke and Eymann, 'The conclusion of contracts by software agents in the eyes of the law', p. 773; P.A. Foriers, 'Les incombances en droit positif belge – L'exemple d' une notion à bannir', in X (ed.), *Le droit du travail au XXIe siècle (Brussels:* Éditions Larcier, 2015), p. 567; M. Petit, 'Décret wallon du 13 décembre 2017 – Addendum sur les donations mobilières aux personnes morales – Pour des tarifs wallons simples, justes et cohérents', *Rec.gén.enr.not.*, 2018, p. 240 (tax law); L. Reyntjens and W. Yperman, 'Terrorisme en internationale mobiliteit: een coherent beleid of nattevingerwerk?', *P&R*, 2019, p. 106 (criminal law); M. Van Hoecke, 'Gezagsargumenten, traditie en coherentie in het recht', in X (ed.), *Liber amicorum Boudewijn Bouckaert* (Bruges: die Keure/la Charte, 2012), p. 369.

12 Other approaches, that we will not discuss in detail, also seem to be possible. One could, for example, research to what extent the declared expression of intent by the AI system should precede over the actual intent of the party employing the AI system.

13 For simplicity of the argument, we presume that the counterparty is a natural person or a company. However, it could well be the case that the counterparty is also an AI system, which would render things even more complicated.

a *per se* precedence of the declared will, or, on the other hand, a precedence of the actual will.[14] In Belgium, the theory of the precedence of the actual will is usually defended. According to this theory, the true will takes precedence over the declared will. As such, the risk that a contract does not bind a party lies completely with the counterparty, who may have been oblivious to the fact that the expressed will differed from the actual will of his or her counterparty. According to the theory of declaration, the declared will takes precedence over the true will. In essence, the risk to be bound by an unwanted contract then resides with the party that poorly expressed his or her will by using an AI system.

The Belgian theory of confidence provides an in-between solution: a party is only bound by a declared will if his or her counterparty could have been 'reasonably' confident that the declared will was also his or her actual will.[15] In our example, this would not be the case. No reasonable counterparty could believe that anyone actually wanted to pay € 100.000 for an economy class plane ticket to Windhoek.

2.3. DEFECT OF CONSENT

9. Once it has been determined whether or not there was a consent to contract, the validity of that consent should be considered (Article 1108 CC; new Article 5.27 CC).[16] A party's consent is said to be valid only in the absence of defects. Often referred to examples of defects are deceit (Article 1116 CC; new Article 5.35 CC) and error (Article 1110 CC; new Article 5.34 CC). For the sake of brevity, we will limit our discussion to the erroneous consent of the AI system's principal.

10. Any party can claim a contract is invalid when they based their consent on an 'error' or an erroneous perception of reality.[17] To be able to do so, a first

---

14 See in general on these theories: J. Bricout, *De theorie der schijnbaarheid inzake nietige rechtshandelingen* (die Keure: Bruges, 1966), pp. 170–172; A. De Boeck, *Informatierechten en -plichten bij de totstandkoming en uitvoering van overeenkomsten* (Antwerp: Intersentia, 2000), p. 131 and following; X. Dieux, 'Réflexions sur la force obligatoire des contrats et sur la théorie de l'imprévision en droit privé (annotation under Kh. Brussels 16 January 1979)', *RCJB*, 1983, p. 386; J. Limpens, 'Rechtsvergelijkende aantekeningen over wil en wilsverklaring', in X (ed.), *Liber amicorum Baron Louis Fredericq* (Ghent: Story-Scientia, 1966), p. 679; M.E. Storme, *De invloed van de goede trouw op de kontraktuele schuldvorderingen* (Brussels: E. Story-Scientia, 1990), p. 57; I. Verougstraete, 'Wil en vertrouwen bij het totstandkomen van overeenkomsten', *TPR*, 1990, pp. 1163–1164; J.H. Nieuwenhuis, *Drie beginselen van contractenrecht* (Deventer: Kluwer, 1979), p. 12; S. Stijns and S. Jansen, 'De basisbeginselen van het contractenrecht: kroniek van de recentste evoluties', *TBBR*, 2013, pp. 3–4; W. Van Gerven, *Algemeen deel* (Antwerp: Standaard Wetenschappelijke Uitgeverij, 1969), p. 301.

15 See very clearly: Verougstraete,' 'Wil en vertrouwen bij het totstandkomen van overeenkomsten', p. 1164.

16 M. Dupont, 'Nullité absolue et nullité relative', in P. Wéry (ed.), *La nullité des contrats* (Brussels: Larcier, 2006), p. 33; R. Timmermans, *Dwaling en bedrog bij de koop en verkoop van onroerend goed* (Mechelen: Kluwer, 2007), p. 48.

17 For examples of error: Court of First Instance Ghent 13 December 2011, *TBO* 2012, p. 205, *T.Not.* 2013, p. 137. See for examples of deception: Liège 19 February 2013, *TBBR* 2018, p. 116.

requirement is that this erroneous perception of reality concerns the subject matter of the contract that prompted the erring party to enter into the contract in the first place.[18] Furthermore, the counterparty should reasonably have been aware of the crucial nature of this subject matter.[19] When the subject matter of the contract is considered objectively crucial, there is no further problem. It may, however, be more challenging when the erring party subjectively determines that a certain subject matter of the contract was decisive for him or her. In that case, this should have been expressly made clear to the counterparty.[20]

The second requirement to be able to apply error as a vice of consent is that the error must be excusable.[21] Circumstances occasionally dictate that a diligent party should have been more thorough or proactive in trying to understand the subject matter about which he or she claims to be mistaken.[22] The burden of proof therefore resides with the erring party.[23]

H. De Page, *Traité élémentaire de droit civil belge, Tome IV: Les principaux contrats*, part I, (Brussels: Bruylant, 1953), p. 117. See for an application: Court of First Instance Brussels 10 March 2017, *TBO* 2018, p. 337. See for France: J. Ghestin and Y.-M. Serinet, 'Erreur', *Répertoire de droit civil*, 2018, no. 54. For The Netherlands: K.L. Maes, 'Over de toepassing én grenzen van de mededelingsplicht bij dwaling', *Bedrijfsjuridische berichten* 2016, no. 10, paragraph 2.1. See for an application: Court of First Instance Overijssel 25 May 2016, ECLI:NL:RBOVE:2016:1929, https://www.rechtspraak.nl.

18 See: Article 1110 Civil Code (new Article 5.34 CC) ('*zelfstandigheid van de zaak*'); Cass. 24 September 2007, *TBBR* 2009, p. 216, annotated D. Philippe, *RW* 2009–10, p. 1735 (excerpt); Cass. 28 November 2013, *TBO* 2014, p. 133; Court of First Instance Leuven 2 November 2016, *TBO* 2017, p. 89; S. Stijns, *Verbintenissenrecht: Boek 1* (Bruges: die Keure, 2015), p. 87; J. Del Corral, *Dwaling* (Brussels: Larcier, 2011), p. 48.

19 See: Cass. 24 September 2007, *TBBR* 2009, p. 216, annotation D. Philippe, *RW* 2009–10, p. 1735 (excerpt); Vred. Leuven 20 October 2015, *RW* 2017–18, p. 71; Del Corral, *Dwaling*, p. 48; Stijns, *Verbintenissenrecht: Boek 1*, p. 87.

20 Del Corral, *Dwaling*, p. 54. For substantial elements that are usually not relevant for the contractual parties: B. Tilleman, *Overeenkomsten, Deel 2: Bijzondere overeenkomsten, A. Verkoop, Deel 1: De totstandkoming en de kwalificatie van de koop* in *Beginselen van Belgisch Privaatrecht* (Mechelen: Wolters Kluwer, 2001), p. 148. There is an additional exception to this rule where the counterparty has stressed a certain quality or element of the contract him- or herself, see, e.g., for the authenticity of a sold piece of art: M. Von Kuegelgen, 'La responsabilité des professionels de la vente d'oeuvres d'art', *Rev.not.b.* 1994, 317; B. Tilleman, 'Dwaling bij de aan- en verkoop van kunst en antiek' in E. Dirix, P. Senaeve, W. Pintens and S. Stijns (eds.), *Liber Amicorum Jacques Herbots* (Mechelen: Kluwer 2002), p. 446, nr. 6. See also B. Demarsin, *Handel in kunstvoorwerpen* (Brugge: die Keure / la Charte 2009), p. 205 and further.

21 In Belgium this requirement is fulfilled if a normal, diligent, foreseeing person would have been a victim of the *error* in similar circumstances. See: Cass. 28 November 2013, *TBO* 2014, p. 133, Brussels 7 September 2009, *T.Not.* 2010, p. 198; A. De Boeck, 'Dwaling in de ban van de precontractuele informatie- en onderzoeksplichten', annotation under Court of First Instance Hasselt 6 January 2000, *RW*, 2001–02, p. 355; F. Van Nuffel, 'De contractuele bescherming tegen het milieurisico bij overdrachten van ondernemingen en van onroerende goederen', *TMR*, 2005, p. 615; Del Corral, *Dwaling*, p. 63; Stijns, *Verbintenissenrecht: Boek 1*, p. 89.

22 See also: De Boeck, 'Dwaling in de ban van de precontractuele informatie- en onderzoeksplichten', p. 354; Del Corral, *Dwaling*, pp. 69–70; S. Stijns, *Verbintenissenrecht*, p. 89. See for an application: Ghent 13 December 2011, *TBO* 2012, p. 205, *T.Not.* 2013, p. 137.

23 Cass. 12 February 2015, *TBO* 2016, p. 119; Court of First Instance Brussels 10 March 2017, *TBO* 2018, p. 337; H. Jacquemin, *Le formalisme contractuel: mécanisme de protection de la partie faible*, (Brussels: Larcier, 2010), p. 463; Stijns, *Verbintenissenrecht*, p. 90.

11. Based on these requirements, it quickly becomes clear that it is not straightforward to apply the theory of error to a contract that was concluded by our AI booking assistant. Imagine the AI system booked a flight to Cape Town instead of the desired flight to Windhoek. At first glance, it is unlikely that this would be considered an excusable error, as a reasonable person would not make the same mistake. It is however not impossible. For instance, imagine the flight to Cape Town has a stopover in Windhoek, which could have led the AI system to presume that you could leave the airplane in Windhoek. Such a mistake seems more likely to be considered excusable, because it is a logical mistake.

However, because we consider this tool purely as a communication device, technically *you* yourself booked the flight to Cape Town. How then could defects of consent help you out of this contract? When we consider the AI system as a mere tool for communication, relying on error seems to imply that the party who delegated the contract formation to the AI system should have somehow had an erroneous perception of reality when concluding the contract with the airline. When we treat AI as a communication tool, the only legal subject we can consider having erred is thus you (the principal). This differs from the case of agency (*infra* no. 20), where an error could be attributed to the agent, here the AI system.

Because we have to determine the existence of a mistake on the level of the principal our theoretical problem persists. This is because it was in fact the AI system and not the principal that made the error. On a more fundamental level we could argue that perhaps the principal has not erred about the actual contract, but that he or she may have been mistaken about the functioning of the AI system.

12. Given the 'black box' character of AI systems, a diligent user should possibly have taken into account that something might go wrong. Should we view this as negligence on behalf of the principal? Did he or she accept this risk by making use of the booking tool? If we accept this reasoning, the cost of the risk is allocated solely to the principal.[24] This kind of unbalanced risk allocation might disconnect contractual doctrine from the commercial advantages of using AI in transactions. Furthermore, the fact that you make use of an AI system in and of itself may in some cases be considered more diligent. After all, AI systems often yield much better results than a human would in a similar situation. It may thus be considered very prudent of a party to delegate tasks to an AI system, even if such systems exceptionally malfunction.[25]

Then again, is it reasonable to hold the counterparty accountable for these mistakes? In some cases, they would not even know that they have been dealing

---

24 R. Yu and G. Spina Ali, 'What's inside the black box? AI challenges for lawyers and researchers', *Legal Information Management*, 2019, p. 5.

25 This is illustrated nicely by Superior Court of Justice Ontario 22 November 2018 (Cass v. 1410088 Ontario Inc., 2018 ONSC 6959), http://canlii.ca/t/hw728.

with an AI system. Shifting the risk to the other contracting party could thus result in a reluctancy to conclude agreements via AI tools, which may stifle the development of these helpful tools.

In line with the new EU approach to AI systems, it could be interesting to create legal sandboxes to prevent new rules from hindering innovation. It is important to balance divergent interests and reduce the regulatory burden. Applying *error* to contracts concluded by AI systems allows us to keep our current doctrine, but it puts an unreasonably high burden on either the principal or their counterparty. We would need a clear justification if we opt for either of these solutions.

13. A particular type of error, the so-called *error in corpore* or 'common mistake', could offer inspiration for a more straightforward solution.[26] *Error in corpore* applies to situations in which there is only an appearance of consensus but no actual agreement between both parties. In our example, there might be a fictitious airport in Cape Town called 'Windhoek Airport'. As a result, one of the parties may believe he or she booked a flight to Windhoek, while the other party believes the contract to concern a flight to Cape Town.

Some jurisdictions accept that no contract was formed in such a case, on the basis that there was no actual meeting of the minds.[27] As a result, the burden of proof for the erring party is significantly reduced, as he or she does not have to show that the error was excusable. Belgian contract law, however, allows the contract to come into existence.[28] Here an *error in corpore* only affects the validity of the contract and the requirements of the standard error regime apply. Given the specific type of errors that AI systems are bound to make, accepting

---

[26] Court of First Instance Charleroi 26 October 1995, *JLMB* 1996, p. 1117; Tilleman, *Overeenkomsten*, p. 143; Timmermans, *Dwaling en bedrog bij de koop en verkoop van onroerend goed*, pp. 116–117; Stijns, *Verbintenissenrecht*, p. 89 (fn. 31).

[27] This is the case in e.g., the Netherlands: M.Y. Schaub, *Wilsgebreken*, (Kluwer: Deventer, 2015), pp. 9 and 97; Maes, 'Over de toepassing én grenzen van de mededelingsplicht bij dwaling', no. 10, paragraph 2.1; J. Hijma, 'Boek 6, titel 5, artikel 228 Burgerlijk Wetboek – Dwaling', in X (ed.), *Groene Serie Verbintenissenrecht*, 2017, no. 12.1.1; F.M. Van Cassel-Van Zeeland, 'Boek 3, titel 2, artikel 33 – Wil en verklaring', in *Groene Serie Vermogensrecht*, 2018, no. 5.9. See for an application: 's-Hertogenbosch (KG) 22 January 2008, ECLI:NL:GHSHE:2008:BC2420, *NJF* 2008, no. 79. In France e.g.: Cass. fr. 1 February 1995, no. 92-16729, *Bull.civ.* 1995, III, no. 36; Cass. fr. 21 May 2008, no. 07-10772, *Bull.civ.* 2008, III, no. 92; J. Ghestin and Y.-M. Serinet, 'Erreur', no. 154; B. Petit and S. Rouxel, 'Fasc. unique: Contrat. Vice du consentement. Erreur', *JCI Civil Code*, 2018, no. 112. This view presumably still applies since the 2016 law reform, as this reform did not explicitly mention the *error in corpore* (see e.g., Petit and Rouxel, 'Fasc. unique: Contrat. Vice du consentement. Erreur', no. 95 and 112).

[28] A judge can, if he or she sees fit to do so, nullify the contract. See also: Tilleman, *Overeenkomsten*, p. 145; Stijns, *Verbintenissenrecht*, p. 89; A. De Boeck, 'De wilsgebreken dwaling en bedrog vandaag: responsabilisering en ankerplaats voor de precontractuele informatieverplichting', in R. Van Ransbeeck (ed.), *Wilsgebreken* (Bruges: die Keure, 2006), p. 41; Timmermans, *Dwaling en bedrog bij de koop en verkoop van onroerend goed*, p. 118.

that an *error in corpore* precludes the existence of a contract would offer a simple solution in some Belgian cases. This solution would bring more granularity to the general *error* regime, because it could easily be applied to the more obvious mistakes made by an AI system.

2.4. EVALUATION

14. First, the use of AI systems is not prevented by the Belgian solution to conflicts between the expressed and the actual will. The existing regime offers a nuanced solution, based on the hypothesis that AI systems are considered mere tools. Secondly, the booking tool example shows that the traditional *error* regime is rather favourable towards third parties. It is rather hard for a principal to prove that his or her error was excusable when the AI tool booked a flight to Cape Town. There is an element of justice to this solution. As stated above, the principal voluntarily opts to use the AI system without supervision and thus accepts the risks involved. This means that the risk resides with the party who is best able to control it. Control could for example be enforced by introducing human checks into the process.[29] The AI system can first find a suitable flight, and in a second phase, the human principal would get involved before closing the contract. Thirdly and most importantly, this approach offers the advantage that our existing contract law framework would not require any major changes.

15. Notwithstanding these advantages, the 'mere tool' approach does come with some significant trade-offs. First, on a substantial level, it completely ignores the autonomy of AI systems. While this may appear to make sense from the perspective of safeguarding the theoretical coherence of our legal system, this perception is only superficial. The classical theoretical paradigm that the binding force of contracts is based on the expression of human intent is hard to maintain when the autonomy of the medium may result in its human user being oblivious to any of the contract's clauses agreed upon by the AI system.[30] Consequently, it is hard to ignore this autonomy when applying the existing rules in practice.

Secondly, this approach places significant risk on the principal who uses the AI system. As such, it does not stimulate the use and development of new and convenient technologies. Considering AI as a mere tool for communication may stifle innovation.

---

29 The value of human oversight is also stressed by Article 14 of the European Commission's Proposal for a Regulation of the European Parliament and of the Council laying down harmonised rules on Artificial Intelligence (Artificial Intelligence Act) and amending certain Union Legislative Acts of 21 April 2021.

30 See also: Cornelis, 'De achtereenkomst', pp. 26–28; W. Decock, 'Theologen en contractenrecht: de morele transformatie van het ius commune (ca. 1500–1650)', *RW*, 2013, pp. 244–245.

Thirdly, and closely related to the previous point, it ignores the significant advantages this technology offers (cf. *supra*, para. 2). While it is true that the principal is best positioned to mitigate the risks presented by an AI system, the fact that he or she fully delegates contract formation to an AI system may ultimately result in significantly cheaper products and services overall. It is thus not logical to award third parties with the benefits of AI system usage (in our example, the AI system may help save the airline on advertisement costs[31]) without making them share in the corresponding risk allocation.

Fourthly, the damage suffered by a third party whose contract with the AI system is annulled seems *a priori* smaller than the damage caused by forcing such a contract on the principal of the AI system. Annulling a contract puts both parties back in the situation they were in before concluding the contract. The airline would still be able to sell its seat, in our example. While this contractual party may suffer additional losses in case of an annulment (as the airline may, for example, be forced to launch new advertisements), it would make more sense to compare such losses *in concreto* to determine the extent of the liability of the principal. Such an approach would be far more equitable than the blind imposition of an undesired contract on the principal, which is what our current legal framework dictates.

3. AI SYSTEMS AS LEGAL PERSONS

3.1. THE SIGNIFICANCE OF LEGAL CAPACITY

16. When we consider conferring legal personality to AI systems, the first question is of course: what is meant by 'legal personality'? In current AI scholarship, this is the million-dollar question and many authors are not clear on this issue. Is AI to be incorporated in a classical legal person, similar to what is used for today's corporations? Or should we entrust AI systems with a legal personality *sui generis*? And is legal personality needed in the first place to achieve the goals legal doctrine aims for? Several of these points require a bit more context before we can formulate a reply.

17. The main objective in considering granting AI legal personality is to ensure that AI has legal capacity and, as a result, possesses the capacity of carrying rights and obligations (cf. *infra*, para. 20). However, it must be noted that full legal personality is by no means the only option in this respect. While most legal scholars tend to focus on this option, other solutions are possible for an AI system to acquire so-called legal capacity (*rechtsbekwaamheid*, *capacité*

[31] On a more general level, if it is the provider of services or goods that uses an AI system, this may result in cheaper services or goods.

juridique).[32] The key aim is in fact the power to 'act', and not legal personality *per se*.

When studying legal capacity, it must be determined what degree of legal capacity should be given to an AI system. Only the capacity to conclude certain contracts?[33] Or also the capacity to be held liable on the basis of torts? And must it be possible to sue an AI system? And how will the separate estate of the AI system be established and payed-up? And will the founders be limited or unlimited liable together with the AI system? These are just a couple of examples of questions that need to be answered. We will return to some of these below.

18. It is interesting to see how this issue is also topical at the European political level. More specifically, the European Parliament seems to favour an approach in which AI systems *c.q.* robots are granted a *sui generis* form of legal personality. In its resolution of 16 February 2017, the parliament stated that 'creating a specific legal status for robots (...), so that at least the most sophisticated autonomous robots could be established as having the status of electronic persons responsible for making good any damage they may cause, and possibly applying electronic personality to cases where robots make autonomous decisions or otherwise interact with third parties independently.'[34]

Historically, granting legal personhood to non-natural beings has been one of the most impactful legal fictions. It has allowed the creation of companies with legal personality, and as such, altered the distribution of risk and helped capitalism develop. However, we must not forget that legal fictions have real-life consequences. Therefore, caution is warranted before putting in place a *sui generis statute* for AI systems. Perhaps, we should remember *Suetonius' Lives of the Twelve Caesars* (121 AD), in which we read about Caligula's folly when he is planning to make his horse, Incitatus, a senator, and 'the horse would invite dignitaries to dine with him in a house outfitted with servants there to entertain such events'.[35] While giving legal personality to animals may nowadays not seem as far-fetched anymore, Caligula's example should warn us that we must avoid creating absurd loopholes to exploit.

19. From the outset, it must be clear that we cannot answer all of the above questions in one chapter. This would require an in-depth analysis of many

---

32 The Belgian civil partnership (*maatschap*, *société de droit commun*), for instance, can be sued, without the necessity to sue the various partners (Article 703, §2 Belgian Procedural Code), although Article 1:5 of the Belgian Corporate Code explicitly states that the partnership does not have legal personality. For this reason, one might say that the Belgian civil partnership is a 'semi-legal person'.

33 Some contracts will be automatically excluded, given the nature of the AI system.

34 European Parliament resolution of 16 February 2017 with recommendations to the Commission on Civil Law Rules on Robotics (2015/2103(INL)) – para. 59, ff.

35 U. Pagallo, 'Vital, Sophia, and Co. – The Quest for the Legal Personhood of Robots', *Information*, 2018, p. 10.

different aspects of this problem, mainly in corporate law, and this falls outside the scope of this research that takes a close look at the contract law issues.

Nevertheless, we aim to study several real-life contractual consequences of granting AI systems legal capacity or legal personality. For the purpose of this analysis, we presume that the legislator would choose to grant AI full legal personality by incorporating the system as a classical legal person, namely a corporation in one of the forms of the Belgian Corporate Code. This starting point has several advantages. First, the meaning of legal personality of the classical legal person is well-known, which contributes to legal certainty. Second, the classical legal person has some characteristics – for instance, its estate – that would presumably also feature in an AI system having some degree of legal capacity or legal personality. As such, we want to guarantee that, would AI systems acquire legal capacity or legal personality in the near future, our contractual analysis will still be relevant.

20. Belgian law typically defines a legal person as 'a carrier of rights and duties that is not a living being, and that is founded to realise an objective that has been determined by its founders'.[36]

An AI legal person could, for instance, be used by its developers or its purchasers to realise an objective that they determine. The AI system in our example would have the objective of purchasing plane tickets for online customers. Various possibilities could be thought of in this respect, but these are not essential for our contractual analysis.

For our purpose, the most compelling element in the definition of a legal person is the fact that it concerns a carrier of rights and duties. In other words: it is a legal subject having legal capacity.[37] As a legal subject, AI systems would possess an estate or a patrimony (*vermogen*, *patrimoine*) in the sense of Articles 3.35 and 3.36 of the Civil Code.[38] After all, every legal subject possesses an estate.[39] The estate would be composed of all the AI system's assets and liabilities and, as such, forms the execution object of its creditors. Consequently, an AI system could effectively be personally liable for the execution of certain contracts, which has specific relevance for this chapter (cf. *infra*, para. 31). It is in this context irrelevant where the estate comes from: it could be payed-up by a myriad of stakeholders, e.g., the developers, the owners, the managers, an obligatory insurer, etc. The most important thing is that the AI legal person effectively has an estate, which is not an empty box.

36 D. Van Gerven, *Rechtspersonen. Deel 1* (Mechelen: Kluwer, 2007), p. 6.

37 Van Gerven, *Rechtspersonen*, pp. 14–15.

38 Balke and Eymann, 'The conclusion of contracts by software agents in the eyes of the law', p. 773. See on the meaning of the notion 'estate' in Belgian law: V. Sagaert, *Goederenrecht* (Mechelen: Kluwer, 2014), p. 52.

39 Sagaert, *Goederenrecht*, p. 53.

21. Considering AI systems as legal persons has various contractual consequences that are dealt with in the following paragraphs.

First, the fact that AI system is a legal subject means that its acts will be attributed to it. How should this be done specifically? A key element is the fact that an AI system has the capacity to act autonomously, contrary to, for instance, a traditional legal person such as a corporation. The fact that the AI system expresses its consent independently also raises the question of the validity of this consent.

Second, given that an AI system – as a legal subject – can conclude contracts, it necessarily follows that its relationship with the party using the system may also be considered a contractual one. The AI system is then to be regarded as an agent and the person making use of that AI system as its principal. Under Belgian law, this contract between a principal and an agent is seen as contractual representation, specifically a mandate. This raises various new questions that are dealt with below.

3.2. CONTRACTUAL CONSEQUENCE 1: ATTRIBUTION OF ACTS TO THE AI SYSTEM

22. Given the fact that AI is an independent legal person in this approach, it is necessary to develop a way of attributing the acts that an AI system undertakes to that AI system. After, all, this attribution is essential for the AI system to be held liable for its acts, which is exactly the objective of this approach (cf. *supra*, para. 17).

In classical legal persons, corporations for instance, this happens by means of representation. The directors or managers of that legal person represent it to the outer world and their acts in the name of the legal person are attributed to that legal person. In this respect, Article 2:49 of the Belgian Corporate Code stipulates that corporations act through their organs, the acts of whom are attributed to and bind that corporation. Contrary to these classical legal persons, AI might not need a representative to close a contract.[40] AI systems have precisely that kind of autonomy to act on their own, which is the essential feature of AI systems why some legal scholars hold that AI systems should have some degree of legal capacity or legal personality.

The legislator granting AI systems legal capacity or legal personality will need to determine how this attribution will be organised in practice.[41] One

---

40 It may however require a representative in a myriad of different situations, *e.g.*, when a dispute arises in the context of a contract to which the AI system was a party. Further, today most AI technology has not yet advanced to this level of autonomy.

41 An interesting paradox is that in the case of corporations a natural person will voluntarily trigger the attribution of acts to a legal person, in the case of AI systems this would be exactly the opposite.

option would be that all the acts of the AI system are automatically attributed to it. This might, however, become problematic in certain situations. Another option would be the application of the theory of confidence, which has already been elaborated on above (cf. *supra*, para. 8).

23. A second consequence of the AI system having legal capacity or being a legal person is that possible defects of consent will need to be judged on the level of the AI system itself. After all, the AI system has the capacity to express its own consent. What happens, if the AI system errs as to what it purchases?

In this respect, we can refer to the requirements of the error regime considered above (cf. *supra* para. 10). The main difference is that these requirements have to be met on account of the AI system and not on the level of the principal. To the extent that we acknowledge that AI systems can formulate expressions of will, it should be examined whether the expressed will was based on an erroneous perception of reality. Upon closer examination, the requirement that the error should be excusable results in the fact that the error regime should be applied in a similar way as it is applied to errors on account of the principal.

Nevertheless, we could ask ourselves if legislative initiative might be useful in this context. This would solve the question of whether classical vices of consent are applicable on AI systems qualifying as legal subjects.

3.3. CONTRACTUAL CONSEQUENCE 2: AI SYSTEM AS A REPRESENTATIVE

24. The second consequence for contract law is the fact that if we consider an AI system to be an independent legal person, it becomes possible to conclude contracts with that system.

The specific contract that is studied here is the contract between the AI system and the person for whom it will act as an agent, i.e., its principal. In Belgian law, the contractual relationship between the AI system and its principal is called a mandate.[42] The AI system is then seen as a representative, the person who charges it to conclude contracts for him or her the principal. In our example above (cf. *supra*, para. 1), the person wishing to have a flight booked to Windhoek is thus the principal. The concept of a mandate requires an in-depth analysis.

3.3.1. Mandate

25. A mandate is a contract between two parties, a principal and a representative, in which the principal mandates the representative to conclude contracts in his or her name and for his or her account (Article 1984 CC,

42 See also for this approach: Balke and Eymann, 'The conclusion of contracts by software agents in the eyes of the law', p. 774.

lastgeving, mandat).[43] Based on this contract, a representative acquires the capacity to represent a principal within the boundaries specified in the contract. As such, the representative can conclude contracts by which the principal is bound (cf. *infra*, paras. 26 and 27).

A mandate is either general or specific (Article 1987 CC) and formulated in general terms or specific terms (Article 1988 CC). A general mandate concerns all business of the person represented, whereas a specific mandate only concerns one (or more) specific matters.[44] A mandate in general terms gives a representative the capacity to perform only administrative acts. If the principal wants the representative to perform dispositive acts, then the mandate must be concluded in specific terms, which means that the possible acts must be explicitly named in the mandate.[45]

As far as the legal consequences of the representative's act are concerned, again two different forms of mandate must be distinguished in Belgian law: either the indirect mandate (cf. *infra*, para. 27) or the direct mandate (cf. *infra*, para. 26). This distinction has a particular importance for our approach towards AI systems as legal persons in contract law, specifically because it is on this basis that the exact legal consequences of the acts of the representative are determined.

26. When there is a direct mandate, the representative acts in the name and for the account of the principal. Any contract that he or she concludes with a third party is considered to bind that third party and the principal (in our example: the ticket buyer) directly. Hence: direct mandate.[46]

In case of any issues surrounding the contract, the principal and the third party must address each other directly (Article 1998 CC), and not the representative, exactly because the contract is created directly between them.[47] This is known as the principle of direct attribution of actions of the representative to the principal.[48]

27. In a situation of indirect mandate, the representative acts in his or her own name, but for the account of the principal. In this case, the third party does not know the principal and sometimes does not even know that the representative acts as a representative. If the representative concludes a contract with a third party, that contract only binds the representative, but not the principal. Hence: an indirect mandate.[49]

---

43 See on representation in general e.g.: B. Tilleman, *Lastgeving* (Ghent: E. Story-Scientia, 1997), p. 2; W. Van Gerven and A. Van Oevelen *Verbintenissenrecht* (Leuven: Acco, 2015), pp. 157–159.

44 See also: Tilleman, *Lastgeving*, p. 142.

45 See also: *Ibid.*, p. 149.

46 See, e.g.: *Ibid.*, p. 171; Van Gerven and Van Oevelen, *Verbintenissenrecht*, p. 158.

47 See also: Tilleman, *Lastgeving*, p. 185.

48 See also: *Ibid.*, p. 187.

49 See, e.g.: *Ibid.*, p. 4, p. 268; Van Gerven and Van Oevelen, *Verbintenissenrecht*, p. 158.

In case of contractual problems, the third party must address the representative with whom he or she has concluded the contract and that representative must subsequently address the principal.[50] Similarly, the principal must address the representative on the basis of the mandate who must subsequently address the third party with whom he or she has concluded a contract.[51]

28. In the hypothesis that an AI system acts via a mandate as a representative for a principal, we can raise some interesting points. Applying the legal concept of a mandate has various compelling advantages and consequences. Below we discuss four key ideas.

29. Firstly, as far as the nature of the mandate between the principal and the AI system is concerned, it is to be expected that, in practice, the mandate stemming from this contract will always be formulated in specific terms (cf. *supra*, para. 25). The principal will not charge an AI system to perform 'all possible' acts, but only to behave in a very specific way. In our introductory example (cf. *supra*, para. 1), the principal charges the AI system to conclude one very specific contract, i.e., the purchase of a plane ticket. In addition, even in the current realm of technological possibility, it is still difficult to imagine an AI tool capable of representing someone in general.[52]

30. Secondly, one might ask whether an indirect mandate is relevant at all in an AI context? It certainly is because in practice it is very well possible that the third party does not even know it is dealing with an AI system. Of course, the legislator could stipulate a disclosure requirement, which would require an AI system to always be transparent about its nature in order for it to legally conclude contracts. However, it might be a good idea to keep the possibility of a certain secrecy. Counterparties might, for instance, differentiate their prices and raise the price if they know they are dealing with an AI system. Furthermore, if that counterparty would be an AI system itself, even more complicated interactions would be possible.[53]

31. Thirdly, as the AI system is an independent legal person in our hypothesis and possesses an estate (cf. *supra*, para. 20), the AI system itself has the same contractual status as a normal person and can thus be held personally liable. This means that a principal should be able to claim contractual damages from

50 See also: Tilleman, *Lastgeving*, p. 271.

51 See also: *Ibid.*, p. 275.

52 Some researchers argue that in the future, so-called 'strong AI' will have this possibility. However, this falls outside the scope of this chapter.

53 An AI tool might for instance be coded in a way to give preference *c.q.* lower prices to other AI tools of the same developer or to other AI tools that it has a certain relationship with. However, such practices bear the risk of market disruption, so it might be useful to develop means to prevent these.

the 'AI representative' if it does not represent him or her to the standards set out in the initial mandate.

32. Fourthly, because the AI system acts as a representative of the principal, its actions will be attributed to the principal insofar as the AI legal person acts within the boundaries of its mandate (Article 1998, para. 1 CC). This means that the principal will be bound by all contracts that are concluded by its representative within the boundaries of the mandate. However, if an AI system acts outside of the scope of its mandate, this will not be the case. If the AI system acts outside of the mandate, the principal is not bound by this contract. Obviously, the principal can still ratify the faulty contract afterwards (Article 1998, para. 2 CC).[54] For example, in our introductory illustration (cf. *supra*, para. 1), the principal will not be bound by a contract that books a plane ticket to Cape Town because the AI system acted well outside the limits of its specific mandate (which only allowed booking a ticket to Windhoek). The *bona fide* third party (the airline) must address the representative acting outside the boundaries of its mandate (the AI legal person) for compensation (Article 1997 *a contrario* CC), but the airline cannot address the principal.[55] This is an application of extra-contractual liability, which proves again that an AI legal person must absolutely be capable of being held liable on the basis of torts (cf. *supra*, para. 17). In our example, the airline will therefore need to address the AI system directly.

The fact that an AI legal person could be held personally liable allocates the contractual risk fully to the counterparty of the AI system. If the AI system acts outside the boundaries of its mandate, the third party will have to address the AI system directly and, as such, run the risk that the AI system is insolvent. It is therefore critical that any AI legal person effectively has an estate of itself that is payed-up by various stakeholders. Furthermore, it will be relevant to know for whom an AI system only creates limited or unlimited liability. All these issues must be taken into account by any legislator that grants legal capacity or legal personality to AI systems (also cf. *supra*, para. 17).

Nevertheless, an exception exists to the principle that the AI system is personally liable in case it acts outside the scope of its mandate. This exception is the so-called 'apparent mandate' and it has as a result that the principal is held directly liable anyway.

3.3.2. Apparent Mandate

33. Under certain conditions, a principal can be directly bound by a contract concluded by a fake representative or a representative acting outside the

[54] See also: Tilleman, *Lastgeving*, pp. 201–203.

[55] See also: *Ibid.*, pp. 198–201.

boundaries of its mandate. In Belgian law, this is called an 'apparent mandate' (*schijnvertegenwoordiging, mandate apparent*).[56] The requirements are the following: the existence of an apparent capacity of representation, a third party acting in good faith and the attributability[57] of this appearance to the principal.[58] It is in this respect not required that the apparent principal made a fault.[59]

34. The apparent mandate theory could be a solution in the case where an AI-representative accidentally – for instance due to a coding error – acts outside its mandate.[60] In our example: the system books a flight the principal does not need or want. After all, in order for parties to trust the AI system, a legal framework must be developed which does not require third parties to check an AI's mandate prior to every transaction. Apparent mandate could be a fitting solution for this. Let us therefore check whether the above-mentioned conditions are met in our hypothesis (cf. *supra*, para. 33).

First, in any new model we must avoid that a party needs to control the exact capacity or mandate of an AI system. In some cases, transactions will be too quick and numerous for such control to be organised. In other cases, the person represented may want to stay anonymous. We could argue that an 'apparent capacity to represent' exists every time an AI system acts and the party it deals with believes (or should know) that it acts on behalf of a principal.

---

56 See on apparent representation in general e.g.: C. Cauffman, 'De vertrouwensleer', in *Comm. Bijzondere Overeenkomsten* (Mechelen: Kluwer, 2005), p. 5 ff.; P.-A. Foriers, 'Aspects de la représentation en matière contractuelle', in *Les obligations contractuelles* (Brussels: Editions du Jeune Barreau de Bruxelles, 2000), p. 253; Tilleman, *Lastgeving*, p. 223; Van Gerven and Van Oevelen, *Verbintenissenrecht*, pp. 158–159; A. Van Oevelen, 'De juridische grondslag en de toepassingsvoorwaarden van de verbondenheid van de lastgever bij een schijnmandaat (note under Cass. 20 juni 1988)' 1989–1990, p. 1426.; Verougstraete, 'Wil en vertrouwen bij het totstandkomen van overeenkomsten', pp. 1189–1193.

57 This third principle has always been heavily discussed. For an overview: X. Dieux, 'Tendances générales du droit contemporain des obligations. Réforme et contre-réforme', in *Les obligations contractuelles* (Brussels: Editions du Jeune Barreau de Bruxelles, 2000), p. 24; P.-A. Foriers, '(noot onder Cass. 20 januari 2000)', *Rev.dr.comm.b.*, 2000, pp. 487–488; P.-A. Foriers, 'Aspects de la représentation en matière contractuelle', in *Les obligations contractuelles*, p. 250; R. Kruithof, F. De Ly, H. Bocken and B. De Temmerman, 'Overzicht van rechtspraak (1981–1992). Verbintenissen', *TPR*, 1994, pp. 225–226; S. Stijns, D. Van Gerven and P. Wery, 'Chronique de jurisprudence. Les obligations: les sources (1985–1995)', *JT*, 1996, p. 694; S. Stijns and I. Samoy, 'La confiance légitime en droit des obligations', in S. Stijns and P. Wery (eds.), *De bronnen van niet-contractuele verbintenissen* (Bruges: die Keure, 2007), p. 85, fn. 184. Nevertheless, this discussion falls outside the scope of this chapter.

58 See also: Tilleman, *Lastgeving*, p. 233; Van Gerven and Van Oevelen, *Verbintenissenrecht*, p. 159.

59 See: Cass. 20 June 1988, *Arr.Cass.* 1987–88, p. 1365, *Pas.* 1988, I, p. 1258, *JT* 1989, p. 547, obs. P.A. Foriers, *RCJB* 1991, p. 45, ann. R. Kruithof, *RW*, 1989–90, p. 1425, ann. A. Van Oevelen, *TRV*, 1989, p. 540, ann. P. Callens. See also earlier: Liege 6 February 1984, *Pas.* 1984, II, p. 112; Antwerp 21 March 1984, *RW*, 1984–1985, p. 1653; See also e.g.: Tilleman, *Lastgeving*, p. 229; P. Van Ommeslaghe, 'L'apparence comme source autonome d'obligations et le droit belge', *Revue de droit international et de droit comparé*, 1983, p. 154.

60 Also see Poullet, 'La conclusion du contrat par un agent elecontrique', pp. 141 ff.

Second, third parties concluding contracts with an AI system will generally act in good faith. If, however, they are aware of the exact mandate of the AI system and are thus in bad faith, they will not be able to invoke apparent mandate.

Third, there is the aspect of attributability. In Belgian law, it is required that a principal has done something to lead a third party to believe he or she was represented by an AI system. Let us clarify this with an example, namely the act of fraud through hacking. Imagine a hacker breaks into an AI system and forces it to buy something in name of an apparent principal. Do we want that principal to be contractually bound in this situation or not? This is essentially a question of risk attribution: does the risk lie with the third party or with the principal? In Belgium, legal scholars may answer that question at the expense of the third party in this example of hacking. They might reason that the condition of attributability has technically not been met, i.e., the principal has done nothing to lead the third party to believe that he or she was represented. Consequently, this theory would put a lot of risk on any third party. It would thus be reasonable to loosen up this strict requirement of attributability in case law, as judges have done in other legal areas.[61]

3.4. EVALUATION

35. Considering AI systems as legal subjects that thus possess an estate offers considerable advantages. First, analogous to the above 'communication tool' hypothesis, contract law as it exists can be applied to contracts involving AI systems.[62] In this hypothesis the AI system is considered an autonomous legal subject, and although some specific rules would have to be altered, most of our existing framework would be applicable.

Second, the legal capacity or legal personality solution is easily understandable for practitioners. AI systems could simply be compared to existing legal persons and nobody would be confused by what that technically means. The development of AI systems in our day-to-day legal traffic would therefore be stimulated by this solution.

Third, this solution reduces the risk for the principal of an AI system, i.e., the person who concludes a contract via AI. If the AI system is a legal subject of itself, then it would be held personally liable. This limits the risk for the user.[63]

---

61 This is for instance the case in the field of sea law. See on this issue: B. Verheye, 'De vertrouwensleer c.q. schijnvertegenwoordiging bij het scheepsbeslag en een nuancering van de toerekenbaarheidsvereiste (noot onder Cass. 30 juni en 26 september 2016)', *TBBR*, 2017, pp. 509–515.

62 Balke and Eymann, 'The conclusion of contracts by software agents in the eyes of the law', p. 773.

63 *Ibid.*, pp. 773–774.

On top of that, a principal held liable on the basis of apparent mandate could address the AI system's estate for damages.

36. Nevertheless, this second approach also has some considerable drawbacks. Most importantly, it still does not automatically solve the risk attribution problem. While the 'mere communication tool' hypothesis is too harsh on the principal, it might very well be that the legal capacity or legal personality hypothesis ends up being too harsh on the third party, because he or she must bear the risk of the AI system acting outside the scope of its mandate and subsequently appearing to be insolvent.

On top of that, the precise extent of an AI's legal capacity or legal personality will still need to be determined. How would this legal personality be constituted? Does it come with limited or unlimited liability for the owner of the AI? Does the legal personality belong to the hardware or the software of the AI?[64]

4. BUILDING BRIDGES

4.1. INTRODUCTION

37. The ability of an AI system to create rights and obligations on behalf of humans or corporations in an increasingly autonomous way could conceivably lead to situations in which an AI system contractually agrees to financially ruin its unaware principal. The novel legal-ethical framework that was developed by the European Commission tries to come up with more granular solutions in the way we are regulating the Fourth Industrial Revolution. Therefore, in the field of contract law specifically, a consensus is growing among scholars that the sharp distinction between considering automated systems as either a mere tool of communication, or else, as a fully independent legal person, is no longer sustainable. Scholars are looking at innovative solutions to spread the risk while still allowing innovation to flourish. Harmonising standards, conformity assessments and regulated access for high-risk-AI systems are a few of the approaches that the EU commission is further preparing.

As such, a more nuanced response to these technological evolutions is needed. Repurposing existing legal doctrines is an oft-suggested solution (cf. *supra*, para. 6 and para. 20): from applying corporate agency theory, over treating AI systems as boats, animals or franchisees, to developing a hybrid type of mandate contract.[65] The overarching conclusion of these legal experiments

64 *Ibid.*

65 See: R. Michalski, 'How to sue a robot', *Utah L. Rev.*, 2018, pp. 1052–1062; S. Chopra and L.F. White, *A legal theory for autonomous artificial agents* (Ann Arbor: University of Michigan Press, 2011), pp. 29–70.

seems to be that none of our existing models gives a fully satisfactory solution on their own, which has also been made clear in our analysis above (cf. *supra*, paras. 15 and 36).

38. Our aim in this short final part is to suggest a creative approach to existing contract doctrine. In a problem-solving mindset we can develop new contracting principles that take alternative forms of accountability, agenthood and liability into account. A self-learning automated system creates a complex web of distributed responsibility for which current Belgian contract law is not equipped. For reasons of brevity, we focus on only one theoretical suggestion in this chapter but note there is a myriad of legal structures and frameworks that could be helpful, e.g., applying common law contract principles or hybrid forms of legal personality. Finding a fitting legal framework would allow us to create an intermediary solution between either a fully independent automated agent or an automated system seen as only a communication tool.

4.2. ROMAN LAW PECULIUM

39. Part of the theoretical solution for this very 21st century problem might be found far back in (legal) history. The Roman law concept of *peculium* could offer a theoretical solution to dovetail our existing contracting practice together with automated systems.[66] Before applying this Roman law theory to our modern-day legal framework, let us first analyse its historical roots and relevance for today's contract law.[67]

In the Digest of Justinian *peculium* was considered a 'sum of money or property granted by the head of the household to a slave or son-in-power'. Although considered a separate legal estate – to allow the creation of a separated business run by a son or a slave – a *peculium* technically remained property of the head of the household, the *pater familias*. The father's liability was capped to the value of the *peculium* in order to limit the risk burden on the father or master.

66 See also: R. Gamauf, 'Slaves doing business: the role of Roman law in the economy of a Roman household', *European Review of History: Revue européenne d'histoire,* 2009, pp. 331–346; U. Pagallo, *The laws of robots: crimes, contracts, and torts* (Dordrecht: Springer, 2013), pp. 103–106; V.A. Kurki and T. Pietrzykowski, *Legal personhood: Animals, artificial intelligence and the unborn* (Dordrecht: Springer, 2017), p. 98; U. Pagallo, 'Vital, Sophia, and Co. – The Quest for the Legal Personhood of Robots', *Information*, 2018, pp. 235–238; R. Michalski, 'How to sue a robot', pp. 1060–1061; S. Nasarre-Aznar, 'Ownership at stake (once again): housing, digital contents, animals and robots', *Journal of Property, Planning and Environmental Law,* 2018, p. 78.

67 We want to reiterate that all forms of slavery are morally wrong and should be condemned. From a legal theoretical perspective, however, the way Roman law dealt with slaves can be of theoretical interest to us today.

40. In the case of a Roman slave, the concept of *peculium* was based on a theoretical contradiction. Roman lawyers toyed with the idea of giving real world agency and autonomy to Roman slaves while staying true to the concept of the *status libertatis* and the *dominica potestas*, i.e., the legal status of a Roman slave as 'property' of the *pater familias*. While Roman slaves themselves were to some extent objects of Roman civil law, and as such legally lacked the capacity to possess or to own, *peculium* gave them a level of independent agency (and thus partly made them a subject of the law).[68] For Roman slaves there was a clear incentive to do well. If you acquired enough money in your *peculium*, you could in some cases buy your own freedom. AI systems obviously do not have that same incentive, but interestingly enough there are some algorithmic similarities in how deep learning technically works.

With the consent of a *pater familias* a Roman slave or son could administer certain funds, run a business, and even manage other slaves. The economic idea behind *peculium* was to allow a slave to act independently in the name of his master, and as such, optimise the master's business operations, without creating too much risk on the master's side.[69] This involved a balancing act between a Roman slave's autonomy and the potential liability for the *pater familias*. This logic can be transposed to today's use of robots and automated agents in a contractual context.

41. A Roman slave could manage the property of his master as if it was his own property. This while it legally always belonged to the master. All acquisitions made via a *peculium* were immediately credited to the *pater familias*. However, the master's liability never exceeded the peculium's value.[70] This had two key consequences: 1) a slave was able to acquire possessions for his master and 2) a master was liable to his slave's creditors.[71] That being said, in Roman law, a slave was not seen as his master's agent. As such, in some cases, a Roman slave became a direct stakeholder in the contract with a third party.[72]

---

68 See also: Michalski, 'How to sue a robot', p. 1060. While we agree with Michalski's view that slavery was a 'morally repulsive' practice, we disagree with his opinion that this contractual model could not be used in modern day practice because of its terrible history. It would perhaps be a small positive outcome of an otherwise utterly inhumane situation if this model would offer the beginning of a fitting solution for this 21st century.

69 P. Temin, 'The economy of the early Roman Empire', *Journal of Economic Perspectives*, 2006, pp. 133–151.

70 Gamauf, 'Slaves doing business', pp. 330–331.

71 See also: Gamauf, 'Slaves doing business', p. 332; Michalski, 'How to sue a robot', p. 1060.

72 This is a point of discussion among Roman law scholars. While this is on its own an interesting discussion, it would be more favourable to decide if an AI becomes a party to the contract based on the broader solution. See for the opposite pint of view: L. Waelkens, 'Gaius IV, 73: Debet ou Debetur', *Tijdschrift voor Rechtsgeschiedenis/Legal History Review*, 2000, pp. 353–354. For an introduction to responsibility and the Roman *familia*: L. Waelkens, L'origine romaine des obligations naturelles, *Revue Historique de Droit Français et Étranger*, 2012, pp. 318–322.

In today's contractual context, *peculium* offers us a theoretical analogy to develop a system that would authorise an AI system to conclude contracts on behalf of its owner, while at the same time avoid creating a fully separate legal entity. Analogous to Roman slaves, an automated AI system could be considered an object of the law, but with machine learning algorithms in mind, will also be able to take (more and more complex) autonomous decisions and has as such an actual independent agency.

42. This raises the question how the *peculium* actually functioned. In Roman times, a master automatically became the owner of any goods that a son or slave bought. It was of no consequence whether or not he approved of the transaction. However, if the acquisition or agreement was not made within the limits of the *peculium*, the master's consent remained crucial. While a son or slave could acquire goods and services virtually without any restrictions, the *pater familias's* liability was strictly limited to the value of the *peculium*.

There is a clear analogy with modern day limited liability companies. Consequently, *peculium* has been called a 'proto-limited liability company' by some legal scholars.[73] The key difference is the fact that the actor had no legal personality. As such, the actions were difficult to grasp. Procedures were brought before the courts based on petitions.[74] A party had to bring this action directly against the *pater familias*. This was called the *actio de peculio*.[75] A closely connected issue that arises from the *actio de peculio* was the problem of assessing the value a *peculium*. This was not necessarily identical to the actual funds in the *peculium*. The judge could make deductions or additions to the funds based on transactions done within the full *domus*.[76]

43. The key take-away from these Roman legal rules for our purpose is that *peculium* was designed for a specific type of legal subjects (sons and slaves) acting without their father or master's supervision, but within a framework of limited liability. Applying this to our booking tool example, we could opt for a system in which all users of an AI have to create a *peculium* account which is attributed to this modern legal actor. A similar set-up, where there is a limited liability, could be achieved via (obligatory) insurance for the use of an AI. This protection would then be used when the AI tool concludes a faulty contract or does something unexpected. In that way, risk could be more evenly balanced between the user, the London start-up and the airline. This is in many ways similar to the capital requirements of a limited liability company. In combination with our previous

---

73 See: Pagallo, *The laws of robots: crimes, contracts, and torts*, pp. 103–104.

74 Waelkens, 'L'origine romaine des obligations naturelles', p. 325.

75 See also: Gamauf, 'Slaves doing business', p. 332; Justinian Digest, book 15, title 1.

76 While these calculations shed an interesting light on the discussion it falls outside of the scope of our research. We can refer to the article of Gamauf, 'Slaves doing business' and Waelkens, 'Gaius IV, 73: Debet ou Debetur', pp. 353–354.

solutions (error and representation) this could be a next step towards a more substantial solution that takes into account the autonomy of an AI system. Of course, many other contractual and non-contractual issues should be clarified, but this falls outside the scope of our first analysis.

5. CONCLUSION

44. Let us, once again, go back to the booking tool and the flight to Namibia. When you make use of an AI system that finds the cheapest flight and books it in your name, the main problem we identified was the following: what happens when the AI does something wrong? Who is bound by the contract? Who is to be held liable? Who bears the risk?

The possible answers to these contractual questions depend on the general approach we take towards AI in contract law. Various solutions are possible, and this chapter wanted to give an overview and appreciation of the various possibilities.

45. The first approach to AI systems in contract law we discussed, was seeing them as a mere communication tool. This approach proved to be rather problematic (cf. *supra*, para. 15). The application of the current Belgian *error* regime to contracts formed by an AI does not seem ideal. The risk of an undesired contract is fully allocated either to the principal (i.e., the buyer of the ticket) or their counterparty. Both solutions are undesirable in practice because the disadvantages outweigh the advantages *in concreto*.

In addition, another major contra-argument is this approach's neglect of one of the key characteristics of AI systems, namely their autonomy. This is the key reason why our current contract law has difficulties with AI systems. It is therefore more useful to shift our attention to alternative approaches.

46. The second approach to AI systems, i.e., granting AI systems (some degree of) legal personality, looked more promising (cf. *supra*, para. 35). This made it possible to apply the existing contractual frameworks of mandate and apparent representation. These legal notions could perfectly be applied *mutatis mutandis* to an AI agent.

Nevertheless, the condition of attributability that must be met before apparent representation can be applied brings the question of risk allocation to the foreground once again. In an AI context, this condition of attributability has not yet been fully clarified. As a result, the question of risk allocation remains unanswered.

This approach has its clear advantages, but also considerable disadvantages. Many points must be taken into account and a myriad of issues must be resolved before this approach could be applied in practice. It is therefore prudent to consider alternative approaches.

47. An intermediary approach could be inspired by Roman law, namely by the legal figure of *peculium*. The *peculium* is a means by which a *pater familias* granted his son or a Roman slave a certain degree of autonomy to conclude contracts in his own name, although it remained the *pater familias* who was limitedly liable for these contracts and was to be addressed in court in case of any issues arising. This theoretical framework could, by analogy, be applied to AI systems. Such a solution circumvents theoretical dogmatism on legal personality and could help to fit AI into contract law.

48. In this chapter, we wanted to make a first exploration of this new topic in Belgian contract law. It is now clear that the question is not whether AI systems constitute a challenge for contract law, but rather how contract law should respond. After all, AI systems create completely new challenges for legal certainty and risk distribution. This may require fundamental changes in our existing contractual framework. A focus on certain prohibitions in combination with harmonised transparency rules should create a solid basis for the interaction of natural persons with AI systems. This chapter has offered a high-level overview of various possibilities and we hope to elaborate on these possibilities in the future. One of the key challenges of legal scholarship is to anticipate changes and prepare ourselves. AI and robotisation will certainly require us to be creative in that regard.

CHAPTER 14

TORT LAW AND DAMAGE CAUSED BY AI SYSTEMS

Jan De Bruyne*, Elias Van Gool**, Thomas Gils***

1. INTRODUCTION

1. Artificial intelligence is becoming increasingly important in our daily professional and social lives. Although the use of AI systems has many benefits for a variety of sectors, different legal challenges remain. Some of these challenges are extensively discussed in this book. In this chapter, we will focus on the application of liability for damage caused by AI systems.[1] The importance of liability and AI systems has already been mentioned in several recent documents issued by the European Union (EU). The White Paper on Artificial Intelligence, for instance, stresses that the main risks related to the use of AI concern the application of rules designed to protect fundamental rights as well as safety and liability-related issues.[2] Scholars have also concluded that '[l]iability certainly represents one of the most relevant and recurring themes'[3] when it comes to AI systems.

* Research expert AI and Law, lecturer e-contracts at KU Leuven Faculty of Law, Centre for IT & IP Law – imec; assistant professor eLaw, Leiden; senior researcher Knowledge Centre Data & Society.

** Doctoral researcher at KU Leuven Faculty of Law, Consumer Competition Market and at Université de Lille, Centre de recherche Droits et Perspectives du Droit (EA no. 4487).

*** Researcher at KU Leuven Faculty of Law, Centre for IT & IP Law – imec, Knowledge Centre Data & Society.

1 See for more information on the typology of the different types of AI systems Chapter 1. See in general on the relationship between different types of robots and civil liability: S. Navas, 'Robot Machines and Civil Liability', in M. Ebers and S. Navas (eds.), *Algorithms and Law* (Cambridge: Cambridge University Press, 2020), pp. 157–174.

2 European Commission, 'White Paper On Artificial Intelligence – A European approach to excellence and trust', COM(2020) 65 final, 19 February 2020, p. 13.

3 E. Palmerini et al., 'Regulating Emerging Robotic Technologies in Europe: Robotics facing Law and Ethics', RoboLaw, 22 September 2014, p. 212, https://www.robolaw.eu/RoboLaw_files/documents/robolaw_d6.2_guidelinesregulatingrobotics_20140922.pdf.

2. This emphasis on liability is not surprising considering that AI systems will increasingly cause damage. Reference can be made to accidents involving autonomous vehicles. The autopilot of a Tesla car, for instance, was not able to distinguish a white tractor-trailer crossing the road from the bright sky above, leading to a fatal crash.[4] A self-driving Uber car recently hit a pedestrian in Arizona. The woman later died in the hospital.[5] A robot also attacked and injured a man at a tech fair in China.[6] A surgical robot at a hospital in Philadelphia malfunctioned during a prostate surgery, thereby severely injuring the patient.[7] In February 2015, a South Korean woman was sleeping on the floor when her robot vacuum 'ate' her hair forcing her to call for emergency help.[8]

These examples show that accidents may happen despite optimising national and supranational safety rules for AI. This is when questions of liability become important.[9] Nevertheless, the application of liability regimes for damage caused by AI systems can be challenging.[10] The characteristics of AI systems such as opaqueness, autonomy, connectivity, data dependency or self-learning abilities make it difficult to trace back potentially problematic decisions made with the involvement of such systems. This in turn may make it challenging for victims to obtain compensation under the current EU and national liability regimes. Moreover, there is also some uncertainty regarding the allocation of responsibilities between different economic operators in the supply chain of AI systems. Several parties can be involved such as the developers of the software/algorithm, the producer of the hardware, owners/keepers of the AI product, suppliers of data, public authorities and the users of the product. Persons who have suffered harm may not have effective access to the evidence that is necessary to build a case in court and may have less effective redress possibilities compared to situations in which the damage is caused by 'traditional' products.[11]

---

4 Tesla's Blog, 'A Tragic Loss', 30 June 2016, https://www.teslamotors.com/blog/tragic-loss.

5 S. Levin and J. Carrie, 'Self-driving Uber kills Arizona woman in first fatal crash involving pedestrian', *The Guardian*, 19 March 2018.

6 X, 'Robots v Humans: AI machine 'attacks' visitor at Chinese tech fair', *RT News*, 8 November 2016.

7 *Mracek v. Bryn Mawr Hospital*, 363 Fed. Appx. 925 (3d Cir. 2010) as reported in T.N. White and S.D. Baum, 'Liability for Present and Future Robotics Technology', in P. Lin et al. (ed.) *Robot Ethics 2.0: From Autonomous Cars to Artificial Intelligence* (New York: Oxford University Press, 2017), pp. 66–79.

8 J. McCurry, 'South Korean woman's hair 'eaten' by robot vacuum cleaner as she slept', *The Guardian*, 9 February 2015.

9 European Commission, 'Report on the safety and liability implications of Artificial Intelligence, the Internet of Things and robotics', COM(2020) 64 final, 19 February 2020, p. 12.

10 See in general: W. Barfield, 'Liability for Autonomous and Artificially Intelligent Robots', *Paladyn, Journal of Behavioral Robotics*, 2018, vol. 9, no. 1, pp. 193–203; E. Tjong Tjin Tai, 'Liability for (Semi)Autonomous Systems: Robots and Algorithms', Tilburg Law School Legal Studies Research Paper Series, No. 09/2018, https://papers.ssrn.com/sol3/papers.cfm?abstract_id=3161962.

11 European Commission, 'On Artificial Intelligence – A European approach to excellence and trust', p. 13; M. Buiten, A. De Streel and M. Peitz, 'EU Liability Rules for the Age of Artificial

It is, however, important that victims of accidents involving AI systems are not confronted with a lower level of protection compared to other products and services for which they would get compensation under national law. Otherwise, societal acceptance of those AI systems and other emerging technologies could be hampered and a hesitance to use them could be the result.[12]

3. Against this background, we will examine whether victims may be successful in claiming recovery for damage caused by AI systems under Belgian tort law. We will limit our research to the application of tort or extra-contractual liability regimes in the context of AI. Contractual[13] and criminal liability[14] for damage caused by AI systems are thus not addressed in this chapter. We restrict our research to tort liability as this is a re-occurring and important topic in several documents that were recently issued by the European Commission,[15] especially in light of the recent Proposals for an AI Liability Directive[16] and for a revised Product Liability Directive (PLD).[17] Extra-contractual liability

---

Intelligence', April 2021, pp. 24–38, https://papers.ssrn.com/sol3/papers.cfm?abstract_id=3817520.

12 European Commission, 'Report on the safety and liability implications of Artificial Intelligence, the Internet of Things and robotics', p. 13.

13 See: H. Jacquemin and J-B. Hubin, 'Aspects contractuels et de responsabilité civile en matière d'intelligence artificielle', in H. Jacquemin and A. De Streel (eds.), *L'intelligence artificielle et le droit* (Brussels: Larcier, 2017), pp. 77–112; K. Swinnen, 'De inpassing van digitale producten in het Belgisch privaatrecht', *TPR*, 2018, pp. 1068–1078; J. De Bruyne and M. Herbosch, 'Artificiële intelligentie, aansprakelijkheid en contractenrecht. Enkele aandachtspunten voor bedrijfsjuristen' in IBJ, *Artificiële intelligentie door de ogen van de bedrijfsjurist / L'intelligence artificielle à travers les yeux des juristes d'entreprise* (Brussels: Larcier, 2022), pp. 45–76. See also some of the chapters in: M. Ebers, C. Poncibo and M. Zou (eds.), *Contracting and Contract Law in the Age of Artificial Intelligence* (London: Bloomsbury Publishing, 2021), 384 p.

14 See: F. Lagiola and G. Sartor, 'AI Systems Under Criminal Law: a Legal Analysis and a Regulatory Perspective', *Philosophy & Technology* 2019, pp. 1–33.

15 See the many references to policy documents and EU studies throughout this chapter. The limited scope of this chapter does not allow for an extensive (comparative) legal analysis. Reference is, therefore, made to the existing national studies on this topic. See in this regard also the legal comparative analysis (France, England and Germany) by R. Janal, 'Extra-Contractual Liability for Wrongs Committed by Autonomous Systems', in Ebers and Navas (eds.), *Algorithms and Law*, pp. 174–205. See more generally on liability and AI: A. Beckers and G. Teubner, *Three Liability Regimes for Artificial Intelligence: Algorithmic Actants, Hybrids, Crowds* (Camden: Hart, 2021), 166 p.; S. Lohsse et al. (eds.), *Liability for Artificial Intelligence and the Internet of Things* (Baden-Baden: Nomos, 2019), 352 p. This (revised) chapter is based on the preliminary research in: E. Van Gool, J. De Bruyne and M. Fierens, 'De regulering van artificiële intelligentie (deel 2) – Een analyse van buitencontractuele aansprakelijkheid', *RW*, 2021, 1003–1024; J. De Bruyne, E. Van Gool and A. Boes, 'Wat bracht 2022 en wat brengt de toekomst op het vlak van artificiële intelligentie en buitencontractuele aansprakelijkheid?', in T. Vansweevelt and B. Weyts, 'Verslagboek van het IVde Interuniversitair Congres Aansprakelijkheids- en Verzekeringsrecht' (Antwerp: Intersentia, 2022), pp. 191-254.

16 Proposal for a Directive of the European Parliament and of the Council on adapting non contractual civil liability rules to artificial intelligence, European Commission, COM(2022) 496 final, 2022, p. 3 ('AI Liability Directive').

17 Proposal for a Directive of the European Parliament and of the Council on liability for defective products, European Commission, COM(2022) 495 final, 2022 ('revised PLD').

also encompasses many of the most fundamental questions and problems that arise in the context of AI and liability. We will focus on fault-based liability for damage caused by AI systems (part 2), product liability (part 3) and liability for defective things (part 4). We will also briefly discuss some re-occurring elements common to all these regimes, namely damage and causation (part 5). The question of giving legal personality to AI systems is also addressed (part 6). Recent developments on liability and AI at the EU level will be included in the analysis when relevant. The most important findings are summarised in a conclusion (part 7).

2. FAULT-BASED LIABILITY

4. The starting point of Belgian tort law is a liability for one's own acts in the form of liability for fault. The statutory basis is Article 1382 of the Old Belgian Civil Code (OBCC).[18] The most important characteristic of fault-based liability is its broad and general scope of application. Liability for fault may apply to any tangible or intangible aspect of any type of AI system. It may also apply to any person directly or indirectly involved in the development, authorisation or operation of AI systems or to persons who may interact with them in both a professional or non-professional capacity. Furthermore, 'fault' itself is a broad and relatively flexible concept that encompasses both intentional and non-intentional conduct and both actions and omissions.[19] Furthermore, an exploration of the most likely cases of possible liability for faults committed by existing persons in the context of damage created by AI systems reveals that most of such faults will be non-intentional in nature and many will consist of omissions rather than actions.[20] Some examples that are further discussed are failures by developers and 'backend operators' to provide safety precautions, updates and adequate monitoring, or failures by users to timely intervene in the autonomous operation of an AI system. These examples already reveal that the involvement of different actors can make it challenging for victims to understand where things may have gone wrong in the AI supply chain.

5. Liability under Article 1382 OBCC requires the proof of three constitutive elements: a fault, damage and causation. We will focus on the first element in the following paragraphs. Damage and causation are discussed separately in

[18] Together with Article 1383 OBCC, which is interpreted as not having a separate meaning. As a consequence, explicit reference is traditionally only made to Article 1382 OBCC. See in this regard also: M. Kruithof, *Tort Law in Belgium* (Kluwer Law International: Alphen aan den Rijn, 2018), p. 45.

[19] See: H. De Page, *Traité élémentaire de droit civil belge: Tome II: Les obligations* (Brussels: Bruylant, 1964), p. 931.

[20] See: Swinnen, 'De inpassing van digitale producten in het Belgisch privaatrecht', pp. 1091–1092.

part 5 as they are constitutive for the other grounds of (tort) liability as well. Notwithstanding the broad scope of application, it will be shown that the actual application of liability for fault within the context of damage created by AI systems can be challenging. The fundamental problem is the autonomous, opaque and interconnected nature of AI systems, which makes it difficult to connect the functioning of an AI system to conduct of existing persons. While this is also true for product liability and liability for things, it is even more true for liability for fault, which depends most heavily on a direct connection with human conduct.[21]

6. A fault under Belgian law consists of a subjective and an objective component. The application of both components can be challenging in an AI-context.

The subjective component requires that the fault can be attributed to the free will of the person who has committed it ('imputability'), and that this person generally possesses the capacity to control and to assess the consequences of his conduct ('culpability').[22] The subjective requirement makes clear that the lack of a purely formally recognised legal personality is not the only obstacle to a direct liability of AI systems.[23] In order to be liable for their own fault, AI systems would also need to obtain a capacity for moral discernment. This, however, appears to be intrinsically human and difficult to reconcile with the technical constitution of AI.[24] If legal personality would ever be awarded to certain AI systems, it is furthermore worth noting that (a) special non-fault liability rules exist for natural persons who lack 'culpability',[25] (b) legal persons are considered to be liable for faults committed by their non-subordinated legal representatives ('organs') when they acted (ostensibly) within the pursuit of their mission[26] and (c) employees, civil servants and volunteers enjoy a partial immunity from

---

21 European Commission, 'Report on the safety and liability implications of Artificial Intelligence, the Internet of Things and robotics', p. 13; Jacquemin and Hubin, 'Aspects contractuels et de responsabilité civile en matière d'intelligence artificielle', pp. 115–118.

22 See: Cass. 30 May 1969, *Arr.Cass.*, 1969, p. 943, *RCJB*, 1970, p. 36; Cass. 16 February 1984, *Arr. Cass.* 1983–84, p. 44; Cass. 3 October 1994, *Arr.Cass.* 1994, p. 807, *RW*, 1996–97, p. 1227; S. Stijns, *Verbintenissenrecht - Boek 1bis* (Bruges: Die Keure, 2013), p. 48 and 58; T. Vansweevelt and B. Weyts, *Handboek Buitencontractueel Aansprakelijkheidsrecht* (Antwerp: Intersentia, 2009), pp. 147–148; M. Kruithof, *Tort Law in Belgium*, p. 53–56. Also see H. De Page, *Traité élémentaire de droit civil belge: Tome II: Les obligations* (Brussels: Bruylant, 1964), pp. 881–884 who refers to 'capacité aquilienne'. See for an analysis on the (lack of this) requirement in the proposal for a new Civil Code dealing with tort liability: G. Jocqué, '[Hervorming van het aansprakelijkheidsrecht] Foutaansprakelijkheid: algemene beginselen - aansprakelijkheid minderjarigen en geesteszieken', *TPR*, 2021, no. 1, p. 36.

23 Also see *infra* part 6.

24 Also see: Jacquemin and Hubin, 'Aspects contractuels et de responsabilité civile en matière d'intelligence artificielle', pp. 116.

25 See: Articles 1384, paragraphs 2 and 5 and 1386*bis* OBCC.

26 Cass. 13 December 1923, *Pas.*, 1923, I, p. 82; Cass. 15 January 1946, *Arr.Cass.*, 1946, p. 22; Cass. 19 December 1991, *Arr.Cass.*, 1991, p. 396, *RW*, 1992–93, p. 397.

liability for their personal fault which corresponds with a similar attribution of liability to the persons for whom they are working.[27] Consequently, awarding legal personality to certain AI systems could raise several new questions on the corresponding 'imputability' and 'culpability' for faults, in addition to possible more fundamental objections.[28] Given that AI systems currently possess no legal personality whatsoever, the discussion below focuses exclusively on faults committed by existing natural or legal persons.

The objective component of a fault refers to the wrongful behaviour in itself. After some general thoughts on the victim's burden of proof for wrongful acts (part 2.1.), we will focus on the two types of wrongs that Belgian law traditionally recognises: a violation of a specific legal rule of conduct (part 2.2.)[29] and the breach of a general duty of care (part 2.3.).[30]

2.1. GENERAL CONSIDERATIONS ON THE BURDEN OF PROOF FOR FAULT-BASED LIABILITY

7. In accordance with traditional Belgian civil evidence law, it is in principle up to the injured party as claimant to prove that each condition of liability for fault is fulfilled.[31] Notwithstanding the possibility to refute evidence submitted by the claimant, the defendant only bears the burden of proof when he/she invokes a ground of exemption from liability.[32] The required standard of proof is 'a reasonable level of certainty'.[33] The individual injured party needs to deliver this proof for each liability condition.[34] The only possible external support consists

---

27 See: Article 18 Act of 3 July 1978 regarding employment contracts, *BS* 22 August 1978, p. 9277; Articles 2–6 Act of 10 February 2003 regarding the liability of and for the personnel employed by public authorities, *BS* 27 February 2003, p. 9558; Article 5 Act of 3 July 2005 regarding the rights of volunteers, *BS* 29 August 2005, p. 37309; Article 1384, paragraph 3 OBCC.

28 Also see *infra* part 6.

29 Cass. 22 March 1957, *Arr.Cass.*, 1957, p. 610; Cass. 13 May 1982, *Arr.Cass.*, 1982, p. 1134; Cass. 22 September 1988, *Arr.Cass.*, 1988–89, p. 94; Cass. 3 October 1994, *Arr.Cass.*, 1994, p. 807; Cass. 10 April 2014, *Arr.Cass.*, 2014, p. 962. This is also true when the illegal act or omission would be considered as non-negligent (see e.g., Cass. 6 June 2011, *Arr.Cass.*, 2011, p. 1478).

30 See: Cass. 30 April 1976, *Arr.Cass.*, 1976, p. 980; Cass. 8 December 1994, *Arr.Cass.*, 1994, p. 1074; Cass. 25 November 2002, *Arr.Cass.*, 2002, p. 2543; Cass. 5 June 2003, *Arr.Cass.*, 2003, p. 1337; H. Bocken and I. Boone with cooperation by M. Kruithof, *Inleiding tot het schadevergoedingsrecht* (Bruges: Die Keure, 2014), pp. 90–92; Stijns, *Verbintenissenrecht – Boek 1bis*, pp. 42–44.

31 Article 8.4, paragraph 1 New Belgian Civil Code (Act of 13 April 2019, *BS* 14 May 2019, p. 46353); Article 870 Belgian Judicial Code.

32 Article 8.4, paragraph 2 New Belgian Civil Code; Article 870 Belgian Judicial Code. The exemption is either a ground of justification or an external cause (W. Vandenbussche, *Bewijs en onrechtmatige daad* (Antwerp: Intersentia, 2017), p. 150–151). See also *infra* part. 2.2.

33 Article 8.5 New Belgian Civil Code.

34 Class actions are generally not allowed under Belgian law (see *infra* part 5.1.). See on the burden of proof in the context of causation also *infra* part 5.2.

of investigatory measures, which a judge may order (e.g., a judicial expertise[35]), and the principle that all parties are required to cooperate in the administration of evidence,[36] which seems difficult to enforce within the opaque and highly complex context of AI technology.

While both parties may have similar knowledge regarding the events and underlying causes in 'traditional' cases of fault liability, this is no longer true when the damage is a result of technology that has been developed, controlled or used by the defendant. AI technology can be especially complex and inaccessible (cf. black box).[37] Moreover, the injured party will likely be a natural person, while the defendant will mostly be a legal person with considerable knowledge on the specific AI system or on AI technology in general.[38] Only when the defendant is not the developer but a non-professional user, for example the user of an individual autonomous car or housekeeping robot, less informational asymmetry exists between the parties. Nevertheless, even these non-professional defendants still enjoy easier access to the AI system's data, its features, developers and service providers when compared with the injured party.

8. Consequently, it will often not be straightforward for injured parties to establish a defendant's wrongful act. Against this background, the European Group on Liability and New Technologies proposes in its report ('Expert Report') to reverse the burden of proof for fault in a number of cases, namely (a) when the claimant generally encounters disproportionate difficulties and costs to prove a fault; (b) when the defendant has violated a safety rule which was meant to avoid the damage;[39] or (c) when 'logging' information has not been recorded or provided in violation of an obligation to do so.[40] The Commission in its report issued in February 2020 explicitly considers the possibility of reversing

35 Articles 962–991*bis* Belgian Judicial Code.

36 Article 8.4, paragraph 3, New Belgian Civil Code. Also see: Cass. 14 November 2013, *Arr. Cass.* 2013, p. 2401; Cass. 4 June 2015, C.14.0479.F; Cass. 7 June 2019, C.18.0523.N.

37 See specifically regarding the 'discreet, diffuse, discrete and opaque' nature of the development of AI systems: M.U. Scherer, 'Regulating Artificial Intelligence Systems: Risks, Challenges, Competencies, and Strategies', *Harvard Journal of Law & Technology*, 2016, pp. 369–373.

38 See regarding asymmetry in access to evidence: Vandenbussche, *Bewijs en onrechtmatige daad*, pp. 221–225.

39 Also see *infra* part 2.2.

40 Expert Group on Liability and New Technologies, New Technologies Formation, 'Liability for Artificial Intelligence and Other Emerging Digital Technologies', November 2019, pp. 47–49 and 52–55. See also on 'logging obligations' as an instrument for *ex post* verification of potential liability in cases involving AI systems: U. Bose, 'The Black Box Solution to Autonomous Liability', *Washington University Law Review*, 2015, pp. 1342–1351. See for a critical analysis on the Expert Report: A. Bertolini and F. Episcopo, 'The Expert Group's Report on Liability for Artificial Intelligence and Other Emerging Digital Technologies: a critical assessment', *European Journal of Risk Regulation*, 2021, vol. 12, no. 3, pp. 652–654.

the burden of proof for liability conditions such as fault.[41] Interestingly, the final section of Article 8.4 of the Belgian Civil Code now allows a judge to reverse the burden of proof 'in light of exceptional circumstances' when the application of the 'normal rules' would be 'manifestly unreasonable'.[42] The judge can allow a reversal of the burden of proof as a matter of last resort once all useful investigatory measures have been ordered and the obligation of all parties to cooperate in the administration of evidence has already been enforced.[43] The proof of an objective fault in cases of damage created by AI systems seems an appropriate scenario for applying this effective but far-reaching technique.[44] However, one can wonder whether strictly limiting it to a measure of last resort may turn out to be too inefficient in this particular context where the informational asymmetry between parties can be extreme from the onset. Efforts by the claimant to provide sufficient proof will often be futile and a judicial expertise will be time- and resource-consuming. It may still lead to a debatable conclusion as well.[45] In cases of liability for AI systems, it may consequently be more attractive to provide a more immediate possibility to reverse the burden of proof.

9. An alternative solution may consist of lowering the required standard of proof. The Belgian civil evidence law again provides for a possibility to do so. Article 8.6 of the Belgian Civil Code allows proof by probability[46] of negative facts and positive facts for which it is impossible or unreasonable to expect proof by the aforementioned reasonable certainty standard. It remains to be seen how

---

41 European Commission, 'Report on the safety and liability implications of Artificial Intelligence, the Internet of Things and robotics', p. 14 and 16.

42 In this regard, the Memorandum of explanation stipulates that the judge will be able to consider an important imbalance in the aptitude for delivering evidence, if obtaining, recording or reporting the required evidence would be excessively onerous or expensive for one of the parties. The existence of an economic imbalance between the parties, for example an individual against a large company, should not automatically result in a reversal of the burden of proof. Nevertheless, the judge can take such imbalance into consideration if the burden of proof incumbent on the individual would require extremely onerous and/ or expensive performances from him (Memorandum of explanation accompanying the Proposed Act to insert Book 8 'Evidence' in the New Civil Code, *Parl.St.* Kamer 2018–19, no. 3349/001, p. 15, own translation).

43 The legislative proposal emphasises that this measure can only be applied as an '*ultimum remedium*' (Memorandum of explanation accompanying the Proposed Act to insert Book 8 'Evidence' in the New Civil Code, *Parl.St.* Kamer 2018–19, no. 3349/001, pp. 14–15).

44 See already arguing in favour of a reversal of the burden of proof for cases of extra-contractual liability with a significant asymmetry between parties in access to evidence: W. Vandenbussche, *Bewijs en onrechtmatige daad*, pp. 697–721.

45 See for example *infra* parts 2.3, 3.2 and 4.

46 The legislative proposal describes the required probability as 75%, which means that there are serious elements in the file which support the allegations and that alternatives, although not entirely impossible, do not seem credible (Memorandum of explanation accompanying the Proposed Act to insert Book 8 'Evidence' in the New Civil Code, *Parl.St.* Kamer 2018–19, no. 3349/001, p. 17, own translation).

this will be applied in practice. Nevertheless, it is conceivable that cases of tort liability for damage caused by AI systems will be likely candidates for the explicit or implicit use of this probability standard. In our opinion, reversing the burden of proof seems more appropriate than lowering the standard of proof because it offers more certainty on a correct application of the relevant tort law rules. A correct application also better safeguards tort law's 'preventive' or 'steering' function,[47] which is particularly important and relevant for an emerging technology such as AI.

10. In addition to procedural mechanisms at the national level, the recent Proposal for an AI Liability Directive is also worth mentioning in this regard. The purpose of the AI Liability Directive is to improve the functioning of the internal market by laying down uniform requirements for certain aspects of non-contractual civil liability for damage caused with the involvement of an AI system. Article 1 defines the scope of the Directive. It lays down common rules regarding 'the disclosure of evidence on high-risk artificial intelligence (AI) systems to enable a claimant to substantiate a non-contractual fault-based civil law claim for damages'.[48] Article 3 of the AI Liability Directive stipulates that a court may, upon the request of a (potential) claimant, order the disclosure of relevant evidence about a specific high-risk AI system that is suspected of having caused damage. Such requests for evidence may be addressed to *inter alia* the provider of an AI system, a person subject to the provider's obligations or its user.[49] With respect to the 'potential' claimant (differentiated from the 'actual' claimant), however, additional requirements apply before the court can order the disclosure of evidence.[50] The potential claimant's request should be supported by facts and evidence sufficient to establish the plausibility of the contemplated claim for damages.[51] A claimant in turn should undertake all proportionate attempts at gathering the relevant evidence from the defendant before the national court can order the disclosure of the evidence.[52] There are several mitigating elements safeguarding the defendant's position and ensuring proportionality (e.g., national courts need to limit the disclosure of evidence to what is necessary and proportionate to support a potential claim or a claim for damages).[53] The Directive also contains a rebuttable presumption of non-compliance. Where a defendant in a claim for damages fails to disclose or

---

47 See: Vansweevelt and Weyts, *Handboek Buitencontractueel Aansprakelijkheidsrecht*, pp. 7–9; Kruithof, *Tort Law in Belgium*, pp. 35–36. See on the deterring effect of tort law with many references: J. De Bruyne, *Third-Party Certifiers* (Alphen aan den Rijn: Kluwer Law International, 2019), pp. 268–286.

48 Article 1 (a) AI Liability Directive.

49 AI Liability Directive, Art. 3.1., first paragraph.

50 AI Liability Directive, Art. 3.1., first paragraph.

51 Article 3.1, second paragraph AI Liability Directive.

52 Article 3.2 AI Liability Directive.

53 Article 3.4, first paragraph.AI Liability Directive.

preserve evidence at its disposal as ordered by a court, a presumption of non-compliance with relevant duties of care is presumed which that evidence was intended to prove. However, the defendant may rebut that presumption by submitting evidence to the contrary.[54]

More importantly, the Directive also deals with the 'burden of proof in the case of non-contractual fault-based civil law claims brought before national courts for damages caused by an AI system'.[55] More specifically, the Directive applies to non-contractual civil law claims for damage caused by an AI system, where such claims are brought under fault-based liability regimes.[56] Article 4.1 contains a rebuttable presumption of a 'causal link between the fault of the defendant and the output produced by the AI system or the failure of the AI system to produce an output'. By doing so, the Directive 'aims to provide an effective basis for claiming compensation in connection with the fault consisting in the lack of compliance with a duty of care under Union or national law'.[57] It has already been mentioned above that it can be challenging for claimants to establish a causal link between such non-compliance and the output produced by the AI system or the failure of the AI system to produce an output that gave rise to the relevant damage. However, this presumption only applies provided that three conditions are met:[58]

- First, the *fault* of the defendant has to be proven by the claimant according to the applicable EU law or national rules, or presumed by the court following the non-compliance with a court order to disclose or preserve evidence.[59] Such a fault can be established, for example, 'for non-compliance with a duty of care pursuant to the AI Act'.[60]
- Second, it can be considered *reasonably likely*, based on the circumstances of the case, that the fault has *influenced the output* produced by the AI system or the failure of the AI system to produce an output.[61]
- Third, the claimant needs to demonstrate that the output produced by the AI system or the failure of the AI system to produce an output gave rise to the *damage*.[62]

Whereas Article 4.1 targets *defendants* in general, Articles 4.2 and 4.3 make a further distinction between (i) claims brought against the *provider* of a high-risk

---

54 Article 3.5 AI Liability Directive.
55 Article 1 (b) AI Liability Directive.
56 Article 1 (2) AI Liability Directive.
57 Article 4.1 (a) AI Liability Directive, see also p. 13.
58 Article 4.1 AI Liability Directive.
59 Article 3.5 AI Liability Directive.
60 Article 4.1. (a) AI Liability Directive, also see p. 13.
61 Article 4.1 (b) AI Liability Directive.
62 Article 4.1 (c) AI Liability Directive.

AI system or against *a person subject to the provider's obligations* under the AI Act and (ii) claims brought against the *user* of such high-risk AI systems.[63]

Article 4.4 establishes an exception to the presumption of causality specifically for high-risk AI systems where 'the defendant demonstrates that sufficient evidence and expertise is reasonably accessible for the claimant to prove the causal link'. This possibility can induce defendants to comply with their disclosure obligations, 'with measures set by the AI Act to ensure a high level of transparency of the AI or with documenting and recording requirements'.[64] A court will eventually have to assess whether the evidence and expertise are 'reasonably' accessible. This could be the case, for instance, with regard to high-risk AI systems where the claimant could reasonably access sufficient and understandable evidence/expertise through documentation and logging requirements pursuant to the AI Act. In such situations, courts should refrain from applying the presumption.[65] In the case of a claim for damage concerning an AI system that is *not* a high-risk AI system, the presumption of causality only applies where the national court considers it excessively difficult for the claimant to prove the causal link.[66] Moreover, in cases where the defendant uses the AI system in the course of a personal non-professional activity, Article 4.6 provides that the presumption of causality should only apply if the defendant has materially interfered with the conditions of the operation of the AI system or if the defendant was required and able to determine the conditions of operation of the AI system and failed to do so. This condition is justified by the need to balance the interests of injured persons and non-professional users, by exempting from the application of the presumption of causality the cases in which non-professional users do not add risk through their behaviour. In any case, a more general way to rebut the burden of proof is included in Article 4.7. It provides that the defendant has the right to rebut the causality presumption following Article 4.1.[67]

In conclusion, it seems that if the current Proposal for an AI Liability Directive is adopted, claimants would under Belgian law receive considerable additional support to overcome the challenge of proving the required elements under a fault-based liability regime with regard to AI. The still relatively new Belgian civil evidence law already codified rules on the proof by probability and on the reversal of the burden of proof, which are generally applicable but

63 See extensively: O. Dheu et al., 'The European Commission's Approach to Extra-Contractual Liability and AI – A First Analysis and Evaluation of the Two Proposals', KU Leuven Centre for IT & IP (CiTiP) Working Paper 2022, 6 October 2022, pp. 10–14, https://papers.ssrn.com/sol3/papers.cfm?abstract_id=4239792.

64 AI Liability Directive, p. 13.

65 Recital 27 AI Liability Directive.

66 Article 4.5. AI Liability Directive.

67 O. Dheu et al., 'The European Commission's Approach to Extra-Contractual Liability and AI – A First Analysis and Evaluation of the Two Proposals', pp. 10–14.

not always easy to apply in practice for a plaintiff. In contrast, the proposed AI Liability Directive's rules on the disclosure of evidence and on the presumption of causality are easier to apply for a plaintiff in the specific context of damage involving AI systems. Such rules can in our view greatly aid a plaintiff's case.

2.2. VIOLATION OF A LEGAL RULE REQUIRING SPECIFIC CONDUCT

11. Under Belgian law, violating a legal rule which requires a specific behaviour without a ground of exemption, is automatically considered to be wrongful. This is the so-called 'unitary theory', which equates illegality and (objective) fault within the context of tort liability.[68] It is not required that the person was aware that his/her conduct would be illegal. Ignorance of the law only exempts from liability if it qualifies as an unsurmountable error, which requires that any reasonable and prudent person would not have realised the illegality in those circumstances.[69] The act or omission that happens to be illegal afterwards should be committed knowingly and willingly.[70] It is necessary that the violated legal rule requires a specific conduct. This condition is often interpreted relatively flexibly.[71] If a violated legal rule requires conduct in a general way or if broad considerations of care are at stake, it is equated with the general duty of care and the corresponding conditions of that category should be fulfilled in order to constitute an objective fault.[72] Additionally, a fault constituted by the violation of a legal rule demanding specific conduct does not require that the actor foresees a possibility of damages.[73]

---

68 While illegal behaviour automatically constitutes an objective fault, the opposite is not true. Conduct in accordance with all applicable legal rules requiring specific behaviour, may still violate the general duty of care (see Bocken and Boone with cooperation by Kruithof, *Inleiding tot het schadevergoedingsrecht*, p. 95).

69 See: Cass. 25 October 1999, *Arr.Cass.*, 1999, p. 1327; M. Van Quickenborne and H. Vandenberghe, 'Overzicht van rechtspraak. Aansprakelijkheid uit onrechtmatige daad (2000–2008)', *TPR*, 2010, pp. 1772–1773.

70 Kruithof, *Tort Law in Belgium*, pp. 50–51.

71 See for example: Cass. 13 May 1982, *Arr.Cass.*, 1982, p. 1134; Cass. 22 February 1989, *Arr. Cass.*, 1989, p. 703; Court of Appeal Antwerp 1 June 2004, *NJW*, 2005, p. 739; Court of Appeal Brussels 23 April 1996, *RW*, 1998–99, p. 296. See, however, Cass. 10 April 2014, *Arr.Cass.*, 2014, p. 962.

72 See for example: Cass. 26 June 1998, *Arr.Cass.*, 1998, p. 343; Court of Appeal Antwerp 11 October 2005, *T.Gez.*, 2005–06, p. 393, *Limb.Rechtsl.*, 2006, no. 3, p. 179; Court of Appeal Ghent 18 April 2002, *RW*, 2003–04, p. 139. See the discussion *infra* part 2.C. See for an application in the context of autonomous vehicles: J. De Bruyne and J. Tanghe, 'Liability for Damage Caused by Autonomous Vehicles: A Belgian Perspective', *Journal of European Tort Law*, 2017, vol. 8, no. 3, pp. 338–339.

73 Bocken and Boone with cooperation by Kruithof, *Inleiding tot het schadevergoedingsrecht*, p. 92; H. Vandenberghe et al., 'Aansprakelijkheid uit onrechtmatige daad. Overzicht van rechtspraak 1994–1999', *TPR*, 2000, p. 1564. As opposed to a violation of the general duty of care, as discussed *infra* part 2.3.

12. The equation under Belgian law of a violation of a legal rule requiring a specific conduct with an objective fault is relatively strong and comprehensive. In the long term, this may constitute an important contribution to the challenge of proving liability for fault when damage is caused by AI systems. This is because the need and importance to develop all sorts of relevant technical and safety rules for AI systems is currently being emphasised at the EU level.[74] Such rules may *inter alia* consist of (a) development requirements, (b) restrictions on autonomy and use in uncontrolled or unsupervised environments, (c) obligations on training, data input, monitoring and cybersecurity and (d) obligations regarding *ex-post* transparency such as 'logging'.[75] Such binding AI-related rules can either be general or sector-specific. It is furthermore possible that they only consist of essential safety requirements, which are further specified by standardisation organisations according to the European 'new legislative framework' for regulating goods.[76] However, binding legal rules requiring specific conduct that are tailored to AI systems do not yet exist.[77] That is one reason why the proposed AI Act is so important. It contains several obligations for providers and users of AI systems. Providers, for instance, have to ensure that their high-risk AI systems are compliant with the applicable requirements included in the AI Act (e.g., on data and data governance). They also have to draw up the technical documentation of high-risk AI systems and keep the logs automatically generated by their high-risk AI systems when under their control.[78] Users of high-risk AI systems have to use such systems in accordance

---

74 European Commission, 'Report on the safety and liability implications of Artificial Intelligence, the Internet of Things and robotics', pp. 3–11 and p. 15; European Commission, 'White Paper on Artificial Intelligence: A European approach to excellence and trust', pp. 12–15; European Parliament Resolution of 16 February 2017 with recommendations to the Commission on Civil Law Rules on Robotics, 2015/2103(INL), recitals 22, 25 and 33; Expert Group on Liability and New Technologies, New Technologies Formation, 'Liability for Artificial Intelligence and Other Emerging Digital Technologies', p. 23 and 48. See also G. Spindler, 'User Liability and Strict Liability in the Internet of Things and for Robots', in S. Lohsse et al., *Liability for Artificial Intelligence and the Internet of Things* (Baden-Baden: Nomos, 2019), p. 138.

75 The Expert Report suggests that AI technologies should embed some kind of logging system which would enable to identify the source of the malfunctioning that caused the damage (Expert Group on Liability and New Technologies, New Technologies Formation, 'Liability for Artificial Intelligence and Other Emerging Digital Technologies', pp. 47–48).

76 European Commission, 'Report on the safety and liability implications of Artificial Intelligence, the Internet of Things and robotics', pp. 3–4. See on the 'new legislative framework': D. Verhoeven, *Productaansprakelijkheid en productveiligheid*, (Antwerp: Intersentia, 2018), p. 85–88 and pp. 375–384. See on standardisation and AI: M. Ebers, 'Standardizing AI – The Case of the European Commission's Proposal for an Artificial Intelligence Act' in L.A. DiMatteo, C. Poncibò en M. Cannarsa (eds.), *The Cambridge Handbook of Artificial Intelligence: Global Perspectives on Law and Ethics* (Cambridge: Cambridge University Press, 2022), pp. 321–344.

77 See as an illustration of current pioneering work in (initially non-binding) AI standardisation: ISO/IEC JTC 1/SC 42, https://www.iso.org/committee/6794475.html.

78 Article 16 Commission proposal for a regulation of the European Parliament and of the Council laying down harmonised rules on artificial intelligence (Artificial Intelligence Act)

with the instructions of use accompanying the systems. They have to keep the logs automatically generated by that high-risk AI system to the extent that such logs are under their control.[79] Such provisions will be important to assess whether one of these actors violated a legal rule, and hence potentially faces liability. At the same time, however, there is a risk that the provisions included in the AI Act may be incomplete or easily become outdated.

13. Naturally, general legal rules requiring specific conduct which are not specific to AI systems already exist. Countless existing legal rules require specific conduct in particular sectors in which AI systems are already being introduced, such as road and air transportation, healthcare or financial services. More general rules suitable for determining liability for fault that are relevant to all types of AI systems are rare. The most prominent examples are likely to be found in general product safety law. Examples are the obligation for producers to provide users with relevant information to enable them to assess a product's safety risks, surveillance and recall obligations imposed on producers and distributors and, more importantly, the obligation of producers to only put safe products on the market.[80] Furthermore, distributors are not allowed to supply products which they know or are supposed to know to be unsafe.[81] These rules will continue to apply to products and associated services that are part of AI systems as long as the same risks are not regulated by more specific safety rules.[82] The Proposal for a new General Product Safety Regulation is also relevant in this regard, especially concerning AI systems not covered by the AI Act (cf. low-risk AI systems). According to Article 5, economic operators are required to place or make available on the Union market only safe products. Article 7 contains aspects for assessing the safety of products. It refers to the evolving, learning and predictive functionalities of a product as well as to the appropriate cybersecurity features necessary to protect the product against external influences, including

and amending certain Union legislative acts, COM(2021) 206, 21 April 2021 (further referred to as 'AI Act').

79 Article 29 AI Act.

80 A safe product means any product which, under normal or reasonably foreseeable conditions of use including duration and, where applicable, putting into service, installation and maintenance requirements, does not present any risk or only the minimum risks compatible with the product's use, considered to be acceptable and consistent with a high level of protection for the safety and health of persons, taking into account several points such as the characteristics of the product or its presentation (Article I.10 °2 Code of Economic Law and Article 2 of Directive 2001/95/EC of the European Parliament and of the Council of 3 December 2001 on general product safety, *OJ L* 11.

81 See: Articles IX.2 and IX.8 Code of Economic Law. Also see: Article IX.9 Code of Economic Law. These rules are the Belgian transposition of Directive 2001/95/EC of 3 December 2001 on general product safety, *OJ L* 11.

82 Article IX.1, section 2 Code of Economic Law. See regarding the associated services covered by Belgian general product safety law: Verhoeven, *Productaansprakelijkheid en productveiligheid*, pp. 28–31. Services are crucial in the digital and interconnected context of AI systems.

malicious third parties, when such an influence might have an impact on the safety of the product.[83]

Regarding the obligation to only put safe products on the market or to only supply such products, it must be noted that the European Court of Justice considers that the Product Liability Directive provides a maximum harmonisation.[84] This could theoretically mean that it is no longer possible to base Belgian liability for fault directly on a violation of these general safety rules.[85] However, it is uncertain whether the European Court of Justice would confirm such interpretation because the violation of a legal rule requiring specific conduct is only an alternative criterion to establish the objective component of Belgian liability for fault. The latter clearly remains a legal basis that is distinct from the product liability regime.[86] And even if the aforementioned restrictive interpretation would be confirmed, it appears relatively simple to qualify the same violations of safety rules also as violations of the general duty of care,[87] which certainly falls outside the harmonisation scope of the Product Liability Directive.

14. Finally, it is necessary to briefly mention the possible presence in certain cases of *force majeure*, an order from the government, state of necessity, lawful

[83] Article 7.1 Proposal for a Regulation on general product safety, amending Regulation (EU) No 1025/2012 of the European Parliament and of the Council, and repealing Council Directive 87/357/EEC and Directive 2001/95/EC of the European Parliament and of the Council, 30 June 2021, COM(2021) 346 final.

[84] Council Directive 85/374/EEC of 25 July 1985 on the approximation of the laws, regulations and administrative provisions of the Member States concerning liability for defective products, *OJ L* 210; ECJ 25 April 2002, no. C-52/00, ECLI:EU:C:2002:252, *Commission v. France*; ECJ 25 April 2002, no. C-154/00, ECLI:EU:C:2002:254, *Commission v. Greece*; ECJ 25 April 2002, no. C-183/00, ECLI:EU:C:2002:255, *Gonzales Sánchez*; ECJ 10 January 2006, no. C-402/03, ECLI:EU:C:2006:6, *Skov Aeg*.

[85] See: M. Kruithof, 'Wie is aansprakelijk voor schade veroorzaakt door onveilige producten?', in I. Claeys and R. Steennot (eds.), *Aansprakelijkheid, veiligheid en kwaliteit – PUC W. Delva nr. 40* (Mechelen: Kluwer, 2015), pp. 170–183. *Contra*: older case law and scholarship accept a violation of these general safety rules as sufficient proof of an objective fault (Court of Appeals Brussels, 23 January 2001, *RGAR*, 2002, no. 13.513; Commercial Court Hasselt, 8 november 1999, *RW*, 2001–02, p. 101; H. Bocken, 'Buitencontractuele aansprakelijkheid voor gebrekkige producten', in X. (ed.), *Bijzondere overeenkomsten – PUC W. Delva nr. 34* (Mechelen: Kluwer, 2008), pp. 353–356).

[86] Also see: Article 13 *juncto* recital 13 Council Directive 85/374/EEC of 25 July 1985 on the approximation of the laws, regulations and administrative provisions of the Member States concerning liability for defective products, *OJ L* 210; G. Howells, 'II. Purpose and Effect of the Directive', in P. Machnikowski (ed.), *European Product Liability. An analysis of the State of the Art in the Era of New Technologies* (Cambridge: Intersentia, 2016), p. 37.

[87] See for example: Court of Appeal Brussels, 9 February 1955, *JT*, 1955, p. 683; Court of Appeal Liège, 7 November 2005, *TBBR*, 2006, p. 620. Kruithof argues that also these decisions are theoretically not allowed when they overlap with the maximally harmonised scope of product liability if they are in practice considered in a way akin to a quasi-objective liability (Kruithof, 'Wie is aansprakelijk voor schade veroorzaakt door onveilige producten?', pp. 184–194). However, it appears in our opinion unlikely that the Court of Justice would prohibit an approach to determine national liability for fault which remains at least formally based on a *rationale* of negligence.

defence, unsurmountable error or duress. It is debated to what extent they impair the subjective or objective component of a fault or causality ('an external cause')[88] and whether some have an excusatory rather than a justificatory nature.[89] Nevertheless, Belgian tort law generally recognises that these 'grounds of exemption' may exempt any person from liability that would otherwise be held liable.[90] A defendant has to prove that the (stringent) conditions of a specific ground of exemption are fulfilled. Although these grounds may be applied to other tort liability regimes as well,[91] they are particularly important with regard to liability for fault. Take the example of an autonomous vehicle that violates traffic regulations (e.g., running a red light) and subsequently causes damage. The driver may try to argue that the violation of the traffic regulations was due to *force majeure*, implying that the vehicle's behaviour could not be foreseen or avoided by the driver. Consequently, it cannot constitute a fault for which he/she can be held personally liable.[92]

2.3. VIOLATION OF THE GENERAL DUTY OF CARE

15. The objective component of fault can also consist of the violation of the general duty of care, which is formulated as the reasonable amount of care that a normal, foreseeing and prudent person ('*bonus pater/mater familias*') would have applied when placed in the same concrete circumstances. Some argue that the Belgian general duty of care is only a standard serving as the yardstick for judging whether conduct is negligent or not, rather than imposing a pre-existing obligation to behave like a fictive person would have done.[93] This nuance may prove useful in the context of damage caused by AI systems because, as we will see below, it is precisely the evaluation through the lens of traditional human conduct that is most difficult to conceptualise in these cases. It has already been mentioned that relevant binding rules to establish liability for fault within the context of AI systems are currently missing and that such rules will never be able to precisely regulate all possible human conduct surrounding the wide diversity of potential AI systems.[94] Against this background, a general and open category

88 See also *infra* part 5.2.

89 See for an overview: I. Claeys, 'Fout, overmacht en rechtvaardigingsgronden. Zoveel hoofden…', in B. Tilleman and I. Claeys (eds.), *Buitencontractuele aansprakelijkheid* (Bruges: die Keure, 2004), pp. 1–42; Vansweevelt and Weyts, *Handboek Buitencontractueel Aansprakelijkheidsrecht*, pp. 299–306.

90 Also see: Kruithof, *Tort Law in Belgium*, pp. 114–117.

91 See for example: Court of Appeal Liège 18 October 1993, *JLMB*, 1994, p. 1322.

92 See: J. Tanghe and J. De Bruyne, 'Aansprakelijkheid voor schade veroorzaakt door autonome motorrijtuigen', *RW*, 2016–17, pp. 971–972; De Bruyne and Tanghe, 'Liability for Damage Caused by Autonomous Vehicles: A Belgian Perspective', pp. 343–344.

93 Kruithof, *Tort Law in Belgium*, p. 47.

94 See *supra* part 2.2.

of negligence will always remain necessary to achieve the comprehensive scope and 'catch all' function of liability for fault.[95]

16. A crucial component of the general duty of care consists of taking into account the same concrete circumstances in which the defendant was placed at the time of committing the alleged wrongful act. This avoids that the abstract standard would become too objective and blunt,[96] which would also diminish the important 'preventive' or 'deterring' function of liability for fault. While 'external circumstances' such as time and place, the surroundings, the expected behaviour of others involved and the technical possibilities should always be taken into account when determining whether the general duty of care has been violated, 'internal' traits of the defendant are traditionally excluded.[97] Nevertheless, case law increasingly considers the (non-)professional capacity of the defendant, his/her factual knowledge, his/her age or the presence of physical or mental impairments in either the defendant or the injured party.[98] These 'internal circumstances' that remain relatively objective and comparable can be important factors in many cases of damage created by AI systems. As opposed to other grounds of liability, claims regarding liability for fault will often be directed against non-professional users of AI systems. The 'internal circumstances' and the extent to which they can be taken into account are in general most relevant when the defendant is a user or 'frontend operator' of an AI system. Frontend operators are the persons who primarily decide on and benefit from the use of an AI system within a specific factual context (e.g., owner or user).

On the other hand, the 'external circumstances' likely become the most important and most challenging aspects of an evaluation of the general duty of care when the defendant is an AI system's producer or 'backend operator'. Backend operators are the persons who continuously define the features of an AI system and who provide essential and ongoing backend support to its functioning within the specific usage contexts decided by individual frontend

---

95 Also see: X. Thunis, 'Théorie de la faute civile, volume 1', in J. Fagnart (ed.), *Responsabilités. Traité théorique et pratique*, (Mechelen: Kluwer, 2017), losbl., Titre II, book 20, p. 27, no. 29 who refers to general legal philosophical observations in H. Hart, *The Concept of Law*, (Oxford: Oxford University Press, 1994), p. 128. Also see the discussion *supra* part 2.1.

96 See: Vansweevelt and Weyts, *Handboek Buitencontractueel Aansprakelijkheidsrecht*, p. 129.

97 Stijns, *Verbintenissenrecht - Boek 1bis*, p. 43–45; M. Van Quickenborne and H. Vandenberghe, 'Overzicht van rechtspraak. Aansprakelijkheid uit onrechtmatige daad (2000–2008)', *TPR*, 2010, pp. 1861–1862; Kruithof, *Tort Law in Belgium*, p. 48–49 with references; Bocken and Boone with cooperation by Kruithof, *Inleiding tot het schadevergoedingsrecht*, pp. 90–92.

98 See for example: Cass. 5 June 2003, *Arr.Cass.*, 2003, p. 1337, *TBBR*, 2005, p. 114, *JLMB*, 2004, p. 543; Court of Appeal Antwerp 30 June 1995, *RW* 1997–98, p. 83, Court of Appeal Ghent 10 September 2004, *TBBR*, 2006, p. 185; Court of First Instance Hasselt 13 November 1995, *De Verz.*, 1997, p. 317; Thunis, 'Théorie de la faute civile, volume 2', pp. 33–35; Van Quickenborne and Vandenberghe, 'Overzicht van rechtspraak. Aansprakelijkheid uit onrechtmatige daad (2000–2008)', pp. 1862–1875.

operators.[99] The importance of backend operations and of the particular 'external circumstances' in which they operate is a result of the factual complexity and interconnected nature of AI systems. They consist of algorithmic codes, datasets, a network-connection for purposes of monitoring, updates and cybersecurity, interconnection with other computer systems or physical objects, etc. Many of these features are possibly provided by third parties. Furthermore, AI technology can be incorporated in its own hardware (e.g., robotic AI applications) integrated in wider internet of things (IoT) systems (e.g., the AI-management of a smart building) or it can be purely 'digital' (e.g., AI systems for management or advice purposes). The latter systems are not necessarily less complex or less interconnected because they still remain part of a public or private network infrastructure, still interact with the user's digital and physical environment and still remain dependent on data and digital services that are possibly provided by third parties. As a consequence, the very complex, interconnected and opaque factual context in which particular AI systems operate[100] is not only challenging for establishing causation[101] but definitely also needs to be considered when determining whether the general duty of care has been violated.

17. A violation of the general duty of care requires that it was reasonably foreseeable for the defendant that his/her conduct could result in some kind of damage.[102] This, at first sight, appears difficult to reconcile with the highly autonomous and opaque nature of many AI systems.[103] However, this requirement can in our opinion already be considered as fulfilled when a person develops, supplies or operates an autonomous system of which he/she should reasonably know that it has a capability to later develop behaviour which can cause damage.[104] The autonomous nature means that it can by definition not be excluded that damage may occur. However, this does not mean that such a

99 See on the distinction between 'frontend' and 'backend' operators: Expert Group on Liability and New Technologies, New Technologies Formation, 'Liability for Artificial Intelligence and Other Emerging Digital Technologies', pp. 39–42. Also see the discussion *infra* part 4.2.

100 See in general: European Commission, 'Report on the safety and liability implications of Artificial Intelligence, the Internet of Things and robotics', pp. 5–8, 13–15; J. Burell, 'How the machine 'thinks': Understanding opacity in machine learning algorithms', *Big Data & Society*, 2016, p. 4–5; Scherer, 'Regulating Artificial Intelligence Systems: Risks, Challenges, Competencies, and Strategies', pp. 369–373.

101 See *infra* part 5.2.

102 It is not required that the particular damage that occurred was reasonably foreseeable (e.g., Cass. 5 May 1971, *Arr.Cass.*, 1971, p. 869, *JT*, 1971, p. 662); Vansweevelt and Weyts, *Handboek Buitencontractueel Aansprakelijkheidsrecht*, p. 134–136; Bocken and Boone with cooperation by Kruithof, *Inleiding tot het schadevergoedingsrecht*, p. 91.

103 See: Jacquemin and Hubin, 'Le robot et l'intelligence artificielle en droit des obligations contractuelles', p. 118; Tanghe and De Bruyne, 'Aansprakelijkheid voor schade veroorzaakt door autonome motorrijtuigen', pp. 973; J. Turner, *Robot Rules – Regulating Artificial Intelligence* (London: Palgrave, 2019), pp. 90–91. See also W. Kowert, 'The Foreseeability of Human-Artificial Intelligence Interactions', *Texas Law Review*, 2017, vol. 96, no. 1, pp. 181–204.

104 See on the concept of damage *infra* part 5.1.

person is automatically held liable for fault when this damage does eventually occur. When he/she has acted after developing, supplying or operating such an autonomous AI system like a normal, foreseeing and prudent person would have done in those circumstances, for example by taking certain precautionary measures, he/she has in the meantime complied with the general duty of care.

18. In order to further pin down the evaluation of the general duty of care within the context of AI systems, we will elaborate on the distinction between users or frontend operators on the one hand and producers and backend operators on the other hand. The former generally seem the easier category, given that it is possible to directly evaluate their human conduct. In contrast, the latter generally present a more difficult category. Ascertaining the conduct of producers and backend operators of an AI system always requires taking into account the system's interconnected, opaque and potentially autonomous functioning through which these persons have interacted with the factual context in which the damage occurred.[105]

19. Concerning the users or frontend operators, we have already mentioned the potential importance of certain 'internal circumstances' such as professional capacity, personal factual knowledge, age and mental and physical capabilities which are to a certain extent accepted in case law. A second possible guiding element are sectoral or general standards of conduct such as rules of craftsmanship or usage principles for a specific AI system. Admittedly, these will be more abundant for producers and backend operators as discussed below. Note that these rules should not be legally binding and precise in order to be relevant. Otherwise, their violation would already constitute an objective fault.[106] A third possible guiding element is the user's or frontend operator's intention to either knowingly apply the AI system in an incorrect or dangerous way or to wilfully cause damage.[107] However, such intention will be relatively rare and difficult to prove.

A more comprehensive approach can consist of two sequential criteria. The first one is to determine whether the user or frontend operator violated the general duty of care when he/she chose the time, location and amount of control which remains available in the environment in which he/she used the AI system. One can think of using an autonomous vehicle in extreme weather conditions[108] or deploying a garden or security robot in an unsupervised way in the presence of a child, mentally impaired person or animal. The second criterion is to determine to what extent the user or frontend operator, when the

105 See on the allocation of liability between different parties *infra* part 5.2.

106 See *supra* part 2.2.

107 See Jacquemin and Hubin, 'Aspects contractuels et de responsabilité civile en matière d'intelligence artificielle', p. 117.

108 See: Tanghe and De Bruyne, 'Aansprakelijkheid voor schade veroorzaakt door autonome motorrijtuigen', p. 966.

threat of damage manifested itself, still possessed the capability to observe this risk and still had an option to intervene and, in doing so, avoid or mitigate the damage. The example of autonomous vehicles can once again be used to illustrate this. These systems have different levels of autonomy. Human drivers are still expected to remain vigilant and capable of taking over the steering wheel when necessary.[109] Naturally, both determinations not only depend on the decisions made by the user of the particular AI system but also on the extent to which the harmful event itself was foreseeable or avoidable.[110]

20. As stated above, producers and backend operators present a more difficult category. This is due to the conflict between the intrinsically human standard of the general duty of care and the highly technical, interconnected and opaque factual context of AI systems that also possess capabilities to act and develop themselves autonomously. AI systems present a challenging but unavoidable technological lens through which the conduct of these persons must be ascertained and evaluated. Several options have already been suggested to overcome this fundamental challenge.

A first potential solution consists of the proposal to replace the human-centred standard of the general duty of care with a 'reasonable algorithm' standard. This approach maintains a negligence-based evaluation but no longer looks at whether human actions meet the standard of a normal, foreseeing and prudent person. Instead, the idea is to look whether the autonomous performance of an AI system meets the standard of a reasonable AI system.[111] The idea appears attractive at first because of the aforementioned difficulties in using the general duty of care and because the behaviour of AI systems will likely become generally safer than human behaviour.[112] The actual implementation of the idea, however, is problematic. It remains unclear what can be considered as 'a reasonable AI' with similar functionalities within the same factual context. Even the comparison with an actually existing 'reference AI system', which already presupposes a mature market, would lead to numerous conceptual and practical difficulties.[113] Furthermore, deep learning AI systems decide on the basis of probabilistic calculations. This means that their behaviour can only be

---

109 See: Swinnen, 'De inpassing van digitale producten in het Belgisch privaatrecht', pp. 1091–1092; Tanghe and De Bruyne, 'Aansprakelijkheid voor schade veroorzaakt door autonome motorrijtuigen', pp. 965–978 and pp. 972–974.

110 Also see regarding grounds of exemption *supra* part 2.2. and *infra* part 5.2.

111 See: K. Chagal-Feferkorn, 'The Reasonable Algorithm', *Journal of Law, Technology & Policy*, 2018, pp. 111–147. Also see: R. Abbott, 'The Reasonable Computer: Disrupting the Paradigm of Tort Liability', *George Washington Law Review*, 2018, vol. 86, no. 1, pp. 35–45.

112 De Bruyne and Tanghe, 'Liability for Damage Caused by Autonomous Vehicles: A Belgian Perspective', p. 325, 360 and 362.

113 See J.-S. Borghetti, 'How can Artificial Intelligence be Defective?', in S. Lohsse, *Liability for Artificial Intelligence and the Internet of Things* (Baden-Baden: Nomos, 2019), pp. 68–71.

described on a statistical basis,[114] which makes comparisons even more difficult. One can also wonder whether it is possible at all for humans to evaluate conduct in accordance with a non-human standard.[115]

A less radical solution consists of maintaining the human-centred general duty of care and supporting its evaluation by means of a multitude of legal and 'soft law' rules and standards related to the proper design, training, monitoring, updating and decommissioning of AI systems.[116] Rules of craftsmanship, technical standards and known professional best practices have always constituted an important element in evaluating the general duty of care.[117] Such an approach also perfectly coincides with the European aim to develop rules and standards that are relevant to the safe functioning of various types of AI systems within our society on the basis of a risk-management approach.[118] In this regard, the Expert Report issued in November 2019 proposes to explicitly recognise a set of general duties of care specific to AI systems.[119] Operators would need to choose the right AI system for a given task and in light of their own capabilities. Operators would also be required to always continue monitoring and maintaining these systems. Producers would need to design and market their AI systems in a way that effectively enables operators to comply with their aforementioned duties of care. They would also need to continue monitoring the systems after putting them into circulation.[120] Providing general guidance indeed seems an appropriate approach. Nevertheless, more sector-specific and detailed standards are necessary as well, especially for high-risk AI systems or for complex AI systems for which the allocation of responsibilities between actors currently remains unclear.

Finally, we have already discussed the possible added value of reversing the burden of proof, the corresponding European proposals and the possibility to already do so on the basis of Article 8.4 of the Belgian Civil Code.[121] A reversal of the burden of proof seems particularly relevant to determine whether a

---

114 Also see: Geistfeld, 'A roadmap for Autonomous Vehicles: State Tort Liability, Automobile Insurance, and Federal Safety Regulation', pp. 1645–1646; H. Zech, 'Liability for Autonomous Systems: Tackling Specific Risks of Modern IT', in S. Lohsse et al. (eds.), *Liability for Artificial Intelligence and the Internet of Things* (Baden-Baden: Nomos, 2019), pp. 188–192. Also see *infra* parts 3.2. and 4.1.

115 See regarding this the 'theory of mind' as referred to in: Tanghe and De Bruyne, 'Aansprakelijkheid voor schade veroorzaakt door autonome motorrijtuigen', p. 973.

116 Also see: Zech, 'Liability for Autonomous Systems: Tackling Specific Risks of Modern IT', p. 191 and 195.

117 Also see: Bocken and Boone with cooperation by Kruithof, *Inleiding tot het schadevergoedingsrecht*, p. 91; Thunis, 'Théorie de la faute civile, volume 2, pp. 30–31.

118 European Commission, 'White Paper On Artificial Intelligence – A European approach to excellence and trust'. Also see *supra* part 2.2. and see Chapter 3 of this book for more information and references.

119 Expert Group on Liability and New Technologies, New Technologies Formation, 'Liability for Artificial Intelligence and Other Emerging Digital Technologies', pp. 44–45.

120 Also see *infra* part 3.4.

121 See *supra* part 2.1. Also see *infra* part 5.2.

professional producer or backend operator of an AI system has violated the general duty of care. Such rule could become even more valuable and effective to the extent that it is combined with regulatory obligations that enhance the 'accountability' for producing and operating AI systems.[122] Such obligations could first of all consist of technical measures that enable accountability such as machine learning algorithms that are open to interpretation and analysis, cryptographic guarantees and AI-forensic software.[123] Such obligations can also be found in (already existing) regulatory frameworks such as EU data and consumer protection regulations, which can increase the transparency of and hence the *ex post* accountability for AI systems.[124] This final strategy reveals a broader picture of how the wider regulatory framework relevant to AI can aid and interact with tort liability for damage created by AI systems.

3. PRODUCT LIABILITY

21. The previous part has demonstrated that the application of fault-based liability on cases of damage caused by AI systems can be challenging. Certain characteristics of AI systems make it hard to impute the damage to human behaviour that qualifies as a fault under Belgian law.[125] Therefore, victims often need alternative grounds of tort liability to recover damage that has been caused by AI systems. An option is to submit a claim against the manufacturer of a defective AI system on the basis of the product liability regime.

In this part, we will focus on the application of the Belgian Product Liability Act (hereafter referred to as Product Liability Act).[126] This Act implements the Directive on Liability for Defective Products (hereafter referred to as the Product

---

122 See generally regarding 'accountable' AI systems: G. Comandé, 'Multilayered (Accountable) Liability for Artificial Intelligence', in S. Lohsse et al. (eds.), *Liability for Artificial Intelligence and the Internet of Things* (Baden-Baden: Nomos, 2019), pp. 180–182; J. Kroll et al., 'Accountable Algorithms', *University of Pennsylvania Law Review*, 2017, vol. 165, pp. 633–706.

123 Also see: Kroll et al., 'Accountable Algorithms', pp. 662–674. It should be noted that there is an emerging research and development field described as 'AI-neuroscience' (see P. Voosen, 'The AI Detectives: As neural nets push into science, researchers probe back', *Science*, 2017, no. 6346, pp. 22–27).

124 Also see: Comandé, 'Multilayered (Accountable) Liability for Artificial Intelligence', pp. 180–181.

125 European Commission, 'Report on the safety and liability implications of Artificial Intelligence, the Internet of Things and robotics', p. 13.

126 Act of 25 February 1991 concerning liability for defective products (*BS* 22 March 1991). See on the application of the PLD in an AI-context: A. Seehafer en J. Kohler, "Künstliche Intelligenz: Updates für das Produkthaftungsrecht?", *Europäische Zeitschrift für Wirtschaftsrecht*, 2020, pp. 213–218; A. Bertolini, 'Robots as Products: The Case for a Realistic Analysis of Robotic Applications and Liability Rules', *Law Innovation and Technology,$* 2013, vol. 5, no. 2, pp. 214–247; T.S. Cabral, 'Liability and artificial intelligence in the EU: Assessing the adequacy of the current Product Liability Directive', *Maastricht Journal of European and Comparative Law*, 2020, vol. 27, pp. 615–635.

Liability Directive).[127] The product liability regime provides a layer of protection that national fault-based liability alone does not provide. It introduces a system of strict liability of producers for damage caused by defects in their products.[128] The liability of the producer is based on putting a defective product into circulation and not on committing allegedly wrongful acts.[129] Four elements deserve particular attention in the context of AI systems. First, it is unclear to what extent software is a product falling within the scope of the Product Liability Directive or Act (part 3.1.). Second, there must be a 'defect' in the product (part 3.2.). Third, the concept of producer needs to be briefly discussed within the context of AI systems (part 3.3.). Fourth, the defect needs to exist at the moment when the product is put into circulation (part 3.4.). We will also evaluate how the revised PLD covers these issues.

3.1. THE NOTION OF 'PRODUCT'

22. A producer will be liable for damage caused by a defect in the product. Technology and industry, however, have evolved drastically over the last decades. First of all, the division between products and services is no longer as clear-cut as it was. Producing products and providing services are increasingly intertwined.[130] Secondly, software and AI systems merit specific attention in respect of product liability. Software is essential to the functioning of a large number of products and affects their safety. It is integrated into products but it can also be supplied separately to enable the use of the product as intended. Neither a computer nor a smartphone would be of particular use without software. Consequently, an essential question is whether stand-alone software can be qualified as a product within the meaning of the Product Liability Directive or Act.[131]

---

127 Council Directive 85/374/EEC of 25 July 1985 on the approximation of the laws, regulations and administrative provisions of the Member States concerning liability for defective products, *OJ L* 210.

128 European Commission, 'Report on the safety and liability implications of Artificial Intelligence, the Internet of Things and robotics', p. 12. Also see: Article 1 Product Liability Directive and Act.

129 See in general: H. Bocken, 'Buitencontractuele aansprakelijkheid voor gebrekkige producten', in X., *Bijzondere overeenkomsten* (Mechelen: Wolters Kluwer, 2008), p. 367; Verhoeven, *Productaansprakelijkheid en productveiligheid*, 732 p.; Bocken and Boone with cooperation by Kruithof, *Inleiding tot het schadevergoedingsrecht*, p. 196; Vansweevelt and Weyts, *Handboek Buitencontractueel Aansprakelijkheidsrecht*, pp. 498–499; Kruithof, 'Wie is aansprakelijk voor schade veroorzaakt door onveilige producten?', p. 148.

130 See B. Keirsbilck, E. Terryn and E. Van Gool, 'Consumentenbescherming bij *servitisation* en product-dienst-systemen (PDS)', *TPR*, 2019, pp. 817–899.

131 European Commission, 'Report on the safety and liability implications of Artificial Intelligence, the Internet of Things and robotics', pp. 13–14. See more extensively: D. Verhoeven, *Productaansprakelijkheid en productveiligheid*, pp. 53–56. Also see: Buiten, De Streel and Peitz, 'EU Liability Rules for the Age of Artificial Intelligence', pp. 50–51; C.

23. There are several reasons why software cannot be seen as a product. For instance, software might be qualified as a service and not as a product.[132] The question whether information incorporated in a physical good constitutes a (part of the) product was discussed in the *Krone* case. The Court upheld the product vs service distinction and found that the information in question (i.e., health advice) was outside the scope of the PLD.[133] However, some scholars argue that software is not a service but the object of a service. It would, therefore, be covered by the Directive.[134] Yet, the fact that software is not qualified as a service does not necessarily mean that it is a product. Article 2 of the Product Liability Directive defines a product as all movables, with the exception of primary agricultural products and game, even though incorporated into another movable or into an immovable. As the Directive mentions 'movables', some argue that it cannot be limited to tangible goods only.[135] Others, by contrast, conclude that it does.[136] It would otherwise make no sense to explicitly include electricity in the scope of the Directive.[137] The Belgian Product Liability Act confirms this final line of reasoning and stipulates that the regime only concerns tangible goods.[138]

This last interpretation is problematic for software used in AI systems. Software is a collection of data and instructions that is imperceptible to the human eye. Therefore, software is often regarded as intangible.[139] As a

Wendehorst, 'Safety and Liability Related Aspects of Software', July 2021, pp. 64–66; B. Koch et al., 'European Commission's Public Consultation on Civil Liability Adapting Liability Rules to the Digital Age and Artificial Intelligence. Response of the European Law Institute', January 2022, pp. 12–15.

132 See for example: A. Zegers, 'Produktenaansprakelijkheid voor software en informatie?', *Computerrecht*, 1989, p. 109. See for additional references and discussion: I. Demuynck et al., *De consument in het recht: verwend, verwaand of miskend* (Antwerp-Apeldoorn: Maklu, 2003), p. 38, fn. 71; A. Bertolini, 'Artificial Intelligence and Civil Liability', Study requested by the JURI committee, July 2020, p. 57.

133 CJEU, case C-65–20, VI v Krone, 10 June 2021, ECLI:EU:C:2021:471, para. 36–37. See for an analysis of the case: E. Van Gool, 'Case C-65/20 Krone: Offering (some) clarity relating to product liability, information and software', Europeanlawblog.eu, 19 January 2022.

134 See for example: M. Flamée, ''Malfunction 54' of het produktkarakter van software', in: X, *Liber Amicorum E. Krings* (Brussels: Story-Scientia, 1991), p. 124, no. 124 *in fine*; T. Vansweevelt, 'De Wet van 25 februari 1991 inzake produktenaansprakelijkheid', *TBBR*, 1992, pp. 96 and 105, no. 17.

135 J. Verlinden, 'Veiligheid van producten en diensten en productaansprakelijkheid', in N. Betsch et al. (eds.), *Huur van diensten – Aanneming van werk: vormingsprogramma* 2005–2006 (Ghent: Larcier, 2007), pp. 62–63.

136 See: Vansweevelt and Weyts, *Handboek Buitencontractueel Aansprakelijkheidsrecht*, p. 503.

137 Article 2 Product Liability Directive.

138 Article 2 Product Liability Act; D. Verhoeven, 'Productveiligheid en productaansprakelijkheid: krachtlijnen en toekomst perspectieven', in R. Steennot and G. Straetmans (eds.), *Wetboek economisch recht en de bescherming van de consument* (Antwerp: Intersentia, 2015), p. 198; Jacquemin and Hubin, 'Aspects contractuels et de responsabilité civile en matière d'intelligence artificielle', pp. 129–130.

139 See for an overview of arguments to qualify software as intangible: C. Stuurman and G.P.V. Vandenberghe, 'Softwarefouten: een 'zaak' van leven of dood?', *NJB*, 1988, pp. 1669–1670.

consequence, it would fall outside the scope of product liability.[140] However, not everyone agrees with this conclusion. Some authors claim that software should be regarded as a product when it is captured on a tangible medium or device (e.g., CD-ROM or USB). The European Commission has in the past expressed this point of view.[141] According to other scholars, software by itself qualifies as a tangible good.[142] Even though codes used in software systems might be imperceptible to humans, they are part of our tangible world according to the standards of physics. Software differs from abstract ideas such as political or philosophical opinions. Human sensory perception is actually an inadequate criterion to determine whether something is a product or not. Note, for instance, that electricity is sensibly perceptible to humans, although explicitly mentioned in the Act and therefore, not considered a product by its nature.[143] Following a teleological interpretation, the Directive can also apply to software even if it is qualified as an intangible good. After all, the inclusion of electricity shows that the drafters of the Directive aimed at a wide material scope. It is not surprising that legislators did not think of software in the early 1980s as personal computers only became commercially widespread during the second half of the 1980s. The inclusion of software in the Directive would reflect the current economic reality in which software is a commercial product just as any other product that may entail risks for users and third parties.[144]

140 E. Tjong Tjin Tai, 'Liability for (Semi)Autonomous Systems: Robots and Algorithms', Tilburg Law School Legal Studies Research Paper Series No. 09/2018, p. 15; Verhoeven, *Productaansprakelijkheid en productveiligheid*, pp. 55–56.

141 See in this regard: Written Question no. 706/88 (5 July 1988) and Answer by Lord Cockfield on behalf of the Commission (15 November 1988), *OJ* 114/42, 8 May 1989; E. Montéro, *La Responsabilité civile du fait des bases de données* (Namur: Presses universitaires de Namur, 1998), p. 223; Jacquemin and Hubin, 'Aspects contractuels et de responsabilité civile en matière d'intelligence artificielle', p. 130. See for additional references: Verhoeven, *Productaansprakelijkheid en productveiligheid*, pp. 54–55.

142 See for example: J.P. Triaille, 'The EEC Directive (25 July 1985) on product liability and its application to databases and information', *Computer Law and Practice,* 1993, p. 217; M. Tenreiro and S. Gomez, 'La Directive 1999/44/CE sur certains aspects de la vente et des garanties des biens de consommation', *Revue Européenne de Droit de la Consommation*, 2000, p. 12. The Criminal Court in Brussels comes to similar conclusions when ruling that "[u]n logiciel – ou programme informatique – indépendamment même de son support – ou disquette – ne constitue pas un bien immatériel, possède une valeur économique propre et est susceptible d'un transfert de possession qui peut être constaté matériellement' (Criminal Court Brussels 24 June 1993, *Jurisprudence de Liège, Mons et Bruxelles*, 1994, p. 444).

143 De Bruyne and Tanghe, 'Liability for Damage Caused by Autonomous Vehicles: A Belgian Perspective', pp. 356–357.

144 B. Koch, 'Product Liability 2.0 – Mere Update or New Version?', in S. Lohsse et al., *Liability for Artificial Intelligence and the Internet of Things* (Baden-Baden: Nomos, 2019), p. 106; G. Wagner, 'Robot Liability', in S. Lohsse et al., *Liability for Artificial Intelligence and the Internet of Things* (Baden-Baden: Nomos, 2019), p. 42; De Bruyne and Tanghe, 'Liability for Damage Caused by Autonomous Vehicles: A Belgian Perspective', p. 357.

24. Although the Belgian Court of Cassation and/or the European Court of Justice have not yet ruled on the matter, the revised PLD specifically qualifies software and digital manufacturing files as products.[145] The inclusion of software is rather surprising, yet essential.[146] Recital (13) of the revised PLD states that it should not apply to 'free and open-source software developed or supplied outside the course of a commercial activity' in order not to hamper innovation or research. However, where software is supplied in exchange for a price or personal data is provided in the course of a commercial activity (i.e., for other purposes than exclusively improving the security, compatibility or interoperability of the software), the Directive should apply.[147] Previously, several EU policy documents already favoured a broad interpretation of the notion of a product. The Report on the safety and liability implications of AI, the IoT and robotics acknowledges that the Product Liability Directive's definition of product is broad. Nevertheless, its scope could be further clarified to better reflect the complexity of emerging technologies, and ensure that compensation is always available for damage caused by products that are defective because of software or other digital features.[148] The New Technology Formation Expert Group also concludes that damage caused by defective digital content should trigger the producer's liability because digital content performs many of the functions tangible movable items used to perform when the Product Liability Directive was adopted. This is all the more true for defective digital elements of other products, some of which come separately from the tangible item or as over-the-air updates after the product has been put into circulation (e.g., security updates), or as digital services provided on a continuous basis during the time the product is being used (e.g., navigation cloud services). In sum, strict liability of the producer should play a key role in indemnifying damage caused by defective products and their components, irrespective of whether they take a tangible or digital form.[149]

145 Revised PLD, Art. 4 (1).

146 See, e.g., C. Twigg-Flesner et al., 'Guiding Principles for Updating the Product Liability Directive for the Digital Age', ELI innovation paper series, 2021, p. 5 ('The definition of 'product' in the PLD should be updated to cover (i) the combination of goods with digital elements and (ii) digital content and digital services supplied as 'digital products''); M. Buiten et al., 'EU Liability Rules for the Age of Artificial Intelligence', Centre on Regulation in Europe, 9 April 2021, p. 51 ('The risks involved in software, irrespective of its medium, therefore support including software in the notion of products'); J. Tanghe and J. De Bruyne, 'Software aan het stuur. Aansprakelijkheid voor schade veroorzaakt door autonome motorrijtuigen', in T. Vansweevelt en B. Weyts (eds.), *Nieuwe risico's in het aansprakelijkheids- en verzekeringsrecht*, Intersentia, 2018, p. 56–57; B. Koch et al., 'European Commission's Public Consultation on Civil Liability Adapting Liability Rules to the Digital Age and Artificial Intelligence. Response of the European Law Institute', p. 12–14.

147 Recital (13) AI Liability Directive. See extensively O. Dheu et al., 'The European Commission's Approach to Extra-Contractual Liability and AI – A First Analysis and Evaluation of the Two Proposals', pp. 24–25.

148 European Commission, 'Report on the safety and liability implications of Artificial Intelligence, the Internet of Things and robotics', p. 14.

149 Expert Group on Liability and New Technologies, New Technologies Formation, 'Liability for Artificial Intelligence and Other Emerging Digital Technologies', November 2019, pp. 42–43.

25. Regardless of the qualification of software, the victim of an accident involving an AI system may have a claim against the producer of a product incorporating software such as an autonomous vehicle, a robot used for surgery or a household robot. Software steering the operations of a tangible product could be considered part or component of that product.[150] This means that an autonomous vehicle or material robot used for surgery is a product in the sense of the Product Liability Act or Directive and can be defective if the software system it uses is not functioning properly.

3.2. THE NOTION OF 'DEFECT'

26. Liability under the Product Liability Act requires a defect in the product.[151] The injured person must prove the damage, the defect and the causal relationship between the defect and damage.[152] A product is defective if it does not provide the safety that a person is entitled to expect, taking all circumstances into account (the so-called 'consumer expectations test').[153] This does not refer to the expectations of a particular person but to the expectations of the general public[154] or the target audience.[155] The criterion of legitimate expectations is normative as well. The question is not what expectations the general public or the audience actually have but what expectations they are entitled to have, in other words which expectations are legitimate.[156] Article 6 of the revised PLD defines the notion of defect in a similar way as the currently applicable PLD.

For a brief discussion: O. Dheu, 'EU report on AI, new technologies and liability: key take-aways and limitations', 9 January 2020, https://www.law.kuleuven.be/citip/blog/eu-report-on-ai-new-technologies-and-liability-key-take-aways-and-limitations/. This report has in the meantime been reflected in a legislative initiative by the European Parliament, 'Resolution of 20 October 2020 with recommendations to the Commission on a civil liability regime for artificial intelligence', 2020/2014(INL), https://www.europarl.europa.eu/doceo/document/TA-9-2020-0276_EN.html.

150 European Commission, 'Report on the safety and liability implications of Artificial Intelligence, the Internet of Things and robotics', pp. 13–14.

151 Article 1 Product Liability Act.

152 Article 7 Product Liability Act.

153 Article 5 Product Liability Act.

154 Recital 6 Product Liability Directive. Bocken argues that it concerns the consumer as part of a group (H. Bocken, 'Buitencontractuele aansprakelijkheid voor gebrekkige producten', p. 367).

155 Cass. 26 September 2003, *Arr.Cass.*, 2003, p. 1765, *RW*, 2004–05, p. 22, annotation by B. Weyts; Court of Appeal Antwerp 13 April 2005, *RW*, 2008–09, p. 803; Court of Appeal Antwerp 28 October 2009, *TBBR*, 2011, p. 381, noot D. Verhoeven; Bocken and Boone with cooperation by Kruithof, *Inleiding tot het schadevergoedingsrecht*, p. 196; B. Dubuisson, 'La notion de défaut dans la directive européenne du 25 juillet 1985 ', *DCCR*, 1989, p. 78; Jacquemin and Hubin, 'Aspects contractuels et de responsabilité civile en matière d'intelligence artificielle', p. 131.

156 Vansweevelt and Weyts, *Handboek Buitencontractueel Aansprakelijkheidsrecht*, p. 510. See on the notion of safety expectations also: Buiten, De Streel and Peitz, 'EU Liability Rules for the Age of Artificial Intelligence', pp. 52–53.

27. The assessment of the legitimate expectations is done in concrete terms.[157] Several elements can be used to determine the legitimate expectations regarding the use of AI systems. These include the presentation of the product, the normal or reasonably foreseeable use of it and the moment in time when the product was put into circulation.[158] This enumeration of criteria, however, is not exhaustive as other factors may play a role as well.[159] Especially the criterion of the presentation of the product is important for manufacturers of autonomous vehicles or medical robots. That is because they often tend to market their products explicitly as safer than existing alternatives.[160] The presentation of the product may on the other hand also provide an opportunity for manufacturers of AI systems to reduce their liability risk through appropriate warnings and user information.[161] Nevertheless, it remains uncertain how technically detailed or accessible such information should be. As already mentioned, the revised PLD also refers to the legitimate safety expectations. A product is deemed defective if it fails to 'provide the safety which the public at large is entitled to expect, taking all circumstances into account'.[162] Yet, the non-exhaustive list of such circumstances that allow to assess the product's defectiveness is expanded and also includes 'the effect on the product of any ability to continue to learn after deployment'.[163] It should, however, be noted that the product cannot be considered defective for the sole reason that a better product, including updates or upgrades to a product, is already or subsequently placed on the market or put into service.[164]

28. The definition of a defect under Belgian law illustrates that the difference between a deficiency in the design, a manufacturing defect or a lack of information is actually not decisive in this context. In each of these cases, the product is defective because it does not meet the legitimate expectations.[165] Some scholars have, however, suggested to clarify the different types of defects

---

157 Bocken and Boone with cooperation by Kruithof, *Inleiding tot het schadevergoedingsrecht*, p. 196; Vansweevelt and Weyts, *Handboek Buitencontractueel Aansprakelijkheidsrecht*, p. 511.

158 Article 5, first paragraph Product Liability Act.

159 Bocken and Boone with cooperation by Kruithof, *Inleiding tot het schadevergoedingsrecht*, p. 196; Kruithof, 'Wie is aansprakelijk voor schade veroorzaakt door onveilige producten?', p. 148, fn. 18.

160 Swinnen, 'De inpassing van digitale producten in het Belgisch privaatrecht', p. 1087.

161 Jacquemin and Hubin, 'Aspects contractuels et de responsabilité civile en matière d'intelligence artificielle', p. 131. See in general: T. Verheyen, 'Modern Theories of Product Warnings and European Product Liability Law', *Utrecht Law Review*, 2019, pp. 44–56.

162 Article 6.1. revised PLD.

163 Article 6.1 revised PLD.

164 Article 6.2. revised PLD.

165 See for more information on the distinction between the three types of defects: Bocken and Boone with cooperation by Kruithof, *Inleiding tot het schadevergoedingsrecht*, pp. 190–191; D. Wuyts, 'Productaansprakelijkheid: een Richtlijn voor (n)iets?, *TBBR*, 2008, p. 12; A.P. Garza, 'Look Ma, No Hands!: Wrinkles and Wrecks in the Age of Autonomous Vehicles', *New England Law Review*, 2012, vol. 46, p. 590.

and potentially differentiate the applicable liability regime. One could, for instance, limit strict liability to manufacturing defects, while a presumption of fault could be applied for defects in design and instructions to users.[166] That being said, the criterion of legitimate expectations remains very vague. It gives judges a wide margin of appreciation.[167] As a consequence, it is difficult to predict how this criterion will be applied in the context of AI systems. The safety expectations will be very high for AI systems used in high-risk contexts such as healthcare or mobility.[168] At the same time, however, the concrete application of this test remains difficult for AI systems because of their novelty, the complexity to compare these systems with human or technological alternatives and the characteristics of autonomy and opacity.[169] The interconnectivity of products and systems also makes it hard to identify the defect. Sophisticated AI systems with self-learning capabilities also raise the question of whether unpredictable deviations in the decision-making process can be treated as defects. Even if they constitute a defect, the state-of-the-art defence[170] may apply. The complexity and the opacity of emerging digital technologies such as AI systems further complicate the chance for the victim to discover and prove the defect and/or causation.[171] In addition, there is some uncertainty on how and to what extent the Product Liability Directive or Act apply in the case of certain types of defects, for example those resulting from weaknesses in the cybersecurity of the product.[172] For these reasons, some authors propose to adhere to the so-called 'risk-utility test' for new technologies. The risk-utility test examines whether the risk linked to a certain design of a product could have been avoided or reduced by alternatives that would not have notably affected the social utility of the product

166 >Buiten, De Streel and Peitz, 'EU Liability Rules for the Age of Artificial Intelligence', p. 54 with further references.

167 Bocken, 'Buitencontractuele aansprakelijkheid voor gebrekkige producten', p. 368; Vansweevelt and Weyts, *Handboek Buitencontractueel Aansprakelijkheidsrecht*, p. 515.

168 See for example: ECJ, 5 March 2015, C-503/13, ECLI:EU:C:2015:148, *Boston Scientific*, consideration 39; De Bruyne and Tanghe, 'Liability for Damage Caused by Autonomous Vehicles: A Belgian Perspective', p. 362. See also: T. Malengreau, 'Automatisation de la conduite: quelles responsabilités en droit belge? (Première partie)', *RGAR*, 2019, no. 5, 15578–15607, no. 27.

169 See: Borghetti, 'How can Artificial Intelligence be Defective?', pp. 68–69; De Bruyne and Tanghe, 'Liability for Damage Caused by Autonomous Vehicles: A Belgian Perspective', pp. 358–362. *Contra* B. Koch, 'Product Liability 2.0 – Mere Update or New Version?', in S. Lohsse et al. (eds.), *Liability for Artificial Intelligence and the Internet of Things* (Baden Baden: Nomos, 2019), pp. 107–109.

170 Under this defence, the producer will not be held liable if he/she proves that the state of scientific and technical knowledge at the time when he/she put the product into circulation was not such as to enable the existence of the defect to be discovered (Article 7, e) Product Liability Directive and Article 8, e) Product Liability Act). Also see *infra* part 3.4.

171 Expert Group on Liability and New Technologies, New Technologies Formation, 'Liability for Artificial Intelligence and Other Emerging Digital Technologies', p. 28.

172 European Commission, 'White Paper on Artificial Intelligence – A European approach to excellence and trust', p. 13.

or would not have increased the cost of production disproportionately. As such, this test determines whether an accident could have caused less damage or been avoided altogether if a (more) reasonable design would have been used.[173]

29. The burden of proof for victims will especially remain difficult when the potential defect does not relate to the presentation of an AI system ('lack of information') or when no relevant safety standards have been breached. In those circumstances, there may be a 'production defect' that will need to be identified by technical experts. Such defects may, on the one hand, lie in the hardware of AI systems such as an assembly or configuration flaw in material components or sensors of autonomous vehicles. Obvious production defects will not be problematic in an AI-context. The defect may, on the other hand, also relate to the AI software itself such as a programming error in the source code. In those circumstances, the discussion will more likely relate to potential 'design flaws' in AI systems for which 'the reasonable design alternative' is the most commonly used criterion.[174]

Comparing an AI system with a human or human-controlled technological alternative, however, is challenging. Over time, AI systems by their very nature may also become safer than existing alternatives.[175] Therefore, it seems appropriate to make the comparison with a functionally comparable reference AI system placed in the same circumstances. Not only the basic algorithm should be considered but also the technical context in which the AI system operates such as the underlying algorithms and the used datasets.[176] Several additional (legal) challenges arise as well. An advanced AI system works with probability calculation and tries to achieve a sufficiently safe behaviour through self-learning training.[177] As such, it cannot be assumed that an AI system that causes damage in a specific case in which another system would not do so would by itself be a more dangerous system than the latter one.[178] Therefore,

173 De Bruyne and Tanghe, 'Liability for Damage Caused by Autonomous Vehicles: A Belgian Perspective', pp. 368–369 with further references; M. Schellekens, 'Self-driving cars and the chilling effect of liability law', *Computer Law & Security Review*, 2015, vol. 31, no. 4, pp. 510–512; Wagner, 'Robot Liability', p. 42–43. Also see: J. Werbrouck, 'De productaansprakelijkheid voor zelfrijdende motorrijtuigen', *TPR*, 2018, pp. 567–570.

174 Borghetti, 'How can Artificial Intelligence be Defective?', pp. 66–68; M.A. Geistfeld, 'A roadmap for Autonomous Vehicles: State Tort Liability, Automobile Insurance, and Federal Safety Regulation', *California Law Review*, 2017, vol. 105, pp. 1635–1636.

175 Borghetti, 'How can Artificial Intelligence be Defective?', pp. 68–69; Wagner, 'Robot Liability', p. 44. Also see: De Bruyne and Tanghe, 'Liability for Damage Caused by Autonomous Vehicles: A Belgian Perspective', pp. 359–360 with further references.

176 See: A. Vedder and L. Naudts, 'Accountability for the use of algorithms in a big data environment', *International Review of Law, Computers & Technology*, 2017, vol. 31, no. 2, p. 209.

177 Geistfeld, 'A roadmap for Autonomous Vehicles: State Tort Liability, Automobile Insurance, and Federal Safety Regulation', p. 1645–1646; Zech, 'Liability for Autonomous Systems: Tackling Specific Risks of Modern IT', pp. 188–192.

178 Borghetti, 'How can Artificial Intelligence be Defective?', p. 70.

the overall safety performance of an AI system should be compared statistically with that of a reference AI system, whereby this performance may be lowered by a certain percentage without resulting in a qualification as a defective product. Indeed, it should be avoided that any AI system that is not the safest on the market is automatically considered to be defective.[179] Nevertheless, the question remains how to identify a reference AI system, how to collect information on the performance of both AI systems and how to determine the percentage of deviation allowed.[180]

30. The revised PLD also contains several relevant provisions in this regard. Article 8 is a key provision with respect to (AI) products. It allows Member States' courts to require the defendant to disclose to the injured person – the claimant – relevant evidence that is at its disposal. The claimant must, however, present facts and evidence that are sufficient to support the plausibility of the claim for compensation.[181] Moreover, the disclosed evidence can be limited to what is 'necessary' and 'proportionate' to support a claim.[182] Again, the 'necessity' and 'proportionality' will be subject to court interpretation. Article 9 is another key provision that provides rules with regard to the burden of proof. It is probably the most important one with respect to damage caused by AI products. It first provides the conditions under which the claimant may claim compensation: he/she shall prove that the product was defective, that he/she suffered a damage and the causal link between the damage and the defectiveness.[183] The revised PLD establishes a presumption of defectiveness under certain conditions.[184] Such conditions include the defendant's failure to disclose relevant evidence, when the claimant provides evidence that the product does not comply with mandatory safety requirements set in EU or national law, or when the claimant establishes that the damage was caused by an 'obvious malfunction' of the product during normal use or under ordinary circumstances. Again, the contours of what is to be considered an 'obvious malfunction' or that of 'ordinary circumstances' will have to be decided and further refined by judges and/or policymakers. Article 9.3 also provides a presumption of causality when 'it has been established that the product is defective and the damage caused is of a kind typically consistent with the defect in question'. In other words, Article 9 contains two presumptions, one of the product's defectiveness and one related to the causal link between the defectiveness of the product and the damage. Article 9.4 also

179 Borghetti, 'How can Artificial Intelligence be Defective?', pp. 70–71; Wagner, 'Robot Liability', pp. 44–45.

180 Van Gool, De Bruyne and Fierens, 'De regulering van artificiële intelligentie (deel 2) – Een analyse van vraagstukken inzake buitencontractuele aansprakelijkheid', pp. 1012–1013.

181 Article 8.1 revised PLD.

182 Article 8.2 revised PLD.

183 Article 9.1 revised PLD.

184 Article 9.2 revised PLD.

contains a more general presumption. Where a national court decides that 'the claimant faces excessive difficulties, due to the technical or scientific complexity, to prove the product's defectiveness or the causal link between its defectiveness and the damage' (or both), the defectiveness of the product or causal link between its defectiveness and the damage (or both) are presumed when certain conditions are met. The claimant must demonstrate, based on 'sufficiently relevant evidence', that the 'product contributed to the damage'[185] and that it is 'likely that the product was defective or that its defectiveness is a likely cause of the damage, or both'.[186] The defendant, however, has the right 'to contest the existence of excessive difficulties' or the mentioned likelihood.[187] Of course, the defendant is allowed to rebut any of these presumptions as well.[188] This provision is particularly relevant in the context of AI systems.[189]

3.3. THE NOTION OF 'PRODUCER'

31. The liability rests with the producer of the product.[190] This is the manufacturer of a finished product, the producer of any raw material or the manufacturer of a component part and any person who presents himself/herself as its producer by putting his/her name, trade mark or other distinguishing feature on the product.[191] Any person who imports a product into the EU for sale, hire, lease or any form of distribution in the course of his business also bears this liability.[192] If the producer (or importer) cannot be identified, each supplier of the product will bear this liability unless he/she informs the victim within a reasonable time of the identity of the producer (or importer) or of the person who supplied him/her with the product.[193]

32. The producer is thus defined in a very broad way to make sure that at least one person who is involved in the product supply chain can incur liability, thereby ensuring compensation to the victim. In situations where several persons could be held liable for the same damage, the principle of consumer protection requires that the injured person should be able to claim full compensation for

185 Revised PLD, Art. 9.4 (a).
186 Revised PLD, Art. 9.4 (b).
187 Revised PLD, Art. 9.4, second paragraph.
188 Revised PLD, Art. 9.5.
189 O. Dheu et al., 'The European Commission's Approach To Extra-Contractual Liability and AI – A First Analysis and Evaluation of the Two Proposals', pp. 25–27.
190 Article 1 Product Liability Act and Article 1 Product Liability Directive. See extensively on the concept of producer: Verhoeven, *Productaansprakelijkheid en productveiligheid*, pp. 59–83.
191 Article 3 Product Liability Act and Article 3.1. Product Liability Directive.
192 Article 4.1. Product Liability Act and Article 3.2. Product Liability Directive.
193 Article 4.2. Product Liability Act and Article 3.3. Product Liability Directive.

the damage from any one of them.[194] However, emerging digital technologies such as AI system or products incorporating software are affected/characterised by complex value chains that involve many actors such as the manufactures of the hardware, material parts, software, etc. Consequently, the 'production' process of an AI system is more dynamic and it is furthermore evolutive due to its self-learning capacities. In addition to the 'traditional' parties involved in the production process – the producer on the one hand and the injured party on the other hand – other parties such as the developers of algorithms intervene in the supply chain of AI systems as well.[195] Moreover, the dividing line between products and services may no longer be as clear-cut as it was. Products and the provision of services are increasingly intertwined.[196] Against this background, Article 7 of the revised PLD lists the types of 'economic operators' that can be held liable for defective products. This list is broader than the one used in the current PLD. These cover different parties based on a layered approach and include amongst others the manufacturer of a defective product or component, the importer, 'fulfilment service providers' or any provider of online platforms allowing consumers to conclude distance contracts with traders and that is not a manufacturer, importer or distributor.[197]

In any case, a victim can claim recovery from the producer who puts the product (e.g., autonomous vehicle or a robot used for surgery) into circulation. Hence, actors involved in the supply chain of digital products will often provide for a contractual allocation of liabilities.[198] The European Commission stipulates that while the producer's responsibility for the final product safety seems adequate for current complex value chains, explicit provisions specifically requesting cooperation between economic operators in the supply chain and the users could provide legal certainty in even more complex value chains. In particular, each actor involved in the supply chain having an impact on the product safety (e.g., software producers) and users (e.g., by modifying the product) should assume their responsibility and provide the necessary information and measures to the next actor in the chain.[199]

---

194 Consideration 4 Product Liability Directive. Also see: J.-B Hubin, 'La responsabilité du fait des robots – Le droit de la responsabilité à l'ère de la révolution numérique', in H. Jacquemin et al. (eds.), *Responsabilités et numérique* (Namur: Anthemis, 2018), p. 269.

195 Jacquemin and Hubin, 'Aspects contractuels et de responsabilité civile en matière d'intelligence artificielle', p. 131.

196 European Commission, 'Report on the safety and liability implications of Artificial Intelligence, the Internet of Things and robotics', pp. 11 and 13. See on the notion of producer in an AI-context also: C. Wendehorst, 'Safety and Liability Related Aspects of Software', pp. 66– 67.

197 Article 7 revised PLD.

198 Hubin, 'La responsabilité du fait des robots – Le droit de la responsabilité à l'ère de la révolution numérique', p. 270.

199 European Commission, 'Report on the safety and liability implications of Artificial Intelligence, the Internet of Things and robotics', p. 11.

3.4. THE DEFENCES FOR THE PRODUCER

33. Under the product liability regime, the victim only needs to prove that the product was defective at the moment of the accident. There are, however, some possibilities for the producer to escape liability.[200] For instance, the manufacturer of the product can escape liability when he/she establishes that it is probable[201] that the defect causing the damage did not exist at the time when the product was put into circulation or that this defect came into being afterwards.[202] According to Article 6 of the Product Liability Act, 'putting into circulation' means the first act embodying the producer's intention to bestow upon the product the usage that he/she intends for it through the transfer of the product to a third party or the use of it for the benefit of that person. According to the European Court of Justice, a product must be considered as having been put into circulation when it leaves the production process operated by the producer, and enters a marketing process in the form in which it is offered to the public to be used or consumed.[203] Despite this broad interpretation, the notion of 'putting into circulation' can be challenging for products incorporating software or AI systems that may change over time.[204] The self-learning and autonomous nature of AI systems has a continuous 'production process', even without external interaction.[205]

34. Some scholars conclude that if software is seen as a product, any update thereof could be considered an act by which the producer brings a new product into circulation. Consequently, the software producer would not be able to escape liability all too easily by referring to the provision in Article 8(b) of the Product Liability Act.[206] It becomes more difficult with self-learning systems as they continually improve themselves. For defects that are created in this way, a moment of putting the product into circulation cannot be indicated as the manufacturer did not perform an act to that end. It is also unrealistic to qualify a software system as defective merely because it is able to adjust itself.[207] Against

200 See: Article 8 Product Liability Act and Article 7 Product Liability Directive.

201 Article 8(b) Product Liability Act and Article 7(b) Product Liability Directive. Also see: Cass, 4 May 2007 *RW*, 2007, pp. 1286–1287 with annotation by D. Wuyts; Bocken and Boone with cooperation by Kruithof, *Inleiding tot het schadevergoedingsrecht*, p. 197.

202 Article 8(b) Product Liability Act.

203 ECJ, 9 February 2006, no. C-127/04, *Declan O' Byrne v. Sanofi Pasteur MSD Ltd & Sanofi Pasteur SA.*, I-1313 at paragraph 27.

204 European Commission, 'Report on the safety and liability implications of Artificial Intelligence, the Internet of Things and robotics', pp. 15.

205 Van Gool, De Bruyne and Fierens, 'De regulering van artificiële intelligentie (deel 2) – Een analyse van vraagstukken inzake buitencontractuele aansprakelijkheid', forthcoming.

206 See for example: De Bruyne and Tanghe, 'Liability for Damage Caused by Autonomous Vehicles: A Belgian Perspective', p. 370.

207 See, however, more nuanced: Hubin, 'La responsabilité du fait des robots – Le droit de la responsabilité à l'ère de la révolution numérique', p. 272; Jacquemin and Hubin, 'Aspects

this background, it may be considered to completely disallow this defence in the context of AI systems. This makes it possible for victims to file a claim against the manufacturer of the software even when the defect is created through the continuous self-development of software.[208] Other scholars, however, are more nuanced and conclude that the potential defect in an AI system should find its origins in the production process. This may eventually lead to the producer's liability.[209]

The possibility of the producer to escape liability by relying on this defence is also a reoccurring topic in many EU studies. The Expert Report on liability and AI issued by the New Technologies Formation is important in this regard. When the defect came into being as a result of the producer's interference with the product after it was already put into circulation (e.g., by way of a software update) or the producer's failure to interfere, it should be regarded as a defect in the product for which he/she can be held liable. The point in time at which a product is placed on the market should not set a strict limit on the producer's liability for defects where, after that point in time, the producer or a third party acting on behalf of the producer remains in charge of providing updates or digital services. The producer should, therefore, remain liable where the defect has its origin (a) in a defective digital component or digital ancillary part or in other digital content or services provided for the product with the producer's assent after the product has been put into circulation; or (b) in the absence of an update of digital content or of the provision of a digital service which would have been required to maintain the expected level of safety within the time period for which the producer is obliged to provide such updates. The producer should thus be strictly liable for defects in emerging digital technologies even if these defects appear after the product was put into circulation, as long as the producer was still in control of updates to or upgrades of the technology.[210] Similar to the currently applicable PLD, Article 10 of the revised PLD contains different defences that allow economic operators to escape liability. An economic operator will, for instance, not be liable when it is 'probable that the defectiveness that caused the damage did not exist when the product was placed on the market, put into service' or made available on the market, 'or that this defectiveness came into being after that moment'.[211] An economic operator, however, will not be

---

contractuels et de responsabilité civile en matière d'intelligence artificielle', p. 135.

208 De Bruyne and Tanghe, 'Liability for Damage Caused by Autonomous Vehicles: A Belgian Perspective', p. 370.

209 See for example: Hubin, 'La responsabilité du fait des robots – Le droit de la responsabilité à l'ère de la révolution numérique', p. 272; Jacquemin and Hubin, 'Aspects contractuels et de responsabilité civile en matière d'intelligence artificielle', p. 135; T. Malengreau, 'Automatisation de la conduite: quelles responsabilités en droit belge? (Deuxième partie)', *RGAR*, 2019, no. 6, 15582–15611, no. 42.

210 Expert Group on Liability and New Technologies, New Technologies Formation, 'Liability for Artificial Intelligence and Other Emerging Digital Technologies', pp. 42–44.

211 Article 10.1 (c) revised PLD.

exempted from liability where the defectiveness of the product is due to any of the following, provided that it is within the manufacturer's control: '(a) related service; (b) software, including software updates or upgrades; or (c) the lack of software updates or upgrades necessary to maintain safety'.[212]

35. The development risk defence may also be relevant in an AI-context. This defence implies that the manufacturer will not be liable when proving that the state of scientific and technical knowledge at the time when he/she put the product into circulation was not such as to enable the existence of the defect to be discovered.[213] Likewise, under the revised PLD a manufacturer will also not be liable if the objective 'state of scientific and technical knowledge at the time when the product was placed on the market, put into service or in the period in which the product was within the manufacturer's control was not such that the defectiveness could be discovered'.[214] Producers of sophisticated AI systems may probably increasingly attempt to invoke it to refute liability.[215]

The question, however, is how this defence should be applied with regard to AI systems. Due to the autonomous nature of AI systems, their behaviour is not entirely foreseeable. Nevertheless, the fact that damage will occur is foreseeable. Judges interpret this defence in a very restrictive way. This defence is not specifically directed at the practices and safety standards in use in the industrial sector in which the producer is operating but, unreservedly, at the state of scientific and technical knowledge including the most advanced level of such knowledge at the time when the product was put into circulation. This defence does not contemplate the state of knowledge of which the producer actually or subjectively was or could have been apprised. Instead, it relates to the objective state of scientific and technical knowledge of which the producer is presumed to have been informed. The relevant scientific and technical knowledge must have been accessible at the time when the product was put into circulation.[216] Therefore, it seems possible to maintain this defence for AI systems.[217] Its assessment should, however, not be limited to the 'traditional' moment of putting

212 Article 10.2 revised PLD.

213 Article 8, e) Product Liability Act and Article 7, e) Product Liability Directive.

214 Article 10.1 (e) revised PLD.

215 Expert Group on Liability and New Technologies, New Technologies Formation, 'Liability for Artificial Intelligence and Other Emerging Digital Technologies', pp. 28–29 and p. 43; Jacquemin and Hubin, 'Aspects contractuels et de responsabilité civile en matière d'intelligence artificielle', pp. 134–137.

216 Court of Justice, 29 May 1997, *Commission of the European Communities v United Kingdom of Great Britain and Northern Ireland*, no. C-300/95, ECLI:EU:C:1997:255, considerations 26–29. See also: Verhoeven, *Productaansprakelijkheid en productveiligheid*, pp. 271–276.

217 Also see: Hubin, 'La responsabilité du fait des robots – Le droit de la responsabilité à l'ère de la révolution numérique', p. 272; T. Malengreau, 'Automatisation de la conduite: quelles responsabilités en droit belge? (Deuxième partie)', *RGAR*, 2019, no. 6, 15582–15611, no. 43. See, however: Jacquemin and Hubin, 'Aspects contractuels et de responsabilité civile en matière d'intelligence artificielle', p. 137.

the product into circulation but should be continuously assessed over time in the light of a producer's update and monitoring obligations. The Expert Report eventually concludes that the development risk defence should not be available in cases where it was predictable that unforeseen developments might occur.[218]

4. LIABILITY FOR DEFECTIVE THINGS

36. In addition to the product liability regime, Belgian tort law also provides for the strict liability of the custodian of defective things following Article 1384, paragraph 1, OBCC.[219] This provision entails that the person who possesses a defective thing is liable for the damage caused by such defective thing, irrespective of whether that person committed any fault.[220] The two essential elements in this context are a defective thing causing damage (part 4.1.) and its custodian (part 4.2.). We will especially examine their application when damage is caused by AI systems. It should, however, already be pointed out that case law on this topic is still highly fact-specific and the (theoretical) concept of defective thing continues to evolve.

4.1. THE NOTION OF 'DEFECTIVE THING'

37. It is commonly accepted that the liability under Article 1384, paragraph 1, OBCC only applies in relation to tangible things.[221] It may, however, also

218 Expert Group on Liability and New Technologies, New Technologies Formation, 'Liability for Artificial Intelligence and Other Emerging Digital Technologies', pp. 42–43; Jacquemin and Hubin, 'Aspects contractuels et de responsabilité civile en matière d'intelligence artificielle', p. 137; P. Machnikowski, 'Conclusions', in P. Machnikowski (ed.), *European Product Liability. An analysis of the State of the Art in the Era of New Technologies* (Cambridge: Intersentia, 2016), p. 704. In this regard, Buiten, De Streel and Peitz conclude that "In light of AI systems, it needs to be assessed what is the 'state of scientific and technical knowledge in relation to machines powered by automated decision making. In a review of the PLD, clarifying the defence could be justified (Buiten, De Streel and Peitz, 'EU Liability Rules for the Age of Artificial Intelligence', p. 56).

219 See for more information: J-L. Fagnart, *La responsabilité du fait des choses* (Waterloo: Wolters Kluwer Belgium 2017), 196 p.; L. Cornelis and R. Bützler, *De buitencontractuele aansprakelijkheid voor schade veroorzaakt door zaken: rechtsvergelijkend onderzoek: België, Frankrijk, Nederland, Bondsrepubliek Duitsland en Engeland* (Antwerp: Kluwer, 1982), 728 p.

220 Cass. 26 May 1904, *Pas.*, 1904, p. 246; Cass. 25 March 1920, *Pas.*, 1920, p. 110; J. Van Zuylen, 'La responsabilité du gardien d'une chose affectée d'un vice (Article 1384, al. 1er, du Code civil)', in G. Cruysmans (ed.), *Actualités en droit de la responsabilité* (Brussels: Bruylant, 2015), p. 9; M. Kruithof, *Tort Law in Belgium*, pp. 91–92. For an overview of the application of (other) strict liability regimes in an AI-context: C. Wendehorst, 'Strict Liability for AI and other Emerging Technologies', *Journal of European Tort Law*, 2020, vol. 11, no. 2, pp. 150–180; M. Diamantis, 'Vicarious Liability for AI', U Iowa Legal Studies Research Paper No. 2021-27, 19 p.

221 Cass. 21 april 1972, *Arr. Cass.*, 1972, p. 789; Bocken and Boone with cooperation by Kruithof, *Inleiding tot het schadevergoedingsrecht*, p. 184.

apply to things that consist of multiple elements or parts ('composed objects'[222]) including the (integrated) software ensuring the functioning of a tangible object.[223] Whether or not software *per se* can be qualified as a thing is still up for debate.[224] Although several authors do not consider stand-alone software to be a thing,[225] others argue that Article 1384, paragraph 1, OBCC should not be restricted to tangible things.[226] Hence, software may fall within its scope of application as long as it is susceptible to custody.[227] This point of view is further strengthened by the explicit inclusion of software in the definition of product in the revised PLD.[228] Regardless of the qualification of software, objects that are composed of several parts including both software and clearly tangible parts can qualify as a thing within the scope of the Article 1384, paragraph 1, OBCC.[229] Taking into account that most AI systems (e.g., robots) are technologies in which software and hardware are typically deeply integrated, we believe that such systems should indeed be regarded as 'composed objects' whereby the software constitutes an integral part of an AI system 'in its entirety'.[230]

38. More importantly, the thing causing the damage needs to be 'defective'.[231] A thing is considered defective when it features, in its entirety, an abnormal characteristic or state causing the thing to be capable of causing harm in certain circumstances.[232] For a characteristic of a thing to be defective, the characteristic

---

222 See for example: Cass. 7 December 1962, *Arr.Cass.*, 1962, p. 432, *Pas.* 1963, I, p. 432; Cass. 29 September 2006, *Arr.Cass.*, 2006, p. 1969, *NJW* 2007, p. 566, annotation I. Boone.

223 Vansweevelt and Weyts, *Handboek Buitencontractueel Aansprakelijkheidsrecht*, p. 457; Kruithof, *Tort Law in Belgium*, p. 91; Stijns, *Verbintenissenrecht – Boek1bis*, p. 37.

224 See in this regard also the discussion *supra* part 3.1.

225 See references in: Malengreau, 'Automatisation de la conduite: quelles responsabilités en droit belge? (Deuxième partie)', no. 48, fn. 112.

226 Vansweevelt and Weyts, *Handboek Buitencontractueel Aansprakelijkheidsrecht*, p. 456.

227 See for example: De Bruyne and Tanghe, 'Liability for Damage Caused by Autonomous Vehicles: A Belgian Perspective', p. 349 with further references. Also see: Malengreau, 'Automatisation de la conduite: quelles responsabilités en droit belge? (Deuxième partie)', no. 48; P. Gryffroy, B. Fiten and D. Surinx, 'Zelfrijdende wagens anno 2019. Waar staan we juridisch en maatschappelijk?', *NJW*, 2019, no. 406, p. 551; J. Van Zuylen, 'La responsabilité du gardien d'une chose affectée d'un vice (Article 1384, al. 1er, du Code civil)', p. 14.

228 Article 4.1. revised PLD.

229 Kruithof, *Tort Law in Belgium*, p. 91.

230 De Bruyne and Tanghe, 'Liability for Damage Caused by Autonomous Vehicles: A Belgian Perspective', p. 349 with further references. Also see: Malengreau, 'Automatisation de la conduite: quelles responsabilités en droit belge? (Deuxième partie)', no. 48; Gryffroy, Fiten and Surinx, 'Zelfrijdende wagens anno 2019. Waar staan we juridisch en maatschappelijk?', *NJW*, 2019, no. 406, p. 551; Jacquemin and Hubin, 'Aspects contractuels et de responsabilité civile en matière d'intelligence artificielle', pp. 124–125.

231 See for an extensive discussion: Vansweevelt and Weyts, *Handboek Buitencontractueel Aansprakelijkheidsrecht*, pp. 458–463.

232 Cass. 4 January 2016, *RGAR*, 2016, p. 334; Cass. 13 March 2015, *Arr. Cass.*, 2015, p. 737; Cass. 30 January 2003, *Arr. Cass.*, 2003, p. 278; Cass. 23 September 1971, *Arr.Cass.*, 1972, p.8; Kruithof, *Tort Law in Belgium*, p. 91; Stijns, *Verbintenissenrecht – Boek1bis*, pp. 37–38; Bocken and Boone with cooperation by Kruithof, *Inleiding tot het schadevergoedingsrecht*, p. 185.

needs to be abnormal. The thing should deviate from the normal 'model' whereby such deviation increases the risk of damage.[233] The defect must be assessed in the context of an ordinary and normal use of the thing and not in the context of an entirely exceptional use or a use which was almost unforeseeable by the designer of the object.[234] This exercise thus supposes the comparison of the defective object with objects of the same kind and type to determine which requirements one could normally expect the object to fulfil.[235] Courts, therefore, sometimes also refer to the reasonable (safety) expectations that society may have in relation to a thing to establish whether or not it is defective.[236]

The notion of defect is quite broad. Judges have a wide margin of interpretation to establish whether a characteristic of the object is abnormal.[237] This ground for liability traditionally related to the intrinsic characteristics of an object affecting its physical structure.[238] Nowadays, however, a defect no longer needs to be intrinsic, nor does it need to affect a structural element which is inherent to the thing.[239] Although it may thus be an extrinsic defect, a mere (temporary) addition to the object will not be sufficient because a (defective) extrinsic element still needs to be part of the thing 'in its entirety'.[240] Elements that should be taken into account to determine whether an external element could be considered as an extrinsic defect are the period of time during which the external element is able to affect the object[241] and the degree of integration of the external element into the object.[242]

---

233 Kruithof, *Tort Law in Belgium*, p. 91; Stijns, *Verbintenissenrecht – Boek1bis*, p. 38–39; Cass. 4 January 2016, *NjW*, 2016, p. 917, annotated by J. Tanghe; Jacquemin and Hubin, 'Aspects contractuels et de responsabilité civile en matière d'intelligence artificielle', p. 125.

234 Cass. 30 January 2003, *Arr. Cass.*, 2003, p. 278; Swinnen, 'De inpassing van digitale producten in het Belgisch privaatrecht', p. 1079.

235 Cass. 11 March 2010, *Arr. Cass.*, 2010, p.715; Cass. 29 September 2006, *NjW* 2007, p. 566.

236 Cass. 4 January 2016, *RGAR*, 2016, no. 15, p. 334, Cass. 11 March 2010, no. 171, *Arr.Cass.*, 2010, p. 715, *Pas.*, 2010, p. 777 as referred to in Kruithof, *Tort Law in Belgium*, p. 92. Also see: De Bruyne and Tanghe, 'Liability for Damage Caused by Autonomous Vehicles: A Belgian Perspective', p. 352 with further references to case law in fn. 111.

237 De Bruyne and Tanghe, 'Liability for Damage Caused by Autonomous Vehicles: A Belgian Perspective', pp. 351–352.

238 De Bruyne and Tanghe, 'Liability for Damage Caused by Autonomous Vehicles: A Belgian Perspective', p. 350 with further references.

239 Cass. 13 March 2015, no. 193, *Arr.Cass.* 2015, p. 737, *Pas.* 2015, p. 721 as referred to in Kruithof, *Tort Law in Belgium*, p. 92; Cass. 31 October 2013, *RW*, 2014–2015, p. 790; Bocken and Boone with cooperation by Kruithof, *Inleiding tot het schadevergoedingsrecht*, p. 188; Jacquemin and Hubin, 'Aspects contractuels et de responsabilité civile en matière d'intelligence artificielle', pp. 125–126. This, however, used to be the case (Stijns, *Verbintenissenrecht – Boek1bis*, p. 38: Swinnen, 'De inpassing van digitale producten in het Belgisch privaatrecht', pp. 1078–1079).

240 Cass. 13 March 2015, *Arr. Cass.*, 2015, p. 737; Cass. 2 January 2009, *Arr. Cass.*, 2009, 3; Kruithof, *Tort Law*, p. 92; Stijns, *Verbintenissenrecht – Boek1bis*, pp. 38–39.

241 Court of First Instance Turnhout 4 September 2003, *RW*, 2006–07, p. 152.

242 Court of First Instance Ghent 14 February 2008, *RW*, 2010–11, p. 711; Court of First Instance Antwerp 1 October 2012, *RW*, 2014–15, p. 793; Swinnen, 'De inpassing van digitale producten in het Belgisch privaatrecht', p. 1080.

39. Although it will be discussed more thoroughly in part 5.2., a causal relation between the defect and the incurred damage is also required. This means that in the absence of the defect, no damage should have been caused or, at least, not in the same way.[243] However, courts tend to be lenient toward the victim if she/he faces difficulty providing positive evidence of the defect that caused the abnormal behaviour of the object that caused the damage.[244] Judges often also accept a negative proof. The victim may then suffice with demonstrating that all other reasonably possible causes for the 'abnormal behaviour' of the thing can be excluded, meaning that a damage-inflicting defect should be present.[245]

40. The application of this liability regime to AI systems is not straightforward. Especially the question when an AI system can be considered 'defective' is challenging.[246] It has already been mentioned that defects can both be intrinsic and extrinsic. With regard to intrinsic defects affecting inherent or structural elements of an AI system, one can imagine that this may cover defective or malfunctioning sensors, chips, buttons or other rather usual parts of (digital) devices and locally installed software (e.g., the underlying code).[247] As to the extrinsic defects, the concept of a 'composed object' comes into play. The software that enables an AI system to function can be considered as a part of the system in its entirety. This should not only apply when software is installed locally but also when it runs 'in the cloud', which judges may consider to be external to an AI system resulting in an extrinsic defect.[248] Other conceivable extrinsic defects could be interoperability defects whereby an AI system (e.g., a self-driving vehicle) working fine on its own turns out to be unable to communicate with other (AI)systems (e.g., smart traffic lights) that function properly on their own as well, while one could reasonably expect that such interoperability would have been guaranteed.[249] After all, one must discern that such defects which are not entirely intrinsic are not a mere coincidence, while the technology needed to

243 Stijns, *Verbintenissenrecht – Boek1bis*, p. 40.

244 Kruithof, *Tort Law in Belgium*, p. 92.

245 Cass. 11 September 2008, *Pas.*, 2008, p. 1916; Cass. 29 January 1987, *Arr.Cass.*, 1986–87, p. 693, *Pas.*, 1987, I, p. 624; Cass. 24 February 2006, *Arr.Cass.*, 2006, p. 443, *RABG*, 2006, p. 1431; Bocken and Boone with cooperation by Kruithof, *Inleiding tot het schadevergoedingsrecht*, p. 187; Jacquemin and Hubin, 'Aspects contractuels et de responsabilité civile en matière d'intelligence artificielle', p. 127.

246 Hubin, 'La responsabilité du fait des robots – Le droit de la responsabilité à l'ère de la révolution numérique', p. 266 concluding that this can become very challenging in the context of robots.

247 De Bruyne and Tanghe, 'Liability for Damage Caused by Autonomous Vehicles: A Belgian Perspective', p. 350; Swinnen, 'De inpassing van digitale producten in het Belgisch privaatrecht', p. 1079.

248 De Bruyne and Tanghe, 'Liability for Damage Caused by Autonomous Vehicles: A Belgian Perspective', p. 350.

249 See: De Bruyne and Tanghe, 'Liability for Damage Caused by Autonomous Vehicles: A Belgian Perspective', pp. 350–351.

ensure interoperability (e.g., API's[250]) is often integrated to a certain extent into the source code.[251]

41. In order to establish whether an AI system is defective, a comparison between the defective AI system and 'objects of the same kind and type' has to be conducted. This analysis will allow to determine which requirements should normally be fulfilled by the AI system.[252] Such comparative exercise entails at least two important difficulties for AI systems.

First, one should be able to come up with a relevant 'model' AI system. As illustrated by Swinnen in relation to self-driving vehicles, this is a (very) complex and non-evident task ensuing many other questions and considerations.[253] Second, a victim would need to prove how the damage-inflicting AI system deviates from the model AI system, pinpointing the intrinsic or extrinsic defect, and how this deviation – the defect – is causally related to the damage. Providing such positive proof may be difficult, especially in relation to software. Source code is often not publicly available, let alone comparable.[254] However, Belgian courts already adopted a 'victim-friendly' stance as they allow for a negative proof of the existence of the defect and of the causal relation between the damage and the defect.[255] Moreover, courts do sometimes also rely on the 'reasonable expectations' that society may have in relation to things (e.g., AI systems).[256] This criterion comes close to legitimate expectation concept already discussed within the product liability regime.[257] It provides more leeway for victims as it reduces

---

250 API stands for Application Programming Interface.

251 Vice versa: Swinnen, 'De inpassing van digitale producten in het Belgisch privaatrecht', p. 1080. This author uses the example of a Tesla on autopilot which urged its driver to take over the wheel as a moth flew onto the radar of the car, severely limiting its functionality. The moth would not be considered as an extrinsic defect in accordance with the criteria set out above. Also see: https://www.thedrive.com/news/3541/a-tesla-model-ss-autopilot-was-knocked-out-by-a-moth. See for an in-depth analysis of the notion of defectives in context of autonomous vehicles: Malengreau, 'Automatisation de la conduite: quelles responsabilités en droit belge? (Deuxième partie)', no. 52–55.

252 Cass. 25 April 2005, *Arr.Cass.*, 2005, p. 928; Cass. 11 March 2010, *Arr.Cass.*, 2010, p. 715.

253 Swinnen, 'De inpassing van digitale producten in het Belgisch privaatrecht', pp. 1080–1083. The main takeaway is that this strict liability regime can only be clearly applied to things that are no longer subject to major technological developments.

254 Moreover, as AI systems are often referred to as being 'opaque' or 'inscrutable' due to their complexity, it might be difficult for a victim to understand the inner workings of an AI system, let alone to establish a convincing argument that the way a certain AI system works or behaves, should be considered as a damage-causing defect. See in this regard: J.A. Kroll, 'The Fallacy of Inscrutability', *Phil. Trans. R. Soc.*, 2018, pp. 1–14; R. van den Hoven van Genderen, 'Algoritmen en AI: distopische black box of glazen bol? Is een wettelijk kader voor transparantie van algoritmen mogelijk en wenselijk?', *Computerrecht*, 2020/5, pp. 30–42.

255 Also see the discussion *supra* part. 4.1 and *infra* part 5.2; De Bruyne and Tanghe, 'Liability for Damage Caused by Autonomous Vehicles: A Belgian Perspective', p. 352 (these authors, however, doubt whether the possibility of negative proof will be effective for autonomous vehicles).

256 Cass. 4 January 2016, *NJW*, 2016, p. 917, annotated by J. Tanghe.

257 See *supra* part 3.2.

the need to elaborate on the specific nature of the defect.[258] Nevertheless, judges should try to avoid that it is 'reasonably expected' that model AI systems work perfectly and that they are (theoretically) equipped to effectively deal with every imaginable situation. Courts should also avoid assuming that model AI systems do not cause damage, because it would then suffice to determine that AI systems merely causing damage are already defective.[259]

4.2. THE CUSTODIAN

42. Article 1384, paragraph 1, OBCC refers to the 'custodian' of a thing as the responsible person when damage occurs.[260] The custodian is liable irrespective of whether he/she has committed any wrongful act and even if he was not aware or could not have been aware of the defect.[261] The concept of custodian should be interpreted broadly and actually refers to the person who possesses the thing/has its under his/her detention and has factual (and not necessarily legal) control over it.[262] This will often be the owner but may also be a borrower or a licensee as long as such persons have the power to lead, control and supervise.[263] The custodian of an AI system will hence be the person who has factual control over the system in the sense that such a person must be able to lead, control and supervise the AI system. Relevant elements to assess this in practice may relate to the person who introduced the system into socio-economic circulation or requested the services of the AI system.[264] The driver of a partly autonomous vehicle who is also its owner, for instance, may be considered as the custodian, except in particular circumstances. Other actors may also be qualified as custodian insofar as they have factual control over the vehicle (e.g., borrowing or renting a car).[265]

---

258 Swinnen, 'De inpassing van digitale producten in het Belgisch privaatrecht', p. 1083.

259 In that sense: De Bruyne and Tanghe, 'Liability for Damage Caused by Autonomous Vehicles: A Belgian Perspective', pp. 352–353.

260 See extensively on the notion custodian with additional references: Vansweevelt and Weyts, *Handboek Buitencontractueel Aansprakelijkheidsrecht*, pp. 479–495.

261 Cass. 3 May 1974, *Arr.Cass.*, 1974, 989, Pas. 1974, p. 914; Cass. 26 April 2013, *Arr.Cass.*, 2013, p. 1010, *Pas.*, 2013, p. 985 as reported in Kruithof, *Tort Law in Belgium*, p. 92.

262 Cass. 13 September 2012, *Arr.Cass.*, 2012, p. 1923; Cass. 25 March 1999, *Arr.Cass.*, 1999, p. 442; Cass. 28 May 2010, *JT*, 2010, p. 438; Cass. 22 January 2009, *Pas.*, 2009, p. 184; Cass. 20 March 2003, *RCJB*, 2006, p. 9 with annotation by B. Dubuisson; M. Van Quickenborne and H. Vandenberghe, 'Overzicht van rechtspraak. Aansprakelijkheid uit onrechtmatige daad (2000–2008) – deel 3', *TPR*, 2011, pp. 441–443; Van Zuylen, 'La responsabilité du gardien d'une chose affectée d'un vice (Article 1384, al. 1er, du Code civil)', pp. 20–23.

263 De Bruyne and Tanghe, 'Liability for Damage Caused by Autonomous Vehicles: A Belgian Perspective', p. 353; Kruithof, *Tort Law in Belgium*, p. 92.

264 Also see: Swinnen, 'De inpassing van digitale producten in het Belgisch privaatrecht', p. 1084.

265 Malengreau, 'Automatisation de la conduite: quelles responsabilités en droit belge? (Deuxième partie)', no. 50.

43. The identification of the custodian of the AI system (e.g., an autonomous vehicle or a care robot) will not be a major problem. Nevertheless, Belgian scholars seem to have different opinions in relation to what 'factual control' over AI systems could entail. Swinnen argues that just as with regular cars, the driver of an autonomous vehicle should be considered as the custodian because the driver is able to overrule or shut down the operating system of the car and take over control.[266] De Bruyne and Tanghe, however, point out that the requirement of factual control cannot be interpreted as controlling or supervising the autonomous vehicle while driving because liability under Article 1384, first paragraph, OBCC is strict and not based on the user's wrongful acts.[267] They further clarify that construing factual control in terms of the ability of the human driver to overrule decisions by the system or operate the vehicle would imply a fault-based liability, as in that case the damage should result from the lack of intervention by the driver. However, this is clearly at odds with the purpose of Article 1384, paragraph 1, OBCC. After all, this provision aims to make a driver and, more broadly speaking, any user of an AI system susceptible to incur liability 'irrespective of whether and to what extent he was able to control the operating system of the vehicle', which should be generalised to all AI systems.[268]

This discussion, however, becomes more complicated in relation to the software integrated into an AI system. On the one hand, the software vendor is responsible for the initial development and will be able to push later (system) updates. On the other hand, the user of the AI system will be responsible for the subsequent use and the related further adaptations in the system's behaviour. Some conclude that this excludes the developer of such software as custodian because he/she in principle no longer controls the driving behaviour of the vehicle once the software was installed in the car.[269] We believe the latter to be a slightly inaccurate assertion as it does not take into account the situation in which software runs in the cloud, effectively ruling out any factual control over such software by the driver/AI user. Hence, it remains to be seen who will eventually be regarded as the 'custodian' of integrated software and be held liable if the software is deemed defective. Jacquemin and Hubin are clear when concluding that autonomous aspects of AI systems and their ability to evolve in a non-foreseeable way may be incompatible with the requirement of a custodian's factual control and ability to lead, control and supervise.[270] In any case, it cannot be excluded that there are multiple custodians.[271]

---

266 Swinnen, 'De inpassing van digitale producten in het Belgisch privaatrecht', pp. 1083–1084.

267 De Bruyne and Tanghe, 'Liability for Damage Caused by Autonomous Vehicles: A Belgian Perspective', p. 353.

268 *Ibid.*, p. 353. Also see *supra* part 2.

269 Swinnen, 'De inpassing van digitale producten in het Belgisch privaatrecht', p. 1084.

270 Jacquemin and Hubin, 'Aspects contractuels et de responsabilité civile en matière d'intelligence artificielle', pp. 127–128.

271 This will necessarily be factual discussion, which will be further complicated if software runs in the cloud. See also: Cass. 24 October 1994, *Arr. Cass.*, 1994, p. 873; De Bruyne and Tanghe,

44. This discussion may be replaced by a proposal set forth by the Expert Group on Liability and New Technologies which is highly similar to the strict liability regime for defective goods. The Expert Group suggests devising a strict liability regime in relation to emerging digital technologies, especially those operated in non-private environments, revolving around the concept of the 'operator'. Such operator would refer to the person who is in control of the risk connected with the operation of digital technologies and who benefits from their operation, which is broader than the owner/user/keeper.[272] Interestingly, the report distinguishes between a frontend operator and a backend operator.[273] Should several operators be involved in the operation, strict liability should lie with the one who has more control over the risks of the operation. Likewise, in October 2020 the European Parliament issued a Resolution with recommendations to the Commission on a civil liability regime for artificial intelligence. It suggested a strict liability regime for operators of high-risk AI systems and a fault-based liability with a reversal of the burden of proof for low-risk AI systems. It also made a distinction between frontend and backend operators.[274]

5. OTHER COMMON AND RELEVANT ELEMENTS IN TORT LIABILITY LAIMS

45. In addition to the specific components related to the different grounds of liability discussed in the previous parts, tort liability claims also require damage and causation. A victim will have to prove that he/she suffered damage and that it was caused by the fault, defective product or defective thing which has been established relating to an AI system.[275] After a brief elaboration on the notion of damage (part 5.1.), we will especially focus on the requirement of causation, which may become increasingly challenging within the context of AI systems (part 5.2.).

5.1. DAMAGE IN AN AI-CONTEXT

46. The different liability regimes discussed above offer the possibility to claim compensation for damage. Belgian tort law has a broad concept of 'damage'

'Liability for Damage Caused by Autonomous Vehicles: A Belgian Perspective', p. 354; Swinnen, 'De inpassing van digitale producten in het Belgisch privaatrecht', p. 1084.

272 Expert Group on Liability and New Technologies, New Technologies Formation, 'Liability for Artificial Intelligence and Other Emerging Digital Technologies', p. 41.

273 See on the difference between the two categories of operators *supra* part 2.3; Expert Group on Liability and New Technologies, New Technologies Formation, 'Liability for Artificial Intelligence and Other Emerging Digital Technologies', p. 39.

274 European Parliament, 'Resolution of 20 October 2020 with recommendations to the Commission on a civil liability regime for artificial intelligence'

275 Also see *supra* part 2.1 regarding the burden of proof.

consisting of any injury to an interest of the claimant.[276] It is not necessary for the claimant to enjoy a subjective right to the infringed interest.[277] A factual interest suffices, although it cannot be an illegitimate interest.[278] As a consequence, there appears less need to amend or adopt new rules in Belgium regarding damage to data as identified and discussed in the Expert Report.[279] When an AI system such as an automated curator of a government database or an advanced fintech platform would delete, contaminate, modify, encrypt or leak data to which one or more persons have a factual interest, these persons may claim compensation for such damages without being required to demonstrate a property or personal right to the aforementioned data.[280] In order to consider it as damage, it is sufficient to demonstrate a legitimate factual interest regarding the data.

47. The damage also needs to be personal.[281] 'Class actions' are generally not allowed under Belgian law, although one exception is relevant in the context of liability for AI systems. Damage suffered by consumers and SMEs and grounded on the basis of product liability can be claimed on their behalf by recognised representative entities on the basis of the 'action for collective redress' established by Articles XVII.35-XVII.70 of the Belgian Code of Economic Law. Although currently rarely applied, this collective action may become a popular instrument to address cases of product liability for mass-damage created by AI systems, given the difficulties for individual persons to prove liability in such cases. It should also be noted that a European collective action for the protection of consumer interests may be possible as well.[282]

48. Finally, damage needs to be certain. In principle, so-called judicial certainty about the damage's existence and its scope are required. Both elements need to be demonstrated by the claimant.[283] New Belgian rules of evidence allow proof by probability and a reversal of the burden of proof under the aforementioned

---

276 See on damage: Bocken and Boone with cooperation by Kruithof, *Inleiding tot het schadevergoedingsrecht*, pp. 46–64.

277 Cass. 16 January 1939, *Pas.*, 1939, I, p. 25.; Cass. 24 March 1969, *Arr.Cass.*, 1969, p. 690; Cass. 4 September 1972, *Arr.Cass.*, 1973, p. 1, *RW* 1972–73, p. 715; Cass. 21 juni 1990, *Arr.Cass.*, 1989–90, p. 1358.

278 Cass. 3 October 1997, *Arr.Cass.*, 1997, p. 921; Cass. 2 April 1998, *Arr.Cass.*, 1998, p. 407, *TBBR*, 1999, p. 251; Cass. 14 May 2003, *Arr.Cass.*, 2003, p. 1163, *RW*, 2005–06, p. 743, *RGAR* 2003, no. 13.767.

279 Expert Group on Liability and New Technologies, New Technologies Formation, 'Liability for Artificial Intelligence and Other Emerging Digital Technologies', pp. 19 and 59–60.

280 Also see regarding injury to reputation and privacy: Kruithof, *Tort law in Belgium*, pp. 68–70.

281 Cass. 6 January 2010, *Arr.Cass.*, 2010, p. 19; Cass. 25 May 2012, *Arr.Cass.*, 2012, p. 1432. Also see: Article 17 Belgian Judicial Code.

282 See: Directive (EU) 2020/1828 of the European Parliament and of the Council of 25 November 2020 on representative actions for the protection of the collective interests of consumers and repealing Directive 2009/22/EC, *OJ* L 409.

283 See: Vandenbussche, *Bewijs en onrechtmatige daad*, pp. 135–149; Vansweevelt and Weyts, *Handboek Buitencontractueel Aansprakelijkheidsrecht*, pp. 638–639.

conditions.[284] In cases of damage caused by AI systems, however, the other requirements of imposing liability (e.g., causation or wrongful act) are likely more difficult to prove. Consequently, they seem more susceptible to meeting the statutory conditions for these evidentiary techniques. The certainty requirement does not prohibit claiming compensation for future damage if it is sufficiently certain that such damage will occur,[285] or for a loss of a chance if the existence of the lost chance can be demonstrated with sufficient certainty.[286]

5.2. CAUSATION IN AN AI-CONTEXT

49. A victim will in one way or another have to demonstrate that the damage was caused by the fact(s) imputable to the defendant.[287] The traditionally accepted theory in Belgium is the doctrine of the equivalence of conditions.[288] Under this rule, courts are required to accept legal causality between a fact and the incurred damage if it has been established that the invoked fact was necessary in the given circumstances for the damage to occur (the so-called *conditio sine qua non* or 'but-for test'). A fact that *in concreto* was necessary for the harm to occur is a cause even if a later intervening fact was also necessary. Moreover, a fact that was necessary for the damage to occur the way it did is a cause even if the damage was not a necessary consequence, not the normal

---

284 See *supra* part 2.1.

285 See: Cass. 18 June 1962, *Arr.Cass.*, 1962, p. 1171; Vansweevelt and Weyts, *Handboek Buitencontractueel Aansprakelijkheidsrecht*, p. 638.

286 See: Cass. 19 January 1984, *Arr.Cass.*, 1983–84, p. 585; Cass. 23 February 2005, *Arr.Cass.*, 2005, p. 451, *RW* 2007–08, p. 62; Cass. 5 June 2008, *Arr.Cass.*, 2008, p. 1462, *RW* 2008–09, p. 795, annotation by S. Lierman; Court of Appeal Antwerp 10 November 2003, *RW*, 2006–07, p. 1524. Also see *infra* part 5.2.

287 Also see *supra* parts 2.1. and 4.1. See for more information on causation and digital products: M. Martin-Casals, 'Causation and Scope of Liability in the Internet of Things', in S. Lohsse et al., *Liability for Artificial Intelligence and the Internet of Things* (Baden-Baden: Nomos, 2019), p. 228; N. Al Ganim and J. De Bruyne, 'De wetten van Asimov en het buitencontractueel aansprakelijkheidsrecht', *NJW*, 2020, no. 422, pp. 374–385.

288 See for example: Vansweevelt and Weyts, *Handboek Buitencontractueel Aansprakelijkheidsrecht*, pp. 763–873 with further references; J.L. Fagnart, 'Petite navigation dans les méandres de la causalité', *RGAR*, 2006, 14.080, no. 3; M. van Quickenborne, *Oorzakelijk verband tussen onrechtmatige daad en schade* (Mechelen: Kluwer, 2007), pp. 31–46 with further references. See, however: M. Kruithof, 'Oorzaak of aanleiding? Geen causaal verband zonder causale bijdrage', in: T. Vansweevelt and B. Weyts (eds), *Actuele ontwikkelingen in het aansprakelijkheidsrecht en verzekeringsrecht. Iste Interuniversitair Congres over Aansprakelijkheids - en Verzekeringsrecht* (Antwerp: Intersentia, 2015), pp. 139–208 (concluding that another rule can better describe Belgian positive law on causation in civil liability. Under this rule a fact is a cause of a loss if (i) the loss would in the given circumstances not have occurred as it specifically occurred without the fact and (ii) the fact has increased the specific risk of which the specific loss occurrence was a realisation). Also see: I. Durant, 'La causalité, simple trait d'union ou véritable variable d'adjustement?', in P. Wéry (ed.), *Droit des obligations: développements récents et pistes Nouvelles* (Liège: Anthémis, 2007), pp. 73–81.

consequence or not a foreseeable consequence of the fact.[289] When applying the *conditio sine qua non test*, a Belgian judge needs to hypothetically reconstruct the event leading to the loss and leave out the defendant's wrongful act. If the loss remains the same, a defendant's wrongful act was not a necessary condition for it to occur. The application of this '*théorie de l'alternative légitime*', however, is not always straightforward.[290]

50. Many actors may be involved in the production, supply and use of goods incorporating software or of AI systems (e.g., manufacturer of the hardware, the software developer, developers of algorithms, the user or the owner of the network infrastructure). This plurality of actors in digital ecosystems makes it increasingly difficult to find out who may be liable for caused damage.[291] Nevertheless, the doctrine of the equivalence of conditions can lead to persons being held liable in a seemingly unfair way for damage they could not have reasonably foreseen. This can be illustrated by some examples. A causal link can be established between the harm that is caused by a robot to a patient during a surgical procedure and the original quarrel between neighbours causing that person to end up in hospital in the first place. Another example is when a driver of an autonomous vehicle does not accept a software update and the vehicle would subsequently cause an accident resulting in the release of toxic substances in a river.[292] In all of these cases, a person (e.g., neighbour or driver) may be held liable as their behaviour/act was a necessary factual condition for the damage that eventually occurred. Judges, however, do not always strictly apply the doctrine of equivalence of conditions. The unpredictability of damage within long causal chains may sometimes lead to an exemption from liability.[293] It is worth noting that the proposed Article 5:162 that may be included in the new Belgian Civil Code would continue to start from the *conditio sine qua non test*. Nevertheless, it would contain an exception for situations where the relationship

---

289 Kruithof, *Tort Law in Belgium*, p. 126 with references to case law.

290 Bocken and Boone with cooperation by Kruithof, *Inleiding tot het schadevergoedingsrecht*, pp. 67–68; Vansweevelt and Weyts, *Handboek Buitencontractueel Aansprakelijkheidsrecht*, pp. 778–779. See for more information: P. Van Ommeslaghe, 'Le concept de l' "alternative légitime" en droit de la responsabilité civile', in X, *Justitie: vraagstukken en perspectieven voor morgen* (Bruges: die Keure, 2013), pp. 131–137; R. Jafferali, 'L'alternative légitime dans l'appréciation du lien causal, corps étranger en droit belge de la responsabilité?', in F. Glansdorff (ed.), *Droit de la responsabilité. Questions choisies* (Brussels: Larcier, 2015), pp. 94–164. See for an application: Police Court Ghent 8 October 2012, *RW*, 2012–2013, p. 955; J. De Bruyne, *Third-Party Certifiers* (London: Kluwer Law International, 2019), pp. 349–350.

291 Expert Group on Liability and New Technologies, New Technologies Formation, 'Liability for Artificial Intelligence and Other Emerging Digital Technologies', pp. 32–33.

292 Examples used in: Van Gool, De Bruyne and Fierens, 'De regulering van artificiële intelligentie (deel 2) – Een analyse van vraagstukken inzake buitencontractuele aansprakelijkheid', forthcoming.

293 See the many references in: Kruithof, 'Oorzaak of aanleiding? Geen causaal verband zonder causale bijdrage', pp. 139–208; H. Bocken and I. Boone, 'Causaliteit in het Belgische recht', *TPR*, 2002, pp. 1646–1670.

between the fact leading to the damage and the suffered damage is so remote that it would be 'manifestly unreasonable' to impose liability on the defendant. It remains to be seen how this would be applied in practice to cases where damage is caused by AI systems.[294]

51. The Expert Report stipulates that proving that some hardware defect caused damage to a person is difficult. It is more difficult to establish that the underlying cause was a flawed algorithm. It is even more complicated if the algorithm suspected of causing harm has been developed or modified by the AI system itself, using machine learning and/or deep learning techniques, while being fuelled by external data that it has collected since the start of its operation.[295] Algorithms often no longer come as easily readable code but as a 'black box', which has evolved through self-learning and that can be tested as to its effects, but cannot be understood. It is, therefore, becoming increasingly difficult for victims to identify such technologies as even a possible source of harm, let alone why and how they have caused it.[296] Considering that the proof of causation can thus be quite challenging and sometimes even impossible, mechanisms have been developed by national judges to overcome this hurdle.[297] An example in Belgium is the 'loss of a chance' doctrine, which has been confirmed by the Court of Cassation. Courts can award compensation for the value of the lost chance the victim had of not suffering the disadvantage. The value of this lost chance will be estimated as a fraction of the value of the disadvantage that the victim ultimately suffered.[298]

52. Several recent EU documents also address the high burden of proof for victims when damage is caused by AI systems, especially in the context of product liability. The Expert Report is relevant in this regard. As a general rule, the victim should continue to be required to prove what caused the damage. Nevertheless, the Report also stresses the importance of alleviating the burden in cases where it becomes unreasonably difficult for the victim to prove such elements. New

---

294 Article 5.162 Voorontwerp van wet houdende invoeging van de bepalingen betreffende buitencontractuele aansprakelijkheid in het nieuw Burgerlijk Wetboek/Avant-projet de loi portant insertion des dispositions relatives à la responsabilité extracontractuelle dans le nouveau Code civil, 1 September 2019. Also see: M. Kruithof, "Een kritische analyse van het concept causaliteit in het ontwerp van de Commissie tot hervorming van het aansprakelijkheidsrecht", *TPR*, 2021, no. 1, pp. 269–321.

295 Expert Group on Liability and New Technologies, New Technologies Formation, 'Liability for Artificial Intelligence and Other Emerging Digital Technologies', p. 20.

296 *Ibid.*, pp. 32–34.

297 *Ibid*, pp. 21–22.

298 Cass. 15 March 2010, *Arr.Cass* 2010, p. 167, *Pas.* 2010, p. 839; Bocken and Boone with cooperation by Kruithof, *Inleiding tot het schadevergoedingsrecht,* pp. 47–50 with further references; Kruithof, *Tort Law in Belgium*, p. 127; D. Philippe, 'Quelques réflexions sur la perte d'une chance et le lien causal', *RDCB-TBH*, 2013, no. 119, p. 1004; De Bruyne, *Third-Party Certifiers*, p. 351.

technologies are by essence complex, dynamic and interconnected. This makes it sometimes extremely challenging to establish causation. The alleviation of the burden of proof may be appropriate if a balancing of several listed factors warrants doing so (e.g., the likelihood that the technology at least contributed to the harm, the degree of *ex-post* traceability and intelligibility of processes within the technology that may have contributed to the cause or the risk of a known defect within the technology, even though its actual causal impact is not self-evident).[299] Likewise, the European Commission examined whether and to what extent it may be required to mitigate the consequences of the complexity of AI systems by alleviating/reversing the burden of proof required by national liability rules through an appropriate EU initiative.[300] Eventually, the European Commission issued two Proposals of Directives in September 2022 covering liability for damage involving AI. Both Proposals introduce a rebuttable presumption of causality when certain requirements are met.[301] The possibilities to lower the standard of proof or to reverse it under new general Belgian civil evidence law have already been discussed.[302] Proving causation in claims of tort liability for damage caused by AI systems appears to be a particularly appropriate application of these techniques.

53. As many parties are generally involved in the supply chain of AI systems, the allocation between all of them will become an important issue. If the damage that occurred can be divided into separate injuries caused by different actors, each of them is liable for the specific injury it caused. The causality requirement applied in Belgium, however, allows for several facts attributable to different persons to be the cause of a single indivisible loss. The victim will be entitled to sue any or all of them for the full amount of his/her damage. Each of them can be held liable in solidum for the whole damage. If one of the liable parties compensated the victim, contribution can be sought from the others. The fraction of the damage each liable party has to bear is measured based on the relative role the fact for which it is liable played in causing the harm. If the victim is also (partly) responsible for the damage-causing event, shared liability applies.

299 Expert Group on Liability and New Technologies, New Technologies Formation, 'Liability for Artificial Intelligence and Other Emerging Digital Technologies', pp. 49–52.

300 European Commission, 'Report on the safety and liability implications of Artificial Intelligence, the Internet of Things and robotics', p. 14. In this regard, several scholars have also warned that reversing the burden of proof may alter the current distribution of risks to the detriment of the manufacturers. Lowering the standard of proof may be a more viable alternative. See Buiten, De Streel and Peitz, 'EU Liability Rules for the Age of Artificial Intelligence', pp. 55–56 with further references.

301 See Article 4 AI Liability Directive and Article 9 revised PLD. Also see the discussion *supra* in nos. 10 and 30.

302 See *supra* part 2.1.

This will result in a reduction of the liability of the third parties to the extent that the victim has contributed to the occurrence of the event.[303]

6. LEGAL PERSONALITY FOR AI SYSTEMS

54. The previous parts showed that applying the existing tort liability regimes to AI systems is not that obvious and entails several legal issues. An often-proposed idea to resolve these issues is the establishment of some sort of legal personality for AI systems.[304] Such a legal fiction may assist in remedying issues relating to the opacity of AI systems (e.g., causation or wrongful acts) and the plurality of potential responsible parties.[305] Moreover, the apparent simplicity of this 'solution' for liability questions is quite attractive: the 'artificial' legal person would be able to directly indemnify victims.

This idea of establishing legal personality for AI became particularly relevant (and concrete) when the European Parliament adopted a Resolution in 2017. Paragraph 59 f) of the Resolution urges the Commission to explore, analyse and consider the implications of all possible legal solutions such as: '[...] creating a specific legal status for robots in the long run, so that at least the most sophisticated autonomous robots could be established as having the status of electronic persons responsible for making good any damage they may cause, and possibly applying electronic personality to cases where robots make autonomous decisions or otherwise interact with third parties independently'.[306] This suggestion, however, was met by fierce criticism, including by a group of AI experts, industry leaders and legal scholars who published an open letter discouraging the Parliament from further looking into the establishment of such legal status.[307]

55. At the current stage of the discussion, one can distinguish two strands of thought. On the one hand, there are proponents of establishing some

---

303 Kruithof, *Tort Law in Belgium*, p. 130 with references to case law; Bocken and Boone with cooperation by Kruithof, *Inleiding tot het schadevergoedingsrecht*, pp. 74–78.

304 Also see *supra* part 2.

305 G. Wagner, 'Robot, Inc.: Personhood for autonomous systems?', *Fordham Law Review*, 2019, vol. 88, pp. 608–609.

306 European Parliament Resolution, 2015/2103(INL)), Civil Law Rules on Robotics, 16 February 2017. See for a discussion of this resolution: J. Bryson et al., 'Of, for and by the People: The legal Lacuna of Synthetic Persons', *Artificial Intelligence & Law*, 2017, vol. 25, pp. 275–276.

307 See: www.robotics-openletter.eu/. The fact that the idea of legal personality for AI surfaced in this resolution does actually not come as a surprise as this possibility has already been debated and studied for a while at the EU level. For instance, two European Commission-funded research projects both discussed the possibility of creating an 'electronic personhood'. See: C. Leroux and R. Labruto (eds.)), 'Suggestion for a green paper on legal issues in robotics', 31 December 2012, pp. 58–63, euRobotics and D6.2 Guidelines on Regulating Robotics', 22 September 2014, pp. 24, 190 and 206, Robolaw.

sort of legal personality for AI systems on the basis of legal and economic arguments.[308] On the other hand, critics including the Expert Group on Liability and New Technologies either refute the need for such legal concept[309] or point out that we are still in the early stages of this (complex) debate whereby further research is needed to make a well-considered decision.[310] We have also referred to some additional legal questions that should already be answered within the context of Belgian tort law if legal personality would be awarded to certain AI systems.[311] As a final observation in this regard, we would like to add that AI systems, although a potentially very disruptive technology, should remain an end and not a goal. This implies that we should not too eagerly devise legal mechanisms (e.g., legal personality) that may overly shield AI developers from their responsibility for the possible negative (and far-reaching) externalities their technology may cause for society.[312] At the same time, however, legal personality remains an available legal tool that may help achieve extra-legal policy goals.[313] In Belgium, this discussion has so far not given rise to much debate.[314]

---

308 J. Turner summarises a variety of these arguments in his chapter on legal personality for AI (J. Turner, *Robot Rules,* pp. 173–205 with additional sources and references). Also see: A. Bensoussan and J. Bensoussan, *Droit des robots* (Brussels: Larcier, 2015), pp. 41–49. Andrea Bertolini also addresses this topic in his extensive study for the European Parliament. The author brings a nuanced evaluation of a perennial hot topic. Although he recognises some flaws in such a concept, he asserts that legal personality may in certain cases be attributed on 'functional grounds' (A. Bertolini, Policy Department for Citizens' Rights and Constitutional Affairs, 'Artificial Intelligence and Civil Liability', July 2020, pp. 33–46); V. Schollaert, 'Rechtspersoonlijkheid voor robots: een Belgische afweging vanuit burgerrechtelijk en strafrechtelijk aansprakelijkheidsoogpunt', *Computerr. (Tijdschrift Computerrecht),* 2022, pp. 177–190.

309 A critical paper in this regard is the previously mentioned paper by Bryson and al. They argue that conferring legal personality on robots is 'morally unnecessary and legally troublesome' (see Bryson et al., 'Of, for and by the People: The legal Lacuna of Synthetic Persons', pp. 273–291).

310 The Expert Group opposes the idea of granting autonomous systems legal personality, arguing that natural persons or existing categories of legal persons should be able to be held liable, and where this is not the case, new laws directed at individuals are a better response than creating a new category of legal person (Expert Group on Liability and New Technologies, New Technologies Formation, 'Liability for Artificial Intelligence and Other Emerging Digital Technologies', pp. 37–39).

311 See the discussion on the subjective component of 'fault' *supra* part 2.

312 In this regard, we refer to: B.-J. Koops, M. Hildebrandt and D.-O. Jaquet-Chiffle, 'Bridging the Accountability Gap: Rights for New Entities in the Information Society?', *MJLST,* 2010, pp. 553–559. These authors discuss the (realistic) three-tiered progression in terms of liability/legal personality for AI. In a first phase, existing laws will be interpreted and extended, followed by a phase in which they envisage the creation of a limited form of legal personality for AI, in conjunction with strict liability regimes. The evolution may culminate in a final phase in which advanced AI could be attributed full legal personality, including 'posthuman rights'.

313 Turner, *Robot Rules*, p. 205.

314 For some exceptions: J.-B Hubin, 'La responsabilité du fait des robots – Le droit de la responsabilité à l'ère de la révolution numérique', p. 279; F. Hendrickx and S. Taes, 'Robots

7. CONCLUDING REMARKS

56. In this chapter, we examined the application of tort liability for damage caused by AI systems. The analysis shows that the application of tort liability regimes may prove to be challenging in an AI-context. Fault-based liability, for instance, in most cases requires a comparison between the intrinsically human standard of the general duty of care and the highly technical and opaque factual context of AI systems. Within the context of defective products, several pressing issues have been identified in EU initiatives. These initiatives show that things are moving ahead at the European level, especially since the adoption of the AI Liability Directive and the revised PLD. Nevertheless, some shortcomings remain and several key concepts may still require additional clarification in the future.

The core of Belgian tort liability is still formulated as rules based on six articles in the OBCC (Articles 1382–1386*bis*) and some additional legislation. However, these provisions are very vague, leaving most of the task of deciding the content of the rules to judges.[315] Arguably, judges will play an (even more) important role to determine the scope of application of these concepts within an AI-context. Policy-makers may also have to addresses several issues in the future, for instance regarding the further refinements of the burden of proof when damage is caused by AI systems. What seems to be missing at the moment are cross-national solutions or decisions and common answers/approaches to the many challenges for tort liability that have been identified (cf. policy prototyping). We would, however, like to stress that every change to the legal framework should be targeted and well-considered, especially as concepts introduced or relied upon in EU liability initiatives and frameworks will need to be interpreted and applied according to national law.[316] Minor changes to

---

en arbeid: vragen voor het arbeidsrecht 4.0', in P. Valcke, *Technologie en recht* (Antwerp: Intersentia, 2019), p. 79; N. Broeckx and C. Lemmens, 'Artificial or Human Intelligence: Who is to Blame?', *JBSR (Journal of the Belgian Society of Radiology)*, 2018, p. 1.

315 Kruithof, *Tort Law in Belgium*, p. 30.

316 Take the example of the regime that has been proposed by the European Parliament in its Resolution of 20 October 2020 with recommendations to the Commission on a civil liability regime for artificial intelligence. As already mentioned, it contains several provisions regarding the liability for operators of AI systems. Pursuant to Art. 4, the operator of a high-risk AI system will be strictly liable for any harm or damage that was caused by a physical or virtual activity, device or process driven by that system. Such operators will not be able to exonerate themselves from liability by arguing that they acted with *due diligence* or that the harm or damage was caused by an autonomous activity, device or process driven by their AI system. Operators will not be held liable if the harm or damage was caused by *force majeure*. A fault-based liability regime for operators of low-risk AI system is included in Art. 8. However, an operator will not be liable if he or she can prove that the harm or damage was caused without his or her fault, relying on either of the following grounds: (a) the AI system was activated without his or her knowledge while all *reasonable and necessary measures* to avoid such activation outside of the operator's control were taken, or (b) *due diligence* was observed by performing all the following actions: selecting a suitable AI-system for the right task and

the existing regulatory framework may in some cases already be sufficient to embrace the benefits of AI, while reducing and preventing the most significant uncertainties and problems under existing tort law.[317]

skills, putting the AI system duly into operation, monitoring the activities and maintaining the operational reliability by regularly installing all available updates. The operator will not be liable if the harm or damage was caused by *force majeure*. National judges will eventually have to interpret concepts such as due diligence, reasonable measures or force majeure, potentially resulting in diverging national case law. Likewise, the AI Liability Directive as well as the revised PLD rely on concepts that will need a national interpretation and application (e.g., 'duty of care', 'reasonably foreseeable', 'reasonably', 'substantial', 'relevant', 'proportionate', 'necessary').

317 De Bruyne and Tanghe, 'Liability for Damage Caused by Autonomous Vehicles: A Belgian Perspective', p. 367.

CHAPTER 15

INSURANCE UNDERWRITING ON THE BASIS OF TELEMATICS: SEGMENTATION AND PROFILING

Jeffrey Amankwah*

1. INTRODUCTION

1. AI and IoT have been rolled out with spectacular speed in an increasing number of areas. It is transforming the way in which society and the economy operate. As a late adopter, the insurance industry is also starting to embrace the digital transformation. Insurance companies are exchanging traditional business models for new paradigms such as 'Connected Insurance',[1] 'Usage-based Insurance' ('UBI'),[2] and 'Smart Underwriting'.[3] In the same vein, consumers of insurance products and services are seeking on-demand, personalised experiences. The types of risks being covered are also evolving, presenting fresh business opportunities for insurers to reimagine their business by building a digital-enabled core to deliver sustainable operational efficiencies. The insurance industry is adopting a wide variety of digital technologies to meet these ever-changing demands. These technologies will help insurers to reduce costs, optimise business processes, launch new innovative product offerings and

* Lawyer at the Bar of the Province of Limburg (Lydian) & research associate at the Institute for Insurance Law of KU Leuven.

1 'Connected insurance' refers to an evolution of the insurance business model based on the adoption of IoT technologies which allow the direct connection between all actors of the ecosystem: customers, insurers, and players from other industries.

2 'UBI' refers to all policies that make premiums dependent on the level of usage by the driver. This broad definition of UBI also includes self-reporting-based insurance. The premium is calculated based on the driver's reported mileage and no telematics device is placed in the car. For more information, consult Ptolemus consulting group, *Usage-based insurance. Global study. Free abstract*, 2016, p. 59.

3 'Smart Underwriting' entails two main components: (i) real-time risk assessment for automated underwriting and direct policy purchase; and (ii) machine learning to improve the traditional statistical models for claims forecasting.

improve customer experience. For all its potential benefits, it bears no doubt that this digital transformation gives rise to legal challenges.

2. This chapter will elaborate on one specific technological development within the insurance sector, namely the use of telematics in policy underwriting. Underwriting involves measuring risk exposure and determining the premium that needs to be charged to insure that risk. The main technological development which will be the subject of this chapter is UBI. In the context of this chapter, UBI is a type of motor vehicle liability insurance (further referred to as 'vehicle insurance') that tracks driving habits and driving behaviour. Basically, UBI means that a driver's behaviour and habits are monitored directly while the person drives, allowing insurers to align driving behaviour and habits more closely with premium rates. Oftentimes, UBI is powered by in-vehicle telecommunication devices (also referred to as 'telematics') which are either integrated by the vehicle manufacturers, self-installed using a plug-in device or available through mobile applications.

3. This chapter will introduce policy underwriting in Belgian insurance in general terms, with a specific focus on the underwriting process in vehicle insurance (part 2). Afterwards, the concept of UBI will be elaborated upon (part 3). What impact does UBI have on the underwriting process? Various possible variations of UBI will be discussed. It will also outline some of the expected benefits to insurers, consumers and society at large. Next, the (legal) challenges of using UBI in vehicle insurance will be addressed (part 4). These challenges are centred around the underwriting policy technique on the one hand and data protection concerns on the other hand. The first set of challenges are related to the principle of solidarity which is one of the cornerstones of insurance. It begs the question whether the use of UBI in vehicle insurance is reconcilable with the general principles of solidarity. Specific attention will also be paid to the rules governing vehicle insurance and antidiscrimination. The issues concerning data protection include issues such as the collection, use, processing and disclosure of personal data, as well as automated decision-making and profiling. Finally, this chapter will conclude with an overview (part 5).

2. POLICY UNDERWRITING IN VEHICLE INSURANCE

2.1. THE BASICS OF INSURANCE UNDERWRITING

4. In an economical context, insurance can be considered as a means of protection from financial loss by spreading the risks of individuals over groups of people.[4] In other words, insurance is based on the association of a certain number of people who are subject to the same risk, with the aim of sharing the burden of claims which affect only a few members of the group among all of them.[5] This group of people is then further divided into distinct risk groups based on certain selection criteria (cf. *infra*), with the aim of arriving at a correct risk assessment and premium calculation. This principle is also called 'segmentation',[6] which boils down to the following: the insurer charges people with a higher risk a higher premium, insures them under stricter conditions or refuses to grant them any coverage. On the other hand, people with a low risk are charged a lower premium or are excluded from fewer types of damage or situations. Accordingly, premiums paid by policyholders should match as closely as possible their risk exposure (i.e., their expected losses).[7]

5. From a legal point of view, an insurance contract is a contract under which one party, the insurer, undertakes, against payment of a fixed or variable premium, vis-à-vis another party, the policyholder, to provide a performance stipulated in the contract when an uncertain event occurs where, as the case may be, the insured or the beneficiary has an interest in such event not occurring.[8] In any case, an insurance coverage requires an uncertain event, or risk. The term 'risk' means an uncertain, future and possible event, of which the realisation is beyond the control of the policyholder, insured or beneficiary.

6. When underwriting an insurance policy, the insurer will want to assess the risk as accurately as possible. The insurer wants to estimate the chance of an uncertain and accidental event (in particular: damage as a result of an accident) and the possible financial loss. In other words, an insurer wants to determine the probability and extent of a claim as accurately as possible. The probability of a claim refers to the ratio between the number of times that an event occurs and the possible number of times that event actually occurs.[9] Based on the doctrine

---

4 L. Schuermans and C. Van Schoubroeck, *Grondslagen van het Belgisch Verzekeringsrecht* (Antwerp: Intersentia, 2015), p. 5; Insurance Europe, *How insurance works*, 2012, p. 5.

5 M. Fontaine, *Verzekeringsrecht* (Brussels: Larcier, 2017), p. 36; Schuermans and Van Schoubroeck, *Grondslagen van het Belgisch Verzekeringsrecht*, p. 11; T. Vansweevelt and B. Weyts (eds), *Handboek Verzekeringsrecht* (Antwerp: Intersentia, 2016), p. 41.

6 H. Cousy, 'Concurrence et solidarité – paradoxe du temps moderne illustré à partir du droit des assurances', in X (ed.), *Liber Amicorum per Francesco D. Busnelli, Il Diritto Civile Tra Principi E Regole* (Milan: Giuffrè Editore, 2008), no. 2.

7 A. Heras, P.-C. Pradier and D. Teira, 'What was fair in actuarial fairness?', *History of Human Sciences*, 2019, p. 2; X. Landes, 'How fair is actuarial fairness?', *Journal of business ethics*, 2015, vol. 128, p. 521; C. Paris, *Les dérives de la segmentation en assurance*, Les Dossiers du Journal des Tribunaux – 49 (Brussels: De Boeck & Larcier, 2005), p. 20; W. Bossert and M. Fleurbaey, 'Equitable insurance premium schemes', *Social Choice and Welfare*, 2002, vol. 19, p. 114.

8 Article 5, 14° Wet van 4 april 2014 betreffende de verzekeringen, *BS* 30 april 2014 ('Insurance Act').

9 Schuermans and Van Schoubroeck, *Grondslagen van het Belgisch Verzekeringsrecht*, p. 20.

of statistics, insurers can calculate the frequency and average cost of claims.[10] In addition, the insurer will want to neutralise a bad risk by a good risk.[11] In order to distinguish the good risks from the bad risks, the insurer uses several criteria. These criteria can differ according to the risk to be insured. Based on that information, the insurer tries to implement an appropriate segmentation policy and thus, among other things, avoid the risk of anti-selection (or adverse selection) as much as possible.[12] Anti-selection refers to the phenomenon that the tendency to insure is greatest for those who realise that they run a higher than average risk. Without segmentation, the group of good risks would in principle be overcharged for underinsurance, and the group of bad risks would be undercharged for overinsurance. This could, of course, have far-reaching consequences for the solvency and stability of the insurer.[13]

2.2. VEHICLE INSURANCE UNDERWRITING

7. Vehicle insurance in the context of this chapter refers to the motor vehicle liability insurance. Since 1956, Belgian legislation has stipulated that the owner of any motor vehicle that enters public roads and areas accessible to the public must ensure that the civil liability of that vehicle is insured.[14] In general, vehicle insurance must cover the compensation of injured parties in the event of civil liability of the owner, of every holder and of every driver of the insured motor vehicle, as well as the passengers of said vehicle. Therefore, the owner of a motor vehicle must apply for an insurance coverage. After receiving the application, the insurer evaluates the risk and determines whether to insure the owner of the vehicle.

8. In order to apply for an insurance coverage, the potential policyholder has to complete an insurance proposal. The insurance proposal is a form issued by the insurer to be completed by the policyholder with the aim of informing the insurer about the nature of the transaction and about the facts and circumstances on which the insurer relies for the purpose of assessing the risk.[15]

---

10 Fontaine, *Verzekeringsrecht*, p. 36.

11 Landes, 'How fair is actuarial fairness?', pp. 522–523.

12 Vansweevelt and Weyts (eds), *Handboek Verzekeringsrecht*, p. 47; C. Devoet, *Les assurances de personnes* (Limal: Anthemis, 2011), p. 58.

13 Y. Thiery, *Discriminatie en verzekering* (Antwerp: Intersentia, 2011), p. 213.

14 The compulsory motor vehicle liability insurance is regulated by the Wet van 21 november 1989 betreffende de verplichte aansprakelijkheidsverzekering inzake motorrijtuigen, *BS* 8 December 1989. This law replaced the Wet van 1 juli 1956 betreffende de verplichte aansprakelijkheidsverzekering inzake motorrijtuigen, *BS* 15 juli 1956.

15 Article 55, 6° Wet van 4 april 2014 betreffende de verzekeringen, *BS* 30 april 2014.

Regarding vehicle insurance specifically, an insurer will request information on elements such as:[16]

- accident history: if the driver has already been held responsible for traffic accidents in the past, the insurer will estimate the risk higher.
- age: younger drivers represent a higher risk for the insurer. Statistically, they have the highest risk of a traffic accident. Older drivers may also pose a higher risk.
- place of residence: drivers who live in areas where statistically more accidents occur (e.g., busy cities) pose a higher risk.
- engine power of the motor vehicle: a motor vehicle with a higher engine power means a higher risk.
- use of the motor vehicle: an insurer considers whether the driver uses the vehicle privately and/or professionally. The use of the vehicle for private and professional purposes means a higher risk.

Once the insurer has collected and analysed the applicant's information, the application is either approved or denied. If approved, the insurer classifies the risk of the application by assigning a score to said risk and determines the corresponding premium. However, it is important to note that the practice of risk assessment and the freedom of segmentation of insurers have come under increasing pressure in recent years due to the Belgian and European legislation on discrimination and the segmentation rules for consumer contracts (cf. *infra*).[17] In addition, with respect to vehicle insurance, these principles are further limited by the intervention of the '*Tariferingsbureau*'. The *Tariferingsbureau* determines the premium and the conditions under which an insurer may be obliged to insure a person to whom coverage has been refused by at least three insurers (cf. *infra*).[18]

9. As mentioned previously, the insurer groups potential policyholders in pools with similar risk profiles (i.e., similar probabilities of making a claim), and premiums are based on the average risk across the pool. This has made it possible to set an adequate premium for each risk. It is important to note that the

---

16 R. Thys, 'Segmentatie in de verzekering B.A. motorrijtuigen', *T.Verz.*, 2004 (dossier nr. 10), pp. 93–111; G. Werner, C. Modlin and W. Towers, 'Basic ratemaking', *Casualty Actuarial Society*, 2016, pp. 15–17; T. Gage, R. Bishop and J. Morris, 'The increasing importance of vehicle-based risk assessment for the vehicle insurance industry', *Minnesota Journal of Law, Science and Technology*, 2015, p. 775; A. Conrad, F.J. Mostert and J.M. Mostert, 'The underwriting process of motor vehicle insurance', *Corporate ownership & control*, 2009, pp. 239–241; G.B. Hey and J.D. Hey, 'Motor insurance in the United Kingdom: a description and an appraisal', *The Geneva Papers on Risk and Insurance*, 1987, pp. 227–228.

17 Articles 42–46 Insurance Act.

18 Articles 9*bis* – 9*quinquies* Wet van 21 november 1989 betreffende de verplichte aansprakelijkheidsverzekering inzake motorrijtuigen (WAM-wet).

pooling of risk profiles comes at a certain cost, which the insurer will balance against the potential profits. Therefore, an individualised risk assessment aimed at creating more specific pools of risk profiles is only beneficial when the cost of individualisation does not exceed the benefit that the insurer derives from pooling the risks. In some cases, certain criteria on which an insurer relies to pool certain risks are easily attainable. This is especially the case with respect to vehicle insurance. An insurer can gather vital information solely based on a completed application form.[19] Traditionally, when assessing the risk and calculating the premium, insurers could only rely on previous statistical models of premium calculation in which only the characteristics of the vehicle and the policyholder (as a driver) were considered. Gathering more information would be very costly. However, the emergence of AI and IoT has created a paradigm shift. The development of new digital technologies allows insurers to carry out more accurate risk assessments. Specifically, due to the increased availability of data, today's technologies allow insurers to carry out more accurate risk assessments, meaning insurance products can be better tailored to each consumer's risks and needs.[20] As such, insurers are now able to perform individualised risk assessments (also referred to as 'refined classification').

3. USAGE-BASED INSURANCE: PARADIGM SHIFT

10. The automotive vehicles we drive presently already hold a wealth of information because of the use of 'telematics'.[21] 'Telematics'[22] refers to the integrated use of telecommunication and information technology in vehicles.[23] The use of telematics allows the insurer to collect information about the driven distance, the location of use of the vehicle and the driving behaviour of the policyholder.[24] Insurers can collect this data by either installing a device in the vehicle or through systems already fitted within the vehicle by the manufacturer. The technology is increasingly being used to provide vehicle insurance. The use of telematics allows the insurer to base the premium on a new set of data (referred

19 K.S. Abraham, 'Efficiency and fairness in insurance risk classification', *Virginia Law Review*, 1985, vol. 71, p. 428.

20 Insurance Europe, *Q&A on the use of big data in insurance*, January 2019, p. 1.

21 K. Noussia, 'Autonomous vehicles: legal considerations and dilemmas', in P. Marano and K. Noussia (eds.) *InsurTech: a legal and regulatory view* (Springer, 2020), p. 264.

22 The term 'telematics' stems from the merged parts of the French words TÉLÉcommunications (telecommunication) and inforMATIQUE (Informatics).

23 Ptolemus consulting group, Usage-based insurance, p. 67.

24 For more information concerning the use of telematics in auto insurance, consult J. Amankwah, 'Nieuwe technologische ontwikkelingen in verzekeringen' in C. Van Schoubroeck and I. Samoy (eds.) *Themis 106 – Aansprakelijkheids- en verzekeringsrecht*, (Bruges: Die Keure, 2018), pp. 77–106; C. Van Schoubroeck and L. Pogarcic Matija, 'Telematics insurance: legal concerns and challenges in the EU insurance market', SSRN, 2017, 54 p.

to as IoT data), namely the actual driving habits and behaviour of the consumer (e.g., distance travelled, speeds used, method of braking and cornering, road used, time of day, etc.). The introduction of telematics technology in the context of vehicle insurance is commonly referred to as insurance telematics or UBI (the concepts of telematics and UBI will be used interchangeably in the context of this chapter). This information can be complemented with external data such as the speed limit and type of street in order to assess whether the consumer respects the driving and traffic rules.[25] Naturally, the use of these new technologies enables the development of new rating factors, leading to smaller risk pools and a larger number of them. The insurer can thus consider dynamic parameters in order to calculate an individualised premium. It is important to note that, at this point in time, insurers do not solely rely on the use of this new set of data. In reality, insurers combine the traditional underwriting process with the additional data provided through telematics.

11. The use of telematics has been on the rise in recent years. The concept of underwriting in vehicle insurance assisted by telematics emerged in the United States of America ('US') in 1997/98.[26] In Europe, telematics-based insurance was first offered by the British insurer Aviva in 2002.[27] The Italian insurance market has also committed to the use of telematics in car insurance. In order to combat insurance fraud, telematics products have been offered on the Italian market since 2002.[28] In fact, the Italian Monti Decree obligates insurers to offer insurance based on telematics in addition to traditional insurance products.[29] In addition, Italian insurers have to offer a lower premium for these insurance products.[30] The Belgian insurance market also features insurance schemes based on telematics. Currently, only a small number of insurers offer vehicle insurance (partly) based on telematics. For instance, in 2016 AXA launched *DriveXperience* geared towards young drivers.[31] Other insurers offering such telematics products

25 EIOPA, *Big data analytics in motor and health insurance: a thematic review*, 2019, p. 12.

26 C.K. Fan and W. Wang, 'A Comparison of Underwriting Decision Making Between Telematics-Enabled UBI and Traditional Auto Insurance', *Advances in Management & Applied Economics*, 2017, vol. 7, no. 1, p. 17; P. Desyllas and M. Sako, 'Profiting from business model innovation: Evidence from Pay-As-You-Drive auto insurance', *Research Policy*, 2013, vol. 42, p. 102.

27 Desyllas and Sako, 'Profiting from business model innovation', p. 111.

28 R. Frisoni, F. Dioniri, L. Casullo, C. Vollath, M. Tavani, L. Devenish, D. Ranghetti and F. Spano, *Technical Development And Implementation Of Event Data Recording In The Road Safety Policy*, Brussels, European Parliament, 2014, p. 39.

29 Decreto-Legge 24 gennaio 2012, n. 1, Disposizioni urgenti per la concorrenza, lo sviluppo delle infrastrutture e la competitivita. (12G0009).

30 Frisoni, Dioniri, Casullo, Vollath, Tavani, Devenish, Ranghetti and Spano, *Technical Development And Implementation Of Event Data Recording In The Road Safety Policy*, p. 39.

31 AXA driveXperience is a formula that works with a smartphone application (AXA Drive 2) and a small device that you install in the insured vehicle car (the AXA drive key). The system continuously evaluates the driving style based on the following four criteria: (i) acceleration; (ii) braking; (iii) cornering and (iv) driving speed. After each drive, the driver/policyholder

on the Belgian insurance market are P&V and Vivium. All these products target young or inexperienced drivers.

12. While the use of telematics is commonly associated with the underwriting process, it is important to highlight that telematics are not only used for assessing risk and pricing insurance policies. Telematic devices allow insurers to offer a wide range of services to consumers which can broadly be classified between assistance services and risk prevention and mitigation services.[32] In addition, the use of telematics can also enhance fraud prevention systems.[33] This will benefit both consumers and insurers alike, as an increased fraud detection rate will decrease unjustified pay outs and individual premiums.[34] However, these additional applications of telematics fall outside the scope of this chapter.

3.1. DIFFERENT TYPES OF TELEMATICS/UBI SCHEMES

13. Insurers can offer insurance coverages based on different types of telematics or UBI schemes. Specifically geared towards the underwriting process, the most commonly used telematics schemes in vehicle insurance are: (i) Pay as you drive ('PAYD') and (ii) Pay how you drive ('PHYD'). The above methods of premium setting differ from each other because of the dynamic data used to determine the premium.[35] A distinction is made between the driving habits of the policyholder on the one hand (targeted by PAYD insurance) and the driving behaviour of the policyholder on the other hand (targeted by PHYD insurance).[36] Generally, the main driving indicators mostly

---

will receive a score and an overview of the strengths and weaknesses of his or her driving style. Each time the overall score is calculated, the policyholder will receive a 20 to 50% discount on the premium.

32 EIOPA, *Big data analytics in motor and health insurance: a thematic review*, 2019, p. 20.

33 Examples of insurance fraud are: (i) providing untruthful or incomplete information in applications for insurance or answers on an insurance proposal form; (ii) submitting a claim for a loss based on misleading or untruthful circumstances, including deliberate causing of loss and exaggerating a genuine claim; and (iii) otherwise being misleading or untruthful in dealings with an insurer with the intention of gaining a benefit under the insurance contract. For more information, consult S. Viaene and G. Dedene, "Insurance Fraud: Issues and Challenges", *The Geneva papers on Risk and Insurance*, 2014, vol. 29, no. 2, pp. 313–333.

34 Insurance Europe, *Q&A on the use of big data in insurance*, January 2019, p. 2.

35 S. Husnjak, D. Perakovic, I. Forenbacher and M. Mumdziev, 'Telematics Systems in Usage Based Motor Insurance', *Procedia Engineering*, 2015, vol. 100, p. 816; P. Handel, I. Skog, J. Wahlstrom, F. Bonawiede, R. Welch, J. Ohlsson and M. Ohlsson, 'Insurance Telematics: Opportunities and Challenges with the Smartphone Solution', *IEEE Intelligent Transportation Systems Magazine*, 2014, vol. 6, p. 57.

36 Van Schoubroeck and Pogarcic Matija, 'Telematics insurance', pp. 6–7; Husnjak, Perakovic, Forenbacher and Mumdziev, 'Telematics Systems in Usage Based Motor Insurance', p. 817; M. Azzopardi and D. Cortis, 'Implementing Automotive Telematics for Insurance Covers of Fleets', *J.Technol.Manag.Innov.*, 2013, vol. 8, Issue 4, p. 61; Desyllas and Sako, 'Profiting from business model innovation', p. 101; J. Ferreira and E. Minikel, 'Measuring Per Mile Risk for

used in UBI for calculating the driving risk of an individual are shown in the following table:[37]

PAYD	PHYD
Total distance driven by the user (the higher the mileage the higher the risk)	Speeding expressed either as a percentage of kilometres/time driving over the speed limit or a percentage of speeding
Road network type (increased accident frequency in the cities, increased accident severity outside)	Harsh braking/acceleration
Risky hours driving (increased accident frequency during a particular hour's range).	Driver's accident history (severity of accidents, the circumstances of the accident)
Trip frequency (a driver is more likely to cause an accident during an infrequent trip)	Cornering
Vehicle type	Swerving

14. As already mentioned, manufacturers are increasingly fitting vehicles with systems which record the driving habits and behaviour.[38] If such systems are not fitted by default, a device can be installed or retrofitted in the vehicle. Insurers can use different devices to collect the required data. The most common devices are:[39] (i) the black box (also known as the Event Data Recorder); (ii) integrated equipment; (iii) a smartphone; (iv) drive key; and (v) a dongle. In Europe, insurers often opt for the so-called black box.[40] In Belgium, insurers use a mix of the black box, smartphone and a dongle. The insurer can have these devices (temporarily) installed in the policyholder's vehicle. Although the costs of the black box and its installation can be high, it provides the insurer with very detailed information about the driving behaviour of the policyholder. Alternatively, insurers can rely on the use of smartphones to register the driving behaviour of the policyholder.[41] The use of smartphones has the advantage that the insurer or the policyholder do not incur additional costs. Installing a simple app allows the insurer to collect the required information. However, it could be argued that the data collected by a smartphone is less reliable than that of a black

Pay-As-You-Drive Automobile Insurance', *Transportation Research Record,* 2012, vol. 2297, p. 97.

37 Table provided by D. Tselentis, G. Yannis and E. Vlahogianni, 'Innovative insurance schemes: pay as/how you drive', *Transportation Research Procedia,* 2016, vol. 14, p. 365.

38 Cognizant, *The New Auto Insurance Ecosystem: Telematics, Mobility and the Connected Car,* 2012, p. 3.

39 Ptolemus consulting group, *Usage-based insurance*, p. 114; Husnjak, Perakovic, Forenbacher and Mumdziev, 'Telematics Systems in Usage Based Motor Insurance', p. 820.

40 F. L. Filipova-Neumann and P. Welzel, 'Reducing asymmetric information in insurance market; Cars with black boxes', *Telematics and Informatics,* 2010, vol. 27, p. 394–403.

41 Azzopardi and Cortis, 'Implementing Automotive Telematics for Insurance Covers of Fleets', p. 61.

box.[42] Finally, several insurers use the so-called dongle. This small and simple device is provided by the insurer and installed in the vehicle by the policyholder. The device remains installed in the vehicle for a limited period of time. It is a reliable device with a relatively limited cost for the insurer.[43]

3.2. POTENTIAL BENEFITS OF TELEMATICS/UBI BASED INSURANCE

15. Telematics or UBI based insurance has the potential to provide a number of benefits to the insurer, policyholder and society as a whole. Several studies point to the commercial benefits to insurers from better alignment of insurance with actual risk and improved customer segmentation.[44] However, it is important to note that there are limits to the ability of any insurance system to predict future risk, including usage-based insurance. Therefore, some lower-risk drivers will still subsidise some higher-risk drivers, to some extent (cf. *infra*). In any case, telematics enable insurers to better assess the risk, offer an individualised premium, attract new (mainly young) customers, counter adverse selection[45] and moral hazard[46] and even possibly influence the driving behaviour of the policyholder.[47] As already mentioned, the biggest advantage that the use

---

42 J. Paefgen, F. Kehr, Y. ZhaI and F. Michahelles, 'Driving behavior Analysis with Smartphones: Insights from a Controlled Field Study', *MUM*, 2012, p. 7.

43 Ptolemus consulting group, *Usage-based insurance. Global study. Free abstract*, 2016, p. 114.

44 K. Antonio, R. Verbelen and G. Claeskens, 'Unraveling the predictive power of telematics data in car insurance pricing', https://lirias.kuleuven.be/bitstream/123456789/552745/3/KBI_1624.pdf, 2017, pp. 29–30; National association of insurance commissioners and the center for insurance policy research, *Usage-based Insurance and Vehicle Telematics: Insurance Market and Regulatory Implications*, 2015, p. 5; Cognizant, *The New Auto Insurance Ecosystem*, p. 3.

45 The risk of adverse selection, as it is applied in the insurance market, comes down to the fact that persons who perceive their risk of incurring a claim as high, will be willing to purchase more extensive insurance cover, or are willing to pay a higher premium than people who perceive their risk to be lower. For more information, consult M. Rotschild and J. Stiglitz, 'Equilibrium in competitive insurance markets: an essay on the economics of imperfect information', *The Quarterly of Economics*, 1976, p. 629.

46 Moral hazard refers to the situation in which a person with insurance takes greater risks than they normally would without insurance. For more information, consult S. Shavell, 'On moral Hazard and insurance', *The quarterly Journal of Economics*, 1979, p. 541.

47 Antonio, Verbelen and Claeskens, 'Unraveling the predictive power of telematics data in car insurance pricing', pp. 29–30; J. Lemaire, S. Park and K. Wang, 'The Use of Annual Millage as a Rating Variable', *ASTIN Bulletin*, 2016, vol. 46, p. 40; National association of insurance commissioners and the center for insurance policy research, *Usage-based Insurance and Vehicle Telematics*, p. 5; J. Paefgen, T. Staake and F. Thiesse, 'Evaluation and aggregation of pay-as-you-drive insurance rate factors: A classification analysis approach', *Decision Support Systems*, 2013, vol. 56, p. 200; Cognizant, *The New Auto Insurance Ecosystem*, p. 3; J. Ferreira Jr. and E. Minikel, 'Pay as you drive auto insurance in Massachusetts, A risk assessment and report on consumer, industry and environmental benefits', *Conservation Law Foundation & Environmental Insurance Agency*, 2010, p. 1.

of telematics offers the insurer is the individualised risk assessment and the premium setting. In turn, this may lead to new customers who assume that they can obtain a better premium based on telematics. Those new customers, who regard themselves as better drivers, often represent a better risk. Furthermore, existing customers could be motivated to adapt their driving behaviour in order to obtain a better premium. By attracting better consumers, the insurer will probably have to pay out fewer claims.[48]

16. Additionally, the policyholder potentially benefits from the use of telematics-based insurance. The benefits on the part of the policyholder are potential cost-savings and enabling young drivers access to affordable insurance. For instance, better drivers could benefit from a lower and individualised premium.[49] The cheaper premium or reduction in costs for the policyholder will often be the result of participation discounts, better driving behaviour and/or a reduction in the number of kilometres driven. In addition, policyholders will become more aware of their driving behaviour. They could improve their driving behaviour in order to obtain the lowest possible premium.[50] Finally, technology that powers UBI enables other vehicle-to-infrastructure solutions including drive-through payments, emergency road assistance, tracing the vehicle whereabouts following an accident, breakdown or theft.

17. Society may also benefit from the use of telematics-based insurance. The benefits can relate to the environment (reduction of CO_2 emissions, reduced fuel consumption, reduction of traffic), safer roads and a reduction of the number of uninsured vehicles.[51] This is because the number of kilometres driven will be considered in the premium calculation. In order to obtain a lower premium, policyholders will try to reduce the number of kilometres driven. If a significant number of policyholders take out telematics-based vehicle insurance, this can lead to a significant reduction in the use of vehicles all around. If the vehicle is used less frequently and for shorter distances, this will have a significant societal impact. Fewer vehicles on the road leads to better road safety and less pollution.[52] Finally, as mentioned previously, the use of telematics could provide more affordable vehicle insurance to people who initially could not obtain an

---

48 Deloitte, *Overcoming speed bumps on the road to telematics, Challenges and opportunities facing auto insurers with and without usage-based programs*, 2013, p. 22.

49 Antonio, Verbelen and Claeskens, 'Unraveling the predictive power of telematics data in car insurance pricing', p. 30.

50 J.W. Bolderdijk, J. Knockaert, E.M. Steg and E.T. Verhoef, 'Effects of Pay-As-You-Drive vehicle insurance on young drivers' speed choice: Results of a Dutch field experiment', *Accident Analysis and Prevention*, 2011, vol. 43, pp. 1181–1186.

51 T. Litman, 'Distance-Based Vehicle Insurance Feasibility, Costs and Benefits, Comprehensive Technical Report', *Victoria Transport Policy Institute,* 2011, p. 83.

52 National association of insurance commissioners and the center for insurance policy research, *Usage-based Insurance and Vehicle Telematics*, p. 46.

affordable premium. As a result, the risk of uninsured vehicles driving on the roads could decrease.[53]

4. LEGAL CHALLENGES

18. It is clear that the use of AI and the IoT in the guise of UBI comes with many potential benefits. However, the development of these new technologies with respect to policy underwriting in vehicle insurance faces some (legal) challenges. There are a few concerns which will considered in this part. These concerns are centred around the possibility of an individualised risk assessment by the insurer. First, a more or fully individualised risk assessment (refined classification) and premium setting by an insurer could be seen as an extensive form of segmentation. It begs the question whether this is technically possible or socially desirable as it could potentially lead to social exclusion of drivers who represent a bad risk when they face uninsurability and discrimination or unaffordability of the premium.[54] In turn, as more data on individual drivers' habits and behaviour are available to insurers, concerns about profiling and potential legal discrimination arise. Telematics-based insurance is based on the use of personal data concerning the driving habits and behaviour of the policyholder. This could give rise to issues concerning privacy and personal data protection infringements, which are potential roadblocks to wide acceptance of telematics insurance.[55] Although privacy and data protection are not the main topic of this chapter, it is imperative to outline some important legal challenges which the insurance sector faces in this respect.[56]

4.1. REFINED CLASSIFICATION: LEGAL AND ECONOMIC CONSIDERATIONS

4.1.1. Principle of Mutualisation and Solidarity

19. In general, insurers enjoy complete freedom in selecting and covering risks.[57] Moreover, insurers also enjoy a large degree of freedom in determining an underwriting (and risk selection) policy. This freedom is based on the principle that it is incumbent on the policyholder to communicate accurately, at the time of the conclusion of the contract, any circumstances known to him which he must reasonably consider as likely to affect the insurer's assessment

---

53 Lemaire, Park and Wang, 'The Use of Annual Millage as a Rating Variable', p. 42.
54 Schuermans and Van Schoubroeck, *Grondslagen van het Belgisch Verzekeringsrecht*, p. 32.
55 Cognizant, *The New Auto Insurance Ecosystem*, p. 9.
56 For more information concerning the legal challenges with respect to privacy, data protection and the rise of robots, AI and IoT, consult Chapter 8.
57 Paris, *Les dérives de la segmentation en assurance*, nos. 37 and following.

of the risk.[58] As mentioned previously, the principle of segmentation enables the insurer to decide whether to insure certain risks and, if so, at what price and under what conditions. In order to develop an *a priori* segmentation, it is necessary to verify whether certain criteria or variables influence the degree of risk of the policyholders. Traditionally for this purpose, the statistical information of an insurance portfolio is used and only the criteria for which data are available per policyholder can be considered.[59] When selecting criteria for *a priori* segmentation, the available criteria should not be considered separately, but in combination with each other. Solely relying on the traditional method of segmentation, it would be practically impossible to select risks on an individual level as this would require that the influence of each of the risk factors can unequivocally be identified. Under the traditional method of risk selection, this is practically impossible for the following reasons, among others:[60] (i) the large number of risk factors and the fact that not even all of them are known; (ii) the fact that many factors are not observable or not objectively measurable; (iii) the dependency that exists between different risk factors; (iv) the changes in risk factors over the duration of the insurance period; and (v) the fact that, for legal or social reasons, some risk factors may not be used as a segmentation criterion.

20. By using the traditional method, it is impossible to take all risk factors into account when determining the premium. This means that in any case there will still be individual differences between the premium a policyholder has to pay and the expected damage he or she will cause. As mentioned previously, an insurer strives to group policyholders with the same risk profile (with a comparable loss probability and loss extent). The ideal situation would be that the obligations of the totality of small contributions of a group are statistically fully compensated for by the totality of the contributions made by this group. Consequently, solidarity (or mutualisation) is intrinsic to the classification of insurance risks.[61] All the policyholders are involved in paying for the costs of future damage without knowing who the particular insured individual is who suffers from the consequences of the accident. This type of genuine insurance solidarity is called 'pure chance solidarity'.[62] Groups that, despite the insurer's efforts, do not consist of members with a comparable risk profile, give rise to the phenomenon of 'subsidising solidarity'.[63] In this situation, low risks are unfairly forced to subsidise high risks. This situation is problematic because if a low risk policyholder is set a higher premium than the premium due for the risk he

58 Article 58 W. Verz.

59 Thys, 'Segmentatie in de verzekering B.A. motorrijtuigen', p. 97.

60 Commissie voor Verzekeringen, *Rapport van de werkgroep segmentering*, Brussels, 1995, p. 7.

61 Y. Thierry and C. Van Schoubroeck, 'Fairness and equality in insurance classification', *The Geneva Papers*, 2006, vol. 31, p. 195.

62 H. Cousy, 'Over ethiek en verzekeringen: ter oriëntatie', in H. Cousy, H. Claassens and C. Van Schoubroeck (eds.) *Competitiviteit, ethiek en verzekering* (Antwerp: Maklu, 1998), p. 24.

63 C. Paris, 'Segmentation et selection des risques', *T. Verz.*, 2005, p. 71.

(assumes to) represent, he would leave the group.[64] This problem is also referred to as 'subsidy-aversion'.

4.1.2. *Refined Classification and Reducing Subsidising Solidarity: Identifying the Issues and Limits*

21. Based on the subsidy-aversion argument, insurers aim to decrease subsidising solidarity as much as possible through increasing classification and extensive segmentation. The pursuit of maximum homogeneity within the risk group or the creation of the largest possible number of groups within which people with the same risk are united could lead to full social benefit.[65] UBI would allow the insurer to calculate the premium at a more individual level and thus create more similar risk (homogenous) groups (cf. *supra*). Several factors that traditionally hampered individual risk assessment are remedied by the use of new technologies. Because of telematics devices, insurers can gather much more information on more risk factors. As such, the risk factors on which a group division is to be based are easily observable. In such a case, extensive classification is perceived as efficient.[66] In a PAYD or PHYD insurance scheme, the use of AI and IoT guarantees that the risk factors used are first and foremost stable, reliable and easy to process administratively. However, it begs the question whether such a form of increasing classification is desirable or feasible from a legal or societal point of view.[67]

A. Legal Safeguards Regarding Segmentation in Belgium

22. While insurers are free to determine their underwriting policy, they must abide by the legal rules concerning pricing, conditions and segmentation enshrined in the Insurance Act. It is important to note that the Insurance Act does not prohibit segmentation, but it aims to safeguard the protection of the policyholder, the insured and/or the beneficiary against arbitrary differentiation.[68] Any segmentation in terms of acceptance, pricing and/or coverage must be objectively justified by a legitimate aim and the means of

---

64 Thierry and Van Schoubroeck, 'Fairness and equality in insurance classification', p. 196.

65 K.J. Arrow, 'Uncertainty and the welfare economics of medical care', *American Economics Review*, 1963, pp. 963–964.

66 K.J. Crocker and A. Snow, 'The efficiency effects of categorical discrimination in the insurance industry', *Journal of Political Economy*, 1986, vol. 2, pp. 327–330.

67 There are several interest groups which have launched policy proposals suggesting to limit the individualization of insurance, for instance by limiting the allowed ratio between the highest and lowest premiums. For more information, consult The Geneva Association, *Promoting responsible artificial intelligence in insurance*, 2020, p. 13; BEUC, *The use of big data and artificial intelligence in insurance*, 2020, p. 16.

68 *Parl.St.* Kamer, Doc. 53, no. 3361/1, p. 31.

achieving that aim must be appropriate and necessary.[69] By a decree deliberated upon in the Council of Ministers, the use of certain criteria can be imposed or prohibited. By imposing or prohibiting certain criteria, for example for reasons of general interest, it is possible to intervene in the insurers' segmentation policy, even if this segmentation policy is based on an objective justification. In addition, insurers are legally obligated to take certain measures with respect to pricing and segmentation.[70] These measures are of general interest. For this reason, they apply to any insurer operating in Belgium, regardless of its origin or status. Otherwise, the application of the measures is limited to those contracts where the risk or commitment is in Belgium. A first measure is that the insurer must publish the segmentation criteria it uses for each type of insurance contract on its website. The insurer must also provide guidance on the division and the segmentation criteria used. In addition, the insurer must mention the segmentation criteria in the insurance proposal. The same applies in the event of amendment of the insurance contract because of a changed risk or in the event of cancellation. In explaining the segmentation criteria used, the insurer makes a distinction between: (i) the criteria used to determine the conditions that will apply at the inception of the contract; and (ii) the criteria that may have an impact on the contract terms in the future. The explanation of criteria which may have an impact on the terms of contracts in the future is intended to provide additional protection for the policyholder.[71] In the case of refusal of insurance coverage, the insurer is obligated to explicitly communicate that decision to the policyholder in writing, stating the reasons, unless this disclosure could cause serious damage to the insurer's business or violate a legal obligation of confidentiality.

23. Failure to comply with the legal obligations regarding segmentation enacted in the Insurance Act, could result in a request from the Financial Services and Markets Authority (FSMA) for withdrawal or conversion of documents of a contractual or publicity nature which it finds contrary to the provisions laid down by or pursuant to the Insurance Act.[72] In addition, the FSMA may impose an administrative fine on an insurer, should it ascertain a violation of the legal obligations regarding segmentation.[73]

69 This legal obligation only applies to the insurance coverages listed in Article 43 of the Insurance Act, which are the following: (i) Compulsory motor vehicle liability insurance (ii) The insurance against fire and other dangers with regard to dwellings which are a simple risk according to Article 5 of the Royal Decree of 31 December 1992 implementing the law of 25 June 1992 on land insurance; (iii) The insurance to cover civil liability outside the scope of the contract with regard to private life; (iv) The legal expenses insurance; and (v) Individual life insurance.

70 These measures are listed in the Articles 45–46 Insurance Act.

71 *Parl.St.* Kamer, Doc. 53, no. 3361/1, p. 33.

72 Article 306 Insurance Act.

73 Article 319 Insurance Act.

B. Pricing Competition

24. Increasing segmentation has the potential to cause a price competition where the insurers with a smaller market share are eliminated and the remaining insurers face smaller profits or larger losses.[74] The same holds true for insurers which are reluctant or unable to adopt a UBI pricing scheme. The price competition is likely to be the result of insurers following each other in their segmentation policy. If a given insurance company does not use a significant segmentation criterion while other companies do, then in an efficient market, only the risks that score worse on that criterion will go to the first company, while the better risks will go to the insurer that adopts an extensive segmentation method. In other words, an insurer offering UBI is likely to attract the better drivers, who represent the better risks. Insurers that are unable or unwilling to jump on the UBI bandwagon, are likely to attract bad drivers, who represent the worse risks. Insurers with less refined classification are therefore faced with an increasing degree of adverse selection.

C. Uninsurability

25. With refined classification, an increasing number of worse risks will no longer be able to obtain insurance cover or will only be able to obtain insurance cover at very high – and therefore unaffordable – premiums.[75] This could leave certain individuals 'uninsurable' and lead to new forms of financial exclusion.[76] As mentioned previously, UBI premium schemes are likely to attract good drivers. An increasing segmentation will lead to very high premiums for bad drivers. As a result, a refined classification may make vehicle insurance sufficiently expensive that candidate-policyholders do not procure it.[77] One potential effect might be that people who would qualify as bad drivers choose not to drive. This could actually result in an efficiency gain for the insurer and for society. Another beneficial effect could be that bad drivers try to improve their driving behaviour and/or habits. However, problems could arise when those drivers who represent a bad risk do not opt out of driving and drive uninsured instead. Uninsured individuals are a risk to themselves and to society. To counter this phenomenon, the Belgian legislator introduced the 'Tariferingsbureau Auto' in 2002 as a means of reducing the number of uninsured drivers (cf. *supra*). Anybody who is obliged to take out vehicle insurance can make a request to the *Tariferingsbureau* if at least three regular insurers have refused to offer coverage or are only willing to provide insurance coverage against a high premium

74 Commissie voor Verzekeringen, *Rapport van de werkgroep segmentering*, p. 18.

75 L. Wortham, 'The economics of insurance classification: the sound of one invisible hand clapping', *Ohio State Law Journal*, 1986, vol.47, p. 878.

76 BEUC, *The use of big data and artificial intelligence in insurance*, 2020, p. 9.

77 EIOPA, *Big data analytics in motor and health insurance: a thematic review*, 2019, p. 29.

or deductible.[78] To assess whether a premium is high, the lowest possible premium that the insurer could calculate (if the most beneficial conditions apply) is multiplied by five. The *Tariferingsbureau* determines the premium considering the risk presented by the candidate-policyholder and the cover of all insured parties. It may impose conditions to limit the risk presented by the candidate-policyholder. In practice, this implies that, for more severe risks, the *Tariferingsbureau* can charge higher premiums, except if this would lead to the uninsurability of the risk. It remains unclear what impact UBI could have on the functioning of the *Tariferingsbureau*.

D. Lack of Transparency and (Indirect) Discrimination

26. An increasing segmented insurance market becomes less transparent for the consumer and gives him less grip on the longer term.[79] By using UBI, insurers collect data on the policyholder's driving habits and/or behaviour. The use of these new risk factors will make it increasingly difficult for the policyholder to see the link between the cover provided and the criteria determining the premium.[80] Comparing insurance products will become more difficult. Therefore, before collecting this data, the policyholder should be informed whether driving in certain areas (e.g., urban/rural) or at certain times of day (e.g., night driving, early morning driving, rush hour) is considered as an increased risk and how the use of the new rating factors will impact the premium (cf. *supra*). This is important for the policyholder, as it is incumbent on him to notify the insurer of the data necessary for the risk assessment. In addition, a greater number of segmentation criteria increase the likelihood that the policyholder will forget to inform the insurer during the contract that one of the criteria has changed. Furthermore, the policyholder could perceive the use of certain segmentation criteria as subjective and arbitrary. This is exacerbated by the fact that insurers could change the criteria (or their importance in the risk assessment), which does not provide a long-term guarantee for the policyholder that his driving habits and/or behaviour will always be classified as good or bad.

27. Moreover, the use of certain new risk factors might raise questions regarding the compatibility with European or national rules prohibiting direct or indirect discrimination.[81] For instance, imagine a situation where less educated individuals work during the night and use roads in urban areas. In a scenario where both elements statistically represent a higher risk and these insured will have the pay more for their insurance, the question could raise whether this would imply an indirect discrimination of less educated

[78] Article 9*ter* WAM-wet.

[79] Commissie voor Verzekeringen, *Rapport van de werkgroep segmentering*, pp. 19–20.

[80] EIOPA, *Big data analytics in motor and health insurance: a thematic review*, 2019, p. 44.

[81] Van Schoubroeck and Pogarcic Matija, 'Telematics insurance', pp. 42–43.

individuals. Another example of potential discrimination manifests itself if certain areas predominantly inhabited by persons of a particular race and/or nationality are marked as risky. Furthermore, discrimination could occur in a vehicle insurance scenario where people share their personal data in order to obtain a lower insurance premium.[82] It is plausible that people who consider themselves as safer drivers will be more lenient towards sharing their personal driver data, while people who are driving more or are more reckless will not opt for such policies. The threat of discrimination lurks for drivers who do not opt for UBI, as they could instantly be labelled as riskier drivers and thus be charged a higher premium.

28. The Belgian legal order contains three legislative instruments which create a legislative framework for combating discrimination and impose a number of criminal and civil sanctions:[83] (i) the Anti-Discrimination Act;[84] (ii) the Gender Equality Act;[85] and (iii) the Anti-Racism Act.[86] With regard to criminal sanctions, only an incitement to discrimination and the discriminatory behaviour of public officials are punishable as a criminal offence.[87] In addition, the aforementioned legislative instruments impose civil penalties, such as (i) the nullity of clauses which are contrary to the Act;[88] (ii) a prohibitory injunction;[89] (iii) liquidated damages;[90] and (iv) a safeguard against retaliation.[91]

E. Data Quality

29. UBI relies on the input data which is gathered by the (equipment in the) vehicle. The correctness and reliability of the risk profile used in UBI is dependent on the quality, accuracy and completeness of the available data, and can be hampered by possible errors. It is, therefore, crucial to ensure the data quality and the suitability of data.[92]

---

82 *Ibid.*, pp. 42–43.

83 For more information, consult Thierry, *Discriminatie en verzekering*, pp. 154–163.

84 Act of 10 May 2007 ter bestrijding van bepaalde vormen van discriminatie.

85 Act of 10 May 2007 ter bestrijding van discriminatie tussen vrouwen en mannen.

86 Act of 30 July 1981 tot bestraffing van bepaalde door racisme of xenophobie ingegeven daden.

87 Articles 22 and 23 Anti-Discrimination Act; Articles 27 and 28 Gender Equality Act; Articles 20 and 23 Anti-Racism Act.

88 Article 15 Anti-Discrimination Act; Article 20 Gender Equality Act; Article 13 Anti-Racism Act.

89 Article 20 Anti-Discrimination Act; Article 20 Gender Equality Act; Article 18 Anti-Racism Act.

90 Article 18 Anti-Discrimination Act; Article 23 Gender Equality Act; Article 16 Anti-Racism Act.

91 Articles 16 and 17 Anti-Discrimination Act; Articles 21 and 22 Gender Equality Act; Articles 14 and 15 Anti-Racism Act.

92 BEUC, *The use of big data and artificial intelligence in insurance*, 2020, p. 13.

4.2. PROTECTION OF PRIVACY AND PERSONAL DATA: LEGAL CONSIDERATIONS

30. The principle of telematics-based insurance requires the policyholder to disclose several details of his private life (e.g., time of travel, location details, etc.) to the insurer. The continuous registration of all kinds of data means a drastic invasion of privacy. The protection of the personal data and the method of processing are of paramount importance to the policyholder. The protection of personal data is a fundamental right which should be respected by the insurer.[93] While there are several (international) instruments granting individuals the fundamental right to privacy and data protection, none are as detailed and technical as the General Data Protection Regulation (GDPR).[94,95]

4.2.1. General Principles of Data Protection

31. The GDPR aims to protect the processing of personal data of natural persons. The term personal data means any information relating to an identified or identifiable natural person.[96] An insurer can only process personal data for specified, explicit and legitimate purposes.[97] Moreover, the processing of personal data needs to be compatible with those purposes.[98] It could be argued that the GDPR distinguishes three types of personal data, each with its own legal consequences:

- sensitive data: personal data revealing racial or ethnic origin, political opinions, religious or philosophical beliefs, or trade union membership, and the processing of genetic data, biometric data for the purpose of uniquely identifying a natural person, data concerning health or data concerning a natural person's sex life or sexual orientation (Article 9 GDPR);

---

93 For more information on the impact of the right to data protection and privacy on the insurance sector, consult J. Amankwah, 'In het licht van de AVG: het verwerken van bijzondere categorieën van persoonsgegevens in de verzekeringssector', *TBH*, 2019, vol. 2, pp. 245–254; N. Stroobants, 'GDPR en het verwerken van gezondheidsgegevens in private ziekteverzekeringen', *DCCR*, 2019, no. 1, pp. 231–272; Amankwah, 'Nieuwe technologische ontwikkelingen in verzekeringen', pp. 77–106.

94 Regulation (EU) 2016/679 of the European Parliament and of the Council of 27 April 2016 on the protection of natural persons with regard to the processing of personal data and on the free movement of such data, and repealing Directive 95/46/EC, *Pb.L.* 4 May 2016, No. 119, 1.

95 In Belgium, the GDPR is further implemented by the Wet van 30 juli 2018 betreffende de bescherming van natuurlijke personen met betrekking tot de verwerking van persoonsgegevens, *BS* 5 september 2018.

96 Article 4.1 GDPR.

97 Article 5.1(b) GDPR.

98 The assessment of compatibility will often imply a multi-criteria evaluation. For more information, consult 29WP, *Opinion 03/2013 on purpose limitation*, 2 April 2013, nr. 00569/13/EN-WP 203, pp. 21–27.

- personal data relating to criminal convictions and offences (Article 10 GDPR);
- residual category of personal data which cannot be categorised under the first or second category.

The EDPB recognises that certain data generated by vehicles which are connected through a telematics device may warrant special attention given their sensitivity (not necessarily in the sense of Article 9 GDPR) or potential impact on the rights and interests of data subjects. At present, the EDPB has identified three categories of personal data warranting special attention, by vehicle and equipment manufacturers, service providers and other data controllers: location data, biometric data (and any special category of data as defined in art. 9 GDPR) and data that could reveal offences or traffic violations (cf. *infra*, 4.2.4).[99]

32. Based on the GDPR, the insurer has to ensure that the personal data is:[100] (a) processed lawfully, fairly and in a transparent manner in relation to the data subject; (b) collected for specified, explicit and legitimate purposes and not further processed in a manner that is incompatible with those purposes; (c) adequate, relevant and limited to what is necessary in relation to the purpose for which they are processed; (d) accurate and, where necessary, kept up to date; (e) kept in a form which permits identification of data subjects for no longer than is necessary for the purposes for which the personal data are processed; (f) processed in a manner that ensures appropriate security of personal data.

The GDPR contains rather strict remedies, liabilities and penalties. As such, any person who has suffered material or non-material damage as a result of an infringement of the GDPR has the right to compensation for the damage suffered.[101] Moreover, infringements of the GDPR could result in the imposition of an administrative fine of up to 20.000.000 EUR, or in the case of an enterprise, up to 4% of the total worldwide annual turnover of the preceding financial year, whichever is higher.[102]

33. In addition to the GDPR, the ePrivacy Directive[103] sets a specific standard for all actors that wish to store or access information stored in the terminal equipment[104] of a subscriber or user in the European Economic Area. As the

---

99 EDPB, *Guidelines on processing personal data in the context of connected vehicles and mobility related applications*, 28 January 2020, p. 12.

100 Article 5 GDPR.

101 Article 82 GDPR.

102 Article 83 GDPR.

103 Directive 2002/58/EC of the European Parliament and of the Council of 12 July 2002 concerning the processing of personal data and the protection of privacy in the electronic communications sector, *OJ L 31 July 2002, no. 201, pp. 37–47.*

104 Article 1(a) Directive 2008/63/CE defines the terminal equipment as "equipment directly or indirectly connected to the interface of a public telecommunications network to send, process

connected vehicles – and every device connected to it – are considered as a terminal equipment, the provisions of article 5(3) ePrivacy Directive apply.[105] Article 5(3) ePrivacy Directive provides that, as a rule, prior consent is required for the storing of information, or the gaining of access to information already stored, in the terminal equipment of a subscriber or user. According to the EDPB, none of the exemptions provided by Article 5(3) ePrivacy Directive implies to the context of telematics insurance.[106] If there is further processing of personal data that has been obtained by accessing information in the terminal equipment, one of the legal bases as provided in Article 6 GDPR should apply.

4.2.2. Establishing an Individualised Risk Profile

34. As mentioned previously, telematics-based insurance allows the insurer to collect data concerning the driving behaviour and driving habits of the policyholder. This personal data fits in the residual category of personal data. The nature of the collected data is neither sensitive, nor is it related to criminal convictions and offences. Based on that data, the insurer creates a risk profile by algorithms and AI. This involves some form of automated processing of personal data or profiling.[107] The GDPR recognizes two legal frameworks applicable on profiling: (i) a legal framework which applies to solely automated decision-making, including profiling; and (ii) another legal framework of general data protection provisions applicable to general profiling and automated decision making.[108]

(i) Solely automated decision-making is the ability to make decisions by technological means without human involvement.[109] To qualify as human involvement, any oversight of the decision must be meaningful, rather than just a token gesture. It should be carried out by someone who has the authority and competence to change the decision.[110] Article 22 GDPR

---

or receive information; in either case (direct or indirect), the connection may be made by wire, optical fibre or electromagnetically; a connection is indirect if equipment is placed between the terminal and the interface of the network; (b) satellite earth station equipment".

105 EDPB, *Guidelines on processing personal data in the context of connected vehicles and mobility related applications*, 28 January 2020, p. 5.

106 EDPB, *Guidelines on processing personal data in the context of connected vehicles and mobility related applications*, 28 January 2020, p. 22.

107 For more information on this, see N. Stroobants and C. Van Schoubroeck, 'Telematics Insurance: Legal Concerns and Challenges in the EU Insurance Market', *European Journal of Commercial Contract Law*, 2021, pp. 73–76.

108 E. Kamenjasevic, 'Profiling in the financial sector under the GDPR (Part I)' CiTiP Blog, 2017, https://www.law.kuleuven.be/citip/blog/profiling-in-the-financial-sector-under-the-gdpr-part-i/ accessed 13 October 2021, 2.

109 Article 4(4) GDPR; 29WP, *Guidelines on Automated individual decision-making and Profiling for the purposes of Regulation 2016/679,*, 6 February 2018, no. 17/EN– WP 251rev.01, p. 8.

110 It could be argued that meaningful human intervention or oversight means that the individuals making the decision should be able to determine whether the fraud score that informs their decision is accurate, fair and non-discriminatory. For more information,

prohibits decisions based solely on automated processing which produces legal effects concerning the data subject or similarly significantly affects him or her. Unfortunately, the GDPR does not define what must be understood by 'legal effects concerning him or her' or 'similarly significantly affects him or her'. According to the Article 29 Working Party, a legal effect requires that the decision affects someone's legal rights. A legal effect may also be something that affects a person's legal status or their rights under a contract (such as the cancellation of a contract or denial of a particular benefit).[111] Even if a decision-making process does not have an effect on people's legal rights it could still fall within the scope of the prohibition if it produces an effect that 'similarly significantly affects him or her'. According to the Article 29 Working Party, this means that the decision must have the potential to: (i) significantly affect the circumstances, behaviour or choices of the individuals concerned; (ii) have a prolonged or permanent impact on the data subject, and (iii) lead to the exclusion or discrimination of individuals.[112] Finally, it is important to mention that Article 22(2) GDPR provides three exceptions to the general prohibition rule on solely automated decision-making, namely if the decision based solely on automated processing (i) is necessary for entering into, or performance of, a contract between the data subject and a data controller; (ii) is authorised by Union or Member State law to which the controller is subject and which also lays down suitable measures to safeguard the data subject's rights and freedoms and legitimate interests; or; (iii) is based on the data subject's explicit consent.

(ii) The GDPR recognizes profiling as a sub-category of automated decision-making.[113] As such, profiling always involves some form of automated processing which still allows for human involvement. Profiling amounts to gathering information and producing statistical deductions about individuals in order to make an analysis and predictions about their ability to perform a task, interests or expected behaviour, such as insurance fraud.[114] Recital 72 of the GDPR stipulates that profiling is subject to the

---

consult F. Kaltheuner and E. Bietti, 'Data is power: towards additional guidance on profiling and automated decision-making in the GDPR' Journal of Information Rights, Policy and Practice, p. 14.

111 For more information on this concept, consult J. Goetghebuer, 'De invloed van artikel 22 AVG op het gebruik van robo-advies binnen de beleggingssector. Met de rug tegen de muur?', *TBH*, 2020, 151–154.

112 29WP, *Guidelines on Automated individual decision-making and Profiling for the purposes of Regulation 2016/679*, 6 February 2018, no. 17/EN- WP 251rev.01, pp. 21–22.

113 Article 4(4) GDPR defines 'profiling' as any form of automated processing of personal data consisting of the use of personal data to evaluate certain personal aspects relating to a natural person, in particular to analyse or predict aspects concerning that natural person's performance at work, economic situation, health, personal preferences, interests, reliability, behaviour, location or movements.

114 29WP, *Guidelines on Automated individual decision-making and Profiling for the purposes of Regulation 2016/679*, 6 February 2018, no. 17/EN- WP 251rev.01, p. 7.

rules of the GDPR governing the processing of personal data, such as the legal grounds for processing or data protection principles. Therefore, insurers are bound to respect data protection principles concerning lawful, fair and transparent processing, purpose limitation and further processing, data minimization, accuracy and storage limitation.

In the case of risk assessment, the insurer uses an algorithm to determine the risk profile by processing any relevant data. Based on that score, automated decisions could be made, resulting in a certain premium or certain contract conditions. In that case, the insurer should strive to comply with one of the three possible exceptions to the prohibition on solely automated decision-making, including profiling. Belgian legislation does not impose a legal obligation on insurers to offer an insurance product based on telematics data. That leaves an insurer with two options: (i) explicit consent and (ii) the entering into or performance of a contract. As they are both valid options, both will be discussed below.

4.2.3. Legitimising UBI

35. In the context of telematics-based insurance, the insurer can create a risk profile and determine a premium if the policyholder has explicitly consented to the processing of his or her personal data. Consent means any freely given, specific, informed and unambiguous indication of the data subject's wishes by which he or she, by a statement or by a clear affirmative action, signifies agreement to the processing of personal data relating to him or her.[115] Consent must be given before the processing starts.[116] Consent includes any indication of a wish, by which the data subject signifies his agreement: it could include a handwritten signature affixed at the bottom of a paper form, but also oral statements to signify agreement, or a behaviour from which consent can be reasonably concluded.[117] The notion of 'indication' is rather broad, but it seems to imply a need for action. The insurer should strive to obtain the consent of the policyholder to process his data at the time of the conclusion or underwriting of the insurance policy, at the latest. A good practice would be for the insurer to obtain an express statement from the policyholder to signify agreement, such as a signed agreement or written statements of the desire to agree. Insurers cannot validly obtain consent using the general terms and conditions attached to an insurance policy.[118] It is important to note that the policyholder has the right

---

115 Article 4 (11) GDPR.

116 29WP, *Opinion 15/2011 on the definition of consent*, 13 July 2011, no. 01197/11/EN-WP187, p. 9.

117 29WP, *Opinion 15/2011 on the definition of consent*, p. 11.

118 B. Bruyndonckx, 'De verwerking van bijzondere categorieën van persoonsgegevens en de toestemming', in CH.-A. Van Oldeneel (ed.) *Data Protection – De Impact van de GDPR in de Verzekering* (Mechelen: Wolters Kluwer, 2017), p. 55.

to withdraw his or her consent at any time.[119] The withdrawal of consent does not affect the lawfulness of processing based on consent before its withdrawal. In other words, decisions or processes previously taken based on this information can therefore not simply be annulled. The consent should comply with the following five conditions.

(i) First, consent should be given freely.[120] Thus, consent can only be valid if the data subject is able to exercise a real choice, and there is no risk of deception, intimidation, coercion or significant negative consequences if the data subject does not consent.[121] No undue influence or pressure (which can be of an economic or other nature) whether direct or indirect, may be exercised on the data subject and consent should not be regarded as freely given where the data subject has no genuine choice or is unable to refuse or withdraw consent without prejudice.[122] The concept of a freely given consent is rather problematic in an insurance context. Can a potential policyholder exercise a real choice, or will he/she face negative consequences by withholding consent? Consent in an insurance context has a strong connection with the performance of a contract and could be regarded as being conditional for the performance of the contract. A conditional consent is by definition not freely given. Thus, the validity of consent in the context of an insurance contract is left hanging in the balance.
(ii) Second, consent must be specific.[123] To be specific, consent must be intelligible: it should refer clearly and precisely to the scope and the consequences of the data processing.[124] Moreover, consent should refer to the processing that is reasonable and necessary in relation to the purpose.[125] It includes which data are processed and for which purposes.
(iii) Third, consent must be informed. For consent to be informed, the data subject should be aware at least of the identity of the controller and the

---

119 Article 7.3 GDPR.

120 Recital 42 and 43 GDPR.

121 29WP, *Guidelines on consent under Regulation 2016/679*, 10 April 2018, no. 17/EN-WP259 rev.01, 5.

122 Council of Europe, *Convention 108 + Convention for the protection of individuals with regard to the processing of personal data*, 2018, p. 20.

123 Also see, CJEU 5 May 2011, C-543/09, *Deutsche Telekom / Bundesrepublik Deutschland*, ECLI:EU:C:2011:279, §65: 'if it is guaranteed that the data in question will not be used for purposes other than those for which the data were collected with a view to their first publication. The consent given under Article 12(2) of the Directive on privacy and electronic communications, by a subscriber who has been duly informed, to the publication of his personal data in a public directory relates to the purpose of that publication and thus extends to any subsequent processing of those data by third-party undertakings active in the market for publicly available directory enquiry services and directories, provided that such processing pursues that same purpose'.

124 29WP, *Guidelines on consent under Regulation 2016/679*, p. 12.

125 *Ibid*, p. 11.

purposes of the processing for which the personal data are intended.[126] In order to ensure appropriate information, the insurer must make sure that:[127] (i) the information is understandable for a regular or average user;[128] and (ii) the information is given directly to individuals in a clearly visible, prominent and comprehensive manner.[129] Before entering into the insurance contract, policyholders should be given clear and comprehensive information so that they know what personal data is collected. Furthermore, the insurer has to provide meaningful information about the logic involved in the risk assessment process, as well as the significance and the envisaged consequences of such processing for the policyholder.[130] They should also be informed of any changes to what data is collected or used or how the data is processed.

(iv) Fourth, consent must be unambiguous. In other words, the indication by which the data subject signifies his agreement must leave no room for ambiguity regarding his/her intent.[131] Insurers are encouraged to have in place procedures and mechanisms that leave no doubt that consent has been given, either on the basis of an express action carried out by the individual or by being clearly inferred from an action carried out by an individual.[132]

(v) Finally, consent should be explicit. Explicit consent encompasses all situations where individuals are presented with a proposal to agree or disagree to a particular use or disclosure of their personal information and they respond actively to the question, orally or in writing.[133] Individuals may give explicit consent, orally and also in writing, by engaging in an affirmative action to express their desire to accept a form of data processing.

36. The insurer can also legitimately process personal data if the processing is necessary for the performance of a contract to which the data subject is party or in order to take steps at the request of the data subject prior to entering into a contract.[134] It goes without saying that the processing of telematics data is necessary to perform the contract or can be considered a pre-contractual measure. Indeed, based on the telematics data, the insurer will draw up a risk profile and

126 Recital 42 GDPR.
127 29WP, *Guidelines on consent under Regulation 2016/679*, pp. 13–14.
128 Recital 42 GDPR states that a declaration of consent preformulated by the controller should be provided in an intelligible and easily accessible form, using clear and plain language and it should not contain unfair terms.
129 CJEU 5 October 2004, Joined cases C-397/01 to C-403/, *Pfeiffer / Deutsches Rotes Kreuz, Kreisverband Waldshut*, ECLI:EU:C:2004:584, §§82–86.
130 Article 15.1(h) GDPR.
131 29WP, *Guidelines on consent under Regulation 2016/679*, p. 16.
132 *Ibid.*, p. 16.
133 29WP, *Opinion 15/2011 on the definition of consent*, p. 25.
134 Article 6.1 (b) GDPR; Article 22.2 (a) GDPR.

determine a premium. The insurer does this at the request of the prospective policyholder who seeks to take out insurance. As mentioned previously, the determination of the risk and premium by the insurer is an essential step that precedes the conclusion of an insurance contract.[135] The insurer cannot be expected to cover a certain risk if he is unable to determine that risk.

37. While the aforementioned legal grounds may suffice to legitimise the processing of personal data of the policyholder, issues might arise when considering that a motor vehicle can be shared between different members of a family. In such a case, the driving habits and/or driving behaviour of those different drivers will also be registered, which could result in an alternation of the premium. In that case, the EDPB states that an insurer needs to pay careful attention to the modalities of obtaining valid consent from the different users of the vehicle.[136] The insurer could overcome this by having the drivers named in the insurance contract, which means the insurer could base the processing on the performance of the contract. However, this is does not seem practical, as drivers do not necessarily have to be named on the policy. Another possibility would be to recognise that the policyholder can provide consent on behalf of other (unknown) drivers. As such, consent given on behalf of third parties would be deemed as valid in the case of an insurance contract.[137] This would require that the EDPB guidelines on consent would specifically allow for this in an insurance context. However, it could be argued that the processing of driving habits and behaviour of unnamed drivers cannot be regarded as personal data as it will be impossible or extremely difficult to identify a merely accidental driver on the sole basis of driving behaviour or location data.[138] This would mean that the insurer could suffice to legitimise the processing on the basis of the policyholder's content or the necessity for the performance of the insurance contract.

4.2.4. Particular Issues Regarding Processing of Personal Data Warranting Special Attention

38. As mentioned, the processing of specific types of personal data in the framework of UBI requires special attention.[139] As UBI is used in motor vehicle

---

135 29WP, *Opinion 06/2014 on the notion of legitimate interests of the data controller under article 7 of directive 95/46/EC*, 9 April 2014, nr. 844/14/EN – WP 217, p. 18.

136 EDPB, *Guidelines on processing personal data in the context of connected vehicles and mobility related applications*, 28 January 2020, p. 10.

137 Insurance Europe, *Position paper: Insurance Europe views on EC report on the review of the GDPR*, 28 April 2020, pp. 11–12.

138 N. Stroobants and C. Van Schoubroeck, 'Telematics Insurance: Legal Concerns and Challenges in the EU Insurance Market', *European Journal of Commercial Contract Law*, 2021, p. 64.

139 For more information on these issues, consult N. Stroobants and C. Van Schoubroeck, 'Telematics Insurance: Legal Concerns and Challenges in the EU Insurance Market', *European Journal of Commercial Contract Law*, 2021, pp. 66–68.

liability insurance, it is quite possible that in the case of a road traffic accident the insurer, when handling claims, needs to process health data of the injured party. The processing of health data is prohibited, unless one of the ten possible legal grounds mentioned in Article 9(2) GDPR applies. An in-depth analysis of this issue goes beyond the scope of this chapter, but in general terms it could argued that the insurer will probably have to rely on the explicit consent of the injured party in order to process his/her health data.[140]

39. It is possible that personal data from connected vehicles could reveal the commitment of a criminal offence or other infractions and therefore be subject to special restrictions according to the EDPB.[141] According to Article 10 GDPR, such data can only be processed under the control of an official authority, or when the processing is authorised by the European Union or Member States law providing for appropriate safeguards for the rights and freedoms of data subjects. Several Member States have authorised the processing of data relating to a criminal convictions or offences. In Belgium, Article 10 of the Act of 30 July 2018 concerning the protection of natural persons with regards to the processing of personal data[142] specifically provides in which cases personal data relating to criminal convictions and offences can be processed. Within the framework of UBI, this means that according to Belgian law, the insurer can only process for instance speeding offences retrieved from telematics data if the insured driver has given explicit written permission for the processing of the data for the specific purpose of UBI.[143] As an additional safeguard, Belgian law requires (i) the designated person(s) who process(es) the data to be bound by confidentiality; and (ii) the insurer to draw up a list (which is kept at the disposal of the competent supervisory authority) of the categories of persons who have access to the personal data, with a description of their capacity with regard to the processing of the personal data relating to criminal convictions and

---

140 For more information on this topic, see J. Amankwah and N. Stroobants, 'GDPR and processing of health data in insurance contracts: opening a can of worms?', in M. Lima Rego and B. Kuschke (eds.) *AIDA Europe Research Series on Insurance Law and Regulation: Insurance and Human Rights* (Springer, 2022), pp. 173–227; N. Stroobants and C. Van Schoubroeck, 'Telematics Insurance: Legal Concerns and Challenges in the EU Insurance Market', *European Journal of Commercial Contract Law,* 2021, p. 67; J. Amankwah, 'Nieuwe technologische ontwikkelingen in verzekeringen' in C. Van Schoubroeck and I. Samoy (eds.) *Themis 106 - Aansprakelijkheids- en verzekeringsrecht,* (Bruges: Die Keure, 2018), pp. 77–106.

141 For instance, the instantaneous speed of a vehicle combined with precise geolocation data or data indicating that the vehicle crossed a white line could be considered offence-related data. For more information, see EDPB, *Guidelines on processing personal data in the context of connected vehicles and mobility related applications,* 28 January 2020, p. 13.

142 *Belgian State Gazette,* 5 september 2018.

143 Article 10, §1 (5) Act of 30 July 2018 concerning the protection of natural persons with regards to the processing of personal data.

offences.[144] The Netherlands have implemented similar rules which allow the insurer to process personal data relating to criminal convictions or offences for UBI purposes on the basis of explicit consent of the insured drivers.[145]

5. CONCLUSION

40. UBI offers the insurer the possibility to collect data on the driving behaviour and habits of the policyholder. The insurer will process the collected data to determine an individualised premium. This new technology has the possibility to revolutionise the way insurers underwrite vehicle insurance policies. Insurers are no longer dependent on information provided to them solely by the prospective policyholder. Through telematics, the insurer can also obtain objective information. This could potentially have several advantages as this allows the insurer to refine the segmentation criteria and classification of risks. By distributing similar risks in more homogenous risk groups, the insurer is able to severely reduce or eliminate subsidising solidarity between policyholders. In addition, society and the policyholder can also benefit from UBI. However, the insurer must consider the legal and economic challenges which go hand in hand with increasing segmentation and classification of risks. The Belgian legislator seeks to protect the policyholder by imposing certain measures on the insurer with respect to pricing and segmentation. Moreover, the very nature of insurance – which is based on (chance) solidarity – could be rocked to its core by the use of an individualised underwriting policy. It is also important to consider that UBI goes hand in hand with the monitoring of the policyholder and could therefore constitute an invasion of privacy and data protection rights. It is up to the insurer to handle the policyholder's data with care. Indeed, the insurer must ensure that the processing of personal data is necessary to achieve the predetermined legitimate aims.

---

144 Article 10, §2 Act of 30 July 2018 concerning the protection of natural persons with regards to the processing of personal data.

145 Article 32 Act of 16 May 2018 houdende regels ter uitvoering van Verordening (EU) 2016/679 van het Europees Parlement en de Raad van 27 april 2016 betreffende de bescherming van natuurlijke personen in verband met de verwerking van persoonsgegevens en betreffende het vrije verkeer van die gegevens en tot intrekking van Richtlijn 95/46/EG (Uitvoeringswet Algemene Verordening Gegevensbescherming).

CHAPTER 16

AI AND CREDITWORTHINESS ASSESSMENTS: THE TALE OF CREDIT SCORING AND CONSUMER PROTECTION. A STORY WITH A HAPPY ENDING?

Julie GOETGHEBUER*

1. INTRODUCTION

1. Recently, the availability and variety of innovative technologies, which support the provision of financial services, have increased considerably. Examples thereof range from biometric technology, virtual currencies, artificial intelligence and cloud computing to distributed ledger technology. During the past few years, we have not only been confronted with such terms, but also with the new buzzword 'FinTech'.[1] FinTech, the abbreviation of 'Financial Technology', is defined as 'technologically enabled financial innovation that could result in new business models, applications, processes or products with an associated material effect on financial markets and institutions and the provision of financial services'.[2] It is, in other words, an umbrella term for all the innovative products, services, processes, functions and distribution channels that have been created in the financial sector in order to respond to the needs of today's consumers.[3] Financial technology – in the shape of algorithms, AI,

---

* PhD researcher and academic assistant, Ghent University, Financial Law Institute.

1 See inter alia: European Banking Authority, 'The EBA's Fintech Roadmap: Conclusions from the Consultation on the EBAs Approach to Financial Technology (FinTech)', 15 March 2018, https://eba.europa.eu; European Banking Authority, 'Discussion Paper on the EBA's Approach to Financial Technology (FinTech)', 4 August 2017, https://eba.europa.eu; Financial Stability Board, 'Monitoring of FinTech', 12 May 2017, https://www.fsb.org.

2 Financial Stability Board, 'Financial Stability Implications from FinTech: Supervisory and Regulatory Issues that Merit Authorities' Attention', 27 June 2017, https://www.fsb.org.

3 European Banking Authority, 'Discussion Paper on Innovative Uses of Consumer Data by Financial Institutions', *EBA/DP/2016/01*, 4 May 2016, https://eba.europa.eu.

ML and/or big data analytics[4] – is frequently used when providing consumer credit. Creditors may use financial technology and automation to provide financial advice to the consumer asking for credit, thus guiding them in making a credit decision.[5]

Before concluding a credit agreement, creditors are obligated to perform a thorough assessment of the creditworthiness of said consumer, based on sufficient information obtained from the consumer, where appropriate and on the basis of a consultation of a relevant database, where necessary.[6] This assessment helps them decide whether this individual should be granted credit and allows them to verify whether the consumer will be able to meet his or her (financial) responsibilities under the credit agreement.[7] The obligation to evaluate the financial and personal situation of each consumer who wants to acquire a loan can be met through automated techniques, which require no or very little human intervention and instead rely on computer-based algorithms. Some of these automated techniques are called 'credit scoring techniques'.

2. This chapter tries to answer the central question of whether consumer protection is fully guaranteed under the European Consumer Credit Directive, given the new digital reality and the extensive use of credit scoring techniques to assess creditworthiness.

First, this article focuses on the Consumer Credit Directive itself and the creditworthiness assessment as expected by the 'responsible lending' requirement (part 2). Afterwards, the meaning of credit scoring and its functioning are clarified, including new 'credit scoring' systems ('credit scoring 2.0'), which apply more sophisticated techniques, such as AI, ML and big data (part 3). Next, this article points out some benefits and challenges credit scoring may entail for consumers. It will tackle the conundrum of whether credit scoring can be part of responsible lending and whether consumers are sufficiently protected against potential risks that may arise (part 4). The main findings are summarised in a conclusion (part 5).

On a side note, it is important to add that, even though there are many privacy aspects involved in this context, the privacy legislation and its relation to credit scoring techniques will not be addressed in this chapter, as discussing this subject thoroughly would lead us too far.

---

4 For more information regarding the meaning and definitions, see Chapter 1 of this book.

5 European Supervisory Authorities, 'Report on automation in financial advice', 16 December 2016, https://esas-joint-committee.europa.eu/; Financial Stability Board, 'Artificial intelligence and machine learning in financial services: Market developments and financial stability implications', 1 November 2017, https://www.fsb.org.

6 See Consumer Credit Directive, recitals 8 and 26.

7 European Supervisory Authorities, 'Report on automation in financial advice', p. 12.

2. THE CREDITWORTHINESS ASSESSMENT

2.1. CREDITWORTHINESS ASSESSMENT AND THE CONSUMER CREDIT DIRECTIVE

3. Before tackling the more technical features of automated creditworthiness assessments, we will look at the legal aspects of the obligation and meaning of the creditworthiness assessment. The Consumer Credit Directive[8] (hereinafter 'CCD' or 'the Directive') contains the aforementioned obligation for the creditor to assess the consumer's creditworthiness prior to the conclusion of a credit agreement. This Directive applies to credit agreements in which a creditor grants or promises to grant a consumer credit in the form of a deferred payment, loan or other similar financial accommodation.[9] The credit must be provided for purposes which are outside the consumer's trade, business or profession,[10] for example for personal, household or domestic purposes.[11] Credit agreements that are secured either by a mortgage or by another comparable security commonly used in a Member State on immovable property or secured by a right related to immovable property, do *not* fall under the scope of the CCD, as they are covered by the Mortgage Credit Directive.[12, 13]

The Directive aims to facilitate the emergence of a well-functioning internal market in consumer credit[14] and to offer a high and equivalent level of consumer protection to ensure consumer confidence and create a genuine internal market.[15] Especially in light of the currently expanding credit market, the CCD focuses on the importance of creditors not engaging in irresponsible lending or handing out credit without a prior assessment of creditworthiness.[16]

---

8 Directive 2008/48/EC of the European parliament and of the council of 23 April 2008 on credit agreements for consumers and repealing Council Directive 87/102/EEC, *L 133*, 66–92. This Directive strives to achieve full harmonisation in order to ensure that all consumers across the European Union enjoy a high and equivalent level of protection. However, this full harmonisation is limited by the scope of the Directive itself. This means that Member States remain free to extend the provisions of the Directive to operations which it does not cover. Where no harmonised provisions exist, Member States are free to maintain or introduce national legislation (see recital 9 of the Directive).

9 Article 2.1 and Article 3(c) CCD.

10 Article 3(a) CCD. See also E. Terryn, 'Consumers, by Definition, Include Us All'... But Not for Every Transaction', *European Review of Private Law*, 2016, vol. 24, no. 2, pp. 271–286.

11 O.O. Cherednychenko and J.M. Meindertsma, 'Irresponsible Lending in the Post-Crisis Era: Is the EU Consumer Credit Directive Fit for Its Purpose?', *Journal of Consumer Policy*, 24 August 2019, vol. 42, p. 485.

12 Directive 2014/17/EU of the European Parliament and of the Council of 4 February 2014 on credit agreements for consumers relating to residential immovable property and amending Directives 2008/48/EC and 2013/36/EU and Regulation (EU) No 1093/2010, *L 60*, 34–85.

13 Article 2.2 CCD.

14 See Consumer Credit Directive, recital 7.

15 See Consumer Credit Directive, recitals 8 and 9.

16 See Consumer Credit Directive, recital 26.

4. When performing a creditworthiness assessment, the creditor has to check whether the consumer will be able to repay the requested credit in a *reasonable* manner. This means that the consumer has to be able to repay the credit without undue financial hardship[17] and the creditor is obligated to assess whether the commitments arising from the credit agreement may have an adverse impact on the customer's financial situation.[18] When a consumer, after receiving a credit, finds himself or herself in a problematic repayment situation, he or she cannot be seen as creditworthy, as this can lead to over-indebtedness. In such circumstances, the consumer may feel the need to take out more credit in order to meet his/her existing repayment obligations and to cover his/her basic living expenses.[19] Moreover, when a consumer has reduced some expenditures to be able to repay the credit to a degree which would be harmful to him/her or his/her household, the creditor has to withhold granting a credit.[20] In other words, the creditor cannot conclude a credit agreement if he or she has not checked whether the consumer will be able to repay the credit in a reasonable way.[21] This obligation aims to make creditors completely accountable and to avoid loans being granted to consumers who are not creditworthy.[22]

It should be noted that the CCD does not contain any provision regarding the course of action to be taken by the creditor in case of doubts as to the creditworthiness of the consumer.[23] The Directive only stipulates that the creditor must assess the consumer's creditworthiness, without clarifying what the consequences are if such an assessment has a negative outcome, or how the creditor should act in case of doubt.[24] Furthermore, the CJEU stated that Member States are free to determine the obligations to be imposed on the creditor following the assessment of creditworthiness. This means that only the obligation to carry out a creditworthiness assessment is fully harmonised by the Directive, but the consequences attached to a negative creditworthiness assessment are not.[25] As such, Member States are not precluded from taking different approaches.[26] Creditors in Belgium, for example, do have the obligation

---

17 Cherednychenko and Meindertsma, 'Irresponsible Lending in the Post-Crisis Era', p. 487.

18 Financial Conduct Authority, 'Understanding consumer credit–Creditworthiness and affordability: common misunderstandings', 26 June 2015, https://www.fca.org.uk, p. 4.

19 F. Ferretti, 'Data protection in credit for consumers', *International Journal for Financial Services*, 2019, p. 72.

20 Cherednychenko and Meindertsma, 'Irresponsible Lending in the Post-Crisis Era', p. 488.

21 See Consumer Credit Directive, recital 26: 'creditors should bear the responsibility of checking individually the creditworthiness of the consumer'.

22 CJEU C-449/13, *CA Consumer Finance SA v. Ingrid Bakkaus and Others*, ECLI:EU:C:2014:2464, para. 35.

23 CJEU C-58/18, *Michel Schyns v. Belfius Bank NV*, ECLI:EU:C:2019:467, para. 42.

24 European Commission, 'Report from the Commission to the European Parliament and the Council on the implementation of Directive 2008/48/EC on credit agreements for consumers', COM(2020) 963 final, 5 November 2020, p. 7, https://eur-lex.europa.eu/.

25 CJEU C-58/18, *Michel Schyns v. Belfius Bank NV*, ECLI:EU:C:2019:467, para. 43.

26 European Commission, 'Report on the implementation of Directive 2008/48/EC on credit agreements for consumers', p. 7; O.O. Cherednychenko, 'Full Harmonisation of Retail

to refrain from concluding a credit agreement unless they can reasonably assume that, in the light of the information they possess or which they should have been able to obtain, the consumer will be able to fulfil his or her obligations under the agreement. The Belgian legislator has introduced an additional duty which cannot be found in the CCD and which enhances responsible lending. Nonetheless, the lack of consequences in the Directive may also result in an absence or a bare minimum of consequences in national law, which generates less or maybe even no protection at all for consumers. However, in June 2021 the European Commission issued a proposal for a new directive on consumer credits repealing and replacing the current Consumer Credit Directive.[27] The proposed new directive strengthens the existing provisions, but also adds new elements of protection. In particular, the Proposal changes abovementioned legal uncertainty by determining the consequences of a negative creditworthiness. Article 18(4) of this Proposal stipulates that credit should only made available to the consumer where the result of the creditworthiness assessment indicates that the obligations resulting from the credit agreement are likely to be met in the manner required under that agreement.

2.2. CREDITWORTHINESS ASSESSMENT AND INFORMATION

5. The creditor has to take into account all relevant factors that could influence the consumer's ability to repay the credit, and this without undue hardship and over-indebtedness.[28, 29] The creditor has the obligation to obtain *all relevant* information regarding the personal and financial situation of the consumer in order to make a thorough assessment of the latter's creditworthiness.[30]

Financial Services Contract Law in Europe: A Success or a Failure?', in S. Grundmann and Y.M. Atamer (eds.), *Financial services, financial crisis and general European contract law: failure and challenges of contracting* (Alphen aan den Rijn: Kluwer Law International, 2011), p. 237.

27 Proposal for a Directive of the European Parliament and of the Council on consumer credits, COM(2021) 347 final (hereinafter: 'Proposal').

28 Over-indebtedness is defined as the situation in which the consumer's existing and foreseeable resources are insufficient to meet the financial commitments without lowering his or her living standards, which has both social and policy implications if this means reducing them below what is regarded as the minimum acceptable standard in the country concerned (see European Commission, 'Research note 4/2010: Over-indebtedness – New evidence from the EU-SILC special module', November 2010, https://ec.europa.eu, p. 4). This may have a significant negative impact on both consumers and the economy at large (see T. Wilson, 'The Responsible Lending Response', in T. Wilson (ed.), *International Responses to Issues of Credit and Over-indebtedness in the Wake of Crisis* (Surrey/Burlington: Ashgate Publishing Limited/ Ashgate Publishing Company, 2013), p. 121).

29 European Banking Authority, 'Final Report – Guidelines on creditworthiness assessment', 1 June 2015, pp. 10–11, https://eba.europa.eu.

30 Cherednychenko and Meindertsma, 'Irresponsible Lending in the Post-Crisis Era', p. 488.

The current Directive only states that the creditworthiness assessment has to be based on *sufficient* information, obtained from the consumer *where appropriate* and on the basis of a consultation of the relevant database *where necessary.*[31] In other words, the creditor has to obtain all relevant and necessary information from the consumer himself/herself and/or consult, if necessary, a relevant database established by credit bureaus.[32] In this respect, it should be noted that the words 'where necessary' in Article 8.1 of the CCD entail that Member States cannot introduce the obligation for creditors to assess creditworthiness – in all cases – on the basis of a consultation of the relevant database. Nevertheless, the second sentence of Article 8.1 states that Member States whose legislation requires creditors to assess the creditworthiness of consumers on the basis of a consultation of the relevant database may retain this requirement. In other words, Member States, like Belgium, whose regulation had required such an obligation even before the Directive came into force, may retain this obligation, but for other Member States the consultation of credit databases must remain non-mandatory.[33]

6. As the CCD leaves much leeway to the Member States to further implement and specify the creditworthiness assessment obligation, it may not come as a surprise that assessments in the area of consumer credit are carried out in ways which differ significantly across Member States.[34, 35] Member States are basically free to choose *how* the creditor should obtain all appropriate and sufficient information. A few Member States solely require attaining information from the consumer, some require attaining information from the consumer and the consultation of external databases and others give creditors the flexibility to decide for themselves. For example, Belgium and the Netherlands have legally obligated the creditor to obtain certain information from the consumer in order to assess his or her financial situation.[36] In fact, creditors are also obligated

31 Article 8.1 of the Consumer Credit Directive.

32 F. Ferretti, 'The Legal Framework of Consumer Credit Bureaus and Credit Scoring in the European Union: Pitfalls and Challenges – Overindebtedness, Responsible Lending, Market Integration, and Fundamental Rights', *Suffolk University Law Review*, 2013, vol. 46, no. 3, p. 794.

33 P. Rott, 'Consumer Credit', in N. Reich, H-W. Micklitz, P. Rott and K. Tonner (eds.), *Understanding EU Consumer Law* (Cambridge: Intersentia, 2014), p. 221; Ferretti, 'The Legal Framework of Consumer Credit Bureaus and Credit Scoring in the European Union', p. 805.

34 European Commission, 'Action plan: Better products, more choice – Communication from the Commission to the European Parliament, the Council, the European Central Bank, the European Economic and Social Committee and the Committee of the Regions', 23 March 2017, https://eur-lex.europa.eu, p. 10.

35 For an overview of the different regulatory approaches: X, 'Mapping of national approaches in relation to creditworthiness assessment under Directive 2008/48/EC on credit agreements for consumers', 9 October 2018, https://ec.europa.eu.

36 In Belgium, Article VII.69, §1 WER ('Wetboek Economisch Recht') states that as part of the assessment of the creditworthiness, the creditor *shall ask* the consumers, applying for a credit agreement, for the accurate and comprehensive information which the creditor considers

to consult the national credit register in Belgium.[37] Conversely, creditors in the United Kingdom and Germany are not obligated to obtain the necessary information from the consumer or an external database, hence they can choose how to attain all the necessary information to carry out an in-depth assessment.[38]

Based on the CCD, creditors may first of all use information provided by the *consumer* in order to assess their creditworthiness. This information can be obtained during the preparation of the credit agreement in question, but also during a longstanding commercial relationship.[39] Moreover, the CJEU ruled that the assessment may be carried out solely on the basis of information of the financial situation offered by the consumer, provided that that information is sufficient and appropriate and that unsupported declarations are accompanied by supporting evidence.[40, 41] Secondly, creditors can obtain consumer data via *(external) databases.* Credit bureaus and credit registers are privately or publicly managed entities that run centralised databases providing positive and/or negative information regarding borrowers in an organised manner. They gather this information through input from the creditors themselves: the members of the credit bureaus and registers will often be obliged (by law) to communicate (certain) credits granted to these entities. Since both publicly-run and privately-run credit bureaus exist in the EU, the state of affairs in Europe is mixed.[42]

necessary to assess their financial situation and their ability to repay (for more information see Federal Public Service Economy, 'Guidelines regarding the creditworthiness assessment, of a consumer, in the context of granting a consumer credit', 10 October 2018, https://economie.fgov.be). In the Netherlands, Article 4:34 Wft ('Wet op het financieel toezicht') states that a credit provider *shall*, before the conclusion of a credit agreement, in the interests of the consumer, *obtain information* on his financial situation and, in order to avoid excessive lending to the consumer, assess whether the conclusion of the agreement is justified.

37 I.e., 'Centrale voor Kredieten aan Particulieren'.

38 In the United Kingdom, the CONC ('Consumer Credit sourcebook') 5.2A.7 states that the creditor must base his or her creditworthiness assessment on sufficient information of which he/she is aware at the time the creditworthiness assessment is carried out, or is obtained, *where appropriate*, from the customer, and *where necessary* from a credit reference agency. This information must enable the creditor to carry out a reasonable creditworthiness assessment. This provision has basically been copied from the Directive.
In Germany, Article §18a KWG ('Kreditwesengesetz') specifies that the credit assessment *can* be based on information provided by the borrower and, *if necessary*, information provided by bodies which collect, store, modify or use personal data for the purpose of transmission for business purposes which may be used to assess the creditworthiness of consumers. This means that the creditor can choose which information he sees as relevant in the creditworthiness assessment.

39 See Credit Consumer Directive, recital 26.

40 CJEU C-449/13, *CA Consumer Finance SA v. Ingrid Bakkaus and Others*, ECLI:EU:C:2014:2464, para. 37.

41 This does not entail that the creditor has the obligation to systematically check the veracity of the information supplied by the consumer, CJEU C-449/13, *CA Consumer Finance SA v. Ingrid Bakkaus and Others*, ECLI:EU:C:2014:2464, para. 38.

42 European Commission, 'Report on the implementation of Directive 2008/48/EC on credit agreements for consumers', p. 7; Ferretti, 'The Legal Framework of Consumer Credit Bureaus and Credit Scoring in the European Union', p. 793.

For example, whereas in Belgium[43] and France[44] only public credit bureaus or credit registers operate, the Netherlands and the United Kingdom use private credit bureaus. Generally speaking, private credit bureaus (or Credit Reference Agencies (CRAs)) are privately managed (usually profit-driven) entities that run centralised databases and provide credit information regarding the consumer to creditors.[45] This stands in contrast to public credit databases or registers, which are supervised by national financial supervisory authorities or the central banks and serve to monitor the health and soundness of a country's overall financial system, including the level of indebtedness of creditors.[46] The information contained in the databases may also differ from Member State to Member State (positive credit data and/or negative credit data).[47]

7. Besides the means by which creditors have to collect the necessary information, the Consumer Credit Directive is vague regarding *which necessary information* the creditor has to obtain. As a result, the obligations adopted may also vary across the EU. Whereas some Member States did lay down more clear and concrete obligations for the creditors, others merely copied the vague CCD obligation into their legal system.[48] For example, in Belgium the creditor is subjected to a minimum information obligation: he or she has to assess the financial situation of the consumer by asking questions that at least address the purpose of the credit, the income, the persons at charge, the existing outstanding financial obligations and the number of credit contracts.[49] Belgium obliges

43 I.e., 'Centrale voor Kredieten aan Particulieren'.

44 I.e., 'Fichier des incidents de remboursement des crédits aux particuliers'.

45 They collect data held by the various creditors on their borrowers and, at the same time, provide the same creditors with reports on consumer credit, making the personal data and reputation of consumer borrowers accessible to other (potential) creditors. In addition, private credit bureaus may also have members located outside the traditional credit sector (i.e., consumer – financial institution), such as telecommunications and other utilities, allowing both financial and non-financial entities to access consumer information across different economic elements. The more members there are, the more complete information on the consumer-borrower the credit bureau will have at its disposal. In addition, private credit agencies aim to offer risk management tools to the financial market in order to optimise economic efficiency and profitability of creditors. These private entities for example create credit scoring models in which consumers are mathematically and statistically assessed on the basis of their credit history and credit profile and other data they have collected. See Ferretti, 'The Legal Framework of Consumer Credit Bureaus and Credit Scoring in the European Union', pp. 798–799.

46 In other words, public credit registers are part of a country's supervisory structure. Unlike private credit bureaus, only traditional (authorised or registered) creditors can obtain (and communicate) information to the central credit database. See N. Jentzsch, *Financial Privacy – An International Comparison of Credit Reporting Systems*, 2nd edn (Berlin/Heidelberg: Springer-Verlag, 2007), p. 115; Ferretti, 'The Legal Framework of Consumer Credit Bureaus and Credit Scoring in the European Union', pp. 793 and 800.

47 European Commission, 'Report on the implementation of Directive 2008/48/EC on credit agreements for consumers', p. 7.

48 European Commission, 'Report on the implementation of Directive 2008/48/EC on credit agreements for consumers', p. 7.

49 Article VII.69, §2 WER.

creditors to ask relevant questions, which at least address the purpose of the credit, the income of the borrower(s), any dependants, the existing financial obligations of which the amount is outstanding and the number of credit contract requests. In other words, Belgium has determined what 'sufficient information' entails in the context of the creditworthiness assessment. Additionally, creditors have the obligation to consult the credit register managed by the Belgian Central Bank[50] in order to assess whether the consumer has defaulted on credit agreements as well as to assess whether the consumer has concluded credit agreements, and if so, how many.[51] Belgian law, case law and legal doctrine presuppose, firstly, that a minimum of information is requested and, secondly, that this information is interpreted in a specific way. For instance, Belgian case law states that the creditor must always exercise greater ('double') caution and vigilance if the consumer indicates that he or she wishes to use the requested credit to repay other credits. A credit agreement concluded to settle another credit or other credits may send a negative signal to the creditor.[52] The Belgian Federal Public Service Economy[53] stipulates that a person will be considered more likely to be creditworthy if he or she did not ask for credit before than someone who has already obtained (multiple) credit(s). Despite these initiatives, other Member States did no such thing.[54] A number of countries (for example: France)[55] give discretion to the creditors to determine which information has to be used in order to perform the creditworthiness assessment. Moreover, as the Directive does not contain an exhaustive list of the information the creditor must obtain to assess a consumer's creditworthiness, nor stipulates any exhaustive rules on how to interpret this information[56], the CJEU has decided that the wording of Article 8.1 CCD – read in the light of recital 26 in the preamble to the Directive – offers the creditor a certain margin of discretion in deciding whether or not the information he or she has already requested from the consumer is sufficient to ascertain the consumer's

---

50 I.e., Nationale Bank van België.

51 Federal Public Service Economy, 'Guidelines regarding the creditworthiness assessment, of a consumer, in the context of granting a consumer credit', 10 October 2018, pp. 19–20, https://economie.fgov.be.

52 Rb. Coutrai (1st Ch.) 11 September 1998, *DCCR* 1999, 73–80; Vred. Sint-Niklaas 6 August 2004, *T. Vred.* 2006, 32–38, note F. de Patoul; Vred. Ghent 6 January 2005, *RABG* 2005, no. 4, 345–349; Vred. Courtrai 6 February 2008, *T.Vred.* 2009, 295–301, note R. Steennot; Vred. Arendonk 12 October 2010, *NjW* 2011, no. 242, 343–344, note R. Steennot.

53 I.e., 'FOD Economie'.

54 For example, Germany exhibits a minimal implementation of EU law and does not apply an extensive sanctioning regime. See F. Ferretti, R. Salomone, H. Sutschet and V. Tsiafoutis, 'The Regulatory Framework of Consumer Over-indebtedness in the UK, Germany, Italy, and Greece: Comparative Profiles of Responsible Credit and Personal Insolvency Law – Part I', *Business Law Review*, 2016, vol. 37, no. 2, p. 67.

55 Article L311-9 Code de la consommation states that the creditor shall check the borrower's creditworthiness on the basis of *sufficient* information, but it omits to indicate exactly which information qualifies as sufficient information.

56 European Commission, 'Report on the implementation of Directive 2008/48/EC on credit agreements for consumers', p. 7.

creditworthiness.[57] Hence, the creditor will have to check on a *case-by-case* basis, taking into account the circumstances in which the credit agreement was concluded, the personal situation of the consumer and/or the amount covered by the agreement, whether the information is appropriate and sufficient to enable a thorough assessment to be made.[58]

That being said, the Proposal for a consumer credit directive will provide some clarification regarding the kind of information that should be used during a creditworthiness assessment. Article 18 of the Proposal requires the creditor to assess the prospect of the consumer to meet his or her obligations on the basis of 'appropriate account of factors relevant to verifying the prospect of the consumer to meet his or her obligations under the credit agreement'. This article states that the assessment of creditworthiness shall be carried out on the basis of 'relevant and accurate information regarding the consumer's *income* and *expenses* and *other financial and economic circumstances* which is necessary and proportionate such as evidence of income or other sources of repayment, information on financial assets and liabilities, or information on other financial commitments (emphasis added)'. In terms of sources of information, the Proposal specifies that the information shall be obtained from relevant *internal* or *external sources*, including the *consumer* and, where necessary, on the basis of a consultation of a *database* referred to in Article 19.[59, 60]

2.3. CREDITWORTHINESS ASSESSMENT AND RESPONSIBLE LENDING

8. It is not laid down by European law *how* the assessment of the consumer's creditworthiness has to be carried out. The CCD only speaks of carrying out an assessment of creditworthiness of the consumer, without clarifying what kind of test is envisaged by it, nor explaining when a consumer can be seen as 'creditworthy'. The only (current European) obligation now in force is thus to carry out an undefined assessment. Nevertheless, in the context of consumer credit, a concept exists that may offer some guidance to national legislators and creditors: *responsible lending*. This concept emerged in the wake of the 2008 global financial crisis, triggered by systemic problems regarding the US housing debt.[61] The creditworthiness assessment is seen as an essential component of responsible lending after the financial crisis has clearly demonstrated the damage that

[57] CJEU C-449/13, *CA Consumer Finance SA v. Ingrid Bakkaus and Others*, ECLI:EU:C:2014:2464, para. 36.
[58] *Ibid.*, para. 37.
[59] I.e., the public and private databases, see, *supra*, no. 6.
[60] See article 18(1) Proposal.
[61] I. Ramsay, 'Consumer Credit Regulation after the fall: international dimensions', *Journal of European Consumer and Market Law*, 2012, vol. 1, p. 24.

irresponsible lending practices can inflict on consumers, creditors, the financial system and the economy (i.e., systemic risks) in general. This concept envisages that all creditors must act in a fair, honest and professional manner and entails that consumer credit products should be designed in a responsible way to prevent the manifestation of potential risks detrimental to the consumer.[62] Responsible lending, which essentially means offering credit products that are appropriate to consumers' needs and tailored to their ability to repay, is key to ensuring a steady and effective credit market[63] and can be achieved by averting the granting of credit to a consumer before a creditworthiness assessment has taken place.[64] Responsible lending and, by extension, the creditworthiness assessment, are intended to protect consumers against the risks of over-indebtedness and bankruptcy.[65]

9. In order to achieve all of the above, creditors should not solely act in their own interests, but should also take into account consumers' interests and needs, and this throughout the whole lifecycle of the credit product.[66] However, the interests of the creditor and those of the consumer do not always coincide, as the gaining revenues for the creditor does not always create benefits for the consumer.[67]

The financial incentives will motivate creditors to make profits or at least reduce their losses. In order to achieve this, the creditor will try to minimise its own credit risk, i.e., the risk to the creditor that he or she will not recuperate his or her money in case of a default.[68] Credit risk can be defined as the potential exposure the creditor risks when the consumer will fail to meet its financial obligations in accordance with the agreed terms and thus the risk that the consumer will not make the required repayments.[69] In other words, when deciding whether to grant credit, irresponsible creditors will solely calculate

---

62 European Commission, 'Financial services: Commission launches consultation on how to ensure responsible lending and borrowing in the EU', 15 June 2009, https://ec.europa.eu.

63 Ferretti, 'The Legal Framework of Consumer Credit Bureaus and Credit Scoring in the European Union', p. 799.

64 See Consumer Credit Directive, recital 26.

65 CJEU C-565/12, *LCL Le Crédit Lyonnais SA v Fesih Kalhan*, ECLI:EU:C:2014:190, pp. 42–43. See also C.M. van Heerden and R. Steennot, 'Pre-Agreement Assessment as a Responsible Lending Tool in South-Africa, the EU and Belgium: Part 2', *Potchefstroom Electronic Law Journal*, 19 March 2018, vol. 21, no. 1, pp. 1–38.

66 Financial Services Users Group, 'Responsible consumer credit lending – FSUG opinion and recommendations for the review of the Consumer Credit Directive', 8 April 2019, https://ec.europa.eu/, p. 6; Ferretti, 'Data protection in credit for consumers', p. 72.

67 L.C. Thomas, 'A survey of credit and behavioural scoring: forecasting financial risk of lending to consumers', *International Journal of Forecasting*, 2000, vol. 16, no. 2, p. 150; Financial Services Users Group, 'Responsible consumer credit lending', p. 6; Ferretti, 'Data protection in credit for consumers', p. 72; Cherednychenko and Meindertsma, 'Irresponsible Lending in the Post-Crisis Era', p. 485.

68 Cherednychenko and Meindertsma, 'Irresponsible Lending in the Post-Crisis Era', p. 485.

69 Basel Committee on Banking Supervision, 'Supervision Principles for the Management of Credit Risk', *Basel Committee Publications*, 27 September 2000, https://www.bis.org.

the probability of default and determine the credit risk of losing their money connected to it. In doing so, they will assess whether they will get their money back in case of the creditor's default on a credit and thus keep on carrying out a credit risk assessment.[70] This means that, given their strong commercial and financial incentives, creditors will always assess the risk of non-repayment associated with a credit and will be less inclined to assess the risk of a credit product having a negative impact on the consumer's financial situation, especially when the latter is still profitable for the creditor.[71] This way, creditors may decide to grant credit to non-creditworthy consumers when they know that the credit risk (i.e., the risk of loss) is limited by the presence of a certain collateral or personal security they can rely on in case of default. In addition, by granting a credit but charging consumers with excessively high interest rates or a penalty rate, creditors may guarantee that they will recover (a large part of) their money, even if this could lead to a financial disadvantage for the consumer.[72]

Apart from these commercial incentives, the probability of default and the credit risk assessment also play a role in the context of prudential supervision and risk management requirements. The Basel Standards obligate the creditor to hold a minimum amount of capital in relation to its credit risk exposure (i.e., the risk-weighted assets), so it can absorb the losses that ensue when their debtors go into default. The creditor should thus first calculate the expected loss ('EL') of the inability of the consumer to repay the credit associated with each consumer (portfolio) in order to determine a rating.[73] These credit risk ratings are based on the probability of default ('DF'), the loss given default ('LGD') and the exposure at default ('EAD').[74] The outcome will depend on several variables, such as the credit or payment history of the consumer. In addition, credit with a certain level of coverage (such as a mortgage or personal securities) implies a lower risk for the creditor and can thus contain a better rating.[75] Furthermore, the credit risk affects credit product pricing. This means that the interest rate granted to a particular credit will depend on the risk associated with the credit product

70 Ferretti, 'Data protection in credit for consumers', p. 72.

71 Financial Services Users Group, 'Responsible consumer credit lending', p. 7; Ferretti, 'Data protection in credit for consumers', p. 72; Cherednychenko and Meindertsma, 'Irresponsible Lending in the Post-Crisis Era', p. 485.

72 Commission Staff Working Document, SWD(2020) 254 final, 5 November 2020, pp. 37–38, https://eur-lex.europa.eu/; Cherednychenko and Meindertsma, 'Irresponsible Lending in the Post-Crisis Era', pp. 485–486.

73 For more detailed explanations on this subject, see Basel III standards (international standards), which are incorporated in the Capital Requirements Directive (Directive 2013/36/EU) or 'CRD' and the Capital Requirements Regulation (Regulation (EU) No 575/2013) or 'CRR'.

74 Basel Committee on Banking Supervision, 'International Convergence of Capital Measurement and Capital Standards: A Revised Framework', *Basel Committee Publications*, 15 November 2005, www.bis.org, pp. 74–75.

75 Basel Committee on Banking Supervision, 'International Convergence of Capital Measurement and Capital Standards', p. 74.

or credit portfolios. The higher the risk of default, the higher the amount the creditor can lose and thus the higher the interest rate that will be charged.[76]

10. In a nutshell, an absence of credit risk does not automatically entail consumer creditworthiness. Whereas a credit risk assessment will be influenced by coverage, the creditworthiness assessment cannot. In addition, the creditworthiness of a consumer has to be unrelated to the interests and penalties attached to the credit. Both assessments try to answer the following question: can the consumer repay the credit or not? Whereas the creditor's assessment of credit risk or risk of default attempts to determine whether or not granting a credit would result in a loss for the creditor itself, the consumer's assessment of creditworthiness aims to determine whether or not the credit will have a negative impact on the consumer and whether he or she can repay the credit without becoming over-indebted.[77] The creditor is therefore obligated to take the other party's interests and needs into account, and not solely act in his or her own interest.[78] All of this means that the assessment of credit risk may be part of a creditworthiness assessment but should not be limited to it. An assessment based solely on gaining potential profits and avoiding potential losses is insufficient and does not entail responsible lending. After all, in this situation the standard execution of the credit agreement is not prioritised, as the assessment takes external factors into account, such as the personal securities granted or the fees charged in the event of default. In other words, creditworthiness assessments and credit risk assessments can be seen as complementary (for a summary comparison see *Table 1*).

Table 1.

Credit risk assessment	Creditworthiness assessment
Creditor's interests assessment	Consumer's interests assessment
Calculating the risk of default and creditor's loss	Calculating the risk of consumer's over-indebtedness and overall detriment
Influence of external factors (e.g. securities or mortgages)	No influence of external factors (e.g. securities or mortgages)
Granting credit when creditors will get their money back and make profit	Granting credit when consumer can repay the credit without becoming over-indebted
Basel/commercial lending	Responsible lending

76 P. Vissers, 'The operational flow of a home loan, a look behind the scenes of Crelan', *BFW*, 2019, vol. 2, p. 132. See also: https://www.ing.be/static/legacy/SiteCollectionDocuments/Tarievenblad_EN.pdf and https://www.thebalance.com/what-are-interest-rates-and-how-do-they-work-3305855.

77 Ramsay, 'Consumer Credit Regulation after the fall', p. 33.

78 *Ibid.*, p. 33.

3. THE AUTOMATION OF CREDITWORTHINESS ASSESSMENT THROUGH CREDIT SCORING

3.1. MEANING AND FUNCTION

11. Credit scoring is usually formulated as a systematic and mathematical method to calculate and predict the credit risk and/or the creditworthiness of potential borrowers. It is the use of statistical models to transform relevant data into numerical measures that guides credit decisions. The general idea of credit scoring is to compare the characteristics of a potential borrower with other (past or current) borrowers from a previous period. If the characteristics of the potential borrower are sufficiently similar to those who have been granted credit and have consequently defaulted, the application will normally be rejected.

In other words, a credit scoring model extracts findings from patterns and correlations identified from data regarding credit performances, financial transactions, and other characteristics obtained from different borrowers, to predict the repayment behaviour and financial solvency of potential *new* borrowers when deciding whether or not to grant credit.[79] The credit scoring process analyses financial (credit) data and consumers' characteristics as well as application form details.[80] This means that credit scoring models will identify a statistical correlation between certain characteristics of borrowers-consumers and their credit repayment situation.[81, 82] This analysis helps creditors to identify the relevant predictive factors of default risk and divides the various borrowers into several categories according to their risk class.[83] Thus, when using this technique, the creditor will not only assess the potential borrower's own data, but will cross-check them with the data he or she possesses regarding other borrowers. The analysis of historical data on financial transactions and the characteristics of several borrowers combined with statistical techniques

79 N. Aggarwal, 'Machine Learning, Big Data and the Regulation of Consumer Credit Markets: The Case of Algorithmic Credit Scoring', in N. Aggarwal, H. Eidenmüller, L. Enriques, J. Payne and K. van Zwieten (eds.), *Autonomous Systems and the Law* (Munich: Beck, 2019), p. 38; Ferretti, 'Data protection in credit for consumers', p. 70; Thomas, 'A survey of credit and behavioural scoring', p. 150.

80 Thomas, 'A survey of credit and behavioural scoring', p. 150.

81 For example: the gross amount of credit, the marriage status, the number of dependants, the place of residence, years of living in the same place of residence, whether the house is rented or owned, education level, total monthly payments on all debts, type of bank accounts, number of years of work, total monthly household income, the debt-to-income ratio, the annual percentage interest on the credit. Each creditor can decide which factors to take into account on the basis of their (potential) influence on the level of credit risk and creditworthiness.

82 Thomas, 'A survey of credit and behavioural scoring', p. 150.

83 F. Ferretti, 'The 'Credit Scoring Pandemic' and the European Vaccine: Making Sense of EU Data Protection Legislation', *Journal of Information, Law & Technology*, 28 May 2009, p. 3; Ferretti, 'Data protection in credit for consumers', p. 70.

allows for an efficient and rapid identification of several characteristics linked to creditworthiness.

In short, credit scoring techniques are using data from past (and/or current) borrowers to analyse creditworthiness and credit risk of new borrowers.

12. Credit scoring is based on statistical research methods.[84] There are many different credit scoring methods and there is not one standardised model used by every creditor worldwide. The statistical tools used by creditors can vary and can for example include linear regression, classification trees or discriminant analysis.[85] In addition, as of late more and more AI- and ML-based credit scoring models are being used. Most credit scoring developers use one of these techniques or a combination thereof.[86]

So how are these various methods applied? Simply put, credit scoring can be subdivided in the following steps. Firstly, different types of consumer data will be processed. In doing so, the model will collect and analyse the collected data[87] from a sample of previously accepted borrowers who already have (had) a credit agreement (*step 1: data collection and data preparation*). During this process, inconsistencies are removed and missing values and outliers are dealt with.[88] Secondly, the creditor will determine, through statistical models, which factors have the most influence on the creditworthiness of the consumer by first determining which borrowers can be classified as 'uncreditworthy' (*step 2: uncreditworthiness definition*). For example, the creditor may determine that all borrowers who are more than 90 days in total overdue with their repayments within a period of one year,[89] missed three consecutive month of payments, or whose credit account has been concluded in a (court) dispute, are considered to be uncreditworthy borrowers.[90] Once the creditor has determined which borrowers he or she considers to be creditworthy or not, the credit model can calculate the most predictive factors (*step 3: variable selection*).[91] In the end, a well-functioning credit scoring model will divide the characteristics of borrowers in 'good' and 'bad'.

84 B.W. Yap, S.H. Ong and N.H.M. Husain, 'Using data mining to improve assessment of credit worthiness via credit scoring models', *Expert Systems with Applications*, 2011, vol. 38, no. 10, p. 13275; Thomas, 'A survey of credit and behavioural scoring', p. 152.

85 Yap et al., 'Using data mining to improve assessment of credit worthiness via credit scoring models', p. 13275.

86 Thomas, 'A survey of credit and behavioural scoring', p. 152.

87 After all, during the application process of the borrowers, the creditor has to obtain all relevant and necessary information from these borrowers himself/herself and/or consult, where necessary, a relevant database from credit bureaus. See *supra* no. 5–7.

88 Thomas, 'A survey of credit and behavioural scoring', p. 152.

89 This is also the definition of 'default' of the Basel Accord.

90 Thomas, 'A survey of credit and behavioural scoring', p. 153.

91 Variable reduction reduces a large number of variables that are eligible for inclusion in the scorecard to a smaller number by using statistical methods like the Weight of Evidence (WoE), the Pearson chi-square test and the Information Value (IV).

A last step is developing the actual model or scorecard (*step 4: model development*) and applying it to new potential borrowers. In other words, the scorecard represents the link between credit performance of former or current borrowers ('good' or 'bad') and their characteristics. This model is then applied to future customers to estimate their creditworthiness. The sum of all weighted points for each variable represents a certain score for each potential borrower. Depending on the final score, a credit will or will not be granted. If the borrower obtains a score that does not reach the minimum ('the bottom score' or 'cut-off score'), it will not be possible to grant a loan. From the various collected data, an algorithm can, for example, establish that a person who carries out his or her professional activity for several years with the same employer will repay a credit on a more regular basis than a person who changes jobs more frequently. Where a higher point will be given for consumers who are in the first situation, it will be much lower for consumers who find themselves in the second situation. The sum of all weighted points will result in a certain score for each borrower. Depending on this final score, the creditor can then decide whether or not to grant credit to each particular borrower. If the borrower obtains a score that does not reach the minimum required by the creditor (the 'bottom score' or 'cut-off score'), no credit shall be granted. If the minimum is reached, the creditor may decide to grant credit. Nevertheless, the creditor can also decide that in certain cases or in a range between certain scores a further assessment should be made. All of this means that a good scoring model should ensure that high scores are given to those consumers who are creditworthy and low scores to those who are uncreditworthy.[92]

13. The most well-known credit scoring model is the FICO model used by the United States.[93] This scoring model was created by the Fair Isaac Corporation (nowadays referred to as 'FICO'), a major analytics software company that provides products and services to both businesses and consumers. This credit scoring model is based on data from three different credit agencies, Experian, TransUnion, and Equifax.[94] It uses various factors in five different areas to determine creditworthiness: payment history, amounts owed, length of credit history, new credit and credit mix. Each category is given a certain percentage. These percentages reflect how important each of the categories is in calculating the FICO scores. For example, the payment history, as the most important factor, will account for 35% of the score. FICO scores vary between 300 and 850 points.

---

92 Yap et al., 'Using data mining to improve assessment of credit worthiness via credit scoring models', p. 13274.

93 Keep, however, in mind that there is not one FICO score. Different creditors use different versions of the FICO score when evaluating credit. For example, a mortgage creditor will probably use a different score than a vehicle creditor.

94 The 'big three' nationwide credit bureaus in the United States. See M. Hurley and J. Adebayo, 'Credit scoring in the era of big data', *Yale Journal of Law and Technology*, 2016, vol. 18, no. 1, p. 154.

The higher the FICO-score, the more reliable a borrower is in repaying the credit and the easier a credit will be granted to this consumer. In general, many creditors treat scores above 670 as an indication that a borrower is creditworthy. In contrast, borrowers with a score below 620 will find it often difficult to obtain funding at favourable rates.[95]

The FICO-scoring system uses five different categories to calculate the final score. The payment history-factor *(i)* refers to the question whether the potential borrower has paid his or her credit accounts on time. Payment history of a consumer thus reveals details regarding late or missed payments. Depending on how late they were, how much was owed, how recently they occurred and how many there are, late payments will have a negative effect on the borrower's score.[96] The credit history of a borrower indicates how many of the consumer's credit accounts are overdue in relation to all his or her accounts on file. This means that if a borrower has ten credit accounts and he or she has had a late payment on five of those accounts, that ratio may affect his or her credit scores. Secondly, how much of the available credit – the 'credit limit' – the consumer is using or the amount of debt on his or her credit accounts *(ii)* may give the borrower a low credit score. When a high percentage of a person's available credit is being used, it can indicate that a person is overextended, and is more likely to make late payments or miss payments. The amount the potential borrower already owes on credit accounts and the portion of his or her available credit that he or she is using together, is worth about a third of the score. In addition, the score increases if the borrower has a long credit history *(iii)*, which means that the borrower needs credit to get credit.[97] The average age of all the borrower's accounts is worth about fifteen percent of the score. Additionally, the FICO credit score considers the different types of credit accounts the potential borrower has and thus takes into account the mix of retail accounts, instalment loans, finance company accounts and mortgage loans *(iv)*. Ten percent of the FICO score is based upon the idea that it is not necessary to have one of each, and that it is not a good idea to open credit accounts that one does not intend to use. However, to obtain high credit scores, individuals need a strong credit mix. Finally, new credit inquiries and recently opened accounts *(v)* will also influence about a tenth of the credit score. So a borrower who has opened several new accounts in a short amount of time, will get a lower score.[98] The FICO scoring

---

95 See https://www.myfico.com/credit-education/whats-in-your-credit-score.

96 *Ibid.*

97 'Like fine wine, whiskey and cheese, most credit histories only get better with age', see https://www.myfico.com/credit-education/whats-in-your-credit-score. For example, a borrower who has a credit history of less than one year will only be able to score 12 points, while the score of a person who already has a credit history of four years or more will increase with 75 points (see https://www.doughroller.net/credit/a-rare-glimpse-inside-the-fico-credit-score-formula/).

98 See https://www.myfico.com/credit-education/whats-in-your-credit-score.

model does not take into account the salary, occupation, employment history of the potential borrower and other items that might suggest creditworthiness.[99]

3.2. NEW CREDIT SCORING TECHNIQUES

14. Traditional credit scoring uses regular statistical techniques in order to draw conclusions from patterns in a limited number of categories of data. Yet, due to current technological evolutions, including the emergence of FinTech, many new credit scoring models are emerging.[100] New credit scoring models differ from traditional ones in two ways: firstly, they use different inputs and secondly, they apply a different process to evaluate the creditworthiness of prospective borrowers.

15. Firstly, new credit models on the market may apply a larger volume and diversity of data, the so-called alternative data or non-traditional data.[101] As the use of smartphones, including social media and electronic methods of payment, has greatly increased, consumer nowadays will leave a digital trail of data behind.[102] Combining this with the fact that it may for some consumers be hard to predict their creditworthiness and credit risk because they have a sparse or a non-existent credit history or payment history,[103] creditors are eager to capture and analyse these alternative data sources (e.g., social media insights or other digital footprints) in order to better predict consumer behaviour.[104] To creditors using this new technique of credit scoring, *all data is credit data*.[105]

---

99 See https://www.myfico.com/credit-education/credit-scores/whats-not-in-your-credit-score.

100 L. Gambacorta, Y. Huang, H. Qiu and J. Wang, 'How do machine learning and non-traditional data affect credit scoring? New evidence from a Chinese fintech firm', *BIS Working Papers*, 19 December 2019, p. 2; Hurley and Adebayo, 'Credit scoring in the era of big data', p. 162.

101 G. Barci, G. Andreeva and S. Bouyon, 'Data sharing in credit markets: Does comprehensiveness matter?', *ECRI Research Report No. 23*, 12 September 2019, pp. 41–42; Gambacorta et al., 'How do machine learning and non-traditional data affect credit scoring?', p. 2; Aggarwal, 'Machine Learning, Big Data and the Regulation of Consumer Credit Markets', p. 38.

102 European Commission, 'Evaluation of Directive 2008/48/EC on credit agreement for consumers', Final Report, February 2020, https://ec.europa.eu/, p. 37; Hurley and Adebayo, 'Credit scoring in the era of big data', p. 151.

103 After all, some credit scoring models, such as the FICO score to a great extent, assess creditworthiness and credit risk on the basis of the borrower's credit history (see Aggarwal, 'Machine Learning, Big Data and the Regulation of Consumer Credit Markets', p. 38), which means that these consumers are seen as 'unscorable' and can thus not access traditional forms of credit (see Hurley and Adebayo, 'Credit scoring in the era of big data', p. 155).

104 Gambacorta et al., 'How do machine learning and non-traditional data affect credit scoring?', p. 2.

105 'All data is credit data', a quote from the CEO of ZestFinance in the *New York Times*, see https://www.ft.com. See also Hurley and Adebayo, 'Credit scoring in the era of big data', p. 151.

These 'big-data' credit scoring models combine traditional financial data points and non-traditional data points collected from the borrower's online and offline activities, such as social media platforms, smartphone records, consumers' retail spending histories and other public platforms,[106] the device type, the operating system (e.g., iOS or Android), the time of day of the purchase (e.g., morning, afternoon, evening, or night) or the email service provider (e.g., Gmail or Hotmail or Yahoo).[107] In addition, creditors may use a consumer's car brand, Facebook friends, educational background and college majors, even the fact whether he or she sends text messages in all capital letters or in lower case.[108] Instead of using traditional credit rating information, Kreditech, a German online creditor, for example, assesses the creditworthiness of their potential borrowers by using their online data such as location data, social graphing (e.g., likes and posts on Facebook), behavioural data (e.g., movement on a webpage or how quickly the applicant scrolls through an online terms-and-conditions disclosure) or e-commerce shopping behaviour.[109] The company Big Data Scoring Ltd has created a credit scoring model that uses up to 10.000 data points, including location-based information, web search results, behavioural tracking, device technical details, mobile app data and much more.[110] Even FICO is implementing new strategies for assessing a consumer's creditworthiness. In addition to looking at the information offered on social networking sites, the scoring model will also assess smartphone records.[111] VisualDNA has even taken things a step further and combined elements of psychology and machine learning to create unique products based on the proven connection between personality and behaviour in credit and insurance.[112] The credit scoring model of VisualDNA asks applicants to choose pictures from a selection. For example, one question offers pictures of several leisure activities. The potential borrower then has to select the picture of the leisure they prefer (e.g., a day out with the family? A night out partying? A good book?). The chosen pictures eventually reflect the attitude the applicant has towards different types of risk.[113]

---

106 Hurley and Adebayo, 'Credit scoring in the era of big data', p. 163.

107 T. Berg, V. Burg, A. Gombović and M. Puri, 'On the Rise of the FinTechs – Credit Scoring using Digital Footprints', *FDIC-CFR Working Paper Series*, September 2018, https://www.fdic.gov, pp. 2–3.

108 G. Roberts, 'Regulator Wades into Big Data Credit Swamp, Bloomberg Law: Banking', 20 April 2017, https://www.bna.com.

109 Robinson + Yu, 'Knowing the Score: New Data, Underwriting, and Marketing in the Consumer Credit Marketplace: A Guide for Financial Inclusion Stakeholders', 29 October 2014, https://www.upturn.org, p. 17.

110 See www.bigdatascoring.com.

111 B. Hardekopf, 'Your Social Media Posts May Soon Affect Your Credit Score', *Forbes*, 23 October 2015, https://www.forbes.com.

112 R. Grétarsson, 'Creditinfo acquires VisualDNA Credit & Risk business for psychometrics and alternative data', press release, 29 August 2016, https://mt.creditinfo.com.

113 P. Jenkins, 'Big data lends new Zest to banks' credit judgments', *Financial Times*, 23 June 2014, https://www.ft.com.

16. Secondly, in addition to their increasing use of big data, some creditors also rely on more sophisticated techniques to analyse the collected (big) data.[114] Due to advances in technology, more intelligent credit scoring models are being developed. Nowadays, a number of credit scoring models use AI and ML to sift through and analyse the (sometimes endlessly available) data points.[115] These techniques make it possible to analyse very large volumes of data at a very high-speed and in an effective manner.[116] Algorithms can *learn* how to make creditworthiness determinations, largely by themselves, instead of merely performing a creditworthiness assessment once the creditor has decided which data points are correlated with creditworthiness and how much weight to give each variable. A credit scoring model based on ML-techniques subsequently mines and analyses the given data (i.e., all the company's data about consumers who previously applied for credit, including whether they were granted credit and if so, whether they repaid their credit in a timely and correct manner). It then decides on its own which variables are relevant for someone's creditworthiness and which ones are the most important in order to calculate how much weight must be given to each one of them.[117]

A prominent ML-technique in credit scoring, for example, is deep learning using neural networks. Neural networks mimic the way in which the human brain works and are mathematical representations inspired by the human brain nerve cells and their communication and processing information methods. In short, credit scoring based on neural networks learns to identify the pattern between numerous data points, through different inner layers. There are three layers: the input layer (i.e., input nodes which represent the variables), the hidden layer (i.e., nodes which facilitate and analyse the flow of information) and the output layer (i.e., the nodes which represent the decision, the result).[118] In other words, neural networks are computer networks of units in which different (input) neurons are analysed by another (hidden) layer of neurons to obtain an output neuron.[119]

17. Although at first creditors used the same type of traditional credit scoring methods to analyse these increased volumes of data inputs, instead of

114 Hurley and Adebayo, 'Credit scoring in the era of big data', p. 151.

115 For more information on the meaning and definitions of AI and ML, see Chapter 1 of this book.

116 Hurley and Adebayo, 'Credit scoring in the era of big data', p. 158; Aggarwal, 'Machine Learning, Big Data and the Regulation of Consumer Credit Markets', p. 38.

117 M.A. Bruckner, 'Regulating Fintech Lending', *Banking & Financial Services Policy Report*, 2018, vol. 37, no. 6, p. 2; M.A. Bruckner, 'The Promise and Perils of Algorithmic Lenders' Use of Big Data', *Chicago-Kent Law Review*, 2018, vol. 93, no. 1, p. 17.

118 A.K. Soni and A.U. Abdullahi, 'Using neural networks for credit scoring', *International Journal of Science, Technology & Management*, 2015, vol. 4, no. 5, p. 26.

119 Aggarwal, 'Machine Learning, Big Data and the Regulation of Consumer Credit Markets', p. 39.

fundamentally changing the underlying process of evaluation, a variety of data cannot easily be analysed without the use of more complex methods.[120] As such, the abovementioned non-traditional ways of credit scoring will operate hand-in-hand with the more traditional means.

The combination of more sophisticated algorithms (i.e., artificial intelligence, machine learning, deep learning and neural networks) and big data can uncover some nonintuitive, non-obvious connections. Moreover, such processes can operate more efficiently.[121] However, this does not automatically mean that non-traditional credit scoring is risk-free (see *infra* no. 21–24).

4. THE IMPACT OF CREDIT SCORING ON CONSUMERS

4.1. THE POTENTIAL EFFECTS ON CONSUMERS-BORROWERS

4.1.1. Benefits

18. First of all, credit scoring helps to increase the speed and consistency of the loan application process and reduces the length of the application approval process.[122] Credit scoring can reduce the average time to assess a credit application to well under an hour (at least in cases where no human intervention or re-evaluation has taken place), and sometimes even less.[123] When effective, such credit scoring may be able to analyse criteria faster, and could even respond in real time[124] to both consumers' data and market conditions. Consumers may benefit from increased efficiency and speed when decision-making is fully automatic, including data collection and analysis.[125] Furthermore, credit

---

120 Bruckner, 'Regulating Fintech Lending', p. 2; Bruckner, 'The Promise and Perils of Algorithmic Lenders' Use of Big Data', p. 14.

121 Bruckner, 'Regulating Fintech Lending', p. 2.

122 A study has shown that a normal, non-automated assessment of a consumer's creditworthiness takes on average about twelve hours per credit application (see L. Mester, 'What Is the Point of Credit Scoring?', *Business Review*, September/October 1997, p. 8).

123 H.Ch. Koh, W.Ch. Tan and Ch.P. Goh, 'A Two-step Method to Construct Credit Scoring Models with Data Mining Techniques', *International Journal of Business and* Information, 2006, vol. 1, no. 1, p. 99; Mester, 'What Is the Point of Credit Scoring?', p. 8.

124 For example, consumers can obtain credit with the purpose of financing a vehicle within mere seconds at KBC, a Belgian credit institution.

125 A. Jabłonowska, M. Kuziemski, A.M. Nowak, H-W. Micklitz, P. Palka and G. Sartor, 'Consumer law and artificial intelligence: challenges to the EU consumer law and policy stemming from the business' use of artificial intelligence: final report of the ARTSY project', *EUI Department of Law Research Paper*, 2018, vol. 11, p. 38; FiCoNet, 'Digitalisation of short-term, high-cost consumer credit Guidance to supervisors', November 2018, https://www.finconet.org, p. 9.

scoring has a cost-reducing impact. It reduces the need for a manual review of the application and human evaluation, and thus lowers the labour cost as credit scoring automatically requires less employees.[126]

19. Secondly, the application of credit scoring could lead to a more objective and more accurate prediction of a consumer's creditworthiness when compared to the assessment based on the intuition of an individual, i.e., the credit officer.[127] A number of academic studies have compared the accuracy of credit scoring and judgmental credit-evaluation carried out by humans. These studies show that credit scoring systems consistently outperform judgmental systems in predicting loan performance. As a result, fewer creditworthy applicants will be rejected, and fewer non-creditworthy applicants will be accepted.[128] Humans lack objective and sometimes rational, judgemental capabilities which is why their decisions will be based on subjective reasoning instead. Humans are prone to numerous cognitive biases and emotion (especially when they personally know the potential borrower).[129] Instead of assessing one's creditworthiness on subjective and personal criteria, a credit scoring system uses objective credit factors in the credit application process.[130]

20. Finally, credit scoring may increase the availability of credit and lead to more financial inclusiveness of consumers.[131] Non-traditional algorithmic credit scoring may, by using both traditional and non-traditional data, increase financial inclusiveness for consumers. That is because many people who have traditionally been denied a credit – because they do not have an extensive credit

---

126 C. Wendel and M. Harvey, 'Credit Scoring: Best Practices and Approaches', *Commercial Lending Review*, 2003, vol. 18, no. 3, p. 6; Koh et al., 'A Two-step Method to Construct Credit Scoring Models with Data Mining Techniques', p. 99; Bruckner, 'The Promise and Perils of Algorithmic Lenders' Use of Big Data', p. 21.

127 K.G. Gunter, 'Computerized Credit Scoring's Effect on the Lending Industry', *N.C. Banking Inst. 443*, 2000, vol. 4, no. 1, p. 449; FiCoNet, 'Digitalisation of short-term, high-cost consumer credit Guidance to supervisors', pp. 28–29; Barci et al., 'Data sharing in credit markets: Does comprehensiveness matter?', p. 50; Bruckner, 'The Promise and Perils of Algorithmic Lenders' Use of Big Data', p. 18; Mester, 'What Is the Point of Credit Scoring?', p. 8.

128 For more information regarding these (American) studies, see Board of Governors of the Federal Reserve System, 'Report to the Congress on Credit Scoring and Its Effects on the Availability and Affordability of Credit', August 2007, https://www.federalreserve.gov, pp. 39–41,

129 C. Castets-Renard, 'Accountability of algorithms in the GDPR and beyond: a European legal framework on automated decision-making', *Fordham Intellectual Property, Media & Entertainment Law*, 2019, vol. 30, no. 1, pp. 96–97; D.A. Zetzsche, D. Arner, R. Buckey and B.W. Tang, 'Artificial Intelligence in Finance: Putting the Human in the Loop', C*FTE Academic Paper Series*, 2020, vol. 1, p. 18; Ferretti, 'Data protection in credit for consumers', p. 71.

130 Gunter, 'Computerized Credit Scoring's Effect on the Lending Industry', p. 450.

131 Board of Governors of the Federal Reserve System, 'Report to the Congress on Credit Scoring', pp. 42–43.

history ('unscorable' or 'thin file' borrowers) – will now be accepted as a borrower by relying on this broader approach to credit scoring.[132, 133] Likewise, credit scoring makes acquiring credit less expensive and more affordable for consumers. It, therefore, becomes more accessible.[134] By reducing costs, creditors may also be more willing to grant small credits.[135] Creditors often refrain(ed) from assessing the creditworthiness of small borrowers because the cost would be too high taking into account that the profit for smaller credits would be lower than the accompanying costs, including the time and energy invested.[136]

4.1.2. Challenges

21. However, as great as these abovementioned benefits may sound, the use of credit scoring is a double-edged sword. On the one hand, credit scoring may ultimately entail some important advantages for consumers, but on the other hand, it could generate significant risks as well.

22. First of all, credit scoring will not always lead to financial inclusiveness, as credit scoring models may also result in and perpetuate biases and discrimination.[137] After all, credit scores are only as free from bias as the data and algorithms relied upon.[138] Even though credit scoring may lead to more objective, bias-free decision-making and the used variables may at first sight appear objective, in reality they may still reflect (racial) biases and therefore perpetuate or increase discrimination.[139, 140] It is clear that scoring models cannot use race, age or gender as creditworthiness factors, as this will lead to

---

132 This is a common practice in the United States, as the credit scoring system in the US is based on the credit and payment history of the consumer. Therefore, consumers who do not have enough information in their credit files to receive a traditional credit score or have an unjustifiably low score, will be excluded from getting credit or will get credit on worse terms (e.g., higher interest or penalty rates).

133 Aggarwal, 'Machine Learning, Big Data and the Regulation of Consumer Credit Markets', p. 39; Barci et al., 'Data sharing in credit markets: Does comprehensiveness matter?', p. 50.

134 Bruckner, 'The Promise and Perils of Algorithmic Lenders' Use of Big Data', p. 21.

135 Koh et al., 'A Two-step Method to Construct Credit Scoring Models with Data Mining Techniques', p. 99; Wendel and Harvey, 'Credit Scoring: Best Practices and Approaches', p. 6.

136 International Monetary Fund (Majid Bazarbash), 'FinTech in Financial Inclusion Machine Learning Applications in Assessing Credit Risk', *IMF Working Papers*, 17 May 2019, p. 24.

137 European Commission, 'Impact assessment report accompanying the Proposal for a Directive of the European Parliament and of the Council on consumer credits', Commission Staff Working Document, SWD(2021) 170 final, 30 June 2021, p. 3 and 27.

138 D.K. Citron and F. Pasquale, 'The Scored Society: Due Process for Automated Predictions', *University of Maryland Francis King Carey School of Law Legal Studies Research Paper*, 2014, vol. 89, no. 8, pp. 13–14; Hurley and Adebayo, 'Credit scoring in the era of big data', p. 167.

139 After all, the Consumer Credit Directive seeks to ensure full respect of the rules on non-discrimination, therefore both direct and indirect discrimination are absolutely prohibited (see recital 45 CCD).

140 Gunter, 'Computerized Credit Scoring's Effect on the Lending Industry', p. 451; Castets-Renard, 'Accountability of algorithms in the GDPR and beyond', p. 6; J.A. Kroll, J. Huey, S.

direct discrimination. But a credit scoring model may be based on factors that have unwanted discriminatory effects and use 'discriminatory proxies'.[141] For example, algorithms may take the income of the consumer into account in order to assess whether he or she is creditworthy. This criterion by itself has no discriminatory effect. However, since differences still exist between the incomes of men and women, the reliance on this criterion may (indirectly) discriminate the latter. Alternatively, a credit scoring system may draw a negative correlation between consumers with a certain low-paying service job and creditworthiness and therefore give low scores to these consumers. If a majority of people who hold these jobs are racial minorities, this job classification may have an indirect but still unfair effect. While this correlation may not reflect intentional bias, it can thus have a (perhaps unforeseen) discriminatory effect on certain protected groups.[142] Even when a credit algorithm is programmed to give higher scores to consumers who graduated from a specific (prestigious) college or university, it may have indirect discriminatory effects when the admission process for those colleges or universities happens to be biased against particular classes of people. In other words, by using seemingly innocuous information such as consumers' postal codes, magazine subscriptions or current work environment as proxies for sensitive and discriminatory attributes including race or gender, credit scoring may have a major negative impact on a consumer's fundamental right not to be discriminated against.[143] As such, this kind of discrimination cannot only occur in creditworthiness assessments carried out by individuals but can also arise when using automated tools in the decision-making process.

In addition, credit scoring may lead to discriminatory results when the underlying algorithms are trained on historical examples that reflect a previously existing prejudice or implicit bias, or on data that reflects a distorted picture of the population (i.e., an overrepresentation or underrepresentation of a minority group).[144] If the credit model is based on prior application decisions and these decisions have systematically disadvantaged certain minorities, this model will have indirect discriminatory effects. Automating a process based on previous discriminatory practices means that these prejudices and biases from the past will be transformed (whether conscious or unconscious) into a formalised rule that systematically and negatively affects all future applicants.[145, 146]

Barocas, E.W. Felten, J.R. Reidenberg, D.G. Robinson and H. Yu, 'Accountable Algorithms', *University of Pennsylvania Law Review*, 24 February 2017, vol. 165, no. 3, p. 680.

141 Gunter, 'Computerized Credit Scoring's Effect on the Lending Industry', p. 451.

142 Gunter, 'Computerized Credit Scoring's Effect on the Lending Industry', p. 451; Bruckner, 'The Promise and Perils of Algorithmic Lenders' Use of Big Data', p. 28.

143 Renard, 'Accountability of algorithms in the GDPR and beyond', p. 6; Hurley and Adebayo, 'Credit scoring in the era of big data', p. 152.

144 Kroll et al., 'Accountable Algorithms', p. 680.

145 Bruckner, 'The Promise and Perils of Algorithmic Lenders' Use of Big Data', p. 26; Bazarbash, 'FinTech in Financial Inclusion Machine Learning Applications in Assessing Credit Risk', p. 28.

146 In addition to discrimination issues, financial exclusion can occur due to the so-called 'cost of privacy'. Privacy-minded consumers may be unwilling to give access to private (non-

23. Beyond discrimination, the opacity of credit scoring systems also needs to be considered. Especially self-learning algorithms are often considered as 'black boxes' because the amount of inferences drawn by a self-learning process makes it difficult for humans to evaluate why a certain conclusion was reached as human intervention is mainly limited to defining the model and selecting the data.[147] This way, the credit scoring system may be able to discover patterns that go well beyond human intuition.[148] This means that individuals (i.e., consumers, creditors or regulators) cannot easily understand, explain, challenge and audit certain credit decisions taken by the credit scoring model and cannot detect errors and correct them.[149] At the same time, it is not always possible to determine whether a rule has discriminatory effects.[150] That is because it can be difficult to predict the effects of an algorithm in advance. The opacity and complexity of credit scoring models may thus make it more difficult to anticipate and *ex ante* detect whether these models contain biases and/or facilitate unlawful discrimination.[151]

24. Finally, creditors using credit scoring systems assume that the data they use is both accurate and complete. Still, data quality may be poor, especially when data was not directly obtained from the consumer himself/herself, but from the latter's digital footprint.[152] When credit scoring models rely on social media to assess one's creditworthiness, we have to remember that such 'social' data can easily be manipulated and is not always an accurate and complete representation of reality. Conversely, consumers may proactively shape their behaviour in order to manipulate the results and obtain a high credit score.[153] For example, the number of friends could be indicative of good creditworthiness thereby causing the credit scoring model to include the number of social media connections as a variable to assess the creditworthiness. However, considering that social media connections do not reflect the depth of those relationships and the fact that

traditional) information, like their digital footprint data, at the expense of still getting credit, but at higher interest or penalty rates. These consumers thus have to pay for their privacy protection, which is the opposite of the purpose of the data protection legislation. See BEUC, 'Big data & financial services – BEUC response to ESAs consultation', 27 March 2017, https://www.beuc.eu, p. 7.

147 Renard, 'Accountability of algorithms in the GDPR and beyond', p. 6; Bruckner, 'Regulating Fintech Lending', p. 2.

148 Bruckner, 'Regulating Fintech Lending', p. 3.

149 *Ibid.*, p. 10.

150 Kroll et al., 'Accountable Algorithms', p. 680.

151 Aggarwal, 'Machine Learning, Big Data and the Regulation of Consumer Credit Markets', p. 39.

152 Gunter, 'Computerized Credit Scoring's Effect on the Lending Industry', p. 455; Bazarbash, 'FinTech in Financial Inclusion Machine Learning Applications in Assessing Credit Risk', p. 29; Hurley and Adebayo, 'Credit scoring in the era of big data', p. 156; Zetzsche et al., 'Artificial Intelligence in Finance: Putting the Human in the Loop', p. 18.

153 Financial Services Users Group, 'Responsible consumer credit lending', p. 13.

applicants could expand the size of their social network in a fairly easy way to achieve a better credit score, this cannot be seen as a proper and effective credit scoring variable.[154] Moreover, one (wrong) like or post on Facebook can lead to a lower credit score. This could eventually result in a chilling effect on the freedom of expression. Furthermore, credit scoring models incorporating the credit scores of members of the social network that are connected to the applicant can easily be interpreted incorrectly, leading to wrong conclusions regarding the applicant himself/herself.[155]

4.2. THE CONFINES OF THE CONSUMER CREDIT DIRECTIVE

4.2.1. Can the Use of Credit Scoring Techniques be Considered a Responsible Lending Practice?

25. An adequate creditworthiness assessment, performed prior to the conclusion of the credit agreement, could be a powerful tool in granting credit based on the principles of responsible lending and of preventing over-indebtedness and detriment to consumers.[156] However, the aforementioned analysis shows that a creditworthiness assessment has to go beyond a mere credit risk assessment or a risk of default assessment. This implies that the creditor has to assess whether granting a credit would have a negative impact on the consumer and whether he or she can repay the credit without the risk of becoming over-indebted.[157] This means that, if a credit scoring system only takes the personal situation of the consumer into account and solely evaluates his or her personal characteristics against the used credit scoring variables, this practice could be in accordance with what is expected from creditors in the context of responsible lending, but only if the credit scoring model does not consider any external factors (e.g., personal securities and interest of penalty fees charged in the event of default). The fact that creditors still grant credit to consumers with low credit scores, thereby ensuring they can recover their money by charging higher rates of interests on top of the charges consumers have to pay in case of default, will further financially penalise vulnerable consumers. This

---

154 Bazarbash, 'FinTech in Financial Inclusion Machine Learning Applications in Assessing Credit Risk', p. 29.

155 Hurley and Adebayo, 'Credit scoring in the era of big data', p. 167.

156 CJEU C-58/18, *Michel Schyns v. Belfius Bank NV*, ECLI:EU:C:2019:467, para. 41. See van Heerden and Steennot, 'Pre-Agreement Assessment as a Responsible Lending Tool in South-Africa, the EU and Belgium: Part 2', pp. 1–38; FiCoNet, 'Digitalisation of short-term, high-cost consumer credit Guidance to supervisors', pp. 28–29.

157 See *supra* no. 8–10.

can in no way be considered as a responsible lending practice.[158] After all, the latest credit that has been granted may easily be the straw that broke the camel's back for the consumer: the potential borrower may be able to prove its ability to repay its existing credit facilities on time (and without financial difficulties), but may be so heavily committed that one additional credit facility could lead to over-indebtedness.

In short, credit scoring models allowing consumers to fall victim to disproportionate credit commitments they are unable to meet do not comply with the principle of responsible lending. Automated creditworthiness assessment models used by actors when providing consumer credit through digital channels taking into account consumers' individual circumstances can thus be sufficiently resilient, and may lead to responsible lending decisions. Credit scoring could in this way be seen as the automation of an individual (i.e., credit officer) who analyses the data of a potential borrower and who evaluates it against the knowledge he or she already has of former borrowers, due to his or her former experiences with assessing creditworthiness.

4.2.2. Are the Provisions of the Consumer Credit Directive Sufficient to Fully Protect Consumers?

26. The question arises whether the obligation to assess one's creditworthiness under the Consumer Credit Directive, including the 'responsible lending' requirement, is sufficient to protect consumers against the potential negative effects of credit scoring. As stated above, besides several important benefits, credit scoring, especially credit scoring 2.0, may entail risks for consumers such as (1) *financial exclusion* due to inaccurate, irrelevant and/or discriminatory data and discriminatory algorithms, (2) *unwanted financial inclusion*, i.e., the risk of granting credit to uncreditworthy consumers, and (3) *the opacity of complex algorithms* leading to extreme difficulties in understanding and contesting credit decisions.

27. The fact that a creditor always has the right to refuse a credit contract[159] coupled with the absence of any provisions in the Directive clarifying what has to be understood under over-indebtedness or (un)creditworthiness could lead to the financial exclusion of creditworthy consumers. The CCD only states that '(...) it is important that creditors should not engage in irresponsible lending or give out credit without prior assessment of creditworthiness and the Member

[158] Ferretti, 'The Legal Framework of Consumer Credit Bureaus and Credit Scoring in the European Union', p. 823.

[159] Access to credit is thus not a right the consumer can enforce in order to obtain a credit agreement. See I. Ramsay, 'Regulation of consumer credit', in Geraint Howells (ed.), *Handbook of Research on International Consumer Law*, 2nd edn (Cheltenham: Edward Elgar Publishing, 2010), p. 368.

States should carry out the necessary supervision to avoid such behaviour',[160] such as ensuring that, before concluding the credit agreement, the creditor assesses the consumer's creditworthiness on the basis of sufficient information, where appropriate obtained from the consumer and, where necessary, on the basis of a consultation of the relevant database.[161] This allows Member States to simply incorporate this vaguely formulated obligation into their legal framework without stating on which information they can or cannot base their credit decision and how to interpret said information. In addition, there is no clear legal basis to decide when a consumer can be considered creditworthy or not. Although the Directive is based on the principle of full harmonisation[162], only a modest degree of harmonisation is likely to be achieved regarding the creditworthiness assessment obligation. As the full harmonisation principle of the CCD is limited to its harmonised area and to the extent the provisions entail specific wording – and taking into account that the concept and the obligation of responsible lending remain unclear – the open-textured wording paves the way for different interpretations of this obligation and for granting different types of consumer protection across the various Member States. This has created the situation in which there is no common acceptance across the EU of what creditworthiness is, which information must be used to perform a creditworthiness assessment, and how to interpret said information. This means that the amount and categories of data collected by creditors, as well as the techniques to assess the collected data, differ greatly.[163] Whereas some Member States did lay down more clear and concrete obligations for the creditors (e.g., Belgium), others merely copied the vague CCD obligation into their legal system and give discretion to the creditors to determine which information has to be used in order to perform the creditworthiness assessment (e.g., Germany). In addition, the Directive does not specifically establish whether the assessment should be creditor-focused (i.e., risk assessment) or borrower-focused (i.e., affordability assessment done in the interest of the consumer).[164]

Consequently, in some countries consumers may not be adequately protected against irresponsible lending practices. Vaguely formulated obligations, for instance, leave room for credit scoring systems grounding their decisions on the (lack of) credit history of consumers[165] and on the fact that the consumer is

---

160 See Consumer Credit Directive, recital 26.

161 See Article 8.1 CCD.

162 See *supra* note no. 8.

163 European Commission, 'Evaluation of Directive 2008/48/EC on credit agreement for consumers', p. 37.

164 European Commission, 'Impact assessment report accompanying the Proposal for a Directive of the European Parliament and of the Council on consumer credits', p. 17.

165 Consumers in Belgium are more protected against the situation in which lower credit scores are awarded when the consumer has no credit or payment history. This situation now occurs in the United States (and possibly in some other EU Member States). After all, attributing a lower score when the consumer has not concluded a credit agreement is in no way consistent

new to the client database. These variables are more useful for estimating credit risk than for assessing the consumer's creditworthiness. In addition, ambiguous formulations or non-existing requirements regarding the data they may or may not use create the possibility for credit scoring models to obtain consumer data that is irrelevant in the context of creditworthiness-assessments (e.g., likes on Facebook or the number of connections on LinkedIn). In short, the fact that personal data is not used within a proper framework regarding (consumer) credit could lead to major financial exclusion entailing great detriment to consumers.[166] Thus, the European legislator has to consider specifying which information is relevant for the creditworthiness assessment and which is not in order to ban these (mal)practices and prevent financial exclusion. In addition to irrelevant or inaccurate data, credit scoring models may use data that lead to (direct or indirect) discriminatory effects for consumers. The question arises whether European financial regulators need to determine whether the way in which creditors use credit data is compliant with anti-discrimination legislation. Nowadays, there are some general regulations[167] regarding the prohibition of any discrimination based on various grounds such as sex, race, colour, ethnic or social origin, genetic features, language, religion or belief, political or any other opinion, membership of a national minority, property, birth, disability, age or sexual orientation. However, as opposed to the situation in the United States,[168]

---

with how the creditworthiness assessment is done in Belgium. Belgian case law states that the creditor must always exercise greater ('double') caution and vigilance if the consumer indicates that he or she wishes to use the requested credit to repay other credits. A credit agreement concluded to settle another credit or other credits may send a negative signal to the creditor (see Rb. Coutrai (1st Ch.) 11 September 1998, DCCR 1999, 73–80; Vred. Sint-Niklaas 6 August 2004, T. Vred. 2006, 32–38, note F. de Patoul; Vred. Ghent 6 January 2005, RABG 2005, no. 4, 345–349; Vred. Courtrai 6 February 2008, T. Vred. 2009, 295–301, note R. Steennot; Vred. Arendonk 12 October 2010, NjW 2011, no. 242, 343–344, note R. Steennot). The Belgian Federal Public Service Economy (i.e., 'FOD Economie') stipulates that a person will be considered more likely to be creditworthy if he or she did not ask for credit before than someone who has already obtained (multiple) credit(s) (see Federal Public Service Economy, 'Guidelines regarding the creditworthiness assessment, of a consumer, in the context of granting a consumer credit', 10 October 2018, https://economie.fgov.be, pp. 19–20).

166 The applicable data protection legislation may be a useful tool to examine credit scoring practices that use irrelevant and disproportionate information. Discussing this legislation does not fall within the scope of this chapter.

167 Such as Directive 2000/43/EC against discrimination on grounds of race and ethnic origin, Directive 2000/78/EC against discrimination at work on grounds of religion or belief, disability, age or sexual orientation, Directive 2006/54/EC regarding equal treatment for men and women in matters of employment and occupation, Directive 2004/113/EC regarding equal treatment for men and women in the access to and supply of goods and services, Directive Proposal (COM(2008)462) against discrimination based on age, disability, sexual orientation and religion or belief beyond the workplace and finally the General Data Protection Regulation (and more specifically, Article 9).

168 In the United States, the Equal Credit Opportunity Act ('ECOA') prohibits creditors from discriminating against credit applicants on the basis of sensitive characteristics such as race, religion, national origin, sex, or marital status (see Hurley and Adebayo, 'Credit scoring in the era of big data', p. 190).

no specific anti-discrimination provisions are included in the CCD.[169] This begs the question whether more specific non-discrimination credit obligations may be useful and even necessary.

As stated above (see, *supra*, no. 7), article 18 of the Proposal requires the creditor to assess the prospect of the consumer to meet his or her credit obligations[170] on the basis of relevant and accurate information on the consumer's income and expenses and other financial and economic circumstances, such as evidence of income or other sources of repayment, information on financial assets and liabilities, or information on other financial commitments. Furthermore, the Proposal specifies that the information shall be obtained from relevant internal or external sources, including the consumer and, where necessary, on the basis of a consultation of a database referred to in Article 19.[171] Recital 47 of the Proposal provides further indications on the types of information the creditor should use in the creditworthiness assessment. Reference is made to the European Banking Authority's guidelines on loan origination and monitoring, which contains guidelines on which categories of data may be used for the processing of personal data for creditworthiness purposes.[172] Moreover, personal data found on social media platforms or health data should not be used when conducting a creditworthiness assessment.[173] Additionally, article 6 entails a credit specific non-discrimination provision preventing credit scoring of systematically disadvantaged groups.

This clarification of the creditworthiness obligation constitutes a real improvement and therefore can only be welcomed. However, it is a shame the European legislator did not seise the opportunity to include a more specific list of categories of relevant and necessary data in the Directive itself. Instead, it only refers to the guidelines of the European Banking Authority. Clarification is thus provided, but only through the guidance of the Proposal[174] and soft law.[175] To fully ensure consumer protection, the Directive must further specify

169 In Belgium, however, Article VII.69, §1 WER clearly states that the creditor cannot obtain information regarding race, ethnic origin, sexual behaviour, health, beliefs or activities in the political, philosophical or religious fields, or membership of a trade union or health insurance fund.

170 I.e., a borrower- assessment and not a credit risk assessment.

171 See Article 18(1)–(2) Proposal.

172 European Banking Authority, 'Final Report: Guidelines on loan origination and monitoring', EBA/GL/2020/06, 29 May 2020, www.eba.europa.eu.

173 See Article 18(2) Proposal.

174 Recitals provide guidance on how to interpret the Articles, but are not themselves legally binding. See R. Baratta, 'Complexity of EU Law in the Domestic Implementing Process', *The Theory and Practice of Legislation*, 2014, vol. 2, no. 3, pp. 293308.

175 One explanation for not clarifying certain matters in the text of the directive itself and referring to the guidelines may be that this offers more flexibility. However, in view of the current advanced technologies, referring to soft law or policy documents containing principles is not sufficient. In addition, in a situation with consumers and asymmetry, it is recommended to use a rules-based regulation rather than a principles-based approach. See, e.g., H.P. Tarbert, 'Rules for Principles and Principles for Rules: Making Sense of Financial

the categories of data to be processed for creditworthiness assessment in the operative part of Proposal.[176] The Proposal itself should include a clear overview of the categories of personal data which can (or cannot) be processed rather than referring to guidance alone. Specifying the categories of data which can be used for creditworthiness assessment, as well as how to interpret said information, would improve consumer protection and would further ensure responsible lending. In addition, the Proposal fails to identify which internal and external sources are deemed relevant in the context of the creditworthiness assessment, and when the information should be obtained from the consumer.

28. The vague and unclear wording of the CCD may not only lead to financial exclusion, but also to *(unwanted) financial inclusion* of uncreditworthy consumers. This is especially the case because the current Directive does not clarify what the consequences of the consumer's lack of creditworthiness are, nor does it address the issue of whether the creditor may provide a credit to uncreditworthy consumers, and if so, which steps the creditor should take prior to concluding such a risky credit agreement. This allows Member States (and therefore creditors) to conclude a credit agreement after a negative outcome of the creditworthiness assessment. In the light of the importance not to engage in irresponsible lending practices and the Member States' responsibility to carry out the necessary supervision to avoid such behaviour, it is opportune that national legal systems include the prohibition[177] to conclude a credit agreement with non-creditworthy consumers (as Belgium has implemented, see, *supra*, no. 4). Stipulating that the creditor cannot grant credit once the consumer is qualified as uncreditworthy is even more important when creditors use credit scoring techniques. In this situation, consumers with low scores may still get credit but under worse conditions, such as very high interest rates or penalty provisions.

Again, regarding this issue, the Proposal will exert impact. In its Proposal, the Commission aims to tighten the rules on creditworthiness assessments by banning lending practices if the result of the assessment is negative. Article 18(4) of the Proposal stipulates that in principle credit should only made available to the consumer where the result of the creditworthiness assessment is positive

Regulation', 2019 Annual Robert Glauber Lecture at Harvard University's Institute of Politics by CFTC Chairman TARBERT, https://www.cftc.gov/.

176 See EDPS, 'Opinion 11/2021 on the Proposal for a Directive on consumer credits', 26 August 2021, https://edps.europa.eu/, p. 7.

177 Some authors argue that the creditor must only warn the consumer that he or she is uncreditworthy and will probably experience difficulties in repaying the credit (see Rott, 'Consumer Credit', p. 190). Nonetheless, in my opinion a mere warning will not guarantee full consumer protection. The consumer-applicant may already be over-indebted and may see this credit contract as his or her last resort for immediate cash. In this scenario, the consumer will not be able to think in a rational manner, and can only be protected against himself or herself by refusing to conclude a credit agreement.

and verifies that the obligations resulting from the credit agreement are likely to be met. If the assessment is negative, the creditor can make credit available in specific and justified circumstances such as when they have a long-standing relationship with the consumer, or in case of loans to fund exceptional healthcare expenses, students loans or loans for consumers with disabilities. In such a case, when deciding on whether or not to make the credit available to the consumer, the creditor should take into account the amount and the purpose of the credit, and the likelihood that the obligations resulting from the agreement will be met.[178] Determining the consequences of a negative creditworthiness assessment could mitigate the unwanted financial inclusion.

29. Another problem is the *opacity* and lack of transparency in the scoring process. This leads to the situation in which consumers may not know why their applications were rejected, existing scoring models cannot (easily) be challenged and new adverse (irrelevant, inaccurate or discriminatory) data is unavoidably being added for future applications. It is even possible that the creditor itself does not know why a consumer's application was rejected, because credit scoring systems may use thousands of variables while complex algorithms assess an applicant's creditworthiness. Creditors must avoid using credit scoring systems that are inadequately transparent to prevent submitting consumers to decisions that they or the creditor no longer understand.

In this regard, the Proposal states in article 18(6) that whenever the creditworthiness assessment involves the use of profiling or other automated processing of personal data, the consumer has the right to obtain human intervention to review the decision. In this situation, the consumer also has the right to request and obtain a clear explanation of the assessment made and of the functioning of the automated processing used, including among others the main variables, the logic and risks involved, as well as a right to express his or her point of view and to contest the assessment of the creditworthiness and the decision.[179] Such a provision may lead to a *de facto* ban on the use of incomprehensible, black box AI systems. In addition, where the credit application is rejected the creditor is required to inform the consumer without delay of the rejection and, where applicable, of the fact that the assessment of creditworthiness is based on automated processing of data (article 18(7) of the Proposal).

To ensure a better consumer protection when credit scoring is applied to assess one's creditworthiness, it is however necessary to clarify that the information regarding the automation must be provided regardless whether the

---

178 See Proposal, recital 47.

179 Recital 48 of the Proposal recalls that the Proposal for Regulation laying down harmonized rules on artificial intelligence ('Artificial Intelligence Act', COM(2021) 206 final) specifies that AI systems used to evaluate the credit score or creditworthiness of natural persons should be classified as high-risk AI systems, since they determine those persons' access to financial resources or essential services such as housing, electricity, and telecommunication services.

credit application is rejected or granted. Consumers should also be informed of their rights under Article 18(6) of the Proposal before concluding a credit agreement or rejecting a credit application.

5. CONCLUSION

30. In summary, the increasing use of automated (AI/ML-based) credit scoring techniques is an undeniable and irreversible truth. The world has evolved tremendously since the time in which a credit manager knew each of his consumer-applicants individually and made credit judgments based upon how long and how well he or she knew the consumer personally, regardless of the information received during the credit application process.

Credit scoring, which is a mathematical and statistical method to calculate and predict the creditworthiness of potential borrowers, may be a satisfying instrument to automatically assess one's creditworthiness. Such a creditworthiness assessment will comply with the principle of responsible lending when it is more than a mere credit risk-estimation. However, the assessment in which the standard execution of the credit agreement is not prioritised, while other external factors (e.g., personal securities granted or the fees charged in the event of default) are considered, cannot be qualified as responsible lending. This also implies that a credit scoring system which only evaluates the personal situation of the consumer and his or her personal characteristics can be seen as a responsible lending practice. It is thus important that the credit scoring model is not limited to assessing external factors, such as personal securities and interest or penalty fees charged in the event of default. Credit scoring models should always take into account the individual circumstances of consumers. When creditors still grant credit to consumers with low credit scores, thereby ensuring that they can recover their money by charging higher rates in addition to the charges consumers have to pay in case of default, financial vulnerable consumers will be further penalised. This situation cannot be considered as a responsible lending practice.

31. Nevertheless, even if credit scoring in fact complies with the requirements of responsible lending, we must not forget that this new reality still leads to many challenges and potential ramifications for consumers. After all, in addition to the potential benefits including cost reduction and efficiency gains, credit scoring may entail several adversarial effects for consumers. Financial exclusion and the opacity of complex algorithms are only two of the identified challenges. This means that regulators must be aware of the potential negative effects that may be caused by the use of credit scoring. Regulators must create an environment in which financial innovation can thrive within the boundaries of adequate consumer protection. As stated above, current European consumer credit legislation is not sufficient to limit and mitigate all (potential) risks associated with the use of credit scoring. However, with the new Proposal, the EU will strengthen consumer protection and will solve some of the problems regarding credit scoring. Some of the measures in the Proposal aim to encourage responsible lending practices as well as measures to prevent and combat over-indebtedness. The Proposal ensures stricter consumer-centric creditworthiness assessments, with a ban on lending to consumers if the outcome of this assessment is negative. It states that the assessment of creditworthiness should be done in the interest of the consumer, to prevent irresponsible lending practices and over-indebtedness.[180] Furthermore, the Proposal contains a *credit-specific* provision adjusted to the ubiquitous credit scoring techniques: where creditworthiness assessments involve profiling or automated processing, consumers will have a right to demand human intervention, to obtain a clear explanation and to contest the decision.[181] This could lead to a *de facto* ban on fully opaque credit scoring systems, and could ensure that creditors only use those credit scoring systems whose outcomes can be fully understood, interpreted and explained.

Although these new provisions are certainly to be encouraged, there are still some issues that the EU did not address. Firstly, the improved Consumer Credit Directive itself still has to specify what 'creditworthiness' and 'ability to pay' exactly mean and when the consumer will meet his or her obligations under the credit agreement. Secondly, the new directive should ensure that only pertinent and well-founded data are used in the right way by creditors when assessing consumers' creditworthiness. There is still a clear need of clarifying which data sources are relevant, which credit relevant data should (at a minimum[182]) be taken into account and how to interpret these data points. The Proposal only states that the creditor must take appropriate account of relevant factors, including information regarding the consumer's income, expenses, and other financial and economic circumstances. This provision remains too vague and needs to be amended. Additionally, it would be worth introducing an explicit ban on the use of certain (e.g., irrelevant, inappropriate or discriminatory) data. Thirdly, to fully be able to exercise their rights when the creditworthiness assessment involves the use of profiling or other automated processing of personal data, consumers must be informed of their rights of human intervention, explanation and protest. This information needs to be part

180 See Proposal, recital 46.

181 The General Data Protection Regulation also contains a provision which states that data subjects have the right not to be subject to a decision based solely on automated processing and can ask for human intervention (see Article 22 GDPR). However, as this is a quite general and ambiguous provision, so this concrete and credit-specific requirement must be celebrated.

182 Bear the principle of proportionality in mind.

of the pre-contractual information listed in article 10 of the Proposal. Lastly, it should be noted that Member States nowadays may decide how to enforce their national provisions that are adopted pursuant to the Consumer Credit Directive. The penalties under national law must, however, be effective, proportionate and dissuasive.[183] Nevertheless, if the European legislator decides to impose sanctions, a balance will have to be found between sanctions that are too strict and those that are too flexible. Sanctions that are too strict may lead to situations in which credit scoring techniques are programmed in such a way that the risk of liability of the creditor is limited. This could imply that more consumers are rejected and that the risk of financial exclusion increases. For example: when the score of a consumer is close to the cut-off score, a cautious algorithm will automatically reject this consumer in order to limit the creditor's liability. That being said, a more serious penalty is certainly recommended in this context to achieve the goal of responsible lending. In situations where there is doubt regarding the creditworthiness of a consumer – 'grey areas' –, a solution could be to oblige the creditor to introduce a (*a priori*) human intervention, which implies that an individual has to evaluate whether or not to grant the credit.

34. In short, in order to ensure that consumer protection lives happily ever after in times where automatic creditworthiness assessment increasingly takes the lead, the current Credit Consumer Directive has to be revised and adjusted to the new digital reality. The Proposal for a new directive on consumer credits has updated the current European consumer credit regulation and introduces various necessary improvements which have a clear positive impact on the protection of consumers. Nonetheless, some additional changes still have to be made to fully adapt the credit regulation to this digital environment. This is the only way in which the cost-benefit analysis regarding consumer credit scoring could have a positive outcome. In other words, even though we are on the brink of ensuring a full consumer protection when it comes to credit scoring systems, we are not quite there *yet*.

[183] See Article 23 CCD.

CHAPTER 17
AI AND THE CONSUMER

Skander BENNIS*

1. INTRODUCTION

1. Business entities currently employ AI and other algorithmic techniques in essentially all sectors of the economy in order to influence potential customers.[1] The concept of AI is discussed elsewhere in this book.[2] This contribution is more concerned with what is happening on the market under the label 'AI' and how this may affect those who are generally labelled as consumers.[3] After all, the focus of legal research is not so much on 'new' technology itself, but rather on the aspects of social life that this technology makes newly salient.[4]

To that end, I will first identify and categorise some of the ways in which business entities employ what is commonly referred to as AI as well as the risks and benefits of such uses (part 2).[5] For this, I will rely on the findings of the ARTificial intelligence SYstems and consumer law & policy project (ARTSY Project) conducted by the European University Institute in Florence under the supervision of professor Hans Micklitz. Subsequently, I will examine how the legislator intends to adapt consumer policy to the changing circumstances created by these previously mentioned developments (part 3). I will limit this

* Former academic assistant in the field of Economic Law at the University of Antwerp.

1 A. Jabłonowska et al., 'Consumer law and artificial intelligence. Challenges to EU consumer law and policy stemming from the business' use of artificial intelligence', *EUI Working Papers 2018/11*, 2018, p. 1.

2 For the concepts, see Chapter 1.

3 Jabłonowska et al., *Consumer law and artificial intelligence*, 2018, p. 1.

4 J.M. Balkin, 'The Path of Robotics Law', *California Law Review*, 2015, vol. 6, p. 45.

5 I will not go into the particularities of business to consumer (B2C) contracts that have AI applications as their object. In this regard, see H. Jacquemin and J.-B. Hubin, 'Aspects contractuels et de responsabilité civile en matière d'intelligence artificielle', in H. Jacquemin and A. de Streel (eds), *L'intelligence artificielle et le droit* (Brussels: Larcier, 2016), pp. 89–100. However, this analysis needs to be supplemented with the new Directive (EU) 2019/770 of the European Parliament and the Council of 20 May 2019 on certain aspects concerning contracts for the supply of digital content and digital services, ELI: http://data.europa.eu/eli/dir/2019/770/oj. The measures the Belgian legislator will need to adopt to transpose this directive into Belgian law must enter into force on 1 January 2022 at the latest.

study to European Union consumer policy as the Belgian legislator is likely to adopt this approach. I will then examine some of the hurdles (AI-driven) autonomous agents present to consumer autonomy as well as the question to what extent and how this can be dealt with within the current consumer law framework (part 4). In particular, I will discuss a number of market practices which are closely related to the advent of autonomous agents. In this regard, I will rely on the key issues in the consumer domain as defined in a briefing document to the European Parliament prepared by one of the researchers of the ARTSY Project.[6] I will not elaborate on consumer privacy as privacy considerations are discussed elsewhere in this book.[7] Finally, I will recapitulate my findings and contemplate on the nature of consumer rights in the era of AI (part 5).

2. BENEFITS AND RISKS OF AI AS A MARKET TOOL

2. A sectoral analysis prepared within the framework of the ARTSY Project shows that the use of AI is booming in several domains.[8] This project study included an inquiry into the business practices in finance and insurance,[9] information services (encompassing the 'digital' business models of social media, online advertising, content hosting and screening as well as facilitating communication), energy and 'smart solutions' (ranging from smartphones to smart homes and even cities), retail, autonomous vehicles,[10] healthcare and legal services.[11]

There are several ways in which we can distinguish these AI-uses. One distinction which I will draw in this contribution is based on the four stages a business goes through while performing its activities[12]:

- In a preparatory stage, AI is mainly used to gather and process large amounts of data in view of several possible goals (e.g., to improve product quality, to develop new goods and services, to improve risk management, to lower costs).

6 Briefing requested by the IMCO committee, *Artificial Intelligence: Challenges for EU Citizens and Consumers*, January 2019. Available at https://www.europarl.europa.eu/RegData/etudes/BRIE/2019/631043/IPOL_BRI(2019)631043_EN.pdf.

7 See Chapter 8.

8 To this end, the researchers analysed more than 100 websites and online media entries. See Jabłonowska et al., 'Consumer law and artificial intelligence', pp. 19–34.

9 Some aspects of which are discussed in Chapters 15 and 16.

10 Tort law is discussed in Chapter 14. See also Jacquemin and Hubin, 'Aspects contractuels et de responsabilité civile en matière d'intelligence artificielle', pp. 112–138.

11 Jabłonowska et al., 'Consumer law and artificial intelligence', pp. 19–34.

12 See in general: M. Ebers et al. (eds), *Contracting and Contract Law in the Age of Artificial Intelligence* (London: Bloomsbury, 2022), 384 p.

- In a pre-contractual stage, AI is used to improve existing techniques of gaining and keeping customers. It concerns the use of AI in advertising and price setting. The use of AI in these stages is already widespread.
- In a contractual stage, when the actual 'purchase'[13] decision occurs, AI is used to facilitate the conclusion of a contract.
- In a post-contractual stage, AI may be used to aid in the performance and, possibly, the enforcement of obligations.[14]

However, keep in mind that this distinction remains somewhat superficial as AI utilities may have broader (and overlapping) uses in each of these stages. Another broader distinction can be drawn between AI-based products and AI applications 'applied' by businesses to improve their relationship with consumers.[15]

3. Business entities invest in AI-driven applications in the hope of gaining several advantages. These efficiency gains can be grouped as follows. Firstly, business entities aim to limit their costs while increasing their profits. In several sectors of the economy, AI-driven applications will decrease the cost of employees.[16] Such applications can also improve the circumstances of workers (whether they are self-employed or employees) by reducing the time and effort they have to invest in minor – yet time- and effort-consuming – tasks (e.g. research, translation and drafting of standard clauses in the field of legal services), which in turn also impacts the overall business costs. Furthermore, certain AI uses (be it complicated algorithms, neural networks or even more advanced technologies) allow business entities to make smarter decisions. Thorough analyses based on real-time information improves merchandising operations. In this sense, a business entity could further optimise its inventory levels, its targeting strategy (advanced targeting and ads personalisation) and its treatment of existing customers (especially as long-term relationships with customers may improve customer support as it provides more data on customers), thereby making smarter investments from a costs-benefits

---

13 In this contribution the term 'purchase decision' denotes the customer's decision to conclude an agreement with a business entity. It covers all types of contracts.

14 S. Bennis, 'Consumentenbescherming bij blockchain en smart contracts', in R. Steennot and G. Straetmans (eds.), *Digitalisering van het recht en consumentenbescherming* (Antwerp: Intersentia, 2019), pp. 262–267, no. 22–23 and 26 (on the term and its use) and pp. 267–268, no. 27 (on the use of smart contracts as an enforcement tool for consumer rights).

15 As opposed to the similar, yet more negatively formulated distinction in A. Jabłonowska and P. Pałka, 'EU Consumer Law and Artificial Intelligence', in L. de Almeida et al. (eds.), *The Transformation of Economic Law. Essays in Honour of Hans-W. Micklitz* (Oxford: Hart Publishing, 2019), p. 105 who warn that 'in reality the boundaries are more difficult to draw'.

16 Jabłonowska et al., 'Consumer law and artificial intelligence', pp. 20–21 (finance and insurance), pp. 23–24 (information services), pp. 25–26 (energy and smart solutions), pp. 27–28 (retail) and p. 33 (legal services).

perspective. In addition, certain AI-based applications give business entities easier access to other geographical markets (e.g. AI-improved translation tools which help overcome language-barriers more cost-efficiently), or help them to create new product markets altogether (e.g. new smart solutions which create additional commercialisation opportunities).[17] Secondly, business entities hope to improve their risk management. Several business entities employ AI-based applications to improve fraud prevention and cybersecurity, risk assessment, the credibility and quality of its online content, the quality of smart products (preventing possible defects and thus the risk of litigation) and the monitoring of the supply chain.[18]

AI-driven applications are not only advantageous for business entities but for consumers as well. These general consumer benefits can also be grouped together. First and foremost, such applications can improve the quality of existing goods and services. Consumers ultimately benefit from better protection against fraud and cyber-attacks, easier and faster communication with business entities through AI-driven chatbots (available 24/7), more accurate machine translation, improved (more user-friendly and safer) smart applications and advices or diagnoses based on more accurate analyses provided by AI-driven applications (over larger data sets).[19] In addition, consumers may experience an easier and more flexible shopping experience. Secondly, AI-based applications can lead to increased and more informed choices. Choices will increase as AI can help to create new products, e.g., new 'smarter' solutions. Furthermore, the use of AI-based applications can lead to a decrease in the price of some goods. Think of more affordable energy through smart-grids (real time AI-based analysis of energy consumption patterns) and more affordable medical advice and therapy through e-health solutions such as Babylon (which provides medical advice based on AI and on a doctor's assessment), Woebot (a mental health chatbot) and Quitxt (which helps the user quit smoking).[20] Moreover, more customised or personalised consumer targeting and treatment can provide consumers with the necessary guidance to make informed choices in a very complex world where they are literally drowning in information. AI-driven interactive catalogues, robo-advisors, chatbots and digital assistants (Amazon's Alexa and Echo) can provide consumers with customised information very quickly. Such AI-based applications can, therefore, be of great use to consumers giving them better access to goods and services (the market) specifically tailored to their needs.

4. Paradoxically, while the use of AI-driven applications may improve the quality of goods and services as well as increase (more informed) choice, such

17 *Ibid.*, pp. 20–33.
18 *Ibid.*
19 *Ibid.*
20 *Ibid.*, pp. 25–26 and pp. 31–32.

applications have great potential to do exactly the opposite. First and foremost, a number of scholars warn about the growing knowledge gap between business entities employing AI-driven data analytics and consumers whose data are processed, which in turn holds the potential for abuse.[21] The assessment of such abuse may become increasingly difficult. One example thereof is the blurring line between efficient commercial personalisation strategies and consumer manipulation (or even harassment). In the same sense, there is a risk of haphazard (uninformed) or erroneous purchases. Furthermore, as consumers become more dependent on AI-based applications to make informed purchase decisions, several other risks emerge. Disinformation constitutes an important risk. After all, AI-driven applications may not always work well. Imagine for example an AI-driven electronic lawyer (or robo-lawyer) providing the wrong legal advice because of an error of judgment. Moreover, greater dependence on successful AI-based applications, such as digital assistants, may actually make consumers more vulnerable as they may become less careful. In addition, pre-verifications could discourage consumers from making critical evaluations.

We also need to be aware of the risks for consumer privacy. In this regard, it must be stated that a number of services that are provided for free are actually paid for in terms of data which fuel AI-driven applications. As consumers value their personal data differently from business entities, a number of them risk to undervalue the price they pay for such 'free' services.

For the sake of completeness, the use of AI-based applications has other effects for society as a whole, which we call 'externalities'.[22] Examples of negative externalities are the costs of job losses, the loss of freedom of expression (when AI preselects information, especially if the criteria are not clear – the black box problem), the cost of a greater amount of consumer information available to be hacked or exploited by third parties and the risk of stabilising existing patterns. An example of positive externalities are the environmental benefits that might follow from the use of certain AI-based applications, such as smart energy meters. While legal research must keep such externalities in mind, we will focus on the consumer in the next parts.

3. BUILDING BLOCKS FOR A CONSUMER POLICY IN THE AGE OF AI

5. Nearly every citizen is expected to be confronted with AI sooner rather than later. A study conducted by Ernst & Young shows that Belgium and Luxemburg

---

[21] *Ibid.*, pp. 20–33.

[22] This term is derived from the works of the neoclassical economist Arthur Cécile Pigou. See A.C. Pigou, *The Economics of Welfare* (London: MacMillan, 1960), 876 p.

have invested more than 100 million euros in AI over the past decade.[23] Another global study conducted by PricewaterhouseCoopers (PWC) shows that 'AI could contribute up to $15.7 trillion to the global economy in 2030'.[24] A study commissioned by the Federal Public Service (FPS) Economy, SMEs, Middle Classes and Energy on the Belgian citizen's perception of AI shows that there is a (potential) market for AI-based goods and services.[25]

On 25 April 2018, the European Commission launched its 'Artificial Intelligence for Europe' agenda.[26] It announced the development of ethical guidelines on AI which would include a look at AI's impact on consumer protection.[27] The Commission also stressed that '[t]he large-scale use of AI-enabled tools in business-to-consumer transactions needs to be fair, transparent and compliant with consumer legislation' and that '[c]onsumers should receive clear information on the use, features and properties of AI-enabled products'. In June 2018, the European Commission set up an Independent High-Level Expert Group on Artificial Intelligence which published its final version of the 'Ethics Guidelines for Trustworthy AI' on 8 April 2019 (AI Guidelines) providing an assessment list for AI projects. The AI Guidelines mention four ethical imperatives: respect for human autonomy, prevention of harm, fairness and explainability. The AI Guidelines state that 'different opportunities and challenges arise from AI systems used in the context of business-to-consumer' without further elaboration and mention of the applicability of current consumer law on AI-based applications.[28]

On 21 January 2020, the European Parliament's Internal Market and Consumer Protection Committee approved a resolution on AI – and, in particular, on automated decision-making – technologies which suggests the need to 'examine the current EU legal framework, including the consumer law acquis, data protection legislation, product safety and market surveillance legislation (..) to check it is able to respond to the emergence of AI and automated decision-making and that it is able to provide a high level of consumer protection as required under Article 38 of the Charter of Fundamental Rights

---

23 This study was commissioned by Microsoft. The full report is available at https://info.microsoft.com/WE-DIGTRNS-CNTNT-FY19-09Sep-27-ArtificialIntelligenceinBelgium-MGC0003166_01Registration-FormінBody.html?wt.mc_id=AID732606_QSG_280351.

24 E.g., a report prepared by PricewaterhouseCoopers indicates that 45% of total economic gains by 2030 will come from product enhancements, stimulating consumer demand. The full report is available at https://www.pwc.com/gx/en/issues/analytics/assets/pwc-ai-analysis-sizing-the-prize-report.pdf.

25 For the results of the study, see https://economie.fgov.be/nl/publicaties/perceptie-van-artificiele.

26 Communication (European Commission) on Artificial Intelligence for Europe, 25 April 2018, COM(2018) 237 final.

27 *Ibid.*, p. 15.

28 Aside from considerations on product safety and liability which will be discussed in another chapter.

of the EU' (para. D).[29] Subsequently, the European Commission published its White Paper on Artificial Intelligence.[30] However, in the chapter regarding 'the possible adjustments to the existing EU legislative framework relating to AI' the European Commission seems to narrow its focus to product safety and liability issues that may arise from employing AI-based applications. It does mention other directives such as the General Data Protection Regulation, some directives prohibiting discrimination and 'a number of consumer protection rules' (e.g. the Unfair Practices Directive and Consumer Rights Directive).[31] Recital (28) of the Proposal for a Regulation on AI, stipulates that '[t]he extent of the adverse impact caused by the AI system on the fundamental rights protected by the Charter is of particular relevance when classifying an AI system as high-risk. Those rights include the right to human dignity, respect for private and family life, protection of personal data, freedom of expression and information, freedom of assembly and of association, and non-discrimination, consumer protection, workers' rights, rights of persons with disabilities, right to an effective remedy and to a fair trial, right of defence and the presumption of innocence, right to good administration'.[32] The European institutions are clearly concerned with consumer policy in the age of AI, although it remains unclear what such policy should look like.

6. Consumer confidence has become a (pre)dominant justification for EU consumer policy.[33] As the previously mentioned White Paper as well as the Proposal for an AI Act indicate, the European Commission seeks to foster (consumer) trust in AI in order to allow everyone concerned to enjoy the benefits of such technologies as well as of the internal market.[34] Certain authors have questioned to what extent such a paradigm is justified.[35] It remains to be seen whether confident consumers will indeed enjoy the benefits of AI applications. Furthermore, while increasing consumer trust in AI applications (and cross-

---

29 Resolution (European Parliament) on Automated decision-making processes: Ensuring consumer protection, and free movement of goods and services, 2019/2915(RSP).

30 White Paper (European Commission) on Artificial Intelligence – A European approach to excellence and trust, COM(2020)65 final.

31 *Ibid.*, p. 13.

32 European Commission, Proposal for an AI Act, COM/2021/206 final. See also Chapter 3 and especially in the consumer context: BEUC, 'Regulating AI to Protect Consumer', Position Paper on the AI Act, October 2021, 42 p.

33 See C. Twigg-Flesner, 'The Importance of Law and Harmonisation for the EU's Confident Consumer', in D. Leczykiewicz and S. Weatherill (eds.), *The Images of the Consumer in EU Law: Legislation, Free Movement and Competition Law* (Oxford: Hart Publishing, 2016), pp. 184–186.

34 E.g. White Paper (European Commission) on Artificial Intelligence – A European approach to excellence and trust, COM(2020)65 final, pp. 2 and 9–10.

35 Jabłonowska and Pałka, 'EU Consumer Law and Artificial Intelligence', p. 109. The 'confident consumer' has already been criticised in the past. See Twigg-Flessner, *The importance of Law and Harmonisation*, with further references.

border transactions) is a commendable goal (especially with regard to product safety), it remains an ambiguous one.

Current European and Belgian consumer law hinges on two paradigms. The weaker party paradigm, which originates from private law, assumes the need for consumer protection to mitigate an imbalance, a disparity of powers. Traces of this paradigm can be found in the traditional definition of the consumer.[36] However, in current 'consumer law' this paradigm is directly linked to the position of the citizen in the market. Citizens are only consumers when they are confronted with an economic activity from a counterpart, the business entity, while they themselves act (predominantly) outside of their profession in order to meet their individual consumption needs.[37] It is also linked to another more dominant paradigm. The information paradigm assumes that consumers will act rationally as long as they receive sufficient information. In this sense, the weaker party is the less informed party.[38] As the information asymmetry between consumers and business entities constitutes a market failure,[39] the use of consumer law is justified to restore the overall balance. However, as behavioural economists have demonstrated,[40] market failures are not merely due to simple information discrepancies, which in theory can easily be resolved by providing the relevant information, but also to cognitive biases which interfere with consumers' autonomy.[41] As a result thereof, (some) consumers may be

---

36 See private international law: CJEU 14 February 2019, C-630/17, *Milivojević*, ECLI:EU:C:2019:123, para. 88; CJEU 25 January 2018, C-498/16, *Schrems*, ECLI:EU:C:2018:37, para. 30; CJEU 19 January 1993, *Shearson Lehmann Hutton*, ECLI:EU:C:1993:15, para. 18; Unfair Contract Terms Directive: CJEU 17 May 2018, C-147/16, *Karel De Grote Hogeschool*, ECLI:EU:C:2018:320, para. 54; CJEU 30 April 2014, C-26/13, *Arpád Kásler*, ECLI:EU:C:2014:282, para. 39; CJEU 26 October 2006, C-168/05, *Mostaza Claro*, ECLI:EU:C:2006:675, para. 25; CJEU 27 June 2000, C-240/98 to C-244/98, *Océano Grupo*, ECLI:EU:C:2009:615, para. 25; Unfair Trade Practices Directive: CJEU 4 October 2018, C-105/17, *Kamenova*, ECLI:EU:C:2018:808, para. 34; CJEU 13 September 2018, C-54/17 and C-55/17, *Wind Tre and Vodafone*, ECLI:EU:C:2018:710, para. 54; Consumer Rights Directive: CJEU 4 October 2018, C-105/17, *Kamenova*, ECLI:EU:C:2018:808, para. 34.

37 See S. Bennis, 'De consument van sociale netwerken en grensoverschrijdende collectieve consumentenvorderingen', *Consumentenrecht*, 2019, pp. 95–117. This close connection between consumer and business has been confirmed in several cases including CJEU 3 October 2013, C-59/12, *BKK Mobil Oil*, ECLI:EU:C:2013:634; CJEU 4 October 2018, C-105/17, *Kamenova*, ECLI:EU:C:2018:808, para. 34 and CJEU 17 May 2018, C-147/16, *Karel De Grote Hogeschool*, ECLI:EU:C:2018:320.

38 This follows from the suggestion that an informed consumer is a strong consumer. In the latter sense: G. Straetmans, *Consument en markt: onderzoek naar de rechtspositie van de consument op de Europese interne markt met de financiële sector als toetssteen* (Deurne: Kluwer, 1998), p. 68.

39 In that regard, see George Akerlof's 1970 article entitled 'The Market for Lemons: Quality Uncertainty and the Market Mechanism'.

40 Such as professors Richard Thaler, Cass Sunstein and Daniel Kahneman. See their most influential popularised works: R. Thaler and C. Sunstein, *Nudge: Improving Decisions about Health, Wealth, and Happiness* (New Haven: Yale University Press, 2008), 312 p. as well as D. Kahneman, *Thinking Fast and Slow* (New York: Yale University Press, 2011), 512 p.

41 Authors in the area of consumer law have thus criticised mere information obligations, see G. Howells, 'The Potential and Limits of Consumer Empowerment by Information', *Journal of*

more vulnerable to certain business practices.[42] Whatever paradigm one may prefer, allowing citizens to exercise their autonomy in the market seems to be the common goal under current European and Belgian consumer law.

The idea that consumer autonomy constitutes the bedrock of consumer law is not new.[43] It aligns very well with the view that the consumer is a market participant, the business' counterpart, and shifts the focus from protecting consumers to empowering them in order to exercise their freedom of choice in a meaningful way on the market. This in turn aligns with the European Commission's confident consumer rationale. Furthermore, it translates the first ethical imperative of the AI Guidelines into consumer policy: respect for human ('consumer') autonomy. An AI consumer policy should thus be supportive of the benefits and respond to the challenges AI presents to consumer autonomy.

The main challenge is our increased dependence on successful autonomous agents to assist us with establishing our preferences and making our purchase decisions. The success of such autonomous agents is connected to big data analytics, which severely alters the dimensions of the information asymmetry between business entities employing such agents and consumers using these. As indicated by the researchers of the ARTSY Project: businesses' 'advantage [over consumers] is no longer limited to the product or service and the overall market experience, but extends to the characteristics of the consumers themselves',[44] e.g. their willingness to pay. Consumer autonomy may be impaired if consumers are approached by 'corporate' autonomous agents (or 'spies') that know the consumers better than they know themselves in terms of preferences and likely market behaviour.[45]

Law and Society, vol. 32, no. 3, 2005, p. 359; O. Ben-Shahar and C.E. Schneider, 'The failure of mandated disclosure', *University of Pennsylvania Law Review*, 2011, vol. 159, pp. 679–729. In their thought-provoking book on European consumer law and policy Howells, Twigg-Flesner and Wilhelmsson stress the need to include behavioural economics in the Union's approach to consumer policy. See G. Howells, C. Twigg-Flesner and T. Wilhelmsson, *Rethinking EU Consumer Law* (Routledge: London, 2017), 350 p.

42 The question remains to what extent these findings should lead us to a re-conceptualised legal consumer image. See the interesting dialogue between professors Oren Bar-Gill and Richard A. Epstein who represent opposing sides of the debate: O. Bar-Gill, 'The Behavioral Economics of Consumer Contracts', *Minnesota Law Review*, 2008, vol. 92, pp. 749–802 and R.A. Epstein, 'The Neoclassical Economics of Consumer Contracts', *Minnesota Law Review*, 2008, vol. 92, pp. 803–835.

43 In Belgium, professor Straetmans defended a similar position in his 1998 doctoral thesis. See Straetmans, *Consument en markt: onderzoek naar de rechtspositie van de consument op de Europese interne markt met de financiële sector als toetssteen*, p. 86, while criticising the existing model proposed by professor Bourgoignie (which departs from the 'weak consumer').

44 Jabłonowska et al., 'Consumer law and artificial intelligence', p. 11.

45 See on consumer autonomy also: J.M. Paterson and Y. Maker, 'AI in the Home: Artificial Intelligence and Consumer Protection', January 2022, pp. 13–14 available at SSRN (to be published in E. Lim and P. Morgan (eds), *The Cambridge Handbook of Private Law and Artificial Intelligence* (Cambridge: Cambridge University Press, 2022).

7. The consumer plays a role that goes far beyond his own purchase decisions. (S)he also serves as a yardstick for evaluating the fairness of market practices and the lawfulness of national laws in view of European market integration.[46] The Court of Justice of the European Union (CJEU) developed[47] this 'average' consumer in its case law regarding the freedom of products in the 1980s and 1990s.[48] The average consumer is a normative concept (much like private law's *bonus pater familias* concept): it reflects how consumers ought to behave considering the circumstances. The 'average' consumer is 'reasonably well-informed and reasonably observant and circumspect'[49] and the concept found

---

[46] For further reading in a number of (related) domains: internal market freedoms law: S.A. De Vries, 'The Court of Justice's 'Paradigm Consumer' in EU Free Movement Law', in D. Leczykiewicz and S. Weatherill (eds.), *The Images of the Consumer in EU Law: Legislation, Free Movement and Competition Law* (Oxford: Hart Publishing, 2016), pp. 401–430. European competition law: A. Albors-Llorens and A. Jones, 'The Images of the 'Consumer' in EU Competition Law', in D. Leczykiewicz and S. Weatherill (eds.), *The Images of the Consumer in EU Law: Legislation, Free Movement and Competition Law* (Oxford: Hart Publishing, 2016), pp. 43–92. European trade mark law: G.B. Dinwoodie and D.S. Gangjee, 'The Image of the Consumer in EU Trade Mark Law', in D. Leczykiewicz and S. Weatherill (eds.), *The Images of the Consumer in EU Law: Legislation, Free Movement and Competition Law* (Oxford: Hart Publishing, 2016), pp. 339–380.

[47] See also G. Howells and G. Straetmans, 'The Interpretive Function of the CJEU and the Interrelationship of EU and National Levels of Consumer Protection', *Perspectives on Federalism*, 2017, vol. 9, no. 2, pp. 1–36.

[48] After establishing in the 1970s that consumer protection could justify obstacles to the freedom of movement within the European Union (CJEU 20 February 1979, 120/78, *Cassis de Dijon*, ECLI:EU:C:1979:42, para. 8), the CJEU went on to reject national laws that involved special requirements with regard to retail and marketing. The argument that (some) consumers would easily be misled by certain packages or promotional statements could not justify such general prohibitive measures discouraging market access by business entities of other Member States. See CJEU 10 November 1982, 261/81, *Rau*, ECLI:EU:C:1982:382 (regarding requirements for the packaging of margarine); CJEU 7 March 1990, 362/88, *GB Inno BM*, ECLI:EU:C:1990:102 (regarding a prohibition to provide certain information regarding promotional sales to consumers) and CJEU 18 May 1993, C-126/91, *Yves Rocher*, ECLI:EU:C:1993:19 (regarding a general prohibition on 'eye-catching' comparative advertising). Neither could the CJEU be convinced that consumers were easily fooled. In *Clinique*, the CJEU rejected the view that using term 'Clinique' for cosmetics would make consumers wrongly believe such cosmetics would have medicinal properties. In this regard, it applied an analysis of the global presentation of the products (CJEU 2 February 1994, C-315/92, *Clinique*, ECLI:EU:C:1994:34). See in the same vein CJEU 13 December 1990, 238/89, *Pall* [1990]; CJEU 6 July 1995, C-470/93, *Mars*, ECLI:EU:C:1995:224. In certain cases the CJEU left it up to the national courts to decide based on a global analysis whether consumers might be misled, e.g. the CJEU's cases *Gutshof-Ei* and *Graffione*, as it explained in *Gut Springenheide and Tusky*. See CJEU 16 July 1998, C-210/96, *Gut Springenheide and Tusky*, ECLI:EU:C:1998:369, para. 33.

[49] See CJEU 16 July 1998, C-210/96, *Gut Springenheide and Tusky*, ECLI:EU:C:1998:369, para. 31, building upon *GB Inno BM*, para. 12 ('average consumer') and *Mars*, para. 24 ('reasonably circumspect'). However, it did not rule out the possible relevance of demographic consumer studies as an auxiliary in order to establish whether this abstract 'average' consumer might be misled by a certain practice as the CJEU established in CJEU 16 January 1992, C-373/90, *Nissan*, ECLI:EU:C:1992:17, para. 16. See in the same vein CJEU 28 January 1999, C-303/97, *Sektellerei Kessler*, ECLI:EU:C:1999:35, para. 36–37.

its way into (the case law on) the secondary legislation of the European Union as consumer protection got increasingly harmonised.[50] This consumer is also a European consumer,[51] although the CJEU did recognise that in some cases social, cultural or linguistic factors might justify national differences.[52] While the bar seems to be set rather high,[53] the CJEU has softened the 'general average consumer' in two ways. Firstly, the CJEU has shown a willingness to take into account the characteristics of certain groups of consumers which may be more vulnerable to certain business practices.[54] This so-called vulnerable consumer[55] was also consolidated in the Unfair Trade Practices Directive (e.g. Articles 5.2, b) and 5.3).[56] Secondly, the CJEU has in recent years become more sensitive to the varying attention levels of consumers depending on the circumstances in

---

50 See in particular Articles 5–9 Unfair Commercial Practices Directive mentioning the 'average consumer' several times. See also cases such as CJEU 16 July 1998, C-210/96, *Gut Springenheide and Tusky*, ECLI:EU:C:1998:369; CJEU 28 January 1999, C-303/97, *Sektellerei Kessler*, ECLI:EU:C:1999:35; CJEU 13 January 2000, C-220/98, *Estée Lauder*, ECLI:EU:C:200:8; CJEU 4 April 2000, C465/98, *Darbo*, ECLI:EU:C:2000:184; CJEU 24 October 2002, C-99/01, *Linhart and Biffl*, ECLI:EU:C:2002:618; CJEU 10 September 2009, C-446/07, *Severi*, ECLI:EU:C:2009:530 and CJEU 21 May 2011, C-122/10, *Ving Sverige*, ECLI:EU:C:2011:299.

51 As argued in T. Wilhelmsson,'The Average European Consumer: a Legal Fiction?', in T. Wilhelmsson, E. Paunio and A. Pohjolainen (eds.), *Private Law and the Many Cultures of Europe* (Alphen aan den Rijn: Kluwer Law International, 2007), pp. 243–268.

52 See CJEU 13 January 2000, C-220/98, *Estée Lauder*, ECLI:EU:C:200:8, para. 29 (regarding the meaning of the term 'lifting' in Germany) and, previously, CJEU 26 November 1996, C-313/94, *Graffione*. ECLI:EU:C:1996:450, para. 22 (regarding the use of the term 'Cotonelle' in France for products that did not actually have cotton in it). The CJEU has reiterated this phrase on occasion in its case law on the Unfair Trade Practices Directive: CJEU 25 July 2018, C-628/17, *Orange Polska*, ECLI:EU:C:2019:480, para. 30; CJEU 7 September 2017, C-310/15, *Deroo-Blanquart*, ECLI:EU:C:2016:633, para. 32; CJEU 21 May 2011, C-122/10, *Ving Sverige*, ECLI:EU:C:2011:299, para. 22.

53 Especially following cases such as *Darbo*. In *Darbo*, the CJEU assumed that the average consumer read and fully understood ingredient lists and that this meant that (s)he 'should' not easily be misled by other eye-catching texts on a package. See CJEU 4 April 2000, C465/98, *Darbo*, ECLI:EU:C:2000:184, para. 22–23, 27–28 and 31–33. See, previously, in the same vein CJEU 26 October 1995, C-51/94, *Commission v Germany*, ECLI:EU:C:352.

54 In *Buet*, the CJEU considered a French prohibition on doorstep selling of educational material a proportionate measure in view of the protection of a group of consumers that are particularly vulnerable to such practices. This eventually gave rise the Directive on doorstep selling, which was later replaced by the Consumer Rights Directive. See CJEU 16 May 1989, 382/87, *Buet*, ECLI:EU:C:1989:198.

55 For further reading on this subject, see N. Reich, 'Vulnerable Consumers in EU Law', in D. Leczykiewicz and S. Weatherill (eds.), *The Images of the Consumer in EU Law: Legislation, Free Movement and Competition Law* (Oxford: Hart Publishing, 2016), pp. 139–158.

56 The CJEU's case law regarding the aforementioned Directive suggests that the practices enlisted in annex I (the black list) are especially prone to exploitation of vulnerabilities of certain groups of consumers. See in particular *Purely Creative* regarding the presentation of a good as a prize if claiming it incurs costs for the consumer (CJEU 18 October 2012, C-428/11, *Purely Creative*, ECLI:EU:C:2012:651, para. 40 and 53–54). This may also explain the CJEU's strict approach in *Lucky4all* (CJEU 15 December 2016, C-667/15, *Lucky4all*, ECLI:EU:C:2016:958).

which they are confronted with certain business practices.[57] The CJEU has been especially strict with regard to the presentation (and omission) of information pertaining to core elements for a consumer decision, such as the price.[58] The CJEU also applies the average consumer benchmark less strictly in cases that involve what it considers to be technical products.[59] In *Citroen Belux*, the CJEU showed more leniency towards a general prohibition (with certain exceptions) of an in itself legitimate market practice, a joint offer, when it involved the offer of at least one financial product.[60] In *Wind Tre Vodafone*, the CJEU did not appear convinced that the average buyer of a SIM card might be aware of pre-loaded and pre-activated services which can incur additional fees, or that (s)he is sufficiently technically capable, on his (or her) own, of making the necessary configurations to deactivate those services, although it left the final decision in this regard to the national court.[61]

The level of assumed knowledge and attention of a consumer dealing with AI applications such as autonomous agents is unclear. A discussion on how AI-driven technology should affect the consumer image is not entirely new. It is partly identical to the discussion about the ever-growing digitalisation of our daily lives. In that regard, a number of scholars have expressed their concern that consumers are more vulnerable on 'digital' markets.[62] Interestingly, an opposing view regards such consumers as more likely to correspond to the 'rational consumer' protected by the European information model of consumer protection.[63] This view was expressed by the Polish Supreme Court in a judgment of 17 January 2014 defending the position that 'digital' consumers

57 In *Teekanne*, the CJEU softened its *Darbo* judgment in the sense that the presentation of the information matters (see CJEU 4 June 2014, C-195/14, *Teekanne*, ECLI:EU:C:2015:361). For a more detailed analysis, see G. Straetmans, 'Over indrukken, misleiding en levensmiddelen met juiste en volledige ingrediëntenlijsten', *Revue européenne de droit de la consommation*, 2016, pp. 51–62. According to some authors the CJEUs judgments in *Teekanne* and *Canal Digital* reflect a tendency to take the 'real life' consumer into account. P. Verbiest, 'Arrest Canal Digital: naar een bescherming van de real life-consument bij oneerlijke handelspraktijken?', *Consumentenrecht*, 2017, no. 6, p. 263. See also the cautious view by G. Straetmans, 'Case Canal Digital Danmark: On misleading practices, the limitations of the communication medium used and the divergent levels of attention of consumers', *Revue européenne de droit de la consummation*, 2016, pp. 329–341.

58 CJEU 13 September 2018, C-54/17 and C-55/17, *Wind Tre Vodafone*, para. 47; CJEU 8 February 2017, C-562/15, *Carrefour Hypermarchés*, ECLI:EU:C:2017:95, para. 35; CJEU 26 October 2016, C-611/14, *Canal Digital*, ECLI:EU:C:2016:800, para. 55; CJEU 7 September 2017, C-310/15, *Deroo-Blanquart*, ECLI:EU:C:2016:633, para. 48.

59 CJEU 25 July 2018, C-628/17, *Orange Polska*, ECLI:EU:C:2019:480, para. 36 (mentioning the considerable information asymmetry); CJEU 13 September 2018, C-54/17 and C-55/17, *Wind Tre and Vodafone*, ECLI:EU:C:2018:710, para. 52 and 54.

60 CJEU 18 July 2013, C-265/12, *Citroën Belux*, ECLI:EU:C:2013:498.

61 CJEU 13 September 2018, C-54/17 and C-55/17, *Wind Tre and Vodafone*, ECLI:EU:C:2018:710, para. 54.

62 E. Mik, 'The erosion of autonomy in online consumer transactions', *Law, Innovation and Technology*, 2016, no. 8, pp. 1–38.

63 *See* Jabłonowska et al., 'Consumer law and artificial intelligence', p. 11.

are more technology-savvy, active, cautious and attentive.[64] The CJEU's case law, whilst sensitive to the possible technological ineptness of the average consumer, does not (yet) provide clear guidance on this matter.[65] In my opinion, a proper consideration of the case takes into account the growing asymmetry in information collection and processing as well as the purpose of many AI-based products for consumers, for instance to make daily life easier (prompting them to be less attentive) or to aid them in making important decisions (requiring them to rely heavily on such products).

4. CONSUMER AUTONOMY VERSUS AUTONOMOUS MACHINES

8. In a briefing in January 2019 addressed to the European Parliament, Giovanni Sartor, one of the researchers who took part in the ARTSY project identified five key issues in the consumer domain: unfair practices in targeted advertising and (hyper)nudging, algorithmic price discrimination, discrimination in advertisements, and AI tools empowering consumers.[66] In what follows, I will discuss these subjects taking into account the stages in which they occur. I will also provide a *prima facie* analysis under the current consumer law framework.

4.1. AI-BASED MARKETING

4.1.1. AI and Personalised Marketing (Targeting)

9. Autonomous agents are being employed in personalised targeting strategies which seek to provide consumers with customised, if not individualised, information about goods and services (e.g., a personalised offer, personalised prices, personalised terms and conditions).[67] Common examples include personalised advertising and ranking. Personalised (also targeted or behavioural) advertising refers to the (business) practice of showing consumers

---

64 See case I CSK 555/13, as referred to in Jabłonowska et al., *Consumer law and artificial intelligence*, p. 11. It concerned the online sale of tickets to football games in 2012. A term in the general conditions stating that the English version should prevail in the event of a discrepancy between the language versions of these conditions (Polish and English), was held to be lawful as these conditions were addressed at a group of (digital) consumers who apparently ought to be familiar with standard terms drafted in English.

65 CJEU 13 September 2018, C-54/17 and C-55/17, *Wind Tre and Vodafone*, ECLI:EU:C:2018:710, para. 52, which can be read in view of the possible regional differences.

66 See https://www.europarl.europa.eu/thinktank/en/document.html?reference=IPOL_BRI(2019)631043.

67 Jabłonowska et al., *Consumer law and artificial intelligence*, p. 48. See also Mik, 'The erosion of autonomy in online consumer transactions', pp. 1–38.

customised advertisements. 'Customised' means that the consumers' estimated preferences are taken into account. Personalised ranking refers to a (business) practice which consists of altering the display of available options to suit consumers' estimated preferences.[68] Personalised targeting itself is not a new phenomenon.[69] However, autonomous agents facilitate these practices, which rely heavily on data collection and analytics, the scale and effectiveness of which is quite unprecedented.[70]

In a (digital) world overflowing with information, personalised advertising and ranking may actually increase informed consumer choice. It prepares the consumer's decision showing a pathway in an overly exposed environment by putting out some of the lights.[71] However, as the researchers of the ARTSY Project point out: 'There is a thin line between showing me what I need, showing me what I think I need, and showing me what I fear I need'.[72] In fact, the market analysis performed by these researchers shows that 'software agents are increasingly being used by business to exert technological influence upon consumers with the aim of steering them towards specific products or services.'[73] In particular, a number of authors raise concerns about (digital market) manipulation.[74] In an environment where autonomous agents are ready to adequately predict consumers' future reactions, fuelled with knowledge about consumers' past behaviour, weaknesses and biases, the risk of such agents exploiting consumers' vulnerabilities, (hyper)nudging them into buying certain products, is not to be taken lightly.[75]

Personalised marketing involving the use of autonomous agents is not prohibited as such. After all, business entities are free to engage in economic activities (Article II.3 CEL), which includes the freedom to choose and implement a marketing strategy. Consequently, businesses are entitled to try and 'nudge' consumers into buying their products. However, there are a number of

68 Organisation for Economic Co-operation and Development (OECD), *Personalised Pricing in the Digital Era*, n° DAF/COMP(2018)13, https://one.oecd.org/document/DAF/COMP(2018)13/en/pdf. (OECD DAF/COMP(2018)13), p. 3.

69 See N.A. Draper and J. Turrow, 'Audience Constructions, Reputations and Emerging Media Technologies: New Issues of Legal and Social Policy', in R. Brownsword, E. Scotford and K. Yeung (eds.), *The Oxford Handbook of Law, Regulation and Technology* (Oxford: Oxford University Press, 2017), pp. 1143–1168.

70 *Ibid.*

71 In more economic terms: in the age of AI such strategies have great potential to subject the consumer to more relevant content, which lowers transactions costs.

72 Jabłonowska et al., *Consumer law and artificial intelligence*, 2018, p. 60.

73 *Ibid.*, p. 48.

74 R. Calo, 'Digital Market Manipulation', *Washington Law Review*, 2014, vol. 82, p. 995; N. Helberger, 'Profiling and Targeting Consumers in the Internet of Things – A New Challenge for Consumer Law', in R. Schulze and D. Staudenmayer (eds.), *Digital Revolution: Challenges for Contract Law in Practice* (Baden-Baden: Nomos, 2016), pp. 135–161. In a similar sense Mik, 'The erosion of autonomy in online consumer transactions', pp. 1–38.

75 See also K. Yeung, 'Hypernudge: Big data as mode of regulation by design', *Information Communication & Society*, 2016, vol. 20, no. 1, pp. 118–136.

express limits. Firstly, Article VI.110 §1 and XII.13 §1 CEL prohibit the use of automated call systems for direct marketing to consumers and direct electronic mailing without prior, free, specific and informed consent. Furthermore, consumers have the means to resist being subjected to a decision based solely on automated processing, such as profiling (Article 22 GDPR).[76] In addition, every business practice can be prohibited under Belgian law if it is deemed unfair in the sense of Article VI.93 CEL. This requires the practice to distort consumers' economic behaviour[77] and to breach the requirements of professional diligence. Providing misleading information, omitting required information or exerting 'undue influence' are clear breaches of professional diligence (see Articles VI.94-VI.99 and VI.101-VI.102 CEL).

Interestingly, examples of 'undue influence' in (published) case law are scarce, in particular in a digital environment where autonomous agents are usually active. Indeed, typical online advertising practices, such as interstitials and pop-up windows, are in themselves usually considered fair (non-aggressive).[78] Yet, the line between very persuasive personalised ads and undue influence may be thin,[79] especially when autonomous agents are aware of personal biases and weaknesses[80] and can target consumers effectively at any time.[81] The concept of 'undue influence' has only recently been explained by the CJEU.[82] It covers the exploitation of a position of power in relation to the consumer in a way which 'significantly' limits the consumer's ability to make an informed decision (e.g. harassment and coercion that are expressly mentioned in Article VI.101 CEL).[83] It is not limited to impermissible influence.[84] The impact of the practice on consumer autonomy is the benchmark. Undue influence means that the consumer's will is actively (i.e., through the application of pressure) and forcibly

76 However, this provision has a limited scope. See Bennis, 'Consumentenbescherming bij blockchain en smart contracts', pp. 276–278.

77 Article VI.93, b) CEL. See also CJEU 19 December 2013, C-281/12, *Trento Sviluppo*, ECLI:EU:C:2013:859, para. 31–34.

78 P. Rott, 'A Consumer Perspective on Algorithms', in L. de Almeida et al. (eds.), *The Transformation of Economic Law. Essays in Honour of Hans-W. Micklitz* (Oxford: Hart Publishing, 2019), p. 52 who refers to a number of German cases.

79 See G. Howells, 'Aggressive commercial practices', in G. Howells, H.-W. Micklitz an T. Wilhelmsson, *European Fair Trading Law. The Unfair Commercial Practices Directive* (London: Routledge, 2016), pp. 167–194.

80 See Hanson and Kysar who would consider such personalisation strategies a source of market failure as it presents the business with an incentive to 'utilise cognitive bias actively to shape consumer perceptions throughout the product purchasing context'. J.D. Hanson and D.A. Kysar, 'Taking Behaviouralism Seriously', *New York University Law Review*, 1999, vol. 74, no. 3, pp. 1420–1572.

81 Helberger, 'Profiling and Targeting Consumers in the Internet of Things – A New Challenge for Consumer Law', pp. 135–161.

82 CJEU 25 July 2018, C-628/17, *Orange Polska*, ECLI:EU:C:2019:480.

83 *Ibid.*, para. 33.

84 *Ibid.*

conditioned.[85] This may be difficult to prove in the context of autonomous agents: the mere fact that autonomous agents exploit their abilities does not necessarily show that an individual's consumer autonomy is 'significantly' impaired.[86] How would consumers even realise that their vulnerabilities are exploited by these invisible agents?

The current framework is not quite adapted to direct marketing through autonomous agents in an AI-fuelled landscape. Jacquemin and Hubin stress the importance of the 'transparance du processus' and they suggest *de lege ferenda* a more general information obligation with regard to AI.[87] Yet, this may not be so easily achieved. It requires the elimination of black box issues and a minimal amount of technical understanding about AI on the part of the consumer (which is currently largely absent from general education in Belgium). Another suggestion, building on the existing limitations to direct automated marketing, is to provide consumers with a general right to 'turn off' personalisation.[88] While this suggestion respects consumer's choice, it remains unclear whether it constitutes a sufficient – or even an effective – guarantee to safeguard consumer autonomy. In practice, it is likely to boil down to an 'all or nothing' choice incentivising consumers to allow personalisation. Moreover, autonomous agents make increasingly better predictions based on increasingly little information. The way forward may lie in the proposal of an updated list of forbidden practices which facilitates demonstration and monitoring of particularly dangerous practices that are commonly used to exploit consumers' vulnerabilities in an online (AI-fuelled) environment. However, this requires further study. As a warning, I would urge policymakers not to attack business practices that consumers merely perceive as unfair, even though they do not hurt their economic interests.[89]

10. The CEL contains a wide range of – partially overlapping – information requirements business entities have to comply with when marketing their products.[90] As previously mentioned, omitting such information or presenting it in a way which misleads consumers is unfair and prohibited. Yet, this does not entirely prevent the use of black boxes in the sense of autonomous agents whose

85 *Ibid.*

86 Compare CJEU 25 July 2018, C-628/17, *Orange Polska*, ECLI:EU:C:2019:480, para. 43–45.

87 Jacquemin and Hubin, 'Aspects contractuels et de responsabilité civile en matière d'intelligence artificielle', pp. 102 and 103 ('De lege ferenda, une obligation plus générale d'information impose par la loi et portant sur le recours à un système automatisé, voire autonome, dans le cadre du processus contractuel, nous parait utile').

88 Briefing requested by the IMCO committee, Artificial Intelligence: Challenges for EU Citizens and Consumers, January 2019.

89 This would go against the logic of the Unfair Trade Practices Directive. See CJEU 3 April 2014, C-515/12, *4finance*, ECLI:EU:C:2014:211, para. 24.

90 The information a business needs to provide a consumer is listed in Books III, VI and XII CEL.

decisions (e.g., to target a certain person) cannot be explained by the business employing them. However, it could be argued that employing such black boxes constitutes a breach of professional diligence[91] (which in itself does not establish the unfairness of a practice).

Nowadays, consumers rely more often on purchase information provided by online intermediaries employing autonomous agents for scoring and ranking purposes, who are themselves not held to the same requirements as the business with regard to the latter's goods and services. However, under the Platform Regulation,[92] online intermediaries will have to provide business entities with information on rankings. Furthermore, the Directive on better enforcement and modernisation of EU consumer protection rules[93] contains additional information requirements for platforms in their relation to consumers with regard to transparency about the status of the actual provider of services or goods, rankings and personalised pricing.[94] Higher ranking of commercial offers is considered to have an important impact on consumers' behaviour. Online platforms will, therefore, have to inform consumers about the main criteria determining the ranking of the offers provided in response to a search query (e.g., price, distance, consumer ratings), and have to clearly indicate when a trader has directly or indirectly paid the platform for a higher ranking.[95]

As a result, these new rules discourage the use of more complex autonomous agents whose actions (decisions) cannot be properly explained (the so-called black box-problem). These new rules align very well with the ethical imperative of explainability listed in the AI Guidelines (no. 5). It can thus be expected that similar rules will eventually apply to nearly all uses of autonomous agents on the market.

11. Autonomous agents are (likely) not without flaws. A great deal of the literature is concerned with the possible erroneous, discriminatory or

---

91 This argument could be further developed based on the AI Guidelines.

92 Regulation (EU) 2019/1150 of the European Parliament and of the Council of 20 June 2019 on promoting fairness and transparency for business users of online intermediation services, ELI: http://data.europa.eu/eli/reg/2019/1150/oj. Date of entry in to force: 12 July 2020.

93 Directive (EU) 2019/2161 of the European Parliament and of the Council of 27 November 2019 amending Council Directive 93/13/EEC and Directives 98/6/EC, 2005/29/EC and 2011/83/EU of the European Parliament and of the Council as regards the better enforcement and modernisation of Union consumer protection rules, ELI: http://data.europa.eu/eli/dir/2019/2161/oj. Date of transposition: 28 May 2022.

94 To ensure that penalties in relation to widespread infringements can be effective, proportionate and dissuasive, national authorities will be able to impose maximum fines of at least 4% of the platform's annual turnover in the Member State or Member States concerned.

95 For 'best practices' in regard to consumer ratings, see OECD (2019), 'Good practice guide on online consumer ratings and reviews: Protecting consumers in e-commerce', *OECD Digital Economy Papers No. 288*, OECD (Publishing: Paris, 2019), https://www.oecd.org/officialdocuments/publicdisplaydocumentpdf/?cote=DSTI/CP(2019)5/FINAL&docLanguage=En.

exploitative outcomes.[96] Discrimination, in particular, is a delicate topic. Autonomous agents (such as automated scoring systems) are not free from historical bias and can produce arbitrary and even discriminatory outcomes.[97] Moreover autonomous agents – using for example ML (see Chapter 1) – are capable of developing their own biases.[98] Arguably, human agents are just as – and perhaps even more – likely to generate discriminatory outcomes. The main difference is the immense scale on which autonomous agents can operate, in many cases even undetected. Several solutions have been proposed, ranging from transparency obligations[99] to policy interventions[100] and from compliance by design[101] to ex post review.[102] The question remains to what extent consumer law should combat such discriminatory practices.

Discrimination – as opposed to a justifiable unequal treatment or differentiation – is undesirable from an internal market (and the connected economic efficiency) perspective as it cuts consumers off from accessing certain goods and/or services without proper (economic) reason.[103] It is explicitly prohibited by Articles III.81 and III.82 CEL (transposing the Services Directive)[104] and Article 5, 1° Belgian Anti-Discrimination Law (for public goods and services).[105] The grounds for discrimination in Articles III.82 and III.83 CEL are limited (nationality and residence), which implies that a barber may choose only to cut men's hair (such a choice may enhance economic efficiency as it

96 See, among others, R. Brauneis and E.P. Goodman, 'Algorithmic Transparency for the Smart City', *Yale Journal of Law & Technology*, 2018, pp. 103–176; O. Bar-Gill, 'Algorithmic Price Discrimination: When Demand is a Function of Both Preference and (Mis)perceptions', *University of Chicago Law Review*, 2019, vol. 86, no. 2, pp. 217–254; P.T. Kim, 'Auditing Algorithms for Discrimination', *University of Pennsylvania Law Review Online*, 2017; S. Barocas and A.D. Selbst, 'Big Data's Disparate Impact', *California Law Review*, 2016, vol. 104, no. 3, pp. 671–732; T.Z. Zarsky, 'Understanding Discrimination in the Scored Society', *Washington Law Review*, 2015, vol. 89, no. 4, pp. 1375–1412; D. Keats Citron and F. Pasquale, 'The Scored Society: Due Process For Automated Predictions', *Washington Law Review*, 2014, vol. 89, pp. 1–32; A.J. Schmitz, 'Secret Consumer Scores and Segmentations: Separating "Haves" From "Have-Nots"', *Michigan State Law Review*, 2014, pp. 1411–1473. For a legal analysis on scoring under (German) consumer law see H. Schulte-Nölke, 'Algorithmen und Verbraucherrecht', in P. Leupold (ed.), *Forum Verbraucherrecht 2019* (Wien: Facultas Verslags- und Buchhandels, 2019), 142 p.

97 Citron and Pasquale, 'The Scored Society: Due Process for Automated Predictions', pp. 1–32.

98 *Ibid.*

99 Schmitz, 'Secret Consumer Scores and Segmentations: Separating "Haves" From "Have-Nots"', pp. 1411–1473.

100 Zarsky, 'Understanding Discrimination in the Scored Society', pp. 1375–1412.

101 See J.A. Kroll et al., 'Accountable Algorithms', *University of Pennsylvania Law Review*, 2017, vol. 165, pp. 633–705 (underlining the limits of *ex post* auditing and transparency).

102 Kim, 'Auditing Algorithms for Discrimination' (stressing the need for audits as an important tool to detect and counter discrimination).

103 In a similar, yet more dogmatic, sense Jabłonowska et al., *Consumer law and artificial intelligence*, pp. 57–59.

104 Directive 2006/123/EC of the European Parliament and of the Council of 12 December 2006 on services in the internal market, ELI: http://data.europa.eu/eli/dir/2006/123/oj.

105 Anti-discrimination Law of 10 May 2007, *Belgian Official Gazette* 30 May 2007, 29016.

leads to specialisation). Furthermore, discriminatory practices could amount to unfair trade practices in so far as they affect consumer autonomy in the sense that a consumer makes a choice (s)he would otherwise not make. In addition, the existing information duties (in Books III, VI and XII) and limits to contractual terms (Articles VI.83-VI.84 CEL) also provide an indirect safeguard against discrimination.

Discrimination through personalised ad delivery is subtle as it merely indirectly hinders access to certain goods and/or services. There is no rule prohibiting a business to present a more favourable offer, of razor blades for example, to men than to women (and there may indeed be justifiable reasons for doing so). Some might argue in favour of new rules prohibiting discrimination in ad delivery.[106] Such rules could be either process- or outcome-based or both.[107] Systematic discrimination – intended or not – through online advertising using autonomous agents must be dealt with, especially if it leads to exploitation of certain consumers' vulnerabilities. However, it is not appropriate to deviate from the general principle that consumers retain responsibility for their own choices in the sense that some effort can be expected from them (e.g., to read and possibly compare online offers (s)he receives).[108]

4.1.2. AI and Personalised Pricing

12. Personalised (or customised) pricing refers to a business strategy aimed at charging the highest price the individual end-consumer is willing to pay, which usually results in heterogeneous prices for homogenous products and requires businesses to obtain reliable data on their consumers' preferences.[109] In economic theory, the term 'personalised pricing' is usually coined as a synonym for first degree price discrimination (or customised pricing) as opposed to second and third degree price discrimination.[110] Second degree price discrimination

---

106 Jabłonowska et al., *Consumer law and artificial intelligence*, pp. 58–59.

107 *Ibid.*

108 This statement is derived from the *De Slegte* case. *See* Belgian Supreme Court 29 April 2004, *Jaarboek voor handelspraktijken* 2004, p. 97. The extent of the study of an offer is debatable. See German Bundesgerichtshof, *Gewerblicher Rechtsschutz und Urheberrecht* 1999, p. 1110 which appeared less strict.

109 OECD DAF/COMP(2018)13, 5; M. Maggiolino, 'Personalized Prices in European Competition Law', *Bocconi Legal Studies Research Paper No. 2984840*, 2017, p. 5. See extensively: R. Owens, 'Personalised Shopping and Algorithmic Pricing: How EU Competition Law Can Protect Consumers in the Digital World', in B. Custers and E. Fosch Villaronga, *Law and Artificial Intelligence – Regulating AI and Applying AI in Legal Practice* (Berlin: Springer, 2022), pp. 395– 413; M. Grochowski et al., 'Algorithmic Price Discrimination and Consumer Protection. A Digital Arms Race?', *Technology and Regulation* (Special Issue: Should Data Drive Private Law?), 2022, pp. 36–47.

110 See H. Varian, 'Price discrimination', in W. Schmalensee (ed.), *Handbook of industrial organization Volume I* (Amsterdam: Elsevier, 1989), p. 601; A.C. Pigou, *The Economics of Welfare*, p. 279. Alternatively, it is used as a synonym for perfect price discrimination as

(versioning or *a la carte* pricing) refers to a scenario where a business offers its customers different versions of the same product at different prices, thereby removing the need for information about individual consumer preferences.[111] Third degree price discrimination (or group pricing) refers to a scenario where a business offers a product at different prices for groups of consumers based on verifiable criteria such as age, occupation or geographical origin.[112] However, the use of algorithms and data analytics in digital markets blurs the line between – the once unachievable ideal[113] of – first degree price discrimination and – the more common – third degree price discrimination.[114]

There is an abundance of literature about the welfare effects of personalised pricing, yet there are no clear answers.[115] In theory, personalised pricing may enhance aggregate surplus by reducing deadweight loss, yet it is likely to reduce aggregate consumer surplus.[116] Studies show that consumers generally tend to perceive personalised pricing as unfair, although this perception can be highly influenced by the specific way personalised pricing is implemented.[117] Common examples are status-based discounts, volume-based or multi-buy discounts, loyalty discounts and new customer discounts.[118]

As a principle, current Belgian law allows business entities to freely set and customise prices (Article II.3) as competition ultimately determines prices on the market (Article V.2 CEL). In addition, the adequacy of the price is excluded from the assessment of the unfair nature of contract terms in so far as these terms are plain and intelligible (Article VI.82, para. 3 CEL). Article VI.116 CEL does

---

opposed to direct and indirect segmentation: see I. Png, *Managerial Economics* (Oxon: Routledge, 2012), pp. 174, 176–178 and 180–182.

111 OECD DAF/COMP(2018)13, p. 9; Maggiolino, 'Personalized Prices in European Competition Law', p. 6 and see Varian, 'Price discrimination', pp. 611–612; Pigou, *The Economics of Welfare*, p. 279.

112 OECD DAF/COMP(2018)13, p. 9; Maggiolino, 'Personalized Prices in European Competition Law', pp. 6–7 and see Varian, 'Price discrimination', p. 617; Pigou, *The Economics of Welfare*, p. 279.

113 OECD DAF/COMP(2018)13, p. 9; Maggiolino, 'Personalized Prices in European Competition Law', p. 5 and see Pigou, *The Economics of Welfare*, p. 280; Varian, 'Price discrimination', pp. 603–604.

114 OECD DAF/COMP/WD(2018)128, pp. 3–4.

115 See e.g. L. Stole, 'Price discrimination and Competition', in M. Armstrong and R. Porter (eds), *Handbook of industrial organization Volume 3* (Amsterdam: Elsevier, 2007), pp. 2221–2299; Varian, 'Price discrimination', pp. 597–654; J. Tirole, *The Theory of Industrial Organization* (Cambridge: MIT Press, 1988), 496 p.; L. Phlips, *The Economics of Price Discrimination*, (Cambridge: Cambridge University Press, 1983), 284p.; J. Robinson, *The Economics of Imperfect Competition* (London: Macmillan & Co, 1969), 352p.; Pigou, *The Economics of Welfare*, 876 p.

116 OECD DAF/COMP(2018)13, pp. 17–23, which discusses the impact on static efficiency, distribution outcomes and dynamic efficiency.

117 See literature and studies mentioned in OECD DAF/COMP(2018)13, pp. 24–26.

118 C. Townley, E. Morrison and K. Yeung, 'Big Data and Personalised Price Discrimination in EU Competition Law', *King's College London Law School Research Paper No. 2017-38*, 2017, vol. 36, pp. 683–748.

prohibit the sale of goods at a loss, save for the exceptions in Article VI.117 CEL. However, this Belgian prohibition is at odds with the Unfair Trade Practices Directive as interpreted by the CJEU in several cases, in particular *Euronics* and *Europamur*.[119]

Personalised pricing as such is not unfair.[120] It could, nonetheless, become unfair when combined with other practices.[121] It might, exceptionally, even constitute an abuse of a dominant position in the sense of Article IV.2 CEL and/or Article 102 TFEU bringing the practice within the scope of competition law.[122] Nonetheless, as long as consumers are adequately informed, personalised pricing appears to be a fair practice under current law. However, it is unclear when consumers are indeed adequately informed. In particular, the question arises whether consumers should be informed about (1) the mere fact that a consumer receives a customised price, (2) the prices which have been proposed to other consumers for homogenous products and (3) the way in which the autonomous agent calculates the price. Such information could impact the consumer's maximal willingness to pay, especially in the event of a misperception. Article VI.99 §4, 3° CEL, which applies to the invitation to purchase, clarifies that the price (including taxes and costs) constitutes core information. However, the limits of the communication medium need to be taken into account.[123] Article VI.97, 4° CEL mentions the requirement to inform consumers about the pricing method. Nonetheless, while the CJEU often stresses the importance of the price as a core element, it tends to be lenient as long as the consumer is sufficiently informed about the total price.[124] Overall, there seems to be no pressing need

---

119 CJEU 19 October 2017, C-295/16, *Europamur*, ECLI:EU:C:2017:782; CJEU 7 March 2013, C-343/12, *Euronics*, ECLI:EU:C:2013:154. However, the Belgian legislator maintains the position that the said Directive has no bearing on Article VI.117 CEL (as it considers it a purely B2B practice). Further information in this regard (including on the divergent views) can be found in G. Straetmans and S. Bennis, *Economisch Recht Leidraad voor Studenten* (Antwerpen: Gompel&Svacina, 2019), pp. 262–264 and pp. 230–248.

120 I. Graef, 'Algorithms and Fairness: What Role for Competition Law In Targeting Price Discrimination Towards End Consumers', *Columbia Journal of European Law*, 2018, vol. 24, no. 3, pp. 551–552.

121 The Commission mentions the example of a trader who falsely claims that only a few tickets are left after finding out that a consumer is running out of time to buy a flight ticket. Commission Staff Working Document – Guidance on the Implementation/Application of Directive 2005/29/EC on unfair commercial practices, 25 May 2016, SWD(2016)163 final, pp. 146 and 149.

122 For analyses under Article 102 TFEU: Graef, 'Algorithms and Fairness: What Role For Competition Law In Targeting Price Discrimination Towards End Consumers', pp. 542–550; Townley, Morrison and Yeung, 'Big Data and Personalised Price Discrimination in EU Competition Law', pp. 32–50.

123 For this reason, the CJEU considered in *Ving Sverige* that the mere mentioning of an entry-level price might be acceptable depending on the communication medium. See CJEU 21 May 2011, C-122/10, *Ving Sverige*, ECLI:EU:C:2011:299.

124 In *Deroo-Blanquart*, the CJEU stressed the importance of the price, yet showed leniency for a common practice, where the seller of a computer equipped with the pre-installed software indicates the total price without indicating the prices of each of those software items (para.

to prohibit price discrimination guided by autonomous agents. Increased transparency might suffice.

4.2. AI-AIDED CONTRACTING

13. The previous part discussed some of the legal challenges posed by autonomous agents that provide consumers with information, and in particular the parameters for their purchase decisions. This part moves on to contractual issues. The importance of this part must be stressed for two reasons. Firstly, the conclusion of a contract impacts the legal positions of the consumer vis-à-vis the business and, secondly, AI's potential benefits in this regard may render consumers increasingly dependent (nos. 3–4).[125]

Consumers have a duty to process the information they receive, and are not as such protected against their own biases while entering into an agreement. Take the example of present bias which refers to the tendency to settle for a smaller present reward than to wait for a larger future reward (as long as they have not been misinformed). To counter the effects of the present bias (and other biases) in online sales, Article VI.47 CEL provides for the right of withdrawal within a period of 14 days. While this provision alleviates the dangers to some extent, autonomous agents (employed in contract ware) risk (ab)using consumers' biases in ways we cannot yet predict. Further examination on this subject is required. Such studies would have to be interdisciplinary and should include insights from behavioural economics.

14. As a counterweight for the use of autonomous agents employed by business entities, Gal and Elkin-Koren propose to employ the same technology for the benefit of consumers.[126] In this sense, 'algorithmic consumers' are autonomous agents which 'make and execute (purchase) decisions for the consumers by directly communicating with other systems through the internet. They automatically identify a need, search for an optimal purchase and execute the transaction on behalf of the consumer'.[127] In Gal's view, algorithmic consumers

48 and 50–51). This mattered little as the trader was under no obligation to sell these items separately. In *Wind Tre Vodafone*, the CJEU seemed less convinced that the sale of SIM cards with pre-loaded and pre-activated services (for which a monthly fee was due) was an acceptable practice in so far as the users were not informed of the fact that those services had been pre-loaded and pre-activated, nor of their cost. See CJEU 13 September 2018, C-54/17 and C-55/17, *Wind Tre and Vodafone*, ECLI:EU:C:2018:710.

[125] See extensively the many contributions in M. Ebers et al. (eds), *Contracting and Contract Law in the Age of Artificial Intelligence* (London: Bloomsbury, 2022), 384 p. Also see Chapter 13.

[126] M.S. Gal and N. Elkin-Koren, 'Algorithmic Consumers', *Harvard Journal of Law & Technology*, 2017, vol. 30, no. 2., pp. 309–353.

[127] M.S. Gal, 'Algorithmic Challenges to Autonomous Choice', *Michigan Telecommunications and Technology Law Review*, 2018, vol. 25, no. 1, p. 4.

would present themselves as individual consumers on the market while representing groups of 'anonymised' consumers.[128] Consumers would thus gain bargaining power as well as regain their anonymity leaving themselves less exposed to exploitation. Furthermore, coordination of the supplier's autonomous agents (which could result in anti-competitive prices) can be circumvented through code (e.g., an algorithm that instructs not to buy if coordination is presumed.[129] In this view, algorithmic consumers would enhance competition and 'consumer welfare' in the long run (although this remains a hypothesis). Gal and Elkin-Koren, nonetheless, remain warry about the pro-competitive effects of algorithmic consumers as they observe that 'mega platforms may attempt to provide and control algorithmic consumers by themselves, given that such algorithms are likely to become consumers' gateway into the digitalised world'.[130]

In any event, Gal and Elkin-Koren argue convincingly that algorithmic consumers will enable speedier decisions based on more sophisticated analyses, while avoiding consumer bias and thereby reducing information and transaction costs.[131] However, convenience comes at a price. When an autonomous agent makes the purchase decision based on its estimation of consumer preferences (e.g., a smart refrigerator which automatically purchases milk as soon as it registers the need for a refill), the consumer is one step removed from his (or her) purchase decision. As Gal and Elkin-Koren correctly observe, 'the algorithmic choice may not always accurately reflect consumers' preferences' and, as previously indicated, such technology may be susceptible to its own biases and errors. When such discrepancies occur, consumers have in essence two types of defence: the lack of sufficient consent or redress against the provider of the autonomous agent.

Consent is paramount for an agreement to exist (Article 1108 Civil code). Safeguarding free consent has resulted in specific duties for businesses that offer goods and/or services online. Business entities are not only required to meet information obligations (in view of establishing informed consent),[132] but also formal – albeit sometimes vaguely formulated – requirements on how to obtain consent (express consent),[133] especially with regard to the acceptance of privacy declarations (e.g., Articles 7–8 General Data Protection Regulation).[134]

---

128 *Ibid.*

129 Gal and Elkin-Koren, 'Algorithmic Consumers', pp. 309–353. A similar stance was defended in J.A.T. Fairfield, 'Smart Contracts, Bitcoin Bots, and Consumer Protection', *Washington and Lee Law Review Online*, September 2014.

130 Gal and Elkin-Koren, 'Algorithmic Consumers', p. 29.

131 See Gal and Elkin-Koren, 'Algorithmic Consumers', pp. 10–13.

132 E.g., Articles VI.45, XII.6 and XII.7 CEL.

133 E.g., Articles VI.46, XII.8, XII.9 and XII.15 CEL.

134 See also I. Domurath, 'Technological Totalitarianism: Data, Consumer Profiling, and the Law', in L. de Almeida, *et al.* (eds), *The Transformation of Economic Law. Essays in Honour of Hans-W. Micklitz* (Hart Publishing: Oxford, 2019), pp. 72–75.

It remains unclear to what extent a consumer can express (binding) consent through an algorithmic consumer (or any autonomous agent). Article 9 of the Directive on electronic commerce requires Belgium to ensure that it 'allows contracts to be concluded by electronic means', a concept broad enough to encompass most – if not all known – autonomous agents.[135] A similar, yet slightly more specific legal basis, can be found in the United Nations Convention on the Use of Electronic Communications in International Contracts.[136] Article 12 states that 'A contract formed by the interaction of an automated message system and a natural person, or by the interaction of automated message systems, shall not be denied validity or enforceability on the sole ground that no natural person reviewed or intervened in each of the individual actions carried out by the automated message systems or the resulting contract'. Jacquemin and Hubin suggest adopting a similar provision into Belgian law.[137] Both consumers and business entities would indeed benefit from such a provision, insofar as such automated systems respect certain standards developed on the basis of the best-known practices. As Jacquemin and Hubin observe, business entities that enter into an agreement with consumers by using autonomous agents, can invoke the doctrine of legitimate expectations.[138] However, such a defence will probably only be successful if the business entity demonstrates that it has taken sufficient precautions (taking into account the state of the art) to protect itself from misrepresentation by autonomous agents.[139] If the interpretation is too strict, it may discourage businesses from entering in fully automated agreements altogether. Conversely, the consumer will need to demonstrate that (s)he did not instruct the autonomous agent to enter into the agreement and that (s)he cannot be held responsible for any misunderstanding.

15. In business to consumer (B2C) contracts (especially in e-commerce), consumers are usually required to accept the general terms and conditions set by businesses. As a result, businesses are usually better placed to estimate the legal and economic consequences of B2C contracts. Therefore, consumer law does not only require business entities to inform consumers as indicated in the previous paragraphs, but also protects consumers against unfair terms (Articles I.8.22°, VI.82 and VI.83 CEL).

---

135 Directive 2000/31/EC of the European Parliament and of the Council of 8 June 2000 on certain legal aspects of information society services, in particular electronic commerce, in the Internal Market, ELI: http://data.europa.eu/eli/dir/2000/31/oj. In addition it states: 'Member States shall in particular ensure that the legal requirements applicable to the contractual process neither create obstacles for the use of electronic contracts nor result in such contracts being deprived of legal effectiveness and validity on account of their having been made by electronic means.'

136 Available at https://www.uncitral.org/pdf/english/texts/electcom/06-57452_Ebook.pdf.

137 Jacquemin and Hubin, 'Aspects contractuels et de responsabilité civile en matière d'intelligence artificielle', p. 107.

138 *Ibid.*, pp. 110–111.

139 This follows from the requirement of an apparent state.

However, as shown by studies, consumers rarely read the terms and conditions until after the conclusion of the contract.[140] Autonomous agents, functioning as digital assistants or robo-helpers, may alleviate this issue. In fact, researchers have already developed a program using ML to automatically detect potentially unfair clauses in online contracts: CLAUDETTE (Automated CLAUse DETecTEr).[141] CLAUDETTE can moreover be used to check whether privacy policies are GDPR-compliant.[142]

4.3. AI-AUTOMATED ENFORCEMENT

16. Enforcement of consumer rights is usually considered a weakness of consumer policy, especially in a global online environment in which unfair practices are more difficult to monitor.[143] AI can be expected to add a layer of complexity to enforcement. However, it can also be used to aid in the enforcement of consumer rights. Firstly, it can help to detect consumer law infringements in a similar way as it can detect tax law infringements.[144] Furthermore, the marriage between AI-based applications and a script that captures legal logic allows for automated protection of consumer rights (e.g. automatic compensation in case of a certain practice such as a flight delay).[145] Nonetheless, the use of autonomous agents in the enforcement stages of a business-to-consumer relation is expected to be limited in the near future.[146]

---

140 This follows from several empirical studies. E.g., T.J. Maronick, 'Do Consumers Read Terms of Service Agreements When Installing Software? -- A Two-Study Empirical Analysis', *The Journal of Business*, June 2014; Y. Bakos, F. Marotta-Wurgler and D.R. Trossen, 'Does Anyone Read the Fine Print? Consumer Attention to Standard-Form Contracts', *Journal of Legal Studies*, 2014, vol. 43, no. 1, pp. 1–35.

141 See: http://claudette.eui.eu. See also Lippi et al., 'CLAUDETTE: an Automated Detector of Potentially Unfair Clauses in Online Terms of Service', *Artificial Intelligence Law*, 2019, vol. 27, pp. 117–139.

142 See: http://claudette.gdpr.eu.

143 O. Borgogno, 'Smart contracts as the (new) Power of the Powerless? The Stakes for Consumers', *European Review of Private Law*, 2019, pp. 893–894. Further on the difficulties of enforcement in a global online environment: R. Koulu, 'Blockchains and Online Dispute Resolution: Smart Contracts As an Alternative to Enforcement', *SCRIPTed*, May 2016, pp. 42–48.

144 At the University of Antwerp, Emma Caeyers is investigating the requirements for the tax administration to employ AI in the fight against tax fraud. The PhD project is entitled 'Artificiële intelligentie gebruikt door de belastingadministratie, balancerend tussen effectiviteit/efficiëntie en het recht op privacy. De afweging gemaakt'.

145 See Bennis, 'Consumentenbescherming bij blockchain en smart contracts', pp. 267–268 with further references.

146 On this subject, see J. Barnett and P. Treleaven, 'Algorithmic Dispute Resolution', *The Computer Journal*, 2018, vol. 61, no. 3, pp. 399–408.

5. CONCLUSION: A TALE ABOUT OPEN-MINDEDNESS AND VIGILANCE

17. AI-based applications offer a great number of benefits to businesses, consumers and society as a whole. Artificial intelligence can even be relied upon in the armoury of consumer law against the difficulties in detecting infringements and to boost overall enforcement (with respect for the rights and legitimate interests of business entities). However, consumer law practitioners should be mindful of the increasing risks of online discrimination, manipulation and even harassment. A more general fundamental question is how to deal with the growing knowledge (or power) imbalance not only between the traditional business and consumer categories, but between those who have the means and those who have not. While these issues must be dealt with appropriately, they are not – and should never become – an excuse for excessive regulation from which neither business entities nor consumers benefit. The questions raised must be dealt with from a coherent multi-layered perspective that includes market-based, technical as well as legal – including consumer, competition, privacy and anti-discrimination – solutions based on careful research of the actual issues. Consumer and privacy legislations in particular – the bedrock of both is identical: consumer autonomy – would have to be more coordinated and I would recommend the institutions in charge of these legislations to cooperate. Ultimately, we will need an open, yet vigilant mindset to reap as many of the benefits AI promises as possible.

CHAPTER 18

ROBOTS AND AI IN THE HEALTHCARE SECTOR: POTENTIAL EXISTING LEGAL SAFEGUARDS AGAINST A(N) (UN)JUSTIFIED FEAR FOR 'DEHUMANISATION' OF THE PHYSICIAN-PATIENT RELATIONSHIP

Wannes BUELENS*

1. INTRODUCTION

1. In this chapter, I will first discuss the rise of robotics and AI in the healthcare sector and the concern of some scholars that this may lead to a dehumanisation of the physician-patient relationship (part 2). I will then elaborate on four potential existing legal safeguards against such dehumanisation: the fact that only qualified persons are allowed to provide healthcare (part 3) and the resulting liability of the physician if things go wrong (part 4); the right of the patient to receive information about his/her health condition and to give his/her prior informed consent under the Belgian Law on Patient Rights (part 5), and finally transparency and informed consent under the General Data Protection Regulation (GDPR) (part 6). In the future, the EU Artificial Intelligence Act[1] may help the physician to live up to the aforementioned obligations (part 7). I will conclude with an overview (part 8).

* Lawyer, teaching assistant University of Ghent and voluntary academic collaborator University of Antwerp.

1 Proposal for a Regulation of the European Parliament and of the Council Laying Down Harmonised Rules on Artificial Intelligence (Artificial Intelligence Act) and Amending Certain Union Legislative Acts, 2021/0106 (COD).

2. THE RISE OF ROBOTICS AND AI TO DEAL WITH INCREASING DEMANDS IN THE HEALTHCARE SECTOR

2. A recent publication commissioned by the European Parliament states that the health sector is facing increasing demands on services brought on by issues such as an ageing population, an increase of chronic diseases, budgetary constraints, and a shortage of qualified workers.[2] Developments in the field of robotics and AI can provide countless opportunities for addressing these challenges, resulting in necessary and significant cost and time savings. These efficiency benefits are the result of the fact the work is done more efficiently, more quickly and at a lower cost than a human actor could do it. According to the same study, the application of robotics and AI could lead to improvements in fields such as medical diagnosis, surgical intervention, prevention and treatment of diseases, and support for rehabilitation and long-term care. They could also contribute to more effective and automated work management processes, while offering continuous training for healthcare workers. It is estimated that the market for AI in healthcare will reach around $6,6 billion by 2021[3] and $8 billion by 2022,[4] with significant cost savings for healthcare systems. According to a recent French study, the health sector is internationally the second most impacted sector by robotics and AI after the telecommunications and technologies sector, but preceding the financial services and automotive sector.[5]

3. A recent PwC study shows that there are indeed already many applications in the healthcare sector that use robotics and AI.[6] This study divides the applications into eight domains: keeping well, early detection, diagnosis, decision-making, treatment, end-of-life care, research and training. Of course, there are also other ways to categorise the various applications.[7]

---

2 Z. Dolic, R. Castro and A. Moarcas, *Robots and healthcare: a solution or a problem?* (Luxemburg: European Parliament, April 2019), p. 7, https://www.europarl.europa.eu/RegData/etudes/IDAN/2019/638391/IPOL_IDA(2019)638391_EN.pdf.

3 See: https://www.accenture.com/us-en/insight-artificial-intelligence-healthcare.

4 See: https://www.sueddeutsche.de/wirtschaft/gesundheidssystem-dr-ki-zur-visite-bitte-1.3665374.

5 C. Nozet, A. Metayer-Mathieu, S. Dahbi, A. Faure and E. Menard, 'Intelligence artificielle – État de l'art et perspectives pour la France', February 2019, p. 112, https://www.cget.gouv.fr/sites/cget.gouv.fr/files/atoms/files/2019-02-intelligence-artificielle-etat-de-l-art-et-perspectives_0.pdf.

6 D. Arnold and T. Wilson, *What doctor? Why AI and robotics will define New Health* (London: PwC, 2017), pp. 4–18, https://www.pwc.com/gx/en/industries/healthcare/publications/ai-robotics-new-health/ai-robotics-new-health.pdf.

7 E.g., M. Butter, A. Rensma, J. van Boxsel, S. Kalisingh, M. Schoone, M. Leis, G. Gelderblom, G. Cremers, M. de Wilt, W. Kortekaas, A. Thielmann, K. Cuhls, A. Sachinopoulou and I. Korhonen, 'Robotics for healthcare', *Ehealthnews*, 2008, pp. 36–60, https://www.ehealthnews.eu/images/stories/robotics-final-report.pdf; M. Fenech, N. Strukelj and O. Buston, *Ethical,*

In the category '*keeping well*' we find consumer health applications that enable people to manage their own healthcare, and keep themselves well through healthier living. Examples of these applications are: Smart Belt,[8] Smart Performance Apparel,[9] Lumo Lift,[10] and Pathway Genomics.[11] The category '*early detection*' consists of consumer health applications making it possible to oversee early-stage diseases, thus enabling doctors to better monitor and detect potentially life-threatening conditions at earlier and thus more treatable stages. For example, in Belgium there is an application called FibriCheck to detect arrhythmias.[12] Another example is the iTBra for breast cancer detection.[13] The applications in these two categories can assist in the creation and management of 'personalised care', allowing patients to feel empowered and in greater control of their own well-being.[14]

The third category is '*diagnosis*', referring to AI systems that enable physicians to diagnose faster and more accurately than a human being. A well-known example of a diagnostic tool that is already used in practice is the Watson Oncology Advisor. This algorithm uses almost 15 million pages of medical literature to advise oncologists on cancer diagnosis with an accuracy of 90%.[15] It can also provide treatment recommendations to physicians. Another example is Google's DeepMind. A recent study shows that DeepMind outperforms specialised radiologists in accurately interpreting mammograms to detect breast

---

Social, and Political Challenges of Artificial Intelligence in Health (London: Future Advocacy, April 2018), pp. 12–24, https://wellcome.ac.uk/sites/default/files/ai-in-health-ethical-social-political-challenges.pdf; Nozet, Metayer-Mathieu, Dahbi, Faure and Menard, 'Intelligence artificielle – État de l'art et perspectives pour la France', p. 183; S. Tian, W. Yang, J.M. Le Grange, P. Wang, W. Huang and Z. Ye, 'Smart Healthcare: making medical care more intelligent', *Global Health Journal*, 2019, vol. 3, no.3, pp. 62–65.

8 This is a belt built to prevent falls from unstable gait patterns, such as abnormal gait speed and symmetry. If a user shows an unstable gait pattern and a higher fall risk, its companion app will send a warning notification to the user's phone. The belt also monitors the waist size of the person and his/her (in)activity and helps to develop healthy eating habits (see https://www.weltcorp.com/).

9 This smart workout clothing offers real-time biometrics, personalised programming and customised reporting to help athletes reach their goals faster (see https://www.liveathos.com/).

10 This is a wearable posture coach that helps to sit straighter, stand taller and look better by buzzing when the person slouches (see https://www.lumobodytech.com/lumo-lift/).

11 This company has developed several applications to provide customised advise based on the person's genetic make-up (see https://www.pathway.com/).

12 This mobile application detects arrhythmias if the patient places his/her finger on the camera for one minute. There is always a doctor in the loop to check the results. It is said that 1 out of 4 people develop arrhythmias during their life, that arrhythmias yearly cause 1.25 million strokes, and that 75% of these strokes can be prevented (see https://www.fibricheck.com/).

13 This bra consists of two wearable, comfortable intelligent breast patches which identify circadian temperature changes over time within breast tissue, enabling early detection of breast cancer (see http://cyrcadiahealth.com/).

14 D. Ross and V. Surgenor, 'Artificial Intelligence and Healthcare', *Business Law Today*, 2019, https://Businesslawtoday.org/2019/02/artificial-intelligence-healthcare-faqs/.

15 See https://www.ascopost.com/new/44214.

cancer, with 5.7% and 1.2% (USA and UK) less false positives and 9.4% and 2.7% less false negatives. This paves the way for clinical trials to improve the accuracy and efficiency of breast cancer screening.[16]

The fourth category is '*decision-making*'. Predictive analytics can support clinical decision-making and actions as well as prioritise tasks. Besides Watson, another example is Bodylogical,[17] which is an application that captures insights in mechanistic modelling to digitally represent the physiology of the human body. This enables the development of accurate simulations to predict the likely progression of chronic diseases in the future based on today's actions and interventions. These simulations help to better understand how daily life choices and therapeutics influence individual patients or population health outcomes and associated costs.[18] In the future, these kind of applications will make it possible to provide treatments that are more tailored to the needs of a patient.[19] This can result in budget savings of 5% to 10%.[20]

'*Treatment*' is the fifth category. AI can certainly help healthcare workers to take a more comprehensive approach towards disease management, better coordinate care plans and help patients to better manage and comply with treatment programs.[21] It also opens possibilities to treat patients at home instead of in hospital. Examples of such algorithms are Innovaccer's Healthcare's Data Activation Platform,[22] Philips' Remote patient monitoring,[23] and IMA.[24] Robots also play an important role in treatment, either by assisting the surgeon

---

16 S.M. McKinney, M. Sieniek and V. Godbole et al., 'International evaluation of an AI system for breast cancer screening', *Nature*, 2020, vol. 577, pp. 89–94.

17 See https://www.pwc.com/us/en/industries/health-industries/library/doublejump/bodylogical-precision.html.

18 Arnold and Wilson, *What doctor? Why AI and robotics will define New Health*, p. 10.

19 Fenech, Strukelj and Buston, 'Ethical, Social, and Political Challenges of Artificial Intelligence in Health', p. 27.

20 Nozet, Metayer-Mathieu, Dahbi, Faure and Menard, 'Intelligence artificielle – État de l'art et perspectives pour la France', p. 186. Cf. Lord Darzi, *Better Health and Care for All. A 10-Point Plan for the 2020s. The Lord Darzi Review of Health and Care*, (London: Institute for Public Policy Research, June 2018), p. 26, https://www.ippr.org/files/2018-06/better-health-and-care-for-all-june2018.pdf.

21 Arnold and Wilson, *What doctor? Why AI and robotics will define New Health*, p. 12.

22 This AI driven platform addresses persistent issues in care and connectivity, ands assures adherence to care plans by tracking deviations and staying updated on post-acute patient needs (see https://innovaccer.com/).

23 This application delivers remote care options to proactively help patients at home. The services are powered by data analytics and connected sensors enabling 24/7 monitoring of an ongoing stream of monitoring data to a remote home-care team (see https://www.usa.philips.com/healthcare/services/population-health-management/patient-engagement/remote-patient-monitoring).

24 This application monitors patients with long-term conditions and help them adhere to medication intake. The application uses a visual recognition system to identify the patient's face and the medication they are taking and to confirm ingestion. The data is then sent back to the physician or to a pharmaceutical company conducting a clinical trial (see https://aicure.com/).

or by performing treatment themselves. The most widely used surgical robot is the Da Vinci robot, which allows the surgeon to perform certain operations more accurately. Robots can also assist with repetitive tasks in hospitals and laboratories or in rehabilitation and physical therapy. They can support those with long-term conditions as well.[25] Examples of such robots are Robear, a robot that can lift and move patients in and out their bed or wheelchair and Veebot, a robot that can draw blood faster and more safely than humans.

There are also robots that focus on *assisting patients*,[26] for example in supporting them with manipulation in day-to-day activities such as eating, brushing teeth, picking up objects, opening doors and mobility during daily activities. These robots can also take the form of intelligent prosthetics, revalidation/rehabilitation tools, or can provide assistance with end-of-life care. These robots can prolong the time that people can live independently in their own home, thereby reducing the pressure on healthcare institutions like hospitals, revalidation centres and nursing homes.

AI could also help to make *research* more time- and cost-efficient. AI techniques have advanced to a level that allows them to be employed in real-life situations to assist human decision-makers.[27] For example, the pharmaceutical industry uses AI for drug discovery – i.e., the search for a new active pharmaceutical ingredient. AI can shorten this pivotal and time-consuming task, assess the eligibility of candidates to participate in a clinical trial as well as monitor patients more effectively during trials.[28] AI also enhances the possibility of re-interrogating clinical and market data to determine whether existing drugs can be remodelled for other purposes. For example, AtomNet found two existing drugs that potentially work against Ebola by using deep learning on 3D models of molecules.[29] AI can also be used to analyse scientific papers in order to provide insights on diseases and their treatment to researchers.[30] This is becoming increasingly important given that the amount of medical literature is

---

25 Arnold and Wilson, *What doctor? Why AI and robotics will define New Health*, p. 12.

26 E. Fosch-Villaronga, *Robots, Healthcare, and the law. Regulating automation in personal care* (Abingdone-New York: Routledge, 2020), pp. 21–35.

27 S. Harrer, P. Shah, B. Antony and J. Hu, 'Artificial Intelligence for Clinical Trial Design', *Trends in Pharmacological Sciences*, 2019, vol. 40, no. 8, p. 577.

28 D. Siegismund, 'Developing deep learning applications for life science and pharma industry', *Drug Res.*, 2018, p. 305; C. Tillmanns and M. Fuderer, 'Artificial intelligence as an emerging technology in the pharmaceutical industry: what are the legal challenges?', *EPLR*, 2019, vol. 3, no. 1, pp. 4–5; A. Zhavoronkov, P. Mamoshina, Q. Vanhaelen, M. Scheibye-Knudsen, A. Moskalev and A. Aliper, 'Artificial intelligence of aging and longevity research: Recent advances and perspectives', *Ageing Research Reviews*, 2019, vol. 49, pp. 51–58.

29 See https://www.atomwise.com/2015/03/24/new-ebola-treatment-using-artificial-intelligence/; Fenech, Strukelj and Buston, *Ethical, Social, and Political Challenges of Artificial Intelligence in Health*, p. 16; Harrer, Shah, Antony and Hu, 'Artificial Intelligence for Clinical Trial Design', pp. 577–591.

30 Nozet, Metayer-Mathieu, Dahbi, Faure and Menard, 'Intelligence artificielle – État de l'art et perspectives pour la France" p. 185.

doubling every three years. It is, therefore, not possible to solely rely on humans to keep up with these literature advancements as it would take 29 hours per workday to stay completely up to date.[31]

Finally, AI and robots can provide *training* for physicians. Indeed, unlike classic computer driven algorithms, AI – often combined with virtual reality, and virtual patients[32] – allows training through real life simulations. This technology is able to challenge trainees more effectively than a human tutor by using a large database of possible scenarios, which can continually be adjusted based on previous responses of other trainees.[33] The content of the training will also change. For example, physicians will learn to navigate the digital world and use decision support and other tools to make better decisions, rather than trying to memorise every symptom and its meaning.[34] Nevertheless, memorisation remains important because nowadays algorithms are trained with a specific available dataset. They are, therefore, only suitable for a specific patient population and are limited in their use, for example only for the analysis of scans (as the sole basis of diagnosing a disease). For now, algorithms will thus not be suitable for automatically diagnosing multifactorial diseases, which is far more common.[35]

4. Many legal questions arise when applying these new technologies in the healthcare sector. One can think of liability for damage caused by products equipped with AI, the application of and compliance with medical devices, clinical trials and data protection regulations, the use and ownership of data (e.g., patients' medical records) and intellectual property.

Apart from these legal issues, one of the concerns expressed by scholars and expert groups with respect to these new technologies is a fear of '*dehumanisation*' of healthcare and the possible negative impact on the personal relationship between a physician and a patient.[36] In this chapter, I will discuss whether this fear of dehumanisation of the physician-patient relationship is justified in light of the current legal framework in Belgium. I will thus focus on the third, fourth and fifth category mentioned above, namely diagnosis, decision-making and treatment. This question is of particular importance as

---

31 A. Curioni-Fontecedro, 'A new era of oncology through artificial intelligence', *ESMO Open*, 2017, https://www.ncbi.nlm.nih.gov/pmc/articles/PMC5519782/.

32 D. Combs and F. Combs, 'Emerging Roles of Virtual Patients in the Age of AI', *Journal of Ethics*, 2019, pp. 153–159.

33 Arnold and Wilson, *What doctor? Why AI and robotics will define New Health*, p. 15.

34 M. Mitchell and L. Kan, 'Digital Technology and the Future of Health Systems', *Health Systems & Reform*, 2019, vol. 5, no. 2, p. 115.

35 Nozet, Metayer-Mathieu, Dahbi, Faure and Menard, 'Intelligence artificielle – État de l'art et perspectives pour la France', p. 188.

36 Dolic, Castro and Moarcas, *Robots in healthcare: a solution or a problem?*, p. 19; D. Schiff and J. Borenstein, 'How Should Clinicians Communicate With Patients About the Roles of Artificially Intelligent Team Members?', *AMA Journal of Ethics*, 2019, vol. 21, no. 2, p. 139.

personal relationships between physicians and patients are still considered to be essential in healthcare.[37] Moreover, a recent study shows that patients are still very attached to a personal relationship with their physician.[38]

5. In my opinion, there are currently at least four possible legal safeguards against the feared dehumanisation of healthcare, and the possible negative impact on the physician-patient relationship, resulting from the increased use of robots and AI. First of all, only qualified persons are allowed to provide healthcare (part 3). A second possible safeguard is the general liability standard. Indeed, the use of a robot or AI does not discharge the physician of the obligation to act in accordance with this standard and may encourage him/her to remain closely involved in the patients' treatment (part 4). Thirdly, a physician has an obligation to provide the patient with information about his/her health condition and to obtain the patient's informed consent before he/she can start treatment (part 5). Finally, the physician also has a transparency obligation towards the patient under the GDPR. The latter will most of the time have to give his/her informed consent for the processing of his/her (health) data (part 6).

Apart from these legal aspects, the use of algorithms and robots may also have a positive impact on the workload of physicians – not only with respect to their medical tasks, but also vis-à-vis their administrative tasks. This can enable them to spend more time with their patients, be more involved in their treatment and focus on tasks needing a human element.[39] A recent study, for instance, shows that the time of healthcare professionals freed up by using algorithms and robots varies between 11% and 57%.[40]

---

37 Conseil National de l'Ordre des Médecins (France), *Médecins et patients dans le monde des data, des algorithms et de l'intelligence artificielle. Analyse et recommandations du Cnom*, (Paris: Cnom, January 2018), p. 6, https://www.conseil-national.medecin.fr/sites/default/files/external-package/edition/od6gnt/cnomdata_algorithmes_ia_0.pdf; EP Resolution 12 February 2019 no. 2018/2088(INI) on a comprehensive European industrial policy on artificial intelligence and robotics, no. 70, https://www.europarl.europa.eu/doceo/document/TA-8-2019-0081_EN.pdf.

38 Arnold and Wilson, *What doctor? Why AI and robotics will define New Health*, p. 18.

39 G. Vallancien, *La médecine sans médecin? Le numérique au service du malade* (Paris: Éditions Gallimard, 2015), p. 13; S. Jha and E. Topol, 'Adapting to Artificial Intelligence, Radiologists and Pathologists as Information Specialists', *JAMA*, 2016, p. 2; Lord Darzi, *Better Health and Care for All. A 10-Point Plan for the 2020s. The Lord Darzi Review of Health and Care*, p. 25; M. Lupton, 'Some ethical and legal consequences of the application of artificial intelligence in the field of medicine', *Trends Med*, 2018, p. 3; E. Topol, *Deep Medicine: how artificial intelligence can make healthcare human again*, (New York: Hachette, 2019), 400 p.; EP Resolution 12 February 2019 no. 2018/2088(INI), no. 70. Cf. A. Murphy and B. Liszewski, 'Artificial Intelligence and the Medical Radiation Profession: How Our Advocacy Must Inform Future Practice', *Journal of Medical Imaging and Radiation Sciences*, 2019, vol. 50, no. 4, p. 3.

40 Lord Darzi, *Better Health and Care for All. A 10-Point Plan for the 2020s. The Lord Darzi Review of Health and Care*, pp. 26–27.

3. ONLY QUALIFIED PERSONS ARE ALLOWED TO PROVIDE HEALTHCARE

6. The fear of dehumanisation has to be tempered by the fact that only qualified persons are allowed to provide 'healthcare services'. In Belgium, this refers to services aiming to enhance, establish, maintain, improve, restore or improve a patient's health condition, to change the patient's physical appearance for mainly esthetical reasons or to assist the patient in dying.[41] Indeed, the Law on the Exercise of the Healthcare Profession stipulates that one must fulfil certain conditions to be allowed to provide (certain aspects of) healthcare.[42] For example, Articles 3, §1 and 25 of this Law stipulate that a person can only practice medicine if he or she: (1) holds the degree of doctor in medicine, surgery and obstetrics; (2) this degree has been certified by the Directorate-General for Health Professions, Medical Surveillance and Welfare at Work of the Federal Public Service Public Health, Food Chain Safety and Environment; and (3) is registered in the register of the Order of Doctors. Other healthcare jobs can only be provided by a qualified person such as a pharmacist, physiotherapist, nurse, midwife, rescue worker in an ambulance, clinical psychologist or paramedic.

7. As long as only the aforementioned *persons* – a robot/algorithm is not a 'person' – are allowed to provide healthcare, robots and algorithms will not be allowed to provide healthcare on their own. In other words, from a legal point of view, a robot/algorithm that provides healthcare cannot act completely autonomously and/or without the supervision and oversight of one of the aforementioned healthcare professionals (each of them in their own field).[43] The robot and algorithm thus remain, at least from a legal point of view, mere (augmenting) tools in the hands of the physician, similar to a scalpel or scanner. It is clear that this principle in itself is an important potential legal safeguard against the dehumanisation of the patient-physician relationship. This is enhanced by the fact that this has important implications for the physician's liability if things go wrong.

4. LIABILITY RULES

8. I will not discuss *all* the liability rules that may come into play when damage is caused by a robot or algorithm.[44] Nor will I discuss the possible problems and

41 Article 2, 3° Law on the Exercise of the Healthcare Profession.

42 *Official Gazette* 18 June 2015, p. 35172.

43 C. Lequillerier, 'L'impact de l'intelligence artificielle sur la relation de soin', *JDSAM*, 2017, vol. 17, p. 15.

44 E. Fosch-Villaronga, *Robots, Healthcare, and the law. Regulating automation in personal care* (Abingdone-New York: Routledge, 2020), p. 174 et. seq.

undesirable effects that may occur when applying the current liability framework to algorithms and robots used by physicians. Think of the allocation of liability between the different actors involved (e.g., manufacturers, physicians, hospitals, distributors and government) based on strict liability principles. Some of these issues are dealt with in another chapter.[45]

In this part, I will only describe from a general perspective how the liability principle of the 'reasonably prudent physician under similar circumstances' may affect the behaviour of a physician using robots or algorithms. Indeed, since the robot and the algorithm are mere (augmenting) tools in the hands of a physician, the latter remains responsible for a robot's or algorithm's actions and omissions, and/or his/her own actions and omissions based on the outcome of the algorithm (e.g., a diagnosis or treatment suggestion).[46] The use of robots or AI does not discharge the physician of the obligation to act as a reasonable prudent physician (of the same specialty) would act in the same circumstances. This may encourage the physician to remain closely involved in the patient's treatment. It may even avoid the dehumanisation of healthcare, and ensure that a human remains in the loop.

9. First of all, when a physician uses an algorithm for a diagnosis or treatment suggestion, he/she must verify the outcome of the algorithm, and assess whether the outcome is correct and in accordance with the specific needs of his/her patient. All relevant elements have to be taken into account.[47] For example, a careful diagnosis generally requires that the physician performs a physical examination of the patient. Such an examination may contradict the outcome of the algorithm.[48] However, some studies conducted in the United States showed that doctors are becoming increasingly reluctant to overrule decisions made by algorithms, as they risk exposing themselves to liability.[49] Some authors have

45 See Chapter 14.

46 N. Price, 'Medical Malpractice and Black-Box Medicine', in G. Cohen, F. Lynch, E. Vayena and U. Gasser (eds.), *Big Data, Health Law, and Bioethics* (Cambridge: Cambridge University Press, 2018), p. 300; J.-P. Beregi, 'Artificial intelligence and medical imaging 2018: French Radiology Community white paper', *Diagnostic and Interventional imaging*, 2018, vol. 99, no. 11, p. 737; Fenech, Strukelj and Buston, *Ethical, Social, and Political Challenges of Artificial Intelligence in Health*, p. 35; Cf. S. O'Sullivan, N. Nevejans, C. Allen, A. Blyth, S. Leonard, U. Pagallo, K. Holzinger, A. Holzinger, M. Imran and H. Ashrafian 'Legal, regulatory, and ethical frameworks for development of standards in artificial intelligence (AI) and autonomous robotic surgery', *The International Journal of Medical Robotics and Computer Assisted Surgery*, 2018, vol. 15, no. 1, p. 7.

47 N. Price, 'Artificial Intelligence in Health Care: Applications and Legal Implications', *The SciTech Lawyer*, 2017, vol. 14, no. 1, p. 12; C. Liew, 'The future of radiology augmented with Artificial Intelligence: A strategy for success', *European Journal of Radiology*, 2018, vol. 102, p. 155.

48 T. Vansweevelt, 'De aansprakelijkheid van de arts en het ziekenhuis voor eigen gedrag', in T. Vansweevelt en F. Dewallens (eds.), *Handboek Gezondheidsrecht* (Antwerp: Intersentia, 2022), p. 1278.

49 Dolic, Castro and Moarcas, *Robots in healthcare: a solution or a problem?*, p. 20.

subsequently argued that it would be undesirable to hold a physician liable for not overruling the algorithm, since the algorithm's suggestion would statistically always be the best option.[50] Others state that the degree of liability should depend on the level of automation. This implies that a physician cannot be held liable for decisions based on the outcomes of algorithms with a very high level of autonomy.[51]

I do not agree with this view. Indeed, according to the general liability standard, the physician will *only* be liable if he did not act as a reasonably prudent physician (of the same specialty) in similar circumstances, taking into account possible urgency and the current state of the art (which may include the autonomy of the algorithm).[52] A physician will not *automatically* be liable if he/she did not verify the outcome of the algorithm or if he did (not) overrule the algorithm[53] but only if a reasonably prudent physician would have verified the outcome of the algorithm and/or would (not) have overruled the algorithm. For example, a physician will be liable if he/she did not take, in the light of the specific circumstances, adequate measures to properly evaluate and/or implement the outcome of the algorithm used in caring for the patient.[54] This implies that physicians must properly inform, educate and train themselves when using these tools. They should also be aware of their limitations.

Furthermore, if one abandons the obligation for a physician to verify the results of the algorithm, even if it has a very high level of autonomy,[55] they risk becoming 'slaves to the machines'. In contrast, 'keeping a human' in the loop ensures a holistic approach towards the patient, rather than only focusing on his/her symptoms. Indeed, an algorithm has no emotions (it does not exert non-verbal communication, does not feel compassion and does not possess common sense). It does not necessarily have a complete image of the patient including the latter's medical antecedents, hobbies, work, general lifestyle, physical condition and other circumstances, which can have an impact on the most desirable

---

50 S. Thomas, 'Artificial Intelligence, Medical Malpractice, and the End of Defensive Medicine', 26 January 2017, https://blog.petrieflom.law.harvard.edu/2017/01/26/artificial-intelligence-medical-malpractice-and-the-end-of-defensive-medicine/.

51 J. Jaremko, M. Azar, R. Bromwich, A. Kum, L.Cheong, M. Gibert, M. Cicero, J. Chong, J. Shaw, F. Rybicki, C. Hurrell, E. Lee and A. Tang, 'Canadian Association of Radiologists White Paper on Ethical and Legal Issues Related to Artificial Intelligence in Radiology', *Canadian Association of Radiologists Journal*, 2019, vol. 70, no. 2, p. 115.

52 Vansweevelt, 'De aansprakelijkheid van de arts en het ziekenhuis voor eigen gedrag', p. 1273.

53 Cf. EP Resolution 12 February 2019 no. 2018/2088(INI), no. 77: 'Stresses the need therefore to ensure that users will not be led invariably to back the diagnostic solution or treatment suggested by a technological instrument for fear of being sued for damages if, on the basis of their informed professional judgement, they were to reach conclusions that diverged even in part.'

54 Price, 'Artificial Intelligence in Health Care: Applications and Legal Implications', p. 12; Liew, 'The future of radiology augmented with Artificial Intelligence: A strategy for success', p. 155.

55 E.g., it may be that an algorithm with a very high autonomy was not fit to use for a specific patient. In such an event, it may be either negligent to use this algorithm or to not verify its outcome.

treatment method or the most probable diagnosis.[56] The physician is the guardian of the machine and should act as an active operator instead of a mere passive user. He remains responsible for the consequences of the diagnostic/treatment strategy applied to the patient, even when this strategy is partially assisted or entirely applied by a robot/AI.[57] One will of course have to find a proper balance for holding the physician liable when failing to verify its result and/or for (not) overruling the algorithm, which will sometimes be difficult.[58]

10. From a more general perspective, the degree of supervision required by the physician will mainly depend on the patient's general health condition and the risks involved for the patient's health.[59] For example, if a surgeon uses a robot to perform surgery – i.e., the robot performs the surgery autonomously, which can be considered to pose severe risks for the patient – he/she must monitor the actions of the robot and the patient's health condition. This will enable him/her to address the patient's particular care needs and to intervene as soon as things go wrong. Given the severe risks to the patient's health, it is also prohibited for a surgeon to conduct multiple surgeries at the same time by using several robots that act autonomously. This is analogous to the prohibition on anaesthetists simultaneously anesthetising multiple patients[60] and the obligation to remain with the patient, as well as to monitor the patient's condition continuously in close vicinity from the moment the patient is anesthetised until the patient is transferred to the post-anaesthesia care unit or the intensive care unit.[61]

11. Physicians must also properly inform, educate and train themselves when using these tools. They should know the limits of their application as well. This is the case when the dataset used to train the algorithm makes it inappropriate to apply to a particular patient population or when it is able to diagnose only a

---

56 D. Britton, 'Automating Surgery: The Law of Autonomous Surgical Robots', *Life Sciences Innovation*, 2016, pp. 20–21; Fenech, Strukelj and Buston, *Ethical, Social, and Political Challenges of Artificial Intelligence in Health*, p. 26; Comité consultative national d'éthique pours les sciences de la vie et de la santé, *Rapport de synthèse du comité consultatif national d' éthique. Opinions du comité citoyen* (Les Ulis Cedex: EDP Sciences, 2018), pp. 100–101.

57 Beregi, 'Artificial intelligence and medical imaging 2018: French Radiology Community white paper', p. 737.

58 Cf. Dolic, Castro and Moarcas, *Robots in healthcare: a solution or a problem?*, p. 20.

59 Antwerp 30 March 1993, *T.Gez.* 1997–98, p. 103; Ghent 14 October 2010, *T.Gez.* 2013–14, p. 185; Price, 'Medical Malpractice and Black-Box Medicine', p. 301.

60 Bergen 28 June 1994, *T.Gez.*, 1995–96, p. 291; Luik 18 September 2000, *T.Gez.*, 2000–01, p. 303; Rb. Bruges 10 November 1986, *Vl.T.Gez.*, 1987, p. 284; Corr. Brussels 17 September 1986, *Vl.T.Gez.*, 1987, p. 384; Rb. Luik 20 October 1998, *T.Gez.*, 1998–99, p. 405; Section IV, Article 2.09 Belgian Standards for patient safety in anesthesia: an update, *Acta Anaesthesiologica Belgica*, 2002, p. 53, no. 1.

61 Section IV, Article 2.07 Belgian Standards for patient safety in anesthesia: an update, *Acta Anaesthesiologica Belgica* 2002, p. 53, no. 1.

limited amount of diseases.[62] Using a robot/AI but not taking into account the patient's health condition and/or not acting according to the current state of the art may trigger the physician's liability.[63] If the use of a robot/AI is not yet scientifically validated – i.e., is still in an experimental phase – the physician is only allowed to use this technique if he/she properly informed the patient of the experimental nature of the treatment, the risks involved and the (scientifically validated) treatment alternatives (if any).[64]

12. Finally, another obligation of a physician that may potentially trigger his/her liability when not complied with is to provide the patient with information about his/her health condition, prognosis and ways to maintain or improve his/her health condition according to Article 7 Belgian Law on Patient Rights. A physician may also incur liability when not having obtained a patient's informed consent before providing healthcare pursuant to Article 8 Belgian Law on Patient Rights. This requires a dialogue between physician and patient.[65]

If a patient is not properly informed about his/her health condition by the physician and the patient suffers damage as a result thereof, the physician is liable to pay damages as well.[66] This can be the case if it was not possible to timely start a treatment to cure the patient or when the patient lost a chance thereto due to the lack of information. The same is true if the physician did not inform the patient about the risks of the patient's way of life[67] or health condition and/or how to improve or maintain the health condition[68] or to deal with these risks. To obtain the patient's prior informed consent, the latter must be informed about the purpose, nature, degree of urgency, duration and frequency of the treatment, as well as the relevant counter-indications, side effects and risks associated with the treatment, the aftercare, possible alternative treatments and financial consequences. For example, if a physician did not inform the patient about the risks of a certain treatment, and one of these risks materialise, the physician will

---

62 S. Carter, W. Rogers, K.T. Win, H. Frazer, B. Richards and N. Houssami, 'The ethical, legal and social implications of using artificial intelligence systems in breast cancer', *The Breast*, 2020, vol. 49, p. 28.

63 N. Nevejans, *Traité de droit et d'éthique de la robotique civile* (Bordeaux: LEH Édition, 2017), p. 653.

64 T. Vansweevelt and S. Tack, 'Het recht op gezondheidstoestandinformatie en geïnformeerde toestemming', in T. Vansweevelt en F. Dewallens (eds.), *Handboek Gezondheidsrecht* (Antwerp: Intersentia, 2022), p. 402 and *infra* no. 21.

65 Articles 7, §2(2) and 8, §1(3) Belgian Law on Patient Rights.

66 E.g., Rb. Dinant 31 May 2005, *T.Gez.*, 2009–10, p. 35, note (a gynaecologist, who is aware of his patient's infection, must inform the patient before the birth and in any case ensure that the information has been passed on to the medical staff. He must also prescribe appropriate treatment if he finds that the infection was not taken into account when the child was born).

67 E.g., Ghent 30 March 1998, *T.Gez.*, 1998–99, p. 296, note B. Weyts; Antwerp 31 March 1998, *T.Gez.*, 1998–99, p. 297, note B. Weyts (driving a car while there is a risk of an epileptic attack).

68 E.g., Luik 24 October 2007, *JLMB*, 2007, p. 1747 (inform the patient about the importance of dental hygiene and to consult a dentist after radiotherapy to avoid tooth decay).

be liable if the patient proves that he/she would not have given consent if he/she had known this risk before the treatment was provided. If the causal link is not established with the required certainty, a patient can still receive compensation for the loss of a chance. The physician will be liable for a percentage of the patient's harm, which is the percentage of the patient's lost chance to recover.[69] If there is no causal link – implying that the patient would certainly have agreed to the treatment even had he/she been properly informed – some judges have in line with French case law[70] been willing to grant damages for 'unpreparedness' if a risk materialises that was not (but should have been) communicated to the patient.[71] If a physician did not obtain the patient's proper prior informed consent, this may also qualify as a criminal offence.[72]

In the next part, I will discuss the extent to which the informed consent obligation and the obligation to inform the patient about his/her health condition under Belgian law is a third legal safeguard against the possible dehumanisation of the physician-patient relationship resulting from the use of AI and robots.

5. THE RIGHT OF THE PATIENT TO RECEIVE INFORMATION ABOUT HIS/HER HEALTH CONDITION AND TO GIVE INFORMED CONSENT UNDER THE BELGIAN LAW ON PATIENT RIGHTS

13. It is an internationally recognised principle that patients have a right to be informed about their health condition. They also have to give their free and informed consent prior to a treatment. This is required to respect the patients' right to self-determination and to avoid a violation of their right to personal autonomy and physical integrity. These rights are protected under Articles 2, 3

69 C. van Dam, *European Tort Law* (Oxford: Oxford University Press, 2013), pp. 337–338; Vansweevelt and Tack, 'Het recht op gezondheidstoestandinformatie en geïnformeerde toestemming', pp. 580–585; G. Genicot, 'Le dommage consécutif à un manquement au devoir d'information du médecin: une valse à trois temps. Plaidoyer pour la reconnaissance du prejudice d'impréparation', in I. Lutte (ed.), *Droit médical. Dommage corporel. État des lieux et perspectives* (Limal: Anthemis, 2014), pp. 101–102.

70 Cass. Fr. 12 July 2012, *Resp.Civ.Ass.*, 2012, p. 314, *JCP G.*, 2012, p. 1036, note P. Sargos, *D.*, 2012, p. 2277, note M. Bacache, *RDT Civ.*, 2012, p. 737, note P. Jourdin, *RTD Eur.*, 2013, p. 292, note N. Rias; Cass. Fr. 23 January 2014, *Resp.Civ.Ass.*, 2012, p. 351, note L. Bloch, RDSS, 2014, p. 295, note F. Arhab-Girardin, *D.*, 2°14, 584; CE 24 September 2012, *JCP G.*, 2012, p. 1252, note F. Vialla; CE 10 October 2012, *D.*, 2012, 2518, note D. Poupeau, *Dict. Bioéthique*, 2012, 10, note C. Caillé, *AJDA*, 2012, 1991, note X. Barella.

71 Antwerp 28 June 2004, *JDJ*, 2006, 40, *NjW*, 2005, 553, *RW*, 2005–06, 906; Rb. Antwerp 13 October 2011, *unpublished.*; Rb. Brussels 5 April 2016, *TBBR*, 2017, p. 424, *JT*, 2016, p. 404, note F. Glansdorff.

72 Article 392 Penal Code; Ghent 11 maart 1992, *T.Gez.*, 1995–96, p. 54, note T. Vansweevelt.

and 8 of the European Convention on Human Rights,[73] and under Articles 5–9 of the Oviedo Convention on Human Rights and Biomedicine. In Belgium, the right to receive information about one's health condition is embedded in Article 7 Belgian Law on Patient Rights.[74] The right to informed consent is embedded in Article 8 of the Belgian Law on Patient Rights,[75] but also in specific legislation.[76]

Pursuant to Article 7 Belgian Law on Patient Rights, the patient has the right to be provided by the physician with all the information that is necessary to understand his/her health condition and the expected evolution thereof. Pursuant to Article 8, §2 Belgian Law on Patient Rights, the physician has to inform the patient about the purpose, nature, degree of urgency, duration and frequency of the treatment, as well as of the relevant counter-indications, side effects and risks associated with the treatment, the aftercare, possible alternative treatments and financial consequences. The patient must also be informed about the possible consequences in the event of refusal or withdrawal of his/her consent, and other details considered relevant by the patient or the physician.

The aforementioned information must be provided through a *dialogue* with the patient. The latter can request to be provided with a written confirmation.[77] A written statement can never replace the conversation between physician and patient.[78] The obligation to inform the patient implies a 'human' contact between physician and patient. This is an important potential legal safeguard against the feared 'dehumanisation' of the patient-physician relationship. It can, however,

---

73 W. Buelens, C. Herijgers and S. Illegems, 'The View of the European Court of Human Rights on competent patients' rights to informed consent. Research in the Light of Articles 3 and 8 of the European Convention on Human Rights', *EJHL*, 2016, vol. 23, no. 5, pp. 481–509.

74 See also Article 11 Law 19 December 2008 on the use of bodily material for medical or scientific use, *Official Gazette* 30 December 2008.

75 For a recent study about this topic refer to: E. Verjans, *Het recht op informatie en toestemming van de patiënt* (Antwerp: Intersentia, 2019), 1224 p.

76 These specific laws specify additional conditions to obtain the patient's informed consent, for example the content of the information, formal requirements for the information and formal requirements for the consent, e.g., Article 8 Law 13 June 1986 on organ donation and transplantation, *Official Gazette* 14 February 1987, p. 2129; Article 6 Law 7 May 2004 on experiments to human persons, *Official Gazette* 18 May 2004, p. 39516; Article 18 Law 23 May 2013 on the regulation of the qualifications required to perform interventions in non-medical aesthetic medicine and aesthetic surgery and regulation of advertising and information relating to those interventions, *Official Gazette* 2 July 2013, p. 4151; Article 2 Law 6 July 2007 on medically assisted procreation and the destination of supernumerary embryos and gametes, *Official Gazette* 17 July 2007, p. 38575; Article 2 Law 15 October 2018 on voluntary termination of pregnancy, to abolish Articles 350 and 351 of the Penal Code, to amend Articles 352 and 383 of the same Code and to amend various legal provisions, *Official Gazette* 29 October 2018, p. 82140; Article 2 Law 28 May 2002 on Euthanasia, *Official Gazette* 22 June 2002, p. 28515.

77 Articles 7, §2(2) and 8, §1(3) Belgian Law on Patient Rights.

78 Vansweevelt and Tack, 'Het recht op gezondheidstoestandinformatie en geïnformeerde toestemming', p. 395; Advies Nationale Raad Orde der Artsen 6 mei 2017, 'Informeren van de atient over zijn gezondheidstoestand en de verstrekte zorg', *TNRI*, 2017, no. 157.

not be excluded that some of these 'dialogues' will take place from a distance (e.g., through videoconference). Nevertheless, the patient can always demand a physical contact).[79]

14. The fact that AI is used to provide healthcare to a patient is without prejudice to the application of the aforementioned principles.[80] Below, I will discuss the most important aspects of the physician's duty to inform the patient in order to obtain his/her informed consent. This information relates to the purpose and nature of the treatment, the relevant risks and the alternative treatments.[81] I will also focus on the patient's right to obtain information about his/her health condition. The question also arises whether the patient must always be informed about the fact that the physician is using AI/robots to provide healthcare or if he/she has to be provided with the technical details of the AI/robot. Finally, the physician may have additional duties when using AI to provide healthcare under the GDPR. Indeed, a distinction should be made between the AI/robots as a caregiver, on the one hand, and as a data processing device, on the other hand.[82]

5.1. PURPOSE AND NATURE OF THE TREATMENT

15. When providing the patient with information, the physician should empower the patient to make a decision about his/her treatment with full knowledge. When providing information about the *nature and purpose* of the treatment, the physician may not overload the patient with the technical and medical details of the treatment (and its alternatives). The patient must be given a general and clear overview of all the relevant aspects of the physician's intervention (e.g., chirurgical intervention, pharmaceutical intervention, diagnostic or therapeutic intervention, painful or invasive/dangerous character of the intervention).[83] The patient should also be informed about the scientifically controversial nature or the new/experimental character of the treatment, and

---

79 Advies Nationale Raad Orde der Artsen 7 februari 2015, 'Artsen en digitale media', *TNRI*, 2015, no. 148.

80 Lequillerier, 'L'impact de l'intelligence artificielle sur la relation de soin', p. 19; D. Schönberger, 'Artificial intelligence in healthcare: a critical analysis of the legal and ethical implications', *Int.Jour.Law and Information Technology*, 2019, vol. 27, no. 2, p. 188.

81 O'Sullivan, Nevejans, Allen, Blyth, Leonard, Pagallo, Holzinger, Holzinger, Imran and Ashrafian 'Legal, regulatory, and ethical frameworks for development of standards in artificial intelligence (AI) and autonomous robotic surgery', p. 8.

82 Fosch-Villaronga, *Robots, Healthcare, and the law. Regulating automation in personal care,* p. 180.

83 Vansweevelt and Tack, 'Het recht op gezondheidstoestandinformatie en geïnformeerde toestemming', p. 353.

why the physician suggests this treatment.[84] This is of particular importance with respect to emerging technologies such as AI. The duty to inform the patient is also more extensive with respect to new and innovative treatments.[85]

5.2. RELEVANT RISKS OF THE USE OF AI

16. A patient must be informed about the 'relevant' risks and counter-indications of the use of AI/a robot.[86] This refers to all risks and counter-indications that are relevant in the eyes of an average and reasonable patient placed in the same circumstances to consent to a treatment with full knowledge. To make this assessment, the physician has to take into account the frequency of the risk, the seriousness of the risk and the personal qualities of the patient (e.g., profession, physical condition, personality).[87]

Some of the risks or counter-indications with respect to tools equipped with AI systems that may be relevant to disclose to a patient include (i) that the algorithm may be biased due to the underlying datasets that are used or that inconclusive correlations exist, (ii) the black-box problem and consequential 'intelligibility', making it impossible for the physician to know how the algorithm arrived at a certain conclusion or how an error may occur, and (iii) the inaccuracy that is inherent to each technology. The fact that robot-assisted surgery takes more time than a classic surgical intervention can also be of particular importance (e.g., for obese patients).[88] These risks are inherent to the use of an algorithm and show the necessity of a physician supervising AI systems and of keeping a human in the loop.

17. The above implies that a physician must be well informed about new (AI) technologies in general, as well as about the opportunities and boundaries of the specific (AI) technology that he/she wants to use to provide healthcare. For example, the physician must know whether the AI system was trained on a dataset that is an accurate representation of a particular patient population. The physician also needs to be informed about the predictive accuracy and error rates of the AI system across patient subgroups, and, by doing so, needs

---

84 P. Henry, B. De Cocquéau, 'L'information et le consentement du patient: les atientt balises', in G. Schamps (ed.), *Evolution des droit du patient, indemnisation sans faute des dommages liés aux soins de santé: le droit atient en atient* (Brussels: Bruylant, 2008), p. 51; G. Genicot, *Droit atient et atientti* (Brussels: Larcier, 2016), p. 196; Verjans, *Het recht op informatie en toestemming van de atient*, pp. 99–102.

85 H. Baeyens, C. Pouppez and P. Slegers, *Towards a guided a phased introduction of high-risk medical devices in Belgium – KCE Report 249*, Brussels, 2015, pp. 31 and 66.

86 Lequillerier, 'L'impact de l'intelligence artificielle sur la relation de soin', p. 19.

87 Vansweevelt and Tack, 'Het recht op gezondheidstoestandinformatie en geïnformeerde toestemming', pp. 356–365.

88 Nevejans, *Traité de droit et d'éthique de la robotique civile*, p. 648.

to ascertain how the system arrived at a decision and how an error may occur.[89] Thus, to reduce the risk to create a black-box – which can never be avoided – physicians who use AI systems must be informed about their construction, the data sets they are built on, and their limitations.[90] In addition, the designer of the AI system must ensure that the results of the algorithm are, as far as possible, interpretable and explainable to its users. This could, for example, be achieved by documenting what they created and how the AI is learning from training data.[91] Medical device companies should detail types of errors and side effects, their likelihood and severity, and differences in predictive accuracy and error rates across demographic subgroups, health conditions and patient histories.[92] Indeed, on many occasions you only know what your supplier informs you about.[93] Manufacturers and suppliers that do not properly inform, educate and/or train physicians, risk liability claims.[94]

5.3. DISCLOSURE OF THE ALTERNATIVE TREATMENTS

5.3.1. Disclosure of Alternatives to AI Systems and Robots

18. Another question that arises is whether the patient has to be informed about an alternative treatment that does not imply the use of AI or a robot (hereafter: '*traditional treatment*'). Some scholars argue that a physician not only has to explain that he/she is subjecting the patient to a 'non-conventional' treatment – I do not fully agree[95] – but also has to disclose which aspects could hypothetically produce a greater risk, as well as all collateral effects of the therapy, together with the reasons why robotic surgery is expected to prove advantageous. This is to ensure that the patient is – at least theoretically and hopefully also in practice – put in a position to estimate the reliability of the scientific data upon which

---

89 Schiff and Borenstein, 'How Should Clinicians Communicate with Patients About the Roles of Artificially Intelligent Team Members?', p. 140.

90 D.S. Char, N.H. Shah and D. Magnus, 'Implementing machine learning in healthcare – addressing ethical challenges', *N.Engl.J.Med.*, 2018, vol. 378, no. 11, p. 982.

91 Comité consultative national d'éthique pours les sciences de la vie et de la santé, *Rapport de synthèse du comité atienttive national d' éthique. Opinions du comité citoyen*, p. 108.

92 Schiff and Borenstein, 'How Should Clinicians Communicate with Patients About the Roles of Artificially Intelligent Team Members?', p. 142.

93 B. Kehoe, 'Serverless IoT @ iRobot', 2018, https://www.infoq.com/presentations/serverless-iot-irobot/.

94 E. Palmerini, F. Azzarri, F. Battaglia, A. Bertolini, A. Carnevale, J. Carpaneto, F. Cavallo, A. Di Carlo, M. Cempini, M. Controzzi, B.-J. Koops, F. Lucivero, N. Mukerji, L. Nocco, A. Pirni, H. Shah, P. Salvini and M. Schellekens, K. Warwick, *Regulating Emerging Robotic Technologies in Europe: Robotics facing Law and Ethics* (Strasbourg: European Commission, 2014), p. 94, https://www.robolaw.eu.

95 See *infra* no. 25.

the physician bases his/her decision. This will allow the patient to opt for a more traditional treatment.[96] This view has to be nuanced.

19. In principle, the physician is free to decide which treatment method/ tool is the most suitable to meet the patient's needs. However, if there are different treatments methods available according to the current state of the art, the physician has to inform the patient about the 'reasonable' alternatives. As a consequence, and taking a more general perspective, the patient has to be informed about the treatment alternatives when there are, according to the current state of the art, various common and accepted treatment methods with different success ratios and/or risks.[97]

Thus, if the use of AI/robots is more successful and poses less risks for the patient's health compared to the conventional treatment, the physician is in principle not obliged to inform the patient about this conventional treatment. The physician must inform the patient about both the AI treatment method and the conventional treatment if, for instance, the AI treatment has high/ severe risks but a high success ratio, and the conventional treatment has no risks but a lower success ratio (or the other way around). If the risks and success ratio of the AI treatment are comparable to the risks and success ratio of the conventional treatment, the physician has to inform patient about both methods. The physician has to give information about the benefits and disadvantages that may be important to the patient, such as costs, duration and frequency of the treatment and the recovery period.[98] If the robot/AI treatment is more expensive – for example because it is not reimbursed by social security – the physician will be obliged to inform the patient about the conventional treatment. According to some scholars, this will often be the case.[99]

20. The question arises whether these general principles apply *mutatis mutandis* to treatments involving the use of AI/robots. A recent study shows that a majority of (Belgian)[100] patients is unwilling to undergo a surgery performed by a robot instead of a human even when evidence showed that a robot could

---

96 Palmerini, Azzarri, Battaglia, Bertolini, Carnevale, Carpaneto, Cavallo, Di Carlo, Cempini, Controzzi, Koops, Lucivero, Mukerji, Nocco, Pirni, Shah, Salvini, Schellekens and Warwick, *Regulating Emerging Robotic Technologies in Europe: Robotics facing Law and Ethics*, p. 649.

97 Vansweevelt and Tack, 'Het recht op gezondheidstoestandinformatie en geïnformeerde toestemming', p. 368.

98 J.-L. Fagnart, 'Information du patient et responsabilité du médecin', in E. Thiry (ed.), *Actualités de droit atient* (Brussels: Bruylant, 2006), p. 68; Vansweevelt and Tack, 'Het recht op gezondheidstoestandinformatie en geïnformeerde toestemming', p. 368. *Contra* Verjans, *Het recht op informatie en toestemming van de atient*, p. 197.

99 Nevejans, *Traité de droit et d'éthique de la robotique civile*, p. 651.

100 It appears from the study that there are big differences between the respondents from another country, e.g., in Nigeria 73% of the respondents was willing to undergo a minor surgery performed by a robot and 69% was willing to undergo a major surgery.

do it better than a physician, for example more quickly, more accurately and with a faster recovery time. Only 39% would be willing to have a robot instead of a surgeon perform a minor non-invasive surgery (e.g., cataract surgery or laser eye surgery). That number drops to 32% for major invasive surgeries (e.g., replacing a knee or hip joint, removing a tumour or heart surgery).[101] When a physician uses AI/robots only to provide advice – e.g., diagnosis or suggestion of a treatment – or to monitor the patient's health condition, a majority of the patients is willing to accept this technology.[102] However, a significant portion of (Belgian)[103] patients (43%) is unwilling to engage with AI and robotics for their general healthcare needs.[104] Furthermore, the Eurobarometer survey of May 2017[105] shows that EU citizens still feel uncomfortable with the idea of robots being used in everyday healthcare.[106]

This outcome can be explained by 'the fear of the unknown' and perhaps by inaccurate perceptions of AI and robots. This study illustrates that it is important that governments and physicians properly educate and inform patients about the risks and benefits attributable to the use of a robot/AI.[107] It also shows that it is important to have a human in the loop when using AI/robots to provide healthcare.

In my opinion, and from a legal point of view, the outcome of this study does not imply that a physician must inform the patient about the alternative surgical procedure or alternative monitoring and diagnostic tool if the robot/AI treatment outperforms the conventional treatment. In any event, a physician cannot be forced to provide the conventional treatment if he/she is convinced that the treatment performed by a robot is a more suitable – better – option. Moreover, if the robot/AI treatment outperforms the conventional treatment, and the physician did perform the robot/AI treatment without informing the patient about the conventional treatment, it will be difficult for the patient to claim compensation if the physician did inform the patient about the risks of the robot/AI treatment.[108] Finally, as mentioned above, it is unlawful under the current legal framework to not have a human in the loop. This is a qualified person who monitors the robot while performing the treatment or verifies the outcome of the algorithm. It remains uncertain whether the respondents

101 Arnold and Wilson, *What doctor? Why AI and robotics will define New Health*, pp. 36 and 38.

102 *Ibid.*, p. 32.

103 It appears from the study that there are large differences between the respondents from another country, *e.g.*, in Nigeria 94% of the respondents was willing engage with AI and robotics for their healthcare needs.

104 Arnold and Wilson, *What doctor? Why AI and robotics will define New Health*, p. 27.

105 Special Eurobarometer 460: Attitudes towards the impact of digitisation and automation on daily life, https://data.europa.eu/euodp/en/data/dataset/S2160_87_1_460_ENG.

106 EP Resolution 12 February 2019 no. 2018/2088(INI), no. 83.

107 Schiff and Borenstein, 'How Should Clinicians Communicate with Patients About the Roles of Artificially Intelligent Team Members?', p. 141.

108 Nevejans, *Traité de droit et d'éthique de la robotique civile*, p. 650.

participating in the above-mentioned study would give the same responses when being aware of this legal safeguard.

5.3.2. *Disclosure of AI as an Alternative*

21. As long as a robot/AI treatment or the use of robots is experimental and/or controversial in a certain field of medicine, the physician has no obligation to inform the patient about it.[109] The physician is allowed to limit himself/herself to common treatments methods in his/her field of medicine. He/she has no obligation to inform the patient about treatment methods that are not standard according to the current state of the art.[110] However, if there is no treatment for the patient's disease, the physician must inform the patient about the existing treatments that are still experimental.[111] The same is true if there are important indications that the experimental treatment method (e.g., AI or the use of a robot) may have significant advantages for the patient compared to the generally accepted treatment method(s).[112] The physician will, however, have to inform the patient about the experimental nature of this treatment.

At some point, the use of a robot/AI will become fully integrated into healthcare and thus become a part of the state of the art in many fields of medicine. From that point onwards, using these techniques will be part of the duty of a reasonably prudent physician. This will probably happen sooner rather than later, as shown by the rapid implementation of automated algorithms for computer vision in radiology and pathology.[113] A failure to use these techniques may lead to liability for the damage that would not have occurred if they had been used.[114]

5.3.3. *Disclosure of AI Treatments in Other Hospitals*

22. The physician also has to inform the patient about the availability of clearly better treatments – i.e., lower/less severe risks and/or higher success ratio – in other care facilities.[115] Algorithms and robots may be part of such treatments,

---

109 Verjans, *Het recht op informatie en toestemming van de patiënt*, p. 202.

110 W. Dijkhoffz, 'Het recht op informatie en geïnformeerde toestemming', *T.Gez.*, 2003–04, p. 110.

111 Vansweevelt and Tack, 'Het recht op gezondheidstoestandinformatie en geïnformeerde toestemming', p. 369.

112 Verjans, *Het recht op informatie en toestemming van de patiënt*, p. 204.

113 K. Johnson, J. Soto, B. Glocksberg, K. Shameer, R. Miotto, M. Ali, E. Ashley and J. Dudley, 'Artificial Intelligence in Cardiology', *Journal of the American College of Cardiology*, 2018, p. 11.

114 S. Bennet and L. Habte, 'Artificial Intelligence in Health Care: Welcome to the Machine' in *Connections for the health and life sciences community*, 2018, vol. 5, pp. 18–19.

115 Henry and De Cocquéau, 'L'information et le consentement du patient: les nouvelles balises', p. 51; G. Schamps, 'Le droit à l'information et le droit au consentement libre et éclaire' in S. Brillon, S. Callens, V. Gauché (eds.), *Mémento des droits du paient et de la responsabilité médicale* (Brussels: Kluwer, 2003), p. 57; Genicot, *Droit médical et biomédical*, p. 197;

especially compared to treatments that rely solely on a human actor.[116] This of course supposes that the physician is aware, or reasonably should have been aware, of the treatment alternatives in other care facilities.[117] A physician has to be aware of the treatments of which every reasonably prudent physician in the same circumstances should have been aware of. These are all usual treatment alternatives and treatments mentioned in the medical literature.[118]

As a consequence, as soon as the use of robots/AI becomes a common treatment practice in a certain field of medicine (i.e., when the use of robots/AI leads to better results than the alternative treatment without robots/AI and has less (severe) risks) the treatment methods that only rely on a human actor will disappear. Healthcare facilities and physicians that do not invest in robots/AI will have a major disadvantage compared to those equipped with such technology and will face liability for damage that could have been prevented by using these techniques.[119]

5.4. RIGHT OF THE PATIENT TO RECEIVE INFORMATION ABOUT HIS/HER HEALTH CONDITION

23. According to Article 7 Belgian Law on Patient Rights, the patient has the right to be provided by the physician with all information that is necessary to understand his/her health condition and the expected evolution thereof. This information includes diagnosis, prognosis and health education. The latter refers to insight into the behaviour that is necessary to maintain a patient's health condition or to prevent deterioration thereof.[120] The goal of this right is to ensure that the patient knows as much about his/her health condition as the physician does. This means that the latter may in principle not withhold any information from the patient.[121] This implies that the physician must also provide the patient with presumptions related to his/her health condition, such as a 'likely diagnosis'

Vansweevelt and Tack, 'Het recht op gezondheidstoestandinformatie en geïnformeerde toestemming', p. 370.

116 O'Sullivan, Nevejans, Allen, Blyth, Leonard, Pagallo, Holzinger, Holzinger, Imran and Ashrafian 'Legal, regulatory, and ethical frameworks for development of standards in artificial intelligence (AI) and autonomous robotic surgery', p. 8.

117 S. Tack and T. Balthazar, *Patiëntenrechten: informed consent in de zorgsector: recente evoluties* (Brussels: Larcier, 2007) p. 164.

118 Dijkhoffz, 'Het recht op informatie en geïnformeerde toestemming', p. 110; Henry and De Cocquéau, 'L'information et le consentement du patient: les nouvelles balises', p. 51; Schamps, 'Le droit à l'information et le droit au consentement libre et éclaire', p. 57; Verjans, *Het recht op informatie en toestemming van de patiënt*, p. 208.

119 Bennet and Habte, 'Artificial Intelligence in Health Care: Welcome to the Machine', pp. 18–19.

120 Parliamentary works law on patient rights, *Parl.St. Chamber*, 2001–02, no. 1642/1, p. 20.

121 Vansweevelt and Tack, 'Het recht op gezondheidstoestandinformatie en geïnformeerde toestemming', p. 333.

('*waarschijnlijkheidsdiagnose*').[122] The physician may incur liability if the patient suffers harm because he/she had not been provided with this information.[123]

24. The fact that a physician chooses to use AI tools to provide healthcare is without prejudice to the patient's right to obtain the aforementioned information. For example, if a patient is diagnosed by an AI system with a 95% risk of getting diabetes, it is not only important that the physician informs the patient of this diagnosis but also on how to prevent further deterioration by explaining the underlying risk factors of this disease (e.g., weight, nutrition, genetic predisposition). The physician also needs to inform the patient on how to deal with these risks (e.g., adapt nutrition and use insulin).

This illustrates the importance for a physician to properly understand the logic of the AI system he/she uses to provide health care. Indeed, this may be necessary to comply with Article 7 Belgian Law on Patient Rights. The physician cannot hide behind the use of an AI system to withhold this information from the patient. The information that is eventually provided to the patient must be the same as if the physician's decision was not based on an AI system. This does not imply that a patient must be informed about the use of the AI system or its internal working. Indeed, as will be argued below, this information will not empower patients to have a better knowledge of his/her health condition, the evolution thereof and of how to adapt his/her behaviour to deal with the possible risks involved.

5.5. INFORMATION ABOUT THE USE OF AI/ROBOTS AND THE UNDERLYING TECHNOLOGY?

25. According to some scholars, a physician must always inform the patient about the mere fact that he/she will use robots and/or AI systems to support him/her when providing healthcare services.[124] Some of them argue that the technology behind AI has to be explained to the patient, and that the understanding of the technology by patients is a prerequisite for their informed

[122] Vansweevelt and Tack, 'Het recht op gezondheidstoestandinformatie en geïnformeerde toestemming', p. 334.

[123] *Supra* no. 12.

[124] Palmerini, Azzarri, Battaglia, Bertolini, Carnevale, Carpaneto, Cavallo, Di Carlo, Cempini, Controzzi, Koops, Lucivero, Mukerji, Nocco, Pirni, Shah, Salvini, Schellekens and Warwick, *Regulating Emerging Robotic Technologies in Europe: Robotics facing Law and Ethics*, p. 95; Nevejans, *Traité de droit et d'éthique de la robotique civile*, pp. 647–648. Cf. Beregi, 'Artificial intelligence and medical imaging 2018: French Radiology Community white paper', p. 735. *Contra* Schönberger, 'Artificial intelligence in healthcare: a critical analysis of the legal and ethical implications', p. 191.

consent.[125] Others suggest that a physician must inform the patient only about the 'basic nature' of the AI system and also must clearly distinguish between the roles human caregivers will play during each part of the treatment and the roles that AI/robots will play.[126]

Some scholars argue that if a physician uses an algorithm to, for example, diagnose a disease and/or to propose a certain treatment, the physician must inform the patient. This means informing the patient about the fact that an algorithm diagnosed the disease and/or suggested the treatment.[127] Information must also be given about the alternatives to the treatment proposed by the algorithm, as well as about the relevant counter-indications, side effects and risks associated with both treatments.[128]

26. In light of Articles 7 and 8 Belgian Law on Patient Rights, I do not fully agree with this conclusion. AI or robots must be considered as mere (augmenting) tools in the hands of a physician to provide healthcare, just like a scalpel or MRI-scanner. In principle, a physician has no obligation to inform the patient about every tool – e.g., AI/robot – that he/she uses to provide healthcare.[129] More precisely, the mere fact that a physician did not inform the patient about the use of AI/robots to provide healthcare does in my opinion not imply that the physician acted negligently as long as he/she did inform the patient about (1) his/her health condition, prognosis and desirable behaviour and (2) the purpose and nature of the treatment, the relevant risks of the treatment and possible alternatives (if any). Indeed, knowledge regarding the origin of the information and/or technical cause of these risks (i.e., the use of AI as such) will not empower the patient to make a more informed choice, nor to have more insight with regard to the health condition. In other words, knowledge about the cause of the risks is subordinate to the knowledge regarding the risks

125 G. Collste, P. Duquenoy, C. George, K. Hedström, K. Kimppa and E. Mordini, 'ICT in Medicine and Healthcare: Assessing Social, Ethical and Legal Issues', in J. Berleur, M.I. Numinen and J. Impagliazzo (eds.), *Social Informatics: An Information Society for All?* (Boston: Springer, 2006), p. 301; C. Bourdaire-Mignot, T. Gründler, 'Intelligence Artificielle et robotisation: la performance de l'IA au prix de la relation humaine?', *Rev.dr.h.*, 2018, p. 2, http://journals.openedition.org/revdh/4669; Schiff and Borenstein, 'How Should Clinicians Communicate with Patients About the Roles of Artificially Intelligent Team Members?', p. 140.

126 Schiff and Borenstein, 'How Should Clinicians Communicate with Patients About the Roles of Artificially Intelligent Team Members?', p. 140.

127 Comité consultative national d'éthique pours les sciences de la vie et de la santé, *Rapport de synthèse du comité consultatif national d' éthique. Opinions du comité citoyen*, p. 108; Lupton, 'Some ethical and legal consequences of the application of artificial intelligence in the field of medicine', p. 5. Cf. Beregi, 'Artificial intelligence and medical imaging 2018: French Radiology Community White Paper', p. 735.

128 Lupton, 'Some ethical and legal consequences of the application of artificial intelligence in the field of medicine', p. 5.

129 Vansweevelt and Tack, 'Het recht op gezondheidstoestandinformatie en geïnformeerde toestemming', p. 353.

themselves.[130] It can, however, be expected that the physician may spontaneously mention that AI/a robot is used to provide healthcare when discussing the patient's health condition or the course of the treatment.

Furthermore, if an algorithm suggests a treatment, a physician has in my opinion no obligation to inform the patient that the algorithm suggested this treatment. Nowadays, a physician will for example also not inform the patient of the fact that one of his/her colleagues suggested to perform a certain treatment. However, I do agree that in principle[131] the physician has to verify the outcome of the algorithm and check whether the proposed treatment is the best treatment option for a specific patient. If this is the case, the physician has to inform the patient about the risks and benefits of the treatment and the alternatives (if any).[132] As already mentioned, an algorithm has no emotions and does not necessarily have a complete overview of the patient's medical antecedents, hobbies, work, general lifestyle, and other circumstances that can have an impact on the most desirable treatment method.[133] Keeping a human in the loop ensures a holistic approach towards the patient, thereby not only focusing on his/her symptoms.[134] This implies that the physician is educated about their construction, the datasets they are built on and their limitations. For example, the dataset used to train the algorithm may make the algorithm inappropriate to apply to a particular patient population or could diagnose only a limited amount of diseases.[135]

The same elements apply when the algorithm suggests a diagnosis. A physician does not necessarily need to inform the patient that an algorithm made the diagnosis. Nevertheless, he/she does in principle[136] need to verify whether the outcome of the algorithm is correct, thereby taking into account all the relevant elements. A physician also needs to provide the patient with information about the health condition, prognosis and how to adapt his/her behaviour to manage the associated risks.[137] As argued above, this implies that the physician is to some extent aware of the internal logic of the AI system.

It may be that a physician is not able to verify the outcome of the algorithm because of the 'black-box-problem'. In those circumstances, a physician should

130 *Ibid.*, p. 353.

131 If a normal, prudent physician in similar circumstances would do so, see *supra* no. 9–10.

132 Lupton, 'Some ethical and legal consequences of the application of artificial intelligence in the field of medicine', p. 5.

133 Britton, 'Automating Surgery: The Law of Autonomous Surgical Robots', pp. 20–21; Fenech, Strukelj and Buston, *Ethical, Social, and Political Challenges of Artificial Intelligence in Health*, p. 26.

134 Comité consultative national d'éthique pours les sciences de la vie et de la santé, *Rapport de synthèse du comité consultatif national d' éthique. Opinions du comité citoyen*, pp. 100–101.

135 Char, Shah and Magnus, 'Implementing machine learning in healthcare – addressing ethical challenges', p. 982 and *supra* no. 17.

136 If a normal, prudent physician in similar circumstances would do so, see *supra* no. 9–10.

137 Article 7 Belgian Law on Patient Rights.

in my opinion be transparent towards the patient. The physician should inform the patient about the fact that the algorithm suggested the diagnosis or treatment but that he/she is not able to verify whether this diagnosis is right or wrong. The potential consequences (e.g., providing the patient with information about possible treatment(s) and risks thereof) or additional tests that can be conducted need to be explained as well. The patient and the physician will then have to assess the risks and benefits of the different actions that can be undertaken based on the AI system's suggestion.

27. *A fortiori*, according to Articles 7 and 8 Belgian Law on Patient Rights, a physician is not obliged to inform the patient about the *technology* relied upon by AI systems. A physician has no obligation to inform the patient about the medical and technical details of the treatment and of the tools that are used to provide a treatment.[138] AI technologies simply represent more advanced techniques for analysing data.[139] An explanation of the internal workings of the algorithm does not empower patients to make an informed choice about a certain treatment. Nor does it give them a better understanding of their health condition and the evolution thereof. Indeed, a physician also does not give the patient an explanation of the decision-making process in the brain[140] or of the highly complex technology behind conventional medical tools and machines.[141]

6. TRANSPARENCY AND INFORMED CONSENT UNDER THE GDPR

6.1. TRANSPARENCY IS KEY UNDER THE GDPR

6.1.1. General

28. The GDPR imposes additional information duties on the physicians as data controllers. Indeed, *transparency* is one of the core principles underpinning the GDPR. Physicians as data-controllers must clearly explain to the patients how a profiling[142] or automated decision-making process works. When the processing

138 Vansweevelt and Tack, 'Het recht op gezondheidstoestandinformatie en geïnformeerde toestemming', p. 353.

139 Schönberger, 'Artificial intelligence in healthcare: a critical analysis of the legal and ethical implications', p. 188.

140 Fenech, Strukelj and Buston, *Ethical, Social, and Political Challenges of Artificial Intelligence in Health*, p. 32.

141 Carter, Rogers, Win, Frazer, Richards and Houssami, 'The ethical, legal and social implications of using artificial intelligence systems in breast cancer', p. 30.

142 Article 4(4) GDPR: 'Any form of automated processing of personal data consisting of the use of personal data to evaluate certain personal aspects relating to a natural person, in particular to analyse or predict aspects concerning that natural person's performance at work,

of personal (health) data involves profiling-based decision-making – which will often be the case when a physician uses AI applications for diagnosis or treatment suggestion[143] – the patient should be informed of several aspects,[144] including that the processing is done for the purpose of profiling *and* making a decision based on the profile generated.[145] In principle, this information must be provided in *writing*,[146] which implies that this information duty as such is not really a safeguard against the (feared) dehumanisation of the physician-patient relationship.

6.1.2. Decisions Solely Based on Automated Processing of Personal (Health) Data

29. In the event of decisions based 'solely' on automated processing, including profiling, which produces legal or 'similarly significant' effects for the patient, the physician has the duty to inform the latter about the existence of automated decision-making. The physician also has to give a patient 'meaningful information' about the logic involved and the significance and envisaged consequences of such processing for the patient.[147] Thus, a physician has to inform the patient about the use of an automated decision before the decision was made (*ex ante*) as well as about its general basic mechanisms/ system functionality. It will ensure that the patient understands the rationale behind or the criteria relied on in reaching the decision[148] (i.e., how and why the patient is classified in a certain way and what consequences result from this classification).[149] This can be achieved by providing the categories of data that have been used and their relevance for the decision-making process, information related to the building of profiles or statistical groups and how they are relevant, and the way in which a profile is used for a decision affecting the patient.[150]

economic situation, health, personal preferences, interests, reliability, behaviour, location or movements.'

143 A. Ferretti, M. Schneider and A. Blasimme, 'Machine Learning in Medicine: Opening the New Data Protection Black Box', *EDPL*, 2018, p. 323.

144 See Articles 13 and 14 GDPR for a full list of the information that must be provided when processing personal data.

145 Articles 13(1)(c) and 14(1)(c); Article 29 Data Protection Working Party, 'Guidelines on Automated individual decision-making and Profiling for the purposes of Regulation 2016/679', 3 October 2017 (revised on 6 February 2018), p. 16.

146 Article 12(1) GDPR.

147 Articles 13(2)(f), 14(2)(g) and 22 (1) GDPR.

148 S. Wachter, B. Mittelstadt and L. Floridi, 'Why a Right to Explanation of Automated Decision-Making Does Not Exist in the General Data Protection Regulation', *IDPL*, 2017, vol. 7, no. 2, p. 83; Article 29 Data Protection Working Party, 'Guidelines on Automated individual decision-making and Profiling for the purposes of Regulation 2016/679', p. 25; Hoeren and Neihoff, 'Artificial Intelligence in Medical Diagnosis and the Right to Explanation', p. 314.

149 E. Bayamlioglu, 'Contesting Automated Decisions: A View of Transparency Implications', *EDPL*, 2018, vol. 4, no. 4, p. 438.

150 Article 29 Data Protection Working Party, 'Guidelines on Automated individual decision-making and Profiling for the purposes of Regulation 2016/679', p. 31; Schönberger, 'Artificial intelligence in healthcare: a critical analysis of the legal and ethical implications', p. 190.

Furthermore, some scholars argue that the patient also has the right to an explanation of the specific automated decision (*ex post*).[151] This right does not entail a 'model-based explanation' – which would force the physician to 'open the black box' and disclose the whole model of an AI system – but rather a 'subject-based explanation'. This implies that the patient has a right to be provided with an explanation about the decision-making process by revealing the key factors that led to the physician's decision (based on the AI system).[152] The right to an *ex post* explanation has been rejected by the majority of the legal doctrine[153] as well as by the Article 29 Data Protection Working Party (WP29).[154] It held that the GDPR only embeds the right to obtain *ex ante* information about the envisaged consequences of the processing, rather than an explanation of a particular decision.[155] As mentioned above, such obligation may, however, exist to some extent under Article 7 Belgian Law on Patient Rights.[156]

Finally, if a decision is based *solely* on automated processing, the physician must also take suitable measures to safeguard the patient's rights, freedoms and legitimate interests. This includes at least the right to a human intervention of someone with the authority to change the decision, to express his/her point of view and to contest the automated decision.[157] To exercise these rights in a meaningful way, the data subject must be provided with the aforementioned information on how the decision has been made and on what basis (notably on factors taken into account for the decision-making process and on their

151 Article 22(3) GDPR in conjunction with recital 71 and Article 15(1)(h) GDPR; B. Goodman an S. Flaxman, 'EU Regulations on Algorithmic Decision-Making and a "Right to Explanation"', p. 6, https://arxiv.org/pdf/1606.08813.pdf; Hoeren and Neihoff, 'Artificial Intelligence in Medical Diagnosis and the Right to Explanation', p. 314.

152 Hoeren and Neihoff, 'Artificial Intelligence in Medical Diagnosis and the Right to Explanation', p. 317.

153 L. Edwards and M. Veale, 'Slave to the Algorithm? Why a 'Right to an Explanation' Is Probably Not the Remedy You Are Looking For', *DL&TR*, 2017, vol. 18, pp. 48–53; Wachter, Mittelstadt and Floridi, 'Why a Right to Explanation of Automated Decision-Making Does Not Exist in the General Data Protection Regulation', p. 83; Article 29 Data Protection Working Party, 'Guidelines on Automated individual decision-making and Profiling for the purposes of Regulation 2016/679', p. 27; Schönberger, 'Artificial intelligence in healthcare: a critical analysis of the legal and ethical implications', pp. 192–193; M. Temme, 'Algorithms and Transparency in View of the New General Data Protection Regulation', *EDPL*, 2017, vol. 3, pp. 482–483.

154 The Article 29 Working Party was an advisory body composed of representatives from the data protection authorities of all EU Member States that existed prior to the entry into force of the GDPR. Since 25 May 2018, it has been replaced by the European Data Protection Board (EDPB). The EDPB has ratified several WP29 opinions and guidelines under the GDPR, including the 'Guidelines on Automated individual decision-making and Profiling for the purposes of Regulation 2016/679', 3 October 2017 (revised on 6 February 2018).

155 Article 29 Data Protection Working Party, 'Guidelines on Automated individual decision-making and Profiling for the purposes of Regulation 2016/679', p. 27.

156 *Supra* no. 23.

157 Article 22(3) and 22(4) GDPR.

respective 'weight' on an aggregate level) it was made.[158] The reviewer (i.e., the physician) should make a thorough assessment of all the relevant data, including any additional information provided by the patient.[159] This right induces human involvement. It is thus an important potential legal safeguard against a dehumanisation of the physician-patient relationship when the physician's decisions are solely based on automated processing of personal health data.

30. The question, however, arises whether the aforementioned duties will often be applied in a physician-patient relationship. There is no discussion that a decision potentially affecting someone's health and life produces legal effects or at least has 'similarly significant' effects for the patient.[160] Yet, it is not entirely clear how a decision based '*solely*' on automated processing should be interpreted in a healthcare setting.

According to the WP29, any oversight of a decision by a human actor implies that the latter must have had a meaningful impact on the final decision, rather than just a token gesture. It must be done by someone who has the authority and competence to change the decision of the algorithm, thereby taking into account all the relevant data.[161] According to the WP29, it is thus sufficient that the physician oversees and scrutinises an AI decision.[162] As a consequence, it is expected that the 'decisions' of the physician will not often be based *solely* on an automated processing of personal health data. This also stems from the fact that only qualified persons are allowed to provide healthcare, which implies that, from a legal point of view, a robot/algorithm that provides healthcare cannot act completely autonomously and/or without the supervision and oversight of a physician. This also implies that the physician has the last call and bears the responsibility for his/her decision (based on the outcome of the algorithm).[163] As mentioned above, the general liability standard may avoid that physicians become 'slaves to the machines'. It may also decrease the number

158 Article 29 Data Protection Working Party, 'Guidelines on Automated individual decision-making and Profiling for the purposes of Regulation 2016/679', p. 27.

159 Article 22(3) and 22(4) GDPR; Article 29 Data Protection Working Party, 'Guidelines on Automated individual decision-making and Profiling for the purposes of Regulation 2016/679', p. 27.

160 Hoeren and Neihoff, 'Artificial Intelligence in Medical Diagnosis and the Right to Explanation', p. 312; R. Pierce, 'Machine Learning for Diagnosis and Treatment: Gymnastics for the GDPR', *GDPL*, 2018, p. 336; Schönberger, 'Artificial intelligence in healthcare: a critical analysis of the legal and ethical implications', p. 191.

161 Article 29 Data Protection Working Party, 'Guidelines on Automated individual decision-making and Profiling for the purposes of Regulation 2016/679', pp. 20–21.

162 Hoeren and Neihoff, 'Artificial Intelligence in Medical Diagnosis and the Right to Explanation', p. 312. These authors demand a higher standard and claim a real, meaningful influence of the human actor. There must be an actual modification of the decision, not just critical oversight.

163 Schönberger, 'Artificial intelligence in healthcare: a critical analysis of the legal and ethical implications', p. 191.

of decisions that are *solely* based on automated processing of personal (health) data in the sense of Article 22(1) GDPR. This, however, does not exclude that a physician's decision may be solely based on automated processing in the sense of Article 22(1) GDPR.

Indeed, whether the physician's decision is based solely on automated processing in the sense of Article 22(1) GDPR depends on the factual circumstances. Thus, if a physician's intervention is *de facto* limited to nominal oversight and the results are automatically/routinely applied to individuals without any actual influence on the result ('rubber-stamping') – which may be justified depending on the patient's health condition and the risks involved[164] – the decision may be qualified as based 'solely' on automated processing of personal (health) data in the sense of Article 22(1) GDPR.[165] In such a case, the physician has to comply with the additional duties described above. However, this is without prejudice to the physician's responsibility for the outcome of such 'decision'.

31. According to the WP29, it is good practice to provide the aforementioned information to the data subject (patient) even if the automated decision-making and profiling do not meet the requirements in Article 22(1) GDPR.[166] However, in a healthcare setting, it will in my opinion be more important that the physician, rather than the patient, understands the logic of the AI system that is used to provide healthcare. This implies that he/she (1) knows whether the system can be used for the specific patient, (2) knows the risks involved, (3) verifies the specific outcome, and (4) informs the patient about his/her health condition and the expected prognosis. The physician also needs to advise the patient to adapt his/her behaviour in order to deal with these risks. In other words, the physician needs to act as a reasonably prudent physician placed in the same circumstances and also has to comply with his/her information duties according to Articles 7 and 8 Belgian Law on Patient Rights.

Indeed, the rationale behind the data subject's right to obtain the information is to give the latter (i.e., the patient) the possibility to exercise the right to contest the AI system's decision solely based on automated processing in a meaningful way.[167] However, in a healthcare setting, the patient is not only confronted with the complexity of the AI system but also with the complexity of medicine itself.

---

164 *Supra* no. 10.

165 Article 29 Data Protection Working Party, 'Guidelines on Automated individual decision-making and Profiling for the purposes of Regulation 2016/679', 3 October 2017 (revised on 6 February 2018), p. 21.

166 *Ibid.*, p. 25.

167 Article 22(3) and 22 (4) GDPR; Article 29 Data Protection Working Party, 'Guidelines on Automated individual decision-making and Profiling for the purposes of Regulation 2016/679', 3 October 2017 (revised on 6 February 2018), p. 27; Bayamlioglu, 'Contesting Automated Decisions: A View of Transparency Implications', p. 434.

This will often imply that the only person that has the (scientific) knowledge to contest the AI system's decision in a meaningful way is the patient's physician. Without the intervention of a physician, the patient's right to contest an AI decision will be meaningless. As mentioned above, the patient can require such intervention if the physician's decision is solely based on automated processing.

32. In any case, although there is no legal right to an *ex post* explanation of a specific decision under the GDPR, especially not in a healthcare setting given the limited decisions solely based on automated processing, it will in my opinion be important that a physician is able to inform the patient about the factors that led to his/her decision based on AI systems. This is not only required to comply with the obligations under Articles 7 and 8 Belgian Law on Patient Rights towards the patient but also to prevent that a patient's trust in the use of AI systems is undermined. A patient's trust in the physician's decision based on the AI system may indeed be affected if the former is not able to provide this information to the patient – just as he/she would do in a purely human decision-making process. This may eventually cause the patient to refuse a treatment and the use of AI systems in the future. This would probably not be in the patient's best interest.

6.1.3. Informed Consent under the GDPR

33. Under the GDPR, personal health data are considered as a 'special category'. The processing of personal health data is in principle prohibited,[168] unless one of the exceptions provided in Article 9(2) GDPR apply.

For example, Article 9(2)(h) GDPR allows the processing of (health) data if such processing is necessary for the purposes of preventive or occupational medicine, medical diagnosis, the provision of health or social care or treatment on the basis of Union or Member State law or pursuant to a contract with a health professional, and the data are processed by or under the responsibility of a person subject to the obligation of professional secrecy. To invoke this basis for the processing of personal health data to provide healthcare, the physician will thus have to justify why the processing is necessary (i.e., it is a reasonable and proportionate way to achieve this purpose).

In the event of decisions solely based on automated processing, processing of personal health data is only allowed if the patient gave his/her explicit consent or if this is necessary for reasons of substantial public interest on the basis of Union or Member State law which shall be proportionate to the aim pursued, respect the essence of the right to data protection and provide for suitable and specific measures to safeguard the fundamental rights and interests of the data subject.[169]

---

168 Article 9(1) GDPR.

169 Article 22(4) GDPR *juncto* Articles 9(2)(a) and 9(2)(g) GDPR.

34. The data subject's (i.e., patient) *explicit, free, specific* and *informed* consent is thus an exception to the principled prohibition to process personal health data. It will generally be the legal basis in the event of decisions based solely on automated processing.[170] This legal basis for processing personal (health) data requires an *express* written or oral statement from the patient after being provided with all relevant information ('opt-in'). This information includes the identity of the controller and the purposes of the processing for which the personal data are intended (e.g., profiling and making a decision (solely or not) based on the profile generated if a physician wants to use an AI tool to perform a diagnosis or to obtain a treatment suggestion).[171]

Valid consent also requires the controller to demonstrate that it is possible for the data subject (patient) to refuse or withdraw consent without detriment. For example, the controller needs to prove that withdrawing consent does not lead to any costs for the data subject and thus no clear disadvantage for those withdrawing consent. Other examples of detriment are deception, intimidation, coercion or significant negative consequences if a data subject does not consent.[172]

The implied consent under which physicians generally operate to provide healthcare under the Belgian Law on Patient Rights would thus not meet the standard of a clear affirmative act – or qualify as explicit consent for special category data – to allow the processing of personal health data under the GDPR. Furthermore, there has to be a clear distinction between the information regarding the healthcare that will be provided on the one hand and the processing of personal health data on the other hand.[173] In a healthcare context, informed consent is often not considered to be a valid/preferred legal basis to process personal data. This is caused by several factors such as the lack of freedom, information or specificity.[174]

---

170 Article 9(2)(a) GDPR. See also EDPB, 'Guidelines 05/2020 on consent under Regulation 2016/679', 4 May 2020, p. 7 *et seq.*

171 According to the corresponding guidelines of the European Data Protection Board an 'informed' consent requires at least the following information: (i) the controller's identity, (ii) the purpose of each of the processing operations for which consent is sought, (iii) what (type of) data will be collected and used, (iv) the existence of the right to withdraw consent, (v) information about the use of the data for decisions based solely on automated processing, including profiling, in accordance with Article 22 (2) GDPR, and (vi) if the consent relates to transfers of data to third countries, about the possible risks of data transfers to third countries in the absence of an adequacy decision and appropriate safeguards (Article 46 GDPR) (EDPB, 'Guidelines 05/2020 on consent under Regulation 2016/679', 4 May 2020, pp. 15–16).

172 EDPB, 'Guidelines 05/2020 on consent under Regulation 2016/679', 4 May 2020, p. 12–13.

173 Articles 7(2) and 7(4) GDPR. Article 7(4) GDPR also indicates that the practice of 'bundling' consent with acceptance of terms or conditions, or 'tying' the provision of a contract or a service to a request for consent to process personal data that are not necessary for the performance of that contract or service, is considered highly undesirable. If consent is given in this situation, it is presumed to be not freely given (EDPB, 'Guidelines 05/2020 on consent under Regulation 2016/679', 4 May 2020, p. 10).

174 See, e.g., G. Verhenneman, *The Patient's Right to Privacy and Autonomy Against a Changing Healthcare Model. Assessing informed consent, anonymization and purpose limitation in light of E-health and personalized care* (Leuven: KU Leuven, 2020), p. 137 and further.

35. It follows from this analysis that, irrespective of the legal basis which is used to process personal health data, the GDPR will likely only have a limited added value in light of the physician's obligations under the Belgian Law on Patient Rights to avoid the feared dehumanisation of the physician-patient relationship. Indeed, the additional information that must be provided by the physician to the patient will most of the times be provided through a form and does as such not trigger additional 'human' contact. Only in the event of decisions solely based on automated processing of personal health data – which will not often be the case – the GDPR may trigger additional 'human' contact between a physician and a patient. That is because the patient has the right to obtain human intervention of someone with authority to change the decision (i.e., the physician).

7. ARTIFICIAL INTELLIGENCE ACT

36. On 21 April 2021, the European Parliament and the Council adopted a proposal for a regulation laying down harmonised rules on AI.[175] If adopted, this new piece of EU legislation will be implementing harmonised rules on artificial intelligence systems and integrate them into existing EU legislative frameworks (the 'Proposal').

In the context of this contribution, it is important to note that according to the Proposal, medical devices using AI, i.e., computer programs having the capacity to perform operations analogous to learning and decision-making in humans,[176] are qualified as 'high-risk AI systems'.[177] In addition, AI systems intended to be used for the 'real-time' and 'post' remote biometric identification of natural persons, AI systems intended to be used to dispatch, or to establish priority in the dispatching of emergency first response services (including by firefighters and medical aid) and AI systems intended to be used by competent public authorities to assess a health risk posed by a natural person who intends to enter or has entered into the territory of a Member State are also high-risk AI systems (also if they do not qualify as a medical device).[178]

For such high-risk AI systems, the Proposal imposes several requirements, which may have an important impact avoiding the 'dehumanization' of the physician-patient-relationship, including, amongst others, transparency and provision of

---

175 Proposal for a Regulation of the European Parliament and of the Council Laying Down Harmonised Rules on Artificial Intelligence (Artificial Intelligence Act) and Amending Certain Union Legislative Acts, 2021/0106 (COD).

176 Defined in article 3 (1) of the Proposal as software that is developed with one or more of the techniques and approaches listed in Annex I and can, for a given set of human-defined objectives, generate outputs such as content, predictions, recommendations, or decisions influencing the environments they interact with.

177 Article 6.1 of the Proposal.

178 Article 6.2 of the Proposal.

information to users (7.1),[179] human oversight (7.2),[180] and accuracy, robustness and cybersecurity (6.3).[181] Below the relevant aspects of these three requirements are summarized. In my opinion, these two requirements may play an important role to allow the physician to live up to his/her legal obligations described above.

7.1. TRANSPARENCY AND PROVISION OF INFORMATION TO USERS

37. According to the Proposal, high-risk AI systems shall be designed and developed in such a way to ensure that their operation is sufficiently transparent to enable users to interpret the system's output and use it appropriately. An appropriate type and degree of transparency shall be ensured, with a view to achieving compliance with the relevant obligations of the user and of the provider set out in Chapter 3 of the Proposal. For that purpose, it shall be accompanied by instructions for use in an appropriate digital format or otherwise that include concise, complete, correct and clear information that is relevant, accessible and comprehensible to users. The Proposal specifies which information has to be provided to the users.

7.2. HUMAN OVERSIGHT

38. High-risk AI systems shall be designed and developed in such a way, including with appropriate human-machine interface tools, that they can be effectively overseen by natural persons during the period in which the AI system is in use. Human oversight shall aim at preventing or minimising the risks to health, safety or fundamental rights that may emerge when a high-risk AI system is used in accordance with its intended purpose or under conditions of reasonably foreseeable misuse, in particular when such risks persist.

Moreover, the users must be enabled to: (a) fully understand the capacities and limitations of the high-risk AI system and be able to duly monitor its operation, so that signs of anomalies, dysfunctions and unexpected performance can be detected and addressed as soon as possible; (b) remain aware of the possible tendency of automatically relying or over-relying on the output produced by a high-risk AI system ('automation bias'), in particular for high-risk AI systems used to provide information or recommendations for decisions to be taken by natural persons; (c) be able to correctly interpret the high-risk AI system's output, taking into account in particular the characteristics of the

179 Article 13 of the Proposal.
180 Article 14 of the Proposal.
181 Article 15 of the Proposal.

system and the interpretation tools and methods available; (d) be able to decide, in any particular situation, not to use the high-risk AI system or otherwise disregard, override or reverse the output of the high-risk AI system; and (e) be able to intervene on the operation of the high-risk AI system or interrupt the system through a "stop" button or a similar procedure.

39. For AI systems intended to be used for the 'real-time' and 'post' remote biometric identification of natural persons, it must be ensured that no action or decision can be taken by the user on the basis of the identification resulting from the system unless this has been verified and confirmed by at least two natural persons. In this regard, the logging capabilities of the high-risk AI system must include the identification of these natural persons.[182] For the avoidance of doubt, the Proposal also imposes logging requirements on high-risk AI systems in general.[183]

7.3. ACCURACY, ROBUSTNESS AND CYBERSECURITY

40. High-risk AI systems shall be designed and developed in such a way that they achieve, in the light of their intended purpose, an appropriate level of accuracy, robustness and cybersecurity, and perform consistently in those respects throughout their lifecycle. The levels of accuracy and the relevant accuracy metrics of high-risk AI systems shall be declared in the accompanying instructions of use.

Furthermore, they shall be resilient with regard to errors, faults or inconsistencies that may occur within the system or the environment in which the system operates, in particular due to their interaction with natural persons or other systems. The robustness of high-risk AI systems may be achieved through technical redundancy solutions, which may include backup or fail-safe plans. High-risk AI systems that continue to learn after being placed on the market or put into service shall be developed in such a way to ensure that possibly biased outputs due to outputs used as an input for future operations ('feedback loops') are duly addressed with appropriate mitigation measures.

Finally, high-risk AI systems shall be resilient with regard to attempts by unauthorised third parties to alter their use or performance by exploiting the system vulnerabilities. The technical solutions aimed at ensuring the cybersecurity of high-risk AI systems shall be appropriate to the relevant circumstances and the risks. The technical solutions to address AI specific vulnerabilities shall include, where appropriate, measures to prevent and control for attacks trying to manipulate the training dataset ('data poisoning'), inputs

[182] Article 12.4(d) of the Proposal.
[183] Article 12 of the Proposal.

designed to cause the model to make a mistake ('adversarial examples'), or model flaws.

8. CONCLUSION

41. AI and robotics will have an enormous impact on the healthcare sector in the coming years. As personal relationships are considered to be essential in healthcare, one of the major concerns that is often raised is the risk of the 'dehumanisation' of the healthcare sector. AI and robotics may also have a potential negative impact on the personal relationship between physicians and patients. In this chapter, I tried to nuance this fear of 'dehumanisation' of the physician-patient relationship in light of the applicable legal framework in Belgium. Indeed, there are good reasons to believe that the current Belgian legal framework provides at least four potential legal safeguards against such dehumanisation. The proposal adopted by the European Parliament and the Council regarding harmonised rules on artificial intelligence systems, may have an important impact enabling the physician to live up to these obligations.

42. First of all, according to the Law on the Exercise of the Healthcare Profession, only qualified persons are allowed to provide healthcare in Belgium. In other words, from a legal point of view, a robot/algorithm that provides healthcare cannot act completely autonomously and/or without a physician's oversight. Thus, the robot and algorithm remain mere (augmenting) tools in the hands of the physician. It is obvious that this principle by itself is an important potential legal safeguard against a dehumanisation of the patient-physician relationship. This is further strengthened by the fact that physicians remain responsible both for the actions and omissions of these tools and/or for his/her own actions and omissions based on the outcome of these tools (e.g., a diagnosis or treatment suggestion). This may encourage the physician to remain closely involved in the patient's treatment and may have a positive impact on avoiding dehumanisation of healthcare, thereby ensuring that a human remains in the loop.

43. As such, the use of robots or AI does not discharge the physician of the obligation to act the way in which a reasonable prudent physician (of the same specialty) placed in the same circumstances would act. This does not imply that a physician will *automatically* be held liable if he/she did not verify the outcome of the algorithm or did (not) overrule the algorithm (e.g., in the event that these tools are used for diagnosis or treatment suggestion). There is only a risk to incur liability if a reasonably prudent physician would have verified the outcome of the algorithm and/or would have (not) overruled the algorithm in the same circumstances. More generally, the physician's required degree of supervision will mainly depend on the patient's general health condition and the risks involved. The general liability standard is thus a second safeguard and may encourage the physician to remain closely involved in the patients' treatment. By doing so, the risk of 'dehumanisation' towards patients is avoided. This may also induce physicians to properly inform, educate and train themselves to use these tools and to become aware of their limitations.

It is, therefore, not desirable to abandon a physician's obligation to verify the results of the algorithm even if it has a very high level of autonomy. Physicians risk becoming 'slaves to the machines' if that would be the case. Moreover, 'keeping a human' in the loop ensures a holistic approach towards the patient rather than only focusing on his/her specific symptoms. An algorithm does indeed not have emotions and does not necessarily have a good overview of the patient. Think of medical antecedents, hobbies, work, general lifestyle, physical condition and other circumstances which can have an impact on the most desirable treatment method or the most probable diagnosis. The physician is the guardian of the machine. He/she should act as an active operator and not as a passive user. Of course, a good balance has to be struck to impose liability on physicians for not having verified its result and/or (not) having overruled the algorithm. This will sometimes be difficult to achieve. However, this is not a convincing reason to abandon the general liability principle. Arguably, this principle is sufficiently flexible to take into account the specific circumstances of each case and to reach a fair decision.

44. A third potential legal safeguard against the feared dehumanisation of healthcare is the physician's obligation to obtain a patient's informed consent to provide healthcare. The most important aspect of this obligation is providing the patient with information about the purpose and nature of the treatment, the relevant risks and the reasonable alternative treatments (if any). Furthermore, the patient has the right to be informed about his/her health condition and the expected evolution. This information includes diagnosis, prognosis and health education. The goal of this right is to ensure that the patient knows as much as the physician about his/her health condition. In principle, the latter may not withhold any information from the patient.

This information must be provided through a dialogue between the physician and patient, which cannot be replaced by an informed consent form. This implies a 'human' contact between physician and patient. It may, therefore, be an important potential safeguard against 'dehumanisation'.

45. Finally, according to the GDPR, and irrespective of the legal basis used to process personal (health) data, the physician must clearly explain to the patients how a profiling or automated decision-making process works. Where the processing of personal (health) data involves profiling-based decision-making,

the patient should be informed of several aspects (e.g., that the processing is for the purpose of profiling). In principle, this information must be provided in writing. It is also possible under the GDPR to legally process personal (health) data without informed consent of the patient. Moreover, informed consent is not considered as an appropriate legal basis to process personal data in a healthcare context. As such, these additional information duties under the GDPR will not provide additional safeguards against the feared dehumanisation of healthcare in addition to the physician's obligations that already exist under the Belgian Law on Patient Rights.

In the event of decisions *solely* based on automated processing – which will not often occur in a healthcare context – the GDPR provides additional obligations to induce the 'personal' intervention of the physician who uses AI to provide healthcare. In such a case, a physician not only has additional information duties – e.g., provide meaningful information about the logic involved and the significance and envisaged consequences of the processing for the patient – but the patient also has a right to obtain the intervention of someone with the authority to overrule the decision. Unlike the additional information duties, this right to a human intervention may be an important safeguard against 'dehumanisation' of the physician-patient relationship.

In a healthcare setting, it will be more important that the physician understands the logic of the AI system that he/she uses to provide healthcare. The physician has to comply with the information duties under Articles 7 and 8 Belgian Law on Patient Rights. The fact that a physician is not able to provide the required information to the patient may compromise a patient's trust in the physician's decision based on the AI system. It has been argued that this may result in a patient's refusal of a particular treatment or of reliance on an AI system in the future.

46. Although it can be expected that robots and AI will have an impact on the relationship between the physician and the patient, it does not necessarily have to be a negative one and result in 'dehumanisation'. Regardless of the potential legal safeguards that have been discussed in the chapter, the use of AI and robots may also have a positive impact on the workload of physicians. This will not only be the case regarding their medical tasks, but also in relation to their administrative duties. This in turn will allow them to spend more time with their patients, be more involved in their treatment and focus on tasks needing a human element. The role of the physician will inevitably evolve in the coming decades. Nevertheless, he/she will (must) remain the 'guardian of the machine' that is used to provide healthcare. The physician must be the patient's guide and guardian to ensure a safe and proper use of the numerous (forthcoming) AI applications in the healthcare sector.

CHAPTER 19

AI AND ANTITRUST: BETWEEN COLLISION AND COLLUSION

Christof KOOLEN* and Bruno VAN DEN BOSCH**

1. INTRODUCTION

1. The algorithmic age is near. Undertakings increasingly rely on artificial intelligence (AI) to steer their commercial behaviour on the market. Contrary to traditional business models, human involvement is reduced to a minimum. For instance, the idea of a bank manager who manually checks and approves loan applications belongs to the past. Instead, firms increasingly derive value from algorithms and automation. AI sets the price on e-commerce platforms, AI recommends songs on Spotify or viewing recommendations on Netflix, and AI determines which consumers qualify for a bank loan. While the age of machine intelligence was ushered in by large entities such as Google, Amazon, Facebook, and Alibaba, smaller entities are now following suit.

Traditional business models are gradually becoming intertwined with digital components in the form of software and code. By tapping into the potential of big data and by subsequently involving AI-based models in a commercial setting, it becomes possible to revolutionise how entrepreneurs conduct business. More particularly, the value proposition offered by AI revolves among others around increased accuracy, detailed insights into the customer base, and the ability to tailor products and services to these insights accordingly. When contrasting traditional processes against AI-driven processes, it quickly becomes clear that an algorithmic approach to commerce offers distinct advantages over a non-algorithmic approach.

---

* Christof Koolen works as a Ph.D. Researcher at Consumer Competition Market (KU Leuven, Belgium). He holds a research fellowship from the Research Foundation Flanders (FWO). For correspondence: christof.koolen@kuleuven.be.

** Bruno Van den Bosch is a former researcher at Consumer Competition Market (CCM) and a former affiliated researcher at the University of Leiden. For correspondence: bruno.van.den.bosch@hotmail.com.

2. It follows that AI has significant potential to disrupt the current means of doing business and the ability to compete on the market. This triggers the following question: *are AI and competition law on a collision course?* This chapter demonstrates that this is true to at least some extent. At the same time, the contribution also argues that some of the difficulties stem from an incomplete understanding of the inner workings of AI and relate to AI taking legal scholars into unfamiliar territory. All in all, algorithms do indeed create new challenges for both national and European competition authorities – tasked with assessing anticompetitive agreements under Article 101 TFEU, curbing abusive market behaviour pursuant to Article 102 TFEU, and conducting merger control[1] under the EU Merger Regulation. However, not all of these challenges are insurmountable.

3. This chapter focusses on the current implications of AI for the field of EU competition law *sensu stricto* (Articles 101 and 102 TFEU) and provides a comprehensive overview of the current state of the art. The underlying theme within this contribution is 'predictability': while AI is often said to function as a black box (i.e., data goes in and solutions come out, but the intermediary steps between input and output are unclear), it should be borne in mind that algorithms essentially perform a set of steps that any individual could also carry out himself. The ability to retrace these steps offers some solace to competition authorities put in a position to judge the anticompetitive nature of machine intelligence, which is affecting the competitive dynamics of a given market.

In terms of content, the chapter adheres to a threefold structure. Firstly, we will focus on *competition for AI*. This part provides the necessary context by illustrating how market dynamics are changing due to the increased possibility to implement AI within undertakings' business models (part 2). We will then discuss *competition with AI*. This part addresses how undertakings currently make use of AI. It explains what AI does and does not do for undertakings. Real-world use cases serve as a point of reference to assess how firms compete against each other and how competition law is adapted to deal with AI-based collusion and abuses of dominance (part 3). Subsequently, we will focus on *AI for competition*. This part explains how the enforcement angle of competition law can also be changed by algorithms. AI not only proves beneficial for undertakings, but also for

---

1 The intersection between artificial intelligence and competition law contains a broad range of subtopics. To bring focus to this book chapter, the choice was made to study Articles 101 and 102 TFEU in particular. Readers interested in EU merger control and algorithms may consider the following literature recommendations: V. Egerton-Doyle and J. Ford, 'Algorithms, Big Data, and Merger Control' in A. Portuese (ed.), *Algorithmic Antitrust* (Cham: Springer, 2022), p. 87; N. Maier, 'Closeness of Substitution for 'Big Data' in Merger Control', *Journal of European Competition Law & Practice* 2019, vol. 10, no. 4, p. 246; J. Modrall, 'Big Data and Merger Control in the EU', *Journal of European Competition Law & Practice* 2018, vol. 9, no. 9, p. 569; B. Holles de Peyer, 'EU Merger Control and Big Data', *Journal of Competition Law & Economics* 2017, vol. 13, no. 4, p. 767.

competition authorities, for instance, in the form of pattern recognition algorithms (part 4). We will end this chapter with some concluding remarks (part 5).

4. The contribution is novel in two ways. Firstly, it comprehensively scrutinises the existing literature on AI and competition law and presents the main findings of the different strands of literature in one concise overview. Secondly, it aspires to deliver added value on top of the existing body of scholarship by remaining grounded in reality. A lot of hype surrounds AI nowadays, and our objective is to add nuance to the debate and to contextualize where necessary, in addition to downplaying some of the buzz surrounding AI. In concluding the topic of AI and competition law, the chapter puts forward the question whether firms and competition authorities are truly trapped in a competitive legal environment that is at least partially governed by AI.

2. COMPETITION FOR AI – THE MARKET FOR AI SYSTEMS

2.1. THEORY OF COMPETITION

5. Underpinning competition law is the idea that society as a whole is better off when firms compete.[2] A competitive market is theorised to give each individual firm the incentive to keep innovating, to lower prices, and to meet consumer demand in the most efficient manner.[3]

6. To maintain effective competition on a given market, competition law specifically targets several market practices, which are considered harmful to the process of competition.[4] Pursuant to Article 101 TFEU, agreements between undertakings[5], decisions by associations of undertakings[6], and concerted practices[7] are prohibited when they have as their object or effect the prevention, restriction, or distortion of competition within the internal market.[8]

---

2 R. Khemani, 'Objectives of Competition Policy' in R. Khemani (ed.), *A Framework for the Design and Implementation of Competition Law and Policy* (Washington, D.C.: World Bank Publications, 1999), p. 2.

3 M. Stucke, 'What is competition?' in D. Zimmer (ed.), *The Goals of Competition Law* (Cheltenham: Edward Elgar Publishing, 2012), p. 33.

4 R. Whish and D. Bailey, *Competition Law*, 8th edn (Oxford: Oxford University Press, 2015), p. 3.

5 CJEU 25 October 1983, no. C-107/82, ECLI:EU:C:1983:293, *AEG-Telefunken*.

6 CJEU 14 July 1972, no. C-48/69, ECLI:EU:C:1972:70, *Dyestuffs*.

7 CJEU 15 September 2005, no. T-325/01, ECLI:EU:T:2005:322, *DaimlerChrysler*.

8 D. Bailey and L. John, *Bellamy & Child: European Union Law of Competition*, 8th edn (Oxford: Oxford University Press, 2018), pp. 87–88; E. Fox and D. Gerard, *EU Competition Law: Cases, Texts and Context* (Cheltenham, Edward Elgar Publishing, 2017), p 33; A. Jones, B. Sufrin and N. Dunne, *EU Competition Law: Test, Cases, and Materials*, 7th edn (Oxford: Oxford University Press, 2019), pp. 137–139; Whish and Bailey, *Competition Law*, pp. 84–85.

This provision specifically precludes competing undertakings from entering into agreements with the aim to fix prices, restrict outputs, share markets, or coordinate their behaviour on the market in general when such an agreement would have an appreciable effect on trade between EU Member States.[9]

Apart from prohibiting anticompetitive agreements between different undertakings, competition law also considers abusive unilateral behaviour to run counter to Article 102 TFEU. Accordingly, any abuse[10] of a dominant position[11] within the internal market shall be prohibited as incompatible with the internal market in so far as it affects trade between EU Member States.[12] This provision is put in place to curb abusive conduct on the market, which can occur by means of leveraging established market power and resources in view of suppressing competition or expanding into other market segments. Typical abuses of dominance caught under Article 102 TFEU include predatory pricing, price discrimination, tying practices, or refusals to supply.

7. The abovementioned aims of competition law have seen extensive coverage in academic scholarship and the core policy objectives underpinning these provisions have been widely accepted.[13] While there is some debate on the scope and reach of competition policy, the normative justifications as to why competition is necessary predominantly revolve around increasing consumer and societal welfare.[14] Although some disagreement exists as to the precise meaning of the phrase 'society being better off as a whole', these discussions have mostly been relegated to the margins.[15] When further addressing the goals of competition law, it should be borne in mind that the early conceptions of antitrust law were mostly aimed at breaking up large economic powers since they were perceived as a threat to core democratic values.[16] Nowadays, however, these

---

9 Established case law on this topic includes: CJEU 30 June 1966, no. C-56/65, ECLI:EU:C:1966:38, *Société Technique Minière*; CJEU 13 July 1966, nos. C-56/64 and C-58/64, ECLI:EU:C:1966:41, *Consten and Grundig*.

10 CJEU 12 December 1991, no. T-30/89, ECLI:EU:T:1991:70, *Hilti AG*.

11 CJEU 14 February 1978, no. C-27/76, ECLI:EU:C:1978:22, *United Brands*.

12 Bailey and John, *Bellamy & Child*, pp. 859–862; Fox and Gerard, *EU Competition Law*, pp. 159–161; Jones, Sufrin and Dunne, *EU Competition Law*, pp. 277–280; Whish and Bailey, *Competition Law*, pp. 183–184.

13 See, for instance, L. Parret, 'The multiple personalities of EU competition law: time for a comprehensive debate on its objectives' in D. Zimmer (ed.), *The Goals of Competition Law* (Cheltenham: Edward Elgar Publishing, 2012), p. 64 ff.

14 A. Ezrachi, 'EU Competition Law Goals and The Digital Economy', *SSRN Scholarly Papers*, 2018, https://papers.ssrn.com/sol3/papers.cfm?abstract_id=3191766, pp. 4–5.

15 L. Kaplow, 'On the choice of welfare standards in competition law' in D. Zimmer (ed.), *The Goals of Competition Law* (Cheltenham: Edward Elgar Publishing, 2012), pp. 3–4 and pp. 18–19: '*For all the debate about the objectives of competition law and, in particular, whether a welfare- based measure should reflect only consumer welfare or encompass total welfare, only modest attention has been given to why the difference matters*'.

16 F. Roosevelt, *The New Deal: Message to Congress on the Concentration of Economic Power*, 29 April 1938, https://publicpolicy.pepperdine.edu/academics/research/faculty-research/new-deal/roosevelt-speeches/fr042938.htm: '*The first truth is that the liberty of a democracy is not safe if the people tolerate the growth of private power to a point where it becomes stronger*

goals have been stretched significantly and, for instance, also address aspects such as sustainability considerations.[17] Nonetheless, the core idea remains the same: competition law aims to foster and protect the process of competition between undertakings.

2.2. THE MARKET FOR AI SYSTEMS

8. From the perspective of an undertaking, facing fierce competition typically implies a reduction in terms of profit margins (i.e., the producer surplus) due to market prices remaining close to marginal costs.[18] Hence, given the need to compete on the market, firms must continuously push for lower prices, better products, increased product choice, or more efficient production methods. This constant strive regularly incites undertakings to engage in anticompetitive behaviour. For instance, competing firms could benefit from coordinating their market conduct with each other by fixing prices at an above-market level or by deciding to stay out of each other's way (i.e., market allocation). Similarly, a firm that maintains a dominant position in a particular market may decide to leverage its established market power to engage in exclusionary[19] (e.g., refusals to supply, exclusive dealing, bundling/tying, predatory pricing, …) or exploitative[20] conduct (e.g., excessive pricing, price discrimination, …).

9. There are several reasons why market conditions are changing following the introduction of AI into undertakings' value chains. One of those reasons is tied to the creation of a new *market for AI systems*.[21] While there is no doubt about the benefits that AI could bring to the market, undertakings often lack the necessary human capital or financial means to create their own AI system. A hospital, for example, would benefit from having access to AI to automatically detect cancer cells in microscopic images.[22] However, developing such a solution

than their democratic state itself. That, in its essence, is fascism – ownership of government by an individual, by a group, or by any other controlling private power'.

17 On this topic, see for instance S. Holmes, 'Climate change, sustainability, and competition law', *Journal of Antitrust Enforcement*, 2020, vol. 8, no. 2, pp. 354–355.

18 Jones, Sufrin and Dunne, *EU Competition Law*, pp. 4–7.

19 Communication from the Commission – Guidance on the Commission's enforcement priorities in applying Article 82 of the EC Treaty to abusive exclusionary conduct by dominant undertakings [2009] OJ C 45/7.

20 M. Botta and K. Wiedemann, 'Exploitative Conducts in Digital Markets: Time for a Discussion after the Facebook Decision', *Journal of European Competition Law & Practice*, 2019, vol. 10, no. 8, p. 465.

21 Proposal for a Regulation of the European Parliament and of the Council laying down harmonized rules on Artificial Intelligence (Artificial Intelligence Act), 2021, COM (2021) 206 final; X, 'New rules for Artificial Intelligence', *European Commission*, 2021, https://ec.europa.eu/commission/presscorner/detail/en/QANDA_21_1683.

22 M. Stumpe, 'An Augmented Reality Microscope for Cancer Detection', *Google AI Blog*, 2018, https://ai.googleblog.com/2018/04/an-augmented-reality-microscope.html.

in-house is often not feasible. For those instances, undertakings could rely on AI systems that are offered 'off the shelf'.[23] Such solutions are usually brought to market by dedicated companies and are tailored to a client's specific needs and wants. Other notable examples of pre-build AI models include chatbots and virtual assistants.

At the other side of the spectrum, there are also undertakings that develop their AI in-house. Such an approach not only calls for access to expertise and know-how, but also requires expensive hardware, which is needed to meet the high computational demands of contemporary AI systems.

10. Barring specific situations, it is worth pointing out that the *barriers to entry* into the market for AI systems are relatively low. Basic information on how to code algorithms or on the fundamentals of complex AI models are readily available online.[24] It is also not unusual to find university-level courses on the topic of AI via online learning platforms.

In terms of hardware, AI is known to be extremely resource-intensive due to the lengthy calculations that need to be performed. Evidently, the more computing power is available to the AI, the less time it will take to train the model. Individuals looking to recreationally use AI would incur roughly 3.000 EUR in hardware costs for an entry-level setup. While such a setup will enable users to solve basic tasks, it will fall short when attempting to tackle more sizeable problems. The computational complexity of a task – expressed in terms of computation time and memory space – therefore acts as a constraint on the entry into the market for AI systems.[25] On that note, AI assignments in a commercial setting will generally involve large datasets, implying that consumer-grade hardware is unsuitable for such tasks.[26]

Training data for the AI model might be difficult to come by. While some machine learning repositories offer extensive datasets for free[27], these data will often lack the necessary specificity to address the practical issues and questions that arise in a commercial setting. Web scraping could be considered as a valid alternative strategy to acquire training data, but this comes with its own set of concerns and shortcomings.

---

23 Amazon, for instance, offers a wide range of pre-build AI models and machine learning services, which can be used for business analytics, language processing, or text analytics. For more details, see the AWS Marketplace at https://aws.amazon.com/marketplace/solutions/machine-learning.

24 E.g., via Coursera or Udemy.

25 P. Louridas, *Algorithms* (Massachusetts: MIT Press, 2020), pp. 30–31.

26 *Ibid.*: '*We don't really care how long it takes to sort 10 items; after all, we can do that by hand. We care how long it takes to sort one million items or more. We want a measure of how we expect an algorithm to perform in problems that are not trivial.*'

27 See, for instance, the UCI Machine Learning Repository at https://archive.ics.uci.edu/ml/index.php. The repository offers datasets suitable for different training tasks (e.g., classification, regression, clustering, ...), various data types (multivariate, univariate, sequential, time-series, ...) and subject matters (life sciences, physics, business, ...).

It follows from the digital nature of AI that the market for such systems remains fairly accessible and that entry barriers are not overly high. At the same time, it is plausible that achieving high market penetration will pose a more significant hurdle, notably due to data access limitations[28] and high hardware costs.

11. While the market for AI systems has some notable players anno 2023 – such as IBM[29], Microsoft[30], Google[31] and Amazon[32] –, the power dynamics on the market have not yet fully crystallised.[33] Yet, it is worth noting that the firms listed here feature a high level of vertical integration, implying that they are active on hardware, software, and service levels of the market. While this could pose potential problems in the future, there does not currently seem to be any clear evidence of anticompetitive behaviour in the market for AI systems. However, given the evolving nature of AI, competition authorities should be mindful of ongoing market trends. Market leaders obviously do not want to fall behind the curve and, thus, face strong incentives to continuously invest in AI-related technology. When such investments take on the form of mergers and acquisitions, this may impact the level of competition on the market.[34]

3. COMPETITION WITH AI – COMPETITIVE DYNAMICS VIA AI

3.1. CONCEPTUALISATION OF AI

12. Apart from creating an entirely novel market for AI systems, AI also affects *how* firms compete on the market. It is especially this dimension that attracts significant attention in scholarly literature.[35] When interacting with the existing

---

28 This topic has been extensively covered in I. Graef, *EU Competition Law, Data Protection and Online Platforms: Data as Essential Facility* (Alphen aan den Rijn: Kluwer Law International, 2016), 418 p.

29 See https://www.ibm.com/watson.

30 See https://www.microsoft.com/en-us/ai.

31 See https://ai.google/.

32 See https://aws.amazon.com/ai/.

33 J. Anderson, 'Do AI markets create competition policy concerns?', *Bruegel*, 2020, https://www.bruegel.org/2020/01/do-ai-markets-create-competition-policy-concerns/.

34 See fn. 1; F. Beneke and M.-O. Mackenrodt, 'Remedies for algorithmic tacit collusion', *Journal of Antitrust Enforcement*, 2021, vol. 9, no. 1, p. 172.

35 Notable contributions include: A. Ezrachi and M. Stucke, 'Artificial intelligence & collusion: When computers inhibit competition', *University of Illinois Law Review*, 2017, vol. 5, p. 1778; J. Harrington, 'Developing competition law for collusion by autonomous artificial agents', *Journal of Competition Law & Economics*, 2018, vol. 14, no. 3, pp. 331–333; N. Petit, 'Antitrust and Artificial Intelligence: A Research Agenda', *Journal of European Competition Law & Practice*, 2017, vol. 8, no. 6, p. 361; F. Beneke and M.-O. Mackenrodt, 'Artificial Intelligence

body of literature, it is useful to briefly reconsider a fundamental question: '*what is AI?*'. It should come as no surprise that numerous pages have been written on the meaning of notions such as machine-learning, artificial intelligence, and algorithms. While certainly meritorious, some important intricacies of AI have been overlooked and some misunderstandings made their appearance in legal scholarship.[36] For those reasons, a careful explanation of the functioning of AI will be provided first.

Figure 1. Visualisation of the relationship between algorithms, artificial intelligence, machine learning and deep learning.

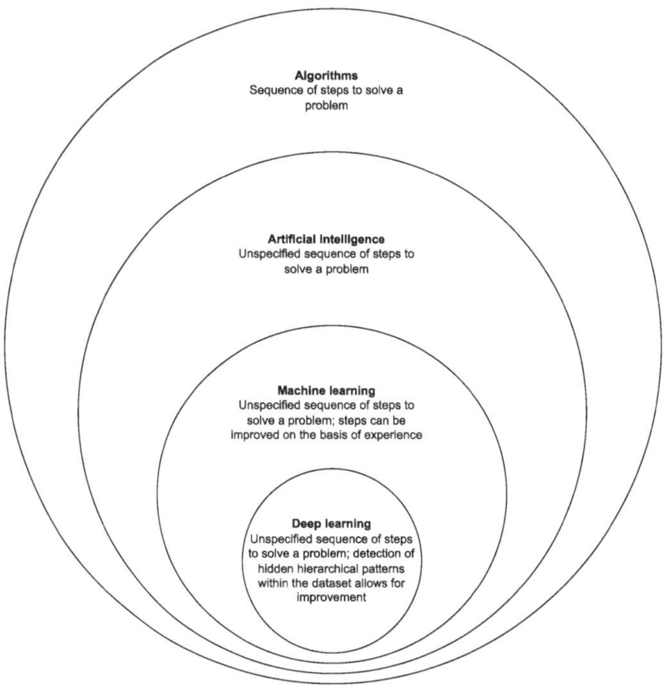

3.1.1 Algorithms

13. At the outset, it should be noted that there is nothing particularly mysterious about an algorithm. For instance – and contrary to popular belief – algorithms have nothing to do with computers.[37] In fact, algorithms have existed long before computers made their appearance on the market. At its core, an

---

and Collusion', *IIC – International Review of Intellectual Property and Competition Law*, 2019, vol. 50, pp. 110–112.

36 Also expressing this view is Petit, 'Antitrust and Artificial Intelligence: A Research Agenda', p. 361, who writes that '*AAI* [Antitrust and AI, ed.] *literature is the closest ever our field came to science-fiction*'.

37 Louridas, *Algorithms*, p. 4.

algorithm embodies nothing more than a set of clearly defined steps to solve a given problem.[38]

14. A good example of an algorithm is the methodology used to discover the greatest common divisor of two numbers, *a* and *b* (i.e., Euclid's algorithm).[39] As with other algorithms, Euclid's algorithm provides a series of sequential steps that involve specifying an input, doing basic calculations – such as additions, subtractions, divisions, and multiplications – on that input, and producing an output. It is useful to keep in mind that the outcome of one step can determine which second step to follow. Moreover, it happens that several steps are put in a *loop* and, in order to arrive at the correct output, it may be necessary to go through multiple *iterations* of that loop.

Figure 2. Visualisation of Euclid's algorithm via a flowchart diagram[40]

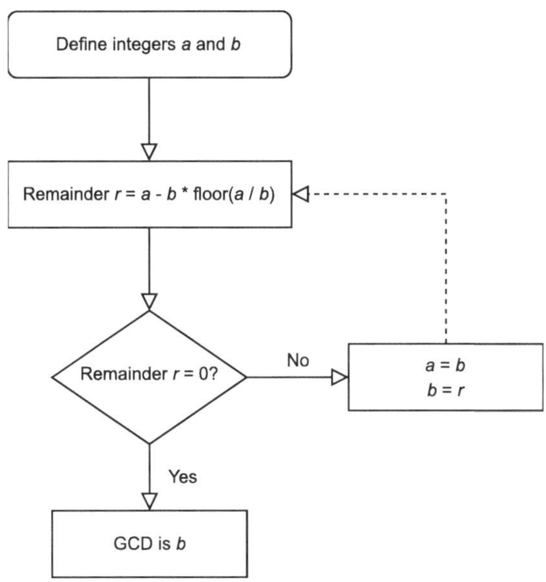

15. A crucial takeaway of any algorithm is that the steps of the algorithm can also be performed with pen and paper, thus confirming that there is nothing revolutionary about it.[41] What is novel, is that algorithms can presently be coded

---

38 See, for instance, the definition provided by Webster's Dictionary: '*a set of steps that are followed in order to solve a mathematical problem or to complete a computer process*'; T. Cormen, C. Leiserson, R. Rivest et al., *Introduction to Algorithms*, 3rd edn (Massachusetts: MIT Press, 2009), pp. 5–6.

39 A more in-depth explanation of this algorithm is provided in the Appendix (see 6.1 Euclid's algorithm).

40 Louridas, *Algorithms*, p. i.

41 Louridas, *Algorithms*, pp. 21–23.

in a computer programming language. Relying on a computer has the added benefit of parsing algorithms much quicker than any human being.[42] Yet, the steps performed by an encoded algorithm are the exact same steps as those performed using pen and paper.

3.1.2. *Artificial Intelligence*

16. According to its dictionary definition, AI is understood as '*an area of computer science that deals with giving machines the ability to seem like they have human intelligence*'.[43] Contrary to the algorithms mentioned above, the involvement of information technology is more apparent when assessing the functioning and performance of AI. The definition mentioned here seems to hint at AI's ability to somewhat act independently and to not require instructions prior to performing a computational step. However, 'seem' is an important operative word in this context. It would be inaccurate to state that AI possesses something that resembles human intelligence.[44] Conversely, it is better to hold that artificial intelligence involves algorithms of a more advanced nature; algorithms where some of the steps to be performed are not obvious at first sight. Whereas algorithms rely on a logic of ones and zeros, AI transcends this realm and introduces more complexity between one and zero.[45] Among others, it involves reasoning under uncertainty and introduces probabilistic reasoning.[46] Yet, as is the case for algorithms, the foundation of AI also hinges on taking a given input, performing a set of computational steps on that input, and producing the most optimal output that can occur within the boundaries of any predefined constraints.

3.2. UNPREDICTABILITY AND RANDOMNESS WITHIN AI SYSTEMS

3.2.1. *Unpredictable AI Systems*

17. AI is typically associated with an element of *unpredictability* or randomness. This unpredictability factor can easily materialize in very simple code snippets. Consider, for instance, the following:

---

42 Thus, significantly reducing the computing time, which is one of the core constraints governing the usefulness of contemporary algorithms: T. Cormen, *Introduction to Algorithms*, pp. 11–12.

43 X, 'Artificial intelligence', *Webster's Dictionary*, 2021, https://www.merriam-webster.com/dictionary/artificial%20intelligence.

44 W. Ertel, *Introduction to Artificial Intelligence*, 2nd edn (London: Springer International, 2017), pp. 1–3: '*The attribute* artificial *might awaken much different associations. It brings up fears of intelligent cyborgs. It recalls images from science fiction novels*'.

45 Ertel, *Introduction to Artificial Intelligence*, pp. 9–10.

46 *Ibid.*

```
import random

possibilities = [1, 2, 3, 4, 5, 6, 7, 8, 9, 10]
print(random.choice(possibilities))
```

18. The function mentioned here is tasked to pick a value from a list that includes all numbers between 1 and 10. As the code already suggests, there seems to be a degree of *randomness* attached to the selection of the number. When studying AI, some competition scholars refer to this unpredictable element of AI to argue that it is impossible to retrace the steps taken by the AI model (i.e., AI's black box).[47] The result is that literature sometimes instils an element of unpredictability on well-known algorithms or AI systems that in reality are more predictable than it may seem (for instance, due to the ability to retrace function calls or due to reverse engineering). Nonetheless, the unpredictable nature of AI is said to tie into notable competition law concerns such as different AI systems tacitly colluding with each other.[48] This triggers the question whether AI and competition law are on a collision course.

19. We are not to question the complexity of AI systems – be it because of the sheer amount of input data (i.e., big data systems) or because of the plurality in decision layers (e.g., the multitude of layers contained in random forests). However, we would like to take the opportunity to shed more light on the functioning of AI systems in order to argue that AI is, in fact, sometimes more predictable than one might think. The reality is that it is not entirely inconceivable to determine how an AI system arrives at a particular decision. Accordingly, while concerns surrounding the compatibility of AI and competition law are valid, the clash between both is occasionally exaggerated in literature.

20. We would like to support the thesis that there is no unpredictable AI, only rigidly trained AI and randomly trained AI.[49] Within this dichotomy,

---

[47] F. Beneke and M.-O. Mackenrodt, 'Artificial Intelligence and Collusion', *IIC – International Review of Intellectual Property and Competition Law*, 2019, vol. 50, no. 1, p. 129; U. Schwalbe, 'Algorithms, Machine Learning, and Collusion', *Journal of Competition Law & Economics*, 2019, vol. 14, no. 4, p. 569; this discussion also regularly surfaces in a consumer context: T. Wischmeyer, 'Artificial Intelligence and Transparency: Opening the Black Box' in T. Wischmeyer and T. Rademacher (eds.), *Regulating Artificial Intelligence* (Cham: Springer, 2020), p. 76.

[48] Ezrachi and Stucke, 'Artificial intelligence & collusion: When computers inhibit competition', p. 1783; U. Schwalbe, 'Algorithms, Machine Learning, and Collusion', p. 575; G. Zheng and H. Wu, 'Collusive algorithms as mere tools, super-tools or legal persons', *Journal of Competition Law & Economics*, 2019, vol. 15, no. 2–3, p. 124; S. Thomas, 'Harmful signals: cartel prohibition and oligopoly theory in the age of machine learning', *Journal of Competition Law & Economics*, 2019, vol. 15, no. 2–3, pp. 159–160; B. Sørensen, 'Digitalisation: An Opportunity or a Risk?', *Journal of European Competition Law & Practice*, 2018, vol. 9, no. 6, p. 349.

[49] Also expressing this view, albeit without referring to it as such, is L. Eliot, 'Antitrust and Artificial Intelligence (AAI): Antitrust Vigilance Lifecycle and AI Legal Reasoning

rigidly trained AI systems are perceived as the typical expert systems, which are completely designed by humans. Their design stage usually revolves around linking a series of '*if...then...else...*'-statements and '*try...except...*'-statements and pairing those statements with several statistical functions. A fitting example are pricing algorithms: undertakings could rely on pricing algorithms to *algorithmically collude* with their competitors and implement price-fixing agreements through computer code.[50]

On the other hand, *randomly trained AI systems* refer to systems that can identify patterns within datasets, learn and improve of their own motion, without human intervention, prior classification or labelling of the available data. Customer segmentation models, aimed at creating personal shopping experiences, are a good example of this second category. The main risk here revolves around algorithmic collusion without any human facilitation, otherwise known as *algorithmic tacit collusion*.[51]

21. The statement that there is currently no 'unpredictable' AI might stir some controversy. However, since it underpins several of the findings of this contribution, some further clarification is needed prior to resuming the legal analysis. As shown above in the code snippet[52], the perceived unpredictability is the result of a specific step in AI's code. The assignment to pick a *random* number between 1 and 10, for instance, intuitively suggests that one value is indeed *randomly* chosen out of all available options. However, from a computer scientific point of view, this is not entirely correct.

22. AI does not perform choice steps on the basis of *true* randomness. In reality, choice steps are taken by relying on so-called randomness sources, usually provided by the computer that runs the AI model.[53] These randomness sources include, for instance, the current date and time (for simple use cases, e.g., random number generators) or mathematical functions (for complex use cases, e.g., cryptography).[54] A random choice step is thus determined through means of *pseudo*-randomness[55]: AI takes certain input data, AI relies on a well-known

---

Autonomy', *ArXiv*, 2020, https://arxiv.org/abs/2012.13016, p. 2: '*the AI can either be established in a means to be directed by human hands while undertaking antitrust behaviors, plus can be ostensibly let loose via the inclusion of Machine Learning and Deep Learning to perform antitrust behaviors without a human hand at the wheel per se*'; A. Deng, 'An Antitrust Lawyer's Guide to Machine Learning', *Antitrust*, 2018, vol. 32, no. 2, p. 82.

50 Deng, 'An Antitrust Lawyer's Guide to Machine Learning', p. 82.

51 *Ibid.*

52 See above at no. 17.

53 More information on these randomness sources can be found in the reference documentation of the Python Random library: X, 'Random – Generate pseudo-random numbers', *Python*, 2021, https://docs.python.org/3/library/random.html.

54 *Ibid.*; note that the reference documentation explicitly specifies not to use the (pseudo-) random generator for security purposes.

55 *Ibid.*

randomness source, and AI outputs a pseudo-random result. The result is that even complex AI systems can yield deterministic outputs once the randomness source has been identified.

3.2.2. Random Seed Values

23. In scientific research communities, the findings of any study need to be reproducible. This implies that, when a study is repeated, the same results should be found. The same reasoning holds true for AI systems. Reliability-wise, it is good practice to pursue reproducibility when working with AI systems. To that end, AI systems have the ability to adhere to a reproducibility requirement.[56] In practice, this entails that the randomness source is predefined by the user rather than relying on the system time and date. A manually specified randomness source is called the 'seed'. A use case is provided below:

```
1 import random
2
3 possibilities = [1, 2, 3, 4, 5, 6, 7, 8, 9, 10]
4 random.seed(13)
5 print(random.choice(possibilities))
```

24. Contrary to the example in no. 17, the code snippet here will consistently yield the same number. Technically speaking however, this number is still chosen in a random manner. However, by specifying the seed value in line 4, it is possible to ensure that the code snippet always uses the same randomness, therefore leading to reproducibility.

3.2.3. Choice Layers, Iterations and Input Value Combinations

25. When using large datasets, it is highly plausible that several choice steps need to occur within the training stage of the AI system. An optimisation AI affords us a good example of this phenomenon and its implications.

Suppose we have the following array of numbers: [1, 2, 3, 4, 5]. Imagine if we now were to task AI to consecutively pick two (unique) numbers and to optimise the sum of these two numbers to approach the value 10. In the first step, the system must choose (pseudo-)randomly between 1 and 5. Assume that the firstchoice step yields the number 2. During the secondchoice step, the system needs to pick from the remaining numbers [1, 3, 4, 5]. This is illustrated below:

---

[56] *Ibid.*: *'Sometimes it is useful to be able to reproduce the sequences given by a pseudo-random number generator. By re-using a seed value, the same sequence should be reproducible from run to run [...]'.*

Figure 3. Overview of two sequential random choice steps

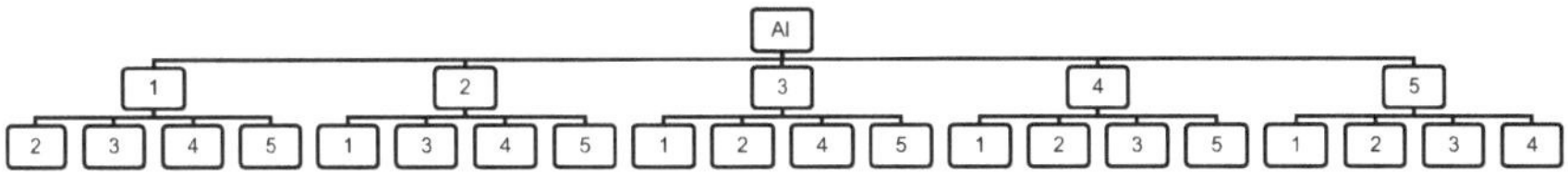

26. A first iteration of the program could result in the combination 2 + 4 = 6. This outcome corresponds to an error value of 10 – 6 = 4. If we were to run the program for a second iteration, it could pick 4 + 3 = 7 and yield an error value of 10 – 7 = 3. It now becomes obvious that this particular system has two layers of choice steps. In order to have a fully trained AI model, which can optimise for the value 10, many iterations through these two layers will be necessary. If the number of iterations is high enough, the optimised output will either be 4 + 5 or 5 + 4. Both combinations have the lowest possible error value of 10 – 9 = 1.

27. The explanation from the previous paragraph describes how any AI model works: optimisation occurs by continuously looping through the different options within the various choice steps until the returned error value is as small as possible. If we apply this reasoning to the abovementioned *rigidly trained AI systems*[57], the choice steps are explicitly integrated in the programme's code. The implication thereof is that the outcome will always squarely fall within the possibilities the programmer had anticipated. For instance, an AI model could produce a signal indicating that an undertaking should lower its product prices after having assessed the price levels of competing firms.

Matters are a bit more complicated for *randomly trained AI systems*[58] since the choice steps are not pre-programmed. Although this gives the appearance of randomness, there are only a finite amount of input variable combinations the AI model can turn into choice steps. It will most certainly require effort to determine where the output value will land, and which parameters will have contributed the most to this output. Nonetheless, this is not an absolute impossibility.

An added detail here is the ability of more complex AI systems to improve and learn from experience. When applied, this could be reflected in the AI model no longer choosing number 1 during any of the choice steps after several iterations because, after a while, the model has 'figured out' that picking number 1 consistently yields larger error values when compared to selecting any of the other four numbers.

---

57 See above at no. 20.

58 See above at no. 20.

3.2.4. About Pebbles and Bouncy Balls

28. If we resort to a metaphorical approach, rigidly trained AI systems can best be compared to *pebbles*: once a pebble is dropped, it will remain still once it has touched the ground. Randomly trained AI systems rather fit the description of *bouncy balls*: once a bouncy ball is dropped, it will keep bouncing around for a while before eventually remaining still on the ground. In both types of AI systems, the area wherein the dropped pebble or bouncy ball can eventually be found, is demarcated.

This is obvious for pebble systems as they can, by definition, not make any decision the creator has not planned for. At the same time, this also holds true for bouncy systems, given that these systems are also leveraging the know-how of its creator. The difference is that for bouncy systems, the creator's relevant know-how does not cover all possible input value combinations, whereas this is the case for pebble systems.

29. In the example from no. 25, where we optimised the sum of two integers to approach 10, it is not useful to know all possible combinations the AI system can make in an attempt to produce the output value with the lowest error. It is only required to have prior knowledge of the possible inputs and to understand the basic principles of the field. Even if 'all possible inputs' includes an enormous number of irrelevant parameters and AI must find the gold nuggets – which is exactly how big data algorithms work – these general principles will apply.

30. Throughout the remainder of this chapter, it is useful to keep in mind that humans can scrutinise the input values AI might use and evaluate how the basic principles of AI take effect. Once choice steps can be identified, it also becomes possible to make projections and estimations about the model's functioning. Understandably, it will take valuable time to fully grasp the intricacies of real-world AI models; time which may need to be committed elsewhere. Nevertheless, recent decisions taken by the European Commission (EC) and judgments rendered by the Court of Justice (CJEU) indicate that technical discussions occasionally come to the forefront as well.[59]

Building further on this, it is a worthwhile effort for undertakings and competition authorities alike to reflect on the functioning of AI models when necessary, in an effort to get a better understanding of what AI does and what it does not do. As shown, seemingly unpredictable outcomes should not be a genuine factor that discourages these efforts. Although an AI model's complexity

[59] See, for instance, Commission Decision of 3 September 2014, Case AT.39574, *Smart Card Chips* and the ensuing discussions during the appellate proceedings on whether SIM card chips and non-SIM card chips are part of the same market in CJEU 15 December 2016, no. T-758/14, ECLI:EU:T:2016:737, *Infineon Technologies v Commission*.

is an important factor as well, it should be borne in mind that it is always possible to uncover the model's functioning, sometimes by literally (re)tracing the model's underlying function calls.

3.3. IMPLICATIONS OF DECISION-MAKING BY AI FOR COMPETITION LAW

3.3.1. How AI Changes Commercial Decision-Making

31. The chapter now turns to the reasons why AI has become such an important tool in steering a firm's commercial decision-making on the market. What algorithmic *loops* and *iterations* are doing, is testing all possible combinations of input variables until the best – or near best – decision is found. The goal of this decision could be anything, ranging from a marketing firm looking to devise a slogan that will attract the most attention (by applying regression models to the performance metrics acquired from previous slogans) to a law boutique attempting to identify the relevant legislation needed to best advise their clients (by resorting to text mining and building a classification tree). In essence, if tasks are of a repetitive nature and if output values can be captured in predeterminable options, it is plausible that those tasks can be fully automated.

32. The topic of the automation and the future of commerce has been repeatedly covered in both scholarly[60] and popular[61] literature. The competition law implications of automation have not been overlooked either.[62] While firms have used algorithms in the past and will continue to do so in the future, it is especially the sheer amount of computing power available to undertakings which regularly thrusts AI into the limelight nowadays. The increased computational capabilities in a commercial context tie into lower entry barriers to work with algorithms and AI systems.[63] When considering the relevant AI legal scholarship on the topic, the focus lies, on the one hand, on plausible risks[64] created by contemporary AI systems and, on the other hand, on potential or

---

60 E.g., W. Wang and K. Siau, 'Artificial Intelligence, Machine Learning, Automation, Robotics, Future of Work and Future of Humanity: A Review and Research Agenda', *Journal of Database Management*, 2019, vol. 30, no. 1, pp. 61–79; J. Wajcman, 'Automation: is it really different this time?', *British Journal of Sociology*, 2017, vol. 68, no. 1, pp. 119–127.

61 E.g., X. 'Free exchange: It's a bot time', *The Economist*, 2021, vol. 438, no. 9228, p. 70.

62 Ezrachi and Stucke, 'Artificial intelligence & collusion: When computers inhibit competition', p. 1778; Eliot, 'Antitrust and Artificial Intelligence (AAI): Antitrust Vigilance Lifecycle and AI Legal Reasoning Autonomy', pp. 6–8.

63 See above at no. 10.

64 A. Ezrachi and M. Stucke, *Virtual Competition: The Promise and Perils of the Algorithm-Driven Economy* (Cumberland: Harvard University Press, 2016), pp. 35–36.

theoretical risks[65] created by AI systems that are on the horizon.[66] The literature is unanimous in at least one respect though: algorithmic competition is on the rise. And with algorithmic competition comes the risk of impeding effective competition.

3.3.2. *Article 101 TFEU and the Risk of Concerted Practices via AI*

33. It is accepted knowledge that cartelisation is harmful to the market. Cartel agreements or concerted practices between undertakings are known for generating strong anticompetitive effects, such as increasing prices above competitive levels and decreasing production volumes. In these instances, consumers are confronted with a situation where they either have to choose not to purchase a particular product or to pay an above-market price for that product. As a result, cartelised products have the effect of transferring wealth from the hands of the consumer into the hands of the cartel members. Additionally, entering into cartel agreements also shields the individual cartel members from the competitive pressure of the market, which under normal circumstances would incite these undertakings to keep innovating to remain effective. For those reasons, cartelisation – whether tacit or not – is caught under Article 101 TFEU.[67]

A. Algorithmic (Tacit) Collusion

34. Many cartel agreements concern either price fixing arrangements or output restrictions between direct (horizontal) competitors active in the same market. Given that the price is an essential element of any product, it should come as no surprise that pricing algorithms and production planning algorithms are well integrated in (online) markets and that they have also been the subject of scholarly research in the past.[68] The underlying principle of these algorithms is that a firm should take both their own production costs and their competitors' prices into consideration when setting a price.[69] When the relevant

---

65 Beneke and Mackenrodt, 'Remedies for algorithmic tacit collusion', p. 155; A. von Bonin and S. Malhi, 'The Use of Artificial Intelligence in the Future of Competition Law Enforcement', *Journal of European Competition Law & Practice*, 2020, vol. 11, no. 8, p. 469.

66 Beneke and Mackenrodt, 'Artificial Intelligence and Collusion', p. 125 capture this discussion quite well under the heading '*What, if Anything, Changes with AI?*'.

67 See the references above at fn. 9.

68 E. Calvano et al., 'Artificial Intelligence, Algorithmic Pricing, and Collusion', *American Economic Review*, 2020, vol. 110, no. 10, p. 3268; Schwalbe, 'Algorithms, Machine Learning, and Collusion', p. 568; Harrington, 'Developing competition law for collusion by autonomous artificial agents', p. 331; Ezrachi and Stucke, 'Artificial intelligence & collusion: When computers inhibit competition', p. 1777; Beneke and Mackenrodt, 'Remedies for algorithmic tacit collusion', p. 164.

69 G. Delporte, *Pricing algorithms in EU competition law* (Apeldoorn: Maklu Publishers, 2019), p. 19, para. 21.

inputs are determinable (e.g., what are the prices of my competitor's products?) and the output is a single number (e.g., what would be my optimal price?), these calculations can be performed by means of computer code.[70]

35. Amazon affords us a rather amusing example of pricing algorithms.[71] In 2011, a researcher at UC Berkeley was looking to purchase an academic textbook. Great was his astonishment when discovering that new copies of the textbook were listed at prices starting from $1,730,045.91 (+ $3.99 shipping), whereas used copies would cost only $35.54. A brief investigation soon followed, which revealed that two vendors of new textbook copies relied on algorithmic pricing.[72] Each day, vendor X would automatically adjust the book's price by a factor 0.9983 on the basis of the price charged by vendor Y. At the same time, vendor Y would also alter its price on a daily basis with a factor 1.270589 by looking at the price charged by vendor X. This pattern continued for some time, with outrageous prices as a result.

36. In competition law literature, the use of pricing algorithms has mostly been studied under Article 101 TFEU.[73] Notable literature on this topic includes the seminal work titled '*Virtual Competition*' by EZRACHI and STUCKE.[74] The book covers several thought-provoking topics such as collusion and behavioural discrimination. One of their main theses revolves around algorithmic tacit collusion, a phenomenon where the interactions between algorithms owned by different competitors will likely generate anticompetitive effects without the need for an explicit cartel agreement.[75] According to the authors, such instances are likely to occur in concentrated markets that are typified by fairly homogenous products (e.g., fruits, chemicals, or metals).[76] These characteristics prove ideal for algorithms to monitor changes in the market and adjust product prices accordingly once deviations (e.g., discounts) are detected.

---

70 A. Capobianco, Algorithms and Collusion – Note from the European Union', *OECD*, 2017, https://one.oecd.org/document/DAF/COMP/WD(2017)12/en/pdf, p. 3, para. 9: '*[O]nline prices are highly transparent. Monitoring can be done at short time intervals and at a low cost. Firms can use software to automatically monitor competitors' prices almost in real time, and adapt prices (or "reprice") accordingly*'.

71 M. Eisen, 'Amazon's $23,698,655.93 book about flies', *Michael Eisen*, 2011, https://www.michaeleisen.org/blog/?p=358; Ezrachi and Stucke, *Virtual Competition: The Promise and Perils of the Algorithm-Driven Economy*, p. 13.

72 *Ibid.*

73 See the references above at fn. 67.

74 A. Ezrachi and M. Stucke, *Virtual Competition: The Promise and Perils of the Algorithm-Driven Economy* (Cumberland: Harvard University Press, 2016), 365 p.

75 *Ibid.*, p. 56 ff.

76 *Ibid.*, p. 60; A. Ezrachi and M. Stucke, 'Algorithmic Collusion: Problems and Counter-Measures', *OECD*, 2017, https://www.oecd.org/officialdocuments/publicdisplaydocumentpdf/?cote=DAF/COMP/WD%282017%2925&docLanguage=En, p. 3, para. 8.

37. Combining views from the available literature suggests that at least three scenarios pertaining to algorithmic collusion are worth reflecting upon[77]:

a. *AI to facilitate explicit coordination.* A first scenario, which clearly falls within the ambit of Article 101 TFEU, is the use of algorithms to explicitly facilitate cartelisation. At the time of writing, several notable decisions are available on this topic. In both *CMA v. Trod and GBE*[78] and *US v. Topkins*[79], conspirator-undertakings agreed to design and adopt price-fixing algorithms with the specific intention to fix, increase, maintain, and stabilise prices, respectively in the market for sports and entertainment merchandise and in the market for posters and wall decoration. In 2018, the EC also fined four consumer electronics manufacturers for engaging in resale price maintenance (RPM) through means of price monitoring and price adjustment software.[80] Retailers that were found to be selling products below a certain price level, were explicitly asked by manufacturers to increase their prices.
b. *AI as a hub-and-spoke arrangement.* A second scenario involves instances where price recommendations or price setting happens through means of an AI system controlled by an intermediary party.[81] Bringing a third-party into the equation may facilitate a hub-and-spoke arrangement that eventually results in above-market prices. Situations susceptible to such AI-based hub-and-spoke dynamics may, for instance, implicate sellers that rely on automatic pricing tools offered by websites such as Amazon, eBay, Uber or Airbnb.[82] Anno 2023, the usage of AI in a hub-and-spoke setting has received some coverage by national competition authorities, but there is presently no case law available on this topic.[83]

---

77 Competition & Markets Authority, 'Algorithms: How they can reduce competition and harm consumers', *CMA*, 2021, https://www.gov.uk/government/publications/algorithms-how-they-can-reduce-competition-and-harm-consumers/algorithms-how-they-can-reduce-competition-and-harm-consumers.

78 CMA 12 August 2016, Case no. 50223, *CMA v. Trod and GBE.*

79 US District Court ND California 21 October 2015, no. CR 15-00201 WHO, *US v. Topkins*; see also S. Mehra, 'US v. Topkins: can price fixing be based on algorithms?', *Journal of European Competition Law & Practice*, 2016, vol. 7, no. 7, p. 471.

80 Commission Decision 24 July 2018, Case AT.40465, *Asus*, para. 27; Commission Decision 24 July 2018, Case AT.40469, *Denon & Marantz*, para. 95; Commission Decision 24 July 2018, Case AT.40181, *Philips*, para 64; Commission Decision 24 July 2018, Case AT.40182, *Pioneer*, paras. 136 and 155.

81 Ezrachi and Stucke, *Virtual Competition*, p. 47; Competition & Markets Authority, 'Pricing algorithms', *CMA*, 2018, https://assets.publishing.service.gov.uk/government/uploads/system/uploads/attachment_data/file/746353/Algorithms_econ_report.pdf, pp. 26–27.

82 Competition & Markets Authority, 'Algorithms: How they can reduce competition and harm consumers', *CMA*, 2021, https://www.gov.uk/government/publications/algorithms-how-they-can-reduce-competition-and-harm-consumers/algorithms-how-they-can-reduce-competition-and-harm-consumers.

83 S. Li, C. Chunying Xie and E. Feyler, 'Algorithms & Antitrust: an overview of EU and national case law', *Concurrences Antitrust Publications & Events*, 2021, https://www.concurrences.

c. *AI to facilitate tacit collusion.* A third and final scenario concerns complex algorithms that can learn and improve on their own and that may engage in autonomous tacit collusion.[84] Stated otherwise, in theory, when using advanced AI models, collusion can occur without explicit communication between undertakings or collusive intentions by their human AI designers. While theories on algorithmic tacit collusion have contributed to an extensive body of literature, it must be noted that no cases involving AI and tacit collusion have been brought yet.

38. The categorisation of algorithmic collusion in three different types offers a refreshing perspective. While scenarios involving explicit coordination and hub-and-spoke dynamics are plausible, literature seems divided as to whether the third type of algorithmic collusion – tacitly colluding price algorithms – is purely theoretical or not.[85] It is accepted that if competitors have fairly homogenous products, then competitors' prices will be more transparent to all market participants and collusion is more likely to occur.[86] However, some scholars argue that this type of 'accidental' collusion – by means of using similar software or similar software settings – does not fall under the cartel prohibition.[87] Another strand of literature refers to the lack of empirical evidence in support of the algorithmic tacit collusion rationale, the rather reductive assumptions about market conditions, or the simplified understanding of price algorithms' operational environment.[88]

39. According to the authors, assessing tacitly colluding algorithms under Article 101 TFEU poses serious challenges. On the one hand, if algorithms respond to each other's (public) signals, there is an argument to be made that

com/en/bulletin/special-issues/algorithms-antitrust-en/general-antitrust-3924/algorithms-antitrust-an-overview-of-eu-and-national-case-law.

84 Ezrachi and Stucke, *Virtual Competition*, p. 56.

85 T. McSweeny, 'Algorithms and Coordinated Effects', *University of Oxford Center for Competition Law and Policy*, 2017, https://www.ftc.gov/system/files/documents/public_statements/1220673/mcsweeny_-_oxford_cclp_remarks_-_algorithms_and_coordinated_effects_5-22-17.pdf, p. 3; G. Delporte, *Pricing algorithms in EU competition law*, p. 37, para. 53; Competition & Markets Authority, 'Algorithms: How they can reduce competition and harm consumers', *CMA*, 2021, https://www.gov.uk/government/publications/algorithms-how-they-can-reduce-competition-and-harm-consumers/algorithms-how-they-can-reduce-competition-and-harm-consumers.

86 Germany's Monopolies Commission, 'Algorithms and collusion', *Monopolkommission*, 2018, https://www.monopolkommission.de/images/HG22/Main_Report_XXII_Algorithms_and_Collusion.pdf, pp. 6–7, paras. 179–181.

87 Schwalbe, 'Algorithms, Machine Learning, and Collusion', p. 597; Beneke and Mackenrodt, 'Remedies for algorithmic tacit collusion', p. 153.

88 A. Deng, 'When Machines Learn to Collude: Lessons from a Recent Research Study on Artificial Intelligence', *SSRN Scholarly Papers*, 2017, https://papers.ssrn.com/sol3/papers.cfm?abstract_id=3029662, p. 1 and pp. 4–5.

tacitly concerted practices are – or could be – happening. This is especially true when algorithms use similar inputs or share commercially sensitive information.

On the other hand, it must be recalled that a high standard of proof applies to the finding of a concerted practice.[89] A close reading of the relevant CJEU case law indicates that a concerted practice involves an element of coordination between undertakings, which cannot be attributable to an agreement or decision, but which is nevertheless caught under Article 101 TFEU.[90] *Dyestuffs*[91] and *Suiker Unie*[92] suggest that the legal test for the finding of a concerted practice revolves around a mental consensus between undertakings – through either direct or indirect contact – where competition is knowingly substituted by cooperation.[93]

40. Especially the criteria of 'mental consensus' and 'knowingly substituting competition' create a significant hurdle for the qualification of AI-driven conduct as a concerted practice. While it may be possible to predict which commercial strategy market rivals might pursue and while these same market rivals may also accurately predict your commercial strategy, the doctrine on *intelligent adaptation*[94] from *Suiker Unie* could offer a valid argument against such qualification: in principle, firms are entitled to intelligently adapt their market strategy to the conduct of their competitors.[95]

For pricing algorithms in particular, the core argument holds that firms signal their intentions via openly communicated prices, which AI models can subsequently pick up. For the most part, these data ripples are created

---

89 M. Gassler, *Information Exchange Between Competitors in EU Competition Law* (Alphen aan den Rijn: Kluwer Law International, 2021), p. 127.

90 CJEU 14 July 1972, no. C-48/69, ECLI:EU:C:1972:70, *ICI v Commission (Dyestuffs)*; CJEU 16 December 1975, no. C-40/73 etc., ECLI:EU:C:1975:174, *Suiker Unie v Commission (Sugar Cartel)*.

91 CJEU 14 July 1972, no. C-48/69, ECLI:EU:C:1972:70, *ICI v Commission (Dyestuffs)*, para. 66: '*[Article 101 TFEU] draws a distinction between the concept of "concerted practices" and that of "agreements between undertakings" or of "decisions by associations of undertakings"; the object is to bring within the prohibition of that article a form of coordination between undertakings which, without having reached the stage where an agreement properly so-called has been concluded, knowingly substitutes practical cooperation between them for the risks of competition*'.

92 CJEU 16 December 1975, no. C-40/73 etc., ECLI:EU:C:1975:174, *Suiker Unie v Commission (Sugar Cartel)*, para. 174: '*[The] requirement of independence does not deprive economic operators of the right to adapt themselves intelligently to the existing and anticipated conduct of their competitors, it does however strictly preclude any direct or indirect contact between such operators, the object or effect whereof is either to influence the conduct on the market of an actual or potential competitor or to disclose to such a competitor the course of conduct which they themselves have decided to adopt or contemplate adopting on the market*'.

93 Whish and Bailey, *Competition Law*, p. 118.

94 CJEU 16 December 1975, no. C-40/73 etc., ECLI:EU:C:1975:174, *Suiker Unie v Commission (Sugar Cartel)*, para. 174.

95 OECD, 'Unilateral disclosure of information with anticompetitive effects', *OECD Working Paper DAF/COMP/WP3(2012)1*, 2012, p. 18.

unintentionally in the normal course of business. For the AI model, acting on the basis of these signals is sufficient to create a mutual understanding between competitors. Further to this, in line with the wording of the Guidelines on Horizontal Cooperation Agreements, such conduct also has strong potential to 'reduce strategic uncertainty' in the market, which is a key element in the assessment of a concerted practice.[96] However, for the company executives, it could be the case that no mental consensus was reached nor that an intentional substitution of competition took place. Therefore, if strictly adhered to the current case law principles, the technological capabilities of AI suggest that algorithmic tacit collusion can occur, but that such conduct may escape the ambit of Article 101 TFEU due to a lack of mental consensus among competitors.

41. Another point of interest also deserves attention, namely the fact that, for concentrated industries in specific, several other conditions must be met in order to prove a concerted practice.[97] These conditions tie into the *oligopoly defence*[98]: in concentrated markets, the theory of oligopolistic interdependence asserts that a certain degree of parallel conduct between competitors is to be expected, given that the possession of extensive market power naturally incites competitor-firms to match each other's conduct.[99] Hence, pursuant to *Airtours*[100], competition authorities can only qualify conduct as tacit coordination when three conditions are met[101]:

(i) Transparency: 'each member of the dominant oligopoly must have the ability to know how the other members are behaving in order to monitor whether or not they are adopting the common policy'.[102]
(ii) Sustainability: 'there must be an incentive not to depart from the common policy on the market'.[103]
(iii) Absence of competitive restraints: 'the foreseeable reaction of current and future competitors, as well as of consumers, would not jeopardise the results expected from the common policy'.[104]

---

96 Communication from the Commission – Guidelines on the applicability of Article 101 of the Treaty on the Functioning of the European Union to horizontal co-operation agreements [2011] OJ C 11/1, paras. 60–63.

97 C. Veljanovski, 'Algorithmic Antitrust: A Critical Overview' in A. Portuese (ed.), *Algorithmic Antitrust* (Cham: Springer, 2022), p. 56.

98 N. Petit, 'The oligopoly problem in EU competition law' in I. Lianos and D. Geradin (eds.), *Handbook on European Competition Law. Substantive Aspects* (Cheltenham: Edward Elgar Publishing, 2013), pp. 289–290.

99 M. Gassler, *Information Exchange Between Competitors in EU Competition Law*, p. 127; R. Posner, *Antitrust Law* (Chicago: University of Chicago Press, 2001), pp. 55–56.

100 CJEU 6 June 2002, no. T-342/99, ECLI:EU:T:2002:146, *Airtours*.

101 Whish and Bailey, *Competition Law*, p. 598.

102 CJEU 6 June 2002, no. T-342/99, ECLI:EU:T:2002:146, *Airtours*, para. 62.

103 *Ibid.*

104 *Ibid.*

As a result, while it is true that AI systems could dispense with human interactions between competitors, it must be prevented that concerted practices become conflated with objective business decisions and conscious parallelism.[105] Consequently, tacit oligopolistic collusion hinges on a set of specific structural and behavioural market conditions.[106] In an oligopolistic setting, the threat of algorithmic tacit collusion must therefore not only consider the technical challenges surrounding the assessment of self-learning and autonomously coordinating algorithms, but also the market-specific circumstances.

42. On balance, it is difficult to make definitive statements on how to handle complex AI models from a competition law point of view. In theory, algorithmic tacit collusion could circumvent Article 101 TFEU given the absence of direct contact or a meeting of minds among competitors. Furthermore, undertakings could invoke the oligopoly defence and plausibly argue that parallel conduct is a natural occurrence when markets are relatively concentrated.

At first sight, this suggests that a gap in the EU rules on cartels exists and that AI systems may provide entrepreneurs with an opportunity to obscure anticompetitive conduct behind the opaqueness of their algorithmic models. Yet, it could also be argued that EU competition law is flexible enough to deal with these instances. As recalled, the conditions apropos mental consensus and the threefold test originating from *Airtours* are not enshrined in the Treaty. Consequently, nothing prevents Europe's highest court from overturning or refining existing case law when the need to do so arises.

Moreover, it must be emphasised again that there is no clear empirical evidence to corroborate the phenomenon of algorithmic tacit collusion. While some computer simulations indicate that tacit collusion between AI systems is theoretically possible[107], real world evidence is lacking.[108] Nonetheless, this does not detract from the fact that the use of complex AI models triggers interesting questions for competition enforcement authorities and that further research into suitable remedies is recommended.

---

105 N. Petit, 'The oligopoly problem in EU competition law', p. 290.

106 C. Veljanovski, 'Algorithmic Antitrust: A Critical Overview', p. 56.

107 T. Klein, 'Autonomous algorithmic collusion: Q-learning under sequential pricing', *The RAND Journal of Economics*, 2021, p. 540: *'[The] main finding is that when the number of discrete prices is limited, competing Q-learning algorithms indeed often coordinate on collusive equilibria. The intuition behind this outcome is that Q-learning first learns the short-run benefit of slightly undercutting its competitor, but then also learns through experimentation the longer-run benefit of "resetting" this gradual price decline with a large price increase once prices become low'*; E. Calvano et al. 'Artificial Intelligence, algorithmic pricing and collusion', *SSRN Scholarly Papers*, 2019, https://papers.ssrn.com/sol3/papers.cfm?abstract_id=3304991, p. 3: *'The results indicate that, indeed, relatively simple pricing algorithms systematically learn to play collusive strategies. The algorithms typically coordinate on prices that are somewhat below the monopoly level but substantially above the static Bertrand equilibrium'*.

108 C. Veljanovski, 'Algorithmic Antitrust: A Critical Overview', p. 55.

B. Removing Information Asymmetries via AI

43. A topic that has received less attention is AI's ability to remove any information asymmetry between firms, not just pricing. Literature suggests that cartels, by definition, are unstable given that each individual cartelist has an incentive to cheat on the other firms involved in the cartel.[109] These dynamics are often compared to a prisoner's dilemma, where all firms eventually end up trying to deceive each other.[110] Yet, this principle only holds true when the individual participants are unaware of each other's moves. This could also provide an explanation as to why cartel decisions often refer to the exchange of commercially sensitive information to corroborate the existence of a cartel.

44. From a cartelist's point of view, managers will likely remain reluctant to commit to a cartel without the exchange of sensitive documents. The effects thereof are twofold. On the one hand, by mutually exchanging sensitive information between cartelists, one firm gains leverage over the other and vice versa, thus generating deterrence effects that somewhat resemble the threat of mutually assured destruction. On the other hand, the exchange of documents takes away any information asymmetry and facilitates the preservation of the cartel.

A similar conclusion can be drawn from an enforcement angle. The EC mostly refers to specific emails[111], employee schedules[112], or internal memos[113] when looking to find and subsequently dismantle cartels. Based on this reasoning – and without having experience running a cartel – we are willing to speculate that these documents are inculpatory precisely because they are aimed at removing information asymmetries around the cartelised object or because they serve to verify or uphold the intentions of the other cartelists.

45. These observations tie into two crucial findings. Firstly, if there are no information gaps between firms – be it vis-à-vis price, quantity, research, or firm expansions – there is no longer a need to 'create evidence' of the cartel by means of exchanging inculpatory documents. Secondly, if there is no need to exchange sensitive information, it also follows that there is no need to check the good faith behaviour of the other cartelists (within the cartel, that is). On balance,

---

109 Ezrachi and Stucke, *Virtual Competition*, p. 35; M. Levenstein and V. Suslow, 'What Determines Cartel Success?', *Journal of Economic Literature*, 2006, vol. 44, no. 1, p. 44.

110 Schwalbe, 'Algorithms, Machine Learning, and Collusion', p. 581; Beneke and Mackenrodt, 'Artificial Intelligence and Collusion', pp. 114–117; A. Deng, 'When Machines Learn to Collude: Lessons from a Recent Research Study on Artificial Intelligence', *SSRN Scholarly Papers*, 2017, https://papers.ssrn.com/sol3/papers.cfm?abstract_id=3029662, p. 3.

111 CJEU 9 September 2019, no. T-84/13, ECLI:EU:T:2015:611, *Samsung SDI and Others v Commission*, para. 69.

112 CJEU 3 September 2009, nos. C-332/07 P, C-327/07 and C-338/07 P, ECLI:EU:C:2009:500, *Papierfabrik August Koehler and Others v Commission*, para. 62.

113 CJEU 16 June 2011, no. T-240/07, ECLI:EU:T:2011:284, *Heineken Nederland and Heineken v Commission*, para. 119.

by removing information asymmetries, AI can facilitate cartelisation without leaving any trace – or at least by making evidence of cartelisation scarce. In turn, this could considerably complicate competition authorities' objective to dislodge cartels.

46. It is worthwhile to consider the overall picture at this point. Firms generate *ripples of information*, which can be picked up by AI systems, regardless of whether these firms have a desire to do so or not. At the extreme, it is conceivable that AI systems can uncover enough ripples – both obvious and non-obvious ones – to allow a firm to find out what its competitor is doing. In other words, the more complex AI systems become, the more difficult it will be to keep information asymmetries in place to facilitate effective competition. As such, complex AI systems provide a means to tacitly collude in a way not thought possible at the time of the drafting of Article 101 TFEU.

47. The configuration and performance of an AI model hinges on two factors: feeding it all possible options for a choice step and providing it with a definition of success. When these prerequisites are met, AI will eventually be able to anticipate some future ripples as well. In high-performance AI models, at least some predictions are likely to classify as 'statistically significant', suggesting that predicted ripples will correspond to the real-world ripples with a certain degree of certainty.[114] Whereas descriptive analytics (i.e., what has happened in the past?) are oftentimes said to belong to the realm of pure statistics, AI goes one step further by facilitating predictive analytics (i.e., what will happen in the future?) and prescriptive analytics (i.e., how to affect future outcomes?).

48. It is not far-fetched to say that competitor firms will also rely on the same – or at least similar – algorithms to determine their best course of action. Thus, a firm's competitors will also attempt to move towards its optimal production configuration and make estimations about other market actors' optimal performance levels. Therefore, in homogenous markets where players possess similar know-how and have a similar understanding of the technical possibilities and limitations of a production process, each individual firm can deduce what competitor firms might do in terms of their behaviour on the market.

C. Exploring the Market for Grenadine – A Code Example

49. It is useful to consider a specific code example to illustrate how these findings play out in real-life and to touch on some of the inner workings of AI systems. These findings also serve the purpose of confirming that the removal of

---

114 The 'error' or 'definition of success' can be anything; it does not need to be a numerical value, but can also be the occurrence of certain facts (e.g., the registration of IP).

information asymmetries via AI is no longer science fiction. Readers can find the annotated pseudo-code of our example in the Appendix.[115]

50. A first step in designing an AI system is establishing what the algorithm should yield as an outcome. For instance, a CEO might be wondering 'will my competitor lower its product prices?', 'has my competitor access to technology that I am unaware of?' or 'is my competitor going to change production methods?'.

A second step revolves around the identification of the events or instances that can or need to happen to trigger a change in competitors' conduct. Especially this second step illustrates that prior, intimate knowledge of the field is crucial for the proper functioning of the AI model.[116] For instance, the second step can be implemented more accurately when the CEO is familiar with the different aspects of the production chain, has an in-depth understanding of the tools and machinery, and has the ability to identify where interruptions in the production process could occur.

51. Detail is important in computer models, which is why the example needs to be more specific as well. For this illustration, we will explore the market for grenadine by tailoring the AI model to a grenadine production corporation. Our AI model, while containing some simplified functions, is fully capable of answering the CEO's three questions from the previous paragraph. However, the reader should keep several limitations of the model in mind. Firstly, the model assumes that the CEO is running his grenadine making operation in a limited market, as applying the model to open market conditions would require several significant modifications. Secondly, the AI model only assesses price competition against what the current ideal price could be, considering the currently available know-how and desired profit targets. Thirdly, all things considered, the model remains a model, which means that the control variable 'price' remains a simplification when compared to a real-world price for grenadine.

52. The AI system calculates the best possible price given a structured array of options (pertaining, for instance, to the production steps or raw inputs).[117] Immediately, the question 'does my competitor know something I don't' can be answered:

a. When the competitor's price is lower than the optimal grenadine price calculated by the AI system, it follows that the competitor knows something the CEO doesn't. More concretely, this ties into situations where, for instance, the competitor has access to cheaper production inputs or where he relies on a more efficient production process. After all, the CEO provided all

[115] See below at no. 93.
[116] In no. 29, we referred to these informational aspects as 'the basic principles of the field'.
[117] See the code example in the Appendix.

information to the model what he thought possible for his competitor as well as the know-how pertaining to his own production process.

b. When the prices set by the competitor lie far below what the model considers possible – while taking a reasonable margin of error into account –, the only possible conclusion is that the competitor is (anticompetitively) selling at a loss.

While the grenadine market model is certainly not free from criticism, especially given the need to simplify, the general principle remains. An AI system can determine optimal configurations for any system when provided with a range of possibilities for each choice step.

53. To reiterate: building a fully functioning model calls for a preliminary stage where information pertaining to the CEO's production facilities, the production facilities of his competitors, and the overall market are aggregated and fed into the model:

a. Data on the functioning and throughput of the CEO's own production plant will usually be readily available, for instance via bookkeeping records.
b. Details relating to the production facilities, system configurations, and product characteristics of competing firms will be difficult, but not impossible, to come by. Certain facts and figures can be found online. Along these lines, one could think of quarterly earnings reports, financial statements, the location of factories, product measurements, and the number of employees. For other elements, attempts could be made to reverse engineer (parts of) competitors' choice steps or to work with estimates in combination with margins of error.
c. Information related to the grenadine market itself – such as the total addressable market and market penetration levels – can be estimated fairly well on the basis of market research and sales intelligence.

By analysing these (often) publicly available *ripples of information*, the AI system can verify whether a competitor is already operating at an optimal level, or whether he is likely to improve in the near future, relative to the CEO's own operating performance.

54. While some readers may rightfully remain wary or sceptical of these systems, the methodology of finding patterns in big data sets is tried and tested.[118] Big data algorithms have already proven their effectiveness in categorising people and predicting their product preferences, and similar

[118] As discussed in M. Broussard, *Artificial unintelligence: How computers misunderstand the world* (Cambridge: MIT Press, 2018), 248 p.; C. O'Neil, *Weapons of Math Destruction: How*

developments are now occurring on the business side of the market as well. To some extent, for instance, a part of a firm's know-how and history can be retraced by simply looking at its decision track record. These public ripples often provide a first step in creating an AI system.

55. Depending on the needs and wants of a particular firm, data scientists might forego some of the more arduous steps in creating a tailor-made AI model. This is especially the case when the necessary data is expensive to come by – timewise or moneywise. In those instances, one could opt to fit system configurations directly to publicly acquired information, albeit with the potential risk of conflating correlation and causation. Such concerns could be overcome by deciding to work with a *rigidly trained AI system*. At the cost of accuracy, human input in these systems can mitigate some of the negative effects of not having access to highly detailed intelligence or big data.

D. Countering Predictability with Inexperience and Complexity

56. The findings from the previous sections indicate that algorithmic conduct may contravene Article 101 TFEU. What is especially noteworthy is that the relevant yardstick for collusion in the context of AI systems seems to revolve around a derivative *requirement of predictability* rather than the traditional benchmark of having a common understanding between competitors. Be that as it may, the competition law toolbox appears flexible and well-equipped enough to cope with instances of algorithmic collusion, given that collusive problems experienced in an algorithmic setting are not fundamentally different from those that occur in a non-algorithmic setting. What is different, though, is that AI systems can parse infinitely more parameters than humans and they can do so without necessarily making those parameters explicit. Hence, as described above, AI systems can inadvertently cast a shroud of fog over collusive conduct whereas colluding entrepreneurs may leave behind a trail of evidence. It is especially this element of attributing collusion to AI that complicates competition enforcement. From a remedial perspective, however, once algorithmic collusion has been established, no significant deviations from established competition law principles are to be expected.

57. Predictability within the market can be counteracted with inexperience and complexity, two approaches which, in effect, are akin to the introduction of new market players and market deconcentration. In those cases, the inexperience of new market entrants and market deconcentration may prevent a common understanding from arising between competitors whilst relying on AI systems.

Big Data Increases Inequality and Threatens Democracy (New York: Crown Publishing, 2017), 254 p.

a. For *experienced players*, it is a given that a firm relies on the assumption that all other market participants will also rely on AI systems, which use similar inputs and which are based on the same general framework. The result is predictability, i.e., the ability to make correct assessments about other actors' commercial conduct.
b. For *inexperienced players*, gaps in terms of know-how are likely to exist. When relying on AI, such models cannot be trained to the same degree of precision than those of experienced players. Inexperienced players' understanding of the market is inherently flawed since they are not yet fully aware of all intricacies and dynamics of the market.

Experienced players may still be able to estimate what a new, inexperienced player is doing on the market given that there is prior knowledge about common pitfalls and challenges that can occur within the sector. Put differently, experience also teaches what can go wrong. This has some notable implications for competition law enforcement.

58. In 2020, the General Court overturned an EC merger decision on the ground that the EC decision was based on the principle that 4-to-3 market player mergers are said to restrict competition by definition.[119] The general principle remains that the (anti)competitive nature of a market is influenced by the number of market players and their respective experience. Given that every market participant influences the available inputs and the market's functioning, the fewer players active in a market, the less complex AI models need to be. Note, however, that this holds true for AI-driven markets as well as non-AI-driven markets and that it corroborates that the finding of an AI infringement poses more serious challenges than resolving the infringement once it is discovered.

59. To further reinforce the market complexity argument, it is useful to briefly venture into the world of chess. In 1997, a chess-playing AI model named Deep Blue was able to defeat reigning world champion Garry Kasparov.[120] While several attempts to dethrone top-tier chess players had already been made in the years preceding the 1997 bout, it wasn't until the late 1990s that AI systems were able to consistently evaluate all chess moves a human player might consider.

Imagine now a three-player chess game. A three-sided game implies that the AI model not only needs to take the reactions of its two human competitors into account, but also how these two players interact with one another. Moreover, the system is further complicated by 'I know that you know' and 'I know that you know that I know' dynamics. This effectively leads to something that can

---

119 CJEU 28 May 2020, no. T-399/16, ECLI:EU:T:2020:217, *CK Telecoms UK Investments Ltd v European Commission.*
120 X, 'Deep Blue', *IBM*, 2012, https://www.ibm.com/ibm/history/ibm100/us/en/icons/deepblue/.

best be described as an algorithmic *three-body problem*.[121] Undoubtedly, these issues can be resolved by allowing AI to optimise for (more plausible) qualitative solutions rather than tasking AI to brute force all possible configurations. Thus, while feedback loops could go on forever, there are diminishing returns for each additional iteration beyond a certain point. The AI model could thus include logic statements to the effect that the model will halt its calculations once an acceptably low error value has been attained.

60. As recalled, it is not necessary to simulate the entire market in order to make assumptions about a competitor's inner workings. Instead, it is sufficient to consider those ripples of information that concern commercial configurations and changes in these configurations. Nevertheless, since all firms influence the available inputs, any AI system would have to take those other market players into account. It is therefore crucial to state that markets are inherently more obscure with more market players.

When a reasonable amount of computing power is available to firms – and assuming that not every firm has access to a supercomputer – a 4-to-3 merger could mean the difference between a competitive market shaped by unreliable AI predictions and an anticompetitive market shaped by complete transparency.

61. In the judgment referenced above in no. 58, the General Court did not argue that the EC was not entitled to invoke the theory of harm associated with 4-to-3 mergers, but it did hold that the EC should demonstrate the anticompetitive effects of such mergers in this specific sector.[122] Based on this reasoning and in light of the prevalence of AI systems in contemporary markets, such discussions may need to shift towards an assessment of the scarcity of data on relevant parameters for competition (e.g., production costs, R&D, product quality and product prices), rather than the level of competitiveness on the market. In this respect, data scarcity ties into a reduced ability to make accurate predictions about the market conduct of a competitor, which in turn lowers the ability to collude algorithmically with that competitor.

62. In conclusion, the advantages of AI significantly manifest themselves when input data is readily available. While it may not always be possible to prevent ripples of information from being picked up by a competitor's AI system, the general principles of competition law can still provide solace. In that sense, it must be recalled that the intensity of competition on a given market is affected by the number of competitors active on that market. Thus, when input data are

[121] While modelling the motion of two objects is relatively straightforward, there is no closed-form solution for modelling the movement of three objects. In this respect, see C. Marchal, *The Three-Body Problem* (Amsterdam, Elsevier Science Publishers, 1990), 592 p.

[122] CJEU 28 May 2020, no. T-399/16, ECLI:EU:T:2020:217, *CK Telecoms UK Investments Ltd v European Commission*, paras. 97 and 118.

divided between many competitors, the accuracy of AI predictions is negatively impacted, given the high computational demands of taking many variables into account. Conversely, when there are only a select number of firms active on the market, those firms can accurately monitor and predict each other's behaviour and anticompetitive effects should be assumed. Once market participants' internal behaviour has become fully transparent, any other competitive effects analyses are largely redundant.

Similar views on this topic are expressed elsewhere in literature as well, with authors hinting at divestitures as a potential remedy to counteract instances of algorithmic tacit collusion.[123] Moreover, for the purpose of identifying harmful algorithmic conduct, firms should also be prepared to explain how their AI systems work.[124]

3.3.3. Article 102 TFEU and Abuses of Dominance via AI

63. Apart from cartelisation, another harm to effective competition is governed by Article 102 TFEU. This provision catches abusive conduct by undertakings that hold substantial market power within a given market.[125] The rationale behind Article 102 TFEU is that in instances where one firm (or a small group of firms) possesses high levels of market power, that firm (or group) can act completely independently on the market. The ability to wholly disregard competitors opens the door for dominant firms to unilaterally abuse their privileged position on the market, to the detriment of consumers and competitors alike.

64. Perhaps surprisingly, algorithmic abuse has seen relatively little coverage compared to algorithmic collusion. Some contributions are available on this topic, which mostly focus on the implications of algorithmic pricing and price discrimination under Article 102 TFEU.[126] Nevertheless, even in the face of limited academic coverage, some aspects of AI are worth addressing under Article 102 TFEU.

---

123 Beneke and Mackenrodt, 'Remedies for algorithmic tacit collusion', p. 168: '*Structural remedies like divestitures can be used to address concerns of tacit collusion in several ways. A divestiture can aim either at creating a higher number of competitors or at rearranging the competition dynamics between present market participants so that tacit collusion is made more difficult to achieve*'.

124 Competition & Markets Authority, 'Algorithms: How they can reduce competition and harm consumers', *CMA*, 2021, https://www.gov.uk/government/publications/algorithms-how-they-can-reduce-competition-and-harm-consumers/algorithms-how-they-can-reduce-competition-and-harm-consumers.

125 See the references above at fn. 12.

126 E.g., I. Graef, 'Algorithms and Fairness: What Role for Competition Law in Targeting Price Discrimination towards Ends Consumers', *Columbia Journal of European Law*, 2018, vol. 24, no. 3, p. 558; A. Gautier, A. Ittoo and P. Van Cleynenbreugel, 'AI algorithms, price discrimination and collusion: a technological, economic and legal perspective', *European Journal of Law and Economics*, 2020, vol. 50, p. 417.

65. For the proper functioning of AI systems, know-how is extremely important. Without the necessary data, the model cannot be adequately trained, and any predictive results will likely fall short of the desired level of accuracy. This points towards two things. Firstly, larger and more experienced firms will have access to more robust AI models, simply due to having access to more extensive or more specific data for training purposes. Consequently, data provide such firms with a competitive advantage over other market actors. Secondly, larger firms will also have an ability to tip a novel market more easily to their advantage. Their significantly larger datasets provide an opportunity to leverage that data for market tipping purposes.

A. Data as a Competitive Advantage

66. In essence, the possession of data can therefore create a competitive advantage for a firm. Although data are typified as non-exclusive and non-rivalrous goods, the ability to prevent certain competitors from having access to a dataset can provide other undertakings with a competitive edge. This can eventually tie into a positive feedback loop: more data enables a firm to make more accurate predictions. These more accurate predictions put the firm in a position to better serve its customers. This ties into an increased ability to attract new customers. These customers will subsequently also start generating data for the firm. As a result, firms that benefit from extensive market power, are likely able to maintain their dominance via ongoing data collection practices.

67. To illustrate this, it is useful to briefly circle back to the grenadine production facilities from no. 49. Suppose that consumer preferences indicate an appreciable interest in apple-flavoured grenadine rather than strawberry-flavoured grenadine. While the CEO has initially focussed exclusively on producing the traditional, strawberry-flavoured red syrup, he contemplates entering the market for apple-flavoured beverages. He subsequently consults his data engineer, who will likely inform him that the firm's (trained) AI model is robust enough to optimise for very specific results; results which were not necessarily foreseen during the programming stages of the AI. Here, for instance, the CEO could adjust the AI's main task in order to yield the best settings to produce a novel sort of grenadine with a certain flavour palette, while also indicating a suitable price strategy to optimise profits. Once the target is defined, the AI system will parse all possible options and configurations to determine which settings are best suited to attain the predefined goal, here being the production of apple-flavoured grenadine.

68. Two important provisos come to mind. Firstly – as reiterated earlier – an AI model is only capable of optimisation if the general production principles have been adequately described and the options for the various choice steps

have been fed into the model. Then, and only then, the model can output the most optimal configuration. This means that an established firm can more rapidly improve their systems and production processes compared to start-ups or small-scale players. Experience in itself will thus allow firms to ramp up their competitiveness with respect to the governing principles of the market. As such, market experience may become a defining barrier to entry into that market, at least in respect of the successful usage of AI.

Secondly, with established firms naturally having more experience (e.g., by virtue of a higher number of client interactions), these firms will encounter more system errors, thus providing them with more opportunities to learn. Again, dominant undertakings will likely have a competitive advantage over smaller players by virtue of their size alone.

69. However, some limitations to this line of reasoning are also worth pointing out. Firstly, even with a high level of technical know-how, one constraint will be the programming complexity of the AI model. With more and more details being added, the model may become unwieldy or computational time might exceed acceptable levels. From that angle, it is fair to assume that the relation between know-how and the performance levels of the AI model cannot be captured by a direct linear relationship. Instead, beyond a certain point, diminishing returns will occur for each additional variable added to the model.

The second limitation lies in the specificity of the model. The fact that know-how of the field is required to train a model also works as a constraint on the model: it will perform well within the sector it was programmed for, but question marks can be put over the transferability of an AI model to a sector that significantly differs in terms of overall structure and functioning. This at least partially does away with concerns about abusive leveraging where dominant firms use their AI models to extend an acquired dominant position to an adjacent market. For completeness's sake, it should be noted that the phenomenon of '*transfer learning*' – i.e., the ability to apply AI's knowledge to a problem that differs from the problem the model was initially trained for – is gaining traction in computer scientific communities.[127]

B. Tipping Markets by Means of Data

70. As the law currently stands, Article 102 TFEU assumes that dominant firms can leverage certain advantages they have obtained by engaging in methods that go beyond competition on the merits. Thus, it is established knowledge that dominant undertakings have a special obligation not to transgress Article 102 TFEU's prohibition of anticompetitive unilateral conduct. Among others, this

[127] F. Zhuang et al., 'A Comprehensive Survey on Transfer Learning', *Proceedings of the IEEE*, 2021, vol. 109, no. 1, p. 43.

suggests that they are prohibited from tipping the market by other means than their productive merits. However, the argument here is that if dominant firms use AI in the ways described above, there would not really be a need to exploit or to leverage on behalf of that firm. Monopolists can quickly outcompete smaller players, simply because they can better assess the importance of certain market characteristics. In other words, those firms can promptly identify which adjustments are necessary in the face of changing market circumstances, whereas smaller, more inexperienced firms do not have this ability.

71. In theory, large undertakings can thus tip markets in their favour without raising any concerns under Article 102 TFEU, since AI allows them to meritoriously optimise their behaviour on the market. This triggers the following question: how should competition law respond? To answer this question, it should first be recalled that the EC does not oppose the existence of large firms – even monopolies – for reasons tied to their size alone.[128] The main criterion is that firms in a dominant position cannot be allowed to harm consumer welfare by means of their commercial conduct.[129] Hence, if a dominant firm can achieve their best results via AI models and without cheating, this should be considered as competition on the merits. Accordingly, the use of AI by a dominant firm does not in itself create a legal ground for competition authorities to intervene. Instead, if 'know-how leveraging' through AI would become a standard practice, it is perhaps useful to reconsider the scope and meaning of the notion 'competition on the merits'.[130]

C. Ongoing Legislative Developments

72. There is increased awareness in both academic and policy circles that data may act as a barrier to market entry.[131] When firms lack the ability to acquire a critical mass of data, there is no real means to effectively compete against incumbent firms. The European legislator has taken note of these challenges and has subsequently launched several initiatives to reassess the balance in digital markets. These legislative proposals attest to a desire to revise the current status quo.

73. The Digital Markets Act (DMA) is a first notable instrument.[132] Among others, the regulation stipulates that firms qualifying as 'gatekeepers'[133] must

---

128 Whish and Bailey, *Competition Law*, p. 202.

129 CJEU 9 November 1983, no. C-322/81, ECLI:EU:C:1983:313, *NV Nederlandsche Banden Industrie Michelin v Commission of the European Communities*, paras. 10 and 57.

130 In the past, the notion of 'competition on the merits' has already been the subject of different interpretations: M. Stucke, 'What is competition', p. 31.

131 L. Abrardi, C. Cambini and L. Rondi, 'Artificial intelligence, firms and consumer behavior: A survey', *Journal of Economic Surveys* 2021, p. 18.

132 Regulation (EU) 2022/1925 of the European Parliament and of the Council of 14 September 2022 on contestable and fair markets in the digital sector and amending Directives (EU) 2019/1937 and (EU) 2020/1828 (Digital Markets Act) [2022] OJ L 265/1.

133 Article 3 DMA.

refrain from using, in competition with business users, data which is generated through activities from those business users and which is not publicly available.[134] In a similar fashion, the DMA also sets out that business should have access to data they generate on the gatekeeper's platform.[135] Other data – pertaining, for instance, to aspects such as rankings, search queries and clicks – must be made available to the business by the gatekeeper on fair, reasonable and non-discriminatory terms.[136] While the scope of the DMA is limited to gatekeepers, it does confirm the EU's desire to seek novel legislative solutions for problems originating in data-driven markets.

74. Another noteworthy initiative is the proposed Data Act.[137] Its contents reveal several data sharing obligations, set out conditions under which data holders must make data available to certain recipients, and prohibit the use of assorted contract terms relating to data access and use. One provision, for instance, asserts an obligation to make data generated by the use of products or related services accessible to its users (Article 3), which is combined with a right of those users to access and use those data (Article 4). Those same users are also entitled to share data with third parties (Article 5). Similar to the abovementioned DMA, the proposed regulation aims to ensure that data holders make data available to recipients under fair, reasonable, and non-discriminatory terms.[138] While some carve-outs[139] for micro and small enterprises exist, it is interesting to see that the scope of application of the proposed Data Act includes both business-to-consumer and business-to-business contexts.[140]

4. AI FOR COMPETITION – IMPLICATIONS OF AI FOR ENFORCEMENT

4.1. THE EC ENFORCEMENT TOOLKIT

75. The enforcement of competition law cannot be reduced to a simple game of cat and mouse. Compliance through cooperation rather than punishment appears to be an important credo. The EC's leniency programme captures this idea quite well: by offering cartel members an opportunity to disclose the existence of the cartel, the firm that comes forward with sufficient

[134] Article 6(2) DMA.
[135] Article 6(10) DMA.
[136] Article 6(11) DMA.
[137] Proposal for a Regulation of the European Parliament and of the Council on harmonised rules on fair access to and use of data (Data Act), 2022, COM/2022/68 final.
[138] Recital 5 Data Act, Article 8 Data Act.
[139] Article 7 Data Act.
[140] Chapter II Data Act.

inculpatory evidence may obtain full immunity.[141] Additionally, the EC can adopt Commitment Decisions under Regulation 1/2003 in view of ensuring an undertaking's compliance with competition law.[142] Hence, the cat and mouse metaphor does not fully hold true, considering the various cooperative tools available to the EC to maintain effective competition on the market. Nevertheless, for the purpose of this chapter it is helpful to make an abstraction of these considerations and to work with the hypothesis of firms acting in bad faith and enforcement authorities seeking to aggressively counteract anticompetitive conduct.

4.2. INVOLVING AI MODELS IN THE ENFORCEMENT OF COMPETITION LAW

76. When pursuing enforcement actions against anticompetitive firms, it is well established that the EC relies on economic computer models.[143] For instance, the EC models the impact of specific mergers, checks for specific competition law infringements, or scrutinises certain markets for suspiciously stable prices.[144] Naturally, as computer techniques evolve beyond simple linear regression models, it is reasonable to assume that the EC will incorporate AI in their enforcement toolkit.

77. Little additional details are needed to understand that the EC can also use the ripples of information generated by firms to seek for specific anticompetitive behaviour. Gun jumping[145] affords us a good example in this regard. Given the number of people and countless hours of administrative work involved in mergers, some derivative effects are very likely to be noticeable.

---

141 Commission Notice on Immunity from fines and reduction of fines in cartel cases [2006] OJ C 298/17; A. Stephan, 'An empirical assessment of the European Leniency Notice', *Journal of Competition Law & Economics*, 2008, vol. 5, no. 3, p. 538.

142 Council Regulation (EC) No 1/2003 of 16 December 2002 on the implementation of the rules on competition laid down in Articles 81 and 82 of the Treaty [2003] OJ L 1/1, article 9.

143 Notable research on this topic has been performed by Wouter Wils: W. Wils, 'The European Commission's 2006 Guidelines on Antitrust Fines: A Legal and Economic Analysis', *World Competition: Law and Economics Review*, 2007, vol. 30, no. 2, p. 14 ff; W. Wils, 'Optimal Antitrust Fines: Theory and Practice', *World Competition*, 2006, vol. 29, no. 2, p. 30–32; see also G. Massarotto and A. Ittoo, 'Gleaning Insight from Antitrust Cases Using Machine Learning', Stanford Computational Antitrust, 2021, vol. 1, p. 37.

144 W. Wils, 'Optimal Antitrust Fines: Theory and Practice', pp. 7–8.

145 Gun jumping encompasses practices relating to the unlawful coordination between firms prior to a merger or the failure to notify the merger to the relevant competition authorities in a timely manner.

4.2.1. *Procedural Limitations*

78. At the same time, the EC will also face some of the constrains experienced by new market entrants or smaller-scale firms: they might lack the industry-specific knowledge to truly grasp which choice steps firms can go through. However, this has always been the case and the proliferation of AI does not introduce new challenges in this respect. This also explains why the EC conducts sector inquiries, dawn raids, and why the EC has the authority to issue requests for information, albeit within the bounds of the relevant procedural restrictions contained in Regulation 1/2003.[146] The limitation vis-à-vis such requests for information is that the EC has to (i) communicate the legal basis for the request, (ii) specify the request's purpose, (iii) indicate which information needs to be provided within a given timeline, and (iv) mention the relevant penalties in case of non-compliance.[147] Furthermore, the prohibition for the EC to engage in fishing expeditions should also be kept in mind.[148] Asking for information without a specific reason would not be permitted. The opposite holds true if the EC has solid reasons to believe it could find evidence of anticompetitive conduct in a firm's AI models.

4.2.2. *Building and Using AI-based Enforcement Tools*

79. While no precedents are available on this topic, there does not seem to be a legal reason barring the EC from inquiring about a firm's AI models and its training data – for the purpose of a competition investigation or perhaps also for the purpose of building their own regulatory AI enforcement tools – save for the requirement to communicate the purpose of the request for information.[149] While a firm can refuse to grant access to the relevant information, such behaviour could prompt the EC to issue a Commission Decision to force the firm to comply. On the one hand, at this point, the targeted firm could try to seek recourse before the European Courts to invalidate the EC Decision. On the other hand, a refusal to cooperate could quality as an aggravating circumstance in the context of infringement cases.

More procedurally oriented research could further describe the conditions under which the EC may overcome its know-how limitations in view of creating a level playing field for competition enforcement purposes. Yet, in doing so, the procedural and practical barriers should not be overlooked. For AI models specifically, the principle remains that you 'learn by doing', implying that

---

146 The different powers of investigation accorded to the EC are listed in Chapter V of Regulation 1/2003. The provisions mentioned there also touch on several procedural limitations.

147 Regulation 1/2003, articles 18.

148 CJEU 18 June 2015, no. C-583/13 P, ECLI:EU:C:2015:404, *Deutsche Bahn and Others v Commission*, para. 67.

149 Regulation 1/2003, article 20.

active firms will likely always have an informational edge over competition enforcement authorities.

80. At an earlier point in this chapter, concerns about evidence of anticompetitive conduct drying up due to AI were addressed.[150] Yet, even if firms no longer produce a paper trail of their cartel, the source code of the AI model still forms part of the firm's records. Thus, once the EC becomes aware that certain firms possess AI systems, they could request information about the source code and verify the model's functioning and performance against flagrant types of cartel abuses. Traditional restrictions by object might still be easily proven this way. This is the case, for instance, when an AI model recommends a specific configuration that would allow a firm to compete on prices more aggressively, yet the firm refuses to lower its prices since it knows other firms will not do so either.

81. Yet, firms are entitled to use publicly available information to determine their competitive strategy.[151] This suggests it may be difficult to confirm anticompetitive conduct by merely referring to the AI's source code and output. For instance, firms' internal AI-based strategic decisions are sometimes difficult to qualify as a concerted practice, simply because the decision is the most rational. If two competing ice cream shops are considering expanding to new locations and they know where the other firm is likely to move – based on preparatory actions generating ripples of information for AI to pick up –, then it would be bad management to not take this information into account when deciding on a new venue. As noted earlier, drawing a line between tacit collusion and intelligent adaptation in such instances remains a difficult task.[152]

82. A final element that needs to be addressed is the predictability of the EC's actions. It is not inconceivable that the EC also generates certain ripples of information, be it by employing staff members with a specific expertise, adopting administrative decisions, or initiating legal actions. From that perspective, firms or their legal counsels might attempt to monitor what the EC is doing in an anticipatory move. A determined cartelist could, for instance, devise a system to assess the risk of a dawn raid or estimate the chances of being targeted via a sector inquiry.

5. CONCLUSION

83. The underlying theme throughout this chapter is predictability. Some confusion and misconceptions exist surrounding the level of predictability of

---

150 See above at no 45.

151 Which is the argument made on the use of pricing algorithms by Schwalbe, 'Algorithms, Machine Learning, and Collusion', pp. 594–596.

152 See above at no. 40.

AI systems. The chapter sets out to do away with this confusion by putting AI's (pseudo)-randomness into context and by arguing that AI does not act inherently unpredictably. Furthermore, it was emphasized that the proper functioning of an AI system hinges on two factors. Firstly, the AI model's programmer should have sufficient knowledge of the principles of the sector wherein the AI model will operate. Secondly, sufficient time needs to be spent on feeding the model with the possible options for the various choice steps. When both conditions are met, the AI model will in principle be able to indicate a firm's optimal commercial strategy in a given market.

84. A first implication of using AI relates to algorithmic collusion. Commercially sensitive decisions are likely to generate ripples of information within the sector. Firms can rely on their AI models to detect such signals and to derive or predict possible decision strategies of their competitors. The use of AI thus puts strain on the existence of information asymmetries on the market. These effects tie into concerns about algorithmic collusion; concerns which are dealt with under Article 101 TFEU and which usually involve the unlawful exchange of information between competitors. Since direct contact between firms is no longer required to identify each other's conduct on the market, little to no evidence exists to corroborate findings of anticompetitive decision-making, except for evidence inferred from the AI model itself.

85. A second implication of the proliferation of AI in commercial settings is that know-how could be leveraged to make a firm and its products objectively best adapted to its market. AI can identify optimal product characteristics and specify how these characteristics can be attained given the constraints within the sector and considering a firm's productive limitations. The result is that established players and large undertakings have a clear advantage compared to new market entrants and small-scale undertakings. Established, dominant players will generally have more experience and knowledge of a sector's inner workings and have a better, more in-depth understanding of how certain choice steps can play out. Hence, such firms will be quicker and more effective in optimising their commercial strategy and products on the market, thereby enabling them to remain in the lead. While interesting to consider these implications under Article 102 TFEU, these firms will have no need to exploit or leverage their market power. Instead, combining AI with dominant firms' superior levels of market know-how will already guarantee their sustained competitive advantage. As the law currently stands, Article 102 TFEU does not prohibit tipping the market via such methods, as the market is objectively won by the dominant firm via competition on the merits.

86. A third implication of AI concerns competition enforcement. In that regard, what applies for firms, also applies for the EC. The EC – as well as NCAs

– could theoretically identify firm's (anticompetitive) conduct on the basis of ripples of information tied to such conduct. However, in this respect, the EC will face some of the constraints that smaller firms also experience, namely that it will have trouble creating AI systems that can attain insider levels of accuracy. Competition authorities could issue a request for information pertaining to the AI model's source code, yet procedural and practical limitations emerge. Additionally, firms could task their AI systems to estimate the risk of being involved in EC antitrust investigations. This, together with the potential dry up of direct evidence of anticompetitive behaviour, might give the EC a hard time in bringing future antitrust cases.

87. The increasing use of AI in commercial settings triggers interesting questions, both from a legal and policy perspective. At present, concerns about 'super AIs' – AIs which are orders of magnitude smarter than humans – are overblown, simply because they are not (yet) on the horizon. However, current conceptualisations of AI give rise to a serious problem for competition law, namely AI's ability to remove information asymmetries for experienced market participants. On the one hand, the core function of AI is to make predictions about competitors' conduct. On the other hand, unpredictability within the market is crucial to the process of effective competition.

88. Despite the challenges created by AI, competition scholars may find solace in knowing that the body of competition law is flexible enough to cope with algorithmic conduct. For algorithmic collusion, it was shown that a deviation from established case law principles may be appropriate in order to prevent future instances of algorithmic tacit collusion from escaping the ambit of Article 101 TFEU. For algorithmic abuses of dominance, it was recalled that the possession of a dominant position is not prohibited as such and that the extensive use of AI remains perfectly legitimate when committing to competition on the merits. Nonetheless, there is increased awareness that data may act as a barrier to market entry and that limited access to data can put strain on the competitive process. Future discussions on this topic are therefore likely to be shaped by legislative initiatives such as the Digital Markets Act and the Data Act, which stipulate data sharing obligations and set out conditions under which data holders must make data available to other market actors. For competition enforcement, topical issues revolve around strengthening the investigative powers of competition authorities and making sure that sufficient resources and know-how are available to effectively respond to threats of anticompetitive practices that occur via AI. The conclusion of this chapter is therefore as follows: *competition law and AI are indeed on a collision course, but a head-on collision can be averted by making minor course corrections.*

APPENDIX

EUCLID'S ALGORITHM

89. In order to discover the greatest common divisor (GCD) of two numbers *a* and *b*, we start by dividing *a* by *b*. This division results into a quotient *q* and a remainder *r*. The value of *a* can subsequently be rewritten as follows: $a = q * b + r$. At this point, two options are possible:

a. If the value of *r* equals zero, the algorithm stops and the GCD of *a* and *b* is found to be *b*.
b. If the value of *r* does not equal zero, the algorithm continues by writing the value of *b* to variable *a*, and by writing the value of *r* to variable *b*. The while-loop will continue with its next iteration, until *r* eventually reaches either 0 (and the *while*-loop stops) or 1 (and *r* triggers the *break*-condition within the *while*-loop).

90. This algorithm – colloquially known as Euclid's algorithm – can be coded in Python as follows.

```
a = int(input("Number 1:"))
b = int(input("Number 2:"))
while 1:
    r = a%b
    if not r:
        break
    a = b
    b = r
print("The greatest common divisor is:", b)
```

91. When the algorithm is applied to $a = 19$ and $b = 8$, it is found that the GCD = 1. Since *r* is constrained to non-zero values, the *break*-condition within the *while*-loop will trigger during an attempted 4th iteration.

Iteration 1: $19 / 8 = 2 * 8 + 3$
Iteration 2: $8 / 3 = 2 * 3 + 2$
Iteration 3: $3 / 2 = 1 * 2 + 1$
Iteration 4: $2 / 1 = 2 * 1 + 0$ (suppressed)

92. When the algorithm is applied to $a = 12$ and $b = 6$, it is found that the GCD = 6. Note that the *break*-condition within the *while*-loop is already triggered during the 1st iteration, given that *r* is zero. No 2nd iteration of the *while*-loop is attempted.

Iteration 1: $12 / 6 = 2 * 6 + 0$ (suppressed)

THE MARKET FOR GRENADINE

93. The pseudo-code for the 'market for grenadine'-AI model. Annotations are listed as triple-quoted strings and typeset in italics.

```
''' An assortment of variables (fruits, supplier_1, equalise_fruit_and_water, ...) is created
and written to memory. These variables concern the relevant production factors and are
subsequently linked to a specific category (inputs, suppliers, production_steps, ...). '''

inputs = (fruits,
          sugar,
          water,
          spices)

suppliers = (supplier_1,
             supplier_2,
             supplier_3,
             farmer_1,
             farmer_2,
             farmer_3,
             shop_1,
             shop_2,
             shop_3)

production_steps = (equalise_fruit_and_water,
                    boil_fruit_and_water,
                    test_fruit_boil,
                    sift_fruit_water,
                    discard_waste,
                    sift_first_extract,
                    boil_extract,
                    add_sugar_extract,
                    boil_sugar_extract,
                    cool_down_warm_grenadine,
                    bottle_grenadine,
                    cool_down_grenadine)

intermediary_steps = (human_action,
                      conveyor_action,
                      external_action)

preparatory_steps = (setup_cauldron,
                     setup_fire_a,
                     setup_fire_b,
                     setup_fire_c,
                     setup_sift,
                     set_new_cauldron,
                     set_cauldron_cool_place,
                     set_empty_bottle,
                     set_trench,
                     set_cool_bottle_place)

''' A well-defined target (executive_target) and target constraints (consumer_preference)
are introduced. At a later stage, the AI model will rely on these parameters to find a
```

```
combination of input variables that is not only deemed 'most suitable', but that also
adheres to specified decision boundaries. '''

executive_target = profit_target

consumer_preference = (flavour,
                       process_appreciation)

''' The section below defines a function (optimal_supply_chain_process) that, considering
all available inputs, determines what the most desirable commercial strategy is. This
process consists of several sub-steps:
    1. Firstly, the system checks which combinations can be formed with the provided
       input values.
    2. Secondly, the system assigns a score to each combination of input values.
    3. Thirdly, the system calculates the difference between the assigned scores and
       the desired outcome.
    4. Fourthly, the system returns as its output the configuration of input values with
       the smallest error, i.e. the configuration of input values with an assigned score
       that best approximates the desired outcome. '''

def optimal_supply_chain_process(inputs,
                                 suppliers,
                                 production_steps,
                                 intermediary_steps,
                                 preparatory_steps,
                                 executive_target,
                                 consumer_preference):
        error = [1,0,2]

        while error[0] > error[1] and error[0] < error[2]:
          for product in inputs:
            product_supplied.append(AI_choose_supplier(product, suppliers))
              for step in production_steps:
                agent_work.append(AI_choose_between_step(step,
                intermediary_steps))
              for preparation in production_steps:
                agent_work_two.append(AI_choose_preparation(preparation,
                intermediary_steps))

        unit_costs = calculcate_grenadine_cost(product_supplied,
                                               agent_work,
                                               agent_work_two)

        appreciation_score = calc_grenadine_appreciation(
                               agent_work.append(
                               agent_work_two),
                               consumer_preference[1])

        grenadine_taste = calc_grenadine_taste_flavor(product_supplied)

        if grenadine_taste.sour_limit > consumer_preference.sour_limit:
          error.insert(0,100)
          next
        elif grenadine_taste.sweet_limit > consumer_preference.sweet_limit:
          error.insert(0,100)
```

```
            next
        else:
            taste_score = taste_overlap(grenadine_taste.key_features,
            consumer_preference[0].key_features)

        for work in agent_work:
            if work.actor == conveyor_action:
                try:
                    automation_dictionary[work.name]
                except:
                    error.insert(0,100)
                    next

        for work in agent_work_two:
            if work.actor == conveyor_action:
                try:
                    automation_dictionary[work.name]
                except:
                    error.insert(0,100)
                    next

        current_variables = (product_supplied,
                             agent_work,
                             agent_work_two)

        most_profitable_configuration = ai_set_price_and_markettest(
                                            unit_costs,
                                            appreciation_score,
                                            taste_score)

        error.insert(0, abs(executive_target – most_profitable_configuration))

        return (current_variables, most_profitable_ configuration)

''' Analogous to the steps performed above, estimated input values for a competitor are specified and parsed by the function 'optimal_supply_chain_process'. The function makes an estimation as to the competitor's ideal price. '''

competitor_ideal_price = optimal_supply_chain_process(inputs,
                                                      suppliers,
                                                      production_steps,
                                                      intermediary_steps,
                                                      preparatory_steps,
                                                      executive_target,
                                                      consumer_preference)
                                                      [1].price

''' The model compares the competitor's ideal price with your own price. Accounting for a margin of error and in light of your own and your competitor's input parameters, the difference between the two resulting values provides an indication as to what the competitor might be doing:
    – The competitor has a production process similar to your own and charges similar
      prices.
    – The competitor has a production process similar to your own and charges lower
      prices. The competitor may be anticompetitively selling at a loss.
```

```
    – The competitor has a better production process relative to your own and charges
      similar prices. The competitor may lower its prices in the future to attract more
      customers.
    – The competitor has a better production process relative to your own and charges
      lower prices. The competitor may have access to technology which you do not
      possess. '''

if competitor_ideal_price!= competing.price + model_margin_up or competitor_
ideal_price!= competing.price – model_margin_down:
    if competitor_ideal_price > competing.price + model_margin_up:
        print("competitor likely has already improved production system by technology we
        are unaware of")
    if competitor_ideal_price < competing.price – model_margin_down:
        print("competitor can improve their production method and is likely to lower its
        prices – or might be acting anticompetitively")
```

CHAPTER 20

AI IN THE BELGIAN MEDIA LANDSCAPE

When Fundamental Risks Meet Regulatory Complexities

Noémie Krack*, Marie Beudels**,
Peggy Valcke*** and Aleksandra Kuczerawy****

1. INTRODUCTION

1. Just like multiple other sectors, AI technologies are permeating the Belgian media sector. The media landscape has considerably evolved with and since the invention of the internet. The impact of digital technologies and social media on communications has been compared to the impact of the printing press invention.[1] Nowadays, AI systems are gradually being implemented at every stage of the media production, aggregation and distribution process.[2] AI systems are used for content creation, dissemination, moderation but also for content storage and for analytical purposes. But these systems are also present in less visible ways such as in (commercial or political) advertising. Indeed, advertisers, through real time bidding processes, buy the online spots to place advertisements for the best suited audience. This contributes to the remuneration

* Researcher at imec - KU Leuven Faculty of Law, Centre for IT & IP Law.

** PhD Candidate at the Université libre de Bruxelles, Centre for Public and Social Law.

*** Professor of Law and Technology at imec - KU Leuven Faculty of Law, Centre for IT & IP Law.

**** Post-doctoral researcher at imec - KU Leuven Faculty of Law, Centre for IT & IP Law.

This chapter received funding from EU Horizon 2020 programme grants n° 951962 – MediaFutures and n° 951911- AI4Media and from FWO grant nr. 1214321N.

1 Y. Mounk, *The people vs. democracy: why our freedom is in danger and how to save it*, (Cambridge: Massachusetts: Harvard University Press, 2018), p. 137.

2 European Parliament, 'What is artificial intelligence and how is it used?', 2020, https://www.europarl.europa.eu/news/en/headlines/society/20200827STO85804/what-is-artificial-intelligence-and-how-is-it-used.

of content producers, uploaders and broadcasters[3] and leads to pop ups, targeted advertisements, like-minded content loops, personalised online experiences and recommendations. In this way, the internet and AI systems have contributed to the realisation of the so-called "attention economy theory"[4], firstly expressed in 1971 (i.e., long before the internet).[5]

2. Media are playing a key role in democratic societies. They enable and support the exercise of the right to freedom of expression and to information. They act as purveyors of information[6], creators of forums for public debate, producers of cultural expressions, and public watchdogs.[7] Technological developments have shaped, and continue to shape, the democratic role of media.[8] Given the major impact of AI technologies on the way media content is produced and disseminated, the question arises to what extent existing media laws can (and should) tackle the resulting societal challenges.

3. Acknowledging that the law is only one instrument to guide the development and use of technological innovations in society, and might not always be the appropriate answer, this chapter will focus on the role of existing and upcoming legislation in coping with challenges arising from the introduction of AI technologies in the media sector. In line with the Council of Europe's Recommendation CM/Rec(2011)7 on a new notion of media[9], the media

---

3 Y. Poullet and N. Bontridder, 'L'Union européenne et la régulation de la désinformation', *Revue du Droit des Technologies de l'information*, 2020/4, p. 33.

4 H. A. Simon, 'Designing Organizations for an Information-Rich World', M. Greenberger (ed.), *Computer, communications and the public interest*, (Baltimore MD: The John Hopkins Press, 1971), pp. 37–72. According to this theory, in a situation of information abundance, the attention of information consumers becomes scarce.

5 H. A. Simon had predicted the reversal of the economic relationship between media producers and media consumers. His theory provides that the abundance, wealth of information would result in a scarcity of attention from information consumer. For the time it was a radical idea when the opposite situation was existing: less information offers compared to the high information consumer demand. With the attention economy, consumer attention would become a precious and pricey commodity. in F. Rose, 'The Attention Economy 3.0.', *The Milken Institute Review – A Journal of Economic Policy*, 2015, p. 42.

6 European Court of Human Rights (ECtHR), 25 March 1985, no. 8734/79, *Barthold v. Germany*, para. 59.

7 ECtHR, 25 March 1985, no. 8734/79, *Barthold v. Germany*, para. 59; ECtHR,8 July 1986, no. 9815/82, *Lingens v. Austria*, para. 44; ECtHR, 14 July 2009, no. 37374/05, *Társaság a Szabadságjogokért v. Hungary*, para. 27.

8 J. Balkin, 'Free Speech in the Algorithmic Society: Big Data, Private Governance, and New School Speech Regulation', *University of California Davis Law Review*, nr. 51, pp. 1151–1210.

9 "The Committee of Ministers, under the terms of Article 15. b of the Statute of the Council of Europe recommends that member states: adopt a new, broad notion of media which encompasses all actors involved in the production and dissemination, to potentially large numbers of people, of content (for example information, analysis, comment, opinion, education, culture, art and entertainment in text, audio, visual, audiovisual or other form) and applications which are designed to facilitate interactive mass communication (for example social networks) or other content-based large-scale interactive experiences (for

sector is broadly understood here as covering various types (print, broadcasting, audiovisual, online, social media), functions (news, entertainment, education, social communication) and actors (content editors, aggregators, distributors). The latter can belong to the private or public sector (e.g., commercial versus public service broadcasters), and cover both institutional actors (like newspaper publishers) and individuals (like journalists[10]). The chapter offers a descriptive and a critical analysis from the perspective of Belgian and European media law. Media law is understood here as the body of sectoral rules that govern the media institutions and actors, as well as their services and infrastructures. These rules can be of a statutory, co-regulatory or self-regulatory nature, and hence, cover legislative acts like the Flemish Media Decree,[11] as well as journalists' codes of ethics.[12] Rules and principles laid down in those normative instruments are further given shape through the case law of courts and the decision practice of independent media authorities[13] and press councils.[14] Other legal frameworks, such as fundamental rights, competition law, data protection law, trade law, consumer protection law, criminal law, intellectual property law, and civil liability law, also have relevance for the media sector. These rules may be referred to throughout this chapter, but will not be systematically analysed.[15] Similarly, we will neither focus on non-legislative policy initiatives, like training, education, media literacy, staff upskilling and recruitment, support to research and awareness campaigns, which are also part of the bundle of measures necessary for addressing the challenges created by the use of AI systems in media.[16]

---

example online games), while retaining (in all these cases) editorial control or oversight of the contents…"; Council of Europe, 'Recommendation CM/Rec(2011)7 on a new notion of media', 2013, https://edoc.coe.int/en/media/8019-recommendation-cmrec20117-on-a-new-notion-of-media.html.

10 For the purpose of this chapter, we interpret the notion of journalist in a broad meaning.

11 Flemish Community Decree on radio broadcasting and television of 27 March 2009, *BS*, 30 April 2009, as amended several times.

12 See, for instance, the 'dictum' on the use of algorithms in journalism of the Finnish self-regulatory body, the Council for Mass Media, presented by A. Alén-Savikko in IRIS – Legal Observations of the European Audiovisual Observatory, 2020–1:1/2; for a more-indepth discussion, see A. Alén-Savikko, 'Transparency in algorithmic journalism: from ethics to law and back' in T. Pihlajarinne and A. Alén-Savikko (eds), *Artificial Intelligence and the Media: Reconsidering Rights and Responsibilities*, (Cheltenham, Northampton: Edward Elgar Publishing, 2022), pp. 33–60.

13 Such as the Flemish Media Regulator (Vlaamse Regulator voor de Media), https://www.vlaamseregulatormedia.be/nl, see footnotes 60 and 61 for the other Belgian media authorities.

14 Such as the *Raad voor de Journalistiek*; https://www.rvdj.nl/ competent for the Flemish Community and the *Conseil de Déontologie journalistique* competent for the French and German Communities https://www.lecdj.be/fr.

15 For a broader perspective on the impact of AI on the media sector through the lenses of various legal instruments, we refer to the following work: T. Pihlajarinne and A. Alén-Savikko (eds), *Artificial Intelligence and the Media: Reconsidering Rights and Responsibilities*, (Cheltenham, Northampton: Edward Elgar Publishing, 2022).

16 C. Beckett, 'JournalismAI Report – New powers, new responsibilities. A global survey of journalism and artificial intelligence', November 2019, https://blogs.lse.ac.uk/

4. To understand the legal challenges created by AI media applications, this chapter starts with a description of the use of AI systems in the media sector (section 2). It then provides a sketch of the complex Belgian institutional structure, to help the reader to navigate between the sources of Belgian media law (section 3). This section will also guide the reader in the understanding of the context in which new rules that are being proposed at European Union (EU) level to cope with the challenges of AI in the media sector will have to be operationalized. The European media law order is fed from two sources of law: the public international law of the Council of Europe, and the law of the European Union. The chapter focuses on a selection of three AI media applications, given their prominence in today's legal discussions: recommender systems (section 4), content moderation systems (section 5) and deepfakes (section 6). These systems will be analysed from the perspective of their impact on the media sector, notably on communication freedoms, and their effect on democracy. We will examine to what extent existing Belgian media law is relevant for these applications (or which shortcomings exist) and discuss relevant existing and forthcoming EU legislations.

2. AI MEDIA APPLICATIONS

5. AI systems have considerably transformed and influenced today's media landscape.[17] They are already omnipresent in the media sector and play an important role at all levels of the media value chain.[18] This goes from the creation stage to content production, edition, organisation, dissemination and consumption stages.[19] First, AI systems are used to facilitate journalistic activities, and to stimulate the creation, edition and production of content. This can include fully automated journalism[20], which can be used for content

polis/2019/11/18/new-powers-new-responsibilities, p. 9.

17 D. Kaye for the United Nations, 'Report of the Special Rapporteur to the General Assembly on AI and its impact on freedom of opinion and expression', 29 August 2018, https://www.ohchr.org/EN/Issues/FreedomOpinion/Pages/ReportGA73.aspx, p. 3.

18 New European Media, 'AI in the media and creative industries', April 2019, pp. 6–33. For a concise overview in Dutch see Tom Van De Weghe, 'Nemen robots de nieuwsredactie van morgen over?', VRT NWS, 25 October 2019; https://www.vrt.be/vrtnws/nl/2019/10/24/nemen-robots-de-nieuwsredactie-van-morgen-over.

19 The Journalism AI report pointed that on 71 news organisations consulted, already under half use AI for newsgathering, two-third used it for production and over half for distribution. In the news sector, most AI systems are primarily used to make journalists' work more efficient and then to deliver more relevant content to users. C. Beckett, 'JournalismAI Report – New powers, new responsibilities. A global survey of journalism and artificial intelligence', November 2019, pp. 6–7, and N. Aronis, 'Artificial Intelligence and Journalism; the future is already here', 10 December 2021, https://lab.imedd.org/en/artificial-intelligence-and-journalism-the-future-is-already-here.

20 The use of AI media applications in the newsroom responds to a changing media environment. AI can enable new forms of investigative, data-driven journalism N. Helberger, S. Eskens, M. van Drunen, M. Bastian, J. Moeller for the Council of Europe, 'Background

requiring only a limited input from the journalist, such as sport results.[21] AI applications can also assist news gathering by journalists. They enable data collection, uncovering useful information from multiple sources, receiving automatically summarised articles to support research, fact-checking, and identifying fake news.[22] In addition, AI systems help automatising processes and leaving time for journalists to focus on the creative, research and writing parts.[23] AI systems enable media companies to conduct thorough analysis of their services, know their audience, produce smarter content and design online-friendly looks.[24]

6. Second, AI media applications are used to enhance the user's online experience. For instance, AI media applications are used during web research to classify the results of the search and, if possible, ensure that the users find what they are looking for. AI media applications are also used for automated translation purposes, when the language of the open window is not the user's language.[25] AI systems can also be used as a tool to support content moderation efforts including detecting illegal or off-topic content.[26]

7. Finally, as the online environment allows individuals to become media content creators, users themselves are in a position to use artificial intelligence.

Paper – Artificial Intelligence-Intelligent Politics Challenges and opportunities for media and democracy', February 2020, https://www.coe.int/en/web/freedom-expression, p. 5. They raise many questions especially when used in the newsroom in terms of editorial liability, journalistic ethics, and deontology. P. Valcke, A. Kuczerawy, P.-J. Ombelet, 'Supervising automated journalists in the newsroom: liability for algorithmically produced news stories', *Revue de droit des technologies de l'information*, 2016, no. 61, pp. 5–19. See also L. Haapanen, 'Media Councils and self-regulation in the emerging era of news automation', Council for Mass Media in Finland, https://www.presscouncils.eu/research.

21 See M. Monti, 'Automated journalism and freedom of information: ethical and juridical problems related to AI in the press field', *Opinio Juris in Comparatione*, no. 1/2018, pp. 139–155.

22 Among the services they can use, we can mention the following services based on AI systems which help to monitor real-time media monitoring (NewsWhip), detect breaking news, understand what matters for their audience (Dataminr) or unveil unexpected stories worldwide (Vocativ), auto-indexing the media assets for archive purposes (Newsbridge), and so forth.

23 Forbes, 'AI making waves in news and journalism', 23 August 2019, https://www.forbes.com/sites/cognitiveworld/2019/08/23/ai-making-waves-in-news-and-journalism.

24 We can name the Belgian company Twipe which help media companies to turn their online activities into success.

25 European Parliament, 'What is artificial intelligence and how is it used?', 2020, https://www.europarl.europa.eu/news/en/headlines/society/20200827STO85804/what-is-artificial-intelligence-and-how-is-it-used. For instance, EuroVox provides a single API access to multiple language tools for transcription and translation purposes.

26 Council of Europe, 'Guidance Note on content moderation adopted by the Steering Committee for Media and Information Society (CDMSI), Best practices towards effective legal and procedural frameworks for self-regulatory and co-regulatory mechanisms of content moderation', May 2021, p. 14.

AI as a tool to develop content has indeed seen a considerable democratisation of its accessibility. This has enabled individuals to easily create deepfakes, sometimes containing disinformation or infringing someone's rights.

8. This widespread presence of AI media applications results in a significant impact on society and individuals. A Council of Europe study has demonstrated the horizontal and transversal impact of AI systems on fundamental rights, democracy and the rule of law.[27] The use of AI systems in the media sphere has, in particular, an impact on the right to privacy, right to data protection, freedom of expression, the right to non-discrimination, the right to an effective remedy and freedom of thought.[28] The profiling and tracking of individuals online, relying on online surfing habits, cookies and social media data, has a potential to impact the right to moral integrity.[29] Furthermore, governments are increasingly operating social media surveillance through AI (e.g., OSINT)[30] which creates serious concerns especially since the target is not aware of the profiling and is not offered any remedies.[31] In addition, legitimacy questions arise, as these AI media applications are almost only developed by major technology companies resulting in power concentration from private stakeholders impacting individuals life without any democratic choice.[32] There is an inherent risk that "AI-driven technologies will be developed to exploit vulnerabilities of users to manipulate, erode privacy, institutionalise intellectual surveillance, and create, intentionally or unintentionally, new digital inequalities".[33] AI media applications can also have both positive and negative implications for freedom of expression. While they enable information structuration, search, access, inclusivity, and

---

27 Council of Europe, ad Hoc Committee on artificial intelligence, 'Report by Catelijne Muller on the impact of artificial intelligence on human rights, democracy and the rule of law', 24 June 2020.

28 D. Kaye for the United Nations, 'Report of the Special Rapporteur to the General Assembly on AI and its impact on freedom of opinion and expression', 29 August 2018, https://www.ohchr.org/EN/Issues/FreedomOpinion/Pages/ReportGA73.aspx, pp. 13–15; Council of Europe, ad Hoc Committee on artificial intelligence, 'Report by Catelijne Muller on the impact of artificial intelligence on human rights, democracy and the rule of law', 24 June 2020.

29 Council of Europe, ad Hoc Committee on artificial intelligence, Report by Catelijne Muller on the impact of artificial intelligence on human rights, democracy and the rule of law, 24 June 2020, p. 9.

30 OSINT stands for Open Source Intelligence, their service focuses on gathering information available on free tools and resources. It could be used to help building a profile about a certain target.

31 The Freedom of the net 2019 Report by Freedom House showed that Governments were increasingly purchasing sophisticated technology to monitor their citizens' behaviour on social media. See Freedom House, 'Freedom on the Net 2019, The crisis of social media', https://freedomhouse.org/report/freedom-net/2019/crisis-social-media.

32 A. Webb, *The Big Nine: How the tech titans and their thinking machines could warp humanity*, (New York: PublicAffairs, 2019).

33 N. Helberger, S. Eskens, M. van Drunen, M. Bastian, J. Moeller for the Council of Europe, 'Background Paper – Artificial Intelligence-Intelligent Politics Challenges and opportunities for media and democracy', February 2020, https://www.coe.int/en/web/freedom-expression, p. 5.

expression[34], they also create new challenges such as private censorship, prior restraint, disinformation amplification and harm to media pluralism. Some put forward that for respecting individual autonomy media users should have knowledge, choice and control over the AI media applications.[35] Hence one can wonder how law could provide appropriate solutions to handle the risks and maximise the opportunities of AI media applications.

3. BELGIAN MEDIA LAW LANDSCAPE

9. Media law is primarily designed to protect and promote freedom of expression. This is the building block of media law and is the primary norm to be respected by those adopting rules for the sector. In the federal state of Belgium, there are multiple levels at which such rules can be adopted. To understand the country's complex federal architecture, this section describes how the principles of freedom of expression apply in Belgium (3.1) and explains the division of powers in relation to media matters (3.2).

3.1. FREEDOM OF EXPRESSION IN BELGIUM

10. Freedom of expression is enshrined and protected at the different jurisdictional levels: international, European (Council of Europe, European Union) and national.[36] Freedom of expression includes the freedom to seek, receive and spread information and ideas of all kinds either orally, in writing, in print or in the form of art or by any other means of choice.[37] Freedom of expression is not only "applicable to information or ideas that are favourably received or regarded as inoffensive or as a matter of indifference, but also to those that offend, shock or disturb the State or any sector of the population. Such are

---

34 E. Llansó, J. Van Hoboken, P. Leerssen and J. Harambam, 'Artificial intelligence, content moderation, and freedom of expression', Transatlantic Working Group paper series, February 2020, www.annenbergpublicpolicycenter.org/twg, p. 9.

35 D. Kaye for the United Nations, 'Report of the Special Rapporteur to the General Assembly on AI and its impact on freedom of opinion and expression', 29 August 2018, https://www.ohchr.org/EN/Issues/FreedomOpinion/Pages/ReportGA73.aspx, p. 19.

36 At international level see Article 19 (1) and (2) of the International Covenant on Civil and Political Rights and article 19 of the Universal Declaration of Human Rights. At European level see Article 10 European Convention of Human Rights and Article 11 Charter of fundamental rights of the European Union. At national level see mainly articles 19 and 25 of the Belgian Constitution. For more information see C. Behrendt for the European Parliamentary Research Service (EPRS), 'Freedom of expression, a comparative perspective, Belgium', October 2019.

37 The freedom of expression key principles were developed by the European Court of Human Rights (ECtHR) and taken up extensively by EU and Belgian case law. For instance, here by the Belgian Constitutional Court, 15 January 2009, case n° 9/2009.

the demands of that pluralism, tolerance and broadmindedness without which there is no democratic society".[38] Nowadays, the internet plays a central part for freedom of expression being one of the main means by which individuals exercise their right to freedom to receive and impart information and ideas.[39] It further provides access to diverse and pluralistic information and constitutes an essential tool for participation in activities and discussions concerning political matters and issues of general interest.[40] Freedom of expression, despite being broadly interpreted, is not an absolute freedom and can be subject to restrictions. This is enshrined in article 10.2 of European Convention of Human Rights (ECHR), which is directly applicable in the Belgian legal order. These restrictions must however meet the principles of *lawfulness, legitimacy and necessity*.

11. Not all parties involved in AI media applications are directly bound by the human rights frameworks. Only the States signatories of the human rights instruments are bound by them. However, some authors are researching on this responsibility gap when it comes to AI and are rethinking this argument.[41] States own a peculiar position as they usually do not create AI media applications but instead rely on private companies to design, develop and deploy them. According to the ECHR framework, Member States such as Belgium are subject to negative and positive obligations to ensure freedom of expression. The former entails that States must refrain from implementing measures constituting an unjustified interference with the exercise of freedom of opinion and expression. The latter involves that States must promote the rights to freedom of opinion and expression including protect its exercise even in the relationships between private parties. Therefore, States have the positive duty to create a favourable

---

38 ECtHR, 7 December 1976, no. 5493/72, *Handyside v. The United Kingdom*, para. 49; we can find comparable ruling by the Court of the Justice of the European Union (CJEU), 6 March 2001, C-274/99 P, *Bernard Connolly v. Commission*, ECLI:EU:C:2001:127, para. 37–39; 49.

39 ECtHR, 10 March 2009, no.3002/03 and no. 23676/03, *Times Newspapers Ltd v. United Kingdom*; ECtHR, 16 June 2015, no. 64569/09, *Delfi v. Estonia*, para. 110; ECtHR, 19 February 2013, no.40397/12, *Neij and Sunde Kolmisoppi v. Sweden*.

40 CJEU, 6 March 2001, C-274/99 P, *Bernard Connolly v. Commission*, ECLI:EU:C:2001:127, para. 39; ECtHR, 18 March 2013, no.3111/10, *Ahmet Yildirim v. Turkey*, para. 54; ECtHR, 1 March 2016, no.48226/10 and no.14027/11, *Cengiz and others v. Turkey*, para. 49, CJEU, 27 March 2014, C-314/12, *UPC Telekabel Wien GmbH c. Constantin Film Verheil GmbH et Wega Filmproduktiongesellschaft mbH*, ECLI:EU:C:2014:192, para. 47.

41 The concept of responsibility in an AI and human rights framework has been researched by K. Yeung, she states that 'the fundamental value of human rights is of such strength and importance that they are increasingly recognised as grounding horizontal effects on non-state actors, including tech developers'; K. Yeung 'A study of the implications of advanced digital technologies (including AI systems) for the concept of responsibility within a human rights framework', MSI-AUT, 2018, n°5, Available at https://ssrn.com/abstract=3286027. This principle has been developed in 2008 in the Ruggie report, UN, 'Report of the Special Representative of the Secretary-General on the issue of human rights and transnational corporations and other business enterprises, John Ruggie: Protect, Respect and Remedy: a Framework for Business and Human Rights', April 2008.

environment allowing all individuals to participate in the public debate.[42] Private actors are hence indirectly bound by human rights frameworks via the legislations that Member States adopt to fulfil their positive obligations. To incentivise private stakeholders on compliance with human rights, soft law and codes of conducts are being developed.[43] We can name the Council of Europe recommendations on the human rights impacts of algorithmic systems and on the impacts of digital technologies on freedom of expression.[44] Moreover, an increasing number of technology-oriented legislations incorporate fundamental rights components in their provisions applicable to private stakeholders.[45]

3.2. THE BELGIAN FEDERALISM AND DIVISION OF POWERS

12. Belgium has a complicated State structure with multiple institutions. Through several State reforms, the country has been shaped into a Federal State composed of the following federated entities: three Regions (the Flemish, the Walloon and the Brussels-Capital Regions) and three Communities (the Flemish,

---

42 ECtHR,14 December 2010, no. 2668/07, 6102/08, 30079/08, 7072/09 and 7124/09, *Dink v. Turkey.*

43 E.g., UN guiding principles on business and human rights. "The Guiding principles require companies, at a minimum, make high-level policy commitments to respect the human rights of their users in all AI applications (principle 16); avoid causing or contributing to adverse human rights impacts through their use of AI technology and prevent and mitigate any adverse effects linked to their operations (principle 13); conduct due diligence on AI systems to identify and address actual and potential human rights impacts (principles 17–19); engage in prevention and mitigation strategies (principle 24); conduct ongoing review of AI-related activities, including through stakeholder and public consultation (principles 20–21), and provide accessible remedies to remediate adverse human rights impacts from AI systems (principles 22, 29 and 31)." in D. Kaye for the United Nations, 'Report of the Special Rapporteur to the General Assembly on AI and its impact on freedom of opinion and expression', 29 August 2018, https://www.ohchr.org/EN/Issues/FreedomOpinion/Pages/ReportGA73.aspx, p. 9.

44 Council of Europe, Recommendation CM/Rec(2020)1 of the Committee of Ministers to member States on the human rights impacts of algorithmic systems, 8 April 2020, and Recommendation CM/Rec(2022)13 of the Committee of Ministers to member States on the impacts of digital technologies on freedom of expression, 6 April 2022.

45 Specific references concerning the respect of fundamental rights can be increasingly found in the recent EU proposals and legislations such as, non-exclusively, in the AI Act explanatory memorandum, in 20 different recitals (such as 1, 2, 5), and in 13 different articles including 7, 10, 13, 14 of the AI ACT proposal (Proposal for a regulation of the European Parliament and the Council laying down harmonised rules on artificial intelligence (AI ACT) and amending certain union legislative acts, 21 April 2021, *OJ* COM(2021) 206 final; in more than 20 DSA recitals and in articles 1, 14, 34, 35, 36, 48 of the DSA (Regulation (EU) 2022/2065 of the European Parliament and of the Council of 19 October 2022 on a Single Market For Digital Services and amending Directive 2000/31/EC (Digital Services Act), OJ L 277/1); finally, in recitals 12, 31, 47 and 58 of the Proposal for a Regulation (EU) on the transparency and targeting of political advertising, 25 November 2021, COM/2021/731 final.

French and German Communities).[46] These federated entities have respective competences and executive and legislative bodies, next to the competences and institutions of the Federal State, which has residual competences. In light of the bilingual status for Brussels-Capital, the French and Flemish Communities are competent for the institutions and organisations speaking their language located in the Brussels-Capital Region. The Federal State is in charge of the institutions or organisations not belonging to one of the Communities within the Brussels-Capital Region.[47]

13. The country's complex institutional history is also reflected in the division of powers relating to media and communications. This is especially true since media reflected the cultural and societal division between the Flemish and French communities. French was the former "dominant and elitist" language in Belgium.[48] This "dominance" gave birth to Flemish linguistic claims and triggered the federalisation process. The competences to regulate the media sector and adjacent sectors, such as telecommunications, are split up between the Federal and Community authorities.[49] The powers for culture (arts, libraries, audio-visual media, cultural heritage, museums, support for the written press and arts training) lie with the Communities.[50] In 1990 and 1991, the Constitutional Court ruled that radio and television broadcasting, as part of the Communities' cultural competences, did not only cover programming aspects, but also technical and transmission aspects.[51] On the occasion of the latest

---

46 Articles 1, 2 and 3 of the Belgian Constitution. There are also four linguistic regions in Belgium: the Dutch language, the French language, the bilingual Brussels-Capital and the German language (Article 4 of the Belgian Constitution). To add on the institutional complexities, the territory of the Communities and the Regions do not correspond and can overlap. This can lead to different federated entities being in charge over the same territory; C. de Visscher and V. Laborderie 'Belgique: stop ou encore? Entre fédéralisme, confédéralisme et séparatisme', *Politique étrangère*, 2013, p. 27, https://doi-org.kuleuven.e-bronnen.be/10.3917/pe.134.0023.

47 This is the case for the Act of 5 May 2017 on audiovisual media services in the bilingual region of Brussels-Capital, *BS* 23 May 2017.

48 Media Landscape, 'Expert Analyses of the State of Media', *Belgium*, https://medialandscapes.org/country/belgium.

49 P. Valcke and E. Lievens, 'Belgium', P. Valcke (ed.), *International Encyclopedia of Laws: Media Law*, (Alphen aan den Rijn: Kluwer Law International, 2010), p. 14; K. Reybrouck and S. Sottiaux, *De federale bevoegdheden*, (Antwerp: Intersentia, 2019), Chapter 26, p. 839.

50 Article 127 para. 1, 1), Article130 para. 1, 1) of the Belgian Constitution and Article 4 of the Special Act on Institutional Reforms of 8 August 1980, *BS* 15 August 1980, as amended, amongst others, by the Act of 6 January 2014, *BS* 31 January 2014 (the "Special Act on Institutional Reforms 8 August 1980").

51 Belgian Constitutional Court, 25 January 1990, n° 7/90 and Belgian Constitutional Court, 7 February 1991, n° 1/91. The motivation behind this ruling was to entrust the Communities to regulate broadcasting entirely and independently from the federal level. Including the technical aspects in the Communitie's competence prevented the Federal level to activate a sort of political control over cultural powers through technical licensing. P. Valcke and E. Lievens, 'Belgium', in: *International Encyclopedia of Laws: Media Law*, (Alphen aan den Rijn:

and sixth institutional State reform, in 2012–2014, the Belgian legislator has codified the Constitutional Court's interpretation modernising the terminology (from "radio and television broadcasting" to "audio and audio-visual media services").[52] The Federal State retains cross-sectoral powers such as competition law, trade law, consumer protection law and intellectual property law.[53] Part of written press regulation and telecommunications also remained Federal competencies.[54] Some powers are shared between the Federal authorities and the Communities, such as journalistic deontology.[55]

14. Another particularity of the Belgian division of powers is the cooperation duty between the federal authorities and the Communities in relation to the converging media and communications landscape. This was initially proclaimed through rulings of the Constitutional Court.[56] It nowadays relies on Title IV*bis* of the Special Act on Institutional Reform.[57]As a result, each Community has its own audio-visual media legislation which sets out rules in relation to licensing of traditional and online radio and television service providers, video platforms, the governance of the public service broadcaster, programme requirements, commercial communications, as well as distribution networks. The main audio-

Kluwer Law International, 2010), p. 17; C. Uyttendaele, *Openbare information. Het juridisch statuut van openbare informatie in een convergerende media-omgeving*, (Anvers: Maklu, 2002), p. 60.

52 Article 4, 6°, Special Act on Institutional Reform 8 August 1980. See R. Debilio, R. Queck, D. Stevens, 'La sixième réforme de l'Etat et les industries de réseau', *Revue du droit des industries de réseau*, 2014, liv. 4, p. 391.

53 Article 6, para. 1, VI, al. 5, 4°, 5° and 7° Special Act on Institutional Reform 8 August 1980, *BS* 15 August 1980.

54 For written press, this includes everything not related to support to written press freedom because this has been attributed to the Communities. At the moment, the federal legislator has regulated journalists' status (Act of 30 December 1963 on the recognition and protection of the title of journalist, *BSBS* 14 January 1964), the secrecy of journalistic sources (Act of 7 April 2005 on the protection of journalist sources, *BS* 27 April 2005) and the right of reply (Act of 23 June 1961 on the right of reply, *BS* 8 July 1961). For telecommunications, it includes the general police for radio waves power to a certain extent, the issuance of federal government communications (See Art 4, 6° of the Special Act on Institutional Reform 8 August 1980, *BS* 15 August 1980). More information in R. Debilio, R. Queck and D. Stevens, 'La sixième réforme de l'Etat et les industries de réseau', *Revue du droit des industries de réseau*, 2014, liv. 4, pp. 394–395.

55 The Communities have the power for creating, acknowledging, or subsidizing instances responsible for monitoring audio-visual operators regarding information objectivity and journalistic ethics' respect. (Art 4, 6° Special Act on Institutional Reform 8 August 1980). The Federal authority keeps power for journalist profession regulation and protection (including journalistic sources) and journalist's deontology. Belgian Senate, Information report concerning the necessary collaboration between the federal authority and the Communities in the fight against fake news, 7-110/2, session 2021–2022, 25 October 2021, p. 20, https://www.senate.be/www/?MIval=/Dossiers/Informatieverslag&LEG=7&NR=110&LANG=fr.

56 Belgian Constitutional Court, 14 July 2004, n° 132/2004 and Belgian Constitutional Court,13 July 2005, n° 128/2005.

57 Article 92*bis*, 4*sexies* Special Act on Institutional Reform 8 August 1980, *BS* 15 August 1980. An illustration of this is the cooperation agreement on communication networks from 16 November 2006.

visual legislations applicable in Belgium are: the "*Vlaams MediaDecreet*"[58] for the Flemish Community, the "*Décret elative aux services de medias audiovisuels et aux services de partage de vidéos*"[59] for the French Community and the "*Dekret über die Mediendienste und die Kinovorstellungen*"[60] for the German Community. Oversight is the responsibility of the respective media regulators[61], which have varying tasks and powers depending on the Community concerned. The regulatory authority which has been established at federal level is in charge of electronic communications in the strict sense (telephony and internet, fixed and mobile networks) and bilingual broadcasting activities in the Brussels-Capital Region.[62] The Conference of Regulators of the electronic communications sector (CRC) provides a forum in which the four regulators cooperate on certain matters. There are also three public service broadcasting institutions *VRT*, *RTBF* and *BRF*[63]; they all receive public subsidies and have their management contract published in the official State Gazette of Belgium. When it comes to self-regulatory bodies, we can name the *Raad voor de Journalistiek* for the Flemish Community and the *Conseil de Déontologie journalistique* for the French and German communities. Their missions include notably to examine complaints against violations of good journalistic practices and codify deontological rules.

15. The Belgian regulation of the use of AI systems in media will depend on the matter at stake and which authority detains powers to legislate, which is not always easy to determine. Some authors have considered that the Federal Authority could be responsible for the internet and social media[64] based on its residual powers[65],

---

58 Flemish Community Decree on radio broadcasting and television of 27 March 2009, *BS* 30 April 2009, as amended several times.

59 French Community Decree relating to audiovisual media services and video sharing services,1 March 2021, *BS* 26 March 2021. The decree transposes the European obligations of three directives concerning audiovisual media services.

60 German Community Decree on Media Services and Cinema Shows, *BS* 1 March 2021.

61 For the French community, the CSA (*Conseil Superieur de l'Audiovisuel;* https://www.csa.be/). For the Flemish community, the VRM (*Vlaamse Regulator voor de media*; https://www.vlaamseregulatormedia.be/). For the German Community, the *Medienrat* (www.medienrat.be/).

62 At the Federal level the regulatory authority is the Belgian Institute for Postal Services and Telecommunications (BIPT). The BIPT's Strategic Plan 2020–2022, explains that when it comes to AI, BIPT is monitoring the digital evolution in order to develop action plans and regulatory framework, https://www.bipt.be/operators/publication/strategic-plan-2020-2022.

63 *Vlaamse Radio en Televisieomroeporganisatie* (VRT), *Radio Télévision Belge de la Communauté Française* (RTBF) and *Belgischer Rundfunk* (BRF).

64 F. Jongen and A. Strowel, *Droit des médias et de la communication*, 1st edn, (Brussels: Larcier, 2017), p. 33.

65 In Belgium, the communities and regions can only execute the powers which are explicitly attributed to them via the Constitution and the special acts on institutional reforms. The rest of the powers are known as residual powers and belong to the Federal Authority. This system should be reversed according to article 35 of the Constitution which shifts the residual powers to the federated entities and the attributed powers to the federal authority. This provision has not been given effect in practice, given that the required special act has not yet been adopted.

while the Communities would be competent for the online presence of radio and television channels.[66] It is doubtful whether this view is in line with established case law of the Constitutional Court, stating that the underlying medium or technology used to convey the media content is irrelevant to determine the competent level; what matters is that the content is meant to be received by a general audience (or a sub-set thereof) and cannot be considered as private communication.[67] The Flemish Media Regulator, for instance, applies the relevant rules on commercial communications also on vloggers and influencers on social media, and recently adopted a 'Content Creator Protocol' in consultation with the sector.[68] As cultural matters are regulated at community level, each Community is entitled to adopt its own vision on the use of AI in media, as long as the matters they touch upon remain within their competences (or can be seen as a necessary corollary thereof) and are in accordance with higher norms (at international or European level, or the Belgian Constitution). The European Union has lately been very active in the area of AI regulation, with recent legislative proposals including (to some extent) the use of AI media applications.[69]

16. The next subsections will focus on a selection of three common uses of AI in the media sector, namely recommender systems, content moderation systems and deepfakes. The risks and opportunities that they create and how Belgian and EU media law address or plan to address them will be analysed.

4. RECOMMENDER SYSTEMS

17. The internet is a "high-choice media environment"[70]; users have the choice to use a search engine or another, to select a certain website or platform and

66 Belgian Senate report, 'Information report concerning the necessary collaboration between the federal authority and the Communities in the fight against fake news', 7-110/2, session 2021-2022, 25 October 2021, pp. 21-23.

67 Belgian Constitutional Court, 14 July 2004, n° 132/2004 and Belgian Constitutional Court,13 July 2005, n° 128/2005.

68 Vlaams Regulator voor de Media, 'Content Creator Protocol', https://www.vlaamseregulatormedia.be/nl/content-creator-protocol.

69 Think of the following proposals: Proposal for a Regulation (EU) laying down harmonized rules on Artificial Intelligence (AI act) and amending certain Union legislative acts, COM(2021) 206 final, 21 April 2021 and the Proposal for a Regulation (EU) on a Single Market for Digital Services (Digital Services Act-DSA) and amending Directive 2000/31/EC, COM/2020/825 final, 15 December 2020 proposal now finalised: Regulation (EU) 2022/2065 of the European Parliament and of the Council of 19 October 2022 on a Single Market For Digital Services and amending Directive 2000/31/EC (Digital Services Act), *OJ* L 277/1.

70 P. Van Aelst et al., 'Political communication in a high-choice media environment: A challenge for democracy?', *Annals of the International Communication Association*, vol. 41, no. 1, pp. 2-27.

then they will be confronted with an impressive amount of content. It is indeed impossible for a single human being to watch all the videos available on YouTube, to read all the information available online or to read all the comments posted by other users. Search engines, websites and (social media) platforms therefore use recommender systems to classify the available content.

4.1. DEFINITION

18. In the framework of this chapter, we propose to use an agnostic definition of recommender systems, such as the one proposed by Jockum Hildén, according to whom "recommender systems are the underlying technologies that enable personalization of content interfaces"; they "filter the existing content database according to a predefined set of rules and organises the content in a specific order".[71] Under this definition, the recommender systems must not necessarily meet the users' expectations or interest and can serve other objectives such as the displaying of content of public interests. The notion of recommender systems does therefore not refer to a single concept but to a set of means that are put in place to classify, according to priority, the content that a user has access to in priority. Hence, all recommender systems are different, depending on the type of filtering set up, the basis on which the filtering takes place and the purpose of the recommender system. There are several types of filtering or recommendations. The most commonly accepted categories are the following[72]:

- Demographic filtering – recommendation is made based on the demographic information of the user such as their language, location, age, or gender.
- Content-based or behavioural filtering – recommendation is based on the passive and active feedback of the user, such as their previous behaviour or content which they have liked in the past.
- Collaborative filtering – recommendation is based on content consumed by similar user.
- Knowledge-based filtering – recommendation is made based on the knowledge that the system has on the needs, constraints and preferences of the users.
- Social-based or community-based filtering – recommendation is based on the social network of the user and the preferences of the members of this network.

---

71 J. Hildén, 'The Public Service Approach to Recommender Systems: Filtering to Cultivate', *Television & New Media*, 2021, pp. 1–20, p. 2.

72 See F. Ricci, *Recommender system handbook*, 2nd edn, (New-York: Springer, 2015), pp. 10–15; J. Hildén, 'The Public Service Approach to Recommender Systems: Filtering to Cultivate', *Television & New Media*, 2021, pp. 1–20.

- Non-personalised filtering – recommendation is based on non-personalised criteria such as the most-viewed videos or the musical hits of the moment.
- Hybrid recommender systems – the recommendation is based on a combination of the abovementioned techniques. Most of the recommender systems are hybrid systems.

19. In addition to the different types of recommendations, recommender systems can also serve different interests or purposes. Most recommender systems will aim at selecting content which may meet the interest of the user, or at least aim at having the user interact with the proposed items.[73] Yet, in doing so, a recommender system also serves the interest of the platform provider and of advertisers on this platform. Finally, recommender systems could be designed in order to serve social or public interests[74] or, in non-democratic states, the government interests.

4.2. RISKS AND BENEFITS

20. The risks caused by recommender systems are often analysed from a data protection and privacy perspective.[75] Indeed, recommendation algorithms[76] heavily rely on personal data, either from the user which receives the recommendation or from other users. In this respect, authors have stressed the likely trade-off between privacy and accuracy.[77]

21. Platforms and website using recommender systems are also criticised for the opacity around the systems they use.[78] Users, when they are aware of

---

73 F. Vasile et al., 'A Gentle Introduction to Recommendation as Counterfactual Policy Learning', in *Proceedings of the 28th ACM Conference on User Modeling, Adaptation and Personalization (UMAP' 20) July14–17, 2020, Genoa, Italy.*

74 See J. Hildén, 'The Public Service Approach to Recommender Systems: Filtering to Cultivate', *Television & New Media*, 2021, pp. 1–20.

75 Unfair commercial practices are also relevant in this context. For a discussion of the EU Unfair Commercial Practices Directive and the relevant case law in the United States, see C. Goanta and G. Spanakis, 'The commercial unfairness of recommender systems on social media', in T. Pihlajarinne and A. Alén-Savikko (eds), *Artificial Intelligence and the Media: Reconsidering Rights and Responsibilities*, (Cheltenham, Northampton: Edward Elgar Publishing, 2022), pp. 148–170.

76 For a (technical) introduction into different recommendation algorithms, see H. Ko, S. Lee, Y. Park, A. Choi, 'A Survey of Recommendation Systems: Recommendation Models, Techniques, and Application Fields', *Electronics* 2022, 11, p. 141. https://doi.org/10.3390/electronics11010141.

77 S. Milano, 'Recommender systems and their ethical challenges', *AI & Society*, 2020, vol. 35, pp. 957–967, p. 962. However, as this issue is not specific to recommender system but common to all AI systems, we refer to Chapter 8 of the present book for further analysis of data protection questions in AI systems.

78 *Ibid.*

the use of recommender systems, usually do not know why they have received a certain recommendation, which type of recommender system is used by the platform and what are the actual parameters which are used for each recommendation. Yet, increasing transparency around recommender systems could help revealing and correcting other risks created by recommender systems such as the reproduction of social categories, the introduction of bias in the recommendation[79] and the perpetuation of existing discrimination.[80] This is why, as it will be further detailed below[81], existing and upcoming legislations introduce transparency obligations around recommender systems.

22. In addition, the effect that recommender systems could have on the diversity of content displayed to a specific user has often been highlighted.[82] Recommender systems would aim at meeting the interests of the user and have them interact with the recommended items. In doing so, recommender systems could create or increase the so-called, echo chambers or filter bubbles[83], namely environments in which only ideas and beliefs commonly shared by the audience are expressed.[84] Yet, as explained above, we use as working definition an agnostic definition of recommender systems, according to which recommender systems relate to the personalisation technologies. This means that recommender systems do not in themselves create risks for content diversity. On the contrary, they could be designed to promote diversity or other

79 *Ibid.*

80 United Nations, 'Report on Artificial Intelligence technologies and implications for freedom of expression and the Information environment of the Special Rapporteur on the promotion and protection of the right to freedom of opinion and expression', 29 August 2018, p. 9, available at https://www.undocs.org/A/73/348.

81 See below from para. 23 until 27.

82 N. Helberger et al., 'Exposure diversity as a design principle for recommender systems', *information, communication & society*, 2018, vol. 21, no 2, pp. 191–207, p. 192; EU High Level Group on Media Freedom and Pluralism, 'report on a free and pluralistic media to sustain European democracy', January 2013, p. 27, available at https://ec.europa.eu/information_society/media_taskforce/doc/pluralism/hlg/hlg_final_report.pdf.

83 The Filter Bubble Theory elaborated by Pariser and investigated by Sunstein showed how algorithms keep suggesting personalised content to users consolidating and confirming their worldview, regardless of the empirical truth behind the story. Users are rarely confronted with opinions differing from their own, which creates a real bubble around them and discourages balanced debate. E. Pariser, *The Filter Bubble: What the Internet is hiding from you*, (Penguin Books, 2012); C.R. Sunstein, *On rumours: How Falsehoods Spread, Why We Believe Them, and What Can Be Done*, (Princeton: Princeton University Press, 2014); R. Klepka, "Information and Disinformation and the transformation of modern democracy- From media bias through the "Echo Chamber" and the "Filter Bubble" to fake news" in G. Terzis et al. (ed.), *Disinformation and digital media as a challenge for democracy, European Integration and Democracies Series*, vol. 6 (Cambridge: Intersentia, June 2020), p. 38; European Commission, 'Study for the "Assessment of the implementation of the Code of Practice on Disinformation, SMART 2019/0041", final report', May 2020, p. 39.

84 E. Dubois and G. Blank, 'The echo chamber is overstated: the moderating effect of political interest and diverse media', *Information, communication & society*, vol. 21, no. 5, 2018, pp. 729–745.

public interest values.[85] The design and development of the systems will only lead to risks for diversity depending on the objectives and aims behind the recommender systems.

4.3. NATIONAL FRAMEWORK

23. Recommender systems are a rather recent phenomenon which explains why specific legal rules are (quasi-) absent in the national framework. Only the French Community has tackled this issue in its Decree on audiovisual media services and video sharing services. The decree creates the obligation for audiovisual media service distributors[86] who offer an electronic programme guide to guarantee the transparency and neutrality of the content recommendation algorithms they use.[87] This obligation intends to tackle the aforementioned risks of opacity, perpetuation of discrimination and of echo-chambers. The obligation of transparency and neutrality does not however prejudice emphasis that would be given by result of the recommendations to European works, including French-language Belgian initiatives. Indeed, article 13 of the Audiovisual Media Services Directive[88] creates an obligation for Members States to ensure that at least thirty percent of the catalogue of on-demand platforms are European works. This obligation was implemented in the three Communities. Yet, this obligation for platforms to have at least 30% of European works in their catalogues could be undermined if the recommender systems only promote other works – because they are designed to or as a consequence of their design.[89] The French

85 N. Helberger et al., 'Exposure diversity as a design principle for recommender systems', *Information, communication & society*, 2018, vol. 21, no 2, pp. 191–207; See also J. Hildén, 'The Public Service Approach to Recommender Systems: Filtering to Cultivate', *Television & New Media*, 2021, pp. 1–20, and J. Vermeulen, 'To Nudge or Not to Nudge: News Recommendation as a Tool to Achieve Online Media Pluralism', *Digital Journalism*, 2022, pp. 1–20.

86 Service distributors (*distributeur de services*) are those who make audiovisual media services available to the public via terrestrial networks, satellite or cable. The one who bears editorial responsibility for an audiovisual media service is called a service editor (*éditeur de services*). Like in the Audiovisual Media Services Directive, audiovisual media services have (as a whole or a dissociable section thereof) as principal purpose the provision, in linear or non-linear (i.e., on-demand) mode, of programmes which fall under the editorial responsibility of a media service provider, to the general public, in order to inform, entertain, educate or provide commercial communication, by means of electronic communications networks; see definitions in Article 1.3–1, 12°, 13° and 52° of the French Community Decree on audiovisual media services and video sharing services.

87 Article 8.3.2–1, para. 2 of the French Community Decree on audiovisual media services and video sharing services.

88 Directive 2010/13 on the coordination of certain provisions laid down by law, regulation or administrative action in Member States concerning the provision of audiovisual media services in view of changing market realities, as amended by Directive 2018/1808 of 14 November 2018, *OJ*, L303/69.

89 For instance, a recommender system could be designed to promote only content similar to previous content consumed by the user. In this case, if the user consumed e.g., only Korean content, European works will be overshadowed by the system.

Community has indirectly acknowledged this risk by creating an obligation to guarantee the neutrality of the recommender system. It went even further by creating an exception to this obligation of neutrality when the recommendation concerns European works.

24. In Belgium, public service media are governed by Community legislation[90], but also through a management contract established by their respective governments. In this respect, both the management contract of the RTBF *(Radio-Télévision belge de la Communauté française)*[91] and the management contract of the VRT *(Vlaamse Radio- en Televisieomroeporganisatie)*[92] include provisions on recommender systems. The VRT contract includes provisions on the promotion of so-called taste-enhancing algorithms, which aim to stimulate the diversity of content consumed by the user, instead of filter bubbles.[93] The RTBF contract states that recommender system algorithms must be designed with public service and public service content provision in mind and must aim at promoting diversity while respecting the users' interest in order not to jeopardise their loyalty.[94]

4.4. EU FRAMEWORK

25. Recommender systems have also raised attention at EU level. Through its Digital Services Act (DSA)[95], the European Commission indeed proposed to regulate some uses of recommender systems. First, the DSA introduces the first legal definition of recommender systems[96], as follows: "'recommender system' means a fully or partially automated system used by an online platform

---

90 See the Decree of the Flemish Community on radio and television broadcasting of 27 March 2009, *BS* 30 April 2009, as amended from time to time and the Decree of the French Community on the status of the Radio-Télévision belge de la Communauté française, *BS* 28 August 1999.

91 See Decree of the Government of the French Community of 12 December 2018 approving the fifth management contract of the Belgian radio and television of the French community for the years 2019 to 2022 included.

92 Beheersovereenkomst 2021–2025 of the VRT available at https://www.vrt.be/nl/over-de-vrt/beheersovereenkomst.

93 See also the annual report of the VRT, p. 75, available at https://www.vrt.be/nl/over-de-vrt/prestaties/jaarverslag.

94 See Article 42*octies* of the RTBF management contract.

95 The DSA aims to harmonize rules on the provision of intermediary services in the internal market. The goal is to create a safer digital space where fundamental rights and European values are respected and protected while ensuring a level playing field to foster innovation, growth and competitiveness. The text revises the twenty years old E-commerce Directive and creates several layers of due diligence obligations for intermediary services. Regulation (EU) 2022/2065 of the European Parliament and of the Council of 19 October 2022 on a Single Market for Digital Services and amending Directive 2000/31/EC (Digital Services Act), OJ L 277/1.

96 S. Schwemer, 'Recommender Systems in the EU: from Responsibility to Regulation?', *FAccTRec Workshop '21, September 27–October 1, 2021, Amsterdam, Netherlands*, p. 1.

to suggest or prioritise in its online interface specific information to recipients of the service, including as a result of a search initiated by the recipient of the service or otherwise determining the relative order or prominence of information displayed".[97]

26. In addition, the DSA introduces several obligations for online platforms,[98] very large online platforms (VLOPs)[99] and very large online search engines (VLOSEs)[100] using recommender systems.[101] Online platforms are expected, firstly, to set out in their terms and conditions in plain and intelligible language the main parameters used in their recommender systems.[102] In addition, they must provide an easily accessible functionality on their platform interface allowing the recipients to modify or influence at any time the main parameters used in the recommender systems. The parameters shall include information about the criteria which are most significant in determining the information suggested to the recipient of the service and the reasons for the relative importance of the parameters.[103] Finally, VLOPs and VLOSEs must provide at least one recommendation option which is not based on profiling, such alternative option should be directly accessible from the interface where the recommendations are presented.[104]

---

97 Article 3, (s) of the DSA.

98 An online platform is defined as "a hosting service that, at the request of a recipient of the service, stores and disseminates information to the public, unless that activity is a minor and purely ancillary feature of another service or a minor functionality of the principal service and, for objective and technical reasons, cannot be used without that other service, and the integration of the feature or functionality into the other service is not a means to circumvent the applicability of this Regulation". Article 3, (i) of the DSA.

99 A very large online platform (VLOP) is defined as an online platform which reach a number of average monthly active users in the European Union of at least 45 million and which is designated as such following a specific procedure detailed in Article 33 of the DSA. See Article 3, (i) *juncto* Article 33 and recital 75–78 of the DSA.

100 An online search engine is defined as " an intermediary service that allows users to input queries in order to perform searches of, in principle, all websites, or all websites in a particular language, on the basis of a query on any subject in the form of a keyword, voice request, phrase or other input, and returns results in any format in which information related to the requested content can be found". See Article 3, (j) of the DSA. A very large online search engine (VLOSEs) is an online search engine which reach a number of average monthly active users in the European Union of at least 45 million and which is designated as such following a specific procedure detailed in Article 33 of the DSA. See Article 3, (j) *juncto* Article 33 of the DSA.

101 Article 27, rec. 70 and Article 38, rec. 94 of the DSA.

102 Initially, this transparency obligation only applied to very large online platforms. The inclusion of online platforms in the final text has broaden the scope and replied to criticisms about the risk of low impact of these transparency and empowerment measures. See Article 29 of the DSA proposal and now Article 27, rec. 70 and Article 38, rec. 94 of the DSA. S. Schwemer has also been quite critical about the VLOP's definition which excludes platforms which do not store information at the request of the recipient of the service, such as Netflix of Spotify or the website of a news outlet, and smaller online platform. See S. Schwemer, 'Recommender Systems in the EU: from Responsibility to Regulation?', *FAccTRec Workshop '21, September 27–October 1, 2021, Amsterdam, Netherlands*, p. 2.

103 Article 27, para. 2 of the DSA.

104 Article 38 and rec. 94 of the DSA.

27. The DSA also introduces a self-assessment obligation for VLOPs and VLOSEs about the systemic risks that their services may cause, e.g., regarding any negative effects for the exercise of fundamental rights linked to family/private life, freedom of speech, freedom and pluralism of the media, prohibition of discrimination and children' rights, or the intentional manipulation of their services, including through inauthentic use or automated exploitation means, that has a negative effect on the protection of public health, minors, civic discourse, or on electoral processes and public security.[105] VLOPs and VLOSEs shall consider, in particular, how the design of their recommender systems and any other relevant algorithmic system influence these risks including the dissemination of illegal content.[106] They must address these risks via mitigation measures adapting their recommender system.[107] These measures can include correcting the criteria used in their recommendations, discontinuing advertising revenue for specific information, improving the visibility of authoritative information sources[108] or measures preventing or minimising biases leading to discrimination of persons in vulnerable situations.[109]

28. Transparency is not only working one way in this approach. VLOPs and VLOSEs can also be requested by researchers, auditors, enforcement authorities to provide access to data to a certain extend and provide information on the algorithms used or the functioning and testing of algorithmic systems including their recommender systems.[110] This can include access to training data and algorithms.[111]

5. CONTENT MODERATION SYSTEMS

5.1. CONCEPTUALISATION OF CONTENT MODERATION AND EU LIABILITY RULES

29. The intermediary services providers gather a considerable amount of online content including user-generated content.[112] Online intermediary services have the power and sometimes the legal obligation to discourage or

105 Article 34, para 1. of the DSA.
106 Article 34 para. 2, a) and rec. 84 of the DSA.
107 Article 34, para. 1, d) and rec. 84 of the DSA.
108 Rec. 88 of the DSA.
109 Rec. 94 of the DSA.
110 Article 40, para 3 and rec. 96, art. 37 and rec. 92, art. 69 para. 2, f) and rec. 141 of the DSA.
111 Rec. 96 of the DSA.
112 E. Llansó, J. Van Hoboken, P. Leerssen and J. Harambam, 'Artificial intelligence, content moderation, and freedom of expression', Transatlantic Working Group paper series, February 2020, https://www.annenbergpublicpolicycenter.org/twg, p. 3.

even block the spread of illegal or unwelcome content.[113] Content moderation is also used to moderate irrelevant or off topic content. Algorithmic systems have become essential tools for scale content moderation on platforms services.[114] Furthermore, the legal provisions setting a limited time window for removal leave no other choice but to rely on automated tools.[115]

30. AI in content moderation is a broad concept. It can refer to the use of diverse automated processes at different content moderation stages. It includes processes, tools and techniques which may be as simple as keyword filters but also those relying on machine learning.[116] Automation can be used to detect, flag content but also to evaluate and enforce governance decisions such as suspending[117], blocking (sometimes geographically based), removing, tagging/labelling, demoting or prioritising. Algorithmic moderation systems help classifying user-generated content based on either matching or prediction techniques, leading to a decision and governance outcome.[118] Regarding the momentum of action, AI systems can be used to "pre-screen uploaded files before they become publicly available and block them".[119] They can also come at a later stage in the moderation process and inspect content already publicly available. Another technique based on AI system enables content de-prioritisation or deindexation and help reducing the visibility of certain content.[120] This could lead to shadow banning practices impacting marginalized communities.[121] As

---

113 Council of Europe, 'Guidance note on content moderation, Best practices towards effective legal and procedural frameworks for self-regulatory and co-regulatory mechanisms of content moderation', June 2021, https://www.coe.int/en/web/freedom-expression, p. 51.

114 T. Flew, F. Martin and N. Suzor, 'Internet regulation as media policy: Rethinking the question of digital communication platform governance', *Journal of Digital Media & Policy*, 2019, vol. 10, no.1, pp. 33, 41, 43.

115 Article 3 (3) of the EU regulation on addressing the dissemination of terrorist content online (also known as TERREG) provides that hosting services shall remove terrorist content or disable access to terrorist content in all Member States as soon as possible and in any event within one hour of receipt of the removal order. Regulation 2021/784 of the European Parliament and of the Council of 29 April 2021 on addressing the dissemination of terrorist content online, *OJ* L 172/79.

116 E. Llansó, J. Van Hoboken, P. Leerssen and J. Harambam, 'Artificial intelligence, content moderation, and freedom of expression.', Transatlantic Working Group paper series, February 2020, www.annenbergpublicpolicycenter.org/twg, p. 3.

117 In 2021, Facebook and Twitter had suspended US President Trump social media account on their respective platforms following an alleged violation of their terms and conditions. https://blog.twitter.com/en_us/topics/company/2020/suspension.

118 R. Gorwa, R. Binns and C. Katzenbach, 'Algorithmic content moderation: Technical and political challenges in the automation of platform governance', *Big Data and Society*, February 2020.

119 V. Golunova, 'Chapter 3 – Intermediary liability and freedom of expression in the algorithmic age: swaying the balance', H. Jacquemin (ed.), *Time to Reshape the Digital Society*, 1st edn., (Brussels: Larcier, 2021), p. 389.

120 Y. Poullet and N. Bontridder, 'L'Union européenne et la régulation de la désinformation', *Revue du Droit des Technologies de l'information.*, 2020/4, p. 35.

121 Shadow banning "consists in for an online social net-work in limiting the visibility of some of its users, without them being aware of it" E. Le Merrer et al., 'Setting the Record Straighter on

acknowledged by some major platforms, algorithmic content moderation is also used to manage the notices for action submitted by individuals, fact-checkers, rightsholders or public authorities.[122]

31. The two main categories of algorithmic content moderation are matching and predictive systems. Matching systems use cryptographic or hashing techniques. A piece of content is transformed into a 'hash' which is a string of data meant to uniquely identify the underlying content. The system then compares user generated content with the hash database containing existing and known content.[123] This system is used by the Global Forum to Counter Terrorism's (GIFCT) database to spot terrorist content [124] and also by ContentID (YouTube) for copyright infringement purposes.[125] Classification systems, also known as predictive systems, consists in the analysis of content with training data in order to identify common features in the content. The training data can contain generalised features such as nudity, blood, weapons leading to "blacklist" and whitelist keywords and vocabulary libraries.[126]

32. Intermediary service providers use AI media applications notably to comply with the intermediary liability rules. The European *lex generalis* for intermediary liability regime is the e-commerce directive[127] until the DSA becomes applicable. The directive provides, in its articles 12, 13 and 14, that their liability should be exempted for the content on their services if the intermediary service providers did not have actual knowledge of the illegal activity/content,

---

Shadow Banning', *IEEE INFOCOM 2021 – IEEE Conference on Computer Communications*, 2021. More information on this practice in C. Middlebrook, 'The Grey Area: Instagram, Shadowbanning, and the erasure of Marginalized Communities', *SSRN: https://ssrn.com/abstract=3539721,* February 2020.

122 V. Golunova, 'Chapter 3 – Intermediary liability and freedom of expression in the algorithmic age: swaying the balance', H. Jacquemin (ed.), *Time to Reshape the Digital Society*, 1st edn, (Brussels: Larcier, 2021), p. 389.

123 G. Sartor and A. Loreggia, 'Study for the European Parliament on the Impact of algorithms for online content filtering or moderation', September 2020, p. 40.

124 Global Internet Forum to Counter Terrorism, 'FAQ- What is the hash-sharing database?', https://gifct.org/explainers.

125 Youtube, Support page entitled: 'Youtube Practical Guide', https://support.google.com/youtube/answer/3244015.

126 H. Sun and W. Ni, 'Design and Application of an AI-Based Text Content Moderation System', *Scientific Programming*, vol. 2022, https://doi.org/10.1155/2022/2576535.

127 Directive 2000/31/EC of the European Parliament and of the Council of 8 June 2000 on certain legal aspects of information society services, in particular electronic commerce, in the Internal Market ('Directive on electronic commerce'), *OJ*, L 178, 17 July 2000, pp. 1–16. In Belgium, the directive has been initially transposed by two legislations: Act of 11 March 2003 on certain legal aspects of information society services referred to in Article 77 of the Constitution, *BS* 17 March 2003, and the Act of 11 March 2003 on certain legal aspects of information society services, *BS* 17 March 2003. But since then, these Acts were abrogated and now the e-commerce Directive implementation was transferred in Book XII in the Belgian Economical Code since 2013. Some aspects of the e-commerce are devoted to the Federal and some to the Communities for the cultural matters.

or if they acted expeditiously to remove or disable access to the information, when they became aware of its illegal character.[128] Providers must, in principle, remain passive to benefit from the liability exemption. Article 15 of the Directive also prohibits EU Member States to impose general monitoring obligations on providers, as opposed to specific monitoring obligations. This regime has now been transplanted in the DSA. Algorithmic content moderation enables proactive search for content, which jeopardises the passive role needed to benefit from the liability exemption. This could prevent providers from conducting algorithmic content moderation by fear of losing their liability exemption while a "refusal or unwillingness to use filters could also be considered as a form of negligence on the part of the intermediary".[129] These contradictory constraints seem to find a solution in the recent encouragements from the European Commission to intermediary services providers to adopt a more proactive approach to content moderation.[130] However, this could lead to potential risks of over blocking lawful content and unduly restricting freedom of expression. So far, content moderation obligations remain confusing and have not received a full answer in legal texts or case-law up until now. There is a call to have regulatory explicit clarification stating that "the mere fact that providers use AI-technologies does not automatically preclude the exemption of responsibility".[131]

33. The general framework is complemented by *lex specialis* addressing specific types of content, such as terrorist content, child sexual abuse material, copyright infringement and so forth.[132] The different types of content subject to

---

128 Transposed in Belgium in Book XII Chapter 6 Liability of intermediary services of the Belgian Economic Code. There is no addition on the use of AI systems for fulling these tasks.

129 E. Llansó, J. Van Hoboken, P. Leerssen and J. Harambam, 'Artificial intelligence, content moderation, and freedom of expression.', Transatlantic Working Group paper series, February 2020, www.annenbergpublicpolicycenter.org/twg, p. 12.

130 The encouragements emanate from several EU initiatives. European Commission, Recommendation 2018/334 on measures to effectively tackle illegal content online, 1 March 2018, *OJ* L 63; The EU Code of conduct on countering illegal hate speech online, June 2016, European Commission, Communication to the European Parliament, the Council, the European Economic and Social Committee and the Committee of the Regions, Tackling Illegal content online-Towards an enhanced responsibility of online platforms, 28 September 2017, COM(2017) 555 final. More information on the evolution of liability rules and the DSA in A. Kuczerawy, 'The Good Samaritan that wasn't: voluntary monitoring under the (draft) Digital Services Act', January 2021, https://www.law.kuleuven.be/citip/blog/the-good-samaritan-that-wasnt.

131 A. De Streel, M. Lognoul, H. Jacquemin and V. Ruelle, 'Study on Potential Policy Measures to Promote the Uptake and Use of AI in Belgium in Specific Economic Domains', for the Belgian Ministry of Economy (FPS Economy), 2022, p. 213.

132 The *lex specialis* regimes include the Copyright in the Digital Single Market Directive (Directive (EU) 2019/790 of the European Parliament and of the Council of 17 April 2019 on copyright and related rights in the Digital Single Market and amending Directives 96/9/EC and 2001/29/EC, *OJ* L 130; the child sexual abuse material Directive (Directive 2011/93/EU of the European Parliament and of the Council of 13 December 2011 on combating the sexual abuse and sexual exploitation of children and child pornography, and replacing Council

lex specialis are fundamentally different, firstly in terms of their illegality, but also their characteristics, the seriousness of their consequences and the legal basis applicable.[133] A one size fits all approach would be detrimental for freedom of expression; appropriate measures depending on the type of content, in the design of the algorithmic content moderation tools are necessary to ensure proportionate restriction.[134]

34. In addition to regulations imposing some form of content moderation, there is a growing number of self-and co-regulatory instruments adopted for addressing certain aspects of content moderation. In the EU, this is notably the case for disinformation and hate speech.[135] At a national level, content moderation is also part of the Belgian self-regulation for medias and journalists.[136] These regulatory approaches stand by their quick design and implementation. Yet, this speed involves a drawback on the checks and balances of a legislative or judicial procedure.[137]

5.2. RISKS AND BENEFITS

35. A constant tension exists between content moderation and freedom of expression. Media pluralism and legitimate content could be negatively impacted

---

Framework Decision 2004/68/JHA, *OJ* L 335); the Regulation preventing the dissemination of terrorist content online (Regulation 2021/784 of the European Parliament and of the Council of 29 April 2021 on addressing the dissemination of terrorist content online, *OJ* L 172/79); the AVMS Directive containing specific obligation for the video sharing platforms (Directive (EU) 2018/1808 of the European Parliament and of the Council of 14 November 2018 amending Directive 2010/13/EU on the coordination of certain provisions laid down by law, regulation or administrative action in Member States concerning the provision of audiovisual media services (Audiovisual Media Services Directive) in view of changing market realities, *OJ* L 303), and the Council framework decisions on illegal hate speech (Council Framework Decision 2008/913/JHA of 28 November 2008 on combating certain forms and expressions of racism and xenophobia by means of criminal law, *OJ* L 328). Some policy initiatives such as the code of conduct on hate speech, code of practice on disinformation are part of this regime even if they do not constitute legislation or binding obligations.

133 Council of Europe, 'Guidance note on content moderation, Best practices towards effective legal and procedural frameworks for self-regulatory and co-regulatory mechanisms of content moderation', June 2021, https://www.coe.int/en/web/freedom-expression, p. 39.

134 *Ibid.*

135 EU Code of practice on disinformation, adopted in April 2018, https://digital-strategy.ec.europa.eu/en/policies/code-practice-disinformation. There is also an EU Code of conduct on countering illegal hate speech online, adopted in May 2016, https://ec.europa.eu/info/policies/justice-and-fundamental-rights/combatting-discrimination/racism-and-xenophobia/eu-code-conduct-countering-illegal-hate-speech-online_en.

136 See the Code of Journalistic Ethics from the Conseil de déontologie journalistique, Article 16 and Code of the Raad voor de Journalistiek, p. 10, 17.

137 Council of Europe, 'Guidance note on content moderation, Best practices towards effective legal and procedural frameworks for self-regulatory and co-regulatory mechanisms of content moderation', June 2021, https://www.coe.int/en/web/freedom-expression, p. 29.

if a fair balance between content moderation and freedom of expression is not achieved.[138] On the positive side, AI systems have contributed on some occasions to quickly spot illegal content and support content moderation decisions.[139] They can indeed help assisting moderators and synthesising data to enlarge training data sets.[140]

36. Despite these beneficial effects, many scholars have underlined the risks that AI-based content moderation poses for the respect and exercise of fundamental rights including freedom of expression.[141] The scrutiny over these tools has increased during the COVID-19 pandemic and showed the overreliance of intermediary services on these AI-based tools and the limits associated with it.[142] The removal of an online post is a limitation of a user's freedom of expression, which needs to be performed in a predictable, legitimate, necessary and proportionate way.[143] This requirement does not however materialise in practice. Several issues arise, as described below.

37. The lack of accuracy is a serious risk of AI content moderation decision making. Used for detecting specific content, AI moderation systems are prone to false positives – i.e., when a legitimate content is qualified as problematic – and false negatives – i.e., when a problematic content is not spotted by the moderation system. Both will impact freedom of expression, including the freedom to impart and receive information. The lack of accuracy problem has several roots.

Primarily, AI content moderation tools cannot react to new contexts. Context[144] is essential to assess whether a specific content violates a legislation or

---

138 E. Llansó, J. Van Hoboken, P. Leerssen and J. Harambam, 'Artificial intelligence, content moderation, and freedom of expression.', Transatlantic Working Group paper series, February 2020, www.annenbergpublicpolicycenter.org/twg.

139 V. Golunova, 'Chapter 3 – Intermediary liability and freedom of expression in the algorithmic age: swaying the balance', H. Jacquemin (ed.), *Time to Reshape the Digital Society*, 1st edn, (Brussels: Larcier, 2021), p. 387.

140 Cambridge Consultants for OFCOM, '2019 Report on the Use of AI in online content moderation', July 2019, https://www.ofcom.org.uk/research-and-data/internet-and-on-demand-research/online-content-moderation.

141 E. Montero and Q. van Enis, 'Enabling freedom of expression in light of filtering measures imposed on Internet intermediaries: squaring the circle?', *Computer Law & Security Review*, 2011, 27, pp. 21 and 34; T. Gillespie, 'Content moderation, AI, and the question of scale', *Big Data & Society*, 2020, 7(2), pp. 1, 2; V. Golunova, 'Chapter 3 – Intermediary liability and freedom of expression in the algorithmic age: swaying the balance'; H. Jacquemin (ed.), *Time to Reshape the Digital Society*, 1st edn, (Brussels: Larcier, 2021), p. 387.

142 C. Shenkman, D. Thakur and E. Llansó, 'Do you see what I see? Capabilities and Limits of Automated Multimedia Content Analysis', Centre for Democracy & Technology, May 2021, p.6.

143 Council of Europe, 'Guidance note on content moderation, Best practices towards effective legal and procedural frameworks for self-regulatory and co-regulatory mechanisms of content moderation', June 2021, https://www.coe.int/en/web/freedom-expression, p. 14.

144 Including social, historical, linguistic contexts.

a policy.[145] They also fail to detect new unwanted content, which they have never encountered in their training or design.[146] In addition, with a fully automated moderating system, no human is kept in the loop of the AI decision. However, and especially for freedom of expression matters, it is essential to consider contextual, linguistic, and cultural elements before imposing any restrictions, to ensure a fair and balanced assessment.[147] Classification systems are specifically known for missing context or nuances. The AI systems could filter out parody, irony, content belonging to a legal exemption to intellectual property rights, journalistic or civil society work using illegal content for illustration, negatively impairing legitimate forms of expression and sometimes even privacy.[148]

Moreover, the strict time requirements to remove certain types of illegal content, such as for terrorist or child sexual abuse material content, have pushed providers, through threats of liability and fines, to heavily rely on algorithmic content moderation systems.[149] These threats can incentivise providers to take disproportionate measures leading to over-compliance impacting legitimate

---

145 E. Llansó, J. Van Hoboken, P. Leerssen and J. Harambam, 'Artificial intelligence, content moderation, and freedom of expression.', Transatlantic Working Group paper series, February 2020, www.annenbergpublicpolicycenter.org/twg, p.7.

146 C. Shenkman, D. Thakur and E. Llansó, 'Do you see what I see? Capabilities and Limits of Automated Multimedia Content Analysis', Centre for Democracy & Technology, May 2021, p. 7. For instance, an algorithm which has been designed to detect Holocaust denial cannot spot other genocide denials. See K. Hao, 'How Facebook got addicted to spreading misinformation', *MIT Technology Review*, March 2021, https://www.technologyreview.com/2021/03/11/1020600/facebook-responsible-ai-misinformation.

147 For instance, the YouTube moderating system has already blocked a chess channel by mistaking moves against black and white pieces as racist content. Wired, 'Why a YouTube Chat About Chess Got Flagged for Hate Speech?', January 2021, https://www.wired.com/story/why-youtube-chat-chess-flagged-hate-speech.

148 A recent investigation by the Irish Council for Civil Liberties showed that AI tools for scanning private communications to detect child sexual abuse material (CSAM) online suffer not only from low accuracy and high rates of false alarms. This has infringed people's data and privacy without reasonable suspicion because AI was not able to recognise the context and detect cases of private distribution among child peers above the age of sexual consent or knowing which legal age(s) of consent apply. Irish Council for Civil Liberties, 'An Garda Síochána unlawfully retains files on innocent people who it has already cleared of producing or sharing of child sex abuse material', 19 October 2022 and EDRI, 'a safe internet for all: upholding private and secure communications – EDRi network position paper on the 'Proposal for a Regulation of the European Parliament and of the Council laying down rules to prevent and combat child sexual abuse,' 2022/0155(COD) (CSA Regulation)', 19 October 2022.

149 We can name several legislatives instruments setting up short time requirements for removing specific content: the EU Regulation preventing the dissemination of terrorist content online: Regulation 2021/784 of the European Parliament and of the Council of 29 April 2021 on addressing the dissemination of terrorist content online, *OJ* L 172/79; the German NetzDG law (Netzwerkdurchsetzungsgesetz), October 2017 or the article 1 and 2 of the French proposal known as AVIA law (Proposition de loi visant à lutter contre la haine sur internet, n° 1785) which were then censored by the French Constitutional Council and do not appear in the adopted version of the legislation LAW n° 2020-766 of June 24, 2020 aimed at combating hateful content on the internet.

content. Platforms adopt strategies where removal is quick and automatic, but reintegration of content requires a specific and successful complaint. This approach echoes the concerns about online content moderation such as private censorship, prior restraint, and due process concerns.[150]

38. Another risk for freedom of expression is to have a (deliberate) censorship of specific group of people. This could be the result of platform prioritisation policy or from private censorship techniques such as preventively removing certain content, keywords or blocking authors from publishing on platforms services.[151] This could also be a result of malicious behaviour by individuals or group of individuals such as by submitting numerous individuals' complaints against content from a certain group of people.[152]

39. Despite efforts being made to improve the explainability of AI decision making, understanding machine learning systems remains a daunting technical task and hardly translate in human reasoning decision.[153] Individuals see their right to freedom of expression affected without being able to investigate or understand the underlying reasons.[154] This opacity prevents research, audits on understanding when and why content is only being flagged or directly removed.

40. Digital private actors are in a better position than public actors to act and address content moderation challenges as they are at the heart of the system and can – except for small players – rely on significant financial, human and technical resources. However, entrusting private stakeholders to take decisions on illegal content puts a great deal of power in their hands without democratic

---

150 E. Llansó, J. Van Hoboken, P. Leerssen and J. Harambam, 'Artificial intelligence, content moderation, and freedom of expression.', Transatlantic Working Group paper series, February 2020, www.annenbergpublicpolicycenter.org/twg, p. 9; J. Cobbe, 'Algorithmic Censorship by Social Platforms: Power and Resistance', *Philosophy & Technology*, 2021, vol. 34; I. A. Hartmann, 'A new framework for online content moderation', *Computer Law & Security Review*, 2020, vol. 36, pp. 7–8.

151 P. Butcher, 'Disinformation and democracy: the home front in the information war', *European Policy Centre*, Brussels, 2019, p. 3.

152 Council of Europe, 'Guidance note on content moderation, Best practices towards effective legal and procedural frameworks for self-regulatory and co-regulatory mechanisms of content moderation', June 2021, https://www.coe.int/en/web/freedom-expression, p. 25.

153 C. Shenkman, D. Thakur and E. Llansó, 'Do you see what I see? Capabilities and Limits of Automated Multimedia Content Analysis', Centre for Democracy & Technology, May 2021, p. 9; M. Ananny and K. Crawford, 'Seeing without knowing: limitations of the transparency ideal and its application to algorithmic accountability', *New Media and Society*, 13 December 2016, vol. 20, no. 3. Available at http://journals.sagepub.com/doi/abs/10.1177/14614448166766 45?journalCode=nmsa.

154 D. Kaye for the United Nations, 'Report of the Special Rapporteur to the General Assembly on AI and its impact on freedom of opinion and expression', 29 August 2018, https://www.ohchr.org/EN/Issues/FreedomOpinion/Pages/ReportGA73.aspx, p. 12.

control.[155] It bypasses the protection normally granted by the legal system when the intervention originates from the State and it renders a less visible speech control compared to classic State intervention.[156] Such delegation of power to platforms also leads to conflict of interests as inflammatory content maximises a platform growth.[157] A potential solution to this legitimacy risk, as suggested by Llansó et al., could be to have greater user controls or Application Programming Interfaces (APIs) that enable users to implement a third-party's content moderation rules on the content they view on a platform.[158]

5.3. NATIONAL FRAMEWORK

41. In Belgium, content moderation triggers the interweaving of the powers of the Federal State[159] and of the Communities in the fight against illegal content on the internet. Such exercise of powers requires cooperation.[160] Belgian legislation is currently silent regarding the use of AI systems in content moderation. No specific provisions can be found in the Belgian Code of Economic Law, nor at the Community level in the various media Decrees.

42. The Flemish public broadcaster VRT explains in its privacy policy that it uses AI to prevent and combat illegal practices, which is always done based on legitimate interest or to comply with their legal obligation to carry out their public broadcasting mission. They further clarify not to use automated decision making with legal or far-reaching consequences without human intervention.[161] Given the global dimension of content moderation systems, some harmonisation measures are put forward at the EU level.

---

155 P. Butcher, 'Disinformation and democracy: the home front in the information war', *European Policy Centre*, Brussels, 2019, p. 10.

156 A. Kuczerawy, 'Fighting online disinformation: did the EU Code of Practice forget about freedom of expression?', in G. Terzis et al. (ed.), *Disinformation and digital media as a challenge for democracy, European Integration and Democracies Series*, vol. 6 (Cambridge: Intersentia, June 2020) p. 301.

157 Inflammatory content trigger's emotional reaction which triggers user engagement and time spent on the services.

158 E. Llansó, J. Van Hoboken, P. Leerssen and J. Harambam, Artificial intelligence, content moderation, and freedom of expression., Transatlantic Working Group paper series, February 2020, www.annenbergpublicpolicycenter.org/twg, p. 11.

159 Book XII on digital economy law in the Belgian Code of Economic Law.

160 Conseil Supérieur de l'Audiovisuel (CSA), 'Guidance note on combating certain forms of illegal content on social media and videos on demand platform, in particular hate speech', 5 February 2020, https://www.csa.be/document/contenus-illicites-sur-les-reseaux-sociaux-et-plateformes-de-partage-video-le-csa-publie-une-note-dorientation, p. 41.

161 VRT, 'Privacy Policy', latest updated on 12 July 2021, https://www.vrt.be/nl/info/privacybeleid.

5.4. EU FRAMEWORK

43. As explained above[162], the European Union has been developing a new set of legislative measures applicable to digital technologies, including AI, in response to the challenge they raise. With respect to automated content moderation, the EU took in its DSA the approach which was proposed in 2018 by the United Nations Special Rapporteur on the promotion and protection of the right to freedom of opinion and expression. The Special Rapporteur, David Kaye, had reported that "radical transparency about the impact of an AI system in the information environment requires disclosure of, for example, data on how much content is removed by AI systems, how often AI-suggested content removals are approved by a human moderator, how often content removals are contested and how often challenges to content removal are upheld".[163]

44. Indeed, transparency from intermediary services on AI content moderation systems is key to the DSA. The text provides that intermediary services must include in their terms and conditions, in a clear and ambiguous language, information on tools used for the purpose of content moderation, including algorithmic decision-making.[164] Decisions from intermediary on content should indicate information on the use of automated means for reaching the decision.[165] AI systems would be allowed for managing complaints on intermediary providers decision on content but only if humans are in the loop.[166] In addition, the text provides for an obligation for intermediary services to draft yearly transparency reports on content moderation.[167] These reports must include meaningful and comprehensible information on any use made of automatic means for the purpose of content moderation and a qualitative description, a specification of the precise purposes, indicators of the accuracy and the possible rate of error of the automated means used in fulfilling those purposes, and any safeguards applied.[168] VLOPs and VLOSEs will have additional elements to report on such as the human resources dedicated to

---

162 See fn. 69.

163 D. Kaye for the United Nations, 'Report of the Special Rapporteur to the General Assembly on AI and its impact on freedom of opinion and expression', 29 August 2018, https://www.ohchr.org/EN/Issues/FreedomOpinion/Pages/ReportGA73.aspx, p. 17.

164 Article 14 combined with rec. 45 of the DSA.

165 Article 17 para. 3, c) of the DSA. For online platforms, the DSA goes one step further and requests online platforms to submit content moderation decision and the statement of the reasons in a database managed by the Commission. (Article 24, para. 5 and recital 66 of the DSA).

166 Article 20 para. 6 of the DSA.

167 Article 23 of the proposal initially only included online platforms but and now Article 15 of DSA widens the scope of the obligation by also including intermediary services.

168 Article 15, para. 1, c) and e) of the DSA.

content moderation, their training, languages expertise and accuracy indicators per official EU languages.[169]

45. VLOPs and VLOSEs will also have to assess and mitigate systemic risks stemming from their content moderation systems.[170] Mitigation measures may include adapting content moderation and decision-making processes.[171] In addition, the DSA introduces a crisis mechanism which enables the Commission to request, where a crisis occur,[172] the adoption of certain specific measures to be taken urgently by VLOPS or VLOSEs including adapting content moderation processes or relevant algorithms systems and increasing the resources dedicated to content moderation.[173]

46. Similarly to recommender systems[174], VLOPs may also be subject to access and explanation requests in relation to the design, the logic, the functioning and the testing of the algorithmic systems for content moderation.[175] This could include data training data and algorithms, or data on processes and outputs of content moderation.[176] With all of these provisions, the EU tried to bring more clarity about proactive measures for content moderation.

6. DEEPFAKES

6.1. DEFINITION

47. Deepfake is a term that first emerged in 2017 to describe realistic photo, audio, video, text[177] and other forgeries generated with artificial intelligence

169 Article 42, para. 2, a) of the DSA.

170 See para. 27 of this chapter. Article 34, para. 2, b) of the DSA.

171 Article 35, para. 1, c) and rec. 84 of the DSA. The mitigation measures may include "content moderation personnel, their training and local expertise" and "the speed and quality of processing notices related to specific types of illegal content and, where appropriate, the expeditious removal of or disabling access to the content notified, in particular for the illegal hate speech or cyber violence; as well as adapting any relevant decision-making processes and dedicated resources for content".

172 Article 36 of the DSA provides that a "crisis shall be deemed to have occurred where extraordinary circumstances lead to a serious threat to public security or public health in the Union or in significant parts thereof".

173 Rec. 91 of the DSA.

174 See para. 28 of this chapter.

175 Article 40 and rec. 96, art. 37 and rec. 92, art. 69 para. 2, f) and rec. 141 of the DSA.

176 Rec. 96 of the DSA.

177 Text based deepfakes can imitate the style of a target from the vocabulary used, the emotional subtleties, intentions expressed. M. van Huijstee et al. for the EPRS, 'Study: Tackling deepfakes in European Policy', July 2021, p. II.

technologies.[178] The name comes from the contraction between deep learning and fake (news). Deepfakes merge, combine, replace and superimpose images and video clips creating a fake content that appears authentic.[179] They were first to generate fake pornographic films of well-known actresses such as Gal Galdot or Scarlett Johansson.[180]

48. Images have an impactful influence on society even more since the beginning of social media era. Indeed, videos and images have become popular means of communication thanks to the social media, stories, video sharing platforms like YouTube or Twitch and video-on-demand platforms like Netflix. Deepfakes can become viral such as the Tom Cruise high quality one created by Chris Umé, a Belgian visual effects expert which gathered rapidly some million views.[181] Image manipulation options are even included in popular social media platforms including Instagram, TikTok and Snapchat. Up until now, it required a high degree of skill to produce very convincing deepfake videos.[182] However, thanks to progress in artificial intelligence, deepfakes are becoming more and more realistic hence difficult to spot to the naked eyes and even more for a non-specialised audience.

6.2. RISKS AND BENEFITS

49. As for nearly every AI media applications, deepfakes may have both positive and negative effects on fundamental rights including freedom of expression. Creative industries such as the entertainment sector (movies, games) but also digital communications are benefitting from this technology capable of enhancing creativity and technical possibilities. Deepfakes support both freedom of the arts[183] and freedom of expression, as they constitute instruments to creatively express satire, personal or artistic expression. Deepfakes can also be

---

178 US Congressional Research Service, 'Deep Fake and National Security', August 2020, https://apps.dtic.mil/sti/pdfs/AD1117081.pdf.

179 M.-H. Maras and A. Alexandrou. 'Determining authenticity of video evidence in the age of artificial intelligence and in the wake of Deepfake videos', *The International Journal of Evidence & Proof*, 2018, vol. 23, no. 3, p. 255.

180 K.A. Pantserev, 'The Malicious Use of AI-Based Deepfake Technology as the New Threat to Psychological Security and Political Stability' in H. Jahankhani, S. Kendzierskyj, N. Chelvachandran and N. Ibarra (eds), *Cyber Defence in the Age of AI, Smart Societies and Augmented Humanity*, (New-York: Springer, 2020).

181 La Libre Belgique, 'Les vidéos deepfakes de Tom Cruise sont l'œuvre d'un belge', 5 March 2021, https://www.lalibre.be/lifestyle/people/2021/03/05/les-videos-deepfake-de-tom-cruise-sur-tik-tok-sont-loeuvre-dun-belge-M2WCHTTFQ5GYFKBRPT6JE4N67U.

182 Europol, 'Report: Malicious use and abuse of artificial intelligence', 19 November 2020, p. 59 https://www.europol.europa.eu/publications-documents/malicious-uses-and-abuses-of-artificial-intelligence.

183 Article 13 of the Charter of fundamental Rights of the European Union.

used in case of speech impediment, for reshooting facility, for the revival of old stars.[184] Furthermore, in an attention economy, deepfakes can be used to catch audience on certain topics. In 2020, the Belgian Prime Minister Sophie Wilmès was subject of a deepfake created by the group Extinction Rebellion to raise environmental and climate awareness.[185]

50. Besides these positive aspects, deepfakes are a matter of concern for various reasons: the outreach they can have, the increasing level of precision which makes them hard to detect, the fact that anybody with a computer or smartphone can become a deepfake creator and that they can be made without the consent of the individuals targeted by the deepfake.[186]

51. Europol has identified eleven malicious and criminal purposes for deepfakes including harming someone's reputation, harassment, spreading disinformation, supporting extremist narratives, spreading incitement to violence and manipulation.[187] A study on deepfakes from 2021 carried out at the request of the European Parliamentary Research Service also provides an overview of the wide and diverse categories of risks (psychological, financial, societal) associated with deepfakes.[188] The "impact of a single deepfake is not limited to a single type or category of risk, but rather to a combination of cascading impacts at different levels", including individual, organisational and

---

184 This would lead to interesting copyrights and neighbouring rights question.

185 Extinction rebellion is a global environmental movement. Extinction Rebellion, '#TellTheTruthBelgium campaign: Press coverage', April 2020, https://www.extinctionrebellion.be/en/news/2020/04/20/tellthetruthbelgium-campaign-press-coverage.

186 M. van Huijstee et al. for the EPRS, 'Study: Tackling deepfakes in European Policy', July 2021.

187 The complete list is: Destroying the image and credibility of an individual, Harassing or humiliating individuals online, Perpetrating extortion and fraud, Facilitating document fraud, Falsifying online identities and fooling KYC (know your customer/client) mechanisms, Falsifying or manipulating electronic evidence for criminal justice investigations, Disrupting financial markets, Distributing disinformation and manipulating public opinion, Inciting acts of violence toward minority groups, Supporting the narratives of extremist or even terrorist groups, and Stoking social unrest and political polarization. In addition, the report indicates that deepfakes are not yet massively used by the criminal community given the costs, necessary technical skills, and short life span of the deepfakes. However, if technological progresses are made and provide more accessible and high quality deepfakes, this trend will change. Europol, 'Report: Malicious use and abuse of artificial intelligence', 19 November 2020, pp. 52 and 56, https://www.europol.europa.eu/publications-documents/malicious-uses-and-abuses-of-artificial-intelligence. Since then, another report further researched on the topic. Europol, 'Facing reality? Law enforcement and the challenge of deepfakes', April 2022, https://www.europol.europa.eu/publications-events/publications/facing-reality-law-enforcement-and-challenge-of-deepfakes.

188 Psychological harm: (s)extortion, defamation, intimidation, bullying, undermining trust. Financial harm: extortion, identity theft, fraud (insurance/payment), stock-price manipulation, brand damage, reputational damage. Societal harm: news media manipulation, damage to economic stability, damage to justice system, damage to the scientific system, erosion of trust, damage to democracy, manipulation of elections, damage to international relations, damage to national security).

societal.[189] In numbers, deepfake pornography is by far the most prevalent kind of deepfake currently being created and circulated, with women almost exclusively being targeted.[190] Even if politically motivated deepfakes are relatively rare, their impact must not be underestimated.[191] Ali Bongo deepfake in Gabon has led to an unsuccessful coup by the Gabonese military.[192] So far, it is also surprising that some of the most prolific deepfake videos which went viral were not created for malicious intent, but rather for the purpose of raising awareness with the goal of highlighting the potential threat of this technology.[193]

52. Before being identified as fake, these deepfakes might have influenced the viewers, especially in presence of a short impact window triggering some immediate emotional response.[194] Trust in information, authorities and media is crucial for the stability of social interactions and structures. Deepfakes, by removing trust in news, lead to doubt on everything.[195] Beside confusing individuals, another major threat is that once published, the deepfakes are reposted in various platforms which makes it almost impossible to delete. In addition, identifying the author seems increasingly complex due to these

189 M. van Huijstee et al. for the EPRS, 'Study: Tackling deepfakes in European Policy', July 2021, pp. IV-V: Here is an illustration, the first impact is an impact on the individual targeted in the deepfake for instance a video aiming to incriminate someone, secondly a group impact such as the need for a Court to adjust its process to verify the deepfake presented as evidence and thirdly a societal impact where the court system could be undermined when incorrectly qualifying an evidence of deep fake. Recently a UK Court received a fake audio recording to influence a custody case; G. Swerling, 'Doctored audio evidence used to damn father in custody battle.', *The Telegraph,* 31 January 2020). https://www.telegraph.co.uk/news/2020/01/31/deepfake-audio-used-custody-battle-lawyer-reveals-doctored-evidence.

190 H. Ajder, G.Patrini, F. Cavalli, and L. Cullen for Deeptrace, 'The State of DeepFakes – Landscape, threats and Impact', September 2019, p. 6–7;15 https://regmedia.co.uk/2019/10/08/deepfake_report.pdf; S. Maddocks, 'A Deepfake Porn Plot Intended to Silence Me: exploring continuities between pornographic and 'political' deep fakes', *Porn Studies*, 2020, p. 415, DOI: 10.1080/23268743.2020.1757499.

191 C. Langlais-Fontaine, 'Démêler le vrai du faux: étude de la capacité du droit actuel à lutter contre les deepfakes', *Revue des droits de l'homme*, 2020, no. 18, p. 4, https://journals.openedition.org/revdh/9747.

192 In this video, the President Ali Bongo was reassuring the population after a cardiac attack, but an opposition leader identified the video as a deepfake and put in question the President's ability to govern. Despite denial from Ali Bongo's crew, this doubt pushed the army to tempt a coup. M. Westerlund, 'The Emergence of Deepfake Technology: A Review', *Technology Innovation Management Review*, 2019, pp. 40–53, http://doi.org/10.22215/timreview/1282.

193 Europol, 'Report: Malicious use and abuse of artificial intelligence', 19 November 2020, p. 56, https://www.europol.europa.eu/publications-documents/malicious-uses-and-abuses-of-artificial-intelligence.

194 For instance, deepfakes seriously incriminating a candidate the night before an election.

195 S. Karnouskos, 'Artificial Intelligence in Digital Media: the era of deepfakes', *EEE Transactions on Technology and Society,* 2020, vol. 1, no. 3, p. 8; Europol, 'Report: Malicious use and abuse of artificial intelligence', 19 November 2020, p. 53, https://www.europol.europa.eu/publications-documents/malicious-uses-and-abuses-of-artificial-intelligence.

successive reuploads but also due to increasingly sophisticated anonymisation and obfuscation techniques.

6.3. NATIONAL FRAMEWORK

53. This section analyses the Belgian legal arsenal applicable to deepfakes and assesses the potential legal grounds for victims to claim back their face, body and voice. Deepfake technology is not only accessible to professionals but also to every individual, which may motivate the existence of legal remedies and *ex post* measures directly available for victims. Belgium currently does not have a legislation specifically tackling deepfakes. In 2019, deepfakes were hotly debated in Belgium at the political level and multiple parliamentary questions were submitted to several Federal Ministers.[196] The answers given in March 2020 explained that there had been no known cases of deepfake leading to major confusion in Belgium. The deepfakes applications were limited to experiments by journalists, media and universities and were used in the entertainment industry.[197]

54. The section presents a selection of legal frameworks, which could help deepfakes victims: on disinformation, data protection, criminal law, personality's rights and right to image and intermediary liability. This analysis does not aim to be exhaustive. Questions relating to intellectual property rights[198], competition, and consumer's law can also be associated to deepfakes but does not fit the framework of this chapter.

55. Deepfakes are often assimilated to a disinformation technique but not all deepfakes can be categorised as disinformation material. Disinformation framework would only apply in some cases. In Belgium, there is also no legal framework on disinformation. This can partly be explained by the 2018 Report

---

196 Senate of Belgium, Written question n° 7-83, 14 October 2019, https://www.senate.be/www/?MIval=/Vragen/SVPrintNLFR&LEG=7&NR=83&LANG=nl; Senate of Belgium, Written question n° 7-82, 14 October 2019, https://www.senate.be/www/?MIval=/Vragen/SVPrint&LEG=7&NR=82&LANG=fr; Senate of Belgium, Written question n° 7-81, 14 October 2019, https://www.senate.be/www/?MIval=/Vragen/SVPrintNLFR&LEG=7&NR=81&LANG=fr.

197 Senate of Belgium, Written question n° 7-81, 14 October 2019, https://www.senate.be/www/?MIval=/Vragen/SVPrintNLFR&LEG=7&NR=81&LANG=fr.

198 Intellectual property rights which raise interesting questions both concerning the original material protection used to produce a deepfake but also as to whether the deepfake itself could be protected under the intellectual property regime – as an original creation or as a parody. As often, "as with new technologies, the law is unequipped to handle these impending issues". See D. Harris, 'Deepfakes: False Pornography Is Here and the Law Cannot Protect You', *Duke Law & Technology Review*, 2019, p. 102.

of the Belgian Expert Group on False Information and Disinformation.[199] The report recommended against adopting specific law as attempts to do so risk undermining freedom of expression. Instead, the group of experts opted for a model of consultation, cooperation and education.[200] This non-legal strategy was both criticised[201] and welcomed[202] by authors. An information report from the Belgian Senate then underlined the multi-territoriality dimension of the phenomenon, which requires uniting forces within Belgium but also with the EU and international organisations.[203] Belgium is currently studying the different recommendations for disinformation regulation provided in the report.[204] These recommendations are organised around two main axis: 1) measures targeting the disseminators of disinformation in collaboration and harmony with EU initiatives and 2) measures aiming at strengthening the citizens' resistance to the disinformation.[205] Regarding the educational and awareness raising aspects of disinformation and deepfakes, Flanders and the French Community have already undertaken some preventive measures through youth education, factchecking and digital transition funds.[206]

56. The data protection regime offers legal grounds to protect individuals against the unconsented use of their personal data. Article 4 of the General Data Protection Regulation (GDPR)[207] provides that personal data are any information relating to an identified or identifiable natural person, this includes information contained in a visual image. To fall in the GDPR scope,

---

199 A. Rouvroy et al., 'Report of the Belgian Expert Group on False Information and Disinformation', July 2018.

200 *Ibid.*, p. 15.

201 E. Marique and A. Strowel, 'La régulation des *fake news* et avis factices sur les plateformes', *Revue internationale de droit économique*, t. XXXIII, 2019/3, pp. 383–398., https://www.cairn.info/revue-internationale-de-droit-economique-2019-3-page-383.htm.

202 F. Ernotte, *Droit des réseaux sociaux*, 1st edn (Brussels: Larcier, 2021), p. 35.

203 Belgian Senate, 'Information report concerning the necessary collaboration between the federal authority and the Communities in the fight against fake news', session 2021–2022, nr. 7-110/2, 25 October 2021, p. 3 https://www.senate.be/www/?MIval=/Dossiers/Informatieverslag&LEG=7&NR=110&LANG=fr.

204 *Ibid.*, pp. 45–48.

205 *Ibid.*

206 The French community created the Higher Council for Media Education (Conseil supérieur de l'éducation aux médias (CSEM), https://csem.be/educationauxmedias) and the Flemish Community created the Flemish Knowledge Center Digital and Media Literacy (Vlaams Kenniscentrum Digitale en Mediawijsheid, https://mediawijs.be/over-ons). Flanders has fact checking projects in place: Factcheck.Vlaanderen and FactRank. Some Funds are also in place to ensure the digital transition of the medias and support the fight against disinformation. The Senate report recommends investing in AI technologies enabling identification and flagging of disinformation. Source: Belgian Senate, Information Report, pp. 18 and 37.

207 European Union, Regulation (EU) 2016/679 of the European Parliament and of the Council of 27 April 2016 on the protection of natural persons with regard to the processing of personal data and on the free movement of such data, and repealing Directive 95/46/EC (General Data Protection Regulation), *OJ* L119, 4 May 2016.

the personal data must be part of a processing activity.[208] Personal data are processed when deepfakes are created.[209] Yet, even if deepfakes are falling in the GDPR scope, individual's' rights[210] enforcement is hard to achieve particularly when identifying authors is a struggle and when content gets easily copied and reuploaded. In addition, data subjects are sometimes not even aware of the processing of their personal data, which prevents them from activating their other GDPR rights such as the right to be forgotten.[211] Even if enforced, the right to be forgotten may not be sufficient to completely remove the deepfake from the internet.[212] However, the GDPR remains a powerful tool at the disposal of a deepfake victim, which can activate their right to object.

57. Criminal law is another area of law that can capture deepfakes. Yet, a common obstacle for the application of criminal law to prosecute deepfakes creators is the difficulty to gather all the constitutive elements of these offences, especially regarding the strict interpretation of criminal law.[213] The criminal offences rarely perfectly fit deepfakes situation and it will be up to the judge to decide. The identity and the intentional character of the author are also hard to demonstrate for victims.[214] They could have various motives including the intention to harm, but also commercial motives.[215] Several criminal provisions could be envisaged:

- Revenge porn. Article 371 of the Belgian Criminal Code (BCC) prohibits taking a visual or audio recordings without permission or knowledge, while the person was nude or engaged in explicit sexual activity, but also disseminating or making this recording or the images available without that person's consent or knowledge, even if that person consented to the making of the images or recordings. However, the criminal code does not address the creation of manipulated pornographic images, audio or video made

208 Commission de la protection de la vie privée, 'Avis n°14/95 Applicabilité de la loi du 8 décembre 1992 relative à la protection de la vie privée à l'égard des traitements de données à caractère personnel à l'enregistrement d'images et ses conséquences', *J.T.*, 1996, pp. 586 and M. Isgour et B. Vinçotte, *Le droit à l'image*, (Brussels: Larcier, 2014), pp. 26–27.

209 B. van der Sloot and Y. Wagensveld, 'Deepfakes: regulatory challenges for the synthetic society', *Computer Law & Security Review*, 2022, p. 7.

210 Chapter III of the GDPR.

211 Article 17 GDPR.

212 N. Debruyne, *Grenzen voorbij*, (Antwerpen: Intersentia, 2020), p. 439.

213 *Nulla poena sine lege* (Article 12 and 14 of the Belgian Constitution, Article 7 of the ECHR, Article 15(1) of the UN International Covenant on Civil and Political Rights).

214 C. Langlais-Fontaine, 'Démêler le vrai du faux: étude de la capacité du droit actuel à lutter contre les deepfakes', *Revue des droits de l'homme*, 2020, no. 18, p. 4.

215 Belgian Senate, 'Information report concerning the necessary collaboration between the federal authority and the Communities in the fight against fake news', 7-110/2, session 2021–2022, 25 October 2021, p. 14 https://www.senate.be/www/?MIval=/Dossiers/Informatieversla g&LEG=7&NR=110&LANG=fr.

from images without any sexual character[216] and without the consent of the victim.[217]

- *Harassment.* Article 442*bis* of the BCC provides the legal ground for harassing. Aggravating circumstances to harassment may be used when the infraction is motivated by hatred, contempt or hostility towards a person because of their sex. As, the majority of pornographic deepfakes are targeting women[218], such behaviour could qualify as harassment motivated by the sex of the victim.
- *Computer Forgery.* Article 210*bis* of the BCC sanctions behaviour that distorts the truth through the use of computers, namely computer forgery. However, to fall in the scope of computer forgery, there must be a situation of deliberate distortion of the truth of data with impaired legal effect.[219] Some authors believe that despite the absence of case-law on deepfakes and computer forgery, this provision could apply to the creation of deepfakes.[220]
- *Defamation.* Article 443 of the BCC provides that anybody who has maliciously imputed to a person a specific fact, which is likely to cause damage to that person's honour or expose them to public contempt can be pursued for defamation. The provision indicates that images also fall in the scope. When deepfakes are used to present an individual - or a company - in a way that could harm their reputation, this provision could be applicable. In the event of pornographic deepfakes, the intention to commit this offence can be presumed by the fact of uploading the video online on a pornographic website or a social media platform. However here as well, once categorised as defamation, the judge will conduct a balancing exercise with other potential clashing rights, including freedom of expression and freedom of the arts. Any interference of the right to private life must take place in compliance with the principles of lawfulness, legitimacy and necessity.

---

216 M.-A. Weiss, 'Deepfakes, Fake News, Mauvais Sosie et Fausses Nouvelles', *Revue Francophone de la Propriété Intellectuelle*, November 2019, no. 9, p. 39. In the United Kingdom, the Law Commission, which is an independent legal body, stated that Deepfake Porn should now be considered a crime, along with Revenge Porn. This Statement came after victims were being denied justice because the existing gaps in the law which has not kept up with new, high-tech forms of abuse and which left victims unprotected. Law Commission (UK), Reforms to laws around intimate image abuse proposed to better protect victims, 26 February 2021, https://www.lawcom.gov.uk/reforms-to-laws-around-intimate-image-abuse-proposed-to-better-protect-victims.

217 C. Langlais-Fontaine, 'Démêler le vrai du faux: étude de la capacité du droit actuel à lutter contre les deepfakes', *Revue des droits de l'homme*, 2020, no. 18, p. 4.

218 H. Ajder, G.Patrini, F. Cavalli and L. Cullen for Deeptrace, 'Report on the State of DeepFakes - Landscape, threats and Impact', September 2019, pp. 6, 7 and 15.

219 Cass., 23 December 1998, *J.L.M.B.*, 1999, p. 393.

220 F. Ernotte, *Droit des réseaux sociaux*, 1st edn (Brussels: Larcier, 2021), p. 210.

- Identity theft. Article 231 of the BCC provides that "anyone who publicly takes a name that does not belong to him shall be punished". This provision only covers deepfakes if the author of the deepfakes has taken the name, the provision does not speak of image or voice. This provision therefore seems too narrow for tackling deepfakes.

Next to these provisions creating offences, the press offence regime could also apply but, as we will see, to textual deepfakes only. Press offence is not a criminal offence as such but is a regime constituting a procedural safeguard for freedom of expression when an offence is committed via press.[221] It is enshrined in the Belgian Constitution.[222] Under such regime, the so-called press offence can only be prosecuted following a burdensome procedure at the *Cour d'Assises*, with a popular jury. However, in 1999 the legislator adopted an exception to this procedure and now press offences on racism or xenophobia are handled by the criminal court.[223] There are four constitutive elements of press offence, which have been developed by the case-law: (1) the expression of an opinion, (2) a punishable opinion; (3) in a text, reproduced by printing or by a similar process, (4) an opinion reproduced and made public. Online publishing has been assimilated as a "similar process".[224] Therefore, press offences do not include the dissemination of oral or audio-visual opinions, as they do not constitute (digitally) printed texts.[225] Hence, deepfakes made of pictures or videos would not be covered but the press offences regime. It would only apply to textual deepfakes (made of text synthesis technologies) and only if the four constitutive elements are met.

58. The right to image is another legal ground which could be used for deepfakes' victims. In Belgium, the right to image derives from the fundamental right to the protection of private life (as protected by article 22 of the Belgian Constitution and article 8 of the ECHR), on the one hand, and from article XI.174 of the Code of Economic Law, on the other hand. According to this provision, the individual must consent[226] to further reproduction, communication or dissemination of their images. The burden of proof

221 *Ibid.*, p. 218.

222 Article 150 of the Belgian Constitution.

223 Article 1 of the law of 7 May 1999 on the amendment to the Constitution, *BS* 29 May 1999.

224 Cass., 6 March 2012, AR P.11 1374.N, www.juridat.be.

225 S. Royer and N. Krack, 'Cour d'appel Liège (chambre des mises en accusation), 01 April 2021 – Comment les incels ont déclenché la compétence de la cour d'assises en matière de délit de presse', *La revue du jurisprudence de Liège, Mons et Bruxelles*, 2021, no. 38, p. 1741.

226 The form of the consent abides by the Belgian civil law rules which means it can be manifested in expressed, explicit, tacit or silent (it is not a solemn act) ways, as long as the consent is certain and non-equivocal. The consent is also specific and must related to determined use and context. F. Jongen and A. Strowel, *Droit des médias et de la communication*, 1st edn, (Brussels: Larcier, 2017), p. 422.

relies on the one who avails themselves of an authorisation unless there is a presumption of manifest consent.[227] The right to image keeps evolving based on new technology developments such as smartphones and drones which enable an increasing exposure of individuals to their image capture.[228] Several conditions must be met to action this right. First, there must be an image enabling the identification of a natural person to third party. This can include the voice and the name, even if these cases are rare.[229] The reproduction mode of someone's image does not matter, it can be a drawing, a photograph, audio-visual images, a verbal description that reliably identifies the person.[230] Second, the image must concern a physical individual. Third, the physical individual must remain recognisable and it does not matter if the image is processed with other images.[231] In addition, contrary to the rights granted under the GDPR, the right to image is still valid for 20 years after the individual's death for its rights holders. *Post mortem* deepfakes could still be punished under this scheme.[232]

59. The scope of someone's right to image and right to private life must be balanced with other fundamental rights such as the right to freedom of expression.[233] and with criteria developed by the case-law.[234] Caricature or other creative work contributing to a general interest purpose can counterbalance someone's right to image.[235] This could be the case of the famous Barack Obama deepfake[236] warning about the danger of new technologies and artificially manipulated videos.[237]

---

227 *Ibid.*, p. 423.

228 *Ibid.*, p. 413.

229 Liège, 10th Chamber, 13 January 2003, *Auteurs & Media*, 2003/3, p. 213, note B. Remiche and R. Dethier, 'L'hôtel Simenon et le droit d'auteur', *La revue de jurisprudence de Liège, Mons et Bruxelles*, 2003/18, p. 778; Civ. Ghent, 19 November 2003, *Auteurs & Media*, 2004/4, p. 384. The former tennis champion Kim Clijsters was also able to object to the use of her first name "Kim" in an advertisement that identified her behind this common name.

230 F. Jongen and A. Strowel, *Droit des médias et de la communication*, 1st edn (Brussels: Larcier, 2017), p. 417.

231 V. Verstraeten and N. Somers, 'Juridische wapens tegen deepfake', *De Juristenkrant*, 2019, no. 400, p. 16.

232 Article XI.174 of the Code of Economic Law and Recital 27 of the GDPR.

233 ECtHR, 7 February 2012, no. 40660/08 and 60641/08, *Van Hannover vs. Germany II.*

234 The public status of the victim, the prior conduct of the victim, the contribution to public interest debate, the behaviours of the journalist or other, the type and reach of the medium, the severity of the sanction imposed, are elements taken into account. F. Jongen and A. Strowel, *Droit des médias et de la communication*, 1st edn (Brussels: Larcier, 2017), p. 420; These criteria are developed by the caselaw in ECtHR, 7 February 2012, no. 39954/08, *Axel Springer AG v. Germany*, para. 101.

235 F. Jongen and A. Strowel, *Droit des médias et de la communication*, 1st ed (Brussels: Larcier, 2017), p. 420.

236 Obama deepfake accessible here: https://www.youtube.com/watch?v=cQ54GDm1eL0.

237 C. Langlais-Fontaine, 'Démêler le vrai du faux: étude de la capacité du droit actuel à lutter contre les deepfakes', *Revue des droits de l'homme*, 2020, no. 18, p. 8.

60. Victims could engage intermediary services liability[238] for deepfakes that can be qualified as illegal based on the various options introduced in this section.[239] This approach can be particularly useful in case of unidentified uploader.[240] Indeed, deepfakes are mostly distributed on platforms including pornographic and social media platforms.[241] Take down request and flagging tools should be employed and documented by victims to prove the actual knowledge from the intermediary services hosting the illegal content.

61. There is a real patchwork of legal grounds which could be of help for individuals or companies victims of deepfakes. The solutions are quite fragmented, and the phenomenon is overlapping different legislation which is preventing a comprehensive and impactful legal solution. Solutions are sometimes hypothetical as they are not yet confirmed by case-law. More guidance from the policymakers is therefore necessary. The European Union has decided to deal specifically with the phenomenon in its new legislative proposal, the AI Act proposal.

62. Not only legal provisions can help fighting the damages of deepfakes. Indeed, Mika Westerlund has pointed out that deepfakes can be combatted via a mix of different measures including legislation and regulation, corporate policies and voluntary actions, education and training, as well as the development of technology for deepfake detection, content authentication, and deepfake prevention.[242] On concrete initiatives from the Belgian media sector, deepfakes have notably been the subject of media literacy initiatives by the VRT.[243] Media literacy organisations have also deepfakes on their agenda and more broadly their link with disinformation.[244]

---

238 See paragraph 31 on intermediary liability for more information.

239 Intermediary Liability regime from the e-commerce Directive implemented in the Belgian Economical Code XII.17 to XII.20.

240 F. Ernotte, *Droit des réseaux sociaux*, 1st edn (Brussels: Larcier, 2021), p. 22.

241 S. Karnouskos, 'Artificial Intelligence in Digital Media: the era of deepfakes', *EEE Transactions on Technology and Society*, 2020, vol.1, no.3, p. 7.

242 M. Westerlund, 'The Emergence of Deepfake Technology: A Review', *Technology Innovation Management Review*, 2019, pp. 39–53. https://doi.org/10.22215/timreview/1282.

243 VRT, '2020 Annual report', p. 56, https://www.vrt.be/nl/over-de-vrt/prestaties/jaarverslag.

244 Here are some Belgian media literacy association active in the education about disinformation but also deepfakes: Mediawijs (https://www.mediawijs.be/nl), Stamp Media (https://www.stampmedia.be), Média Animation (https://media-animation.be), Action Médias Jeune (https://www.actionmediasjeunes.be).

6.4. EU FRAMEWORK

63. The AI Act proposal[245] categorises deepfakes as part of the limited risks category. The proposal, which is based on a risk-based approach only imposes transparency requirement for circulating on the EU market to this category of risk. Article 52.3 of the proposal provides that "users of an AI system that generates or manipulates image, audio or video content that appreciably resembles existing persons, objects, places or other entities or events and would falsely appear to a person to be authentic or truthful ('deepfake'), shall disclose that the content has been artificially generated or manipulated". Textual deepfakes seem to have been forgotten from the scope of the provision. Recital 70 further clarifies that the disclosure should be done by labelling the artificial intelligence output accordingly and disclosing its artificial origin. Disclosing the nature of the deepfake is a crucial element to enable people to trust content online and make informed decision and appreciation about the content that they see online. However, the scope of the provision is rather limited given several limitations. Firstly, article 52 only applies to "user" of AI systems; concept which excludes the individuals using the AI system in their personal non-professional activities from the scope of the regulation.[246] Then, two further exceptions are foreseen by article 52 namely when the deepfake is used for authorised law enforcement purpose or when it is necessary to exercise the rights to freedom of expression and the right to freedom of the arts and sciences as guaranteed in the Charter of Fundamental Rights of the EU.

64. Additionally, the strengthened EU code of practice on disinformation published in June 2022 contains new commitments for signatories including one on deepfakes.[247] Relevant signatories commit to take into consideration the transparency obligations and the list of manipulative practices prohibited under the AI Act proposal. To implement this commitment, the code indicates that they will have to establish or confirm their policies in place about deepfakes, which can include measures such as warning users and proactively detect deepfake.[248]

---

245 European Commission, Proposal for a Regulation of the European Parliament and of the Council laying down harmonized rules on artificial intelligence Artificial Intelligence Act) and amending certain union legislative acts, *OJ* COM(2021) 206 final, 21 April 2021.

246 Article 3, para. 4 of the AI Act proposal. This transparency obligation would not be mandatory for individuals creating deepfakes in the course of their personal activities.

247 Commitment 15 of the strengthened Code of practice on disinformation 2022, 16 June 2022, https://digital-strategy.ec.europa.eu/en/library/2022-strengthened-code-practice-disinformation. The Code is open for different type of signatories. They can be providers of online services such as platforms that participate in the dissemination of content to the public such as social media, private messaging applications and search engines; players from the online advertising industry; providers of e-payment services, e-commerce platforms, …

248 "Signatories will provide the European Commission with baseline reports detailing how they have implemented their commitments under the Code", Preamble, o), of the strengthened code of practice on disinformation. Therefore, "relevant Signatories will have to report on

The code was initially a self-regulatory instrument, but it is now backed by the DSA which introduces a co-regulatory mechanism. Indeed, adherence to and implementation of codes of conducts is a criterion which should be considered to assess if systemic risks are well managed and mitigated.[249] It will help to determine whether there is an infringement of the DSA obligations which can trigger financial sanctions.[250]

7. CONCLUSION

65. This chapter described how AI technologies are being integrated in different media activities, ranging from content production to search and dissemination, and legal challenges arising from it. It offered an overview of relevant rules in Belgian and European media law (and related frameworks) to address the challenges associated with the use of three AI media applications: recommender systems, content moderation systems and deepfakes. It described both the opportunities and risks, including for fundamental rights, resulting from AI-systems in the media sector. Like in other sectors, AI technologies deployed in media are not neutral. They are designed by individuals or companies willing to protect and promote their own interests. Companies use AI systems to maximise user engagement, hence revenues, by keeping individuals as long as possible on their platform, even if it implies recommending controversial content that is on the brink of illegal or harmful speech. They also use AI systems to moderate content in line with the intermediary liability rules. The consequence of this, as illustrated in this chapter, is that the use of AI in the media field can create drawbacks. Such challenges are of particular importance, given the crucial role that media represent for democracy and fundamental rights including freedom of expression.

66. Our analysis of Belgian media law has highlighted the complexities involved in addressing the challenges created by the use of AI media applications. The division of powers between the Communities and the Federal State of Belgium creates a complex architecture of legislators and regulatory authorities with sometimes exclusive, sometimes shared competences in the sphere of media and communications. In addition, while challenges in relation to the use of AI systems in the media often present common features, they also present distinct risks depending on the type of systems. Recommender systems, content

their policies in place for countering prohibited manipulative practices for AI systems that generate or manipulate content" (deepfakes), Commitment 15 of the strengthened code of practice on disinformation.

249 Article 45 combined with rec. 80 which relates to Article 34 of the DSA.

250 Articles 45, 52 and rec. 104 of the DSA.

moderation systems and deepfakes require tailor-made provisions tackling their specific issues. This requires a fine balance between enshrining general principles and formulating detailed provisions to regulate AI in the media field.

67. Although existing Belgian legislation hardly contains any specific provisions on AI technologies in the media sector, several existing rules which have been phrased in a technology-neutral manner continue to apply. At least to some extent, they can mitigate risks, for instance through liability and damage schemes. This is especially the case for deepfakes because the technology is available not only to professionals but to all individuals which creates an unprecedented level of outreach. Furthermore, in light of the difficulties to identify deepfakes authors and successive reuploads, providing *ex post* remedies to victims of deepfakes is crucial.

68. Moreover, several legislative initiatives, mainly (but not only) at EU level[251], are being developed and focus on *ex ante* provisions. These provisions intend to prevent harm to fundamental rights, stemming from recommender systems, content moderation systems and deepfakes. In terms of *ex ante* obligations, the trend is mainly towards imposing transparency measures, but also responsibilities for (very large online) providers to be more vigilant in anticipating long-term and major risks, e.g., for freedom of expression, that their services may cause – hence, the obligation to carry out annual systemic risk assessments and adopt measures to mitigate these risks.

69. The major impact of AI technologies on the media sector is beyond question, and new AI applications will continue to reshape the media landscape also in Belgium. The law is a key instrument to set out clear rules ensuring that these technologies respect human rights and fundamental values, including democracy. At the same time, legislators need to be careful that the law does not become itself an instrument of censorship...

---

[251] It includes the previously cited Digital Services Act, the draft AI Act, the draft Regulation on the transparency and targeting of political advertising. We can also add the European Commission's Communication on Europe's Media in the Digital Decade: An Action Plan to Support Recovery and Transformation (also known as the Media Action Plan), 3 December 2020, COM(2020) 784 final and the European Commission's Communication on the European democracy action plan, 3 December 2020, COM/2020/790 final. At the level of the Council of Europe, negotiations on a Treaty on AI will start in Q2 of 2022 via the Committee on Artificial Intelligence; https://www.coe.int/en/web/artificial-intelligence/cai.

KU Leuven Centre for IT & IP Law

The KU Leuven Centre for IT & IP Law Series brings together the results of research activities of the Centre for IT & IP Law. The central research themes of the series concern the legal and ethical aspects of information technology, innovation and intellectual property.

Each book in the series focuses on the essential developments in the current legal framework, necessitated by the rapid evolution of technology in various fields, such as government, media, health care, informatics, digital economy, banking, transport and culture. The research is characterised by an interdisciplinary approach, constantly cross-fertilising legal, technical, economic, ethical and socio-cultural perspectives.

Books are published in English, Dutch and/or French.

Recently published in this series:

1. Rán Trygvadóttir, *European Libraries and the Internet: Copyright and Extended Collective Licences*, 2018.
2. Niels Vandezande, *Virtual Currencies*, 2018.
3. Aleksandra Kuczerawy, *Intermediary Liability and Freedom of Expression in the EU: From Concepts to Safeguards*, 2018.
4. Letizia Paoli, Jonas Visschers Cedric Verstraete, Elke van Hellemont, *The Impact of Cybercrime on Belgian Businesses*, 2019.
5. Niels Vandezande, *When An Original Is Not Original. The Originality Requirement in Belgian Law*, 2019.
6. Brendan Van Alsenoy, *Data Protection Law in the EU: Roles, Responsibilities and Liability*, 2019.
7. A. Vedder, J. Schroers, C. Ducuing and P. Valcke (eds.), *Security and Law. Legal and Ethical Aspects of Public Security, Cyber Security and Critical Infrastructure Security*, 2019.
8. M-C. Janssens, *Handboek Merkenrecht*, tweede editie, 2022.
9. KU Leuven Centre for IT & IP Law (ed.), *Rethinking IT and IP Law. Celebrating 30 Years CiTiP*, 2019.
10. Valerie Verdoodt, *Children's Rights and Commercial Communication in the Digital Era*, 2020.
11. Pieter-Jan Aerts, Frank Hoogendijk, Niels Vandezande, *Smart contracts. Een overzicht vanuit juridisch perspectief*, 2020.
12. Griet Verhenneman, The *Patient, Data Protection and Changing Healthcare Models. The impact of e-health on informed consent, anonymisation and purpose limitation*, 2021.

13. Jan De Bruyne en Cedric Vanleenhove, *AI and the Law,* second edition, 2022.
14. Ana Maria Corrêa, *Discrimination in Online Platforms. A Comparative Law Approach to Design, Intermediation and Data Challenges*, 2022.